Human Rights Law
in Scotland

Third Edition

Robert Reed and Jim Murdoch

Bloomsbury Professional

Bloomsbury Professional Ltd
Maxwelton House
41–43 Boltro Road
Haywards Heath
West Sussex
RH16 1BJ

First edition (Butterworths LexisNexis) 2001
Second edition (Tottel Publishing Ltd) 2008

British Library Cataloguing-in-Publication Data

A CIP Catalogue record for this book is available from the British Library.

ISBN 978 1 84766 556 0

Typeset by Etica Press Ltd, Malvern, Worcestershire

Printed in Great Britain by Antony Rowe Limited, Chippenham, Wilts

Preface

Three and a half years ago, in the preface to the second edition of this book, we said that a more thorough rewriting would be necessary at some point. In preparing this edition, it became apparent that rewriting could no longer be postponed. The Strasbourg jurisprudence has continued to develop at a daunting pace, and the domestic case law has grown exponentially. The work of the House of Lords and the Supreme Court, in particular, has become dominated by questions of human rights, and such questions are also at the forefront of the work of the intermediate appellate courts, including the Inner House of the Court of Session and (in relation to devolution issues) the High Court of Justiciary.

One development that has become increasingly apparent is the establishment of an effective dialogue between the House of Lords and the Privy Council – whose functions in relation to Convention rights are now brought together in the Supreme Court – and the European Court of Human Rights. When Sir Nicolas Bratza, the UK judge (and now President) of the European Court of Human Rights, delivered the Slynn lecture in 2007, he described what he saw as the 'major and distinctive contribution of the United Kingdom courts', and particularly of the House of Lords, to the Strasbourg case law, 'enriching the jurisprudence by the clarity and cogency of the analysis of the Convention issues'. That has become even more apparent in recent years. UK judgments are discussed in the judgments of the Strasbourg Court, often in detail, and in some important cases the court has responded to criticisms made by the House of Lords and the Supreme Court, or has adopted views expressed in those courts: as, for example, in *McCann v United Kingdom* (2008), where the Court's judgment was based on the minority view of Lord Bingham in an earlier case in the House of Lords. At the same time, the domestic jurisprudence on Convention rights has focused almost entirely on the Strasbourg case law, and has responded to findings that domestic decisions were not in conformity with the Convention: as, for example, when Lord Rodger stated, '*Argentoratum locutum, iudicium finitum*: Strasbourg has spoken, the case is closed' (*Secretary of State for the Home Department v AF (No 3)* [2010] 2 AC 269). This reflects the fact that the duty under the Human Rights Act to 'take into account' the Strasbourg jurisprudence has been interpreted as meaning that, in the absence of some special circumstance, any clear and constant jurisprudence of the Strasbourg Court should be followed. That approach has reflected the intention behind the Act to 'bring rights home': to enable a remedy to be obtained in the domestic courts without the necessity to go to Strasbourg. The resultant focus on the Convention case law may have increased the influence of domestic courts upon the Strasbourg Court. It has however also exposed the domestic legal systems to the possibility of major change as a consequence of decisions taken by an international court (as, for example, in the *Cadder* case).

Two other developments should be noted. First, although the Human Rights Act continues to be blamed for many of the ills in society (including, most recently, the riots in English cities during the summer of 2011), the prospect of its being repealed – other than, possibly, to clear the way for a more extensive protection of fundamental rights ('ECHR plus', in the jargon) under a UK Bill of Rights – appears to have retreated for the time being, following the election of the Coalition government. Secondly, concern about the Strasbourg Court – in particular, the quality and independence of some of the judges, and the extent to which the Court intervenes in promoting its vision of the Convention as a pan-European constitutional instrument – has become more widely shared by European governments, and is reflected in the Interlaken process described in Chapter 2. Reforms designed to improve the overall quality and independence of the Strasbourg judges, and to focus their work on significant breaches of human rights, have now come into effect under Protocol no 14. It remains to be seen whether those reforms, and the Interlaken process, will bring about changes in the approach adopted by the Court, such as a greater commitment to subsidiarity and the recognition of a wider margin of appreciation for national authorities.

In preparing this edition, we have again received invaluable assistance from a number of recent Glasgow law graduates including Gavin Baird, Eleanor Deeming, Gavin Law, Neale McDonald, and Andy Sirel, and in particular from Jim Gaughan (who helped with Chapter 5). Once again, we benefited from the helpfulness of the staff of the Library of the European Court of Human Rights. The usual disclaimers continue to apply.

This edition is dedicated to the memory of Lord Rodger of Earlsferry, who died when it was nearing completion. Alan Rodger was a graduate of Glasgow University and an honorary professor in the School of Law. As a law officer, he was responsible for a change in practice whereby Scottish counsel were normally instructed to represent the United Kingdom in proceedings concerning Scotland before the European Court of Human Rights, and he himself took part in several important cases there. As Lord President, Lord of Appeal in Ordinary and Justice of the Supreme Court, he made an important contribution to the development and understanding of human rights law in this country. As a judge and a teacher, but above all as a friend, he is greatly missed.

We have generally attempted to state the law as at 31 March 2011.

Robert Reed and Jim Murdoch

September 2011

Contents

CHAPTER 1

Contents

Contents

Contents

Contents

Contents

Table of statutes

Table of statutory instruments

Table of international and European treaties and domestic legislation

Table of United Kingdom cases

Table of cases of other domestic courts and international tribunals

Table of judgments and decisions of the European Court of Human Rights

For a discussion of citation of decisions and reports, see paras 2.101-2.102. A case selected for publication is shown thus: eg '2008-...' (but note that allocated volume numbers for 2007 cases are provisional).

A

D

PARA

F

Q

Table of Commission decisions on admissibility and reports on the merits – alphabetical list

For a discussion of citation of decisions and reports, see paras 2.99-2.100.

A

PARA

X

Table of Commission decisions on admissibility and reports on the merits – numerical list

For a discussion of citation of decisions and reports, see paras 2.99-2.100.

Abbreviations

A	Series A Publications of the European Court of Human Rights [see para 2.99]
AC	Appeal Cases Law Reports
AJIL	American Journal of International Law
All ER	All England Law Reports
asp	Act of the Scottish Parliament
B	Series B Publications of the European Court of Human Rights [see para 2.99]
BCLC	Butterworths Company Law Cases
BCLR	Butterworths Constitutional Law Reports
BYBIL	British Yearbook of International Law
CA	Court of Appeal
CD	Collection of Decisions of the European Commission of Human Rights [see para 2.99]
CETS	Council of Europe Treaty Series
CFLQ	Child and Family Law Quarterly
Ch	Chancery Division Law Reports
ChD	Chancery Division
CIL	Contemporary Issues in Law
CJEU	Court of Justice of the European Union
CLJ	Cambridge Law Journal
Colum Hum Rts L Rev	Columbia Human Rights law Review
Colum J Transnat'l L	Columbia Journal of Transnational Law
Comms L	Communications Law
CP(S)A	Criminal Procedure (Scotland) Act 1995
CPT	European Committee for the Prevention of Torture and Inhuman and Degrading Treatment or Punishment
Cr App R	Criminal Appeal Reports
Crim LR	Criminal Law Review
Ct of S	Court of Session
Dalloz Jur	Répertoire Dalloz de Juriprudence Générale
DR	Decisions and Reports of the European Commission of Human Rights [see para 2.99]
E Europ HRRev	East European Human Rights Review
EAT	Employment Appeal Tribunal
ECHR	European Convention on Human Rights
ECJ	European Court of Justice
ECR	European Court Reports

ECRI	European Commission against Racism and Intolerance
ECSR	European Committee of Social Rights
ECtHR	European Court of Human Rights
Ed Law	Education and the Law
EdinLR	Edinburgh Law Review
EEA	European Economic Area
EFTA	European Free Trade Association
EHRC	Equality and Human Rights Commission
EHRLR	European Human Rights Law Review
EJIL	European Journal of International Law
Elec St	Electoral Studies
ELRev	European Law Review
EMLR	Entertainment and Media Law Reports
EMRK	Konvention zum Schutze der Menschenrechte und Grundfreiheiten
EPL	European Public Law
ERevPL	European Review of Public Law
ESC	European Social Charter
ET	Employment Tribunal
ETS	European Treaty Series
EuGRZ	Europäische Grundrechte Zeitschrift
EuroCLY	European Current Law Yearbook
EYMI	European Yearbook of Minority Issues
Fam Law	Family Law
Fam	Family Division Law Reports
FCR	Family Court Reporter
FLR	Family Law Reports
'FYRO Macedonia'	'The Former Yugoslav Republic of Macedonia'
GYIL	German Yearbook of International Law
Harv Hum Rts Jo	Harvard Human Rights Journal
Harv Int LJ	Harvard International Law Journal
HCJ	High Court of Justiciary
HL	House of Lords
HLR	Housing Law Reports
HR & UKP	Human Rights and UK Practice
HRA	Human Rights Act 1998
HRLJ	Human Rights Law Journal
HRLR	Human Rights Law Reports
HRQ	Human Rights Quarterly
ICC	International Criminal Court

ICCPR	International Covenant on Civil and Political Rights
ICLQ	International and Comparative Law Quarterly
ICR	Industrial Case Reports
ICTY	International Criminal Tribunal for the former Yugoslavia
IFLJ	International Family Law Journal
IH	Inner House, Court of Session
IJHR	International Journal of Human Rights
IJL	International Journal of Law
ILO	International Labour Organisation
Imm A R	Immigration Appeal Reports
Int J Minor Group Rights	International Journal of Minorities and Group Rights
Int Jo Children's Rights	International Journal of Children's Rights
Int Jo Constit Law	International Journal of Constitutional Law
Interights Bull	Interights Bulletin
IR	Irish Reports
IRLR	Industrial Relations Law Reports
J Env L	Journal of Environmental Law
J L & Ed	Journal of Law and Education
JC	Justiciary Cases
JCHR	Joint Committee on Human Rights
JCPC	Judicial Committee of the Privy Council
JDI	Journal du Droit International
JEnvL	Journal of Environmental Law
JL&Ed	Journal of Law and Education
JLSS	Journal of the Law Society of Scotland
JPL	Journal of Planning and Environment Law
JR	Juridical Review
KB	King's Bench Law Reports
LQR	Law Quarterly Review
Maastricht J	Maastricht Journal of European and Comparative Law
Med L Rev	Medical Law Review
Med Sci Law	Medicine, Science and the Law
MLR	Modern Law Review
NJW	Neue Juristische Wochenschrift
NLJ	New Law Journal
Nott L J	Nottingham Law Journal
NQHR	Netherlands Quarterly of Human Rights
NV	Naamloze Vennootschap
OH	Outer House, Court of Session

OJEC	Official Journal of the European Communities
OJLS	Oxford Journal of Legal Studies
OSCE	Organisation for Security and Co-operation in Europe
PACE	Parliamentary Assembly of the Council of Europe
PL	Public Law
QB	Queen's Bench Law Reports
QBD	Queen's Bench Division
RDTE	Revue Trimestrielle de Droit Européene
REDP	Revue Européenne de Droit Public
RGDIP	Revue Générale de Droit International Public
RIPA	Regulation of Investigatory Powers Act 2000
RIPSA	Regulation of Investigatory Powers (Scotland) Act 2000
RTDH	Revue Trimestrielle des Droits de l'Homme
RTR	Road Traffic Reports
RUDH	Revue Universelle des Droits de l'Homme
SA	Scotland Act 1998
SC	Session Cases
SCC	Supreme Court Cases [Canada]
SCCR	Scottish Criminal Case Reports
SCHRA	Scottish Commission on Human Rights Act 2006
SI	Statutory Instrument
SIAC	Special Immigration Appeals Commission
SLPQ	Scottish Law and Practice Quarterly
SLT	Scots Law Times
SSI	Scottish Statutory Instrument
Stat Law Rev	Statute Law Review
STC	Simons Tax Cases
Tech and Con Ct	Technology and Construction Court
TEU	Treaty on European Union
TFEU	Treaty on the Functioning of the European Union
UDHR	Universal Declaration of Human Rights
UFR	Ugeskrift for Retsvæsen
UNHCR	United Nations High Commissioner for Refugees
Web JCLI	Web Journal of Current Legal Issues
WLR	Weekly Law Reports
YB	Yearbook of the European Convention on Human Rights
YEL	Yearbook of International Law

Chapter 1

The ECHR and Scots law

INTRODUCTION

1.01 This book considers human rights law in Scotland. It is principally concerned with the rights guaranteed by the European Convention on Human Rights (ECHR)[1], as interpreted by the European Court of Human Rights and by the courts of the UK. The present chapter considers how those rights are given effect in our domestic law. The following chapter considers how they are given effect in international law. Subsequent chapters consider the content of those rights, as interpreted by the European Court of Human Rights and by the courts of the UK.

---

1   There are of course many other international instruments concerned with human rights, but they are generally of less significance than the ECHR in the domestic law of the UK, since they have not been made directly enforceable by any equivalent of the Human Rights Act (HRA) 1998. In so far as they have been implemented by domestic legislation, it is that legislation which is enforceable rather than the international instrument itself, although the latter may well be relevant as an aid to interpretation. In practice, international human rights instruments other than the ECHR are most often referred to by UK courts, as by the European Court of Human Rights, as part of the matrix of standards and rules in which the ECHR operates: see, for example, the discussion of the UN Convention on the Rights of the Child in *Dyer v Watson* 2002 SC (PC) 89; and para **3.44** below. It has, however, also been said of the latter convention that its requirements are 'a relevant consideration which should be taken into account by the state and its emanations in determining upon their actions': *E v Chief Constable of the Royal Ulster Constabulary* [2009] 1 AC 536 at para 60 per Lord Carswell.

1.02 The ECHR is a treaty made between member states of the Council of Europe, by which the High Contracting Parties undertake to 'secure to everyone within their jurisdiction the rights and freedoms defined in Section 1 of this Convention'. Article 19 establishes the European Court of Human Rights 'to ensure the observance of the engagements undertaken by the High Contracting Parties'. It has jurisdiction under Article 32 to decide 'all matters concerning the interpretation and application of the Convention'. By Article 46, the High Contracting Parties undertake 'to abide by the final judgment of the Court in any case to which they are parties'. Respondents to proceedings before the Court are the states themselves, not the particular bodies whose conduct may have infringed the guaranteed rights. The judgments of the Court are enforced at an international level, by the Committee of Ministers of the Council of Europe. The ECHR is thus an international treaty, and the European Court of Human Rights is an international court with jurisdiction under international law to interpret and apply it. An international treaty such as the ECHR does not form part of Scots law[1], although it can be taken into account as an aid to the interpretation of statutes and in the development of the common law[2].

1   *J H Rayner (Mincing Lane) Ltd v Department of Trade and Industry* [1990] 2 AC 418; *Whaley v Lord Advocate* 2008 SC (HL) 107. The position may be different to the extent that a treaty merely repeats a rule of customary international law, since customary international law forms part of the common law.

2   See paras **1.04** and **1.23–1.24** below.

1.03 Parliament may pass a law which mirrors the terms of a treaty and in that sense incorporates the treaty into domestic law. In such a case, the courts will try to construe the legislation in a way which does not put the United Kingdom in breach of its international obligations[1]. But it is not the treaty but the statute which forms part of domestic law. And the courts will not be bound to give effect to interpretations of the treaty by an international court, unless and to the extent that the statute so provides[2]. As Lord Hoffmann said of the HRA 1998 in *Re McKerr*:

> 'What the Act has done is to create domestic rights expressed in the same terms as those contained in the Convention. But they are domestic rights, not international rights. Their source is the statute, not the Convention. They are available against specific public authorities, not the United Kingdom as a state. And their meaning and application is a matter for domestic courts, not the court in Strasbourg.'[3]

At the same time, since the purpose of the HRA 1998 is, in the words of its long title, 'to give further effect to rights and freedoms guaranteed under the European Convention on Human Rights', the domestic rights created by the Act are interpreted by reference to the corresponding rights under the ECHR[4].

1   *In re G (Adoption: Unmarried Couple)* [2009] AC 173 at para 35 per Lord Hoffmann.

2   Cf *R v Lyons* [2003] 1 AC 976 at para 27 per Lord Hoffmann.

3   *Re McKerr* [2004] 1 WLR 807 at para 63. See also at para 25 per Lord Nicholls of Birkenhead.

4   *R (S and Marper) v Chief Constable of West Yorkshire* [2004] 1 WLR 2196 at para 66 per Lord Rodger of Earlsferry.

1.04 The rights with which the ECHR is concerned have long been protected in Scotland – and continue to be protected – by the common law or by statute. Indeed, the ECHR owes much to the British constitutional tradition and to common law concepts[1]. For example, the independence of the judiciary has been protected by statute since the end of the seventeenth century and the beginning of the eighteenth. The 110 day rule, ensuring that persons held in custody are tried within a reasonable time, dates from the same era. Most of the law of criminal evidence and procedure has its roots far in the past, and has been designed to ensure a fair trial. Similarly, the law of delict is designed to protect people's bodily integrity, their reputation, and their freedom to live free of unlawful interferences of all kinds. The law of property protects their possessions. Freedom from illegal searches of premises or correspondence has been protected since at least the English case of *Entick v Carrington*[2] in the eighteenth century. When the House of Lords recently rejected the admission of evidence obtained by torture, they did so on the basis of the English common law and on the basis of one of the earliest statutes passed by Parliament after the Union, which put an end to the use of torture in Scotland[3]. One can find similar domestic origins for other rights protected by the Convention. As Dicey wrote in 1885 in his *Introduction to the Study of the Law of the Constitution*, 'the general principles of the constitution (as for example the right to personal liberty, or the right of public meeting) are with us the result of judicial decisions'.

Neither the common law nor statutory law stands still. The development of the common law can in particular be influenced by international treaties, including the ECHR. Equally, the interpretation of statutes may be influenced by the Convention and other international instruments. As Lord Bingham observed in *R v Lyons*:

> 'Even before the Human Rights Act 1998 the Convention exercised a persuasive and pervasive influence on judicial decision-making in this country, affecting the interpretation of ambiguous statutory provisions, guiding the exercise of discretions, bearing on the development of the common law.'[4]

The influence of international law, including the ECHR, on statutory interpretation and on the development of the common law continues to be relevant. As was said by Lord Penrose in *Robertson and Gough v HM Advocate*[5]:

> '…the common law retains the flexibility necessary to its continuing development, drawing on all relevant and appropriate sources, including international instruments such as the European Convention on Human Rights and Fundamental Freedoms.'

---

1   In *A v Secretary of State for the Home Department* [2005] 1 AC 98, a case concerned with the right to liberty under Art 5 of the Convention, Lord Hoffmann remarked at para 88: 'I would not like anyone to think that we are concerned with some special doctrine of European law. Freedom from arbitrary arrest and detention is a quintessentially British liberty, enjoyed by the inhabitants of this country when most of the population of Europe could be thrown into prison at the whim of their rulers. It was incorporated into the European Convention in order to entrench the same liberty in countries which had recently been under Nazi occupation. The United Kingdom subscribed to the Convention because it set out the rights which British subjects enjoyed under the common law.' Lord Hoffmann also however acknowledged at para 90 that, until the HRA 1998, the question whether a threat to the nation was sufficient to justify the suspension by Parliament of ordinary liberties could not have been the subject of judicial decision.

2   *Entick v Carrington* (1765) 2 Wils KB 275; 95 ER 807.

3   *A v Secretary of State for the Home Department* [2006] 2 AC 221.

4   *R v Lyons* [2003] 1 AC 976 at para 13.

5   *Robertson and Gough v HM Advocate* 2008 JC 146 at para 115. See also *Dickson v HM Advocate* 2008 JC 181 at para 31 per Lord Justice General Hamilton.

1.05 In addition to the influence of international law on judicial decision-making, Parliament legislated in 1998 to impose duties on public authorities in domestic law reflecting the obligations undertaken by the UK under international law by its ratification of the ECHR. It did so by creating 'Convention rights', as the domestic counterpart of the rights guaranteed under international law by the ECHR. The HRA 1998 makes it unlawful for a public authority to act in a way which is incompatible with a Convention right[1]. Although the HRA 1998 may be regarded as reproducing as rights in domestic law the guarantees found in certain Articles of the ECHR and its Protocols, it is important not to lose sight of the distinction between the obligations which the UK accepted by accession to the ECHR and the duties under domestic law which were imposed upon public authorities in the UK by the HRA 1998. It is possible, for example, for the UK to be in breach of the ECHR without there being any breach of a Convention right under the HRA 1998[2]. Equally, it has been suggested that legislation which might not be regarded by the European Court of Human Rights as resulting in a violation of the ECHR, on the basis that it fell within the state's margin of appreciation, may nevertheless be incompatible with a Convention right under the HRA 1998[3].

1   HRA 1998, s 6.

2   For example, because the latter is narrower in its temporal and territorial effect.

3   *In re G (Adoption: Unmarried Couple* [2009] AC 173 at paras 29–38 per Lord Hoffmann, para 50 per Lord Hope of Craighead, paras 119–120 per Baroness Hale of Richmond and paras 126–130 per Lord Mance; contrast paras 79 and 82 per Lord Walker of Gestingthorpe.

1.06 In addition to the HRA 1998, the Scotland Act (SA) 1998 provides that a provision of an Act of the Scottish Parliament is not law so far as it is incompatible with any of the Convention rights[1], and that a member of the Scottish Executive has no power to make any subordinate legislation, or to do any other act, so far as the legislation or act is incompatible with any of the Convention rights[2]. Similar provision was made by the devolution statutes for Northern Ireland[3] and Wales[4].

1   SA 1998, s 29.

2   SA 1998, s 57.

3   Northern Ireland Act 1998.

4   Government of Wales Act 1998, as amended by the Government of Wales Act 2006.

1.07 Human rights are also protected by EU law[1], to which effect is given in domestic law by the European Communities Act 1972. In consequence, EU law provides, within its scope, an important means of invoking fundamental rights, including those guaranteed by the ECHR, before UK courts. The protection of fundamental rights in EU law, and the relationship in that regard between EU law and the ECHR, are discussed in Chapter 2[2].

EU law is reflected in the SA 1998, in terms of which a provision of an Act of the Scottish Parliament is not law so far as it is incompatible with EU law[3], and a member of the Scottish Executive has no power to make any subordinate legislation, or to do any other act, so far as the legislation or act is incompatible with EU law[4].

1   See eg Case 29/69 *Stauder v City of Ulm* [1969] ECR 419; Case 11/70 *Internationale Handelsgesellschaft* [1970] ECR 1125; Case 4/73 *Nold v Commission* [1974] ECR 491; Case 222/84 *Johnston v Chief Constable of the RUC* [1986] ECR 1651.

2   See paras **2.12–2.29** below.

3   SA 1998, s 29.

4   SA 1998, s 57.

1.08 The focus of this work is on the ECHR, and on the domestic statutes designed to give effect to the Convention rights: in particular , the HRA 1998 and the SA 1998. Nevertheless, it is important at the outset not to overlook the extent to which the rights guaranteed by the ECHR continue to be protected by the common law[1], by other statutes and by EU law. That is so for a number of reasons. First, there is no need to investigate the often difficult questions which arise in connection with Convention rights if the act in question is in any event unlawful under domestic law. The Convention rights are primarily protected by our own domestic law. It is only if it fails to meet the requirements of the Convention that it is necessary to go beyond it. Secondly, the rights afforded by the common law or by statute may be more extensive than those arising under the ECHR. For example, the duty to act fairly at common law applies in contexts, such as immigration and tax, which have traditionally not been regarded as falling within the scope of the right to a fair hearing under Article 6 of the ECHR; and a statute such as the Equality Act 2006 may provide greater protection from discrimination than the ECHR[2]. Thirdly, the remedies which are available may depend on the source of the right in question. For example, a statute of the UK Parliament which is incompatible with EU law must to that extent be disapplied[3], whereas the incompatibility of such a statute with Convention rights can result only in a declaration of that incompatibility: the statute remains effective and must be applied. Fourthly, reliance on the HRA 1998 or, more especially, on the SA 1998 has certain procedural consequences, as explained below. These include time limits for the commencement of proceedings under the HRA 1998, or for the raising of a 'devolution issue' under the SA 1998, which do not apply to proceedings brought under the common law.

---

1   Cf *Robertson and Gough v HM Advocate* 2008 JC 146 at paras 64–65 per Lord Justice-Clerk Gill. It also has to be borne in mind that, if the HRA 1998 were to be repealed, the common law protection of human rights would be of obvious importance.

2   For example, contrast *R (ABCIFER) v Ministry of Defence* [2003] QB 1397 and *R (Elias) v Secretary of State for Defence* [2006] 1 WLR 3213.

3   *R v Secretary of State for Transport ex parte Factortame Ltd (No 2)* [1991] AC 603.

1.09 More fundamentally, the common law bearing on fundamental rights, much of which is common to the UK jurisdictions (and is also shared with other jurisdictions such as Canada, Australia and New Zealand) remains of enduring significance[1], and its continued development is a responsibility of the courts. As Lord Cooke of Thorndon observed in *R (Daly) v Secretary of State for the Home Department*[2], a case concerned with legal professional privilege:

'... while this case has arisen in a jurisdiction where the European Convention for the Protection of Human Rights and Fundamental Freedoms applies, and while the case is one in which the Convention and the common law produce the same result, it is of great importance, in my opinion, that the common law by itself is being recognised as a sufficient source of the fundamental right to confidential communication with a legal adviser for the purpose of obtaining legal advice ... The truth is, I think, that some rights are inherent and fundamental to democratic civilised society. Conventions, constitutions, bills of rights and the like respond by recognising rather than creating them.'

Most matters falling within the scope of the ECHR can and should be satisfactorily resolved under the common law or statute, taking the ECHR into account as and when may be appropriate.

1   Not least because of the possibility that the HRA 1998 might be repealed.

2   *R (Daly) v Secretary of State for the Home Department* [2001] 2 AC 532 at para 30. This dictum was cited by the Inner House in *Narden Services Ltd v Inverness Retail and Business Park Ltd* 2008 SC 335 at para 11.

1.10 At the same time, the common law and statute have limitations as means of protecting fundamental rights. First, in the case of some rights (such as the right to respect for one's private life), the protection afforded by the common law or statute has proved to be more limited than that required by the ECHR[1]. Secondly, Parliament may legislate in terms which fail to meet ECHR requirements, even when construed in accordance with common law principles of interpretation (principles which themselves protect human rights, by presuming that retroactivity is not intended, that penal statutes are to be narrowly construed, and so on and so forth). Thirdly, common law rules as to standing in judicial review, or as to the principles of judicial review, may in some circumstances be too restrictive to provide the degree of protection for such rights which the ECHR requires. It was in such circumstances that, prior to the HRA 1998, the courts began to refer to the ECHR as an aid to the interpretation of statutes and the development of the common law, as explained below; and it was in such circumstances that individuals began to make applications to the Strasbourg institutions.

1   See eg *Malone v Metropolitan Police Commissioner (No 2)* [1979] Ch 344; *Malone v United Kingdom* (1985) A 82.

1.11 This chapter will consider the ECHR and Scots law under the following headings:

*   Scottish cases in Strasbourg;
*   The ECHR in the Scottish courts prior to the 1998 Acts;
*   The Human Rights Act 1998;
*   The Scotland Act 1998;
*   The relationship between the Human Rights Act 1998 and the Scotland Act 1998; and
*   Promoting awareness of human rights.

SCOTTISH CASES IN STRASBOURG

1.12 A survey of cases in Strasbourg which have originated in Scotland may be of some value, particularly as the issues raised by Scottish applicants have often arisen from a distinctively Scottish context. Scottish cases in Strasbourg do not, however, always have a distinctively Scottish dimension. Where the law and practice in Scotland are similar to that elsewhere in the United Kingdom, the national background of a case is of no particular importance. This is reflected in the fact that the law in Scotland has often been altered in response to Strasbourg judgments in cases from other parts of the UK, just as the law in England and Wales and Northern Ireland has sometimes required alteration in consequence of a Strasbourg decision in a Scottish case[1]. As well as those cases which have resulted in judgments or decisions of the European Court of Human Rights, some of the earlier Scottish cases which were considered by the European Commission on Human Rights, prior to its discontinuance in November 1998, remain of some relevance and are noted below. Broad categories have been used in the following survey to indicate the principal subject matter of the cases, but it should be appreciated that these are not watertight compartments.

---

1   Eg the abolition of corporal punishment in state schools by the Education (No 2) Act 1986, following the judgment in *Campbell and Cosans v United Kingdom* (1982) A 48.

Criminal procedure

1.13 Several of the Scottish cases decided by the European Court of Human Rights have concerned aspects of criminal procedure: notably the absence of reasons in the jury's verdict[1]; the composition of a jury[2]; the examination of witnesses before the Appeal Court[3]; legal aid for criminal appeals[4]; legal representation in criminal appeals[5]; delay in the determination of a criminal appeal[6]; the 'sifting' procedure whereby the court decides whether to grant leave to appeal[7]; the retention of personal data[8]; whether the definition of breach of the peace was sufficiently clear[9]; restrictions on the right to call and cross-examine witnesses[10]; restrictions on the admission of evidence as to the sexual history and character of complainers in sexual offences[11]; and the adequacy of facilities for interpretation[12]. The Court has also considered the extent to which the media may challenge restrictions placed upon the right to broadcast details of criminal proceedings[13].

---

1   *Judge v United Kingdom* (dec) (8 February 2011).

2   *Pullar v United Kingdom* 1996-III.

3   *Pullar v United Kingdom* 1996-III.

4   *Granger v United Kingdom* (1990) A 174.

5   *Boner v United Kingdom* (1994) A 300-B; *Maxwell v United Kingdom* (1994) A 300-C.

6   *Mellors v United Kingdom* (17 July 2003); *Henderson v United Kingdom* (dec) (6 February 2007).

7   *Martin v United Kingdom* (dec) (7 September 1999).

8   *Donnan v United Kingdom* (dec) (8 November 2005).

9   *Lucas v United Kingdom* (dec) (18 March 2003).

10   *Mellors v United Kingdom* (dec) (30 January 2003).

11   *Judge v United Kingdom* (dec) (8 February 2011).

12   *Ucak v United Kingdom* (dec) (24 January 2002).

13   *MacKay and BBC Scotland v United Kingdom* (7 December 2010).

1.14 A number of cases were also considered by the European Commission on Human Rights. These included cases concerning the availability of legal aid for trials[1] or appeals[2], and the related problem of appellants being unrepresented. In relation to pre-trial procedure, cases have concerned: the questioning of a suspect by the police without a solicitor being present[3]; detention without access to a solicitor[4]; detention under prevention of terrorism legislation[5]; the adequacy of time and facilities for the preparation of the defence[6]; absence of access to police statements and Crown precognitions[7]; the late instruction of counsel[8]; the refusal of an adjournment of the trial[9]; the obtaining ex parte of a warrant to take hair samples[10]; the forcible execution of such a warrant[11]; and conviction on a charge of obstructing the execution of a warrant to obtain bodily samples and teeth impressions[12]. In relation to trial procedure, cases have concerned: the composition of the jury[13]; the impartiality of the jury[14]; newspaper reporting of the trial[15]; the adequacy of legal representation at the trial[16]; alleged errors of fact in the judge's charge[17]; deletions from the indictment[18]; conviction on a basis of concert rather than as an actor[19]; and conviction on an individual basis under an indictment libelling mobbing and rioting[20]. In relation to appeal procedure, cases have concerned: the handcuffing of an appellant during the hearing of his appeal[21]; access to the transcript of the trial[22]; access to a translation of the trial judge's charge and report to the appeal court[23]; the withdrawal of counsel[24]; the increasing of a sentence by the appeal court[25]; its refusal to allow an appeal to be abandoned[26]; its impartiality[27]; its refusal of an adjournment[28]; its alleged refusal to allow an appeal to be presented[29]; its receipt of a witness statement[30]; its substitution of a conviction in amended terms[31]; the absence of a right of appeal to the House of Lords[32]; and the absence of a right to compensation[33]. Other cases concerned delay in bringing a case to trial[34] (where 'just satisfaction' was also considered); an increase in statutory sentencing powers[35]; the ability of a Secretary of State's reference of a case to the Appeal Court to cure defects in an earlier appeal hearing[36]; a prohibition, by an order made under the *nobile officium*[37], of the broadcasting of a television programme until the completion of a criminal trial[38]; and the question whether a person has a right to have criminal proceedings instituted against other persons[39].

1   11711/85, *McDermitt v United Kingdom* (1987) DR 52, 244; 12322/86, *Bell v United Kingdom* (13 October 1987); 12370/86, *S v United Kingdom* (9 December 1987); 12917/87, *Drummond v United Kingdom* (9 December 1987).

2   16212/90, *R v United Kingdom* (17 April 1991); 14778/99, *Higgins v United Kingdom* (1992) DR 73, 95; 18711/91, *B v United Kingdom* (4 May 1993); 25523/94, *Murdoch v United Kingdom* (12 April 1996); 23934/94, *Middleton v United Kingdom* (12 April 1996); 22112/93, *Wotherspoon v United Kingdom* (12 April 1996); 24487/94, *Given v United Kingdom* (12 April 1996); 25648/94, *Robson v United Kingdom* (15 May 1996); 28891/95, *McAteer v United Kingdom* (2 July 1997); 31021/96, *Taylor v United Kingdom* (22 October 1997); 28944/95, *Faulkner v United Kingdom* (4 March 1998).

3   25648/94, *Robson v United Kingdom* (15 May 1996).

4   13081/87, *Windsor v United Kingdom* (14 December 1988); 25648/94, *Robson v United Kingdom* (15 May 1996).

5   11641/85, *C v United Kingdom* (12 July 1986); 15096/89, *McGlinchey v United Kingdom* (2 July 1990).

6   13081/87, *Windsor v United Kingdom* (14 December 1988); 23934/94; *Middleton v United Kingdom* (12 April 1996).

7   22112/93, *Wotherspoon v United Kingdom* (12 April 1996).

8   12834/87, *Boyle v United Kingdom* (3 March 1988).

9   26282/95, *Burns v United Kingdom* (4 September 1996).

10   34723/97, *Mellors v United Kingdom* (21 May 1998).

11   34723/97, *Mellors v United Kingdom* (21 May 1998).

12   34723/97, *Mellors v United Kingdom* (21 May 1998).

13   24399/94, *Mennie v United Kingdom* (16 October 1994).

14   23934/94, *Middleton v United Kingdom* (12 April 1996).

15   23934/94, *Middleton v United Kingdom* (12 April 1996).

16   25523/94, *Murdoch v United Kingdom* (12 April 1996); 23934/94, *Middleton v United Kingdom* (12 April 1996); 25648/94, *Robson v United Kingdom* (15 May 1996).

17   32874/96, *Moore v United Kingdom* (11 September 1997).

18   24399/94, *Mennie v United Kingdom* (16 October 1994).

19   12323/86, *Campbell v United Kingdom* (1988) DR 57, 148.

20   21266/93, *K v United Kingdom* (30 June 1993).

21   12323/86, *Campbell v United Kingdom* (1988) DR 57, 148.

22   18077/91, *Montes and Lopez v United Kingdom* (2 December 1992).

23   18077/91, *Montes and Lopez v United Kingdom* (2 December 1992).

24   12834/87, *Boyle v United Kingdom* (3 March 1988).

25   12002/86, *Grant v United Kingdom* (1988) DR 55, 218.

26   12002/86, *Grant v United Kingdom* (1988) DR 55, 218.

27   12002/86, *Grant v United Kingdom* (1988) DR 55, 218.

28   25523/94, *Murdoch v United Kingdom* (12 April 1996).

29   24487/94, *Given v United Kingdom* (12 April 1996); 26282/95, *Burns v United Kingdom* (4 September 1996); 28944/95, *Faulkner v United Kingdom* (4 March 1998).

30   24399/94, *Mennie v United Kingdom* (16 October 1994), applying *Pullar v United Kingdom* 1996 III, 783.

31   24399/94, *Mennie v United Kingdom* (16 October 1994).

32   24399/94, *Mennie v United Kingdom* (16 October 1994).

33   24399/94, *Mennie v United Kingdom* (16 October 1994).

34   21437/93, *Dougan v United Kingdom* 1997 SCCR 56.

35   14099/88, *Gillies v United Kingdom* (14 April 1989).

36   16732/90, *WK v United Kingdom* (11 January 1993).

37   The High Court of Justiciary's equitable jurisdiction.

38   34324/96, *BBC Scotland, McDonald, Rodgers and Donald v United Kingdom* (23 October 1997).

39   13081/87, *Windsor v United Kingdom* (14 December 1988); 18077/91, *Montes and Lopez v United Kingdom* (2 December 1992).

Prisoners' rights

1.15 Several Court judgments have concerned aspects of prisoners' rights, such as correspondence[1], visits[2], leave[3] and prison conditions[4]. The Court has also considered the removal from association of a prisoner who subsequently committed suicide[5]. The Commission also examined a range of issues, including interference with correspondence with a solicitor[6] or with the court[7]; restrictions on lawyers' visits[8]; restrictions on television interviews[9]; solitary confinement[10]; imprisonment in a remote location[11]; the transfer of prisoners to Scotland[12]; denial of access to a telephone[13]; lockdown conditions[14]; parole, in particular the system of periodical reviews and the withdrawal of a release recommendation following an incident which resulted in the prisoner's being charged and acquitted[15]; the suspension of invalidity benefits during imprisonment[16]; and the position of child offenders in relation to remission[17]. The law governing mentally disordered offenders was considered in a case concerned with the absence of a judicial remedy allowing the periodic review of detention[18].

1   *Boyle and Rice v United Kingdom* (1988) A 131; *McCallum v United Kingdom* (1990) A 183; *Campbell v United Kingdom* (1992) A 233-A.

2   *Boyle and Rice v United Kingdom* (1988) A 131.

3   *Boyle and Rice v United Kingdom* (1988) A 131.

4   *McCallum v United Kingdom* (1990) A 183.

5   *Bollan v United Kingdom* (dec) 2000-V.

6   10621/83, *McComb v United Kingdom* (1986) DR 50, 81 (friendly settlement); 20075/92, *Leech v United Kingdom* (31 August 1994) (considering *Leech v Secretary of State for Scotland* 1993 SLT 365).

7   11392/85, *Hodgson v United Kingdom* (4 March 1987).

8   12323/86, *Campbell v United Kingdom* (1988) DR 57, 148.

9   12656/87, *K v United Kingdom* (13 May 1988).

10 12323/86, *Campbell v United Kingdom* (1988) DR 57, 148.

11 14462/88, *Ballantyne v United Kingdom* (12 April 1991).

12 15817/89, *Wakefield v United Kingdom* (1990) DR 66, 251.

13 18077/91, *Montes and Lopez v United Kingdom* (2 December 1992).

14 18942/91, *Windsor v United Kingdom* (6 April 1993); 25525/94, *Advic v United Kingdom* (6 September 1995).

15 20755/92, *Howden v United Kingdom* (10 October 1994), applying *Wynne v United Kingdom*.

16 27537/95, *Carlin v United Kingdom* (3 December 1997).

17 11077/84, *Nelson v United Kingdom* (1986) DR 49, 170.

18 10213/82 *Gordon v United Kingdom* (1985) DR 47, 36 (following *X v United Kingdom* (1981) A 46).

Civil procedure

1.16 The Court has considered excessive length of proceedings in the Court of Session[1] and in the processing of applications for social security benefits[2]. Aspects of civil procedure were also considered by the Commission in a number of cases. These included cases concerned with: a vexatious litigant order[3]; summary warrant procedure[4]; child maintenance review procedures[5]; directors' disqualification proceedings[6]; an unfair dismissal hearing before an industrial tribunal following acquittal in criminal proceedings[7]; the Warsaw Convention[8]; the treatment of a party litigant[9]; the adequacy of rights of appeal from the Lands Tribunal for Scotland[10]; procedure at public inquiry[11]; and the effect of developments in the common law on prior transactions[12].

1   *Richard Anderson v United Kingdom* (9 February 2010) (violation of fair hearing guarantees in respect of the length of proceedings in a dispute concerning the share of common repair costs).

2   *Wilson v United Kingdom* (dec) (10 March 2009).

3   11559/85, *H v United Kingdom* (1985) DR 45, 281.

4   25373/94, *Smith v United Kingdom* (29 November 1995); 25602/94, *ANM & Co v United Kingdom* (29 November 1995).

5   24875/94, *Logan v United Kingdom* (1996) DR 86, 74.

6   28530/95, *X v United Kingdom* (19 January 1998).

7   11882/85, *C v United Kingdom* (1987) DR 54, 162.

8   37650/97, *Manners v United Kingdom* (21 May 1998); 38698/97, *Sykes v United Kingdom* (21 May 1998).

9   13475/87, *Kay v United Kingdom* (2 May 1989).

10 13135/87, *S and Others v United Kingdom* (1988) DR 56, 268.

11 22301/93, *McKenzie v United Kingdom* (1 December 1993).

12 37857/97, *Bank of Scotland v United Kingdom* (21 October 1998), considering *Smith v Bank of Scotland* 1997 SC (HL) 10.

Parents and children

1.17 The Court has considered procedure at a children's hearing and parental rights in relation to an illegitimate child[1]; corporal punishment in schools[2]; procedures in the Court of Session for the enforcement of a contact order made by an English court[3]; custody proceedings[4]; and the failure of a local authority to protect children from serious abuse[5]. The Commission also considered the effects of a child maintenance order on access to the children and on religious observance[6]; corporal punishment in schools and 'philosophical convictions'[7]; the failure of the state to provide financial assistance for private education[8]; and the taking of children into care[9].

1   *McMichael v United Kingdom* (1995) A 307-B.

2   *Campbell and Cosans v United Kingdom* (1982) A 48 (merits); *Campbell and Cosans v United Kingdom* (1983) A 60 (just satisfaction).

3   *Glaser v United Kingdom* (19 September 2000).

4   *ML v United Kingdom* (dec) (20 March 2001).

5   *E and others v United Kingdom* (26 November 2002).

6   24875/94, *Logan v United Kingdom* (1996) DR 86, 74.

7   8566/79, *X, Y and Z v United Kingdom* (1982) DR 31, 50.

8   9461/81, *X and Y v United Kingdom* (1982) DR 31, 210.

9   19579/92, *B Family v United Kingdom* (4 April 1993).

Property

1.18 The protection of property has been considered in one Court judgment concerning the nationalisation of an industry, the adequacy of compensation and the assessment of compensation by a statutory tribunal[1].

1   *Lithgow v United Kingdom* (1986) A 102.

Miscellaneous issues

1.19 Two Court judgments arising from the participation of servicemen in nuclear tests raised a wide variety of issues concerning the duties of the Government to protect both the servicemen themselves and their future children; access to records; the recovery of documents; and (before the Commission) the interception of communications and the effectiveness of domestic remedies[1]. In another judgment, the Court considered mental health provisions and found that the imposition of the burden of proof upon a patient to show that detention was no longer necessary, together with the delay in determining a challenge to the deprivation of liberty, gave rise to violations of the Convention[2]. Another case concerned discrimination against widowers in connection with the grant of bereavement allowances for income tax purposes[3]. The Court has also considered the admissibility of cases concerning a failure to hold a fatal accident inquiry[4], the denial of criminal injuries compensation[5], the lawfulness of bridge tolls[6], the impact of the Gender Recognition Act 2004 upon an existing relationship[7], and anti-hunting legislation[8]. More recently, the Court applied its 'pilot judgment' procedure in respect of the blanket denial of the right to vote to convicted prisoners[9].

1   *McGinley and Egan v United Kingdom* 1998-III; 23413/94, *LCB v United Kingdom* 1998-III. The Commission's decision on admissibility in *McGinley and Egan* is 21825/93 (28 November 1995). Its decision on admissibility in *LCB* is reported at (1995) DR 83, 31. An application for revision of the *McGinley and Egan* judgment was refused in *McGinley and Egan v United Kingdom* (revision) 2000-I.

2   *Hutchison Reid v United Kingdom* 2003-IV.

3   *Smith v United Kingdom* (20 May 2008).

4   *Boyd and McColm v United Kingdom* (dec) (29 June 1999).

5   *Stuart v United Kingdom* (dec) (6 July 1999).

6   *Anderson v United Kingdom* (dec) (5 November 1999).

7   *R and F v United Kingdom* (dec) (28 November 2006).

8   *Friend v United Kingdom* (dec) (24 November 2009).

9   *Greens and MT v United Kingdom* (23 November 2010), discussed at para **2.81.** below.

1.20 A wide range of topics was considered by the Commission. One case concerned immigration law and Article 8 in respect of re-admission as a returning resident[1]: no special issue of Scots law arose. Other cases concerned a variety of issues, including: the interception of communications[2]; a closed shop.agreement[3]; compensation for the compulsory purchase of land[4]; differences between valuation for rating in Scotland and in England[5]; the security vetting of prospective employees[6]; the keeping of dossiers on individuals by the Security Services and others[7]; an employer's right to reprimand an employee who wrote to a newspaper without permission[8]; dismissal for a theft of which the employee had not been convicted[9]; the loss of tied accommodation[10]; privilege under the law of defamation[11]; the Crown's refusal to disclose a post-mortem report to a relative of the deceased[12]; and issues relating to company law[13].

1   25525/94, *Advic v United Kingdom* (6 September 1995).

2   21482/93, *Christie v United Kingdom* (1994) DR 78, 119.

3   9520/81, *Reid v United Kingdom* (1983) DR 34, 107.

4   13135/87, *S v United Kingdom* (1988) DR 56, 268.

5   13473/87, *P v United Kingdom* (11 July 1988).

6   12015/86, *Hilton v United Kingdom* (1988) DR 57, 108. This decision contains a discussion of the status of the BBC under the ECHR.

7   12015/86, *Hilton v United Kingdom* (1988) DR 57, 108.

8   16936/90, *Todd v United Kingdom* (7 November 1990).

9   28530/95, *X v United Kingdom* (19 January 1998).

10   28530/95, *X v United Kingdom* (19 January 1998).

11   22301/93, *McKenzie v United Kingdom* (1 December 1993).

12   11516/85, *B v United Kingdom* (13 May 1986).

13   11413/85, *A v United Kingdom* (13 May 1986).

THE ECHR IN THE SCOTTISH COURTS PRIOR TO THE 1998 ACTS

1.21 The Scottish courts were relatively slow to make use of the ECHR. In *Kaur v Lord Advocate* Lord Ross expressed the view (obiter[1]) that a Scottish court was not entitled to have regard to the ECHR, either as an aid to construction or otherwise, unless and until its provisions were given statutory effect[2]. That view was approved by the Inner House (again, obiter) in *Moore v Secretary of State for Scotland*[3]. These decisions discouraged reference to the ECHR in Scottish cases for many years (although such references appeared in the speeches in the House of Lords in *Lord Advocate v Scotsman Publications Ltd*[4]), and contrasted with the approach adopted in England and Wales, not least by Scottish judges sitting in the House of Lords[5].

1   There was conceded to be no ambiguity in the legislation in issue, and thus no room for the use of the Convention as an aid to interpretation.

2   *Kaur v Lord Advocate* 1980 SC 319. The presumption that Parliament does not intend to legislate in a manner inconsistent with the treaty obligations entered into by the Crown had previously been accepted in Scots Law: see eg *Mortensen v Peters* (1906) 8 F (J) 93.

3   *Moore v Secretary of State for Scotland* 1985 SLT 38.

4   *Lord Advocate v Scotsman Publications Ltd* 1989 SC (HL) 122.

5   Eg *Waddington v Miah* [1974] 1 WLR 683 at 694 per Lord Reid; *Attorney-General v British Broadcasting Corporation* [1981] AC 303 at 352 per Lord Fraser of Tullybelton.

1.22 The ECHR nevertheless began to have an impact upon the Scottish courts, particularly through a number of decisions of the European Court of Human Rights concerned with Scottish criminal proceedings. The first of these decisions, *Granger v United Kingdom*[1], resulted in the issue of a Practice Note by Lord Justice-General Emslie, providing for a procedure whereby the High Court of Justiciary (as a court of appeal) could recommend the review of a decision of the legal aid authorities to refuse legal aid for representation at an appeal hearing. Subsequently, the cases of *Boner v United Kingdom*[2] and *Maxwell v United Kingdom*[3] resulted in a major alteration of the criminal appeal system in Scotland, so as to end the automatic right of appeal against conviction or sentence and to introduce a requirement that leave to appeal must be obtained. The High Court's awareness of the implications of the ECHR was reflected in *Anderson v HM Advocate*, where Lord Hope of Craighead referred to Article 6 as describing

'... principles which ... have, for a long time, been established as part of the law of this country'[4].

1   *Granger v United Kingdom* (1990) A 174.

2   *Boner v United Kingdom* (1994) A 300-B.

3   *Maxwell v United Kingdom a:* (1994) A 300-C.

4   *Anderson v HM Advocate* 1996 JC 29 at 34.

1.23 Following his appointment as Lord President and Lord Justice-General, Lord Hope made clear extra-judicially his concerns over the difference in approach to the ECHR between the Scottish and English courts, and the consequent reluctance of Scottish counsel to make use of the ECHR in argument[1]. Subsequently, in *T, Petitioner*, he took the opportunity to review the status of the ECHR in Scots law[2]. In relation to *Kaur*[3], he stated:

'Lord Ross's opinion, although widely quoted in the textbooks as still representing the law of Scotland on this matter, has been looking increasingly outdated in the light of subsequent developments, and in my opinion, with respect, it is time that it was expressly departed from.'[4]

Lord Hope then reviewed the series of English cases in the House of Lords, culminating in *R v Secretary of State for the Home Department, ex p Brind*[5], which had established that in construing any provision in domestic legislation which is ambiguous in the sense that it is capable of a meaning which either conforms to or conflicts with the ECHR, the courts will presume that Parliament intended to legislate in a manner compatible with the ECHR. Lord Hope concluded:

'I consider that the drawing of a distinction between the law of Scotland and that of the rest of the United Kingdom on this matter can no longer be justified. In my opinion the courts in Scotland should apply the same presumption as that described by Lord Bridge [in *ex p Brind*], namely that, when legislation is found to be ambiguous in the sense that it is capable of a meaning which either conforms to or conflicts with the Convention, Parliament is to be presumed to have legislated in conformity with the Convention, not in conflict with it.'[6]

1   1991 JR 122 at 126–127; 'From Maastricht to the Saltmarket', Society of Solicitors in the Supreme Courts of Scotland, Biennial Lecture 1992, at 16–17. See also Lord Hope of Craighead 'Devolution and Human Rights' [1998] EHRLR 367.

2   *T, Petitioner* 1997 SLT 724.

3   *Kaur v Lord Advocate* 1980 SC 319.

4   *T, Petitioner* 1997 SLT 724 at 733.

5   *R v Secretary of State for the Home Department, ex p Brind* [1991] 1 AC 696.

6   *T, Petitioner* 1997 SLT 724 at 734.

1.24 Following *T, Petitioner* the ECHR was cited with increasing frequency in the Scottish courts, and was applied in the same way as in England and Wales[1]. The Convention was thus influencing the law in Scotland before the commencement of the SA 1998 or the HRA 1998, and can continue to do so, in appropriate cases, even where those statutes do not apply.

1   See eg *McLeod v HM Advocate (No 2)* 1998 JC 67; *Cox and Griffiths, Petitioners* 1998 JC 267; *Ucak v HM Advocate* 1998 JC 283; *Shaw, Petitioner; Milne, Petitioner* 1998 SCCR 672; *Megrahi v Times Newspapers Ltd* 1999 JC 22; *Gayne v Vannet* 2000 JC 51; *Abdadou v Secretary of State for the Home Department* 1998 SC 504; *Ward v Scotrail Railways Ltd* 1999 SC 255; *Booker Aquaculture Ltd v Secretary of State for Scotland* 2000 SC 9; *Akhtar v Secretary of State for the Home Department* 2001 SLT 1239.

THE HUMAN RIGHTS ACT 1998

1.25 The Government elected in May 1997 had a manifesto commitment to a programme of constitutional reform, including the 'incorporation' of the ECHR into UK law. The White Paper *Rights Brought Home* announced the Government's intention to

'... give people in the United Kingdom1 opportunities to enforce their rights under the ECHR in British Courts rather than having to incur the cost and delay of taking a case to the European Human Rights Court in Strasbourg.'[2]

1   Despite the language used at this time, it is clear that the HRA 1998 may in certain circumstances have extra-territorial scope: *R (Al-Skeini and Others) v Secretary of State for Defence* [2008] 1 AC 153.

2   Cm 3782 (1997) p 1.

1.26 The Human Rights Act 1998, which came into force on 2 October 2000, seeks to fulfil that intention through, in particular, the introduction of the following obligations:

1.   So far as it is possible to do so, primary legislation and subordinate legislation must be read and given effect in a way which is compatible with the Convention rights[1].

2.   If the court is satisfied that a provision of primary legislation is incompatible with a Convention right, it may make a declaration of that incompatibility[2]. In that event, a Minister of the Crown may by order make such amendments to the legislation as he considers necessary to remove the incompatibility[3].

3.   It is unlawful for a public authority (including a court or tribunal) to act in a way which is incompatible with a Convention right, unless the authority could not have acted differently as the result of primary legislation, or it was acting so as to give effect to or enforce primary legislation (or provisions made under such legislation) which cannot be read or given effect in a way which is compatible with the Convention right[4].

4.   A Minister of the Crown in charge of a Bill in either House of Parliament must, before the Second Reading of the Bill, make a statement about the compatibility of the Bill with Convention rights[5].

1   HRA 1998, s 3.
2   HRA 1998, s 4.
3   HRA 1998, s 10.
4   HRA 1998, s 6.
5   HRA 1998, s 19.

1.27 The significance of the HRA 1998 was explained by Lord Rodger of Earlsferry in *Wilson v First County Trust Ltd (No 2)*:

'Although the Act is not entrenched, the Convention rights that it confers have a peculiar potency. Enforcing them may require a court to modify the common law. So far as possible, a court must read and give effect to statutory provisions in a way that is compatible with them. Rights that can produce such results are clearly of a higher order than the rights which people enjoy at common law or under most other statutes ... The 1998 Act is unusual – perhaps unique – in its range. Whilst most statutes apply to one particular topic or area of law, the 1998 Act works as a catalyst across the board, wherever a Convention right is engaged. It may affect matters of substance in such areas as the law of property, the law of marriage and the law of torts. Or else it may affect civil and criminal procedure, or the procedure of administrative tribunals.'[1]

1   *Wilson v First County Trust Ltd (No 2)* [2004] 1 AC 816 at paras 180 and 182.

1.28 It has been observed that it is undesirable that there should be conflicting decisions in Scotland and in England on the interpretation of the HRA 1998; and the High Court of Justiciary has therefore followed a decision of the House of Lords on an English appeal, in the interests of consistency, where the English interpretation was not clearly wrong[1]. A further safeguard against inconsistency is provided by the possibility of an appeal to the Supreme Court.

1   *Dickson v HM Advocate* 2008 JC 181.

Convention rights

1.29 The HRA 1998, s 1 defines the Convention rights to which effect is given. These are the rights and fundamental freedoms set out in Articles 2 to 12 and 14 of the Convention; Articles 1 to 3 of Protocol no 1, and Article 1 of Protocol no 13, as read with Articles 16 to 18 of the Convention[1]. The definition of 'Convention rights' may be amended to reflect the effect of an additional protocol which the United Kingdom has ratified (or has signed with a view to ratification)[2]. The 'Convention rights' therefore do not include Articles 1 and 13 of the ECHR. That is because the HRA 1998 is intended itself to give effect to Articles 1 and 13[3]. The articles setting out Convention rights are to have effect for the purposes of the HRA 1998 subject to any designated derogation or reservation, as provided by ss 14 and 15 of the Act[4]. In addition, the term 'Convention' is defined by s 21 as meaning the ECHR 'as it has effect for the time being in relation to the United Kingdom'. Convention rights therefore do not include the rights under the ECHR and its Protocols which have been extended by the UK under Article 56 (or equivalent provisions in the protocols) to other territories[5]. Similarly, to the extent that the UK's obligations under the ECHR are qualified by its obligations under the UN Charter, the Convention right in question does not have 'effect ... in relation to the United Kingdom' for the purposes of the HRA 1998[6].

The Convention rights in Sch 1 are distinct obligations in the domestic legal systems of the United Kingdom. The Act does not incorporate into our domestic law the international law obligations under the ECHR as such[7].

1   HRA 1998, s 1(1), as amended (with effect from 22 June 2004) by the Human Rights Act (Amendment) Order 2004, SI 2004/1574. As originally enacted, s 1 referred to Arts 1 and 2 of the Sixth Protocol, but those provisions (which abolished the death penalty in most circumstances) were superseded by the UK's ratification of the Thirteenth Protocol.

2   HRA 1998, s 1(4). The power is now exercisable by the Lord Chancellor: Transfer of Functions (Miscellaneous) Order 2001, SI 2001/3500.

3   Article 1 bears on the territorial application of the HRA 1998: see paras **1.75** and **3.03–3.14** below. As to Art 13, see *Montgomery v HM Advocate* 2001 SC (PC) 1 at 16 per Lord Hope of Craighead; *Brown v Stott* 2001 SC (PC) 43 at 70 per Lord Hope of Craighead; *Re S (Minors) (Care Order: Implementation of Care Plan)* [2002] 2 AC 291 at paras 60–61 per Lord Nicholls of Birkenhead (legislation which fails to provide an effective remedy for an infringement of a Convention right is not for that reason incompatible with a Convention right; but HRA 1998, ss 7 and 8 seek to provide such a remedy); and *Aston Cantlow and Wilmcote with Billesley Parochial Church Council v Wallbank* [2004] 1 AC 546 at para 44 per Lord Hope of Craighead. It should be borne in mind that HRA 1998 itself has to be interpreted in accordance with the ECHR in so far at least as it may be ambiguous, given the purpose of the HRA 1998, and bearing in mind the principle in *T, Petitioner* (see paras **1.23** and **1.24** above); cf *R (Al-Skeini) v Secretary of State for Defence* [2008] 1 AC 153 at paras 147–149 per Lord Brown of Eaton-under-Heywood.

4   HRA 1998, s 1(2). As to ss 14 and 15, see paras **1.106** and **1.107** below.

5   *R (Quark Fishing Ltd) v Secretary of State for Foreign and Commonwealth Affairs* [2006] 1
     AC 529; *R (Barclay) v Lord Chancellor and Secretary of State for Justice* [2010] 1 AC 464. *A
     fortiori,* they do not apply where there has been no extension under Art 56: *R (Bancoult) v
     Secretary of State for Foreign and Commonwealth Affairs (No 2)* [2009] 1 AC 453.

6   *R (Al-Jedda) v Secretary of State for Defence* [2008] 1 AC 332, especially per Lord Rodger of
     Earlsferry at paras 54 and 112.

7   See paras **1.02–1.03** and **1.05** above.

The duty to 'take into account' Strasbourg jurisprudence

1.30 The HRA 1998, s 2 provides that a court or tribunal determining a question
which has arisen in connection with a Convention right must take into account
any judgment, decision or declaration or advisory opinion of the European Court
of Human Rights[1], any opinion of the Commission given in a report adopted under
Article 31 of the ECHR (ie any opinion on the merits of an application), any
opinion of the Commission in connection with Articles 26 or 27(2) (ie any decision
on admissibility) or any decision of the Committee of Ministers taken under Article
46, so far as relevant to the proceedings. In practice, the most important of these
sources are judgments of the European Court of Human Rights on the merits of
applications, and decisions of the Court on their admissibility. The Commission
ceased to exist under the revised structure established by Protocol 11 to the
ECHR (with effect from 1 November 1998). Its admissibility decisions and Article
31 reports can be a useful source, but have less authority than judgments and
decisions of the Court. Decisions of the Committee of Ministers (which are taken
under Article 46 in connection with its supervision of the implementation of a
judgment) are unlikely to be of practical significance. Any authoritative report is
sufficient evidence of a judgment, etc. Judgments of the Grand Chamber take
precedence under the ECHR case law over those of Chambers, and equally
carry the greatest weight under the HRA 1998, s 2. Similarly, under the system
which existed until 1 November 1998, judgments of a plenary court carry greater
authority than those of a chamber.

1   For discussion as to the relevance of comparative material, see eg *R (Daly) v Secretary of State
     for the Home Department* [2001] 2 AC 532 at para 30 per Lord Cooke of Thorndon; and *R v
     Lambert* [2002] 2 AC 545 at para 40 per Lord Steyn. Such material can only be of persuasive
     effect: see *Brown v Stott* 2001 SC (PC) 43 at 78 per Lord Hope of Craighead.

1.31 It is apparent from the terms of the HRA 1998, s 2 that a court or tribunal is
not bound to follow Strasbourg case-law:

'[A] court adjudicating in litigation in the United Kingdom about a domestic
"Convention right" is not bound by a decision of the Strasbourg court. It must take
it into account.'[1]

At the same time, it has been said that in the absence of some special
circumstances any clear and constant jurisprudence of the European Court of

Human Rights should be followed[2]. In particular, a court should not without good reason depart from the principles laid down in a carefully considered judgment of the Grand Chamber[3]. The domestic court can, however, decline to follow a Strasbourg judgment where the Strasbourg Court appears to have misunderstood domestic law[4], or where the domestic court has concerns as to whether a decision of the Strasbourg Court sufficiently appreciates or accommodates particular aspects of the domestic process[5]. Where the jurisprudence of the European Court of Human Rights is not consistent, particular weight is likely to be accorded to judgments of the Grand Chamber[6].

1   *Re McKerr* [2004] 1 WLR 807 at para 64 per Lord Hoffmann.

2   *R (Ullah) v Special Adjudicator* [2004] 2 AC 323 at para 20 per Lord Bingham of Cornhill. See also *R (Alconbury Developments Ltd) v Secretary of State for the Environment, Transport and the Regions* [2003] 2 AC 295 at para 26 per Lord Slynn of Hadley; *R (S) v Chief Constable of South Yorkshire* [2004] 1 WLR 2196 at para 29 per Lord Steyn; *R (SB) v Governors of Denbigh High School* [2007] 1 AC 100 at para 29 per Lord Bingham of Cornhill; *Huang v Secretary of State for the Home Department* [2007] 2 AC 167 at para 18; *Manchester City Council v Pinnock* [2010] 3 WLR 1441.

3   *R (Anderson) v Secretary of State for the Home Department* [2003] 1 AC 837 at para 18 per Lord Bingham of Cornhill; *Secretary of State for the Home Department v AF (No 3)* [2010] 2 AC 269 ('*Argentoratum locutum, iudicium finitum* – Strasbourg has spoken, the case is closed', per Lord Rodger JSC at para 98).

4   *R v Lyons* [2003] 1 AC 976 at para 46 per Lord Hoffmann; *R v Spear* [2003] 1 AC 734 at para 12 per Lord Hoffmann; *Kay v Lambeth London Borough Council* [2006] 2 AC 46 at para 28 per Lord Bingham of Cornhill; *Doherty v Birmingham City Council* [2009] 1 AC 367.

5   *R v Horncastle* [2010] 2 AC 373 at para 11 per Lord Phillips PSC, paras 117–120 per Lord Brown JSC.

6   See eg *R (Al-Skeini) v Secretary of State for Defence* [2008] 1 AC 153.

1.32 The fact that the ECHR is an international treaty has certain consequences. One is that the role of a national court in interpreting the ECHR is limited. In particular, the court should not expand domestic protection, by means of interpretation of the ECHR, beyond the law as developed by the Strasbourg Court:

> 'This reflects the fact that the Convention is an international instrument, the correct interpretation of which can be authoritatively expounded only by the Strasbourg court … It is of course open to member states to provide for rights more generous than those guaranteed by the Convention, but such provision should not be the product of interpretation of the Convention by national courts, since the meaning of the Convention should be uniform throughout the states party to it. The duty of national courts is to keep pace with the Strasbourg jurisprudence as it evolves over time: no more, but certainly no less.'[1]

On the other hand, where the question is one falling within the margin of appreciation allowed to states by the European Court of Human Rights, it may be open to UK courts to exercise that appreciation in their interpretation of the scope of the Convention rights protected by the HRA 1998. It was said by Lord Mance in *In re G (Adoption: Unmarried Couple)*:

'It would be contrary to the Strasbourg court's purpose, and circular, if national authorities were to take the view that they should not consider any question other than whether a particular solution was within the United Kingdom's margin of appreciation. Under the 1998 Act, United Kingdom authorities (legislators and courts) have domestically to address the impact of the domestically enacted Convention rights in the particular context of the United Kingdom.'[2]

1 *R (Ullah) v Special Adjudicator* [2004] 2 AC 323 at para 20 per Lord Bingham of Cornhill; cf *Brown v Stott* 2001 SC (PC) 43 at 59 per Lord Bingham of Cornhill: '... the process of implication [of terms into the ECHR] is one to be carried out with caution, if the risk is to be averted that the contracting parties may, by judicial interpretation, become bound by obligations which they did not expressly accept and might not have been willing to accept'; *N v Secretary of State for the Home Department* [2005] 2 AC 296 at para 25 per Lord Hope of Craighead: 'It is for the Strasbourg court, not for [domestic courts], to decide whether its case law is out of touch with modern conditions ... We must take its case law as we find it, not as we would like it to be'; and *M v Secretary of State for Work and Pensions* [2006] 2 AC 91 at para 136 per Lord Mance: national courts may 'provide for rights more generous than those guaranteed by the Convention, though not as the product of interpretation of the Convention'. See also *R (Al-Skeini) v Secretary of State for Defence* [2008] 1 AC 153, especially at para 90 per Baroness Hale of Richmond and at paras 105–107 per Lord Brown of Eaton-under-Heywood; and *R (Smith) v Oxfordshire Assistant Deputy Coroner* [2011] 1 AC 1 at para 60 per Lord Phillips. It has been noted that, 'in an evolving area, a domestic court may perhaps have to consider whether relatively elderly jurisprudence reflects the result that the court would still reach': *M v Secretary of State for Work and Pensions* [2006] 2 AC 91 at para 131 per Lord Mance.

2 *In re G (Adoption: Unmarried Couple)* [2009] 1 AC 173 at para 130; see also paras 29–38 per Lord Hoffmann, para 50 per Lord Hope of Craighead and paras 119–120 per Baroness Hale of Richmond; contrast paras 79 and 82 per Lord Walker of Gestingthorpe. This matter is discussed further at paras 3.142–3.147 and below.

1.33 There may also on occasion be a difference in approach between domestic courts and the European Court of Human Rights as to the interpretation of particular guarantees. In *R (RJM) v Secretary of State for Work and Pensions,* the House of Lords held that lower courts should continue to follow any binding decision of the House of Lords, even if the precedent was considered to be in conflict with the case law of the European Court of Human Rights, unless there were 'wholly exceptional circumstances'[1]. On the other hand, where the Court of Appeal concluded that one of its own previous decisions was inconsistent with a subsequent decision of the European Court of Human Rights, it was free (but not obliged) to depart from that decision[2]. In *Doherty v Birmingham City Council*[3], the House of Lords decided that it should follow its own recent decision notwithstanding that the European Court of Human Rights had subsequently disagreed with its reasoning[4]. The Supreme Court subsequently departed from the decision in *Doherty* when it became unambiguously clear that the decision was incompatible with the Convention as interpreted by the Strasbourg Court[5].

1 *R (RJM) v Secretary of State for Work and Pensions* [2009] 1 AC 311 at para 64 per Lord Neuberger of Abbotsbury. As to what would constitute exceptional circumstances, Lord Neuberger referred to the exceptional features identified by Lord Bingham of Cornhill in *Kay v Lambeth London Borough Council* [2006] 2 AC 46 at para 45 as justifying the approach taken by the Court of Appeal in *D v East Berkshire Community NHS Trust* [2004] QB 558.

2   *R (RJM) v Secretary of State for Work and Pensions* [2009] 1 AC 311 at para 66 per Lord Neuberger of Abbotsbury.

3   *Doherty v Birmingham City Council* [2009] 1 AC 367.

4   In *McCann v United Kingdom* 2008-....

5   *Manchester City Council v Pinnock* [2010] 3 WLR 1441. The decision followed the Strasbourg court's judgment in *Kay and Others v United Kingdom* (21 September 2010).

Legislation and the Human Rights Act

Legislative proposals: statements of compatibility

1.34 The HRA 1998, s 19 requires a Minister of the Crown[1] in charge of a Bill in either House of Parliament to make a statement[2], before the second reading of the Bill, either to the effect that in his view the provisions of the Bill are compatible with the Convention rights ('a statement of compatibility') or to the effect that although he is unable to make a statement of compatibility the Government nevertheless wishes the House to proceed with the Bill[3]. A statement of compatibility has been made in respect of almost every Bill introduced since the HRA 1998 received Royal Assent[4]. An analogous practice has been adopted in respect of statutory instruments[5].

1   As defined by HRA 1998, s 21(1).

2   The statement must be in writing and be published in such manner as the Minister making it considers appropriate: HRA 1998, s 19(2).

3   HRA 1998, s 19(1). Although this provision does not apply to the Scottish Parliament, analogous provision is made by the SA 1998, s 31(1). A statement made to the Westminster Parliament probably does not give rise to a justiciable issue, by virtue of Parliamentary privilege under the Bill of Rights 1688. That privilege does not, however, apply to the Scottish Parliament: *Whaley v Watson* 2000 SC 340. As to the possible effects of a compatibility statement in legal proceedings, see *A v Scottish Ministers* 2002 SC (PC) 63 at 66–67 per Lord Hope of Craighead. For discussion, see Lester, 'Parliamentary Scrutiny of Legislation under the Human Rights Act 1998' [2002] EHRLR 432.

4   There have been two exceptions. One was the Local Government Bill 1999, because clause 91 sought to reaffirm the provisions of s 2A of the Local Government Act 1986 (concerning sex education in schools), which appeared to be incompatible with Convention rights (eg possibly those of homosexuals and their families, under Art 8, or those of teachers under Art 10). The other exception concerned the Communications Act 2003, s 321, which prohibits political advertising. The Government's hesitation arose from the judgment of the European Court of Human Rights in *VgT Verein gegen Tierfabriken v Switzerland* 2001-VI. In the event, s 321 was held to be compatible with Convention rights: *R (Animal Defenders International) v Secretary of State for Culture, Media and Sport* [2008] 1 AC 1312.

5   See House of Lords Select Committee on Delegated Powers and Deregulation, 1st Report, Session 1999–2000, Annex 6; also 608 HL Official Report (5th series) written answers col 76 (10 January 2000).

The Joint Committee on Human Rights

1.35 Parliamentary consideration of the compatibility of Bills with human rights (and of other matters concerning human rights in the UK) has also been greatly strengthened by the establishment of the Joint Committee on Human Rights[1].

1   This is a committee of both Houses of Parliament whose terms of reference include consideration of matters relating to human rights in the UK (excluding individual cases) and proposals for remedial orders under HRA 1998, s 10. The reports of the Committee have been discussed in numerous cases: see eg *YL v Birmingham City Council* [2008] 1 AC 95 and *R (Animal Defenders International) v Secretary of State for Culture, Media and Sport* [2008] 1 AC 1312.

Statutory interpretation

1.36 The HRA 1998, s 3 requires primary legislation and subordinate legislation[1] to be read and given effect in a way that is compatible with the Convention rights[2], so far as it is possible to do so[3]. This provision is of great significance. It applies to legislation whenever enacted[4], and may therefore require established interpretations to be re-examined. Lord Nicholls of Birkenhead has observed that s 3 is:

'... a powerful tool whose use is obligatory. It is not an optional canon of construction. Nor is its use dependent on the existence of ambiguity.5 Further, the section applies retrospectively.'[6]

1   The question whether this might cover rules made under a private Act of Parliament was considered, but not decided, in *Royal Society for the Prevention of Cruelty to Animals v Attorney General* [2002] 1 WLR 448. 'Legislation' means legislation enacted in Great Britain and Northern Ireland: *R (Al-Skeini) v Secretary of State for Defence* [2008] 1 AC 153 at para 139 per Lord Brown of Eaton-under-Heywood. The Immigration Rules are not 'subordinate legislation' as defined by s 21(1): *Pankina v Secretary of State for the Home Department* [2011] QB 376.

2   That is to say, so as to avoid a breach of a Convention right under domestic law. There may be a breach of the ECHR without there being a breach of a Convention right under domestic law eg by reason of the non-retrospectivity of the HRA 1998: see *R (Hurst) v London Northern District Coroner* [2007] 2 AC 189 at paras 43–44 per Lord Brown of Eaton-under-Heywood.

3   HRA 1998, s 3(1).

4   HRA 1998, s 3(2)(a). Thus it has been applied to override the intention of Parliament when enacting legislation subsequent to the HRA 1998: see eg *Sheldrake v Director of Public Prosecutions* [2005] 1 AC 264 at para 53, per Lord Bingham of Cornhill. It has been said that s 3 applies to the interpretation of the HRA itself: *R v Lambert* [2002] 2 AC 545 at para 110, per Lord Hope of Craighead; *R (Al-Skeini) v Secretary of State for Defence* [2008] 1 AC 153 at paras 146–147 per Lord Brown of Eaton-under-Heywood; *contra*, para 15 per Lord Bingham of Cornhill. The SA 1998 must be construed in accordance with the HRA 1998, s 3. The new interpretation of legislation, consequent on an application of s 3, does not however apply to pre-HRA 1998 events, and in particular does not alter rights which had accrued or vested before s 3 came into force (on 2 October 2000): see *Wilson v First County Trust Ltd (No 2)* [2004] 1 AC 816. Nor can s 3(1) be applied to invalidate a decision which was good at the time when it was made: *Aston Cantlow and Wilmcote with Billesley Parochial Church Council v Wallbank* [2004] 1 AC 546 at para 29 per Lord Hope of Craighead.

5   See eg *R v A (No 2)* [2002] 1 AC 45.

6   *Re S (Minors) (Care Order: Implementation of Care Plan)* [2002] 2 AC 291 at para 37.

1.37 The obligation imposed by s 3 does not affect the validity, continuing operation or enforcement of any incompatible primary legislation, or of any incompatible subordinate legislation if (disregarding the possibility of revocation) primary legislation prevents removal of the incompatibility[1]. The HRA 1998 therefore does not impliedly repeal previous legislation enacted by the UK Parliament which is incompatible with Convention rights, or prevent the enactment of subsequent legislation by the UK Parliament which is incompatible with Convention rights. Nor does it affect subordinate legislation which cannot, by reason of primary legislation, be interpreted compatibly with the Convention. Subject to that proviso, however, the courts are generally required (by virtue of their obligation to act compatibly with Convention rights, under the HRA 1998, s 6) to disregard subordinate legislation which cannot be interpreted or given effect in a way which is compatible with Convention rights[2]. It has been said that a finding that delegated legislation is *ultra vires* should normally result in the legislation being quashed[3].

1   HRA 1998, s 3(2)(b) and (c).

2   *In re G (Adoption: Unmarried Couple)* [2009] 1 AC 173. For an example, see *Miller v Bull* [2010] 1 WLR 1861. See also *Francis v Secretary of State for Work and Pensions* [2006] 1 WLR 3202, where a declaration was granted. In relation to issues arising in relation to legal certainty, see paras **1.115**, **1.153** and **3.63** below. In relation to special provisions concerning Scottish subordinate legislation, see paras **1.39** and **1.154** below.

3   *R (C) (A Minor) v Secretary of State for Justice* [2009] QB 657. In relation to the status of statutory instruments whose vires are challenged, see generally such authorities as *Smith v East Elloe RDC* [1956] AC 736, *Agricultural etc Training Board v Aylesbury Mushrooms Ltd* [1972] 1 WLR 190 and *Boddington v British Transport Police* [1999] AC 143.

1.38 Since the object of the HRA 1998, s 3 is to avoid, where possible, action by a public authority which would be unlawful under s 6 as incompatible with Convention rights, the interpretative duty under s 3 arises only where there would otherwise be a breach of Convention rights under domestic law. It follows that the same legislation may be interpreted differently in different cases, depending on whether or not the ordinary construction of the legislation would result in a breach of Convention rights in the particular case in question. For example, since s 6 did not apply to a coroner in respect of deaths occurring prior to 2 October 2000, and applied in relation to subsequent deaths only if they involved actual or potential state responsibility under Article 2 of the ECHR, it was only in relation to the latter category of deaths that s 3 could be relevant to the interpretation of the legislation applicable to coroners[1].

1   *R (Hurst) v London Northern District Coroner* [2007] 2 AC 189.

1.39 Acts of the Scottish Parliament, and certain instruments made by Scottish Ministers, are 'subordinate legislation' as defined in the HRA 1998[1], and must therefore be construed in accordance with s 3.[2] The principle of interpretation contained in s 3 is different from that which has to be applied under the SA 1998 in determining whether Acts of the Scottish Parliament are within the legislative competence of the Parliament, or whether subordinate legislation is within the powers conferred on Scottish Ministers by that Act: where any provision in such legislation could be read in such a way as to be outside competence, it is to be read as narrowly as is required for it to be within competence, if such a reading is possible[3]. The relationship between the two principles of interpretation is discussed below[4].

1   HRA 1998, s 21(1).

2   *DS v HM Advocate* 2007 SC (PC) 1 at para 24 per Lord Hope of Craighead.

3   SA 1998, s 101. It should also be borne in mind that the Interpretation Act 1978 applies only in part to Acts of the Scottish Parliament: see SA 1998, Sch 8, para 16.

4   See para **1.121** below.

1.40 The HRA 1998, s 3 has been considered in a number of cases by the House of Lords and the Supreme Court. In *R (Wardle) v Crown Court at Leeds*, Lord Hope of Craighead drew attention to the need first to consider the ordinary construction of legislation before resorting to s 3:

> 'Section 3(1) of the 1998 Act provides that, so far as it is possible to do so, primary legislation and subordinate legislation must be read and given effect in a way which is compatible with Convention rights. This means that, if according to its ordinary construction1 [a provision] is incompatible with any of the Convention rights, a possible meaning for [the provision] must be found that will prevent the need for a declaration of incompatibility. But one must first be satisfied that the ordinary construction of the [provision] gives rise to an incompatibility.'[2]

Where the ordinary construction gives rise to an incompatibility, s 3 requires the legislation to be read and given effect in a way which is compatible with Convention rights 'so far as it is possible to do so'. As Lord Nicholls of Birkenhead asked in *Ghaidan v Godin-Mendoza*:

> 'What is the standard, or the criterion, by which "possibility" is to be judged? A comprehensive answer to this question is proving elusive. The courts ... are still cautiously feeling their way forward as experience in the application of section 3 gradually accumulates.'[3]

1   'Ordinary principles of statutory construction include a presumption that Parliament does not intend to legislate in a way which would put the United Kingdom in breach of its international obligations': *Ghaidan v Godin-Mendoza* [2004] 2 AC 557 at para 60 per Lord Millett.

2   *R (Wardle) v Crown Court at Leeds* [2002] 1 AC 754 at para 79.

3   *Ghaidan v Godin-Mendoza* [2004] 2 AC 557 at para 27.

1.41 Guidance as to the effect of s 3 was given by Lord Nicholls in *Re S (Minors) (Care Order: Implementation of Care Plan)*, in a speech with which the other members of the House expressed agreement:

> 'Section 3 is concerned with interpretation ... Section 4 (power to make declaration

of incompatibility) and, indeed, section 3(2)(b) presuppose that not all provisions in primary legislation can be rendered Convention compliant by the application of section 3(1) ...

In applying section 3 courts must be ever mindful of this outer limit. The Human Rights Act reserves the amendment of primary legislation to Parliament. By this means the Act seeks to preserve parliamentary sovereignty. The Act maintains the constitutional boundary. Interpretation of statutes is a matter for the courts; the enactment of statutes, and the amendment of statutes, are matters for Parliament.

... The area of real difficulty lies in identifying the limits of interpretation in a particular case. This is not a novel problem. If anything, the problem is more acute today than in past times. Nowadays courts are more "liberal" in the interpretation of all manner of documents. The greater the latitude with which courts construe documents, the less readily defined is the boundary ... For present purposes it is sufficient to say that a meaning which departs substantially from a fundamental feature of an Act of Parliament is likely to have crossed the boundary between interpretation and amendment. This is especially so where the departure has important practical repercussions which the court is not equipped to evaluate. In such a case the overall contextual setting may leave no scope for rendering the statutory provision Convention compliant by legitimate use of the process of interpretation. The boundary line may be crossed even though a limitation on Convention rights is not stated in express terms ...

I should add a further general observation ... When a court, called upon to construe legislation, ascribes a meaning and effect to the legislation pursuant to its obligation under section 3, it is important the court should identify clearly the particular statutory provision or provisions whose interpretation leads to that result. Apart from all else, this should assist in ensuring the court does not inadvertently stray outside its interpretation jurisdiction.'[1]

---

1   *Re S (Minors) (Care Order: Implementation of Care Plan)* [2002] 2 AC 291 at paras 38–41. For this reason, the decision at first instance in *Re Deep Vein Thrombosis* [2003] 1 All ER 935 that s 3 applies to the interpretation of an international convention, such as the Warsaw Convention, which has been given effect in the UK by incorporating it into legislation, appears to be questionable (cf *Abnett v British Airways plc* 1997 SC (HL) 26). The point was not considered on appeal. Contrast the decision in *ITP SA v Coflexip Stena Offshore Ltd* 2005 1 SC 116.

1.42 It has been said on a number of occasions that s 3 cannot be deployed if the legislation contains provisions which expressly, or by necessary implication, contradict the meaning which the enactment would have to be given to make it compatible with Convention rights[1]. That approach was clarified in *Ghaidan v Godin-Mendoza*, where the House of Lords decided that s 3 permits a court to read words into a legislative provision that otherwise would be unambiguously inconsistent with a Convention-compliant meaning (in the case in question, so as to treat homosexual partnerships in a manner similar to heterosexual partnerships), provided the Convention-compliant meaning is not inconsistent with a fundamental feature or underlying principle of the provision or of the legislation as a whole, and provided it does not require the court to address issues falling outside its province[2]. The principal focus of attention, in identifying the boundary between interpretation and amendment, is therefore not the linguistic form of the legislation in question, but rather its substance. In *Ghaidan*, Lord Rodger of Earlsferry observed:

> 'If the court implies words that are consistent with the scheme of the legislation but necessary to make it compatible with Convention rights, it is simply performing the duty which Parliament has imposed on it and on others. It is reading the legislation in a way that draws out the full implications of its terms and of the Convention rights. And, by its very nature, an implication will go with the grain of the legislation. By contrast, using a Convention right to read in words that are inconsistent with the scheme of the legislation or with its essential principles as disclosed by its provisions does not involve any form of interpretation, by implication or otherwise. It falls on the wrong side of the boundary between interpretation and amendment of the statute.
>
> ... The key to what is possible for the courts to imply into legislation without crossing the border from interpretation to amendment does not lie in the number of words that have to be read in. The key lies in a careful consideration of the essential principles and scope of the legislation being interpreted. If the insertion of one word contradicts those principles or goes beyond the scope of the legislation, it amounts to impermissible amendment. On the other hand, if the implication of a dozen words leaves the essential principles and scope of the legislation intact but allows it to be read in a way which is compatible with Convention rights, the implication is a legitimate exercise of the powers conferred by section 3(1) ...
>
> ... What matters is not so much the particular phraseology chosen by the draftsman as the substance of the measure which Parliament has enacted in those words ...
>
> Sometimes it may be possible to isolate a particular phrase which causes the difficulty and to read in words that modify it so as to remove the incompatibility. Or else the court may read in words that qualify the provisions as a whole. At other times the appropriate solution may be to read down the provision so that it falls to be given effect in a way that is compatible with the Convention rights in question. In other cases the easiest solution may be to put the offending part of the legislation into different words which convey the meaning that will be compatible with those rights ... It is enough that the interpretation placed on the provision should be clear, however it may be expressed and whatever the precise means adopted to achieve it.'[3]

In the same case, Lord Nicholls said:

> 'Section 3 may require a court to depart from the unambiguous meaning the legislation would otherwise bear ... that is, depart from the intention of the Parliament which enacted the legislation. The question of difficulty is how far, and in what circumstances, section 3 requires a court to depart from the intention of the enacting Parliament. The answer to this question depends upon the intention reasonably to be attributed to Parliament in enacting section 3.
>
> On this the first point to be considered is how far, when enacting section 3, Parliament intended that the actual language of a statute, as distinct from the concept expressed

in that language, should be determinative. Since section 3 relates to the "interpretation" of legislation, it is natural to focus attention initially on the language used in the legislative provision being considered. But once it is accepted that section 3 may require legislation to bear a meaning which departs from the unambiguous meaning the legislation would otherwise bear, it becomes impossible to suppose Parliament intended that the operation of section 3 should depend critically upon the particular form of words adopted by the parliamentary draftsman in the statutory provision under consideration. That would make the application of section 3 something of a semantic lottery. If the draftsman chose to express the concept being enacted in one form of words, section 3 would be available to achieve Convention-compliance. If he chose a different form of words, section 3 would be impotent.

From this the conclusion which seems inescapable is that the mere fact the language under consideration is inconsistent with a Convention-compliant meaning does not of itself make a Convention-compliant interpretation under section 3 impossible. Section 3 enables language to be interpreted restrictively or expansively. But section 3 goes further than this. It is also apt to require a court to read in words which change the meaning of the enacted legislation, so as to make it Convention-compliant. In other words, the intention of Parliament in enacting section 3 was that, to an extent bounded only by what is "possible", a court can modify the meaning, and hence the effect, of primary and secondary legislation.

Parliament, however, cannot have intended that in the discharge of this extended interpretative function the courts should adopt a meaning inconsistent with a fundamental feature of legislation. That would be to cross the constitutional boundary section 3 seeks to demarcate and preserve. Parliament has retained the right to enact legislation in terms which are not Convention-compliant. The meaning imported by application of section 3 must be compatible with the underlying thrust of the legislation being construed. Words implied must, in the phrase of my noble and learned friend, Lord Rodger of Earlsferry, "go with the grain of the legislation". Nor can Parliament have intended that section 3 should require courts to make decisions for which they are not equipped. There may be several ways of making a provision Convention-compliant, and the choice may involve issues calling for legislative deliberation.'[4]

---

1   *R v A (No 2)* [2002] 1 AC 45 at para 108 per Lord Hope of Craighead; *R (Anderson) v Secretary of State for the Home Department* [2003] 1 AC 837 at para 59 per Lord Steyn.

2   *Ghaidan v Godin-Mendoza* [2004] 2 AC 557.

3   *Ghaidan v Godin-Mendoza* [2004] 2 AC 557 at paras 121–124. See also *R v Lambert* [2002] 2 AC 545 at para 81 per Lord Hope of Craighead.

4   *Ghaidan v Godin-Mendoza* [2004] 2 AC 557 per Lord Nicholls of Birkenhead at paras 29–33. See also *R (Wilkinson) v Inland Revenue Commissioners* [2005] 1 WLR 1718 at paras 17–18 per Lord Hoffmann, whose approach is perhaps more readily understood as one of interpretation of the text of the legislation: 'the interpretation which the reasonable reader would give to the statute read against its background, including, now, an assumption that it was not intended to be incompatible with Convention rights'.

1.43 The circumstances in which an incompatibility can, or cannot, be resolved by recourse to s 3 are illustrated by the decided cases. In *Ghaidan v Godin-*

Mendoza, the social policy underlying the legislation giving security of tenure to the survivor of couples living together as husband and wife was equally applicable to the survivor of homosexual couples living together in a close and stable relationship[1]. In *R v A (No 2),* the legislation required the exclusion of evidence of prior sexual contact between the complainer and the defendant. Since such evidence could be relevant to the issue of consent, its exclusion could be incompatible with the Convention right to a fair trial. The statute was interpreted under s 3 as being subject to an implied proviso that such evidence was admissible if it was so relevant to the issue of consent that to exclude it would endanger the fairness of the trial[2]. In *R v Offen,* a provision requiring the imposition of an automatic life sentence unless there were 'exceptional circumstances' could be rendered Convention-compliant by giving that phrase a less restrictive interpretation[3]. In *R v Lambert,* the legal burden of proof placed on the defendant by the phrase 'if he proves' was incompatible with the ECHR. The phrase was therefore to be read as though it imposed only an evidential burden[4]. In *R (Sim) v Parole Board,* the provision in question was read as requiring the Parole Board to direct a recalled prisoner's release unless it was satisfied that the interests of the public required that his confinement should continue[5]. In *Manchester City Council v Pinnock,* a provision relating to possession orders which enabled the court to check that the statutory procedure had been followed was interpreted as enabling the court to check that the procedure had been 'lawfully' followed in accordance with Convention rights[6]. In *DS v HM Advocate,* in a particularly bold use of s 3, a statutory presumption to be applied by the court 'in entertaining an objection' by the accused to the disclosure of his previous record (namely, that its disclosure was in the interests of justice) was read as setting out the default position that would apply if the accused failed to make any objection: the presumption was to be disregarded when the court considered an objection which had been made[7]. In *R (Wright) v Secretary of State for Health,* a provision which enabled the Secretary of State to include care workers in a list of individuals considered unsuitable to work as carers of vulnerable adults was read as requiring the Secretary of State to afford workers an opportunity to make representations before being included in the list, unless she reasonably considered that the resultant delay would place a vulnerable adult at risk of harm[8]. In *Principal Reporter v K,* a definition of persons entitled to participate in a children's hearing, which was too restrictive to be compatible with Convention rights, was rendered Convention-compliant by reading in additional words[9].

1   *Ghaidan v Godin-Mendoza* [2004] 2 AC 557.

2   *R v A (No 2)* [2002] 1 AC 45. A similar approach was adopted to analogous Scottish legislation in *DS v HM Advocate* 2007 SC (PC) 1, eg at paras 46–48 per Lord Hope of Craighead. Other examples of implied qualifications being read into unqualified provisions include *R (Hammond) v Secretary of State for the Home Department* [2006] 1 AC 603 and *Secretary of State for the Home Department v MB* [2008] 1 AC 440. Contrast *R v Lyons* [2003] 1 AC 976 at para 45 per Lord Hoffmann: a provision that answers given by defendants under compulsion 'may be used in evidence' could not be interpreted so as to make it possible for such answers to be excluded.

3   *R v Offen* [2001] 1 WLR 253.

4   *R v Lambert* [2002] 2 AC 545. Similarly *R v Carass* [2002] 1 WLR 1714 (burden of proof on defendant accused of concealing debts in anticipation of winding up); *Sheldrake v Director of Public Prosecutions* [2005] 1 AC 264 (burden of proof on defendant under s 11(2) of the Terrorism Act 2000).

5   *R (Sim) v Parole Board* [2004] QB 1288. 6 *Manchester City Council v Pinnock* [2010] 3 WLR 1441.

7   *DS v HM Advocate* 2007 SC (PC) 1.

8   *R (Wright) v Secretary of State for Health* [2008] QB 422.

9   *Principal Reporter v K* 2011 SLT 271. Other examples of interpretation under s 3 include *R (Van Hoogstraten) v Governor of Belmarsh Prison* [2003] 1 WLR 263; and *R (Middleton) v West Somerset Coroner* [2004] 2 AC 182.

1.44 In other cases, however, the incompatibility could not be removed by recourse to s 3. In *International Transport Roth GmbH v Secretary of State for the Home Department,2:* for example, a fixed penalty scheme could not be rendered compatible with Convention rights without creating a wholly different scheme[1]. In *Re S (Minors) (Care Order: Implementation of Care Plan),* the proposed interpretation was inconsistent with an important aspect of the scheme of the legislation, and had far-reaching practical ramifications for local authorities[2]. In *R (Anderson) v Secretary of State for the Home Department,* the provision in question could not be read in a Convention-compliant way without giving it a meaning inconsistent with an important feature expressed clearly in the legislation[3]. Similarly in *Doherty v Birmingham City Council* it was said that s 3 'does not enable the court to change the substance of a provision from one where it says one thing into one that says the opposite'[4]. In *Bellinger v Bellinger,* the removal of the incompatibility would have involved problems of great complexity (such as where the line was to be drawn to mark the transition from one sex to the other), which had to be left to Parliament[5]. Similarly in *Smith v Scott* the court declined to 'read down' s 3(1) of the Representation of the People Act 1983 so as to modify the blanket ban on voting which applied to all convicted prisoners serving custodial sentences[6], observing that to do so:

'would be, in the phrase used by Lord Nicholls of Birkenhead in *Re S*[7], to depart substantially from a fundamental feature of the legislation. Without the benefit of consultation or advice, this Court would, in a real sense, be legislating on its own account, especially in view of the wide range of policy alternatives from which a "possible" solution would require to be selected.'[8]

1   *International Transport Roth GmbH v Secretary of State for the Home Department* [2003] QB 728.

2   *Re S (Minors) (Care Order: Implementation of Care Plan)* [2002] 2 AC 291.

3   *R (Anderson) v Secretary of State for the Home Department* [2003] 1 AC 837. For similar reasons, any incompatibility in the provisions of the Children (Scotland) Act 1995 considered in *Dundee City Council v GK* 2006 SC 326 could not have been resolved by recourse to s 3: see at para 22 per Lord President Hamilton. Similarly, in *Gunn v Newman* 2001 SC 525 it was held that it was not possible to construe a provision which was subject to an exception in such a way that the exception invariably applied. In *ITP SA v Coflexip Stena Offshore Ltd* 2005 1 SC 116 it was not possible to invoke s 3 so as to qualify a statutory provision giving effect to

decisions of the Board of Appeal established under the European Patent Convention in accordance with that Convention.

4   *Doherty v Birmingham City Council* [2009] 1 AC 367 at para 49 per Lord Hope of Craighead.

5   *Bellinger v Bellinger* [2003] 2 AC 467.

6   *Smith v Scott* 2007 SC 345.

7   *Re S* [2002] 2 AC 291.

8   *Smith v Scott* 2007 SC 345, at para 27. See also *R (Wright) v Secretary of State for Health* [2009] 1 AC 739.

Declarations of incompatibility

1.45 The HRA 1998 does not affect the validity of Acts of Parliament which are incompatible with the ECHR. On the contrary, the Act preserves the traditional supremacy of Parliament. It recognizes that the United Kingdom can, by reason of legislation on the statute book, be in breach of the ECHR if Parliament should so choose, and it is the statute which must be upheld and applied by the courts. This situation is confirmed by the HRA 1998, s 4[1], which enables certain courts to make a declaration that a provision of primary legislation is incompatible with a Convention right. Such a declaration can also be made in respect of a provision of subordinate legislation where primary legislation prevents removal of the incompatibility. A declaration of incompatibility may be made if the provision in question is 'incompatible with a Convention right'. 'That will normally mean a real Convention right in issue in the proceedings, not a hypothetical Convention right which the claimant or someone else might have if the facts were different'[2]. The making of a declaration of incompatibility is a measure of last resort, since the obligation in respect of statutory interpretation contained in s 3 provides the prime remedial remedy[3]. Lord Hoffmann explained the structure of the provisions in *R (Nasseri) v Secretary of State for the Home Department*:

'The structure of the 1998 Act suggests that a declaration of incompatibility should be the last resort in a process of inquiry which begins with the question raised by section 6(1), namely, whether a public authority is acting in a way which is incompatible with a Convention right. If the answer is no, that should ordinarily be the end of the case. There will be no need to answer the hypothetical question of whether a statutory provision would have been incompatible with a Convention right if the public authority had been infringing it. On the other hand, if the answer is yes, the next question is whether, as a result of primary legislation, the public authority "could not have acted differently" or was acting "so as to give effect to or enforce" such primary legislation: see section 6(2). If the answer is yes, the public authority will not be acting unlawfully. In answering this question, the court is required by section 3 to interpret the primary legislation, so far as it is possible to do so, in a way which is compatible with Convention rights. If, despite such interpretation, the primary legislation makes the infringement of Convention rights lawful, the court may then make a declaration of incompatibility under section 4(2).'[4]

The court's powers under s 4 accordingly do not arise in a case where s 3 is inapplicable[5]. In practice, declarations of incompatibility have been granted in a considerable number of cases[6].

1   It is also confirmed by s 6(2).

2   *R (Nasseri) v Secretary of State for the Home Department* [2010] 1 AC 1 at para 17 per Lord Hoffmann.

3   *Wilson v First County Trust Ltd (No 2)* [2004] 1 AC 816; *Ghaidan v Godin-Mendoza* [2004] 2 AC 557 at paras 39 and 50 per Lord Steyn.

4   *R (Nasseri) v Secretary of State for the Home Department* [2010] 1 AC 1 at para 18.

5   *Wilson v First County Trust Ltd (No 2)* [2004] 1 AC 816.

6   A list was appended to the speech of Lord Steyn in *Ghaidan v Godin-Mendoza* [2004] 2 AC 557. For more recent examples, see eg *A v Secretary of State for the Home Department* [2005] 1 AC 98 (in respect of the indefinite detention of suspected international terrorists under the Anti-terrorism, Crime and Security Act 2001, s 23; *R (Morris) v Westminster City Council* [2006] 1 WLR 505 (in respect of a nationality requirement under s 185(4) of the Housing Act 1996); *R v Holding* [2006] 1 WLR 1040 (in relation to the Representation of the People Act 1975, s 75); and *Smith v Scott* 2007 SC 345.

1.46 Although an Act of the Scottish Parliament falls within the definition of 'subordinate legislation', the Parliament has no power to enact legislation which is incompatible with the Convention rights[1]. A declaration of incompatibility is accordingly not the appropriate remedy. The same would appear to apply to subordinate legislation made by a Scottish Minister, notwithstanding that it may fall within the definition of 'subordinate legislation' in the HRA 1998, since a Scottish Minister has no power to make subordinate legislation which is incompatible with Convention rights[2].

1   SA 1998, s 29.

2   SA 1998, s 57(2).

1.47 In Scottish proceedings, the courts which have the power to make a declaration of incompatibility are the Supreme Court, the Courts-Martial Appeal Court, the High Court of Justiciary sitting otherwise than as a trial court[1], and the Court of Session[2]. The expression 'Court of Session' has been construed in this context as extending to any court in Scotland consisting of judges of the Court of Session sitting in their capacity as such (eg the Registration Appeal Court)[3].

1   In relation to procedure, see *Stevens v HM Advocate* 2001 SCCR 948, discussed at para **1.150** below. The expression 'trial court' may not be confined to trial diets, bearing in mind that a preliminary diet takes place before the trial court: *Montgomery v HM Advocate* 2001 SC (PC) 1 at 14 per Lord Hope of Craighead.

2   HRA 1998, s 4(5) as amended by the Constitutional Reform Act 2005, Sch 9, para 66.

3   *Smith v Scott* 2007 SC 345.

1.48 A declaration of incompatibility does not affect the validity, continuing operation or enforcement of the provision in respect of which it is given, and is not binding on the parties to the proceedings in which it is made[1]. It has no effect in law other than to provide a minister with the opportunity, by way of delegated legislation, to use the powers conferred by the HRA 1998, s 10 and Sch 2. The award of expenses in cases in which a declaration of incompatibility is sought may raise difficult questions[2].

1   HRA 1998, s 4(6).
2   Cf *Motsepe v IRC* (1997) 6 BCLR 692 at 705 per Ackermann J [Constitutional Court of South Africa].

1.49 Rather than imposing a duty, the HRA 1998, s 4(2) confers a discretion on the court to make a declaration of incompatibility if it is satisfied that a provision is incompatible with a Convention right[1]. The court will ordinarily grant a declaration only to a person who is a victim of an actual or proposed breach of a Convention right[2]. The House of Lords did not, however, exclude the possibility that 'in a case in which a public authority was not, on the facts, acting incompatibly with a Convention right, the court might consider it convenient to make a declaration that if he had been so acting, a provision of primary legislation which made it lawful for him to do so would have been incompatible with Convention rights.'[3]

1   See *R (Rusbridger) v Attorney-General* [2004] 1 AC 357.
2   *Re S (Minors) (Care Order: Implementation of Care Plan)* [2002] 2 AC 291 at para 88 per Lord Nicholls of Birkenhead; *Lancashire County Council v Taylor* [2005] 1 WLR 2668; *Dundee City Council v GK* 2006 SC 326 at paras 17 and 24 per Lord President Hamilton.
3   *R (Nasseri) v Secretary of State for the Home Department* [2010] 1 AC 1 at para 19 per Lord Hoffmann. His Lordship added that 'such cases, in which the declaration is, so to speak, an obiter dictum not necessary for the decision of the case, will in my opinion be rare'.

1.50 The granting of such a declaration may not be sought by the parties to the proceedings in question, for whom it might well have no practical effect. In *S v Miller*, where a correcting Bill had been presented to the Scottish Parliament, the court was invited simply to indicate a view that the provision in question was incompatible with the Convention, without making a formal declaration. The court however observed that such an approach would in effect circumvent the provisions of the HRA 1998, s 5(1), requiring notice to be given to the Crown, for whom an indication of the court's view that the UK was in breach of its obligations under the ECHR would be a matter of significance. It would also have the effect of depriving the responsible authorities of the powers which Parliament intended they should have (under the HRA 1998, s 10 and Sch 2) to deal with incompatible legislation. It was said to be unsurprising that, during the passage of the Human Rights Bill through Parliament, the Lord Chancellor had indicated that he expected that, where a court had found a provision to be incompatible, it would declare that incompatibility[1].

In *Bellinger v Bellinger,* the House of Lords rejected an argument that a declaration of incompatibility would serve no useful purpose where the Government's powers to amend the offending legislation under s 10 had already been triggered by a decision of the European Court of Human Rights, and where the Government had already announced its intention to bring forward correcting legislation[2]. In *Doherty v Birmingham City Council,* on the other hand, the House found that the making of a declaration of incompatibility was unnecessary, since amending legislation had already been passed[3].

Where legislation discriminated against a person, contrary to her Convention rights, by preventing her from being assisted under statutory powers relating to homeless persons with a priority need, the existence of other means of assisting her was not regarded as a reason for withholding a declaration of incompatibility[4].

1   *S v Miller* 2001 SC 977.

2   *Bellinger v Bellinger* [2003] 2 AC 467. See also *Ghaidan v Godin-Mendoza* [2004] 2 AC 557 at para 56 per Lord Millett.

3   *Doherty v Birmingham City Council* [2009] 1 AC 367.

4   *R (Morris) v Westminster City Council* [2006] 1 WLR 505.

1.51 The HRA 1998, s 5 entitles the Crown to notice where a court is considering whether to make a declaration of incompatibility. In such a case, a Minister of the Crown, or member of the Scottish Executive, or Northern Ireland Minister or Department, is entitled to be joined as a party to the proceedings. The court can fix a diet for a hearing on the question of incompatibility as a separate hearing from any other hearing in the proceedings, and can sist the proceedings if it considers it necessary to do so while the question of incompatibility is being determined[1].

1   For the procedure in the High Court of Justiciary, see the Criminal Procedure Rules 1996, SI 1996/513, Ch 41 inserted by the Act of Adjournal (Criminal Procedure Rules Amendment No 2) (Human Rights Act 1998) 2000, SSI 2000/315. For the procedure in the Court of Session, see RCS 1994, Ch 82, inserted by the Act of Sederunt (Rules of the Court of Session Amendment No 6) (Human Rights Act 1998) 2000, SSI 2000/316. These arrangements were criticised in *Dundee City Council v GK* 2006 SC 326 at para 29 per Lord President Hamilton. For procedure in the Supreme Court, see the Supreme Court Rules 2009, SI 2009/1603, and Supreme Court Practice Direction 9.

1.52 It has been held in an English case that the court must direct *ex proprio motu* that notice be given under s 5 if there is an apparent incompatibility which has not been raised by the parties to the case. In such a case, it was said that an *amicus curiae* should be appointed to put before the court the argument for making the declaration of incompatibility if it is opposed by the Crown[1]. The court also proceeded on the basis that notice should be given to the Crown before the court decided how the statutory provision in question should be interpreted in the light of s 3, the question whether a declaration might be made under s 4 being dependent on the court's decision as to the interpretation of the provision. The same approach was adopted in a Scottish case where it was considered that the issue of interpretation under s 3 and the issue of incompatibility might be so bound up with one another as to mean that, in substance, when determining the interpretation question the court was already engaged in part of the process of 'considering whether to make a declaration of incompatibility', with the result that the Crown was entitled to notice in terms of s 5(1)[2].

---

1   *Wilson v First County Trust Ltd (No 1)* [2001] QB 407. This was criticised by Lord Hobhouse
      of Woodborough in the House of Lords: [2004] 1 AC 816 at para 127.
2   *Gunn v Newman* 2001 SLT 776.

1.53 The purpose of the HRA 1998, s 5 is to ensure that the appropriate minister
has an opportunity to address the court on the objects and purposes of the legislation
in question and any other matters that may be relevant[1]. Given that that is the
purpose of s 5, it would be unsatisfactory, and possibly productive of injustice, if
the court were to determine the question of interpretation of the provision in
question having heard only the parties to the action, subsequently to find that it
changed its mind, after notice had been given to the Crown and in the light of
additional arguments presented by the Crown in a hearing about a declaration of
incompatibility[2]. There is also a danger that delay and inefficiency will result if
the Crown is not involved at an appropriately early stage of proceedings where
the court may have to consider whether to make a declaration of incompatibility[3].
It has also been said, in an English case, that so as to give the Crown as much
notice as possible, whenever a party is seeking a declaration of incompatibility or
acknowledges that a declaration of incompatibility may be made, it should give
the Crown as much informal notice as practical of the proceedings and the issues
involved; and at the same time should send a copy of such informal notice to the
court, so that the court is alerted to the fact that it will have to consider whether
a formal notice should be given, and to the other parties[4].

---

1   *R v A* [2001] 1 WLR 789 at para 13.
2   *Gunn v Newman* 2001 SLT 776.
3   *Gunn v Newman* 2001 SLT 776.
4   *Poplar Housing and Regeneration Community Association Ltd v Donoghue* [2002] QB 48.

Statutory incompatibility

1.54 'The essence of the word "incompatible" is that there is an inconsistency
between one thing and another. It is in this sense that the word "compatible" is
used in section 3 of the Human Rights Act 1998'[1]. The concept of 'incompatibility'
with Convention rights, as applied to legislation[2], is not however straightforward.
The possibility that a public authority may exercise a statutory power in a manner
which is incompatible with a Convention right does not necessarily mean that the
legislation is itself incompatible with the Convention right[3]. It seems that the question
might depend on whether the violation of a Convention right was compelled, or at
least countenanced, by the legislation[4]. Nor does the fact that legislation fails to
provide an effective remedy in the event of a violation of a Convention right
mean that the legislation is itself incompatible with a Convention right, since a
failure to provide an effective remedy for a violation of a Convention right is not
itself a violation of a Convention right[5] (Article 13 of the ECHR not being among
the Convention rights).

---

1   *Montgomery v HM Advocate* 2001 SC (PC) 1 at 18 per Lord Hope of Craighead.

2   Its application to acts and omissions is discussed below: see paras **1.78** and **1.141–1.146**.

3   *Re S (Minors) (Care Order: Implementation of Care Plan)* [2002] 2 AC 291 at para 56 per Lord Nicholls of Birkenhead. Another illustration is *R (Fuller) v Chief Constable of the Dorset Police* [2003] QB 480 (power to move on trespassers not incompatible with Art 8).

4   *Re S (Minors) (Care Order: Implementation of Care Plan)* [2002] 2 AC 291 at para 57.

5   *Re S (Minors) (Care Order: Implementation of Care Plan)* [2002] 2 AC 291 at paras 59 and 85–86.

1.55 Compatibility with Convention rights may depend on the proportionality of the means employed by the statute to achieve its policy objective. In such a case, it is the current effect and impact of the legislation which matter, not the position when the legislation was enacted or came into force[1].

1   *Wilson v First County Trust Ltd (No 2)* [2004] 1 AC 816 at para 62 per Lord Nicholls of Birkenhead.

USE OF HANSARD AND OTHER BACKGROUND MATERIAL

1.56 The decision on the compatibility with Convention rights of any legislative provision (or of any action of a public authority) does not depend on the anterior reasoning of the body concerned[1]. 'In human rights adjudication, the court is concerned with whether the human rights of the claimant have in fact been infringed, not with whether the administrative decision-maker properly took them into account'[2]. If the court examines the matter objectively and comes to the conclusion that a provision or action is indeed compatible with Convention rights, the fact that the reasoning of the decision-maker may have been flawed is irrelevant for Convention purposes[3].

When the court is considering the compatibility of legislation with Convention rights, the purpose and effect of the legislation will usually be self-evident[4]. In the minority of cases where it is not, the court can take into account relevant background material, such as a White Paper, explanatory notes published with the Bill, and information provided by a minister or any other member of either House of Parliament in the course of a debate on the Bill. Ministerial or other statements should not however be treated as indicative of the objective intention of Parliament. Nor should a ministerial statement be given determinative weight. Beyond the use of Hansard as a source of background information, Parliamentary debates are not a proper matter for investigation or consideration by the courts. In particular, the proportionality of a statutory measure is not to be judged by the quality of the reasons advanced in support of it in the course of Parliamentary debate, or by the subjective state of mind of individual ministers or other members[5].

1   *R (SB) v Denbigh High School Governors* [2007] 1 AC 100; *Belfast City Council v Miss Behavin' Ltd* [2007] 1 WLR 1420.

2   *Belfast City Council v Miss Behavin' Ltd* [2007] 1 WLR 1420 at para 31 per Baroness Hale of Richmond.

3   *DS v HM Advocate* 2007 SC (PC) 1 at para 82 per Lord Rodger of Earlsferry.

4   *Wilson v First County Trust Ltd (No 2)* [2004] 1 AC 816 at para 61 per Lord Nicholls of
     Birkenhead; *Lancashire County Council v Taylor* [2005] 1 WLR 2668 at para 57 per Lord
     Woolf LCJ; *DS v HM Advocate* 2007 SC (PC) 1 at para 79 per Lord Rodger of Earlsferry.

5   *Wilson v First County Trust Ltd (No 2)* [2004] 1 AC 816 at paras 63–67 per Lord Nicholls of
     Birkenhead, and at para 118 per Lord Hope of Craighead. See also *Lancashire County Council
     v Taylor* [2005] 1 WLR 2668; *R (Morris) v Westminster City Council* [2006] 1 WLR 505; *R
     (Wilson) v Wychavon District Council* [2007] QB 801.

1.57 The foregoing observations apply to legislation passed by the Westminster
Parliament, whose proceedings attract Parliamentary privilege in accordance with
Article 9 of the Bill of Rights 1689. The proceedings of the Scottish Parliament
are not in the same position[1]. Nevertheless, the considerations underlying the
foregoing observations[2] apply also to the Scottish Parliament[3]. In practice,
background material has sometimes been considered[4].

1   The privilege attaching to statements made in proceedings of the Parliament under the SA
     1998, s 41 is solely for the purposes of the law of defamation.

2   In particular, that the courts and the legislature should respect each other's sphere of operations;
     that it is the intention of Parliament, not of the executive, that defines the policy and objects
     of its legislation; and that the courts should evaluate the proportionality of the legislation, not
     the adequacy of the reasons advanced in its support in the course of Parliamentary debate.

3   See eg *DS v HM Advocate* 2007 SC (PC) 1 at paras 79 and 82 per Lord Rodger of Earlsferry.

4   See eg *Whaley v Lord Advocate* 2008 SC (HL) 107.

Remedial action in relation to statutory provisions

1.58 The HRA 1998, s 10 enables the Government[1] to take urgent action to
amend legislation declared to be incompatible with a Convention right. It also
applies where there has been an adverse finding of the European Court of Human
Rights in proceedings against the UK. Broadly similar powers are vested in the
Scottish Ministers by the Convention Rights (Compliance) (Scotland) Act 2001,
ss 12–14, although these powers can be exercised in a wider range of
circumstances[2].

The HRA 1998, s 10 applies in two situations:

(a) where a provision of legislation has been declared under s 4 to be
    incompatible with a Convention right and, if an appeal lies, all persons who
    may appeal have stated in writing that they do not intend to do so; or the
    time for bringing an appeal has expired and no appeal has been brought
    within that time; or an appeal brought within that time has been determined
    or abandoned; or

(b) it appears to a Minister of the Crown[3] or Her Majesty in Council that,
    having regard to a finding of the European Court of Human Rights made
    after the coming into force of s 10 in proceedings against the UK, a provision
    of legislation is incompatible with an obligation of the UK arising from the
    ECHR[4].

In these circumstances, if a Minister of the Crown considers that there are compelling reasons for proceeding under s 10, he may by order[5] make such amendments to the legislation as he considers necessary to remove the incompatibility[6]. This power extends to legislation enacted by the Scottish Parliament. In the case of subordinate legislation, if the Minister considers it necessary to amend the primary legislation under which the subordinate legislation was made, in order to enable the incompatibility to be removed, and if he considers that there are compelling reasons for proceeding under s 10, then he may by order make such amendments to the primary legislation as he considers necessary[7]. The HRA 1998, s 10 also applies where the provision in question is in subordinate legislation and has been quashed, or declared invalid, by reason of incompatibility with a Convention right and the Minister proposes to make a remedial order under para 2(b) of Sch 2[8]. Schedule 2 makes further provision about remedial orders, and indicates that such an order may have retrospective effects and may make 'different provision for different cases'[9].

1   It seems that powers under the HRA 1998, s 10 can also be exercised by a Scottish Minister in relation to matters falling within devolved competence: see the complex provisions of the SA 1998, s 53 and Sch 4, paras 1, 12 and 13.

2   It is necessary that any legislation (or provision) whether of the UK Parliament or of the Scottish Parliament, or any subordinate legislation, 'is or may be incompatible with any of the Convention rights', and that the Scottish Ministers are of the opinion that there are compelling reasons for making a remedial order as distinct from taking any other action: Convention Rights (Compliance) (Scotland) Act 2001, ss 12(1) and (2). The procedure for making such an order is laid down in s 13, and provides for a period of public notice and consultation prior to the order being laid before the Scottish Parliament for approval; s 14 enables the order to be made immediately in urgent cases, but the order will fall after 120 days unless it has been approved by the Scottish Parliament (s 14(6)).

3   Defined by the HRA 1998, s 21(1) as having the same meaning as in the Ministers of the Crown Act 1975. A member of the Scottish Executive is not a Minister of the Crown: see *Beggs v Scottish Ministers* 2007 SLT 235.

4   HRA 1998, s 10(1).

5   That is, by statutory instrument: HRA 1998, s 20(1).

6   HRA 1998, s 10(2). If the legislation is an Order in Council, the power conferred by s 10(2) or (3) is exercisable by Her Majesty in Council: s 10(5).

7   HRA 1998, s 10(3).

8   HRA 1998, s 10(4).

9   HRA 1998, Sch 2, para 1. The exercise of such a power could give rise to issues under the ECHR (eg under Art 6(1)), but it may be that HRA 1998, s 6 would not apply (see s 6(3) and (6)). Judicial review of the exercise of the s 10 power may nevertheless be available. The exercise of s 10 powers falls within the ambit of the Joint Select Committee on Human Rights.

Public authorities and the Human Rights Act

1.59 The HRA 1998, s 6 makes it generally unlawful for a public authority to act in a way which is incompatible with a Convention right. An 'act' is defined by s 6(6) as including a failure to act (thus giving effect to the ECHR concept of positive obligations), but does not include a failure to:

(a) introduce in, or lay before, Parliament a proposal for legislation; or

(b) make any primary legislation or remedial order.

These exceptions preserve the principle of Parliamentary sovereignty. It follows from s 6(6) that the HRA 1998 imposes no duty to keep a given situation under review in order to decide whether to promote primary legislation[1]. Although an 'act' includes a failure to act, it does not include a refusal by a public authority to do something which it has no power to do: s 6(1) is concerned with acts which are otherwise lawful but are made unlawful by the HRA 1998 on Convention grounds[2]. If an act is 'unlawful' by virtue of s 6(1), it follows that it cannot lawfully be done[3]. In so far as the concept of competence or *vires* can be applied to the act in question, such acts would appear to be acts which the public authority has no power to do[4].

It has been said that the broad purpose of s 6(1) is not in doubt:

'The purpose is that those bodies for whose acts the state is answerable before the European Court of Human Rights shall in future be subject to a domestic law obligation not to act incompatibly with Convention rights. If they act in breach of this legal obligation victims may henceforth obtain redress from the courts of this country. In future victims should not need to travel to Strasbourg.'[5]

---

1   *R (Nasseri) v Secretary of State for the Home Department* [2010] 1 AC 1 at para 21 per Lord Hoffmann.

2   *R (Pretty) v Director of Public Prosecutions* [2002] 1 AC 800 at para 76 per Lord Hope of Craighead, with whom Lords Steyn and Scott of Foscote agreed.

3   See the speeches of the majority in *Attorney-General's Reference (No 2 of 2001)* [2004] 2 AC 72.

4   *Attorney-General's Reference (No 2 of 2001)* [2004] 2 AC 72 at para 78 per Lord Hope of Craighead; see also at para 130 per Lord Millett.

5   *Aston Cantlow and Wilmcote with Billesley Parochial Church Council v Wallbank* [2004] 1 AC 546 at para 6 per Lord Nicholls of Birkenhead.

1.60 In terms of the HRA 1998, s 6(2), s 6(1) does not apply to an act if:

(a) as the result of one or more provisions of primary legislation, the authority could not have acted differently; or

(b) in the case of one or more provisions of, or made under, primary legislation which1 cannot be read or given effect in a way which is compatible with the Convention rights, the authority was acting so as to give effect to or enforce those provisions.

These exceptions are again designed to preserve Parliamentary sovereignty:

'... in the final analysis, if primary legislation cannot be interpreted in a way that is compatible with them, parliamentary sovereignty takes precedence over the Convention rights.'[2]

1   In relation to secondary legislation, it appears that 'which' is governed by 'primary legislation'
     rather than by 'provisions': cf HRA 1998, s 4(3) and (4).

2   *R (Hooper) v Secretary of State for Work and Pensions* [2005] 1 WLR 1681 at para 70 per
     Lord Hope of Craighead.

1.61 The exception provided by s 6(2)(a) applies where the public authority is
required by primary legislation to act in a manner which is incompatible with a
Convention right: in other words, it is concerned with statutory duties[1]. For example,
a judge's act in admitting evidence is not unlawful if the judge is required by
statute to admit the evidence in question[2]. On the other hand, s 6(2)(a) cannot
apply if the public authority could have acted differently. For example, a prosecutor
could have acted otherwise than to proceed with a trial before a judge who did
not constitute an independent and impartial tribunal[3].

1   *R (Hooper) v Secretary of State for Work and Pensions* [2005] 1 WLR 1681 at para 71 per
     Lord Hope of Craighead.

2   *R v Kansal (No 2)* [2002] 2 AC 69 at para 86 per Lord Hope of Craighead; *R v Lyons* [2003]
     1 AC 976.

3   See *Starrs v Ruxton* 2000 JC 208 at 231 per Lord Justice-Clerk Cullen, and at 255–256 per
     Lord Reed.

1.62 The exception provided by s 6(2)(b) applies where the public authority,
although not required by statute to act as it did, was acting so as to give effect to
legislation which cannot be read in a way that is compatible with the Convention
rights: in other words, it is concerned with statutory powers and discretions[1]. For
example, a prosecutor gave effect to a provision that statements given under
compulsion 'may be used in evidence' by tendering evidence of such a statement[2].
A landlord gave effect to a provision entitling it to recover possession by seeking
a possession order (and the court gave effect to the provision by granting the
order), notwithstanding that the grant of the order violated Convention rights[3]. In
Re S (Minors) (Care Order: Implementation of Care Plan), it was observed
that judicial review of decisions concerning children which were taken by local
authorities under statutory powers might not meet the requirements of Article 6
of the ECHR, but that s 6 did not enable the court to make good any shortcoming:

> 'In failing to provide a hearing as guaranteed by article 6(1) the court is not acting
> unlawfully for the purposes of section 6. The court is simply giving effect to the
> Children Act: see section 6(2)(a)4 of the Human Rights Act. The court has no power
> to act otherwise. Section 6 is prohibitory, not enabling.'[5]

It has been held that in prosecuting an offender before a temporary sheriff the
prosecutor was not giving effect to or enforcing the statutory provision which
provided for the appointment of temporary sheriffs[6]. A prosecutor moving for
sentence did not give effect to legislation which prohibited convicted prisoners
from voting[7].

1   *R (Hooper) v Secretary of State for Work and Pensions* [2005] 1 WLR 1681 at para 49 per

Lord Hoffmann, and at paras 72–73 per Lord Hope of Craighead; *Doherty v Birmingham City Council* [2009] 1 AC 367 at paras 21 and 39–40 per Lord Hope of Craighead. The public authority's exercise of its discretion, in deciding to act as it has done, may still be reviewable at common law on judicial review grounds: see eg *Doherty* at paras 52–55 per Lord Hope of Craighead. See also at paras 108–109 per Lord Walker of Gestingthorpe and at paras 134–135 per Lord Mance.

2   *R v Kansal (No 2)* [2002] 2 AC 69 at para 88 per Lord Hope of Craighead. See also *R (Anderson) v Secretary of State for the Home Department* [2003] 1 AC 837 and *Aston Cantlow and Wilmcote with Billesley Parochial Church Council v Wallbank* [2004] 1 AC 546.

3   *Doherty v Birmingham City Council* [2009] 1 AC 367.

4   *Sic*: s 6(2)(b) appears to be meant.

5   *Re S (Minors) (Care Order: Implementation of Care Plan)* [2002] 2 AC 291 at para 80 per Lord Nicholls of Birkenhead.

6   *Millar v Dickson* 2002 SC (PC) 30. In a subsequent decision it was held that, in so acting, the prosecutor was giving effect to a provision entitling a temporary sheriff to exercise the jurisdiction and powers attaching to the office of sheriff: *Dickson v HM Advocate* 2008 JC 181. This may be questionable: see the commentary by Sir Gerald Gordon QC at 2008 SCCR 81.

7   *XY v Scottish Ministers* 2007 SC 631.

1.63 Where domestic law on a particular topic is an amalgam of common law and statute it may be difficult to decide whether s 6(2) applies or not. It has been said that the paramount consideration is whether the composite legal scheme in general, and the incompatible provision in particular, clearly represents the considered intention of Parliament[1]. It has been held that the Secretary of State gave effect to legislation which restricted the receipt of statutory payments to widows by declining to exercise his common law power to make similar extra-statutory payments to widowers[2]. Similarly, a public authority is not required by s 6 to use a statutory power for the purpose of circumventing or replacing another statutory provision which is incompatible with Convention rights[3].

1   *Doherty v Birmingham City Council* [2009] 1 AC 367 at para 104 per Lord Walker of Gestingthorpe (with whom Lord Rodger of Earlsferry agreed); see also para 132 per Lord Mance.

2   *R (Hooper) v Secretary of State for Work and Pensions* [2005] 1 WLR 1681.

3   *R (Morris) v Westminster City Council* [2006] 1 WLR 505.

The meaning of 'public authority'

1.64 Since the ECHR is concerned with the obligations of states in international law, it does not define the domestic bodies whose acts engage the liability of the state[1]. For the purposes of the HRA 1998, however, it is necessary to identify the public authorities whose acts fall within the ambit of s 6. In terms of s 6(3), the expression 'public authority' includes:

(a) a court or tribunal[2], and

(b) any person certain of whose functions are functions of a public nature, but does not include either House of Parliament or a person exercising functions in connection with proceedings in Parliament[3]. In addition, s 6(5) provides that, in relation to a particular act, a person is not a public authority by virtue only of s 6(3)(b) if the nature of the act is private.

1   Indeed, states may be responsible for acts of private bodies eg for corporal punishment administered in private schools: *Costello-Roberts v United Kingdom* (1993) A 247-C.
2   'Tribunal' is defined as meaning any tribunal in which legal proceedings may be brought: HRA 1998, s 21(1). As to the effect of s 6 on courts and tribunals, see paras **1.76–1.77** below.
3   'Parliament' did not include the House of Lords in its judicial capacity: HRA 1998, s 6(4).

1.65 It is implicit in s 6(3), read with s 6(5), that a distinction has to be drawn for the purposes of s 6 between two types of public authority: 'core' public authorities who are to be so regarded in relation to all their functions, and 'hybrid' persons with functions both of a public and of a private nature who are only to be regarded as public authorities when the nature of their particular act under consideration is public rather than private[1].

1   *YL v Birmingham City Council* [2008] 1 AC 95 at para 81 per Lord Mance.

1.66 Core public authorities fall within s 6 without reference to s 6(3). A core public authority is bound to respect Convention rights in the discharge of all of its responsibilities. That is so notwithstanding that

'… it is a fallacy to regard all functions and activities of a core public authority as inherently public in nature. All such functions and activities are subject to the Convention, because the authority is a core public authority. It only becomes necessary to analyse their nature, if and when they are contracted out to a person who is not a core public authority. Some of them may then on analysis be private in nature.'[1]

It follows from the latter observations that a person to whom a function or activity of a core public authority is delegated or contracted out does not necessarily constitute a public authority either generally or in respect of the performance of the function in question.

   In deciding whether a body is a core public authority, it is therefore necessary to consider whether Parliament can have intended that the body in question should be subject to s 6(1) in all that it does and should itself have no Convention rights[2]. Since a body which would be regarded as a non-governmental organisation within the meaning of Article 34 of the ECHR can be a 'victim' of a violation of Convention rights[3], it follows that such a body ought not to be regarded as a 'core' public authority for the purposes of s 6[4].

1   *YL v Birmingham City Council* [2008] 1 AC 95 at para 81 per Lord Mance.
2   *Aston Cantlow and Wilmcote with Billesley Parochial Church Council v Wallbank* [2004] 1 AC 546 at para 8 per Lord Nicholls of Birkenhead, and at para 41 per Lord Hope of Craighead.
3   Since a victim can be 'any person, *non-governmental organisation* or group of individuals': ECHR, Art 34 (emphasis added). Article 34 is given effect by the HRA 1998, s 7(7).

4   *Aston Cantlow and Wilmcote with Billesley Parochial Church Council v Wallbank* [2004] 1 AC
     546 at para 47 per Lord Hope of Craighead.

1.67 Hybrid public authorities are brought within the scope of s 6, by virtue of
s 6(3)(b), by including within the phrase 'public authority' any person whose
functions include 'functions of a public nature'; but, by virtue of s 6(5), this extension
of the expression 'public authority' does not apply to a person if the nature of the
act in question is 'private'[1]. Hybrid public authorities are not absolutely disabled
from having Convention rights[2].

1   A hybrid authority may, however, come under an obligation to observe Convention rights in
     relation to its acts of a private nature by reason of the 'horizontal' impact of the HRA 1998:
     see paras **1.76–1.77** below.
2   For example, the BBC is bound to act compatibly with Convention rights (eg under Art 10) in
     so far as it acts as a public authority (as in *Pro-Life Alliance v BBC* [2004] 1 AC 185), but it
     can also claim the protection of Art 10 when there is an interference with its own freedom to
     broadcast.

1.68 The application of these provisions is by no means straightforward. In
principle, the purpose of s 6 is that those bodies for whose acts the UK is
answerable before the European Court of Human Rights shall in future be subject
to a domestic law obligation not to act incompatibly with Convention rights[1]. In
one leading case, it was said that the relevant question was whether the body in
question

> '… is a public authority in the sense that it carries out, either generally or on the
> relevant occasion, the kind of public function of government which would engage
> the responsibility of the United Kingdom before the Strasbourg organs.'[2]

The body in question must be a UK public authority, rather than one for which the
UK is responsible by virtue of a territorial extension of the ECHR beyond the
UK[3].

   Strasbourg case law may offer guidance on the scope of state responsibility in
a particular field. In relation to hybrid public authorities, in particular, Strasbourg
case law suggests that there may be certain essentially state or governmental
functions, particularly involving the exercise of duties or powers, for the manner
of exercise of which the state will remain liable, notwithstanding that it has
delegated them to a private body[4].

1   *Aston Cantlow and Wilmcote with Billesley Parochial Church Council v Wallbank* [2004] 1 AC
     546 at para 6 per Lord Nicholls of Birkenhead; similarly *YL v Birmingham City Council* [2008]
     1 AC 95 at para 87 per Lord Mance.
2   *Aston Cantlow and Wilmcote with Billesley Parochial Church Council v Wallbank* [2004] 1 AC
     546 at para 163 per Lord Rodger of Earlsferry.
3   Under ECHR, Art 56 or equivalent provisions in the protocols). See paras **1.75** and **3.04**
     below.
4   *YL v Birmingham City Council* [2008] 1 AC 95 at para 99 per Lord Mance. See para **3.20**
     below.

1.69 In relation to core public authorities, it has been said that the most obvious examples are government departments, local authorities, the police and the armed forces:

> 'Behind the instinctive classification of these organisations as bodies whose nature is governmental lie factors such as the possession of special powers, democratic accountability, public funding in whole or in part, an obligation to act only in the public interest, and a statutory constitution.'[1]

Other examples include health authorities and NHS trusts[2]. It has been held that the Church of England is not a core public authority, although some of its emanations discharge functions (such as education through church schools, and the conduct of marriage services) which may qualify as governmental. It is, however, essentially a religious organisation, and undoubtedly has Convention rights (notably under Article 9)[3].

1   *Aston Cantlow and Wilmcote with Billesley Parochial Church Council v Wallbank* [2004] 1 AC 546 at para 7 per Lord Nicholls of Birkenhead.

2   *R (Wilkinson) v Broadmoor Special Hospital Authority* [2002] 1 WLR 419 at para 61 per Hale LJ.

3   *Aston Cantlow and Wilmcote with Billesley Parochial Church Council v Wallbank* [2004] 1 AC 546.

1.70 In relation to hybrid public authorities, it has been said that there are situations where in the interests of efficiency and economy or otherwise, functions of a governmental nature are discharged by non-governmental bodies, sometimes as a consequence of privatisation, and sometimes not. Examples include the running of prisons by commercial organisations and the discharge of regulatory functions by organisations in the private sector. It has been said that 'essentially the contrast being drawn is between functions of a governmental nature and functions, or acts, which are not of that nature'[1]. In a number of cases, emphasis has been placed on whether the legal context of the act in question was private law or public law[2].

1   *Aston Cantlow and Wilmcote with Billesley Parochial Church Council v Wallbank* [2004] 1 AC 546 at para 10 per Lord Nicholls of Birkenhead.

2   See eg *Aston Cantlow and Wilmcote with Billesley Parochial Church Council v Wallbank* [2004] 1 AC 546 per Lord Hope of Craighead and Lord Hobhouse of Woodborough; *YL v Birmingham City Council* [2008] 1 AC 95 per Lord Scott of Foscote.

1.71 In *Aston Cantlow and Wilmcote with Billesley Parochial Church Council v Wallbank,* Lord Nicholls of Birkenhead suggested a factor-based approach to the application of s 6(3)(b):

> 'What, then, is the touchstone to be used in deciding whether a function is public for this purpose? Clearly there is no single test of universal application. There cannot be, given the diverse nature of governmental functions and the variety of means by which these functions are discharged today. Factors to be taken into account include the extent to which in carrying out the relevant function the body

is publicly funded, or is exercising statutory powers, or is taking the place of central government or local authorities, or is providing a public service.'[1]

In *YL v Birmingham City Council,* Lord Mance developed that approach:

'... as both *Aston Cantlow* and *R (West) v Lloyds of London*[2] show, the mere possession of special powers conferred by Parliament does not by itself mean that a person has functions of a public nature. Such powers may have been conferred for private, religious or purely commercial purposes. Conversely, there can be bodies without special statutory powers amenable to judicial review, as shown by *R v Panel on Take-overs and Mergers, Ex p Datafin plc*[3] and *R v Code of Practice Committee of the British Pharmaceutical Industry, Ex p Professional Counselling Aids Ltd*[4] ... In *Datafin,* the panel was as a matter of fact entrusted with an extensive and vital regulatory role in the public interest, and that was sufficient to make it susceptible to judicial review. In *Code of Practice Committee*, applying *Datafin*, judicial review was available in respect of the administration by a trade association of a code of practice which it had voluntarily developed in conjunction with the Department of Health, and which was obligatory for members and followed in practice by non-members. I do not doubt that such bodies would in respect of their regulatory functions also constitute a public authority under section 6(3)(b).

... it should be no surprise that the usual source of the "functions of a public nature" addressed by section 6(3)(b) is legislative or governmental, when section 6(3)(b) is intended to reflect in domestic law the scope of the state responsibility which the Convention addresses ... The existence and source of any special powers or duties must on any view be a very relevant factor when considering whether state responsibility is engaged in Strasbourg or whether section 6(3)(b) applies domestically.

Typical State or governmental functions include powers conferred and duties imposed or undertaken in the general public interest. I shall not attempt to identify the full scope of the concept of "functions of a public nature", any more than Lord Nicholls did in *Aston Cantlow*. But some further consideration is appropriate of his suggested hallmarks of a public authority. As stated, these were, in the case of a core public authority and in addition to special powers, democratic accountability, public funding in whole or in part, an obligation to act only in the public interest and a statutory constitution. All these factors can readily be understood to throw light on the nature of a person's functions. When considering section 6(3)(b), Lord Nicholls suggested as factors, again in addition to statutory powers, the extent that a body is publicly funded or is "taking the place" of central government or local authorities or is providing a public service: [2004] 1 AC 546, para 12. These are more generally expressed factors, to which I address some further comments.

... That powers or duties may in some circumstances be delegated to others is clear – witness the examples, given by Lord Nicholls, of privately run prisons and the regulation (at that time) of the solicitors' profession by the Law Society or the example of the private contractor entrusted with responsibility for enforcing the Road Traffic Regulation Act 1984. Section 101 of the Local Government Act 1972 enables a limited form of delegation, whereby arrangements may be made for the discharge of local authority functions by a committee or subcommittee or an officer of the authority or by any other local authority. More significantly, under section 70 of the Deregulation and Contracting Out Act 1994, the Secretary of State may specify statutory functions which may be discharged by a person other than the authority primarily responsible for them. Section 72 provides that any acts or omissions of a person so authorised shall be treated for all purposes as done or omitted to be done by or in relation to the authority … In such cases, while the acts or omissions are by statute attributed to the authority, there is a clear basis for regarding the authorised delegate as a person having functions of a public nature within section 6(3)(b) …

Democratic accountability, an obligation to act only in the public interest and (in most cases today) a statutory constitution exclude the sectional or personally motivated interests of privately owned, profit earning enterprises. Public funding and the provision of a public service are most easily understood in a similar sense. In a much looser sense, the self-interested endeavour of individuals usually works to the general benefit of society, as Adam Smith noted. But more than that is required under section 6(3)(b). The difficulty is where to draw the line. Public funding takes various forms. The injection of capital or subsidy into an organisation in return for undertaking a non-commercial role or activity of general public interest may be one thing; payment for services under a contractual arrangement with a company aiming to profit commercially thereby is potentially quite another. In every case, the ultimate focus must be upon the nature of the functions being undertaken.'[5]

---

1   *Aston Cantlow and Wilmcote with Billesley Parochial Church Council v Wallbank* [2004] 1 AC 546 at para 12.

2   *R (West) v Lloyds of London* [2004] 3 All ER 251.

3   *R v Panel on Take-overs and Mergers, Ex p Datafin plc* [1987] QB 815.

4   *R v Code of Practice Committee of the British Pharmaceutical Industry, ex p Professional Counselling Aids Ltd* (1990) 3 Admin LR 697.

5   *YL v Birmingham City Council* [2008] 1 AC 95 at paras 101–105. There are also helpful analyses of the authorities in *R (Weaver) v London and Quadrant Housing Trust* [2010] 1 WLR 363.

1.72 It has been held that a private operator of care homes, providing care and accommodation to residents under a contract with the local authority (which was itself under a statutory duty to arrange care and accommodation for the residents), and under agreements with the residents themselves, was not performing a function of a public nature[1]. The operator was a commercial enterprise which received no public funding (although its fees were paid wholly or in part by the local authority), possessed no special statutory powers and was at liberty to accept or reject residents as it chose. Lord Mance observed:

'In providing care and accommodation, [the company] acts as a private, profit-earning company. It is subject to close statutory regulation in the public interest. But so are many private occupations and businesses, with operations which may impact on members of the public in matters as diverse for example as life, health, privacy or financial well-being. Regulation by the state is no real pointer towards the person regulated being a state or governmental body or a person with a function of a public nature, if anything perhaps even the contrary. The private and commercial motivation behind [the company's] operations does in contrast point against treating [the company] as a person with a function of a public nature. Some of the particular duties which it has been suggested would follow ... fit in my view uneasily with the ordinary private law freedom to carry on operations under agreed contractual terms ...'[2]

Following a broadly similar approach, Railtrack was held not to have been a public authority at the time of the Potters Bar rail crash[3]. On the other hand, s 6(3)(b) covered the functions performed by a privately operated mental nursing home in which the claimant was compulsorily detained under statutory powers[4]. In another case, a county council, which had previously run farmers' markets under statutory powers, set up a non-profit making company to run such markets on a contractual basis on publicly owned land to which the public had, and at common law had the right of, access for the sale of goods. The Court of Appeal held that, despite the lack of any statutory source or underpinning for the company's role, the company was performing a function of a public nature under s 6(3)(b). An important element in the decision was the common law right of access of the public to such markets, which was being regulated by the company in succession to the council[5].

1   *YL v Birmingham City Council* [2008] 1 AC 95. The decision was reversed by statute: Health and Social Care Act 2008, s 145(1). That does not affect the binding nature of the reasoning in the case.

2   *YL v Birmingham City Council* [2008] 1 AC 95 at para 116.

3   *Cameron v Network Rail Infrastructure Ltd* [2007] 1 WLR 163. The RSPCA is not a public authority: *Royal Society for the Prevention of Cruelty to Animals v Attorney General* [2002] 1 WLR 448. An adjudicator acting under the system of adjudication established by the Housing Grants, Construction and Regeneration Act 1996 has also been held not to be a public authority: *Austin Hall Building Ltd v Buckland Securities Ltd* [2001] BLR 272. In relation to the Advertising Standards Authority, see *R (Matthias Rath BV) v Advertising Standards Authority Ltd* [2001] HRLR 22.

4   *R (A) v Partnerships in Care Ltd* [2002] 1 WLR 2610.

5   *R (Beer (trading as Hammer Trout Farm)) v Hampshire Farmers' Markets Ltd* [2004] 1 WLR 233.

1.73 In relation to s 6(5), it has been held that the termination of an agreement between a private care home and a resident provided with accommodation there at the cost of the local authority was an act of a private nature[1]. On the other hand, the termination of a tenancy of social housing by a registered social landlord was held by a majority of the Court of Appeal not to be an act of a private nature[2]. The enforcement by a parochial church council of a repairing obligation in respect of the parish church, which was a burden arising from the ownership of glebe land, was an act of a 'private' nature[3].

1   *YL v Birmingham City Council* [2008] 1 AC 95.

2   *R (Weaver) v London and Quadrant Housing Trust* [2010] 1 WLR 363.

3   *Aston Cantlow and Wilmcote with Billesley Parochial Church Council v Wallbank* [2004] 1 AC 546.

1.74 The Scottish Parliament and the Scottish Ministers are 'public authorities' within the meaning of s 6. The application of s 6 to these bodies is, however, more complicated than in respect of most other bodies, and depends on the interplay of the SA 1998 and the HRA 1998. Any question as to the compatibility with Convention rights of the acts or omissions of these bodies[1] constitutes a 'devolution issue' within the meaning of the SA 1998[2]. The Parliament has no power to enact legislation which is incompatible with a Convention right[3]. Scottish Ministers have no power to make any subordinate legislation which is incompatible with a Convention right[4]. Subject to one exception, Scottish Ministers have no power to do any other act which is incompatible with a Convention right. That exception is an act of the Lord Advocate in prosecuting an offence or in his capacity as head of the system of criminal prosecution and investigation of deaths in Scotland which, because of the HRA 1998, s 6(2), is not unlawful under s 6(1)[5]. At the time of writing, it is anticipated that the relevant provisions of the SA 1998 will be amended by the Scotland Act 2011.

1   Scotland Act 1998, Sch 6, para 1. At the time of writing, it is anticipated that this provision may be amended by the Scotland Act 2011 so as to exclude from the scope of 'devolution issues' an act or omission of the Lord Advocate in prosecuting any offence, or in the capacity of head of the system of criminal prosecution in Scotland.

2   *Somerville v Scottish Ministers* 2008 SC (HL) 45 at para 108 per Lord Rodger of Earlsferry.

3   SA 1998, s 29.

4   SA 1998, s 57(2).

5   SA 1998, s 57(3). At the time of writing, it is anticipated that this provision may be amended by the Scotland Act 2011 so as to extend the exception to any act of the Lord Advocate in prosecuting an offence or in his capacity as head of the system of criminal prosecution and investigation of deaths in Scotland. In relation to the provision as originally enacted, see *Starrs v Ruxton* 2000 JC 208; *Millar v Dickson* 2002 SC (PC) 30; *Dickson v HM Advocate* 2008 JC 181. Such acts fall however within the HRA 1998, s 6.

'Public authorities': extra-territorial application of the HRA 1998, s 6

1.75 The duty under the HRA 1998, s 6 to act in a manner compatible with Convention rights can apply not only when a UK public authority acts within the UK, but also when it acts outside the UK where the victim is within the jurisdiction of the UK for the purposes of Article 1 of the ECHR[1]. In *R (Al- Skeini and Others) v Secretary of State for Defence*[2], the House of Lords considered the question whether actions of British military personnel in Iraq gave rise to responsibilities under s 6, and held that liability could be engaged, but only in circumstances where it could be said that the UK had such effective control over an area as to enable it to provide the full package of rights and freedoms guaranteed by Article 1 of the ECHR to everyone within that area. Since the UK's presence in Iraq fell far short of such control, most of the claims were ill-founded; but the exception recognised in respect of embassies and consular officials[3] could be extended to the military base where the son of one of the claimants was alleged to have been killed. On the other hand, British soldiers serving in Iraq were not within the jurisdiction of the UK within the meaning of Article 1 when they were outside their army base[4].

The HRA 1998 is concerned with the Convention only as it applies to the United Kingdom[5]. Section 6 did not therefore apply to the Foreign Secretary when he refused a licence to fish in the waters of South Georgia and the South Sandwich Islands[6]. Nor did the HRA 1998 apply to an Order in Council made for the governance of the British Indian Ocean Territory[7].

---

1   See paras **3.05–3.10** below.

2   *R (Al-Skeini) v Secretary of State for Defence* [2008] 1 AC 153, at paras 54–57. See also *R (Al-Saadoori v Secretary of State for Defence* [2010] QB 486. See now *Al-Skeini v United Kingdom* [GC] (7 July 2011).

3   As, for example, in *R (B) v Secretary of State for Foreign and Commonwealth Affairs* [2005] QB 643, discussed at para **3.11** below.

4   *R (Smith) v Oxfordshire Assistant Deputy Coroner* [2011] 1 AC 1.

5   See para **1.29** above.

6   *R (Quark Fishing Ltd) v Secretary of State for Foreign and Commonwealth Affairs* [2006] 1 AC 529.

7   *R (Bancoult) v Secretary of State for Foreign and Commonwealth Affairs (No 2)* [2009] 1 AC 453. See also *R (Barclay) v Lord Chancellor and Secretary of State for Justice* [2010] 1 AC 464. Contrast *R (Al-Jedda) v Secretary of State for Defence* [2008] 1 AC 332 (since UK forces in Iraq were not operating under the auspices of the United Nations, the UK remained responsible for their conduct under the ECHR, Art 1, and also under the HRA 1998).

The courts as 'public authorities'

1.76 The court is itself a public authority for the purposes of s 6. It is therefore unlawful for the court to act in a way which is incompatible with a Convention right. The court cannot therefore knowingly act in such a way[1]. There is no doubt that this prohibition applies to the court's conduct of proceedings before it. Its practices and procedures must be Convention-compliant. Section 6 also affects the remedies which the court can provide: it is, for example, the source of the court's power to make anonymity orders where necessary to protect Convention rights[2]. Whether, and in what circumstances, the court's obligation under s 6 affects the substantive law to be applied by the court, still awaits authoritative decision[3]. The question is of particular importance in relation to proceedings between private parties.

The principles which have been developed by the Court of Appeal were summarised by Baroness Hale of Richmond in *Campbell v MGN Ltd*:

> 'The 1998 Act does not create any new cause of action between private persons. But if there is a relevant cause of action applicable, the court as a public authority must act compatibly with both parties' Convention rights.'[4]

On this approach, one private party cannot bring (or defend) proceedings against another private party on the basis of a Convention right. The court cannot invent new rights or remedies in the absence of existing domestic principles[5], but can reflect Convention principles in developing existing rights and remedies. As has been explained[6], even prior to the enactment of the HRA 1998 the ECHR had an influence on the development of the common law and on the interpretation of legislation. That influence continues, and has in practice been strengthened by the HRA 1998.

1   *Attorney-General's Reference (No 2 of 2001)* [2004] 2 AC 72.

2   *In re Guardian News and Media Ltd* [2010] 2 AC 697.

3   *Kay v Lambeth London Borough Council* [2006] 2 AC 465 at para 61 per Lord Nicholls of Birkenhead; *Doherty v Birmingham City Council* [2009] 1 AC 367 at paras 92 and 99 per Lord Walker of Gestingthorpe and at paras 129–130 per Lord Mance. A wide approach was suggested by Lord Hope of Craighead in *R v Lambert* [2002] 2 AC 545 at para 114. See also the discussion in *X v Y* [2004] ICR 1634.

4   *Campbell v MGN Ltd* [2004] 2 AC 457 at para 132.

5   Cf *Wainwright v Home Office* [2004] 2 AC 406.

6   See paras **1.04**, **1.08** and **1.23–1.24** above.

1.77 The question has arisen mainly in the context of protection against intrusion by the media into private life[1]. In that context, the English courts have re-fashioned the tort of breach of confidence, to the extent that it has been said that 'articles 8 and 10 are now the very content of the domestic tort that the English court has to enforce'[2].

1   See eg *Venables v News Group Newspapers* [2001] Fam 430; *A v B plc* [2003] QB 195; *Douglas v Hello! Ltd (No 3)* [2006] QB 125; *McKennitt v Ash* [2008] QB 73; *Wales v Associated Newspapers Ltd* [2008] Ch 57; *Browne v Associated Newspapers Ltd* [2008] QB 103.

2   *McKennitt v Ash* [2008] QB 73 at para 11 per Buxton LJ; *Browne v Associated Newspapers Ltd* [2008] QB 103 at para 22 per Sir Anthony Clarke MR.

The meaning of 'incompatible'[1]

1.78 Under the ECHR, the question is whether there has been a violation by the state of one of the guaranteed rights: it is unnecessary to identify any specific act which resulted in the violation, or any specific agency of the state which was responsible for that act. Under the HRA 1998, s 6, on the other hand, it is necessary to decide whether a specific act of a specific public authority is incompatible with a Convention right. As explained above, the term 'incompatible' has been likened to 'inconsistent'[2]. It appears that the inconsistency must be proximate rather than indirect. The making of an order for the recall to prison of a convicted prisoner who had been released on licence was not incompatible with his Convention right to vote, notwithstanding that legislation prohibited convicted prisoners from voting: it was the legislation, not the order recalling him to prison, which was incompatible with his Convention right[3].

1   See also paras **1.54–1.55** above and paras **1.141–1.146** below.

2   See para **1.54** above.

3   *XY v Scottish Ministers* 2007 SC 631. This result followed from the scheme of the HRA 1998. Although the legislation was incompatible with Convention rights, it was nevertheless to be implemented in accordance with s 6(2). It could not have been the intention of Parliament in enacting the HRA 1998 that such legislation should be subverted indirectly, by rendering unlawful any acts which would result in circumstances in which the legislation could be implemented (acts which would not themselves be protected by s 6(2)).

Making use of Convention rights in proceedings involving public authorities

1.79 The consequences of a breach of the HRA 1998, s 6 are dealt with in ss 7–9. The HRA 1998, s 7(1) provides that a person who claims that a public authority has acted (or proposes to act) in a way which is made unlawful by s 6(1) may:

(a) bring proceedings against the authority under the Act in the appropriate court or tribunal[1], or

(b) rely on the Convention right or rights concerned in any legal proceedings;

but in each case only if he is (or would be) a victim of the unlawful act.

The appropriate form of proceedings will depend upon the context. 'In some cases, for example where delegated legislation or the policy of a public authority is in question, then the appropriate remedies will only be available in judicial review. But in others, where specific invasions of individuals' rights are in question, an ordinary action would be more appropriate'[2]. If the proceedings are made by way of a petition for judicial review in Scotland, the applicant is to be taken to have title and interest to sue in relation to the unlawful act only if he is, or would be, a victim of that act[3].

1   Defined by HRA 1998, s 7(2) as meaning 'such court or tribunal as may be determined in accordance with rules' (as to which, see s 7(9)–(13)). See para **1.80** below, and *R (Hurst) v Chief Commissioner of the Metropolis* [2007] 2 AC 189, paras 60–64.

2   *R (Wilkinson) v Broadmoor Special Hospital Authority* [2002] 1 WLR 419 at para 442 per Hale LJ. The question whether a declaration can be sought under HRA 1998, s 7 as to the legality of a proposed course of action was considered (in the context of English law) in *R (Pretty) v Director of Public Prosecutions* [2002] 1 AC 800 and *R (Rusbridger) v Attorney General* [2004] 1 AC 357.

3   HRA 1998, s 7(4). See para **1.87** below. Interventions can however be made by other persons, where a matter of public interest is raised, in accordance with RCS 1994, r 58.8A, inserted by the Act of Sederunt (Rules of the Court of Session Amendment No 5) (Public Interest Intervention in Judicial Review) 2000, SSI 2000/317. In practice, interventions were unknown in Scottish proceedings prior to the HRA 1998 and the SA 1998. The first appears to have been that of JUSTICE in *Brown v Stott* 2001 SC (PC) 43. Separate provision is made for interventions by the Scottish Commission for Human Rights and by the Commission for Equality and Human Rights.

1.80 The HRA 1998, s 7(1)(a) enables the victim of the unlawful act to bring proceedings under the Act against the authority. It has been said that s 7(1)(a) (and consequently the time bar imposed by s 7(5)) applies to claims brought for breach of Convention rights, by whatever procedure they are pursued and whether or not they are pursued alone or in conjunction with other claims[1]. The appropriate court or tribunal (in so far as not determined by any other enactment[2]) is any civil court or tribunal which has jurisdiction to grant the remedy sought[3]. Proceedings under s 7(1)(a) are therefore civil proceedings[4]. There is no set form of proceedings which must be adopted. The HRA 1998, s 7(2) defines 'proceedings against an authority' as including a counterclaim or similar proceeding[5], and s 9(1) envisages that proceedings under s 7(1)(a) in respect of a judicial act may be brought by way of an appeal or on an application for judicial review. A defence of *ex turpi causa non oritur actio* does not apply to a claim brought under s 7[6].

1　*Somerville v Scottish Ministers* 2008 SC (HL) 45 at para 175 per Lord Mance. See also at para 40 per Lord Hope of Craighead and para 71 per Lord Scott of Foscote.

2　The appropriate tribunal in relation to a wide variety of matters concerning the intelligence services, HM forces, the police, the National Criminal Intelligence Service, the National Crime Squad and HM Revenue and Customs is the Investigatory Practices Tribunal established under s 65 of the Regulation of Investigatory Powers Act 2000: see *R (A) v Director of Establishment of the Security Service* [2010] 1 AC 1. The appropriate tribunal in respect of a refusal by the Secretary of State to remove an organisation from Sch 2 to the Terrorism Act 2000 (as amended), or a refusal to provide for a name to cease to be treated as a name for an organisation listed in that Schedule, is the Proscribed Organisations Appeal Commission: see the Proscribed Organisations Appeal Commission (Human Rights Act 1998 Proceedings) Rules 2006, SI 2006/2290. The appropriate tribunal in relation to proceedings which call into question a control order under the Prevention of Terrorism Act 2005 or a 'derogation matter' as defined by that Act, is the Outer House of the Court of Session where the controlled person is a person whose principal place of residence is in Scotland, or otherwise the High Court in Northern Ireland or in England and Wales: Prevention of Terrorism Act 2005, ss 11(2) and 15.

3　Human Rights Act 1998 (Jurisdiction) (Scotland) Rules 2000, SSI 2000/301, r 3.

4　*R v Kansal (No 2)* [2002] 2 AC 69 at para 63 per Lord Hope of Craighead; *R (A) v Director of Establishment of the Security Service* [2010] 1 AC 1 at para 45 per Lord Hope DPSC; *Beck, Petitioner* 2010 SCCR 222; *Beggs, Applicant* [2011] HCJAC [49].

5　See *R (A) v Director of Establishment of the Security Service* [2010] 1 AC 1 at para 47 per Lord Hope DPSC.

6　*Al Hassan-Daniel v Revenue and Customs Commissioners* [2011] 2 WLR 488.

1.81 Apart from bringing proceedings under s 7(1)(a), s 7(1)(b) makes it possible for the victim of the unlawful act[1] to rely on the Convention rights in any legal proceedings[2] (for example, as part of a defence to a criminal prosecution or a civil action brought by a public authority). 'Legal proceedings' are defined for the purpose of s 7(1)(b) by s 7(6) to include proceedings brought by or at the instigation of a public authority, and an appeal against the decision of a court or tribunal. It has been said that the purpose of s 7(1)(b) is to enable persons against whom proceedings have been brought by a public authority to rely on the Convention rights for their protection[3].

　　In relation to s 7(1)(b), it has been said by the House of Lords, in an English case concerned with criminal proceedings, that where the very fact of *proceeding* with a criminal trial would constitute a breach of a Convention right, there is no discretion as to whether to continue with the trial as to do so would thereby constitute an unlawful act[4]. On the other hand, a finding on appeal that there has been a breach of a Convention right will not necessarily result in the quashing of the conviction, whether the point is raised under the HRA 1998[5] or the SA 1998[6]. In cases concerned with violations of Article 6 that affected the way the trial was conducted, the critical question is whether the trial as a whole was unfair. That will be the case, where the trial proceeded on indictment, if there is a real possibility that, but for the breach of the Convention right, the jury would have arrived at a different verdict[7].

1   Or the Commission for Equality and Human Rights: Equality Act 2006, s 30(3).

2   Section 7(1)(b) can therefore confer on a court or tribunal a jurisdiction which it would not otherwise possess: *Manchester City Council v Pinnock* [2010] 3 WLR 1441. See also *Customs and Excise Commissioners v Newbury* [2003] 1 WLR 2131.

3   *R (A) v Director of Establishment of the Security Service* [2010] 1 AC 1 at para 45 per Lord Hope DPSC. A petition to the *nobile officium* of the High Court of Justiciary is a form of proceeding initiated by the petitioner and therefore does not fall within the scope of s 7(1)(b), even if the petition stems from or is consequential upon proceedings brought by the Crown: *Beck, Petitioner* 2010 SCCR 222.

4   *Attorney-General's Reference (No 2 of 2001)* [2004] 2 AC 72 at paras 33–34.

5   See eg *R v Forbes* [2001] 1 AC 473 at para 30; *R v Lambert* [2002] 2 AC 545 at para 159 per Lord Clyde; *R v Loveridge* [2001] EWCA Crim 973 (admission of evidence obtained in breach of Article 8).

6   See eg *Holland v HM Advocate* 2005 SC (PC) 3, *Sinclair v HM Advocate* 2005 1 SC (PC) 28 and *McInnes v HM Advocate* 2010 SC (UKSC) 28 (disclosure).

7   *McInnes v HM Advocate* 2010 SC (UKSC) 28 .

1.82 The appropriate stage in proceedings at which a Convention issue should be raised will depend on the circumstances. It has been said that as a general rule a question as to whether the admission or exclusion of evidence at a criminal trial is incompatible with the right to a fair trial under Article 6 is best considered after the trial has been completed. This is so that the question of fairness can be considered in the context of the trial as a whole. It is, however, undesirable that vulnerable witnesses such as the complainant in a rape trial should be exposed to the risk of having to give evidence again at a re-trial, as would happen if the verdict of the first trial were to be quashed on the ground that the accused did not receive a fair trial. In such a case, it is desirable that the issue should be determined before the trial. Similarly, if the issue is one of general public importance which is likely to affect other trials, it should be determined as soon as possible[1].

1   *R v A* [2001] 1 WLR 789 at para 11 per Lord Hope of Craighead. See also *Moir v HM Advocate* 2005 1 SC (PC) 1; *Holland v HM Advocate* 2005 1 SC (PC) 3 at para 41 per Lord Rodger of Earlsferry.

1.83 By virtue of the HRA 1998, s 22(4), s 7(1)(b) applies to proceedings brought by or at the instigation of a public authority whenever the act in question took place, but otherwise does not apply to an act taking place before s 7 came into force[1]. To that limited extent, s 6 can have retroactive effect.

---

1   The HRA 1998 was brought fully into force on 2 October 2000. For s 22(4), see paras **1.111–1.114** below.

Time limitation

1.84 The HRA 1998, s 7(5) provides that proceedings under s 7(1)(a) must be brought before the end of:

(a) the period of one year beginning with the date on which the act complained of took place; or

(b) such longer period as the court or tribunal considers equitable having regard to all the circumstances,

but that is subject to any rule imposing a stricter time limit in relation to the procedure in question[1]. There is no time limit imposed by the Act in respect of s 7(1)(b). It has been suggested that, in so far as any common law claim existing independently of the HRA 1998 is conjoined with a claim within s 7(1)(a), it will have its own limitation or prescriptive period, which will continue to apply[2]; that, if Convention rights are relied on in the development or application of common law principles in civil proceedings brought for a cause of action not arising under the HRA 1998, the time limits applicable to that cause of action will apply[3]; and that the time limit in s 7(5) is purely procedural in nature[4].

---

1   No such time limit originally applied if the point was raised under the SA 1998: *Somerville v Scottish Ministers* 2008 SC (HL) 45. This difference was, however, removed by the Convention Rights Proceedings (Amendment) (Scotland) Act 2009, in relation to proceedings brought on or after 2 November 2009. See para **1.152** below.

2   *Somerville v Scottish Ministers* 2008 SC (HL) 45 at para 175 per Lord Mance.

3   *Somerville v Scottish Ministers* 2008 SC (HL) 45 at para 175 per Lord Mance.

4   *Somerville v Scottish Ministers* 2008 SC (HL) 45 at para 112 per Lord Rodger of Earlsferry.

1.85 The wording of s 7(5) contemplates that an 'act' is a single event which occurred on a particular date. Different views have been expressed, *obiter*, as to how s 7(5) applies to what might be described as a continuing act (or failure to act), or as an act (or failure to act) which has continuing consequences[1]. In a case concerned with delay in holding a hearing, it was said that time ran from the time when the hearing was eventually held[2].

---

1   *Somerville v Scottish Ministers* 2008 SC (HL) 45 at paras 51–52 per Lord Hope of Craighead, para 81 per Lord Scott of Foscote, paras 89 and 112 per Lord Rodger of Earlsferry and paras 196–197 per Lord Mance. See also *A v Essex County Council* [2011] 1 AC 280 at para 113 per Baroness Hale JSC.

2   *Dunn v Parole Board* [2009] 1 WLR 728 at para 39 per Thomas LJ.

1.86 In relation to s 7(5)(b), it has been said that it would not be helpful to list the factors to be taken into account or to state which should have greater or lesser weight: it is for the court to examine in the circumstances of each case all the relevant factors and then decide whether it is equitable to provide for a longer period[1]. The disproportionality of the cost of the proceedings, relative to any benefit to the claimant or the wider public, has been held to be a good reason for holding that it was not equitable to extend the limitation period[2]. The Supreme Court declined on that basis to permit an extension of time where the applicant's case was arguable but, even if successful, would resolve no issue of principle and be unlikely to sound in significant damages[3]. The absence of prejudice to the respondent party has not been treated as decisive[4]. It has been said that the burden lies on the claimant to prove that there are circumstances which make it equitable that the defendant should not be able to take advantage of the limitation provisions[5].

1   *Dunn v Parole Board* [2009] 1 WLR 728.
2   *A v Essex County Council* [2011] 1 AC 280 at paras 167–169 per Lord Kerr of Tonaghmore JSC.
3   *A v Essex County Council* [2011] 1 AC 280.
4   *Weir v Secretary of State for Transport* [2004] EWHC 2772 (Ch).
5   *Cameron v Network Rail Infrastructure Ltd* [2007] 1 WLR 163. Such circumstances were held to be absent in that case, where the claimant was a solicitor who had done nothing to investigate the legal position for more than a year following the defendants' denial of liability. See also *Dobson v Thames Water Utilities Ltd* [2008] 2 All ER 362 (reversed on a different point, [2009] 3 All ER 319).

The meaning of 'victim'

1.87 The HRA 1998, s 7(7) provides that, for the purposes of s 7, a person is a victim of an unlawful act only if he would be a victim for the purposes of Article 34 of the ECHR if proceedings were brought in the European Court of Human Rights in respect of that act. The relevant principles established by the Strasbourg institutions, and the relevant domestic case law, are discussed in Chapter 2[1].

1   See paras **2.64–2.74** below.

Remedies against 'public authorities'

1.88 The HRA 1998, s 8 enables the court (defined as including a tribunal[1]) to grant appropriate remedies in relation to any act (or proposed act) of a public authority which the court finds is (or would be) unlawful under s 6(1). Where the court finds that any act (or proposed act) of a public authority is (or would be) unlawful, it may grant such relief or remedy, or make such order, within its powers as it considers just and appropriate[2]. The appropriate remedy will depend on the nature of the breach of Convention rights and all the circumstances[3]. It has been said that a remedy will be just and appropriate if it constitutes the kind of effective remedy required by Article 13 of the ECHR[4].

It has been held in an English case that s 8 does not allow a court to hold a criminal trial if the trial itself would be unfair[5].

1   HRA 1998, s 8(6).

2   HRA 1998, s 8(1). The Lord Chancellor could not be held liable for wasted expenses incurred when a hearing had to be aborted due to a lack of impartiality, because the Court of Appeal had ordered a re-hearing and no breach of a Convention right had therefore occurred: *In re Medicaments and Related Classes of Goods (No 4)* [2002] 1 WLR 269.

3   *Attorney-General's Reference (No 2 of 2001)* [2004] 2 AC 72 at para 24 per Lord Bingham of Cornhill. The remedies which have been given in respect of breaches of different Convention rights are discussed in subsequent chapters in the context of the discussion of the particular rights in question.

4   *Attorney-General's Reference (No 2 of 2001)* [2004] 2 AC 72 at para 175 per Lord Rodger of Earlsferry.

5   *Attorney-General's Reference (No 2 of 2001)* [2004] 2 AC 72.

Damages

Introduction

1.89 The focus of the ECHR is on the protection of human rights and not the award of compensation. Although the ECHR makes provision in Article 41 for affording just satisfaction to the victim of a violation, the award of compensation is far from being an automatic consequence of a finding that a violation has occurred. This approach is reflected in the HRA 1998, s 8. Damages[1] may be awarded only by a court which has power to award damages, or to order the payment of compensation in civil proceedings[2]. The purpose of this provision is to ensure that a claim for damages as a result of a criminal prosecution is brought in a civil court[3]. It has been said that s 8 does not give rise to a delictual action for breach of statutory duty, but gives the court a special statutory discretion, modelled in relation to damages on the European Court of Human Rights[4]. The remedy has novel features, in so far as it is discretionary, residual and to be awarded taking account of the principles applied by the Strasbourg Court, some of which are unfamiliar to our law of damages[5].

It is undecided whether s 8 is applicable where a pursuer invokes a Convention right in reply to a defence which would otherwise exist to the claim (eg statutory authority)[6]. Where a public authority is found liable in damages under s 8, the law of contribution (under the Law Reform (Miscellaneous Provisions) (Scotland) Act 1940) applies in relation to joint and several liability[7].

1   Ie for an act of a public authority which is unlawful under HRA 1998, s 6(1): HRA 1998, s 8(6).

2   HRA 1998, s 8(2). For example, the High Court of Justiciary is unable to award damages. HRA 1998, s 8(1) in any event keeps the court 'within its powers', which presumably refers to the powers of the court in the context of the proceedings before it.

3   *R v Kansal (No 2)* [2002] 2 AC 69 at para 60 per Lord Hope of Craighead.

4   *Somerville v Scottish Ministers* 2008 SC (HL) 45 at para 176 per Lord Mance. See also *Dobson v Thames Water Utilities Ltd* [2009] 3 All ER 319.

5   Eg whether the applicant is viewed as deserving or not, or whether the breach of the Convention was procedural or substantive, technical or flagrant. In a discrimination case, damages may be inappropriate because non-discriminatory treatment would have left the applicant no better off (although the person who benefited from the discrimination would have been worse off): *R (Wilkinson) v Inland Revenue Commissioners* [2005] 1 WLR 1718.

6   *Somerville v Scottish Ministers* 2008 SC (HL) 45 at paras 176–178 per Lord Mance (who considered it 'very arguable' that s 8 would apply).

7   HRA 1998, s 8(5).

Whether an award of damages should be made

1.90 No award of damages is to be made under the HRA 1998, s 8 unless, taking account of all the circumstances of the case, including any other relief or remedy granted, or order made, in relation to the act in question (by that or any other court) and the consequences of any decision in respect of that act, the court is satisfied that the award is necessary to afford just satisfaction to the person in whose favour it is made[1]. This echoes the language of Article 41 of the ECHR.

1   HRA 1998, s 8(3).

1.91 In determining whether to award damages, or the amount of an award, the court must take into account the principles applied by the European Court of Human Rights in relation to the award of compensation under Article 41 of the ECHR[1]. The approach adopted by the European Court depends to some extent on the particular ECHR guarantee which has been violated. It is possible to identify some basic principles which appear to be of general application: that the victim of a violation should as far as possible be put in the position he would have enjoyed had the requirements of the ECHR been complied with[2]; that compensation is not awarded unless the loss or damage complained of was caused by the violation in question[3]; that the burden lies on the applicant to prove his damage, unless damage was a necessary consequence of the breach; that, if damages are awarded, they will take account of any conduct of the applicant which contributed to his damage or injury[4]; and that the award of compensation is not based on the principles or scales of assessment used by domestic courts[5]. One can also infer from the case law that compensation is not awarded where the finding of a violation constitutes sufficient just satisfaction; that compensation can be (but is not always) awarded for non-pecuniary loss, including mental distress; that exemplary damages are not awarded; that compensation is not usually awarded for the loss of an opportunity[6], although it has been awarded in certain cases for the loss of an opportunity to present a meritorious case[7]; and that interest on compensation can be awarded (but rarely is)[8]. In practice, the European Court of Human Rights tends to carry out a broad equitable assessment of the facts of the individual case and decide whether compensation is appropriate in those circumstances. It takes account of a wider range of factors than a court in the UK would ordinarily do[9].

1   HRA 1998, s 8(4). The approach of the Strasbourg court is discussed at paras 2.76–2.77 below.

2   *Kingsley v United Kingdom* [GC] 2002-IV.

3   *Kingsley v United Kingdom* [GC] 2002-IV.

4   *Johnson v United Kingdom* 1997-VII; *DG v Ireland* 2002-III.

5   *Osman v United Kingdom* 1998-VIII. For example, £1500 was awarded for ten years of 'frustration, uncertainty and anxiety' in *Curley v United Kingdom* (28 March 2000).

6   *Ezeh and Connors v United Kingdom* [GC] 2003-X. For domestic discussion, see *R (KB) v Mental Health Review Tribunal* [2004] QB 936 and *R (Greenfield) v Secretary of State for the Home Department* [2005] 1 WLR 673.

7   See for example *Osman v United Kingdom* 1998-VIII.

8   See *Damages under the Human Rights Act 1998* (Scot Law Com No 180; Law Com No 266; Cm 4853).

9   Eg whether the applicant is viewed as deserving or not, or whether the breach of the Convention was procedural or substantive, technical or flagrant.

1.92 Since the European Court may decline to award damages, on the basis that a finding that there has been an infringement of a Convention guarantee is sufficient and just satisfaction, the national court must have the same power under the HRA 1998, s 8. This has been held, in particular, in cases concerned with Articles 5[1], 6[2] and 8[3]. In a case concerned with Article 5, it has been said that not every feeling of frustration and distress will justify an award of damages: it must be of such intensity as to justify such an award[4]. In relation to Article 6, it has been observed that compensation is not usually awarded by the European Court for a violation of that article[5].

In practice, there have been few cases in which damages have been awarded under s 8[6].

1   *R (KB) v Mental Health Review Tribunal* [2004] QB 936.

2   *R (Greenfield) v Secretary of State for the Home Department* [2005] 1 WLR 673.

3   *Anufrijeva v London Borough of Southwark* [2004] QB 1124; *Dobson v Thames Water Utilities Ltd* [2009] 3 All ER 319.

4   *R (KB) v Mental Health Review Tribunal* [2004] QB 936.

5   See the discussion in *R (Greenfield) v Secretary of State for the Home Department* [2005] 1 WLR 673.

6   See eg *R (Bernard) v Enfield London Borough Council* [2003] LGR 423 (breach of Art 8); *R (KB) v Mental Health Review Tribunal* [2004] QB 936 (Art 5); *R (B) v Director of Public Prosecutions* [2009] 1 WLR 2072 (Art 3); and *Greens, Petitioner* 2011 SLT 549 (Art 8). The awards in the first two of these cases were made following an approach which was disapproved in *R (Greenfield) v Secretary of State for the Home Department* [2005] 1 WLR 673. In *Napier v Scottish Ministers* 2005 1 SC 229 the court held that its award of damages under the common law, together with its finding of a violation of Art 3, constituted just satisfaction, rendering any further award of damages under the HRA 1998, s 8 or the SA 1998, s 100 unnecessary.

Level of damages

1.93 In relation to the level of damages, the HRA 1998, s 8(4) requires the court to take into account the principles applied by the European Court under Article 41 not only in determining whether to award damages but also in determining the amount of an award. This is consistent with the object of the Act, namely to enable domestic courts to give remedies which would otherwise have been available in Strasbourg. Courts in the UK should therefore look to Strasbourg for guidance as to the amount of awards, and not to domestic precedents[1].

1   *R (Greenfield) v Secretary of State for the Home Department* [2005] 1 WLR 673. Contrary
     statements in earlier cases were disapproved.

1.94 As has been mentioned, the European Court often makes no award of compensation under Article 41, on the basis that the finding of a violation is in itself sufficient to afford the victim just satisfaction. When compensation is awarded by the European Court, it tends to be in the form of a global sum, without any breakdown between different heads of loss, or sometimes even any distinction between damages and the expenses of the proceedings[1].

1   As, for example, in *Van der Leer v Netherlands* (1990) A 170-A.

1.95 In relation to s 8, Lord Bingham of Cornhill said in *R (Greenfield) v Secretary of State for the Home Department*:

> 'First, the 1998 Act is not a tort statute. Its objects are different and broader. Even in
> a case where a finding of violation is not judged to afford the applicant just
> satisfaction, such a finding will be an important part of his remedy and an important
> vindication of the right he has asserted … The [European] court routinely describes
> its awards as equitable, which I take to mean that they are not precisely calculated
> but are judged by the court to be fair in the individual case. Judges in England and
> Wales must also make a similar judgment in the case before them. They are not
> inflexibly bound by Strasbourg awards in what may be different cases. But they
> should not aim to be significantly more or less generous than the court might be
> expected to be, in a case where it was willing to make an award at all.'[1]

1   *R (Greenfield) v Secretary of State for the Home Department* [2005] 1 WLR 673 at para 19.

Challenges to judicial determinations

1.96 The HRA 1998, s 9 concerns judicial acts. A 'judicial act' is defined[1] to mean a judicial act of court[2], including an act done on the instructions, or on behalf, of a judge[3]. Proceedings under s 7(1)(a) in respect of a judicial act may be brought only:

(a) by exercising a right of appeal;

(b) on a petition for judicial review; or

(c) in such other forum as may be prescribed by rules[4].

That does not affect any rule of law which prevents a court from being the subject of judicial review[5]. Nor does it exclude reliance on Convention rights in proceedings falling within the scope of s 7(1)(b), such as an appeal (civil or criminal) against the decision of a court or tribunal.

1   HRA 1998, s 9(5).

2   'Court' includes a tribunal: HRA 1998, s 9(5).

3   'Judge' includes a member of a tribunal, a justice of the peace and a clerk or other officer entitled to exercise the jurisdiction of a court: HRA 1998, s 9(5).

4   HRA 1998, s 9(1).

5   HRA 1998, s 9(2). For example, the High Court of Justiciary is not subject to the supervisory jurisdiction of the Court of Session.

1.97 Since proceedings under s 7(1)(a) are civil proceedings, the right of appeal to which s 9(1)(a) refers must be a civil appeal[1]. In relation to s 9(1)(c), the relevant rule[2] prescribes the Court of Session in cases where proceedings in respect of the judicial act in question could not, at any time since the date of that act, have competently been brought under s 9(1)(a) or (b).

1   *R v Kansal (No 2)* [2002] 2 AC 69 at paras 63–64 per Lord Hope of Craighead; *Beck, Petitioner* 2010 SCCR 222.

2   Human Rights Act 1998 (Jurisdiction) (Scotland) Rules 2000, SI 2000/301, r 4. Proceedings under s 9(1)(c) cannot therefore be brought in the High Court of Justiciary: *Beck, Petitioner* 2010 SCCR 222.

1.98 The HRA 1998, s 9 preserves judicial immunity except to the extent required by Article 5(5) of the ECHR. Damages cannot be awarded in proceedings under the HRA 1998 in respect of a judicial act done in good faith, otherwise than to compensate a person to the extent required by Article 5(5)[1]. Any such award of damages is to be made against the Crown, but no award may be made unless the appropriate person, if not a party to the proceedings, is joined[2], ie made a party to the proceedings.

1   HRA 1998, s 9(3). Exemplary damages therefore cannot be awarded. As to ECHR, Article 5(5), see para **4.241** below.

2   HRA 1998, s 9(4). The 'appropriate person' means the minister responsible for the court concerned, or a person or government department nominated by him: HRA 1998, s 9(5).

Miscellaneous provisions

Safeguarding existing rights, etc

1.99 The HRA 1998, s 11 safeguards existing human rights by providing that a person's reliance on a Convention right does not restrict any other right or freedom conferred on him by or under any law having effect in any part of the UK, or his right to make any claim or bring any proceedings which he could make or bring apart from ss 7–9[1]. Nothing in the Act creates a criminal offence[2].

---

1   For judicial discussion, see *R(S) v Chief Constable of the South Yorkshire Police* [2002] 1 WLR
     3223, CA per Lord Woolf at para 34; *Whaley v Lord Advocate* 2008 SC (HL) 107 at para 14
     per Lord Hope of Craighead.
2   HRA 1998, s 7(8).

Freedom of expression; and freedom of thought, conscience and religion

1.100 The HRA 1998, ss 12 and 13 respond to concerns expressed by, respectively, the media and the churches during the progress of the Bill, as to the impact which its provisions might have upon their activities.

1.101 The HRA 1998, s 12 applies if a court[1] is considering whether to grant any relief[2] which, if granted, might affect the exercise of the Convention right[3] to freedom of expression[4]. In terms of s 12(2), if the person against whom the application for relief is made ('the respondent') is neither present nor represented, no such relief is to be granted unless the court is satisfied that the applicant has taken all practicable steps to notify the respondent, or that there are compelling reasons why the respondent should not be notified.

---

1   Including a tribunal: HRA 1998, s 12(5).
2   'Relief' includes any remedy or order, other than in criminal proceedings: HRA 1998, s 12(5).
3   ECHR, Art 10.
4   HRA 1998, s 12(1).

1.102 In terms of s 12(3), no such relief is to be granted so as to restrain publication before trial unless the court is satisfied that the applicant is likely to establish that publication should not be allowed. It has been explained in an English case that the purpose of this provision is to set a higher threshold for the grant of interlocutory injunctions against the media than the *American Cyanamid* guideline of a 'serious question to be tried' or a 'real prospect' of success at the trial[1]: *mutatis mutandis,* it is likewise intended to set a higher test for the grant of interim interdict than would be imposed by the customary Scottish approach to the question whether a prima facie case has been established. At the same time, in order to be Convention-compliant, s 12(3) must be sufficiently flexible in its application to give effect to countervailing Convention rights. The effect of s 12(3) was explained by Lord Nicholls of Birkenhead in *Cream Holdings Ltd v Banerjee* as follows:

> 'There can be no single, rigid standard governing all applications for interim restraint orders. Rather, on its proper construction the effect of section 12(3) is that the court is not to make an interim restraint order unless satisfied the applicant's prospects of success at the trial are sufficiently favourable to justify such an order being made in the particular circumstances of the case. As to what degree of likelihood makes the prospects of success "sufficiently favourable", the general approach should be that courts will be exceedingly slow to make interim restraint orders where the applicant has not satisfied the court he will probably ("more likely than not") succeed at the trial. In general, that should be the threshold an applicant must cross before

the court embarks on exercising its discretion, duly taking into account the relevant jurisprudence on article 10 and any countervailing Convention rights. But there will be cases where it is necessary for a court to depart from this general approach and a lesser degree of likelihood will suffice as a prerequisite. Circumstances where this may be so include those ... where the potential adverse consequences of disclosure are particularly grave, or where a short-lived injunction is needed to enable the court to hear and give proper consideration to an application for interim relief pending the trial or any relevant appeal.'[2]

1   *Cream Holdings Ltd v Banerjee* [2005] 1 AC 253 at para 15 per Lord Nicholls of Birkenhead.

2   *Cream Holdings Ltd v Banerjee* [2005] 1 AC 253 at para 22; applied in *Browne v Associated Newspapers Ltd* [2008] QB 103. Scottish examples of the application of s 12(3) include *Dickson Minto v Bonnier Media* 2002 SLT 776, *Response Handling Ltd v BBC* 2008 SLT 51 and *Scottish National Party v British Broadcasting Corporation* 2010 SC 495.

1.103 In terms of s 12(4), the court must have particular regard to the importance of the Convention right to freedom of expression and, where the proceedings relate to material which the respondent claims, or which appears to the court, to be journalistic, literary or artistic material (or to conduct connected with such material[1]), the court must also have particular regard to:

(a) the extent to which the material has, or is about to, become available to the public; or it is, or would be, in the public interest for the material to be published[2];

(b) any relevant privacy code[3].

In relation to s 12(4), it has been observed that one cannot have particular regard to Article 10 of the Convention without having equally particular regard at the very least to Article 8; and s 12 does not give either article pre-eminence over the other[4].

1   Cf *Goodwin v United Kingdom* 1996-II, 483.

2   This reflects Convention jurisprudence: see para 7.56 below.

3   Privacy is addressed in cl 3 of the Code of Practice ratified by the Press Complaints Commission in November 1997. The effect of cl 3 in relation to s 12(4) was discussed in *Douglas v Hello! Ltd (No 1)* [2001] QB 967.

4   *Campbell v MGN Ltd* [2004] 2 AC 457 at para 111 per Lord Hope of Craighead. Section 12(4) was also applied in such cases as *Attorney General v Times Newspapers Ltd* [2001] 1 WLR 885 and *X (A Woman formerly known as Mary Bell) v O'Brien* [2003] EMLR 37 (restraints upon publication in the media of details concerning a high-profile prisoner after her release), and was discussed in *Attorney General v Punch Ltd* [2003] 1 AC 1046.

1.104 The HRA 1998, s 13 provides that if a court's[1] determination of any question arising under the Act might affect the exercise by a religious organisation (itself or its members collectively) of the Convention right to freedom of thought, conscience and religion[2], it must have particular regard to the importance of that right[3].

1   Including a tribunal: HRA 1998, s 13(2).

2   Ie Art 9.

3   This provision was mentioned, but did not add anything of substance to the discussion, in *R (Amicus) v Secretary of State for Trade and Industry* [2007] ICR 1176. See also para **7.05** below.

Derogations and reservations

1.105 The HRA 1998, ss 14–17 deal with designated derogations or reservations from the ECHR[1]. Article 15 of the ECHR enables a contracting state to derogate from certain of its obligations under the ECHR in specified circumstances. Article 57 of the ECHR enables a contracting state, when signing the ECHR or when depositing its instrument of ratification, to make a reservation in respect of any provision to the extent that any law then in force in its territory is not in conformity with the provision. Derogations and reservations can also be made in respect of Protocols to the ECHR[2].

1   Cf HRA 1998, s 1(2): see para **1.29** above.

2   Where permitted by the terms of the Protocols. See eg Art 5 of Prot 1; Art 7 of Prot 7; contrast Arts 3 and 4 of Prot 6.

1.106 The HRA 1998, s 14 as amended[1] defines the expression 'designated derogation' to mean any derogation by the UK from an article of the ECHR, or of any protocol to the ECHR, which is designated for the purposes of the Act in an order[2] made by the Secretary of State[3]. The effect of the order, under s 1(1) and (2) of the HRA 1998, is to restrict the effect of the Convention right in question in the domestic law of the UK. Further provisions are designed to ensure that designated derogations for the purposes of the Act continue to reflect the UK's international obligations from time to time under the ECHR and its protocols[4]. The validity of a derogation order has been challenged in judicial proceedings, under anti-terrorism legislation which provided for the bringing of such a challenge[5].

1   See Secretary of State for Constitutional Affairs Order 2003, SI 2003/1887. For discussion of UK derogations in respect of Art 5 of the ECHR, see paras **4.147–4.148** below.

2   That is to say, a statutory instrument: HRA 1998, s 20(1) and (3).

3   HRA 1998, s 14(1). The order ceases to have effect unless approved by Parliament.

4   HRA 1998, s 14(3)–(6).

5   See *A v Secretary of State for the Home Department* [2005] 2 AC 68 (in relation to the Human Rights Act 1998 (Designated Derogation) Order 2001, SI 2001/3644, which concerned the detention of non-nationals who were suspected terrorists but could not be deported).

1.107 The HRA 1998, s 15 defines the expression 'designated reservation' to mean the UK's reservation to Article 2 of Protocol 1 to the ECHR[1], and any other reservation by the UK to an article of the ECHR, or of any Protocol to the ECHR, which is designated for the purposes of the Act in an order[2] made by the Lord Chancellor[3]. Further provisions are designed to ensure that designated reservations for the purposes of the Act continue to reflect the UK's international obligations from time to time under the ECHR and its Protocols[4].

1   This relates to the education of children in accordance with the wishes of their parents. The
     reservation is set out in the HRA 1998, Sch 3, Pt II.
2   Ie a statutory instrument: HRA 1998, s 20(1) and (3).
3   HRA 1998, s 15(1); Secretary of State for Constitutional Affairs Order 2003, SI 2003/1887.
4   HRA 1998, s 15 (3)–(5).

1.108 The HRA 1998, s 16 as amended[1] provides for a designated derogation to cease to have effect for the purposes of the Act after a period of five years[2], unless extended by an order made by the Secretary of State[3]. This reflects the emergency nature of derogations under Article 15 of the ECHR. The HRA 1998, s 17 makes similar provision in respect of designated reservations.

1   By the Human Rights (Amendment) Order 2001, SI 2001/1216; see also Secretary of State for
     Constitutional Affairs Order 2003, SI 2003/1887.
2   HRA 1998, s 16(1).
3   HRA 1998, s 16(2). See also s 20(1) and (4).

Appointment of judges

1.109 The HRA 1998, s 18 makes provision in respect of the appointment of serving UK judges to the European Court of Human Rights[1].

1   As amended by the Constitutional Reform Act 2005, Sch 4 para 278.

Miscellaneous

1.110 Most of the remaining provisions of the HRA 1998 are supplemental and can be discussed briefly. The HRA 1998, s 20 concerns the order-making powers contained in the Act[1]. The HRA 1998, s 21 defines certain terms used in the Act[2], and also abolishes the death penalty for military offences. The HRA 1998, s 22 is the commencement section[3].

1   Amended by the Secretary of State for Constitutional Affairs Order 2003, SI 2003/1887.
2   See para **1.29** above as to the meaning of 'Convention'.
3   As amended (in respect of Wales) by the Government of Wales Act 2006, Sch 10.

Extent of retroactive application of the HRA 1998

1.111 The extent to which the HRA 1998 has retroactive effect, so as to enable Convention rights to be enforced in respect of past events, has proved to be a difficult question[1]. The provisions of the Act came into force on 2 October 2000[2], in accordance with s 22. The only provision in the Act which gives retroactive effect to any of its provisions is s 22(4), which provides that s 7(1)(b):

'applies to proceedings brought by or at the instigation of a public authority whenever the act in question took place; but otherwise that subsection does not apply to an act taking place before the coming into force of that section'.

1   See in particular *Wilson v First County Trust Ltd (No 2)* [2004] 1 AC 816 at paras 186 ff per Lord Rodger of Earlsferry.

2   With the exception of ss 18, 20, 21(5) and 22, which came into force on 9 November 1998.

1.112 In general, therefore, the HRA 1998, ss 6–9 are directed at post-Act conduct and post-Act events[1]. An application for judicial review of a decision taken by a public authority prior to 2 October 2000 cannot in general be brought on the basis that the decision was incompatible with a Convention right[2]. Nor do the duties of investigation of deaths imposed by s 6 apply in respect of deaths occurring prior to 2 October 2000[3]. Nor can the Act be relied upon retrospectively so as to create a right of action in respect of conduct which was lawful at the time when it took place[4], or so as to alter rights of private parties which had accrued or vested prior to 2 October 2000[5].

1   *Wilson v First County Trust Ltd (No 2)* [2004] 1 AC 816 at para 12 per Lord Nicholls of Birkenhead.

2   *R (Ben-Abdelaziz) v Haringey London Borough Council* [2001] 1 WLR 1485; *Advocate General v Macdonald* 2003 SC (HL) 35; *DJS v Criminal Injuries Compensation Appeal Tribunal* 2007 SC 748.

3   *Re McKerr* [2004] 1 WLR 807; *R (Hurst) v London Northern District Coroner* [2007] 2 AC 189; *Jordan v Lord Chancellor* [2007] 2 AC 226. Otherwise, as Lord Hoffmann observed in *Re McKerr,* 'it would in principle be necessary to investigate the deaths by state action of the Princes in the Tower'.

4   Cf *Wainwright v Home Office* [2004] 2 AC 406.

5   *Wilson v First County Trust Ltd (No 2)* [2004] 1 AC 816.

1.113 An exception to this scheme is created by s 22(4). Its effect is that, in response to proceedings brought by or at the instigation of a public authority, a victim of an unlawful act may rely on a Convention right 'whenever the act in question took place'. So this provision enables a victim to assert and rely on a Convention right in respect of conduct which was not unlawful under domestic law when it took place. The scope of s 22(4) is, however, limited. In particular, an appellant cannot rely on the HRA 1998 in an appeal (whether civil or criminal) against a decision of a court or tribunal which was taken before the Act came into force[1]. The same approach applies also to references by the Criminal Cases Review Commission (since they are required to be treated as appeals)[2]. An inquest does not constitute proceedings brought by or at the instigation of a public authority, since inquest proceedings are not brought against those participating in them[3].

1   *R v Lambert* [2002] 2 AC 545; *R v Kansal (No 2)* [2002] 2 AC 69; *R v Lyons* [2003] 1 AC 976; *R v Benjafield* [2003] 1 AC 1099; *Advocate General v Macdonald* 2003 SC (HL) 35; *Hoekstra v HM Advocate (No 6)* 2002 SCCR 135; *DJS v Criminal Injuries Compensation Appeal Tribunal* 2007 SC 748; *Dickson v HM Advocate* 2008 JC 181. The remarks of Lord Hope of Craighead (who dissented in *Lambert* and *Kansal*) in *Aston Cantlow and Wilmcote with Billesley*

Parochial Church Council v Wallbank [2004] 1 AC 546 at para 32 suggest a limitation to this approach, but were *obiter dicta* and were not supported by the other members of the House.

2   *R v Kansal (No 2)* [2002] 2 AC 69.

3   *R (Hurst) v London Northern District Coroner* [2007] 2 AC 189.

1.114 The HRA 1998, s 3 expressly applies to legislation 'whenever enacted'. It may therefore have the effect of changing the interpretation and effect of legislation already in force. Subject to the retroactive effect given to s 7(1)(b) of the Act by s 22(4), however, any new interpretation of legislation consequent on an application of s 3 cannot alter rights or obligations which had been acquired or entered into prior to 2 October 2000[1]. Nor can s 3(1) be applied to invalidate a decision of a court or tribunal which was good at the time when it was made[2]. Equally, no question can arise of the court making a declaration of incompatibility under s 4 in a case where s 3 is not available as an interpretative tool[3].

1   *Wilson v First County Trust Ltd (No 2)* [2004] 1 AC 816; *Jordan v Lord Chancellor* [2007] 2 AC 226.

2   *Aston Cantlow and Wilmcote with Billesley Parochial Church Council v Wallbank* [2004] 1 AC 546 at para 29 per Lord Hope of Craighead; *R v Lambert* [2002] 2 AC 545 at para 142 per Lord Clyde.

3   *Wilson v First County Trust Ltd (No 2)* [2004] 1 AC 816 at para 23 per Lord Nicholls of Birkenhead.

1.115 The principle of legal certainty requires that the retrospective effect of a judicial decision is generally excluded from cases that have been finally determined[1]. Cases which have been finally determined should not therefore ordinarily be re-opened in consequence of a decision in a subsequent case which implies that Convention rights may have been violated[2].

1   *Cadder v HM Advocate* 2010 SCCR 951.

2   *Cadder v HM Advocate* 2010 SCCR 951, following the approach adopted by the Irish Supreme Court in *A v Governor of Arbour Hill Prison* [2006] IR 88. As to late grounds of appeal based on a change in understanding of the law, see *R v Cottrell* [2007] 1 WLR 3262; *Interfact Ltd v Liverpool City Council* [2011] 2 WLR 396 (discussed at paras **3.72** and **5.229** below).

THE SCOTLAND ACT 1998

Introduction

1.116 Another aspect of the programme of constitutional reform to which the Government elected in May 1997 was committed was devolution to Scotland, Northern Ireland and Wales. The White Paper on Scottish devolution[1], published in July 1997, left open the precise implications for devolution of giving further domestic effect to the ECHR, although making it clear that the Scottish Executive[2] and Parliament would implement the UK's international obligations. Although Acts of the Scottish Parliament were to have the status of subordinate legislation for the purposes of the HRA 1998[3] and would therefore fall within the scope of s 6 of that Act, and the acts and omissions of the Scottish Government would equally fall within the ambit of s 6, that Act could not be relied on, initially at least, to ensure their compatibility with the ECHR, since the Scotland Act 1998 was to come into force in advance of most of the provisions of the HRA 1998. There were two broad approaches by means of which the risk of incompatibility with the ECHR could be avoided: by enabling the UK Government to override Acts of the Scottish Parliament (or subordinate legislation, or executive action) which would contravene the ECHR, or by making it impossible for the Scottish Parliament or Government competently to legislate or act in a manner which was incompatible with the ECHR. The White Paper on the Human Rights Bill[4], published in October 1997, made it clear that the latter approach was to be adopted:

'The Government has decided that the Scottish Parliament will have no power to legislate in a way which is incompatible with the Convention; and similarly that the Scottish Executive will have no power to make subordinate legislation or to take executive action which is incompatible with the Convention. It will accordingly be possible to challenge such legislation and actions on the ground that the Scottish Parliament or Executive has incorrectly applied its powers. If the challenge is successful then the legislation or action would be held to be unlawful.'[5]

These proposals were reflected in the provisions of the Scotland Bill, which were enacted (with substantial modifications) in the SA 1998.

1   *Scotland's Parliament* (Cm 3658) (1997).

2   As it was then referred to. At the time of writing, it is anticipated that the Scotland Act 2011 will re-name the Scottish Executive as the Scottish Government, and the latter usage has been generally adopted in the present work.

3   HRA 1998, s 21(1).

4   *Rights Brought Home* (Cm 3782) (1997).

5   *Rights Brought Home* (Cm 3782) (1997), para 2.21.

1.117 The SA 1998 therefore addresses questions concerning the Convention rights primarily in the form of questions as to the competence or *vires* of Acts of the Scottish Parliament and acts of members of the Scottish Government. Formally similar questions arise in relation to the other limitations on the powers of the Scottish Parliament and Government: in particular, questions as to whether legislation or executive action falls within the devolved areas of responsibility or is incompatible with EU law. Such questions are termed 'devolution issues'. After 1999, when the SA 1998 came into force, the courts were called upon to determine numerous such issues, most of which concerned questions of criminal procedure. At the time of writing, it is anticipated that, as a result of amendments to be made to the SA 1998 by the Scotland Act 2011, acts and omissions of the Lord Advocate in prosecuting any offence or in the capacity of head of the systems of criminal prosecution and investigation of deaths in Scotland may be excluded from the definition of devolution issues, but will continue to fall within the scope of the HRA 1998 and of a number of provisions of the SA 1998, as explained below.

1.118 The devolution statutes for Northern Ireland[1] and Wales[2], although establishing systems of devolved government which differ in various ways from the Scottish system, contain similar provisions in relation to Convention rights. Under each statute, the final power of decision in relation to devolution issues is held by the Supreme Court of the United Kingdom[3]. The legal issues arising under the SA 1998, the Northern Ireland Act and the Government of Wales Act cannot therefore be viewed in isolation from one another: the devolution statutes are designed to form a coherent scheme, with uniformity of approach being ensured by the Supreme Court. Although the Scottish case law is currently more developed than that concerned with Northern Irish or Welsh devolution, the latter should not be overlooked when questions under the SA 1998 require to be considered.

1   Northern Ireland Act 1998.

2   Government of Wales Act 1998, as amended by the Government of Wales Act 2006.

3   Constitutional Reform Act 2005, s 40 and Sch 9, paras 93–107. Prior to the entry into force of these provisions, the corresponding power was held by the House of Lords in relation to Scottish civil cases, and by the Judicial Committee of the Privy Council in relation to Scottish criminal cases.

1.119 The consequence of rendering it incompetent for the devolved institutions to act incompatibly with Convention rights, when those institutions are also public authorities within the meaning of the HRA 1998, is that Convention rights are to that extent protected under both the devolution statutes and the HRA 1998. The scheme for protecting Convention rights under the SA 1998 (and the other devolution statutes) differs, however, in important respects from the scheme established by the HRA 1998.

Acts of the Scottish Parliament

Limitations on competence

1.120 The SA 1998, s 29(1) provides that an Act of the Scottish Parliament is not law so far as any provision of the Act is outside the legislative competence of the Parliament. The SA 1998, s 29(2) provides that a provision is outside that competence in a number of circumstances, including where it is incompatible[1] with any of the Convention rights or with EU law[2]. The expression 'Convention rights' is defined[3] as having the same meaning as in the HRA 1998[4].

1   As to 'incompatibility', see paras **1.54–1.55** and **1.78** above and paras **1.140–1.145** below.

2   SA 1998, s 29(2)(d).

3   SA 1998, s 126(1).

4   HRA 1998, s 1. See para **1.29** above. The Strasbourg jurisprudence must therefore be taken into account under the SA 1998 also: *R v HM Advocate* 2003 SC (PC) 21 at para 54 per Lord Hope of Craighead.

Interpretation of legislative proposals and provisions

1.121 In terms of the SA 1998, s 101(2), a provision of an Act of the Scottish Parliament, or of a Bill for such Act, or of subordinate legislation made[1] by a member of the Scottish Government, is to be read as narrowly as is required for it to be within competence, provided such a reading is possible. In contrast, the HRA 1998, s 3(1) requires Acts of the Scottish Parliament and certain instruments made by Scottish Ministers[2] to be read and given effect in a way that is compatible with the Convention rights, so far as it is possible to do so[3]. In *DS v HM Advocate*, Lord Hope of Craighead observed:

> 'The explanation for the choice of language in sec 101(2) is to be found in the way the limits of the legislative competence of the Scottish Parliament are defined in sec 29(2). The matters listed there extend well beyond incompatibility with the Convention rights. They include legislation relating to reserved matters as defined in sch 5 and legislation which is in breach of the restrictions in sch 4. An attempt by the Scottish Parliament to widen the scope of its legislative competence as defined in those schedules will be met by the requirement that any provision which could be read in such a way as to be outside competence must be read as narrowly as is required for it to be within competence.
>
> It is otherwise in the case of the Convention rights. The proper starting point is to construe the legislation as directed by sec 3(1) of the Human Rights Act. If it passes this test, so far as the Convention rights are concerned it will be within competence. The obligation to construe a provision in an act of the Scottish Parliament so far as it is possible to do so in a way that is compatible with the Convention rights is a strong one. The court must prefer compatibility to incompatibility. This enables it to look closely at the legislation to see if it can be explained and operated in a way that is compatible and, if it is not, how it can be construed so as to make it so.'[4]

1   Or confirmed or approved (or purporting to be made, confirmed or approved) by a member of the Scottish Government: SA 1998, s 101(1).

2   HRA 1998, s 21(1).

3   See paras **1.36–1.44** above.

4   *DS v HM Advocate* 2007 SC (PC) 1 at paras 23–24.

Scrutiny of Bills

1.122 The SA 1998 contains provisions designed to ensure that Bills are scrutinised before their introduction in the Scottish Parliament, and to allow for their further scrutiny prior to their submission for Royal Assent. Under s 31, a member of the Scottish Government[1] in charge of a Bill must, on or before introduction of the Bill in the Parliament, state that in his view the provisions of the Bill would be within the legislative competence of the Parliament[2]. In addition, the Presiding Officer of the Parliament must, on or before the introduction of the Bill, decide whether or not in his view the provisions of the Bill would be within the legislative competence of the Parliament and state his decision. These provisions do not influence the determination by the courts of a legal challenge to a statutory provision enacted by the Scottish Parliament: decisions by the Minister[3] in charge of a Bill and by the Presiding Officer that a Bill is within the vires of the Scottish Parliament are 'no more than statements of opinion which do not bind the judiciary'[4]. Such statements may conceivably be challengeable on common law grounds (such as unreasonableness), if title and interest to sue can be demonstrated, but the courts might be reluctant to interfere in the legislative process. It is difficult to see how a challenge could be brought on Convention grounds, given the need to satisfy the 'victim' test and the fact that these are no more than statements of opinion. Legal proceedings can in principle be taken against a Law Officer or a member of the Scottish Government; and the SA 1998 provides for proceedings against the Parliament or the Presiding Officer, although only a restricted range of remedies is available[5].

1   At the time of writing, it is anticipated that the reference to a member of the Scottish Government may be amended by the SA 2011 to 'a person'.

2   Standing Orders rule 9.3.3a specifies that in relation to Public Bills, 'A Member's Bill shall, and a Committee Bill may, also be accompanied by a Policy Memorandum, as defined in paragraph 3(c) (but with the reference [to an assessment of the effects, if any, of the Bill on equal opportunities, human rights, etc] to the Scottish Ministers read as a reference to the member introducing the Bill)'. In respect of Private Bills, see rule 9A.2.2.

3   See fn 1 above.

4   *A v Scottish Ministers* 2002 SC (PC) 63 at 66–67 per Lord Hope of Craighead.

5   SA 1998, s 40. The Crown Proceedings Act 1947, s 21, would also be relevant to the remedies available: see SA 1998, Sch 8, para 7. See also *Davidson v Scottish Ministers* 2006 SC (HL) 41 and *Beggs v Scottish Ministers* 2007 SLT 235.

1.123 These statutory requirements are reflected in the Standing Orders of the Scottish Parliament[1]. Rule 9.3.1 requires a Bill, on its introduction, to be accompanied by a written statement signed by the Presiding Officer indicating whether or not in his or her view the provisions of the Bill would be within the legislative competence of the Parliament and, if in his or her view any of the provisions would not be within such competence, indicating which those provisions are and the reasons for that view. Rule 9.3.3 requires a Bill introduced by a member of the Scottish Government also to be accompanied by a written statement signed by the member of the Scottish Government in charge of the Bill which states that in his or her view the provisions of the Bill would be within the legislative competence of the Parliament. The statement must also include explanatory notes summarising the effect of the Bill and a Policy Memorandum which sets out (i) the policy objectives of the Bill; (ii) whether alternative ways of meeting those objectives were considered and, if so, why the approach taken in the Bill was adopted; (iii) the consultation, if any, which was undertaken on those objectives and the ways of meeting them or on the detail of the Bill and a summary of the outcome of that consultation; and (iv) an assessment of the effects, if any, of the Bill on human rights and other matters.

1   Available at http://www.scottish.parliament.uk/business/so/sto-c.htm.

1.124 Scrutiny of Bills takes place in committees, with the general principles of a Bill considered at stage 1 and detailed amendments at stage 2. Human rights issues can be considered by the committees (possibly with the assistance of the Scottish Commission for Human Rights[1]), but there is no separate human rights committee equivalent to the UK Parliament's Joint Committee on Human Rights.

1   See para **1.181** below.

1.125 Once a Bill has been passed, it is for the Presiding Officer to submit it for Royal Assent[1]. There is a period of four weeks beginning with the passing of a Bill during which the Advocate General, the Lord Advocate or the Attorney General can refer to the Supreme Court the question whether a Bill or any provision of a Bill would be within the legislative competence of the Parliament[2]. A Law Officer cannot however make a reference if he has notified the Presiding Officer that he does not intend to make a reference in relation to the Bill[3]. The Presiding Officer cannot submit a Bill for Royal Assent at any time when any of the Law Officers is entitled to make a reference, or when any such reference has been made but has not been decided or otherwise disposed of by the Supreme Court[4]. If the Supreme Court decides that the Bill or any provision of it would not be within the legislative competence of the Parliament, then the Presiding Officer cannot submit the Bill for Royal Assent in its unamended form[5]. The Bill can, however, be reconsidered by the Parliament following an adverse decision by the Supreme Court; and any Bill amended on reconsideration can then be approved or rejected by the Parliament[6]. Where a Bill is approved following its reconsideration, there is then a further four-week period during which it can again be referred by a Law Officer to the Supreme Court[7]. In the event that a reference to the Supreme Court results in a reference to the European Court of Justice for a preliminary ruling, special provisions apply[8]. The fact that a Law Officer has decided not to refer a Bill to the Supreme Court is not of consequence in determining a subsequent challenge to the compatibility of the Act in legal proceedings[9].

1   SA 1998, s 32(1).

2   SA 1998, s 33(1) and (2)(a), as amended by the Constitutional Reform Act 2005, Sch 9. The difficulties which may be involved in attempting to determine the compatibility of a Bill with Convention rights without a concrete factual setting are evident.

3   SA 1998, s 33(3).

4   SA 1998, s 32(2). At the time of writing, it is anticipated that s 32(2) may be amended by the SA 2011 so that the words 'any such reference has been made' become 'a general reference has been made in relation to the Bill under section 33'. The proposed s 33A will enable a Law Officer to make a limited reference, ie a reference which does not affect provisions specified in the reference as the unaffected provisions.

5   SA 1998, s 32(3).

6   SA 1998, s 36(4).

7   SA 1998, s 33(2).

8   SA 1998, s 34, read with SA 1998, ss 32(3)(B) and 36(4)(B). At the time of writing, it is anticipated that s 34 may be amended by the SA 2011.

9   *A v Scottish Ministers* 2002 SC (PC) 63 at 66–67 per Lord Hope of Craighead.

1.126 Under the SA 1998, s 35 the Secretary of State can make an order prohibiting the Presiding Officer from submitting a Bill for Royal Assent if it contains provisions which he has reasonable grounds to believe would be incompatible with any international obligations or the interests of defence or national security, or (in the case of modifications of the law as it applies to reserved matters) would have an adverse effect on the operation of the law as it applies to reserved matters. Such an order can be made within the period of four weeks following the passing of the Bill, the date of any decision or disposal by the Supreme Court on a reference, or the approval of the Bill following reconsideration by the Parliament. Standing Orders provide for the reconsideration of the Bill in the event that such an order is made[1]. The Secretary of State has a similar power under s 58 to intervene where he has reasonable grounds to believe that any action proposed to be taken[2] by a member of the Scottish Government would be incompatible with any international obligations. For the purposes of these provisions, the expression 'international obligations' excludes compatibility with the ECHR or EU law[3]; but it would include obligations under other human rights treaties ratified by the UK.

1   Rules 9.9.2 and 9.9.3; see also SA 1998, s 36(4)(c).

2   This has been said to include the proposed introduction of a Bill in the Parliament: *Whaley v Lord Advocate* 2008 SC (HL) 107 at para 9 per Lord Hope of Craighead.

3   SA 1998, s 126(10).

Post-enactment remedial powers

1.127 The SA 1998, s 107 provides for subordinate legislation to make 'such provision as the person making the legislation considers necessary or expedient' in consequence of an Act of the Scottish Parliament which is not, or may not be, within its competence, or any purported exercise by a member of the Scottish Government of his functions which is not, or may not be, an exercise or a proper exercise of those functions[1]. Such subordinate legislation can have retrospective effects[2]. The exercise of these powers may be liable to give rise to a variety of issues under the Convention.

Further powers to make remedial orders are conferred on the Scottish Ministers by the Convention Rights (Compliance) (Scotland) Act 2001, ss 12–14[3].

1   SA 1998, s 107.

2   SA 1998, s 114(3).

3   See para **1.58** above.

Challenges to Acts of the Scottish Parliament

1.128 There have been a number of challenges to legislation passed by the Scottish Parliament on the ground that statutory provisions are incompatible with Convention rights. They have concerned inter alia the Mental Health (Public Safety and

Appeals) (Scotland) Act 1999[1], the Protection of Wild Mammals (Scotland) Act 2002[2], the Convention Rights (Compliance) (Scotland) Act 2001[3], the Sexual Offences (Procedure and Evidence) (Scotland) Act 2002[4], the Damages (Asbestos-related Conditions) (Scotland) Act 2009[5] and the Tobacco and Medical Services (Scotland) Act 2010[6]. In one case the challenge had a measure of success, as a provision was 'read down' under the HRA 1998, s 3 in order to avoid an incompatibility with Convention rights[7]. As in cases where a declaration of incompatibility is sought under the HRA 1998, similarly in a challenge to legislation under the SA 1998, s 29 the court is concerned with the effect of the legislation rather than with the background material which preceded it or the anterior reasoning of the Parliament or of the Scottish Government[8].

1   *A v Scottish Ministers* 2002 SC (PC) 63.

2   *Adams v Scottish Ministers* 2004 SC 665; *Whaley v Lord Advocate* 2008 SC (HL) 107.

3   *Flynn v HM Advocate* 2004 SC (PC) 1.

4   *DS v HM Advocate* 2007 SC (PC) 1.

5   *AXA General Insurance Ltd v Lord Advocate* 2011 SLT 439. An appeal was heard by the Supreme Court during June 2011.

6   *Sinclair Collis Ltd v Lord Advocate* 2011 SLT 620.

7   A statutory presumption to be applied by the court 'in entertaining an objection' by the accused to the disclosure of his previous record (namely, that its disclosure was in the interests of justice) was read as setting out the default position that would apply if the accused failed to make any objection; it was to be disregarded when the court was considering an objection which had been made: *DS v HM Advocate* 2007 SC (PC) 1 at para 48 per Lord Hope of Craighead.

8   *DS v HM Advocate* 2007 SC (PC) 1 at paras 79 and 82 per Lord Rodger of Earlsferry.

Acts of Members of the Scottish Government

The Scottish Government

1.129 In order to understand how the Convention applies under the SA 1998 to administrative acts, it is necessary to begin with a rather complicated taxonomy. The Scottish Administration comprises the Scottish Government (whose members are referred to collectively as the Scottish Ministers[1]), junior Scottish Ministers[2], the holders of certain non-ministerial offices[3] and the staff of the Scottish Administration[4] (ie civil servants). The members of the Scottish Government are the First Minister, Ministers appointed by the First Minister under the SA 1998, s 47, the Lord Advocate and the Solicitor General for Scotland[5]. Statutory functions (ie functions conferred by any enactment, including an Act of the Scottish Parliament or an Act of the UK Parliament[6]) may be conferred on the Scottish Ministers as a whole, or on the First Minister alone, or on the Lord Advocate alone[7]. Statutory functions conferred on the Lord Advocate alone after he ceases to be a Minister of the Crown, together with any functions exercisable by him immediately before he ceases to be a Minister of the Crown, comprise his 'retained functions'[8].

1   SA 1998, s 44(2).

2   SA 1998, s 49.

3   SA 1998, s 126(8).

4   SA 1998, s 51.

5   SA 1998, s 44(1).

6   SA 1998, ss 52(7) and 126(1).

7   SA 1998, s 52(1), (2), (5)(A) and (6)(B).

8   SA 1998, s 52(6).

Civil servants and junior Ministers

1.130 Since junior Scottish Ministers are appointed 'to assist the Scottish Ministers in the exercise of their functions'[1], their acts are presumably to be treated as those of the Scottish Ministers, and therefore as those of the members of the Scottish Government. The *Carltona*[2] principle applies to the Scottish Ministers, so that the acts of civil servants, acting in the name of a Scottish Minister and on his behalf, will be treated as his acts[3]. The acts of members of the Procurator Fiscal Service have, by concession of the Crown, been treated as the acts of the Lord Advocate[4]. The acts of a person who is not a member of the Scottish Government, and is not acting on behalf of a member of the Scottish Government in exercising a given function, will not be treated as those of the Scottish Ministers (even if the person is also a member of the staff of the Scottish Administration)[5].

1   SA 1998, s 49.

2   *Carltona v Works Comrs* [1943] 2 All ER 560.

3   See eg *Napier v Scottish Ministers* 2005 1 SC 229; *Somerville v Scottish Ministers* 2008 SC (HL) 45; *Beggs v Scottish Ministers* 2007 SLT 235.

4   See eg *Starrs v Ruxton* 2000 JC 208, *Buchanan v McLean* 2002 SC (PC) 1 and *Millar v Dickson* 2002 SC (PC) 30.

5   *Somerville v Scottish Ministers* 2008 SC (HL) 45 (prison governor exercising function conferred by Prison Rules on holder of that office); *Goatley v HM Advocate* 2008 JC 1 and *La Torre v HM Advocate* 2008 JC 23 (Crown Agent acting as designated authority for purposes of extradition legislation). Contrast *Napier v Scottish Ministers* 2005 1 SC 229 (decision that remand prisoners be housed in particular hall was result of policy adopted by Scottish Ministers, not exercise of discretion by prison governor).

Powers transferred to Scottish Ministers: limits on competence

1.131 The SA 1998, s 53 provides for the general transfer of existing ministerial functions of the UK Government to the Scottish Ministers. It applies to three specified categories of function which appear to cover all the functions exercisable by a Minister of the Crown[1] – subject to the important exception of the retained functions[2] of the Lord Advocate – and provides that those functions 'shall, so far as they are exercisable within devolved competence', be exercisable by the Scottish Ministers.

---

1   Subject to specified exceptions, eg functions exercisable in relation to cross-border public authorities: SA 1998, s 88(1).

2   Defined by s 52(6) as comprising any function that was exercisable by the Lord Advocate immediately before he ceased to be a UK Minister, and any other function conferred on him alone after that time.

1.132 The expression 'within devolved competence' is explained in s 54. This provides first, by s 54(2), that the making of any provision by subordinate legislation is outside devolved competence if the provision would be outside the legislative competence of the Parliament if it were included in an Act of the Scottish Parliament. In relation to any function other than a function of making, confirming or approving subordinate legislation, s 54(3) provides that it is outside devolved competence to exercise the function (or exercise it in any way) so far as a provision of an Act of the Scottish Parliament conferring the function (or, as the case may be, conferring it so as to be exercisable in that way) would be outside the legislative competence of the Parliament. These provisions have the effect that the functions transferred to the Scottish Ministers – other than the retained functions of the Lord Advocate – do not include any function which would be outside the legislative competence of the Scottish Parliament, and do not include any power to exercise a function in a way which would be outside the legislative competence of the Parliament. Accordingly, in broad terms, if the exercise of an existing function of a Minister of the Crown is incompatible with any Convention right, then the function is not transferred to the Scottish Ministers. Equally, if the exercise in a particular way of an existing function of a Minister of the Crown is incompatible with any Convention right, then the power to exercise it in that way is not transferred to the Scottish Ministers.

1.133 One effect of these provisions is that the power to exercise Crown powers incompatibly with the Convention rights – for example, where that was required by an Act of the UK Parliament – was not devolved by the SA 1998, but was retained by the Crown, ie by the United Kingdom Government. For example, if the Sheriff Courts (Scotland) Act 1971 conferred on the Secretary of State a power to appoint temporary sheriffs which was incompatible with the Convention rights, that power was not transferred to the Scottish Ministers (or abolished by an implied repeal) but remained with the Secretary of State[1].

---

1   *Starrs v Ruxton* 2000 JC 208 at 230 per Lord Justice-Clerk Cullen and at 251 per Lord Reed.

1.134 Prosecution functions were, however, treated differently, since they were not to be retained by the UK Government. They continue to be exercised by the Lord Advocate; but because he is now a member of the Scottish Government, his retained functions were excluded from the scope of the limitation on competence imposed by ss 53 and 54. Similarly, although the Lord Advocate's acts fall within the scope of the provision (discussed below) in the SA 1998, s 57(2) that a member of the Scottish Government has no power to do any act incompatible with

Convention rights, an exception was created (in s 57(3)) to enable him, and him alone, to act in breach of Convention rights when that is necessary to implement UK legislation[1]. At the time of writing, it is anticipated that s 57(3) may be amended by the SA 2011 so as to exclude from the scope of s 57(2) any act or omission of the Lord Advocate in prosecuting any offence or in the capacity of head of the systems of criminal prosecution and investigation of deaths in Scotland.

1   SA 1998, s 57(3). In *Goatley v HM Advocate* 2008 JC 1 and *La Torre v HM Advocate* 2008 JC 23 it was said that, when the Lord Advocate exercised a retained function under extradition legislation, he did not do so as head of the system of criminal prosecution in Scotland, with the implication that he did not do so in a capacity which fell within SA 1998, s 57(3). That would seemingly entail that the Lord Advocate might be prevented by s 57(2) from implementing UK primary legislation which was incompatible with the Convention, notwithstanding SA 1998, s 57(3) and HRA 1998, s 6(2). It seems unlikely that such a result was intended by Parliament.

1.135 The SA 1998, s 53, read with s 54, provides a basis for proceedings challenging the competency of the exercise of functions of the Scottish Ministers under (or purportedly under) pre-devolution legislation and prerogative powers[1].

1   *Somerville v Scottish Ministers* 2008 SC (HL) 45 at paras 28 and 46 per Lord Hope of Craighead and at paras 97 and 103 per Lord Rodger of Earlsferry.

'Acts' of a Member of the Scottish Government: limits on competence

1.136 Compatibility with Convention rights is further addressed in the SA 1998, s 57(2). It provides that a member of the Scottish Government has no power to make any subordinate legislation, or to do any other act, so far as the legislation or act is incompatible with any of the Convention rights. Compliance with Convention rights is thus a question of vires[1].

1   It has been suggested that SA 1998, s 57(2) is essentially different in this respect from HRA 1998, s 6: see eg *R v HM Advocate* 2003 SC (PC) 21 at paras 126–128 per Lord Rodger of Earlsferry; *Somerville v Scottish Ministers* 2008 SC (HL) 45 at paras 13–16 per Lord Hope of Craighead (and contrast para 73 per Lord Scott of Foscote). This approach may be open to question, particularly in the light of the discussion of s 6 in *Attorney-General's Reference (No 2 of 2001)* [2004] 2 AC 72. See para **1.59** above.

1.137 It has been said that if the Lord Advocate (or, presumably, any other member of the Scottish Government) threatens to act in a way which is incompatible with Convention rights, the court has no discretion to withhold a remedy[1]. In general, however, an element of discretion is involved in the granting of remedies (such as interdict, specific performance or reduction) in respect of ultra vires acts[2]; and it has been held, in particular circumstances, that reduction should be refused, as a matter of discretion, notwithstanding that the Scottish Ministers had acted incompatibly with Convention rights[3]. The right to challenge the competence of an act under s 57(2) can in addition be waived[4] or barred by acquiescence[5].

1   *Dyer v Watson* 2002 SC (PC) 89 at para 131 per Lord Millett; *R v HM Advocate* 2003 SC (PC) 21 at paras 69–70 per Lord Hope of Craighead. So far as the Lord Advocate is concerned, this was said in relation to s 57(2) of the SA 1998 as originally enacted: as explained in para **1.134** above, it is anticipated at the time of writing that a material amendment may be made by the Scotland Act 2011.

2   See eg Clyde and Edward, *Judicial Review,* 628; cf *Somerville v Lord Advocate* 2008 SC (HL) 45 at para 17 per Lord Hope of Craighead.

3   *Ramzan Bibi, Petitioner* [2007] CSOH 151.

4   *Millar v Dickson* 2002 SC (PC) 30.

5   *Robertson v Higson* 2006 SC (PC) 22.

1.138 The term 'act' in the SA 1998, s 57(2) has been given a wide interpretation. It has been said that the implementation of any executive or administrative decision must involve an 'act'[1]. In the context of criminal proceedings, it was held in *R v HM Advocate* that the term 'act' as a matter of statutory interpretation fell to be read as capable of extending to all acts performed by the Lord Advocate in the exercise of his functions as prosecutor[2]. This approach is consistent with the intention that (subject to the exception provided by s 57(3)) the Scottish Government should have no power to take executive action which is incompatible with Convention rights[3]. It has the consequence that any allegation that an act of the Lord Advocate is incompatible with the accused's Convention rights must be raised as a devolution issue[4]. Other functions (including those which are not devolved functions) discharged by the Lord Advocate will similarly involve 'acts' within the meaning of s 57(2)[5]. It has been said that the word 'act' in s 57(2) should be construed in the same way as the same word in s 6(1) of the HRA 1998to:[6]. On that basis, s 57(2), like s 6(1) of the HRA 1998, is concerned with acts which are otherwise lawful but which are made incompetent on Convention grounds[7].

As explained above[8], it is anticipated at the time of writing that material amendments may be made by the SA 2011.

1   *HM Advocate v Burns* 2001 JC 93. See also *Napier v Scottish Ministers* 2005 1 SC 229, per Lord Bonomy at paras 84 and 85 (the decision to detain a prisoner in particular conditions of detention involved a 'positive act of detaining him there, and continuing to detain him there when he requested a move' while '[e]ven in the wider context of government policy, the decision to detain the petitioner [in these conditions] can be seen as the result of positive choices made by the respondents in the knowledge that there was an urgent need to address slopping out and the prison conditions associated with it'); and *XY v Scottish Ministers* 2007 SC 631 (the recall of a convicted person to prison was an exercise of a devolved competence; the resultant disenfranchisement from participation in an election involved a reserved matter not within the competence of the Scottish Ministers). On the other hand, it has been doubted whether merely indicating support for a third party's initiative constitutes an 'act' or (for the purposes of SA 1998, Sch 6) the 'exercise of a function': *BBC, Petitioners (No 2)* 2000 JC 521.

2   *R v HM Advocate* 2003 SC (PC) 21, per Lord Hope of Craighead at paras 38–52.

3   *R v HM Advocate* 2003 SC (PC) 21, per Lord Hope of Craighead at para 42.

4   *R v HM Advocate* 2003 SC (PC) 21, per Lord Rodger of Earlsferry at para 118. This was said in relation to s 57 as originally enacted: as explained in para **1.134** above, it is anticipated at the time of writing that a material amendment may be made by the SA 2011.

5   *Goatley v HM Advocate* 2008 JC 1.

6   *R (Pretty) v Director of Public Prosecutions* [2002] 1 AC 800 at para 75 per Lord Hope of Craighead.

7   See para **1.59** above.

8   See para **1.134** above.

1.139 The question whether s 57(2) applies where it is submitted that the Scottish Ministers have failed to act (for example, so as to reform an aspect of the legal system which is said to be incompatible with the Convention) was discussed in *R v HM Advocate*, where the view was expressed by Lord Hope of Craighead and by Lord Rodger of Earlsferry that 'act' does not include a failure to act[1]. It is however not entirely clear how the distinction between acts and omissions might be drawn in this context. The matter would appear to have been clarified by the Convention Rights Proceedings (Amendment) (Scotland) Act 2009, which amended s 100 of the SA 1998 so as to impose a time limit on the bringing of proceedings by virtue of that Act. As amended, s 100 envisages that such proceedings may be brought on the ground that an act of the Scottish Ministers or a member of the Scottish Government is incompatible with Convention rights; and 'act' is defined as including a failure to act (including a failure to make legislation)[2].

1   *R v HM Advocate* 2003 SC (PC) 21, at para 47 per Lord Hope of Craighead and at para 125 per Lord Rodger of Earlsferry. A failure to act by a member of the Scottish Government which was incompatible with Convention rights would, however, be unlawful under HRA 1998, s 6. It would also involve a devolution issue in terms of SA 1998, Sch 6 para 1(e). The failure might also be challengeable under reference to SA 1998, s 54(3). A failure to act does not include a failure to do something which the authority in question has no power to do: see para **1.59** above.

2   SA 1998, s 100(3D).

1.140 The general rule laid down in the SA 1998, s 57(2) is subject to an important qualification in terms of s 57(3): it does not apply to an act of the Lord Advocate in prosecuting any offence, or in the capacity of head of the system of criminal prosecution and investigation of deaths in Scotland[1] which, because of the HRA 1998, s 6(2), is not unlawful under s 6(1). In other words, if, as the result of primary legislation, the Lord Advocate could not have acted differently, or if he was acting so as to give effect to or enforce provisions of primary legislation (or provisions made under primary legislation) which cannot be read or given effect in a way which is compatible with the Convention rights, then it is not unlawful for him so to act[2]. The reason for the creation of this exception, and for its being confined to the Lord Advocate, has been explained above[3]. The effect of the exception provided by s 6(2) of the HRA 1998, as it applies to the Lord Advocate, has been considered in a number of cases[4]. It is to be noted that the HRA 1998 has opened the possibility of review of the Lord Advocate's exercise of his discretionary powers as head of the systems of prosecution and investigation of deaths[5].

At the time of writing, it is anticipated that s 57(3) may be amended by the SA 2011 so as to exclude from the scope of s 57(2) any act of the Lord Advocate in prosecuting any offence, or in the capacity of head of the system of criminal prosecution and investigation of deaths in Scotland. In the event of such an amendment, the compatibility of such acts and omissions of the Lord Advocate with Convention rights will be governed by s 6 of the HRA 1998, and by the procedural provisions contained in the SA 1998.

1   See *Goatley v HM Advocate* 2008 JC 1, discussed at para **1.134** above.

2   On the interpretation of HRA 1998, s 6(2), see paras **1.60–1.63** above.

3   At para **1.134** above.

4   See *Starrs v Ruxton* 2000 JC 208, *Millar v Dickson* 2002 SC (PC) 30 and *Dickson v HM Advocate* 2008 JC 181. The possible implications of the inability of the Scottish Ministers (other than the Lord Advocate) to rely on HRA 1998, s 6(2) were commented on by Lord Hope of Craighead in *Bellinger v Bellinger* [2003] 2 AC 467.

5   Cf *Fayed v Lord Advocate* 2004 SC 568; *Kennedy v HM Advocate* 2008 SLT 195; *Emms, Petitioner* 2011 SLT 354. Judicial review, which is a residual remedy, will not, however, be appropriate where a decision to prosecute is in breach of a Convention right and that decision can be challenged in the trial process or on appeal: *Montgomery v HM Advocate* 2001 SC (PC) 1 at 14–15 per Lord Hope of Craighead.

'Incompatibility'

1.141 Although the term 'act' has been given a wide construction, there remains the critical question whether the act is incompatible with the Convention rights. As discussed above[1], however, what is meant by 'incompatible' has proved to be a difficult question. Although it has been said on a number of occasions that the essence of the word 'incompatible' is that there is an inconsistency between one thing and another[2], that explanation does not resolve all the difficulties that have arisen. Whether an act is 'inconsistent' with a Convention right may not be obvious: it may not depend on a 'but for' causal test (ie 'but for' the act under challenge, there would be no infringement)[3], or involve a 'remoteness' test (ie whether any infringement of Convention rights will be the direct or proximate result of the act under challenge)[4]. Other approaches have been to ask whether the act under challenge is precluded by the Convention right in question[5], or whether the act involves an infringement of the Convention right[6]. The latter formulations have the advantage of requiring analysis of the precise bearing of the Convention right, as understood in the Strasbourg and domestic jurisprudence, on the specific act under challenge, rather than falling back on concepts, such as those of causation or remoteness, borrowed from other areas of domestic law.

1   See paras **1.54–1.55** and **1.78**. The term has the same meaning in SA 1998 as in the HRA 1998: *R v HM Advocate* 2003 SC (PC) 21 at para 141 per Lord Rodger of Earlsferry.

2   *Montgomery v HM Advocate* 2001 SC (PC) 1 at 18 per Lord Hope of Craighead. Similar formulations were employed by Lord Steyn, Lord Hope of Craighead and Lord Clyde in *R v HM Advocate* 2003 SC (PC) 21.

3   See eg *XY v Scottish Ministers* 2007 SC 631, where the Inner House decided that the act of the
    Scottish Ministers in recalling a convicted prisoner to prison was not incompatible with the
    right to vote in free elections under Art 3 of Prot 1, notwithstanding that the recall would have
    the consequence that the prisoner would be unable to vote in an imminent election. See also
    HM Advocate v Robb 2000 JC 127, 131–132; *Campbell v HM Advocate* 1999 SCCR 980;
    McKenna v HM Advocate 2000 JC 291; *HM Advocate v Burns* 2001 JC 93; and *McCall v
    Scottish Ministers* 2006 SC 266.

4   See eg *HM Advocate v Robb* 2000 JC 127, 131–132 (tendering of evidence); *Campbell v HM
    Advocate* 1999 SCCR 980 (lodging of production); *McKenna v HM Advocate* 2000 JC 291
    (service of notice of intention to lead evidence); *BBC, Petitioners (No 2)* 2000 JC 521 (court's
    authorisation of restricted CCTV transmission of proceedings); *HM Advocate v Burns* 2001
    JC 93 (lodging of statement of assets preliminary to confiscation proceedings); *Monterroso v
    HM Advocate* 2000 SCCR 974 (making of legal submissions to court); *McCall v Scottish
    Ministers* 2006 SC 266; *XY v Scottish Ministers* 2007 SC 631.

5   *R v HM Advocate* 2003 SC (PC) 21 at para 7 per Lord Steyn.

6   *R v HM Advocate* 2003 SC (PC) 21 at para 140 per Lord Rodger of Earlsferry.

1.142 This question has been discussed, in particular, in relation to the compatibility
of acts of the prosecution with the Convention rights guaranteed by Article 6(1).
An important consideration in that context is that the court is itself obliged by the
HRA 1998, s 6 to ensure that Article 6 rights are protected. If the apprehended
breach of Article 6 is one which the court will be able and obliged to prevent
(bearing in mind its obligations under the HRA 1998), then arguably the act of the
prosecutor which is subject to challenge cannot result in an infringement of the
Convention right. The issue is of practical significance because an appeal lies
from the High Court of Justiciary to the Supreme Court in respect of any question
relating to the compatibility with Convention rights of an act or omission of the
Lord Advocate in prosecuting any offence or in the capacity of head of the system
of criminal prosecution in Scotland, but not in relation to any question relating to
the compatibility with Convention rights of an act or omission of the court. At the
time of writing, it is uncertain whether this will remain the position under the
Scotland Act 2011.

1.143 The question was discussed by the Privy Council (without any concluded
view being reached) in *Montgomery v HM Advocate,* where it was argued that
the Lord Advocate was acting incompatibly with the Convention rights by
prosecuting the accused in circumstances where a fair trial was not possible
(because of pre-trial publicity)[1]. Lord Nicholls of Birkenhead observed that there
might be a non sequitur involved in the view that, because a fair trial was not
possible, the Lord Advocate had acted incompatibly with the Convention[2].
Developing the point, Lord Hoffmann suggested that the right under Article 6(1)
to have a criminal charge 'determined' at a fair and public hearing could not be
infringed by the prosecutor, since criminal charges are determined by courts and
not by prosecutors: the acts of the Lord Advocate in bringing and maintaining the
prosecution, tendering evidence and so forth were 'capable of creating the
conditions for an unfair determination of the charge but they cannot in themselves
cause such an event and therefore infringe the provisions of Article 6(1)'

guaranteeing the right to a fair trial[3]. On the other hand, Lord Hope of Craighead suggested that s 57(2) of the SA 1998 (which at that time applied to the acts of the Lord Advocate in prosecuting any offence) should be interpreted as prohibiting the Lord Advocate (or any other member of the Scottish Government) from acting in a manner which is inconsistent with the obligations which the United Kingdom has assumed under the ECHR, whether the act is one which gives rise to a present and immediate incompatibility or is one which will inevitably lead to an incompatibility in the future[4]. Lord Clyde doubted whether the bringing or maintaining of a charge fell within the scope of Article 6(1)[5].

1   The case raised an issue which would be dealt with under the common law by way of a plea in bar of trial. Article 6 was treated by the High Court of Justiciary (which heard the case before HRA 1998, s 6 came into force) as re-shaping that area of the common law, and therefore as raising (in that respect) an analogous plea: 2000 SCCR 1044 at 1073 per Lord Justice-General Rodger.

2   *Montgomery v HM Advocate* 2001 SC (PC) 1 at 5–6.

3   *Montgomery v HM Advocate* 2001 SC (PC) 1 at 7–8.

4   *Montgomery v HM Advocate* 2001 SC (PC) 1 at 18.

5   *Montgomery v HM Advocate* 2001 SC (PC) 1 at 33–34.

1.144 The question was discussed again in *Brown v Stott*, concerned with the leading in evidence of an answer obtained from the accused under compulsory powers. A majority of the Privy Council expressly left open the question whether, even if the admission of the evidence in question had been incompatible with the accused's Convention rights, the prosecutor could nevertheless lawfully (as far as the Scotland Act was concerned) lead such evidence[1]. Lord Hope of Craighead reiterated the view which he had expressed in *Montgomery,* and observed that 'the fact that [another] person has the last word or has the power to intervene in such a way as to preserve or give effect to the Convention rights may enable the question as to incompatibility to be answered in the negative'[2]. Lord Clyde again dealt with the question as one turning on the interpretation of Article 6(1), which he construed as covering the leading of evidence of the kind in issue[3].

1   *Brown v Stott* 2001 SC (PC) 43. The case had been decided in the High Court of Justiciary before the HRA 1998, s 6 was in force, and therefore at a time when the court could not have excluded the evidence in question, other than under the SA 1998, s 57(2), even if its admission would have been incompatible with a Convention right.

2   *Brown v Stott* 2001 SC (PC) 43, at 71–72.

3   *Brown v Stott* 2001 SC (PC) 43, at 81.

1.145 The question was again raised and left unanswered in *McIntosh, Petitioner*[1]. In *Mills v HM Advocate* it was not argued before the Privy Council[2]. In *R v HM Advocate*, concerned with delay in bringing an accused person to trial[3], Lord Steyn considered that the Lord Advocate would be unable to continue with a prosecution only if a Convention right precluded him from doing so[4]. Lord Hope reiterated his previous observations, while Lord Clyde and Lord Rodger each expressed the opinion that an act would be incompatible with the Convention rights if the act would involve an infringement of a Convention right. In *Clark v Kelly*, it was accepted that the Lord Advocate could not prosecute the accused before the district court if to do so would 'inevitably' infringe his Convention rights (because, it was argued, the court was not an independent and impartial tribunal)[5]. In *McDonald v HM Advocate,* Lord Hope of Craighead said, obiter, that he would 'be willing to accept that it would be incompatible with the appellant's rights under Article 6(1) for the Lord Advocate to seek to support the conviction if the appellant was able to demonstrate that there was a reasonable possibility of unfairness as a result of the non-disclosure'[6]. This seems to imply that merely opposing an appeal can be incompatible with Convention rights, notwithstanding that the court would be bound under the HRA 1998 to allow the appeal if to do otherwise would be incompatible with Convention rights.

1   *McIntosh, Petitioner* 2001 SC (PC) 89. The point was also raised, and left open, by Lord Hamilton in *Dickson v HM Advocate* 2001 JC 202 at para 5.

2   *Mills v HM Advocate* 2003 SC (PC) 1.

3   *R v HM Advocate* 2003 SC (PC) 21. The case raised an issue which would be dealt with under the common law by way of a plea in bar of trial.

4   As, for example, where the accused person would not receive a fair trial, or where the court was not an independent and impartial tribunal, but not where there had been an unreasonable delay.

5   *Clark v Kelly* 2003 SC (PC) 77 at para 76 per Lord Rodger of Earlsferry.

6   *McDonald v HM Advocate* 2010 SC (PC) 1 at para 37. Contrast paras 69, 75 and 77 per Lord Rodger of Earlsferry.

1.146 There may also be circumstances where there has been or will be an infringement of Convention rights in the course of criminal proceedings, but the continuation of the prosecution is nevertheless not itself an act which is incompatible with Convention rights. For example, a delay in criminal proceedings which violates Article 6(1) does not entail that the continued prosecution of the accused is itself incompatible with the Convention rights[1].

1   *Spiers v Ruddy* 2009 SC (PC) 1.

Legal proceedings

Devolution issues

1.147 The SA 1998, Sch 6 contains provisions[1] for dealing with 'devolution issues'. These are defined by para 1 as meaning:

(a) a question whether an Act of the Scottish Parliament or any provision of such an Act is within the legislative competence of the Parliament;

(b) a question whether any function (which a person has purported, or is proposing, to exercise) is a function of the Scottish Ministers, the First Minister or the Lord Advocate;

(c) a question whether the purported or proposed exercise of a function by a member of the Scottish Government is, or would be, within devolved competence;

(d) a question whether a purported or proposed exercise of a function by a member of the Scottish Government is, or would be, incompatible with any of the Convention rights or with EU law[2];

(e) a question whether a failure to act by a member of the Scottish Government is incompatible with any of the Convention rights or with EU law[3];

(f) any other question about whether a function is exercisable within devolved competence or in or as regards Scotland and any other question arising by virtue of the Act about reserved matters.

At the time of writing, it is anticipated that para 1 may be amended by the SA 2011 so as to add that a question whether an act or omission is, or would be, incompatible with any of the Convention rights or with EU law is not a devolution issue if it is an act or omission of the Lord Advocate in prosecuting any offence or in the capacity of head of the systems of criminal prosecution and investigation of deaths in Scotland.

It follows that a question as to the compatibility of an Act of the Scottish Parliament with Convention rights under s 29(2)(d), or a question as to whether the exercise of a function by a member of the Scottish Government is within devolved competence under s 54(3), or whether a member of the Scottish Government has no power under s 57(2), will be a devolution issue.

Para 2 of Sch 6 provides that a devolution issue is not to be taken to arise merely because of a contention which appears to the court to be frivolous or vexatious[4].

---

1   Similar provisions are contained in Sch 8 to the Government of Wales Act 1998 and Sch 10 to the Northern Ireland Act 1998.

2   Plainly, such a question may arise even if the answer to the question is in the negative, for example because some other public authority, such as the court, has the last word or has the power to intervene in such a way as to preserve or give effect to the Convention rights: *Brown v Stott* 2001 SC (PC) 43 at 71–72 per Lord Hope of Craighead.

3   This possibly goes beyond the scope of SA 1998, s 57(2): see para **1.139** above.

4   More widely, there must be a point of substance that needs to be addressed. The raising of the issue may be premature, or the question which has been raised may not be a devolution issue at all: *Montgomery v HM Advocate* 2001 SC (PC) *Brown v Stott* 2001 SC (PC) 43 at 72 per Lord Hope of Craighead.

1.148 In practice, prior to the amendment of the SA 1998 by the SA 2011, the great majority of devolution issues have arisen in criminal proceedings and have concerned the compatibility of acts of the prosecution with Convention rights. That was perceived by some members of the judiciary as giving rise to certain practical difficulties, arising in particular from the requirement that devolution issues be dealt with in accordance with a potentially cumbersome procedure, involving intimation to the Advocate General. It is anticipated that that problem, in so far as it exists , may be addressed by amendments to the SA 1998 which may be effected by the SA 2011.

The distinction between acts of the prosecution (which can give rise to appeals from the High Court of Justiciary) and acts of the court or of the police (which cannot[1]) in determining questions as to compatibility with Convention rights can be artificial[2]. In logic it might be preferable if there were a possibility of appeal to the Supreme Court whenever a question of Convention rights arises in criminal proceedings in Scotland. In practice, a similar result is being achieved by adopting a broad approach to the question whether an act of the Lord Advocate is compatible with Convention rights, so as to elide any distinction which might otherwise have been drawn between acts of the Lord Advocate and acts of the court.

1   In relation to the courts, see eg *BBC, Petitioners (No 2)* 2000 JC 521; *Monterroso v HM Advocate* 2000 SCCR 974; *Hoekstra v HM Advocate (No 3)* 2001 SC (PC) 37. As to the police, see *McGibbon v HM Advocate* 2004 JC 60. It may also be necessary in criminal proceedings to distinguish between acts of the Lord Advocate and acts for which other Scottish Ministers are responsible: see eg *Monterroso v HM Advocate* 2000 SCCR 974. It is of course also necessary to distinguish between acts of the Scottish Ministers and acts of UK Ministers: *Monterroso v HM Advocate* 2000 SCCR 974.

2   The distinction sought to be drawn in such cases between acts of the judiciary and acts of the prosecutor has not been adopted under the HRA 1998. It was described in one case as 'not only artificial in a case like the present but also likely to lead to infinite arguments as to the application of the distinction': *R v Kansal (No 2)* [2002] 2 AC 69 at para 9 per Lord Slynn of Hadley; also at para 15 per Lord Lloyd of Berwick.

1.149 One noteworthy aspect of the procedure is that the Supreme Court is the final court of appeal in respect of devolution issues, and issues concerning the compatibility with Convention rights of acts or omissions of the Lord Advocate in prosecuting any offence, that arise in Scottish criminal proceedings[1]. Although the Supreme Court has been careful to confine itself to issues concerning Convention rights, it is nevertheless in the nature of those rights that they can have significant implications for criminal law and procedure. As Lord Justice-General Rodger observed in *Montgomery v HM Advocate*:

> 'it would be wrong ... to see the rights under the European Convention as somehow forming a wholly separate stream in our law; in truth they soak through and permeate the areas in our law in which they apply.'[2]

One effect of the SA 1998 has consequently been to make the Supreme Court the final appellate court on many questions affecting Scottish criminal law and procedure. This has attracted some criticism from Scottish legal nationalists[3]. There are, however, three points which it is necessary to bear in mind.

First, the issues which the Supreme Court has decided, in relation to such matters as unreasonable delay, disclosure of material in the possession of the Crown, access to a solicitor after detention, and pre-trial publicity, have depended upon the interpretation and application of Convention rights rather than upon home-grown Scots law. The decisions of the Supreme Court in such cases may consequently have implications for the whole of the United Kingdom. That is reflected in the fact that the Lord Advocate has sometimes intervened in English cases before the House of Lords or the Supreme Court concerned with Convention rights, as happened in the *Alconbury* case[4] and in a case concerned with the registration of sex offenders[5]. Important cases on Convention rights have implications which spill over the boundaries of the UK's three jurisdictions.

Secondly, it is important to remember that it is not Scotland which is a party to the Convention, but the UK. The international obligations of the United Kingdom do not vary according to whether the issue arises in Scotland, England, Wales or Northern Ireland. The jurisdiction of the Supreme Court enables the United Kingdom to ensure that fundamental rights enshrined in international obligations and given effect in domestic law are secured in a consistent manner throughout the UK. That is true of Convention rights, and it is also true of the obligations which arise (or may arise in the future) under EU law. The jurisdiction of the Supreme Court in relation to Scottish criminal cases is thus a constitutional jurisdiction, in the sense that it is limited to questions of compatibility with the international obligations of the United Kingdom as given effect in domestic law, so as to ensure protection of Convention rights and compliance with EU law, and questions concerning the terms of the devolution settlement. If there is a failure to protect Convention rights, the United Kingdom may be brought before the European Court of Human Rights. In the case of non-compliance with EU law, the United Kingdom may be faced with infringement proceedings before the European Court of Justice. It is the function of the Supreme Court to prevent that happening. That is reflected in the fact that its decisions on devolution matters are binding in all legal proceedings throughout the UK, whereas its decisions on all other matters are to be regarded as the decisions of a Scottish, English or Northern Irish court (depending on the origins of the appeal).[6]

Thirdly, dissatisfaction with the present system derives in part from a sense that Scottish criminal law and procedure are subject to scrutiny by a court whose members do not all have previous experience of that system. As has been explained, however, the issue for decision will not be one of home-grown Scots law but of compliance with rights guaranteed in international law. The objection is in any event somewhat naïve. Judges are appointed to the High Court of Justiciary who have no previous experience of Scottish criminal proceedings, and then sit on their own, without two or three experienced Scottish criminal judges to assist them. Furthermore, if a case were to go to Strasbourg or Luxembourg, those courts do not at present include any judge who is familiar with Scots criminal law and procedure. In practice, the most significant developments resulting from appeals to the Supreme Court have been in areas of criminal procedure where Scots law had failed to keep up with developments elsewhere. Without a right of appeal to the Supreme Court, unsuccessful Scottish appellants would have had to take their cases to Strasbourg, to be decided (after a prolonged delay) by judges none of whom would have any experience of Scots law (and few of whom would have experience of any common law system), if innovations such as a modern system for the disclosure of Crown materials, or access to a solicitor during police detention, were to be introduced. For that practical reason in particular, as well as the constitutional reasons emphasised by other commentators[7], opinion within the legal profession has generally been supportive of an appeal from the High Court of Justiciary to the Supreme Court.

1　Final jurisdiction in respect of devolution issues was conferred by the SA 1998 upon the Judicial Committee of the Privy Council, and was transferred to the Supreme Court with effect from 1 October 2009 by the Constitutional Reform Act 2005, s 40 and Sch 9.

2　*Montgomery v HM Advocate* 2000 JC 111 at 117. See also *Robertson and Gough v HM Advocate* 2008 JC 146. It appears that if a trial is alleged to have been unfair as a result of the conduct of the Crown, there is a devolution issue.

3　See for example the statements made by the Cabinet Secretary for Justice during discussion of the Criminal Procedure (Legal Assistance, Detention and Appeals) Bill, *The Scottish Parliament – Official Report* 27 October 2010). See also the representations submitted in 2010 to the Advocate General for Scotland (available at www.oag.gov.uk/oag/225).

4　*R (Alconbury Developments Ltd and Others) v Secretary of State for the Environment, Transport and the Regions* [2003] 2 AC 295.

5　*R (F (A Child)) v Secretary of State for the Home Department* [2011] 1 AC 331.

6　Constitutional Reform Act 2005, s 41.

7　See eg the Report of the Advocate General's Expert Group, chaired by Sir David Edward (2010), and the First Report of the Review Group appointed by the First Minister, chaired by Lord McCluskey (2011).

1.150 It was held in the case of *Stevens v HM Advocate* that an application for a declaration of incompatibility under the HRA 1998, s 4, made in criminal proceedings where the Crown is relying on the statutory provision in question, implicitly raises a devolution issue and must be dealt with in accordance with the procedure governing devolution issues[1]. This approach has been followed in practice, but may be open to question[2].

1　*Stevens v HM Advocate* 2001 SCCR 948.

2　The approach adopted is based on the assumption that for the prosecution to perform any act in the course of criminal proceedings, on the basis of a statutory provision which is incompatible with Convention rights, is itself an act which is incompatible with Convention rights. As discussed at paras **1.142–1.145** above, however, there may be room for argument, at least in some circumstances, as to whether any infringement of Convention rights can properly be said to be the result of the act of the prosecutor. It should also be noted that declarations of incompatibility cannot be made by the High Court of Justiciary sitting as a trial court (HRA 1998, s 4(5); and the expression 'trial court' may have encompassed preliminary diets as well as trial diets, since a preliminary diet takes place before the trial court: *Montgomery v HM Advocate* 2001 SC (PC) 1 at 14 per Lord Hope of Craighead.

The Lord Advocate: questions as to compatibility

1.151 As has been explained, it is anticipated, as at the time of writing, that questions as to whether acts and omissions of the Lord Advocate in prosecuting any offence or in the capacity of head of the systems of criminal prosecution and investigation of deaths in Scotland are compatible with Convention rights or EU law may be excluded from the scope of devolution issues as a result of amendments made to the SA 1998 by the SA 2011[1]. In that event, it will, however, be possible to raise such questions, so far as relating to the Lord Advocate's acts or omissions as head of the system of investigation of deaths, under the HRA 1998 in the same way as questions relating to the acts or omissions of other public authorities. , with an appeal lying from the Court of Session to the Supreme Court. Questions relating to acts and omissions of the Lord Advocate in prosecuting any offence, or in the capacity of head of the system of criminal prosecution, will be dealt with differently from other acts or omissions of Scottish Ministers, because of the absence of a general appeal from the High Court of Justiciary to the Supreme Court. It is anticipated that such an appeal may, however, be provided, specifically in relation to such questions, by a new provision of the SA 1998, as amended by the SA 2011. It is anticipated that an appeal may lie under that provision against a determination as to compatibility by a court of two or more judges of the High Court of Justiciary, but only with the permission of that court or, failing such permission, with permission of the Supreme Court[2]. It is anticipated that, in such an appeal, the provisions of ss 106(3) to (3D) and 175(5) to (5D) of the Criminal Procedure (Scotland) Act 1995, relating to miscarriages of justice, may apply to the Supreme Court. It is anticipated that, in relation to such an appeal, the Supreme Court may have all the powers of the court below, and may be able to affirm, set aside or vary order or judgment given by that court, remit any issue for determination by that court, or order a new trial or hearing.

1   See para **1.147** above.

2   At the time of writing, it is uncertain whether there may in addition be a requirement that the High Court of Justiciary certify that the case raises a point of law of general public importance.

Time limitation

1.152 Proceedings brought under s 100 of the SA 1998 are not subject to the limitation period imposed by s 7(5) of the HRA 1998[1]. A time limit is however imposed by s 100 of the SA 1998, as amended by the Convention Rights Proceedings (Amendment) (Scotland) Act 2009. At the time of writing, it is anticipated that further amendments will be made by the SA 2011, but will not apply to any proceedings brought before the amending provisions are brought into force.

In terms of s 100(3A) and (3B), any proceedings brought on or after 2 November 2009 by virtue of the SA 1998 against the Scottish Ministers or a member of the Scottish Government in a court or tribunal, on the ground that an act[2] of the Scottish Ministers or a member of the Scottish Government is incompatible with the Convention rights, must be brought within one year of the date on which the act complained of took place, or such longer period as the court or tribunal considers equitable having regard to all the circumstances. That time limit is subject to any rule imposing a stricter time limit in relation to the procedure in question. The time limit does not apply to proceedings brought by a Law Officer[3]. Nor does it apply to the making of any legislation, but it does include any other act or failure to act (including a failure to make legislation)[4]. Differing views have been expressed as to whether the time limit applies to appeals in criminal proceedings, or is confined to civil proceedings[5].

1   *Somerville v Scottish Ministers* 2008 SC (HL) 45.

2   Including an act done before that date: SA 1998, s 100(3E).

3   SA 1998, s 100(3C).

4   SA 1998, s 100 (3D).

5   Contrast *Cadder v HM Advocate* 2010 SCCR 951 at para 60 per Lord Hope and paras 105–106 per Lord Rodger (with one or both of whom the other justices agreed) and *Jude v HM Advocate* [2011] HCJAC 46 at para 37–39 per Lord Justice Clerk Gill.

1.153 The principle of legal certainty requires that the retrospective effect of a judicial decision is generally excluded from cases that have been finally determined[1]. Cases which have been finally determined should not therefore ordinarily be re-opened in consequence of a decision in a subsequent case which implies that Convention rights may have been violated.

1   *Cadder v HM Advocate* 2010 SCCR 951. See also para **1.115** above, and paras **3.72** and **5.229** below.

Retroactivity

1.154 In the event that a court or tribunal decides that an Act of the Scottish Parliament is beyond its competence, or that subordinate legislation is ultra vires, the court or tribunal has a power under the SA 1998, s 102 to make an order removing or limiting any retrospective effect of the decision, or suspending the effect of the decision for any period and on any conditions to allow the defect to be corrected. This power 'enables the court to give the Scottish Parliament time to reconsider the legislation and to amend it in such a way as to remove the incompatibility'[1]. It might be thought that this power should only be exercised on compelling grounds, since it results in the denial of an immediate or fully effective remedy to a person who has been found to be the victim of a violation of Convention rights[2]. Section 102, as originally enacted, does not give the court power to remove or limit the effect of a decision that an act of a Scottish Minister was one that, in terms of s 57(2), the Minister had no power to make[3].

At the time of writing, it is anticipated that s 102 may be amended by the Scotland Act 2011 so as also to apply in the event of a decision that any other purported exercise of a function by a member of the Scottish Government was outside devolved competence. This form of words may exclude acts or omissions of the Lord Advocate in prosecuting any offence, or in the capacity of head of the systems of criminal prosecution and investigation of deaths in Scotland, if such acts or omissions are excluded from the scope of the *vires* control imposed by SA 1998, s 57(2).

1   *A v Scottish Ministers* 2002 SC (PC) 63 at 67 per Lord Hope of Craighead. See also *McCall v Scottish Ministers* 2006 SC 266 and *Somerville v Lord Advocate* 2008 SC (HL) 45 at para 35 per Lord Hope of Craighead.

2   Reference might be made to the use made of analogous powers in other jurisdictions. For
     Canada, see *Reference Re Manitoba Language Rights* [1985] 1 SCR 721, *R v Swain* [1991] 1
     SCR 933, *Schachter v Canada* [1992] 2 SCR 679, *R v Demers* [2004] 2 SCR 489 and *Attorney-
     General of Canada v Hislop* [2007] 1 SCR 429. Comparable provisions are also contained in
     the South African Constitution: see *Zuma v State of South Africa* [1995] ZACC 1, *S v
     Bhulwana* 1996 (1) SA 388 (CC), *Fraser v Children's Court, Pretoria North* 1997 (2) SA 261
     (CC), *First National Bank of SA Ltd v Minister of Finance* 2002 (4) SA 768 (CC), *Bhe v
     Magistrate, Khayelitsha* 2005 (1) SA 580 and *Minister of Home Affairs v Fourie* 2006 (1) SA
     524 (CC). For Hong Kong, see *Koo Sze Yiu v Chief Executive of the Hong Kong Special
     Administrative Region* [2006] 9 HKCFAR 441. See also para **3.72** below.

3   *Cadder v HM Advocate* 2010 SCCR 951.

Standing to rely on Convention rights

1.155 Under the SA 1998, s 100(1), nothing in the Act enables a person to bring
legal proceedings on the ground that any Act of the Parliament or any act is
incompatible with the Convention rights, or to rely on any of the Convention rights
in such proceedings, unless he would be a victim for the purposes of Article 34 of
the ECHR[1]. The relevant principles established by the Strasbourg institutions,
and the relevant domestic case law, are discussed in Chapter 2[2].

1   SA 1998, s 100(1). See eg *Grampian University Hospitals NHS Trust v Frame* 2004 JC 117;
     Axa General Insurance Ltd v Lord Advocate 2011 SLT 439 (in which an appeal was heard by
     the Supreme Court in June 2011). This provision does not apply to the Law Officers: s
     100(2).

2   See paras **2.64–2.74**, below.

Procedure for determining devolution issues

1.156 Devolution issues may arise in any proceedings before courts or tribunals
anywhere in the UK. They may, for example, arise in proceedings for judicial
review instituted for the purpose of challenging legislation of the Scottish Parliament
or acts of Scottish Ministers, or collaterally (eg by way of defence in criminal
proceedings). They can thus arise in proceedings at any level in the judicial
hierarchy. Although devolution issues arising under the SA 1998 are most likely to
arise in proceedings in Scotland, they may also arise in proceedings in England
and Wales or in Northern Ireland[1]. The SA 1998, Sch 6 contains separate provisions
in respect of each jurisdiction. They are, however, broadly similar. The present
discussion will focus on the Scottish provisions. The provisions cover both
proceedings for the determination of a devolution issue[2] and other proceedings in
which a devolution issue arises[3]. In each case, provision is made for the involvement
in the proceedings of the Advocate General and the Lord Advocate.

1   Cf *R (Horvath) v Secretary of State for Environment, Food and Rural Affairs* [2007] EuLR
     770.

2   SA 1998, Sch 6, para 4.

3   SA 1998, Sch 6, para 5.

1.157 The SA 1998 provides for subordinate legislation for prescribing such matters as the stage in proceedings at which a devolution issue is to be raised or referred, the sisting of proceedings for the purpose of a reference, and the manner and time within which any intimation is to be given[1]. Rules have been issued, and are discussed below.

1   SA 1998, Sch 6, para 37.

1.158 When a devolution issue arises in civil proceedings before a court other than the Supreme Court or any court consisting of three or more judges of the Court of Session, that court has a discretion (subject to any rules made under the Scotland Act) to refer the devolution issue to the Inner House[1]. Alternatively, the court can decide the issue itself, and it can thereafter come before the higher courts by way of appeal. Similarly, tribunals must make a reference if there is no appeal from their decision, but otherwise have a discretion[2]. The position in criminal proceedings is similar: a court other than any court consisting of two or more judges of the High Court of Justiciary has a discretion (subject to any rules made) either to refer the devolution issue to the High Court of Justiciary, or to decide the issue itself[3]. The reference procedure is designed to allow a court, when faced with an issue of difficulty or of some general importance, to refer the issue to a higher court[4]. It is a stage in the proceedings before the original court, rather than a free-standing procedure. If the proceedings come to an end (eg because the indictment falls) the reference comes to an end along with the proceedings[5]. It is for the court, and not the parties, to decide whether to make the reference[6].

1   SA 1998, Sch 6, para 7. This is subject to rules made under SA 1998, Sch 6, para 37.

2   SA 1998, Sch 6, para 8.

3   SA 1998, Sch 6, para 9.

4   *HM Advocate v Touati* 2001 SCCR 392.

5   *HM Advocate v Touati* 2001 SCCR 392.

6   *HM Advocate v Touati* 2001 SCCR 392.

1.159 The court to which the issue is referred cannot refer the issue to a yet higher court[1]. The court to which the reference is made responds to the reference[2]. It is, however, for the original court to make the operative decision, using the guidance given by the court to which the reference was made. When the Inner House decides a devolution issue on a reference by a lower court, an appeal lies to the Supreme Court[3]. Similarly, when the High Court of Justiciary decides a devolution issue on a reference by a lower court, an appeal again lies to the Supreme Court, but in this instance it is necessary to obtain the permission of the High Court or, failing such permission, the permission of the Supreme Court[4]. The reason why permission is required in this instance, but not from a decision of the Inner House, is that an appeal ordinarily lies from any final decision of the Inner House to the Supreme Court without leave, whereas prior to the Scotland Act there was no right of appeal in criminal proceedings beyond the High Court of Justiciary.

1   This is implicit in SA 1998, Sch 6, paras 10 and 11.

2   See para **1.162** below, fn1.

3   SA 1998, Sch 6, para 12.

4   SA 1998, Sch 6, para 13.

1.160 If, on the other hand, a devolution issue arises in proceedings before a court consisting of three or more judges of the Court of Session, or two or more judges of the High Court of Justiciary (typically, but not necessarily, on appeal from a lower court or tribunal), then they can either refer the issue to the Supreme Court[1] or decide the issue themselves. If they decide the issue themselves, an appeal will normally lie in civil proceedings to the Supreme Court; but where in civil proceedings there is no right of appeal to the Supreme Court, and in all criminal proceedings, an appeal will lie to the Supreme Court with permission of the court concerned or, failing such permission, with permission of the Supreme Court[2]. It has been said that reasons ought to be given for the refusal of permission[3]. Permission cannot be granted unless there has been a determination of a devolution issue[4]. If the devolution issue was argued before a lower court but not before the appellate court it cannot be resurrected by means of a further appeal to the Supreme Court[5]. If a devolution issue is raised, but the court refuses to allow a devolution minute to be received, that is a determination of the devolution issue[6]. Equally, if a devolution issue is raised in an application for leave to appeal, the refusal of leave is the determination of a devolution issue[7].

1   SA 1998, Sch 6, paras 10 and 11.

2   SA 1998, Sch 6, para 13.

3   *Follen v HM Advocate* 2001 SC (PC) 105.

4   *Hoekstra v HM Advocate (No 3)* 2001 SC (PC) 37.

5   *Follen v HM Advocate* 2001 SC (PC) 105.

6   *McDonald v HM Advocate* 2010 SC (PC) 1; *Fraser v HM Advocate* 2011 SLT 515.. The Supreme Court may grant permission, notwithstanding a failure to observe the procedural rules of the lower court, if there is a point of general public importance: *McDonald* at para 15 per Lord Hope of Craighead.

7   *Cadder v HM Advocate* 2010 SCCR 951.

1.161 The jurisdiction of the Supreme Court is not confined to answering the question which constitutes the devolution issue, but extends also to any other questions which are preliminary to or consequential upon the determination of the devolution issue[1]. In *Montgomery v HM Advocate,* for example, having determined the devolution issue against the appellants, the Privy Council ordered that publication of the proceedings in the appeal should be postponed until the conclusion of the trial[2]. In *Robertson v Higson,* the Privy Council decided that appellants whose Convention rights had been breached were barred by acquiescence from challenging their convictions[3]. In *McInnes v HM Advocate,* the Supreme Court held that the question of remedy forms part of the devolution issue, as also does the test to be applied in determining whether the appellant is entitled to that remedy. The Supreme Court can therefore examine the reasoning of the High Court of Justiciary to see whether it applied the correct test[4].

1 *Mills v HM Advocate* 2003 SC (PC) 1 at para 34 per Lord Hope of Craighead; *Robertson v Higson* 2006 SC (PC) 22 at para 5 per Lord Hope of Craighead. Examples given were the question whether a person was a 'victim' for the purposes of SA 1998, s 100(1), and the question as to the appropriate remedy for breach of a Convention right. See also *R v HM Advocate* 2003 SC (PC) 21 at paras 34–37 per Lord Hope of Craighead. The last point was, however, based on the doubtful characterisation of 'delay' cases such as *R* as being concerned with remedies, rather than with the compatibility of an act with Convention rights. In relation to remedies, a more restricted approach was suggested by Lord Bingham of Cornhill in *Spiers v Ruddy* 2009 SC (PC) 1 at para 16.

2 *Montgomery v HM Advocate* 2001 SC (PC) 1.

3 *Robertson v Higson* 2006 SC (PC) 22.

4 *McInnes v HM Advocate* 2010 SC (UKSC) 28; *Fraser v HM Advocate* 2011 SLT 515.

1.162 The Lord Advocate, the Advocate General, the Attorney General or the Attorney General for Northern Ireland may require any court or tribunal to refer to the Supreme Court any devolution issue which has arisen in proceedings before it to which he is a party[1]. A Law Officer may also refer to the Supreme Court any devolution issue which is not the subject of proceedings[2].

1 SA 1998, Sch 6, para 33. This occurred in *Clark v Kelly* 2003 SC (PC) 77, where the High Court of Justiciary had previously considered the same issue in earlier proceedings between the same parties. It occurred again in *Spiers v Ruddy* 2009 SC (PC) 1, where the Crown wished to resolve the conflict between *R v HM Advocate* 2003 SC (PC) 21 and *Attorney-General's Reference (No 2 of 2001)* [2004] 2 AC 72. The Privy Council declined to decide one of the questions referred to it: para 3, per Lord Bingham of Cornhill. A reference was also made in *HM Advocate v Murtagh* 2010 SC (PC) 39, concerned with disclosure. The Supreme Court is not bound by the terms of the questions referred: *Clark v Kelly* at para 76 per Lord Rodger of Earlsferry.

2 SA 1998, Sch 6, para 34.

Procedural rules

1.163 Subordinate legislation has been made regulating the procedure to be followed where a devolution issue is sought to be raised. The present discussion will focus on the rules applicable to criminal proceedings in Scotland[1], and to civil proceedings before the Court of Session[2]. There are also rules in respect of civil proceedings in the sheriff court[3] and in respect of proceedings before the Supreme Court[4].

1 Act of Adjournal (Devolution Issue Rules) 1999, SI 1999/1346, as amended. This inserted a new Ch 40 in the Act of Adjournal (Criminal Procedure Rules) 1996, SI 1996/513.

2 Act of Sederunt (Devolution Issue Rules) 1999, SI 1999/1345, as amended. This inserted a new Ch 25A in the Act of Sederunt (Rules of the Court of Session) 1994, SI 1994/1443.

3 Act of Sederunt (Proceedings for Determination of Devolution Issues Rules) 1999, SI 1999/1347, as amended.

4   The Supreme Court Rules 2009, SI 2009/1603. See also Supreme Court Practice Direction 10.

1.164 So far as criminal proceedings are concerned, the rules are contained in Chapter 40 of the Act of Adjournal (Criminal Procedure Rules) 1996 (as amended). In relation to proceedings on indictment, the Act of Adjournal requires a party to those proceedings who proposes to raise a devolution issue to give notice within seven days of service of the indictment[1]. The minute of notice must give sufficient specification of the alleged devolution issue to enable the court to determine whether any devolution issue actually arises[2]. It is sufficient, for the minute competently to raise a devolution issue, that it raises a question falling within one of the descriptions set out in para 1 of Sch 6 to the SA 1998, such as a question as to whether or not a purported or proposed exercise of a function by a member of the Scottish Government is incompatible with a Convention right[3]. A devolution minute in an appeal process must be linked to the grounds of appeal raised: it is not free-standing[4].

1   Act of Adjournal (Criminal Procedure Rules) 1996, SI 1996/513, Rule 40.2(1). This rule applies to appellate proceedings on indictment as well as to proceedings at first instance: *McDonald v HM Advocate* 2010 SC (PC) 1. Leave of the court is therefore required to raise an issue on appeal which was not raised earlier, even if it arises out of events at the trial.

2   Rule 40.6. See *Montgomery v HM Advocate* 2001 SC (PC) 1 at 20 per Lord Hope of Craighead; *Brown v Stott* 2001 SC (PC) 43 at 72 per Lord Hope of Craighead; *McCarthy v HM Advocate* 2008 SCCR 902.

3   *Brown v Stott* 2001 SC (PC) 43. Differing views on the point had been expressed in the earlier case of *Montgomery v HM Advocate* 2001 SC (PC) 1.

4   *Walls v Brown* 2009 JC 375; *Russell v Thomson* 2011 SCCR 77; *Beggs, Applicant* 2011 SCCR 347.

1.165 Notice has to be given to the court, the other parties to the proceedings and the Advocate General[1]. The devolution issue is then to be considered at a hearing held in accordance with the procedure followed under existing law[2]. A challenge to a provision in an Act of the Scottish Parliament as being incompatible with any of the Convention rights might, for example, take the form of a plea to the competency or relevancy of an indictment based on the provision. In some circumstances, a plea in bar of trial might be appropriate. In either case, the issue could (and normally should) be dealt with, in solemn proceedings in the High Court, at a preliminary hearing[3]. A broadly similar procedure applies where a party wishes to raise a devolution issue in summary proceedings[4] or in other types of criminal proceedings[5]. A devolution issue cannot be raised in criminal proceedings except in accordance with the prescribed time limits, unless the court on cause shown otherwise determines[6].

1   Rule 40.2(1).

2   *HM Advocate v Montgomery* 2000 JC 111. The court need not wait until the period of notice has expired before holding the hearing: *HM Advocate v Montgomery* 2000 JC 111 at 118.

3   Under the Criminal Procedure (Scotland) Act (CP(S)A) 1995, s 72. See *HM Advocate v Montgomery* 2000 JC 111. In solemn proceedings in the sheriff court, the issue could be dealt

with at a first diet: CP(S)A 1995, s 71(2). As to the granting of leave to appeal against a pre-trial decision of a devolution issue, see *HM Advocate v Montgomery* 2000 JC 111 at 121.

4   Rule 40.3.

5   Rule 40.4. This would cover petitions to the nobile officium. It may also cover appeals. It does not cover extradition proceedings: cf *Allen v HM Advocate* 2010 SCCR 861.

6   Rule 40.5. As to what constitutes 'cause shown', see *HM Advocate v Montgomery* 2000 JC 111. As that case indicates, 'ordinary' time limits or rules may apply as well as the particular requirements imposed by Chapter 40 of the Act of Adjournal.

1.166 Following the service of the notice, the court may determine that no devolution issue in fact arises[1]. If a devolution issue does arise, then the court can determine it, or it can make a reference to the High Court of Justiciary (unless the court itself consists of two or more judges of the High Court of Justiciary[2], in which case a reference can be made to the Supreme Court[3]). The one exception is that where a court determines that a devolution issue may be raised during a trial, it cannot make a reference, but must determine the issue itself. This avoids the inconvenience and undesirability of interrupting a trial for longer than is necessary. Where there is a reference to the High Court, the court has a wide power to make appropriate orders, including orders postponing any trial diet[4]. The scheme of the Act of Adjournal is directed towards ensuring that devolution issues are raised prior to trial, whenever possible. This partly reflects the practical problems which are liable to arise, as just mentioned, if devolution issues are raised during a trial. It may also reflect the fact that an erroneous determination of a devolution issue during a trial leading to an acquittal in proceedings on indictment could not be appealed so as to affect the acquittal[5]. A challenge to the Act of Adjournal, on the basis inter alia that the time limits were incompatible with the Convention, was unsuccessful[6].

1   Rules 40.2(2), 40.3(2) and 40.4(3). See eg *BBC, Petitioners (No 2)* 2000 JC 521; *Hoekstra v HM Advocate (No 3)* 2001 SC (PC) 37.

2   Rule 40.7(1).

3   Rule 40.9(1).

4   Rule 40.8. The power of postponement is not subject to the time limits ordinarily applying to adjournments: *HM Advocate v Touati* 2001 SCCR 392. Rule 40.8(1) does not enable the court to make any order in criminal proceedings after the accused has been acquitted: *HMA v K* 2010 SCCR 163.

5   *Montgomery v HM Advocate* 2001 SC (PC) 1 at 15 per Lord Hope of Craighead. A decision taken prior to trial can be appealed: CP(S)A 1995, s 74.

6   *HM Advocate v Dickson* 2000 JC 93; affd *Dickson v HM Advocate* 2001 JC 202.

1.167 The rules applicable to civil proceedings in the Court of Session[1] adopt a broadly similar scheme. The devolution issue must be specified in detail in pleadings. The issue must be raised before any evidence is led, unless the court on cause shown otherwise determines[2]. Intimation of the devolution issue must be given to the Lord Advocate and to the Advocate General[3], who then have 14 days to decide whether to take part in proceedings[4], and a further seven days to lodge written submissions[5]. The issue is then dealt with at a hearing before proof or trial.

1 Act of Sederunt (Devolution Issue Rules) 1999, SI 1999/1345, as amended. As to the sheriff court, see the Act of Sederunt (Proceedings for Determination of Devolution Issues Rules) 1999, SI 1999/1347.
2 SI 1999/1345, Rule 25A.3(1).
3 Rule 25A.5(1).
4 Rule 25A.5(4).
5 Rule 25A.6(1).

1.168 In both criminal and civil procedure, then, the rules aim to ensure, as far as possible, that devolution issues are raised and determined prior to trial. In practice, however, this may not be possible or appropriate: there may be situations where the devolution issue cannot reasonably be identified in advance of trial; and even if the devolution issue can be identified prior to trial, it may not always be possible (or necessary) to determine it until the significance of the point raised can be assessed in the context of the trial. This applies particularly to the fair trial guarantee in Article 6, which requires a consideration of the trial as a whole. Questions under Article 6 as to the fairness of a trial should therefore generally be considered after the trial[1]. There are, however, circumstances in which a devolution issue relating to the fair trial guarantee can be raised and determined prior to trial[2].

1 *Moir v HM Advocate* 2005 1 SC (PC) 1; *Holland v HM Advocate* 2005 1 SC (PC) 3 at para 41 per Lord Rodger of Earlsferry.
2 See eg *Brown v Stott* 2001 SC (PC) 43; *R v A* [2001] 1 WLR 789.

Remedies

1.169 It has been held to be implicit in the SA 1998, s 100 that proceedings can be brought on the basis of that Act by a person whose Convention rights have been infringed by an Act of the Scottish Parliament or by conduct of the Scottish Government[1]. The appropriate remedies are generally determined in accordance with common law principles[2]. There are, however, restrictions on the remedies which can be granted against the Parliament[3].

1 *Somerville v Scottish Ministers* 2008 SC (HL) 45.
2 See eg *R v HM Advocate* 2003 SC (PC) 21 at para 60 per Lord Hope of Craighead and at paras 121–122 per Lord Rodger of Earlsferry.
3 SA 1998, s 40.

1.170 The question whether the SA 1998 enables a court to award damages, or a pecuniary award by way of 'just satisfaction', in respect of an act which is incompatible with Convention rights (and, if so, on what basis), has divided judicial opinion. The prevailing view is set out in the speeches of the majority of the House of Lords in *Somerville v Scottish Ministers*[1]. It was considered to be implicit in the SA 1998, s 100(3) that 'damages for just satisfaction' may be claimed in respect of an act which is outside devolved competençe because it is incompatible with a Convention right[2]. It was also implicit that a common law claim for damages for breach of statutory duty was excluded. The remedy was limited to what was necessary to afford just satisfaction. The conditions imposed by the HRA 1998, s 8(3) and (4) were applicable.

1 *Somerville v Scottish Ministers* 2008 SC (HL) 45.

2 Damages cannot be awarded by the criminal courts, but they may be able to provide an effective remedy by other means: *R v HM Advocate* 2003 SC (PC) 21 at paras 61–62 per Lord Hope of Craighead.

1.171 Since acts or failures to act which are incompatible with Convention rights are both 'outside competence', in the language of the SA 1998, and unlawful for the purpose of the HRA 1998, it follows that there are two equally valid ways of addressing the incompatibility:

> 'It is open to the litigant to choose which of two alternative remedies he should pursue, even if the effect of doing so is to enable him to avoid a time bar that excludes one of them.'[1]

Indeed, there is no need for the litigant to choose, since he can bring proceedings under both Acts[2]. Even if proceedings are brought under the HRA 1998, they will still involve a devolution issue in terms of para l(d) of Sch 6 to the SA 1998 and will be subject to the procedural requirements of that Schedule[3].

1 *Somerville v Scottish Ministers* 2008 SC (HL) 45 per Lord Hope of Craighead at para 31.

2 *Somerville v Scottish Ministers* 2008 SC (HL) 45 per Lord Rodger of Earlsferry at para 108 and Lord Mance at para 180.

3 *Somerville v Scottish Ministers* 2008 SC (HL) 45 per Lord Rodger of Earlsferry at para 108.

THE RELATIONSHIP BETWEEN THE HUMAN RIGHTS ACT 1998 AND THE SCOTLAND ACT 1998

1.172 The relationship between the HRA 1998 and the SA 1998 is complex. Both statutes require domestic courts to consider 'Convention rights', but the manner in which compatibility with these treaty obligations is examined proceeds upon two contrasting approaches. As Lord Hope of Craighead explained in *Somerville v Scottish Ministers*, the Human Rights Act has two fundamental features:

> 'The first is that it does not disturb the principle of the sovereignty of Parliament. A finding that primary legislation is incompatible with a Convention right does not affect its validity (sec 3(6) HRA). Subject to the power that is given to ministers to make remedial orders under sec 10, it is left to Parliament to decide, in the light of a declaration of incompatibility, what should be done about it. An act or failure to act of a public authority is not unlawful if, as a result of primary legislation, the public

authority could not have acted differently or it was acting so as to give effect to primary legislation which cannot be read in a way that is compatible with the Convention rights (sec 6(2) HRA). The second feature is that the language that it uses to describes acts or failures to act that are incompatible with the Convention rights is that they are "unlawful" (secs 6(1), 7(1), 8(1)). Unlawfulness in terms of the Human Rights Act has certain consequences with regard to what can be obtained by way of a remedy. This is because the Human Rights Act makes the acts or failures to act unlawful in domestic law.

The Scotland Act, on the other hand, is concerned with the consequences of devolving legislative and executive power to institutions which have limited competence. Sections 29 and 30 and schs 4 and 5 define the legislative competence of the Scottish Parliament. The executive competence of the Scottish Ministers is limited in exactly the same way as that of the Scottish Parliament. Section 52 enables statutory functions to be conferred on the Scottish Ministers by the Scottish Parliament within its area of devolved competence. Section 29(1) SA provides that an Act of the Scottish Parliament is not law so far as any provision of the Act is outside the legislative competence of the Parliament. The effect of this provision is that the Scottish Ministers have no power to exercise functions that may be conferred on them which are outside the legislative competence of the Scottish Parliament. Section 53 provides for the transfer of functions previously exercisable by Ministers of the Crown to the Scottish Ministers, but only in so far as they are exercisable within devolved competence. The expression "devolved competence" is defined by sec 54. Subsection (2) of that section restricts the devolved competence of the Scottish Ministers with regard to making, confirming or approving of subordinate legislation to what would be within the legislative competence of the Scottish Parliament. Subsection (3) imposes the same restriction on the devolved competence of the Scottish Ministers in the case of the exercise of any other function that they may exercise under a pre-commencement statute.

Section 57(2) SA reinforces, in the context of provisions about the devolved competence of the Scottish Ministers generally, the restriction that sec 29(2)(d) imposes on the legislative competence of the Scottish Parliament. It provides that a member of the Scottish Executive "has no power" to make any subordinate legislation, or to do any other act, so far as the legislation or other act is incompatible with any of the Convention rights or with Community law. Section 57(3) qualifies that restriction in the case of an act of the Lord Advocate in prosecuting an offence or in his capacity as head of the systems of criminal prosecution ... and investigation of deaths in Scotland, so as to align his position with that of the equivalent authorities in England and Wales. It does so by providing that sec 57(2) does not apply to an act of the Lord Advocate in that capacity ... if, because of sec 6(2) HRA, it would not be unlawful under sec 6(1) HRA[1]. That qualification on the limits of devolved competence does not apply to any other member of the Scottish Executive or to the Lord Advocate acting in any other capacity. It is not open to them to claim that the act or the failure to act was within devolved competence because, as a result of primary legislation, they could not have acted differently or they were acting so as to give effect to primary legislation which cannot be read in a way that is compatible with the Convention rights ...

Fundamental, therefore, to a proper understanding of the Scotland Act is its concentration on the limits of devolved competence ... So an act by a member of the

Scottish Executive which is incompatible with the Convention rights is not described by the Scotland Act as "unlawful"[2]. It is described instead as "outside devolved competence" in sec 54(3), and as something that he has "no power" to do in sec 57(2). The machinery described in sec 98 and sch 6 SA is available for the resolution of questions as to whether a failure to act by a member of the Scottish Executive is incompatible with any of the Convention rights or with Community law and any other questions as to whether a function is exercisable within devolved competence.'[3]

1   This was said prior to the amendments to s 57 which, it is anticipated, may be made by the SA 2011.

2   As to the significance, of the choice of language, cf paras **1.59** and **1.136** above.

3   *Somerville v Scottish Ministers* 2008 SC (HL) 45 at paras 13–16.

1.173 There are further distinctions between these two statutes. Devolution issues can be dealt with by a preliminary reference, whereas issues raised under the HRA 1998 cannot. The SA 1998 confers statutory powers on the courts and on the Scottish Government, in the event that Acts of the Scottish Parliament or acts of members of the Scottish Government are ultra vires, which are not available under the HRA 1998[1]. On the other hand, the inherent power of a court to limit the retrospective effect of its decisions, which may be applicable under the HRA 1998, is implicitly excluded by the statutory regime provided by the SA 1998[2].

1   See paras **1.127** and **1.154** above.

2   *Cadder v HM Advocate* 2010 SCCR 951 at paras 57–59 per Lord Hope.

1.174 The SA 1998 contains a number of provisions which help ensure broad congruence with the HRA 1998. First, in relation to standing, the SA 1998 does not enable a person to bring any proceedings on the ground that an act is incompatible with the Convention rights, or to rely on the Convention rights in proceedings, unless he would be a victim for the purposes of Article 34 of the ECHR (within the meaning of the HRA 1998) if proceedings in respect of the act were brought in the European Court of Human Rights[1]. This imports the same test as the HRA 1998, s 7(7). Secondly, in relation to damages, the SA 1998 does not enable a court or tribunal to award any damages in respect of an act which is incompatible with the Convention rights which it could not award if the HRA 1998, s 8(3) and (4) applied[2]. Thirdly, in relation to time limits, s 7(5) of the HRA 1998 and s 100(3B) of the SA 1998 are in similar terms. Nevertheless, the decision of the majority of the House of Lords in *Somerville v Scottish Ministers* that the SA 1998, s 100 implicitly enables the court to grant any remedy or relief which it considers appropriate in the case of acts or failures to act which are outside devolved competence, including damages, is capable of giving rise to a number of questions[3].

1   SA 1998, s 100(1).

2   SA 1998, s 100(3).

3   Including those mentioned by Lord Mance in his dissenting speech: see *Somerville v Scottish Ministers* 2008 SC (HL) 45 at paras 182–192.

PROMOTING AWARENESS OF HUMAN RIGHTS

National human rights institutions

1.175 The establishment of national human rights institutions – whether in the form of commissions, committees, ombudsmen, institutes or the like – is supported by the United Nations as helping to ensure the effective implementation of international obligations entered into by nation states[1]. To this end, the adoption of the 'Paris Principles' by the United Nations in 1993 envisages such institutions as having a role to promote and to protect human rights[2]. At the level of the European Union, the European Union Agency for Fundamental Rights was established in 2007 with the functions of collecting information and data, providing advice to the European Union and its member states, and raising public awareness of fundamental rights[3]. Within the UK, the first human rights institution was the Northern Ireland Human Rights Commission, which was established by the Northern Ireland Act 1998 with a statutory duty to review the adequacy and effectiveness of human rights law and practice, and with the power to represent individuals in cases against public authorities and to intervene in proceedings[4]. The Northern Ireland Act also established an Equality Commission for Northern Ireland, charged with developing 'equality schemes' for the guidance of public authorities[5].

---

1   For discussion of the use of such offices in domestic human rights protection, see Burdekin and Gallagher 'The United Nations and National Human Rights Institutions' in Alfredsson, Gudmundur et al (eds) *International Human Rights Monitoring Mechanisms: Essays in Honour of Jakob Th Möller* (2001). For domestic discussion, see O'Brien 'Human Rights Accountability in the UK: Deliberative Democracy and the Role of the Ombudsman' [2010] EHRLR 504.

2   'Principles Relating to the Status of National Institutions for the Promotion and Protection of Human Rights' UN General Assembly Resolution 48/134, 20 December 1993, UN Doc A/RES/48/134. See also Committee of Ministers Rec R (97) 14 on the establishment of independent national human rights institutions.

3   See Reg (CE) No 168/2007. For discussion, see Alston and de Schutter (eds) *Monitoring Fundamental Rights in the EU: the Contribution of the Fundamental Rights Agency* (2005), passim; Howard 'The European Agency for Fundamental Rights' [2006] EHRLR 445; and De Beco 'National Human Rights Institutions in Europe' (2007) 7 HRLR 331.

4   Northern Ireland Act 1998, ss 68–71. See also *R (Northern Ireland Human Rights Commission) v Greater Belfast Coroner* [2002] NI 236. See further Lester and Pannick *Human Rights Law and Practice* (3rd d edn, 2009), 746–52 .

5   Northern Ireland Act 1998, s 75.

The Commission for Equality and Human Rights

1.176 The Equality and Human Rights Commission (EHRC) was established by the Equality Act (EA) 2006. Since October 2007, it has combined the functions of the previous Commission for Racial Equality, the Disability Rights Commission and the Equal Opportunities Commission, which it replaces. In addition, it has a responsibility for promoting equality and combating unlawful discrimination in respect of sexual orientation, religion or belief, and age. The EHRC also has responsibility for the promotion of human rights[1].

1   See further Lester and Beattie 'The New Commission for Equality and Human Rights' [2006] PL 197; and Klug 'Breaking New Ground: the Joint Committee on Human Rights and the Role of Parliament in Human Rights Compliance' [2007] EHRLR 231.

1.177 In relation to human rights, the statute provides that the EHRC may not take human rights action[1] in relation to a matter, or consider the question whether a person's human rights have been contravened, if the Scottish Parliament has legislative competence to enable a person to take action of that kind in relation to that matter, or to consider that question. That general prohibition does not prevent the EHRC from taking action with the consent of a person established by an Act of the Scottish Parliament whose principal duties relate to human rights (such as the Scottish Human Rights Commission).

1   EA 2006, s 7; 'human rights action' is defined by s 7(2).

1.178 The EA 2006 sets out the Commission's duties in relation to human rights[1]. The provisions require the EHRC to promote awareness, understanding and protection of human rights and to encourage good practice in relation to human rights. In addition, the EHRC is required to encourage public authorities[2] to comply with the HRA 1998, s 6. However, in relation to the more general duties under this section, the EHRC is not limited to dealing with public authorities. It is, for example, also able to provide encouragement to the voluntary and commercial sectors to adopt appropriate human rights standards as the basis of their relationship with their clients and customers in the provision of their services. The statute makes clear that the EHRC may take action under this section in respect of human rights other than the 'Convention rights' set out in the HRA 1998, Sch 1[3]. However, the EHRC is required to have particular regard to the importance of exercising its powers in relation to the Convention rights[4]. The Commission must also take account of relevant human rights when fulfilling its wider duties[5].

1   EA 2006, s 9.
2   'Public authorities' are as defined in the HRA 1998, s 6: see para **1.59** above.
3   EA 2006, s 9(2).
4   EA 2006, s 9(3).
5   Ie, under EA 2006, ss 8 and 10: EA 2006, s 9(4).

1.179 The Commission has certain obligations and powers to keep the equality and human rights enactments (including the HRA 1998) under review and to provide advice and recommendations on the law and proposed changes to the law[1]. The general powers available to the EHRC and the general activities it can undertake to carry out any or all of its duties involve publishing or disseminating ideas and information, giving advice and guidance, undertaking research and providing education or training[2]. The EHRC also has a power to conduct inquiries into matters relating to its duties in respect of equality and diversity, human rights and groups[3]. These inquiries may be thematic (for example into the causes of unequal outcomes), sectoral (looking at inequality in, for example, the uptake of health screening services or at the employment of disabled people in particular sectors, eg the retail sector) or relate to one or more named parties. The EHRC may also co-operate with other people or organisations within the UK and abroad when undertaking its human rights duties[4]. In particular, this allows the EHRC to co-operate with the Scottish and Northern Ireland Human Rights Commissions, and to give its opinion to international bodies about the compliance of the UK with its international human rights obligations.

1   EA 2006, s 11. For equality legislation, see now the Equality Act 2010.

2   EA 2006, s 13.

3   EA 2006, s 16.

4   That is, in terms of EA 2006, s 9: EA 2006, s 18.

1.180 The EHRC has capacity to institute or intervene in legal proceedings where the proceedings are relevant to any of the Commission's functions[1]. The procedure is regulated by rules of court[2]. The EHRC is deemed to have the necessary title and interest in relation to any such legal proceedings in Scotland[3]. The EHRC may rely on the HRA 1998, s 7(1)(b) in any legal proceedings which it has instituted (or in which it has intervened), even if it is not itself a victim or potential victim of the breach of Convention rights in question, provided there are one or more persons who are (or, for a potential future breach, would be) victims[4]. No award of damages may be made to the EHRC in relation to a breach of the Convention rights[5].

1   EA 2006, s 30. For examples of successful interventions, *see R (JL) v Secretary of State for Home Department* [2009] 1 AC 588 (duty to hold ECHR, Art 2-compliant investigation of near deaths in custody); *R (C) v Secretary of State for Justice* [2009] QB 657 (restraint measures in secure training centres incompatible with Art 3); *R (N) v Secretary of State for Health and R(E) v Nottinghamshire Healthcare NHS Trust* [2009] EWCA Civ 795 (mental illness or other mental disability constitutes a 'personal characteristic' in terms of Art 14); *R (RJM) v Secretary of State for Work and Pensions* [2009] 1 AC 311 (disability premium falls within scope of Prot 1, Art 1; and homelessness constitutes a 'personal characteristic' in terms of Art 14); *R (G) v Governors of X School* [2010] 1 WLR 2218 (circumstances when Art 6 calls for legal representation in employment tribunals); and *HJ (Iran) v Secretary of State for Home Department* [2011] 1 AC 596 (return of asylum seekers to countries where persecution on grounds of their sexual orientation would violate Art 3).

2   For the Court of Session, see Ch 94 of the Rules of Court, inserted by Act of Sederunt (Rules of the Court of Session Amendment No 8) (Miscellaneous) 2007, SSI 2007/449. For the Sheriff Court: see Ch 13A of the Ordinary Cause Rules, Ch 14A of the Summary Cause Rules, rules 2.37–2.38 of the Summary Application Rules and Ch 13A of the Small Claim Rules, inserted by Act of Sederunt (Sheriff Court Rules) (Miscellaneous Amendments) 2008, SSI 2008/223.

3   EA 2006, s 30(2).

4   EA 2006, s 30(3).

5   EA 2006, s 30(3)(d).

Scottish Commission for Human Rights

1.181 The Scottish Commission for Human Rights[1] was established by the Scottish Commission for Human Rights (SCHRA) Act 2006[2]. It has a general duty to promote awareness and understanding of, and respect for, human rights and, in particular, to encourage best practice in relation to human rights[3]. To this end, it may publish or otherwise disseminate information or ideas, provide advice or guidance, conduct research, and provide education or training[4]. It may also review and recommend changes to any area of the law of Scotland, or to any policies or practices of any Scottish public authorities[5]. In the exercise of any of its functions, the Commission may consult, act jointly with, co-operate with, or assist any other person, and it must seek to ensure, so far as practicable, that any activity undertaken by it does not duplicate unnecessarily any activity undertaken by any other person under any other enactment[6]. It is precluded, however, from providing assistance (including giving advice, guidance and grants) to, or in respect of, any person in connection with any claim or legal proceedings to which that person is or may become a party[7]. The Commission must prepare and lay before the Scottish Parliament once every four years its strategic plan setting out information as to how it proposes to fulfil its general duty during that period[8].

1   The Commission consists of a member to chair the Commission appointed by Her Majesty on the nomination of the Scottish Parliament, and not more than four other members appointed by the Scottish Parliament Corporate Body, each member holding office for a period of up to five years (but eligible for reappointment): Scottish Commission for Human Rights Act 2006, Sch 1, paras 1 and 5. The Commission is not a servant or agent of the Crown, and has no status, immunity or privilege of the Crown: Sch 1 para 2. It is not to be subject to the control of any member of the Scottish Parliament, any member of the Scottish Executive or the Parliamentary corporation: Sch 1, para 3. For further provisions concerning its constitution, etc, see Sch 1. The SCHRA 2006 came fully into force on 1 April 2008.

2   This followed a consultation exercise by the Scottish Executive which began in 2001: see *Protecting our Rights: A Human Rights Commission for Scotland?* (2001); *The Scottish Human Rights Commission* (2003); and MacDonald and Thompson, *The Scottish Human Rights Commission: Analysis of Responses* (2004). A review was also commissioned into the use of the Convention in the Scottish courts: see Greenhill et al *The Use of Human Rights Legislation in the Scottish Courts* (2004).

3   SCHRA 2006, ss 1 and 2. 'Human rights' in this context means the Convention rights within the meaning of s 1 of the HRA 1998, and other human rights contained in any international convention, treaty or other international instrument ratified by the UK: s 2(2). In deciding what action to take in pursuance of its general duty, the Commission must have regard, in particular, to the importance of exercising its functions in relation to Convention rights and human rights of those groups in society whose human rights are not, in the opinion of the Commission, otherwise being sufficiently promoted: s 2(4).

4   SCHRA 2006, s 3(1).

5   SCHRA 2006, s 4(1). The Commission must consult the Scottish Law Commission before undertaking any such review of an area of Scots law: s 4(2).

6   SCHRA 2006, s 5.

7   SCHRA 2006, s 6.

8   SCHRA 2006, s 7. An annual report is also to be submitted to the Scottish Parliament, which is to include a summary of any inquiries conducted by the Commission and of any other

activities undertaken by it in pursuance of its general duty: s 15. The Commission must arrange for the publication of all reports laid before the Scottish Parliament: s 16(1). The first strategic plan was laid before the Scottish Parliament in July 2009.

1.182 In relation to any matter relevant to its general duty, the Commission may conduct an inquiry into the policies or practices of a particular Scottish public authority, Scottish public authorities generally, or Scottish public authorities of a particular description[1]. However, this power is subject to certain restrictions: an inquiry into the policies and practices of a particular Scottish public authority may only be conducted if the authority is the only Scottish public authority with functions in relation to the subject matter of the inquiry, or if the subject matter of the inquiry is about whether human rights[2] are being respected by the authority[3]. Nor may an inquiry be conducted into the policies and practices of any Scottish public authority in relation to a particular case, but such policies and practices may be taken into account in the course of an inquiry[4]. The Commission may not, in the course of an inquiry (including the report of the inquiry), question the findings of any court or tribunal[5]. An inquiry is to be conducted in public, except to the extent that the Commission considers it necessary or expedient that any part of it should be conducted in private[6]. The Commission may require any Scottish public authority, or any member, officer or member of staff of such an authority, to give oral evidence, produce documents or otherwise provide information[7], may take into account any evidence, information or document relevant to the subject matter of the inquiry which it has obtained otherwise than by virtue of such a requirement[8], and may enter any place of detention, inspect it and conduct interviews in private with any detainee with that person's consent[9]. The Commission can seek the assistance of the Court of Session in order to enforce its powers[10]. At the conclusion of an inquiry (other than an inquiry into whether specified human rights are being respected), a report of the inquiry including the Commission's findings and any recommendations must be laid before the Scottish Parliament[11].

---

1 'Scottish public authority' is defined in SCHRA 2006, s 19 as '(a) any body or office which, or office-holder who, is (i) a part of the Scottish Administration, or (ii) a Scottish public authority with mixed functions or no reserved functions, and (b) any other person who is a public authority within the meaning of the Human Rights Act 1998, but only in so far as the public functions exercisable by the person (i) are exercisable in or as regards Scotland, and (ii) do not relate to reserved matters'. Before taking any step in the conduct of an inquiry, the Commission must draw up terms of reference for the proposed inquiry and a summary of the procedure to be followed in the conduct of the inquiry; it must also give notice of the proposed inquiry and its terms of reference and procedure to the relevant Scottish public authority and publicise such details in such manner as it considers appropriate to bring them to the attention of any other persons likely to be affected by the inquiry: s 8(4). Provision regarding notice is made in s 18.

2 SCHRA 2006, s 9(3) and 9(4). 'Human rights' are as specified by SCHRA 2006, s 9(6): that is, the human rights (so far as ratified by the UK) contained in the United Nations Convention against Torture and Other Cruel, Inhuman or Degrading Treatment or Punishment (1984); the European Convention for the Prevention of Torture and Inhuman or Degrading Treatment or Punishment (1987); any Protocol to those conventions; and such other international conventions, treaties or international instruments as may be specified by order. The United Nations Convention on the Rights of Persons with Disabilities was so specified by the Scottish

Commission for Human Rights (Specification) Order 2008, SSI 2008/355. The Commission has been designated a 'National Reporting Mechanism' within the meaning of the Optional Protocol on the Convention against Torture, along with HM's Inspectorate of Prisons for Scotland, HM's Inspectorate of Constabulary for Scotland, the Mental Welfare Commission for Scotland, and the Care Commission.

3   SCHRA 2006, s 8(5).

4   SCHRA 2006, s 9(3) and (4).

5   SCHRA 2006, s 9(1).

6   SCHRA 2006, s 8(5): otherwise, the procedure to be followed is to be such as the Commission may determine: s 8(6).

7   SCHRA 2006, s 8(4).

8   SCHRA 2006, s 10(3). However, a person is not required to answer any question, produce any document or provide any information which he would be entitled to refuse to answer, produce or provide in proceedings in a court in Scotland: s 10(4).

9   SCHRA 2006, s 11(1). 'Place of detention' is defined by s 11(2) as meaning any premises, vehicle or other place in or at which an individual is or may be detained by, or with the authority or consent of, a Scottish public authority.

10   SCHRA 2006, Sch 2, para 3(3) and Sch 3, para 3(1). The procedure is regulated by Ch 95 of the Rules of Court, inserted by Act of Sederunt (Rules of the Court of Session Amendment No 4) (Miscellaneous) 2008, SSI 2008/123.

11   SCHRA 2006, s 12(1) and (2). The report is subsequently to be published: s 16(1). The report is not to make reference to the activities of a specified or identifiable person unless the Commission considers that it is necessary to do so in order for the report adequately to reflect the results of the inquiry: s 12(3). If an individual is to be identified in a report, the Commission must provide the person concerned with a draft of the report and an opportunity to make representations concerning it, and thereafter consider any representations made: s 12(4). Provision is made for confidentiality of information gained in the course of an inquiry not constituting an authorised disclosure: s 13. Any statement made by the Commission in conducting an inquiry, in communicating with any person for the purposes of an inquiry, or in a report of an inquiry has absolute privilege; any other statement made for or in pursuance of the purposes of the Act has qualified privilege: s 17(1).

1.183 The Commission is also empowered to intervene in civil proceedings (other than children's hearings proceedings) for the purpose of making a submission to the court on an issue arising in the proceedings which is considered relevant to its general duty and raising a matter of public interest[1]. Such interventions may only be made with leave of the court or at the invitation of the court, and the court may grant leave or invite the Commission to intervene only if satisfied that such intervention is likely to be of assistance to the court[2]. The procedure is regulated by rules of court[3]. It has been observed that leave to intervene may be given to bodies such as the Commission in the expectation that their fund of knowledge or particular point of view will enable them to provide the court with a more rounded picture than it would otherwise obtain, but that an intervention is of no assistance if it merely repeats points which the parties have already made, and that it is not the role of an intervener to be an additional counsel for one of the parties[4].

The relationship between the Commission and the Commission for Equality and Human Rights, discussed above, is addressed in a memorandum of understanding.

---

1   SCHRA 2006, s 14(1)–(3). 'Court' means the Court of Session and sheriff court, both as
     courts of first instance and appeal, and the Land Court; and 'civil proceedings' and 'children's
     hearing proceedings' are defined in s 14(9). It is envisaged that the Commission might also
     intervene in proceedings in the European Court of Human Rights: see para **2.37** below.

2   SCHRA 2006, s 14(2) and (6). When applying for leave, the Commission must set out the
     issue arising in the proceedings which it intends to address, and a summary of the submission
     that it intends to make: s 14(4). An invitation from a court to intervene must set out the issue
     arising in the proceedings upon which the court seeks a submission: s 14(5).

3   For the Court of Session, see Ch 95 of the Rules of Court, inserted by Act of Sederunt (Rules
     of the Court of Session Amendment No 4) (Miscellaneous) 2008, SSI 2008/123. For the
     Sheriff Court, see Ch 13B of the Ordinary Cause Rules, Ch 14B of the Summary Cause Rules,
     rules 2.39–2.41 of the Summary Application Rules and Ch 13A of the Small Claim Rules,
     inserted by Act of Sederunt (Sheriff Court Rules) (Miscellaneous Amendments) 2008, SSI
     2008/223.

4   *E v Chief Constable of the Ulster Constabulary* [2009] AC 536.

Parliamentary institutions

1.184 There is now a growing awareness of the importance of national parliaments
in ensuring the effective protection of human rights. While there is significant
involvement of national parliamentarians in the work of the Parliamentary Assembly
of the Council of Europe, the role of domestic legislatures remains under-developed
both in implementing judgments of the European Court of Human Rights and also
in proactive scrutiny of legislative proposals[1]. The Scottish Parliament lacks both
engagement with Strasbourg human rights work[2] and any dedicated committee
specifically charged with human rights issues.

---

1   See Drzemczewski and Gaughan 'Implementing Strasbourg Court Judgments: the Parliamentary
     Dimension' in Benedek, Karl and Mihr (eds) 2010 EYHR, vol 2, 247–258.

2   Two MSPs are members of the Committee of the Regions of the Congress of Local and
     Regional Authorities of the Council of Europe, but this body is charged with furthering local
     democracy rather than engaging in human rights work.

The Joint Committee on Human Rights

1.185 The Joint Committee on Human Rights has made a significant contribution
to the protection of human rights in the United Kingdom[1]. It is comprised of 12
members drawn from both Houses of Parliament, and is charged with considering
matters relating to human rights in the United Kingdom, but is precluded from
taking up individual cases. Its work has three main aspects. First, it may undertake
thematic inquiries on human rights issues. Secondly, it scrutinises Government
Bills, paying particular attention to legislative proposals that appear to have
implications for human rights awareness. Thirdly, it examines Government action
to deal with judgments of domestic courts and of the European Court of Human
Rights where breaches of human rights have been established[2]. Parliamentary
consideration of the compatibility of Bills with human rights (and of other matters

concerning human rights in the UK) has also been greatly strengthened by the establishment of the Joint Committee on Human Rights[3].

1   For discussion of the work of the Committee, see Hiebert 'Parliament and the Human Rights Act: Can the JCHR help facilitate a Culture of Rights?' (2006)1 Int Jo Constit Law 11. Current inquiries concern the work of the Equalities and Human Rights Commission, and counter-terrorism policy and human rights. See also Joint Committee on Human Rights *Enhancing Parliament's Role in relation to Human Rights Judgments*, Fifteenth Report of Session 2009–10, HL 85/HC 455 (2010).

2   The Committee thus considers proposals for remedial orders and draft remedial orders including remedial orders made by the Government and laid before Parliament by virtue of the Human Rights Act 1988, s 10 and Sch 2: see para **1.58** above. In respect of draft remedial orders and remedial orders, it must consider whether the special attention of the House should be drawn to them on any of the grounds specified in Standing Order 73 (Joint Committee on Statutory Instruments).

3   See eg Joint Committee on Human Rights *Monitoring the Government's response to Court Judgments finding Breaches of Human Rights*, Sixteenth Report of Session 2006–07, HL 128/ HC 728 (2007); and *Counter-terrorism Policy and Human Rights,* Sixteenth Report of Session 2009–10, HL86/HC111 (2010).

Chapter 2

European protection of human rights

THE COUNCIL OF EUROPE AND THE PROTECTION OF HUMAN RIGHTS

A developing international concern for human rights

2.01 Before 1945, legal protection for the individual against state interference with what now would be termed 'human rights' was still largely a matter for domestic law. By the early part of the nineteenth century, international law had begun to develop an interest in the prohibition of slavery, in the treatment of aliens, and in humanitarian intervention. Later that century, issues such as the care of injured combatants and prisoners of war were being addressed by multilateral treaties. While the establishment of the League of Nations and the International Labour Organisation after the 1914–18 war gave additional impetus to the international protection of minorities and employees' rights[1], the individual continued to be unable to rely directly upon international law for relief. The excesses of totalitarianism before and during the 1939–45 war, however, prompted a more dynamic concern for human rights through the establishment of innovative charters of guarantees and new institutions for their enforcement. Of key importance in the development of this new international legal order was the Atlantic Charter of 1941, which sought to give prominence to international law and to human rights, and promised a fresh start in the post-war era.

---

1   Covenant of the League of Nations, Arts 22 and 23. For a brief overview of the historical development of international human rights, see Steiner and Alston *International Human Rights in Context* (3rd edn, 2007), pp 56–135. It goes without saying that there is considerable disagreement on the philosophical and historical origins of human rights. The brief treatment here takes a distinctly Euro-centric (or western) approach.

2.02 Subsequently, the Charter of the United Nations of June 1945 specifically sought to 'reaffirm faith in fundamental human rights' by 'promoting and encouraging respect for human rights and for fundamental freedoms for all without distinction as to race, sex, language or religion'[1]. To this end, the United Nations adopted the Universal Declaration of Human Rights in December 1948. In international law, this marked a fundamental shift in approach by appearing to limit nation-state sovereignty through the recognition that a state's treatment of its citizens within its territorial boundaries was of legitimate concern. Together with the Convention on the Prevention and Punishment of Genocide adopted at the same time, this instrument gave expression to a new global emphasis on the protection of individual liberty and the meeting of basic economic and social needs. The theme of the Declaration was universal. It involved a common conception of human rights capable of commanding wide acceptance throughout the world despite significant differences between countries in culture, in religion and in political systems[2].

1   UN Charter, Preamble; and Art 1(3). Arts 55 and 56 further commit states to take joint and separate action with a view to promoting economic and social development and universal observance of human rights 'without distinction as to race, sex, language or religion'.

2   See Johnson and Symonides *The Universal Declaration of Human Rights: A History of its Creation and Implementation 1948–1998* (1998), p 39; and Glendon *A World Made New* (2001), p 176.

2.03 The Universal Declaration of Human Rights tended, however, to blur an important distinction. Civil and political rights are grounded in Western liberal democratic tradition, and stress protection for personal integrity (through respect for the right to life, protection against torture or inhuman treatment, and guarantees against arbitrary deprivation of liberty), procedural propriety in the determination of civil rights and criminal liability, protection for democratic processes (including participation in political activities, association with others, and freedom of expression), and the promotion of religious tolerance and plurality of belief. These rights are usually deemed 'first generation' rights, in the sense that they constitute what may be deemed the 'classic' freedoms as developed and expressed in constitutional documents from the late eighteenth century onwards. The first constitutional catalogues of civil and political rights had appeared in the American states (in 1776 and in 1780, Virginia and Massachusetts respectively incorporated Bills of Rights), and had been followed by the French Declaration of the Rights of Man and the Citizen of 1789, and Amendments I–X of the Constitution of the United States of America of 1791.

On the other hand, claims for economic and social rights – 'second generation' rights, since historically they appeared later than claims to civil and political rights – formed the basis of socialist conceptions of human rights. These rights are concerned with the satisfaction of human needs, such as the rights to housing, to minimum standards of income or social welfare provision, to work, to education, and to health care. From a European perspective, claims to economic and social rights emerged from the Industrial Revolution. In 1792, for example, Thomas Paine in *The Rights of Man* proposed social welfare insurance and provision of employment for the poor. By 1848, working-class movements (such as the Chartists in Britain) were advocating not only universal (male) suffrage but also the rights to fair remuneration and fair working conditions. These calls were replicated in other countries undergoing industrialisation and urbanisation. Ferdinand Lassalle, the founder of the German Labourers' Association, argued that civil and political rights were empty concepts from the perspective of the labourer, who would only achieve political freedom through education; economic security, in turn, would come through the nationalisation of industry, which would allow the state to effect social equality and shared prosperity. In time, states came to accept that they had responsibilities in respect of the satisfaction of the economic, social and cultural well-being of their citizens. Ultimately, writers such as Karl Marx adopted a more radical stance towards entitlements to economic and social rights.

2.04 These conceptually differing approaches towards human rights resulted in the adoption of two separate international human rights instruments in 1966. Both instruments entered into force ten years later. The International Covenant on Civil and Political Rights focuses upon the protection of the individual against state encroachment on physical integrity and political liberties[1], while the International Covenant on Economic, Social and Cultural Rights emphasises state responsibility to meet human needs such as housing, public health, education and employment. International legal and political initiatives could not however bridge the widening gulf between liberal democracy and communism after 1945. The dichotomy between these competing concepts of human rights became more marked as each side sought to advance its own distinct philosophy, leading to a weakening of the notion of the universal applicability of human rights and its gradual replacement by the view that human rights were to some extent culturally specific. This view was strengthened by arguments advanced by Third World countries from the 1970s onwards that human rights could also be considered as group or community rights. These states sought to advance claims to self-determination, development and peace as part of their struggles for political, social and economic advancement, thus producing a 'third generation' of rights[2]. The lack of intellectual clarity and philosophical agreement at an international level[3] was to some extent masked by the welter of international treaties under the auspices of the United Nations which appeared in the years before the fall of communism in Europe[4], but the continuation of these ideological fault-lines and lack of effective enforcement machinery prevented the establishment of a genuinely universal human rights legal order.

1   There are two additional Optional Protocols: the first (which also entered into force in 1976) provides for a system of individual complaint, and the second (which entered into force in 1991) for abolition of the death penalty. See further Nowak *UN Covenant on Civil and Political Rights: CCPR Commentary* (2nd edn, 2005).

2   For discussion of group rights, see Alston, ed *Peoples' Rights* (2001). For discussion of protection in Europe of the rights of members of minority groups (a notion distinct from group rights), see paras **2.88–2.91** below.

3   See further Nowak *Introduction to the International Human Rights Regime* (2003), pp 215–234; and Costa 'Les Droits de l'Homme en Europe: Sources Culturelles et Idéalogiques' (2005) 17 REDP 851.

4   Including conventions on the prevention and punishment of genocide (1948); the treatment of prisoners of war (1949); status of refugees (1951); political rights for women (1952); slavery (1956); forced labour (1957); consent to marriage (1962); racial discrimination (1965); apartheid (1973); discrimination against women (1979); torture (1984); children's rights (1989); and persons with disabilities (2008). As well as treaty-based norms, rights may also be established by customary international law (and although it can be difficult to determine what forms of state action are prohibited by such custom, it is normally accepted that slavery, torture, genocide and racial discrimination so qualify). For materials and background, see Steiner and Alston *International Human Rights in Context* (3rd edn, 2007). Arguably, the crucial issue in international human rights is not the existence of standards but defective implementation: for example, acceptance that the UN's Human Rights Commission had become too politicised a body led to its replacement in 2006 by a Human Rights Council. In general, the promotion of international human rights is advanced by a range of techniques including standard-setting,

state reporting and technical assistance, while their protection involves investigation, fact-finding, individual and group complaint mechanisms, and individual criminal responsibility. Some of these techniques are judicial (such as the International Court of Justice, and those international criminal courts established after armed conflict).

2.05 Against this background, the Helsinki Final Act of 1975 may be seen as a milestone in the development of a common approach to human rights between east and west. The Act arose out of the Conference on Security and Co-operation in Europe, and was accepted by all European states on both sides of the Iron Curtain (with the exception of Albania), together with Canada and the USA. It established what is now known as the Organization for Security and Co-operation in Europe (the OSCE)[1]. Subsequently, the fall of communism and the beginnings of the establishment of democracy in east European states by the close of the twentieth century permitted the importance of economic and social rights to be reassessed in a climate of greater material prosperity, free of such acute political confrontation. There is now a greater recognition of the importance of the aims behind such rights. In particular, the Vienna Declaration and Programme of Action of 1993 affirmed that 'all human rights are universal, indivisible and interdependent and interrelated', with the consequence that 'the international community must treat human rights globally in a fair and equal manner, on the same footing, and with the same emphasis'[2]. Economic and social rights, though, cannot as readily be protected through judicial means as is the case with civil and political rights[3]. Nevertheless, the increasing stress being placed upon economic and social rights not only in domestic constitutions but also now in the Charter of Fundamental Rights of the European Union (enjoying a status of primary source of EU law by virtue of the Lisbon Treaty) has led to an enhanced awareness of the relevance of social rights. At the same time the importance of group or minority rights (or 'solidarity rights') – so-called 'third generation' approaches to human rights – has become more marked on account of societal responses to immigration and a greater awareness of the inherent limitations in the use of the right of individual complaint in tackling discriminatory attitudes and practices[4].

---

1   The OSCE was originally known as the Conference on Security and Co-operation in Europe (CSCE) until the 1994 Budapest Conference. It became a permanent institution by virtue of the Charter of Paris, 1990. Its membership includes the 47 member states of the Council of Europe together with Belarus, Canada, the Holy See, Kazakhstan, Kyrgyzstan, Tajikistan, Turkmenistan, the USA, and Uzbekistan. The OSCE was originally concerned with three separate issues – *détente* and disarmament, economic co-operation, and human rights. Its current focus is upon consolidation of democracy, the rule of law, and conflict prevention. A strong human rights focus is found in its 'human dimension' activities which take the form of practical assistance to states in drafting legislation compatible with international norms and in the provision of training. The OSCE's aims are essentially achieved by a political process and intergovermental conferences rather than by creating legally binding norms and principles or establishing any more formal machinery. Certain of its approaches, however, are at odds with Council of Europe standards (above all, in relation to the death penalty where OSCE efforts are primarily directed at securing 'transparency' in its use rather than its outright abolition); but see the Third Summit of Heads of State and Government of the Council Of Europe: Action Plan (2005), heading IV and Appendix 2 (Declaration on co-operation between the two organisations). For an overview of the human rights aspects of the OSCE system, see Binder

The Human Dimension of the OSCE: From Recommendation to Implementation (2001). See further http://www.osce.org.

2   Vienna Declaration and Programme of Action (1993), para 5.

3   Note, though, that the link between economic, social and cultural rights and (certain) civil and political rights guaranteed by the ECHR permits the European Court of Human Rights to interpret the ECHR in light of the Charter: see further para **3.44** below. At a Council of Europe level, the monitoring of economic, social and cultural rights contained in the European Social Charter is undertaken by the European Committee of Social Rights: see para **2.93** below.

4   See further paras **2.88–2.91** below for discussion of Council of Europe initiatives.

2.06 As advances in international human rights were taking place, new regional arrangements were also being established[1]. New developments in human rights law also continued. The *Pinochet* judgment in the United Kingdom[2] was one key landmark; and the steps taken to establish an International Criminal Court another[3]. The legacy of a century marked by armed conflict and systematic violation of human rights was a fresh determination to enforce respect for human dignity at national, regional and international levels.

1   For discussion of other regional systems of human rights protection, see eg Burgorgue-Larsen and de Torres *The Inter-American Court of Human Rights: Case-law and Commentary* (2011); Okafor *The African Human Rights System, Activist Forces and International Institutions* (2007). The principal regional systems outside Europe are the Inter-American (in terms of the American Convention on Human Rights) and the African (under the African Charter on Human and Peoples' Rights). Additionally, there is an Arab Charter on Human Rights (in force since 2008), and in South East Asia (ASEAN), an Intergovernmental Commission on Human Rights was established in 2009.

2   See *R v Bow Street Metropolitan Stipendiary Magistrate ex p Pinochet Ugarte (No 3)* [2000] 1 AC 147.

3   For discussion of these developments in international law, see Cassese *International Criminal Law* (2003); and Henckaerts and Doswald-Beck *Customary International Humanitarian Law* (2005).

2.07 Even if considerable advances have been made since 1945 in the protection of both civil and political rights and also economic, social and cultural rights, by the start of the twenty-first century it was clear that there was no room for complacency. New threats both to communities and also to the firm establishment of human rights in legal and political discourse have emerged, in particular from terrorism and from organised crime and its involvement in human trafficking and the drugs trade. The source of interferences with human rights guarantees is increasingly from non-state parties, not state officials, and thus requiring the development of positive obligations upon states to ensure the effective protection of human rights in the private sphere. At the same time, advances in technology have brought with them new challenges in ensuring continuing respect for private life, particularly when it is presumed that such technologies can help provide that very protection for individuals[1].

1   For case law on surveillance and DNA-retention, see paras **6.88–6.102** and **6.105–6.106** below. For a perspective on recent developments in British law, see Ewing *Bonfire of the Liberties: New Labour, Human Rights, and the Rule of Law* (2010).

The work of the Council of Europe

2.08 The Council of Europe is an intergovernmental organisation founded upon the principles of pluralist democracy, respect for human rights, and the rule of law. Established in 1949 in the aftermath of the 1939–45 war and in a period when the Cold War was rapidly escalating, it was one of several European initiatives which sought to bring western liberal democracies closer together on the basis of shared values and to resist the further spread of totalitarianism. As a result of the increase in its membership after the fall of communist regimes, the Council of Europe now has 47 member states[1].

Its founding charter refers to the furtherance of European co-operation not only in the political sphere but also in respect of economic and social progress[2]. The activities of the Council of Europe include the promotion of Europe's cultural identity and diversity, the consolidation of democratic stability through legislative and constitutional reform, and the finding of common solutions to contemporary challenges facing the continent in such matters as terrorism, organised crime and trafficking in human beings[3]. Its work thus covers a broad range of activities, leading to a number of European initiatives[4] in the areas of legal co-operation[5], media[6], local democracy[7], environmental and regional planning[8], economic, social and health issues[9], and education, culture and heritage[10]. Many of these topics also have a human rights dimension[11]. There are three key approaches to its work: first, standard-setting (in particular, by means of securing agreement to international treaties, but also through the making of recommendations and resolutions and the gradual emergence of standards in the course of the work of monitoring bodies); secondly, monitoring of implementation of state obligations (in particular, through the work of bodies established by treaty); and thirdly, co-operation with member states and non-governmental organisations (for example, in promoting institutional capacity-building and legislative reform through training and compatibility studies)[12].

---

1   The original ten members of the Council of Europe were Belgium, Denmark, France, Ireland, Italy, Luxembourg, Netherlands, Norway, Sweden and the United Kingdom. Greece and Turkey also joined in 1949, followed by Iceland and Germany (1950), Austria (1956), Cyprus (1961), Switzerland (1963), Malta (1965), Portugal (1976), Spain (1977), Liechtenstein (1978), San Marino (1988) and Finland (1989). The organisation rapidly expanded after 1989 with the membership of Hungary (1990), Poland (1991), Bulgaria (1992), Estonia, Lithuania, Slovenia, the Czech Republic, Slovakia and Romania (1993), Latvia, Albania, Moldova, Ukraine and the Former Yugoslav Republic of Macedonia (1995), Russia and Croatia (1996), Georgia (1999), Armenia and Azerbaijan (2001), Bosnia and Herzegovina (2002), Serbia (2003), and Monaco (2004). Canada, the Holy See, Japan the USA and Mexico also enjoy observer status. Montenegro was formerly a constituent part of Serbia and Montenegro until its declaration of independence in 2006, and became the 47th member of the Council of Europe in 2007. Authority to admit European states as members of the Council of Europe rests with the Committee of Ministers (Statute of the Council of Europe, Arts 4–6), and it may also suspend or terminate membership (Statute, Art 8). The process of admission must be initiated by a proposal put forward by at least one representative (Rules of Procedure of the Committee of Ministers, Rule 25(a)). The Committee of Ministers then consults the Parliamentary Assembly, which will adopt an opinion (Statutory Resolution (51) 30). If the Committee decides that a

state is to be admitted, it adopts a resolution inviting that state to become a member. The invitation, sent through the Secretary General (Rules of Procedure, Art 25(b)), specifies the number of seats that the state will have in the Assembly as well as how much it will contribute to the budget (Statute, Art 6). Recent invitations have included a number of conditions concerning the implementation of human rights and respect for the rule of law. Once invited, a state becomes a member by depositing an 'instrument of accession' with the Secretary General. Membership requires a commitment to human rights, parliamentary democracy and the rule of law. Monaco's application for membership was delayed pending clarification of its constitutional relationship with France. Belarus has been an applicant state since 1993, but its observer status was suspended in 1997 amid concerns that its constitution was unlawful and did not respect minimum democratic and constitutional standards; a request for restoration of its status was refused in 2004, and application of the death penalty in Belarus in 2010 and 2011 has further delayed membership. In 1969, Greece's military dictatorship denounced the ECHR and withdrew from the Council of Europe shortly before a decision was to have been taken to exclude it, but Greece was readmitted in 1974 following the reestablishment of democracy. Following a military coup d'état in 1981, the Parliamentary Assembly withdrew the Turkish parliamentary delegation's right to their seats, the delegation only resuming its place in 1984 after the holding of free elections.

2   Statute of the Council of Europe, Art 1. For the background and early development of the Council of Europe, see Robertson *The Council of Europe* (1961), pp 1–24, 160–184; and Huber *A Decade Which Made History – The Council of Europe 1989–1999* (1999).

3   The current political mandate was defined by the third Summit of Heads of State and Government in 2005.

4   Statute of the Council of Europe, Art 15(a) requires the Committee of Ministers to 'consider the action required to further the aim of the Council of Europe, including the conclusion of conventions and agreements'. Adoption of treaties requires both a two-thirds majority of representatives in the Committee of Ministers casting a vote and a majority of those entitle to vote (Statute, Art 20). Conventions are only binding on those member states that choose to ratify them. There are now some 210 European conventions which are published in the European Treaty Series (ETS Nos 001–193), and from 2004, continued in Council of Europe Treaty Series (CETS No 194 onwards). These are available at http://conventions.coe.int/. The European Court of Human Rights may refer to relevant treaties in its judgments: see paras **2.32**, **2.92** and **3.44** below.

5   Through, in particular, harmonisation of domestic legislation in line with the principles of human rights, democracy and the rule of law by improving the delivery of justice. Of particular note is the European Commission for Democracy through Law (the 'Venice Commission') established in 1990. This body considers constitutional and administrative measures of assistance in the consolidation of democratic stability. The Commission publishes a Bulletin on Constitutional Case-Law summarising constitutional developments and judgments in European states, which is available at http://www.venice.coe.int/site/interface/english.htm. In addition, several treaties regulate medical law issues, including the European Convention on Human Rights and Biomedicine (ETS 164 (1997)) and co-operation in penal matters (cf Co-operation in Penal Matters – Conventions (vol 1) (1997)). See also the European Convention on the Suppression of Terrorism (ETS 90 (1980) and amending Protocol (ETS 190 (2001)), and the Convention on the Prevention of Terrorism (CETS 196 (2005)).

6   In particular, by seeking to strengthen freedom of expression and the free flow of information: see eg the European Convention on Transfrontier Television (ETS 132 (1989)) and the amending Protocol (ETS 171 (1998)), and the European Convention Relating to Questions on Copyright Law and Neighbouring Rights in the Framework of Transfrontier Broadcasting by Satellite (ETS 153 (1994)). See further http://www.humanrights.coe.int/media.

7   That is, with a view to promoting local democracy and regional diversity: see in particular the European Charter of Local Self-Government (ETS 122 (1985)) and the European Outline

Convention on Transfrontier Co-operation between Territorial Communities or Authorities (ETS 106 (1983)) and its additional Protocols (ETS 159 (1995)) and (ETS 169 (1998)). See further http://www.local.coe.int.

8   Through promoting international co-operation with a view to protecting the natural environment and promoting the development of spatial planning: see in particular the Convention on Conservation of European Wildlife and Natural Habitats (ETS 104 (1982)) and the Convention on Civil Liability for Damage Resulting from Activities Dangerous to the Natural Environment (ETS 150 (1993)).

9   By aiming to promote social rights and equality of treatment through, for example, guaranteeing adequate social welfare protection, the promotion of employment and training, combating discrimination, and the harmonisation of health policies: see in particular the European Social Charter discussed further at para **2.92** below.

10   The Convention on the Recognition of Qualifications concerning Higher Education in the European Region (ETS 165 (1997)) seeks to facilitate movement in higher education. The European Cultural Convention (ETS 18 (1954)) provides a framework for international co-operation in the fields of culture, heritage, education and youth. See also the European Convention on the Protection of Archaeological Heritage (ETS 143 (1992)).

11   For example, treaties relating to the media, and treaties such as the European Convention for the Protection of Individuals with regard to Automatic Processing of Personal Data (ETS 108 (1981)) and Additional Protocol (ETS 181 (2001)), the European Convention on Recognition and Enforcement of Decisions concerning Custody of Children and on Restoration of Custody of Children (ETS 105 (1980)), the European Convention on Contact concerning Children (ETS 192 (2003)), and the European Convention on Action against Trafficking in Human Beings (CETS 197 (2005)).

12   See further www.coe.int/capacitybuilding.

The Committee of Ministers

2.09 The Council of Europe is headed by a Secretary General[1] who supervises the work of the organisation's civil service[2]. Its executive decision-making body is the Committee of Ministers[3]. The Committee comprises the foreign ministers of member states, or their permanent diplomatic representatives[4], and plays a key role in the protection and promotion of human rights. In particular, the Committee of Ministers is charged with supervising the action taken by a state consequent upon a finding by the Court that a state has breached its legal responsibilities[5]. It also has a wider remit to help express agreed approaches to problems confronting Europe and, to this end, the Committee of Ministers may make recommendations to member states on matters where the Committee has agreed 'a common policy'[6]. In addition, regular summits of heads of state seek to give strategic direction and fresh impetus to the work of the organisation[7].

1   The Secretary General may require states to furnish reports on domestic compliance with the ECHR in terms of ECHR, Art 52 (see para **2.34** below); additionally, by virtue of Art 15(3), states must notify the Secretary General of any derogation lodged (see paras **4.147–4.148** below, and in terms of Art 56 of any application of the treaty to dependent territories (see para **3.04** below). The deposit of instruments of ratification, and notification of denunciation of the ECHR, must also be made to the Secretary General: Arts 58 and 59.

2   Day-to-day activities of the Council of Europe are carried out by an international civil service or secretariat comprising some 2,000 officials and employees under the authority of the Secretary General.

3   Its responsibilities include determination of membership: see para **2.08**, fn 1 above. The Committee of Ministers may discuss any matter of mutual interest with the exception of national defence (Statute of the Council of Europe, Art 1(d)). Meetings at Ministerial level tend to be dominated by political dialogue. As the Council of Europe's decision making body, it is the Committee of Ministers that decides on the activities of the Council of Europe (Statute, Art 16) and considers the action required to further the aim of the Council of Europe, including the conclusion of conventions or agreements (Statute, Art 15). Since 1966 the Council of Europe has organised, planned and budgeted its activities according to an annual work programme (published as the 'Intergovernmental Programme of Activities'). The Committee of Ministers adopts the programme towards the end of each year and is entrusted with overseeing its implementation. The Committee of Ministers also adopts the budget for the Council of Europe following the submission of a draft budget by the Secretary General (Statute, Art 38(c)).

4   The Committee of Ministers meets at ministerial level once a year to provide the necessary political impetus to the Council's activities. Generally these meetings are held in private in Strasbourg (Statute, Art 21). When a Foreign Minister is unable to attend a meeting, an alternate member of the same Government (Statute, Art 14) may be nominated to act on his behalf. Each representative on the Committee of Ministers appoints a Deputy to act on his behalf when the Committee is not in session (Rules of Procedure of the Committee of Ministers, Art 14). The Deputies meet once a week on behalf of the Ministers, and it is they who conduct most of the day-to-day business of the Committee of Ministers. All of these permanent representatives are based in Strasbourg, and are usually senior diplomats with Ambassadorial rank. Decisions taken by the Deputies have the same force and effect as decisions taken by the Committee of Ministers meeting at the level of the Ministers for Foreign Affairs (Rules of Procedure for Meetings of the Ministers' Deputies, Rule 2(2)).

5   See paras **2.79 and 2.82–2.83** below.

6   Statute of the Council of Europe, Art 15(b). The adoption of a recommendation requires a unanimous vote of all representatives present and a majority of those entitled to vote (Statute, Art 20(a)) but by virtue of a non-binding agreement reached in 1994 the Ministers' Deputies decided not to apply this rule in practice. While recommendations are not binding on member states, the Committee of Ministers may ask member governments 'to inform it of the action taken by them' (Statute, Art 15(b)). Recommendations adopted before 1979 were issued in the 'Resolution' series of texts adopted. Recommendations are available at http://www.coe.int/T/CM/documentIndex_en.asp. Treaties, declarations and conclusions, resolutions, recommendations and decisions of the Committee of Ministers, and opinions, recommendations, resolutions and orders of the Parliamentary Assembly are published in the *Official Gazette* of the Council of Europe (and see http://www.coe.int/t/cm).

7   Summits of heads of state and governments have been held in Vienna (1993), Strasbourg (1997) and Warsaw (2005). The 1997 Summit led to the establishment of the office of the Council of Europe Commissioner for Human Rights (see para **2.94** below), while the 2005 Summit's 'action plan' identified the need to take future action to improve the effectiveness of the Convention at domestic level, to support other European human rights mechanisms, and to help combat terrorism and other serious crime.

The Parliamentary Assembly

2.10 The Parliamentary Assembly of the Council of Europe ('PACE') is the deliberative organ of the Council of Europe. Under the Statute of the Council of Europe, it is tasked with debating matters within its competence[1] and presenting its conclusions to the Committee of Ministers[2]. It is comprised of representatives from each member state, the number being determined by the size of each country[3]. The Assembly also has a part to play in the appointment of judges and others with a responsibility for the protection of human rights[4]. The Assembly can adopt its own recommendations (in the form of proposals addressed to the Committee of Ministers for implementation of action within the competence of member states) and resolutions (which embody decisions by the Assembly on issues which it is empowered to put into effect or to give a considered view upon)[5]. The Committee of Ministers works closely with the Parliamentary Assembly. At each session of the Parliamentary Assembly, the Committee of Ministers provides an account of its activities[6], and this report is then debated[7]. A Joint Committee[8] (consisting of the Bureau of the Parliamentary Assembly, a representative of each member government and one representative of each parliamentary delegation of member states not represented on the Bureau) seeks to coordinate the activities of – and maintain good relations between – the Committee of Ministers and the Assembly[9]. The Assembly's Rules of Procedure also provide that members of the Committee of Ministers have a right of access to the Assembly and its committees, and may be called to speak if they so request[10].

1   Defined as including questions of common concern in economic, social, cultural, scientific, legal and administrative matters and the maintenance and further realisation of human rights and fundamental freedoms (Statute of the Council of Europe, Art 1). Under Art 1(d), matters relating to national defence are specifically excluded from the scope of the Council of Europe.

2   Statute of the Council of Europe, Art 22. The Assembly can adopt three types of texts: recommendations to the Committee of Ministers, resolutions expressing the Assembly's view on a subject (under Statute, Art 29, resolutions require a two-thirds majority of those representatives casting a vote), and opinions on questions posed by the Committee of Ministers. Work is prepared by the committee within whose remit the issue falls. In general, it is a motion for a recommendation or resolution that generates a report. This motion has to be tabled by ten or more members of the Assembly belonging to at least five national delegations. It is then referred to a committee for report and may also be referred to other committees for their opinion. The main committee then appoints a Rapporteur who drafts, with the help of the Assembly secretariat, a report which is divided into two parts: the operational draft resolution, recommendation or opinion, and the explanatory memorandum. Both parts are discussed in committee, but only the operational part is voted on. Although the explanatory memorandum is drafted in the name of the Rapporteur, he has to take into account dissenting opinions voiced in the committee. When a report has been adopted in the committee it is tabled for discussion by the Assembly either at a part-session or at a meeting of the Standing Committee.

3   Statute of the Council of Europe, Art 29. The Assembly is composed of 318 members, all of whom serve as national parliamentarians in their own member state (Statute, Art 25(a)) with the number from each member state varying from 2 to 18 as specified (Statute, Art 26). Each representative may have a substitute who can, in the absence of the representative, sit, speak and vote in his place (Statute, Art 25(c)). Members are elected or appointed by their national parliaments, and it is open to the national parliament to decide the manner in which these appointments are made. Insofar as the number of their members allows, national delegations should be composed so as to ensure a fair representation of the political parties or groups in their parliaments, and should include the under-represented sex at least in the same percentage as is present in their parliaments and in any case one representative of each sex. Each national parliament is required to inform the Assembly of the methods used to appoint seats on the delegation and of the number of its women members (Rules of Procedure of the Assembly, Rule 6(2)). The UK has 18 representatives. In order to develop a non-national but European

outlook, the Assembly has five political groups: the Group of the Unified European Left; the European Democratic Group; the Liberal, Democratic and Reformers' Group; the Group of the European People's Party; and the Socialists Group. Parliamentarians are free to choose whether or not to belong to any one group. Political groups must commit themselves to respect the promotion of the values of the Council of Europe (ie, political pluralism, human rights and the rule of law) (Rules of Procedure of the Assembly, Rule 18(1)). It is open to Parliamentarians to form new political groups through submissions to the Bureau of the Parliamentary Assembly, but they are required to have 20 members from at least six national delegations to do so (Rules, Rule 18(2)). The work of the Parliamentary Assembly is primarily done by ten separate thematic committees (Rules, Rule 42): Political Affairs; Legal Affairs and Human Rights; Economic Affairs and Development; Social, Health and Family Affairs; Migration, Refugees and Population; Culture, Science and Education; Environment, Agriculture and Local and Regional Affairs; Equal Opportunities for Women and Men; Honouring of Obligations and Commitments by member states of the Council of Europe ('Monitoring Committee'); and Rules of Procedure, Immunities and Institutional Affairs. All of these are composed of 84 members, with the exception of the latter Committee which has 27 seats. All Committees except the Monitoring Committee have an equal number of alternate members of the same nationality as the primary member of the Committee, and they can replace absent members. Committees are formed following nominations by national delegations, and these are ratified by the Parliamentary Assembly. Committees are re-formed in January of each year and may examine any matter within their terms of reference (Rules, Rule 43(1)). The Assembly meets four times a year in Strasbourg for a week long plenary session. A President is elected by secret ballot (Rules, Rule 14).

4   The Parliamentary Assembly elects judges to the European Court of Human Rights from a list of three candidates nominated by the relevant member state (ECHR, Art 22), and the Bureau of the Parliamentary Assembly is responsible for preparing a list of names from which the Committee of Ministers elects new members to the Committee for the Prevention of Torture (Convention for the Prevention of Torture and Inhuman and Degrading Treatment or Punishment, Art 5(1)). The Parliamentary Assembly is also responsible for appointing the Secretary General and Deputy Secretary General following a recommendation of the Committee of Ministers (Statute, Art 36(b). In addition, the Assembly elects the Commissioner for Human Rights (Resolution 99(50) of the Committee of Ministers, Art 9(1)).

5   The Committee of Ministers may also request the Parliamentary Assembly for an opinion or further consideration on a specific issue, and this may result in either an opinion or a new recommendation to the Committee of Ministers (Rules of Procedure of the Parliamentary Assembly, Rule 56.) Members of the Parliamentary Assembly may also address written questions to the Committee of Ministers on any matter within the competence of the Committee of Ministers, but it is for the President of the Assembly to decide whether these questions are to be sent to the Committee of Ministers (Rules of Procedure of the Parliamentary Assembly, Rule 57). Opinions, recommendations, resolutions and orders of the Parliamentary Assembly are published in the *Official Gazette* of the Council of Europe and see http:// www.assembly.coe.int. For discussion of the work of the Parliamentary Assembly in respect of human rights, see para **2.85** below.

6   Statute of the Council of Europe, Art 19,

7   Rules of Procedure of the Parliamentary Assembly, Rule 55.

8   Rules of Procedure of the Parliamentary Assembly, Rule 54.

9   The Bureau (which includes the President, 20 Vice-Presidents, the Chairpersons of the political groups or their representatives, and the Chairpersons of the general PACE Committees or their substitutes) co-ordinates the activities of the Assembly and of its committees and prepare the Assembly's agenda, arrange day-to-day business, and guide and develop relations with other bodies. The President of the Assembly is the President of the Joint Committee. For the discussion of a particular item, the Bureau of the Assembly and the Committee of Ministers

may decide by agreement to set up a mixed working party: Rules of Procedure of the Parliamentary Assembly, Rule 54.

10   Rules of Procedure of the Parliamentary Assembly, Rule 53.

The Council of Europe and the European Union

2.11 The Council of Europe has been able to achieve innovative systems of effective protection of human rights at a regional level. Its success in promoting respect for civil and political rights, first through the establishment and progressive development of an enforcement machinery under the ECHR[1] and then through the entry into force of the European Convention for the Prevention of Torture or Inhuman and Degrading Treatment or Punishment, is without parallel. The Council of Europe has also been mindful of the need to promote social cohesion through the promotion of social standards under the European Social Charter, and to encourage equality of treatment of members of national minorities through its Framework Convention for the Protection of National Minorities and the work of the European Commission against Racism and Intolerance[2]. Its success is in part attributable to a number of disparate factors which emerged in Europe over a 60-year period: the constitutional willingness of emerging democracies (after both 1945 and 1989) to incorporate international human rights treaties into domestic law as a safeguard against any repetition of the excesses of the past; a political desire to follow basic tenets of liberal democracy as outward symbols of shared values (after 1945, in opposition to the continuing totalitarianism in East Europe, and for states which joined after 1989, as members of a new and democratic Europe); recognition that assumption of the responsibilities required by membership of the Council of Europe was a prerequisite of membership of the European Union[3]; and – perhaps most significantly – growing trust in the European enforcement machinery itself which encouraged the assumption of unilateral obligations by states.

1   For discussion of the ECHR's impact upon international legal developments elsewhere, see Buergenthal 'The European and Inter-American Human Rights Courts: Beneficial Interaction' in Mahoney, Matscher, Petzold and Wildhaber (eds) *Protecting Human Rights: The European Perspective* (2000), pp 123–133; Cassese 'The Impact of the European Convention on Human Rights on the International Criminal Tribunal for the Former Yugoslavia' in Mahoney, Matscher, Petzold and Wildhaber (eds) *Protecting Human Rights: The European Perspective* (2000), pp 213–236; and Lester 'The Export of the Convention to the Commonwealth', in Mahoney, Matscher, Petzold and Wildhaber *Protecting Human Rights: The European Perspective* (2000), pp 753–762.

2   See further paras **2.88–2.93** below. In this work, the importance of international non-governmental organisations (INGOs) and national non-governmental organisations (NGOs) is crucial: for example, a Conference of International Non-governmental Organisations with participatory status with the Council of Europe meets annually. See further Committee of Ministers Resolutions (2003) 8 and (2003) 9; and http://www.coe.int/ngo.

3   Cf TEU, Art 49 which confirms that accession is dependent upon respect for democracy, human rights and the rule of law. For discussion of the impact of the European Court of

Human Rights on the development of the rule of law in new member states of the Council of Europe, see Pellonpää 'Der europäische Gerichtshof für Menschenrechte und der Aufbau des Rechtsstaats in den neuen Demokratien' in Donatsch, Forster and Schwarzenegger (eds) *Strafrecht, Strafprozessrecht und Menschenrechte: Festschrift für S Trechsel zum 65. Geburtstag* (2002), 79–92.

Protection of human rights in the European Union

2.12 The Council of Europe and the European Union were conceived in the same political climate, share common aspirations, and have institutional structures which at first sight have common features: decision-making bodies comprising ministers of member states, consultative and deliberative parliamentary assemblies, and judicial organs exercising European jurisdiction. But the Council of Europe and the EU diverge in membership, organisation and emphasis. The EU – the 'Europe of the 27' – currently affects the lives of 500 million Europeans, while the Council of Europe's 47 member states contain a population of some 820 million. The Council of Europe is an organisation of nation states whose structures reflect the retention of national sovereignty: its Committee of Ministers can only make recommendations or approve conventions for further determination by member states, and the Parliamentary Assembly is deliberative only and has no legislative authority[1]. Above all, the EU's principal focus is upon economic and political integration, while the Council of Europe's most significant success lies in the promotion of human rights.

1   See para **2.10** above.

2.13 Greater convergence between both institutions has been evident for some time. The Council of Europe's aims of closer legal and political co-operation and the strengthening of pluralist democracy were given greater urgency after 1989 with the increase in membership of central and eastern European states. More significantly, the EU has embraced enhanced expectations in the protection of human rights[1]. Although the Treaty of Rome did not refer to fundamental rights, the European Court of Justice has upheld the need for respect for such rights since the European Union's early days[2]. This was essential if member states were to give full effect to EU law, as national constitutional courts made clear[3]. Since then, both the Court's jurisprudence[4] and the treaties concluded by the member states[5] have given increasing prominence to the protection of fundamental rights as guaranteed by the ECHR and as they result from the constitutional traditions common to the member states. In consequence, national constitutional courts have accepted that, as long as EU law guarantees an effective protection of fundamental rights, actions challenging the legal acts of the EU will be dismissed unless the applicant shows that the development of EU law falls below a proper level of protection of fundamental rights[6]. It is to be noted that the duty in EU law to respect fundamental human rights applies not only to the EU institutions but also to national authorities when interpreting and implementing EU law[7].

1   See further, Rosas 'Fundamental Rights in the Luxembourg and Strasbourg Courts' in
      Baudenbacher, Tresselt, Thorgen-Örlyggson (eds) *The EFTA Court: Ten Years On* (2005), pp
      163–175; Douglas-Scott 'A Tale of Two Courts: Luxembourg, Strasbourg and the Growing
      Human Rights Acquis' (2006) 43 CMLRev 629; Pellonpää 'The European Court of Human
      Rights and the European Union' in Caflisch, Callewaert, Liddell, Mahoney and Villiger (eds)
      Liber Amicorum Luzius Wildhaber: Human Rights – Strasbourg Views (2007), pp 347–370;
      and Greer and Williams 'Human Rights in the Council of Europe and the EU' (2009) 15 ELJ
      462. For discussion of recent developments in assimilating procedural rights of suspects in
      criminal cases, see para **5.11** below. For a more sceptical approach, see Callewaert 'The
      European Convention on Human Rights and European Union Law: a Long Way to Harmony'
      [2009] EHRLR 768. See generally http://eeas.europa.eu/human_rights/index_en.htm.

2   See eg Case 29/69 *Stauder v Ulm* [1969] ECR 425; Case 11/70 *Internationale Handelsgesellschaft
      mbH v Einfuhr und Vorratstelle für Getreide und Futtermittel* [1970] ECR 1125. Member
      states were only bound to respect human rights when acting within the context of EU law:
      Case 5/88 *Wachauf v Germany* [1989] ECR 2609. For EU documents on human rights (including
      annual reports), see http://europa.eu/pol/rights/index_en.htm.

3   See eg the *Solange I* judgment of the German Constitutional Court, (1974), BVerfGE 37, 271
      and the *Frontini* judgment judgment of the Italian Constitutional Court: *Frontini v Ministero
      delle Finanze* [1974] 2 CMLR 372.

4   See eg Case C–105/03, *Maria Pupino* [2005] ECR I-6427, para 59 (Framework Decision of 15
      March 2001 on victim standing in criminal proceedings to be interpreted in accordance with
      ECHR, Art 6); and Case C-283/05 *ASML Netherlands BV v Semiconductor Industry Services
      GmbH* [2006] ECR I-12041.

5   See eg the development of Article 6 TEU from the Maastricht Treaty (Article F) via the
      Treaty of Amsterdam to its current version as amended by the Treaty of Lisbon.

6   See eg the *Solange II* and *Bananenmarktordnung* judgments of the German Constitutional
      Court (1986 and 2000, respectively), and the *Fragd* judgment of the Italian Constitutional
      Court: *SpA Fragd v Amministrazione delle Finanze dello Stato* (case 33/84) (1989) [Italy].

7   See eg Case 222/84 *Johnston v Chief Constable of the RUC* [1987] ECR 1651; Case C–109/01
      Home Secretary v Akrich [2003] ECR I-9607.

2.14 In recent years, the Court of Justice has developed a practice of citing the
case law of the European Court of Human Rights: a notable development, as the
Court rarely refers to the decisions of any other court. The Strasbourg Court in
turn has acknowledged the extent of review by the Court of Justice for compliance
with the ECHR, and has treated that review as limiting the need for it to carry out
an independent scrutiny. In its *Bosphorus* judgment, concerned with a complaint
brought against a member state whose implementation of an EC Regulation was
alleged to have violated rights guaranteed under the ECHR, the Court stated that
state action taken in compliance with the obligations flowing from membership of
an international organisation is justified as long as the relevant organisation protects
fundamental rights, as regards both the substantive guarantees offered and the
mechanisms controlling their observance, in a manner which can be considered
at least equivalent to that for which the ECHR provides. The Court found that the
system of protection of fundamental rights in EU law could be considered equivalent
to that of the ECHR system[1].

1   *Bosphorus Hava Yollari Turizm ve Ticaret Anonim ^irketi v Ireland* [GC] 2005-VI, discussed
      at paras **2.29** and **3.18** below.

2.15 In this regard, Article 6 of the Treaty on European Union (TEU), as amended by the Treaty of Lisbon[1], contains three important provisions. First, Article 6(1) provides that the EU recognises the rights, freedoms and principles set out in the Charter of Fundamental Rights of the European Union, 'which shall have the same legal value as the Treaties'. Secondly, Article 6(2) provides that the EU shall accede to the ECHR[2]. Thirdly, Article 6(3) provides that fundamental rights, as guaranteed by the ECHR and as they result from the constitutional traditions common to the member states, shall constitute general principles of EU law. The latter provision reflects the previous text of the TEU and the jurisprudence of the Court of Justice.

---

1   Given effect in the UK by the European Union (Amendment) Act 2008.

2   The EU has legal personality: Art 47, TEU.

The Charter of Fundamental Rights

2.16 The EU Charter of Fundamental Rights was originally proclaimed in Nice in December 2000, and sought to provide in a single text the range of rights enjoyed by EU citizens (and others resident in the EU) under six chapters: dignity; freedoms; equality; solidarity; citizens' rights; and justice[1]. These rights are of both a civil and political as well as an economic and social nature, and are based upon sources which include the ECHR and the European Social Charter, as well as the EU Charter of Fundamental Social Rights of Workers and other international conventions ratified by the EU or member states. Prior to the entry into force of the Treaty of Lisbon, the Charter of Fundamental Rights had no legally binding force, but was nevertheless an instrument of some significance[2]. The Court of Justice referred to the Charter in some of its judgments, although by way of confirmation rather than as a source of rights[3]. As explained above, the Treaty of Lisbon has altered the status of the Charter, so as to give it the same legal value as the Treaties. It has also adapted the text of the 'horizontal' provisions in Title VII of the Charter, and revised the Explanations prepared by the Bureau of the Charter Convention[4]. Reflecting these changes, the amended Article 6(1) TEU provides that 'the provisions of the Charter shall not extend in any way the competences of the Union as defined in the Treaties', and that the 'rights, freedoms and principles' in the Charter are to be interpreted in accordance with the provisions of Title VII and with 'due regard' to the revised Explanations. Similar provisions are contained in the Charter itself[5].

---

1   See further eg de Búrca 'The Drafting of the European Union Charter of Fundamental Rights' (2001) 26 ELRev 126–138; Hervey and Kenner (eds) *Economic and Social Rights under the EU Charter of Fundamental Rights* (2006); and Barcz et al *Fundamental Rights Protection in the European Union* (2009).

2   It indirectly influenced the preparation of EU legislative proposals by the Commission, which undertook in 2005 to ensure that its proposals complied with the Charter. The EU Fundamental Rights Agency, established in 2007, was also required to have particular regard to the ECHR and the Charter when carrying out pre-legislative scrutiny of Commission proposals.

3 See eg Case C-540/03 *Parliament v Council* [2006] ECR I-5769; Case C-432/05 *Unibet (London) Ltd* [2007] ECR I-2271.

4 The adapted Charter and the revised Explanations were published at OJ C 303/1 and 303/17 of 14.12.2007.

5 See Charter, Arts 51 and 52.

2.17 Despite its title, the Charter is not an all-purpose human rights instrument for the EU, but on the contrary is intended to have a limited scope. Article 51(1) provides that the Charter is addressed to the institutions of the Union, and to the member states only when they are implementing EU law. Article 51(2) states that the Charter does not extend the field of application of EU law beyond the powers of the Union or establish any new power or task for the Union. The Charter therefore has no application to situations involving only domestic law.

2.18 The Charter is not an easy document to interpret. It sets out 50 'rights, freedoms and principles'. Rights and freedoms are given a legally enforceable status by Article 52(1):

'Any limitation on the exercise of the rights and freedoms recognised by this Charter must be provided for by law and respect the essence of those rights and freedoms. Subject to the principle of proportionality, limitations may be made only if they are necessary and genuinely meet objectives of general interest recognised by the Union or the need to protect the rights and freedoms of others.'

Principles have a more limited effect. Article 52(5) states that the provisions of the Charter containing principles 'may be implemented by legislative and executive acts taken by ... the Union, and by acts of Member States when they are implementing Union law'. Such provisions 'shall be judicially cognisable only in the interpretation of such acts and in the ruling on their legality'. They therefore do not in themselves give rise to enforceable rights, but they may affect the interpretation and validity of EU or national legislation or administrative action. Despite the importance of the distinction between rights and principles, and the possibility of confusion when provisions of such differing character are included in the same instrument, the Charter and its revised Explanations fail to identify which provisions contain rights and freedoms and which contain principles, or how the distinction should be drawn[1]. It appears that the classification of the various articles will have to be worked out in future cases by the courts, and ultimately by the Court of Justice. The Court will also have to decide the scope of the Charter rights, which in some cases is far from clear[2].

1 The Explanations give as examples of principles Charter, Art 25 (confusingly headed 'The rights of the elderly'), Art 26 (integration of persons with disabilities) and Art 37 (environmental protection). They also state that some provisions may contain elements of rights and principles, giving as examples Art 23 (equality between men and women), Art 33 (family and professional life) and Art 34 (social security and social assistance). The status of many articles is left obscure.

2 See for example Charter, Art 13 ('The arts and scientific research shall be free of constraint. Academic freedom shall be respected').

2.19 The tenor of the recitals and the Explanations is that the Charter is declaratory of rights resulting from 'the constitutional traditions and international obligations common to the Member States, the ECHR, the Social Charters adopted by the Union and by the Council of Europe and the case law of the Court of Justice … and the European Court of Human Rights'. It is questionable whether this adds anything to the content of the rights protected by Article 6(3) TEU, ie 'fundamental rights, as guaranteed by the ECHR and as they result from the constitutional traditions common to the Member States'. On one view, the legal effect given to the Charter by Article 6(1) TEU amounts to a consolidation of existing EU law in relation to fundamental rights. That view is supported by the Protocol on the Application of the Charter to Poland and the UK, whose recitals state that 'the Charter reaffirms the rights, freedoms and principles recognised in the Union and makes those rights more visible, but does not create new rights or principles'. So understood, the Charter renders more visible to institutions and citizens alike the EU's commitment to respect the rights and principles set out in the Charter. It does so, however, at the price of an increase in the complexity of the framework of fundamental rights in EU law. From a UK perspective, it is noteworthy that the Charter gives effect to rights and principles derived from treaties which have not been ratified by the UK (such as Protocol no 4 to the ECHR) or have not been incorporated into domestic law (such as the ICCPR).

2.20 As mentioned earlier, the UK and Poland have secured a Protocol on the application of the Charter in those member states. In terms of Article 51 TEU, the Protocol has the same legal status as the EU Treaties. It is popularly referred to as an 'opt-out', but that description is inaccurate: it is concerned primarily with the interpretation of the Charter. Its recitals state that the Charter has to be applied by the courts of the UK and Poland in accordance with Article 6 TEU: in other words, in the same way as in other member states. They go on to state that the purpose of the Protocol is to 'clarify' the application of the Charter. Article 1(1) provides that the Charter does not extend the ability of the Court of Justice or any UK or Polish court to find the laws and practices of the UK or Poland inconsistent with the fundamental rights, freedoms and principles that the Charter reaffirms. Article 1(2) provides, for the avoidance of doubt, that nothing in Title IV of the Charter (the 'Solidarity' rights) creates justiciable rights applicable to Poland or the UK except in so far as such rights are provided for in their national law. That provision brings a degree of clarity as to the effect of Title IV, not only in relation to the UK and Poland[1]. Article 2 provides that 'to the extent that a provision of the Charter refers to national laws and practices[2], it shall only apply to Poland or the United Kingdom to the extent that the rights or principles that it contains are recognised in the law or practices of Poland or of the United Kingdom'. The relevance of this approach to interpretation may, again, not be confined to the UK and Poland[3].

---

1   Since Title IV does not create rights which are justiciable in the UK or Poland (unless already recognised in national law), as the Protocol makes clear, it seems unlikely that the Court of Justice would reach a different conclusion as to the effect of Title IV in relation to other member states.

2   See Arts 9, 10(2), 14(3), 16, 27, 28, 30, 34, 35, 36 and 52(7) of the Charter.

3   It is consistent with the approach already followed by the Court of Justice: see eg Case C-438/
     05 *International Transport Workers' Federation v Viking Line ABP* [2007] ECR I-10779 at
     paras 43–44; and Case C-341/05 *Laval un Partneri Ltd v Svenska* [2007] ECR I-11767 at
     paras 90–92.

2.21 A number of questions arise as to the relationship between the Charter and
the ECHR. The recitals to the Charter indicate that one of the sources of the
rights which it 'reaffirms' is the ECHR. Article 52(3) states that, in so far as the
Charter contains rights which correspond to rights guaranteed by the ECHR, 'the
meaning and scope of those rights shall be the same as those laid down by the
Convention'. It adds that this provision does not prevent EU law providing more
extensive protection. As the Explanations state, Article 52(3) is intended to ensure
the necessary consistency between the Charter and the ECHR. The Charter
does not make clear where and how far it is intended to add to the ECHR. In so
far as it may be intended to reproduce rights contained in the ECHR, it does so in
a manner which for several reasons, including the use of different language, is
liable to cause confusion.

2.22 The Explanations provide a list of rights 'which may at the present stage,
without precluding developments in the law, legislation and the Treaties, be regarded
as corresponding to rights in the ECHR'. The implication is that correspondence,
for the purposes of Article 52(3), may change over time. Confusingly, in the light
of Article 52(3), the Explanations distinguish between 'Articles of the Charter
where both the meaning and the scope are the same as the corresponding Articles
of the ECHR'[1] and 'Articles where the meaning is the same as the corresponding
Articles of the ECHR, but where the scope is wider'[2]. In one case, more than
one Charter article corresponds to a single provision of the ECHR[3]. In another
case, a single article of the Charter corresponds to more than one provision of the
ECHR[4]. In one case, the correspondence is subject to a qualification[5]. Besides
the articles of the Charter which 'correspond' to articles of the ECHR, there are
Charter provisions which are said to be related in other ways to the ECHR[6]. The
Charter articles corresponding to qualified ECHR rights, such as those guaranteed
by Articles 2, 5 and 8–11 of the ECHR, do not themselves contain any express
qualification. As the Explanations indicate, the implication of Article 52(3) of the
Charter is that the same qualifications apply as in the ECHR. The Explanations
also explain how Articles 15 and 16 of the ECHR apply in the context of the
Charter[7].

1   This category comprises the Charter article corresponding to ECHR, Arts 2, 3, 4, 5, 6(2) and
     (3), 7, 8, 9 and 10, and Art 1 of Prot 1, and Art 4 of Prot 4.

2   This category comprises the Charter provisions corresponding to Arts 6(1), 11 and 12 of the
     ECHR, Art 2 of Prot 1, and Art 4 of Prot 7. It is said that Art 47(2) and (3) of the Charter (right
     to an effective remedy and to a fair trial) correspond to ECHR, Art 6(1), but that the limitation
     to the determination of civil rights and obligations or criminal charges does not apply as
     regards EU law and its implementation. Art 12(1) of the Charter (freedom of assembly and
     association) corresponds to ECHR, Art 11, but 'its scope is extended to European Union

level'. Art 9 of the Charter (right to marry and right to found a family) covers the same field as ECHR, Art 12, but 'its scope may be extended to other forms of marriage if these are established by national legislation'. Art 14(1) of the Charter (right to education) corresponds to ECHR, Art 2 of Prot 1, but expressly includes access to vocational and continuing training. Art 50 of the Charter applies the *non bis in idem* principle to the courts of the member states as a whole.

3   Art 4 of the Charter imposes a general prohibition of torture and inhuman or degrading treatment or punishment, corresponding to ECHR, Art 3. Art 19(2) of the Charter, which prohibits removal, expulsion or extradition to a state where the person 'would be' subjected to the death penalty, torture or other human or degrading treatment or punishment, is also said to correspond to Art 3 of the ECHR, since it is regarded as incorporating the relevant case law (eg *Soering v United Kingdom* (1989) A 161, discussed at para **4.56** below).

4   In relation to ECHR, Art 2, the Explanations state that the relevant Charter provision also corresponds to Art 1 of Prot 6.

5   Art 11 of the Charter (freedom of expression and information), which corresponds to ECHR, Art 10, is said to be without prejudice to any restrictions which EU law may impose on member states' right to introduce the licensing arrangements permitted by the third sentence of ECHR, Art 10(1), ie licensing of broadcasting, television or cinema enterprises.

6   Art 13 of the Charter (freedom of the arts and sciences) is said to be 'deduced from' the right to freedom of thought and expression, which (as expressed in Arts 10 and 11 of the Charter) is said to correspond to ECHR, Arts 9 and 10. Article 21(1) of the Charter (non-discrimination) is said to 'draw on' ECHR, Art 14. The right of collective action guaranteed by Art 28 of the Charter is said to have been recognised by the Strasbourg Court as one of the elements of ECHR, Art 11. Article 47(1) of the Charter (right to an effective remedy and to a fair trial) is said to be 'based on' ECHR, Art 13, but to provide more extensive protection, since it guarantees the right to an effective remedy before a court.

7   The Explanations state that 'the Charter does not affect the possibilities of Member States to avail themselves of Article 15' (which allows derogations from ECHR rights in times of emergency). ECHR, Art 16 (which permits states to impose restrictions on the political activity of aliens, notwithstanding Arts 10, 11 and 14) is said not to apply to EU citizens, since it would be incompatible with the prohibition of discrimination on grounds of nationality.

2.23 One implication of Article 52(3) of the Charter is that the Court of Justice has to interpret the ECHR. It is also required to do so by Article 6(3) TEU, which (as earlier explained) provides that fundamental rights as guaranteed by the ECHR constitute general principles of EU law. There is a consequent risk of inconsistent interpretations by the Court of Justice on the one hand and the Strasbourg Court on the other. In practice, each court pays close attention to the case law of the other, and conflict has generally been avoided[1]. There have, however, been occasions when divergent interpretations have emerged (eg in relation to the privilege against self-incrimination under Article 6 ECHR, and the applicability of Article 8 to searches of business premises). Such situations can present a problem, particularly in jurisdictions where both EU law and the ECHR are legally binding.

1   See eg Case C-145/04 *Spain v United Kingdom* [2006] ECR I-7917, where the ECJ avoided a direct conflict with the Strasbourg Court's judgment in *Matthews v United Kingdom* [GC] 1999-I.

2.24 In the domestic law of the UK, EU law takes precedence over inconsistent national law by virtue of s 2 of the European Communities Act 1972[1]. In addition, s 3 of that Act requires UK courts to determine questions of EU law in accordance with any relevant decision of the Court of Justice. The ECHR on the other hand does not form part of the domestic law of the UK. Although the Human Rights Act 1998 has created 'Convention rights' which are derived from the ECHR, those rights do not take precedence over inconsistent national law in the same way as EU law: their effect, although important, is more limited. EU law therefore takes precedence, in the event of conflict, over the Human Rights Act 1998 and the Scotland Act 1998. If a UK court considered that there might be a conflict between EU law and the ECHR, it would be likely to refer the issue to the Court of Justice (as happened, for example, in a case concerned with an EC Directive which permitted the compulsory destruction of diseased fish, but failed to provide for compensation[2]). It would then be obliged to follow the decision of the Court of Justice rather than any judgment of the Strasbourg Court. That follows from the overriding effect given to EU law by the European Communities Act and the statutory direction, mentioned earlier, to apply decisions of the Court of Justice. It has been suggested by some commentators that any conflict could raise an acute problem in the context of devolution, since devolved institutions such as the Scottish Parliament and Executive cannot act incompatibly with either EU law or the Convention rights[3]. If such a conflict were to occur, it seems likely that the devolution legislation would have to yield to the European Communities Act. The supremacy of EU law in the domestic legal system does not, however, absolve the UK of its responsibility under international law for a violation of the ECHR. A difficulty would therefore arise if a conflict with one regime could only be avoided by producing a conflict with the other. The accession of the EU to the ECHR would reduce the risk of inconsistency, by making the EU and its institutions subject to the jurisdiction of the Strasbourg Court.

1   *R v Secretary of State for Transport Ex p Factortame Ltd* [1990] 2 AC 85.

2   Case C-64/00, *Booker Aquaculture Ltd v The Scottish Ministers* [2003] ECR I-7411.

3   See paras **1.120** and **1.132–1.136** above.

The effect of accession of the EU to the ECHR

2.25 From the perspective of the Council of Europe, Protocol no 14 which entered into force in June 2010 makes provision for accession by the EU to the European Convention on Human Rights[1]. It thus envisages the European Court of Human Rights adjudicating upon a complaint involving the compatibility of acts taken by the EU, but only after an applicant has sought to exhaust available remedies in EU law. However, it is possible to question whether the accession of the EU to the ECHR will, in reality, greatly strengthen the protection of human rights in the EU[2]. The exercise of the EU's powers in relation to individuals and undertakings, either by member states or by EU institutions, can normally be reviewed by the Court of Justice. That review can include an examination of the conformity of the measure or act in question with the ECHR. The conduct of member states in implementing EU law can be further reviewed by the Strasbourg Court. Moreover, in its *Bosphorus* judgment, the Court held in effect that further scrutiny by that court was unnecessary so long as the EU's judicial system continued to ensure the effective protection of human rights[3]. In so far as there are situations where the EU system fails to provide effective judicial protection of fundamental rights[4], either at national or at EU level, it might be argued that the logical answer is to extend the jurisdiction or remedies available to the EU courts, rather than to look to a different international body for judicial protection.

1   Prot 14, Art 17, inserting a new Art 59(2). Accession would thus result in the appointment of an additional judge, presumably with expertise in EU law. See further de Schutter 'L'Adhésion de l'Union Européenne à la Convention Européenne des Droits de l'Homme' (2010) 83 RTDH 535.

2   See further Harpaz 'The European Court of Justice and its Relations with the European Court of Human Rights: the Quest for Enhanced Reliance, Coherence and Legitimacy' (2009) 46 CMLRev 1055.

3   See paras **2.14** above and paras **2.29** and **3.18** below.

4   See para **2.29** below. The Treaty of Lisbon has extended the jurisdiction of the Court of Justice, by abolishing the three pillar structure. The Court's jurisdiction is however limited in relation to certain areas, such as the common foreign and security policy. In addition, the restrictive rules of locus standi applicable to direct actions may prevent an individual from challenging an EU measure on ECHR grounds unless it is implemented at national level.

2.26 Nevertheless, accession is not merely of symbolic significance. As has been mentioned, there is a risk of inconsistent interpretations by the Court of Justice and the Strasbourg Court. That risk is likely to increase as EU law becomes increasingly significant in areas where fundamental rights are engaged, such as immigration, asylum and crime, and as increasing use is made of databases in relation to those areas. There is also a question as to the degree to which the Court of Justice can be expected to deal with questions of fundamental rights, particularly in the context of preliminary references, where the Court may not have the benefit of detailed discussion of the issue in any national court, and may be given little explanation of the factual or legal background. It appears in principle to be preferable that fundamental rights should be placed on a consistent foundation throughout the EU, and therefore that a single court, with expert knowledge of the legal subject-matter, should be recognised as having final authority in that field.

2.27 Accession is not, however, without difficulties. One which existed until recently arose from the absence of any provision in the ECHR for the accession of non-states. That difficulty has been removed by the entry into force of Protocol no 14 to the ECHR, which amends Article 59 so as to provide that the EU may accede to the ECHR. Some other areas of difficulty are identified in Protocol no 8 to the TEU and the Treaty on the Functioning of the European Union (TFEU). These require the accession agreement to make provision with regard to the arrangements for the EU's possible participation in the control bodies of the ECHR, and the mechanisms necessary to ensure that proceedings are correctly directed against member states and/or the EU as appropriate. Other issues arise which are not mentioned in the Protocol. One question is how the Strasbourg Court will cope with any additional case load resulting from accession, notwithstanding the changes in procedure instituted by Protocol no 14. The Court is already greatly overburdened. The Interlaken Declaration of 19 February 2010 has drawn attention to other issues relating to the Court, such as the clarity and consistency of its case law and the independence of the judges[1].

---

1   See further para **2.43** below, and Däubler-Gmelin 'The Future of the Strasbourg Court and Enforcement of ECHR Standards: Reflections on the Interlaken Process', Document AS/Jur (2010)06; and Mowbray 'The Interlaken Declaration: the Beginning of a New Era for the European Court of Human Rights?' (2010) 10 HRLRev 519.

2.28 Work is under way to address these and other questions[1]. The most fundamental question, however, may be whether accession to the ECHR will endanger the autonomy of the EU's legal order and the authority of the Court of Justice. If the validity of EU acts depends on conformity with the ECHR, and the Strasbourg Court is the authoritative judge of such conformity, it might be argued that accession is incompatible with the role of the Court of Justice as the final interpreter of EU law. That may, however, be an over-simplified view. The Strasbourg Court will have the last word on what the ECHR requires in any case brought before it. Subject to that important qualification, the Court of Justice will remain the final judge on questions of EU law, and on the validity and lawfulness of EU acts.

---

1   On 26 May 2010 the Committee of Ministers of the Council of Europe gave a mandate to its Steering Committee for Human Rights to elaborate with the EU the necessary legal instrument for accession to the ECHR. On 4 June 2010 EU Justice Ministers gave the Commission a mandate to conduct negotiations on their behalf. Official talks started on 7 July 2010. See further Draft agreement on the accession of the EU to the Convention, doc CDDH-UE(2011) 4 (March 2011).

Challenge under the ECHR to national measures that apply or implement EU law

2.29 The extent to which Council of Europe member states can be held accountable for action taken in relation to obligations arising from membership of the EU was addressed – at least in relation to what were at that time known as 'first pillar' competencies – in *Bosphorus Hava Yollari Turizm ve Ticaret Anonim Şirketi v Ireland,* the 'Bosphorus Airways' case. The Irish authorities had seized an aircraft belonging to the applicant company following a European Council regulation implementing UN-approved sanctions against the former Federal Republic of Yugoslavia and a preliminary ruling from the European Court of Justice. The Grand Chamber rejected the applicant company's argument that the significant financial loss sustained by it through the manner in which the sanctions regime had been applied by the respondent state had constituted an excessive burden and thus a violation of the right to property under Article 1 of Protocol no 1. The state's obligation to comply with EU law had been a legitimate aim. Further, in the opinion of the Court there is a presumption that the protection of fundamental rights by EU law is equivalent to that of the Convention system, a presumption rebuttable only where it can be shown that the level of protection of an applicant's rights by EU law has been manifestly deficient[1].

However, national authorities may not merely assume that other states bound by EU law will treat individuals in conformity with ECHR standards. In *MSS v Belgium and Greece*, the applicant had been removed to Greece from Belgium in accordance with the Dublin II Regulation requiring asylum claims in the EU to be determined in the country of first arrival. The applicant had sought to argue in Belgium that the Greek authorities would fail to honour their obligations in asylum matters if he were returned to Greece, and further that detention centres in that country were exceptionally poor. However, the expulsion order had been issued even although under the EU Regulation it would have been permissible for Belgium to have made an exception and to have refused the applicant's transfer. The Court ruled that the transfer had knowingly exposed the applicant to detention conditions that amounted to degrading treatment within the meaning of Article 3[2].

---

1 *Bosphorus Hava Yollari Turizm ve Ticaret Anonim Şirketi v Ireland* [GC] 2005-VI, paras 149–158. For discussion of the judgment, see Costello 'The *Bosphorus* Ruling of the European Court of Human Rights: Fundamental Rights and Blurred Boundaries in Europe' (2006) 6 HRLR 87; Eckles 'Does the European Court of Human Rights Provide Protection from the European Community?' (2007) 13 EPL 47; Conforti 'Le Principe d'Équivalence et le Contrôle sur les Actes Communautaires dans la Jurisprudence de la Cour Européenne des Droits de l'Homme' in Caflisch, Callewaert, Liddell, Mahoney and Villiger (eds) *Liber Amicorum Luzius Wildhaber: Human Rights – Strasbourt Views* (2007), pp 173–182; and Callewaert 'Les Voies de Recours Communautaires sous l'Angle de la Convention Européenne des Droits de l'Homme: la Portée Procédurale de l'Arrêt *Bosphorus*' in Caflisch, Callewaert, Liddell, Mahoney and Villiger (eds), above, pp 115–131; and for discussion of the possible application to the Agreement on the European Economic Area extending the common market of the EU to Iceland, Norway and Liechtenstein, see Björgvinsson 'The EEA Agreement and Fundamental Rights' in Caflisch, Callewaert, Liddell, Mahoney and Villiger (eds), above, pp 25–40. EU member states were initially not considered responsible by the Strasbourg organs for actions taken in respect of EU obligations: see, eg 13258/87, *M & Co v Germany* (1990) DR 64, 138 (writ of execution issued by domestic authorities to give effect to judgment of European Court of Justice upholding Commission imposition of fine: inadmissible); cf *Waite and Kennedy v Germany* [GC] 1999-I, paras 67–74 (restrictions on access to court on account of immunity of the applicants' employer, the European Space Agency, were appropriate); and *Senator Lines GmbH v 15 Member States* (dec) [GC] 2004-IV (penalty subsequently quashed by Court of First Instance: inadmissible). A similar principle applied in respect of other international obligations entered into by member states: eg 21090/92, *Heinz v The Contracting States also Parties to the European Patent Convention* (1994) DR 76, 125. However, in *Matthews v United Kingdom* [GC] 1999-I, the Grand Chamber examined the question of whether states which were bound by the ECHR had positive responsibilities in determining the manner in which they discharged their rights or duties under EU law within the context of electoral law: see further para **7.139** below.

2 *MSS v Belgium and Greece* [GC] (21 January 2011), paras 362–368.

THE EUROPEAN CONVENTION ON HUMAN RIGHTS

Introduction

2.30 The ECHR[1] was opened for ratification in November 1950 and entered into force in September 1953[2]. It is currently in force in 47 states[3], and is applied by the courts in Kosovo[4]. Its preamble affirms the Council of Europe's aim of achieving greater unity between states inter alia through 'the maintenance and further realisation of human rights and fundamental freedoms'. Such rights are considered to be 'the foundation of justice and peace in the world [which] are best maintained on the one hand by an effective political democracy and on the other by a common understanding and observance of the human rights upon which they depend'. To these ends, the ECHR involves 'the first steps for the collective enforcement of certain of the rights stated in the Universal Declaration'[5]. The ECHR, however, embodied in some respects a narrower view of human rights than the Universal Declaration. The framers of the ECHR required a shorter and uncontroversial text which would secure general acceptance among European nations. Thus the ECHR contains, unlike the Universal Declaration, no guarantees of economic, social and cultural rights. A further illustration relates to the guarantees of equality in the two texts. The guarantee in the Universal Declaration is free standing and comprehensive[6]. In the ECHR the provision is parasitic: it is linked with other Convention rights[7]. While the text of the ECHR thus is influenced by international legal norms, the case law of the European Court of Human Rights in turn has influenced the jurisprudence of other international and regional tribunals, helping establish the universality of human rights norms[8].

1   The formal name of the treaty is 'The Convention for the Protection of Human Rights and Fundamental Freedoms'. For current ratifications etc see http://conventions.coe.int.

2   For further background, see Beddard *Human Rights and Europe* (3rd edn, 1993), pp 19–32; Blackburn and Polakiewicz (eds) *Fundamental Rights in Europe: the European Convention on Human Rights and its Member States, 1950–2000* (2001); and Bates *The Evolution of the European Convention on Human Right* (2010). For critical analysis of achievements, see Greer *The European Convention on Human Rights: Achievements, Problems and Prospects* (2006).

3   Before 2004, the ECHR was also applied in Bosnia and Herzegovina by virtue of Annexe VI of the Dayton Accord, and by an Ombudsperson office and a Human Rights Chamber. Chamber judgments are available at http://www.hrc.ba/english/default.htm. For an overview of the case law of the former Bosnian Human Rights Chamber, see Human Rights Chamber for Bosnia and Herzegovina *Digest: Decisions on Admissibility and Merits 1996–2002*.

4   Kosovo was part of the national territory of Serbia and Montenegro (and subsequently, of Serbia), but by virtue of regulations made under the authority of UN Security Council Resolution 1244 (1999), this province was administered by the United Nations Interim Administration Mission in Kosovo (UNMIK) and latterly by the European Union Rule of Law Mission in Kosovo. UNMIK Regulation 1999/1 and the Constitutional Framework for Provisional Self Government, s 3(2)(b) provided that those exercising public duties were bound by the ECHR which is directly applicable in Kosovo. Domestic courts were thus expected to apply Convention guarantees in proceedings. The Republic of Kosovo declared its independence in 2008 (but this has not been recognised by all Council of Europe member states), and Art 22 of the Constitution provides that the ECHR is directly applicable. Applicants in Kosovo continue

to have problems in obtaining redress from the Strasbourg Court: while Serbia and Montenegro ratified the Convention in 2004 without territorial reservation, it would have been inappropriate to hold Serbia responsible for human rights violations in what was a province administered on an interim basis by the United Nations following *Behrami and Behrami v France and Saramati v France, Germany and Norway* (dec) [GC] 2007-... (actions of the Kosovo Force and UNMIK were not attributable to states).

5   For discussion of the preamble, see van Boren 'The Preamble of the Convention on Human Rights and Fundamental Freedoms' in Coomans and others (eds) *Human Rights from Exclusion to Inclusion: Principles and Practice* (2000), pp 401–412. The Court may refer to the preamble for guidance in interpreting substantive guarantees: see, eg *Brumrescu v Romania* [GC] 1999-VII, para 61 (principle of the rule of law implies legal certainty).

6   UDHR, Art 7.

7   ECHR, Art 14. Note, however, the provisions of Prot 12 (not yet ratified by the United Kingdom), discussed at para **3.86** below.

8   See generally Cohen-Jonathan and Flauss (eds) *Le Rayonnement International de la Jurisprudence de la Cour Européenne des Droits de l'Homme* (2005); and in particular the following chapters in this work: Cassese 'La Prise en Compte de la Jurisprudence de Strasbourg par les Jurisdictions Pénales Internationales', pp 29–82; Cançado Trindade 'Approximations and Convergences in the Case-Law of the European and Inter-American Courts of Human Rights', pp 101–138; and de Schutter 'L'Influence de la Cour Européenne des Droits de l'Homme sur la Cour de Justice des Communautés Éuropéennes,' pp 189–242.

2.31 The drafters of the ECHR were concerned to ensure that the treaty protected those substantive rights which commanded general support. There was lengthy consideration at the drafting stage as to whether the treaty should include certain rights which had more of an economic or social than a civil and political flavour, such as the rights to marry and to found a family (which ultimately were included in the ECHR as Article 12) and to the peaceful enjoyment of property and to education (two provisions which were eventually rejected)[1]. The approach adopted involved a decision to exclude rights which did not command support from each of the original member states. Later additions to the catalogue of protected human rights were not however precluded, and were to be secured by means of additional optional protocols[2]. In consequence, ECHR guarantees reflect values which are the common currency of European legal systems: equality before the law, fair hearings, impartiality of judges, no retroactive lawmaking, protection against discrimination and against wrongful deprivation of liberty, recognition of the concept of marriage, freedom of conscience and expression, respect for privacy and belief, and protection of property rights. Such ideas had been articulated and developed by the judiciary in domestic legal systems long before the ECHR's ratification, but were to be given heightened status and enhanced protection through international protection. The rights to property and to education (along with the right to free elections) were thus eventually secured by Protocol no 1[3], opened for signature in 1952. Additional substantive guarantees were provided in 1963 through Protocol no 4, which protects freedom of movement and prohibits imprisonment for debt, expulsion of nationals and the collective expulsion of aliens; in 1983 through Protocol no 6, which abolishes the death penalty except in time of war; and in 1984 through Protocol no 7, which provides for additional procedural safeguards relating to the expulsion of aliens, rights of appeal in criminal matters, compensation for wrongful conviction, protection against being tried or punished twice, and the principle of equality between spouses. Protocols nos 4 and 7 have not been ratified by the UK, and consequently these rights are not incorporated into domestic law by virtue of the HRA 1998 or SA 1998[4]. Protocol no 12, which strengthens protection against discrimination, was opened for signature in November 2000 and entered into force in April 2005[5]. This, too, has not yet been ratified by the United Kingdom. Protocol no 13 of 2002 abolishes the death penalty in all circumstances and was promptly ratified by the British Government[6].

1   For the background to the drafting of the ECHR, see Robertson *Human Rights in Europe* (3rd edn, 1993), pp 1–24; Marston 'The United Kingdom's Part in the Preparation of the European Convention on Human Rights' (1993) 42 ICLQ 796; Janis, Kay and Bradley *European Human Rights Law: Text and Materials* (2nd edn, 2000), pp 16–22; and Simpson *Human Rights and the End of Empire: Britain and the Genesis of the European Convention* (2001), ch 14. See too Council of Europe *Collected Edition of the Travaux Préparatoires of the European Convention on Human Rights* (7 vols, 1975–1985).

2   ECHR, Prots 1, 4, 6, 7, 12 and 13 are concerned with substantive guarantees, while Prots 2, 3, 5, 8, 9 and 11 made amendments to the Convention's enforcement machinery. Prot 10 did not enter into force, and has been superseded by the procedural reforms occasioned by Prot 11. Proposals for further developments are normally considered by a Steering Committee for Human Rights, a Committee of Experts for the Improvement of Procedures for the Protection of Human Rights (currently examining means of improving further the Court's working methods) and a Committee of Experts for the Development of Human Rights.

3   Opened for signature in March 1952. As at 31 March 2011, Prot 1 had been ratified by all member states with the exception of Monaco and Switzerland.

4   Prot 4, opened for signature in September 1963. As at 31 March 2011, Prot 4 had been ratified by all states other than Greece, Switzerland Turkey and the United Kingdom; and Prot 7, opened for signature in November 1984, has not been ratified by Belgium, Germany, the Netherlands, Turkey and the United Kingdom.

5   The Protocol provides for a general prohibition of discrimination by providing (in Art 1, para (1)) that 'the enjoyment of any right set forth by law shall be secured without discrimination on any ground such as sex, race, colour, language, religion, political or other opinion, national or social origin, association with a national minority, property, birth or other status'; and (in para (2)) that 'no one shall be discriminated against by any public authority on any ground such as those mentioned in paragraph 1'. The Protocol entered into force in 2005. For discussion of Art 14's prohibition of discrimination in the enjoyment of Convention rights, see paras **3.87–3.128** below.

6   Prot 6, opened for signature in April 1983, has now been ratified by all member states with the exception of Russia. As at 31 March2011, Prot 13 (which entered into force in 2004) had been ratified by all member states other than Armenia, Azerbaijan, Latvia, Poland and Russia. For further discussion, see para **4.54** below.

2.32 The primary focus of the ECHR is thus upon civil and political rights rather than upon economic and social rights, and – more particularly – upon those civil and political rights which are recognised and shared by developed western legal systems. However, the Court has stressed that the distinction between these two categories of human rights is by no means clear cut[1]. A number of judgments have addressed aspects of economic, social and cultural rights, including cases involving environmental pollution[2], the rights of persons with disabilities[3], the homeless[4], and economic migrants[5], the rights to work[6] and to form a trade union[7], and denial of educational provision[8].

1   Cf *Airey v Ireland* (1989) A 32, at para 26: 'Whilst the ECHR sets forth what are essentially civil and political rights, many of them have implications of a social or economic nature. The Court therefore considers, like the Commission, that the mere fact that an interpretation of the ECHR may extend into the sphere of social and economic rights should not be a decisive factor against such an interpretation; there is no water-tight division separating that sphere from the field covered by the Convention.' See also *Sidabras and Džiautas v Lithuania* 2004-VIII, para 47. For further discussion, see Van Bueren 'Including the Excluded: the case for an Economic, Social and Cultural Human Rights Act' [2002] PL 456; and Tomuschat 'Social Rights under the European Convention on Human Rights' in Breitenmoser, Ehrenzeller, Sassòli, Stoffel and Pfeifer (eds) *Human Rights, Democracy and the Rule of Law: Liber Amicorum Luzius Wildhaber* (2007), pp 837–863.

2   See paras **6.125–6.128** below.

3   See para **6.47**, fn 2 below.

4   Eg *Moldovan and Others v Romania (no 2)* 2005-VII, paras 93–101 (continuing and serious violation of Art 8 rights involving perpetuation of insecurity affecting Roma villagers forced to sleep in livestock premises after the destruction of their homes by a mob which included state officials). See also para **4.05** fn 3, below.

5   See paras **6.67–6.70** below.

6   See para **7.28** below.

7   See para **7.132** below.

8   See paras **6.154–6.155** and **6.167** below.

Enforcement mechanisms under the ECHR

2.33 The ECHR 'creates, over and above a network of mutual, bilateral undertakings, objective obligations [which] benefit from a 'collective enforcement''[1]. It is, however, up to each state to decide the extent of the obligations it wishes to accept, and thus the level of human rights protection available to individuals can vary between European states[2]. Three distinct mechanisms to ensure that states respect their obligations are found. First, a reporting procedure requires states to furnish the Secretary General of the Council of Europe with details of the implementation of Convention guarantees in domestic law on receipt of a request under Article 52 (formerly Article 57); secondly, a state may bring an allegation of a violation by another state to the notice of the Strasbourg institutions under Article 33 (formerly Article 24); and thirdly, individuals and other non-governmental bodies may raise complaints of violations directly under Article 34 (formerly Article 25). While the first two methods of enforcement existed elsewhere in international law at the time of the Convention's entry into force, the latter right of individual application was at the time an innovation which remedied the traditional lack of standing of individuals in international law.

1   *Ireland v United Kingdom* (1978) A 25, at para 239.

2   This will not only be dependent upon state ratification of optional protocols, but also any declarations or reservations made at the time of ratification and any subsequent use of the right

to derogate under Art 15. In addition, the recognition of a 'margin of appreciation' by the Court will influence the practical level of domestic human rights protection: see paras **3.134–3.141** below.

Reporting procedures

2.34 Reporting procedures involve the scrutiny of periodic or ad hoc reports by independent agencies (or 'treaty bodies'). This is an established way of monitoring the progressive implementation of rights (such as economic, social and cultural rights) which are open-textured in nature, of overcoming problems with reliance upon inter-state complaint (which may be weakened by political practicalities), and of providing a more adequate assessment of compliance with international obligations than could be achieved by piecemeal examination of particular issues highlighted by individual complaints. To these ends, reporting procedures exist under a number of international treaties[1]. In particular, substantial use has been made of these by the (former) Human Rights Committee under the International Covenant on Civil and Political Rights[2]. The ECHR, Article 52[3] makes provision for the Secretary General of the Council of Europe to request a ratifying state to 'furnish an explanation of the manner in which its internal law ensures the effective implementation of any of the provisions of this Convention'. While Article 52 is succinct, 'the conclusion must ... be that the Secretary General has an independent, autonomous and discretionary power of investigation conferred upon him'. In making any use of this power he would be expected to proceed 'in an objective and impartial manner'[4]. This is, however, an under-utilised and (in comparison with equivalent provisions in other treaties) a relatively weak measure[5], with no provision for formal scrutiny of the information supplied, presumably because the drafters considered that reliance upon domestic implementation of Convention guarantees, and the right of individual application, would fill the lacuna traditionally found in human rights enforcement machinery[6].

1　These include procedures under the International Covenant on Civil and Political Rights, Art 40; the International Covenant on Economic, Social and Cultural Rights, Art 16; the Convention on the Rights of the Child, Art 44; and the European Social Charter, Art 21.

2　See Alston (ed) *The United Nations and Human Rights* (2000), *passim*.

3　ECHR, Art 57 (original treaty).

4　Mahoney 'Does Article 57 of the European Convention on Human Rights Serve any Useful Purpose?' in Matscher and Petzold (eds) *Protecting Human Rights: The European Dimension* (2nd edn, 1990), pp 373–393 at 380 and 385.

5　ECHR, Art 52 has been used on eight occasions to date. On six of these occasions, the request was addressed to all state parties: that is, in 1964 in relation to all provisions of the ECHR and Prot 1; in 1970 in respect of Art 5(5); in 1975 to review state obligations under Arts 8–11; in 1983 with regard to guarantees for children and minors in care; in 1988 in respect of fair trial guarantees under Art 6; and in 2005 in relation to alleged illegal detention and rendition flights in Europe (with a further request to most states to clarify and complement the information supplied). Responses are summarised and circulated to the Parliamentary Assembly. In 2006, the Secretary General held a press conference to report upon the outcomes of the inquiry into rendition flights. On two occasions, requests have been addressed to individual states: in 1999 the Russian Federation was requested to furnish a report on the manner in which the Convention was being implemented in Chechnya, and in 2002, Moldova was required to report upon restrictions upon political parties.

6   Cf Dimitrijevic 'The Monitoring of Human Rights and the Prevention of Human Rights Violations through Reporting Procedures' in Bloed, Leicht, Nowak and Rosas (eds) *Monitoring Human Rights in Europe* (1993), pp 7–10, who suggests that an enhanced system of monitoring compliance through reporting and scrutinising under the ECHR would be desirable, first to ensure compliance with rights which may not necessarily be 'cognisable under contentious proceedings' (such as the rights to education and to free elections at reasonable intervals under Prot 1) and secondly to help assimilate central and eastern European states which have recently ratified the Convention. Mahoney 'Does Article 57 of the European Convention on Human Rights Serve any Useful Purpose?' in Matscher and Petzold (eds) *Protecting Human Rights: The European Dimension* (2nd edn, 1990) at pp 391–392 suggests that 'the lack of precision in the text as to the exercise of the function conferred needs to be cured by rules of application laying down set procedures to be followed by the Secretary General' before Art 52's potential can be realised.

Inter-state cases

2.35 Inter-state complaint is similarly a recognised method of calling states to account for failure to discharge their obligations under the treaty[1]. Under what is now Article 33 of the ECHR[2], a contracting state is able to complain of an alleged violation of the treaty by any other state, and also accepts the jurisdiction of the Strasbourg Court to consider such a complaint brought against it. In bringing an application against another state alleging breach of any provision of the ECHR, the state 'is not to be regarded as exercising a right of action for the purposes of enforcing its own rights but rather as [raising] an alleged violation of the public order of Europe', since the responsibilities assumed upon ratification by states 'are essentially of an objective character, being designed rather to protect the fundamental rights of individual human beings ... than to create subjective and reciprocal rights' between ratifying states[3]. Unlike most other multilateral treaties, the aim of a human rights treaty is to seek to confer rights directly upon non-state beneficiaries who need not even be nationals of the states in question. Nevertheless, although individuals and groups are the beneficiaries of such treaties, states are responsible in international law to other state parties. Enforcement can thus become a matter for other contracting states that may have no particular link with the victims of state violations, although this may be unlikely in practice unless the nature of the violation is compelling and the state interest in upholding the responsibility coincides with other diplomatic interests[4]. Probably on account of the political nature of such a remedy, the use of inter-state complaint under the ECHR has been limited[5], despite less rigorous requirements of admissibility[6]. The reluctance of governments to make use of Article 33 reflects the dominance of political over human rights considerations[7].

1   See further Rogge 'Inter-state Cases under Article 33 of the European Convention on Human Rights' in Hartig, ed *Trente Ans de Droit Européen des Droits de l'Homme: Études à la Mémoire de Wolfgang Strasser* (2007), pp 289–306.

2   ECHR, Art 24 (original treaty).

3   788/60, *Austria v Italy* (1961) YB 4 112 at 140. In consequence, inter-state applications may challenge a law *in abstracto*, for a breach may result 'from the mere existence of a law which introduces, directs or authorises measures incompatible with the rights and freedoms safeguarded' provided that the law in question 'is couched in terms sufficiently clear and precise to make the breach immediately apparent; otherwise, the decision of the Convention institutions must be arrived at by reference to the manner in which the respondent State interprets and applies in concreto the impugned text or texts': *Ireland v United Kingdom* (1978) A 25, at para 240.

4   Dimitrijevic 'The Monitoring of Human Rights and the Prevention of Human Rights Violations through Reporting Procedures' in Bloed, Leicht, Nowak and Rosas (eds) *Monitoring Human Rights in Europe* (1993), p 1.

5   The 26 interstate applications lodged (and considered in 15 separate decided cases after the joining of related applications) involved complaints against the United Kingdom in relation to Cyprus and to Northern Ireland; a complaint against Italy in respect of the trial of German-speaking nationals; complaints against Greece in response to action taken by its military dictatorship; complaints against Turkey after the occupation of northern Cyprus; and complaints against Turkey in respect of violations by its military dictatorship and of the infliction of torture. Three have led to Court judgments, and another case has been struck out the list by the Court. *Ireland v United Kingdom* (1978) A 25, discussed at para **4.68** below, led to a finding of violation of Art 3 by the Court. *Denmark v Turkey* (friendly settlement) 2000-IV was struck out by the Court after a friendly settlement was achieved (allegations of ill-treatment in violation of Art 3 inflicted against a Danish citizen detained in Turkey and that the interrogation techniques allegedly applied in the individual's case formed part of a widespread practice in the state: the settlement took the form of an *ex gratia* payment, acknowledgment of 'occasional and individual' *(sic)* infliction of torture and ill-treatment, recognition that training of police officers is crucial in preventing violations of Art 3, and establishment of a bilateral dialogue between the two states with a view to improving human rights). *Cyprus v Turkey* [GC] 2001-IV involved challenges to the occupation of northern Cyprus by Turkey since 1974 and led to the Court's finding of multiple violations of ECHR guarantees (including Turkey's failure to carry out effective investigations into the fate of Greek Cypriots who had disappeared while in custody; the continuing refusal to allow the return of any Greek Cypriot displaced persons to their homes; degrading discriminatory treatment; limiting access to places of worship and participation in religious life through restrictions on movement; censorship of school books destined for use by Greek Cypriot primary schoolchildren; lack of provision of secondary school facilities; and (in respect of Turkish Cypriots) violations of fair trial guarantees through authorisation of the trial of civilians by military courts). Two inter-State cases are currently pending: *Georgia v Russia (no 1)* (dec) (30 June 2009) (alleged harassment of the Georgian immigrant population in Russia involving deportation of Georgian nationals: admissible); and jurisdiction to determine the merits subsequently relinquished in favour of the Grand Chamber) and *Georgia v Russia* (no 2) (complaints arising out of the invasion of Georgia by Russian troops in 2008). A third complaint was struck off the list following the release of minors detained in South Ossetia: *Georgia v Russia (no 3)* (dec) (16 March 2010).

6   Cf ECHR, Arts 33 and 35. There is no need to establish any particular state interest in the complaint (for example, that any of its nationals are a victim); and the only admissibility requirements to be satisfied are exhaustion of domestic remedies and the six-month rule.

7   For further discussion see Van Dijk and van Hoof *Theory and Practice of the European Convention on Human Rights* (4th edn, 2006), pp 47–51.

The right of individual application

2.36 Although states are generally reluctant to enforce inter-state obligations, individuals and groups may be given the right to instigate complaints directly. In international law, recognition of the right of a person or body to challenge national legislation or administrative practice before an international forum was an innovation with far-reaching potential. Not all states found it easy to accept that an individual should enjoy equality of status with state parties[1]. Recognition of this right initially came somewhat reluctantly[2]. Under the ECHR, states could accept the optional right of individual application (either without limit of time or for a specified period) in terms of what is now Article 34[3], whereby 'any person, non-governmental organisation or group of individuals claiming to be a victim of a violation' of an ECHR guarantee[4] could bring a complaint before the Strasbourg organs. Such a provision marked a fundamental change in the relationship between the individual and the state. The United Kingdom first recognised the right of individual application in 1966 in respect of any act or decision occurring after the date of this recognition[5]. The potential afforded by this innovation in international human rights protection was soon exploited by individual applicants. Its success led to incremental reforms of judicial procedures, and ultimately in 1998 to radical reform when Protocol no 11 entered into force.

---

1   Other international and regional human rights instruments have extended the use of recognition of individual complaint, and in particular, under the Optional Protocol to the International Covenant on Civil and Political Rights the ability of the (former) Human Rights Committee to deal with 'communications' from individuals and groups has now been recognised by the majority of contracting states (but not by the United Kingdom).

2   In general, northern (west) European states were the first to recognise the right of individual petition: Sweden, Iceland, Denmark, Belgium, Germany, Norway, Luxembourg and the Netherlands all had done so by the end of 1960. France and Spain only recognised this right in 1981, while Greece and Turkey only did so in 1985 and 1987 respectively.

3   Art 25 (original treaty).

4   For discussion of 'victim', see paras **2.64–2.73** below. The provision also specifies that states 'undertake not to hinder in any way the effective exercise of this right': see para **2.49** below.

5   That is, 14 February 1966: cf *LCB v United Kingdom* 1998-III, para 35 (no jurisdiction to determine events taking place before this date). The UK thereafter renewed recognition at five-yearly intervals. See further Lester 'UK Acceptance of the Strasbourg Jurisdiction: What Really went on in Whitehall in 1966' [1998] PL 237. After the Court's judgment in *Tyrer v United Kingdom* (1978) A 26, however, the right of individual petition was not renewed in relation to the Isle of Man until 1993.

Overview of the machinery established to deal with inter-state cases and individual complaints

2.37 The original treaty provided for shared responsibility between a Commission responsible for scrutiny of admissibility, fact-finding, conciliation and a preliminary opinion on the merits; a Court whose jurisdiction was optional and (where this was recognised) charged with giving a binding judgment and determination of an award of 'just satisfaction'; and the Committee of Ministers, which would give a final decision on cases not brought before the Court and supervise state compliance with obligations where a violation had been established. Both the Commission and the Court were judicial institutions[1]; the Committee of Ministers on the other hand was a political body[2]. These arrangements reflected the innovative nature of the ECHR when it first entered into force, for states were naturally cautious in subjecting themselves to international enforcement machinery.

The entry into force of Protocol no 11 on 1 November 1998 resulted in a significant overhaul of the enforcement machinery provided by the ECHR. This was made necessary by a dramatic increase in individual applications to Strasbourg[3], reflecting both a growing awareness of the ECHR on the part of individuals and legal practitioners and a significantly enlarged membership of the Council of Europe. The new procedures were designed to improve efficiency in the disposal of applications: a full-time Court replaced a part-time Commission and Court[4], eliminating much of the duplication of effort inherent in the original arrangements, which had to some extent reflected a need initially to secure state confidence in international supervision.

The reforms introduced by Protocol no 11 were not sufficient, however, to deal with an ever-increasing workload and backlog of applications[5], highlighting systemic failures in certain member states to ensure the provision of effective remedies at domestic level to allow individuals to challenge alleged shortcomings in law and practice[6]. Further amendment of the enforcement machinery came in June 2010 with the entry into force of Protocol no 14[7] which seeks to improve the efficiency of the court through the use of new single-judge and committee procedures and greater opportunity to concentrate upon cases considered as requiring more in-depth examination[8].

---

1   Members of the Commission and Judges of the Court were elected by the Committee of Ministers from a list drawn up by the Parliamentary Assembly of persons of 'high moral character' who possessed the qualifications required for high judicial office or who were of recognised competence in national or international law: Arts 21(3) and 39 (original treaty, as amended by Prot 8).

2   See further para **2.09** above. Cf Opsahl's comments that 'if control mechanisms are to be just, the legal ones should be allowed to do their job; but if they are to be effective, the political ones are better', in Eide and Hagtvet (eds) *Human Rights in Perspective: A Global Perspective* (1992), pp 60–65, discussed by van Boven 'General Course on Human Rights' *Collected Courses of the Academy of European Law vol IV–2* (1995), pp 62–65 who concludes that the legal and the political processes should be seen as complementary, not contradictory.

3   The number of applications lodged (and provisional files opened) annually had reached almost 600 (and over 2,700 respectively) by 1982, some 1,000 (and 4,100) by 1988, and over 2,000 (and 9,300) by 1993. The majority of applications continued to be introduced without legal assistance: in 1998, of the 5,981 applications registered by the Commission, 45% had been introduced through a lawyer (a percentage which had, however, increased significantly from the period 1955–1970 when the average figure was around 10%). In contrast, the number of applications made by persons detained had decreased. Well over a third (and on occasion one half) of applications in most years until 1978 concerned individuals who were detained: the figure for 1998 was 10%. See further (1998) YB 41, 18–19.

4   The Commission continued to function under transitional arrangements until the end of October 1999 to deal with cases which had been declared admissible before the entry into force of Prot 11 in November 1998.

5   In 2009, ten years after the entry into force of Prot 11, the number of applications lodged annually had reached over 57,000 (an increase of 15% on the 2008 figure), and this in turn had resulted in a backlog of some 120,000 applications still awaiting disposal: *European Court of Human Rights, Annual Report 2009* (2010), p 5.

6　　In 2009, 28% of pending cases were in respect of Russia (33,500), 11% in respect of Turkey (13,100), and some 8% in respect of Ukraine and Romania (some 10,000). That year, the highest number of judgments (and accounting for more than half of all judgments) concerned Turkey (356), Russia (219), Romania (168) and Poland (133), while half of the Contracting States had less then 10 judgments against them: *European Court of Human Rights, Annual Report 2009* (2010), pp 144–145. The failure of Eastern European countries to ensure domestic realisation of Convention guarantees is discussed in Maruste 'The Impact of Accession of Eastern Block Countries on the Convention Machinery and its Case-Law' in Caflisch, Callewaert, Liddell, Mahoney and Villiger (eds) *Liber Amicorum Luzius Wildhaber: Human Rights – Strasbourg Views* (2007), pp 285–308 (typical problems giving rise to findings of violation include poor prison conditions, judicial control and legal grounds for detention, and relevant and sufficient grounds and unreasonable length of preliminary detention (ECHR, Art 5); non-respect of legal certainty, unreasonable length of judicial proceedings (Art 6), prohibition of retroactive criminalisation (Art 7); censorship of prisoners' correspondence; and application of *res judicata* in property cases (Prot 1, Art 1)).

7　　But note that certain provisions of Prot 14 were applied under agreement or by virtue of Prot 14 *bis* between 2009 and 2010: see para **2.44** below.

8　　See Explanatory Reports to Prots 11, 14 and 14 *bis*.

Enforcement procedure before November 1998

Functions of the European Commission on Human Rights

2.38 Some understanding of the original enforcement machinery remains necessary in order to appreciate the relative importance of the case law of the Commission and Court, and the role formerly played by the Committee of Ministers. The Commission was responsible for consideration of the admissibility of any application lodged and thereafter for examination of the merits of the complaint[1]. The Commission was first established in 1954, and was a part-time institution serviced by its Secretariat, normally holding some eight sessions per annum. Members held office for an initial period of six years, sitting in their individual capacities and not as representatives of states[2]. The vast majority of applications lodged – almost 90% – were rejected by the Commission as inadmissible, either at the outset of the proceedings or after the observations of the relevant state had been considered[3]. Where admissibility criteria had been satisfied, the Commission's task was thereafter threefold: first, it would establish the facts (and, to this end, in exceptional cases could undertake an investigation); secondly, it would place itself at the disposal of the parties with a view to securing a friendly settlement (achieved in some 10% of cases declared admissible, normally in the form of an offer by the state to pay financial compensation or to amend domestic law or practice); and thirdly, where no friendly settlement was effected, it would issue a report on the facts as established, giving its opinion as to whether there had been a violation[4]. Most of this work took place through the consideration of written submissions. Committees (of three members) would examine admissibility; Chambers (of seven members) would normally determine more difficult questions of admissibility and the merits of applications declared admissible[5]. A decision that an application was inadmissible was final. The Commission's report on the merits of a complaint, however, was only an opinion and thus not binding. The Committee of Ministers could ultimately decide (by a two-thirds majority) whether there had been a violation of the treaty and, if so, the time by which the state had to take satisfactory measures to comply with the decision[6]. However, within three months from the date of transmission of the report to the Committee of Ministers, the case could be referred to the European Court of Human Rights if the respondent state had recognised the Court's optional jurisdiction[7]. A referral could be made either by the Commission or by the state against which the complaint was lodged or, in an appropriate case, by the state whose national was alleged to be a victim[8]. From 1994 onwards, additionally, an individual applicant could refer the case to the Court with leave of a screening panel where the relevant state party had recognised this additional optional provision[9].

1   See further Fribergh and Villiger 'The European Commission of Human Rights' in Macdonald, Matscher and Petzold (eds) *The European System for the Protection of Human Rights* (1993), pp 605–620.

2   ECHR, Arts 21–23 (original treaty as amended by Prots 5 and 8).

3   By the end of the Commission's work, 39,047 applications had been registered and 33,123 decisions taken. The number of applications declared inadmissible (or struck off the list *de plano*) was 26,226; and a further 2,733 applications had been declared inadmissible after communication to the respondent government. Only 4,161 applications were declared admissible (of which a further 12 were rejected in the course of examination of the merits): (1998) YB 41, 20. For discussion of admissibility criteria, see paras **2.58–2.63** below.

4   ECHR, Arts 28–31 (original treaty as amended by Prots 3 and 8). For friendly settlements, see para **2.75** below.

5   ECHR, Prot 8.

6   ECHR, Art 32 (original treaty). The Committee met *in camera*. Prot 10 would have reduced the majority required for such a decision to that of a simple majority, but never entered into force.

7   Under ECHR, Art 46 (original treaty).

8   ECHR, Art 48 (original treaty).

9   In terms of ECHR, Prot 9.

The European Court of Human Rights

2.39 The Court was first established in 1959. The optional nature of its jurisdiction and the relative paucity of applications to the Commission in the early years (reflecting the optional nature of recognition of the right of individual application) resulted in a slow start to its work: the first case was referred to it in 1960[1], and between then and the end of 1975, only another 10 cases followed. In time, all states had come to recognise its jurisdiction or had indicated (in the case of new member states of the Council of Europe) an intention of doing so as a condition of membership[2]. The corresponding exponential growth in workload is remarkable. In the next ten years – 1976 until 1985 – the Court was seised of a further 81 cases; and in the final full year of the 'old' Court alone – 1997 – of 119 cases. Before implementation of the reforms of Protocol no 11, no less than 837 judgments had been delivered[3]. The vast majority of referrals were made by the Commission, where it considered that an authoritative ruling by the Court was appropriate; less than 40 cases were on account of state referrals alone[4]. Its additional function of giving advisory opinions on interpretation of the ECHR at the request of the Committee of Ministers was never exercised[5].

1 That is, *Lawless v Ireland* (1960–1961) A 1–3.

2 Cf the formula used by the Parliamentary Assembly in considering commitments undertaken as a condition of membership that it attached 'great importance' to recognition of the right of individual application: see further doc Monitor/Inf (99) 1.

3 As well as 190 decisions rejecting applications under Prot 9, Art 5(2): European Court of Human Rights *Survey; Forty Years of Activity 1959–1998* (1999), p 25.

4 European Court of Human Rights *Survey: Forty Years of Activity* (1999), p 3. Only two of those cases involved a referral by a state whose national was alleged to have been a victim.

5 In terms of ECHR, Prot 2. This function was first exercised by the 'new' Court in 2004: see para **2.46**, fn 3 below.

2.40 This steady growth in workload was reflected in organisational and procedural reforms. As the number of member states grew, so did the Court. The Court was essentially a part-time institution comprised of a number of judges equal to that of member states[1] and serviced by its full-time Registry. It normally sat in Chambers of seven (and subsequently nine) judges, which would include the judge appointed in respect of the respondent state; in certain cases, however, a case would be considered by a Grand Chamber of 17 (and subsequently 21) judges or, in exceptional cases, by the plenary court[2]. The first stage in any case was the submission of written memorials or other documentation by the parties (and, in certain cases, by other states or organisations where the President of the Court determined that this would be in the interests of the proper administration of justice)[3]. At any subsequent hearing, the Commission was not formally a party to the proceedings but appeared through its delegates to assist the Court in its deliberations. Any applicant who had indicated a wish to take part in the proceedings was normally legally represented by a practising or academic lawyer. The state concerned was heard last. The Court was able to reconsider whether a decision that an application was admissible had been correctly decided by the Commission, to re-open deliberations on the merits of an application, and in certain cases to deliberate upon the application of a treaty provision which had not been considered by the Commission[4]. Judgments were given by simple majority. They were binding upon states but were essentially declaratory. Supervision of the implementation of measures required by any judgment (and of any Court determination as to the payment of costs and expenses and payment of compensation by way of 'just satisfaction') was a matter for the Committee of Ministers[5].

1 ECHR, Art 38 (original treaty). Judges were elected (or re-elected) by the Parliamentary Assembly for a period of nine years from a list of three persons drawn up by member states, and sat in their own individual capacity: Arts 39 and 40 (original treaty, as amended).

2 ECHR, Art 43 (original treaty); and (former) Rule of Court 'A' 51.

3 In terms of (former) Rule of Court 'A' 37(2).

4 *De Wilde, Ooms and Versyp v Belgium* (1971) A 12, paras 47–52. A decision of the Commission that an issue was inadmissible could not, however, be reopened: see eg *Fusco v Italy* 1997-V,

para 16. See further van Dijk and van Hoof *Theory and Practice of the European Convention on Human Rights* (3rd edn, 1998), pp 203–213. See also *Guzzardi v Italy* (1980) A 39, paras 58–63 (identification of Art 5 issue by the Commission and the Court which had not been specifically raised by the applicant).

5   ECHR, Arts 52–54 (original treaty).

Reform of the control machinery and Protocol no 11

2.41 By the early 1990s there was substantial recognition that the existing procedures were inefficient, with needless duplication between Commission and Court, and productive of excessive delay[1]. The Commission's increasing willingness to refer cases to the Court for determination led to a situation where it was not uncommon for applications to take some five years between Commission registration and Court judgment. Protocol no 11 in essence abolished the Commission, restricted the functions of the Committee of Ministers to supervision of the enforcement of judgments, and made significant reforms to the Court, which became a full-time body. Applications were normally assigned to a particular Chamber (or 'Section'), whose President allocated it to a particular judge (the 'judge rapporteur') who was responsible for preparing the case[2]. The application was thereafter considered by a Committee comprising three judges who could (by unanimous vote) decide to declare an individual application inadmissible or strike it from its list[3]. Alternatively, the rapporteur could decide that the application should be dealt with by a Chamber from the outset. Any application not considered inadmissible by unanimous vote of a committee was transferred to a Chamber for further examination of admissibility[4]. The Chamber was able to declare the application inadmissible or strike it from its list, or to seek further information or to 'communicate' the case by inviting the state to submit written observations on the admissibility and merits. The merits of the case were thereafter determined by a Chamber or by the Grand Chamber.

1   See further Council of Europe Report of the Committee of Experts for the Improvement of Procedures for the Protection of Human Rights, Doc H (89) 2, reproduced in Janis, Kay and Bradley *European Human Rights Law: Text and Materials* (1st edn, 1995), pp 88–105; and Explanatory Report to Protocol no 11, Doc H (94) 5.

2   The name of the judge rapporteur was kept confidential.

3   ECHR, Art 28 (before entry into force of Prot 14). The judge appointed in respect of the respondent state was not necessarily a member of the committee deciding admissibility. If a Committee declared an application inadmissible, no reasons for doing so were given; the vast majority of applications were disposed of by Committees (under 'summary procedure'). These decisions were final. Only a Chamber could (and still can unless it relinquishes jurisdiction to the Grand Chamber) decide the question of admissibility of any inter-state application: Art 29(2).

4   Determination of admissibility on occasion depended upon examination of the merits, and the two issues were often conjoined: eg *Ferrazzini v Italy* [GC] 2001-VII, paras 18–19 (opportunity taken by Grand Chamber to review existing case law on the applicability of Art 6 to tax proceedings). However, it was increasingly the case that admissibility and merits issues were disposed of at the same time. While Art 29(3) provided that this could occur 'in exceptional

cases', Rule of Court 54A permitted the joint examination of admissibility and merits. This practice became formally recognised with the entry into force of ECHR, Prot 14.

Protocol no 14 and current arrangements

The need for further reform

2.42 From the very inception of the 'new' full-time Court in November 1998, its workload continued to grow at a rate which reflected both the heightened awareness of the ECHR on the part of applicants and also the failure of domestic legal systems to provide effective relief for applicants without the need for recourse to Strasbourg[1]. If the increase was not entirely unexpected in light of the accession of new and t:'emerging' democracies, it threatened to overwhelm the Court. The Ministerial Conference on Human Rights held in Rome in November 2000 and marking the 50th anniversary of the opening for signature of the ECHR, was the first in a series of initiatives seeking to address the Court's increasing incapacity to deal with the growing volume of cases. The outcomes included the opening for signature of Protocol no 14 in 2004[2], the adoption of procedural measures by the Court in respect of cases revealing an underlying systemic problem at domestic level[3], and the provision of additional resources for the Court[4].

1   During the three years which followed the entry into force of Prot 11, the Court's case-load grew at an unprecedented rate. The number of applications registered rose from 5,979 in 1998 to 13,858 in 2001, an increase of approximately 130%. This increase has been maintained. In the ten-year period between 1995 and 2006, applications lodged annually rose from 11,200 to 51,300; the number of cases declared inadmissible rose from 2,182 to 28,160, and the number of judgments delivered rose from 56 to 1,560: *European Court of Human Rights Annual Report 2006* (2007), Appendix XI. In 2009, the number of applications allocated to a judicial formation had reached 57,100, an increase of 15% over 2008, but only 35,460 cases had been disposed of by the end of that year: *European Court of Human Rights, Annual Report 2009* (2010), p 135. Provisional statistics for 2010 indicate a further increase of 7% in comparison to 2009. The number of judgments has also increased significantly. Between 1 November 1998 and 5 December 2000, the new Court had delivered 838 judgments – one more than the previous, part-time Court had delivered in the 40 years between its establishment in 1959 and its demise on 31 October 1998. By December 2009, it had delivered 11,362 judgments (1,625 in 2009 alone).

2   The proposal for Prot 14 arose from the Activity Report on the reinforcement of the human rights protection mechanism of the Reflection Group of the Steering Committee for Human Rights (CDDH) (June 2001), its interim report of October 2002, its Proposals of April and November 2003, and its Final Activity Report of April 2004 (containing a draft Prot 14); the Report of the Evaluation Group set up by the Committee of Ministers on the European Court of Human Rights (September 2001) leading to Committee of Ministers Declarations in November 2001, November 2002, and May 2003; and the opinion of the Parliamentary Assembly on the draft Prot 14 in April 2004.

3   See *European Court of Human Rights, Annual Report 2009* (2010), p 11: 'At the end of 2009, 119,300 allocated applications were pending before the Court. Four States account for over half (55.7%) of its docket: 28.1% of the cases are directed against Russia, 11% of the cases concern Turkey, 8.4% Ukraine and 8.2% Romania'; and *European Court of Human Rights, Annual Report 2010* (provisional edition, 2011), p 6: 'By the end of [2010, the backlog] had

reached approximately 140,000 applications, which is an increase of 17%. The deficit at the end of 2010 amounted to more than 1,600 applications per month.' See generally *Reforming the European Convention on Human Rights: A Work in Progress* (2009). See in particular the Action Plan adopted at the Third Summit of Heads of State and Government of the Council of Europe, Heading 1.1, in 2005 (commitment to ensuring the long-term effectiveness of the Court through in particular ensuring proactive scrutiny of the compatibility of law and practice and of the provision of effective domestic remedies and adequate professional training at domestic level); CDDH's Activity Report of April 2006; and the Committee of Ministers Declaration on 'Sustained action to ensure the effectiveness of the implementation of the European Convention on Human Rights at national and European levels'. External input has come from the Report of the 'Group of Wise Persons' (November 2006) (which envisaged easier reform of the judicial machinery by way of unanimously adopted resolutions without formal amendment through Protocol, the introduction of a new judicial filtering mechanism, improvements to the dissemination of the Court's case law, the introduction of advisory opinions submitted by national courts, improvements to domestic remedies for redressing violations of the Convention, promotion of the use of 'pilot judgments', greater use of friendly settlements and encouragement of mediation, and extending the duties of the Council of Europe Commissioner for Human Rights); the joint response to this report from key NGOs in January 2007; and the San Marino colloquy on the report in March 2007. For further discussion, see eg Council of Europe, *Reform of the European Human Rights System: Proceedings of the High-Level Seminar, Oslo, 18 October 2004*, (2004); Cohen-Jonathan, Flauss, and Lambert Abdelgawad (eds) *De l'Effectivité des Recours Internes dans l'Application de la Convention Européenne des Droits de l'Homme* (2006); and Wolfrum and Deutsch (eds) *The European Court of Human Rights Overwhelmed by Applications: Problems and Possible Solutions* (2009) *passim*. For more radical suggestions for reform, see Caflish and Keller 'Le Protocole Additionel no 15 à *La Convention Européenne des Droits de l'Homme* in Caflisch, Callewaert, Liddell, Mahoney and Villiger (eds), *Liber Amicorum Luzius Wildhaber: Human Rights – Strasbourg Views* (2007), pp 91–113.

4   The Court's budget for 2010 was €58.6m (some 27% of the overall budget of the Council of Europe).

2.43 Protocol no 14 does not seek to make significant amendments to the enforcement machinery, but rather aims to streamline the decision-making process, primarily by permitting a single judge assisted by rapporteurs from the Court Registry[1] to declare applications inadmissible, and by enabling a three-judge committee to deal with both the admissibility and the merits of an application simultaneously. The Protocol also amends the term of office of judges (now elected for a single, non-renewable period of nine years), allows the Court to request the Committee of Ministers to reduce the size of Chambers from seven members to five, and permits the Council of Europe Commissioner for Human Rights to submit written comments and take part in hearings in all cases before a Chamber or the Grand Chamber. However, the Protocol also introduces a new admissibility criterion by allowing an application to be deemed inadmissible if 'the applicant has not suffered a significant disadvantage, unless respect for human rights [within the meaning of the Convention] requires an examination of the application on the merits and provided that no case may be rejected on this ground which has not been duly considered by a domestic tribunal'[2]. This is likely to have an impact upon the ability of the Court to be more selective in determining the types of cases it wishes to consider with greater care[3]. Protocol no 14 will not in itself, however, solve the problem of overload. In advance of its entry into force, the

'Interlaken Declaration' made in early 2010 sought to emphasise the responsibility of states in ensuring effective domestic protection[4], at the same time recognising the need for further action to address the problem of repetitive or 'clone' cases on the part of the Court and the Committee of Ministers.

1   The Registry now comprises some 640 staff (around half of whom are on permanent contracts, and of whom 270 are lawyers) and is headed by a Registrar and Deputy Registrar elected by the Plenary Court in terms of Art 25; each Section also has a Section Registrar and a Deputy Section Registrar. The Registry is divided into case-processing divisions (currently 31) with cases assigned on the basis of knowledge of the language and legal system concerned, and service divisions (information technology; case law information and publications; research and the library; just satisfaction; press and public relations; language department and internal administration). See further Fribergh 'The Authority over the Court's Registry within the Council of Europe' in Breitenmoser et al (eds) *Human rights, Democracy and the Rule of Law: Liber Amicorum Luzius Wildhaber* (2007), pp 145–158.

2   ECHR, Prot 14, inserting a new Art 35(3)(b). See further para **2.62** below.

3   See further paras **2.64–2.73** below.

4   See Committee of Ministers Recommendations Rec (2004) 5 on the verification of the compatibility of draft laws, existing laws and administrative practice with the standards laid down in the ECHR; Rec (2004) 6 on the improvement of domestic remedies; and Rec (2008) 2 on efficient domestic capacity for rapid execution of judgments of the European Court of Human Rights. Other Council of Europe activities include verification of the ECHR compatibility of draft laws, existing laws and administrative practices and professional training. The unwillingness or inability of certain states to address systemic problems has also led to the introduction of the 'pilot judgment' procedure: see paras **2.80–2.81** below. Certain states, in particular, appear chronically weak in their commitments. See *European Court of Human Rights, Annual Report 2009* (2010), p 12 (the highest number of judgments concerned Turkey (356), Russia (219), Romania (168) and Poland (133) which together accounted for more than half (52%) of all judgments, while half of all states had less than 10 judgments against them).

2.44 The opening of signature of Protocol no 14 in May 2004 was followed within a relatively short time by its ratification by all member states with the exception of Russia, whose reluctance could only be explained as a political gesture in the face of repeated findings of violations of ECHR guarantees[1]. Exasperation at Russia's intransigence led to the introduction as a temporary measure of Protocol no 14 *bis*[2] which allowed the Court to implement for cases involving those states which had ratified the protocol (or had declared that they accepted its provisional application)[3] the single judge procedure and the three-judge committee for cases that could be disposed of on the basis of well-established case law[4]. By the entry into force of Protocol no 14, only 18 states had accepted these procedures before these temporary arrangements lapsed.

1   Certain judgments have caused difficulty. See eg *Ilaşcu and Others v Moldova and Russia* [GC] 2004-VII, at para 392: (determination that the 'republic' in question 'remains under the effective authority, or at the very least under the decisive influence, of the Russian Federation, and in any event that it survives by virtue of the military, economic, financial and political support given to it by the Russian Federation'). See also Committee of Ministers Interim Resolution Res DH(2006)26 (profound regret that Russia has not 'actively pursued all effective avenues to comply with the Court's judgment'). See further Leach 'Strasbourg's Oversight of Russia – an Increasingly Strained Relationship' [2007] PL 640; and Leach 'The Chechen

Conflict: Analysing the Oversight of the European Court of Human Rights' [2008] EHRLR 732.

2   CETS 204 (no longer in force). See Flauss 'Le Protocole N° 14 bis de la Convention Européenne des Droits de l'Homme' (2009) 113 RGDIP 621.

3   In terms of the 'the Madrid Agreement' of May 2009. The single judge formation was introduced in July 2009; Prot 14 *bis* entered into force in October 2009.

4   See further Explanatory Memorandum to Protocol no 14 *bis*, paras 3–6.

Functions and organisation of the European Court of Human Rights

2.45 With the entry into force of Protocol no 14 in June 2010, the appointment, organisation and functions of the Court are now governed by Articles 19–51 of the revised ECHR (that is, the ECHR as amended by Protocols nos 11 and 14) as supplemented by Rules of Court and practice directions[1]. The Court has jurisdiction in both inter-state cases and individual applications[2] (that is, applications from any person, non-governmental organisation or group of individuals claiming to be a victim of a breach of the ECHR)[3], and to this end will give a decision on the admissibility of an application and a judgment on its merits. A judgment on the merits is essentially declaratory of the law, and the monitoring of action taken by the state as a consequence of a finding of a violation (including the payment of any award of 'just satisfaction') still remains the responsibility of the Committee of Ministers. However, in certain cases the Court is now prepared to indicate what specific action it considers indispensable in light of a judgment[4]. The Court continues to be able to give advisory opinions[5].

1   The current Rules of Court are dated 1 April 2011, and are available at http://www.echr.coe.int/ECHR/EN/Header/Basic+Texts/Other+texts/Rules+of+Court/.Practice directions are made by the President in terms of Rule 32, and seek to provide guidance and to standardise procedures to facilitate the processing of cases. Half of the judges appointed in 1998 had prior experience as members of the 'old' Court or Commission (with this expertise drawn in equal numbers from each institution). For further discussion, see Bratza and O'Boyle 'Opinion: The Legacy of the Commission to the New Court under the Eleventh Protocol' [1997] EHRLR 211.

2   ECHR, Art 33.

3   ECHR, Art 34. For discussion of 'victim' see paras **2.64–2.73** below.

4   See paras **2.79–2.81** below.

5   ECHR, Art 47–49. Requests for advisory opinions are considered by the Grand Chamber: Art 31 (and see further paras **2.46**, fn 3 and **2.54** below). The Council of Europe Convention on Human Rights and Biomedicine (ETS 164(1997)), Art 29 also permits the Court to give advisory opinions at the request of states when the treaty enters into force (this Convention has neither been signed nor ratified by the United Kingdom).

2.46 The Court consists of a number of judges equal to that of state parties to the ECHR[1]. Judges are to be 'of high moral character and must either possess the qualifications required for appointment to high judicial office or be jurisconsults of recognised competence'[2]. States are required to nominate three candidates, one of whom is selected by the Parliamentary Assembly[3]. Until 2010, judges were elected for renewable periods of six years, but now serve for one, non-renewable period of nine years[4]. Judges must retire when they reach 70[5].

1   ECHR, Arts 20 and 22. Each state nominates three candidates (with or without indicating a ranking of preference); the Parliamentary Assembly selects one candidate by a majority of votes following interviews of candidates by a committee: see Parliamentary Assembly Committee on Legal Affairs and Human Rights *Procedure for Electing Judges to the European Court of Human Rights: Information Document* (2010). Judges need not be nationals of the state in respect of which they have been elected: currently, the judge elected in respect of Liechtenstein is Swiss. Not until 1998 did the United Kingdom Government nominate a Scottish qualified candidate for this office (although one Scot, Professor AE Anton, did serve albeit for a matter of weeks as a member of the Commission in the early 1980s). A Scottish judge first sat on the Court, on an *ad hoc* basis, in *Hashman and Harrup v United Kingdom* [GC] 1999-VIII. Following the Interlaken Conference of 2010, a new Panel of Experts is being established to help ensure appointments are of suitable quality. For discussion of appointments, see eg Schermers 'Election of Judges to the European Court of Human Rights' (1998) 23 EL Rev 568; Flauss 'L'Assemblée Parlementaire du Conseil de l'Europe et l'Élection de la Nouvelle Cour Européenne des Droits de l'Homme' in Haller, Krüger and Petzold *Law in Greater Europe: Towards a Common Legal Area* (2000), pp 190–207; Coomber 'Judicial Independence: Law and Practice of Appointments to the European Court of Human Rights' [2003] EHRLR 486; Hedigan 'The Election of Judges to the European Court of Human Rights' in Kohen (ed) *Promoting Justice, Human Rights and Conflict Resolution through International Law: Liber Amicorum Lucius Caflisch* (2007), pp 235–253; and Mowbray 'The consideration of Gender in the Process of Appointing Judges to the European Court of Human Rights' (2008) 8 HRLRev 549.

2   ECHR, Art 21(1). Judges sit in their individual capacity, and must not engage in any activity which is incompatible with their independence or impartiality: paras (2) and (3). The Court adopted a resolution on judicial ethics in 2008.See the *Sixth Protocol to the General Agreement on Privileges and Immunities of the Council of Europe* (ETS 162(1996)) for privileges and immunities of judges. Rule of Court 29 makes provision for the appointment by a state of an *ad hoc* judge if there is no judge elected in respect of a respondent state, or where the judge is unable to sit, withdraws, or is exempted.

3   The extent of the powers of the Parliamentary Assembly in this regard has been raised in two advisory opinions. See *Advisory Opinion on Certain Legal Questions concerning the Lists of Candidates Submitted with a View to the Election of Judges to the European Court of Human Rights* [GC] 2008-..., paras 36–37 (question whether the Parliamentary Assembly could reject a list of candidates submitted by Malta for the post of judge solely on the ground that the list did not include any female candidate: while the criterion derived from a gender-equality policy supported by the Committee of Ministers, the Committee had deliberately not acted upon an Assembly proposal to amend ECHR, Art 22: the Assembly had no power so to reject); and *Advisory Opinion on Certain Legal Questions concerning the Lists of Candidates Submitted with a View to the Election of Judges to the European Court of Human Rights (no 2)* [GC] 2010-..., paras 37–57 at para 37 (withdrawal of list and its replacement by Ukraine: the ECHR must be interpreted in such a way as to ensure their effectiveness and the authority and proper functioning of the Court, and while both states and the Parliamentary Assembly have a certain latitude in discharging their obligations under Art 22 so that states may withdraw or replace a list of candidates during the initial period of the procedure, the interests of legal certainty and the transparency and efficacy of the election procedure requiring that a time-limit should be set for doing so, beyond which a state may not withdraw the list).

4   ECHR, Art 23(1). Judges may be removed on a vote of two-thirds of the remainder of the Court: Art 23(4).

5   ECHR, Art 23(2). Note transitional arrangements for judges in office in June 2010 who will have their term of office increased to a total of nine years if they are serving their first term and by two years otherwise.

2.47 The procedures are largely written, and oral argument is required only in exceptional cases where the Court feels this is helpful for the proper disposal of a difficult or novel issue[1]. Rules of Court provide that such hearings will be held in public unless the Court in exceptional circumstances decides otherwise[2]. The Court is 'master of the characterisation to be given in law to the facts of a case', and thus is not constrained by the choice of provision in the written application or in pleadings[3].

1   See Rules of Court 59(2) and 63. Oral hearings thus may be held where in the opinion of the respondent government the outcome of the case may have a significant impact upon domestic law or practice: see Reid *A Practitioner's Guide to the European Convention on Human Rights* (3rd edn, 2007), p 13. The tendency is for oral hearings in Grand Chamber cases, and for Chambers normally not to hold such hearings (in 2009, 18 cases before the Grand Chamber involved hearings, but only 10 oral hearings were held by Chambers). Since mid 2007, public hearings are broadcast on the internet (at http://www.echr.coe.int/ECHR/EN/Header/Press/Multimedia/Webcasts+of+public+hearings/latestwebcastEN.htm).

2   For example, the hearing in the related cases of *T v United Kingdom* [GC] (16 December 1999) and *V v United Kingdom* [GC] 1999-IX were held in private. There is a requirement that an applicant is legally represented after an application has been communicated and at oral hearing: see para **2.49**, fn 3 below.

3   *Phillips v United Kingdom* (5 July 2001) at para 38. See also *Guzzardi v Italy* (1980) A 39, paras 58–63 (identification of Art 5 issue by the Commission and the Court which had not been specifically raised by the applicant).

2.48 Considerable use is made of devolution of authority. In terms of Protocol no 11, the Court sat in committees (of three judges), Chambers (of seven judges, including the President of the Section, together with substitute judges), a Grand Chamber (of 17 judges), or in plenary[1]. Protocol no 14 now allows the use of the single judge procedure, and accordingly, the Court now sits in single-judge formation, committees (of three judges), Chambers (of seven judges, but with the proviso that the number of judges may be reduced to five), a Grand Chamber (of seventeen judges), or in plenary[2]. Reasons for admissibility decisions and for judgments on the merits must be given; any judge who considers the judgment does not represent in whole or in part the unanimous opinion of the Court is entitled to deliver a separate opinion[3].

1   ECHR, Art 26 and 27 (before the entry into force of Prot 14).

2   ECHR, Arts 25 and 26. The plenary Court meets to elect its President and one or two Vice-Presidents for a period of three years; to adopt its Rules of Court; to set up Chambers; and to elect Chamber Presidents, the Court Registrar and Deputy Registrars. To this extent the plenary Court is essentially a managerial body. The plenary Court can now also request the Committee of Ministers to reduce the number of judges in a Committee to five. See further Rules of Court 24–30. Rule of Court 9A provides that the President of the Court will be assisted in the discharge of his administrative tasks by a Bureau composed of the President of the Court, the Vice Presidents of the Court and the Section Presidents

3   ECHR, Art 45. Abstentions are not permitted in final votes on the admissibility and merits of cases: Rule of Court 23(2). For discussion of the use of separate opinions, see Sudre *Les Opinions Séparées des Juges à la Cour Européene de Droits de l'Homme* (2004).

Making an application

2.49 Rules of Court specify that an individual application must be made in writing, and prescribe the information and documents that must be supplied[1]. The application will be assigned to one of the Court's Sections[2]. The parties may be requested to submit further information, and the Court may also decide to 'communicate' the case by inviting the respondent state to submit written observations on the admissibility and merits[3]. An applicant need only be legally represented once an application has been communicated to the respondent state[4]. The right of individuals and non-governmental organisations to make use of their rights is carefully protected by the Court. Article 34 specifically provides that contracting states 'undertake not to hinder in any way the effective exercise of this right'. Intimidation of an applicant, or deliberate attempts to prevent effective communication with the Strasbourg Court, may result in a finding of a violation[5]. Sensitivity to the practical difficulties facing persons deprived of their liberty is evident. For example, in *Cotleţ v Romania*, the intimidation of the prisoner, the failure of the prison authorities to provide writing materials for his correspondence with the Court, and the delay in forwarding and the systematic opening of his mail were held to have 'constituted a form of illegal and unacceptable pressure which infringed the applicant's right of individual application', a conclusion 'all the more imperative having regard to the particular vulnerability of the applicant who had few contacts with his close relatives or with the outside world while in custody'[6].

1   See in particular Rule of Court 47. Rule 45(3) provides that an application submitted by a representative must be accompanied by a duly-signed power of attorney: see *Post v Netherlands* (dec) (20 January 2009). An application may be lodged by post or by fax. Electronic filing of written communications is restricted to governments that have opted for this system. However, receipt of any prior communication and which contains a brief outline of the facts sufficient to indicate the nature of the complaint will interrupt application of the six-month admissibility requirement (see para **2.60** below). The expectation is that a formal application will thereafter be lodged within six weeks. See further Practice Direction on Institution of Proceedings, Annex 6; and Leach *Taking a Case to the European Court of Human Rights* (2nd ed, 2005), pp 20–23.

2   Rule of Court 52(1).

3   Rule of Court 54(2). Communication takes place where an issue is considered to require further examination. An application may also be communicated in part (that is, after certain aspects have been declared inadmissible). Governments are expected to respond within three months, and applicants thereafter within one month, although these periods may be extended: Rule 38 and Practice Direction on Written Pleadings. The state's written observations are in turn circulated to the applicant who is invited to submit written observations in reply. Chambers may decide to hold a hearing on admissibility, although this is now exceptionally rare in practice. Since June 2007, communicated applications (together with the questions the Court wishes answered) have been published on the Court's website. In 2009, just under 9% of applications allocated to a Committee or Chamber were communicated; in 2010, a further rise (of some 8%) in the number of cases communicated (to almost 6,700 in that year) was recorded.

4   After a case has been communicated, an applicant must be legally represented by a practising lawyer from any Council of Europe member state, although the relevant Section President may authorise other suitably-qualified legal representatives to act: Rule of Court 36. Note also Rule of Court 36(3) (the Section President 'exceptionally [may grant] leave to the applicant to

present his or her own case, subject, if necessary, to being assisted by an advocate or other approved representative') an applicant thus has no right to address the Court directly. An applicant who has insufficient means to meet all or part of the costs in bringing an application may be awarded legal aid after an application has been communicated and where this is necessary or the proper conduct of a case: Rules of Court 100–105. See also Rule of Court 42 (joinder and simultaneous examination of applications).

5   For example of findings of violation of Art 34, see *Akdivar and Others v Turkey* 1996-IV, paras 103–106 (police questioning, videoing etc of individuals in respect of applications made to the Commission); *Assenov and Others v Bulgaria* 1998-VIII, paras 169–171; *Petra v Romania* 1998-VII, paras 43–44 ('*I'll* give you Council of Europe!'); *Colibaba v Moldova* (23 October 2007), paras 65–69 (threats by Prosecutor-General to instigate criminal investigations for making 'false' human rights allegations to international organisations and thus leading to 'grave prejudice' to the country's image); and *Ryabov v Russia* (31 January 2008), paras 56–65 (enquiry into financial arrangements between the applicant and his lawyer lacking any legal or factual basis had specifically targeted the applicant's representative in order to prevent her from participating in Court proceedings). Cf *Öcalan v Turkey* [GC] 2005-IV, paras 199–202 (no indication that lawyers were hindered in preparation of application): and *Sisojeva and Others v Latvia* [GC] 2007-II, paras 115–126 (insufficient evidence to draw conclusion that police questioning involved pressure that may have induced the withdrawal or modification of an application). See also *European Agreement Relating to Persons Participating in Proceedings of the European Court of Human Rights* (ETS 161 (1996)) (covering immunity from legal process in respect of documents etc submitted to the Court, and the freedom of movement of applicants; and ratified by the United Kingdom in 2001).

6   *Cotleţ v Romania* (3 June 2003), para 71.

Interim measures

2.50 An applicant, state party or any other person concerned in the proceedings may request that interim measures be taken to protect the interests of the parties or of the proper conduct of the proceedings; alternatively, the Court may of its own motion indicate what interim measures should be taken to these ends pending determination of the complaint[1]. 'Interim measures play a vital role in avoiding irreversible situations that would prevent the Court from properly examining the application and, where appropriate, securing to the applicant the practical and effective benefit of the Convention rights asserted', but such an indication will only be made if there is an imminent risk of irreparable damage[2]. A state's failure to adhere to any such indication may now be treated as a violation of the right of individual petition where there has been a failure to take steps which could reasonably have been taken in order to comply with interim measures indicated by the Court[3].

1   Rule of Court 39. For guidance on the making of a request for an interim measure, see Practice Direction: Requests for Interim Measures (July 2011). An interim measure may be sought at the request of a party or of any other person concerned, or made by the Court of its own motion: cf *Ilaşcu and Others v Moldova and Russia* [GC] 2004-VIII, para 11 (one applicant urged under Rule of Court 39 to end his hunger strike). For one month in 2010, the Court automatically applied Rule 39 in cases involving the Netherlands, Sweden and the United Kingdom where applicants were seeking to prevent their return to central Iraq in light of a deterioration of the security situation in this area, but at the end of the period the Court decided that it would again examine Rule 39 requests with reference to the applicant's individual

circumstances. Notice of any measure indicated is given to the Committee of Ministers, and parties may be requested to supply information concerning its implementation. For an example of such an interim measure, see *Öcalan v Turkey* [GC] 2005-IV (indication by way of an interim measure that the respondent state should not execute the applicant who had been sentenced to death for terrorist crimes until the Court had determined the issues raised in the application). Rule 39 requests tend in practice to concern Arts 2 and 3 and family life under Art 8, and most requests are made in respect of threatened immediate expulsion, but see eg *Prežec v Croatia* (dec) (28 August 2008) (Rule 39 indication to provide the applicant with psychiatric treatment). Measures are made for defined but renewable periods of time. The number of applications for an interim measure has risen considerably in recent years: in 2009, some 2,400 requests were made under Rule of Court 39, of which just over 650 were successful. By 2010, the number of requests had reached some 4,790, prompting the President of the Court in February 2011 to issue a statement reminding applicants and states of their responsibilities to co-operate with the Court and reminding parties of the Court's 'proper but limited role in immigration and asylum matters'. See further van Dijk, van Hoof, van Rijn and Zwaak, eds *Theory and Practice of the European Convention on Human Rights* (4th edn, 2006), pp 110–120; and Harby 'The Changing Nature of Interim Measures Before the European Court of Human Rights' [2010] EHRLR 73.

2   *Al-Saadoon and Mufdhi v United Kingdom* 2010-..., at para 160.

3   Eg *Paladi v Moldova* [GC] 2009-..., paras 94–106. Thus the state must demonstrate that it complied with the interim measure, or alternatively (and exceptionally), that there was an objective impediment which prevented compliance and that all reasonable steps were taken to remove the impediment and to keep the Court informed. Whether an 'objective impediment' exists is assessed by reference to the legal and factual circumstances which prevail at the time. Each case must be determined on its own facts: eg *Öcalan v Turkey* [GC] 2005-IV, paras 197–202 (no violation of Art 34 despite failure to observe interim measures); *Aleksanyan v Russia* (22 December 2008), paras 228–232 (interim measures under Rule 39: delay in implementing transfer of seriously-ill prisoner to a specialist medical institution and refusal to permit examination by a medical commission had amounted to an attempt to hinder application under Art 34); and *Al-Saadoon and Mufdhi v United Kingdom* 2010-..., paras 160–165 (no indication that any steps – let alone all reasonable steps – had been taken to seek to comply with the Rule 39 indication to prevent the transfer of two prisoners to the Iraqi authorities in circumstances in which there was a substantial risk of imposition of the death penalty, the Court rejecting the state's argument that compliance was not possible as the UN mandate was due to expire and thus the lawful basis of detention would lapse). A state's failure to respect any interim measures indicated under Rule of Court 39 was not in the past considered to give rise in itself to a violation of the right of individual application under Art 34 but merely to aggravate any subsequent finding of violation of ECHR, Art 3: see *Cruz Varas v Sweden* (1991) A 201, paras 99–103. In *Čonka and Others v Belgium* (dec) (13 March 2001), the Court gave notice that it would now consider whether failure to apply interim measures could give rise to a violation of the right of individual petition under Art 34. In *Mamatkulov and Abdurasulovic v Turkey* [GC] 2005-I, para 132, the Grand Chamber agreed with the Chamber's conclusion ((6 February 2003) paras 96–111) that 'in the light of the general principles of international law, the law of treaties and international case law, the interpretation of the scope of interim measures cannot be dissociated from the proceedings to which they relate or the decision on the merits they seek to protect', and that extradition contrary to interim measures ordered by the Court had 'rendered nugatory the applicants' right to individual application' in violation of Art 34.

Procedure for determining an application

2.51 Applications were generally dealt with in the order in which they become ready for examination unless a case was particularly urgent[1]. However, the ever-increasing backlog was resulting in lengthy delays before particularly serious applications could be determined. This in turn was leading to yet more applications being lodged on account of a failure to identify and to address the underlying causes of many violations. Amendments to Rules of Court in 2009 now require the Court to have regard to the importance and urgency of the issues raised in deciding the order in which cases are to be addressed[2].

1   For an example of a particularly urgent case, see *Pretty v United Kingdom* 2002-III, discussed at para **4.53** below (applicant suffering from terminal illness: the time from lodging of application to judgment was just over 4 months).

2   Rule of Court 41. The Court's current policy is to give priority on the basis of categories as follows: (1) urgent applications (risk to life or health of the applicant or other circumstances linked to the personal or family situation of the applicant and especially where the well-being of a child is at issue, or where 'Rule 39' interim measures have been applied); (2) applications giving rise to questions of effectiveness of the Convention system (especially structural or endemic situations not yet examined and application of pilot-judgment procedures) or applications raising an important question of general interest or capable of having major implications, and inter-state cases; (3) complaints involving direct threats to the physical integrity and dignity involving the 'core rights'(Arts 2–5(1)); (4) potentially well-founded applications based on other Articles; (5) applications raising issues already dealt with in a pilot/leading judgment ('repetitive cases'); and (6) applications 'manifestly inadmissible'. The expectation is that the Court's workload will decrease by prioritising the most serious cases and those disclosing the existence of widespread problems capable of generating large numbers of additional cases. See European Court of Human Rights *The Court's Priority Policy* (2010). For a recent example of prioritisation, see *Al-Saadoon and Mufdhi v United Kingdom* (dec) (30 June 2009) (interim measure indicated, but further application refused but decisions to give the case priority under Rule 41 and to expedite the procedure).

2.52 An application will now normally be considered initially by a single-judge formation, that is, by a single judge assisted by rapporteurs from the Court's Registry[1]. A single judge may declare inadmissible or strike out of the Court's list of cases the application where such a decision can be taken without further examination[2]. Such a decision is final[3]. It is likely that substantial numbers of applications will be declared inadmissible by single-judge formations[4]. When sitting as a single judge, the judge may not examine any case involving the state in respect of which that judge has been elected[5]. If the application is not declared inadmissible or is not struck out, the judge will forward it to a committee of three judges or to a Chamber for further examination[6]. If the application is forwarded to a committee[7], the committee may declare it inadmissible or strike it out of its list of cases by a unanimous vote where such decision can be taken without further examination; alternatively, it may declare it admissible and at the same time render a judgment on the merits of the case if the underlying issue 'is already the subject of well-established case-law of the Court'. Such decisions and judgments are final[8].

1   ECHR, Art 27, and 24(2). The rapporteurs function under the authority of the Court President. See also Rule of Court 52A(1). Note that the Court is master of the characterisation to be given to the facts: *Guzzardi v Italy* (1980) A 39, para 61.

2   ECHR, Prot 14, inserting new Art 27 (1): 'A single judge may declare inadmissible or strike out of the Court's list of cases an application submitted under Article 34, where such a decision

can be taken without further examination. A single judge may declare inadmissible or strike out of the Court's list of cases an application submitted under Article 34, where such a decision can be taken without further examination.'

3   ECHR, Art 27(1)–(2).

4   *See European Court of Human Rights, Annual Report 2010* (provisional edition, 2011), at p 6: more than 19,000 decisions were given by single judges with and 149 applications ended with a judgment of a three-judge Committee between June and December 2010: 'the number of decisions given by single judges is impressive, but a comprehensive analysis of the application of Protocol No. 14 will not be able to be done before the end of 2011.'

5   ECHR, Art 26(3).

6   ECHR, Art 27(3).

7   Ie, there is no possibility of referral to the Grand Chamber. If the committee does not include the judge elected in respect of the respondent state concerned, the committee may at any stage of the proceedings invite that judge to take the place of one of the members of the committee, having regard to all relevant factors (including whether the respondent state has contested the application): ECHR, Art 28(3). If the committee cannot obtain unanimity, the case will be referred to a Chamber.

8   ECHR, Art 28(1)–(2).

CHAMBERS

2.53 In the remainder of cases, the admissibility and merits of an application will be determined by a Chamber (unless the case is relinquished by the Chamber in favour of the Grand Chamber). Membership of the Chambers (or 'Sections') is fixed for three years and seeks to achieve gender and geographical balance[1] and representation of the different legal traditions found across the continent. The Chamber consists of seven judges, although the Committee of Ministers may decide that the size of membership should be five judges[2]. The judge elected in respect of a respondent state sits as an *ex officio* member of the Chamber[3]. When an application has been admitted by a Chamber, the parties may be invited to submit further evidence and written observations (including any claim for just satisfaction under Article 41)[4]. The President of the Chamber may invite or grant leave to any other state or person not a party to the proceedings to submit written pleadings (and, exceptionally, to address the Court) where this is in the interests of the proper administration of justice[5]. The Council of Europe Commissioner for Human Rights may also submit written comments and take part in hearings[6].

1   Rule of Court 25.

2   ECHR, Art 26(2): the request for a reduction of size must be made by the plenary Court to the Committee of Ministers (see Art 25) and any decision by the Committee of Ministers must be unanimous and for a fixed period.

3   ECHR, Art 26(4).

4   See further Rules of Court 59 and 60. For discussion of 'just satisfaction', see para **2.50** below.

5   ECHR, Art 36(2) and Rule of Court 44(3). The Scottish Commission for Human Rights would appear to be competent to seek to intervene: see para **1.183** above. Leave is normally restricted to the submission of written observations, but in exceptional cases can extend to oral pleadings. For examples, see *Pretty v United Kingdom* 2002-III, discussed at para **4.53** below (leave given to the Voluntary Euthanasia Society and the Catholic Bishops' Conference of England and

Wales to intervene in the written procedure); *Emesa Sugar NV v Netherlands* (dec) (13 January 2005) (intervention by European Commission in examination of the question as to whether the respondent state could be held responsible for an alleged violation by a EU organ); and *Al-Saadoon and Mufdhi v United Kingdom* 2010-... (leave granted to the Equality and Human Rights Commission, the Bar Human Rights Committee of England and Wales, British Irish Rights Watch, the European Human Rights Advocacy Centre, Human Rights Watch, the International Commission of Jurists, the International Federation for Human Rights, JUSTICE, Liberty and REDRESS). An individual whose rights a state sought to protect in taking action which forms the subject of the application may also be permitted to submit comments: eg *T v United Kingdom* [GC] (16 December 1999), and *V v United Kingdom* [GC] 1999-IX (leave given to parents of murdered child to make written and oral submissions); and *Feldek v Slovakia* 2001-VIII, paras 68–71 (defamation action raised by a minister against the applicant in respect of statements concerning the minister's background). Where the applicant is a national of a Council of Europe state other than the respondent state, this state will be invited to submit observations. From 2007, communicated applications (together with the questions the Court wishes answered) are now published on the Court's website, an initiative designed primarily to assist NGOs to seek permission to intervene within the time limits specified. For discussion of NGO interventions, see Nowicki 'Non-Governmental Organisations (NGOs) before the European Commission of Human Rights' in de Salvia and Villiger (eds) *The Birth of European Human Rights Law* (1998), pp 267–273.

6   ECHR, Art 36(3); and Rule of Court 44(2).

GRAND CHAMBER

2.54 The Grand Chamber includes the President of the Court, the Vice-Presidents and Section Presidents, together with other judges chosen in accordance with Rules of Court[1]. The judge elected in respect of the respondent state in a case sits as an *ex officio* member of the Grand Chamber[2]. The Grand Chamber has three functions. First, it may give advisory opinions to the Committee of Ministers on legal questions (but not on matters concerning substantive guarantees under the ECHR)[3]. To date, only three such advisory opinions have been sought[4]. Secondly, it considers all inter-state cases, and individual applications where a Chamber has decided to relinquish jurisdiction. A Chamber may so decide where it feels that the case pending before it raises a serious question of interpretation or 'where the resolution of a question before it might have a result inconsistent with a judgment previously delivered by the Court', but may not do so if one of the parties to the case objects within one month[5]. The provision is designed to help ensure consistency in jurisprudence, but the 'veto' power seems inconsistent with this aim[6]. Thirdly, the Grand Chamber acts in effect as an appellate court when a case is referred to it following a judgment of a Chamber. As with proceedings before a Chamber, the parties may be invited to submit further evidence and written observations[7].

1   ECHR, Art 26(5). However, when a case has been referred to the Grand Chamber in terms of Art 43, no judge who took part in the Chamber judgment may sit with the exception of the President and the judge elected in respect of the respondent state.

2   ECHR, Art 26(4). See also Rules of Court 24(2) and 26(1). Rule of Court 30 provides that where two or more respondent states have a common interest of a 'common-interest' judge who will sit *ex officio*.

3   ECHR, Arts 31, 47–49 (cf Art 47(2): opinions may not deal with issues as to the content or scope of substantive rights and freedoms).

4   *Decision on the Competence of the Court to give an Advisory Opinion* [GC] 2004-VI (issue whether the Human Rights Commission for the Commonwealth of Independent States should be considered another procedure of international investigation within the meaning of ECHR, Art 35(2)(b): the Court declined to give an opinion as the question was one which could arise in the context of actual proceedings in future so that its competence to rule on this was excluded); and *Advisory Opinion on Certain Legal Questions Concerning the Lists of Candidates Submitted with a View to the Election of Judges to the European Court of Human Rights* [GC] 2008-...; and *Advisory Opinion on Certain Legal Questions Concerning the Lists of Candidates Submitted with a View to the Election of Judges to the European Court of Human Rights (no 2)* [GC] 2010-..., discussed at para **2.46**, fn 3 above.

5   ECHR, Art 30. Objections have to be 'duly reasoned': Rule of Court 72(2). In 2009, the sections referred only 7 cases: *European Court of Human Rights, Annual Report 2009* (2010), pp 135–136.

6   For an assessment, see Mowbray 'An Examination of the Work of the Grand Chamber of the European Court of Human Rights' [2007] PL 507.

7   See para **2.53**, fn 5 above.

REFERRAL OF CASES TO THE GRAND CHAMBER

2.55 A request for a referral of a Chamber judgment to the Grand Chamber should be made only 'in exceptional cases', and must be considered by a panel of five judges of the Grand Chamber to determine whether the case 'raises a serious question affecting the interpretation or application of the Convention ... or a serious issue of general importance'[1]. Since too liberal use of this provision will result in further delay in the final disposal of applications[2], referral is made in relatively few cases[3]. The practical result is that judgments of Chambers do not become final until the expiry of the three-month period or until the parties have confirmed that they do not intend to request a referral to the panel: consequently, care must be taken with the use of recent judgments of a Chamber. Where a case is referred, the Grand Chamber will proceed to examine afresh all aspects of the application declared admissible[4]. The composition of the Grand Chamber which will re-hear the case is somewhat contentious, for both the President of the Chamber and the 'national' judge (who will have been involved in the Chamber proceedings) will again sit[5].

1   ECHR, Art 43, and Rule of Court 73. The panel of five judges is determined by Rule 24 and comprises the President of the Court, two Presidents of Sections (determined by rotation), and two other judges from other Sections. It is open to the Grand Chamber to take into account new material not previously submitted as well as fresh arguments: cf *K and T v Finland* [GC] 2001-VII, para 147. It is clear that referral requests are indeed granted only in exceptional cases. For discussion of Art 43, see Costa 'Les Arrêts de la Grande Chambre rendus après Renvoi' in Caflisch, Callewaert, Liddell, Mahoney and Villiger (eds) *Liber Amicorum Luzius Wildhaber: Human Rights – Strasbourg Views* (2007), pp 133–144 at 135–139 (between 2002 and 2005, there were 572 requests (about 13% of all judgments) of which 49 (or about 8% of all requests) were accepted by the committee, implying that only about 1% of all judgments are reconsidered by the Grand Chamber; only in one case was the reference solely concerned with just satisfaction (*Kingsley v United Kingdom* [GC] 2002 IV); and in half the cases the

disposal by the Chamber was essentially confirmed, in 14% partly reversed, and in 36% entirely reversed).

2   Drzemczewski and Meyer-Ladewig 'Principal Characteristics of the New ECHR Control Mechanism, as Established by Protocol No 11' (1994) 15 HRLJ 81 at p 85.

3   For example, in 2009, the panel referred only 14 cases to the Grand Chamber, although requests were made in 359 cases (176 by the respondent states, and in five cases, by both the applicant and the Government): *European Court of Human Rights, Annual Report 2009* (2010), p 135.

4   *Göç v Turkey* [GC] 2002-V, at para 36 ('there is no basis for a merely partial referral of the case to the Grand Chamber'). Note that the Chamber judgment has no legal standing once a referral has been made, although it may serve as a 'source of guidance', at least where the Grand Chamber has ultimately deemed a case inadmissible: *Banfield v United Kingdom* (dec) 2005-XI.

5   ECHR, Art 26(5).

FACT-FINDING BY THE EUROPEAN COURT OF HUMAN RIGHTS

2.56 Under the original machinery, fact-finding was the responsibility of the Commission[1]. Article 38 of the ECHR provides that the Court is to 'pursue the examination' of any case declared admissible 'together with the representatives of the parties, and if need be, undertake an investigation, for the effective conduct of which the States concerned shall furnish all necessary facilities'. Both the applicant and the respondent state are expected to assist the Court, and the failure to do so may be taken into account. Thus a state may not determine unilaterally whether or not documents are relevant where an application contains a complaint that there has not been an effective investigation into an allegation of ill-treatment or unlawful killing[2]. While the Court's task is not to substitute its own assessment of the facts, it is not bound by determinations made by domestic courts, and remains free to make its own assessment depending upon all the evidence before it[3]. In normal circumstances, the Court makes use of any appropriate domestic evidence such as official reports[4], transcripts of inquiries[5], and similar sources. In exceptional cases where the facts are in dispute, the Court may carry out an investigation, again making use of existing documentary evidence and also where necessary by holding an inquiry, an on-site investigation or the taking of evidence[6], but there is no power to secure the production of evidence or to compel the attendance of witnesses and, on occasion, the assessment of facts can present particular difficulties[7].

1   ECHR, Arts 28(1) and 31 (original treaty). While the Court remained free to arrive at its own assessment, it would only depart from the Commission's findings in exceptional circumstances: eg *Akdivar and Others v Turkey* 1996-VI, para 78; *Kaya v Turkey* 1998-I, para 75.

2   *Khashiyev and Akayeva v Russia* (24 February 2005), paras 136–138 (inferences drawn by the Court, but no need to consider whether Art 34 responsibility engaged in view of the submission of two-thirds of the investigation file). Cf *Boicenco v Moldova* (11 July 2006), para 158 (refusal of access for a lawyer to a client's medical file involved interference with the right of individual petition).

3   *Ribitsch v Austria* (1995) A 336, para 32. However, it will only depart from the findings of domestic courts in the most compelling of cases: cf *Klaas v Germany* (1993) A 269, para 29.

4   Eg *Yaşa v Turkey* 1998-VI, paras 95–96.

5   Eg *McCann and Others v United Kingdom* (1995) A 324, paras 107–121.

6   See Rules of Court, Annex, Rules A1 – A7. Rule A5(4) provides, however, that a state party 'shall further take all reasonable steps to ensure the attendance of persons summoned who are under its authority or control'. For an example, see *Ilaşcu and Others v Moldova and Russia* [GC] 2004-VII, paras 12–15 (on-the-spot investigations into whether Moldova and the Russian Federation had jurisdiction in respect of Transdniestria; relations between Transdniestria, Moldova and the Russian Federation; and the applicant's conditions of detention). Obstruction of an investigation may lead to a finding of a violation of the right of individual petition under Art 38: see eg *Shamayev and Others v Georgia and Russia* 2005-III, para 504. A delegation may also be assisted by 'any person or institution ... in such manner as [the Court] sees fit': Rule A1(3). See eg *Hun v Turkey* (dec) (2 September 2004) (re-imprisonment of the applicant who was suffering from Wernicke-Korsakoff's syndrome following upon a hunger strike: this application (and some 17 other related applications) resulted in a fact-finding mission which also included a medical examination by a committee of experts appointed by the Court).

7   Cf *Denizci and Others v Cyprus* 2001-V at para 315: 'In a case where there are contradictory and conflicting factual accounts of events, the Court is acutely aware of its own shortcomings as a first instance tribunal of fact. [There are] problems of language ...; there is also an inevitable lack of detailed and direct familiarity with the conditions pertaining in the region. In addition, [there are no] powers of compulsion as regards attendance of witnesses'. For discussion, see Smith 'The Adjudicatory Fact-finding Tools of the European Court of Human Rights' [2009] EHRLR 206; and Leach et al 'Human Rights Fact-Finding: the European Court of Human Rights at a Crossroads' (2010) 28 NQHR 41.

2.57 The Court will generally arrive at its assessment of the facts free from issues of onus or standards of proof. However, in Article 2 cases involving deprivation of life and in Article 3 cases alleging ill-treatment, the requisite standard of proof is one of beyond reasonable doubt[1]. Further, when an individual suffers ill-treatment or dies while in the custody or control of the authorities, the burden of proof lies upon the state to furnish a satisfactory explanation, and failure to do so may give rise to a factual presumption. For example, where an individual in good health has been detained by state authorities but is released suffering from injuries, the state must provide a 'plausible explanation' to avoid an issue arising under Article 3[2]. In such cases, the requisite standard of proof may be reached through the co-existence of sufficiently strong, clear and concordant inferences or presumptions which the state has not been able to rebut[3], bearing in mind the seriousness and nature of the allegations made and the particular circumstances of each case[4].

1   *Ireland v United Kingdom* (1978) A 25, at paras 160–161. See further *Nachova and Others v Bulgaria* [GC] 2005-VII, at para 147 (establishment of whether racism was a causal factor in a fatal shooting):

'... in assessing evidence, the Court has adopted the standard of proof "beyond reasonable doubt". However, it has never been its purpose to borrow the approach of the national legal systems that use that standard. Its role is not to rule on criminal guilt or civil liability but on Contracting States' responsibility under the Convention. The specificity of its task under Article 19 of the Convention – to ensure the observance by the Contracting States of their engagement to secure the fundamental rights enshrined in the Convention – conditions its approach to the issues of evidence and proof. In the proceedings before the Court, there are no procedural barriers to the admissibility of evidence or pre-determined formulae for its assessment. It adopts the conclusions that are, in its view, supported by the free evaluation of all evidence, including such inferences as may flow from the facts and the parties' submissions. According to its established case-law, proof may follow from the coexistence of sufficiently strong, clear and concordant inferences or of similar unrebutted presumptions of fact. Moreover, the level of persuasion necessary for reaching a particular conclusion and, in this connection, the distribution of the burden of proof are intrinsically linked to the specificity of the facts, the nature of the allegation made and the Convention right at stake. The Court is also attentive to the seriousness that attaches to a ruling that a Contracting State has violated fundamental rights....'

2   Eg *Aksoy v Turkey* 1996-VI, para 61; *Hugh Jordan v United Kingdom* 2001-III, at para 103; *Salman v Turkey* [GC] 2000-VII, para 100. But note *Avsar v Turkey*, para 284 (domestic criminal law liability is distinct from international law responsibility of a state for the acts of its organs and agents, and thus the Court is not concerned with reaching any findings as to guilt or innocence).

3   *Aydin v Turkey* 1997-VI, at para 70.

4   *Yaşa v Turkey* 1998-VI, at para 96.

Admissibility criteria

2.58 ECHR, Article 35 details the criteria for admissibility of an application lodged by an individual. Detailed discussion of these criteria is beyond the scope of this work, as is consideration of the practicalities of lodging an application[1]. The vast majority of registered applications are declared inadmissible, and thus fall at this stage of proceeding[2]. A decision declaring an application inadmissible is final[3]. The principal issues considered in determining admissibility include: prior exhaustion of available domestic remedies; lodging an application within six months of the taking of the final decision; and compatibility *ratione temporis*, *ratione loci*, *ratione personae*, and *ratione materiae*. In addition, the Court will not deal with any application which is anonymous[4], or is substantially the same as a matter that has already been examined and which contains no relevant new information, or is 'manifestly ill-founded' or considered an abuse of the right of petition[5]. A new admissibility criterion has been introduced by Protocol no 14 permitting the Court to reject an application where the victim has not 'suffered a significant disadvantage'[6].

1   For a fuller discussion of the practicalities of making an application to the Court, see Leach *Taking a Case to the European Court of Human Rights* (2nd edn, 2005), pp 19–160; Reid *A Practitioner's Guide to the European Convention on Human Rights* (3rd edn, 2007), pp 10–43; van Dijk and van Hoof *Theory and Practice of the European Convention on Human Rights* (4th edn, 2006), pp 121–204; and European Court of Human Rights *Practical Guide on Admissibility Criteria* (2010).

2   In 2009, for example, some 93% of admissibility decisions adopted involved applications being declared inadmissible (with another 3% being struck out): *European Court of Human Rights, Annual Report 2009* (2010), p 139.

3   But note the Court's power under Art 37(2) to restore an application to the list: Reid *A Practitioner's Guide to the European Convention on Human Rights* (3rd edn, 2007), at p 42 notes this power is exercised where the Court has made an error of fact of relevance in determination of admissibility, and possibly, where new circumstances have arisen.

4   See eg *'Blondje' v Netherlands* (dec) 2009-....

5   ECHR, Art 35(1) requires an applicant to have exhausted domestic remedies and to have made a complaint within six months of the date on which the final decision was taken. These requirements apply to all applications, including inter-state applications. The additional requirements apply in respect of individual complaints. Thus an inter-state case cannot be declared inadmissible for being substantially the same as a previous application or as an abuse of the right of petition: 8007/77, *Cyprus v Turkey* (1978) DR 13, 85; and (1983) DR 72, 5.

6   ECHR, Art 35(3)(b), discussed at para **2.62** below.

EXHAUSTION OF DOMESTIC REMEDIES

2.59 The requirement that an applicant has sought to exhaust domestic remedies is further recognition of the supervisory nature of the Strasbourg Court. The purpose is to afford an opportunity to states to prevent or put right an alleged violation of an ECHR guarantee before the matter is considered by an international institution[1]. However, an applicant need only have recourse to 'remedies which are available and capable of remedying the breaches alleged'. In other words, 'the existence of the remedies in question must be sufficiently certain not only in theory but in practice'[2]. Further, the 'remedy' in question must be binding on the authorities, with the consequence that a declaration of incompatibility made under the HRA 1998 does not qualify[3]. Where a new remedy has been introduced following the lodging of an application, an applicant will also be expected to have recourse to this remedy[4]. The burden is upon the state which claims that this requirement has not been met by an applicant to establish that an effective remedy existed; but once this has been achieved, the onus is then on the applicant to show why the remedy advanced by the state was not an effective one in the circumstances. In examining this matter, the Court takes a realistic account 'not only of the formal remedies in the legal system of the Contracting Party concerned but also of the context in which they operate and the personal circumstances of the applicant'[5]. Further, since the context in which the requirement of exhaustion is being considered is that of human rights protection, the rule is applied 'with some degree of flexibility and without excessive formalism'[6]. Thus an applicant need only seek to utilise challenges capable of furnishing him with a remedy, and cannot be criticised for any reasonable determination by him in this regard[7]. Nor need the Convention right be raised explicitly in domestic proceedings, for as long as the issue was raised in substance, the requirement will be deemed to be met[8]. The requirement may be waived by the state[9].

1   *Akdivar and Others v Turkey* 1996-IV, para 66.

2   *Beïs v Greece* 1997-II, para 32. Determination of the character of the remedy is for the Court: *Jeličić v Bosnia and Herzegovina* (dec) 2005–XII (BiH Human Rights Chamber involved 'domestic' proceedings). An application already considered by an international tribunal will be inadmissible in terms of Art 35(2)(b): see para **2.63** below.

3   *Hobbs v United Kingdom* (dec) (18 June 2002): 'In particular, a declaration is not binding on the parties to the proceedings in which it is made. Furthermore, by virtue of section 10(2) of the 1998 Act, a declaration of incompatibility provides the appropriate minister with a power, not a duty, to amend the offending legislation by order so as to make it compatible with the

Convention. The minister concerned can only exercise that power if he considers that there are "compelling reasons" for doing so.' See also eg *Walker v United Kingdom* (dec) (16 March 2004).

4   *Brusco v Italy* (dec) 2001-IX. For discussion of 'pilot judgments' requiring the implementation of an effective remedy, see paras **2.80–2.81** below.

5   *Beïs v Greece* 1997-II, at para 32. See also *Isayeva and Others v Russia* (24 February 2005), para 150 (special circumstances existed which affected the applicants' obligation to exhaust remedies in that law-enforcement bodies were not functioning properly in Chechnya at the time). Exceptionally, the Court may take notice itself of domestic remedies: see eg 20946/92 *Veenstra v United Kingdom* (31 August 1994) cited in Reid *A Practitioner's Guide to the European Convention on Human Rights* (3rd edn, 2007), p 30. See further Robertson 'Exhaustion of Local Remedies in International Human Rights Litigation: the Burden of Proof Reconsidered' (1990) 39 ICLQ 191.

6   *Akdivar and Others v Turkey* 1996-IV, at para 69; *Aksoy v Turkey* 1996-VI, paras 53 and 54.

7   See eg *Airey v Ireland* (1979) A 32, para 23; 19092/91 *Yaÿiz v Turkey* (1993) DR 75, 207; and *Hilal v United Kingdom* (dec) (8 February 2000).

8   *Castells v Spain* (1992) A 236, para 32; and *Azinas v Cyprus* [GC] 2004-III, paras 40–41.

9   *De Wilde, Ooms and Versyp v Belgium* (1971) A 12, para 55. The respondent government's failure to argue exhaustion of domestic remedies will also bar it from relying upon this point subsequently, in contrast to the six months rule: see eg *Steel and Others v United Kingdom* 1998-VII, paras 62–65 (withdrawal of a prosecution against the applicants who had been arrested during a peaceful protest and who in turn had not sought to bring an action of civil damages for false imprisonment: in view of the respondent government's failure to raise a preliminary objection on the grounds of failure to exhaust domestic remedies, the Court itself decided to consider the lawfulness of the detention, and concluded that this had been unlawful in domestic law since there had been no indication that the protest had been anything other than peaceful).

THE SIX MONTHS RULE

2.60 The primary purpose of the requirement that an application must be made within six months from the taking of a final decision or act is to help ensure legal certainty and assist in the establishment of the facts. The rule is closely related to the admissibility requirement of exhaustion of domestic remedies, but only remedies which are normal and effective can be taken into account (and thus an applicant cannot extend the strict time-limit imposed under the Convention by seeking to make inappropriate or misconceived applications to bodies or institutions which have no power or competence to offer effective redress for the complaint)[1]. An application is lodged on the date of the applicant's first letter (rather than on the date of formal registration by the Court), provided that the letter or other form of written communication sufficiently indicates the purpose of the application[2]. The period begins to run from the point when the final outcome of domestic procedures is made known to the applicant or to his legal representative[3]. Where there are no effective domestic remedies, the period will begin to run from the date of the state action[4] or, in certain cases, from the date of the applicant's knowledge of an interference[5]. The rule is inapplicable where there is a continuing situation giving rise to an interference, for example in the form of a legislative provision[6] (rather than a situation attributable to a particular decision or event)[7]. The rule is an absolute one which cannot be waived and will be applied even if the respondent state does not raise the issue[8].

1   *Fernie v United Kingdom* (dec) (5 January 2006).

2   *Papageorgiou v Greece* 1997-VI, at para 32; *Otto v Germany* (dec) 2009-… (six-month period ran from day after the final domestic decision reached the applicant and the last day of the period fell on a Saturday, but the application was not lodged until the following Monday: inadmissible as lodged out of time, even although the applicant may well have believed that the deadline was extended to the next working day). Cf *Arslan v Turkey* (dec) 2002-X (date of posting taken as relevant date rather than date purporting to be when the letter was written where the unexplained difference was several days).

3   *Worm v Austria* 1997-V, at para 32. See also *O'Hara v United Kingdom* (dec) (14 March 2000) (domestic proceedings challenging the lawfulness of detention in 1986 which, if successful, would have resulted in the payment of compensation concluded in 1996: six-month period in the circumstances ran from the dismissal of the appeal and not from the date of release from detention); and *Sapeyan v Armenia* (13 January 2009), paras 20–27 (decision by appeal court to consider final and binding decision: running of the six-month period was interrupted only in relation to issues examined in the extraordinary appeal).

4   Eg 14807/89, *Agrotexim and Others v Greece* (1992) DR 72, 148.

5   *Gongadze v Ukraine* 2005-XI, para 155. Cf 12015/86, *Hilton v United Kingdom* (1988) DR 57, 108 (applicant became aware of possible subjection to vetting process only nine years after the event: six-month rule ran from the date of knowledge).

6   Eg *Dudgeon v United Kingdom* (1981) A 45, para 42 (applicant directly affected by legislation penalising homosexual conduct); and 8440/78 *Christians against Racism and Fascism v United Kingdom* (1981) DR 21, 138 (period ran from date the applicant was actually affected in the case of a continuing prohibition against processions, not start date of general measure).

7   Eg 12659/87, *Gama da Costa v Portugal* (1990) DR 65, 136.

8   See for example 10416/83, *K v Ireland* (1984) DR 38, 158.

COMPATIBILITY WITH ECHR GUARANTEES

2.61 An application which is incompatible with a state's international obligations will be rejected. There are four aspects to compatibility (that is, whether a complaint falls within the scope of the state's obligations): compatibility *ratione temporis*, *ratione loci*, *ratione personae*, and *ratione materiae*. Compatibility *ratione temporis* concerns the question whether the facts giving rise to an allegation of violation occurred after the state's acceptance of the obligation (or recognition of the right of individual petition where this is expressly limited to events occurring after the relevant date)[1]. Compatibility *ratione loci* requires the violation to have taken place within the jurisdiction of the respondent state or over territory effectively controlled by the state[2]. Compatibility *ratione personae* requires that the alleged violation can be imputable to a state and thus rules out complaints not directed against a state authority or public body or involving the exercise or failure to exercise state responsibility[3], or complaints by individuals who cannot qualify as 'victims'[4] or complaints brought against international agencies that are not contracting states[5]. Compatibility *ratione materiae* excludes a complaint seeking to enforce a right which is not included in the ECHR[6] or one which falls outside the scope of a particular provision[7].

1   An act or fact taking place before the date of entry into force or any situation which ceased to exist before this date thus cannot be considered by the Court: eg *LCB v United Kingdom* 1998-III, para 35 (no jurisdiction to examine complaints under Arts 2, 8 and 13 concerning monitoring of exposure to radiation since these were based on events occurring before the UK's acceptance of the right of individual petition). See further *Blečič v Croatia* [GC] 2006-III, paras 63–92; and *Teren Aksakal v Turkey* 2007-X, paras 61–77. But note *Šilih v Slovenia* [GC] (9 April 2009), paras 140–167 (clarification of temporal jurisdiction to hear complaints under Art 2 procedural limb where death had occurred before the entry into force of the ECHR: since the obligation to carry out an effective investigation had evolved into a separate and autonomous duty which could thus be considered a detachable obligation binding the state even when the death took place before the entry into force of the Convention). For discussion of continuing violations following upon acceptance of Convention responsibility, see paras **5.160–5.161** below (in respect of fair hearing guarantees). See also Vaji 'Ratione Temporis Jurisdiction of the (new) European Court of Human Rights' in Caflisch, Callewaert, Liddell, Mahoney and Villiger (eds) *Liber Amicorum Luzius Wildhaber: Human Rights – Strasbourg Views* (2007), pp 483–505 at 495–504.

2   For further discussion of Art 1, see paras **3.03–3.10** below. Note ECHR, Art 56 (a state may extend the territorial application of the Convention to dependent territories by means of a declaration), discussed at para **3.04** below.

3   In other words, the alleged violation must be attributable in some manner to the State, either through direct action or a failure to discharge a positive obligation (for example, in ensuring domestic law regulates the behaviour of private parties in a manner compatible with Convention guarantees): see further paras **3.11–3.12** below. If the complaint involves a particular optional protocol, the state must have ratified this protocol. For discussion of imputability, see *Assanidze v Georgia* [GC] 2004-II, paras 144–150; and *Hussein v Albania and 20 Other Contracting States* (dec) (14 March 2006).

4   For discussion of 'victim' status, see paras **2.64–2.73** below.

5   See paras **3.15–3.19** below.

6   Eg *Johnston v Ireland* (1986) A 112, paras 51–54 (Art 12 does not support a right to divorce). Note also *Haase and Others v Germany* (dec) (12 February 2008) (it is not for the Court to verify whether a state has complied with the obligations imposed on it by one of the Court's judgments).

7   Eg *Botta v Italy* 1998-I, at para 35 (asserted right to gain access to the beach during holidays involved 'interpersonal relations of such broad and indeterminate scope' which fell outwith Art 8).

No 'significant disadvantage'

2.62 With the entry into force of Protocol no 14, the Court may now declare an application inadmissible if the applicant has not 'suffered a significant disadvantage' unless 'respect for human rights' requires an examination of the application on the merits, but always provided that no case can be rejected on this admissibility criterion if it has not been 'duly considered by a domestic tribunal'[1]. It is not yet clear how 'significant disadvantage' will be interpreted: the financial impact of the matter in dispute is one relevant factor[2]. The essence is that the matter 'should attain a minimum level of severity to warrant consideration by an international court'; but 'the severity of a violation should be assessed, taking account of both the applicant's subjective perceptions and what is objectively at stake in a particular case'[3].

1   ECHR, Art 35(3)(b).

2   *Ionescu v Romania* (dec) (1 June 2010) (sum involved was €90: inadmissible).

3   *Korolev v Russia* (dec) 2010-… (issue involved less than €1: inadmissible)

ADDITIONAL ADMISSIBILITY REQUIREMENTS

2.63 In addition, Article 35 requires the Court to reject an application which is anonymous[1], or is substantially the same as a matter that has already been examined by the Court and which contains no relevant new information[2], or one that is considered an abuse of the right of petition[3]. Further, significant numbers of applications are rejected on preliminary examination as 'manifestly ill-founded', that is the facts are unsubstantiated or do not disclose an interference with a ECHR right or the interference can be considered as justifiable[4]. Nor may the Court deal with a complaint which has already been submitted to another procedure of international investigation and settlement, if the complaint contains no relevant new information[5].

1   Eg 10983/84, *Confédération des Syndicats Médicaux Français et la Fédération Nationale des Infirmiers v France* (1986) DR 47, 225 (application on behalf of unidentified individuals, the association itself lacking victim status); but cf 8118/77, *Omkarananda and Divine Light Zentrum v Switzerland* (1981) DR 25, 105 (a church body or an association with religious and philosophical objects is capable of possessing and exercising the rights contained in Art 9 in its own capacity as a representative of its members).

2   *Manuel v Portugal* (dec) (25 September 2003). An application is only 'substantially the same' as another if it concerns substantially not only the same facts and complaints but is introduced by the same persons: *Varnava and Others v Turkey* [GC] 2009-…, paras 162–172 (an inter-state application does not deprive individual applicants of the possibility of introducing their own applications). However, if no formal decision has been given, the matter can be examined: *Sürmeli v Germany* (dec) (29 April 2004).

3   Thus applications seeking to deceive the Court by failing to disclose the full facts may be considered an abuse of the right of individual complaint: *Al-Nashif v Bulgaria* (20 June 2002), para 89. See too 11208/84, *McQuiston v United Kingdom* (1986) DR 46, 182 (an application may be an abuse of the right of petition if motivated by the desire for publicity and not supported by any facts); cf *Sidiropoulos and Others v Greece* 1998-IV, paras 28–29 (objection that the applicants were seeking to raise a question concerning the political relations between two countries rejected).

4   Eg 37664/97, *RC and AWA and Others v United Kingdom* (1998) DR 94, 119 (prohibition of possession of small-calibre pistols involved a complaint relating to the right to pursue a hobby and not one falling within the scope of Prot 1, Art 1: manifestly ill-founded). See European Court of Human Rights *Practical Guide on Admissibility Criteria* (2010), para 344: 'Manifestly ill-founded complaints can be divided into four categories: "fourth-instance" complaints [attempts to have the Court address errors of fact or law], complaints where there has clearly or apparently been no violation, unsubstantiated complaints and, finally, confused or far-fetched complaints'.

5   ECHR, Art 35(2)(b). The applications must relate to the same persons, facts and complaints: 24872/94, *Pauger v Austria* (1995) DR 80A, 170 (complaint to UN Human Rights Committee declared inadmissible precluded application under the ECHR); cf *Jeličić v Bosnia and Herzegovina* (dec) 2005-XII (BiH Human Rights Chamber did not constitute an 'international procedure'); *Mikolenko v Estonia* (dec) (5 January 2006) (previous application concerned

'1503 procedure' and had not involved examination of an individual complaint); and *Celniku v Greece* (5 July 2007), paras 38–41 (previous use of '1503 procedure' to examine the incident had been raised by another complainant). See also *Folgerø and Others v Norway* [GC] 2007-VIII (discussion in minority opinions as to whether the application should be considered inadmissible on this heading). See Wildhaber 'The Case-Law of the European Court on Human Rights' in Delas, Côté, Crépeau and Leuprecht *Les Jurisdictions Internationales: Complémentarité ou Concurrence?* (2005), pp 3–4 (wording of ICCPR, Optional Protocol, Art 5(2)(a) and ECHR, Art 35(2)(b) suggest that an applicant who raises an issue first under the Optional Protocol is precluded from raising the matter before the Court, but not vice versa, noting 17512/90, *Fornieles and Mato v Spain* (1992) DR 73, 214, where the Commission declared inadmissible a complaint since this was simultaneously being examined by the UN Human Rights Committee). Problems of forum-shopping and inconsistent decisions from international tribunals are discussed in O'Boyle '*Ne Bis in Idem* For the Benefit of States?' in Caflisch, Callewaert, Liddell, Mahoney and Villiger (eds) *Liber Amicorum Luzius Wildhaber: Human Rights – Strasbourg Views* (2007), pp 329–346 at 331–334 (discussion of *De Matos v Portugal* (dec) 2001-XII (complaint under Art 6(3)(c) concerning refusal to allow accused to defend himself dismissed as manifestly ill-founded; subsequently, his communication to the Human Rights Committee, Communication 1123/2002 (28 March 2006) was examined under First Optional Protocol to International Covenant on Civil and Political Rights, the Committee holding that his rights under ICCPR, Art 14(3)(d) had not been respected)).

Meaning of 'victim'

2.64 In terms of Article 34, the Court 'may receive applications from any person, non-governmental organisation or group of individuals claiming to be the victim' of a violation of a substantive ECHR guarantee by a state. This is irrespective of nationality[1]. A person can claim to be a 'victim' of an interference with the exercise of a right guaranteed under the Convention 'in the absence of an individual measure of implementation, [also] if they run the risk of being directly affected by it'[2]. The issue of whether a person has actually been a victim of a violation may be one which can only be determined after consideration of the merits of the application[3]. However, only exceptionally can an applicant claim to be a 'victim' on account of the risk of a future violation of the Convention, and reasonable and convincing evidence of the likelihood that a violation affecting the applicant personally will occur is necessary[4]. Bearing in mind the need to ensure that ECHR guarantees are practical and effective, the necessary standing to qualify as a 'victim' is interpreted broadly, and the term is thus given an autonomous meaning[5].

1 For consideration of applications brought by non-nationals, see Dembour 'Human Rights Law and National Sovereignty in Collusion: the Plight of Quasi-Nationals at Strasbourg' (2003) 21 NQHR 63.

2 *Norris v Ireland* (1988) A 142, at para 31. See also *Klass and Others v Germany* (1978) A 28, paras 32–34. For discussion of recognition of 'victim' in respect of specific articles, see further para **4.06** (Art 2), para **4.62** (Art 3), para **7.20** (Art 9), para **7.128** (Art 11) and para **8.07** (Prot 1, Art 1) below.

3 *Marckx v Belgium* (1979) A 31, para 27.

4 *Rossi and Others v Italy* (dec) 2008-... (challenges involving decision to authorise discontinuation of artificial nutrition and hydration in respect of severely disabled persons).

5 *Gorraiz Lizarraga and Others v Spain* 2004-III, para 38. For a fuller account, see eg Van Dijk and Van Hoof *Theory and Practice of the European Convention on Human Rights* (4th edn,

2006), pp 55–81. See also the House of Lords case of *R (Rusbridger) v Attorney General* [2004] 1 AC 357 (courts will not accommodate litigation seeking to found a declaration as to the Convention compatibility of manifestly outdated legislation which imposed no real threat to the applicants as this was a matter for Parliament.)

DIRECT VICTIMS

2.65 The ECHR does not permit an *actio popularis*. Individuals, associations or campaigning groups cannot therefore complain against a law *in abstracto* simply because they feel that it contravenes the ECHR[1]. The applicant must be directly affected in some way by the matter complained of[2].

1   *Klass and Others v Germany* (1978) A 28, para 33.
2   *Amuur v France* 1996–III, para 36.

2.66 A 'victim' need not be prejudiced by the act or omission in question, provided that he is directly affected by it[1]. The existence of injury is thus not relevant, although the existence of prejudice is, however, relevant to the award of just satisfaction under Article 41[2].

1   *Eckle v Germany* (1982) A 51, para 66; *Lüdi v Switzerland* (1992) A 238, paras 31–34.
2   *Eckle v Germany* (1983) A 65, paras 20–24; *Lüdi v Switzerland* (1992) A 238, para 52.

2.67 The range of persons directly affected by a legal situation can, however, be extremely wide. For example, all users or potential users of a state's postal or telecommunication services could claim to be directly affected by legislation which provided for secret surveillance[1]. In another case, all women of childbearing age could claim to be victims of an injunction against the provision of information about abortion facilities[2].

1   *Klass and Others v Germany* (1978) A 28, para 33. See also *The Association for European Integration and Human Rights and Ekimdzhiev v Bulgaria* (28 June 2007), paras 58–62 (since all users of the postal and telecommunications services potentially could be subjected to surveillance, a legal person such as an association could also establish 'victim' status for the purposes of Art 8).
2   *Open Door and Dublin Well Woman v Ireland* (1992) A 246, para 44.

2.68 The term 'victim' is not restricted to persons who can establish that their rights have actually been violated. A person who establishes that there is a reasonable likelihood that his rights have been violated can be treated as a 'victim'[1]. It can also suffice if persons run the risk of being directly affected by the legal situation of which complaint is made[2]. Thus persons can be 'victims' even if they have not been individually affected by the implementation of the law complained of. Individuals have been held to be 'victims' by virtue of legal situations which, for example, criminalised homosexual behaviour or stigmatised untraditional families, even in the absence of the practical enforcement of the laws in question[3]. On the other hand, where there will be no violation of a convention right unless a particular decision is taken (eg as to deportation), a person cannot claim to be a 'victim' unless and until such a decision is in fact made[4].

1   *Halford v United Kingdom* 1997-III, paras 47–48; *Klass v Germany* (1978) A 28, paras 30–32; 12015/86, *Hilton v United Kingdom* (1988) DR 57, 108.

2   *Campbell and Cosans v United Kingdom* (1982) A 48, para 26; *Soering v United Kingdom* (1989) A 161, paras 81–91; *Marckx v Belgium* (1979) A 31, paras 25–27.

3   *Dudgeon v United Kingdom* (1981) A 45, para 41; *Marckx v Belgium* (1979) A 31, paras 25–27; cf *X, Y and Z v United Kingdom* 1997-II, paras 36–43.

4   *Vijayanathan and Pusparajah v France* (1992) A 241–B, para 46; 9214/80, 9473/81 and 9474/81, *X, Cabales and Balkandali v United Kingdom* (1982) DR 29, 176; contrast *Soering v United Kingdom* (1989) A 161.

INDIRECT VICTIMS

2.69 A person may be a 'victim' in his own right if he is directly affected by the violation of another person's rights (eg the spouse of a person who is to be deported, allegedly in breach of Article 8)[1]. A person may also be an 'indirect victim' if, broadly speaking, he is prejudiced by the violation of another person's rights (notably, if he is the spouse or parent of a person killed in violation of Article 2)[2]. However, there must be a personal and specific link between the direct victim and the applicant[3]. The status of 'indirect victim' should be distinguished from the question whether a person is entitled, under Strasbourg procedure, to bring proceedings in a representative capacity (eg if he is the parent of a young child or the guardian of a person of unsound mind[4] or a close relative or heir following the death of the applicant[5]). These categories tend to merge, and clear principles are difficult to state with confidence.

1   9214/80, 9473/81 and 9474/81, *X, Cabales and Balkandali v United Kingdom* (1982) 29 DR 176, para 65; *X, Y and Z v United Kingdom* 1997-II.

2   Eg, *McCann and Others v United Kingdom* (1995) A 324, para 151.

3   Cf *Çakıcı v Turkey* [GC] 1999-IV, paras 98–99 (brother of 'disappeared' person not a 'victim'); and *Dupin v Croatia* (dec) (7 July 2009) (application had been filed by widow on behalf of her late husband and after his death: the case had not been brought by a person who could be regarded as an applicant for the purposes of Art 34: incompatible *ratione personae*).

4   Eg *Campbell and Cosans v United Kingdom* (1980) A 48, Comm Rep para 112. Note that a child may also bring an application in his own right: eg 13134/87, *Costello-Roberts v United Kingdom* (13 December 1990) (no question that his mother had waived his rights under Arts 3 and 8).

5   *Karner v Austria* 2003-IX, para 25. See also *Micallef v Malta* [GC] 2009-…, paras 44–51 (applicant's sister had died while her constitutional claim concerning the allegation of unfair trial right to a fair trial was pending: victim status of brother upheld).

LEGAL PERSONS AND VOLUNTARY ASSOCIATIONS

2.70 Legal persons, such as companies, can be 'victims'[1]. Shareholders cannot claim to be 'victims' in respect of a violation of the rights of the company, other than in exceptional circumstances (for example, if it is impossible for the company to bring a complaint)[2]. A company can be a 'victim' even if dissolved or in receivership[3].

1   Eg *Observer Ltd and Guardian Newspapers Ltd v United Kingdom* (1991) A 216, para 49. For discussion of whether a shareholder rather than the company can qualify as a 'victim' in property rights cases, see para **8.07** below. A company is also protected by Art 8 in respect of privacy: *Société Colas Est and Others v France* 2002-III, paras 40–42. See further Fura-Sandström 'Business and Human Rights – Who Cares? In Caflisch, Callewaert, Liddell, Mahoney and Villiger (eds) *Liber Amicorum Luzius Wildhaber: Human Rights – Strasbourg Views* (2007), pp 159–176.

2   *Agrotexim and Others v Greece* (1995) A 330-A, paras 59–72. For domestic discussion, see *Humberclyde Finance Group Ltd v Hicks and Others* (14 November 2001, unreported) ChD (following *Agrotexim*, shareholders' Convention rights were not infringed on account of decisions taken by the state).

3   *Pine Valley Developments Ltd and Others v Ireland* (1991) A 222, paras 40–43.

2.71 Associations can be 'victims' if their own rights are violated[1]. Further, the Court now recognises that associations are often established by individuals with a view to defending their interests, particularly in respect of complex administrative decision-making, and thus associations are permitted to bring complaints on behalf of their members[2]. The refusal of domestic law to recognise the legal personality of an organisation (in the particular case, a church) can itself constitute a violation of the ECHR[3].

1   Eg 11603/85, *Council of Civil Service Unions v United Kingdom* (1987) DR 50, 228. See also *Unédic v France* (18 December 2008), paras 48–58 (association responsible for managing an insurance scheme covering employees' claims qualified as a non-governmental organisation).

2   *Gorraiz Lizarraga and Others v Spain* 2004-III, para 39. Cf 7805/77, *X and Church of Scientology v Sweden* (1979) DR 16, 68; 10581/83, *Norris v Ireland* (1988) DR 44, 132.

3   *Catholic Church of Canea v Greece* 1997-VIII, paras 32–42. See further para **7.20** below.

2.72 Governmental organisations, such as local authorities, cannot be 'victims'[1]. This follows from the terms of Article 34, which permits applications to be received from 'any person, non-governmental organisation or group of individuals claiming to be a victim of a violation by one of the High Contracting Parties of the rights set forth in the Convention or the protocols thereto'. However, certain public institutions not exercising governmental powers may also qualify as 'victims'[2].

1   13252/87, *Rothenthurm Commune v Switzerland* (1989) DR 59, 251; and *The Municipal Section of Antilly v France* (dec) 1999-VIII.

2   *Radio France and Others v France* (dec) 2003-X. See also *Österreichischer Rundfunk v Austria* (7 December 2006), paras 46–53 (Austrian Broadcasting Corporation could qualify as a non-governmental organisation in light of its editorial and journalistic independence, ability to set its own programme fees, and lack of governmental control); and *MacKay and BBC Scotland v United Kingdom* (7 December 2010), paras 18–19 (public broadcasting corporations). Cf 34324/96, *BBC Scotland, McDonald, Rodgers and Donald v United Kingdom* (23 October 1997) (question whether a state public service broadcaster could qualify as a 'victim' left open). See also *Islamic Republic of Iran Shipping Lines v Turkey* 2007-XIV, paras 80–81

(state-owned company was financially and legally independent of the state of Iran and could qualify as a 'victim').

LOSS OF VICTIM STATUS

2.73 The question whether an applicant can claim to be the victim of the violation alleged is relevant at all stages of the proceedings[1]. A person may not be treated as a 'victim' if the violation of his Convention rights has been acknowledged and redressed by the domestic authorities[2]. A case will thus be struck out if there has been settlement of the case by the domestic authorities[3], always providing there has been explicit or substantial recognition of the violation as well as appropriate and sufficient redress[4] dependent on all the circumstances of the case and having regard to the nature of the Convention violation at stake[5]. An applicant's 'victim' status may thus depend on the level of compensation awarded at domestic level. However, in respect of cases of wilful ill-treatment, 'the breach of Article 3 cannot be remedied only by an award of compensation to the victim... because if the authorities could confine their reaction to incidents of wilful ill-treatment by State agents to the mere payment of compensation, while not doing enough to prosecute and punish those responsible, it would be possible in some cases for agents of the State to abuse the rights of those within their control with virtual impunity, and the general legal prohibition of torture and inhuman and degrading treatment, despite its fundamental importance, would be ineffective in practice'[6]. As noted, a case may be continued after an applicant's death when it raises an important question of public interest relevant to human rights[7].

1   *Gäfgen v Germany* [GC] 2010-..., para 115.

2   Eg *Eckle v Germany* (1982) A 51. See for recent discussion *Cocchiarella v Italy* [GC] 2006-V, paras 70–72 (deprivation of victim status needs state acknowledgment of violation expressly or in substance and redress).

3   Eg *Sisojeva and Others v Latvia* [GC] 2007-II.

4   Eg *Normann v Denmark* (dec) (14 June 2001); and *Bazhenov v Russia* (20 October 2005), paras 37–41 (no loss of victim status unless the authorities acknowledge the violation expressly or in substance and then provide compensation).

5   *Gäfgen v Germany* [GC] 2010-..., para 116.

6   *Gäfgen v Germany* [GC] 2010-..., paras 118–119 at para 119.

7   See para **2.69**, fn 3 above.

DECISIONS OF DOMESTIC COURTS CONCERNING 'VICTIMS'

2.74 The Human Rights Act 1998, s 7(7) provides that a person is to be regarded as a victim of an unlawful act under the statute only if he would be a 'victim' for the purposes of Article 34 of the Convention if proceedings were brought in the European Court of Human Rights in respect of that act. The same test is applied by s 100(1) of the Scotland Act 1998. Article 34 has therefore been considered in numerous decisions of the domestic courts of the United Kingdom. It has been held, consistently with the Strasbourg jurisprudence, that it is sufficient to establish a claim to victim status that the person advancing that claim be a member of a class of people who risk being directly affected by the legislation, and that in order to determine whether a person is a member of such a class it is appropriate to look at the reality of the situation. Insurers who had provided employers' liability insurance were accordingly 'victims' of alleged breaches of Convention rights resulting from legislation which imposed retrospective liabilities on employers[1]. A trade association (as distinct from its members) cannot be regarded as a victim where it is not itself directly affected by the act in question[2]. A local authority cannot be a victim, since it is not a non-governmental authority[3]; nor can an NHS trust, for the same reason[4]. It has been said that a parochial church council, on the other hand, is a non-governmental authority, since it was not established with a view to public administration as part of the process of government[5]. Different views were expressed, *obiter,* as to whether a newspaper qualified as a 'victim' in respect of a law prohibiting the publication of articles urging the abolition of the monarchy, where the risk of prosecution was so remote as to be fanciful[6]. It has been suggested that the fact that someone has been awarded compensation by the European Court of Human Rights as 'just satisfaction' for a violation of a Convention obligation may not necessarily mean that he has ceased to be a 'victim' within the meaning of s 7 of the Human Rights Act[7]. A person cannot be the victim of an unlawful act for the purposes of the Act if the act or omission in question took place before the Act came into force[8]. It has been accepted that the meaning of 'victim' can extend to close relatives of an individual who had allegedly fallen victim to a violation of his or her Convention rights[9].

1   *Axa General Insurance Ltd v Lord Advocate* [2011] SLT 439.

2   *In re Medicaments and Related Classes of Goods (No 4)* [2002] 1 WLR 269.

3   *R (Westminster City Council) v Mayor of London* [2002] EWCA 2440.

4   *Grampian University Hospitals NHS Trust v Napier* 2004 JC 117.

5   *Aston Cantlow and Wilmcote with Billesley Parochial Church Council v Wallbank* [2004] 1 AC 546 at para 50 per Lord Hope of Craighead and at paras 164–166 per Lord Rodger of Earlsferry.

6   *R (Rusbridger) v Attorney General* [2004] 1 AC 357.

7   *In re McKerr* [2004] 1 WLR 807 per Lord Nicholls of Birkenhead and Lord Steyn.

8   *In re McKerr* [2004] 1 WLR 807; *R (Hooper) v Secretary of State for Work and Pensions* [2005] 1 WLR 1681.

9   *Al Hassan-Daniel v Revenue and Customs Commissioners* [2011] 2 WLR 488.

Friendly settlements; and striking out

2.75 At any stage of the proceedings, the Court may make itself available to assist the parties to achieve a friendly settlement[1]. If a friendly settlement is reached, the case will be struck out. It is also possible for a case to be struck out where the Court concludes that the matter has been resolved, or that the applicant does not intend to pursue the application, or that continuation of the examination of the application is no longer justified unless respect for human rights requires its continuation[2]. Provision is also made for the Court to restore a case to the list[3], to allow revision of a judgment upon the discovery of a fact which might by its nature have had a decisive influence (but which was unknown to the Court and could not reasonably have been known to the party requesting revision of the judgment)[4], and to clarify by way of interpretation any part of the operative part of a judgment[5].

1   ECHR, Art 39(3) and Rule of Court 62(3). A friendly settlement normally involves an agreement between the parties in the form of an undertaking to issue a formal apology, to pay compensation, to take specific action such as the restitution of property or the issue of a residence visa, or to amend domestic law or practice). The consent of the Court is required. Negotiations with a view to friendly settlement are confidential, and may not subsequently be referred to in contentious proceedings: Art 39(2) and Rules of Court 43 and 62(2). The Committee of Ministers is responsible for supervision of the execution of any friendly settlement reached: Art 39(4). Failure to comply with the terms of friendly settlement will result in the case being restored to the list: *Katić v Serbia* (dec) (20 July 2009). See further Myjer 'It's Never Too Late for the State – Friendly Settlements and Unilateral Declarations' in Caflisch, Callewaert, Liddell, Mahoney and Villiger eds, *Liber Amicorum Luzius Wildhaber: Human Rights – Strasbourg Views* (2007), pp 309–327; and Keller, Forowicz and Engi *Friendly Settlements before the European Court of Human Rights* (2010) (at p 65 noting that there is often a tendency for the Court Registry to suggest slightly higher amounts of compensation than would be received in ordinary proceedings). See also *Review of the Working Methods of the European Court of Human Rights* (2005), para 4.6 (proposal to establish a 'Friendly Settlement Unit'), and *Report of the Group of Wise Persons to the Committee of Ministers* (2006), para 106 (encouragement of greater attempts to secure friendly settlements).

2   ECHR, Art 37(1). See eg *Gagiu v Romania* (24 February 2009) (continuation of examination of application concerning detention regime made by prisoner who had died and in absence of any request from a relative); and *Léger v France* (striking out) [GC] 2009-..., paras 43–51 (no evidence produced either of status as heir or close relative, or of any legitimate interest: struck out). Striking out may occur where a state unilaterally offers a settlement considered acceptable to the Court (normally referred to as a 'unilateral declaration') and is not dependent upon acceptance of the offer by the applicant.   See for example, *Akman v Turkey* (striking out) 2001–VI, paras 23–32 (acceptance that the state had violated Art 2; and *ex gratia* offer of payment to the victim's father); *Van Houten v Netherlands* (striking out) 2005-IX, paras 34–38; and *El Majjaoui and Stichting Touba Moskee v Netherlands* (striking out) [GC] (20 December 2007), paras 27–35 (refusal of work permit for position of imam struck out after subsequent application for permit had been successful); but note *Tahsin Acar v Turkey* [GC] 2004-III, paras 74–77 (minimum expectation of acknowledgment of failure to carry out an effective investigation in cases of disappearances). A failure by an applicant to take advantage of an offer may result in striking out: *Shevanova v Latvia* (striking out) [GC] (7 December 2007), paras 44–51 (failure by applicants to act upon proposals to regularise immigration status).

3   ECHR, Art 37(2). See also Rule of Court 43(5); and *Glinov v Ukraine* (dec) (25 September 2006).

4   Rule of Court 80. For an example, see *Giuseppi Tripodi v Italy* (just satisfaction) (23 October 2001) (revision of award of just satisfaction upon fact of death of applicant). Cf *Gustafsson v Sweden* (revision) (30 July 1998) paras 25–32 (evidence adduced would not have had any decisive impact); *McGinley and Egan v United Kingdom* (revision) (28 January 2000) para 36 (facts relied upon in request 'could reasonably have been known'). Rule of Court 81 also provides for the rectification of errors or obvious mistakes in decisions and judgments.

5   Rule of Court 79. For an example, see *Ringeisen v Austria* (interpretation) (23 June 1973) (payment of just satisfaction). Cf *Allenet de Ribemont v France* (interpretation) (10 February 1995) (rejection of request from Commission for clarification).

'Just satisfaction'

2.76 In terms of Article 41[1], the Court 'shall, if necessary, afford just satisfaction'[2] to a person whose Convention rights have been found to have been violated 'if the internal law of the [state concerned] allows only partial reparation to be made'[3]. Such an award is thus appropriate where domestic law does not provide for *restitutio in integrum*[4], although the Court in exceptional cases may now also indicate in the operative part of its judgment what specific action is expected of a respondent state[5].

---

1   ECHR, Art 50 (original treaty).

2   See further Bottigliero *Redress for Victims of Crimes under International Law* (2004) pp 155–159; Mahoney 'Thinking a Small Unthinkable: Repatriating Reparation from the European Court of Human Rights to the National Legal Order' in Caflisch, Callewaert, Liddell, Mahoney and Villiger (eds) *Liber Amicorum Luzius Wildhaber: Human Rights – Strasbourg Views* (2007), pp 263–283 (Art 41 case law provides little clear guidance other than in relation to costs, but 'the call for in-depth treatment of just satisfaction is misconceived'); de Salvia 'La Satisfaction Équitable au Titre des Mesures Individuelles et la Pratique des Organes de la Convention Européenne des Droits de l'Homme: Qu'en est-il du Principe de Sécurité Juridique?' in Hartig (ed) *Trente Ans de Droit Européen des Droits de l'Homme: Études à la Mémoire de Wolfgang Strasser* (2007), pp 45–53; Birsan 'Les Aspects Nouveaux de l'Application des Articles 41 et 46 de la Convention dans la Jurisprudence de la Cour Européenne des Droits de l'Homme' in Hartig (ed) *Trente Ans de Droit Européen des Droits de l'Homme: Études à la Mémoire de Wolfgang Strasser* (2007), pp 19–44; and Loucaides 'Reparation for Violations of Human Rights under the European Convention and *Restitutio in Integrum*' [2008] EHRLR 182.

3   Cf *Papamichaloupoulos v Greece* (Art 50) (1995) A 330-B, para 34 (return of property will constitute 'just satisfaction').

4   See *Papamichaloupoulos v Greece* (Art 50) (1995) A 330-B, para 34.

5   See para **2.79** below.

2.77 In Strasbourg, an award of just satisfaction must be specifically requested by an applicant[1]. It is granted at the discretion of the Court, normally at the same time as a violation is established, unless the Court deems it more appropriate to dispose of all or part of the Article 41 issue at a later stage[2]. 'Just satisfaction' covers pecuniary damage, non-pecuniary damage, and costs and expenses. The Court makes its assessment 'on an equitable basis, and having regard to its usual criteria'[3]. In respect of pecuniary damage, there must be a causal connection between the violation established and the loss alleged by an applicant, and the Court will not speculate as to what the outcome of a matter would have been had there not been a breach of a state's obligations[4]. A wide range of factors may be relevant in assessing pecuniary damage, including, for example, depreciation in the value of property on account of pollution[5], real (rather than speculative) loss of development opportunities[6] or of earnings[7] or rental income[8], the costs of publishing a court judgment in a newspaper[9], criminal fines imposed upon an applicant[10], and depreciation in the real value of a compensation award on account of delay in payment[11]. However, the calculation of actual loss sustained may often be a difficult exercise for the Court, and in such circumstances it is likely to proceed upon the basis of what is 'equitable' in all the circumstances[12]. Non-pecuniary damage is awarded to compensate for anxiety, pain and suffering arising from, for example, violation of respect for private life[13], unlawful detention[14], ill-treatment of detainees[15] or failure to carry out an investigation into their disappearance[16], undue delay in the administration of justice[17], and interference with freedom of religion[18]. The Court again seeks to determine what is 'a just and equitable amount of compensation' in all the circumstances of the case[19]. This is reflected in a tendency to deny claims for compensation in Article 6 cases which have involved only procedural breaches of fair hearing guarantees, and in other cases where applicants are considered not to be worthy, for example if they had been involved in terrorist activities[20]. The Court does not expressly award aggravated damages, but may take into account the seriousness of violations established and reflect this in the amount of compensation awarded for non-pecuniary damage[21]. However, in many instances the Court will simply conclude that the finding of a violation is in itself sufficient compensation[22], in particular if the aim of the applicant in bringing a case was to secure a change in domestic law[23]. Further, the Court may aggregate pecuniary and non-pecuniary damage without specifying how its assessment has been reached[24]. Finally, an award of costs and expenses may be made where an applicant has incurred these in order to prevent or to rectify a violation of Convention guarantees before the Strasbourg Court, as long as it can be shown that the costs were 'actually and necessarily incurred and that they are reasonable as to quantum'[25].

1   Cf *FE v France* 1998-VIII, paras 63–65 (award of non-pecuniary damage made, but no ruling on costs and expenses as the applicant had not submitted any such claim).

2   Eg *Guillemin v France* 1997-I, paras 62–63 (issue in respect of pecuniary damage not ready for resolution; but sum awarded in respect of non-pecuniary damage since the applicant had indisputably sustained such); *Cyprus v Turkey* [GC] 2001-IV (question of damage not ready for resolution after the establishment of widespread and serious violations of rights in northern Cyprus). See also Rules of Court 43(2) and 62(3).

3   *Aït-Mouhoub v France* 1998-VIII, at para 68.

4   Eg *Mauer v Austria* 1997-I, para 40 (allegation that the applicant's plans for expanding his business had suffered: since the applicant had not established the existence or extent of such damage, no pecuniary damage awarded); *Findlay v United Kingdom* 1997-I, paras 84–85 (impossible to speculate what the outcome of court-martial proceedings might have been, and thus no award in respect of pecuniary and non-pecuniary damage); *Radio ABC v Austria* 1997-VI, para 41 (claim based upon speculative assumption that the applicant company would have received a licence); *Kopp v Switzerland* 1998-II, para 83 (causal connection between telephone interception and alleged loss not established).

5   *Lopèz Ostra v Spain* (1994) A 303-C, paras 62–65.

6   Eg *De Geoffre de la Pradelle v France* (1992) A 253-B, para 39 (exploitation of land hindered by lack of access to a court to challenge planning restrictions); cf *Podbielski v Poland* 1998-VIII, para 44 (claim based on lost business opportunities which were speculative in nature).

7   Eg *Young, James and Webster v United Kingdom* (Art 50) (1982) A 55, para 11.

8   Cf *Pammel v Germany* 1997-IV, para 78 (pecuniary loss of interest only which could not be calculated precisely but would be made on an equitable basis).

9   *De Haes and Gijsels v Belgium* 1997-I, paras 61–63.

10   Eg *Jersild v Denmark* (1994) A 298, paras 42–43.

11   *Akkuş v Turkey* 1997-IV, paras 35–36.

12   Cf *Sporrong and Lönnroth v Sweden* (1982) A 85, paras 27–32. The problem is most obvious where *restitutio in integrum* cannot be made: see eg *The Former King of Greece v Greece* (just satisfaction) [GC] (28 November 2002), paras 72–102 (at para 78: 'in case of non-restitution, the compensation to be fixed … need not… reflect the idea of wiping out all the consequences of the interference in question. As the lack of any compensation, rather than the inherent illegality of the taking, was the basis of the violation found, the compensation need not necessarily reflect the full value of the properties); *Beyeler v Italy* (just satisfaction) [GC] (28 May 2002), paras 23–26 at paras 20 and 23 ('nature of the breach found in the principal judgment does not allow of *restitutio in integrum*', but 'depreciation in value between 1977 and 1983 must be borne by the applicant on account of his failure to act openly and honestly during that period').

13   Eg *Z v Finland* 1997-I, para 122 (disclosure that the applicant was HIV positive without the consent of the patient); *Halford v United Kingdom* 1997-III, para 76 (interception of telephones); but cf *Kopp v Switzerland* 1998-II, para 80 (finding of a violation of Art 8 on account of interception of communications constituted sufficient compensation in itself); *Smith and Grady v United Kingdom* (just satisfaction) 2000-IX, paras 12–13 (dismissal of homosexuals from the armed forces).

14   *Johnson v United Kingdom* 1997-VII, para 77 (mental health detention: applicant's behaviour taken into account in the calculation of the award); but cf *Nikolova v Bulgaria* [GC] 1999–II, paras 70–76 (unlawful detention on remand; finding of violation of Art 5(3) and (4) was sufficient compensation since the Court was not prepared to speculate whether the applicant would have been detained had there been no violations).

15   Eg *Aydin v Turkey* 1997-VI, para 131 (rape of the applicant while in police custody).

16   Eg *Kaya v Turkey* 1998-I, para 122.

17   Eg *Stamoulakatos v Greece (no 2)* 1997-VII, paras 46–49; *Pailot v France* 1998-II, para 76.

18   Eg *Larissis and Others v Greece* 1998-I, para 74.

19   *Halford v United Kingdom* 1997-III, at para 76. See eg *A and Others v United Kingdom* [GC] 2009-…, paras 249–253 (reduced award of just satisfaction appropriate in case where unlawful detention had been the result of a public emergency and where the state had been unable to deport the applicants for fear of ill-treatment).

20   Reid *A Practitioner's Guide to the European Convention on Human Rights* (3rd edn, 2007), p 617, citing eg *McCann and Others v United Kingdom* (1995) A 324, para 219.

21   Eg *Selçuk and Asker v Turkey* 1998-II, paras 117–118 (destruction of houses and other property by armed forces).

22   Eg *Mantovanelli v France* 1997-II, para 40.

23   Eg *Dudgeon v United Kingdom* (1981) A 59, para 21.

24   Eg *Tsirlis and Kouloumpas v Greece* 1997-III, para 80 (compensation for unlawful detention).

25   *Niederöst-Huber v Switzerland* 1997-I, at para 40. Legal fees will be scrutinised with care: e g *Z v Finland* 1997-I, paras 123 and 126 (certain costs and expenses awarded, but other legal expenses were not necessarily incurred); cf *Robins v United Kingdom* 1997-V, paras 42–44 (an applicant sought compensation for the time spent preparing the case at the level equivalent to that of a solicitor or barrister: the Court's award appears to have included a token award in this respect). The applicant's attendance at Strasbourg will be reimbursed under this heading where this serves a useful purpose: *Sunday Times v United Kingdom (no 1)* (1980) A 38, para 33; but cf *Halford v United Kingdom* 1997-III, para 79 (attendance of the applicant in Strasbourg covered by an award of pecuniary loss).

2.78 The HRA 1998, s 8 provides that a court cannot award damages in relation to any act by a public authority which is found to be unlawful under section 6(1) unless it is satisfied that the award is necessary to afford just satisfaction to the person in whose favour it is made[1]. In determining whether to award damages, or the amount of an award, the court must take into account the principles applied by the Strasbourg court in relation to the award of compensation under Article 41[2]. Article 41 'just satisfaction' awards can often be significantly lower than awards made by domestic courts, since the Court determines its assessments in line with its own principles rather than with the scales used by domestic courts[3]. The problem for domestic courts is that Strasbourg case-law on this issue is not always consistent[4].

1   HRA 1998, s 8(3).

2   HRA 1998, s 8(4). As to the UK law, see paras **1.89–1.95** above.

3   *Osman v United Kingdom* 1998-VIII, para 164. For a domestic example see *R (Greenfield) v Secretary of State for the Home Department* [2005] 1 WLR 673.

4   For discussion, see *Damages under the Human Rights Act* (Law Com Discussion Paper no 266 and Scot Law Com Paper no 180) (Cm 4853) (2000); and Reid *A Practitioner's Guide to the European Convention on Human Rights* (3rd edn, 2007), pp 603–662.

The consequences of a finding of a violation of an ECHR guarantee

2.79 Final judgments are binding on the state which is a party to a case[1]. Where the Court has established a breach of an ECHR guarantee, that finding 'imposes on the respondent State a legal obligation to put an end to the breach and make reparation for its consequences in such a way as to restore as far as possible the situation existing before the breach'[2]. The expectation is that there should be *restitutio in integrum,* but the choice of means for achieving this is for the respondent state[3], and the Court cannot require the taking of any specific measure. The obligation to comply with a judgment of the Court may involve payment of any sum of money which has been awarded to an applicant in the form of just satisfaction[4]. However, the general principle that the Court cannot dictate to a state the action it should take is now subject to two important qualifications. First, in exceptional cases, the Court is prepared to indicate in the operative part of its judgment what action it considers necessary in light of the finding of a violation[5]. Secondly, where the underlying problem is 'a systemic problem connected with the malfunctioning of domestic legislation' (ie, legislation which is incompatible with the ECHR and where in consequence there is (or could be) a significant number of applications of a similar nature), the Court has now determined that it is appropriate to make use of 'a 'pilot judgment' procedure which in essence directs a state to take action to remedy the defect[6]. Neither innovation should be seen as usurping the functions of the Committee of Ministers in respect of enforcement of judgments; rather, each is more properly considered an attempt by the Court to assist the Committee of Ministers in ensuring the proper execution of judgments by the state concerned[7]. More particularly, each development emphasises that the primary responsibility for securing Convention guarantees lies with the state authorities and that the role of the Court should be a subsidiary one.

1   ECHR, Art 46(1); Arts 32 and 54 (original treaty).

2   *Papamichaloupoulos v Greece* (Art 50) (1995) A 330-B, at para 34.

3   *Papamichaloupoulos v Greece* (Art 50) (1995) A 330-B, at para 34. See also *Haase and Others v Germany* (dec) (12 February 2008) (it is not for the Court to verify whether a state has complied with the obligations imposed on it by one of the Court's judgments).

4   See paras **2.76–2.77** above.

5   See in particular *Assanidzé v Georgia* [GC] 2004-II, at paras 202–203 (applicant was not released after being awarded a pardon in respect of one offence and being acquitted in respect of a second; the Grand Chamber noted that the finding of violations 'does not leave any real choice as to the measures required to remedy it' and thus 'the Court considers that the respondent State must secure the applicant's release at the earliest possible date'.). This appears to be the first example where the Court in the operative part of a judgment indicated the action to be taken. In *Papamichaloupoulos v Greece* (Art 50) A 330-B, at paras 38–39, the Court noted that the return of land and buildings 'would put the applicants as far as possible in a situation equivalent to the one in which they would have been' if no violation of Prot 1, Art 1 had taken place, but were this not to occur, payment of pecuniary damages would be appropriate. In a series of cases in which violations of fair hearings were established involving Turkey, the Court also was prepared to indicate that it considered that the appropriate outcome should be a retrial by an independent tribunal: see eg *Gençel v Turkey* (23 Oct 2003) para 27. Cf *Iskandarov v Russia* (23 September 2010), paras 160–162 (inappropriate to indicate any individual measure sought that would require the respondent government to interfere with the internal affairs of another sovereign state). For a survey of the effects of judgments or cases in domestic law, see European Court of Human Rights *Survey: Forty Years of Activities 1959–1998* (1999), pp 86–113; and See further Lambert Abdelgawad *The Execution of Judgments of the European Court of Human Rights* (2nd edn, 2008).

6   *Broniowski v Poland* [GC] 2004-V, discussed at para **2.80** below.

7   See eg Committee of Ministers Resolution Res (2004) 3 (inviting the Court in its judgments to indicate if the case indicates an underlying structural problem and the source of that problem), and Res (2004) 6 (on the improvement of domestic remedies by national states).

'PILOT JUDGMENT' PROCEDURE

2.80 The 'pilot-judgment' procedure represents an attempt by the Court to force the early resolution of structural or widespread underlying problems in domestic legal systems resulting in the lodging of significant number of identical applications. Such 'repetitive cases' now constitute a significant proportion of the Court's workload. The procedure first involves the selection of one or more of these cases for priority treatment with the view to seeking a solution to all of these similar cases (and also with the possibility of the adjournment or 'freezing' of other related applications in the meantime but for a set period of time and normally upon the condition that the state will act promptly and effectively on any conclusions drawn in the pilot judgment). In the actual 'pilot judgment', the Court will identify the particular dysfunction or incompatibility at the root of the violation and determine whether there has been a violation of the Convention in the particular case, but then – and crucially – also indicate to the state in the operative part of the judgment that it must take action to eliminate the dysfunction so as to permit the settlement of all similar cases by bringing about the creation of a domestic remedy[1]. The Court may, additionally, indicate the time-scale by which the prescribed action is to be taken[2]. The pilot-judgment procedure was first used in 2004 in the 'Bug River case', *Browniowski v Poland*. Here, the potential number of victims was some 80 thousand[3], but instead of adjudicating upon the merits of the application, the state was encouraged to introduce amending legislation allowing the settlement of property claims[4]. The success of this first use of the 'pilot judgment' procedure in obtaining swifter resolution of disputes for individuals while simultaneously avoiding the significant use of Court resources could have been expected to have resulted in frequent use of the procedure in repetitive cases, but so far the Court seems to have used the procedure with some restraint[5], restricting its initial use to applications involving the right to property (under Article 1 of Protocol no 1) and the right to a fair hearing (under Article 6). In any event, not all categories of repetitive cases will readily permit use of a pilot judgment[6], and the adjournment of cases pending resolution will not be appropriate where the underlying issue concerns 'core' fundamental rights of the person under the Convention[7].

---

1   See further Rules of Court, Rule 61; and European Court of Human Rights 'Information Note: The Pilot-Judgment Procedure' (undated), paras 2–3.

2   Eg, *Burdov v Russia (no 2)* 2009-…, paras 141 and 143 (six months, with adjournment of one year in other cases pending).

3   *Broniowski v Poland* [GC] 2004-V, at para 189; *Broniowski v Poland* (just satisfaction – friendly settlement) [GC] 2005-IX, at paras 34–36, citing the Court's position paper on proposals for reform of the European Convention on Human Rights and other measures as set out in the report of the Steering Committee for Human Rights of 4 April 2003 (CDDH(2003)006 Final, and Response by the Court to the CDDH Interim Activity Report, 2004).

4   Eg *Wolkenberg and Others v Poland* (dec) 2007-XIV; *Witkowska-Tobola v Poland* (dec) (4 December 2007); and *EG v Poland* (dec) 2008-… (new legislation and other general measures to remedy systemic problem identified in *Broniowski* pilot judgment procedure: applications struck out).

5   For further applications, see *Hutten-Czapska v Poland* [GC] 2006-VIII, paras 231–239 (law affecting some 100,000 landlords through the imposition of significant restrictions upon rental income); *Viaşu v Romania* (9 December 2008), paras 75–83 (inability to secure enforcement of decisions or compensation for land or for delays on account of changes to legislation governing the restitution process and which had created a climate of legal uncertainty and thereby a whole category of individuals had been or were being deprived of the peaceful enjoyment of their possessions); *Burdov v Russia (no 2)* 2009-…, paras 71–88 (non-enforcement of domestic judgments concerning entitlement to sickness benefits following Chernobyl disaster); *Yuriy Nikolayevich Ivanov v Ukraine* 2009-…, paras 78–101 (failure to enforce judgments concerning retirement pension payments); *Suljagić v Bosnia and Herzegovina* (3 November 2009), paras 60–65 (significant delays in implementation of repayment scheme for foreign currency deposited before the dissolution of Yugoslavia); *Olaru and Others v Moldova* (15 November 2009), paras 53–54 (failure to implement rights to housing entitlement); and *Rumpf v Germany* (2 September 2010), paras 59–75 (excessive length of civil proceedings in domestic courts). See further Garlicki 'Broniowski and After: On the Dual Nature of 'Pilot Judgments', and Gattini 'Mass Claims at the European Court of Human Rights', in Caflisch,

Callewaert, Liddell, Mahoney and Villiger (eds) *Liber Amicorum Luzius Wildhaber: Human Rights – Strasbourg Views* (2007), pp 177–192 and pp 271–294; and Leach, Hardman, Stephenson and Blitz, *Responding to Systemic Human Rights Violations – An Analysis of Pilot Judgments of the European Court of Human Rights and their Impact at National Level* (2010).

6   For example, no use was made of the 'pilot judgment' technique in certain cases in which the existence of a systemic problem was discussed: eg *Sejdovic v Italy* [GC] 2006-II, paras 119–127 (absence of fair trial on account of trial in absentia: while legislative measures had been taken, it was considered premature to examine their effect). See also European Court of Human Rights 'Information Note: The Pilot-Judgment Procedure' (undated), para 5: 'Where cases are adjourned in this way, the importance of keeping applicants informed of each development in the procedure is fully recognised by the Court. It should be stressed that the Court may at any time resume its examination of any case that has been adjourned if this is what the interests of justice require, for example where the particular circumstances of the applicant make it unfair or unreasonable for them to have to wait much longer for a remedy.'

7   European Court of Human Rights 'Information Note: The Pilot-Judgment Procedure' (undated), para 7. See also *Fatullayev v Azerbaijan* (22 April 2010), para 177 (immediate release of applicant from custody required).

2.81 The 'pilot-judgment' procedure was first used in relation to the United Kingdom in the case of *Greens and MT v United Kingdom*. Here, two convicted prisoners complained that their voter registration application forms had been rejected as their address in each case had been given as HMP Peterhead, and in consequence they had been unable to vote in the 2009 European Parliamentary election and the 2010 General Election. Noting that 'it was a cause for regret and concern' that the British Government had failed to introduce amending legislation following the judgment in *Hirst v United Kingdom (no 2)*[1] some five years earlier (but acknowledging that the new coalition Government elected in 2010 was actively considering how to do so), the Court held that there had been a violation of Article 3 of Protocol no 1, and applied its pilot judgment procedure in view of the significant number of applications already received (some 2,500). While it was not appropriate for the Court to determine what statutory amendments were appropriate, the Court required the United Kingdom Government to introduce legislative proposals within six months (a timescale reflecting the pending 2011 elections to the Scottish Parliament). In a significant development to the 'pilot-judgment' procedure, the Court considered that further examination of comparable cases on an individual basis was not required since the only possible relevant remedy was amendment of the statutory prohibition preventing convicted prisoners to vote. It thus resolved to strike out all other registered applications on the basis that no advantage would be gained by further examination (and indeed, discontinuation would prevent a significant drain on Court resources), but without prejudice to its right to restore the applications to its list should the United Kingdom fail to comply with this judgment[2].

1   *Hirst v United Kingdom (no 2)* [GC] 2005-IX, discussed at para **7.142** below.

2   *Greens and MT v United Kingdom* 2010-…, paras 110–122 (noting at para 111 that the UK prison population was some 70,000 convicted prisoners).

Role of the Committee of Ministers in the supervision of the execution of judgments

2.82 The Committee of Ministers is charged with the supervision of the necessary action taken by a state following a judgment by the Court that a provision of the ECHR has been breached[1]. The execution of judgments forms an important but often overlooked part of the machinery for the protection of human rights[2]. While there may be compelling political factors which will limit a state's readiness to take the necessary action to comply with a Court judgment[3], a state is obliged to take specific and also general measures to address the causes of the violation established by the Court. To this end, a judgment will remain on the agenda of the Committee of Ministers until it is satisfied that appropriate action has been taken[4]. In certain cases, interim resolutions may be adopted which seek to assess the extent to which progress is being made[5]. Specific measures taken for the benefit of an individual may include, for example, the release of an individual in detention[6], the re-opening of a criminal case by re-examination of the evidence[7], an undertaking not to execute a criminal sentence and to annul the record of a conviction[8], and the granting of indefinite leave to remain in a country to an individual facing expulsion[9]. A judgment may also require the implementation of general measures involving constitutional, legislative or administrative reform[10].

---

1   ECHR, Art 46(2).

2   The task is discharged by the Committee of Ministers working in co-operation with the Directorate General of Human Rights and Legal Affairs and the relevant national authorities. From 2001, the agenda of meetings indicating cases to be considered by the Committee has been published. It appears that several states have challenged individual judgments of the Court at this stage in respect to 'just satisfaction' or to specific measures required although ECHR, Art 46(1) clearly specifies that judgments are binding: see *Report of the Evaluation Group to the Committee of Ministers on the European Court of Human Rights* doc EG Court (2001) 1. See also Rules of the Committee of Ministers for the Supervision of the Execution of Judgments and of the Terms of Friendly Settlements' (2006). On occasion, the Committee of Ministers will also seek to examine underlying structural problems in a domestic legal system: see eg Doc CM/Inf/DH (2006) 19 rev 3 (non-enforcement of domestic judicial decisions in Russia: general measures to comply with the European Court's judgments). Since 2007, the Committee has published an annual report on the supervision of execution of judgments: see http://www.coe.int/execution/. See further van Dijk, van Hoof, van Rijn and Zwaak (eds) *Theory and Practice of the European Convention on Human Rights* (4th edn, 2006), pp 295–317; Leach 'The Effectiveness of the Committee of Ministers in Supervising the Enforcement of Judgments of the European Court of Human Rights' [2006] PL 443; and Barreto 'Les Effets de la Jurisprudence de la Cour Européenne des Droits de l'Homme sur l'Order Juridique et Judiciaire Portugais' in Caflisch, Callewaert, Liddell, Mahoney and Villiger (eds) *Liber Amicorum Luzius Wildhaber: Human Rights – Strasbourg Views* (2007), pp 65–89 at 65–77.

3   It has on occasion been difficult to see how an extreme political situation such as the Turkish occupation of northern Cyprus, which gave rise to findings of violations in *Loizidou v Turkey* (preliminary objections) 1996-VI, and in *Cyprus v Turkey* [GC] 2001-IV, could be remedied: the Convention system is not equipped to deal with serious and systematic violations of human rights. For many observers, the only outcomes in this situation would ultimately have been state denunciation of the Convention in terms of Art 58 (as occurred after the Commission's report in 4448/70, *Denmark, Norway and Sweden v Greece* (1970) YB 13, 108) or a decision to expel the country from the Council of Europe. However, after sustained pressure from the

Committee of Ministers (see Interim Resolutions DH (99) 680, DH (2000) 105, and DH (2001) 80) and the Parliamentary Assembly, Turkey eventually made payment of the just satisfaction awarded by the Court in the *Loizidou* case at the end of 2003.

4   Eg Resolution DH (88) 3 (in relation to the judgment in *Marckx v Belgium* in 1979 concerning establishment of maternal affiliation and discrimination in inheritance rights on the grounds of illegitimacy: period of eight years and nine months between judgment and final resolution which noted various amendments to domestic law).

5   Eg Resolution DH (2009) 160 (concerning the judgment in *Hirst v United Kingdom (no 2)*: noting that the United Kingdom will introduce draft legislation to implement the judgment, and expressing hope that elections scheduled for 2011 in Scotland, Wales and Northern Ireland 'can be performed in a way that complies with the Convention'. See also Interim Resolution DH (99) 680 (concerning the judgment in *Loizidou v Turkey*: the resolution 'deplor[ed]' Turkey's failure to pay the sums awarded as just satisfaction, 'stress[ed]' the nature of the obligation, and 'strongly urg[ed]' Turkey to review its position; a note by the Directorate General of Human Rights indicated that the failure to pay just satisfaction was a situation which was 'unprecedented'). The amount awarded was finally paid more than five years late: Resolution ResDH(2003)190.

6   See eg Resolutions DH (2005) 42, DH (2005) 84, DH (2006) 11, and DH (2006) 26 (in relation to the *Ilaşcu and Others v Moldova and Russia* judgment: while both countries had paid the sums specified by way of just satisfaction, there was condemnation of the continued refusal of the Russian authorities to comply with the Court's judgment to secure the arbitrary release of two individuals).

7   Eg Resolution DH (89) 2 (in relation to the judgment in *Unterpertinger v Austria*).

8   Eg Resolution DH (85) 4 (in relation to the Commission's report in 9193/80, *Marijnissen v Netherlands* (29 June 1980)).

9   Eg Resolution DH (98) 10 (concerning the judgment in *D v United Kingdom*).

10   Eg Resolution DH (2004) 32 (concerning the judgment in *Stefanov v Bulgaria*: decriminalisation of conscientious objection and introduction of alternative to military service); and Resolution DH (2004) 88 (concerning the judgment in *Saunders v United Kingdom*: prohibition of use of evidence obtained under compulsion in criminal trials).

2.83 The responsibilities of the Committee of Ministers are also being strengthened. First, Protocol no 14 has introduced the ability of the Committee of Ministers to refer a case back to the Court where it considers that a state 'refuses to abide by' a final judgment of the Court[1]. Such 'infringement proceedings' will require a two-thirds majority of the Committee of Ministers, and is likely to be used only in exceptional circumstances[2]. Secondly, the Committee will prioritise its scrutiny of the execution of judgments by introducing 'enhanced' supervision in judgments requiring individual urgent measures; pilot judgments and other judgments involving structural or complex issues, and in inter-state cases[3]

1   ECHR, Art 46(4). Note that there is no provision for any order of 'just satisfaction' in such cases.

2   See Explanatory Report to Protocol no 14, para 100.

3   See in general, Council of Europe *Impact of the Council of Europe's Monitoring Mechanisms*, CM/Inf/DH(2010)37 (2010).

OTHER COUNCIL OF EUROPE HUMAN RIGHTS INITIATIVES

2.84 The Council of Europe's work in human rights extends beyond the ECHR. Additional instruments and initiatives complement the protection of the individual, and it is now possible to refer to a Council of Europe *acquis* of standards and expectations. Some understanding of these treaties and bodies (and of other international human rights provisions)[1] is necessary, for the Court may refer to these in its deliberations[2]. As well as the institutions considered below, the Steering Committee for Equality between Women and Men seeks to promote equal treatment[3], while the European Commission for Democracy through Law (the 'Venice Commission') assesses constitutional developments and provides assistance in upholding the rule of law and democratic values[4]. The promotion of human rights at a regional level thus involves a number of techniques, including standard-setting, reporting, investigating and fact-finding, as well as interstate, individual and group complaints mechanisms[5].

1   The key international instruments of relevance in civil and political rights include the International Convention on the Elimination of All Forms of Racial Discrimination (1965); the International Covenant on Civil and Political Rights (1966); the Convention on the Elimination of All Forms of Discrimination against Women (1979) (and the Optional Protocol of 1999); the Declaration on the Elimination of All Forms of Intolerance and of Discrimination Based on Religion or Belief (1981); the Convention Against Torture and other Cruel, Inhuman or Degrading Treatment or Punishment (1984); the United Nations Convention on the Rights of the Child (1989); and the Declaration on the Rights of Persons Belonging to National or Ethnic, Religious and Linguistic Minorities (1992). For examples of the use of such instruments, see eg *Streletz, Kessler and Krenz v Germany* [GC] 2001-II, paras 98–106 (the applicants' conduct also constituted offences under international law).

2   Eg *Van der Mussele v Belgium* (1983) A 70, para 32 (reference to ILO Convention in discussion of Art 4); *Sigurður A Sigurjónsson v Iceland* (1993) A 264, para 35 (references to the Universal Declaration of Human Rights, European Social Charter and ILO Conventions in discussion of Art 11). See further, para **3.44** below. For discussion of the use of European Committee against Torture (CPT) reports, see paras **4.121–4.122** below. Discussion of other conventions, etc in Strasbourg case law has received little academic attention. It can be justified on occasion to ensure that a state which enters into other international obligations does not thereby infringe existing responsibilities under the ECHR: cf 21072/92, *Gestra v Italy* (1995) DR 80, 89; and *Matthews v United Kingdom* [GC] 1999-I, discussed below at para **7.139**. More positively, however, it can help ensure a 'progressive' interpretation of Convention guarantees 'plus ample que celle qui était manifestement dans l'intention des auteurs du texte': Conforti 'Quelques Réflexions sur les Rapports de la Convention Européenne des Droits de l'Homme avec d'Autres Conventions' in de Salvia and Villiger (eds) *The Birth of European Human Rights Law* (1998), pp 47–52 at 48. Regular liaison between Council of Europe organs and UN treaty-based bodies takes place: Weitzel and Strasser 'The Relationship between the European Convention on Human Rights and Other International Enforcement Mechanisms', in de Salvia and Villiger (eds) above, at pp 348–349.

3   For examples of initiatives, see eg Recommendation Rec (2002) 5 of the Committee of Ministers to member States on the protection of women against violence adopted on 30 April 2002; Recommendation Rec (2003) 3 of the Committee of Ministers to member states on balanced participation of women and men in political and public decision making; and Council of Europe Convention on Action against Trafficking in Human Beings (CETS 197(2005)).

4   Eg Venice Commission Opinion no 363/2005 on the International Legal Obligations of Council of Europe Member States in respect of Secret Detention Facilities and Inter-State Transport

of Prisoners, Doc CDL-AD(2006)009. For examples where submissions from the Venice Commission have been considered by the Court, see *Jeličić v Bosnia and Herzegovina* (dec) 2005-XII; and *Hirst v United Kingdom (no 2)* [GC] 2005-IX. See further van Dijk 'The Venice Commission on Certain Aspects of the Application of the European Convention on Human Rights *Ratione Personae*' in Breitenmoser, Ehrenzeller, Sassòli, Stoffel and Pfeifer (eds) *Human Rights, Democracy and the Rule of Law: Liber Amicorum Luzius Wildhaber* (2007), pp 183–202.

5 Other human rights initiatives, in addition to the bodies and treaties considered below, include in central and eastern Europe the Council's Programmes for Democratic Stability, which seek to raise awareness of human rights amongst judges, lawyers and police officers, and provide expert opinions on the compatibility of legislation with European human rights norms. The Council of Europe publishes a regular *Human Rights Information Bulletin*: see further para **2.106** below. For concrete examples of outcomes on domestic law and practice, see *Practical Impact of the Council of Europe Human Rights Mechanisms* doc H/Inf (2007) 2.

2.85 The compliance of a member state of the Council of Europe with its obligations may also be raised before the Committee of Ministers by another member state, the Secretary General or the Parliamentary Assembly of the Council of Europe[1]. In cases requiring 'specific action', the Committee of Ministers may take action including requesting the Secretary General to collect information or to issue an opinion or recommendation, or forward a communication to the Parliamentary Assembly[2]. These monitoring powers have been used in relation to the situation in the Chechen Republic on two occasions[3]. Additionally, the Committee of Ministers may carry out post-accession monitoring in respect of individual countries[4], and thematic monitoring in all member states[5].

1 Committee of Ministers, Declaration on Compliance with Commitments (1994), para 1 'the situation of democracy, human rights and the rule of law in any member State'. See further http://www.dsp.coe.int/DSP/monitoring/. For further discussion, see Drzemczewski 'The Parliamentary Assembly's Involvement in the Supervision of the Judgments of the Strasbourg Court' (2010) 28 NQHR 164.

2 Declaration on Compliance with Commitments (1994), para 4.

3 In 2000, at the request of the Secretary General, and in 2003, at the request of the Parliamentary Assembly (Recommendation 1600 (2003)).

4 This has been used in respect of Armenia and Azerbaijan in respect of allegations of the detention of political prisoners, while Bosnia and Herzegovina, Serbia and Montenegro and Georgia were each subjected to quarterly and bi-annual reporting.

5 Topics have included capital punishment, effectiveness of judicial remedies, functioning of democratic institutions, police and security forces, freedom of expression and information, non-discrimination, and sexual equality.

Furthering protection for physical integrity

The European Committee for the Prevention of Torture and Inhuman or Degrading Treatment or Punishment

2.86 European states have accepted a number of obligations with a view to furthering the protection of persons deprived of their liberty[1], and in particular, have allowed access to places of detention to an international body charged with the responsibility for reporting its conclusions and recommendations. The European Convention for the Prevention of Torture and Inhuman or Degrading Treatment or Punishment[2] established the European Committee for the Prevention of Torture and Inhuman or Degrading Treatment or Punishment (the CPT). The work of the CPT has prompted the Court to adopt a more critical approach to the assessment of poor material conditions of detention[3]. The Committee achieves its goal not through a system of complaint and confrontation but through the process of dialogue and discussion with state officials following visits to places of detention[4]. The key to its success lies in this power to visit. While in general reporting systems rely primarily upon the good faith of state parties, the strategy of allowing an independent body to investigate detention conditions is of particular value where the primary goal is the prevention of human rights violations. The work of the Committee is surrounded by a guarantee of confidentiality, and information on discussions during meetings with officials or on Committee findings and recommendations may not be disclosed. However, states now invariably request publication of reports and governmental responses[5]. In its work, the CPT has also developed codes of standards or expectations which it employs during visits to help assess existing practices and to encourage states to meet its criteria of acceptable arrangements and conditions. These emerging standards are for the most part more detailed and more demanding than those found in other international obligations, and are now having some impact through the implementation of recommendations for the introduction of legislative, administrative and organisational reforms at domestic level[6].

---

1   See in general Murdoch *The Treatment of Prisoners: European Standards* (2006). The CPT may also conclude agreements with non-Member States (in respect of Kosovo, an agreement with the relevant UN authorities in 2004, and an exchange of letters was concluded with NATO in 2006, with the first visit taking place in March 2007 (see CPT/Inf (2009) 3). Other Council of Europe initiatives seeking to promote protection for detainees include recommendations and resolutions of the Committee of Ministers on such matters as the recruitment and training of prison staff (Resolution (66) 26); prison overcrowding and prison population inflation (Rec (99) 22); and the management of life-sentence and other long-term prisoners (Rec (2003) 23).

2   ETS 126 (1987). The inspiration for the Committee is drawn from the work of the International Committee of the Red Cross which pioneered the notion of protecting detained persons through a system of visits to places of detention by an expert and impartial body. The proposal for a European treaty was made to the Council of Europe by the International Commission of Jurists and by the Swiss Committee against Torture. Prompt ratification followed the Convention's adoption in 1987, and the treaty came into force in 1989. See, further, Evans and Morgan 'The CPT: An Introduction' in Morgan and Evans *Protecting Prisoners: The Standards of the CPT in Context* (1999), pp 3–30. See further http://www.cpt.coe.int.

3   See paras **4.121–4.122** below. For an example of the CPT's influence in the disposal of fair trial issues under Art 6, see para **5.126** below; and in promoting family contact, see **6.151** below.

4   The CPT has authority to visit places of detention where individuals – of whatever age, or whatever nationality, or on whatever ground – have been deprived of their liberty on account of official or state action. This will thus include deprivation of liberty which takes place in private as well as in public institutions such as police stations, prisons, mental hospitals

holding patients subject to compulsory detention, immigration centres, and military detention centres. Visits may take place even in times of war or other public emergency (although in certain circumstances where there is armed conflict visits by the International Committee of the Red Cross may replace those by the CPT). The Committee has visited Scottish prisons and police stations on two occasions, in 1994 (CPT/Inf (96) 11) and in 2003 (CPT/Inf (2005) 1. The CPT also carries out monitoring on behalf of the International Criminal Tribunal for the former Yugoslavia (ICTY), and in 2010, carried out two visits to prisons in England in which three prisoners convicted by the ICTY were being held (the second visit related to one of these prisoners who had been seriously assaulted by other inmates after the first visit).

5   But with the exception of the Russian Federation, which has authorised publication of only one report. Turkey authorised the publication of early reports only in 2007 (see eg CPT/Inf (2007) 1, in respect of the 1990 visit by the CPT). The Committee's report of its first visit to Kosovo (administered under a UN mandate) was published in 2009 (see CPT/Inf (2009) 3). In certain circumstances, the Committee may also issue a public statement on conditions in any particular country, a power exercised on two occasions in respect of Turkey and on three occasions in respect of Russia (see eg CPT/Inf (2007) 17). Reports (and further information on the CPT) are available at http://www.cpt.coe.int.

6   See further paras **4.128** and **6.151** below; and 'CPT Standards', doc CPT/Inf/E (2002) 1 – Rev 2010.

The Convention on Action against Trafficking in Human Beings

2.87 The Council of Europe Convention on Action against Trafficking in Human Beings[1] which entered into force in 2008 is the most recent human rights treaty and the first international legally binding instrument in this area. The treaty aims to prevent trafficking, to provide protection to victims of trafficking and to prosecute traffickers. State responsibilities are monitorred by the independent Group of Experts on Action against Trafficking in Human Beings (GRETA), with the Committee of the Parties (comprising state representatives) having the authority to adopt recommendations to states on measures which should be taken to implement GRETA's conclusions[2].

1   CETS 197 (2005). 'Trafficking in human beings' is defined by Art 4 as meaning 'the recruitment, transportation, transfer, harbouring or receipt of persons, by means of the threat or use of force or other forms of coercion, of abduction, of fraud, of deception, of the abuse of power or of a position of vulnerability or of the giving or receiving of payments or benefits to achieve the consent of a person having control over another person, for the purpose of exploitation. Exploitation shall include, at a minimum, the exploitation of the prostitution of others or other forms of sexual exploitation, forced labour or services, slavery or practices similar to slavery, servitude or the removal of organs'. As at 31 March 2011, this treaty had been ratified by 34 states. In respect of the United Kingdom, it entered into force on 1 April 2009. The Convention is open to non-member states and the EU. The Convention requires assistance and protection to be given to victims (and cf Art 11(3) which requires states to consider 'adopting, in accordance with Article 10 [case law] measures aimed at encouraging the media to protect the private life and identity of victims through self-regulation or through regulatory or co-regulatory measures'. For other measures in this area, see in particular Committee of Ministers Recommendations Rec (2000) 11 on action against trafficking in human beings for the purpose of sexual exploitation; Rec (2001) 11 concerning guiding principles on the fight against organised crime; Rec (2001) 16 on the protection of children against sexual exploitation; Rec (2002) 5 on

the protection of women against violence; and Parliamentary Assembly Recommendations Rec 1325 (1997) on traffic in women and forced prostitution; Rec 1450 (2000) on violence against women in Europe; Rec 1523 (2001) on domestic slavery; Rec 1526 (2001) on the campaign against trafficking in minors, etc; Rec 1610 (2003) on migration connected with trafficking in women and prostitution; and Rec 1663 (2004) on domestic slavery, etc. See generally 'Council of Europe's Action to Combat Trafficking in Human Beings' doc CM/Inf(2008)28.

2   See Council of Europe Convention on Action against Trafficking in Human Beings, Arts 36–38. The first round of monitoring commenced in 2010. See further http://www.coe.int/t/dghl/monitoring/trafficking/default_EN.asp?.

Protecting minorities and combating racism

2.88 European state boundaries contain – as they have for centuries in the past – minorities which are ethnically linked with the population of other nation states or which (as with Romany gypsies or the *Sama* of Lapland) share a distinct racial origin without a 'homeland'. The first attempts in Europe in the 17th century to protect minority rights had focused upon religious minorities[1], but the re-drawing of the boundaries of nation states after the 1914–18 war promoted new international legal concern for the protection of the rights of ethnic or cultural minorities in order to try to advance peace and security[2]. After 1945, however, international law sought to emphasise the universality of human rights, and minority-specific legal provision was largely replaced by instruments which were based upon the notion of the enjoyment of individual rights free from discrimination. A revival of interest in minority rights came with the collapse of communism in central and eastern Europe. The establishment of new independent states gave political expression to the democratic aspirations of ethnic groups, but also led to renewed xenophobia and racism. While diversity, broadmindedness and the enjoyment of rights free from discrimination are values stressed in human rights instruments (and particularly in the ECHR), it is now accepted that further steps are required to help address the problem of how best to protect members of minorities. In Europe, the protection of cultural pluralism and tolerance is again of some concern[3].

1   Evans *Religious Liberty and International Law in Europe* (1997), caps 1–2.

2   That is, through peace treaties, bilateral treaties or League of Nations treaties concluded with states which were formerly part of the Austro–Hungarian empire, or through declarations made before admission to the League of Nations: Robertson and Merrills *Human Rights in the World* (4th edn, 1996), pp 20–23; and Evans *Religious Liberty and International Law in Europe* (1997), pp 75–171.

3   See further Thornberry and Estebanez *Minority Rights in Europe* (2004). International law makes specific provision for minorities in a number of instruments: eg, Declaration on the Rights of Persons Belonging to National or Ethnic, Religious and Linguistic Minorities (1992): see Trechsel 'Human Rights and Minority Rights – Two Sides of the Same Coin?' in Mahoney, Matscher, Petzold and Wildhaber (eds) *Protecting Human Rights: The European Perspective* (2000), pp 1437–1453.

The Framework Convention for the Protection of National Minorities

2.89 The Framework Convention for the Protection of National Minorities, which entered into force in 1998, is the first binding treaty in international law to seek to protect national minorities in states[1]. The Preamble acknowledges the historical background and political impetus behind the treaty: the disintegration of former central and eastern European states, and the realisation that there are limits to the extent to which emerging democracies would promote pluralism within their frontiers. Implicit, too, is the concern that a charter of civil and political rights such as the ECHR is not an appropriate instrument for the protection of minority groups[2]. The Preamble specifically refers to the consideration that 'a pluralist and genuinely democratic society should not only respect the ethnic, cultural, linguistic and religious identity of each person belonging to a national minority, but also create appropriate conditions enabling them to express, preserve and develop this identity', and further, that cultural diversity should be seen as a matter of enrichment rather than division[3]. In these respects, the Framework Convention echoes the underlying assumption found in the ECHR that pluralism and tolerance are hallmarks of a democratic society. Article 1 of the Framework Convention refers to 'the protection of national minorities and of the rights and freedoms of persons belonging to national minorities'. No collective rights are thus envisaged, although it is recognised that 'the protection of a national minority can be achieved through protection of the rights of individuals belonging to such a minority'[4]. There is no definition, however, of what constitutes a national minority since the framers found it difficult to arrive at a formulation which would have commanded general political support[5]. The substantive provisions are found in Articles 4–19, and comprise a range of undertakings including the promotion of effective equality and of the conditions necessary for the preservation and development of religion, language and cultural traditions. The Framework Convention also makes provision for freedoms of assembly, association, expression, thought, conscience and religion, access to the media and to education, linguistic freedoms, and participation in public, cultural and social life. These rights are not directly applicable, and are best considered as a series of programme goals assumed by states[6]. An Advisory Committee comprising persons with recognised expertise in the field of the protection of national minorities and who serve in their individual capacities for four years is charged with the monitoring of the implementation of action taken by states based upon periodic reports submitted by state parties[7].

---

1   ETS 157 (1995). As at 31 March 2011, the treaty has been ratified by all Council of Europe states with the exception of Andorra, Belgium, France, Greece, Iceland, Luxembourg, Monaco, and Turkey. In respect of the United Kingdom, the treaty entered into force in May 1998. See further http://www.coe.int/minorities/. The Vienna Declaration of Heads of State and Government of 1993 provided the impetus for the treaty. See further further Weller (ed) *The Rights of Minorities: A Commentary on the European Framework Convention for the Protection of National Minorities* (2005); and Arraiza 'Blueprints for Babel: Legal Policy Options for Minority and Indigenous Languages' (2011) 17 EPL 111. For discussion of languages and the ECHR, see Medda-Windischer 'The ECHR and Language Rights' (2009) 8 EYMI 95.

2   Cf Explanatory Report, para 1, which notes that as early as 1961 the Parliamentary Assembly had recommended that guarantees for national minorities be included by way of an additional

Protocol to the ECHR. The Court's decision in the *Belgian Linguistic case* (1968) A 6, illustrates the limits of the ECHR in this respect: see para **3.125** below. In *Cyprus v Turkey* [GC] 2001-IV, however, the Court found multiple violations of the rights of the enclaved Greek Cypriot community living in northern Cyprus. The Strasbourg Court has determined many other cases which have a minority-*related* aspect, of which the most prominent currently involve members of the Kurdish minority in Turkey or Chechens living in Russia (see, further, paras **4.12** and **4.17** below for discussion of applications raising the right to life).

3   The inspiration for this comes from the United Nations Declaration on the Rights of Persons belonging to National or Ethnic, Religious and Linguistic Minorities of 1992: Commentary, para 24.

4   Commentary, at para 31. Art 3 guarantees to every person belonging to a national minority the right to decide whether to be treated as so belonging: that is, it is open to individuals to decide whether they wish to seek the protection of the Framework Convention: Explanatory Report, para 34.

5   Commentary, para 12. The recognition of a 'national minority' is left to each state, and this may explain why countries such as France and Turkey which politically do not recognise themselves as having minorities (on the grounds that citizenship or nationality is the only constitutional criterion) have failed to ratify the treaty. It is generally accepted that there are both objective (ethnic, cultural, linguistic or religious differences; non-dominance and numerical inferiority) and subjective (sense of solidarity or shared history; and a demand to preserve the group's own traditions and identity) criteria in determining the existence of a minority. The first United Kingdom Report adopts a distinctly Anglo-centric view: the British Government's report proceeds upon the basis that 'national minorities' are to include 'our ethnic communities (or visible minorities) and the Scots, Irish and Welsh, who are defined as a racial group by virtue of their national origins': doc ACFC/SR (99) 13, at para 2. This broad approach, which recognises not only three of the four constituent nationalities of the UK but also other minority groups, was commended by the Advisory Committee: doc ACFC/INF/OP/I(2002)006, at para 14. The second report, on the other hand, commented that 'national minority' 'has no legal meaning in the UK and so there is no mechanism under any of the UK's legal jurisdictions to grant 'national minority status' to any particular group': doc ACFC/SR/II(2007)003 rev. In its third report, the UK Government stated it was 'committed to building a fundamentally inclusive and cohesive society by creating a sense of inclusion and shared British identity, defined by common opportunities and mutual expectations on all citizens to contribute to society and respect others': doc ACFC/SR/III(2010)003 at para 3.

6   Explanatory Report, para 11. Assistance may also be provided to national governments in relation to the identification of discrimination in domestic legislation and in developing bilateral co-operation programmes.

7   Framework Convention, Arts 24–26. See further Committee of Ministers Resolution (97) 10; and *Rules of Procedure of the Advisory Committee on the Framework Convention for the Protection of National Minorities* (1998). The Advisory Committee's first opinion concerning the United Kingdom was made public in 2002. Co-operation in this area with other relevant international bodies is the responsibility of the European Committee of Experts on Issues relating to the Protection of National Minorities which was re-established in 2004.

The European Charter for Regional or Minority Languages

2.90 The European Charter for Regional or Minority Languages, adopted in 1992 and entering into force in 1998[1], encourages states to undertake to base legislative and administrative policies on principles designed to protect regional and minority languages[2], and to adopt measures to promote their use in public life (that is, in education and judicial proceedings, by administrative authorities and the public service, in respect of the media, and in cultural, economic and social life)[3]. States submit periodic reports on policies and measures adopted which are scrutinised by a committee of experts who prepare a report for consideration by the Committee of Ministers[4].

1   ETS 148 (1992). See further http://.www.coe.int/minlang/.Work on this treaty predates the fall of communism, and was prompted by West European concerns to attempt to protect languages considered at risk, rather than by ethnic tensions. See further Woehrling *The European Charter for Regional or Minority Languages: a Critical Commentary* (2005); and Varennes et al *The European Charter for Regional or Minority Languages: Legal Challenges and Opportunities* (2008). For an international perspective, see de Varennes *Language, Minorities and Human Rights* (1996). As at 31 December 2010, the treaty had been ratified by 25 member states including the United Kingdom.

2   Defined by Art 1(a) as those languages that are 'traditionally used within a given territory of a State by nationals of that State who form a group numerically smaller than the rest of the State's population, and different from the official language(s) of that State; [but] it does not include either dialects of the official language(s) of the State or the languages of migrants'. It is estimated by the Council of Europe that there are probably some 230 indigenous languages in Europe.

3   European Charter for Regional or Minority Languages, Arts 7–14.

4   European Charter for Regional or Minority Languages, Arts 15 and 16. Committee members are appointed in accordance with Art 17, and serve for a renewable period of six years and are to be persons of 'the highest integrity and recognised competence'. State reports are made public, and the reports of the committee of experts may be made public by the Committee of Ministers. For Advisory Committee reports in respect of the United Kingdom, see docs ECRML (2004) 1 and ECRML (2007) 2.

The European Commission against Racism and Intolerance

2.91 The European Commission against Racism and Intolerance (ECRI) seeks to combat racism, xenophobia, anti-semitism and intolerance by combating discrimination and prejudice on grounds of race, colour, language, religion, nationality and national or ethnic origin[1]. The Commission, which is composed of independent members, is a monitoring body. It examines the relevant situation in states on a four or five-year cycle and prepares reports with recommendations for action by governments. Initially, draft texts of these reports are communicated to aid what will be a process of confidential dialogue; the final report is made public two months after it has been transmitted unless the state concerned expressly requests that this should not take place[2]. Thereafter, the Commission will monitor what action is taken by national authorities in respect of any proposals made[3]. The Commission also makes policy recommendations on general themes and disseminates examples of good practice to states[4] while also seeking to promote intercultural understanding and respect in civil society. It may also issue statements on matters of contemporary concern[5].

1   The decision to establish the Commission was taken at the Summit of Heads of State and Government in Vienna in 1993, and the Committee began its work in 1994. Members of the

Commission are nominated by states on the basis of recognised expertise in the area of tackling intolerance. See further http://www.coe.int/ecri/.

2   For reports to the United Kingdom, see Docs CRI (99) 5; CRI (2001) 6 (this report recommended action to address a hostile climate concerning asylum seekers and refugees, to make effective criminal law provisions on incitement to racial hatred and civil rules on anti-discrimination, to tackle institutionalised racism in the police service, and to ensure the education system reflects the needs of a diverse society); CRI (2005) 27 (this report noted a failure to implement a number of recommendations made in the 2001 report, the continuation of racism and discrimination in particular affecting Roma/Gypsies, asylum seekers and refugees, and Muslims in connection with the implementation of legislation against terrorism, and the continued responsibility of the media for the climate of hostility towards such groups); and CRI (2010) 4 (this report focused upon the extent to which recommendations made in earlier reports had been implemented, noting an increase in racist attacks, the election of two BNP MEPs, continuing concerns over anti-terrorism legislation, and the funding of the Equality and Human Rights Commission).

3   The Commission arranges contact visits to states to allow its rapporteurs to meet government officials and non-governmental organisations. See further ECRI annual reports available at http://www.coe.int/ecri.

4   Including general policy recommendations on intolerance against Roma and Muslims, the establishment of specialised bodies at national level, combating the dissemination of racist etc material on the internet, and combating racism in fighting terrorism.

5   See eg statements on the ban of the construction of minarets in Switzerland (December 2009) and on the situation of Roma migrants in France (August 2010).

Economic and social rights

The European Social Charter

2.92 Guarantees for social and economic human rights concerning conditions of employment and social cohesion are found in the revised European Social Charter of 1996[1], which is gradually superseding the original 1961 Charter and its three additional Protocols[2]. The revised Charter contains a broad range of economic and social rights in the workplace, and more generally, in the areas of housing, health, education, and social protection[3]. States may decide at the time of ratification which obligations they wish to undertake, although there is a 'hard core' of rights (as well as a minimum number) to which they must subscribe[4].

1   ETS 163 (1996). This treaty was opened for signature in 1996 and entered into force on 1 July 1999. See further Burca and Bruno de Witte, eds *Social Rrights in Europe* (2005); and de Schutter *The European Social Charter: A Social Constitution for Europe* (2010). See further http://www.coe.int/socialcharter/; and

2   That is, ETS 35 (1961), ETS 128 (1988), ETS 142 (1991) and ETS 158 (1995).

3   That is, the rights: to work, just conditions of work, safe and healthy working conditions, and fair remuneration (including the right of women and men to equal pay for work of equal value) (Arts 1–4); to organise and bargain collectively (ESC Arts 5–6); of children and young persons to protection and of employed women to protection of maternity (Arts 7–8); to vocational guidance and training (Arts 9–10); to protection of health (Art 11); to social security, social and medical assistance and social welfare services (Arts 12–14); of disabled persons to social integration and of the family and of children and young persons to social, legal and economic

protection (Arts 16–17); to engage in gainful occupation elsewhere in Europe (Art 18); of migrant workers and their families to protection (Art 19); to equal treatment in employment without sexual discrimination (Art 20); of workers to information and consultation and to take part in determining working conditions and environment (Arts 21–22); of elderly persons to social protection (Art 23); to protection upon termination of employment, to protection of workers' claims in insolvency and to dignity at work (Arts 24–26); of workers with families to equal treatment (Art 27); of workers' representatives to protection; (to information and consultation in collective redundancies (Art 29); to protection against poverty and social exclusion (Art 30); and to housing (Art 31). The Court may refer to the European Social Charter in its judgments: see para **3.44** below.

4   ESC Arts A and B. The United Kingdom has accepted 60 of the 72 provisions (ie, all obligations except for Arts 2(1), 4(3), 7(1), (4), (7) and (8), 8(2)–(4) and 12 (2)–(4)). It has not as yet ratified the Additional Protocol of 1988 or the Amending Protocol of 1991, the Collective Complaints Protocol of 1995, or the Revised European Social Charter of 1996.

2.93 Supervision is by means of international monitoring and scrutiny of reports submitted annually by states. These are initially considered by the European Committee of Social Rights (the ECSR) whose reports in turn provide a legal assessment of the extent of state compliance with their obligations under the Charter. This report is then transmitted to a Governmental Committee which may prepare a recommendation for the Committee of Ministers to adopt by way of recommendations to a state to amend domestic law and practice if it appears that there has been non-compliance with a conclusion[1]. An additional enforcement procedure since 1998 has involved the examination of collective complaints by the European Committee of Social Rights which may in turn result in the adoption of a resolution by the Committee of Ministers[2].

1   ESC, Art C. Since 1992, the Parliamentary Assembly has also based social policy reports on the conclusions of the European Committee of Social Rights. Reports are submitted annually and the Committee issues 'conclusions', ie decisions on whether it considers situations in states are in conformity with the Charter. If no action is taken, the Committee of Ministers may issue a recommendation to the state concerned.

2   ESC, Art D. Complaints may now be lodged by recognised European management (the European Trade Union Confederation, BUSINESSEUROPE and the International Organisation of Employers), labour and non-governmental organisations (NGOs), and by employers' organisations and trade unions in the country concerned (and where a state has agreed, by national NGOs). If a complaint is declared admissible, a written procedure is instigated, and a public hearing may be held. The decision on the merits is transmitted to the Committee of Ministers which is thereafter made public. The Committee of Ministers will thereafter adopt a resolution and may recommend the state takes specific measures necessary to ensure compliance with the Charter. The first decision on admissibility of a collective complaint was taken in 1999 (1/1998 *International Commission of Jurists v Portugal* (1 February 1999)); as at 31 March 2011, it had received 66 collective complaints. A database of collective complaints is available at http://www.coe.int/T/E/Human_Rights/Esc/. See further European Committee on Social Rights *Collective Complaints Procedure: Summaries of Decisions on Admissibility: 1998–2010*; and *Summaries of Decisions on the Merits: 1998–2010* (2010). For discussion of standard-setting, see Malinverni 'La Cour Européenne des Droits de l'Homme et le Comité Européen des Droits Sociaux: Rapprochements et Convergences' in Breitenmoser et al (eds) *Neue Herausforderungen und Perspektiven für den Schutz der Menschenrechte: Kolloquium zu Ehren von Professor Dr Luzius Wildhaber* (2008), pp 3–13.

Promoting awareness of and respect for human rights

The Council of Europe Commissioner for Human Rights

2.94 The Council of Europe Commissioner for Human Rights was first appointed in 1999[1] and is charged with the promotion of human rights by raising awareness of human rights and ensuring their effective respect in Council of Europe member states. This office is designed to complement existing institutions and to play a preventive role (for example, by identifying shortcomings in domestic law and practice). The Commissioner is expected to exercise his functions with complete independence and impartiality while at the same time respecting the competence of the various Council of Europe supervisory bodies. He is thus a non-judicial officer who does not investigate individual complaints but can still act (within the general authority of promoting human rights) on any relevant information made available to him. He submits an annual report on his work to the Committee of Ministers and the Parliamentary Assembly of the Council of Europe, and takes into account views expressed by these institutions concerning the Commissioner's activities. The Commissioner may also issue recommendations, opinions and reports on any matters within his competence[2].

---

1   The office was approved at the Summit of Heads of State and Government in 1997, and the resolution setting out the Commissioner's terms of reference was adopted by the Committee of Ministers in 1999 (Resolution (99)50). The Commissioner for Human Rights is elected by the Parliamentary Assembly, by a majority of votes cast, from a list of three candidates drawn up by the Committee of Ministers and holds office for a non-renewable term of office of six years. Candidates must be nationals of a Council of Europe member state and have recognised expertise in the field of human rights.

2   Documents concerning the work of the Commissioner are available at http://www. commissioner.coe.int. For an example of a thematic report, see doc CommDH(2006)1 (on the human rights situation of the Roma, Sinti and Travellers in Europe); for reports in relation to the United Kingdom, see docs CommDH(2005)6/08 (visit of November 2004) (concerning anti-terrorism legislation, immigration and asylum, criminal justice, age of criminal responsibility, discrimination and race relations, anti-social behaviour orders, identity cards, the proposed Equality Commission, and human rights in Northern Ireland); CommDH(2008)23 (asylum and immigration); CommDH(2008)27 (rights of the child with focus on juvenile justice, and criticism again of the age of criminal responsibility, overuse of child detention and high re-offending rates); and CommDH(2008)28 (corporal punishment). The Commissioner may now intervene in cases before the Court: ECHR, Art 36(3): see para **2.53** above).

RESEARCHING HUMAN RIGHTS LAW

Strasbourg case law

2.95 The HRA 1998, s 2 requires a court or tribunal determining a question which has arisen in connection with a Convention right to take into account any judgment, decision or declaration or advisory opinion of the European Court of Human Rights, any decision on the admissibility of an application or any report on the merits of an application made by the former Commission, or any decision of the Committee of Ministers in relation to supervision of a judgment in so far as relevant to the proceedings[1]. The most important of these sources of ECHR law will be Court judgments and decisions: as the Court's case law has developed (and significantly increased), Commission decisions and reports are now of limited assistance[2]. Further, the substantial increase in the Court's workload is generating considerable opportunities for the clarification of the admissibility criteria, and the Court's decisions reflect the current interpretation.

1   HRA 1998, s 2, and SA 1998, s 129(2) (which requires courts to apply HRA 1998, s 2). See further paras **1.30–1.33** above.

2   For example, Court judgments cover most aspects of the interpretation of Arts 5 and 6 (although Commission decisions on admissibility are still of importance in determining what constitutes a 'deprivation of liberty': see paras **4.149–4.155** below). In contrast, Prot 1, Art 3's guarantees of fair elections required considerable discussion of Commission jurisprudence until comparatively recently. Similarly, Arts 2 and 3 had generated little in the way of Court discussion, but the relative importance of Commission decisions and reports in these areas has now been weakened considerably following a number of cases involving (in particular) Turkey, Russia and the United Kingdom.

Names of applicants

2.96 Court decisions on admissibility and judgments are cited by the name of the applicant and the respondent state, but rules of court provide that 'applicants who do not wish their identity to be disclosed to the public shall so indicate and shall submit a statement of the reasons justifying such a departure from the normal rule of public access to information in proceedings before the Court', and that anonymity may be authorised by the President of the Chamber 'in exceptional and duly justified cases'[1]. In such instances, applicants will be identified by the letters of their surnames (or, in earlier practice, by the use of a formula such as *X v United Kingdom*). A judgment is cited by the surname of the applicant, and with the addition of the applicant's first name where this is necessary to distinguish it from an earlier case[2].

1   Rule of Court 47(3).

2   Thus *Murray v United Kingdom* (1994) A 300-A; and *John Murray v United Kingdom* 1996-I. Cases involving the same applicant are distinguished thus eg *Olsson v Sweden (no 1)* (1988) A 130, and *Olsson v Sweden (no 2)* (1992) A 250. Note *Witold Litwa v Poland* 2000-III (citation of first name of applicant necessary to prevent the suggestion this case was an inter-state application, 'Litwa' being the Polish for 'Lithuania').

Primary sources

2.97 Official publications of the Council of Europe are generally available in print. However, most significant documents are now available on the Internet or on DVD, and since only a selection of the 'new' Court's judgments and reports on admissibility will now be available in printed reports, use of the Council of Europe's electronic database – HUDOC – is now indispensable[1]. Strasbourg case law is also reported in *European Human Rights Reports, European Human Rights Law Review, Human Rights Law Journal*, and in looseleaf format, in *Human Rights Practice*.

1   The HUDOC database contains relevant texts of supervisory organs under the Convention, including (most) decisions and reports of the former Commission, Court decisions and judgments, and (most) resolutions of the Committee of Ministers. It is accessible at http://echr.coe.int/echr/en/hudoc, and now available on a subscription-based (and regularly updated) DVD (for further information, see http://www.echr.coe.int/hudoccd). All sites referred to in this chapter are as accessed at 31 March 2011.

Travaux préparatoires

2.98 In interpreting the ECHR, limited use is made of the 'travaux préparatoires', that is, the documentation concerning the drafting of the treaty and Protocol no 1, in light of the insistence that the Convention should be seen as a 'living instrument'[1]. Discussions in the Parliamentary Assembly and Committee of Ministers and committees are reported in the *Collected Edition of the 'Travaux Préparatoires' of the European Convention on Human Rights*[2]; additionally, an incomplete (and possibly inaccurate) set of reports is now avaiable on-line[3].

1   For discussion of the Vienna Convention on the Law of Treaties and principles of interpretation, see paras **3.40–3.46** below.

2   Council of Europe *Collected Edition of the 'Travaux Préparatoires' of the European Convention on Human Rights*, 8 vols (1975–1985).

3   At http://www.echr.coe.int/Library/COLENTravauxprep.html.

Commission decisions and reports, and citations

2.99 Until 1999, the Commission gave *decisions* on the admissibility of applications, and issued *reports* on their merits. The case law of the former Commission is still of some (but declining) importance (the frequent references to its decisions and reports by the Court may indeed reflect the number of Judges who were formerly members of the Commission and the number of members of the Registry who previously worked in the Commission Secretariat).

A selection of key cases is found in *Collection of Decisions* (from 1959 until 1974) in 46 volumes and in *Decisions and Reports* (from 1975 until 1998): in 94 volumes (volumes 76 onwards appeared in two versions: the 'A' volume contained the text in the official working language for the application (that is, in either English or French) with volume 'B' appearing subsequently with translations). In addition, the *Yearbook of the European Convention on Human Rights* contains certain decisions and reports not readily accessible elsewhere. Further, *Series B* reports include the Commission's report in cases considered by the Court (as well as other relevant documents including written submissions to the Court), but this series terminated with volume 104 in 1995. Commission reports thereafter appear as an appendix to Court judgments in the *Series A* reports (and their continuation in *Reports of Judgments and Decisions*).

2.100 Citation of decisions and reports is thus somewhat complex[1]. Where a decision or report appears in more than one publication, only one reference is required, with the preferred citation in the case of decisions that of the *Collection* or *Decisions and Reports*. All applications are allocated a reference number, and *decisions* are normally cited by this number alone, unless it is considered necessary to specify the name of the respondent state. Decisions are cited in the following manner, eg:

> *Moreira de Azevedo v Portugal*, No 11296/84, Commission decision of 14 April 1988, Decisions and Reports 56, p 126

> *Garnieri v Italy*, No 22256/88, Commission decision of 18 May 1992, unreported

Reports may appear in a variety of official publications as follows, and are generally cited without the application number (although, in this work, the number is also given):

> *Köplinger v Austria*, Comm Report 1.10.68, para 24, Yearbook 12, p 484

> *Jespers v Belgium*, Comm Report 14.12.81, para 55, D.R. 27, p 87

> *Golder v United Kingdom*, Comm. Report 1.6.73, para 53, Eur Court HR, Series B no 16, p 38 [for a report published solely in the Series B reports]

> *Benthem v the Netherlands*, Comm. Report 8.10.83, para 95, Eur Court HR, Series A no 97, p 24 [for reports published in Series A and appended to the judgments of the Court]

> *FE v France*, Comm. Report 22.4.1998, para 46, Eur Court HR, Reports 1999, p 3362 [for a report published in *Reports of Judgments and Decisions* and appended to the judgments of the Court].

In this work, Commission decisions and reports are cited by application number and names of the parties: eg 9267/81, *Moureaux and Others v Belgium* (1983) DR 33, 97. Where a decision or report is unpublished, the date is given[2]: eg 21221/93, *LJ v Finland* (28 June 1995). Fuller citations (and relevant references to *European Human Rights Reports*) appear in the list of cases.

---

1   See Council of Europe 'Directive Concerning Quotations, References and Abbreviations in the Decisions and Reports of the Commission' (December 1996); and 'Memorandum on citation of judgments and decisions' (undated).

2   All judgments and decisions of the Court with the exception of decisions taken by committees of three judges (ECHR, Art 28: see para **2.52** above) are available on the HUDOC website (http://echr.coe.int/echr/en/hudoc) and DVD..

Court judgments and decisions on admissibility, and citations

2.101 Judgments of the Court from 1961 onwards appear in English and French in the *Series A* reports of the European Court of Human Rights and, from 1996 onwards, in the continuation of this series in *Reports of Judgments and Decisions*. From November 1998, the formal reports series of *Reports of Judgments and Decisions* (now cited as 'ECHR') has contained a selection of decisions on admissibility and judgments considered as being of some significance. There is now a delay between the date of decision or judgment and the appearance of the official report of cases selected for publication of approximately five years[1]. Since the vast majority of decisions and judgments are not officially reported, use of the Court's website is likely to be indispensable; but note that many decisions and judgments will not be translated into both official languages, and thus some material will be available only in French[2]. Remember, too, that judgments given by Chambers remain provisional for up three months[3], so that care must be taken in relying upon very recent cases.

1   A decision or judgment selected for future publication appears as eg '2010-…'.

2   Note that the *European Human Rights Reports* may contain English translations of French-language decisions and judgments. These translations are unofficial. Where a case is selected for publication in the official set of reports, it will appear in both languages in approved translations.

3   ECHR, Art 43 provides that any party to the case may, within three months from the date of a Chamber judgment, request that the case be referred to the Grand Chamber of the Court. The request is considered by a panel of five judges who will examine whether the case raises a serious question affecting the interpretation or application of the Convention or any other serious issue of general importance which would justify referral to the Grand Chamber. Chamber judgments thus become final only upon a rejection of any such request, on the expiry of the three-month period, or earlier if the parties declare that they do not intend to make a request to refer: see para **2.55** above. When a case has been referred, the Chamber judgment thus lapses, but may still serve as a 'source of guidance', at least where the Grand Chamber has ultimately deemed a case inadmissible: *Banfield v United Kingdom* (dec) 2005-XI.

2.102 Cases (and relevant judicial observations) before 1999 are cited by the Court in its judgments in the following format[1]:

Plattform 'Ärtze für das Leben' v Austria, 21 June 1988, § 31, Series A No 139

Delta v France (Article 50), 30 January 1990, § 38, Series A No 191-A

Allenet de Ribemont v France (interpretation), 7 August 1996, § 17, Reports of Judgments and Decisions 1996-III

National & Provincial Building Society, Leeds Permanent Building Society and Yorkshire Building Society v the United Kingdom, 23 October 1997, § 118, Reports 1997-VII

Gautrin and Others v France (friendly settlement), 20 May 1998, § 57, Reports 1998-III

Gustafsson v Sweden (revision – merits), 30 July 1998, § 28, Reports 1998-V

The official citation of decisions and judgments of the Court as from November 1998 is as follows[2]:

- Chamber judgment on merits

  Campbell v Ireland, *no 45678/98, §24, ECHR 1999-II.*

- Grand chamber judgment on merits

  Campbell v Ireland *[GC] no 45678/98, §24, ECHR 1999-II.*

- Chamber decision on admissibility

  Campbell v Ireland *(dec.), no 45678/98, ECHR 1999-II.*

- Grand chamber decision on admissibility

  Campbell v Ireland *(dec.) [GC], no 45678/98, ECHR 1999-II.*

- Chamber judgment on preliminary objections

  Campbell v Ireland *(preliminary objections), no 45678/98, §15, ECHR 1999-II.*

- Chamber judgment on just satisfaction

  Campbell v Ireland *(just satisfaction), no 45678/98, §15, ECHR 1999-II.*

- Chamber judgment on revision

  Campbell v Ireland *(revision), no 45678/98, §15, ECHR 1999-II.*

- Chamber judgment on interpretation

  Campbell v Ireland *(interpretation), no 45678/98, §15, ECHR 1999-II.*

Unreported cases (with paragraphs) are cited as follows:

Dupont v France, No 43568/98, § 24, 3 May 1999

Durand v France (striking out), No 45678/98, § 24, 5 September 1999

Martin v France (dec.), No 48666/98, § 22, 13 September 1999

In this work, Court judgments are cited for the sake of brevity as, for example, *T v Italy* (1992) A 245-C (the reference to the number of the report); or *Texeira de Castro v Portugal* 1998-IV (the year and volume of the report). Cases since 1998 are cited in the format *Campbell v Ireland* (dec) (in respect of an admissibility decision); *Campbell v Ireland* (in respect of a Chamber judgment); *Campbell v Ireland* (dec) [GC] (in respect of a Grand Chamber decision); and *Campbell v Ireland* [GC] (in respect of a Grand Chamber judgment), together with the date of the decision or judgment if a decision or judgment has not been selected for inclusion (in the official reports), or alternatively the year and volume number of the *Reports of Judgments and Decisions*. Note that the page number of the published report is not cited. If the case has been reported in *European Human Rights Reports*, the reference also appears in the list of cases.

---

1   See 'Memorandum on citation of judgments and decisions' (undated).

2   Court Instruction on Citation of Case-law of 3 April 2000; and 'Memorandum on citation of

judgments and decisions' (undated). Where the title includes the name of a newspaper or other publication, no italics are used: eg The Sunday Times *v the United Kingdom* (Article 50), 6 November 1980, § 22, Series A no. 38.

Resolutions of the Committee of Ministers

2.103 Where it is necessary to consider resolutions of the Committee of Ministers, these are available in printed collections[1] and in the appropriate volume of the *Yearbook of the European Convention on Human Rights*. This material is also available on-line on HUDOC (or in the HUDOC DVD). The Yearbook also contains relevant texts from the Parliamentary Assembly of the Council of Europe.

---

1   Collection of Resolutions adopted by the Committee of Ministers in the Application of Arts 32 and 54 of the European Convention for the Protection of Human Rights and Fundamental Freedoms: 1959–1983 (and subsequent volumes).

Websites

2.104 Most Strasbourg jurisprudence is available electronically. The Council of Europe's human rights home page is at http://www.coe.int/t/dghl/. Ready access to information on the Court and to the texts of Court decisions and judgments and Resolutions of the Committee of Ministers is available on HUDOC (but note that some early Commission decisions and reports are absent, and some decisions and judgments may be available only in French).

Digests

2.105 Virtually all material available in digests is now considerably out of date. The *Digest of Strasbourg Case-Law Relating to the European Convention on Human Rights* was published in looseleaf format (1984–1985; 6 volumes), while an earlier *Digest of Case Law Relating to the European Convention on Human Rights 1955–1967* (1970) is unlikely now to be of any practical assistance. A useful aid containing relevant extracts from Court judgments before 1999 is Kempees *A Systematic Guide to the Case-Law of the European Court of Human Rights* (1996–2000), published in 4 volumes (vols 1 and 2: 1960–1994; vol 3: 1995–1996; and vol 4 1997–1998).

Secondary sources

2.106 *Human Rights Information Bulletins* are published by the Directorate General of Human Rights some four times per year. The Court also (from November 1998 onwards) publishes monthly *Information Notices on the Case-Law of the Court*, now available on subscription, and an annual report giving statistical information. These documents may be accessed respectively at: http://www.coe.int/t/dghl/publications/index_publications_en.asp.

The *Yearbook of the European Convention on Human Rights* contains summaries of Court judgments. Case summaries (together with useful bibliographies) of judgments up until 1993 appear in Berger *Case Law of the European Court of Human Rights* (1989–1995) in 3 volumes (vol 1: 1960–1987; vol 2: 1988–1990; and vol 3: 1991–1993), and with key judgments in later cases in *Jurisprudence de la Cour Européenne des Droits de l'Homme* (10th edn, 2007).

The influential NGO based in London, the Aire Centre, represents applicants from across Europe before the Strasbourg Court, and publishes useful bulletins on the European Convention on Human Rights at http://www.airecentre.org .

2.107 The leading textbooks on the Convention appear in English, French or German; most are written (or co-written) by lawyers working in the Council of Europe, former members of the Commission, or past or current judges of the Court. See in particular:

- Charrier *Code de la Convention Européenne des Droits de l'Homme* (2005).

- Frohwein and Peukert *Europäische Menschenrechtskonvention: EMRK-Kommentar* (3rd edn, 2009).

- Grabenwarter *Europäische Menschenrechtskonvention* (3rd edn, 2008).

- Harris, O'Boyle, Bates and Buckley *Law of the European Convention on Human Rights* (2nd edn, 2009).

- Meyer-Ladewig *Konvention zum Schutz der Menschenrechte und Grundfreiheiten: Handkommentar* (2nd edn 2006).

- Reid *A Practitioner's Guide to the European Convention on Human Rights* (3rd edn, 2008).

- Renucci *Droit Européen des Droits de l'Homme* (2007).

- Van Dijk, van Hoof, van Rijn and Zwaak (eds) *Theory and Practice of the European Convention on Human Rights* (4th edn, 2006).

Several journals now contain discussion of substantive Convention guarantees and summaries of recent decisions and judgments. Most of this commentary is in English, French or German. The leading English-language publications include *European Human Rights Law Review* and *European Law Review*. The *Human Rights Law Journal* and its two foreign-language counterparts, *Revue Universelle des Droits de l'Homme* and *Europäische Grundrechte Zeitschrift,* contain articles and notes of recent judgments. The *European Law Review, International and Comparative Law Quarterly, Netherlands Quarterly of Human Rights* and *Revue Trimestrielle des Droits de l'Homme* all carry regular articles and commentary on Strasbourg case law.

Other human rights treaties and instruments; and related jurisprudence

2.108 Access to other human rights instruments[1] and reports may provide assistance in addressing issues of Convention rights in domestic tribunals. The Court itself makes reference to other relevant international treaties in its judgments[2]; and the Scottish courts have themselves proved willing to consider other Commonwealth jurisprudence[3].

The following websites in particular provide access to a range of international, regional and national materials: http://www1.umn.edu/humanrts ; http://www.hri.ca and http://www.hrdc.net/accesshr. The impressive search engine facility Human Rights Documentation Systems International is found at http://www.huridocs.org.

---

1   For a survey, see *United Nations Human Rights: a Compilation of International Instruments. Vol 1, Universal Instruments* (2002); and Marie 'International Instruments Relating to Human Rights' 17 RUDH 133 (2005)

2   See para **2.92** above and para **3.44** below.

3   Eg *Brown v Stott* 2001 SC (PC) 43 (observations by Lord Bingham at 61 and by Lord Hope of Craighead at 78–79). The growth in the use of comparative human rights law and practice in domestic proceedings is a phenomenon found in many jurisdictions. For recent discussion, see McCrudden 'A Common Law of Human Rights? Transnational Judicial Conversations' (2000) 20 OJLS 499; and Örücü, ed *Judicial Comparativism in Human Rights Cases* (2003) *passim*.

Jurisprudence of European domestic courts

2.109 Domestic human rights case law from other European countries is of particular relevance in the application of the Convention, but linguistic difficulties may prove a practical barrier to easy access. However, the work of the Council of Europe's Venice Commission may be of some assistance, and in particular its CODICES on-line database on jurisprudence of national courts: see http://www.codices.coe.int. The *Yearbook of the European Convention on Human Rights* also contains summaries to the use of the ECHR in influencing or implementing domestic legislation and executive acts in member states, and of decisions of domestic courts concerning Convention guarantees. The *Human Rights Law Journal* (and particularly its two foreign-language counterparts *Revue Universelle des Droits de l'Homme,* and *Europäische Grundrechte Zeitschrift*) also contain human rights decisions of European domestic courts. An additional source of assistance is *European Current Law* which includes summaries of domestic developments.

Many websites now give direct access to decisions of constitutional courts (and equivalent bodies) in English, French, German, Italian or Spanish[1]. The website of the Court of Justice of the European Union is available at: http://curia.europa.eu.

---

1   See http://www.venice.coe.int/site/dynamics/N_Court_Links_ef.asp?L=E.

Commonwealth, etc jurisprudence

2.110 The *Commonwealth Human Rights Law Digest* provides a summary of key Commonwealth judgments. The Interights website at http://www.interights.org provides access to the Commonwealth Human Rights Case Law database. Sites providing access to Commonwealth courts' interpretation of human rights treaties and domestic human rights charters include:

- Australia: http://www.austlii.edu.au/databases.html
- Canada: http://www.scc-csc.gc.ca and http://www.canlii.org/en/index.html
- New Zealand: http://www.austlii.edu.au/nz/cases/NZCA
- South Africa: http://www.concourt.gov.za

International and other non-Commonwealth jurisprudence

2.111 The leading English language periodicals and reports (each of which also contains material on the ECHR) include *Netherlands Quarterly of Human Rights,* the *Human Rights Quarterly,* and *International Human Rights Reports.* The UN's main portal is at http://www.un.org. Materials from the Human Rights Committee is accessed via http://www1.umn.edu/humanrts/undocs/undocs.htm; the home page of the UN Human Rights Council (established in 2006) is at http://www2.ohchr.org/english/bodies/hrcouncil. The website of the International Court of Justice in The Hague is available at http://www.icj-cij.org; that of the UN High Commissioner for Refugees at http://www.unhcr.ch; and that of the International Labour Organisation at http://www.ilo.org. Decisions of the Inter-American Court of Human Rights can be found at: http://www.corteidh.or.cr.

Other potentially useful sites include:

- Amnesty International: http://www.amnesty.org
- Human Rights Watch: http://www.hrw.org
- INTERIGHTS: http://www.interights.org

Chapter 3

Applying the European Convention on Human Rights

THE OBLIGATIONS OF THE UNITED KINGDOM

Ratification of the European Convention on Human Rights by the United Kingdom

3.01 The European Convention on Human Rights (ECHR) and its protocols guarantee a range of rights and freedoms designed to secure a minimum level of protection against arbitrary state authority. The extent of a state's obligations is, however, dependent upon the application or otherwise of any declaration, reservation or derogation made by the state in question, as well as the range of optional protocols ratified. In other words, although there is one system of European human rights protection enforceable before the European Court of Human Rights, state responsibility is dependent upon the extent of state assumption of such responsibility. In this sense, then, although there is a scheme for the protection of human rights within Europe, the scope of the rights protected varies across the continent[1].

---

1   Prior to the entry into force of Prot 11, the nature of the enforcement machinery available to individuals to challenge states was also dependent upon individual state acceptance of the right of individual application and of the Court's optional jurisdiction but, since November 1998, one universal system of enforcement machinery has existed: see paras **2.41–2.48** above. The state of signatures and ratifications of the ECHR and its protocols is found in the most recent *Human Rights Information Bulletin* of the Council of Europe's Directorate of Human Rights or on the internet at: www.conventions.coe.int. Another factor is the status of the ECHR in domestic law in European states, on which see Sciotti-Lam, *L'Applicabilité des Traités Internationaux Relatifs aux Droits de l'Homme en Droit Interne* (2004); and Keller and Stone Sweet *A Europe of Rights* (2008).

3.02 So far as the UK is concerned, the substantive rights conferred on individuals under international law derive in the first place from the ECHR, Articles 2–18, which was ratified on 8 March 1951 and came into force on 23 September 1953. Further rights derive from Protocol no 1, which was ratified on 3 November 1952 and came into force on 18 May 1954; Protocol no 6, which came into force on 1 March 1985 and was ratified by the United Kingdom on 27 January 1999; and Protocol no 13, which came into force on 1 July 2003 and was ratified by the United Kingdom on 10 October 2003. These ECHR Articles and Protocols are also reflected in the 'Convention rights' created in domestic law by the Human Rights Act 1998 and the Scotland Act 1998[1].

1   See paras **1.03–1.04** and **1.06** above. Ireland adopted the model of the Human Rights Act 1998 when it introduced the European Convention on Human Rights Act 2003 [Ireland] following a commitment made under the Good Friday Agreement (the 'Belfast Agreement'), but the range of rights contains additional restrictions and is itself subject to the provisions of the Irish Constitution. See eg Besson 'The Reception Process in Ireland and the United Kingdom' in Keller and Stone Sweet *A Europe of Rights* (2008) pp 31–106; and de Londras *European Convention on Human Rights Act: Operation, Impact and Analysis* (2010).

Territorial scope of responsibilities of state parties

The concept of 'jurisdiction'

3.03 The ECHR, Article 1 provides that 'the High Contracting Parties shall secure to everyone within their jurisdiction' the rights contained in the treaty, and thus the exercise of jurisdiction is a necessary condition for a state's responsibility for acts or omissions imputable to it[1]. The concept of 'jurisdiction' is given its meaning in public international law, with the consequence that a state's jurisdictional competence is primarily territorial, other bases of jurisdiction being exceptional and requiring special justification in the circumstances of each case. The Convention operates, subject to Article 56, in an essentially regional context and notably in the legal space (*espace juridique*) of the contracting states (ie within the area of the Council of Europe countries)[2].

1   *Ilaşcu and Others v Moldova and Russia* [GC] 2004-VII, para 311.

2   *Banković and Others v Belgium and 16 Other Contracting States* (dec) [GC] 2001-XII, paras 59–61, 80; *Assanidzé v Georgia* [GC] 2004-II, para 137. See also *Hussein v Albania et al* (dec) (14 March 2006) (detention and trial by Iraqi officials did not engage responsibilities of domestic states, the allegation that Iraq was under foreign control being insufficient to establish jurisdictional links with any state); and *Ben El Mahi v Denmark* (dec) 2006-XV (application by resident Moroccan national and associations based in Morocco concerning publication in Denmark of cartoons considered offensive: no jurisdictional link and thus inadmissible). For discussion of considerations applying in the case of threatened deportation or extradition from a state which has ratified the ECHR, see paras **4.54–4.59** and **4.130–4.137** below. British judges have noted the impossibility of attempting to apply the ECHR, at least in its entirety, in the context of societies with different cultures and values: see eg *R (Al-Skeini) v Secretary of State for Defence* [2008] 1 AC 153 at para 78 per Lord Rodger of Earlsferry; and *EM (Lebanon) v Secretary of State for the Home Department* [2009] 1 AC 1198 at para 42 per Lord Bingham of Cornhill. As was however noted in *R (Smith) v Oxfordshire Assistant Deputy Coroner* [2011] 1 AC 1, a state might in some circumstances be required to meet ECHR requirements in so far as it exercises an extra-territorial jurisdiction, without having to secure the whole package.

3.04 The ECHR, Article 56[1] however provides that a state may declare by notification to the Secretary General of the Council of Europe that the ECHR applies to any territory for whose international relations it is responsible. Under Article 56, the United Kingdom has notified its acceptance of the application of the ECHR to certain of its territories. Separate notification is required under each optional protocol[2]. The failure of a state to lodge notification cannot be overcome by arguing that it is in effective control of the territory in question[3]. Any territorial extension of the ECHR's application is subject to due regard being taken of 'local requirements'[4]. The meaning of that expression was considered in *Tyrer v United Kingdom*, where the respondent government attempted to justify the continuation of judicially-authorised corporal punishment on the grounds that its use was supported by public opinion and was necessary to deter crime and uphold public order. The Court considered such arguments to be more to do with 'circumstances and conditions' than 'local requirements', since it could not be shown that the maintenance of law and order specifically required such a punishment[5].

1   Formerly ECHR, Art 63.

2   The United Kingdom has accepted the extension either on a permanent or renewable basis of ECHR obligations to Anguilla, Bermuda, British Virgin Islands, Cayman Islands, Falkland Islands, Gibraltar, the Bailiwick of Guernsey, Isle of Man, the Bailiwick of Jersey, Montserrat, St Helena, St Helena Dependencies, South Georgia and South Sandwich Islands, Turks and Caicos Islands, and (from March 2004) the Sovereign Base Areas of Akrotiri and Dhekelia in Cyprus. For an example, see *Matthews v United Kingdom* [GC] 1999-I (application to Gibraltar). Cf *Gillow v United Kingdom* (1986) A 109, para 62 (no express declaration had been made under Prot 1 to extend these provisions to Guernsey, and thus the Court had no jurisdiction to consider arguments based upon the right to property). See also 16137/90, *Bui Van Thanh v United Kingdom* (1990) DR 65, 330 (complaint that threatened deportation from Hong Kong involved exercise of UK policy declared inadmissible as the UK had not made a declaration extending the ECHR to the colony); and *Yonghong v Portugal* (dec) 1999-IX (proposed extradition from Macao to China).

3   *Quark Fishing Ltd v United Kingdom* (dec) 2006-XIV (refusal of a licence permitting fishing in the waters of South Georgia and the South Sandwich Islands: no extension of Prot 1 to this territory had been made, and the 'effective control' principle could not replace the system of declarations particularly in light of the regional basis of the ECHR and the exceptional nature of extensions beyond that legal space). For domestic discussion of Art 56, see *R (Quark Fishing Ltd) v Secretary of State for Foreign and Commonwealth Affairs* [2006] 1 AC 529 at para 24 per Lord Bingham of Cornhill and at paras 35–44 per Lord Nicholls of Birkenhead, *R (Al-Skeini) v Secretary of State for Defence* [2008] 1 AC 153, at paras 111–114 per Lord Brown of Eaton-under-Heywood; *R (Bancoult) v Secretary of State for Foreign and Commonwealth Affairs (No 2)* [2009] 1 AC 453; and *R (Barclay) v Lord Chancellor and Secretary of State for Justice* [2010] 1 AC 464.

4   ECHR, Art 56(3).

5   *Tyrer v United Kingdom* (1978) A 26, para 38: the Court also ruled that even were a local requirement to have been established (that is, that corporal punishment was indeed necessary to maintain law and order), this would not in any case have allowed a state to make use of such a punishment since states cannot derogate from Art 3 which contains an absolute prohibition of torture or inhuman or degrading treatment.

3.05 Jurisdiction is presumed to be exercised throughout the state's territory unless it can be shown on account of exceptional circumstances that a state is unable to exercise its authority. However, 'a constraining de facto situation, such as obtains when a separatist regime is set up, whether or not this is accompanied by military occupation by another State', does not mean that a state ceases to have jurisdiction for the purposes of Article 1, as a positive obligation to seek to secure ECHR guarantees will continue[1]. In *Ilaşcu and Others v Moldova and*

Russia, Moldova claimed that it was not in control of an area of its territory in which a self-styled 'Moldavian Republic of Transdniestria' had been established with the support of Russia, but the Court considered that the Moldovan Government could still be held responsible in terms of Article 1 in respect of complaints of ill-treatment and arbitrary deprivation of liberty, since the government had not taken all appropriate measures (diplomatic, economic, judicial or otherwise) to seek to re-establish control or to secure the release of those applicants still imprisoned[2]. This presumption of competence and control over national territory is justified on the grounds of the maintenance of equality between states and the effectiveness of the ECHR[3], but is rebuttable in certain circumstances[4].

---

1   *Ilaşcu and Others v Moldova and Russia* [GC] [2004]-VII, para 333. See also *Loizidou v Turkey* (preliminary objections) (1995) A 310; and *Cyprus v Turkey* [GC] 2001-IV, paras 76–80; *Banković and Others v Belgium and 16 Other Contracting States* (dec) [GC] 2001-XII, paras 70–71.

2   *Ilaşcu and Others v Moldova and Russia* [GC] [2004]-VII, paras 322–353.

3   *Assanidzé v Georgià* [GC] 2004-II, para 142 (judgment and presidential decrees granting pardon ignored by the local authorities in the 'Ajarian Autonomous Republic').

4   One example would have been Kosovo which, although part of Serbia's national territory, was administered until recently under UN auspices in terms of UN Resolution 1244.

Extra-territorial application

3.06 The concept of 'jurisdiction' is not necessarily restricted to a state's national territory, as acts performed or which produce effects outside a state's territory ('extra-territorial acts') may amount to the exercise of a state's jurisdiction in terms of international law. As has been said in the House of Lords, however, in relation to this issue:

> '... the judgments and decisions of the European court do not speak with one voice. If the differences were merely in emphasis, they could be shrugged off as being of no great significance. In reality, however, some of them appear much more serious and so present considerable difficulties for national courts which have to try to follow the jurisprudence of the European court.'[1]

---

1   *R (Al-Skeini) v Secretary of State for Defence* [2008] 1 AC 153 at para 67 per Lord Rodger of Earlsferry.

3.07 In this context, particular importance attaches to the unanimous decision of the Grand Chamber in *Banković and Others v Belgium and 16 Other Contracting States*. In that case the Court could find no jurisdictional link between the persons who were the victims of the aerial bombing of a television station in Belgrade by NATO forces, that action being taken as part of NATO's campaign against the Federal Republic of Yugoslavia following the failure to resolve the situation in Kosovo by diplomatic means, and those countries which were members both of NATO and of the Council of Europe. The applicants' assertion that a positive obligation existed to secure Convention rights in a manner proportionate to the level of control exercised in any given extraterritorial situation was tantamount, the Court considered, to holding that the phrase 'within their jurisdiction' in Article 1 was superfluous and devoid of any purpose. Such a reading would also be inconsistent with the Court's view that the rights and freedoms in the Convention cannot be 'divided and tailored'[1]. It would also be inconsistent with existing state practice, since earlier instances of military intervention had not led any state to make a derogation under Article 15, thus suggesting a lack of apprehension of extraterritorial responsibility in military contexts. Nor did the Court consider that declaring the complaint inadmissible would defeat the *ordre public* mission of the ECHR, since the Court's obligation was to have regard to the special character of the ECHR as a constitutional instrument of European public order operating in the legal space (*espace juridique*) of member states: it was not designed to be applied throughout the world, even in respect of the conduct of contracting states[2]. It appears therefore that recognition of extraterritorial jurisdiction is confined to exceptional circumstances in which the principle of 'effective control' applies. Where there is no 'effective control' over a territory or an individual, there can be no 'jurisdiction' for the purposes of Article 1.

---

1   *Banković and Others v Belgium and 16 Other Contracting States* (dec) [GC] 2001-XII, at para 75.

2   *Banković and Others v Belgium and 16 Other Contracting States* (dec) [GC] 2001-XII. For domestic discussion, see *R (Al-Skeini) v Secretary of State for Defence* [2008] 1 AC 153; *R (Gentle) v Prime Minister* [2008] 1 AC 1356; *R (Al-Saadoon) v Secretary of State for Defence* [2010] QB 486; and *R (Smith) v Oxfordshire Assistant Deputy Coroner* [2011] 1 AC 1. The decision in *Banković* can be contrasted with *Markovic and Others v Italy* [GC] 2006-XIV, paras 49–56 at para 54, a case arising out of the same NATO air strike, but here relatives of those killed had brought a civil action in the Italian courts, as they considered that Italy's involvement in the military operations had been more extensive than that of other NATO states. In this instance, the Grand Chamber ruled that once the applicants had raised such proceedings, there then existed the requisite jurisdictional link (in respect of those proceedings) irrespective of what effect the extraterritorial nature of the challenged events would have on the final determination of the proceedings, for 'if civil proceedings are brought in the domestic courts, the State is required by Article 1 of the ECHR to secure in those proceedings respect for the rights protected by Article 6'.

3.08 As to what is meant by 'effective control', it has been suggested by Lord Rodger of Earlsferry that

'… the obligation under article 1 can arise only where the contracting state has such effective control of the territory of another state that it could secure to everyone in the territory all the rights and freedoms in section 1 of the Convention.'[1]

Lord Brown of Eaton-under-Heywood observed in the same case:

'Except where a state really does have effective control of territory, it cannot hope to secure Convention rights within that territory and, unless it is within the area of the Council of Europe, it is unlikely in any event to find certain of the Convention rights it is bound to secure reconcilable with the customs of the resident population'[2].

As Lord Brown commented[3], the imposition of Convention guarantees by an occupying force in a society with very different values (such as in Iraq) would in addition be incompatible with the obligations of the state responsible for that force under other rules of international law.

1   *R (Al-Skeini) v Secretary of State for Defence* [2008] 1 AC 153 at para 79. See also *R (Al Rawi) v Secretary of State for Foreign and Commonwealth Affairs* [2008] QB 289 (no obligation on UK under Art 1 to take steps to protect persons detained by USA at Guantanamo Bay detention centre).

2   *R (Al-Skeini) v Secretary of State for Defence* [2008] 1 AC 153 at para 129.

3   *R (Al-Skeini) v Secretary of State for Defence* [2008] 1 AC 153 at para 129.

3.09 Where a state exercises de facto effective control of an area situated outside national boundaries, for example as a consequence of military action, Article 1 responsibility may be engaged. In particular, the Court recognises Article 1 jurisdiction in order to avoid a 'vacuum in human rights' protection' when the territory 'would normally be covered by the Convention' ie in a Council of Europe country, where otherwise the inhabitants 'would have found themselves excluded from the benefits of the Convention safeguards which they had previously enjoyed'[1].

1   *Banković and Others v Belgium and 16 Other Contracting States* (dec) [GC] 2001-XII, para 80.

3.10 The circumstances in which the Court has exceptionally recognised the extraterritorial exercise of jurisdiction by a state appear to be three in number[1].

First, where the state 'through the effective control of the relevant territory and its inhabitants abroad as a consequence of military occupation or through the consent, invitation or acquiescence of the government of that territory, exercises all or some of the public powers normally to be exercised by [the government of that country]'[2]. An example is Northern Cyprus. In *Loizidou v Turkey*, an individual resident in southern Cyprus had been denied access on several occasions to her property in the northern part of the island, occupied by the respondent state. The Court accepted that Turkey had a responsibility in terms of Article 1 for 'securing' the Convention rights and freedoms of those affected by the occupation of northern Cyprus, an obligation arising directly from its control of the territory, whether or not the military action was lawful[3]. Further, a situation of occupation and control engages state responsibility not merely in respect of action taken by its officials and agents (such as its military), but also a more general responsibility to ensure that the rights contained in the ECHR are secured throughout the territory. The e:'acquiescence or connivance' of the authorities (including authorities which are not internationally recognised) in the acts of private individuals which violate the Convention rights of other individuals will give rise to interferences with Convention guarantees[4]. A further consequence is that, exceptionally, two states may be deemed to have responsibility for complaints of human rights violations in the same territory. Thus in *Ilaşcu and Others v Moldova and Russia* the Court held that the responsibility of Russia was engaged in terms of Article 1 on account of its military, political and economic contribution to the survival of the separatist regime in the Moldovan region of Transdniestria, a regime which remained under the effective authority (or at the very least under the decisive influence) of Russia[5].

1 This analysis reflects that of Lord Brown of Eaton-under-Heywood in *R (Al-Skeini) v Secretary of State for Defence* [2008] 1 AC 153 at para 109, with which the other members of the majority agreed. See also *R (Smith) v Oxfordshire Assistant Deputy Coroner* [2011] 1 AC 1 at paras 267–269 and 305 per Lord Collins JSC.

2 *Banković and Others v Belgium and 16 Other Contracting States* (dec) [GC] 2001-XII, para 80.

3 *Loizidou v Turkey* (preliminary objections) (1995) A 310, para 56. See further Matscher 'Bemerkungen zur extraterritorialen oder indirekten Wirkung der EMKR' in Donatsch, Forster and Schwarzenegger (eds) *Strafrecht, Strafprozessrecht und Menschenrechte: Festschrift für S Trechsel zum 65. Geburtstag* (2002), pp 25–45; Costa 'L'Etat, le Territoire et la Convention Européenne des Droits de l'Homme' in Kohen (ed) *Promoting Justice, Human Rights and Conflict Resolution through International Law: Liber Amicorum Lucius Caflisch* (2007), pp 179–195; and Larsen '"Territorial Non-Application" of the ECHR' (2009) 78 NJIL 73.

4 *Cyprus v Turkey* 2001-IV, para 81.

5 *Ilaşcu and Others v Moldova and Russia* [GC] 2004-VII, paras 376–394.

3.11 Second, a state will also be responsible in 'cases involving the activities of its diplomatic or consular agents abroad and on board craft and vessels registered in, or flying the flag of, that state [where] customary international law and treaty provisions have recognised the extraterritorial exercise of jurisdiction'[1].

1 *Banković and Others v Belgium and 16 Other Contracting States* (dec) [GC] 2001-XII, para 73. In *R (B) v Secretary of State for Foreign and Commonwealth Affairs* [2005] QB 643 it was held that the British Embassy in Melbourne was within the jurisdiction of the UK and that the HRA 1998 was therefore capable of applying to the actions of diplomatic and consular officials.

3.12 Third, there are certain other exceptional cases where a state's responsibility 'could, in principle, be engaged because of acts ... which produced effects or were performed outside their own territory'[1]. A number of cases concerned with irregular extraditions can be regarded as illustrations of this principle. For example, in *Öcalan v Turkey*, the Court noted that the applicant had been arrested by members of the Turkish security forces inside a Turkish-registered aircraft in the international zone of Nairobi airport, and that from that point onwards he had been under effective Turkish authority and therefore within the 'jurisdiction' of Turkey[2]. In *Issa and Others v Turkey*, which concerned a military operation conducted by the Turkish army in northern Iraq, since Turkish forces had not exercised effective control of all or part of the territory it was not possible to draw the conclusion that particular individuals had been within the jurisdiction of Turkey at the relevant time[3]. The Court however accepted that Article 1 jurisdiction could also arise where an individual was under the authority and control of agents of a state who were operating, either lawfully or unlawfully, outside the territory of that state[4]. The latter observations are not easily reconciled with *Banković.*

1   *Banković and Others v Belgium and 16 Other Contracting States* (dec) [GC] 2001-XII, para
     69. See eg *Drozd and Janousek v France and Spain* (1992) A 240, para 91 (if a French judge
     exercised jurisdiction in Andorra in his capacity as a French judge, anyone complaining of a
     violation of his Convention rights by that judge would be regarded as being within France's
     jurisdiction). Scottish judges sat as such in the Netherlands in the Lockerbie case.

2   *Öcalan v Turkey* [GC] 2005-IV, paras 89 and 91. See also 28780/95, *Illich Sanchez Ramirez v
     France* (1996) DR 86, 155; *Medvedyev and Others v France* [GC] 2010-…. In *Al-Saadoon
     and Mufdhi v United Kingdom* (dec) (30 June 2009), detainees in British detention centres in
     Iraq were held to be within UK jurisdiction by reason of the UK authorities' control over the
     premises in question.

3   *Issa and Others v Turkey* (16 Nov 2004), paras 72–82. In *R (Al Skeini) v Secretary of State for
     Defence* [2008] 1 AC 153 the House of Lords held that the HRA 1998 had extra-territorial
     applicability in respect of Art 2 obligations applying to the death of a prisoner in a British
     detention facility in Iraq, by analogy with the cases concerned with diplomatic missions and
     vessels: see para **1.75** above. It did not however apply to the deaths of Iraqi civilians in the
     course of military operations in Iraq. Nor did it apply to the deaths of British soldiers in the
     course of such operations: *R (Gentle) v Prime Minister* [2008] AC 1356; *R (Smith) v Oxfordshire
     Assistant Deputy Coroner* [2011] 1 AC 1.

4   *Issa and Others v Turkey* (16 Nov 2004), para 71.

3.13 Certain ECHR guarantees also have a potential extraterritorial application
in prohibiting the removal of an individual from a Council of Europe member state
to another state, for example where that person would face a serious risk to life
or where there would be a significant risk that the person would be subjected to
torture or to inhuman or degrading punishment, whether at the hands of state or
non-state actors[1]. These cases involve action by the state while the person
concerned is 'on its territory, clearly within its jurisdiction' and not, therefore, the
exercise of the state's jurisdiction abroad[2].

1   See eg *Bader v Sweden* 2005-XI, paras 41–49 (substantial grounds for believing that the first
     applicant would be exposed to a real risk of being executed if returned to Syria, and deportation
     would violate Art 2); *Soering v the United Kingdom* (1989) A 161, paras 88–91 (return to the
     USA would expose the applicant to detention conditions on 'death row' and to treatment in
     violation of Art 3). See further paras **4.54–4.59** and **4.130–4.137** below.

2   *Banković and Others v Belgium and 16 Other Contracting States* (dec) [GC] 2001-XII, para
     68.

Domestic consideration of 'jurisdiction'

3.14 The territorial scope of the UK's obligations under Article 1 has been
considered in several domestic cases concerned with the ambit of the HRA 1998.
Some of the cases concern territories which have been the subject of a notification
under Article 56[1]; others concern British diplomatic or other establishments
overseas[2]; others again concern the activities of British forces overseas[3]. These
cases are discussed in chapter 1[4].

1   *R (Quark Fishing Ltd) v Secretary of State for Foreign and Commonwealth Affairs* [2006] 1
     AC 529; *R (Barclay) v Lord Chancellor and Secretary of State for Justice* [2010] 1 AC 464.

2   *R (B) v Secretary of State for Foreign and Commonwealth Affairs* [2005] QB 643.

3   *R (Al-Skeini) v Secretary of State for Defence* [2008] 1 AC 153; *R (Al Jedda) v Secretary of State for Defence* [2008] 1 AC 332; *R (Gentle) v Prime Minister* [2008] 1 AC 1356; *R (Al-Saadoori) v Secretary of State for Defence* [2010] QB 486; *R (Smith) v Oxfordshire Assistant Deputy Coroner* [2011] 1 AC 1.

4   Above, para **1.75**.

International organisations and the responsibilities of state parties

3.15 The *Banković* case raised but did not resolve the question whether state responsibility was engaged under the ECHR in respect of acts of international organisations of which Council of Europe states are members. Such organisations are not responsible under the ECHR, even as the holders of sovereign power transferred to them by contracting states, unless they are themselves contracting parties to the ECHR. Contracting states, on the other hand, are in principle responsible under the ECHR for all acts and omissions of their organs, regardless of whether the act or omission in question was a consequence of domestic law or of the necessity to comply with international legal obligations[1]. One question which therefore arises is whether the acts in question are attributable to the contracting state or to the international organisation. This is not a question as to the territorial scope of the state's responsibility: in the language used by the Court, it raises a question of jurisdiction *ratione personae* rather than *ratione loci*[2].

1   *Bosphorus Hava Yollari Turizm ve Ticaret Anonim Şirketi v Ireland* [GC] 2005-VI, paras 152–153.

2   See para **2.61** below.

3.16 This question was considered by a Grand Chamber in the conjoined case of *Behrami and Behrami v France and Saramati v France, Germany and Norway*, which related to events in Kosovo. The applicants in *Behrami* complained of death and injury caused to children by the explosion of undetonated cluster bombs previously dropped by NATO forces. They blamed French KFOR troops for failing to clear the mines. Mr Saramati complained of his extra-judicial detention by troops acting on the orders of KFOR. The Court held that the acts and omissions in question were attributable to the UN, since the UN had retained ultimate authority and had delegated only operational command. The ECHR could not be interpreted in a manner which would subject the acts and omissions of contracting states which were covered by UN Security Council resolutions to the scrutiny of the Court, since to do so would interfere with the fulfilment of the UN's mission. This reasoning equally applied to voluntary acts of contracting states, such as the vote of a member of the Security Council in favour of a resolution and the contribution of troops to the security mission, since such acts also were crucial to the fulfilment of the UN's mission. The applicants' complaints were accordingly incompatible *ratione personae* with the provisions of the ECHR[1].

1   *Behrami and Behrami v France and Saramati v France, Germany and Norway* (dec) [GC]

2007-.... See also 6231/73, *Hess v the United Kingdom* (1975) DR 2, 72 (participation in four-power administration of Spandau Prison in Berlin did not mean that Art 1 jurisdictional responsibility was engaged).

3.17 In the domestic case of *R (Al Jedda) v Secretary of State for Defence*, on the other hand, it was held that the detention of the appellant by British forces in Iraq was not attributable to the UN and was not therefore on that basis outside the scope of the Convention, since the multi-national force in Iraq was not established at the behest of the UN, was not mandated to operate under UN auspices and was not a subsidiary organ of the UN[1].

1   *R (Al Jedda) v Secretary of State for Defence* [2008] 1 AC 332.

3.18 A further question is whether the acts in question, if attributable to the contracting state, can be justified under the ECHR by the state's compliance with obligations flowing from an international organisation to which it has transferred part of its sovereignty. This question arose in *Bosphorus Hava Yollari Turizm ve Ticaret Anonim Şirketi v Ireland* (the '*Bosphorus Airways*' case), which concerned the impoundment of an aircraft by Irish authorities in compliance with an EU regulation implementing a UN Security Council resolution imposing sanctions on Serbia. The applicant's challenge concerned the absence of compensation for the impoundment. The Court found, on the basis of an earlier decision of the European Court of Justice, that the failure of the Irish authorities to pay compensation was in compliance with the state's obligations under EU law. The Court confirmed the existence of a rebuttable presumption of compatibility of acts adopted by states in fulfilment of the obligations imposed upon them as members of an international organisation (here, the European Union) with those obligations assumed in ratifying the ECHR, always providing that these acts may be adequately reviewed for compatibility with fundamental rights within the system set up in the organisation in question:

> 'State action taken in compliance with such legal obligations [arising out of commitments undertaken in ratifying a treaty concluded subsequently to accession to the Convention] is justified as long as the relevant organisation is considered to protect fundamental rights, as regards both the substantive guarantees offered and the mechanisms controlling their observance, in a manner which can be considered at least equivalent to that for which the Convention provides. ... By 'equivalent' the Court means 'comparable'; any requirement that the organisation's protection be 'identical' could run counter to the interest of international co-operation pursued ... If such equivalent protection is considered to be provided by the organisation, the presumption will be that a State has not departed from the requirements of the Convention when it does no more than implement legal obligations flowing from its membership of the organisation. However, any such presumption can be rebutted if, in the circumstances of a particular case, it is considered that the protection of Convention rights was manifestly deficient.'[1]

The Court thereafter found that the protection of fundamental rights by EU law could be considered to be equivalent to that of the Convention system.

1   *Bosphorus Hava Yollari Turizm ve Ticaret Anonim Şirketi v Ireland* [GC] 2005-VI, paras
    155–156. See also *KRS v United Kingdom* (dec) 2008-… (removal of asylum seeker from UK
    to Greece in accordance with Dublin II Regulation: presumption that Greece would act
    compatibly with Art 3); *Cooperatieve Producentenorganisatie van de Nederlandse
    Kokkelvisserij UA v Netherlands* (dec) 2009-… (not shown that procedure before the ECJ
    was 'manifestly deficient' in that there was no opportunity to respond to the opinion of the
    Advocate General and thus the applicant had failed to rebut the presumption that the procedure
    before the ECJ provided equivalent protection of its rights); but cf *Emesa Sugar NV v
    Netherlands* (dec) (13 January 2005) (argument of unfair hearing before the ECJ avoided as the
    issue did not concern a 'civil' right); and *MSS v Belgium and Greece* [GC] (21 January 2011),
    noted at para **4.133** below.

3.19 A related question is whether the obligations of a contracting state under the
ECHR may be qualified by its obligations under some other international treaty[1].
Article 103 of the UN Charter, in particular, provides that in the event of a conflict
between the obligations of the members of the UN under the Charter and their
obligations under any other international instrument, their obligations under the
Charter shall prevail. This was applied in *R (Al Jedda) v Secretary of State for
Defence,* where the House of Lords held that British forces could lawfully exercise
a power of detention without trial in Iraq, authorised by UN Security Council
resolutions, but must ensure that the detainees' rights under the ECHR, Article 5
were not infringed to any greater extent than was inherent in such detention[2].

1   For cases involving proceedings of international judicial organs in the context of labour conflicts
    involving international civil servants and employing international organisations in which
    respondent states had neither directly nor indirectly intervened, see eg *Boivin v 34 Member
    States of the Council of Europe* (dec) 2008-… (European Organisation for the Safety of Air
    Navigation ('Eurocontrol'); *Rambus Inc v Germany* (dec) (16 June 2009) (European Patent
    Office)). See further Angelet and Weerts 'Les Immunités des Organisations Internationales
    face à l'Article 6 de la Convention Européenne des Droits de l'Homme: la Jurisprudence
    Strasbourgeoise et sa Prise en Compte par les Juridictions Nationales' (2007) 134 JDI 3;
    Verdirame 'Breaches of the ECHR Resulting from the Conduct of International Organisations'
    [2008] EHRLR 209; Starmer 'Responsibility for Troops Abroad: UN Mandated Forces and
    Issues of Human Rights Accountability' [2008] EHRLR 318; Benoît-Rohmer 'Bienvenue aux
    enfants de Bosphorus: la Cour Européenne des Droits de l'Homme et les Organisations
    Internationales' 21 RTDH 19 (2010); and Drzemczewski 'Look 'Beyond Bosphorus: the
    European Court of Human Rights' Case Law on the Responsibility of Member States of
    International Organisations under the European Convention on Human Rights' (2010) 10
    HRLRev 529.

2   *R (Al Jedda) v Secretary of State for Defence* [2008] 1 AC 332; see also *R (Al-Saadoori) v
    Secretary of State for Defence* [2010] QB 486. See also *Behrami and Behrami v France; and
    Saramati v France, Germany and Norway* (dec) [GC] 2007-… at para 147. It was accepted in
    Al Jedda that, to the extent that Art 5 was 'trumped' by the UN Charter, it did not have effect
    as a Convention right for the purposes of the HRA 1998.

Extent of state responsibilities in the private sector

3.20 The acts and omissions of private individuals and bodies may engage the
responsibility of the state under the Convention[1]. Two broad principles appear

from the case law, although they are not always clearly distinguished. First, the state may in some circumstances be responsible for its own failure to take positive steps to regulate or control the activities of private persons where there will otherwise be a direct and immediate adverse impact on a person's Convention protected interests. As explained below[2], the state has positive obligations under many articles of the Convention. Such obligations may involve taking general steps, such as enacting laws to punish and deter violations[3], and establishing systems of supervision and control where necessary to prevent and detect violations[4]. They may also involve making effective use of the steps which the law provides[5]. Equally, where the Convention imposes a positive obligation on the state, the state cannot absolve itself of responsibility by delegating the performance of the obligation to a private body. Cases concerning the provision of legal aid[6] and education[7] may be regarded as illustrating this principle. Secondly, the state may in some circumstances be responsible for the manner of performance of essentially governmental functions or powers which it has chosen to delegate to a private law institution[8]. The state is not, however, generally responsible for acts which cannot be imputed to a public authority and which do not involve a breach of any positive obligation of the state[9].

1   This analysis is based upon that of Lord Mance in *YL v Birmingham City Council* [2008] 1 AC 95 at paras 92–98. See also Hunter-Henin 'Horizontal Application and the Triumph of the European Convention on Human Rights' in Oliver and Fedtke *Human Rights and the Private Sphere: a Comparative Study* (2007), pp 98–124.

2   See paras **3.26–3.30** below.

3   As in *X and Y v Netherlands* (1985) A 91, where Dutch law did not afford an effective remedy to a mentally disabled girl who had been raped by a relative of the directress of the care home where she lived.

4   As in *Storck v Germany* 2005-V, discussed at para **4.155** below, where there was no system of state supervision of the lawfulness and conditions of confinement of persons treated in private psychiatric hospitals, and where the police had in addition assisted in the illegal detention of a woman in such a hospital.

5   As in *Z and Others v United Kingdom* [GC] 2001-V, discussed at para **4.92** below (local authority's failure to use its powers to protect children known to be at risk of serious abuse and neglect); and *Calvelli and Ciglio v Italy* [GC] 2002-I, discussed at para **4.31** below (Art 2 responsibility to investigate death applies to patient in private hospital).

6   As in *Van der Mussele v Belgium* (1983) A 70, where the provision of legal aid was delegated to the Belgian bar, which required young advocates to provide their services *pro bono*.

7   As in *Costello-Roberts v United Kingdom* (1993) A 247-C, where the state's responsibility was engaged in respect of corporal punishment in private schools.

8   As in *Woś v Poland* (dec) 2005-IV, where the Polish government delegated to a private body the task of allocating compensation received from the German Government after World War II; and *Sychev v Ukraine* (dec) (11 October 2005), where the state had established a private law commission to which were delegated powers relating to the execution of court judgments.

9   As in *Nielsen v Denmark* (1988) A 44, paras 67–73, discussed at para **4.152** below, where a parent was responsible for the hospitalisation of a child.

3.21 The way in which the concept of a 'public authority' has been interpreted in domestic case law, for the purposes of the HRA 1998, has been discussed in chapter 1[1].

---

1   Above, paras **1.64–1.74**.

Reservations and derogations

3.22 The ECHR, Article 57[1] permits any state, when signing the ECHR or when depositing its instrument of ratification, to make a reservation in respect of any particular provision of the ECHR to the extent that any law then in force in its territory is not in conformity with the provision. Reservations of a general character are not permitted, and any reservation must contain a brief statement of the law concerned[2]. This provision applies also to protocols to the ECHR. Effect is given to reservations, under the domestic law of the UK, by virtue of the HRA 1998, ss 1(2), 15 and 17[3]. The UK has made a reservation in respect of Protocol 1, Article 2[4].

---

1   Formerly ECHR, Art 64.

2   As to these requirements, see *Belilos v Switzerland* (1988) A 132, paras 58–59; *Weber v Switzerland* (1990) A 177; *Chorherr v Austria* (1993) A 266-B, para 19.

3   As to which, see paras **1.29**, **1.107** and **1.108** above.

4   The reservation is set out in the HRA 1998, Sch 3, Pt 2. It is discussed at para **6.166** below. In the light of the *Belilos* judgment, it may be questionable whether the UK reservation complies with Art 57(2). See also 28915/95, *SP v United Kingdom* (17 January 1997).

3.23 The ECHR, Article 15 permits any contracting state, 'in time of war or other public emergency threatening the life of the nation'[1] to take measures derogating from its obligations under the ECHR 'to the extent strictly required by the exigencies of the situation'[2], provided that such measures are not inconsistent with its other obligations under international law[3]. No derogation can however be made from Article 2, except in respect of deaths resulting from lawful acts of war, or from Articles 3, 4 (paragraph 1) and 7. This provision applies also to protocols to the ECHR. A state availing itself of the right of derogation must inform the Secretary General of the Council of Europe of the measures it has taken and the reasons for them. It must also tell the Secretary General when the measures have ceased to operate and the provisions of the Convention are again being fully executed. Effect is given to derogations, under the domestic law of the UK, by the HRA 1998, ss 1(2), 14 and 16[4].

---

1   For further discussion, see paras **4.147** and **4.148** below.

2   See *Ireland v United Kingdom* (1978) A 25; *Brannigan and McBride v United Kingdom* (1993) A 258-B.

3   See further van Dijk, van Hoof, van Rijn and Zwaak (eds) *Theory and Practice of the European Convention on Human Rights* (4th edn, 2006) at p 1068 (relevance of International Covenant

on Civil and Political Rights, Geneva Conventions and Additional Protocols, and customary international law in assessment of compatibility with 'international law').

4   See paras **1.29**, **1.106** and **1.108** above.

3.24 The validity of a derogation can be reviewed by the European Court of Human Rights. It is accepted by the Court that Article 15 leaves the national authorities a wide margin of appreciation in deciding on the presence of an emergency and on the nature and scope of derogations necessary to avert it. Nevertheless, the Court is empowered to rule on whether the states have gone beyond the 'extent strictly required by the exigencies' of the crisis[1]. In exercising its supervision the Court must give appropriate weight to such relevant factors as the nature of the rights affected by the derogation, the circumstances leading to, and the duration of, the emergency situation[2].

1   *Ireland v United Kingdom* (1978) A 25, para 207. For discussion, see paras **4.147–4.148** below.
2   *Brannigan and McBride v United Kingdom* (1993) A 258-B, para 43.

Derogations made by the United Kingdom

3.25 The UK has made use of Article 15 from time to time to prevent challenges arising under Article 5 to extended powers of detention conferred by anti-terrorism legislation[1]. In particular, a notice of derogation was made in 1988 following the decision of the European Court of Human Rights in *Brogan and Others v United Kingdom*[2] that the detention of the applicants for more than four days under the Prevention of Terrorism (Temporary Provisions) Act 1984 contravened Article 5(3). The validity of the derogation was subsequently upheld by the European Court of Human Rights[3]. This derogation was listed as a 'designated derogation' in Schedule 3 to the HRA 1998, but in 2001 the UK gave notice that this derogation would be withdrawn following upon the entry into force of the Terrorism Act 2000. A further derogation was lodged at the end of that year[4] following upon the enactment of the Anti-terrorism, Crime and Security Act 2001, which made provision for the indefinite detention of non-UK nationals suspected of involvement in terrorism, a derogation which was subsequently withdrawn in 2005[5]. The derogation was upheld both by the domestic courts[6] and by the Strasbourg Court[7].

1   See further paras **4.147–4.148** below.
2   *Brogan and Others v United Kingdom* (1988) A 145-B.
3   *Brannigan and McBride v United Kingdom* (1993) A 258-B.
4   Human Rights Act 1998 (Designated Derogation) Order 2001 (SI 2001/3644).
5   Human Rights Act 1998 (Amendment) Order 2005 (SI 2005/1071).
6   *A v Secretary of State for the Home Department* [2005] 2 AC 68.
7   *A and Others v United Kingdom* [GC] 2009-....

Positive and negative obligations

3.26 Under the ECHR, Article 1 contracting states undertake to '*secure* to everyone within their jurisdiction' the rights and freedoms set out in the ECHR (and its protocols) upon ratification. In consequence, the state is under a negative obligation to refrain from interfering with the protected rights; and that negative obligation is reflected, for example, in the language used in several of the articles of the ECHR:

'No-one shall be deprived of his life intentionally ...' (Art 2).

'No-one shall be subjected to torture ...' (Art 3).

'No-one shall be held in slavery ...' (Art 4).

'No-one shall be deprived of his liberty except ...' (Art 5).

'No-one shall be held guilty ...' (Art 7).

'There shall be no interference by a public authority ...' (Art 8).

'Freedom to manifest one's religion or beliefs shall be subject only to such limitations as ...' (Art 9).

'Everyone has the right to freedom of expression ... without interference by public authorities' (Art 10).

'No restrictions shall be placed on the exercise of these rights ...' (Art 11).

'No-one shall be deprived of his possessions except ...' (Prot 1, art 1).

The overarching obligation to secure rights is not, however, confined to a requirement that states refrain from interfering with protected rights: it can also place the state under an obligation to take positive steps. This too is reflected in the language used in some of the articles of the ECHR:

'Everyone's right to life shall be protected by law' (Art 2).

'Everyone charged with a criminal offence has ... [the right] to be given [legal assistance] free when the interests of justice so require' (Art 6).

The key principle that ECHR rights must be 'practical and effective' has also allowed the Court to interpret the text of the ECHR in such a way as to imply certain positive obligations. Whether a positive obligation exists does not, however, depend on the semantic form in which a guarantee is expressed, but upon whether it is necessary to construe the guarantee as imposing a positive obligation in order to secure effective protection of the right in question[1].

---

1   As to the 'effectiveness principle' of interpretation, see para **3.42** below; and *Young, James and Webster v United Kingdom* (1981) B 39, comments of the Acting President of the Commission. For further discussion, see Mowbray *The Development of Positive Obligations under the European Convention on Human Rights by the European Court of Human Rights* (2004); Akandji-Kombe *Positive Obligations under the ECHR: A Guide to ther Implementation of the ECHR* (2007); Fredman *Human Rights Transformed: Positive Rights and Positive*

Duties (2008); and Costa 'The European Court of Human Rights: Consistency of its Case-law and Positive Obligations' (2008) 26 NQHR 449.

3.27 Positive obligations can arise in a variety of circumstances and can take a variety of forms, both of a substantive and of a procedural nature. The state – which includes national courts, as well as the legislature, the executive and other public authorities – may be under an obligation to take positive steps to alter domestic law or practice so as to ensure that the legal system meets the standards of the ECHR, for example in relation to the system of criminal prosecution[1], the substance of the criminal law[2], criminal procedure[3] or private law[4]. The scope of the ECHR to impose positive obligations on the state (including the courts) in respect of questions of private law entails that the ECHR, and the Human Rights Act1998, can be relevant to disputes between private individuals[5]. The duty to secure ECHR rights can also impose upon the state (including the courts) a duty to take some positive step of an executive or operational nature: for example, to undertake a criminal investigation[6], or to obtain an expert report before depriving a father of his right to access to his child[7], or to ensure that a prisoner can correspond with the Strasbourg Court[8]. The fact that the ECHR imposes positive as well as negative obligations is reflected in the terms of the HRA1998[9].

1   Eg *MC v Bulgaria* 2003-XII, paras 169–187. See also *Kaya v Turkey* 1998-I, para 93; *Yasa v Turkey* 1998-VI, paras 113–115. See further paras **4.18–4.20**, **4.83–4.86**, and paras **6.120–6.121** below.

2   Eg *MC v Bulgaria*, 2003-XII, paras 169–178. See also *Dudgeon v United Kingdom* (1981) A 45, para 49 (prohibition of homosexual conduct in private), discussed at para **6.140** below; *A v United Kingdom* 1998-VI, paras 23–24 (breach of Art 3 through domestic recognition of a defence of 'reasonable chastisement'), discussed at para **4.86** below.

3   Eg *V v United Kingdom* [GC] 1999-IX.

4   Eg *Marckx v Belgium* (1979) A 31, para 44 (differential status of illegitimate children); *Young, James and Webster v United Kingdom* (1981) A 44, para 49 (domestic law permitted employer to dismiss employees in contravention of Art 11); *Hoffmann v Austria* (1993) A 255-C, para 29 (decision of court in resolving dispute concerning custody of children amounted to 'interference' with Art 8 rights, despite private nature of litigation); *Von Hannover v Germany* 2004-VI paras 61–81 (duty to ensure domestic law protects private life); and *Verein gegen Tierfabriken Schweiz (VgT) v Switzerland (no 2)* [GC] 2009-…, at para 97 (judicial systems must be organised in such a way that domestic courts can meet the requirements of the ECHR including the execution of Court judgments).

5   In an Art 8 case, the Court observed: 'These obligations may even involve the adoption of measures designed to secure respect for private life even in the sphere of the relations of individuals between themselves': *X and Y v Netherlands* (1985) A 91, para 23. The relevant case law under the HRA 1998 is discussed at paras **1.76–1.77** above.

6   Eg *Aydin v Turkey* 1997-VI, paras 103–109.

7   *Elsholz v Germany* [GC] 2000-VIII, paras 62–66.

8   *Cotleţ v Romania* (3 June 2003), para 71.

9   HRA 1988, s 6(6).

3.28 It may be difficult on occasion to determine whether a positive obligation exists, for the Court has not considered it 'desirable, let alone necessary, to elaborate a general theory concerning the extent to which the Convention guarantees should be extended to relations between private individuals *inter se*[1]. In deciding whether or not a positive obligation exists, 'the Court will have regard to the fair balance that has to be struck between the general interest of the community and the competing private interests of the individual, or individuals, concerned'[2].

---

1   *VgT Verein gegen Tierfabriken v Switzerland* 2001-VI, at para 46. See also *Christine Goodwin v United Kingdom* [GC] 2002-VI, para 72: 'the notion of "respect" as understood in Article 8 is not clear cut, especially as far as the positive obligations inherent in that concept are concerned: having regard to the diversity of practices followed and the situations obtaining in the Contracting States, the notion's requirements will vary considerably from case to case and the margin of appreciation to be accorded to the authorities may be wider than that applied in other areas under the Convention'.

2   *McGinley and Egan v United Kingdom* 1998-III, para 98.

3.29 Positive obligations have been found to exist in a variety of situations. In *Osman v United Kingdom*[1] the European Court of Human Rights held that the ECHR, Article 2 imposed a positive obligation on the state to 'secure the right to life by putting in place effective criminal law provisions to deter the commission of offences against the person, backed up by law enforcement machinery for the prevention, suppression and sanctioning of breaches of such provisions'[2]. In the particular circumstances of that case, the police were therefore under an obligation to take reasonable steps to prevent a foreseeable murderous attack. However, the Court also said that this obligation had to be 'interpreted in a way which does not impose an impossible or disproportionate burden on the authorities'[3], and in a manner which was consistent with the rights of suspects. The scope of a positive obligation must thus reflect other ECHR principles and also the material resources realistically available to the authorities. In *Öneryildiz v Turkey,* the Grand Chamber considered the extent of a state's substantive and procedural obligations in respect of the risks known to have existed in respect of hazardous waste, holding that a state is required to take practical measures to address such a situation, including providing necessary information on the risks to the public and carrying out an effective investigation into the circumstances leading to any loss of life[4]. Article 3 has also been held to impose a positive obligation of a similar character[5]. In *Aydin v Turkey*, for example, the Court held that, where an individual made a complaint of torture or inhuman or degrading treatment, the state was under a positive obligation to carry out 'a thorough and effective investigation capable of leading to the identification and punishment of those responsible, and including effective access for the complainant to the investigatory procedure'[6]. Article 6 imposes a number of positive obligations: for example, to establish independent and impartial courts which deal with proceedings within a reasonable time, and to provide legal aid[7] and interpreters where necessary. The right of access to a court, which is implicit in Article 6[8], can also have implications for the courts in their development of the law, including private law[9]. The obligation to 'respect' private and family life, under Article 8, is also capable of imposing specific positive obligations depending on the particular circumstances. For example, it can impose on the state an obligation to give legal recognition to a change of gender by a post-operative transsexual[10], or to provide access to social work records of a person's childhood[11], or to amend the law of succession[12]. Positive obligations have also been held to arise from Articles 9[13] and 10[14]. Article 11 can impose on the state a positive obligation to protect peaceful demonstrators from violent counter-demonstrators[15], while Articles 1[16] and 2[17] of Protocol no 1 each impose specific duties upon domestic authorities.

1   *Osman v United Kingdom* 1998-VIII.

2   *Osman v United Kingdom* 1998-VIII, para 115. See also *McCann and Others v United Kingdom* (1996) A 324, para 161; and *Z v United Kingdom* 2001-V.

3   *Osman v United Kingdom* 1998-VIII, para 116.

4   *Öneryildiz v Turkey* [GC] 2004-XII, paras 97–118.

5   *A v United Kingdom* 1998-VI.

6   *Aydin v Turkey* 1997-VI, para 103. See also *X and Y v Netherlands* (1985) A 91, para 23 (positive obligation to prosecute rapist, in order to secure rights of victim).

7   This is an express obligation in respect of criminal proceedings, but also on implied obligation in respect of civil proceedings: *Airey v Ireland* (1979) A 32, para 26.

8   Eg *Ashingdane v United Kingdom* (1985) A 93, para 55.

9   See eg *Osman v United Kingdom* 1998-VIII and *Z v United Kingdom* 2001-V. An example involving private individuals is *Fayed v United Kingdom* (1994) A 294-B.

10   *Christine Goodwin v United Kingdom* [GC] 2002-VI, paras 89–93.

11   *Gaskin v United Kingdom* (1989) A 160, paras 42–49.

12   *Marckx v Belgium* (1979) A 31, para 31.

13   33490/96 and 34055/96, *Dubowska and Skup v Poland* (1997) DR 89, 156.

14   *Gaskin v United Kingdom* (1989) A 160.

15   *Plattform Ärtze für das Leben v Austria* (1988) A 139, para 32.

16   Eg, *Broniowski v Poland* [GC] 2004-V, paras 189–194 (taking of practical measures to ensure effective protection for property).

17   *Kjeldsen, Busk Madsen and Pedersen v Denmark* (1976) A 23, para 53 (duty to respect parents' philosophical convictions in educational provision where this exceeds the transmission of factual knowledge).

3.30 In some circumstances it may be difficult to distinguish between positive and negative obligations. Whether the state has interfered with a protected right or has failed to protect it can in some cases appear to be a distinction without a difference. In such cases the result should not depend on a semantic classification. The principles applicable are 'broadly similar', however the issue is described[1].

1   *López Ostra v Spain* (1994) A 303-C, para 51; *Rees v United Kingdom* (1986) A 106, para 37.

LIMITS TO THE ENJOYMENT OF CONVENTION RIGHTS

Abuse of rights

3.31 The ECHR, Article 17 provides:

'Nothing in this Convention may be interpreted as implying for any State, group or person any right to engage in any activity or perform any act aimed at the destruction of any of the rights and freedoms set forth herein or at their limitation to a greater extent than is provided for in the Convention.'

This provision prevents the ECHR from being used as a basis for asserting a right to act in a way which is aimed at destroying the Convention rights of others. For example, the ECHR cannot be used as a basis for asserting the right to distribute racist pamphlets or to stand as candidates in elections on a racist platform[1]. On the other hand, those who have acted in a way which was aimed at destroying the Convention rights of others are not thereafter generally barred from asserting their own Convention rights, such as their right to a fair trial[2]. As the text of the provision emphasises, Article 17 must be applied in a proportionate manner[3].

1   8348/78, *Glimmerveen and Hagenbeek v Netherlands* (1979) DR 18, 187; *Lehideux and Isorni v France* 1998-VIII, para 53. On Art 17 generally, see van Dijk, van Hoof, van Rijn and Zwaak (eds) *Theory and Practice of the European Convention on Human Rights* (4th edn, 2006), pp 1083–1092.

2   *Lawless v Ireland (no 3)* (1961) A 3, para 7; *SW v United Kingdom* (1995) A 355-B (and cf the reasoning of Mrs Liddy in the Commission's report in 20166/92, *SW v United Kingdom* (27 June 1994) that a husband charged with the rape of his wife could not claim protection under Art 7). The Court takes account of the conduct of applicants in deciding whether to award compensation under Art 41: see paras **2.76–2.77** above.

3   214/56, *De Becker v Belgium* (1960) B2, para 279 (bar on exercise of freedom of expression placed upon Nazi collaborator); and *Refah Partisi (The Welfare Party) and Others v Turkey* [GC] 2003-II, at para 96: 'some compromise between the requirements of defending democratic society and individual rights is inherent in the Convention system', and thus an assessment of the compatibility of an interference with a substantive ECHR provision is first required, for 'only when that review is complete will the Court be in a position to decide, in the light of all the circumstances of the case, whether Article 17 of the Convention should be applied': here, it was unnecessary to consider Art 17). For further discussion, see paras **7.87** and **7.99** below.

Waiver and acquiescence

3.32 The waiver of Convention rights (and its counterpart, acquiescence in the violation of Convention rights) is an issue which has not been greatly explored in the Strasbourg jurisprudence, possibly because of the requirement that applicants must exhaust domestic remedies if their complaints are to be admissible[1]. The law on waiver and acquiescence is correspondingly lacking in clarity, and raises difficult questions[2]. Certain Convention rights cannot be waived[3]. It is doubtful, for example, whether the right to liberty guaranteed by Article 5 can be waived[4]. It also seems unlikely that waiver could operate in respect of other basic rights such as those guaranteed by Articles 2, 3 and 4[5]. The right to education insofar as it involves discriminatory treatment under Article 2 of Protocol no 1 cannot be waived[6]. On the other hand, some at least of the rights guaranteed by Article 6 are capable of being waived. In general, it appears that a Convention right can be waived where a:'neither the letter nor the spirit of [the] provision prevents a person from waiving [the right] of his own free will', provided that the waiver is 'made in an unequivocal manner, and [does] not run counter to an important public interest'[7]. In the area of employment, the Court has generally accepted that an employee can be taken to have waived certain rights, such as those to freedom of religious belief under Article 9[8] or freedom of expression under Article 10[9].

---

1   ECHR, Art 35. See paras **2.58–2.63** above.

2   See further Frumer La Renonciation aux Droits et Libertés: la Convention Européenne des Droits de l'Homme à l'Epreuve de la Volonté Individuelle (2001); and Aall 'Waiver of Human Rights: Setting the Scene' (2010) 28 NJHR 300.

3   *Albert and Le Compte v Belgium* (1983) A 58, para 35.

4   *De Wilde, Ooms and Versyp v Belgium* (1971) A 12, para 65.

5   In relation to Art 4, see *Van der Mussele v Belgium* (1984) A 70.

6   *DH and Others v Czech Republic* [GC] 2007-..., paras 202 and 204 (and at para 204: 'no waiver of the right not to be subjected to racial discrimination [in general] can be accepted'). See also *Oršuš and Others v Croatia* [GC] 2010-..., paras 178–179 (parents' passivity and lack of objections to segregation of Roma children in schools).

7   *Schüler-Zraggen v Switzerland* (1993) A 263, para 58; *Hakansson and Sturesson v Sweden* (1991) A 171, para 66.

8   See paras **7.26–7.28** below.

9   Eg 11308/84 *Vereinigung Rechtswinkels Utrecht v Netherlands* (1986) DR 46, 200.

3.33 Most of the Strasbourg case law on waiver has concerned Article 6 of the Convention. Neither the letter nor the spirit of Article 6 prevents a person from waiving of his own free will, either expressly or tacitly, the entitlement to the guarantees of a fair trial, but such a waiver must 'be established in an unequivocal manner and be attended by minimum safeguards commensurate with its importance ... and must not run counter to any important public interest'[1]. The requirement that a criminal trial be before a tribunal 'established by law' has been said to be 'of essential importance and its exercise cannot depend on the parties alone'[2]. The requirement that the tribunal be 'independent and impartial' gives rise to complex questions. In *Bulut v Austria*, the Court found that, as a matter of domestic law, there had been an effective waiver of the right to object to a judge with a prior involvement in the case: the domestic court was therefore 'established by law'. The Court considered, however, that, 'regardless of whether a waiver was made or not' it had still to decide whether, from the standpoint of the ECHR, the domestic court was 'impartial'. In that regard, the Court accepted that the judge in question was subjectively impartial; and, applying the objective test, it was not open to the applicant to complain that he had legitimate reasons to doubt the court's impartiality, given his failure to object to its composition[3]. In the subsequent case of *McGonnell v United Kingdom*, the judgment (of a Chamber of the Court) might be understood as accepting that the right to an independent and impartial tribunal could be waived[4]. The right to a hearing in public can be waived[5], as can also the right to be legally represented[6]. The right to have a criminal charge determined by a tribunal (rather than 'settled' by payment of a fiscal fine) can be waived[7].

1   *Hermi v Italy* [GC] 2006-XII, at para 73.

2   *Pfeifer and Plankl v Austria* (1992) A 227, at para 38 (circumstances suggested the applicant as a layman was not fully able to appreciate the implications of the situation, and 'the waiver of rights expressed there and then in such circumstances appears questionable, to say the least'.)

3   *Bulut v Austria* 1996-II, paras 29, 30 and 32–36. See also *Millar v Dickson* 2002 SC (PC) 30 per Lord Clyde at para 81. In the earlier case of *Oberschlick v Austria* (1991) A 204, the Court did not determine whether the right to an independent and impartial tribunal could be waived, but held that there had not been an effective waiver.

4   *McGonnell v United Kingdom* 2000-II, paras 44 and 45. See also *Deweer v Belgium* (1980) A 35, paras 49 (arbitration contract).

5   *Albert and Le Compte v Belgium* (1983) A 58, para 35; *Hkansson and Sturesson v Sweden* (1990) A 171, para 66. This principle was applied, in the context of a construction contract adjudication, in *Austin Hall Building Ltd v Buckland Securities Ltd* [2001] BLR 272, Tech and Con Ct.

6   *Melin v France* (1993) A 261-A, para 25.

7   *Deweer v Belgium* (1980) A 35, para 49.

3.34 As already mentioned, the waiver of a right guaranteed by the ECHR – in so far as it is permissible – must be established in an unequivocal manner[1]. In the case of procedural rights a waiver, in order to be effective, requires 'minimum guarantees commensurate to its importance'[2]. For example, a purported waiver of a procedural right without the benefit of legal advice is unlikely to be valid[3]. Waiver need not be express: 'tacit' waiver can be inferred from conduct[4].

1   *Pfeifer and Plankl v Austria* (1992) A 227, para 37.

2   *Pfeifer and Plankl v Austria* (1992) A 227, para 37.

3   *Pfeifer and Plankl v Austria* (1992) A 227, para 38.

4   See eg *Colozza and Rubinat v Italy* (1985) A 89, para 28; *Hakansson and Sturesson v Sweden* (1991) A 171, para 67; *McGonnell v United Kingdom* 2000-II, paras 44–45.

Domestic consideration of waiver of rights

3.35 In a number of cases under the HRA 1998 and the SA 1998 the courts have considered the issue of waiver of the right under the ECHR, Article 6 to an independent and impartial tribunal or acquiescence in a violation of that right. In *Millar v Dickson,* it was accepted by a majority of the Privy Council that the right to an independent and impartial tribunal could be waived. As Lord Hope of Craighead observed, waiver of the right is not uncommon in practice, as in the case where the parties agree to the resolution of their dispute by private arbitration or the payment of a fixed penalty is tendered in composition of a criminal charge. The Privy Council however made it clear that waiver depends on the making of an informed choice, and that waiver could not be imputed to a party on the basis that he or his agent was deemed to know the law. Lord Clyde was not persuaded that a lack of independence in a criminal court could be waived[1].

The question of acquiescence was considered by the Privy Council in *Robertson v Higson*, where the appellants had delayed for about two years before challenging the regularity of criminal proceedings which had been taken against them before temporary sheriffs. The Privy Council noted that a time-limit for taking proceedings was not incompatible with the Convention: under Article 35 an application to the European Court of Human Rights must be made within six months from the date when the final domestic decision was taken[2]. The HRA 1998 similarly imposed a time limit for the bringing of proceedings[3]. Since the SA 1998 did not specify any time within which proceedings were to be taken, the ordinary rules of domestic law relating to the procedure adopted to vindicate the right in question must apply[4]. The bringing of a bill of suspension, in particular, could be barred by lapse of time unless the defect was so fundamental that a remedy must be given. Since the defect in question could be waived, however (as had been held in *Millar v Dickson*), it did not fall into that category. Like waiver, acquiescence must be voluntary, informed and unequivocal[5].

---

1   *Millar v Dickson* 2002 SC (PC) 30. See also *Warren v Random House Group Ltd* [2009] QB 600 (acceptance of offer in settlement of action constituted waiver of right of access to a court).

2   See para **2.60** above.

3   HRA 1998, s 7(5). See paras **1.84–1.86** above.

4   *Robertson v Higson* 2006 SC (PC) 22 at para 28.

5   *Dickson v HM Advocate* 2006 SCCR 637.

THE INTERPRETATION OF THE ECHR

Introduction

3.36 The ECHR is an international convention, and as such falls to be interpreted in accordance with the principles set out in the Vienna Convention on the Law of Treaties, Articles 31a:–33. These principles are discussed below. In practice, one of these principles has proved to be especially important: that the Convention should be interpreted 'in the light of its object and purpose'[1]. That principle has been elaborated in the Convention jurisprudence under reference to three particular expressions: that the ECHR should guarantee rights that are 'practical and effective'; that certain of its terms should be interpreted as 'autonomous concepts'; and that it should be interpreted and applied as a 'living instrument'. The limitations flowing from the international nature of the Convention, and of the Strasbourg Court, are also reflected in three further principles: the subsidiarity principle, the margin of appreciation doctrine and the fourth instance doctrine. These principles will be discussed separately, for ease of exposition, under the heading of the relationship between Strasbourg and national authorities. They are not however truly distinct from the other principles of interpretation: the margin of appreciation doctrine, in particular, can be regarded to some extent as the other side of the same coin as the 'living instrument' principle.

---

1   Vienna Convention, Art 31(1).

3.37 To approach the ECHR purely as an international convention would not, however, reflect the approach of the Strasbourg institutions. As explained below[1], the Commission and the Court have treated the Convention as not merely creating reciprocal engagements between contracting states, but as a constitutional instrument representing 'the public order of Europe'[2]. The Court appears to view the Convention as having evolved from a purely international law instrument towards becoming Europe's constitutional bill of rights.

---

1   See para **3.34** above.

2   See eg *Loizidou v Turkey* (preliminary objections) (1995) A 310.

3.38 The Convention jurisprudence also manifests a number of other general principles, derived from continental administrative law, including those of legal certainty and proportionality. These are particularly (but not exclusively) related to provisions in the ECHR which call for interferences with protected rights to be 'prescribed by law' (or some equivalent formulation) and 'necessary'. There is in addition a general principle of non-discrimination, which is an express requirement under Article 14 of the Convention.

3.39 For ease of exposition, the guiding principles of interpretation can therefore be discussed under a number of headings:
–   the Vienna Convention
–   the search for balance
–   the effectiveness principle
–   autonomous concepts
–   a living instrument
–   legal certainty
–   necessity and proportionality
–   non-discrimination.
–   subsidiarity
–   margin of appreciation
–   the fourth instance doctrine

The Vienna Convention

3.40 Although the Vienna Convention postdates the ECHR, and does not have retroactive effect, it expresses the pre-existing principles of international law governing the interpretation of treaties. It has been accepted by the European Court of Human Rights that it should be guided by the Vienna Convention Articles 31–33[1].

1   *Golder v United Kingdom* (1975) A 18, para 29; *Banković and Others v Belgium and 16 Other Contracting States* (dec) [GC] 2001-II, paras 55–58.

3.41 Those articles are in the following terms:

Article 31

General rule of interpretation

1. A treaty shall be interpreted in good faith in accordance with the ordinary meaning to be given to the terms of the treaty in their context and in the light of its object and purpose.

2. The context for the purpose of the interpretation of a treaty shall comprise, in addition to the text, including its preamble and annexes:

(a)   any agreement relating to the treaty which was made between all the parties in connection with the conclusion of the treaty;

(b)   any instrument which was made by one or more parties in connection with the conclusion of the treaty and accepted by the other parties as an instrument related to the treaty.

3. There shall be taken into account, together with the context:

(a)   any subsequent agreement between the parties regarding the interpretation of the treaty or the application of its provisions;

(b)   any subsequent practice in the application of the treaty which establishes the agreement of the parties regarding its interpretation;

(c)   any relevant rules of international law applicable in the relations between the parties.

4. A special meaning shall be given to a term if it is established that the parties so intended.

Article 32

Supplementary means of interpretation

Recourse may be had to supplementary means of interpretation, including the preparatory work of the treaty and the circumstances of its conclusion, in order to confirm the meaning resulting from the application of article 31, or to determine the meaning when the interpretation according to article 31:

(a)   leaves the meaning ambiguous or obscure; or

(b)   leads to a result which is manifestly absurd or unreasonable.

Article 33

Interpretation of treaties authenticated in two or more languages

1. When a treaty has been authenticated in two or more languages, the text is equally authoritative in each language, unless the treaty provides or the parties agree that, in case of divergence, a particular text shall prevail.

2. A version of the treaty in a language other than one of those in which the text was authenticated shall be considered an authentic text only if the treaty so provides or the parties so agree.

3. The terms of the treaty are presumed to have the same meaning in each authentic text.

4. Except where a particular text prevails in accordance with paragraph 1, when a comparison of the authentic texts discloses a difference of meaning which the application of articles 31 and 32 does not remove, the meaning which best reconciles the texts, having regard to the object and purpose of the treaty, shall be adopted.

3.42 The Vienna Convention, Article 31(1) contains the fundamental principle that the Convention must be interpreted in accordance with the ordinary meaning of its terms in their context[1] and in accordance with its object and purpose. As regards the 'object and purpose' of the Convention, the European Commission on Human Rights said in *Golder v United Kingdom*:

'The over-riding function of this Convention is to protect the rights of the individual and not to lay down as between States mutual obligations, which are to be restrictively interpreted having regard to the sovereignty of these States. On the contrary, the role of the Convention and the function of its interpretation is to make the protection of the individual effective.'[2]

The Court has also emphasised that the Convention is 'an instrument designed to maintain and promote the ideals and values of a democratic society'[3]. More generally, the Court's approach, and its insistence upon a progressive and realistic application of the Convention, is encapsulated in its description of the Convention as 'a constitutional instrument of European public order'[4]. The Court has tended therefore to resist a traditional treaty-based approach to the interpretation of the Convention: that is to say, an approach which is based on an assessment of the obligations which the contracting states agreed with each other when they entered into the Convention. Its prevailing approach, influenced by the fact that the Convention, unusually for a treaty, admits individual enforcement, has been rather to treat it as if it were a European bill of rights[5]. As the Court put it in *Rantsev v Cyprus and Russia,* 'the increasingly high standards required in the area of the protection of human rights and fundamental liberties correspondingly and inevitably require greater firmness in assessing breaches of the fundamental values of democratic societies'[6].

---

1   Eg *Johnston v Ireland* (1987) A 112, and *Rees v United Kingdom* (1986) A 106, para 49 ('right to marry') (but note revisal of *Rees* in *Christine Goodwin v United Kingdom* [GC] 2002-VI); and *Campbell and Cosans v United Kingdom* (1982) A 48, para 30 ('inhuman or degrading treatment').

2   *Golder v United Kingdom* (1973) B 16 at 40.

3   *Kjelsden, Busk Madsen and Pedersen v Denmark* (1976) A 23, para 53.

4   *Loizidou v Turkey* (preliminary objections) (1995) A 310, para 75.

5   See further Cohen-Jonathan 'La Fonction Quasi Constitutionnelle de la Cour Européenne des Droits de l'Homme' in Bon et al *Renouveau du Droit Constitutionnel: Mélanges en l'Honneur*

de Louis Favoreu (2007), pp 1127–1153; and Dubout 'Interprétation Téléologique et Politique Jurisprudentielle de la Cour Européenne des Droits de l'Homme' (2008)19 RTDH 383.

6   *Rantsev v Cyprus and Russia* 2010-…, at para 277 (scope of Art 4 included the phenomenon of human trafficking).

3.43 The Vienna Convention, Article 31(3)(b) requires the Court to consider 'any subsequent practice in the application of the treaty which establishes the agreement of the parties regarding its interpretation'[1]. Article 31(4) contains the principle that terms can be 'autonomous concepts'.

1   See eg *Loizidou v Turkey* (preliminary objections) (1995) A 310, para 73.

3.44 In accordance with the Vienna Convention, Articles 31(2) and (3), the Convention also has to be interpreted in the light of any relevant rules and principles of international law applicable in relations between the contracting states. Council of Europe measures and other international instruments may therefore be relevant to the interpretation of the ECHR[1]. More generally, the Convention is to be interpreted as far as possible in harmony with other principles of international law of which it forms part[2]. In practice, international instruments are often referred to by the European Court of Human Rights and can be an important source of guidance, whether or not they have been signed or ratified by all or most or any of the Council of Europe states[3] or are binding in international law[4]. These have included United Nations instruments[5], International Labour Organisation instruments[6], EU instruments[7] and other international conventions[8]. The Court has also considered European Union standards[9]. In interpreting the ECHR as a 'living instrument'[10] and taking account of prevailing attitudes within the Council of Europe, the Court has had regard to a wide range of instruments, including resolutions of the European Parliament and of the Parliamentary Assembly of the Council of Europe[11], and a report of the World Council of Churches[12]. These various sources are said to be an aid to the interpretation of the language used in the ECHR: in theory they cannot be used to 'read into' the Convention a right which it does not contain[13]. Furthermore, although the existence or absence of a generally shared approach to an issue among contracting states is often highly relevant to the application of the Convention, this does not mean that absolute uniformity is required[14]. The Court also recognises the growing importance of international co-operation and of the consequent need to secure the proper functioning of international organisations[15]. The Court has accordingly accepted that compliance with European Union obligations by contracting states which are also EU member states can be presumed to be compatible with their obligations under the ECHR[16]. The Court may also refer to and draw upon the standards of other international tribunals[17].

1   As in *Marckx v Belgium* (1979) A 31 (reference to Committee of Ministers Resolution (70) 15 on Social Protection of Unmarried Mothers and their Children); *Autronic AG v Switzerland* (1990) A 178 (European Convention on Transfrontier Television); *National Union of Belgian Police v Belgium* (1975) A 19, *Sigurður A Sigurjónsson v Iceland* (1993) A 264, and *Sidabras*

and Džautas v Lithuania 2004-VIII, para 47 (European Social Charter); and *S v Switzerland* (1991) A 220 (Standard Minimum Rules for the Treatment of Prisoners). See further (for discussion of European Social Charter standards) Tomuschat 'Social Rights under the European Convention on Human Rights' in Breitenmoser et al (eds) *Human rights, Democracy and the Rule of Law: Liber Amicorum Luzius Wildhaber* pp 837–863 (2007); Malinverni 'La Cour Européenne des Droits de l'Homme et le Comité Européen des Droits Sociaux: Rapprochements et Convergences' in Breitenmoser et al (eds) *Neue Herausforderungen und Perspektiven, etc* pp 3–13; Malinverni 'La Cour Européenne des Droits de l'Homme et le Comité Européen des Droits Sociaux: Rapprochements et Convergences' in Breitenmoser et al (eds) *Neue Herausforderungen und Perspektiven, etc*, pp 3–13; and Tulkens and van Drooghenbroeck 'La Place des Droits Sociaux dans la Jurisprudence de la Cour Européenne des Droits de l'Homme: la Question de la Pauvreté' in *La Déclaration Universelle des Droits de l'Homme, 1948–2008: Réalité d'un Idéal Commun?* (2009), pp 105–116.

2   *Al-Adsani v United Kingdom* [GC] 2001-XI, para 60.

3   See eg *Marckx v Belgium* (1979) A 31, para 41; *S v Switzerland* (1991) A 220, para 48.

4   Many UN instruments are supported only by a General Assembly resolution, and are therefore not binding. See further Wildhaber 'The European Convention on Human Rights and International Law' (2007) 56 ICLQ 217.

5   As in *Soering v United Kingdom* (1989) A 161, and *Al Adsani v United Kingdom* 2001-XI [GC] (UN Convention against Torture); *Costello-Roberts v United Kingdom* (1993) A 247 (UN Convention on the Rights of the Child); *V v United Kingdom* [GC] 1999-IX (UN Convention on the Rights of the Child; Standard Minimum Rules for the Administration of Juvenile Justice); *Glass v United Kingdom* 2004-II (Oviedo Convention on Bioethics); *Taskin v Turkey* 2004-X (Aarhus Convention on Access to Information, etc on Environmental Matters); and *Brannigan and McBride v United Kingdom* (1993) A 258-B (International Covenant on Civil and Political Rights); *Funke v France* (1993) A 256-A (International Covenant on Civil and Political Rights); *Saunders v United Kingdom* 1996-VI (International Covenant on Civil and Political Rights); *K-HW v Germany* [GC] 2001-II (International Covenant on Civil and Political Rights; Universal Declaration on Human Rights; the Nuremberg principles adopted by General Assembly Resolution 95 (I) of 1946); *Sigurður A Sigurjónsson v Iceland* (1993) A 264 (International Covenant on Economic, Social and Cultural Rights); and *Jersild v Denmark* (1994) A 298 (International Convention on the Elimination of All Forms of Racial Discrimination).

6   As in *Van der Mussele v Belgium* (1983) A 70 (ILO Convention on Forced or Compulsory Labour), *Siliadin v France* 2005-VII; and *Demir and Baykara v Turkey* [GC] 2008-....

7   See eg *Vilho Eskelinen and Others v Finland* [GC] 2007-IV (EU Charter on Fundamental Rights).

8   Eg *Marckx v Belgium* (1979) A 31 (Brussels Convention on the Establishment of Maternal Affiliation of Natural Children); *Autronic AG v Switzerland* (1990) A 178 (International Telecommunication Convention); *Powell and Rayner v United Kingdom* (1990) A 172 (the Rome Convention on Damages caused by Foreign Aircraft to Third Parties on the Surface).

9   As in *Christine Goodwin v United Kingdom* [GC] 2002-VI.

10   See paras **3.52–3.56** below.

11   *Cossey v United Kingdom* (1990) A 184.

12   *Kokkinakis v Greece* (1993) A 260-A, para 48. For recent examples, see *Mamatkulov and Askarov v Turkey* [GC] 2005-I, paras 109–129 (nature of Rules of Court, Rule 39 interim measures determined by reference to developments in international law); *Blečić v Croatia* [GC] 2006-III, paras 45–91 (issue when termination of tenancy took place considered with respect to international law and general principle concerning non-retroactivity).

13   See eg 8945/80, *S v Germany* (1983) DR 39, 43, and compare the International Covenant on Civil and Political Rights, Art 14(7).

14   See eg *F v Switzerland* A 128 (1987) para 33; and cf the margin of appreciation doctrine, discussed at paras **3.134–3.140** below. For an example where the Court considered both national law and international agreements, see *Vo v France* [GC] 2004-VIII, paras 75–95. See further Popovi 'Le Droit Comparé Dans l'Accomplissement des Tâches de la Cour Européenne des Droits de l'Homme' in Caflisch, Callewaert, Liddell, Mahoney and Villiger (eds) *Liber Amicorum Luzius Wildhaber: Human Rights – Strasbourg Views* (2007), pp 371–386.

15   See eg *Waite and Kennedy v Germany* [GC] 1999-I, paras 63 and 72.

16   See eg *Bosphorus Hava Yollari Turizm v Ticaret Anonim Şirketi v Ireland* [GC] 2005-VI, paras 150–151, discussed at para **3.18** above, and *KRS v United Kingdom* (dec) 2008-....

17   See eg *Rantsev v Cyprus and Russia* 2010-..., para 280 (recognition by the International Criminal Tribunal for the Former Yugoslavia that the traditional concept of 'slavery' now encompasses various contemporary forms of slavery).

3.45 Article 32 permits reference to be made to the *travaux préparatoires*[1] with a view to confirming any meaning resulting from the application of Article 31 or to determining the meaning when the interpretation under Article 31 leaves the meaning 'ambiguous or obscure' or leads to a result which is 'manifestly absurd or unreasonable': this is unusual in practice, in part because of the 'living instrument' principle derived from the need to fulfil the Convention's object and purpose, but it is not unknown[2]. It has been said that no recourse is permissible where the text is sufficiently clear[3]. The Court has however held, even in the absence of any evidence in the *travaux préparatoires*, that an apparently clear wording in the text could be overridden by the presumed intention of the drafting states[4].

1   See the Collected Edition of the Travaux Préparatoires of the European Convention on Human Rights, 8 vols, 1975–1985; see also para **2.98** above, and para **8.01**, fn 5 below.

2   Eg *Johnston v Ireland* (1987) A 112; *Lithgow v United Kingdom* (1986) A 102, para 117. See further Nicol 'Original Intent and the ECHR' [2005] PL 152.

3   *Lawless v Ireland (no 3)* (1961) A 3, Law, para 14.

4   *Pretto v Italy* (1983) A 71 (requirement in Art 6(1) that judgment be 'pronounced publicly' did not apply to courts of cassation).

3.46 In relation to Article 33, it is important to remember that the English and French texts of the Convention are equally authoritative. If the different language versions are capable of different interpretations, Article 33(4) requires them to be given the meaning which best reconciles the texts, having regard to the object and purpose of the Convention[1].

1   *Wemhoff v Germany* (1968) A 7, Law, para 8; *Pakelli v Germany* (1983) A 64, para 31. See further para **4.203** below (texts of Art 5(3)).

The search for balance

3.47 The Court's approach to the interpretation of the Convention has also reflected an appreciation that the fundamental right asserted by one individual may conflict with that asserted by another: for example, free speech may conflict with the protection of privacy[1]. Equally, as Lord Steyn observed in *Brown v Stott*:

> '... a single-minded concentration on the pursuit of fundamental rights of individuals to the exclusion of the interests of the wider public might be subversive of the ideal of tolerant European liberal democracies. The fundamental rights of individuals are of supreme importance but those rights are not unlimited: we live in communities of individuals who also have rights. The direct lineage of this ancient idea is clear: the European Convention (1950) is the descendant of the Universal Declaration of Human Rights (1948) which in art 29 expressly recognised the duties of everyone to the community and the limitation on rights in order to secure and protect respect for the rights of others. It is also noteworthy that art 17 of the European Convention prohibits, among others, individuals from abusing their rights to the detriment of others[2]. Thus, notwithstanding the danger of intolerance towards ideas, the Convention system draws a line which does not accord the protection of free speech to those who propagate racial hatred against minorities: art 10; *Jersild v Denmark*[3], para 31. This is to be contrasted with the categorical language of the First Amendment to the United States Constitution which provides that "Congress shall make no law ... abridging the freedom of speech." The European Convention requires that where difficult questions arise a balance must be struck. Subject to a limited number of absolute guarantees, the scheme and structure of the Convention reflects this balanced approach.'[4]

Accordingly, the Court has repeatedly said that 'inherent in the whole of the Convention is a search for a fair balance between the demands of the general interest of the community and the requirements of the protection of the individual's fundamental rights'[5]. Thus in the political sphere, 'pluralism and democracy are based on a compromise that requires various concessions by individuals or groups of individuals, who must sometimes agree to limit some of the freedoms they enjoy in order to guarantee greater stability of the country as a whole'[6]. This approach is reflected in particular in the concept of proportionality, discussed below[7]. The search for a fair balance may also be relevant in determining the relationship between private individuals, for example where a positive obligation exists upon state authorities under Article 8 to ensure respect for private life[8].

---

1   See further Mowbray 'A Study of the Principle of Fair Balance in the Jurisprudence of the European Court of Human Rights' (2010) 10 HRLRev 289.

2   See para **3.31** above.

3   *Jersild v Denmark* (1994) A 298.

4   *Brown v Stott* 2001 SC (PC) 43 at page 63. See further the discussion of necessity and proportionality at paras **3.73–3.82** below.

5   *Soering v United Kingdom* (1989) A 161; see also, eg, *Sporrong and Lönnroth v Sweden* (1982) A 52 at para 69; *Sheffield and Horsham v United Kingdom* 1998-V at para 52.

6   *Refah Partisi (The Welfare Party) and Others v Turkey* [GC] 2003-II, at para 99.

7   See para **3.76** below.

8   See eg *Van Kück v Germany* 2003-VII, paras 73–86, discussed at para **6.146**, fn 1 below; and *Schüth v Germany* 2010-..., discussed at para **7.28** below.

3.48 This approach has been regarded by UK courts as having a number of important implications. One is that it has to be remembered, when interpreting and applying the Convention, that:

'... it is dealing with the realities of life and it is not applied in ways which run counter to reason and common sense ... If the Convention was to be applied by the courts in ways which would seem absurd to ordinary people then the courts would be doing dis-service to the aims and purposes of the Convention and the result would simply be to prejudice public respect for an international treaty which seeks to express the basic rights and freedoms of a democratic society.'[1]

A second implication is that, where difficult choices have to be made between the rights of the individual and the needs of society, it will in some circumstances be appropriate for the courts to defer to the judgment of the democratically-elected legislature or democratically-accountable executive as to how the balance should be struck[2].

1   *Brown v Stott* 2001 SC (PC) 43 at page 81 per Lord Clyde. See also *R v HM Advocate* 2003 SC (PC) 21 at para 18 per Lord Steyn: 'The moral authority of human rights in the eyes of the public must not be undermined by allowing them to run riot in our justice systems'.

2   See paras **3.142–3.147** below.

The effectiveness principle

3.49 The European Court of Human Rights has said, on many occasions, that the ECHR 'is intended to guarantee not rights that are theoretical or illusory but rights that are practical and effective'[1]. This has a number of consequences. In the first place, the Convention is concerned with the reality of a situation rather than its formal appearance: 'the Court is compelled to look behind the appearances and investigate the realities of the procedure in question'[2]. This is one of the reasons why the Court has given an autonomous meaning to many of the terms of the Convention, rather than adopting the formal classification given by national legal systems. For example, the commencement of criminal proceedings, for the purpose of the 'reasonable time' guarantee in Article 6, depends on the application of tests developed by the Strasbourg Court, rather than upon the moment at which proceedings formally commence under domestic law[3]. Secondly, the principle of effectiveness has resulted in the Court's interpreting the Convention as including numerous implied rights, without which the express rights conferred would be less effective. Article 6, for example, has been interpreted as including an implied right of access to a court, without which the procedural guarantees applicable to court proceedings under Article 6 might be rendered pointless[4]; and, for the same reason, as including an implied right to legal aid where necessary in civil proceedings[5]. Similarly, the right to legal representation in criminal proceedings, under Article 6(3)(c), has been interpreted as including an implied right to be represented by a lawyer who is competent[6]. Thirdly, the principle of effectiveness is reflected in the Court's interpretation of the Convention as imposing positive objections on contracting states (including their courts) to alter their law (including their private law) and practice and to take executive action in certain circumstances[7]. Fourthly, the principle of effectiveness is reflected in the Court's willingness, in certain circumstances, to consider an alleged violation of the Convention on the basis of the facts existing at the time of its own decision, rather than confining itself to a review on the basis of the facts existing at the time of the decision complained of[8]. More generally, the principle of effectiveness pervades the interpretation and application of the Convention.

1   See eg *Airey v Ireland* (1979) A 32, para 24; *Artico v Italy* (1980) A 37, para 33.

2   *Deweer v Belgium* (1980) A 35, para 44.

3   See eg *Deweer v Belgium* (1980) A 35, paras 41–42.

4   *Golder v United Kingdom* (1975) A 18, paras 26–36.

5   *Airey v Ireland* (1979) A 32, para 26.

6   *Artico v Italy* (1980) A 37, para 36.

7   See paras **3.26–3.30** above.

8   Eg *Chahal v United Kingdom* 1996-V (deportation).

Autonomous concepts

3.50 Many of the terms contained in the ECHR have been interpreted by the European Court of Human Rights as having a specific meaning in the context of the Convention, independent of any meaning which they might have in domestic legal systems. This approach not only secures uniformity of interpretation of the terms in question throughout the contracting states: it also ensures that the effectiveness of the Convention cannot be compromised by contracting states' interpreting or applying its provisions in a restrictive manner. An example is the expression 'criminal charge' in Article 6 of the Convention[1]. The relationship between the interpretation of Convention terms as autonomous concepts and the need to look at the realities of a situation in accordance with the effectiveness principle is illustrated by the judgment in *V v United Kingdom* that the Home Secretary's fixing of the tariff to be served by juvenile offenders sentenced to detention during Her Majesty's Pleasure contravened Article 6. The Government argued that the offender was sentenced by the judge, and that the fixing of the tariff was merely an aspect of the administration of the sentence already imposed by the court. The European Court of Human Rights considered that the fixing of the tariff amounted in reality to a sentencing exercise, however it was formally classified under English law, and therefore formed part of the 'determination' of the criminal charge and attracted the safeguards of Article 6[2].

1   See eg *Öztürk v Germany* (1984) A 73, para 53. See further Letsas 'The Truth in Autonomous Concepts: How to Interpret the ECHR' (2004) 15 EJIL 234.

2   *V v United Kingdom* [GC] 1999-IX.

3.51 Certain expressions used in the ECHR can be regarded as a hybrid between autonomous concepts and terms interpreted according to domestic law. For example, the expression 'prescribed by law' (or its equivalents) refers to domestic law in order to determine whether the act in question was in accordance with domestic law, but is also interpreted as requiring that the domestic law in question must satisfy certain requirements implicit in the Convention[1]. A particularly complex concept is that of 'civil rights and obligations' (Article 6). 'Civil' has an autonomous meaning, so that the classification of the right or obligation under domestic law is not conclusive[2]. Domestic law, on the other hand, determines the content of the right in question[3]. Domestic law's denial that there is a right (eg because of an immunity or defence pleaded by the defender) will not, however, prevent there being a civil right for the purposes of Article 6 if the domestic law in question is so disproportionately restrictive as to be incompatible with the right of access to a court[4]. This is another illustration, of particular difficulty, of the Court's insistence on looking at the practical realities of the situation and interpreting the Convention so as to make it practical and effective.

1   See para **3.65** below.

2   *König v Germany* (1978) A 27, para 88. See further paras **5.12–5.30** below.

3   *König v Germany* (1978) A 27, para 89. See further paras **5.17–5.18** below.

4   Eg *Fayed v United Kingdom* (1994) A 294-B.

A 'living instrument'

3.52 In 1950 the Lord Chancellor observed, in relation to the recently concluded European Convention on Human Rights:

> 'Vague and indefinite terms have been used just because they were vague and indefinite, so that all parties, hoping and expecting that these terms will be construed according to their separate points of view, could be induced to sign them.'[1]

In the event, the open texture of the language used in the Convention has enabled the European Court of Human Rights to adopt a particular approach to its interpretation. The court has described the Convention, in a phrase which it has often repeated, as 'a living instrument which ... must be interpreted in the light of present-day conditions'[2]. Another way of expressing the same idea is to say that the Convention must be given a 'dynamic' or 'evolutive' interpretation. In other words, the practical application of the general expressions used in the Convention is considered to change over time, reflecting changes in European society and its prevailing ideas, values and standards.

1   Cabinet Office memorandum CAB 130/64. Sir Hartley Shawcross, the Attorney General, similarly attributed the lack of clarity in the drafting to a compromise to accommodate the different legal systems involved: see Marston, 'The United Kingdom's Part in the Preparation of the European Convention on Human Rights, 1950' (1993) 42 ICLQ 796 at 818–819.

2   *Tyrer v United Kingdom* (1978) A 26, para 31. The case concerned the use of corporal punishment on the Isle of Man. The 'living instrument' approach does not apply to Art 1 of

the ECHR: *Bankovic and Others v Belgium and 16 Other Contracting States* (dec) [GC] 2001-XII, paras 64–65.

3.53 An example is the expression 'necessary in a democratic society', which is one of the tests of the compatibility with the Convention of interferences with the rights guaranteed by Articles 8–11. What is 'necessary in a democratic society' is considered to change as society changes. This has been reflected in an evolution in the court's approach to certain issues, such as the treatment of homosexuals. In one such case, concerned with the criminalisation of homosexual acts, the Court stated:

'… there is now a better understanding, and in consequence an increased tolerance, of homosexual behaviour to the extent that in the great majority of the member states of the Council of Europe it is no longer considered to be necessary or appropriate to treat homosexual practices of the kind now in question as in themselves a matter to which the sanctions of the criminal law should be applied; the Court cannot overlook the marked changes which have occurred in this regard in the domestic law of the member states.'[1]

Similarly, the Court made it clear, when upholding a state's failure to recognise an individual's change of sexual identity, that the treatment of transsexuals should be kept under review, observing:

'Since the Convention has always to be interpreted and applied in the light of current circumstances, it is important that the need for appropriate legal measures in this area should be kept under review.'[2]

Some years later, the Court noted the international trend in favour of increased social acceptance of post-operative transsexuals and of the legal recognition of their new sexual identity, and decided that there was now an obligation to ensure that domestic law made arrangements for gender re-assignment[3]. Many other examples could be given[4]. The 'living instrument' principle is one which pervades the interpretation and application of the Convention.

1   *Dudgeon v United Kingdom* (1981) A 45, para 60. The case concerned Northern Ireland.
2   *Cossey v United Kingdom* (1990) A 184, para 42. Similar comments had been made in the earlier case of *Rees v United Kingdom* (1986) A 106, para 47 and were repeated in the later case of *Sheffield and Horsham v United Kingdom* 1998-V, para 60.
3   *Goodwin v United Kingdom* [GC] 2002-VI, paras 74–93.
4   Eg *Marckx v Belgium* (1979) A 31, para 41 ('family'); *Winterwerp v Netherlands* (1979) A 33 ('persons of unsound mind'); *Borgers v Belgium* (1991) A 214-B ('fair trial'); *Stafford v United Kingdom* [GC] 2002-IV ('lawful detention').

3.54 In principle, evolutive interpretation respects the text of the treaty and reflects changes in understanding of how the language used in the text should be applied in practice. The way in which a concept such as 'inhuman and degrading treatment' is understood changes over time[1], and such changes can be reflected in the application of a treaty or a constitution. The principle is not understood as entitling a judicial body to introduce new concepts into an international treaty which makes no mention of them, simply because it would be more in accordance with the spirit of the times. As the Court said in a case in which it was invited to imply into Articles 8 or 12 a right to divorce:

> 'It is true that the Convention and its protocols must be interpreted in the light of present-day conditions. However, the Court cannot, by means of an evolutive interpretation, derive from these instruments a right that was not included therein at the outset.'[2]

The distinction is not, however, always easy to draw. The point can be illustrated by the case of *Hirst v United Kingdom (no 2)*, where UK legislation which prevents most categories of convicted prisoner from voting was held by a majority of the court to be incompatible with Article 3 of Protocol no 1. The judges in the minority commented:

> 'We do not dispute that it is an important task for the Court to ensure that the rights guaranteed by the Convention system comply with "present-day conditions", and that accordingly a "dynamic and evolutive" approach may in certain situations be justified. However, it is essential to bear in mind that the Court is not a legislator and should be careful not to assume legislative functions. An "evolutive" or "dynamic" interpretation should have a sufficient basis in changing conditions in the societies of the Contracting States, including an emerging consensus as to the standards to be achieved. We fail to see that this is so in the present case.'[3]

---

1   *Tyrer v United Kingdom* (1978) A 26, para 31. Other relevant Article 3 cases include *Soering v United Kingdom* (1989) A 161 (extradition to face capital punishment); and *V v United Kingdom* [GC] 1999-IX (age of criminal responsibility).

2   *Johnston v Ireland* (1986) A 112, para 53. See also *Soering v United Kingdom* (1989) A 161; cf *Emonet and Others v Switzerland* 2007-XIV, para 66.

3   *Hirst v United Kingdom (no 2)* [GC] 2005-IX, Joint Dissenting Opinion of Judges Wildhaber, Costa, Lorenzen, Kovler and Jebens, para 6. This might be contrasted with *Hatton and Others v United Kingdom* [GC] 2003-VIII, joint dissenting opinion of Judges Costa, Ress, Türmen, Zupančič and Steiner, paras 1–2, concerned with the evolution of Art 8 to encompass environmental rights.

3.55 The principle of evolutive interpretation is closely related to the establishment of common European standards, reflecting the Court's conception of the ECHR as 'a constitutional instrument of European public order'[1]. The court therefore takes account of law and practice throughout the contracting states, and of relevant international instruments. For this purpose, the court has a research division which studies questions of comparative and international law that arise in cases before a Grand Chamber. The court does not always wait until a given approach has been adopted by all, or the great majority, of contracting states[2]. In the absence of a sufficient degree of European consensus to apply the 'living instrument' principle, the Court accommodates variations in the practice of contracting states by applying the 'margin of appreciation' doctrine. The 'living instrument' principle, and the 'margin of appreciation' doctrine, are to that extent complementary to one another.

1   *Loizidou v Turkey* (preliminary objections) (1995) A 310, para 75. The qualification 'European' is important. As Lord Rodger of Earlsferry observed in *R (Al-Skeini) v Secretary of State for Defence* [2008] 1 AC 153 at para 78, the result of the 'living instrument' approach 'is a body of law which may reflect the values of the contracting states, but which certainly does not reflect those in many other parts of the world. So the idea that the United Kingdom was obliged to secure observance of all the rights and freedoms as interpreted by the European court in the utterly different society of southern Iraq is manifestly absurd ... If it went further, the court would run the risk not only of colliding with the jurisdiction of other human rights bodies but of being accused of human rights imperialism.'

2   See eg *F v Switzerland* (1987) A 128, para 33; *Christine Goodwin v United Kingdom* [GC] 2002-VI, para 85.

3.56 It follows from the 'living instrument' principle that no strict doctrine of precedent applies to decisions or judgments of the European Court of Human Rights or of the Commission. Nevertheless, the Court refers to its previous decisions and generally builds upon them incrementally, in much the same way as a British court. A former President of the Court has referred to the situation as a 'moderated doctrine of precedent' applying to a situation of 'continuity in the framework of an evolutive jurisprudence' in which examples of 'dynamic interpretation' are readily discernible but against a background in which precedent is followed 'except where cogent reasons [impel] it to adjust the interpretation of the Convention to changes in societal values or in present-day conditions'[1]. In practice, a heavy onus usually lies on a party seeking to persuade the Court to depart from its previous case law[2].

1   *European Court of Human Rights, Annual Report 2005* (2006), per Judge Wildhaber at pp 22–23.

2   See eg *Cossey v United Kingdom* (1990) A 184, para 35; *Wynne v United Kingdom* (1994) A 294-A, para 36. See further Wildhaber 'Precedent in the European Court of Human Rights' in Mahoney, Matscher, Petzold and Wildhaber (eds) *Protecting Human Rights: The European Perspective* (2000), pp 1529–1545; and Pellonpää 'Continuity and Change in the Case-law of the European Court of Human Rights' in Kohen (ed) *Promoting Justice, Human Rights and Conflict Resolution through International Law: Liber Amicorum Lucius Caflisch* (2007), pp 409–420.

Evolutive interpretation and domestic courts

3.57 Evolutive interpretation is not a concept which is peculiar to Convention jurisprudence. In the British courts, cases sometimes arise where changed social conditions require that a statutory provision should be given a different application than it would have had when enacted. The point can be illustrated by the decision in *Fitzpatrick v Sterling Housing Association Ltd* where the House of Lords held that a statutory provision of 1920, giving security of tenure to a member of the tenant's 'family', had come by 1994 to include a long-term homosexual partner[1]. This approach is explained on the basis that a statute is 'always speaking'. A distinction is, however, drawn in domestic law, as in the Convention jurisprudence, between the interpretation of a concept whose application is liable to change as circumstances change, and the introduction of a wholly new concept[2]. A 'living instrument' approach has also been adopted by the Privy Council when construing the written constitutions of Commonwealth states[3].

1   *Fitzpatrick v Sterling Housing Association Ltd* [2001] 1 AC 27.

2   See eg *Birmingham City Council v Oakley* [2001] 1 AC 617 at 631 per Lord Hoffmann.

3   See eg *Boyce v The Queen* [2005] 1 AC 400 at para 28 per Lord Hoffmann.

3.58 For domestic courts applying the legislation creating Convention rights, the evolutive interpretation of the Convention raises numerous issues: for example, the limits of evolutive interpretation, and its relationship to the doctrine of the margin of appreciation; the implications of evolutive interpretation for the use of the Court's judgments as precedents; the assessment of just satisfaction in cases involving an evolutive interpretation; the ascertainment of Convention law in areas which are in a particularly marked state of evolution; and evolutive interpretation of Convention rights by domestic courts[1]. One issue of particular importance is the temporal implications, as they might be described, of evolutive interpretation.

The evolutive interpretation of the Convention may raise two issues in relation to time. First, a question may arise as to the date as from which the application of the Convention had evolved to the extent that a given domestic law or practice should be regarded as having been incompatible with Convention rights. Secondly, a question may arise as to whether it is possible, compatibly with Convention rights, to leave undisturbed transactions or legal decisions which were in conformity with domestic law as it stood at the time of those transactions or decisions, if it is subsequently decided that the law or practice on which they were based was not in conformity with Convention rights. The second of these questions is discussed below in the context of legal certainty[2].

1   See eg *R (Ullah) v Special Adjudicator*[2004] 2 AC 323 at para 20 per Lord Bingham of Cornhill; *M v Secretary of State for Work and Pensions* [2006] 2 AC 91 at para 30 per Lord Nicholls of Birkenhead and at para 131 per Lord Mance; *Jones v Ministry of the Interior of the Kingdom of Saudi Arabia* [2007] 1 AC 270 at para 18 per Lord Bingham; cf *N v Secretary of State for the Home Department* [2005] 2 AC 296 at para 25 per Lord Hope of Craighead.

2   See paras **3.62–3.72** below.

3.59 In relation to the first question, the nature of the problem in domestic law can be illustrated by two cases decided by the House of Lords. First, the case of *Chief Constable of the West Yorkshire Police v A (No 2)* concerned the decision of the Chief Constable in March 1998 not to accept the application of A, a post-operative transsexual, to join his force as a constable. The decision was based in part on the fact that A, a male-to-female transsexual, remained in law a man. In July 1998, four months after the Chief Constables's decision, the Strasbourg court held in *Sheffield and Horsham v United Kingdom*[1] that refusal to recognise a transsexual's reassigned gender did not violate the applicant's rights under Article 8. The case against the Chief Constable was heard by the House of Lords in 2004, after *Christine Goodwin v United Kingdom*[2] had been decided. On the basis that the state of Convention law in 1998 was settled by *Sheffield and Horsham,* the House of Lords rejected the argument that the Chief Constable's decision had violated the Convention[3].

A similar type of problem arose in *M v Secretary of State for Work and Pensions.* The case concerned the liability of a woman to contribute financially during 2000 and 2001 to the support of her children, who lived with her former husband. The woman lived with a female partner. Her liability under the relevant legislation would have been less if she had been living with a man, as she would then have benefited from allowances available to 'families'. She argued that her rights under Article 8 had been violated. Hearing the case in 2006, the House of Lords rejected her argument in the light of the Strasbourg jurisprudence of the relevant period, although it acknowledged that the Strasbourg Court might by 2006 have taken a different view[4].

1   *Sheffield and Horsham v United Kingdom* 1998-V, discussed at para **6.145** below.
2   *Christine Goodwin v United Kingdom* [GC] 2002-VI, discussed at para **6.145** below.
3   *Chief Constable of the West Yorkshire Police v A (No 2)* [2005] 1 AC 51.
4   *M v Secretary of State for Work and Pensions* [2006] 2 AC 91.

3.60 In cases where the Strasbourg Court has invoked the 'living instrument' doctrine, its finding that a given state of affairs had violated the Convention has generally indicated a date by which, at latest, the relevant evolution in the law had occurred. In *Dudgeon v United Kingdom*, for example, the Court did not reject the Government's contention that the legislation in question had at one time been compatible with the Convention, but awarded damages by way of just satisfaction in respect of a criminal investigation of the applicant's homosexual activities in 1976[1]. In *Stafford v United Kingdom,* the Court made an award of just satisfaction in respect of imprisonment from July 1997, on the basis that the application of Article 5(1) to life prisoners had evolved by that date to the extent that the Court's earlier judgment in *Wynne v United Kingdom*[2] (in 1994) should be departed from[3]. In *Christine Goodwin v United Kingdom*, the Court held in July 2002 that the United Kingdom could 'no longer claim' that its refusal to recognise a transsexual's reassigned gender fell within its margin of appreciation, and that the fair balance inherent in the Convention 'now' tilted in favour of the applicant[4]. Running through the Court's reasoning, it seems, was an acceptance that the earlier, contrary judgments of the Court remained correct statements of the interpretation and application of the Convention as at the time when they were given. Consistently with this, the Court held that the finding of violation 'with the consequences which will ensue for the future' was just satisfaction[5]. This series of cases is notable for the Court's having given warning of its direction of travel. Developments in the Court's jurisprudence have not always been so clearly signposted.

1   *Dudgeon v United Kingdom* (1983) A 59, discussed at para **6.140** below.
2   *Wynne v United Kingdom* (1994) A 294-A, discussed at para **4.227** below.
3   *Stafford v United Kingdom* [GC] 2002-IV, discussed at paras **4.172** and **4.227** below.

4   *Christine Goodwin v United Kingdom* [GC] 2002-VI, at para 93, discussed at para **6.145** below.

5   *Christine Goodwin v United Kingdom* [GC] 2002-VI, para 120.

3.61 In practice, domestic courts may have to assess how far the interpretation of the Convention had evolved by a given date without the benefit of a Strasbourg judgment which is clearly intended to operate only prospectively, as in *Christine Goodwin,* or a series of judgments which enable the evolution of the jurisprudence to be tracked with some precision over a period of time, as in *Stafford.* This may be a difficult matter: in addition to the difficulty which domestic courts may experience in obtaining adequate information about developments in comparative and international law, there may also be a delicate judgment involved in deciding at what point in time the interpretation of the Convention can be said to have evolved to the stage at which a different approach to its application is required. This is amply demonstrated by the Strasbourg jurisprudence. At the domestic level, there is the additional consideration that the precise moment at which, for example, the different treatment of a particular group ceases to be justifiable may depend on a judgment of economic, social or political matters falling within the competence of the legislature or the executive: that is to say, falling within an area of discretion forming a domestic counterpart to the margin of appreciation recognised at the international level.

Legal certainty

3.62 Legal certainty might be defined, in broad terms, as the ability to act within a settled framework without fear of arbitrary or unforeseeable state interference. As such, it is a fundamental aspect of the constitutional order of the contracting states, reflected for example in the British concept of the rule of law, the French concept of the *état de droit,* and the German concept of the *Rechtsstaat.* It is expressed in numerous more precise principles of national law, such as (in the United Kingdom) the principles of interpretation of criminal statutes, the presumption against retroactivity and the protection of legitimate expectations[1]. It is a fundamental principle of EU law. It also forms an important element of Convention law. It finds particular expression in a number of articles of the ECHR which are discussed below. It is not, however, confined to those provisions. Those specific provisions, as the Court has said, require domestic law 'to be compatible with the rule of law, a concept inherent in all the articles of the Convention'[2].

1   Partly under the influence of EU law, itself influenced by the German principle of *Vertrauenschutz.*

2   *Amuur v France* 1996-III, at para 50.

3.63 In *R (Gillan) v Commissioner of Police of the Metropolis,* Lord Bingham of Cornhill said:

'The lawfulness requirement in the Convention addresses supremely important features of the rule of law. The exercise of power by public officials, as it affects members of the public, must be governed by clear and publicly-accessible rules of law. The public must not be vulnerable to interference by public officials acting on any personal whim, caprice, malice, predilection or purpose other than that for which the power was conferred. This is what, in this context, is meant by arbitrariness, which is the antithesis of legality. This is the test which any interference with or derogation from a Convention right must meet if a violation is to be avoided.'[1]

---

1   *R (Gillan) v Commissioner of Police of the Metropolis* [2006] 2 AC 307 at para 34 (police stop and search powers under the Terrorism Act 2000,ss 44–45, did not constitute an interference with Arts 10 and 11; and even if they did, they were justified under Arts 10(2) and 11(2)). The principle of legality was also discussed in *R v Shayler* [2003] 1 AC 247 at para 56 per Lord Hope of Craighead.

3.64 A number of provisions in the ECHR contain an express requirement that measures interfering with protected rights must be lawful. A number of different expressions are used in the English text[1]: 'in accordance with law'[2], 'prescribed by law'[3], 'provided for by law'[4] and 'in accordance with law'[5]. No significance has been given to those differences in wording[6]. In order to satisfy the Convention texts, the interference must be in accordance with domestic law, and that law must itself meet certain Convention requirements. The texts therefore call for scrutiny of both the extent to which state activity is covered by domestic legal rules, and also the quality of those rules themselves.

---

1   The French text uses the phrase 'prévues par la loi' throughout.

2   Art 8.

3   Arts 9–11.

4   Prot 1, Art 1.

5   Prot 4, Art 2.

6   *Sunday Times v United Kingdom (no 1)* (1979) A 30, paras 48–49.

3.65 First, the act in question must have a basis in domestic law. This includes not only legislation, but also common law[1] and European Union law[2]. It does not necessarily include non-statutory guidance or codes of practice[3]. Secondly, the law must meet certain requirements, notably of accessibility and foreseeability. These are essentially aspects of a single objective: legal certainty. In relation to accessibility, the European Court of Human Rights said in the *Sunday Times* case:

'First, the law must be adequately accessible: the citizen must be able to have an indication that is adequate in the circumstances of the legal rules applicable to a given case.'[4]

In relation to foreseeability, the Court said in the same case:

'Secondly, a norm cannot be regarded as a "law" unless it is formulated with sufficient precision to enable the citizen to regulate his conduct: he must be able – if need be with appropriate advice – to foresee, to a degree that is reasonable in the circumstances, the consequences which a given action may entail. Those consequences need not be foreseeable with absolute certainty: experience shows this to be unattainable. Again, whilst certainty is highly desirable, it may bring in its train excessive rigidity and the law must be able to keep pace with changing circumstances. Accordingly, many laws are inevitably couched in terms which, to a greater or lesser extent, are vague and whose interpretation and application are questions of practice.'[5]

The level of precision required will be dependent on 'the content of the instrument in question; the field it is designed to cover and the number and status of those to whom it is addressed'[6]. The law can confer a discretion, but in order to conform to the notion of the rule of law there must be some safeguard against arbitrariness in its application[7]:

'A law which confers a discretion is not in itself inconsistent with [the requirement of foreseeability], provided that the scope of the discretion and the manner of its exercise are indicated with sufficient clarity, having regard to the legitimate aim in question, to give the individual adequate protection against arbitrary interference.'[8]

1   Eg *Sunday Times v United Kingdom (no 1)* (1979) A 30, para 47.

2   *Groppera Radio AG v Switzerland* (1990) A 173.

3   27237/95, *Govell v United Kingdom* (14 January 1998); *Khan v United Kingdom* 2000-V. Contrast *Silver and Others v United Kingdom* (1983) A 61, paras 85–88. See also *R (Matthias Rath Bv) v Advertising Standards Authority* [2001] HRLR 22 (ASA codes of practice: prescribed by law).

4   *Sunday Times v United Kingdom (no 1)* (1979) A 30, at para 49.

5   *Sunday Times v United Kingdom (no 1)* (1979) A 30, at para 49.

6   *Rekvényi v Hungary* [GC] 1999-III, para 34. Particular issues arise in the context of secret surveillance: see *Malone v United Kingdom* (1984) A 82; *Kruslin v France* (1990) A 176-A; *Kopp v Switzerland* 1988-II, para 34.

7   *Malone v United Kingdom* (1984) A 82, paras 67–68.

8   *Margareta and Roger Andersson v Sweden* (1992) A 226-A, at para 75.

3.66 These requirements do not give rise to any particular difficulty in relation to the common law. Indeed, as the European Court of Human Rights has pointed out, 'it would be wrong to exaggerate the difference between common-law countries and Continental countries'[1]. The development of a common law offence, for example, is not inconsistent with legal certainty, provided that any development is reasonably foreseeable and consistent with the essence of the offence[2]. Nor are jury awards of damages in defamation cases inconsistent with legal certainty: although there are no specific legal guidelines, that is 'an inherent feature of the law of damages', which has to make allowances for 'an open-ended variety of factual situations'; and an irrational award could be set aside by the appeal court[3]. The Court has accepted that the English concept of breach of the peace is defined with sufficient precision for the foreseeability criterion to be satisfied[4]. On the other hand, the power of the English courts to bind persons over to be of good behaviour (ie not to act *contra bonos mores*) did not satisfy that criterion, because of its complete lack of precision[5]. These cases also indicate that the surrounding factual circumstances, as well as the legal definition in question, can be taken into account in assessing whether the foreseeability criterion is satisfied[6].

1   *Kruslin v France* (1990) A 176-A, para 29.

2   *SW v United Kingdom* (1995) A 355-B. See further paras **5.227–5.228** below.

3   *Tolstoy Miloslavsky v United Kingdom* (1995) A 316-B, paras 37–44. On the other hand, the award in the case in question was disproportionate to the aim of protecting reputation and therefore failed the requirement of being 'necessary in a democratic society'. This case illustrates how the Convention can impact upon litigation between private parties.

4   *McLeod v United Kingdom* 1998-VII, para 42; *Steel v United Kingdom* 1998-VII, paras 55–57.

5   *Hashman and Harrup v United Kingdom* [GC] 1999-VIII, discussed further at para **7.69** below.

6   *Hashman and Harrup v United Kingdom* [GC] 1999-VIII, paras 35 and 40.

3.67 The requirement of legal certainty is also reflected in Article 5, which requires any deprivation of liberty to be 'lawful' and 'in accordance with a procedure prescribed by law'[1]. The principles already discussed apply also to these requirements:

> '[T]he expressions "lawful" and "in accordance with a procedure prescribed by law" in art 5(1) stipulate not only full compliance with the procedural and substantive rules of national law, but also that any deprivation of liberty be consistent with the purpose of art 5 and not arbitrary. In addition, given the importance of personal liberty, it is essential that the applicable national law meets the standard of "lawfulness" set by the Convention, which requires that all law, whether written or unwritten, be sufficiently precise to allow the citizen – if need be, with appropriate advice – to foresee, to a degree that is reasonable in the circumstances, the consequences which a given action may entail.'[2]

1   See further paras **4.161–4.168** below.

2   *Steel and Others v United Kingdom* 1998-VII, at para 54.

3.68 Legal certainty is now also considered an inherent aspect of a fair hearing in terms of Article 6[1]. Inconsistent decisions in the interpretation of domestic law may be such as to deprive individuals of the possibility of a fair determination of their rights[2], although it is recognised that courts may require time to provide settled guidance in statutory interpretation[3]. Legal certainty also requires that of a final and binding judgment of the domestic courts should not be called into question through a fresh examination of the merits, and the powers of review of higher courts should be restricted to the correction of judicial errors or miscarriages of justice[4].

1   See paras **5.100–5.101** below.

2   *Iordan Iordanov and Others v Bulgaria* (2 July 2009). Differences in treatment of analogous situations may thus also give rise to findings of a violation of Art 14 taken in conjunction with Art 6: see eg *Beian v Romania (no 1)* 2007-XIII, paras 32–40 and 59–65 (entirely conflicting

series of decisions of the supreme court on compensatory measures with divergent opinions even being issued on the same day: violation of Art 6, and of Art 14 taken with Prot 1, Art 1).

3   *Schwarzkopf and Taussik v Czech Republic* (dec) (2 December 2008), discussed at para **5.100** below.

4   *Ryabykh v Russia* 2003-IX, at para 52.

3.69 In the context of the criminal law, the need for legal certainty is reflected in Article 7:

'Article 7(1) of the Convention is not confined to prohibiting the retrospective application of the criminal law to an accused's disadvantage. It also embodies, more generally, the principle that only law can define a crime and prescribe a penalty (*nullum crimen, nulla poena, sine lege*) and the principle that the criminal law must not be extensively construed to an accused's detriment, for instance by analogy: it follows from this that an offence must be clearly defined in law.'[1]

This requirement embodies the criteria already discussed: accessibility and foreseeability[2]. It is not incompatible with the development of common law or other offences by judicial case law:

'However clearly drafted a legal provision may be, in any system of law, including criminal law, there is an inevitable element of judicial interpretation. There will always be a need for elucidation of doubtful points and for adaptation to changing circumstances. Indeed, in the United Kingdom, as in the other Convention states, the progressive development of the criminal law through judicial law-making is a well entrenched and necessary part of legal tradition. Article 7 of the Convention cannot be read as outlawing the gradual clarification of the rules of criminal liability through judicial interpretation from case to case, providing the resultant development is consistent with the essence of the offence and could reasonably be foreseen.'[3]

In the opinion of the Commission, Article 7 implies that the consistent elements of an offence (eg 'the particular form of culpability required for its completion') may not be essentially changed to the detriment of the accused by judicial decision, but does not prevent the clarification of the existing elements of the offence or their adaptation to new circumstances which can reasonably be brought within the original concept of the offence[4]. Article 7 is considered more fully in chapter 5 below[5].

1   *Kokkinakis v Greece* (1993) A 260-A, para 52.

2   *SW v United Kingdom* (1995) A 355-B, para 32. The exceptional problems arising from the prosecution of former East German officials and border guards, following German reunification, are discussed in *Streletz, Kessler and Krenz v Germany* [GC] 2001-II, and in *K-H W v Germany* [GC] 2001-II, discussed at para **5.228** below.

3   *SW v United Kingdom* (1995) A 355-B, para 36 (marital rape).

4   8710/79, *X Ltd and Y v United Kingdom* (1982) DR 28, 77, para 9.

5   See paras **5.225–5.237** below.

3.70 Legal certainty also has more general implications. Judgments of the Strasbourg Court, or decisions of domestic courts which are based on the Strasbourg jurisprudence, may effect an abrupt change in what until then the relevant law was generally thought to be, with a consequent risk of uncertainty and disruption. Difficulties of this kind have arisen from time to time in the United Kingdom in relation to Strasbourg judgments[1]. There is also a related question whether, once it has become apparent that domestic law is no longer in conformity with evolving standards, the state should be allowed a reasonable time to address the problem before the Convention is held to have been infringed. It has been observed, in a domestic case concerned with the equal treatment of men and women, that

> '... if one has a form of discrimination which was historically justified but, with changes in society, has gradually lost its justification, a period of consultation, drafting and debate must be included in the time which the legislature may reasonably consider appropriate for making a change. Up to the point at which that time is exceeded, there is no violation of a Convention right.'[2]

---

1   Examples include *Salduz v Turkey* [GC] 2008-..., (access to a lawyer during police detention); cf *Cadder v HM Advocate* 2010 SCCR 951; and Criminal Procedure (Legal Assistance, Detention and Appeals (Scotland) Act 2010); and also *Bouchacourt v France* (17 December 2009) (registration of sex offenders; cf *R (F) v Secretary of State for the Home Department* [2011] 1 AC 331; Sexual Offences Act 2003 (Remedial) (Scotland) Order 2010, SSI 2010/370).

2   *R (Hooper) v Secretary of State for Work and Pensions* [2005] 1 WLR 1681 at para 62 per Lord Hoffmann. In a similar case, Lord Mance commented on 'the unreality of supposing that all aspects of any exercise in achieving complete equality in every area of United Kingdom law could have been addressed by the courts and/or Parliament at one and the same moment': *M v Secretary of State for Work and Pensions* [2006] 2 AC 91 at para 155.

3.71 The Strasbourg Court has recognised that there may be a tension between evolutive interpretation and legal certainty[1]. In the *Marckx v Belgium* case, in particular, the Court addressed the possibility that its decision that 'illegitimate' and 'legitimate' children were entitled to equal treatment could have retrospective implications for inheritance rights. It stated:

> '... the principle of legal certainty, which is necessarily inherent in the law of the Convention as in Community Law, dispenses the Belgian State from re-opening legal acts or situations that antedate the delivery of the present judgment.'[2]

That approach was followed by the Commission in a case concerned with a national measure which ended discrimination against 'illegitimate' children in the law of succession, but only in respect of children born after a specified date. The Commission rejected a complaint based on Article 14 in conjunction with Article 8[3]. The same approach was also followed by the Court in the later case of *Walden v Liechtenstein*, concerned with sexual discrimination in relation to old age pensions. The question was whether the national court had acted incompatibly with the Convention when it did not annul the discriminatory legislation with retroactive effect, but allowed time for amending legislation to be introduced. The Court stated:

' ... the principle of legal certainty, which is necessarily inherent in the law of the Convention, may dispense States from questioning legal acts or situations that antedate judgments of the Court declaring domestic legislation incompatible with the Convention. The same considerations apply where a constitutional court annuls domestic legislation as being unconstitutional ... Moreover, it has also been accepted, in view of the principle of legal certainty that a constitutional court may set a time-limit for the legislator to enact new legislation with the effect that an unconstitutional provision remains applicable for a transitional period.'

The Court concluded that the national court's decision, 'which had the effect that unconstitutional legislation remained applicable to the applicant for a limited period, served the interests of legal certainty', and that there was therefore no violation of Article 14 taken in conjunction with Article 1 of Protocol no 1[4]. The Strasbourg Court also appears to accept that a reasonable time may be allowed for legislative change[5].

1   See eg *Stafford v United Kingdom* [GC] 2002-IV at para 68; *Christine Goodwin v United Kingdom* [GC] 2002-VI at para 74.

2   *Marckx v Belgium* (1979) A 31, para 58.

3   17750/91, *HR v Germany* (30 June 1992). See also 22651/93, *JR v Germany* (1995) DR 83, 14.

4   *Walden v Liechtenstein* (dec) (16 March 2000).

5   *Petrovic v Austria,* 1998-II, paras 40–41; *Sheffield and Horsham v United Kingdom,* 1998-V.

3.72 These problems are also recognised in the domestic law of the United Kingdom. There are a considerable number of dicta to the effect that the court (or at least the Supreme Court) has an inherent power to limit the retrospective effect of its decisions[1]. The *Marckx v Belgium* judgment suggests that there would be no objection to this on Convention grounds. Section 102 of the SA 1998 also gives effect to the principle recognised in the *Walden v Liechtenstein* decision, by enabling the court to limit the temporal effect of a decision that legislation made by the devolved institutions is beyond their competence (by reason, *inter alia,* of being incompatible with Convention rights): the court can make an order removing or limiting any retrospective effect of its decision, or suspending the effect of its decision to enable the defect to be corrected[2]. The court can thus make its decision prospective only, or can declare (seemingly[3]) that the legislation was invalid only from a particular date, or without prejudice to particular transactions. The principle of legal certainty requires that the retrospective effect of a judicial decision is generally excluded from cases that have been finally determined[4].

These principles were applied in the domestic case of *Interfact Ltd v Liverpool City Council,* which concerned defendants who had been convicted of offences relating to pornography, contrary to a 1984 Act of Parliament. It subsequently emerged in 2009 that the Act of Parliament was unenforceable, as the Government had failed to comply with an EU directive which required such legislation to be notified to the European Commission. Notification was then effected, following which identical legislation was brought into force, but without retrospective effect.

Leave to appeal out of time was sought by the defendants, on the basis that their convictions were incompatible with Articles 7 and 10 of the Convention. Leave was refused. The convictions had been in accordance with Articles 7 and 10, since the 1984 Act was valid and in force, notwithstanding that domestic courts would have been obliged under the European Communities Act 1972 to disapply it if the failure to comply with the notification requirement had been known about. The conduct prohibited by the 1984 Act was clearly defined. Enforceability was not an essential element of the concept of law in Articles 7 or 10. In any event, the case law of the European Court of Human Rights did not require contracting states to undo all the consequences of a national law which was later held to be incompatible with the Convention, but acknowledged that the principle of legal certainty dispensed with any such need[5].

1   See *Cadder v HM Advocate* SCCR 951, at para 58 per Lord Hope of Craighead DPSC.

2   Scotland Act 1998, s 102; Government of Wales Act 1998, s 110; Northern Ireland Act 1998, s 88. For detailed discussion, see para **1.154** above. At the time of writing, it is anticipated that the scope of the SA 1998 s 102 may be extended by the Scotland Act 2011.

3   Cf *Ahmed v HM Treasury* [2010] 2 WLR 378.

4   *Cadder v HM Advocate* 2011 SCCR 951.

5   *Interfact Ltd v Liverpool City Council* [2011] 2 WLR 396.

Necessity and proportionality

3.73 The concept of 'necessity' is involved (expressly or implicitly) in several articles of the ECHR, but it has subtly different connotations in different contexts. A broad distinction can be drawn between those articles which guarantee rights principally of a civil and political nature, that are subject to widely expressed qualifications, and those articles which guarantee rights (primarily those concerning physical integrity and human dignity) which are either subject to no express qualification or subject only to stringent qualifications. Rights of the former kind are found in the Articles 8–11. Paragraph 1 of each of these articles guarantees, in turn, respect for private and family life, home and correspondence; freedom of thought, conscience and religion; freedom of expression; and freedom of assembly and association. Paragraph 2 of each of these articles, however, goes on to identify particular interests or 'legitimate aims' which may justify interference with the protected rights, always provided that any such interference is 'in accordance with the law' (or 'prescribed by law') and 'necessary in a democratic society'[1]. Questions arising under these articles are determined using a well-established checklist:

1   What is the scope of the particular guarantee?

2   Has there been any interference with the right guaranteed?

3   Does the interference have a legitimate aim?

4   Is the interference 'in accordance with the law'?

5   Is the interference 'necessary in a democratic society'?

1   The same formula is used in the ECHR, Prot 4, Art 2(3) concerning free movement of persons. This protocol has not been ratified by the United Kingdom.

3.74 In relation to the first and second of these questions, interpretation of the ECHR has clarified the scope of each guarantee and the circumstances in which an interference will be considered to have been established. In relation to the third question, the legitimate aims, so far as Articles 8–11 are concerned, are listed in paragraph 2 of each of the articles in question: the interests of national security, public safety or the economic well-being of the country, the prevention of disorder or crime, the protection of health or morals, and the protection of the rights and freedoms of others. In practice, an interference purporting to have a legitimate aim will be accepted as falling within the scope of one of the listed objectives. In relation to the fourth question, the concept of 'accordance with the law' has been discussed earlier[1].

1   See para **3.65** above.

3.75 In most cases, the real difficulty lies in the fifth question, ie in deciding whether an interference is 'necessary in a democratic society'. In considering this phrase, it is important to bear in mind both the word 'necessary' and the words 'in a democratic society'. The Strasbourg Court has said:

> 'The Court has noted that, whilst the adjective "necessary", within the meaning of art 10(2), is not synonymous with "indispensable", neither has it the flexibility of such expressions as "admissible", "ordinary", "useful", "reasonable" or "desirable" and that it implies the existence of a "pressing social need".'[1]

The Court has also identified certain characteristics of a 'democratic society', for example describing pluralism, tolerance and broadmindedness as the hallmarks of such a society[2], and describing freedom of expression as one of the essential foundations of a democratic society[3]. Deciding whether an interference is 'necessary in a democratic society' may involve considering whether the law or practice in question is out of line with standards generally prevailing elsewhere in the Council of Europe states (either domestically, or in international conventions which they have accepted), as it is more difficult to justify a measure as being 'necessary in a democratic society' if the great majority of other Council of Europe states adopt a different approach.

1   *Sunday Times v United Kingdom (no 1)* (1979) A 30, para 59; *Handyside v United Kingdom* (1976) A 24, para 48. This formulation has been repeated in the context of Art 8(2): *Dudgeon v United Kingdom* (1981) A 45.

2   *Handyside v United Kingdom* (1976) A 24, para 49; *Dudgeon v United Kingdom* (1981) A 45, para 53.

3   *Handyside v United Kingdom* (1976) A 24, para 49; *Bowman v United Kingdom* 1998-I, paras 42–43.

3.76 The question whether an interference is necessary in a democratic society is thus ineluctably a question of judgment. In the domestic law of the United Kingdom, questions of this nature, arising in the exercise of the courts' supervisory jurisdiction, have traditionally been resolved by applying what has come to be known as the *Wednesbury* test of unreasonableness[1]. Under the ECHR, the test applied is a more searching one: the requirement of 'proportionality'. This concept has its origins in continental administrative law: it is found in German law, in the principle of *Verhältnissmässigkeit*, and a similar principle can also be seen in French law. It is also a well-established principle of EU law. Proportionality is a question of degree, and so involves a judicial evaluation of the situation in question. Accordingly, the requirements of proportionality will vary according to the circumstances of the case. In particular, proportionality does not require the effects of a general measure to be precisely tailored to each individual case affected where that would impose an unreasonable burden on the authorities involved. Proportionality involves a closer examination of the merits of the case than is traditional in the administrative law of the United Kingdom: it is directed towards determining whether there has in fact been a violation of the Convention, rather than with whether a decision-making process was flawed. As the Strasbourg Court has said:

> '[a wide margin of appreciation] does not mean that the [Court's] supervision is limited to ascertaining whether the respondent state has exercised its discretion reasonably, carefully and in good faith: what the Court has to do is to look at the interference complained of in the light of the case as a whole and determine whether it was "proportionate to the legitimate aim proposed" and whether the reasons adduced by the national authorities to justify it are "relevant and sufficient".'[2]

Indeed the *Wednesbury* test applied by UK courts led the European Court of Human Rights to decide (in particular circumstances) that judicial review was not an 'effective remedy' within the meaning of Article 13, the Court observing that the threshold for review:

> 'was placed so high that it effectively excluded any consideration by the domestic courts of the question whether the interference with the applicants' rights answered a pressing social need or was proportionate to the national security and public order aims pursued, principles which lie at the heart of the Court's analysis of complaints under art 8 of the Convention.'[3]

The difference between the approach to judicial review which must be adopted by UK courts when dealing with cases under the HRA 1998 and the approach adopted in other contexts is discussed further below[4].

---

1   From *Associated Provincial Picture Houses Ltd v Wednesbury Corporation* [1948] 1 KB 223.

2   *Vogt v Germany* (1995) A 323, para 52.

3   *Smith and Grady v United Kingdom* 1999-VI, para 138 (commenting on *R v Ministry of Defence, ex p Smith* [1996] QB 517).

4   See paras **3.143–3.147** below.

3.77 In the context of the ECHR, Articles 8–11, every interference with a protected right must be proportionate to the legitimate aim pursued. In order to determine this question, the Strasbourg Court decides, in the light of the arguments and evidence available to it, 'whether the reasons given by the national authorities to justify the actual measures of "interference" they take are relevant and sufficient'[1]. In a case concerned with Article 10, the Court summarised its approach as follows:

> 'The Court will look at the interference complained of in the light of the case as a whole and determine whether the reasons adduced by the national authorities to justify it are relevant and sufficient and whether the means employed were proportionate to the legitimate aim pursued. In doing so the Court has to satisfy itself that the national authorities did apply standards which were in conformity with the principles embodied in art 10 and, moreover, that they based themselves on an acceptable assessment of the relevant facts.'[2]

1 *Handyside v United Kingdom* (1976) A 24, para 50.
2 *Jersild v Denmark* (1995) A 298, at para 31. See also eg *Vogt v Germany* (1995) A 323, para 52.

3.78 'Sufficiency' requires that there be not only a rational connection between the means employed and the aim sought to be achieved, but also that a fair balance be struck between the demands of the general interest of the community and the requirements of the protection of the individual's fundamental rights. For example, a measure which involves a grave interference with an important right, such as a parent's right to contact with a child, will not be regarded as proportionate if some less drastic measure would have achieved the desired objective[1]. Similarly, the reading of prisoners' correspondence, when they were not present, was not proportionate when the desired objective (to ensure that no prohibited material was included with letters) could have been achieved by merely opening the correspondence in the prisoner's presence[2]. In addition, for an interference to meet such requirements procedural safeguards may be necessary to ensure due protection of the individual's interests[3].

1 Eg *Olsson v Sweden (no 1)* (1988) A 130, para 72; cf *Olsson (no 2) v Sweden* (1992) A 250, paras 87–91.
2 *Campbell v United Kingdom* (1992) A 233-A.
3 *McMichael v United Kingdom* (1995) A 308, para 87; *Buckley v United Kingdom* 1996-IV, para 76.

3.79 The search for a fair balance between the demands of the general interest of the community and the requirements of the protection of the individual's fundamental rights is, of course, not confined to the ECHR, Articles 8–11. As the Court has said, 'The search for this balance is inherent in the whole of the Convention'[1]. In that sense, proportionality can be regarded as a concept which permeates the entirety of the Convention. It is relevant, for example, to the question whether a difference in treatment can be justified under Article 14[2], or whether an interference with property rights violated the right guaranteed by Article 1 of

Protocol no 1[3]. For example, an interference with property rights will not be regarded as compatible with the latter right if it imposes an individual and excessive burden without the possibility of compensation[4]. Proportionality is also the basis upon which the Court determines whether the Convention should be construed as imposing a positive obligation upon a contracting state in a particular situation[5]. It is also the principal basis upon which the Court sets limits to rights which are implicit in the Convention, such as the right under Article 6 to access to a court[6].

1   *Sporrong and Lönnroth v Sweden* (1982) A 52, para 69.

2   *Belgian Linguistic case* (1968) A 6.

3   *Sporring and Lönnroth v Sweden* (1982) A 52, para 69. See further paras **8.29–8.32** below.

4   *Sporring and Lönnroth v Sweden* (1982) A 52, para 73. This approach has antecedents in French administrative law.

5   Eg *Rees v United Kingdom* (1986) A 106, para 37; *R (Pretty) v Director of Public Prosecutions* [2002] 1 AC 800 at para 90 per Lord Hope of Craighead.

6   Eg *Ashingdane v United Kingdom* (1985) A 93, para 57. See further paras **5.55–5.58** below.

3.80 The onus of establishing that an interference is justified, and therefore the onus of establishing that an interference is proportionate, rests on the state[1]. The standard of justification required depends, in practice, on the particular context. In principle, the stronger the 'pressing social need', the less difficult it will be to justify the interference. For example, national security is in principle a powerful consideration[2]. Certain legitimate aims, such as national security, also require the state to be allowed (at the international level) a wide margin of appreciation, making it more difficult for the Strasbourg court to determine that the interference was unjustified. The concept of the 'margin of appreciation' is discussed below[3]. On the other hand, interferences with certain types of right are more difficult to justify than others. For example, where the case concerns 'a most intimate aspect of private life', such as sexual behaviour, 'there must exist particularly serious reasons before interferences on the part of the public authorities can be legitimate for the purposes of art 8(2)'[4]. Similarly, interferences with correspondence with a legal adviser, or with the confidentiality of such correspondence, require a compelling justification[5]. Interferences with freedom of expression, particularly in respect of the discussion of matters of public interest, similarly require a convincing justification[6]. In addition to the nature of the right interfered with, the degree of interference is of course another material factor[7].

1   Eg *Smith and Grady v United Kingdom* 1999-VI, para 99.

2   See eg *Leander v Sweden* (1987) A 116, para 59; but contrast *Smith and Grady v United Kingdom* 1999-VI, para 89, where the counteracting factor was the serious nature of the interference with an intimate aspect of private life.

3   At paras **3.133–3.140** below.

4   *Dudgeon v United Kingdom* (1981) A 45, at para 52.

5   Eg *Campbell v United Kingdom* (1992) A 233-A; *Niemietz v Germany* (1992) A 251-B.

6   Eg *Barthold v Germany* (1985) A 90, para 55.

7   Eg *Smith and Grady v United Kingdom* 1999-VI, para 91.

3.81 The foregoing discussion has been concerned with rights which are subject to widely expressed qualifications, and especially with those conferred by the ECHR, Articles 8–11, where interferences must be 'necessary in a democratic society'. Other rights are subject to qualifications which are more stringently expressed, or to no express qualification at all. For example, Article 2 of the Convention guarantees the right to life, subject to an exception where the deprivation of life results from the use of force which is 'no more than absolutely necessary' for certain specified purposes. In that context, it has been said that the words 'absolutely necessary' indicate that 'a stricter and more compelling test of necessity must be employed from that normally applicable when determining whether State action is "necessary in a democratic society" under paragraph 2 of Articles 8–11 of the Convention'[1]. Similarly, although Article 3 (which prohibits torture) contains no reference to necessity, there are circumstances in which treatment (eg of prisoners, or of the mentally ill) which would otherwise be inhuman or degrading can be justified by necessity; and so the Court has said that 'in respect of a person deprived of his liberty, any recourse to physical force which has not been made *strictly necessary* by his own conduct diminishes human dignity and is in principle an infringement of the right set forth in Article 3 of the Convention'[2]. Article 5, on the other hand, permits the lawful arrest or detention of a person 'when it is *reasonably considered necessary* to prevent his committing an offence or fleeing after having done so'. Article 6, which guarantees the right to a fair trial, in principle requires a public hearing, but permits the exclusion of the press and the public 'in the interests of morals, public order or national security in a democratic society, where the interests of juveniles or the protection of the private life of the parties so require, or to the extent *strictly necessary* in the opinion of the court in special circumstances where publicity would prejudice the interests of justice'. This qualification has been applied in a realistic manner, the Court emphasising the strictness of the requirements only in circumstances where a strict approach was appropriate to the nature of the proceedings in issue[3]. Similarly, although Article 15 permits derogations in times of emergency 'to the extent strictly required by the exigencies of the situation', the Court has construed that phrase as meaning 'reasonably considered to be strictly required'[4]. In practice, accordingly, the Court has had regard to the nature of the context, as well as to the language of the text, in deciding how strict a test of necessity is appropriate. To the extent that a strict test of necessity is imposed, the test of proportionality is correspondingly stringent. In relation to Article 2(2), for example, any force used 'must be *strictly* proportionate to the achievement of the aims' specified[5].

1   *McCann and Others v United Kingdom* (1996) A 324, para 149.

2   *Ribitsch v Austria* (1995) A 336, para 38.

3   Eg *Diennet v France* (1995) A 325-A. Contrast *Campbell and Fell v United Kingdom* (1984) A 80, para 87; and, in relation to juveniles, *V v United Kingdom* [GC] 1999-IX, paras 76–77, 90.

4   *Ireland v United Kingdom* (1978) A 25, paras 213–220.

5   *McCann and Others v United Kingdom* (1996) A 324, para 149.

3.82 Finally, proportionality is employed as a general supervisory principle which can be used as a yardstick in determining whether a measure is compatible with the ECHR. For example, the Court has suggested on a number of occasions that a criminal sentence which was disproportionate might constitute inhuman or degrading treatment, contrary to Article 3[1]. Under Article 4 (which prohibits slavery and forced labour), the Court has held that a requirement that intrants to the legal profession provide free legal services could amount to forced labour only if the burden imposed was disproportionate[2]. Under Article 6, for example, the Court has held that a system of 'fiscal fines' operating in Belgium was incompatible with the right to a fair trial because of a 'flagrant disproportion' between the modest sum demanded and the alternative consequences of lengthy criminal proceedings during which the applicant's business would have been closed down[3].

1   *Soering v United Kingdom* (1989) A 161, para 104 (the death sentence); cf *V v United Kingdom* [GC] 1999-IX, para 97.

2   *Van der Mussele v Belgium* (1984) A 70, para 37.

3   *Deweer v Belgium* (1980) A 35, para 51.

Non-discrimination

Introduction

3.83 The nature of discrimination, and the reasons why discriminatory laws and administrative practices are objectionable, were explained in a nutshell by Lord Walker of Gestingthorpe in *R (Carson) v Secretary of State for Work and Pensions*:

> 'In the field of human rights, discrimination is regarded as particularly objectionable because it disregards fundamental notions of human dignity and equality before the law. Discrimination on the ground of sex or race demeans the victim by using a sexual or racial stereotype as a sufficient ground for unfavourable treatment, rather than treating her as an individual to be judged on her own merits.'[1]

Although racial and sexual discrimination have for many years been prohibited by statute in the United Kingdom, the common law has dealt with discrimination by applying more general concepts of administrative law, such as reasonableness and the duty not to be influenced by irrelevant considerations: indeed, the classic example given of unreasonable behaviour, in the *Wednesbury* case, was of discrimination[2]. Some other European legal systems recognise a more specific principle of non-discrimination: in Germany, for example, equality is guaranteed by the Basic Law (Grundgesetz) of 1949, Article 3; in France, equality is one of the *principes généraux du droit*. Non-discrimination is also an unwritten principle of EU law, belonging to 'that philosophical, political and legal substratum common to the Member States from which through the case law an unwritten Community law emerges'[3]. In EU law, as in national systems, the principle requires a consideration of differential treatment in the light of the reasons for the measure in question: 'it is thus only within the sphere of the ends pursued that the principle must be respected; it will be infringed only if one treats differently two situations which are similar with regard to their ends'[4]. The approach adopted under the ECHR is similar, and turns upon an assessment of the comparability of situations in the light of the objectives of the measure in question, and an assessment of the justification for their differential treatment in the light of those objectives, applying the principle of proportionality[5] (and, at the Strasbourg level, the doctrine of the margin of appreciation)[6]. In accordance with the principle of effectiveness[7], the focus is upon substantive equality rather than formal equality.

1   *R (Carson) v Secretary of State for Work and Pensions* [2006] 1 AC 173 at para 49. See also *Ghaidan v Godin-Mendoza* [2004] 2 AC 557 at para 9 per Lord Nicholls of Birkenhead and at paras 130–132 per Baroness Hale of Richmond; *A v Secretary of State for the Home Department* [2005] 2 AC 68 at para 46 per Lord Bingham of Cornhill.

2   *Associated Provincial Picture Houses Ltd v Wednesbury Corporation* [1948] 1 KB 223 at 229 per Lord Greene MR. See also *Matadeen v Pointu* [1999] 1 AC 98 at 109 per Lord Hoffmann: '… treating like cases alike and unlike cases differently is a general axiom of rational behaviour'.

3   Case 11/70 *Internationale Handelsgesellschaft* [1970] ECR 1125 at 1146 per Dutheillet de Lamothe AG.

4   Case 13/63 *Italy v Commission* [1963] ECR 165, 190 per Lagrange AG.

5   See paras **3.73–3.82** above.

6   See paras **3.134–3.140** below.

7   See para **3.49** above.

3.84 The principle of non-discrimination is expressed in three provisions[1]. First, Article 14 of the ECHR provides:

'The enjoyment of the rights and freedoms set forth in this Convention shall be secured without discrimination on any ground such as sex, race, colour, language, religion, political or other opinion, national or social origin, association with a national minority, property, birth or other status.'

1   The Commission has also considered discriminatory treatment, taken with the intention of humiliating or debasing an individual, as treatment sufficiently degrading to violate Art 3: 4403/70, *East African Asians v United Kingdom* (1970) CD 36, 92; (1973) DR 78, 5: see further para **4.82** below. Other Council of Europe initiatives also seek to tackle prejudice, eg the European Commission against Racism and Intolerance: see paras **2.88–2.91** above.

3.85 Secondly, Article 5 of Protocol no 7 provides that 'spouses shall enjoy equality of rights and responsibilities of a private law character between them, and in their relations with their children, as to marriage, during marriage and in the event of its dissolution'.[1] The United Kingdom has not ratified this protocol.

1   This provision specifically does not 'prevent States from taking such measures as are necessary in the interests of the children' of a marriage. No violation of this provision has yet been established by the Court.

3.86 Thirdly, Article 1 of Protocol no 12 makes provision for a general prohibition of discriminatory treatment:

'(1) The enjoyment of any right set forth by law shall be secured without discrimination on any ground such as sex, race, colour, language, religion, political or other opinion, national or social origin, association with a national minority, property, birth or other status.

(2) No one shall be discriminated against by any public authority on any ground such as those mentioned in paragraph 1.'[1]

Protocol no 12 entered into force in April 2005, but has not been ratified by the United Kingdom. The intention was that the provision will establish a free-standing (as opposed to accessory) protection against discriminatory treatment, but the text is likely to be interpreted in a manner consistent with Article 14, that is, as imposing an obligation upon public bodies not to discriminate between individuals unless an objective and reasonable justification can be shown to exist. It is clear that Protocol no 12 has a potentially wide scope. In *Sejdić and Finci v Bosnia and Herzegovina,* the first judgment concerning the guarantee, constitutional arrangements which restricted eligibility to stand for parliament or for the presidency to those declaring affiliation to one of the three dominant ethnic groups in the state were held to have violated Article 14 taken with Article 3 of Protocol no 1 (in respect of parliamentary elections) and Protocol no 12 (in respect of elections to the presidency). These arrangements had derived from the Dayton Peace Agreement which had brought about an end to hostilities in the country[2]. In its second judgment on the Protocol, *Savez Crkava 'Riječ Žlvota' and Others v Croatia*, the inability of Reformed churches to provide religious education in public schools or to conclude state-recognised marriage ceremonies was found to have violated Article 14 taken in conjunction with Article 9, thus allowing the Court to consider it unnecessary to rule on the Protocol no 12 issue. The judgment did, however, allow discussion of the applicability of the provision. The text indicated that the prohibition of discrimination was not restricted to 'any right set forth by law' but also extended to the prohibition of discrimination by a public authority, and explicit reference to the Explanatory Report suggested that four categories of cases could fall within the scope of the provision:

'i. in the enjoyment of any right specifically granted to an individual under national law;

ii. in the enjoyment of a right which may be inferred from a clear obligation of a public authority under national law, that is, where a public authority is under an obligation under national law to behave in a particular manner;

iii. by a public authority in the exercise of discretionary power (for example, granting certain subsidies);

iv. by any other act or omission by a public authority (for example, the behaviour of law enforcement officers when controlling a riot).'[3]

---

1   See further Khaliq 'Protocol 12 to the ECHR: a Step Forward or a Step too Far?' [2001] PL 458.

2   *Sejdić and Finci v Bosnia and Herzegovina* [GC] 2009-..., paras 42–56.

3   *Savez Crkava 'Riječ Žlvota and Others v Croatia* (9 December 2010), paras 103–115 (decisions whether to enter agreements with religious authorities were a matter for state discretion and thus did not concern 'rights specifically granted to them under national law', but the issue did fall within the third category specified in the Explanatory Report; and noting the Explanatory Report's comment that it was not necessary to specify which elements fell to be considered under each of the paragraphs as the paragraphs were complementary, the distinctions not clear-cut, and 'domestic legal systems may have different approaches as to which case comes under which category'.

Article 14: the prohibition of discrimination in the 'enjoyment' of ECHR rights

3.87 In the context of Article 14, 'discrimination means treating differently, without an objective and reasonable justification, persons in relevantly similar situations … [The Court] has also accepted that a general policy or measure that has disproportionately prejudicial effects on a particular group may be considered discriminatory notwithstanding that it is not specifically aimed at that group, and that discrimination potentially contrary to the Convention may result from a *de facto* situation'[1]. Normally, the European Court of Human Rights will consider it unnecessary to examine a complaint of discrimination under Article 14 when it has already established that there has been a violation of a substantive guarantee raising substantially the same point[2], unless 'a clear inequality of treatment in the enjoyment of the right in question is a fundamental aspect of the case'[3]. Where the facts suggest that an additional and separate issue of discriminatory treatment arises, for example, where the difference in treatment has been as a result of legal uncertainty caused by conflicting jurisprudence such as to give rise to a denial of the right to a fair hearing[4], then further consideration of any Article 14 issue will be appropriate. Once an applicant has established that a difference in treatment has occurred, it is then for the respondent government to show why this was justified[5]. An individual cannot waive his right not to be subjected to discriminatory treatment[6].

1   *DH and Others v Czech Republic* [GC] 2007-..., at para 175.

2   Eg in *Smith and Grady v United Kingdom* 1999-VI; and *Lustig-Prean and Beckett v United Kingdom* (27 September 1999), concerned with the policy of excluding homosexuals from the armed forces, the Court declined to consider the Art 14 issue, noting that this matter 'amounts in effect to the same complaint [as under Art 8], albeit seen from a different angle' (at para 108). Similarly a complaint of racial bias on the part of a jury was disposed of under Art 6 alone: *Gregory v United Kingdom* 1997-I, paras 43–50.

3   *X and Y v Netherlands* (1985) A 91, at para 32; and *Aziz v Cyprus* 2004-V, at para 35. See eg *Alekseyev v Russia* 2010-..., paras 68–88 and 106–110 (repeated refusals to permit 'gay pride' parades on public order grounds following statements by local officials indicating no such parade would ever be permitted: violation of Art 11 since the issue had been determined by the prevailing moral values of the majority and no measures had been taken to assess or to address public safety risks; and violation of Art 14 taken with Art 11 as the main reason for the bans on the gay marches was the authorities' disapproval of demonstrations which they considered promoted homosexuality).

4   See eg *Beian v Romania (no 1)* 2007-XIII, paras 32–40 and 59–65 (conflicting decisions of the supreme court on compensatory measures for conscripts assigned to forced labour during military service, with divergent opinions even being issued on the same day: violation of Art 6, and of Art 14 taken with Prot 1, Art 1 as there had been a legitimate expectation that his claim would be recognised, but contradictory case law had resulted in a difference of treatment between the applicant and other people in a similar situation).

5   *DH and Others v Czech Republic* [GC] 2007-…, para 177. See further para **3.98** below.

6   *DH and Others v Czech Republic* [GC] 2007-…, at para 204: 'no waiver of the right not to be subjected to racial discrimination can be accepted').

3.88 Article 14 may not be confined to discrimination by the state, for in certain cases, the national authorities will also have positive obligations under Article 14 to protect against discrimination by private parties. In one case, for example, the state was found to have violated Article 14 when a court gave effect to a will which excluded children who were illegitimate or adopted[1]. The failure of relevant national authorities to provide an appropriate response to the threat of domestic violence against women may give rise to issues under Article 14 in conjunction with Articles 2 or 3[2].

1   *Pla and Puncernau v Andorra* 2004-VIII.

2   *Opuz v Turkey* 2009-…, paras 131–153, 158–176 and 183–202, discussed at para **4.85** below. For further discussion of the notion of positive obligations arising under Art 14, see van Dijk, van Hoof, van Rijn and Zwaak (eds) *Theory and Practice of the European Convention on Human Rights* (4th edn, 2006) at p 1051 (suggestion that Art 14 in this respect essentially requires public authorities to act in a non-discriminatory way if they decide to take any specific action in an area connected with Convention rights, although the case law indicates that action taken to remedy existing inequality will escape censure).

Application by the domestic courts

3.89 The effect of Article 14 is limited in two respects. First, it has a restricted list of the matters in respect of which discrimination is forbidden. They are 'the enjoyment of the rights and freedoms set forth in [the] Convention'. Secondly, it has a restricted list of the grounds upon which discrimination is forbidden. They are 'any ground such as [the enumerated grounds] or other status'. It follows from the first of these restrictions that Article 14 'only complements'[1] other provisions:

'Unlike article 1 of the 12th Protocol, article 14 of the Convention does not confer a free-standing right of non-discrimination. It does not confer a right of non-discrimination in respect of all laws. Article 14 is more limited in its scope. It precludes discrimination in the "enjoyment of the rights and freedoms set forth in this Convention". The court at Strasbourg has said this means that, for article 14 to be applicable, the facts at issue must "fall within the ambit" of one or more of the Convention rights. Article 14 comes into play whenever the subject matter of the disadvantage "constitutes one of the modalities" of the exercise of a right guaranteed or whenever the measures complained of are "linked" to the exercise of a right guaranteed.'[2]

255

The meaning of these expressions was considered by the House of Lords in *M v Secretary of State for Work and Pensions*. Lord Nicholls of Birkenhead observed:

'The approach of the ECtHR is to apply these expressions flexibly. Although each of them is capable of extremely wide application, the Strasbourg jurisprudence lends no support to the suggestion that any link, however tenuous, will suffice. Rather, the approach to be distilled from the Strasbourg jurisprudence is that the more seriously and directly the discriminatory provision or conduct impinges upon the values underlying the particular substantive article, the more readily will it be regarded as within the ambit of that article; and vice versa.'[3]

1   *EB v France* [GC] 2008-…, at para 47.

2   *Ghaidan v Godin-Mendoza* [2004] 2 AC 557 at para 10 per Lord Nicholls of Birkenhead, referring to *Petrovic v Austria* 1998-II.

3   *M v Secretary of State for Work and Pensions* [2006] 2 AC 91 at para 14, referring to *Sidabras and Džiautas v Lithuania* 2004-VIII. The issue was considered in detail, in relation to Art 8 and Art 1, Prot 1 by Lord Walker of Gestingthorpe at paras 56–90. It was observed that some articles have a better defined ambit or scope than others.

3.90 Article 14 can only be considered in conjunction with one or more of the substantive guarantees contained in Articles 2 to 12 of the Convention or in one of the protocols. For example, the lack of access for disabled persons to a beach did not fall within the ambit of any substantive Convention right, and therefore did not violate Article 14[1]. It has been held in a domestic case that Article 14 does not therefore concern the right to compensation for infringement of a Convention right[2]. Similarly, in the domestic case of *R (Pretty) v Director of Public Prosecutions*, it was held that the criminal prohibition on assisting suicide did not discriminate, contrary to Article 14, against a disabled woman who could not commit suicide without assistance: none of the substantive Convention articles was engaged, and the criminal law in any event applied equally to all[3]. Article 14 is nevertheless of fundamental importance. In particular, 'a measure which in itself is in conformity with the requirements of the article enshrining the right or freedom in question may however infringe this Article when read in conjunction with art 14 for the reason that it is of a discriminatory nature'[4]. This is so because 'the notion of discrimination includes in general cases where a person or group is treated, without proper justification, less favourably than another, even though the more favourable treatment is not called for by the Convention.'[5] However, it is important to recognise the potential impact of the provision in widening the scope of Convention protection. In particular, if a state goes beyond its core obligations and creates additional rights falling within the wider ambit of any Convention provision, Article 14 will also apply to those additional rights[6].

1   *Botta v Italy* 1998-I, paras 37–39.

2   *R (Hooper) v Secretary of State for Work and Pensions* [2005] 1 WLR 1681.

3   *R (Pretty) v Director of Public Prosecutions* [2002] 1 AC 800. For other domestic illustrations, see eg *DJS v Criminal Injuries Compensation Appeal Tribunal* 2007 SC 748 (criminal injuries compensation did not fall within scope of Arts 3, 8 or Prot 1, Art 1); *Dove v Scottish Ministers*

2002 SC 257 (whether schools were self-governing or under the management of a local authority did not fall within the scope of Art 2 of Prot 1, and thus Art 14 was not engaged by a difference in the management arrangements of different schools); *R (Douglas) v North Tyneside Metropolitan Borough Council* [2004] 1 WLR 2363 (student loans did not fall within the scope of Prot 1, Art 2, and thus Art 14 was not engaged by an age bar in the regulations governing eligibility for such loans); *Watson v King* 2009 SCCR 323 (under-age sex with girl an offence of strict liability unless man aged under 24: no violation of Art 14 read with Art 6, since Art 6 was not concerned with substance of criminal law); *R (Barclay) v Lord Chancellor* [2010] 1 AC 464 (prohibition on aliens from standing for election did not infringe Art 14 read with Prot 1, Art 3, since the rights under Art 3 belonged to citizens only).

4   *Belgian Linguistic case* (1968) A6, Law, para 9.

5   *Zarb Adami v Malta* 2006-VIII, para 73. For example, discrimination in sentencing could contravene ECHR, Art 14 read in conjunction with Art 5, although each sentence considered in isolation might be unobjectionable: 22761/93, *RM v United Kingdom* (1994) DR 77, 98 (the Commission observed (at 105) that the position is 'as though art 14 formed an integral part of each of the provisions laying down the specific rights and freedoms'). Even if a state exceeds its obligations under the Convention, it will contravene Art 14 in conjunction with the substantive provision in issue if it does so in a discriminatory fashion: *Belgian Linguistic case* (1968) A6, Law, para 9. The Court has left open the question whether Art 8 guarantees a right to adopt a child. If, however, domestic law confers a right to apply for an adoption order, then Art 14, read with Art 8, prohibits discrimination in relation to that right, for example by restricting it to heterosexuals: *EB v France* [GC] 2008-..., paras 70–98, discussed at para **6.144** below. See also *Abdulaziz, Cabales and Balkandali v United Kingdom* (1989) A 94, paras 70–89. A domestic illustration is *R (Clift) v Secretary of State for the Home Department* [2007] 1 AC 484 (although there was no requirement under the ECHR to establish an early release scheme, where provision was so made, the right to seek early release fell within the scope of Art 5, and any differential treatment could give rise to issues under Art 14): note, however, the Strasbourg Court's determination in *Clift v United Kingdom* (13 July 2010), discussed at para **3.93** below. The complaint of discrimination must however relate to something that the state itself has provided: *R (Countryside Alliance) v Attorney General* [2008] AC 719; t:*Whaley v Lord Advocate* 2008 SC (HL) 107.

6   *Savez Crkava 'Riječ Žlvota' and Others v Croatia* (9 December 2010), para 58, discussed at para **7.12** below.

3.91 The approach which domestic courts should follow in respect of Article 14 was explained, in line with the case law of the European Court of Human Rights[1] in *R (Carson) v Secretary of State for Work and Pensions*. Lord Nicholls of Birkenhead said:

'Article 14 does not apply unless the alleged discrimination is in connection with a Convention right and on a ground stated in article 14. If this prerequisite is satisfied, the essential question for the courts is whether the alleged discrimination, that is, the difference in treatment of which complaint is made, can withstand scrutiny. Sometimes the answer to this question will be plain. There may be such an obvious, relevant difference between the claimant and those with whom he seeks to compare himself that their situations cannot be regarded as analogous. Sometimes, where the position is not so clear, a different approach is called for. Then the court's scrutiny may best be directed at considering whether the differentiation has a legitimate aim and whether the means chosen to achieve the aim is appropriate and not disproportionate in its adverse impact.'[2]

It was emphasised that a sequential approach is not always appropriate. Lord Rodger of Earlsferry, for example, said:

> '... a court faced with a case of alleged discrimination should not go mechanically through a series of questions. Rather, it should look at the facts of the case as a whole and identify the particular issue or issues which will have to be resolved in order to decide whether there has been discrimination contrary to article 14.'[3]

In particular, the real issue in many cases may be why the complainant has been treated as he has been treated. If it was on a proscribed ground, the important question may then be whether the difference in treatment is justifiable.

1   In such cases as *Rasmussen v Denmark* (1984) A 87.

2   *R (Carson) v Secretary of State for Work and Pensions* [2006] 1 AC 173 at para 3. This judgment effectively superseded the guidance given in the earlier case of *R (S) v Chief Constable of the South Yorkshire Police* [2004] 1 WLR 2196.

3   *R (Carson) v Secretary of State for Work and Pensions* [2006] 1 AC 173 at para 43. See also the detailed discussion at paras 63–70 per Lord Walker of Gestingthorpe.

The existence of a 'relevantly similar' position

3.92 Subject to the foregoing, if the facts fall within the ambit of a Convention right, and there is established to be a difference in the treatment of two situations, the application of Article 14 may turn in the first place upon an assessment of the comparability of the situations in question. The persons in question must be in a 'relevantly similar'[1] position. This issue has been considered in numerous cases[2]. If no analogous situation arises, there can be no application of Article 14. In *Burden v United Kingdom*, for example, the Grand Chamber considered that the ineligibility of cohabiting sisters to exemption from inheritance tax enjoyed by surviving spouses or civil partners involved a qualitatively different nature of a relationship, for the very essence of the connection between siblings was consanguinity rather than (as with married couples and homosexual civil partners) the existence of a public undertaking, carrying with it a body of rights and obligations of a contractual nature[3]. In *Carson and Others v United Kingdom*, a challenge to the failure to index-link pensions of former British residents was considered under Article 14 taken in conjunction with Article 1 of Protocol no 1. The argument that the applicants had been the victims of discrimination based on residence as pensioners living in the United Kingdom or in other countries where up-rating was available were treated more favourably did not succeed. The Grand Chamber did not consider that a relevantly similar position existed for the purposes of Article 14: state pension arrangements differed from private pension schemes as there was no exclusive link between National Insurance contributions and retirement pensions on account of the 'complex and interlocking system of the benefits and taxation systems'; and further, the system of pensions had an essentially national character designed to ensure certain minimum standards for those resident in particular countries[4].

Nevertheless, in most cases the Strasbourg Court glosses over the question of comparability and focuses on the question of justification. In consequence, it was suggested by Baroness Hale of Richmond in *AL (Serbia) v Secretary of State for the Home Department* that 'unless there are very obvious relevant differences between the two situations, it is better to concentrate on the reasons for the difference in treatment and whether they amount to an objective and reasonable justification'[5].

1 *National and Provincial Building Society v United Kingdom* 1997-VII, para 88.

2 A great variety of comparisons have been considered, eg Scottish prisoners compared with prisoners elsewhere in the United Kingdom: 11077/84, *Nelson v United Kingdom* (1986) DR 49, 170; married couples compared with unmarried couples: 11089/84, *Lindsay v United Kingdom* (1986) DR 49, 181: domiciled persons, seeking to rely upon a foreign divorce, compared with non-domiciled persons: *Johnston v Ireland* (1986) A 112, para 60; trainee barristers compared with intrants to other professions: *Van der Mussele v Belgium* (1983) A 70; victims of negligent delicts compared with victims of intentional delicts: *Stubbings v United Kingdom* 1996-IV; citizens compared with non-citizens: *Gaygusuz v Austria* 1996-IV, paras 46–50, *Koua Poirrez v France* 2003-X; former employees of the KGB as opposed to other ex-employees: *Sidabras and Džiautas v Lithuania* 2004-VIII, paras 38–41; and *Andrejeva v Latvia* [GC] 2009-..., para 78; but cf *Moustaquiem v Belgium* (1991) A 193, para 49; homosexuals compared with heterosexuals: 25186/94, *Sutherland v United Kingdom* (1 July 1997); illegitimate compared with legitimate children: *Marckx v Belgium* (1997) A 31; transsexuals compared with persons of a given biological sex: *Sheffield and Horsham v United Kingdom* 1998-V, paras 75–77, but cf *Christine Goodwin v United Kingdom* [GC] 2002-VI: persons convicted in absentia and accused present at a trial: *Eliazer v Netherlands* 2001-X, paras 37–42; children conceived in adulterous relationships and other children: *Sahin v Germany* [GC] 2003-VIII, paras 85–95, *Merger and Cros v France* (22 December 2004); and persons in receipt of Russian military pensions and other groups eligible for an Estonian pension: *Tarkoev and Others v Estonia* (4 November 2010), paras 58–67. For a domestic example, see *R (Al Rawi) v Secretary of State for Foreign and Commonwealth Affairs* [2008] QB 289 (UK nationals and non-nationals not in analogous situations in relation to the UK's right to make a state-to-state claim).

3 *Burden v United Kingdom* [GC] 2008-..., paras 58–66.

4 *Carson and Others v United Kingdom* [GC] 2010-..., paras 83–90 (the conclusion was not affected by the fact that the UK had entered into bilateral agreements to secure reciprocity of state welfare benefits as these agreements would be undermined if considered as obliging a state to confer similar advantages on persons living in all other countries).

5 *AL (Serbia) v Secretary of State for the Home Department* [2008] 1 WLR 1434 at para 25.

Prohibited grounds

3.93 If there is differential treatment of analogous situations, the next question is whether the basis of the differential treatment falls within the scope of Article 14. The list of prohibited grounds for discrimination is qualified by the phrase 'any ground such as', and is not exhaustive but merely illustrative[1]. An applicant must show that a personal characteristic or status is involved in the difference of treatment. Certain prohibited grounds are straightforward: sexual orientation, marital status[2], and illegitimacy have readily been held to so qualify. Different application of the same pensions legislation to persons depending on their residence or presence abroad will involve personal characteristics or status[3], but the application of different legislation depending upon geographical location may not do so[4]. Thus the fact that a suspect obtained access to his solicitor at a later stage in Northern Ireland than he would have in England and Wales did not entail a violation of Article 14 (read with Article 6), since the difference in treatment had nothing to do with personal characteristics[5]. The fact that convicted terrorists are treated less favourably in relation to parole than other criminals does not entail a violation of Article 14 in *Gerger v Turkey*, since 'the distinction is made not between different groups of people, but between different types of offence'[6].

'Status', though, is not necessarily dependent upon a characteristic that is innate or inherently linked to the identity or the personality of the individual (such as sex, race or religion). In *Clift v United Kingdom*, the question involved differences in early release arrangements between prisoners serving determinate sentences of more than 15 years' imprisonment and those sentenced to imprisonment for less than 15 years or to indeterminate sentences. In this case, the Court was satisfied that the present instance did involve treatment falling within the scope of Article 14 as the differences were not based on the gravity of the offence but rather on the sentences imposed. While previous case law indicated Article 14 was limited to different treatment based on characteristics which were inherent or innate, the Court clarified that the test was whether the difference of treatment is based upon 'a personal or identifiable characteristic', a matter which has to be assessed 'taking into consideration all of the circumstances of the case and bearing in mind that the aim of the Convention is to guarantee not rights that are theoretical or illusory but rights that are practical and effective ...'.[7]

---

1   *Engel v Netherlands* (1976) A 22, para 72. See eg *McMichael v United Kingdom* (1995) A 307-B (married and unmarried fathers); and *Danilenkov and Others v Russia* 2009-..., paras 120–125 (discrimination on the basis of trade union membership).

2   Eg *Wagner and JMWL v Luxembourg* 2007-VII, paras 118–136 and 150–160 (domestic prohibition of single-person adoption resulting in refusal to enforce a foreign adoption order: violation of Art 8, and of Art 14 taken with Art 8 as there had been no justification for the discrimination particularly since other such adoption orders had been recognised).

3   *Carson and Others v United Kingdom* [GC] 2010-..., para 70. See also *Andrejeva v Latvia* [GC] 2009-..., paras 81–92 (refusal of pension in respect of employment in the former USSR on the ground that the applicant did not have Latvian citizenship: violation of Art 14 taken with Prot 1, Art1).

4   8364/78, *Lindsay and Others v United Kingdom* (1979) DR 15, 247 (electoral arrangements).

5   *Magee v United Kingdom* 2000-VI, paras 50–51.

6   *Gerger v Turkey* [GC] (8 July 1999), para 69. See also *Budak and Others v Turkey* (dec) (7 September 2004) (different criminal procedure for different types of offence); and *Beale v United Kingdom* (dec) (12 October 2004) (different investigatory procedures for police and trading standards officers). *Gerger* was distinguished in *Clift v United Kingdom* (13 July 2010) on account of differences accountable to different types of offence according to their gravity, while in *Clift* the allegation was based on the position of being a prisoner serving a particular sentence.

7   *Clift v United Kingdom* (13 July 2010), paras 55–62, discussed further at para **4.230** below. For the earlier approach, see eg *Jones v United Kingdom* (dec) (13 September 2005) (the proscribed grounds are not however unlimited: Article 14 'is not concerned with all differences

in treatment but only with differences having as their basis or reason a personal characteristic by which persons or groups of persons are distinguishable from each other', citing *Kjelsden, Busk Madsen and Pedersen v Denmark* (1976) A 23). In domestic proceedings in the House of Lords, the difference in treatment in the applicant's case had not been found to be the result of 'status' such as to fall within the prohibition on discrimination in Art 14 as it had been considered that this provision 'aims to strike down the offensive singling out of an individual or members of a particular group on their personal attributes': *R (Clift) v Secretary of State for the Home Department* [2007] 1 AC 484 at para 57 per Baroness Hale of Richmond.

3.94 The concept of a 'personal characteristic' has been considered in greater detail by the domestic courts[1]. They have considered it to include such matters as nationality or national origin[2], immigration status[3], physical or mental capacity[4], being married or unmarried[5], homelessness[6], residence[7], age[8], being the natural or adoptive parent of a child[9], or being a foster parent or a family member caring for a child[10]. It has been said that 'a generous meaning should be given to the words "or other status"'[11]. On the other hand, legislation which treated differently tenants who were in breach of their obligations, depending on the nature of the obligation breached, did not discriminate on the basis of 'status'[12], nor did legislation which was said to affect adversely members of the hunting community[13]. The House of Lords has considered that legislation which treated prisoners differently depending on the length of their sentence did not involve a 'personal characteristic'[14], but subsequently the Strasbourg Court in *Clift v United Kingdom* took a different approach to this issue[15].

1   See in particular *R (Clift) v Secretary of State for the Home Department* [2007] 1 AC 484 at paras 52–61 per Baroness Hale of Richmond; *AL (Serbia) v Secretary of State for the Home Department* [2008] 1 WLR 1434 at paras 20–35 per Baroness Hale of Richmond; *R (RJM) v Secretary of State for Work and Pensions* [2009] 1 AC 311 at para 5 per Lord Walker of Gestingthorpe and at paras 36–46 per Lord Neuberger of Abbotsbury.

2   *A v Secretary of State for the Home Department* [2005] 2 AC 68, following *Gaygusuz v Austria*, 1996-IV; *R (Clift) v Secretary of State for the Home Department* [2007] 1 AC 484.

3   *A v Secretary of State for the Home Department* [2005] 2 AC 68; and *R (Morris) v Westminster City Council* [2006] 1 WLR 505.

4   *R (Pretty) v Director of Public Prosecutions* [2002] 1 AC 800 at 847 per Lord Hope of Craighead.

5   *In re G (Adoption: Unmarried Couple)* [2009] AC 173.

6   *R (RJM) v Secretary of State for Work and Pensions* [2009] AC 311.

7   *R (Carson) v Secretary of State for Work and Pensions* [2006] 1 AC 173.

8   *R (Carson) v Secretary of State for Work and Pensions* [2006] 1 AC 173; and *M's Guardian v Advocate General for Scotland* 2010 SLT 621.

9   *Francis v Secretary of State for Work and Pensions* [2006] 1 WLR 3202.

10   *V v South Lanarkshire Council* 2004 SLT 372.

11   *R (Clift) v Secretary of State for the Home Department* [2007] 1 AC 484 at para 48 per Lord Hope of Craighead; *R (RJM) v Secretary of State for Work and Pensions* [2009] AC 311 at para 42 per Lord Neuberger of Abbotsbury.

12   *Taylor v Lancashire County Council* [2005] 1 WLR 2668.

13   *R (Countryside Alliance) v Attorney General* [2008] AC 719; *Whaley v Lord Advocate* 2008 SC (HL) 107. See also *Goatley v HM Advocate* 2008 JC 1 and *La Torre v HM Advocate* 2008 JC

23 (differences between Scottish and English criminal procedure not related to any personal characteristic of the accused).

14   *R (Clift) v Secretary of State for the Home Department* [2007] 1 AC 484. See also *R (S) v Chief Constable of Yorkshire Police* [2004] 1 WLR 2196 (the difference between people whose fingerprints or DNA samples are held by the police and other people does not give rise to a 'status' within the meaning of Art 14). Being a person who has started legal proceedings is not a relevant status: *R (Hooper) v Secretary of State for Work and Pensions* [2005] 1 WLR 1681. Failure to qualify for criminal injuries compensation because a change to the scheme was not retrospective did not entail discrimination on basis of 'other status': Criminal Injuries Compensation Appeal Tribunal 2007 SC 748.

15   *Clift v United Kingdom* (13 July 2010), paras 55–62, discussed at para **3.93** above.

Justification for differences in treatment

3.95 If there has been differential treatment of analogous situations, falling within the ambit of a Convention right, on a ground falling within the scope of Article 14, the remaining question which may arise is whether the difference in treatment has an 'objective and reasonable'[1] justification. A difference in treatment is not necessarily discriminatory: public authorities 'are frequently confronted with situations and problems which, on account of differences inherent therein, call for different legal solutions: moreover, certain legal inequalities tend only to correct factual inequalities'[2]. A difference in treatment will be discriminatory only if it does not pursue a legitimate aim, or if there is no 'reasonable relationship of proportionality between the means employed and the aim sought to be realised'[3]. As always, the assessment of proportionality requires the court to strike a fair balance between the protection of the interests of the community and respect for the rights and freedoms safeguarded by the Convention. It is also necessary to bear in mind the 'living instrument' principle: distinctions in treatment which were formerly acceptable may come to be considered no longer compatible with Article 14[4]. The European Court of Human Rights will also apply the 'margin of appreciation' doctrine where appropriate.

1   Eg *EB v France* [GC] 2008-…, at para 70.

2   *Belgian Linguistic case* (1968) A 6 at Law, para 10. See eg 11089/84, *Lindsay v United Kingdom* (1986) DR 49, 181.

3   *Belgian Linguistic case* (1968) A 6, at Law, para 10. See eg 11089/84, *Lindsay v United Kingdom* (1986) DR 49, 181; *Darby v Sweden* (1990) A 187, para 31; *Weber v Germany* (dec) (23 October 2006) (differential treatment of owners of property seized by the Nazi regime, as between property in the subsequent FRG and the GDR: inadmissible); and *Sidabras and Džiautas v Lithuania* 2004-VIII, paras 51–62 (restrictions upon employment rights of ex-KGB employees not justifiable: loyalty to the state was not an inherent condition for private employment).

4   Eg as to the status of illegitimate children: *Inze v Austria* (1987) A 126, para 41; or the age of consent for homosexual relations: 25186/94, *Sutherland v United Kingdom* (1 July 1997).

3.96 It has been said that 'very weighty reasons' are required to justify differential treatment based on such factors as race or ethnic origin[1], nationality[2], sex[3], sexual orientation[4] and illegitimacy or adopted status[5].

1   *DH and Others v Czech Republic* [GC] 2007-..., at para 196.

2   *Gaygusuz v Austria* 1996-IV, at para 42.

3   *Abdulaziz, Cabales and Balkandali v United Kingdom* (1989) A 94, at para 78.

4   *EB v France* [GC] 2008-..., at para 91.

5   *Inze v Austria* (1987) A 126, at para 41; *Pla and Puncernau v Andorra* 2004-VIII, at para 61.

APPLICATION BY THE DOMESTIC COURTS

3.97 The same test – whether the difference in treatment is based on the pursuit of a legitimate objective and, if so, whether there is a reasonable relationship of proportionality between the means employed by the state and the objective that it is attempting to achieve – has also been followed in the domestic case law[1]. As in the Strasbourg case law, 'where the alleged violation comprises differential treatment based on grounds such as race or sex or sexual orientation the court will scrutinise with intensity any reasons said to constitute justification. The reasons must be cogent if such differential treatment is to be justified'[2].

1   See for example *R (Carson) v Secretary of State for Works and Pensions* [2006] 1 AC 173 (refusal to award cost of living increases to individuals entitled to pensions payments but living abroad: no violation of Art 14 taken with Art 1 of Prot 1, since emigration was voluntary, and the difference in treatment could be justified in any event on the ground that the primary purpose of the pension scheme is to provide a basic standard of living to persons living in the UK); *R (Wilson) v Wychavon District Council* [2007] QB 801 (planning controls in respect of residential caravans had indirect discriminatory impact on gipsies but were proportionate means of protecting environment); *AL (Serbia) v Secretary of State for the Home Department* [2008] 1 WLR 1434 (indefinite leave to remain granted to asylum seekers with children in order to reduce administrative and financial burden represented by such cases: differential treatment of single young adult asylum seekers justified); *R (D) v Secretary of State for Work and Pensions* [2010] 1 WLR 1782 (differential treatment, under social security legislation, of convicted prisoners transferred to hospitals and other patients held to be justified).

2   *Ghaidan v Godin-Mendoza* [2004] 2 AC 557 at para 19 per Lord Nicholls of Birkenhead. See also para 136 per Baroness Hale of Richmond; *R (RJM) v Secretary of State for Work and Pensions* [2009] AC 311 at para 14 per Lord Mance; *R (Carson) v Secretary of State for Work and Pensions* [2006] 1 AC 173 at paras 15–17 per Lord Hoffmann and at paras 55–60 per Lord Walker of Gestingthorpe (discrimination on basis of residence or age in a less sensitive category).

Establishing a difference of treatment

3.98 The onus of establishing that the applicant has been treated differently from another person in an analogous position rests on the applicant[1]. It is then for the state to establish an objective and reasonable justification for the difference in treatment[2]. In its more recent case law, however, the Court has implicitly acknowledged that it may in practice be difficult to establish a prima facie case of discrimination even where such discrimination exists, if for example a non-discriminatory rule is applied in a discriminatory manner. In *DH and Others v Czech Republic,* the Court said that 'the level of persuasion necessary for reaching a particular conclusion and, in this connection, the distribution of the burden of proof are intrinsically linked to the specificity of the facts, the nature of the allegation made and the Convention right at stake'[3]. In the same case, the Court stated that 'less strict evidential rules' should apply in the field of discrimination in order to guarantee those concerned 'the effective protection of their rights'[4]. In particular, the Court accepted that 'when it comes to assessing the impact of a measure or practice on an individual or group, statistics which appear on critical examination to be reliable and significant will be sufficient to constitute the *prima facie* evidence the applicant is required to produce'. Thus statistics demonstrating that over 50% of Roma children were placed in special schools for less able children, compared with less than 2% of non-Roma children, were sufficient to shift the burden of proof to the Czech government to establish that there was an objective and reasonable justification for this situation: a burden which the government could not discharge. The Court refused to accept that the educational tests on which the placements were based were not unbiased against Roma children[5].

1   See eg *Menteş v Turkey* 1997-VIII, para 95: *Fredin v Sweden (no 1)* (1991) A 192.

2   See eg 25186/94, *Sutherland v United Kingdom* (1 July 1997); *Markcx v Belgium* (1979) A 31, paras 32–43.

3   *DH and Others v Czech Republic* [GC] 2007-..., at para 178.

4   *DH and Others v Czech Republic* [GC] 2007-..., at para 186.

5   *DH and Others v Czech Republic* [GC] 2007-..., paras 188–195 at para 188. See also *Zarb Adami v Malta* 2006-VIII, para 77 (statistics revealed that jury service was performed predominantly by men, and state could not justify the difference in treatment).

Indirect discrimination

3.99 Article 14 is not confined to direct discrimination: it also covers indirect discrimination. As the European Court of Human Rights said in the case of *DH and Others v Czech Republic*, 'a difference in treatment may take the form of disproportionately prejudicial effects of a general policy or measure which, although couched in neutral terms, discriminates against a group'[1]. There is therefore no need to establish any intention to discriminate.

1   *DH and Others v Czech Republic* [GC] 2007-..., at para 184.

3.100 Article 14 can impose an obligation to treat differently persons whose situations are significantly different. This can be illustrated by *Thlimmenos v Greece*, which concerned a person who had been refused admission as a chartered accountant because of a criminal conviction arising from his refusal to wear military uniform due to his religious beliefs as a Jehovah's Witness. In a key passage in the judgment, the Court indicated that Article 14 may impose a positive duty to treat individuals differently in certain situations: that is, that discrimination can occur when the same treatment is accorded to individuals who ought to be treated differently. While the state had a legitimate interest in excluding certain convicted persons from the profession of chartered accountant, 'a conviction for refusing on religious or philosophical grounds to wear the military uniform cannot imply any dishonesty or moral turpitude likely to undermine the offender's ability to exercise this profession'. Exclusion on this ground was therefore disproportionate and unjustified. In other words, 'there existed no objective and reasonable justification for not treating the applicant differently from other persons convicted of a serious crime'[1].

---

1   *Thlimmenos v Greece* [GC] 2000-IV, paras 39–49 at para 47.

3.101 The majority of cases under Article 14, however, concern more familiar situations, such as discrimination based on gender or sexual orientation. There have also been a significant number of cases concerned with 'illegitimate' children. These and other issues are discussed in the following paragraphs.

Discrimination on the grounds of race or ethnic origin

3.102 Combating discrimination on the grounds of race or ethnic origin is a clear objective of the Council of Europe[1]. The European Court of Human Rights has said that where a difference in treatment is based on race or ethnic origin, 'the notion of objective and reasonable justification must be interpreted as strictly as possible'[2]. In practice, however, the Court has often appeared reluctant to find a violation of Article 14 where allegations are made of discrimination by a state against minorities. This reluctance may reflect a combination of difficulties in proving the allegations in the particular instance beyond reasonable doubt, combined with an acknowledgment of the sensitive political issues at stake. This is illustrated by a number of cases taken by applicants alleging discrimination against the Kurdish minority by the Turkish authorities. In *Tanrikulu v Turkey*, for example, the applicant claimed that her husband had been killed because he was a Kurd. Although the Court found a violation of Article 2, it considered that there was no evidence to support a finding that there had been a violation of Article 14[3]. In contrast, in *Nachova and Others v Bulgaria,* the Grand Chamber held that there had been a violation of Article 14 taken together with Article 2 in respect of the failure to hold an effective investigation into allegations of racially-motivated killing. While it had not been shown that racist attitudes had played a part in the killings, the failure of the authorities to investigate allegations of racist verbal abuse with a view to uncovering any possible racist motives in the use of force against members of an ethnic or other minority had been 'highly relevant to the question whether or not unlawful, hatred-induced violence has taken place'[4]. Even where there is evidence of general prejudice on the part of officials towards certain ethnic groups, there must be some particular and concrete indication of actual prejudice to give rise to the obligation in an individual case[5]. A similar obligation to carry out an effective investigation exists in respect of allegations of ill-treatment motivated by racial discrimination[6].

---

1   For further discussion of human rights initiatives of the Council of Europe in this area, see paras **2.88–2.91** above.

2   *DH and Others v Czech Republic* [GC] 2007-…, para 176.

3   *Tanrikulu v Turkey* [GC] 1999-IV, paras 122–125. See similarly *Anguelova v Bulgaria* 2002-IV, paras 163–168.

4   *Nachova and Others v Bulgaria* [GC] 2005-VII, paras 144–168.

5   *Ognyanova and Choban v Bulgaria* (23 February 2006), paras 143–149.

6   *Balogh v Hungary* (20 July 2004), paras 69–75.

ROMA

3.103 The European Court of Human Rights has also had to consider the treatment of Roma or gypsies. Several judgments have concerned application of planning controls in the United Kingdom. In *Buckley v United Kingdom*, for example, the applicant was a gypsy living with her children on land which she owned. Her land was one of a number of plots which had been occupied by gypsies without planning permission, and the occupants had been subject to enforcement proceedings. The applicant alleged that she was thereby prevented from following the traditional lifestyle of a gypsy, contrary to Article 8. The Commission held that the measures taken were disproportionate and that there had been a violation of Article 8. The Court however disagreed, holding that the measures had been proportionate. The Court considered the applicant's complaint that there had been a violation of Article 14 in conjunction with Article 8, but held that it did not appear that the applicant was at any time penalised or subject to any detrimental treatment for attempting to follow a traditional gypsy lifestyle[1]. In *Chapman v United Kingdom* (and in four other related cases), the Court again considered that environmental concerns leading to measures for the removal of gypsy families from land occupied without planning permission had been proportionate[2].

1   *Buckley v United Kingdom* 1996-IV, at para 88. For discussion of EU provisions, see Xanthaki 'Hope Dies Last: An EU Directive on Roma Integration' (2006) 11 EPL 515.

2   *Chapman v United Kingdom* 2001-I, paras 105–116 and 129–130 (no violation of Art 8, or of Art 14 with 8; and at para 99, no positive obligation under Art 8 to provide individuals with a home). See similarly *Jane Smith v United Kingdom* [GC] (18 January 2001); *Coster v United Kingdom* [GC] (18 January 2001); *Lee v United Kingdom* [GC] (18 January 2001); and *Beard v United Kingdom* [GC] (18 January 2001). Cf *Connors v United Kingdom* (27 May 2004), paras 85–95 (summary eviction from gypsy site where the family had lived permanently for more than 12 years: violation of Art 8): see further para **6.52** below. For further discussion, see Pogany 'Refashioning Rights in Central and Eastern Europe: Some Implications for the Region's Roma' (2004) 10 EPL 85; Liégeois *Roma in Europe* (3rd edn, 2007); and Sandland 'Developing a Jurisprudence of Difference: the Protection of the Human Rights of Travelling Peoples by the European Court of Human Rights' (2008) 8 HRLRev 475.

3.104 Widespread hostility to Roma in certain European countries[1] and evidenced by official attitudes suggesting discriminatory motives, for example, through the expression of judicial prejudice[2] or in policy determinations have given rise to several other challenges. Several cases – such as *Nachova and Others v Bulgaria*, discussed above – have examined the possibility of biased investigations by national authorities[3], while the refusal to recognise the validity of a Roma marriage for the purposes of awarding a survivor's pension was considered to have amounted to a violation of Article 14 when taken with Article 1 of Protocol no 1 in *Muñoz Díaz v Spain*[4]. The Court has also been called upon to examine attacks upon Roma and destruction of their property. In *Moldovan and Others v Romania (no 2),* for example, attacks by villagers aided by police officers had resulted in the deaths of three individuals and the destruction of 13 homes belonging to Roma families. The applicants had been forced to live in livestock premises, and only ten years later had the domestic courts ordered the payment of compensation. Violations of Article 14 taken with Article 6 and Article 8 were established[5].

Arguably the most significant judgment of the Court to date in connection with Roma, and arguably the most important of all the Court's judgments under Article 14, is *DH and Others v Czech Republic*, which has already been discussed[6]. In that case, the Court rejected the argument that the parents had, by consenting to the placements, waived their right not to be discriminated against. The Court held that, even if (contrary to its conclusion) the parents had given their informed consent to the discriminatory treatment, 'no waiver of the right not to be subjected to racial discrimination can be accepted, as it would be counter to an important public interest'[7]. In *Sejdić and Finci v Bosnia and Herzegovina*, constitutional arrangements deriving from the Dayton Peace Agreement which brought the war in Bosnia and Herzegovina to an end but which restricted eligibility to stand for parliament or the presidency to those declaring affiliation to one of the three dominant ethnic groups were held to have violated Article 14 taken with Article 3 of Protocol no 1 (in respect of parliamentary elections) and Protocol 12 (in respect of elections to the presidency), one of the applicants being a Roma[8].

---

1 For consideration of this topic by the European Commission against Racism and Intolerance, see para **2.91** above. A pending case seeks to challenge the recent removals of Roma from France: *Winterstein and Others v France* [communicated].

2 *Paraskeva Todorova v Bulgaria* (25 March 2010), paras 35–46 (refusal to impose suspended sentence as 'members of minority groups … consider that a suspended sentence is not a sentence': violation of Art 14 taken with Art 6(1)). See also *Aksu v Turkey*, case pending before the Grand Chamber (anti-gypsy sentiments expressed in a dictionary and in an academic study, both government-funded publications) [the Chamber (27 July 2010), paras 47–58, determined there had been no resultant discrimination].

3 *Nachova and Others v Bulgaria* [GC] 2005-VII, paras 144–168, discussed at para **3.102** above and para **4.47** below. See also *Angelova and Iliev v Bulgaria* 2007-IX, paras 114–117; *Cobzaru v Romania* (26 July 2007), paras 88–101; and *Bekos and Koutropoulos v Greece* 2005-XIII, paras 53–55 (allegations of physical and verbal ill-treatment of Roma allegedly on grounds of race: violation of procedural requirement under Art 3 to carry out an investigation into racist motives). This line of case law revises earlier reluctance to find that Art 14 was engaged: cf *Velikova v Bulgaria* 2000-VI, at para 94 (the material before the Court did not enable it to 'conclude beyond reasonable doubt' that a death and the lack of a meaningful investigation into it had been motivated by racial prejudice: violation of Art 2 on account of lack of effective investigation, but not of Art 14 taken with Art 2).

4 *Muñoz Díaz v Spain* 2009-…, paras 51–71.

5 *Moldovan and Others v Romania (no 2)* 2005-VII, paras 136–140. See also the similar cases of *Gergely v Romania* (26 April 2007), and *Kalanyos and Others v Romania* (26 April 2007).

6   See para **3.98** above.

7   *DH and Others v Czech Republic* [GC] 2007-..., at para 204.

8   *Sejdić and Finci v Bosnia and Herzegovina* [GC] 2009-..., paras 42–56.

Discrimination on the ground of nationality

3.105 It has been said that 'very weighty reasons would have to be put forward before the Court could regard a difference of treatment based exclusively on the ground of nationality as compatible with the Convention'[1]. The issue has been of some importance in respect to access to welfare entitlements[2]. The domestic courts have also had the opportunity to consider a number of cases involving allegations of discriminatory treatment based on nationality or immigration status[3], including cases concerned with anti-terrorism legislation[4].

1   *Gaygusuz v Austria* 1996-IV, para 42 (refusal to grant emergency social security assistance to non-nationals).

2   Eg *Luczak v Poland* 2007-XIII, paras 49–60 (refusal to affiliate non-national self-employed farmer to the farmers' social security fund as domestic law provided that only Polish nationals could be admitted: violation of Art 14 taken with Prot 1, Art 1 on account of the failure to present a convincing explanation for the refusal); and *Fawsie v Greece* (28 October 2010), paras 26–28 and 31–40, and *Saidoun v Greece* (28 October 2010), paras 28–29 and 33–42 (refusal to grant welfare benefits to political refugees from non-EU states: Art 8 applicable as the granting of an allowance for large families enabled the State to show its respect for family life; violation of Art 14 taken with Art 8, for while the aim was to address the country's demographic problem, the criterion chosen was based mainly on Greek nationality or origin, nor had this been uniformly applied). Cf *Epstein and Others v Belgium* (dec) 2008-... (only limited extension of rights to annuities for war victims: inadmissible *ratione materiae*, for a wide margin of appreciation applies where a state decides to make amends for damage for which it bore no responsibility).

3   For domestic discussion, see eg *R (Morris) v Westminster City Council* [2006] 1 WLR 505 (Housing Act 1996, s 185(4) found to be incompatible with Art 14 read in conjunction with Art 8 when it required a dependent child of a British citizen who was subject to immigration control to be disregarded when determining whether the citizen had a priority need for accommodation: since the statutory provisions were intended to promote family life, Art 8 was engaged; and the difference in treatment on the grounds of nationality was not a reasonable and proportionate way of achieving the result that the provision sought to achieve); *R (Wilson) v Wychavon District Council* [2007] QB 801, CA (discretionary area of judgment accorded the legislature in the review of legislation under the HRA 1998 was narrower in relation to discrimination on grounds of sex or race than for social or economic policy); and *R (Barclay) v Lord Chancellor* [2010] 1 AC 464 (prohibition on aliens from standing for election did not infringe Art 14 read with Prot 1, Art 3, since the rights under Art 3 belonged to citizens only).

4   *A v Secretary of State for the Home Department* [2005] 2 AC 68 (the indefinite detention without trial of non-UK nationals suspected of involvement in terrorism could not be justified under Art 14 when no such measures were taken against UK nationals who were the subject of similar suspicion). See further Arden 'Human Rights in the Age of Terrorism' (2005) 121 LQR 604; and Tomkins 'Readings of *A v Secretary of State for the Home Department*' [2005] PL 259. For CPT consideration of the detention of individuals held under the 2001 Act, see CPT/ Inf (2005) 10.

Sex discrimination

3.106 The European Court of Human Rights has frequently expressed the view that the advancement of the equality of the sexes is a major goal in the member states of the Council of Europe. It has stated that very weighty reasons would have to be put forward before the Convention organs could regard as compatible with the Convention a difference in treatment based exclusively on the ground of sex[1]. This approach underpins much of the Court's jurisprudence. In *Burghartz v Switzerland*, for example, the Court held that a Swiss law which permitted a wife to prefix her married name with her maiden name, but which prohibited her husband from using the same name, lacked an objective and reasonable basis, and therefore constituted discrimination based on sex which was incompatible with Articles 8 and 14[2]. In *Karlheinz Schmidt v Germany*, the Court considered a German law which obliged men, but not women, to serve in the fire brigade or to make a financial contribution[3]. The Court noted that in view of the continuing existence of a sufficient number of volunteers, no man was obliged in practice to serve in a fire brigade: payment of the financial contribution had become the only effective duty. In the imposition of such a financial burden, a difference of treatment based on sex could not be justified. There had therefore been a violation of Article 14 taken in conjunction with Article 4, paragraph 3[4]. Discrimination may also arise from a *de facto* situation as in *Zarb Adami v Malta*, where the Court found a similar violation in light of the absence of a justification for the striking discrepancy between the percentage of men as opposed to women called upon to serve as jurors[5].

These cases can be contrasted with the decision of the Commission in *Spöttl v Austria*, where the applicant argued that the obligation of men to perform military service constituted discrimination prohibited by Article 14 in conjunction with Article 4, since women were not subject to such a duty. The Commission held that the complaint was inadmissible. It observed that the difference in treatment was justified by objective reasons, which were within the broad margin of appreciation available to states in respect of their national defence policy. The Commission distinguished the judgment of the Court in *Karlheinz Schmidt* on the basis that the Court's finding in that case was limited to the assertion that a difference in treatment on the ground of sex in the imposition of a financial burden could not be justified[6].

---

1   *Schüler-Zgraggen v Switzerland* (1993) A 263, para 67; *Burghartz v Switzerland* (1994) A 280-B, para 27; *Karlheinz Schmidt v Germany* (1994) A 291-B, para 24. For domestic consideration, see *R (Wilson) v Wychavon District Council* [2007] QB 801.

2   *Burghartz v Switzerland* (1994) A 280-B. See also *Ünal Tekeli v Turkey* 2004-X, paras 55–69 (impossible for married woman to use her maiden name in official documents: violation). For recent application see eg *Losonci Rose and Rose v Switzerland* (9 November 2010), paras 42–53 (arrangements permitting couples to request use of surnames dependent upon whether the husband or the wife was Swiss: violation of Art 14 taken with Art 8).

3   *Karlheinz Schmidt v Germany* (1994) A 291-B, paras 21–30.

4   *Karlheinz Schmidt v Germany* (1994) A 291-B, paras 28–29.

5   *Zarb Adami v Malta* 2006-VIII, paras 75–84.

6   22956/93, *Spöttl v Austria* (1996) DR 85, 58.

3.107 Ensuring equality between the sexes has also been an important consideration underlying many of the Strasbourg authorities' judgments in relation to the allocation of social security benefits. In *Van Raalte v Netherlands*, the applicant was an unmarried man with no children. He complained that a law which exempted childless women over the age of 45 from paying social security contributions towards child benefit, but which had no such provision for exempting men, was discriminatory[1]. The European Court of Human Rights held that while states enjoyed a certain margin of appreciation as regards exemptions from such contributory obligations, Article 14 requires that such a measure 'applies even-handedly to both men and women unless compelling reasons have been adduced to justify a difference in treatment'[2]. The Court was not persuaded that such reasons existed, and held that there had been a violation of Article 14 when taken together with Article 1 of Protocol no 1. In *Schuler-Zgraggen v Switzerland*, which concerned the decision of the domestic court to refuse the applicant invalidity benefit, the applicant alleged that the domestic court had violated Article 14 in conjunction with Article 6 when it based its judgment on the assumption that many married women gave up their job when their first child was born. The domestic court had inferred that the applicant would similarly have given up work even if she had not had health problems. The applicant considered that if she had been a man, the court would not have made such an assumption, which was in any case contradicted by several scientific studies. The Court noted that this assumption was 'the sole basis for the reasoning', and introduced a difference in treatment based on the grounds of sex only that lacked any reasonable and objective justification[3]. In *MacGregor v United Kingdom*, a case which concerned personal tax allowances, the Commission held admissible a complaint that a woman with a young child and an incapacitated husband was unable to claim an additional personal allowance which was granted to men in similar circumstances. A friendly settlement was reached when the United Kingdom accepted that there were no grounds for the discrimination[4]. In contrast, in *Stec and Others v United Kingdom*, the Grand Chamber ruled that differences between the entitlement of men and women to work-related injury benefits pursued a legitimate aim and were reasonably and objectively justified. The differences reflected the difference in the pensionable retirement age, which was intended to correct the economic disadvantage suffered by women as a result of their traditional (and unpaid) role of family carer[5]. There have been many other cases brought against the United Kingdom relating to discrimination in social security and related fields[6]. Related issues have also been raised under the HRA 1998[7].

1   *Van Raalte v Netherlands* 1997-I, paras 32.

2   *Van Raalte v Netherlands* 1997-I, paras 41–45 at 42.

3   *Schüler-Zgraggen v Switzerland* (1993) A 263, para 67.

4   30548/96, *MacGregor v United Kingdom* (1 July 1998).

5   *Stec and Others v United Kingdom* [GC] 2006-VI, paras 50–66. See also *Duchez v France* (dec) 2002-VIII (military allowances payable to 'head of family' payable only to the husband

where both spouses were serving: inadmissible). Cf *Wessels-Bergervoet v Netherlands* 2002-IV, paras 46–55 (reduction in pension award on ground that applicant had not been insured when her husband had been working abroad, but this condition did not apply to married men: violation).

6   See eg *Cornwell v United Kingdom* (friendly settlement) (25 April 2000) (discrimination as between widows and widowers); *Willis v United Kingdom* 2002-IV, *Leary v United Kingdom* (friendly settlement) (25 April 2000), and *Michael Matthews v United Kingdom* (friendly settlement) (15 July 2002) (ages at which men and women qualified for bus passes); cf *Walker v United Kingdom* (24 August 2006), paras 30–39 (differential contribution periods for national insurance contributions fell to be considered on a similar basis to *Stec*).

7   See eg *R (Hooper) v Secretary of State for Work and Pensions* [2005] 1 WLR 1681 (it was not incompatible with Convention rights under the HRA 1998 for the Secretary of State to refuse widowers' claims arising from bereavements which occurred before the commencement of the amending legislation); *R (Wilkinson) v Inland Revenue Commissioners* [2005] 1 WLR 1718 (the Inland Revenue had not acted incompatibly with Convention rights by refusing to interpret 'widow' so as to include widowers).

3.108 The cases in which the European Court of Human Rights has not held differences in the treatment of the sexes to be a violation of Article 14 have generally concerned issues on which there is no common standard among member states, and where states therefore have a wide margin of appreciation. These are evolving areas of Convention jurisprudence.

One of the most contentious areas has concerned distinctions in treatment between mothers and unmarried fathers. The Convention does not thus require that an unmarried father should enjoy equality of treatment with a mother in the recognition of parental rights[1]. Since Article 5 of Protocol no 7 specifically provides that 'spouses shall enjoy equality of rights and responsibilities', the implication has been drawn that where a state has not ratified this protocol certain differences in treatment are not incompatible with the Convention.

Another such area has concerned paternal leave allowances. Initially, a broad margin of appreciation was accorded states in determining policy. Thus in its 1998 judgment in *Petrovic v Austria*, the Court ruled that the rejection of a father's claim for parental leave allowance as domestic law specified that only mothers could qualify did not give rise to a violation of the ECHR on account of the lack of any common European standard in social security provision for paid parental leave to be granted to fathers. The Court accepted that payment of the allowance was intended to promote family life and that Article 8 was therefore applicable, but did not accept that the discrimination violated Article 14[2]. At the time of writing, this issue is pending before the Grand Chamber[3].

1   See eg *McMichael v United Kingdom* (24 February 1995).

2   *Petrovic v Austria* 1998-II, paras 22–43. The Commission had determined a violation by a majority of 25 to 5; for the two dissenting judges on the Court, the lack of any standard European norm 'was not conclusive'; while states were not under a duty in terms of Art 8 to pay any such allowance, if they chose to do so it would not be appropriate to do so in a discriminatory manner.

3   *Konstantin Markin v Russia*. [In the Chamber judgment (2010-..., paras 45–59), the Court noted that such a consensus now exists. In this instance, differences in the treatment in parental leave rights of mothers and fathers serving in the military (in contrast to the rights

accorded non-military civilians) were found to have given rise to a violation of Art 14 taken with Art 8. The difference in treatment had involved a combination of both gender and military status, but as parental leave seeks to enable both parents to provide home care rather than assist mothers to recover from the rigours of childbirth and as the respondent state had not been able to show that operational requirements justified a prohibition on allowing servicemen to take parental leave, the Court concluded there was no reasonable or objective justification for the difference in treatment.]

3.109 In relation to the positive obligation upon national authorities to protect individuals at risk from the threat of violence or loss of life, Article 14 may also be engaged in cases of domestic violence against women. The justification for this principle is that such violence is gender-based, and thus where there has been a failure to provide an adequate response on the part of relevant authorities (including police, prosecutors and the judiciary), this involves breach of a woman's right to equal protection of the law[1].

1   *Opuz v Turkey* 2009-..., paras 183–202, discussed at para **4.85** below; cf *A v Croatia* 2010-..., paras 55–80 and 94–104 (failure to protect the applicant's physical integrity against assaults from her husband by implementing measures to address his psychiatric condition: violation of Art 8, but complaint under Art 14 inadmissible as the applicant had not produced sufficient evidence to show that the adoption or effects of domestic measures or practices in the context of domestic violence were discriminatory).

Discriminatory arrangements in family law

3.110 A variety of issues have arisen under Article 14 in relation to fathers and their children. A number of cases have concerned the position of fathers who were not married to the mother of the child, and have made it clear that differences in treatment on the basis of marital status can have a reasonable justification. In *McMichael v United Kingdom*, for example, the European Court of Human Rights upheld the distinction which then existed in Scots law between the automatic conferment of parental rights on a married father and the requirement placed upon an unmarried father to take some form of positive step (such as an application to a court) in order to acquire such rights. The reason for the requirement was that unmarried fathers varied in their commitment towards (or even knowledge of) their children. The Court held that this requirement was a proportionate response to achieve the legitimate aim of distinguishing between fathers who had some justifiable claim and those whose status lacked sufficient merit[1]. On the other hand, in *Sahin v Germany* and in *Sommerfeld v Germany,* the Grand Chamber held that a difference between the treatment of applications for access to children, between on the one hand fathers of children born of a relationship where the parties were living together out of wedlock, and on the other hand parents of children born in wedlock, constituted a violation of Article 14 in conjunction with Article 8. The difference in treatment was not supported by sufficiently weighty reasons to justify the assumption that access should only be permitted in the former case where it could be established that this would have beneficial effects upon the particular child's well-being[2]. In *PM v United Kingdom*, the Court held that a rule which restricted tax relief for child maintenance payments to fathers who had been married to the mother of the child was incompatible with Article 14 in conjunction with Article 1 of Protocol no 1[3]. In *Paulik v Slovakia,* the impossibility of challenging a judicial determination of paternity on the basis of additional DNA evidence was considered to be a violation of Article 8, and also of Article 14 in conjunction with Article 8, since such a bar did not exist in respect of presumed (rather than judicially-determined) paternity[4].

1   *McMichael v United Kingdom* (1995) A 308, para 98. The weaker standing of an unmarried father was found elsewhere in Europe: eg 9639/82, *B, R & J v Germany* (1984) DR 36, 130 (differences in treatment could be justified by the greater protection afforded to the family based on marriage in light of Art 12).

2   *Sahin v Germany* [GC] 2003-VIII, paras 50–61; *Sommerfeld v Germany* [GC] 2003-VIII, paras 84–98.

3   *PM v United Kingdom* (19 July 2005), paras 26–29.

4   *Paulik v Slovakia* 2006-XI, paras 41–47 and 51–59.

3.111 As the case of *McMichael v United Kingdom*[1] indicates, differential treatment based on marital status can have a reasonable justification. Unmarried couples are not generally considered to be in a comparable situation to married couples for the purposes of Article 14: as the Court said in *Nylund v Finland,* 'marriage continues to be characterised by a corpus of rights and obligations that differentiate it markedly from the situation of a man and woman who cohabit'. In that case, the complaint of an applicant who claimed to have fathered a child born to a married woman, and who could not obtain a paternity test without her agreement, was held to be inadmissible[2].

1   See para **3.110** above.

2   *Nylund v Finland* (dec) 1999-VI. See also 11089/84 *Lindsay v United Kingdom* (1986) DR 49, 181 (different tax rules for married and unmarried couples); *Shackell v United Kingdom* (27 April 2000) (dec) (social security benefits for widows and unmarried partners); and *Burden v United Kingdom* [GC] 2008-..., paras 58–66 (succession to property on death).

3.112 In the domestic case of *In re G (Adoption: Unmarried Couple)* a provision which allowed only married couples to apply for an adoption order was held to be incompatible with Article 14 in conjunction with Article 8[1]. The House of Lords acknowledged that the European Court of Human Rights might not have reached the same decision.

1   *In re G (Adoption: Unmarried Couple)* [2009] 1 AC 173. On the other hand, difference in treatment between married and unmarried couples in the tax and social security systems have been allowed: *Shackell v United Kingdom* (27 April 2000); *Burden v United Kingdom* [GC] 2008-..., discussed at para **3.92** above.

ILLEGITIMACY AND ADOPTION

3.113 Distinctions based upon the 'illegitimacy' of children are seldom considered to a have a legitimate aim. In *Marckx v Belgium,* domestic law required an unmarried mother to follow certain legal procedures in order to establish a legal bond with her child; further, the rights of inheritance on intestacy of a recognised illegitimate child were less than those of a child recognised as legitimate. The European Court of Human Rights noted that the text of Article 8 did not distinguish between family units constituted through marriage and those outside wedlock. Moreover it considered that to imply any such interpretation would have been inconsistent with the general principle that Convention guarantees apply to 'everyone', as well as contrary to the prohibition under Article 14 of any discrimination in the enjoyment of Convention rights on grounds including 'birth'[1]. The Court confirmed this approach in *Camp and Bourimi v Netherlands*, which concerned the right of a child to inherit from his father. The child had been born illegitimate, and the father had died without recognising the child. Although letters of legitimation had been granted, domestic law prevented the child inheriting. The Court held that there had been no violation of Article 8 when considered alone, but that matters of intestate succession between near relatives fell within the scope of Article 8 as they represented a feature of family life. It was therefore appropriate to consider Article 14 in conjunction with Article 8. The Court accepted that the protection of the rights of other heirs might constitute a legitimate aim, but noted that the child was treated differently not only from children born in wedlock, but also from children who although born out of wedlock had been recognised by their father. In these circumstances, the child's exclusion from his father's inheritance was held to be disproportionate and in breach of Article 14 when taken together with Article 8[2]. In *Merger and Cros v France,* the Court determined that legal restrictions placed upon the rights of children conceived in adulterous relationships to receive gifts from their parents could not be considered to be a justified under Article 8 taken together with Article 14[3].

---

1   *Marckx v Belgium* (1979) A 31, paras 36–62 (various violations of Art 8 taken alone, of Art 14 taken in conjunction with Art 8, and of Art 14 taken in conjunction with Prot 1, Art 1). See also *Inze v Austria* (1987) A 126.

2   *Camp and Bourimi v Netherlands* 2000-X, paras 25–39. See also *Mazurek v France* 2000-II, paras 48–55.

3   *Merger and Cros v France* (22 December 2004), paras 40–50.

3.114 Similarly, distinctions in the rights of children based upon adoption rather than biological criteria must satisfy the requirements of Article 14. This was decided in a case, *Pla and Puncernau v Andorra,* concerned with the interpretation of a will which stipulated that the estate was to pass to a son or grandson of a lawful and canonical marriage. The domestic courts had interpreted the will as excluding an adopted child. The Court, emphasising the 'living instrument' doctrine and the importance of eliminating discrimination against children born out of wedlock, held that there had been a violation of Article 14. The state had violated the applicant's rights by giving effect to the will in accordance with the testator's intention[1].

---

1   *Pla and Puncernau v Andorra* 2004-VIII, discussed in Kay 'The European Convention on Human Rights and the Control of Private Law' [2005] EHRLR 466.

Sexual orientation

3.115 Differences in treatment based upon sexual orientation are subject to particular scrutiny. 'When the distinction in question operates in this intimate and vulnerable sphere of an individual's private life, particularly weighty reasons need to be advanced before the Court to justify the measure complained of' and in such cases a state's margin of appreciation is narrow: 'the principle of proportionality does not merely require the measure chosen to be suitable in general for realising the aim sought; it must also be shown that it was necessary in the circumstances'[1]. Although many of the judgments of the European Court of Human Rights in this area have not concerned Article 14 directly, they have often had discriminatory treatment at their core, and in consequence have had a considerable impact on the approach to discrimination based on sexual orientation[2]. The case law thus reflects a growing European consensus in this area that differences in treatment on account of sexual orientation are unlikely to have any legitimate aim[3], although at least in the area of child care there may be less consensus and a corresponding greater willingness to defer to domestic decision-making[4].

1   *Kozak v Poland* (2 March 2010), at para 92.

2   Examples include *Dudgeon v United Kingdom* (1981) A 45; *Norris v Ireland* (1988) A 142; *Modinos v Cyprus* (1993) A 259; *Lustig-Prean and Beckett v United Kingdom* (27 September 1999); and S*mith and Grady v United Kingdom* 1999-VI. See further paras **6.140–6.144** below.

3   Cf Parliamentary Assembly Opinion no 216 (2000) on draft ECHR Prot 12, at para 6: 'the enumeration of grounds in Article 14 is, without being exhaustive, meant to list forms of discrimination which it regards as being especially odious. Consequently the ground "sexual orientation" should be added [to the draft Protocol]'. The proposal was not followed, 'because such an inclusion was considered unnecessary from a legal point of view since the list of non-discrimination grounds is not exhaustive, and because inclusion of any particular additional ground might give rise to unwarranted a contrario interpretations as regards discrimination based on grounds not so included' (Prot 12, Explanatory Report, at para 20). See also Committee of Ministers Recommendation Rec (2010) 5 on measures to combat discrimination on grounds of sexual orientation or gender identity; and Commissioner for Human Rights *Discrimination on Grounds of Sexual Orientation and Gender Identity in Europe* (2011).

4   Eg *PV v Spain* (30 November 2010), paras 26–37 (restriction on transsexual's access to her young child on account of best interests of the child: no violation of Art 14 in combination with Art 8). For discussion of same-sex adoption, see para **3.118** below, and for same-sex marriage, para **6.04** below.

HOMOSEXUALITY

3.116 Many of the cases which the Strasbourg authorities initially had to consider concerned the criminalisation of same-sex relations[1]. In *Sutherland v United Kingdom*, for example, the Commission considered that the fact that the age of consent for homosexual activity differed from that for heterosexual activity violated Article 8 when taken along with Article 14. Domestic law prohibited homosexual acts between males over the age of 16 but under the age of 18 years, while the minimum age for heterosexual activity was 16. The Commission could find no objective and reasonable justification for the distinction, even after attaching some weight to recent deliberations by Parliament which had considered the argument that certain young men between the ages of 16 and 18 did not yet have a settled sexual orientation and thus required protection, and further that society was entitled to indicate its disapproval of homosexual conduct and its preference that children follow a heterosexual way of life: neither reason was considered sufficient. The Commission noted that current medical findings suggested sexual orientation was already fixed in both sexes by the age of 16 and thus the suggestion of recruitment was inadequate. Moreover, the Commission reiterated the Court's statement in *Dudgeon v United Kingdom* that preference for a heterosexual lifestyle could not constitute an objective or reasonable justification[2].

---

1   *Dudgeon v United Kingdom* (1981) A 45; *Norris v Ireland* (1988) A 142; *Modinos v Cyprus* (1993) A 259 (all concerned the criminalisation of sex between men).

2   25186/94, *Sutherland v United Kingdom* (1 July 1997) paras 55–66; see also *Sutherland v United Kingdom* (striking out) [GC] (22 March 2001). See also *L and V v Austria* 2003-I, paras 34–55 (no convincing case established for distinctions in age of consent between homosexuals and heterosexuals in light of research conclusions on establishment of sexuality and European practice of equal ages: violation); and *SL v Austria* 2003-I, paras 27–47.

3.117 Subsequent cases concerned with sexual orientation have resulted in an expansion of the Court's jurisprudence into other areas of the law. The judgment of the Court in *Smith and Grady v United Kingdom*, concerning employment, although not based on Article 14, is instrumental in demonstrating the Court's commitment to the prohibition of discrimination in the application of any Convention right on the ground of sexual orientation. In that case, the Court held that the dismissal of military personnel on the basis of their sexual orientation violated the right to respect for private life protected by Article 8[1]. The Court took another important step in *Salgueiro da Silva Mouta v Portugal*, when it held for the first time that discrimination on the ground of homosexuality violated Article 14. It ruled that the refusal to grant custody of the daughter of a marriage to her father, who was living in a homosexual relationship, on the ground that such an environment could not be a healthy one in which to raise a child, violated the father's right to respect for his family life under Article 8 when taken together with Article 14[2]. In *Karner v Austria,* the state's failure to justify restriction of the right to succeed to a tenancy to heterosexual couples was considered unwarranted discriminatory treatment, the Court noting that there had to be convincing and weighty arguments showing why it was necessary to exclude homosexuals[3], while in *JM v United Kingdom,* the Court could find no sufficient justification for treating absent parents who had entered into new long-term relationships with same-sex partners differently when calculating the amount of the contribution payable under child-support regulations[4]. In a different context, the Court held in *Bączkowski and Others v Poland* that the refusal of permission to hold a demonstration against discrimination against homosexuals had itself violated Article 14 in conjunction with Article 11[5]. Prohibitions of 'gay pride' parades were also found to have given rise to violations of Article 11 and of Article 14 taken with Article 11 in *Alekseyev v Russia,* in which the Court readily rejected the suggestion that restrictions on the rights of homosexuals to campaign for substantive rights could be justified on the grounds of incompatibility with religious doctrines and public morals or for the protection of others. Noting that there was now indeed a European consensus on a range of matters concerning substantive rights for homosexuals, the Court stressed that the present case concerned the attempts by officials to close down public debate through the expression of populist and uninformed views[6].

1   *Smith and Grady v United Kingdom* 1999-VI. See also *Lustig-Prean and Beckett v United Kingdom* (27 September 1999). See further paras **6.142–6.144** below.

2   *Salgueiro da Silva Mouta v Portugal* 1999-IX.

3   *Karner v Austria* 2003-IX, paras 29–43. Contrast *Mata Estevez v Spain* (dec) 2001-VI, where a claim that a homosexual was discriminated against when he was refused a social security allowance as a surviving 'spouse' was held to be manifestly unfounded. It was held that a homosexual relationship 'does not fall within article 8 in so far as that provision protects the right to respect for family life.' Although the Court accepted that the right to private life might be engaged, it held that the legislation had a legitimate aim, 'the protection of the family based on marriage', and that the difference in treatment was within the state's margin of appreciation. In *Karner*, the Court expressly did not decide whether the applicant's case fell within the scope of 'family life' or 'private life': see para 33. The decision was based on the 'home' limb of Art 8.

4   *JM v United Kingdom* (28 September 2010), paras 54–58.

5   *Bączkowski and Others v Poland* 2007-VI, paras 93–101.

6   *Alekseyev v Russia* 2010-…, paras 68–88 and 106–110.

3.118 Greater caution, though, is evident in the restricted number of situations where no strong European consensus exists and in consequence where a margin of appreciation is recognised[1]. Child care is one such area, although even here cautious advances are evident. In *EB v France,* for example, the state's refusal to give an unmarried homosexual woman the necessary prior approval before she could adopt a child was held to constitute discrimination contrary to Article 14 together with Article 8[2]. On the other hand, the Convention does not require states to recognise the right of same-sex couples to marry[3].

1   *Alekseyev v Russia* 2010-…, at para 83: 'This, however, does not dispense the Court from the requirement to verify whether in each individual case the authorities did not overstep their margin of appreciation by acting arbitrarily or otherwise.'

2   *EB v France* [GC] 2008-…, paras 70–98. See further para **6.144**, fn 2 below.

3   *Schalk and Kopf v Austria* 2010-…, paras 54–64 (a cohabiting same-sex couple living in a stable partnership fell within the notion of 'family life' and were in a relevantly similar situation to a similarly-situated different-sex couple as regards the need for legal recognition of their relationship, but Art 12 did not impose an obligation to recognise marriage, and similarly no obligation to recognise same-sex civil partnerships could be derived from Art 14 taken in conjunction with Art 8). See further para **6.04** below.

DOMESTIC CONSIDERATION

3.119 Discrimination on the ground of sexual orientation has also been considered in a number of domestic cases. In *Ghaidan v Godin-Mendoza*, a provision in landlord and tenant legislation which guaranteed security of tenure to the surviving spouse or heterosexual partner of a deceased tenant, but not to a same-sex partner, was held to be incompatible with Article 8 and Article 14 taken with Article 8, and was therefore read (applying s 3 of the HRA 1998) as extending to same-sex partners[1]. In *M v Secretary of State for Work and Pensions*, on the other hand, a rule governing financial responsibility for the maintenance of children required the income and outgoings of the non-resident parent to be combined with that person's partner only if the partnership was heterosexual. It was held that the issue fell outside the scope of Article 8, as it had at best only a tenuous link with respect for family life, and that the rule in any event sought to strike a fair balance by limiting the impact on new households of the breakdown of relationships between couples with children. It was also emphasised, in connection with the margin of appreciation, that it takes time in a democracy before profound cultural changes, such as the treatment of same-sex couples in the same way as heterosexual couples, are reflected in legislation[2].

1   *Ghaidan v Godin-Mendoza* [2004] 2 AC 557.

2   *M v Secretary of State for Work and Pensions* [2006] 2 AC 91.

TRANSSEXUALS

3.120 The treatment of transsexuals has necessitated consideration of the discrimination provisions. In *Sheffield & Horsham v United Kingdom*, the applicants, who were both transsexuals, claimed that the failure of the Government to recognise in law that they were of the female sex constituted a violation of the ECHR, Article 8 alone and Article 14 in conjunction with Article 8. The Court held, however, that the United Kingdom was entitled to rely on the margin of appreciation to defend its refusal to recognise in law a post-operative transsexual's sexual identity. Minimal inquiries as to pre-operative status were held not to be a disproportionate interference with the applicants' Article 8 rights. The Court also ruled that there had been no violation of Article 14 taken together with Article 8. Relying again on the margin of appreciation, the Court held that the measures taken by the state had struck a fair balance between safeguarding the interests of transsexuals and the interests of the community and were not disproportionate. Moreover, it noted that these considerations 'which are equally encompassed in the notion of "reasonable and objective justification" for the purpose of Article 14 of the Convention, must also be seen as justifying the difference in treatment which the applicants experienced'[1]. This approach rested on the assumption that there was at this time no consensus within Europe on the status of transsexuals, and consequently that it was preferable to allow states some latitude in regulating this area[2], an assumption questioned in the joint dissenting opinion of several of the judges who noted that only the United Kingdom, Ireland, Albania and Andorra expressly prohibited any changes to birth certificates in such circumstances, and indeed that the majority of European countries allowed such amendments[3]. In this instance, neither the Commission nor the strong dissenting opinions focused expressly on Article 14. When the Grand Chamber in 2002 eventually reversed previous jurisprudence and held in *Christine Goodwin v United Kingdom* that there was now a positive obligation on states to alter the register of births or to issue modified birth certificates in the case of post-operative transsexuals, it did so solely upon the basis of Article 8, holding that examination of this matter under Article 8 and the consequent finding of a violation meant that no separate issue arose under Article 14[4]. However, in exceptional circumstances, interferences with Convention rights based upon a person's transsexuality may nevertheless be considered justified[5].

1   *Sheffield and Horsham v United Kingdom* 1998-V, at para 76.

2   *Sheffield and Horsham v United Kingdom* 1998-V, at paras 55–61.

3   *Sheffield and Horsham v United Kingdom* 1998-V, joint partly dissenting opinion of Judges Bernhardt, Thorvilhjalmsson, Spielmann, Palm, Wildhaber, Makarczyk and Voicu.

4   *Christine Goodwin v United Kingdom* [GC] 2002-VI, para 108.

5   *PV v Spain* (30 November 2010), paras 26–37 (restriction on transsexual's access to her young child on account of best interests of the child: no violation of Art 14 in combination with Art 8).

Religious discrimination

3.121 The European Court of Human Rights has on several occasions ruled on differential treatment on the ground of religion. National authorities are under a duty to remain neutral in exercising any regulatory power in the sphere of religious freedom and must remain impartial in their relations with different religions, denominations and beliefs[1]. However, a difference in treatment between religious groups on account of official recognition of a specific legal status resulting in the conferment of privileges is not in itself incompatible with the Convention as long as a framework establishing criteria for conferring legal personality is in place and also providing that each religious group has a fair opportunity to apply for this status[2]. Application of the criteria for any recognised privilege in a non-discriminatory manner – for example, in respect of exemption from military service for those discharging leadership responsibilities in a religious community – will thus give rise to a violation of Article 14 taken with Article 9[3].

1   *Metropolitan Church of Bessarabia and Others v Moldova* 2001-XII, para 116.

2   *Koppi v Austria* (10 December 2009), para 33. See also *Religionsgemeinschaft der Zeugen Jehovas and Others v Austria* (31 October 2008), paras 87–99 (substantial time taken to determine question of recognition of Jehovah's Witnesses: violation of Art 14 with Art 9). See further paras **7.36–7.43** below.

3   *Lang v Austria* (19 March 2009), paras 22–32 (failure to exempt a Jehovah's Witness who served as an elder for his religious community through providing pastoral care and conducting religious services); see similarly *Gütl v Austria* (12 March 2009), paras 30–40; and *Löffelmann v Austria* (12 March 2009), paras 45–55; but cf *Koppi v Austria* (10 December 2009), paras 25–35 (no violation of Art 14 taken with Art 9, the religious community not having applied for recognition as a religious society as required for exemption purposes). See further para **7.12** below.

3.122 An issue as to whether there has been differential treatment on the ground of religion may arise in a wide range of circumstances: for example, the question may arise in respect of educational provision[1]. However, in several of the cases Article 14 has been considered not in conjunction with Article 9, the provision guaranteeing freedom of religion, but in conjunction with other substantive provisions. That has been because the complaint was of discrimination in relation to the enjoyment of a Convention right, other than the right conferred by Article 9, on the ground of religion. In *Hoffman v Austria*, for example, the applicant had been denied custody of her child because of her involvement with the Jehovah's Witnesses. The Court held that it was unacceptable for a domestic court to base a decision on the ground of a difference in religion. Although the point at issue was essentially one of religion, the Court considered it under Articles 8 and 14 as it concerned the determination of child custody, an aspect of family life. As it had already considered the matter under Articles 8 and 14, the Court held that there was no need to consider the point under Article 9[2]. In *Canea Catholic Church v Greece* the Court had to consider a situation where the applicant church could not take legal proceedings in order to protect its property rights, although the Orthodox Church and the Jewish Community were able to do so. The Court found that there could be no objective and reasonable justification for this discriminatory treatment and that there was a violation of Article 14 taken in conjunction with Article 6(1)[3]. A domestic example is the case of *R (Baiai) v Secretary of State for the Home Department (Nos 1 and 2),* in which a declaration of incompatibility was granted under the HRA 1998 in respect of immigration legislation designed to address the problem of marriages of convenience, which applied only to civil marriages, and not to Anglican marriages[4]. In the proceedings before the Strasbourg Court, these statutory provisions were found to have given rise to a violation of Article 14 taken together with Article 12 in relation to one of the applicants who had both been unwilling (on account of his faith) and unable (as he was resident in Northern Ireland) to get married in the Church of England. The Court considered that no objective and reasonable justification for the difference in treatment had been provided[5]. The Court has also extended the principle that a state is under a positive obligation to carry out an effective investigation into serious assaults motivated by discriminatory attitudes: as is the case with racially-motivated attacks, the failure to investigate assaults carried out on the basis of religious belief may constitute a violation of Article 14 in conjunction with Article 3[6].

---

1   Eg *Grzelak v Poland* (15 June 2010), paras 84–101 (failure of education authorities to organise a class in ethics and to give a pupil a mark in his school report, leading to harassment and discrimination for not following religious education classes: violation of Art 14 taken with Art 9).

2   *Hoffman v Austria* (1993) A 255-C, paras 43–47. Cf UN Delaration on the Elimination of All Forms of Intolerance and of Discrimination Based on Religion or Belief (1981), Art 3: 'discrimination between human beings on grounds of religion or belief constitutes an affront to human dignity and a disavowal of the principles of the Charter of the United Nations'. See also 1990 Document of the Copenhagen Meeting of the Conference on the Human Dimension of the CSCE which 'clearly and unequivocally condemns totalitarianism, racial and ethnic hatred,

anti-Semitism, xenophobia and discrimination against anyone as well as persecution on religious and ideological grounds'.

3   *Canea Catholic Church v Greece* 1997-VIII, paras 44–47.

4   *R (Baiai) v Secretary of State for the Home Department (Nos 1 and 2)* [2009] 1 AC 287.

5   *O'Donoghue and Others v United Kingdom* 2010-…, paras 101–107 and 110 (the government conceded there had also been a violation of Art 14 taken with Art 9; additionally, the Court found a violation of Art 12). See also (for rights of religious bodies to conduct officially-recognised marriages) *Savez Crkava 'Riječ Žlvota' and Others v Croatia* (9 December 2010), paras 85–93 (unequal application of criteria: violation of Art 14 taken with Art 9).

6   *Milanović v Serbia* (14 December 2010), paras 87–91 and 96–101 (failure to carry out effective investigation into religiously-motivated attacks by private individuals upon leading member of Hare Krishna sect: violation of Art 3, and of Art 14 taken with Art 3). Cf *Alekseyev v Russia* 2010-…, para 76 (statements calling for violence against protestors made by a Muslim cleric could have led to prosecutions but instead were relied upon by the authorities to prohibit a procession: violation of Art 11).

3.123 Questions under Article 14 relating to discrimination on the ground of religion may also arise in the context of employment. In *Thlimmenos v Greece*, discussed above[1], the applicant had been refused admission as a chartered accountant on the ground of a conviction for insubordination. As a Jehovah's Witness professing pacifism, he had refused to wear military uniform at a time of general mobilisation for which he had been imprisoned for more than two years. While the European Court of Human Rights noted that access to a profession is not covered by the Convention, the applicant's complaint concerned the lack of distinction between convictions based upon religious beliefs and other convictions for criminal offences. In effect, the complaint alleged discrimination on the basis of the exercise of freedom of religion. While states could legitimately exclude certain classes of offenders from various professions, any conviction for refusing to wear military uniform on the basis of religious convictions could not suggest dishonesty or moral turpitude. The disqualification did not therefore have a legitimate objective, and was in the nature of an additional and disproportionate sanction. There was accordingly a violation of Article 14 taken in conjunction with Article 9[2].

1   At para **3.100** above.

2   *Thlimmenos v Greece* [GC] 2000-IV, paras 39–53.

Discrimination in educational provision

3.124 The right to education, protected by the ECHR, Article 2 of Protocol no 1, has many facets. It encompasses not only the right of access to educational institutions but also the right to effective education and official recognition of the successful completion of studies[1]. As explained below[2], the Strasbourg institutions have recognised that national authorities enjoy a wide margin of appreciation in relation to educational provision, so as to reflect the needs and resources of the community in question. As a result, complaints of discrimination in relation to such matters as the level of provision for children with special needs, or transport to schools, have generally been rejected[3]. Complaints of that nature, based on the HRA 1998, have been equally unsuccessful before the domestic courts[4]. There have however been a number of cases raising more fundamental issues of discrimination in relation to the provision of education.

1   *Belgian Linguistic case* (1968) A 6.

2   See paras **6.153–6.157** below.

3   See eg 25959/94, *Cohen v United Kingdom* (28 February 1996) (refusal of local authority to pay cost of transport of a child with special needs to school of parents' choice, when another suitable school was closer: inadmissible); and 29046/95, *McIntyre v United Kingdom* (21 October 1998) (complaint by physically disabled applicant that she had been denied the right to education as a result of school's refusal to install a lift to allow her to access the same facilities as her able-bodied peers: inadmissible). For an examination of how the discrimination provisions affect special needs students, see Black-Branch, 'Equality, Non-Discrimination and the Right to Special Education; From International Law to the Human Rights Act' [2000] EHRLR 297.

4   See eg *Dove v Scottish Ministers* 2002 SC 257 (restoration of a self-governing school to the control of the local education authority did not violate Art 14 in conjunction with Prot 1, Art 2: the right to education was a right to such educational institutions as the state may provide, and to be able to make effective use of that access, and the change of status did not fall within the ambit of the provision); *Douglas v North Tyneside Metropolitan Borough Council* [2004] 1 WLR 2363 (refusal by a local education authority of a loan to a mature student for tertiary education did not give rise to an issue falling within Prot 1, Art 2, and thus Art 14 was not engaged); and *R (R) v Leeds City Council* [2005] EWHC 2495 (Admin) (refusal to provide free transport from claimants' home to the nearest Jewish school some 45 miles away, although transport to other faith schools outside the administrative area up to six miles distant was provided: there was no proper comparator and thus no discriminatory treatment; Art 8 was neither engaged nor infringed, since the claimants were attending the school of their choice; Art 9 was not engaged since the claimants were attending the faith schools; and even if Prot 1, Art 2 were engaged, the refusal would fall within the terms of the United Kingdom's reservation).

3.125 One of the most important judgments in outlining the scope of Article 14 in this area is the *Belgian Linguistic case*. In this case the Court held that Article 14, even when read in conjunction with Article 2 of Protocol no 1, did not have the effect of guaranteeing to a child or his parents the right to obtain education in the language of his choice. The Court stated that the object of the provision was more limited, and was 'to ensure that the right to education shall be secured by each Contracting State to everyone within its jurisdiction without discrimination on the ground, for instance, of language'. The Court also stated that 'to interpret the two provisions as conferring on everyone within the jurisdiction of a State a right to obtain education in the language of his own choice would lead to absurd results, for it would be open to anyone to claim any language of instruction in any of the territories of the Contracting Parties'[1].

1   *Belgian Linguistic case* (1968) A 6, para 11. See also *Skender v Former Yugoslav Republic of Macedonia* (dec) (22 November 2001). Cf *Folgerø and Others v Norway* [GC] 2007-VIII, discussed at para **6.165** below (in view of finding of violation of Article 2 of Protocol 1, it was not necessary to examine the complaint under Art 14 in conjunction with Arts 8 and 9 or Article 2 of Protocol 1).

3.126 In *DH and Others v Czech Republic,* on the other hand, the placement of Roma children in special schools designed to assist children with learning difficulties was found to have involved a violation of Article 14 taken in conjunction with Article 2 of Protocol no 1. Although no issue was taken with the legislation governing placements in special schools, statistical evidence demonstrated that the manner in which it was applied in practice resulted in a disproportionate number of Roma children being placed in such schools. The burden of proof therefore shifted to the state to show that the difference in the impact of the legislation was the result of objective factors unrelated to ethnic origin. The Court concluded that the tests on which the state relied could not justify the difference in treatment[1].

1   *DH and Others v Czech Republic* [GC] 2007-..., paras 182–210. See paras **3.98** and **3.104** above for further discussion of this case.

3.127 The issue of discrimination has also arisen in connection with the content of education. In *Kjeldsen, Busk Madsen and Pedersen v Denmark*, the European Court of Human Rights had to consider a Danish law which introduced compulsory sex education into primary schools[1]. The applicants, who were all parents with school age children, complained that the law violated Article 2 of Protocol no 1 when taken alone, and Article 14 in conjunction with this Article. The applicants noted that Danish law made provision to allow parents to have their children exempted from religious education, and the failure to permit such an exemption with regard to sex education constituted discrimination contrary to Article 14. The Court rejected this argument, holding that there was a difference in kind between religious instruction, which necessarily disseminated tenets, and sex education, which was concerned with 'mere knowledge'[2]. Accordingly the discrimination objected to by the applicants was founded on dissimilar factual circumstances and was consistent with the requirements of Article 14.

1   *Kjeldsen, Busk Madsen and Pedersen v Denmark* (1976) A 23, discussed at para **6.164** below.
2   *Kjeldsen, Busk Madsen and Pedersen v Denmark* (1976) A 23, para 56.

3.128 The issue of religious education in schools has also provoked some controversy. The Commission has acknowledged that Article 2 of Protocol no 1 entitles parents to have their children excused from lessons or acts of worship on the grounds of faith or religion[1]. It is, however, unlikely that the Court would hold that a state has a positive obligation under that provision to provide alternative acts of worship for such children. It has been suggested that non-discrimination provisions may be relevant in this context[2].

1   4733/71, *Karnell and Hardt v Sweden* (1971) YB 14, 676 at 690.
2   See Cumper 'School Worship: Praying for Guidance' [1998] EHRLR 45.

THE RELATIONSHIP BETWEEN STRASBOURG AND NATIONAL AUTHORITIES

Introduction

3.129 In applying the ECHR, the European Court of Human Rights adopts an approach which to some extent reflects a traditional view of its character as an international court enforcing an instrument of international law. Certain general principles are characteristic of that approach: the principle of subsidiarity; the doctrine of the margin of appreciation; and the fourth instance doctrine. These principles are however limited by the extent to which the Convention is being treated by the Court as a constitutional guarantee for Europe[1].

1   See para **3.55** above.

The principle of subsidiarity

3.130 The European Court of Human Rights has often referred to 'the fundamentally subsidiary role of the Convention'[1]. The principle of subsidiarity describes three related aspects of the Convention system. First, the ECHR represents a floor rather than a ceiling – in other words, a minimum level of protection of fundamental rights, rather than a maximum – and in that sense is intended to be subsidiary to any higher level of protection adopted by contracting states under domestic or international law. This is reflected in Article 53:

'Nothing in this Convention shall be construed as limiting or derogating from any of the human rights and fundamental freedoms which may be ensured under the laws of any High Contracting Party or under any other agreement to which it is a Party.'

This approach is also reflected, under United Kingdom law, in the HRA1998, s 11[2].

1   See eg *Hatton and Others v United Kingdom* [GC] 2003-VIII, at para 97.
2   See para **1.99** above.

3.131 Secondly, the ECHR sets minimum standards, but does not prescribe the means by which those standards are to be achieved. The choice of means remains within the competence of national authorities. Thus, in a case concerned with a complaint of discriminatory treatment contrary to Article 14, the Court said:

'In attempting to find out, in a given case, whether or not there has been an arbitrary distinction, the Court cannot disregard those legal and factual features which characterise the life of the society in the State which, as a Contracting Party, has to answer for the measure in dispute. In so doing, it cannot assume the role of the competent national authorities, for it would thereby lose sight of the subsidiary nature of the international machinery of collective enforcement established by the

Convention. The national authorities remain free to choose the measures which they consider appropriate in those matters which are governed by the Convention. Review by the Court concerns only the conformity of these measures with the requirements of the Convention.'[1]

---

1   *Belgian Linguistic case* (1968) A 6; *Handyside v United Kingdom* (1978) A 24.

3.132 Thirdly, the ECHR looks primarily to national authorities, and national courts, in particular, as the means by which the substantive rights conferred by the Convention should be protected. Thus Article 1 places on contracting states the obligation to 'secure to everyone within their jurisdiction the rights and freedoms defined in Section 1 of this Convention' (ie Articles 2–18). Article 13 guarantees a right to an effective remedy at the national level:

'Everyone whose rights and freedoms as set forth in this Convention are violated shall have an effective remedy before a national authority notwithstanding that the violation has been committed by persons acting in an official capacity.'

Article 35 permits the European Court of Human Rights to deal with an application only after all domestic remedies have been exhausted. These provisions are not incorporated into the HRA 1998 (where Article 35 would have no place in any event), but the Act itself gives effect to Articles 1 and 13[1].

---

1   See paras **1.29** and **2.58–2.63** below.

3.133 Finally, and perhaps most importantly, the principle of subsidiarity is reflected in the margin of appreciation[1] and fourth instance doctrines[2].

---

1   See paras **3.134–3.140** below.
2   See para **3.141** below.

The margin of appreciation

3.134 In accordance with the principle of subsidiarity, the European Court of Human Rights exercises a degree of restraint in determining whether the judgment made by national authorities (including national courts) is compatible with the state's obligations under the Convention. That restraint is exercised by means of the doctrine of the margin of appreciation: a translation of the French expression 'marge d'appréciation'. The concept of the margin of appreciation is thus one of the means by which the European Court of Human Rights recognises, to some extent, the right of free societies to choose for themselves the human rights policies that suit them best[1]. The concept is therefore the basis for the allocation of responsibility for protecting human rights between national courts (and other national institutions) and the Strasbourg Court. The doctrine does not appear in the Convention, and is one which has been developed by the Strasbourg Court itself. It is an essential tool for applying the Convention, given the diversity of

285

societies and situations to which the Convention applies. It is a concept which is difficult to apply in practice and is apt to give rise to controversy. It suffers from a lack of clarity and analysis, and underlies a lack of consistency in the case law.

1   See Ryssdall 'The Coming of Age of the European Convention on Human Rights' [1996] EHRLR 18, 24–26.

3.135 The concept was first explained by the European Court of Human Rights in the case of *Handyside v United Kingdom*, which concerned the prosecution of a publisher for obscenity. The issue was whether that interference with freedom of expression was 'necessary in a democratic society ... for the protection of morals', as required by Article 10(2). The Court said:

> 'The Court points out that the machinery of protection established by the Convention is subsidiary to the national systems safeguarding human rights. The Convention leaves to each Contracting State, in the first place, the task of securing the rights and freedoms it enshrines. The institutions created by it make their own contribution to this task but they become involved only through contentious proceedings and once all domestic remedies have been exhausted [art 35].

> These observations apply, notably, to art 10(2). In particular, it is not possible to find in the domestic law of the various Contracting States a uniform European conception of morals. The view taken by their respective laws of the requirements of morals varies from time to time and from place to place, especially in our era which is characterised by a rapid and far-reaching evolution of opinions on the subject. By reason of their direct and continuous contact with the vital forces of their countries, State authorities are in principle in a better position than the international judge to give an opinion on the exact content of these requirements as well as on the "necessity" of a "restriction" or "penalty" intended to meet them ... [I]t is for the national authorities to make the initial assessment of the reality of the pressing social need implied by the notion of "necessity" in this context.

> Consequently, art 10(2) leaves to the Contracting States a margin of appreciation. This margin is given both to the domestic legislator ("prescribed by law") and to the bodies, judicial amongst others, that are called upon to interpret and apply the laws in force.

> Nevertheless, Article 10(2) does not give the Contracting States an unlimited power of appreciation. The Court, which, with the Commission, is responsible for ensuring the observance of those States' engagements, is empowered to give the final ruling on whether a "restriction" or "penalty" is reconcilable with freedom of expression as protected by Article 10. The domestic margin of appreciation thus goes hand in hand with a European supervision. Such supervision concerns both the aim of the measure challenged and its "necessity"; it covers not only the basic legislation but also the decision applying it, even one given by an independent court ...

> It follows from this that it is in no way the Court's task to take the place of the competent national courts but rather to review under art 10 the decisions they delivered in the exercise of their power of appreciation.'[1]

What this 'European supervision' that 'goes hand-in-hand' with the margin of appreciation entails in many cases is the scrutiny of domestic decision-making procedures to ensure that these have given due respect to the rights protected by the Convention. 'Whenever discretion capable of interfering with the enjoyment of a Convention right is conferred on national authorities, the procedural safeguards available to the individual will be especially material in determining whether the respondent State has, when fixing the regulatory framework, remained within its margin of appreciation.'[2] Due process requirements help protect against arbitrary decision-making by public authorities in a range of areas[3]. The Court is thus accorded an opportunity to examine whether at domestic level there has been a convincing explanation of the proportionality of any interference, thus permitting it to respect the outcome of decisions taken by domestic authorities.

1   *Handyside v United Kingdom* (1976) A 24, at paras 48–50.

2   *DH and Others v Czech Republic* [GC] 2007-…, at para 206.

3   See eg para **6.52** below.

3.136 The concept of the margin of appreciation reflects a recognition on the part of the European Court of Human Rights that in certain circumstances, and to a certain extent, national authorities (including national courts) are better placed than the court itself to determine the outcome of the process of balancing individual and community interests, by reason of 'their direct and continuous contact with the vital forces of their countries'[1]. This reflects both the principle of subsidiarity – the primary role of national authorities in ensuring the effective securing of Convention guarantees – and the 'fourth instance' doctrine: that the Court exercises a supervisory jurisdiction at an international level, rather than being a final court of appeal of a domestic character. The Court has however been at pains to emphasise that the margin (where it exists) is limited, and that the Court itself takes the final decision when it reviews the assessment of the national authorities[2].

1   *Handyside v United Kingdom* (1976) A 24, at para 48.

2   *Klass and Others v Germany* (1978) A 28, para 49.

3.137 The existence and width of any margin of appreciation depends on the context. The doctrine has been applied when determining whether an interference with the rights protected by Articles 8–11 has been justified, and in determining whether a state has done enough to comply with its positive obligations under these and other articles[1]. It has also been applied in deciding whether an interference with the property rights protected by Article 1 of Protocol no 1 been justified[2], and in other contexts where an element of judgment by national authorities is involved (as in parts of Articles 5[3] and 6[4], and Articles 14[5] and 15[6]). In some contexts, such as Articles 2 and 3, the Court has not as yet recognised any margin of appreciation at all, and the scope for the doctrine would appear to be extremely limited in a context of that kind, since it does not normally require a balance to be struck between the interests of the individual and a wider public interest.

1   See eg *Abdulaziz, Cabales and Balkandali v United Kingdom* (1985) A 94, para 67; *Keegan v Ireland* (1994) A 290, para 49.

2   See eg *James and Others v United Kingdom* (1986) A 98.

3   See eg *Weeks v United Kingdom* (1987) A 114.

4   See eg *Osman v United Kingdom* 1998-VIII.

5   See eg *Rasmussen v Denmark* (1984) A 87, para 40.

6   See eg *Ireland v United Kingdom* (1978) A 25.

3.138 The width of the margin of appreciation depends fundamentally upon the extent to which it is appropriate for an international court to respect the view taken by the national authorities. That depends upon a number of factors, notably the language of the Convention provision, the existence or not of consensus among the majority of contracting states, the nature of the right protected, the nature of the obligation placed upon the state, the nature of the activity interfered with, the nature of the aim pursued by the restriction and the surrounding circumstances. A wide margin of appreciation therefore tends to be recognised in situations where national authorities must be allowed a wide measure of discretion, for example in dealing with public emergencies or issues of national security[1]. For the same reason, a wide margin tends to be recognised in contexts in which the Strasbourg Court accepts that widely differing views can legitimately be held, consistently with the ECHR: for example, in relation to sensitive moral issues such as the censorship of books or films[2], or issues of economic policy[3], or issues of social policy on which there is no European consensus such as abortion[4]. Thus, in a case concerned with the reform of the law of landlord and tenant, the Court said (in relation to Article 1 of Protocol no 1):

> 'Because of their direct knowledge of their society and its needs, the national authorities are in principle better placed than the international judge to appreciate what is "in the public interest". Under the system of protection established by the Convention, it is thus for the national authorities to make the initial assessment both of the existence of a problem of public concern warranting measures of deprivation of property and of the remedial action to be taken. Here, as in other fields to which the safeguards of the Convention extend, the national authorities accordingly enjoy a certain margin of appreciation.
>
> Furthermore, the notion of "public interest" is necessarily extensive. In particular, as the Commission noted, the decision to enact laws expropriating property will commonly involve consideration of political, economic and social issues on which opinions within a democratic society may reasonably differ widely. The Court, finding it natural that the margin of appreciation available to the legislature in implementing social and economic policies should be a wide one, will respect the legislature's judgment as to what is "in the public interest" unless that judgment be manifestly without reasonable foundation. In other words, although the Court cannot substitute it own assessment for that of the national authorities, it is bound to review the contested measures under art 1 of protocol 1 and, in so doing, to make an inquiry into the facts with reference to which the national authorities acted.'[5]

Even where a broad margin of appreciation is permitted, it is often said that the 'very essence' of the right must be protected. It is not clear what the doctrine of the 'very essence' of a right adds to the doctrine of proportionality.

1   See eg *Leander v Sweden* (1987) A 116, para 67.

2   See eg *Handyside v United Kingdom* (1976) A 24; *Wingrove v United Kingdom* 1996-V.

3   See eg *James and Others v United Kingdom* (1986) A 98, para 46; *Hatton and Others v United Kingdom* [GC] 2003-VIII.

4   See in particular *A, B and C v Ireland* [GC] 2010-..., paras 231–241 (recognition of a margin of appreciation as regards the balancing of the conflicting interests of a and its mother in light of the lack of European consensus on the scientific and legal definition of the beginning of life since the right of the foetus and mother were inextricably linked; the strong consensus among European states that abortion should be available to women either on request or for health-related or well-being reasons was not sufficient to narrow decisively this broad margin of appreciation).

5   *James and Others v United Kingdom* (1986) A 98, para 46.

3.139 On the other hand, the Court tends to adopt a more intrusive approach in contexts where it considers that there is less justification under the ECHR for allowing national authorities a wide discretion, for example in cases concerned with intimate aspects of private life[1] or freedom of political debate[2]. In relation to freedom of expression, for example, the Court has proceeded on the basis that the width of the margin of appreciation depends on the context, and in particular on the nature of the expression restricted and on the nature of the justification for the restriction. In a case concerned with blasphemy, the Court said:

'Whereas there is little scope under article 10(2) of the Convention for restrictions on political speech or on debate on questions of public interest, a wider margin of appreciation is generally available to the Contracting States when regulating freedom of expression in relation to matters liable to offend intimate personal convictions within the sphere of morals or, especially, religion. Moreover, as in the field of morals, and perhaps to an even greater degree, there is no uniform European conception of "the requirements of the protection of the rights of others" in relation to attacks on their religious convictions. What is likely to cause substantial offence to persons of a particular religious persuasion will vary significantly from time to time and from place to place, especially in an era characterised by an ever-growing array of faiths and denominations. By reason of their direct and continuous contact with the vital forces of their countries, State authorities are in principle in a better position than the international judge to give an opinion on the exact content of these requirements with regard to the rights of others as well as on the "necessity" of a "restriction" intended to protect from such material those whose deepest feelings and convictions would be seriously offended.'[3]

Where the justification for the interference is a less subjective concept, on which a broad consensus exists at a European level, such as the need to maintain the authority of the judiciary, the Court will exercise stricter supervision[4].

1   See eg *Dudgeon v United Kingdom* (1981) A 45. Note that the specific subject-matter, rather than the category of discrimination, is crucial: see (in relation to sexuality) *Alekseyev v Russia* 2010-..., at para 83:

'There is ample case-law reflecting a long-standing European consensus on such matters as abolition of criminal liability for homosexual relations between adults, homosexuals' access to service in the armed forces, the granting of parental rights, equality in tax matters and the right to succeed to the deceased partner's tenancy; more recent examples include equal ages of consent under criminal law for heterosexual and homosexual acts. At the same time, there remain issues where no European consensus has been reached, such as granting permission to same-sex couples to adopt a child and the right to marry, and the Court has confirmed the domestic authorities' wide margin of appreciation in respect of those issues. This, however, does not dispense the Court from the requirement to verify whether in each individual case the authorities did not overstep their margin of appreciation by acting arbitrarily or otherwise … The Government's reference to the concept of a "court of fourth instance" cannot prevent the Court from exercising its duties in that regard in accordance with the Convention and established case-law.'

2   See eg *Bowman v United Kingdom* 1998-I.

3   *Wingrove v United Kingdom* 1996-V, para 58.

4   *Sunday Times v United Kingdom (no 1)* (1979) A 30, para 59; *Rasmussen v Denmark* (1984) A 87, paras 40–41.

3.140 The margin of appreciation doctrine is essential in order to maintain the confidence of national institutions, including national courts, in the Strasbourg Court. There is, however, a view amongst national judges[1] in the UK and elsewhere that the doctrine has not been taken far enough. The doctrine proceeds on the basis that the Court is in principle competent to decide any question about the law of a contracting state which is touched by human rights law, but sometimes abstains from exercising this vast jurisdiction on the ground that domestic courts and other institutions are likely to have a better knowledge of local conditions. This approach is criticised, particularly in the UK, partly on the basis that it undermines democratic processes. In that regard, it is relevant to note that the long tradition of Parliamentary sovereignty in the UK legal order has no parallel elsewhere in Europe. The Strasbourg Court's approach is also criticised on the basis that domestic courts always have a better knowledge of local circumstances and legal traditions – and greater constitutional legitimacy – than an international court, enabling them to be the best judges, in general, of how the balance between the competing values protected by the ECHR should be struck in a particular society. One of the core values of the Convention is said to be the maintenance of a pluralist, democratic society subject to the rule of law. National courts are interlocutors for their individual systems and societies. They potentially have an important role, in the Convention system, in explaining why a particular rule exists in their particular system. There are signs that the Strasbourg Court is willing to engage in a dialogue with national courts, such as the UK Supreme Court, with developments in the jurisprudence being winnowed out through a process in which the national court sets out its view of the relationship between the existing Strasbourg case law and the UK legal systems, and the issue is then re-considered by the Strasbourg Court in the light of the national court's observations[2]. The dialogue can, of course, also result in a modification of the approach adopted by the national court[3].

1   See eg Lord Hoffmann 'The Universality of Human Rights' (2009) 125 LQR 416; and Pinto-Duschinsky *Bringing Rights Home: Making Human Rights Compatible with Parliamentary Democracy in the United Kingdom* (2011).

2   See eg *Bellinger v Bellinger* [2003] 2 AC 467; and *Christine Goodwin v United Kingdom* [GC] 2002-VI.

3   See eg *Manchester City Council v Pinnock* [2010] 3 WLR 1441, which followed the Strasbourg Court's judgment in *Kay and Others v United Kingdom* (21 September 2010).

The fourth instance doctrine

3.141 By the 'fourth instance' doctrine is meant the principle that the European Court of Human Rights will not act as an appellate court[1] (the expression 'fourth instance' derives from there being typically two levels of appellate court, beyond the court of first instance, within national legal systems). The Court therefore treats the assessment of national law as primarily a matter for the national courts[2]; and it will not interfere with their findings of fact, unless they have drawn arbitrary conclusions from the evidence before them[3].

1   See eg *García Ruiz v Spain* [GC] 1999-I, para 28.

2   See eg *Winterwerp v Netherlands* (1979) A 33, para 46; contrast *Van Kuck v Germany* 2003-VII; and *Von Hannover v Germany* 2004-VI.

3   See eg *Edwards v United Kingdom* (1992) A 247-B, para 34.

Proportionality, the margin of appreciation and national courts

3.142 The doctrine of the margin of appreciation reflects the way in which the function of an international court differs from that of a national court. The doctrine is essentially a basis for demarcating between the area in which an international court will interfere and the area in which it will not interfere. More specifically, it is a basis for judging the extent to which proportionality – the balance between individual rights and the community interest – should be assessed at the national level rather than the international level. Since the doctrine of the margin of appreciation is a principle relevant to the exercise of jurisdiction at the international level, it is not directly relevant to the application of Convention rights under the HRA 1998 or the SA 1998. It has been said that domestic courts applying Convention rights must, however, decide how the area of judgment allowed by that margin should be distributed between the legislative, executive and judicial branches of government[1].

1   *R (SB) v Governors of Denbigh High School* [2007] 1 AC 100 at para 63 per Lord Hoffmann, with whom Lord Bingham of Cornhill and Lord Scott of Foscote agreed. See also *In re G (Adoption: Unmarried Couple)* [2009] AC 173, eg at paras 32 and 37 per Lord Hoffmann. See further para **3.142–3.147** below.

3.143 Domestic courts deciding questions relating to Convention rights under the HRA 1998 or the SA 1998 'must themselves form a judgment whether a Convention right has been breached'[1]. The consequent distinction between the approach to be adopted under the HRA 1998 and the approach adopted in domestic administrative law was explained by Lord Hoffmann in *R (Nasseri) v Secretary of State for the Home Department*:

'It is understandable that a judge hearing an application for judicial review should think that he is undertaking a review of the Secretary of State's decision in accordance with normal principles of administrative law, that is to say, that he is reviewing the decision-making process rather than the merits of the decision. In such a case, the court is concerned with whether the Secretary of State gave proper consideration to relevant matters rather than whether she reached what the court would consider to be the right answer. But that is not the correct approach when the challenge is based upon an alleged infringement of a Convention right. In the *Denbigh High School* case,[2] which was concerned with whether the decision of a school to require pupils to wear a uniform infringed their right to manifest their religious beliefs, Lord Bingham of Cornhill said, in para 29:

"the focus at Strasbourg is not and never has been on whether a challenged decision or action is the product of a defective decision-making process, but on whether, in the case under consideration, the applicant's Convention rights have been violated."

Likewise, I said, in para 68:

"In domestic judicial review, the court is usually concerned with whether the decision-maker reached his decision in the right way rather than whether he got what the court might think to be the right answer. But article 9 is concerned with substance, not procedure. It confers no right to have the decision made in any particular way. What matters is the result: was the right to manifest a religious belief restricted in a way which is not justified under article 9(2)?"

The other side of the coin is that, when breach of a Convention right is in issue, an impeccable decision-making process by the Secretary of State will be of no avail if she actually gets the answer wrong. That was the basis of the decision of the House of Lords in *Huang v Secretary of State for the Home Department*,[3] in which the question was whether the removal of a migrant would infringe his right to respect for family life under article 8. The Appellate Committee said, in para 11:

"the task of the appellate immigration authority, on an appeal on a Convention ground against a decision of the primary official decision-maker refusing leave to enter or remain in this country, is to decide whether the challenged decision is unlawful as incompatible with a Convention right or compatible and so lawful. It is not a secondary, reviewing, function dependent on establishing that the primary decision-maker misdirected himself or acted irrationally or was guilty of procedural impropriety."'[4]

---

1   *R (Daly) v Secretary of State for the Home Department* [2001] 2 AC 532 at para 23 per Lord Bingham of Cornhill; similarly *A v Secretary of State for the Home Department* [2005] 2 AC 68 at para 40.

2   *R (SB) v Governors of Denbigh High School* [2007] 1 AC 100.

3   *Huang v Secretary of State for the Home Department* [2007] 2 AC 167. Proportionality is not a pure question of fact, and therefore falls within the scope on an appeal on the ground of error of law: *A v Secretary of State for the Home Department* [2005] 2 AC 68 at para 44 per Lord Bingham of Cornhill.

4   *R (Nasseri) v Secretary of State for the Home Department* [2010] 1 AC 1 at paras 12–14. The
     distinction was also discussed in *R v Shayler* [2003] 1 AC 247 at para 33 per Lord Bingham of
     Cornhill and at paras 75–78 per Lord Hope of Craighead; in *R (SB) v Governors of Denbigh
     High School* [2007] 1 AC 100 at paras 29–31 per Lord Bingham of Cornhill and at para 68 per
     Lord Hoffmann; and in *Huang v Secretary of State for the Home Department* [2007] 2 AC 167.

3.144 Guidance as to the approach to be adopted in assessing proportionality
under domestic law has been given in numerous cases under the HRA 1998[1].
The court should ask itself:

> '... whether: (i) the legislative objective is sufficiently important to justify limiting a
> fundamental right; (ii) the measures designed to meet the legislative objective are
> rationally connected to it; and (iii) the means used to impair the right or freedom are
> no more than is necessary to accomplish the objective.'

Lord Hope of Craighead observed in the later case of *R v Shayler*:

> '... it is not enough to assert that the decision that was taken was a reasonable one.
> A close and penetrating examination of the factual justification for the restriction is
> needed if the fundamental rights enshrined in the Convention are to remain practical
> and effective for everyone who wishes to exercise them.'[2]

It has also been observed that the need to balance the interests of society with
those of individuals and groups must never be overlooked: the judgment on
proportionality:

> 'must always involve the striking of a fair balance between the rights of the individual
> and the interests of the community which is inherent in the whole of the Convention.
> The severity and consequences of the interference will call for careful assessment
> at this stage.'[3]

Applying this approach, the application of blanket rules which interfere with
Convention rights without regard to individual circumstances has been found
difficult to justify in contexts where individual circumstances were of critical
importance[4]. On the other hand, there are situations where, for administrative or
other reasons, 'bright line' rules may be justifiable. In a case concerned with a
provision in consumer credit legislation designed to protect consumers, Lord
Nicholls of Birkenhead observed:

> 'Parliament may consider the response should be a uniform solution across the
> board. A tailor-made response, fitting the facts of each case as decided in an
> application to the court, may not be appropriate.'[5]

1   See eg *R (Daly) v Secretary of State for the Home Department* [2001] 2 AC 532; *R v A (No 2)*
     [2002] 1 AC 45; *R (Pretty) v Director of Public Prosecutions* [2002] 1 AC 800; *R v Shayler*
     [2003] 1 AC 247; *A v Secretary of State for the Home Department* [2005] 2 AC 68. In so far as
     some dicta in domestic cases appear to suggest that proportionality requires the adoption of
     the 'least onerous measure' or 'less restrictive alternative', it has been correctly observed that
     that is not a general element of the test of proportionality under the ECHR. See eg *R (Clay's
     Lane Housing Co-operative Ltd) v Housing Corporation* [2005] 1 WLR 2229; *R (Wilson) v
     Wychavon District Council* [2007] QB 801 at paras 61 and 62 per Richards LJ:

'The "less restrictive alternative" test is not an integral part of the analysis of proportionality under Art. 14. [...] It does not follow that the existence of a less restrictive alternative is altogether irrelevant in the context of Art.14. It seems to me that in an appropriate case it can properly be considered as one of the tools of analysis in examining the cogency of the reasons put forward in justification of a measure; and the narrower the margin of appreciation or discretionary area of judgment, or the more intense the degree of scrutiny required, the more significant it may be that a less restrictive alternative could have been adopted. It is not necessarily determinative, but it may help in answering the fundamental question whether there is a reasonable relationship of proportionality between the means employed and the aim sought to be realised.'

See also paras **3.60–3.63** above.

2   *R v Shayler* [2003] 1 AC 247 at para 61.

3   *Huang v Secretary of State for the Home Department* [2007] 2 AC 167 at para 19.

4   See eg *R (Daly) v Secretary of State for the Home Department* [2001] 2 AC 532 (rule requiring prisoners' absence whenever legally privileged correspondence examined); *R v A (No 2)* [2002] 1 AC 45 (statutory provision relating to trials for sexual offences which excluded evidence of previous sexual relationship between complainant and defendant); *In re G (Adoption: Unmarried Couple)* [2009] AC 173 (provision allowing only married couple to apply for an adoption order). Contrast *R v Shayler* [2003] 1 AC 247 (prohibition on disclosure of confidential information by members and former members of the security services unless authorised: safeguards built into system).

5   *Wilson v First County Trust Ltd (No 2)* [2004] 1 AC 816 at para 74. See also *R (Hooper) v Secretary of State for Work and Pensions* [2005] 1 WLR 1681 at para 16 per Lord Hoffmann (social security benefits: 'No doubt means testing would have been more discriminating but the use of more complicated criteria increases the expense of administration and reduces take-up by those entitled'); *R (Carson) v Secretary of State for Work and Pensions* [2006] 1 AC 173 (social security benefits); *R (Animal Defenders International) v Secretary of State for Culture, Media and Sport* [2008] AC 1312 at para 33 per Lord Bingham of Cornhill; *R (RJM) v Secretary of State for Work and Pensions* [2009] AC 311 at para 54 per Lord Neuberger of Abbotsbury (social security).

3.145 Although national courts must decide whether, in their judgment, the requirement of proportionality is satisfied, there is at the same time nothing in the Convention, or in the HRA 1998, which requires national courts to substitute their own views for those of other public authorities on all matters of policy, judgment and discretion. As Lord Bingham of Cornhill observed in *Brown v Stott*:

'Judicial recognition and assertion of the human rights defined in the Convention is not a substitute for the processes of democratic government but a complement to them. While a national court does not accord the margin of appreciation recognised by the European Court as a supra-national court, it will give weight to the decisions of a representative legislature and a democratic government within the discretionary area of judgment accorded to those bodies.'[1]

1   *Brown v Stott* 2001 SC (PC) 43 at pp 58–59 per Lord Bingham of Cornhill.

3.146 The approach of the courts to the 'discretionary area of judgment', as Lord Bingham described it in *Brown v Stott*, has developed over time. In the earlier case of *R v Director of Public Prosecutions, ex p Kebilene*, Lord Hope of Craighead had referred to:

'... an area of judgment within which the judiciary will defer, on democratic grounds, to the considered opinion of the elected body or person whose act or decision is said to be incompatible with the Convention ... the area in which these choices may arise is conveniently and appropriately described as the "discretionary area of judgment". It will be easier for such an area of judgment to be recognised where the Convention itself requires a balance to be struck, much less so where the right is stated in terms which are unqualified. It will be easier for it to be recognised where the issues involve questions of social or economic policy, much less so where the courts are especially well placed to assess the need for protection.'[1]

In the later case of *R (ProLife Alliance) v British Broadcasting Corporation* Lord Hoffmann criticised the use of the term 'deference' and explained that the issue was one of law:

'... although the word 'deference' is now very popular in describing the relationship between the judicial and the other branches of government, I do not think that its overtones of servility, or perhaps gracious concession, are appropriate to describe what is happening. In a society based upon the rule of law and the separation of powers, it is necessary to decide which branch of government has in any particular instance the decision-making power and what the legal limits of that power are. That is a question of law and must therefore be decided by the courts.

... The principles upon which decision-making powers are allocated are principles of law. The courts are the independent branch of government and the legislature and executive are, directly and indirectly respectively, the elected branches of government. Independence makes the courts more suited to deciding some kinds of questions and being elected makes the legislature or executive more suited to deciding others. The allocation of these decision-making responsibilities is based upon recognised principles. The principle that the independence of the courts is necessary for a proper decision of disputed legal rights or claims of violations of human rights is a legal principle. It is reflected in article 6 of the Convention. On the other hand, the principle that majority approval is necessary for a proper decision on policy or allocation of resources is also a legal principle. Likewise, when a court decides that a decision is within the proper competence of the legislature or executive, it is not showing deference. It is deciding the law.'[2]

Similarly in *A v Secretary of State for the Home Department* Lord Bingham declined to use the term 'deference' and stated:

'It is perhaps preferable to approach this question as one of demarcation of functions or ... "relative institutional competence". The more purely political (in a broad or narrow sense) a question is, the more appropriate it will be for political resolution and the less likely it is to be an appropriate matter for judicial decision. The smaller, therefore, will be the potential role of the court. It is the function of political and not judicial bodies to resolve political questions. Conversely, the greater the legal content of any issue, the greater the potential role of the court, because under our constitution and subject to the sovereign power of Parliament it is the function of the courts and not of political bodies to resolve legal questions.'[3]

Lord Bingham also explained in the same case the democratic role of the courts, rejecting a distinction which had been drawn in argument between democratic institutions and the courts:

'It is of course true that the judges in this country are not elected and are not answerable to Parliament. It is also of course true … that Parliament, the executive and the courts have different functions. But the function of independent judges charged to interpret and apply the law is universally recognised as a cardinal feature of the modern democratic state, a cornerstone of the rule of law itself. The Attorney General is fully entitled to insist on the proper limits of judicial authority, but he is wrong to stigmatise judicial decision-making as in some way undemocratic. It is particularly inappropriate in a case such as the present in which Parliament has expressly legislated [in the HRA 1998] to render unlawful any act of a public authority, including a court, incompatible with a Convention right … The effect is not, of course, to override the sovereign legislative authority of the Queen in Parliament, since if primary legislation is declared to be incompatible the validity of the legislation is unaffected (section 4(6)) and the remedy lies with the appropriate minister (section 10), who is answerable to Parliament. The 1998 Act gives the courts a very specific, wholly democratic, mandate.'[4]

It is by determining the appropriate demarcation of functions that the domestic courts decide how the area of judgment allowed by the Strasbourg Court, applying the margin of appreciation doctrine, should be distributed between the courts and the elected branches of government[5].

1   *R v Director of Public Prosecutions, ex p Kebilene* [2000] 2 AC 326 at p 386 per Lord Hope of Craighead.

2   *ProLife Alliance v British Broadcasting Corporation* [2004] 1 AC 185 per Lord Hoffmann at paras 75–76.

3   *A v Secretary of State for the Home Department* [2005] 2 AC 68 at para 29. See also *Huang v Secretary of State for the Home Department* [2007] 2 AC 167 at para 16.

4   *A v Secretary of State for the Home Department* [2005] 2 AC 68 at para 42. See also per Lord Hope of Craighead at paras 113–114.

5   See *A v Secretary of State for the Home Department* [2005] 2 AC 68 at paras 113–114 and 131 per Lord Hope of Craighead and at para 176 per Lord Rodger of Earlsferry.

3.147 The intensity of review involved in deciding whether the test of proportionality is met will therefore depend on the context[1]. It has been said that 'the best guide as to whether the courts should deal with the issue is whether it lies within the field of social or economic policy on the one hand or of the constitutional responsibility which resides especially with them on the other'[2]. The legislature's or executive's decision is less likely to be interfered with 'where the Convention itself requires a balance to be struck than where the right is stated in terms which are unqualified'[3]. In a pre-HRA 1998 case in which an illegal entrant challenged the refusal of exceptional leave to remain on the basis that the Secretary of State had wrongly rejected his claim that he would, if returned to his country of origin, be subjected to treatment contrary to Article 3 of the Convention, Simon Brown LJ observed:

'This is not an area in which the court will pay any especial deference to the Secretary of State's conclusion on the facts. In the first place, the human right involved here – the right not to be exposed to a real risk of art 3 ill-treatment – is both absolute and fundamental: it is not a qualified right requiring a balance to be struck with some competing social need. Secondly, the court here is hardly less well placed than the Secretary of State himself to evaluate the risk once the relevant material is placed before it ... In circumstances such as these, what has been called the "discretionary area of judgment" ... is a decidedly narrow one.'[4]

Similarly, the court is qualified to make its own judgment as to the requirements of a fair trial[5]; and 'courts are specialists in the protection of liberty'[6]. Discrimination in an area of social policy has also been said to lie within the constitutional responsibility of the courts[7]. Thus, even where Parliament has legislated on a question of social policy, the court may intervene. In *In re G (Adoption: Unmarried Couple)*, for example, legislation allowed only married couples to apply for an adoption order. It was argued that this reflected a belief that married couples were more likely to be suitable adoptive parents than unmarried ones. The legislation was held to be incompatible with Convention rights. Lord Hoffmann stated:

'The judge and the Court of Appeal both emphasised that the question of whether unmarried couples should be allowed to adopt raised a question of social policy and that social policy was in principle a matter for the legislature. That is true in the sense that where questions of social policy admit of more than one rational choice, the courts will ordinarily regard that choice as being a matter for Parliament ... But that does not mean that Parliament is entitled to discriminate in any case which can be described as social policy. The discrimination must at least have a rational basis. In this case, it seems to me to be based upon a straightforward fallacy, namely, that a reasonable generalisation can be turned into an irrebuttable presumption for individual cases.'[8]

On the other hand, in a case concerned with consumer credit legislation, where no issue of discrimination was raised, Lord Nicholls of Birkenhead said:

'Parliament is charged with the primary responsibility for deciding whether the means chosen to deal with a social problem are both necessary and appropriate. Assessment of the advantages and disadvantages of the various legislative alternatives is primarily a matter for Parliament ... The court will reach a different conclusion from the legislature only when it is apparent that the legislature has attached insufficient importance to a person's Convention right. The readiness of a court to depart from the views of the legislature depends upon the circumstances, one of which is the subject matter of the legislation. The more the legislation concerns matters of broad social policy, the less ready will be a court to intervene.'[9]

---

1   *R (Daly) v Secretary of State for the Home Department* [2001] 2 AC 532 at para 28 per Lord Steyn. See also *ProLife Alliance v British Broadcasting Corporation* [2004] 1 AC 185 per Lord Walker of Gestingthorpe at paras 131–144; *A v Secretary of State for the Home Department* [2005] 2 AC 68 at para 80 per Lord Nicholls of Birkenhead and at paras 107–108 per Lord Hope of Craighead; *Huang v Secretary of State for the Home Department* [2007] 2 AC 167 at para 17; and *R (RJM) v Secretary of State for Work and Pensions* [2009] AC 311 at para 56 per Lord Neuberger of Abbotsbury .

2   *In re G (Adoption: Unmarried Couple)* [2009] AC 173 at para 48 per Lord Hope of Craighead.

3   *R v Director of Public Prosecutions, ex p Kebilene* [2000] 2 AC 326 at p 381 per Lord Hope of Craighead; *ProLife Alliance v British Broadcasting Corporation* [2004] 1 AC 185 per Lord Walker of Gestingthorpe at paras 136–137.

4   *R (Turgut) v Secretary of State for the Home Department* [2001] 1 All ER 719, 729.

5   *R v A (No 2)* [2002] 1 AC 45 at para 36 per Lord Steyn: '[W]hen the question arises whether in the criminal statute in question Parliament adopted a legislative scheme which makes an excessive inroad into the right to a fair trial the court is qualified to make its own judgment and must do so.'

6   *A v Secretary of State for the Home Department* [2005] 2 AC 68 at para 178 per Lord Rodger of Earlsferry (quoting La Forest J in *RJR-MacDonald Inc v Attorney General of Canada* [1995] 3 SCR 199 at 277).

7   *In re G (Adoption: Unmarried Couple)* [2009] AC 173 at para 48 per Lord Hope of Craighead.

8   *In re G (Unmarried Couple)* [2009] AC 173 at para 20 per Lord Hoffmann.

9   *Wilson v First County Trust Ltd (No 2)* [2004] 1 AC 816 at para 70.

Chapter 4

Physical integrity: life, torture and inhuman treatment, servitude, and liberty of person

INTRODUCTION

4.01 Protection of the physical integrity of the individual[1] is a central concern of any system of protection of civil rights. The widespread loss of life, use of torture and inhuman treatment, imposition of enforced labour, and arbitrary use of detention occasioned by totalitarianism provided compelling justification for the ECHR's first four substantive guarantees: the right to life (Art 2), prohibition of torture or inhuman or degrading treatment or punishment (Art 3), prohibition of slavery and forced or compulsory labour (Art 4), and the right to liberty and security of person (Art 5)[2]. These articles are seen as having a close inter-relationship[3]. However, while the inclusion and textual formulation of each of these guarantees can be explained by the past, they are interpreted in accordance with modern requirements: the European Court of Human Rights gives the highest priority to these guarantees and there is little scope for application of any state margin of appreciation[4]. The Court has also proved capable of creative interpretation, extrapolating from the text positive duties such as carrying out adequate investigations into death or allegations of ill-treatment, and providing opportunities for periodic review of continuing detention. Further developments are by no means improbable since the ECHR requires to be interpreted as a 'living instrument'[5].

---

1   'Physical integrity' here implies a general concern for the protection of the human body (for example, Berger *Jurisprudence de la Cour Européenne des Droits de l'Homme* (10th edn, 2007) deals with ECHR, Arts 2–5 and Art 2 of Prot 4 under the title of 'La Liberté Physique'); alternatively, in a narrower sense the idea may refer solely to infliction of physical or psychological harm, and thus Gomien, Harris and Zwack in *Law and Practice of the European Convention on Human Rights* (1996) use the term as a shorthand reference for torture or inhuman or degrading treatment or punishment. Cf the Charter of Fundamental Rights of the European Union: Art 1 provides that 'human dignity is inviolable [and] must be respected and protected', while Art 3(1) provides that '[e]veryone has the right to respect for his or her physical and mental integrity': in this context, 'dignity' appears to be a foundation for claims for human rights, and 'physical and mental integrity' may also encompass issues falling within the scope of ECHR, Arts 8 and 9. The only explicit reference in the ECHR to 'human dignity' is in the preamble to Prot 13 (in noting that the abolition of the death penalty is 'essential... for the full recognition of the inherent dignity of all human beings'; and see also *Pretty v United Kingdom* 2002-III, para 65: 'The very essence of [the ECHR] is respect for human dignity and human freedom'. For discussion of the concept of 'dignity' in human rights, see eg McCrudden 'Human Dignity and Judicial Interpretation of Human Rights' (2008) 19 EJIL 655.

2   The historical legacy of these guarantees is still reflected in the text (in particular, in its references to capital punishment and compulsory military service, both of which were

commonplace at the time of drafting but which are now subject to significant qualification: see paras **4.54–4.58** and **4.143** below). ECHR, Art 15, which protects, inter alia, the most crucial aspects of Arts 2, 3 and 4 from state derogation in time of emergency, represents a further example of the central importance of physical integrity to the framers of the ECHR. For discussion of the extent to which contemporary practice and heightened expectations may influence textual provision, see para **4.61** below.

3   Cf *Kurt v Turkey* 1998-III, at para 123: 'Prompt judicial intervention [under Arts 5(3) and (4)] may lead to the detection and prevention of life-threatening measures or serious ill-treatment which violate the fundamental guarantees contained in Articles 2 and 3 of the Convention. ... What is at stake is both the protection of the physical liberty of individuals as well as their personal security in a context which, in the absence of safeguards, could result in a subversion of the rule of law and place detainees beyond the reach of the most rudimentary forms of legal protection.'

4   In *McCann and Others v United Kingdom* (1995) A 324, paras 146 and 147, the European Court of Human Rights offered justification for strict construction of Arts 2 and 3 by identifying their paramount importance in the scheme of Convention protection. This approach to interpretation was extended to include the right not to be subjected to the death penalty in *Al-Saadoon and Mufdhi v United Kingdom* 2010-..., para 118, discussed at para **4.58** below. Cf Callewaert 'Is there a Margin of Appreciation in the Application of Articles 2, 3 and 4 of the Convention?' (1998) 19 HRLJ 6. The detailed text of Art 5 also provides restricted latitude for states in decision-making: Mahoney 'The Doctrine of the Margin of Appreciation under the European Convention on Human Rights: Its Legitimacy in Theory and Application in Practice' (1998) 19 HRLJ 1 at p 5.

5   For discussion of the evolution of the right not to be subjected to the death penalty and recent developments, see para **4.54–4.58** below. There has been no common European consensus on abortion, and until now this has been difficult to bring within the sphere of Convention protection: see further paras **4.51** and **6.55** below.

4.02 Advances in the protection of personal integrity have also been achieved through additional optional protocols, as with Protocols nos 6 and 13 which provide for the right not to be subjected to the death penalty, and Article 1 of Protocol no 4, which removes inability to fulfil a contractual obligation from being a legitimate ground for deprivation of liberty[1]. The United Kingdom has ratified Protocols nos 6 and 13[2], but not Protocol no 4. Additionally, applicants have successfully relied upon Article 8's guarantee of respect for private and family life to broaden protection of physical integrity[3], and this provision has now a close relationship with (and may on occasion now be indistinguishable from) Article 3 in certain circumstances[4]. These provisions are in addition to any principles of international human rights law applied in domestic legal systems[5].

1   The United Kingdom has not ratified Prot 4. See para **4.174** below.

2   The White Paper, *Rights Brought Home* (Cm 3782) originally proposed that ratification of Prot 6 would proceed on a free vote in Parliament. Consequently, the Human Rights Bill at first did not propose to include abolition of the death penalty in its scope. However, the Government subsequently proposed an amendment to the Bill during its parliamentary stages to include this Protocol, and formally ratified it in May 1999 (with entry into force on June 1999). The United Kingdom ratified Prot 13 in October 2003 (with entry into force in February 2004). Protocol 13, Arts 1 and 2 are 'Convention rights' for the purposes of the Human Rights Act 1998: The Human Rights Act 1998 (Amendment) Order 2004 (SI 2004/1574). Art 1 of Prot 13 was invoked, unsuccessfully, in *Al-Saadoon v Secretary of State for Defence* [2010] QB 486.

3   In particular, in respect of physical assault and failure to provide protection against environmental pollution: see paras **6.119–6.121** and **6.125–6.128** below.

4   See eg *VC v Slovakia* (dec) (16 June 2009) (sterilisation of Roma woman in a public hospital during the delivery of her second child and allegedly without her informed consent: admissible under Arts 3, 8 12, 13 and 14); and *ES and Others v Slovakia* (15 September 2009), paras 43–44 (failure to provide protection to wife and children: violation of Arts 3 and 8).

5   Cf *R v Bow Street Metropolitan Stipendiary Magistrate, ex p Pinochet Ugarte (No 3)* [2000] 1 AC 147.

RIGHT TO LIFE: ARTICLE 2 AND PROTOCOL NO 13

Scope of the right to life

4.03 The formulation of Article 2 reflects a deliberate determination to provide a more detailed elaboration than the equivalent phrase in the Universal Declaration of Human Rights that 'everyone has the right to life, to liberty and security of person'[1]. The fundamental purpose of Article 2 is to protect individuals from unlawful killing and other real threats to life. Both positive and negative obligations arise. Paragraph (1) requires that the right to life 'shall be protected by law', and the guarantee thus imposes positive duties of a substantive nature involving the provision of an appropriate legal or administrative framework regulating the right to life and backed up by appropriate sanction in case of breach as well as the taking of reasonable measures to counteract threats to life. Paragraph 2 further defines the limited circumstances in which the deprivation of life by state officials may be considered justified and establishes a demanding test whereby any force deployed by the state must not have been in excess of what was 'absolutely necessary'[2]. These substantive obligations are supplemented by a procedural obligation to carry out an investigation into loss of life, a separate and autonomous duty that may be considered as a 'detachable obligation'[3].

1   Universal Declaration of Human Rights, Art 3. For general discussion of Art 2, see Korff *The Right to Life: a Guide to the Implementation of Article 2 of the European Convention on Human Rights* (2006).

2   See paras **4.08–4.13** below.

3   *Šilih v Slovenia* [GC] (9 April 2009), at para 159 (thus the procedural obligation to carry out an effective investigation into loss of life is capable of binding a state even when the death took place before the entry into force of the ECHR).

4.04 No derogation from Article 2 by a state in time of war or other public emergency is permissible except in the case of deaths resulting from lawful acts of war[1]. A strict construction is necessary of Articles 2, 3 and Article 1 of Protocol 13 on account of their recognition as fundamental rights enshrining the basic values of the democratic societies making up the Council of Europe[2].

1   ECHR, Art 15(2), discussed at paras **4.147** and **4.148** below. Cf *Isayeva v Russia* (24 February 2005) at para 191: 'the use of indiscriminate weapons such as heavy free-falling high-explosion aviation bombs in a populated area, outside wartime and without prior evacuation of civilians,

is impossible to reconcile with the degree of caution expected from a law-enforcement body in a democratic society. No martial law and no state of emergency has been declared in [the region], and no derogation has been made under Article 15 of the Convention.' See also *Varnava and Others v Turkey* [GC] 2009-..., para 185 (Art 2 had to be interpreted in the light of the general principles of international law (including international humanitarian law), and thus states were under an obligation in a zone of international conflict to protect the lives of those not or no longer engaged in hostilities, including providing of medical assistance to the wounded, information on the identity and fate of those concerned, and proper disposal of remains of the dead).

2   *McCann and Others v United Kingdom* (1995) A 324, para 147; and *Al-Saadoon and Mufdhi v United Kingdom* 2010-..., para 113.

4.05 Much of the jurisprudence of the European Court of Human Rights in this area is of comparatively recent origin, but judgments in which a finding of a violation of Article 2 is established are now not infrequent[1]. Article 2 issues are likely to arise in respect of intentional or negligent killing of individuals by state officials, effective protection against risks to life, the investigation and prosecution of homicides, and the threatened deportation or extradition of individuals where there would be a real risk to life. However, it has not yet been accepted that this article can be implemented to require the prohibition or punishment of abortion or euthanasia or assisted suicide[2]. Further, the Court seems reluctant to interpret the provision in such a way as to place restrictions upon decision-making in economic or social spheres, and Article 2 cannot be used readily to found any claim of an essentially economic or social nature, for example, to require the provision of adequate social welfare benefits or housing necessary to sustain life[3]. On the other hand, where a state has undertaken to make health care available generally within a state, the denial of health care may possibly give rise to an issue under Article 2 where this can be shown to place an individual's life at risk[4]; additionally, state authorities may be under a positive obligation to protect life by taking preventive measures in the delivery of health care (for example, against the spread of HIV through blood transfusions)[5]. In any event, Article 2 cannot be used to seek to challenge decision-making concerning political or economical policy which has no direct impact upon an individual[6].

1   The first judgment establishing a violation of Art 2 was that of *McCann and Others v United Kingdom* (1995) A 324, discussed at para **4.11** below. Between 1999 and 2009, violations of deprivation of life were established in 217 judgments and of the lack of an effective procedural investigation in 304 judgments. Most of these violations have been established in the period since 2006. These cases have only involved a handful of states, in particular Russia (19 in this period), Bulgaria (11), and the United Kingdom, with the highest number of violations involving Turkey (139 of the total number of 190). A significant number of pending applications involves the situation in the Chechen Republic in Russia, including enforced disappearances and unlawful killings by officials, with little indication that adverse Court judgments are leading to action on the part of the state: see Report on Legal Remedies for Human Rights Violations in the North Caucasus, PACE doc 12276 and Parliamentary Assembly Recommendation 1738 (2010). See further Abresch 'A Human Rights Law of Internal Armed Conflict: the European Court of Human Rights in Chechnya' (2005) 16 EJIL 741.

2   See paras **4.51–4.53** below.

3   The ECHR cannot be interpreted as requiring particular economic or social measures: 40772/

98, *Pancenko v Latvia* (28 October 1999) (complaint concerning precarious economic and social situation arising from refusal of residence permit declared inadmissible: the ECHR does not guarantee the right to a rent-free residence, the right to work, or the right to medical assistance or financial assistance). See also (in respect of Art 3) *Budina v Russia* (dec) 2009- … (level of old-age pension alleged to be insufficient to maintain adequate standard of living, but while state responsibility could arise for 'treatment' where an applicant wholly dependent on state support found herself faced with official indifference when in a situation of serious deprivation or want, here it could not be said that the level of benefits available were insufficient to protect her from damage to her physical or mental health or from a situation of degradation incompatible with human dignity: inadmissible); and *N v United Kingdom* [GC] 2008-…, discussed at para **4.137** below. However, deliberate action such as eviction leading to the threat of loss of life may fall within the scope of Art 2: 5207/71, *X v Germany* (1971) YB 14, 698 (question whether eviction may of chronically ill applicant from her home could give rise to Art 2 considerations left open); 35638/97, *WM v Germany* (2 July 1997) (question of risk of suicide upon eviction from property sufficiently examined before order granted); *Mikayil Mammadov v Azerbaijan* (17 December 2009), paras 106–121 (no violation of the substantive aspect of Art 2 in respect of the suicide of the appellant's wife during the family's eviction from their home); and *Watts v United Kingdom* (dec) (4 May 2010) ('a badly managed transfer of elderly residents of a care home could well have a negative impact on their life expectancy as a result of the general frailty and resistance to change of older people' and thus Art 2 was applicable, but 'the extent of any obligation to take specific measures … and in particular the proportionality of any measures called for by the applicant, must be assessed in light of the equivocal medical evidence as to the extent of any risk to life'. Cf *Apostolakis v Greece* (22 October 2009), paras 35–43 (automatic loss of pension rights and welfare benefits as a result of a criminal conviction with no causal link with retirement rights: violation of Prot 1, Art 1, as total forfeiture of any right to a pension and social cover both amounted to a double punishment and extinguished the principal means of subsistence of a person). For Commonwealth discussion, see *Government of the Republic of South Africa v Grootboom* 2001 (1) SA 46 (CC) [South Africa] (temporary accommodation for evicted squatters ordered).

4   Cf 32647/96, *Passannante v Italy* (1998) DR 94, 91 (where a state has assumed responsibilities for health care, an excessive delay in treatment which is likely to have an impact on a patient's health may give rise to an Art 8 issue); *Cyprus v Turkey* 2001-IV, para 219 (no violation established under Art 2, and issue of access to medical facilities considered under Art 8; no need in this case to consider the extent of any possible positive duty under Art 2 to make available a certain standard of health care); *Nitecki v Poland* (dec) (21 March 2001) (not excluded that Art 2 responsibility may be engaged in certain cases in relation to health care policy); and *Sieminska v Poland* (dec) (29 March 2001) (responsibility to have regulations in place for protection of patients). Note, though, the recognition of a wide margin of appreciation in cases involving allocation of resources in medical treatment: *Pentiacova and Others v Moldova* (dec) 2005-I, noted below at para **6.44** n 2. For domestic discussion see para **4.33** below.

5   *Oyal v Turkey* (23 March 2010), paras 53–61 (Art 2 applicable).

6   9833/82, *H v United Kingdom* DR 43, 53; 22869/93, *Tugar v Italy* (1995) DR 83, 26 (no state responsibility for sale of mines to Iraq); and 28204/95, *Tauira and Others v France* (1995) DR 83, 112 (resumption of nuclear testing: the applicants were not 'victims').

The meaning of 'victim' for the purposes of Article 2

4.06 Applications involving alleged violations of the ECHR may be brought by those who can claim legitimately to qualify as 'victims' in terms of Article 34[1]. In the context of Article 2, applications may normally be brought by a deceased's spouse[2], children[3] or sibling[4], or even nephew[5]. A violation may also be alleged by an individual who has been the subject of an attempted homicide[6].

1   See further paras **2.64–2.73** above. Cf *Sanles Sanles v Spain* (dec) 2000-XI (application by heir of a tetraplegic who had tried unsuccessfully to seek legal recognition of his right to end his life with the help of others and who had been refused permission to carry on domestic proceedings after the tetraplegic's death: inadmissible as the heir could not be recognised in such circumstances as a 'victim' within the meaning inter alia of Art 2); and cf 45305/99 *Powell v United Kingdom* (dec) 2000-V (failure to pursue appeal and settlement of civil claim in respect of alleged failure to provide vital medical treatment to a child deprived the applicants of status of 'victim').

2   Eg *Aytekin v Turkey* 1998-VII.

3   Eg *Osman v United Kingdom* 1998-VIII.

4   Eg *Ergi v Turkey* 1998-IV, at para 61 (application of brother of deceased who had complained about murder of sister involved a 'genuine and valid exercise' of right of individual application).

5   Eg *Yaşa v Turkey* 1998-VI, paras 61–66 (person sufficiently concerned to wish to complain of the murder of a close relation met the 'victim' requirement in the particular circumstances of the case).

6   Eg *Osman v United Kingdom* 1998-VIII, (discussed at para **4.23** below); *Yaşa v Turkey*, 1998-VI, (attempted murder of applicant).

State use of lethal or potentially lethal force

4.07 The first substantive obligation arising under Article 2 is negative in character in that it requires the state to refrain from the taking of life unless this occurs in narrowly prescribed circumstances recognised in paragraph (2). The use of force by state agents[1] such as police officers or military personnel which results in the intentional loss of life, or in situations where it is permitted to use force which leads to death as an unintended outcome[2], will thus give rise to considerations as to the purpose of the use of force and the level of force used. Further, Article 2 may also apply to the use of potentially lethal force even when this does not result in death where there has been recklessness in its deployment[3].

1   State liability may be engaged under Art 1 even where state officials are acting ultra vires or contrary to explicit instructions as a state is strictly liable for the conduct of its agents: cf *Ireland v United Kingdom* (1978) A 25, para 159. Note also *Medova v Russia* 2009-..., paras 95–100 (abduction by a group of armed men thought to be state officials in life-threatening circumstances and the subsequent absence of any news for four years supported the assumption of death, and even although the evidence was insufficient to establish to the requisite standard of proof that the abductors were state officials, this did not necessarily exclude state responsibility under Art 2 in light of the failure to take appropriate steps to safeguard life through preventing the release of the armed men with their captives). See further International Law Commission's Draft Articles, Art 7, on the responsibility of States for internationally wrongful acts. Cf *Behrami and Behrami v France; and Saramati v France, Germany and Norway* (dec) [GC] (2 May 2007) (alleged negligence of French KFOR troops in Kosovo resulting in the death of a child in the explosion of an undetonated cluster bomb through their failure to mark the site or to defuse the bombs which they knew to be in the area: inadmissible, since the impugned action and inaction were attributable to the United Nations which has a

legal personality separate from that of its member states). For further discussion of extra-territorial jurisdiction, see paras **3.03–3.13** above.

2   The scope of Art 2 is thus much wider than mere deliberate killing: 1044/82, *Stewart v United Kingdom* (1984) DR 39, 162, reversing an earlier decision that Art 2 required any killing to have been carried out intentionally.

3   *Makaratzis v Greece* [GC] 2004-XI, paras 49–55, discussed at para **4.10** below; and *Isayeva, Yusupova and Bazayeva v Russia* (24 February 2005), para 171. Cf also *Ilhan v Turkey* 2000-VI, paras 73–78 (the applicant suffered brain damage following at least one blow to the head by a rifle butt inflicted by gendarmes who were seeking to arrest him: the degree and type of force used and the unequivocal intention or aim behind the use of force were relevant factors in assessing whether infliction of injury short of death was incompatible with the object and purpose of Art 2, but here the European Court of Human Rights was not persuaded that the force was of such a nature or degree as to breach Art 2, noting that disposal of such allegations was more appropriate under Art 3 in such cases).

The use of lethal force in police or security operations

4.08 The four sets of circumstances outlined in paragraph (2) involve situations in which the state may use force which results in the deprivation of life: to protect against violence, to effect an arrest, to prevent escape of a prisoner, or to quell rioting or insurrection. At first glance, these categories appear potentially wide; but a more careful reading of the text and recent jurisprudence narrow considerably the extent of permitted state authority. The provision 'does not primarily define instances where it is permitted intentionally to kill an individual, but describes the situations where it is permitted to 'use force' which may result, as an unintended outcome, in the deprivation of life'[1]. There are three further qualifications. First, each of the recognised categories justifying the use of lethal or potentially-lethal force has a particular 'lawful' test to be met (for only action 'lawfully taken' to quell a riot, or force used against 'unlawful' violence in defence of oneself or another, or to effect a 'lawful' arrest or to prevent the escape of one 'lawfully detained' may be justified). In respect of the latter two categories, the requirement of 'lawful' deprivation of liberty is obviously to be determined by reference to Article 5[2]. Secondly, the force used must be able to be show to have been no more than that which was 'absolutely necessary' in the circumstances. The principles developed in the case law are of general applicability, and even 'anti-terrorist operations should be planned and controlled by the authorities so as to minimise to the greatest extent possible recourse to lethal force'[3]. Thirdly, the use of lethal force must be attributable to the respondent state[4].

In practice, the key issue in an Article 2 issue is likely to be whether any use of force falling within one of the recognised categories and resulting in the loss of life (or near-loss of life) can be shown to have met the test of absolute necessity. As the Court put it in *McCann and Others v United Kingdom*:

'In this respect the use of the term 'absolutely necessary' in Article 2 para. 2 indicates that a stricter and more compelling test of necessity must be employed from that normally applicable when determining whether State action is 'necessary in a democratic society' under paragraph 2 of Articles 8 to 11 of the Convention. In particular, the force used must be strictly proportionate to the achievement of the aims set out in sub-paragraphs 2 (a), (b) and (c) of Article 2.'[5]

1   *McCann and Others v United Kingdom* (1995) A 324, at para 148.

2   *Gül v Turkey* (14 December 2000), at para 84.

3   *McCann and Others v United Kingdom* (1995) A 324, at para 149. The central issue is thus whether the facts indicate that force has been shown to have been no more than 'absolutely necessary', rather than the legal standard of justification for the use of force: paras 154–155. The dissenting judgments placed weight on the conclusions of the inquiry jury which had enjoyed the benefits of hearing the witnesses involved and which had thereafter considered that the killings had been lawful; the minority also considered that it had not been shown that the planning and control of the operation had been faulty.

4   See also *Avşar v Turkey* 2001-VII, at para 284: 'criminal law liability is distinct from international law responsibility under the ECHR. The responsibility of a State under the ECHR, arising for the acts of its organs, agents and servants, is not to be confused with the domestic legal issues of individual criminal responsibility under examination in the national criminal courts. The Court is not concerned with reaching any findings as to guilt or innocence in that sense'; and *Timurtaş v Turkey* 2000-VI, at para 66: 'the Court would emphasise that Convention proceedings do not in all cases lend themselves for rigorous application of the principle of *affirmanti incumbit probatio* (he who alleges something must prove that allegation)'. Accordingly while there may be prima facie evidence that an individual has been killed by state agents, if there is insufficient evidence upon which to prove beyond reasonable doubt that a death is attributable to the state, the allegation remains more a matter of assumption and speculation: see eg *Ekinci v Turkey* (18 July 2000), paras 70–76 (prima facie evidence that killing may have been by state agents but this remained assumption and speculation since there was insufficient evidence upon which to prove beyond reasonable doubt that the victim's death was so attributable); and *Celniku v Greece* (5 July 2007), paras 51–59 (fatal shot not triggered by deliberate act of a police officer, and the use of lethal force was not attributable to the state; but violation of Art 2 in respect of inadequate planning and firearms regulation).

5   For examples, see *Gül v Turkey* (14 December 2000), para 89; and *Avşar v Turkey* 2001-VII, para 283.

4.09 The assessment of the use of lethal force will thus require consideration of the regulatory framework concerning the use of force, of the training, planning and operational control of any police or security service operation, and of the particular circumstances surrounding the actual use of force in order to ascertain whether the force used was strictly proportionate. In principle, this assessment is a matter for the domestic courts, and the European Court of Human Rights will only depart from the findings of national tribunals where 'cogent' reasons suggesting domestic proceedings have been defective in examining such matters. Where necessary, though, the Court will itself examine these questions by assessing all the evidence placed before it and, if thought desirable, will carry out its own investigation[1]. The conduct of the parties may be a relevant factor in any assessment: in particular, the failure of a respondent government to provide active assistance by furnishing all necessary assistance without satisfactory explanation may allow inferences to be drawn[2].

1   See further paras **2.56** and **2.57** above. In respect of an allegation of a premeditated plan to kill, 'convincing evidence' is required (*McCann and Others v United Kingdom* (1995) A 324 para 179). Where lack of diligence calls into question whether the killing was 'absolutely necessary',

the evidentiary standard to be met seems lower: *McCann and Others v United Kingdom*, above, at paras 171–173 (this exercise does not involve assessment of criminal liability, and thus there is no onus upon the state to prove beyond reasonable doubt that the operation was in accordance with Art 2). Note also *Yaşa v Turkey*, 1998-VI, para 96 (attainment of the required evidentiary standard of beyond reasonable doubt may follow from the co-existence of sufficiently strong, clear and concordant inferences or unrebutted presumptions, with the evidential value assessed in the light of the circumstances of the individual case and the seriousness and nature of the charges). For further examples of instances where the requisite standard of proof has not been reached, see *Tahsin Acar v Turkey* [GC] 2004-III, paras 211–219, (contradictory evidence of eyewitness); *Tekda v Turkey* (15 January 2004) paras 72–77 (no eyewitnesses to the alleged incidents); and *Nesibe Haran v Turkey* (6 October 2005), paras 68–69 (alleged detention at place of work and subsequent killing remained speculation). But note also the partly dissenting judgment of Judge Bratza in *Ağdaş v Turkey* (27 July 2004): where it is an undisputed fact that police officers have shot and killed an individual 'so far from the burden of proof resting on the applicant, it seems to me that it must in principle be for the respondent State to establish on the evidence … that the deprivation of life resulted from the use of force which was no more than "absolutely necessary"'. The majority's determination that there was insufficient factual and evidentiary basis on which to conclude that the applicant was deprived of his life as a result of the use of force which was more than absolutely necessary 'is to apply the wrong test and to reverse the burden of proof [since] the test to be applied is not whether there is a sufficient evidence to satisfy the Court that the use of force was more than absolutely necessary; rather, it is whether the evidence is such as to satisfy the Court that the use of force was no more than absolutely necessary in self-defence.'

2   See *Timurtaş v Turkey* 2000-VI, para 66: 'It is inherent in proceedings relating to cases of this nature, where an individual applicant accuses State agents of violating his rights under the Convention, that in certain instances solely the respondent Government have access to information capable of corroborating or refuting these allegations. A failure on a Government's part to submit such information which is in their hands without a satisfactory explanation may not only reflect negatively on the level of compliance by a respondent State with its obligations …, but may also give rise to the drawing of inferences as to the well-foundedness of the allegations'. See also eg *Kaya v Turkey* 1998-I, paras 76–78 (failure by the applicant and witness to attend to give evidence to the Commission); *Orhan v Turkey* (18 June 2002), paras 330–332 (failure to submit information in the possession of the state without adequate explanation); and *Isayeva v Russia* (24 February 2005), para 182 (failure by the respondent state to make available key documentation). The issue may also be of relevance in respect of ECHR, Art 34: see para **2.56** above.

4.10 Domestic law thus must adequately regulate the use of potentially lethal force by state officials to ensure this is only employed as a strictly proportionate measure[1]. To this end, states must have in place a regulatory or administrative framework defining the limited circumstances in which law-enforcement officials may use force and firearms. This framework should reflect relevant international standards and have the aim of securing 'a system of adequate and effective safeguards against arbitrariness and abuse of force and even against avoidable accident' in police operations[2], including basic restraint techniques[3]. A 'shoot to kill' policy or instruction is inherently suspect[4]. In *Nachova and Others v Bulgaria,* the Court was critical of unpublished regulations which effectively permitted military police to use lethal force when arresting a member of the armed forces for even minor offences and which thus failed to contain safeguards to prevent the arbitrary deprivation of life[5]. In *Makaratzis v Greece,* police officers had fired several shots at a driver of a car who had driven through a red traffic light and several police barriers, seriously wounding but not killing him. For the Court, the 'chaotic way' in which the firearms had been used 'in a largely uncontrolled chase' in terms of an 'obsolete and incomplete' regulation of the use of firearms had amounted to a violation of Article 2. In particular, the failure of the authorities to put in place an adequate legislative and administrative framework meant that law-enforcement officials lacked clear guidelines and criteria governing the use of force with the unavoidable result in this case that the police officers involved had 'enjoyed a greater autonomy of action and were able to take unconsidered initiatives, which they would probably not have displayed had they had the benefit of proper training and instructions'. Such 'unregulated and arbitrary action' was incompatible with effective respect for human rights[6].

---

1   Cf *McCann and Others v United Kingdom* (1995) A 324, paras 154–155 (assessment of force used in domestic proceedings by the test of 'reasonable' rather than 'actual' necessity, but the Court accepted that in practice there was no significant difference between these standards in light of actual application by domestic courts).

2   *Makaratzis v Greece* [GC] 2004-XI, paras 58–59, citing the United Nations Force and Firearms Principles. See also *Nachova and Others v Bulgaria* [GC] 2005-VII, at para 93; and *Celniku v Greece* (5 July 2007), paras 51–59 (fatal shot not triggered by deliberate act of a police officer, and the use of lethal force was not attributable to the state; but violation of Art 2 in respect of inadequate planning and firearms regulation). See also *Yaşarolu v Turkey* (20 June 2006), paras 47–55 (accidental discharge of firearm during police chase: no violation).

3   See eg *Saoud v France* 2007-XI, paras 88–104 (use of a face-down immobilisation technique by police officers to arrest a man suffering from schizophrenia: while police intervention had been justified and proportionate under Art 2(2) for the protection of others' physical safety, his subsequent physical restraint for 35 minutes resulting in asphyxia in the circumstances constituted a violation of Art 2, the Court noting that no precise instructions had been issued as regards the immobilisation technique). See further De Sanctis 'What Duties Do States Have with Regard to the Rules of Engagement and the Training of Security Forces under Article 2 of the ECHR?' (2006) 10 IJHR 31.

4   See *McCann and Others v United Kingdom* (1995) A 324, para 202–214.

5   *Nachova and Others v Bulgaria* [GC] 2005-VII, at para 99.

6   *Makaratzis v Greece* [GC] 2004-XI, paras 57–72.

4.11 Planning and operational control of an incident in which actual or potentially lethal force is used must minimise the risk of loss of life. In *McCann and Others v United Kingdom,* the European Court of Human Rights questioned whether the control and organisation of an anti-terrorist operation involving military personnel against an active service unit of the IRA in Gibraltar had taken adequate account of the terrorists' rights under Article 2, and concluded not only that there had been less onerous alternatives available to prevent a terrorist outrage, but also that there had been a failure to make sufficient allowance for erroneous intelligence assessments. Further, the reflex action of soldiers in shooting to kill had lacked 'the degree of caution in the use of firearms to be expected from law enforcement personnel in a democratic society'. Consequently, in the eyes of the majority of the Court, the killing of the suspects had not been shown to have been 'absolutely necessary'[1]. Proportionality between means and end sought to be achieved may thus require selection of an appropriate range of weapons to ensure that the use of force is not disproportionate[2].

1　*McCann and Others v United Kingdom* (1995) A 324, paras 195–214 (at para 200: use of lethal force on account of an honestly held belief albeit one which subsequently turns out to be a mistaken belief is acceptable, since to approach the matter otherwise 'would be to impose an unrealistic burden on the State and its law enforcement personnel in the execution of their duty, perhaps to the detriment of their lives and those of others'). See also *Oğur v Turkey* [GC] 1999-III, paras 73–84 (death of night watchman during military operation). In 17579/90, *Kelly v United Kingdom* (1993) DR 74, 139, the Commission accepted that the shooting of an individual in a stolen car as he tried to drive through a security checkpoint in Belfast could be justified as having been for the purpose of apprehending individuals reasonably believed to be terrorists. The Commission was also influenced by the speed at which the situation arose and which had given the soldiers little or no warning, and by the political background of terrorist killings. See also *Bubbins v United Kingdom* 2005-II, paras 134–152 (planning and control of a police operation satisfied Art 2 requirements: the conduct of the operation had remained under the control of senior officers, the deployment of the armed officers had been reviewed and approved by tactical firearms advisers, and domestic provisions regulated the use of firearms and the conduct of police operations and provided adequate and effective safeguards to prevent arbitrary use of lethal force).

2　*Güleç v Turkey* 1998-IV, paras 69–73 at para 71 (use of armoured vehicles because of an 'incomprehensible and unacceptable' lack of less powerful weapons (such as truncheons, riot shields, water cannon, rubber bullets or tear gas) against violent demonstration resulting in death had not been 'absolutely necessary'). See also *Nachova and Others v Bulgaria* [GC] 2005-VII, paras 98–109 (planning and control of the operation had 'betrayed a deplorable disregard for the pre-eminence of the right to life', and 'grossly excessive force' had been used: violation); and *Şimşek and Others v Turkey* (26 July 2005) para 108 (crowd dispersal by shooting directly at demonstrators without initial recourse to less life-threatening methods). Cf *Oya Ataman v Turkey* 2006-XIV, paras 25–27 (use of 'pepper spray' against 40–50 peaceful demonstrators, but no evidence submitted of any side-effects: no violation).

4.12 States must also take steps to minimise the risk of incidental loss of life to civilians caught up in an operation. *In Ergi v Turkey*, the Court was not satisfied that the state had taken 'all feasible precautions in the choice of means and methods' to avoid the risk of death as the location security forces had selected had been such as to place others at substantial risk of being caught up in cross-fire[1]. The principle also applies to military operations, as illustrated by the judgment in *Isayeva, Yusupova and Bazayeva v Russia*. In this case, the Court condemned an aerial missile attack upon a convoy of civilians trying to leave the capital of Chechnya to escape heavy fighting. While the situation in Chechnya may have called for exceptional measures including the employment of military aviation equipped with heavy combat weapons, the respondent state had failed to provide any evidence that the aircraft had been under attack by illegal armed groups; but even if this evidence had been available, the bombing could still not be shown to have been 'absolutely necessary' in view of the absence of steps to evaluate any target, the failure to alert relevant military personnel to the announcement of a humanitarian corridor to allow civilians to leave the capital, the prolonged nature of the attack, and the type of weapons used[2].

1　*Ergi v Turkey* 1998-IV, paras 79–81 at para 79.

2   *Isayeva, Yusupova and Bazayeva v Russia* (24 February 2005), paras 174–200. See also *Isayeva v Russia* (24 February 2005), paras 179–201 (aerial bombing of town during an operation against armed insurgents but no steps taken to warn the population of possible dangers, and the 'massive use of indiscriminate weapons ... cannot be considered compatible with the standard of care prerequisite to an operation of this kind involving the use of lethal force by State agents').

4.13 In any evaluation of the actual force used, consideration of actions of state officials facing split-second decision-making as to whether to use potentially lethal force is not without difficulty. A state official such as a police officer, too, has the right to respect for life, and to use self-defence to protect himself[1]. The European Court of Human Rights has recognised that it would be inappropriate for it to seek to substitute its own detached assessment for that of the officers involved[2], but its appraisals have not always achieved a convincing consensus. In *McCann and Others v United Kingdom,* a bare majority of the Court was prepared to accept that the decisions of the soldiers to open fire had been justified on the basis of the information which had been given to them which had led them honestly to believe that this action was absolutely necessary to protect the lives of others[3]. In *Andronicou and Constantinou v Cyprus*, where it had been considered that the planning and control of a police operation against a gunman involved in a domestic dispute had been carried out in such a manner as to minimise as far as possible any risk of death, a majority of the Court also accepted that the police officers who had opened fire on the gunman had honestly believed that there was a real and immediate danger to the life of another individual and to themselves, even though this belief proved to have been mistaken[4]. In contrast, the situation in *Gül v Turkey* provides an illustration of the use of lethal force which the Court was satisfied could not have been considered as 'absolutely necessary'. As part of a security operation, police officers had sought entry to a flat in order to carry out a search, but as the occupier was unlocking the door, the police officers had opened fire and thereby fatally injured the occupier who had been behind the door. As far as the planning of the operation was concerned, the Court considered that there was insufficient evidence to establish that the officers had been under instructions to use lethal force. However, it also held that the firing of shots at the door could not have been justified by any reasonable belief on the part of the officers that their lives were at risk from the occupants of the flat, let alone that that this had been required to secure entry to the flat. In short, their reaction in opening fire with automatic weapons on an unseen target in a residential block inhabited by innocent civilians could only be considered as a grossly disproportionate response[5]. Similarly, in *Kakoulli v Turkey,* the shooting of an individual by soldiers patrolling the border in northern Cyprus could not be deemed to have been justified as the deceased had posed no imminent risk of death or serious harm to anyone. While it was recognised that the patrolling of frontiers can present special problems, in this case the final shot had been fired several minutes after two earlier shots had already neutralised the individual who thus could easily have been arrested[6].

1   See *Giuliani and Gaggio v Italy* [GC] (24 March 2011), paras 211–218, and 252–262 (death

of protestor killed during violent clashes between anti-globalisation militants and law-enforcement officers through discharge of weapon by injured police officer: no violation of Art 2 as the use of lethal force had not exceeded the limits of what was absolutely necessary in order to avert what the officer honestly perceived to be a real and imminent threat to his life and to the lives of his colleagues; nor was it possible to determine that there had been shortcomings in respect of the preparation and conduct of the long and somewhat unpredictable operation, even although certain questions remained unanswered). Cf 2758/66, *X v Belgium* (1969) YB 12, 174; 10044/82, *Stewart v United Kingdom* (1984) DR 39, 162; and 11257/84, *Wolfgram v Germany* (1986) DR 49, 213.

2   *Andronicou and Constantinou v Cyprus* 1997-VI, para 192.

3   *McCann and Others v United Kingdom* (1995) A 324.

4   *Andronicou and Constantinou v Cyprus* 1997-VI, at paras 181–186, and 191–194. The principal concern of the dissenting judges appears to have been the specialised nature of the police response team involved in the operation. For further examples where the use of force has been deemed to have been no more than was 'absolutely necessary', see 10044/82, *Stewart v United Kingdom* (1984) DR 39, 162 (discharge of a plastic baton round during a riot: inadmissible); 17579/90, *Kelly v United Kingdom* (1993) DR 74, 139 (shooting of a joyrider who failed to stop at an army checkpoint: inadmissible); *Scavuzzo-Hager and Others v Switzerland* (7 February 2006), paras 80–86 (physical restraint used by police in arresting a violent drug addict who had lost consciousness and died three days later: no violation of Art 2 as regards the use of force at the time of arrest, nor of the positive obligation under Art 2 to protect life as paramedics had been summoned immediately, but violation of procedural aspect as the initial phase of the investigation had been carried out by the arresting officers); *Perk and Others v Turkey* (28 March 2006), paras 53–73 (shooting of armed suspects planning a terrorist attack); and *Ramsahai v Netherlands* [GC] 2007-VI, paras 286–289 (shooting of suspect after police officer had drawn his service weapon only as the suspect had begun to raise his loaded pistol towards him causing the officer to believe that a real threat to his life existed: the use of lethal force was no more than what had been 'absolutely necessary').

5   *Gül v Turkey* (14 December 2000), paras 81–83. See also *Oğur v Turkey* [GC] 1999-III, at para 83 (even if the death had been caused by the firing of a gun as a warning, 'the firing of that shot was badly executed, to the point of constituting gross negligence, whether the victim was running aaway or not'); and *Şimeşk and Others v Turkey* (26 July 2005), paras 107–113 (while demonstrations had not been peaceful, police officers had shot directly at the demonstrators without first having recourse to less life-threatening methods).

6   *Kakoulli v Turkey* (22 November 2005), paras 111–121.

Deaths in custody

4.14   States bear the burden of providing plausible explanations for injuries and deaths of individuals within their custody[1]. This responsibility is related to the principle developed under Article 3 that a state must account for injuries sustained by a detainee while in custody[2], an obligation which in terms of Article 2 is 'particularly stringent' in the case of death[3].

1   *Salman v Turkey* [GC] 2000-VII, paras 99–103, and *Tanli v Turkey* 2001-III, paras 139–154 (deaths of individuals who had been in good health during interrogation: respondent state was deemed responsible for the deaths because of its failure to provide such an explanation; and in each instance there was a further violation of Art 2 because of the state's failure to carry out an effective investigation). For discussion of the responsibilities of authorities for preventing severe violence inflicted by other detainees, see paras **4.26** and **4.89–4.91** below.

2   See para **4.79** below.

3   *Taş v Turkey* 2000-XI, at para 63.

'Disappeared persons'

4.15 Similarly, cases involving persons who were last seen in the custody of state officers and who subsequently 'disappear' in circumstances where there is sufficient evidence to support a conclusion that a detainee must be presumed to have died while in custody will give rise to issues under Article 2. The failure of state authorities to provide a plausible explanation for the fate of a detainee or other individual within their exclusive control will thus give rise to issues which go beyond merely the question of unlawful deprivation of liberty under Article 5es:[1]. 'Disappeared persons' thus constitute a distinct phenomenon characterised by ongoing uncertainty and unaccountability and lack of information or deliberate concealment[2]. In consequence, the issue may potentially also give rise to responsibility under Article 3[3]. There may also be a continuing obligation to carry out an effective investigation[4]. Sufficient circumstantial evidence must exist 'based on concrete elements, from which it may be concluded to the requisite standard of proof that a detainee must be presumed to have died while in custody'[5]. The requisite standard in such cases is one of beyond reasonable doubt[6]. However, since information about the events in question will lie wholly, or to a large extent, within the exclusive control of the authorities, a failure to provide this information may allow the drawing of inferences[7].

1   *Taş v Turkey* 2000-XI, para 64. Initially, the Court had treated 'disappeared persons' cases under Art 5 rather than under Arts 2 and 3: cf *Kurt v Turkey* 1998-III, paras 106–109, 126–129 (at para 128: the failure of the state authorities to offer any credible and substantiated explanation for the whereabouts or the fate of the applicant's son who had last been seen in the custody of security forces led to the conclusion that he had been held 'in unacknowledged detention in the complete absence of the safeguards contained in Article 5'). In *Timurtaş v Turkey* 2000-VI, paras 99–106, the Court (in addition to establishing a violation of Art 2) found that the disappearance of the applicant's son during an unacknowledged detention disclosed a particularly grave violation of Art 5 in particular because of the lack of a prompt and effective inquiry into the circumstances of the disappearance and the lack of accurate and reliable records of detention of persons taken into custody by police officers.

2   *Varnava and Others v Turkey* [GC] 2009-…, at para 148.

3   Eg *Osmanolu v Turkey* (24 January 2008), paras 70–99 (violations of Art 2 in respect of death of son; and of Art 3 on account of distress and anguish as a result of the witnessed disappearance of his son and inability over 11 years to find out what had happened).

4   *Varnava and Others v Turkey* [GC] 2009-…, paras 180–194 (and thus while a 34 year period without news of the whereabouts of disappeared persons can provide strong circumstantial evidence of intervening death, it does not preclude application of the procedural obligation under Art 2 even although the deaths may have occurred before temporal jurisdiction arises a distinction has to be drawn between the making of such a factual presumption and the legal consequences that flowed from it as the duty to investigate disappearances cannot end on discovery of the body or the presumption of death since the obligations to account for the disappearance and death and to identify and prosecute any perpetrator of unlawful acts will normally continue; in any event, there is a crucial distinction between the obligation to

investigate a suspicious death and the obligation to investigate a suspicious disappearance as the latter is a distinct phenomenon characterised by ongoing uncertainty and unaccountability and lack of information or deliberate concealment rather than an instantaneous act, and the procedural obligation potentially persists as long as the fate of the missing person is unaccounted for even where death is presumed). See further paras **4.35–4.47** below.

5   *Çakici v Turkey* [GC] 1999-IV, at para 85. See also *Cyprus v Turkey* [GC] 2001-IV, paras 129–136 (detention of Greek Cypriots at a time when military operations involving Turkish or Turkish Cypriot forces were accompanied by widespread arrests and killings); *Betayev and Betayeva v Russia, Gekhayeva and Others v Russia, Ibragimov and Others v Russia,* and *Sangariyeva and Others v Russia* (29 May 2008) (series of linked cases involving failure of criminal investigations to identify armed men wearing camouflage uniforms and using military vehicles who had abducted close relatives in night raids: violation of Art 2 in light of the *prima facie* evidence that service personnel had been involved and the drawing of inferences from the refusal to provide the Court with key documents and the absence of any other plausible explanation, the presumption being that the relatives were now dead following unacknowledged detention); and *Palić v Bosnia and Herzegovina* (15 February 2011), paras 63 and 71 (authorities to conduct an official investigation into an arguable claim that a person, who was last seen in their custody, subsequently disappeared in a life-threatening context, but after the identification of remains, an independent and effective criminal investigation had taken place, and taking into account the special circumstances prevailing in BiH, no violation of Art 2).

6   *Avşar v Turkey* 2001-VII, para 282.

7   See eg *Akkum and Others v Turkey* 2005-II, at para 209: 'where it is solely the respondent Government who have access to information capable of corroborating or refuting allegations made by an individual applicant, a failure on that Government's part – without a satisfactory explanation – to submit such information may give rise to the drawing of inferences as to the well-foundedness of the applicant's allegations'. See also *Anguelova v Bulgaria* 2002-IV, discussed below at para **4.41** below (implausible explanation proffered for death during police custody).

4.16 The obligation upon the state to provide a plausible explanation in such circumstances is supported by – but distinct from – the procedural aspect of Article 2 which requires an independent investigation into the particular circumstances of the case, a duty which will also almost inevitably arise in instances where it is alleged that state agents have either been responsible for unlawful killings or have colluded with those responsible. In practice, the two obligations may both be of significance in such cases. In *Cakici v Turkey,* the security forces had claimed to have found the body of the applicant's brother amongst the corpses of a group of suspected terrorists, while the applicant claimed his brother had last been seen some 15 months before being taken into custody. The European Court of Human Rights held that there had been violations of Article 2 both on the basis of a presumption of death after unacknowledged detention by state officials, and also on account of an inadequate investigation into the disappearance and alleged discovery of the body[1]. A similar outcome is possible even in the absence of a victim's body or acknowledged detention. In *Timurtaş v Turkey*, the applicant's son had been taken into custody and then had disappeared, but the state had disputed the fact that he had ever been detained. The Court accepted that upon the facts established by the Commission there was sufficient evidence for to it to conclude beyond all reasonable doubt that he had died while in the custody of the security forces[2]. In *Taş v Turkey*, the state conceded that an individual had been taken into custody but had been unable to provide any custody or other records showing where he had been subsequently detained, claiming that he had escaped from custody. However, since the report of this alleged escape was unsubstantiated and the signatories of the report had not been traced, the Court held that no plausible explanation for what had happened had been provided. Given the length of time which had elapsed since his disappearance and also the political situation in that part of Turkey, the Court considered that the individual must be presumed dead following his detention by the security forces, and thus liability for his death was attributable to the state[3].

1   *Çakici v Turkey* [GC] 1999-IV, paras 85–87.

2   *Timurtaşv Turkey* 2000-VI, paras 81–86 (a further violation of Art 2 was established because of the inadequacy of the official investigation: paras 87–90). See too *Ertak v Turkey* 2000-V; and *Çiçek v Turkey* (27 February 2001).

3   *Taşv Turkey* 2000-XI, paras 62–67 (it was not known when exactly the victim died; there was no hospital record of his death; and the government had failed to produce the doctor who pronounced him dead; adequate nor effective). See further *Taşv Turkey* (14 November 2000), paras 62–72 (the post-mortem examination of an individual who had been in good health at the start of the period of detention had revealed extensive bruising, while additional evidence pointed to the cause of death as mechanical asphyxiation through strangulation or the application of severe pressure to the chest: the Court accepted that death had occurred as the result of violence inflicted while in police custody, and a further violation of the procedural aspect of Art 2 was established as the investigation was neither prompt nor adequate nor effective). Cf partly dissenting opinion of Judge Gölcüklü, the ad hoc Turkish judge, who was of the opinion that it had not been proved beyond reasonable doubt that the applicant's son had died in police custody; and further that the Court should not have departed from its judgment in *Kurt v Turkey* 1998-III to approach such cases solely under ECHR, Art 5. See also *Nuray Şen v Turkey (no 2)* (30 March 2004), paras 169–180 (the applicant had been advised that her husband's body was lying in a hospital mortuary four days after contacting a police anti-terrorism department after eye-witnesses reported that her husband had been abducted and murdered by state officials but the government had claimed that he had been abducted by persons known to him as he had not put up any physical resistance: the Court could only conclude that the applicant's husband had been abducted and murdered by unknown persons as the main eye-witnesses had failed to give evidence and the only evidence implicating state agents was the applicant's hearsay statements, but the significant shortcomings in the investigation into the abduction and killing led to the conclusion that there had been a violation of the procedural aspect of Art 2).

Persons found dead in an area within the exclusive control of state authorities

4.17 The Court applies the same test to situations in which individuals are found dead in an area within the exclusive control of the authorities and where it can thus be supposed that information about the events in question lies wholly or at least to a large extent within the exclusive knowledge of the authorities. States thus bear the burden of providing plausible explanations for deaths taking place in facilities within their exclusive control such as military bases[1] or sobering-up centres[2]. Similarly, there is a responsibility to account for deaths occurring in areas of conflict under the control of the authorities. Thus in *Akkum and Others v Turkey,* the failure of the respondent government to account for the killings of the applicant's relatives who had been found dead after a military operation in a region of Turkey allowed the drawing of inferences as to the well-foundedness of the applicants' allegations. The withholding of key documentary evidence indispensable for the correct and complete establishment of the facts and the failure to provide any explanation for this, together with omissions and contradictory material found in reports submitted to the Court, supported such a determination. The Court also noted that it was legitimate to draw a parallel between the situation of detainees for whose well-being the authorities are held responsible and with that of individuals found injured or dead in an area within the exclusive control of the state authorities[3]. In *Khashiyev and Akayeva v Russia*, the bodies of the applicants' relatives had been discovered with bullet wounds and signs of beating after heavy fighting between government troops and rebel soldiers. The refusal of the respondent government to provide the Court with a copy of the complete criminal investigation into what had been deemed the 'mass murder' of civilians allowed it to draw inferences of fact of significance in determining that there had been a violation both of the substantive guarantee of the right to life and also of the procedural aspect: government forces had been in firm control of the area and they alone could have conducted identity checks, and in any event the investigation had neither been held with due expedition nor pursued with sufficient rigour[4].

1   *Beker v Turkey* (24 May 2009), paras 39–53 (inexplicable facts seemingly contradicting official findings that a soldier had shot himself: the government had failed to account for the death and thus consequently had to bear the responsibility for it).

2   *Mojsiejew v Poland* (24 March 2009), paras 54–65 (death by asphyxia in a sobering-up centre of a person immobilised with belts and left alone without medical supervision: lack of effective investigation and also a failure to provide a convincing explanation as to whether the centre's employees had carried out periodic checks and had complied with domestic regulations aiming to protect life).

3   *Akkum and Others v Turkey* 2005-II, paras 185–204 et seq.

4   *Khashiyev and Akayeva v Russia* (24 February 2005), paras 115–124 and 156–166. (There was a further violation of Art 2 on account of serious flaws in the investigation into the killings, and of a failure to carry out a thorough and effective investigation into credible allegations of torture as required by Art 3). See also *Isayeva v Russia* (24 February 2005), and *Isayeva, Yusupova and Bazayeva v Russia* (24 February 2005) (complaints concerning the indiscriminate bombing by Russian military planes of civilians), discussed at para 4.12 above.

Positive obligations: (i) ensuring the effective protection of the right to life through effective domestic law and punishment

4.18 As well as prohibiting the intentional and unlawful taking of life by state officials, 'the first sentence of Article 2(1) enjoins the State … also to take appropriate steps to safeguard the lives of those within its jurisdiction'. A number of issues may thus arise. Domestic law is expected clearly to define both lawful killing and unlawful killing, to ensure that no person is immune from prosecution, and to provide for appropriate sanctions[1]. Domestic law must thus as a first and most obvious requirement have in place effective criminal law provisions to deter the commission of offences against the person, backed up by law enforcement machinery for the prevention, suppression and punishment of breaches of such provisions[2]. There is also an expectation that states have in place a regulatory or administrative frameworks defining such matters as the limited circumstances in which law-enforcement officials may use force (including the use of firearms)[3], and ensuring the protection of life from environmental or industrial hazard[4]. The obligation is closely related to the 'procedural aspect' of the guarantee: 'where lives have been lost in circumstances potentially engaging the responsibility of the State, Article 2 entails a duty for the State to ensure, by all means at its disposal, an adequate response – judicial or otherwise – so that the legislative and administrative framework set up to protect the right to life is properly implemented and any breaches of that right are repressed and punished'[5]. In short, the right to life requires protection both in substantive law and through effective implementation[6].

---

1 For consideration of euthanasia and assisted suicide, see paras **4.52** and **4.53** below.

2 *LCB v United Kingdom* 1998-III, at para 36; *Makaratzis v Greece* [GC] 2004-XI, at para 57. See also 23412/94, *The Taylor, Crampton, Gibson and King Families v United Kingdom* (1994) DR 79, 127 (death of applicants' children through actions of a mentally ill nurse: the criminal prosecution of the nurse and the holding of an independent but private inquiry which published its findings satisfied the requirements of Art 2).

3 See para **4.10** above.

4 See para **4.36** below.

5 *Kats and Others v Ukraine* 2008-..., at para 115. See paras **4.35–4.47** below.

6 Eg *Opuz v Turkey* 2009-..., paras 131–153 (criminal law system had had no deterrent effect, nor could the authorities rely on the victims' attitude for the failure to take adequate measures to protect them).

4.19 These obligations are of particular importance in combating the impunity of state officials. In *Akkoç v Turkey,* the Court concluded that while the legal system prohibited homicide and while it also had an infrastructure of police, prosecutors and courts in place, there had been crucial defects (including restrictions on the competence of prosecutors) in the implementation of the criminal law in respect of acts involving security forces in a particular region which in turn had 'permitted or fostered a lack of accountability of members of the security forces for their actions which ... was not compatible with the rule of law in a democratic society'[1].

---

1 *Akkoç v Turkey* 2000-X, paras 87–91 at para 91. See also *Teren Aksakal v Turkey* 2007-X, paras 89–100 (criminal proceedings against police officers had been far from rigorous and had not been capable of acting as an effective deterrent in such cases: violation of Art 2). Cf *Van Melle and Others v Netherlands* (dec) (29 September 2009) (alleged failure to prosecute ministers following death of detainees in a fire in a detention centre for aliens: inadmissible in light of the lack of suggestion of personal criminal responsibility warranting prosecution). See also van Dijk, van Hoof, van Rijn and Zwaak (eds) *Theory and Practice of the European Convention on Human Rights* (4th edn, 2006) at pp 297–8: 'The protection provided by the law, however, is a reality only if that law is implemented. Omission on the part of the authorities to trace and prosecute the offender in case of an unlawful deprivation of life is, therefore, in principle subjected to review by the Court'.

4.20 The importance of combating impunity supports the principle that a sentence for unwarranted loss of life should reflect the gravity of the conviction[1]. However, the mere fact that state officials who have been held to account for the loss of life are subsequently reinstated in their posts does not amount in itself to a flagrant rejection of a criminal conviction or even a cynical approbation of the conduct giving rise to the conviction[2].

1   *Nikolova and Velichkova v Bulgaria* (20 December 2007), paras 65–76 (conviction of police officers for death through intentional grievous bodily harm punished by three-year suspended prison sentence: violation, as the force used for effecting arrest had not been 'absolutely necessary', and a sentence of this nature supported contention of police officers that they had not been responsible). See similarly *Vo v France* Cf 16734/90, *Dujardin and Others v France* (1992) DR 32, 190 (discontinuation of prosecutions for murder following upon an amnesty as an 'exceptional measure' in New Caledonia consequent upon a political settlement: inadmissible).

2   *McBride v United Kingdom* (dec) 2006-V.

4.21 It is clear from the case law, however, that in certain instances the provision of civil remedies for loss of life will be deemed to provide adequate protection for life, and that the failure to prosecute or the absence of criminal sanction will thus not necessarily give rise to a violation of Article 2. Whether protection of life may be secured by means of civil remedies alone will depend on the circumstances[1]. In *Calvelli and Ciglio v Italy*, the Grand Chamber confirmed that this provision did not guarantee a right to have criminal proceedings instituted against third parties if the loss of life is not caused intentionally, and a civil remedy allowing the resolution of liability and the provision of appropriate civil redress in such cases would satisfy the requirements of Article 2 provided that this was available 'effectively in practice within a time-span such that the courts can complete their examination of the merits of each individual case'[2]. In *Öneryildiz v Turkey,* the Grand Chamber reiterated that Article 2 did not 'entail the right for an applicant to have third parties prosecuted or sentenced for a criminal offence ... or an absolute obligation for all prosecutions to result in conviction, or indeed in a particular sentence', for not every case would require criminal proceedings as the provision of civil, administrative or disciplinary remedies to victims may suffice. However, if as in the present case the failure to take the requisite action to prevent loss of life had gone beyond an error of judgment or mere carelessness, 'the fact that those responsible for endangering life have not been charged with a criminal offence or prosecuted may amount to a violation of Article 2, irrespective of any other types of remedy which individuals may exercise on their own initiative'[3].

1   See eg *Menson v United Kingdom* (dec) 2003-V (allegations of failure to take proper post-incident measures to secure evidence from the victim of a racially-motivated attack before he died two week later, and delay in determining whether to take criminal proceedings against police officers in respect of the investigation: manifestly ill-founded in light of the prosecution and conviction of the perpetrators, but the Court noted the distinction drawn between Art 2 obligations and the accountability and civil liability of police officers and the issue of availability of a remedy which fell within the scope of Art 6). Cf *McCann and Others v United Kingdom* (1995) A 324, paras 160–164, where the Court did not find it necessary to decide whether a right of access to a court to bring civil proceedings could be inferred from Art 2 since this was an issue better determined under Arts 6 and 13, neither of which had been invoked by the

applicants; nor was it necessary to determine what form an investigation into the taking of life should assume since the domestic proceedings in the present case seemed satisfactory).

2   *Calvelli and Ciglio v Italy* [GC] 2002-I, paras 48–57 at para 53 (claim that the failure of a private clinic to make appropriate arrangements in light of information as to the mother's health and medical history had significantly reduced a baby's chance of survival: the possibility of raising criminal proceedings for involuntary homicide had become time-barred, but an action for civil damages against the doctor concerned had been instigated and settled between the parties permitting the Court to conclude there had been no violation of Art 2).

3   *Öneryildiz v Turkey* [GC] 2004-XII, at paras 93 and 96. See also *Vo v France* [GC] 2004-VIII, para 89.

Positive obligations: (ii) the duty to protect life through the taking of specific action

4.22 The duty upon a state under Article 2(1) to ensure that the right to life is 'protected by law' also can extend to the taking of practical steps to address situations where there is an identifiable and real threat to life. Such an obligation may arise when it is alleged there has been delay or negligence in the discharge of public responsibilities or where a particular duty of care is deemed to arise, for example, in respect of vulnerable persons, detainees or children. Failure to take steps which could be reasonably expected to address the risk will thus give rise to a violation of Article 2, although a simple error of judgment or negligent co-ordination between agencies will not necessarily do so[1]. Inevitably, whether or not a substantive obligation exists, the procedural obligation to carry out an effective investigation into the circumstances with a view to establishing any responsibility is likely to apply[2]. Article 2 thus has implications not only for the quality of domestic law, but also for the discharge of a wide range of public service responsibilities.

1   *Dodov v Bulgaria* 2008-..., paras 79–98 (disappearance of nursing-home patient following negligent act resulting in presumed death: while a simple error of judgment on the part of a health professional or negligent co-ordination would not give rise to positive obligations under Art 2, an examination of availability of legal remedies was necessary to consider whether these could have secured legal means capable of establishing the facts, holding accountable those at fault and providing appropriate redress to the victim; here, lengthy periods of inactivity and shortcomings in basic investigative measures and prosecution procedures had resulted in a violation of Art 2).

2   See eg *Dodov v Bulgaria* 2008-..., fn 1 above; and *Mikayil Mammadov v Azerbaijan* (17 December 2009), paras 106–121 (no violation of the substantive aspect of Art 2 in respect of the suicide of the appellant's wife during the family's eviction from their home as the authorities could not be considered to have intentionally put her life risk or otherwise caused her to commit suicide, conduct that was not a reasonable or predictable reaction; further, it had not been shown that the authorities were aware of a real and immediate risk of suicide requiring them as a matter of a positive obligation to do all that could reasonably have been expected of them to avert that risk: but violation of the procedural aspect on account of the inadequacy of the investigation into the death as it had not address all relevant issues in assessing state responsibility).

4.23 The positive obligation to take appropriate steps to safeguard life may involve the taking of preventive operational measures to protect an individual[1]. For such a positive obligation to arise, it has to be established that the authorities know or ought to know that there exists a real and immediate risk to life from the criminal acts of another. However, Article 2 does not impose any general duty upon the state to provide indefinite police protection to individuals against threats of violence[2]; rather, the duty will only arise where the threat is identifiable[3] and can be addressed by the use of reasonable measures[4], for the positive obligation to take appropriate steps to try to protect life 'must be interpreted in such a way which does not impose an impossible or disproportionate burden on the authorities'[5]. In *Osman v United Kingdom*, the applicant alleged that the police had taken insufficient measures to provide protection in the face of threats of violence from an unstable teacher who had developed an unhealthy attraction for a pupil. On the particular facts of the case (which involved the shooting of the boy and his father by the teacher, the father being killed as a result), the Court eventually considered that the police could not be assumed to have known of any real and immediate risk to the life of the deceased. Nor could it reasonably have been assumed that any action taken by the police would have neutralised any such risk. Consequently, no violation was established in the circumstances[6]. However, the Court confirmed that Article 2 imposed a positive obligation on states to respond effectively in situations where authorities knew (or ought to have known at the time) of 'the existence of a real and immediate risk to the life of an identified individual or individuals from the criminal acts of a third party' where it can be established 'that they failed to take measures within the scope of their powers which, judged reasonably, might have been expected to avoid that risk'[7]. Indeed, in respect of Article 5, a relevant ground for considering whether pre-trial detention is justified is the need to protect an accused person against threats of violence through public disorder were his release to be ordered[8].

---

1   Thus where it cannot be established whether state officials were involved in an unlawful killing, the circumstances may still engage state responsibility: see eg *Medova v Russia* 2009-..., paras 95–100 (abduction in life-threatening circumstances by a group of armed men thought to be state officials and the subsequent absence of any news for four years supported the assumption of death, and even although the evidence was insufficient to establish to the requisite standard of proof that the abductors were state officials, this did not necessarily exclude state responsibility under Art 2 in light of the failure by other state officials to take appropriate steps to safeguard life by preventing the release of the armed men with their captives).

2   6040/73, *X v Ireland* (1973) YB 16, 338 at 392 (withdrawal after three years of police protection against a terrorist organisation which had attempted to kill the applicant: Art 2 'cannot be interpreted as imposing a duty on a State to give protection of this nature, at least not for an indefinite period of time. ...'); and 9348/81, *W v United Kingdom* (1983) DR 32, 190, at para 12 (claim that the state had not provided adequate and effective security for the population of Northern Ireland rejected on account of level of presence of security forces: Art 2 could not require 'positive obligation to exclude any possible violence').

3   The duty to take specific action may thus include a duty not to place life at risk, for example, by releasing a prisoner in circumstances where indications exist that this would pose a danger to the community, although some recognition of rehabilitation purposes is recognised: see

Mastromatteo v Italy [GC] 2002-VIII, paras 69–79 (murder of the applicant's son by prisoners on home leave after being released by judges without seeking background information or a prescribed psychological report: no violation, the Grand Chamber recognising (at para 72) measures which permit 'the social reintegration of prisoners even where they have been convicted of violent crimes'; but cf *Maiorano and Others v Italy* 2009-..., paras 110–122 (court-authorised day release of dangerous prisoner who thereafter had committed two murders: violation of Art 2 on account of breach of the duty of care in respect of the protection of life in light of indicators of risk and the failure to forward information to court of non-compliance with release conditions).

4   For discussion of resource issues, see O'Sullivan 'Allocation of Scarce Resources and the Right to Life under the ECHR' [1998] PL 389; and McBride 'Protecting Life: A Positive Obligation to Help' (1999) 24 EL Rev HR 43.

5   *Osman v United Kingdom* 1998-VIII, at para 116.

6   *Osman v United Kingdom* 1998-VIII, at paras 119–121. Discussion of application of any procedural aspect of Art 2 was addressed rather in the context of access to court in terms of Art 6, although the Court later revised its approach in a subsequent judgment: see para **5.59** below.

7   *Osman v United Kingdom* 1998-VIII, at para 116. Cf 22998/93, *Danini v Italy* (1996) DR 87, 24 (not foreseeable that the applicant's daughter was in real and imminent danger of being killed by an individual who had made threats against her); *Denizci and Others v Cyprus* 2001-V, paras 375–377 (nothing to suggest an individual's life was at real and immediate risk: no violation of Art 2 on this account).

8   Eg *IA v France* 1998-VII, para 108 circumstances in which detention may be justified to protect a suspect); see para **4.211** below.

4.24 This principle has also been applied in cases where the Court has accepted that the state has failed to take reasonable measures to counter real and immediate threats to the lives of individuals at particular risk on account of their political activities[1], the social context in which the risk arises being a potentially relevant factor in the assessment[2]. However, the positive obligation cannot be extended to cover loss of life arising from incidents which arise in reality from mere chance[3].

1   Eg *Akkoç v Turkey* 2000-X, paras 77–94 (failure to protect the applicant's husband who was at particular risk of falling victim to an unlawful attack because of his political activities; state authorities had been aware of this risk since the public prosecutor had been informed that threats to the lives of the applicant and her husband had been made, and ought further to have been aware of the possibility that this risk derived from the activities of persons acting with the acquiescence of elements in the security forces: conclusion that in the circumstances the authorities had failed to take reasonable measures available to them to prevent a real and immediate risk to the life of the applicant's husband and accordingly there had been a violation of ECHR, Art 2). See also *Kiliç v Turkey* 2000-III, paras 62–77; and *Mahmut Kaya v Turkey* 2000-III, paras 85–101).

2   *Gongadze v Ukraine* 2005-XI, paras 164–171 (failure of the authorities to respond to a specific request for protection made by a political journalist who had received threats to his life had involved a breach of Art 2, the assessment of the circumstances being made against the general background of vulnerability facing such journalists in the country at that time). See also *Dink v Turkey* 2010-..., paras 66–75 (failure to protect life of a journalist following death threats after publication of a series of articles concerning Turkish-Armenian relationships: violation).

3   *Berü v Turkey* (11 January 2011), paras 42–50 (fatal attack by stray dogs, even although previous incidents had occurred, had not involved the positive obligation to protect life).

Domestic violence

4.25 There is a particular responsibility upon the authorities to address domestic violence, for failure to protect individuals known to be at risk from a violent member of the household may engage Article 2[1]. Where the violence is gender-based, Article 14 may also be of relevance in the assessment. In *Opuz v Turkey*, for example, the Court ruled that there had been a violation of Article 2 since a lethal attack had been foreseeable in light of the history of violent behaviour against the deceased and her daughter. Article 14 had also been engaged as the Turkish judicial system's general passivity in cases of domestic violence mainly affected women, and this in turn had amounted to a form of discrimination[2].

1   Eg *Kontrová v Slovakia* (31 May 2007), paras 48–55 (failure to address long-standing physical and psychological abuse by father who eventually shot dead his children and himself: violation in light of failures by police to take prescribed action to prevent risk to family); *Branko Tomašić and Others v Croatia* 2009-…, paras 49–65 (failure to take all reasonable steps to protect lives of mother and child from threat posed by the child's father who had previously been convicted of threatening to kill them: violation); and *ES and Others v Slovakia* (15 September 2009), paras 43–44 (failure to provide immediate protection to wife and children: violation of Arts 3 and 8).

2   *Opuz v Turkey* 2009-…, paras 192–198 (and at paras 132 and 149: 'the issue of domestic violence, which can take various forms ranging from physical to psychological violence or verbal abuse … is a general problem which concerns all member States and which does not always surface since it often takes place within personal relationships or closed circuits and it is not only women who are affected; here, the conclusion was that 'the national authorities cannot be considered to have displayed due diligence' and thus had failed 'in their positive obligation to protect the right to life of the applicant's mother'). See para **4.85** below for discussion of the facts and the Article 3 disposal; see para **3.109** above for discussion of Art 14. The judgment reflects the opinion of the UN Committee on the Convention on the Elimination of All Forms of Discrimination against Women in its General Recommendation no 19 that 'gender-based violence is a form of discrimination that seriously inhibits women's ability to enjoy rights and freedoms on a basis of equality with men' and is thus prohibited under CEDAW, Art 1, and its reiteration in its combined fourth and fifth periodic report on Turkey that violence against women, including domestic violence, is a form of discrimination (CEDAW/C/TUR/4–5 and Corr.1, 15 February 2005, para 28). The judgment also reflects the CEDAW Committee's decisions in Communications 2/2003, *AT v Hungary* (decision of 26 January 2005) and 6/2005, *Fatma Yÿldÿrÿm v Austria* (decision of 1 October 2007). See also *Kontrová v Slovakia*, (31 May 2007), paras 46–55 (failure by the police to take appropriate action to protect the lives of her children in light of knowledge of the threat posed by his abusive behaviour in the home). For further Council of Europe standard-setting, see Committee of Ministers Rec (2002) 5 on the protection of women against violence. Note also the suggestion of the UN Special Rapporteur on Violence against Women to the Commission on Human Rights of the UN Economic and Social Council (E/CN.4/2006/61) that there is now a rule of customary international law requiring states 'to prevent and respond to acts of violence against women with due diligence'.

Persons in the care or custody of the state

4.26 The positive obligation to protect life applies in particular to those persons in the care or custody of the state who by virtue of their deprivation of liberty are in a vulnerable position. Thus detainees must receive adequate protection against other prisoners known to pose a threat. In *Paul and Audrey Edwards v United Kingdom*, the applicants' son had been killed in a police cell by another prisoner who suffered from paranoid schizophrenia. In finding a violation of Article 2, the Court accepted the state had failed to discharge its responsibility to protect the life of the son while in custody. Information had been available which should have meant that the authorities knew or ought to have known that the other prisoner posed an extreme danger on account of mental illness, but shortcomings in the transmission of this information combined with the brief and cursory nature of the examination carried out by the screening health worker supported a determination that there had been a breach of the state's obligation to protect the prisoner's life. For the Court, it was 'self-evident that the screening process of the new arrivals in a prison should serve to identify effectively those prisoners who require for their own welfare or the welfare of other prisoners to be placed under medical supervision'[1]. The responsibility is of particular importance in respect of detainees with disabilities[2]. The substantive obligation to protect life may extend to a duty to take steps to prevent self-harm by vulnerable prisoners, for example, through the force-feeding of detainees[3] or by placing prisoners on suicide watch[4]. The responsibility for ensuring the well-being of detainees also extends to the provision of adequate medical care when a prisoner's health dictates such[5]. The issue of protection of prisoners from infectious diseases is considered below[6].

1   *Paul and Audrey Edwards v the United Kingdom* 2002-II, paras 57–64 at para 62 (the Court also found a violation of the procedural aspect of Art 2 as the authorities were under a duty to initiate and carry out an investigation: while there had been a comprehensive inquiry, the lack of power to compel witnesses and the private character of the proceedings from which the applicants were excluded except when giving evidence thus rendered the proceedings inadequate for the purposes of the provision). Cf 26561/95, *Rebai v France* (1997) DR 88, 72 (no indication that prisoner who set fire to a cell resulting in his death and that of two other prisoners posed a danger to others; nor had authorities failed to protect the lives of cellmates who died); *Scavuzzo-Hager and Others v Switzerland* (7 February 2006), paras 80–86 (physical restraint used by police in arresting a violent drug addict who had lost consciousness and died three days later: no violation of the positive obligation under Art 2 to protect life as paramedics had been summoned immediately); and *Dodov v Bulgaria* (17 January 2008), noted at para **4.22**, fn 1 above.

2   *Jasinskis v Latvia* 2010-..., paras 58–68 (death of deaf and mute detainee in sobering-up facilities in police station: failures to have him medically examined when taken into custody as required by CPT standards, to provide an opportunity to advise on his state of health by the very least providing pen and paper to communicate concerns, reference being had to UN Convention on the Rights of Persons with Disabilities). For discussion of detention conditions of persons with disabilities, see *Price v United Kingdom* 2001-VII, discussed at para **4.123** below.

3   *Nevmerzhitsky v Ukraine* 2005-II, paras 93–99 (measures such as force-feeding where these can be shown to be medically necessary in order to save life could not in principle be regarded as inhuman and degrading providing that they are accompanied by procedural guarantees protecting against arbitrariness and that the measures do not go beyond a minimum level of severity: here, force-feeding of the applicant had constituted torture within the meaning of Art 3 in light of the lack of any proof of medical justification and the restraints and equipment used); and *Ciorap v Moldava* (dec) (19 June 2007) (force feeding of prisoner involving severe pain and not shown to have been for medical necessity and without procedural safeguards:

violation of Art 3). See also *Horoz v Turkey* (31 March 2009), paras 22–31 (death of a pre-trial detainee following lengthy hunger strike following refusal of judicial authorities to follow a recommendation to order his release: no indication that he had been deprived of treatment in prison that could have been provided upon release, and no violation of Art 2 as no causal link between the refusal to release and his death).

4   *Renolde v France* 2008-..., paras 85–110 and 119–130 (suicide in disciplinary cell of mentally disturbed prisoner who had previously self-harmed: violations of Arts 2 and 3); and *Jasińska v Poland* (1 June 2010), paras 63–79 (failure of prison authorities to have given thought to the risk of suicide by drugs overdose and renewal of drug prescriptions despite being aware of deterioration in mental state). Cf *Keenan v United Kingdom* 2001-III, paras 88–101 (not possible to conclude that the applicant's son had been at immediate risk of suicide, and the prison authorities had done all that could have been reasonably expected of them: no violation of Art 2; but a violation of Art 3 because of defects in health care); and *Tanribilir v Turkey* (16 November 2000), paras 68–80 (no negligence on the part of police officers in preventing the suicide of a prisoner which could not have been reasonably foreseeable; and the authorities had carried out an effective investigation). Note the authorities must have actual or imputed knowledge that a real and immediate suicide risk exists: *Younger v United Kingdom* (dec) 2003-I (authorities are not expected to start from the supposition that all prisoners are potential suicide risks as such a stance would place a disproportionate burden on the authorities as well as unduly restrict the liberty of the individual); *Trubnikov v Russia* (5 July 2005), paras 67–79 (prisoner displaying no acute psychiatric symptoms despite tendency to self-harm when in disciplinary confinement: not possible to conclude that suicide could have reasonably been foreseen); and *Akdoğdu v Turkey* (2005), paras 36–51 (no evidence of intentional killing, but nor could it be shown that routine monitoring measures had not been followed or that it was reasonably foreseeable the prisoner would commit suicide); and see Appendix to Committee of Ministers Recommendation Rec (93) 6, para 58: 'The risk of suicide should be constantly assessed both by medical and custodial staff.' For domestic consideration, see *Orange v Chief Constable of West Yorkshire* [2002] QB 347 (duty of care owed to detainee at common law was similar to Art 2 responsibilities), and the authorities discussed at para **4.34** below.

5   *Anguelova v Bulgaria* 2002-IV, paras 125–131 (delay of the provision of medical assistance by police officers contributed decisively to the death of the detainee, and the case-file contained no trace of criticism of the procedure adopted in the case: violation of the obligation to protect the life of persons in custody); and *Tarariyeva v Russia* 2006-XV, paras 79–89 (inadequate medical care for acute ulcer resulting in death: violation). See also *Taïs v France* (1 June 2006), paras 82–104 (death in sobering-up cell in police station of inebriated prisoner suffering from Aids: gross shortcomings and negligence in care and supervision by police); and *Jasinskis v Latvia* 2010-..., paras 58–68 (deficiencies in health care of an individual who was deaf and mute and who had fallen down a flight of stairs after drinking with friends). Responsibilities may possibly extend to the protection of detainees from the risks posed by passive smoking, not under Art 2 but either under Arts 3 or 8: see para **4.122** below.

6   See para **4.122** below (in terms of Art 3). See also *Shelley v United Kingdom* (dec) (4 January 2008) (prisoners in institutions where there was a significantly higher risk of infection of, eg, HIV could claim to be affected by the prison's health policy and thus had 'victim' status for the purposes of Art 8, but not in terms of Arts 2 and 3 unless they can show they are personally at real or immediate risk of infection).

4.27 An analogous responsibility to exercise special diligence and to take preventive measures to protect life from identifiable harm also applies in relation to the armed services. This is of particular importance in respect of compulsory military service where it is expected that the authorities secure high professional standards among regular members of the armed forces in relation to the treatment of conscripts[1]. The positive obligation may also involve ensuring that vulnerable individuals do not have access to lethal weapons[2].

---

1   *Kilinç and Özsoy v Turkey* (7 June 2005), paras 40–57 (suicide of conscript with mental health problems: inadequate regulation of supervision of those considered vulnerable: violation of Art 2); and *Abdullah Yilmaz v Turkey* (17 June 2008), paras 59–76 (suicide of conscript during military service following injuries inflicted by a non-commissioned officer: violation).

2   *Ataman v Turkey* (27 April 2006), paras 54–70 (military service involved handling of weapons and thus a state should provide treatment for soldiers with psychological disorders: here, reasonable steps to prevent the deceased from getting access to weapons had not been taken: violation of Art 2, and also of the procedural aspect on account of the failure to investigate the circumstances giving rise to the suicide); and *Lütfi Demirci and Others v Turkey* (2 March 2010), paras 30–36 (suicide of soldier with known psychological disorders: violation of positive obligation to exercise special diligence and afford treatment appropriate to military conditions for soldiers with psychological problems through preventive practical measures to protect from the risk of suicide).

Environmental hazards

4.28 The responsibility of the state to address serious risks to health may in certain cases also fall within the scope of Article 2 where an environmental hazard poses a real threat to life. The emergence of such a duty is an extension of, and closely related to, the requirement under Article 8 to take steps to ensure effective respect for family life, for example by providing protection against significant environmental pollution[1]. In certain cases, it may also be appropriate to consider application the right to property under Article 1 of Protocol no 1[2]. The positive obligation under Article 2 arises in 'the context of any activity, whether public or not, in which the right to life may be at stake, and *a fortiori* in the case of industrial activities, which by their very nature are dangerous'[3]. The positive obligation to safeguard the right to life may involve such responsibilities as maintaining an adequate infrastructure to counteract known environmental hazards and setting up a warning system[4]. In *Öneryildiz v Turkey,* the Grand Chamber considered the extent of a state's obligations in respect of hazardous waste. The applicant and his family had lived in a shantytown comprising a collection of slums haphazardly built on land surrounding a municipal rubbish tip. Methane gas given off by the decomposing refuse had exploded resulting in the destruction of houses and the deaths of nine members of the applicant's family. In deciding that Article 2 imposed substantive positive obligations in the public sphere, the Court emphasised that a basic duty of the state was the provision of a legislative and administrative framework governing the licensing, setting up, operation, security and supervision of any dangerous activity such as the storage of waste. Further, practical measures such as the provision of necessary information on the risks posed by such an activity to the public were necessary. Here, the authorities had known that there was a specific danger caused by the tip, and while they had not encouraged the applicant to set up home near this site, they had not dissuaded him from doing so. Neither had they passed on information concerning the specific risks of methane gas or of landslides, information which ordinary citizens could not reasonably have been expected to possess without official dissemination[5].

---

1   See *López Ostra v Spain* A303-C, para 51; *Guerra and Others v Italy* 1998-I, paras 56–60; and *Fadeyeva v Russia* 2005-IV, paras 79–88. See further paras **6.125–6.128** below. In the *Guerra* case, paras 60–62, while the Commission had considered that the applicants had been denied the right to receive adequate information on relevant environmental issues as required by Art 10, the Court rather considered the failure to provide applicants who lived within 1 km of the factory with essential information allowing them to assess the risks of living in this area as a violation of Art 8's requirement of effective protection of respect for private and family life and declined to examine the merits in terms of Art 2. This appears to ignore the fact that employees of the polluting factory had died of cancer through the release of highly toxic substances. This case needs now to be read in the light of the Grand Chamber's judgment in *Öneryildiz v Turkey* [GC] 2004-XII, at para 71–74.

2   *Öneryildiz v Turkey* [GC] 2004-XII, at paras 124–129; cf consideration of natural disasters as in *Budayeva and Others v Russia* 2008-..., paras 171–185 (no violation of Prot 1, Art 1 as it was not clear to what extent proper maintenance or warning systems could have mitigated the exceptional force of the mudslides).

3   *Öneryildiz v Turkey* [GC] 2004-XII, at paras 71–74. Relevant European standards relating to 'dangerous activities' cited by the Court include those connected with the disposal and management, treatment, recycling and marketing of urban and industrial waste, and on civil and criminal responsibilities in respect of the environment. Cf 32165/96, *Wöckel v Germany* (1998) DR 93, 82 (Art 2 does not require a general prohibition on smoking to protect life); but note Harris, O'Boyle and Warbrick *Law of the European Convention on Human Rights* (2nd ed, 2009), at p 43 'there is a margin of appreciation left to the state in balancing the competing interests of smokers and non-smokers: a complete ban on smoking in public places to protect non-smokers is not required; a state that limits cigarette advertising, prohibits smoking in certain public area, and campaigns to inform the public of the injurious effect of smoking complies with Article 2.' Note the cases on passive smoking noted at para **4.122** below.

4   *Budayeva and Others v Russia* 2008-..., paras 147–165 (violation of Art 2; and a further violation established in respect of the inadequate judicial response to a disaster caused by a mudslide).

5   *Öneryildiz v Turkey* [GC] 2004-XII, paras 97–118. For discussion of application of the 'procedural aspect' of Art 2 in this case, see para **4.36** below.

4.29 The essence of this obligation is thus to prevent life from being avoidably put at risk by taking such steps within the scope of state authority as can be considered reasonably to be expected in the light of the information available[1]. While the case law concerns particular risks associated with exposure to radiation and the risk to life caused by a build up of methane gas, the principle clearly applies to other avoidable environmental hazards. The extent to which the responsibility will be extended in time to require action to minimise other risks to daily life that can be reduced by public authorities (for example, by taking appropriate measures at identified road traffic accident blackspots) remains unclear. Certainly, the obligation to take effective action can potentially arise in respect of public transportation[2]. However, the Court will be unwilling to extend the obligation to cover risks to life which are in reality matters of chance and thus not foreseeable[3].

---

1   *LCB v United Kingdom* 1998-III, para 36 (issue determined under Art 2; no need to consider Art 8). Presumably, the exercise of state authority must be consistent with ECHR guarantees

such as Arts 5 and 8: in *Osman v United Kingdom* 1998-VIII, para 121, discussed at para **4.23** above, it was considered that there had been insufficient evidence available to the police to justify arrest.

2   *Kalender v Turkey* (15 December 2009), paras 42–58 (deaths substantially attributable to the authorities' failure to take the most elementary safety measures involving failure of the positive obligation to implement regulations for the purpose of protecting the lives of passengers: violation of substantive aspect of Art 2, and also of the procedural limb on account of the lack of appropriate protection 'by law' ensuring respect for the right to life through deficiencies in the response of the criminal justice system).

3   *Berü v Turkey* (11 January 2011), paras 42–50 (fatal attack by stray dogs, even although previous incidents had occurred, had not involved the positive obligation to protect life).

4.30 An applicant must always be able to show that the responsibilities of the state have been engaged. In *LCB v United Kingdom*, the applicant's father had taken part as a conscript serviceman in nuclear weapon testing some eight years before her birth. At four years old, the applicant had been diagnosed as having leukaemia, and medical records indicated that there was a possibility that the condition was linked to her father's exposure to radiation. She complained that there had been a failure on the part of state authorities to warn and advise her parents and to monitor her health. The European Court of Human Rights accepted that such positive action on the part of state officials could have been required, but only if it had appeared likely that her father's exposure to radiation had indeed endangered risk to her health. Here, however, it was not possible to establish any causal link between the applicant's illness and the exposure, and consequently there was no violation of Article 2[1].

1   *LCB v United Kingdom* 1998-III, paras 35–41. The Court had no jurisdiction to examine complaints under Arts 2, 8 and 13 concerning the monitoring of her father's exposure to radiation since these were based on events before the UK's acceptance of the right of individual petition. Cf International Covenant on Civil and Political Rights, Art 7: 'No one shall be subjected to torture or to cruel, inhuman or degrading treatment or punishment. In particular, no one shall be subjected without his free consent to medical or scientific experimentation.' Cf *McGinley and Egan v United Kingdom* 1998-III, paras 85–90 (Art 6 issue could arise in relation to access to documents relevant to determination of pension rights). See also *D v United Kingdom* 1997-III (threat of deportation which would have hastened death on account of lack of medical facilities), discussed in relation to Art 3 at para 4.137 below.

Medical treatment and the right to life

4.31 Article 2 is applicable in cases where it is alleged that health care has been denied[1], or that medical negligence has resulted in avoidable death. Allegations of failure to provide necessary medical treatment may thus give rise to Article 2 issues[2], but domestic decisions involving allocation of limited health care resources are covered by a margin of appreciation[3]. While the case law initially proceeded upon the basis that medical staff in public hospitals were agents of the state and thus potentially may carry responsibility for loss of life, in *Calvelli and Ciglio v Italy,* the Grand Chamber confirmed that Article 2 obligations apply equally to the private health care sector[4]. The Article imposes both 'a requirement for hospitals to have regulations for the protection of their patients' lives and also an obligation to establish an effective judicial system for establishing the cause of a death which occurs in hospital and any liability on the part of the medical practitioners concerned'[5]. The justification for an investigation into deaths is not only to ensure the accountability of medical staff, but to help prevent future deaths: 'apart from the concern for the respect of the rights inherent in Article 2 of the Convention in each individual case, more general considerations also call for a prompt examination of cases concerning death in a hospital setting. This is because the knowledge of facts and possible errors committed in the course of medical care should be established promptly in order to be disseminated to the medical staff of the institution concerned so as to prevent the repetition of similar errors and thereby contribute to the safety of users of all health services.'[6]

1   *Cyprus v Turkey* [GC] 2001-IV, at para 219: 'an issue may arise under Article 2 of the Convention where it is shown that the authorities of a Contracting State put an individual's life at risk through the denial of health care which they have undertaken to make available to the population generally. [In this case, it is not] 'necessary to examine in this case the extent to which Article 2 of the Convention may impose an obligation on a Contracting State to make available a certain standard of health care' (but it had not been established that the authorities had deliberately withheld or delayed providing medical treatment, nor that problems in travel had placed the lives of any patients in danger).

2   Eg *Oyal v Turkey* (23 March 2010), paras 67–77 (failure to protect life by taking preventive measures against the spread of HIV through blood transfusions, civil compensation awarded being insufficient in the circumstances: violation of Art 2). For early discussion, see 7154/75, *Association X v United Kingdom* (1978), DR 14, 31 (vaccination scheme resulting in deaths by the state health services, which had led to the deaths of a number of young children: while finding no violation of Art 2 on the facts, the Commission observed that Art 2 'enjoins the State not only to refrain from taking life intentionally, but further, to take appropriate steps to safeguard life'. For discussion of health care of detainees, see para 4.26 above.

3   *Pentiacova and Others v Moldova* (dec) 2005-I (allegations of chronic under-funding of health services and long-term failure to provide anything other than basic medication and treatment in respect of chronic renal failure: manifestly ill-founded). Cf *Powell v United Kingdom* (dec) 2000-V (failure by parents of child who died after alleged failure to provide recommended treatment: inadmissible in the light of abandonment of appeal and settlement of civil case).

4   *Calvelli and Ciglio v Italy* [GC] 2002-I, paras 48–57 (no requirement under Art 2 that criminal proceedings had to be available where an action for civil damages against the doctor concerned had been instigated and settled and disciplinary measures were envisaged).

5   *Erikson v Italy* (dec) (26 October 1999) (death from condition not diagnosed after x-ray in a public hospital, but criminal investigations failed to identify the doctor responsible for the error: but manifestly ill-founded in light of a significant criminal investigation and the failure of the applicant to instigate civil proceedings); and *Eugenia Lazăr v Romania* (16 February 2010), paras 66–92 (death of applicant's son after hospital operation: requirement under Art 2 of promptness and reasonable expedition implicit in cases of medical negligence examined not satisfied; and significant shortcomings in the conduct of the investigation involving a lack of co-operation between the forensic experts and investigating bodies and lack of reasons given in the experts' opinions: violation). See also 20948/92 *Işiltan v Turkey* (1995) DR 81, 35.

6   *Byrzykowski v Poland* (27 June 2006), paras 104–118 at para 117 (death of mother and severe brain damage to health of her child during delivery by caesarean section: violation of procedural aspect of Art 2).

Domestic cases involving protection of the right to life through the taking of specific action

4.32 In the English case of *Venables v News Group Newspapers Ltd*, the risk to the safety of two individuals (who had, as children, been convicted of a horrific murder) was held to justify the grant of an injunction preventing the press from revealing their identities or whereabouts, following their release. Reliance was placed by the court upon the *Osman* judgment in extending the existing common law to give effect to the state's positive duties under Articles 2 and 3[1].

Article 2 also formed part of the basis for a decision that the Bloody Sunday inquiry should sit outside Londonderry when hearing the evidence of British soldiers, as the witnesses would otherwise be at risk of life-threatening harm[2].

---

1   *Venables v News Group Newspapers Ltd* [2001] Fam 430. Cf *X (A Woman formerly known as Mary Bell) and Y v O'Brien* [2003] EMLR 37 (lifetime protection of the identity of a person convicted of manslaughter and her daughter from media disclosure granted after balancing the press's right of freedom of expression under Art 10 with Art 8 rights, but Arts 2 and 3 arguments were insufficiently strong in this case); *Carr v News Group Newspapers Ltd* [2005] EWHC 971 (QB) (continuation of injunction against media disclosure based on Art 8 considerations on the grounds of a risk of serious physical and psychological harm, it being accepted that the existing injunction had been effective in reducing that risk and aiding treatment and rehabilitation); and *Re Times Newspapers Ltd* [2009] 1 WLR 1015 (defendants anonymised because of risk to life).

2   *R (A) v Lord Saville of Newdigate* [2002] 1 WLR 1249. The Court of Appeal did not regard as appropriate the test in *Osman v United Kingdom* 1998-VIII, where it was held that there had to be a real and immediate threat to life known to the authorities, observing that 'such a degree of risk is well above the threshold that will engage article 2 when the risk is attendant upon some action that an authority is contemplating putting into effect itself'. The decision was based on the common law requirement that the procedure should be fair, as well as accommodating the requirements of Art 2.

4.33 Article 2 has also been considered in a number of medical contexts. In *Re A (Children) (Conjoined Twins: Surgical Separation)*, the issue was whether the court should grant a declaration that a hospital could lawfully carry out an operation to separate twins who were conjoined at the pelvis and shared a common aorta. In the absence of such an operation, it was clear that both twins would die within three to six months. If the operation were carried out, one twin had a reasonable prospect of a worthwhile life, but the other was certain to die within minutes. The parents were opposed to the operation. The court's decision, granting the declaration, was primarily concerned with domestic civil and criminal law, but also considered the issue in relation to Article 2. It was held that the word 'intentionally' in Article 2(1) should be given its natural and ordinary meaning. So construed, it applied only to cases where the purpose of the prohibited action was to cause death. The purpose of the operation was to save life, even though the earlier extinction of another life was a virtual certainty. English law adequately protected the right to life, notwithstanding that in such exceptional circumstances it regarded an act which had as its foreseen consequence the earlier ending of one twin's life (for the sake of saving the other twin's life) as justified by the doctrine of necessity[1].

In *NHS Trust A v M,* the court had to consider the compatibility with Article 2[2] of the withdrawal of feeding from patients in a permanent vegetative state. The court proceeded on the basis that the principles laid down in *Airedale NHS Trust v Bland*[3] had to be reconsidered in the light of the Human Rights Act 1998 (and the same would apply, in a Scottish context, to the principles laid down in *Law Hospital NHS Trust v Lord Advocate*[4]). The court accepted that a patient in a permanent vegetative state continued to be protected by Article 2. It also accepted that the intention of the withdrawal of treatment was to bring about the death of the patient. The court considered that the issue was whether, in such a case, Article 2 imposed upon the state a positive obligation to take steps to prolong the patient's life. In that regard, reference was made to the opinion of the Commission in the *Osman* case:

> 'Whether risk to life derives from disease, environmental factors or from the intentional activities of those acting outside the law, there will be a range of policy decisions, relating, inter alia, to the use of State resources, which it will be for Contracting States to assess on the basis of their aims and priorities, subject to these being compatible with the values of democratic societies and the fundamental rights guaranteed in the Convention.'[5]

The court concluded:

> 'In a case where a responsible clinical decision is made to withhold treatment, on the grounds that it is not in the patient's best interests, and that clinical decision is made in accordance with a respectable body of medical opinion, the state's positive obligation under Article 2 is, in my view, discharged.'[6]

This issue was considered more generally in *R (Burke) v General Medical Council,* where the issue was whether guidance given by the General Medical Council on withdrawal of artificial nutrition and hydration was incompatible with a patient's Convention rights[7]. The court stated:

> 'In so far as the law has recognised that the duty to keep a patient alive by administering ANH or other life-prolonging treatment is not absolute, the exceptions have been restricted to the following situations: (1) where the competent patient refuses to receive ANH and (2) where the patient is not competent and it is not considered to be in the best interests of the patient to be artificially kept alive. It is with the second exception that the law has had most difficulty. The courts have accepted that where life involves an extreme degree of pain, discomfort or indignity to a patient, who is sentient but not competent and who has manifested no wish to be kept alive, these circumstances may absolve the doctors of the positive duty to keep the patient alive. Equally the courts have recognised that there may be no duty to keep alive a patient who is in a persistent vegetative state. In each of these examples the facts of the individual case may make it difficult to decide whether the duty to keep the patient alive persists.
>
> No such difficulty arises, however, in the situation that has caused Mr Burke concern, that of the competent patient who, regardless of the pain, suffering or indignity of

his condition, makes it plain that he wishes to be kept alive. No authority lends the slightest countenance to the suggestion that the duty on the doctors to take reasonable steps to keep the patient alive in such circumstances may not persist. Indeed, it seems to us that for a doctor deliberately to interrupt life-prolonging treatment in the face of a competent patient's expressed wish to be kept alive, with the intention of thereby terminating the patient's life, would leave the doctor with no answer to a charge of murder.'[8]

1   *Re A (Children) (Conjoined Twins: Surgical Separation)* [2001] Fam 147. The court also considered the matter under Arts 3 and 8. Cf 7154/75, *Association X v United Kingdom* (1978) DR 14, 31 (deaths of children as side-effect of vaccination scheme not 'intentional' deprivation of life). For discussion, see Black-Branch 'Being Over Nothingness: The Right to Life under the Human Rights Act' (2001) 26 ELRev HR/22.

2   And also Arts 3 and 8.

3   *Airedale NHS Trust v Bland* [1993] AC 789.

4   *Law Hospital NHS Trust v Lord Advocate* 1996 SC 301.

5   *Osman v United Kingdom* 1998-VIII, Opinion of the Commission, at para 91.

6   *NHS Trust A v M* [2001] Fam 348. This approach, based upon the distinction between acts and omissions, has been criticised as excessively formal: Bainham 'Dehydration and Human Rights' [2001] 60 CLJ 53. Whether there is an obligation on a state to provide life-preserving medical treatment must, however, depend on the scope of the positive obligation imposed by Art 2.

7   Including Arts 3 and 8.

8   *R (Burke) v General Medical Council* [2006] QB 273 at paras 33–34. As to assisted suicide, see *R (Purdy) v Director of Public Prosecutions* [2010] 1 AC 345, discussed at para **6.38** below, and *Pretty v United Kingdom* 2002-III, discussed at para **4.53** below. See further Dupre 'Human Dignity and the Withdrawal of Medical Treatment: a Missed Opportunity?' [2006] EHRLR 678.

4.34 A number of domestic cases have concerned the effect of Article 2 in the context of the law of delict or tort. In *Van Colle v Chief Constable of Hertfordshire Police*, the claimants' son had been shot dead by the person at whose trial (on minor charges) he was due to testify. There had been threatening telephone calls and other incidents prior to the shooting. The claim was brought on the basis that the police had been under a duty to protect the claimant's son by virtue of Article 2. The claim was rejected. The House of Lords held that to establish a violation of the positive obligation under Article 2 it had to be shown that a public authority had, or ought to have, known at the time of the existence of a real and immediate risk to the life of an identified individual from the criminal acts of a third party and that it had failed to take measures within the scope of its powers which, judged reasonably, might have been expected to avoid that risk. Since neither the accused's criminal record nor his approaches to witnesses indicated that he was given to violence, and since some incidents had not been reported and the reported incidents had not involved explicit death threats, it could not reasonably have been anticipated from the information available to the police at that time that there was a real and immediate risk to the claimant's son's life[1]. That approach was followed in the subsequent case of *Mitchell v Glasgow City Council,* which concerned a local authority tenant who had been killed by his neighbour. The landlord had been aware of previous incidents, but had no reason to anticipate a real and immediate risk to life[2].

The same approach was followed in a different context in *Savage v South Essex Partnership NHS Foundation Trust,* which concerned a detained mental patient who absconded from hospital and committed suicide. An action of damages was brought by her daughter, based upon Article 2. The House of Lords held that authorities were under an obligation to adopt appropriate general measures to protect the lives of patients in hospitals, which included ensuring that competent staff were recruited, high professional standards maintained and suitable systems of work put in place. With regard to mental patients, and especially detained mental patients, that obligation required the authorities to take account of their particular vulnerability, including the heightened risk of suicide, and to have in place appropriate systems to protect them. If the hospital authorities had performed those obligations, casual acts of negligence by members of staff would give rise to a domestic claim in damages but not a breach of Article 2. Where, however, members of staff knew or ought to have known that a particular detained mental patient presented a real and immediate risk of suicide, Article 2 imposed a further operational obligation on hospital authorities, distinct from and additional to their more general duties, which required the staff to do all that could reasonably be expected of them to prevent the patient committing suicide[3].

---

1   *Van Colle v Chief Constable of Hertfordshire Police* [2009] 1 AC 225.

2   *Mitchell v Glasgow City Council* 2009 SC (HL) 21.

3   *Savage v South Essex Partnership NHS Foundation Trust* [2009] 1 AC 681.

Positive obligations: (iii) protection of life through effective domestic investigation, etc – the procedural aspect of Article 2

4.35 The prohibition against unlawful or arbitrary deprivation of life would be largely meaningless without the imposition of a stringent requirement of domestic procedural investigation in order to help secure the effectiveness of domestic laws which seek to protect life. Accordingly, Article 2 also contains a so-called 'procedural aspect', imposing a positive obligation upon authorities to carry out a thorough, diligent and comprehensive inquiry, conducted in a prompt and expeditious manner and with guarantees of sufficient public scrutiny, permitting the participation of the deceased person's relations, and held by a body independent of the persons implicated in the events. The obligation extends to situations in which the carrying out of an investigation is necessary to ensure the effectiveness of domestic legal provisions seeking to protect life, and so may arise in cases of suspicious death attributable to the acts or omissions of private parties[1]. An investigation must be carried out when the fact of such a death has come to the attention of the authorities, rather than being dependent upon the taking of any specific initiative by the next of kin[2]. This procedural obligation is properly considered as a separate and autonomous duty (and thus a 'detachable obligation') capable of binding a state even when a death has taken place before the entry into force of the

Convention[3]. The consequence is that there may often be a finding of a violation of the procedural aspect of Article 2 even where it has not been established that lethal force used in the circumstances was unjustified[4].

1   *Menson v United Kingdom* (dec) 2003-V.

2   *İlhan v Turkey* [GC] 2000-VII, para 63; *Tahsin Acar v Turkey* [GC] 2004-III, para 221 (holding of an investigation cannot be left to the initiative of a deceased's next of kin eg to lodge a formal complaint or to take responsibility for the conduct of any investigative procedures). See further Chevalier-Watts 'Effective Iinvestigations under Article 2 of the European Convention on Human Rights: Securing the Right to Life or an Onerous Burden on a State?' (2010) 21 EJIL 701.

3   *Šilih v Slovenia* [GC] (9 April 2009), para 159; and *Varnava and Others v Turkey* [GC] 2009-..., paras 187–194 (it is thus immaterial that this procedural obligation under Art 2 has only developed in the Court's case law after Turkey's acceptance of the right of individual petition; and the obligation to investigate a suspicious disappearance involves ongoing uncertainty and unaccountability and lack of information or deliberate concealment rather than an instantaneous act, and thus the procedural obligation potentially persists as long as the fate of the missing person is unaccounted for even where death is presumed).

4   Eg *Kaya v Turkey* 1998-I, paras 74–78 and 86–92 (allegation of deliberate killing by security forces in the face of government claims that the individual had died during a skirmish between terrorists and security forces, but there were strong inferences that had not been properly investigated).

4.36 The procedural aspect of Article 2 is of particular relevance where state officials have been responsible for the taking of life, or where it is alleged that they have colluded with others to bring about a death[1] or a disappearance[2], or where there are indications of negligence in the discharge of public responsibilities leading to loss of life[3]. Additionally, the 'procedural aspect' of Article 2 will arise whenever lives have been lost in circumstances potentially engaging state responsibility, including situations where public officials are under an obligation to take positive steps to protect the life of an individual from another person known to pose a real threat to life[4], and also in certain circumstances where death has resulted from medical treatment[5]. Death caused by environmental hazard may also give rise to procedural obligations. In *Öneryildiz v Turkey*, the Grand Chamber considered that the loss of life caused by an explosion of methane gas had called for an adequate judicial or other appropriate response to ensure that the legislative and administrative framework protecting the right to life had been properly implemented and that 'any breaches of the right to life [were] repressed and punished'. Domestic criminal proceedings taken after the explosion had precluded any examination of the aspects of the case involving a danger to life, a situation leading to a determination that there had also been a violation of the procedural aspect of Article 2[6].

1   See *Finucane v United Kingdom* 2003-VIII, paras 72–84 (despite several official inquiries, a police investigation and an inquest, there had been a failure to hold a prompt and effective investigation into allegations that police officers had colluded with a loyalist paramilitary group which had claimed responsibility for the murder); and *Brecknell v United Kingdom* (27 November 2007), paras 65–75 at para 71 (decision by prosecutor not to pursue charges relating to murder of applicant's husband by loyalist gunmen on account of lack of a reasonable

prospect of securing a conviction but despite new evidence suggesting collusion between security forces and terrorists: the positive obligation to carry out further investigative measures arose when new 'plausible, or credible, allegation, piece of evidence or item of information relevant to the identification, and eventual prosecution or punishment of the perpetrator of an unlawful killing' came to light). Cf *Xhavara and Others v Italy and Albania* (dec) (11 January 2001) (responsibility of state authorities for a collision at sea which resulted in the deaths of 58 Albanian illegal immigrants: inadmissible, there being no evidence that the boat carrying the immigrants had been deliberately sunk by the Italian warship, and no reason to believe that the Italian investigation had been inefficient).

2   *Varnava and Others v Turkey* [GC] 2009-..., paras 187–194 (there is a crucial distinction between the obligation to investigate a suspicious death and the obligation to investigate a suspicious disappearance, for the latter is a distinct phenomenon characterised by ongoing uncertainty and unaccountability and lack of information or deliberate concealment rather than an instantaneous act, and the procedural obligation potentially persists as long as the fate of the missing person is unaccounted for even where death is presumed).

3   See eg *Maiorano and Others v Italy* 2009-..., paras 110–132 (while criminal proceedings had been taken against the perpetrator of murders, the accountability of officials involved in authorising and monitoring the perpetrator's release from prison in light of indicators of the risk he still posed had not been secured by the disciplinary proceedings subsequently brought: violation of Art 2).

4   See eg *Opuz v Turkey* 2009-...,, paras 131–153 (ineffective investigation into a killing, despite the prerpetrator's confession, and which lasted without being concluded for more than six years).

5   See *Byrzykowski v Poland* (27 June 2006), paras 104–118 (death of mother and severe brain damage to health of her child during delivery by caesarean section).

6   *Öneryildiz v Turkey* [GC] 2004-XI, paras 150–155.

4.37 The essential purpose of the procedural aspect of Article 2 is thus to combat impunity by holding to account those responsible for the loss of life. This duty can be characterised as 'not an obligation of result, but of means' in that the investigation should help secure the accountability of officials and ensure that they cannot act with impunity[1]. There is no requirement that an investigation must result in a prosecution[2]. The application of the procedural aspect will thus require scrutiny of the adequacy of proceedings as well as of the appropriateness of the outcomes of criminal, civil or disciplinary proceedings[3].

1   *Shanaghan v United Kingdom* 2001-III, at para 90. See also *McCann and Others v United Kingdom* (1995) A 324, at para 161: 'a general legal prohibition of arbitrary killing by the agents of the State would be ineffective, in practice, if there existed no procedure for reviewing the lawfulness of the use of lethal force by State authorities'. This principle derives in part from international legal standards: *McCann and Others*, paras 138–140; and see *Shanaghan*, paras 69–74; *Hugh Jordan v United Kingdom* 2001-III, paras 87–92; *McKerr v United Kingdom* 2001-III, paras 92–97; and *Kelly and Others v United Kingdom* 2001-III, paras 75–80 (consideration inter alia of relevant international law and practice including the UN Principles on the Effective Prevention and Investigation of Extra-Legal, Arbitrary and Summary Executions and the UN Basic Principles on the Use of Force and Firearms by Law Enforcement Officials). For general discussion see Aldana-Pindell 'An Emerging Universality of Justiciable Victims' Rights in the Criminal Process to Curtain Impunity for State-Sponsored Crimes' (2004) 26 HRQ 605.

2   Eg *Brecknell v United Kingdom* (27 November 2007), paras 79–81 (no significant oversights or omissions in the inquiry as key witnesses had been interviewed and available evidence

collected and reviewed, and any prosecutions against relatively minor participants were doomed to failure or could be considered unduly oppressive).

3   Eg *Gül v Turkey (14 December 2000), paras 76–95* (only brief oral evidence had been heard from the police officers charged with the fatal shooting of a householder, and their acquittal had been based upon expert reports proceeding upon the assumption that the police officers were not at fault rather than upon any apparent technical expertise: the decision to acquit without explanation as to why these reports had been considered sufficient indicated that the domestic court had 'effectively deprived itself of its jurisdiction to decide the factual and legal issues of the case').

4.38 In most cases, domestic proceedings will have terminated before the Court will adjudicate on whether these have met the requirements of Article 2, but in certain instances it may be appropriate to determine that there have been significant shortcomings in the investigation while these proceedings are still pending. This is illustrated by a series of four related cases, *Hugh Jordan v United Kingdom, McKerr v United Kingdom, Kelly and Others v United Kingdom* and *Shanaghan v United Kingdom.* The cases related to the deaths of 14 individuals arising out of four separate incidents in Northern Ireland. Three of these involved the use of lethal force by police officers and soldiers, and the fourth concerned allegations of collusion between state officials and terrorists through the disclosure of intelligence to those responsible for the murder of another terrorist suspect. The Court wished to avoid duplicating proceedings examining the state's responsibility for these deaths as the domestic civil courts were better placed and equipped to establish factual matters. It was nevertheless possible to assess whether Northern Irish procedures into the allegations of unlawful killings had been capable in any event of leading to the identification and punishment of those responsible under the procedural aspect of Article 2. Here, significant shortcomings in transparency and effectiveness were obvious. These ran counter to the state's aim of allaying suspicions and rumours through proper investigation, and indeed had helped fuel allegations of a shoot-to-kill policy[1].

1   *Hugh Jordan v United Kingdom* 2001-III, paras 110–145; *McKerr v United Kingdom* 2001-III, paras 116–161; *Kelly and Others v United Kingdom* 2001-III, paras 99–139; and *Shanaghan v United Kingdom* 2001-III, paras 93–125. The inadequacies identified in several or all of the cases variously included a lack of independence of the police officers investigating the incident from police officers or security force personnel involved in the incidents; lack of public scrutiny (and information to the deceased's family) of reasons by the public prosecutor not to proceed against any police officer or soldier; police officers or soldiers who had used lethal force could not have been required to attend the inquests as witnesses; inquest procedures had not allowed any verdict or findings which could play an effective role in securing a prosecution; inquest proceedings had not commenced promptly and had not been not pursued with reasonable expedition; and the non-disclosure of witness statements prior to the appearance of the deceased's families at inquests had prejudiced their ability to participate in proceedings (and, in two of the cases, had contributed to long adjournments in the proceedings). Additional failings in individual cases had included the absence of legal aid for the representation of the deceased's family; the effect of a public interest immunity certificate which had prevented the inquest examining crucial matters; and (in the fourth case) the inquest had been excluded from considering concerns of security force collusion in the targeting and killing of the deceased. The Court also considered the CPT's Report on its visit to the United Kingdom in 1999 which was critical of the effectiveness of police and Police Complaints Authority investigations into

allegations of police ill-treatment of individuals in England and Wales: *Report to the United Kingdom*, CPT/Inf (2000) 1, paras 9–58. The UK Government's response is published at CPT/Inf (2000) 7. This report was referred to in *R (Manning) v Director of Public Prosecutions* [2001] QB 330, where the Divisional Court quashed the DPP's decision not to prosecute prison officers who had forcibly searched a prison inmate immediately before his death, and ordered the DPP to reconsider the matter. See further Aolain, 'The Right to Life in Northern Ireland' (2002) 27 ELRev HR 572.

4.39 While applicants are expected to act with reasonable expedition in bringing an application alleging failure to carry out an effective investigation, in certain cases considerable delay between the events giving rise to the application and the making of the application itself may be considered understandable. In *Varnava and Others v Turkey*, the applicants had complained of a continuing failure to investigate the disappearance of members of the Greek-Cypriot forces who had had last been seen in an area under (or about to come under) the control of Turkish forces during the occupation of northern Cyprus in 1974. The Grand Chamber considered that it had not been unreasonable for the applicants to await the outcome of governmental and United Nations initiatives since these could have resulted in the investigation of known sites of mass graves. This in turn could have provided the basis for further measures in light of the exceptional circumstances of the case, for normal investigative procedures could not have resulted in the discovery of the graves or in other information accounting for the fate of the applicants' relatives[1].

1   *Varnava and Others v Turkey* [GC] 2009-…, paras 187–194 (while a lapse of over 34 years without any news of the whereabouts of disappeared persons can provide strong circumstantial evidence of intervening death, this does not preclude application of the procedural obligation under Art 2 even although the deaths may have occurred before temporal jurisdiction arises; and while recognising the considerable difficulty in carrying out an investigation so long after the events and that an investigation might prove inconclusive, such an outcome was not inevitable; nor was the fact that both sides in the conflict may have preferred a 'politically-sensitive' approach relevant in application of Art 2: violation on account of a continuing failure to effectively investigate the fate of missing individuals).

Availability and exhaustion of domestic remedies

4.40 As cases such as *Gül v Turkey* illustrate, the responsibility to carry out an adequate investigation is closely related to the issue as to the existence of an effective remedy in domestic law to enforce the substance of the guarantee in terms of Article 13[1], and initially, as to whether an applicant has exhausted any such remedies in terms of Article 35[2]. However, a state's responsibilities under Article 2 cannot be satisfied merely by awarding civil damages for a deliberate and wrongful taking of life, and it is crucial that an investigation can have the possibility of leading to the identification and punishment of those responsible for the killing. This is not only required by Article 2 but also by the obligation to ensure that there exists an effective remedy to challenge the loss of life in terms of Article 13[3]. The consequence is that the failure to carry out an investigation sufficient to meet the requirements of Article 2 will give rise to a finding of a violation of both provisions as well as excusing applicants from the need to exhaust domestic remedies as a condition of the admissibility of the application in terms of Article 35 of the ECHR[4]. A claim for compensation for unlawful killing by state officials may also fall within Article 6's guarantee of access to a court for determination of civil rights and obligations[5].

1   *Yaşa v Turkey* 1998-VI, at para 114 (Art 13 imposes obligation to carry out 'a thorough and effective investigation capable of leading to the identification and punishment of those responsible and in which the complainant has effective access to the investigation proceedings'). See also *Tanrıkulu v Turkey* [GC] 1999-IV, at para 119 'the requirements of [Art 13] are broader than the obligation to investigate imposed by Article 2'; but in the related cases of *Hugh Jordan v United Kingdom* 2001-III, paras 159–165; *McKerr v United Kingdom* 2001-III, paras 170–176; *Kelly and Others v United Kingdom* 2001-III, paras 153–159; and *Shanaghan v United Kingdom* 2001-III, paras 134–140, the Court found that no separate issue arose under Art 13, noting that civil proceedings were still pending (or had been settled or discontinued) and that complaints concerning the investigation into the deaths had already been examined under the procedural aspect of Art 2.

2   *Gül v Turkey* (14 December 2000), para 95 (decisions of the criminal court meant that no effective criminal investigation could have been considered to have been conducted, and thus the applicant was denied both an effective remedy in respect of his son's death as well as access to any other available remedies including a claim for compensation); *Aytekin v Turkey* 1998-VII, at paras 82 and 84 (domestic remedies must be 'accessible', 'capable of providing redress', and offering 'reasonable prospects of success'; but an alleged violation of ECHR, Art 2 'cannot be remedied exclusively through an award of damages to the relatives of the victim'); and *Tanrıkulu v Turkey* [GC] 1999-IV, at para 117 ('the remedy required by Article 13 must be "effective" in practice as well as in law, in particular in the sense that its exercise must not be unjustifiably hindered by the acts or omissions of the authorities').

3   *Kelly and Others v United Kingdom* 2001-III, para 105.

4   See eg *Makaratzis v Greece* [GC] 2004-XI, at para 73: (actual circumstances of the death will be 'largely confined within the knowledge of State officials or authorities' and thus the bringing of appropriate proceedings such as 'a criminal prosecution, disciplinary proceedings and proceedings for the exercise of remedies available to victims and their families, will be conditioned by an adequate official investigation, which must be independent and impartial'). See also *Khashiyev and Akayeva v Russia* (24 February 2005), para 117 (applicants were not required in terms of Art 35 to pursue certain redress such as civil remedies that could not lead to the identification and punishment of the perpetrators); and *Salman v Turkey* [GC] 2000-VII, paras 107–109.

5   *Kaya v Turkey* 1998-I, para 107 (the applicant alleged that he would have been unable to seek compensation in the Turkish courts on account of the state's untested but firm contention that his brother had been a terrorist, but since the applicant had never attempted to raise any such action, the Court considered that it was not possible to determine the substance of this complaint, but that in any case this issue was more appropriately considered as falling within the scope of Art 13). Similar considerations apply to allegations of violations of Art 3: see *Aksoy v Turkey* 1996-VI, para 98.

Allegations that the use of lethal force was motivated by ethnic origins, etc

4.41 Applicants have in many cases alleged that the use of lethal force by state agents has been motivated by the victim's racial or ethnic origin. Until recently, the Court appeared reluctant to examine such allegations, preferring instead to resolve the issues raised solely by reference to Article 2, a disinclination doubtless attributable to difficulties in proving the allegations of discrimination beyond reasonable doubt. In *Tanrıkulu v Turkey*, for instance, the applicant claimed that her husband had been killed because of his membership of the Kurdish minority in south-east Turkey, and thus that he had been a victim of discrimination on the ground of national origin. Although the Court found a violation of Article 2, it considered that there was no evidence to support a finding that there had also been a violation of Article 14[1]. Similarly, in *Anguelova v Bulgaria*, the Court did not find it established beyond reasonable doubt that the actions of the police and the investigation authorities had been motivated by discriminatory treatment, even though inter-governmental and human rights organisations had noted widespread evidence of racism and hostility displayed by law-enforcement bodies in Bulgaria[2].

However, it is now clear that an obligation arises to investigate whether discriminatory attitudes were of relevance where concrete indications exist that racist or religious attitudes[3] on the part of officials may have played a part in the use of lethal force by officials. In *Nachova and Others v Bulgaria,* the Grand Chamber ultimately determined that there had been a violation of Article 14 taken together with Article 2 in respect of the requirement to hold an effective investigation into allegations of racially-motivated deprivation of life, since 'racial violence is a particular affront to human dignity and, in view of its perilous consequences, requires from the authorities special vigilance and a vigorous reaction'. The killing of two military conscripts of Roma origin after they had absconded had required a proper investigation into the allegation that the shootings had been racially motivated. While it had not been shown that racist attitudes had actually played a part in the shootings, the failure of the authorities to investigate the allegations of racist verbal abuse with a view to uncovering any possible racist motives in the use of force against members of an ethnic or other minority had been 'highly relevant to the question whether or not unlawful, hatred-induced violence has taken place'. In such circumstances, 'the authorities must use all available means to combat racism and racist violence, thereby reinforcing democracy's vision of a society in which diversity is not perceived as a threat but as a source of its enrichment'[4]. It is important to stress that the duty to investigate whether discrimination was a feature in a particular case will arise only where strong indications arise on the particular facts, even although there may exist considerable data on the existence of prejudicial attitudes on the part of officials towards certain ethnic groups[5].

---

1   *Tanrıkulu v Turkey* [GC] 1999-IV, paras 122–125.

2   *Anguelova v Bulgaria* 2002-IV, paras 163–168. (Note the partly dissenting opinion of Judge Bonello (it was 'particularly disturbing that the Court, in over fifty years of pertinacious judicial scrutiny, has not, to date, found one single instance of violation of the right to life (Article 2) or the right not to be subjected to torture or to other degrading or inhuman treatment or punishment (Article 3) induced by the race, colour or place of origin of the victim'.)

3   Cf *97 Members of the Gldani Congregation of Jehovah's Witnesses and Others v Georgia* 2007-…, paras 138–142; and *Milanović v Serbia* (14 December 2010), paras 96–101 (cases in which violations of Art 3, and of Art 14 taken with Art 3 were established).

4   *Nachova and Others v Bulgaria* [GC] 2005-VII, paras 144–168 at para 151, but note at para 157: 'While in the legal systems of many countries proof of the discriminatory effect of a policy or decision will dispense with the need to prove intent in respect of alleged discrimination in employment or the provision of services, that approach is difficult to transpose to a case where it is alleged that an act of violence was racially motivated. The [Court] does not consider that the alleged failure of the authorities to carry out an effective investigation into the alleged racist motive for the killing should shift the burden of proof to the respondent Government with regard to the alleged violation of Article 14 in conjunction with the substantive aspect of Article 2 of the Convention'.

5   See eg *Ognyanova and Choban v Bulgaria* (23 February 2006), paras 96–116 (death of Roma suspect from a fall from a third-floor window of police station while handcuffed and failure to account for injuries and inconsistencies in police evidence: violations of substantive and procedural obligations under Art 2, but not shown that discriminatory motives were present); and *Mižigárová v Slovakia* (14 December 2010), paras 119–123 (no evidence that officer's behaviour had been racially motivated).

Effectiveness of domestic investigation

4.42 In short, 'where lives have been lost in circumstances potentially engaging the responsibility of the State, Article 2 entails a duty for the State to ensure, by all means at its disposal, an adequate response – judicial or otherwise – so that the legislative and administrative framework set up to protect the right to life is properly implemented and any breaches of that right are repressed and punished'[1]. It follows that 'the kind of investigation that will achieve those purposes may vary according to the circumstances'[2]. While it is not for the Court to specify in detail what procedures should be adopted at domestic level, nor to conclude that one unified procedure which combines fact-finding, investigation and prosecution is necessary, certain crucial features are indispensable for maintaining public confidence in the rule of law and helping prevent suggestions of official collusion in or tolerance of unlawful acts[3]. First, the investigation must be carried out by a body independent of those implicated in the death. Secondly, the investigation must be adequate (that is, capable of gathering evidence to determine whether police behaviour complained of was unlawful and if so, to identify and punish those responsible for the death). Thirdly, the investigation must be carried out promptly and with reasonable expedition. Fourthly, there must be a sufficient element of public scrutiny of the investigation or its results, although the degree of public scrutiny required will be dependent upon the circumstances. Fifthly, the deceased's next of kin must be involved in the procedure to the extent necessary to safeguard their legitimate interests[4].

1   *Kats and Others v Ukraine* 2008-..., at para 115.

2   *Mikayil Mammadov v Azerbaijan* (17 December 2009), at para 103.

3   See eg *Hugh Jordan v United Kingdom* 2001-III, paras 110–145; *McKerr v United Kingdom* 2001-III, paras 116–161; *Kelly and Others v United Kingdom* 2001-III, paras 99–139; and *Shanaghan v United Kingdom* 2001-III, paras 93–125: the applicants specifically referred to the Scottish system of inquiry conducted by a judge of criminal jurisdiction as an appropriate model for satisfying the procedural aspect of ECHR, Art 2, but the Court merely noted that this is not the only method available (at paras 143; 159; 137; and 123 respectively).

4   See also Opinion of the Council of Europe Commissioner for Human Rights Concerning
     Independent and Effective Determination of Complaints against the Police (12 March 2009).
     The requirements of Art 2 mirror those under Art 3: these are discussed at paras **4.103–4.108**
     below.

Independence

4.43 The test of whether the body charged with the investigation is sufficiently
independent calls for examination of whether there has been both institutional or
hierarchical and also practical independence in terms of connections between the
investigators and the officer or public official against whom the complaint is made[1].
In short, independence must exist 'in law and in practice'[2]. The supervision of an
investigation by another authority is not in itself a sufficient safeguard of
independence[3]. In *Ramsahai and Others v Netherlands*, for example, the initial
investigation into a fatal shooting had included forensic examinations and the
questioning of witnesses, but these had been carried out by the same police service
involved in the incident. While the investigation subsequently had been under the
responsibility of an external agency, the Grand Chamber concluded this had been
insufficient 'to remove the taint of the force's lack of independence'. There thus
had been a violation of Article 2. An inquiry carried out by an independent
prosecutor, or the supervision of a police investigation by a public prosecutor, may
satisfy the requirements of the guarantee. In the *Ramsahai and Others* case,
the prosecutor who ultimately had supervised the investigation had been responsible
for policing carried out at the station at which the officers involved in the shooting
had been based, and while it would have been better if the supervision had involved
a prosecutor not connected with the police service, it was not appropriate to
conclude that prosecutors in the Netherlands lack sufficient independence as
regards the police in light of the degree of independence of prosecutors in the
country, the fact that the head of the prosecution service was ultimately responsible
for the investigation, and the possibility of review by an independent tribunal[4].

1   *McKerr v United Kingdom* 2001-III, paras 124–129 (and at para 112, in relation to
     investigations into deaths caused by state agents, it is generally 'for the persons responsible
     for and carrying out the investigation to be independent from those implicated in the events.
     This means not only a lack of hierarchical or institutional connection but also a practical
     independence.'). An administrative body carrying out an investigation into killings by police
     or security forces which is hierarchically subordinate to executive authority will thus not be
     considered 'independent': *Güleç v Turkey* 1998-IV, paras 80–82; *Gül v Turkey* (14 December
     2000), para 91. See also *Paul and Audrey Edwards v United Kingdom* 2002-II, para 70. This
     seems to be a different test of 'independence' from that imposed elsewhere in the ECHR: see
     for example *Assenov and Others v Bulgaria* 1998-VIII paras 104–105 and 148 (the prosecutor
     was not 'independent' in respect of the requirements of Art 5(3), but in regard to the carrying
     out of an investigation required by Art 3, the issue was the prosecutor's inadequate response,
     not independence).

2   *Nachova and Others v Bulgaria* [GC] 2005-VII, at para 112 (also referring to a duty of
     impartiality). For an unusual example of lack of both independence and impartiality, see
     Kolevi v Bulgaria (5 November 2009), paras 195–215 (supervision of the investigation into a
     murder by the chief public prosecutor suspected by the family of masterminding the victim's
     murder, and inability to prosecute the chief prosecutor in large measure on account of the

hierarchical structure of the prosecution service). See also *Celniku v Greece* (5 July 2007), paras 64–71 (police officers in charge of investigation into use of lethal force attached to the same police office as were the officers involved in the incident).

3   *Hugh Jordan v United Kingdom* 2001-III, para 120; and *McKerr v United Kingdom* 2001-III, para 128. See also *Brecknell v United Kingdom* (27 November 2007), para 76 (initial inquiries had been carried out by a police service whose officers had been heavily implicated in the allegations of collusion, and while the conduct of the investigation had been taken over by an institutionally distinct organisation and other bodies whose independence was not in doubt, there had been a failure to comply with this requirement for a considerable period of time).

4   *Ramsahai and Others v Netherlands* [GC] 2007-VI, paras 333–346. Note also the CPT's insistence that involvement by prosecutors in investigating allegations of ill-treatment under Art 3 constitutes a significant means for combating impunity: *14th General Report* CPT/Inf (2004) 28. The same would doubtless hold true for investigations into deaths.

Adequacy

4.44 The effectiveness of an investigation is assessed in accordance with whether it is capable of gathering evidence sufficient to determine whether the behaviour or inactivity complained of was unlawful and if so, to identify and to punish those who were responsible for loss of life, and thus 'the authorities must take whatever reasonable steps they can to secure the evidence concerning the incident, including, inter alia, eyewitness testimony, forensic evidence[1] and, where appropriate, 'an autopsy which provides a complete and accurate record of possible signs of ill-treatment and injury and an objective analysis of clinical findings, including the cause of death'[2]. The lack of rigour in the gathering of evidence is often the cause of a finding of a violation. Significant inadequacies in the carrying out of an effective domestic investigation have been established in a number of cases[3].In *Ramsahai and Others v Netherlands*, for example, the Grand Chamber was critical of certain key failings, including failures to examine the officers' firearms, to test for gunshot residue, to stage a reconstruction of the incident, to keep the two officers separated after the shooting, and to question the officers promptly after the shooting[4].

1   *Mikayil Mammadov v Azerbaijan* (17 December 2009), at para 104.

2   *Salman v Turkey* [GC] 2000-VII, at para 105 (and note at para 73 the reference to the Model Autopsy Report included in the UN Manual on the Effective Prevention and Investigation of Extra-legal, Arbitrary and Summary Executions). See also *Giuliani and Gaggio v Italy* [GC] (24 March 2011), paras 307–326 (particularly serious shortcomings in autopsy incapable of providing a starting point for an effective investigation of the use of lethal force during violent counter-demonstrations; further, it was highly regrettable that authorisation of the cremation of the body had taken place well in advance of the results of the autopsy).

3   See eg *Kaya v Turkey* 1998-I, paras 89–90 (failure to collect evidence at the locus, and to check custody records); *Nuray Şen v Turkey (no 2)* (30 March 2004), paras 22–24 (statements from eyewitnesses not taken and ballistic enquiries had been ordered late and were incomplete); *Akkum and Others v Turkey* 2005-II, para 262 (significant omissions in ballistic examinations and in the conduct of the autopsy); and *Celniku v Greece* (5 July 2007), para 67 (no steps taken to secure evidence in the immediate aftermath of the incident). For an example where an investigation was considered adequate, see eg *Bayrak and Others v Turkey* (12 January 2006),

paras 48–56 (judicial investigation into attacks undertaken by Hizbullah organisation in the region had required far-reaching efforts).

4   *Ramsahai and Others v Netherlands* [GC] 2007-VI, paras 326–332.

Promptness and reasonable expedition

4.45 The investigation must be carried out promptly and with reasonable expedition in order to maintain confidence in the rule of law and to help prevent the appearance of collusion in or tolerance of unlawful acts. Promptness also assists in securing evidence. The investigation should thus take place as soon as the matter is brought to the attention of the authorities in order to establish the cause of death[1], although 'it must be accepted that there may be obstacles or difficulties which prevent progress in an investigation in a particular situation'[2].

1   *McKerr v United Kingdom* 2001-III, para 114; and *Çakıcı v Turkey* [GC] 1999-IV, paras 80–87 and 106.

2   *Mikayil Mammadov v Azerbaijan* (17 December 2009), at para 105. See also *Varnava and Others v Turkey* [GC] 2009-..., noted at para **4.39** above.

Public scrutiny

4.46 There must also be a sufficient element of openness and transparency to secure accountability. The degree of public scrutiny required will be dependent upon the circumstances. In particular, domestic arrangements must strike an appropriate balance when seeking to take into account other legitimate interests such as national security or the protection of material relevant to other investigations in ensuring that Article 2 safeguards are provided in an accessible and effective manner[1].

1   *McKerr v United Kingdom* 2001-III, at para 159. In England, an inquiry in public was also considered appropriate in *R (Wright) v Secretary of State for the Home Department* [2001] EWHC Admin 520 concerned with the death of a prisoner, and see the similar case of *R (Amin) v Secretary of State for the Home Department* [2004] 1 AC 653 (racist attack by prisoner known to be violent). See also *R (Wagstaff) v Secretary of State for Health* [2001] 1 WLR 292 (successful application for judicial review of the decision to hold in private the inquiry into the killing of patients by Dr Harold Shipman, based in part on ECHR, Art 10); cf *Persey v Secretary of State for the Environment, Food and Rural Affairs* [2002] EWHC 371.

Involvement of next of kin

4.47 The next of kin must be involved in the procedure 'to the extent necessary to safeguard his or her legitimate interests'[1]. As noted, an investigation must take place as soon as the death comes to the attention of the authorities, and the next-of-kin cannot be required to take the initiative in lodging a formal complaint or assuming responsibility for investigation proceedings[2]. However, there is no requirement for applicants to have access to police files or copies of documents during an ongoing inquiry, or for them to be consulted or informed about every step[3].

1   *Güleç v Turkey* 1998-IV, para 82.

2   *Slimani v France* 2004-IX, paras 45–50 (death of a detainee held in a centre for foreign nationals where medication and general care for his mental health condition had been given by police officers rather than by doctors; a domestic investigation had indicated that death had been caused by acute pulmonary oedema, and since no criminal action had been involved, the conclusion was that no further action needed to be taken: the refusal to allow the applicant access to the investigation file and to advise her of the outcome of the investigation had resulted in a violation of the procedural aspect of Art 2).

3   *Brecknell v United Kingdom* (27 November 2007), para 77 (efforts had been made by the police to meet with members of the family, and any limitation on available information seemed to result from a lack of any concrete results).

Domestic discussion of the procedural aspect of Article 2

4.48 The procedural aspect of Article 2 has been considered in numerous domestic cases. One group of cases has concerned deaths in custody. The case of *R (Amin) v Secretary of State for the Home Department*, for example, concerned the death of a prisoner who had been murdered by a cell-mate who had a history of violent and racist behaviour. The Director General of the Prison Service immediately wrote to the deceased's family accepting responsibility for the death. A number of investigations into the death were commenced. An inquest was opened but adjourned when the cellmate was charged with murder and not resumed after he was convicted. An internal prison service investigation recommended changes to the regime but that no individual member of staff could be disciplined. A police investigation advised that no prosecution should be brought against the Prison Service. The Commission for Racial Equality conducted an investigation into racial discrimination in the Prison Service, with the circumstances of the deceased's death as one of the terms of reference, but declined to hold most of the inquiry's hearings in public or to permit the family to participate. The Secretary of State refused the family's request for a public inquiry into the death on the grounds that such an inquiry would add nothing of substance and would not be in the public interest. The House of Lords held that an independent public investigation, with the deceased's family legally represented, provided with the relevant material and able to cross-examine the principal witnesses, should be held in order to satisfy the state's procedural duty under Article 2. That article required the state to take steps to protect the lives of those involuntarily in its custody from the criminal acts of others, and, where death occurred, the state's procedural obligation to carry out an effective investigation of the circumstances required, as a minimum standard of review, sufficient public scrutiny to secure accountability and an appropriate level of participation by the next-of-kin to safeguard their legitimate interests[1].

The subsequent case of *R (L) (A Patient) v Secretary of State for Justice* concerned a prisoner whose attempted suicide resulted in permanent brain damage. The Prison Service appointed a retired prison governor to investigate the incident. No relative or representative of the claimant was aware of the investigation. The investigator submitted a written report, which was not published. The claimant challenged the Secretary of State's decision not to conduct an investigation which complied with the requirements of Article 2. The Secretary of State resisted the claim on the ground that the investigative obligation imposed by Article 2 did not arise unless there was an arguable case that the prison authorities were in breach of their substantive duty to protect life and that, since that threshold had not been reached, an internal investigation was appropriate. It was conceded that if Article 2 would have imposed an investigative obligation if the suicide attempt had succeeded, the obligation also arose, in the circumstances of the case, notwithstanding that the attempt had failed. The House of Lords held that, since prisoners as a class present a particular risk of suicide, the state's positive obligation under Article 2 to protect life had special application, requiring prison authorities to put in place systemic measures to prevent suicide, and to take operational measures when they knew or ought to have known of a real and immediate risk that a prisoner might commit suicide. Whenever a prisoner killed himself, it was at least possible that the prison authorities had failed, either in their obligation to take general measures to diminish the opportunities for prisoners to harm themselves, or in their operational obligation to try to prevent the particular prisoner from committing suicide. Given the closed nature of the prison world, without an independent investigation you might never know. So there must be an investigation of that kind to find out whether something did indeed go wrong. In that respect a suicide was like any other violent death in custody. The essential ingredients of such an investigation were that it should be initiated by the state, be promptly and expeditiously conducted by a person who was independent of those implicated in the relevant events, involve the victim's family and provide for a sufficient element of public scrutiny. Since the internal investigation initiated by the Prison Service lacked the requisite independence and had not involved the claimant's family or representatives, and since the resulting report had not been published, it had not satisfied those requirements[2].

---

1   *R (Amin) v Secretary of State for the Home Department* [2004] 1 AC 653 (and see Lord Hope's discussion of the Scottish model of fatal accident inquiries at paras 55–63).

2   *R (L) (A Patient) v Secretary of State for Justice* [2009] 1 AC 588. This case might be contrasted with *R (P) v Secretary of State for Justice* [2010] QB 317, where self-harm had resulted in serious injury but had not posed a real and immediate risk to life, and where Art 2 was therefore held not to be engaged. Other cases concerned with deaths in custody include *R (Middleton) v HM Coroner for the Western District of Somerset* [2004] 2 AC 182 (necessary for an inquest to culminate in the formal expression of a jury's conclusion on the facts in dispute in order for the investigation to be compatible with the state's procedural obligations under Art 2); *R (Sacker) v West Yorkshire Coroner* [2004] 1 WLR 796 (inquests into prisoners' deaths had to address not only the means of death but also the circumstances in which these took place to address the positive obligation to protect life); *R (Lewis) v Mid and North Shropshire Coroner* [2010] 1 WLR 1836.

4.49 Another group of cases has concerned deaths in NHS hospitals. The case of *R (Takoushis) v Inner North London Coroner* concerned a person who was brought into an NHS hospital after being seen preparing to jump off a river bridge in an attempt to commit suicide. The hospital operated an emergency triage system for assessing the needs of patients which prioritised those with mental health problems and under which the person, having been identified as a suicide risk, should have been seen by a doctor within ten minutes. He was initially seen by a nurse but was then left unattended for half an hour before a doctor came to see him, by which time he had absconded from the hospital. He made his way back to the river and committed suicide. The Court of Appeal distinguished the cases concerned with deaths in custody, and observed that that where a person died as a result of what was arguably medical negligence in an NHS hospital, the state must have a system which provided for the practical and effective investigation of the facts and for the determination of civil liability. An inquest which carried out a full and fair investigation would satisfy that requirement[1].

1   *R (Takoushis) v Inner North London Coroner* [2006] 1 WLR 461. Subsequent cases concerned with deaths in NHS hospitals or under NHS care have included *Kennedy v Lord Advocate* 2008 SLT 195 (obligation to hold inquiry into deaths following infection with hepatitis C during course of receiving blood products and blood transfusions); and *Emms, Petitioner* 2011 SLT 354 (no obligation to hold inquiry into death of hospital patient where no material supportive of serious concern that there had been a breach of the substantive obligation under Art 2).

4.50 Another group of cases has concerned deaths in the context of armed conflict. The case of *R (Gentle) v Prime Minister* concerned the deaths of two British servicemen killed while on active service in Iraq. Although inquests were to be held which would investigate the circumstances surrounding the deaths, the claimants sought judicial review of the defendants' refusal to hold a separate independent inquiry to examine the wider question, which would not be considered at the inquests, whether the United Kingdom Government had taken reasonable steps to be satisfied that the invasion of Iraq was lawful under the principles of international law. The House of Lords held that Article 2 imposed no obligation to hold such an inquiry. Article 2 was not an absolute guarantee that nobody would be exposed by the state to situations where his life was in danger, whatever the circumstances, and was not violated simply by deploying service personnel on active service overseas as part of an organised military force, even though there was an inherent risk of their being killed. The legality of military action under international law had no immediate bearing on the risk of fatalities. Nor did the Convention provide a suitable framework for resolving questions about the resort to war, for which the United Nations Charter provided the relevant code and means of enforcement. Since Article 2 did not impose the substantive obligation for which the claimants contended, it followed that it did not impose a procedural obligation to investigate whether there had been a breach of such a substantive obligation. The procedural obligation under Article 2 was parasitic upon the existence of the substantive right, and could not exist independently[1].

That decision might be contrasted with two other decisions. In *R (Al-Skeini) v Secretary of State for Defence* it was held that there was an obligation under Article 2 to investigate the death of a person who had been arrested by British forces in Iraq and taken into custody at a British military base, where he had died allegedly as a result of torture carried out by soldiers at the base[2]. The case of *R*

(Smith) v Secretary of State for Defence concerned a soldier who had died on a British army base in Iraq as a result of heat stroke. It was held that, since the investigative obligation under Article 2 arose only in circumstances where there was ground for suspicion that the state might have breached a substantive obligation under Article 2, and the death of a soldier on active service did not of itself raise a presumption of such a breach, it followed that such a death did not automatically give rise to an obligation to hold an investigation which complied with the procedural duty under Article 2. In the case of the deceased, however, the evidence raised the possibility of systemic failure by the military authorities to protect soldiers from the risk posed by the extreme temperatures in which they had to serve. On the assumption that the deceased had been within UK jurisdiction for the purposes of Article 1 (an assumption which, it was held, would be correct only if he had been within premises under the control of the army at the time of the events which led to his death), there was therefore an arguable breach of the substantive obligation under Article 2, which was sufficient to trigger the need for an inquiry which complied with the requirements of Article 2[3].

1   *R (Gentle) v Prime Minister* [2008] 1 AC 1356. The latter proposition might have provided a more straightforward answer in the case of *Niven v Lord Advocate* 2009 SLT 876, where there was no suggestion that the state bore any responsibility for the death of the deceased (death had been the subject of a murder trial followed by a successful appeal by the accused: no obligation to hold an inquiry).

2   *R (Al-Skeini) v Secretary of State for Defence* [2008] 1 AC 153. There was held to be no obligation to investigate the deaths of persons who had been shot in armed incidents in Iraq involving British troops, as the incidents had not occurred on territory within UK jurisdiction for the purposes of Art 1 of the ECHR. A similar approach has been adopted in other cases concerned with deaths occurring overseas: see eg *Fayed v Lord Advocate* 2004 SC 568.

3   *R (Smith) v Secretary of State for Defence* [2011] 1 AC 1.

Particular issues arising under Article 2

Abortion

4.51 The lack of clarity under the ECHR as to when any right to life begins is shared by other international instruments[1] and reflects a lack of general agreement on this issue which justifies a wide margin of appreciation[2]. On this account, the abortion of an unborn foetus has not yet been considered as a violation of Article 2. The question has been essentially avoided by the Strasbourg organs, either since the issue has not been argued directly by applicants[3], or where directly argued, domestic law has been deemed not to exceed the discretion available to national authorities in determining when life begins[4], or the applicants have not been recognised as 'victims'[5]. There may also in particular cases be a need to include countervailing interests – in particular, that of the woman carrying the foetus – in any assessment[6], as in certain circumstances the failure to make provision for therapeutic abortion may indeed give rise to a finding of a violation of other Convention provisions, in particular, Article 8[7]. An opportunity to rule on the matter - albeit indirectly - arose in *Vo v France*, but the actual circumstances of the case again allowed the Court to avoid doing so. In this case the applicant had been forced to undergo an involuntary therapeutic abortion as a consequence of medical error. Her unborn child was expected to have been viable, but no prosecution of the doctors for unintentional homicide was possible in French law as a foetus was not recognised as a potential victim in such circumstances. Her application raised the issue whether the failure to punish the unintentional destruction of a foetus through criminal prosecution constituted a failure on the part of the state to protect the right to life. While reaffirming the existence of positive obligations to ensure that regulations compelled hospitals to protect patients' lives and to provide effective judicial procedures to hold those responsible to account, the Court nevertheless clarified that these do not necessarily require the provision of a criminal law remedy in non-intentional deaths of patients, for these obligations can equally be satisfied by means of a civil remedy or even disciplinary measures. Since an action for damages had been available and the applicant had not made use of this, no violation of Article 2 was established[9]. The conclusion must be that abortion is not necessarily exclusively a matter that falls within the scope of the private life of the mother under Article 8[10] and thus abortion is not categorically excluded from Article 2 consideration, but that it may be difficult to identify circumstances in which a violation will be deemed to have occurred perhaps other than in a case of an involuntary termination not justified on health grounds.

1   Cf UN Convention on the Rights of the Child, Art 6(1): 'Every child has the inherent right to life.' 'Child' is defined by Art 1 as 'every human being below the age of eighteen years'. Attempts to extend the convention to include foetuses were resisted since international consensus was lacking: see Alston 'The Unborn Child and Abortion under the Draft Convention on the Rights of the Child' (1990) 12 HRQ 156. Cf the American Convention on Human Rights, Art 4: 'Every person has the right to have his life respected. This right shall be protected by law, and in general, from the moment of conception.' See further Domien, Harris and Zwaak *Law and Practice of the European Convention on Human Rights and the European Social Charter* (1996), pp 102–103; van Dijk, van Hoof, van Rijn and Zwaak (eds) *Theory and Practice of the European Convention on Human Rights* (4th edn, 2006), pp 387–391.

2   *Vo v France* [GC] 2004-VIII, at para 85: 'it is neither desirable, nor even possible as matters stand, to answer in the abstract the question whether the unborn child is a person for the purposes of Article 2 of the Convention'. At para 87, the Court noted that '[this] issue has not been resolved within the majority of the Contracting states themselves...there is no European consensus on the scientific and legal definition of the beginning of life'. See also 17004/90, *H v Norway* (1992) DR 73, 155 (challenge to the decision of the applicant's partner to abort the child she was carrying: while Art 2 required a state to take appropriate steps to safeguard life, because of differences in their domestic laws, member states 'must have a certain discretion' in the regulation of abortion, and while the possibility of a foetus receiving protection under the ECHR could not be excluded, here the regulation by domestic law of abortion did not exceeded the discretion available to states). This approach was confirmed in *Boso v Italy* (dec) 2002-VII in which the Court again avoided but left open the question whether a foetus could qualify for protection.

3   As in *Open Door and Dublin Well Woman v Ireland* (1992) A 246-A, paras 66–79 (at paras 78–79: question essentially concerned right to receive and impart information on abortion under ECHR, Art 10; but the Court declined to consider whether restrictions could be justified by the state as protecting the 'rights of others'). See also *Tokarczyk v Poland* (dec) (31 January 2002) (conviction for facilitating abortion through practical steps including newspaper

advertisements did not fall within Art 10 freedom of expression as the applicant had not been engaged in any kind of public debate expressing his opinions).

4   *A, B, and C v Ireland* [GC] 2010-..., paras 233–238, discussed at para **6.55** below.

5   Certain applicants have been deemed to lack 'victim' status: eg 867/60, *X v Norway* (1961) YB 4, 270 and 7045/75, *X v Austria* (1976) DR 7, 87 (applicants unable to qualify as a 'victim' in a general challenge to abortion legislation). Other cases have taken a different approach: thus in 8416/79, *X v the United Kingdom* (1980) DR 19, 244, the Commission did accept that while the father of the foetus was 'so closely affected' by the termination of his wife's pregnancy that he could qualify as a 'victim', the term 'everyone' could not normally apply prenatally and thus the applicant could not challenge the decision to have an abortion on health grounds), while in *Open Door and Dublin Well Woman v Ireland* (1992) A 246-A, para 44, the Court considered for the purposes of Art 8 that women of child-bearing age could qualify as 'victims' since they could be affected by the restrictions on the availability of material on abortion. See also the observation in *Vo v France* [GC] 2004-VIII, at para 86, that 'the life of the foetus was intimately connected with that of the mother and could be protected through her' at least in circumstances where alleged negligence had led to the involuntary termination of pregnancy. In Scots civil law, no legal personality is recognised until birth, although a child is entitled to raise an action in delict for injuries sustained while *in utero*: *Hamilton v Fife Health Board* 1993 SC 369. However, this principle cannot be extended to give a father who would qualify as a legal guardian of a child upon its birth the right to prevent any damage to the foetus, at least not to prevent the termination of the pregnancy by way of abortion: *Kelly v Kelly* 1997 SC 285 (husband sought to prevent his wife from seeking an abortion but the court considered he lacked title to sue: an unborn foetus had no rights which could be vindicated). See also *P's Curator Bonis v Criminal Injuries Compensation Board* 1997 SLT 1180 (for the purposes of the criminal injuries compensation scheme, a foetus is not recognised as a person who may qualify). For English discussion, see *R (Smeaton) v Secretary of State for Health* [2002] EWHC 610 Admin.

6   See *A, B, and C v Ireland* [GC] (16 December 2010), at paras 213 and 250: 'Article 8 cannot be interpreted as meaning that pregnancy and its termination pertain uniquely to the woman's private life as, whenever a woman is pregnant, her private life becomes closely connected with the developing foetus'; and 'the establishment of any such relevant risk to [the life of a woman in remission from cancer] caused by her pregnancy clearly concerned fundamental values and essential aspects of her right to respect for her private life'. For earlier discussion, see 6959/75, *Brüggeman and Scheuten v Germany* (1977) DR 10, 100, paras 60–61 (challenge to restrictions on availability of abortion under Art 8 since domestic law required specific situations of distress to the pregnant women to be shown before abortion was lawful: the Commission could not accept that pregnancy pertained exclusively to the sphere of private life since the foetus has some claim to consideration, and thus that not every regulation of abortion constituted an interference with respect for private life, but the Commission avoided consideration whether the foetus was an entity permitting interference 'for the protection of others'). See also 8416/78, *X v United Kingdom* (1980) DR 19, 244 (the Commission in this case also ruled out any interpretation which would recognise an absolute right of the life of the foetus, since this would mean that 'an abortion would have to be considered as prohibited even where the continuance of the pregnancy would involve a serious risk to the life of the pregnant woman [and thus] the "unborn life" of the foetus would be regarded as being of a higher value than the life of the pregnant woman.').

7   The lack of availability of abortion has been raised under Art 8: see *Tysiąc v Poland* 2007-IV, paras 114–130 (refusal to terminate pregnancy of a woman suffering from severe myopia despite concerns that continuing with the pregnancy could have a significant impact upon her eyesight, concerns which in fact were borne out: violation of Art 8). See also *A, B, and C v Ireland* [GC] 2010-..., paras 158–159, 163–165, discussed at para **6.55** below (complaints that that the impossibility of abortion in Ireland except in highly particular circumstances and thus necessitating travel to England had rendered the procedure unnecessarily expensive,

complicated and traumatic, had stigmatised and humiliated the applicants, had risked damaging their health and – in respect of the third applicant was in remission from cancer – had posed a threat to life: complaints under Art 2 rejected as there had been no legal obstacle to any of the applicants travelling abroad for an abortion and the third applicant had not claimed that post-abortion complications had represented a threat to life; and complaints under Art 3 rejected as the undoubted psychological and physical burden of necessary travel abroad had not been sufficiently grave to represent inhuman or degrading treatment; but issues exhaustively examined under Art 8, and finding of a violation in respect of the third applicant only on account of lack of effective and accessible procedures allowing her to establish her right to a lawful abortion).

8   *Vo v France* [GC] 2004-VIII, paras 81–95 (existing jurisprudence was summarised at para 80). See also 24844/94, *Reeve v United Kingdom* (1994) DR 79, 146 (issue of access to court under ECHR, Art 6(1) for the mother of a child born with severe defects and who had been prevented from suing a health authority which allegedly had failed to diagnose defects in the foetus before birth, but the Commission accepted that a law 'based on the premise that a doctor cannot be considered as being under a duty to the foetus to terminate it and that any claim of such a kind would be contrary to public policy as violating the sanctity of human life' pursued the aim of upholding the right to life and further fell within the state's margin of appreciation: manifestly ill-founded).

9   *A, B, and C v Ireland* [GC] 2010- ..., paras 222–241 (despite the undisputed European consensus on the *availability* of abortion, this was insufficient to narrow the broad margin of appreciation accorded states in determining when life begins as there was no similar European consensus on the scientific and legal definition of the beginning of life: further, since the rights of the foetus and of its mother were inextricably linked, a similar margin of appreciation as regards the balancing of the conflicting interests of the foetus and the mother is recognised: and noting that the prohibition on abortion for health or well-being reasons was based on the profound moral values of the Irish people).

Euthanasia and assisted suicide

4.52 Issues concerning the medical treatment of a mentally competent individual seeking to end his life may give rise to consideration of a state's obligations under Article 2 of the ECHR. The general duty of the state is to preserve life, and thus in certain circumstances a positive responsibility to take steps to prevent an individual from harming or killing himself will arise, for example where that individual is in the custody of state authorities[1]. Whether state authorities may approve the ending of life by doctors to avoid further suffering contrary to the wishes of the patient or his family[2], or whether doctors may provide palliative care which is likely to have the unintended effect of shortening life[3], remain to be addressed by the Court. The lack of European consensus on such issues would suggest that states should be accorded a margin of appreciation in this respect, but doubtless subject to the crucial proviso that each instance be considered on a case-by-case basis and determined by a process in which full and careful examination of the circumstances has taken place and the decision has been solely motivated by the best interests of the patient[4].

1   110565/83 *X v Germany* (9 May 1984) (forcible feeding of hunger striker could involve degrading elements within the meaning of Art 3, but Art 2 also imposed duty to take positive action to protect life, particularly in respect of detainees). See para **4.119** below.

2   Cf Parliamentary Assembly Recommendation 1418 (1999) 'mercy killings' are not regarded as acceptable).

3   For domestic support for the principle that, unless the patient chooses otherwise, a terminally ill or dying person should receive adequate pain relief and palliative care even if this treatment as a side-effect may contribute to the shortening of the individual's life, see para **4.33** above.

4   See further 6839/74, *X v Ireland* DR 7, 78; 20527/92, *Widmer v Switzerland* (10 February 1993); 100083/82, *R v United Kingdom* DR 33, 270. Cf Harris, O'Boyle and Warbrick *Law of the European Convention on Human Rights* (1st edn, 1995), at p 38: the authors suggested that while passive euthanasia (eg by withdrawing treatment) is unlikely to give rise to an Art 2 issue; 'a different answer would be likely in the case of active euthanasia, whereby death is accelerated by a positive act'; and cf (2nd edn, 2009), at p 39: 'Less clear [than the involuntary killing of individuals] is the case of voluntary active euthanasia, which is now permitted, subject to stringent safeguards, by the law of at least two European states'. See further Council of Europe *Ethical Eye – Euthanasia* (vols 1 & 2) (2003).

4.53 Whether a state may condone or assist in the taking of action by non-state actors resulting in the ending of the life of an individual suffering from an incurable disease was addressed in *Pretty v United Kingdom*. In this case, the applicant was in advanced stages of motor neurone disease, a degenerative and incurable illness which had rendered her incapable of decipherable speech and had left her paralysed from the neck down. However, the illness had not affected her intellectual capacity to make decisions, and she had attempted to obtain assurances that her husband would not be prosecuted if he were to assist her in her resolve to end her life. The refusal of the public prosecutor to give any such assurance had been upheld by the domestic courts. The Strasbourg Court confirmed that such a refusal was compatible with Article 2 since the guarantee 'cannot, without a distortion of language, be interpreted as conferring the diametrically opposite right, namely a right to die; nor can it create a right to self-determination in the sense of conferring on an individual the entitlement to choose death rather than life'. In other words, the provision 'is unconcerned with issues to do with the quality of living or what a person chooses to do with his or her life' and is 'first and foremost a prohibition on the use of lethal force or other conduct which might lead to the death of a human being and does not confer any right on an individual to require a State to permit or facilitate his or her death'. This was so even where it could be argued that the failure to allow life to be terminated would result in a deterioration of health sufficiently serious as to amount to 'degrading treatment' within the meaning of Article 3, for this particular provision had to be construed in harmony with the right to life[1]. On the other hand, the Court was 'not prepared to exclude' that consideration of a wish to end one's own life would not give rise to an issue under Article 8 in so far as this provision recognises the notion of personal autonomy. However, the Court found no violation of Article 8 in the circumstances. It was neither arbitrary 'for the law to reflect the importance of the right to life, by prohibiting assisted suicide while providing for a system of enforcement and adjudication which allows due regard to be given in each particular case to the public interest in bringing a prosecution', nor was the prosecutor's refusal to give an advance undertaking that no prosecution would be brought against her husband a disproportionate response bearing in mind the seriousness of the act for which immunity was sought and the implications for the rule of law of excluding individuals or classes from the operation of the criminal law[2].

1   *Pretty v United Kingdom* 2002-III, paras 37–42 and 49–56 at paras 39 and 54, citing Parliamentary Assembly Recommendation 1418 (1999) (but note observation at para 41 that 'even if circumstances prevailing in a particular country which permitted assisted suicide were found not to infringe Article 2 of the Convention, that would not assist the applicant in this case, where the very different proposition – that the United Kingdom would be in breach of its obligations under Article 2 if it did not allow assisted suicide – has not been established'). See also *Sanles Sanles v Spain* (dec) 2000-XI (application by heir of a tetraplegic who had tried unsuccessfully to seek legal recognition of his right to end his life with the help of others and who had been refused permission to carry on domestic proceedings after the tetraplegic's death: inadmissible as the heir could not be recognised in such circumstances as a 'victim').

2   *Pretty v United Kingdom* 2002-III, paras 61–67 and 87–90. See also at para 89: an objective and reasonable justification exists 'for not distinguishing in law between those who are and those who are not physically capable of committing suicide' as 'the borderline between the two categories will often be a very fine one and to seek to build into the law an exemption for those judged to be incapable of committing suicide would seriously undermine the protection of life ... and greatly increase the risk of abuse'. For domestic consideration, see *R (Purdy) v Director of Public Prosecutions* [2010] 1 AC 345, discussed at para **6.38** below. For further discussion, see Marshall 'A Right to Personal Autonomy at the European Court of Human Rights' [2008] EHRLR 337.

The right not to be subjected to the death penalty

4.54 The specific reference to capital punishment in Article 2(1) is an historical legacy rather than an indication of contemporary practice. Many European states permitted and applied the death penalty in the middle of the twentieth century; 60 years on, the practice has been almost entirely abandoned[1]. Protocol no 6 abolished the death penalty but retained the right of any state to make legal provision for capital punishment 'in respect of acts committed in time of war or of imminent threat of war', providing always that any such sentence 'shall be applied only in the instances laid down in the law and in accordance with its provisions'[2]. Protocol no 13 removed this exemption by simply providing that capital punishment 'shall be abolished' (and thus no derogation under Article 15 is possible in time of war or other public emergency)[3]. Only two states have not yet signed Protocol no 13, and only three states that have signed have yet to ratify it[4]. In consequence, any issue concerning the death penalty is now likely to be restricted to the question of extradition or deportation to a state where there is a real risk of the imposition of capital punishment.

1   Of the 47 Council of Europe member states, all have abolished the death penalty entirely or in peacetime with the exception of Russia which still retains the death penalty for some five crimes although a moratorium has been in place since 1996. A decision of the Russian Constitutional Court in 1999 prohibited the passing of death sentences until such time as jury trials would be introduced throughout Russia, a move now apparently delayed. The last judicial executions in Council of Europe member states appear to have taken place in Ukraine in 1997 and despite the moratorium in the Chechen Republic in Russia in 1999 where several executions were broadcast on television. However, capital punishment sentences continue to be passed in the internationally-unrecognised regions of Abkhazia, the Dnestr Moldavian

Republic, Nagorno-Karabakh and South Ossetia, although *de facto* moratoria on executions may be in place. The only European non-member state of the Council of Europe still to carry out executions is Belarus where it is estimated that, between 1991 and 2011, some 400 persons were executed. The secrecy surrounding the imposition of these sentences in Belarus was condemned by the UN Human Rights Committee in 2003: see *Bondarenko v Belarus* (CCPR/C/77/D886/1999 (11 March 2003), and *Lyashkevich v Belarus* (CCPR/C/77/D887/1999 (24 April 2003). See further Parliamentary Assembly Recommendation 1760 (2006). For consideration of EU policy towards non-member states, see Guidelines to EU Policy towards Third Countries on the Death Penalty, General Affairs Council, Luxemburg, 29 June 1998; and EU Charter on Fundamental Rights, Arts II–2 and II–19.

2   Prot 6, Arts 1 and 2. 'War or of imminent threat of war' should be interpreted narrowly, and clearly excludes a 'public emergency threatening the life of the nation'. (Cf the wording of Art 15.) It thus suggests international rather than domestic armed conflict and excludes non-legal usage (as in the so-called 'war on terror'). No derogation or reservation is possible: Prot 6, Arts 3 and 4. Gomien, Harris and Zwaak *Law and Practice of the European Convention on Human Rights and the European Social Charter* (1996), at p 96 conclude that any legislation permitting the death penalty in time of war would require to have been enacted during peacetime, and could not be altered during war. Prot 6 opened for signature in April 1983, and entered into force in March 1985. It was ratified by the United Kingdom on 20 May 1999 with effect from 1 June 1999. Ratification followed acceptance in May 1998 by the Commons of a backbench amendment inserting Prot 6 in the Human Rights Bill. The Government had wished to retain the right of Parliament to consider whether the death penalty should be used and was concerned that any ratification of Prot 6 would prevent reintroduction of capital punishment at a later stage without renunciation of the Convention as a whole: see (1998) NLJ 810. The Crime and Disorder Act 1998, s 36 abolished the death penalty for treason, and the Human Rights Act 1998, s 21(5) in respect of military offences. See further Council of Europe *The Death Penalty – Beyond Abolition* (2004). For general discussion, see Hood and Hoyle *The Death Penalty: a Worldwide Perspective* (4th edn, 2008); and Yorke 'The Right to Life and Abolition of the Death Penalty in the Council of Europe' [2009] ELRev 205. For examples of Privy Council disposal of Commonwealth cases involving the death penalty since a more critical appraisal was adopted in *Pratt and Morgan v Attorney-General of Jamaica* [1994] 2 AC 1, see *Guerra v Baptiste* [1996] 1 AC 397; *Lewis v A-G of Jamaica* [2001] 2 AC 50; *R v Hughes* [2002] 2 AC 259; and *Griffith v The Queen* [2005] UKPC 58. Arguments concerning the death penalty are considered in the case of *The State v Makwanyane and Mchunu* (1995) 16 HRLJ 4 [South Africa].

3   Prot 13, Arts 1 and 2. Prot 13, Arts 1 and 2 are 'Convention rights' for the purposes of the Human Rights Act 1998: The Human Rights Act 1998 (Amendment) Order 2004 (SI 2004/1574). Art 1 of Prot 13 was invoked, unsuccessfully, in *Al-Saadoon v Secretary of State for Defence* [2010] QB 486.

4   As at 31 March 2011, only Russia had not ratified Prot 6. Prot 13 was still to be signed by Azerbaijan and by Russia, while Armenia, Latvia and Poland had signed but not yet ratified. Presumably, a state wishing to reintroduce the death penalty would require to denounce the Convention in its entirety rather than merely Prots 6 and 13. See also European Convention on Extradition (ETS 24 (1957)), Art 11 (extradition to a state in respect of an offence which carries the death penalty may be refused if this penalty is not provided for or not normally carried out in the requested state unless sufficient assurances are given that the death penalty shall not be carried out); and Resolution 1271 (2002), para 7 ('prior to the extradition of suspected terrorists to countries that still apply the death penalty, assurances must be obtained that this penalty will not be sought').

4.55 The death penalty constitutes 'the deliberate and premeditated destruction of a human being by the State authorities', and inevitably involves not only 'some physical pain' but also 'intense psychological suffering' on account of 'the foreknowledge of death at the hands of the State'[1]. Whether it would still be permissible to impose or to execute a sentence of capital punishment or to transfer an individual to another state where the death penalty may be imposed even in the absence of ratification of either or both Protocols no 6 and no 13 is now highly dubious. Three judgments in particular mark the progression of the right not to be subjected to the death penalty to the status of a fundamental right on a par with Articles 2 and 3. These judgments plot the interplay between Articles 2 and 3 (for if Article 2 were to be read as permitting capital punishment, Article 3 may possibly be interpreted as prohibiting it), the near-unanimous ratification of optional Protocols no 6 and no 13, and the interpretation of the Convention as a 'living instrument'. A number of factors may now be of relevance in any assessment of the compatibility of the death penalty with the ECHR. These include the fairness of the criminal process, the personal circumstances of the condemned person, the proportionality of the sentence to the gravity of the crime committed, the conditions of detention of a condemned person awaiting execution, and the manner in which the death penalty is executed.

1   *Al-Saadoon and Mufdhi v United Kingdom* 2010-..., at para 115.

4.56 In the first of these cases, *Soering v United Kingdom,* a German national had been detained in the United Kingdom pending determination of a request by the United States of America for his extradition to face two charges of murder allegedly committed when the applicant was 18. There was a substantial likelihood that, if convicted, the sentence would have been one of capital punishment. The Court's ruling that extradition would lead to an Article 3 violation focused upon condemnation of the holding conditions pending execution (or 'death row phenomenon') rather than of the sentence. The Court declined to accept that the imposition of a sentence of death would in itself violate the prohibition of inhuman or degrading treatment under Article 3. However, it ruled that detention on 'death row' in detention facilities in the USA would do so, and thus it was impermissible for the United Kingdom to allow the extradition without firm assurances that this penalty would not be carried out[1]. The rationale for this approach was that European states had chosen to abolish the death penalty not through judicial interpretation but by 'the normal method of amendment', that is, by optional ratification of Protocol no 6. The Court thus concluded that Article 3 could not be interpreted as imposing any general prohibition against infliction of the death penalty[2]. Subsequently, while the Court was not prepared to rule that Article 2 had to be interpreted as precluding application of the death penalty, the Court did accept that Protocol no 6 (and therefore also now Protocol no 13) could indeed be engaged in cases of threatened extradition or deportation to a country where an individual faced a serious risk of being executed, whether on account of the imposition of the death penalty or otherwise[3]. In *Soering,* the possibility of challenge to extradition to face the death penalty was extended to include denial of fair hearings[4]; in later cases, the Court indicated it was also prepared to consider other disproportionate sentences imposed by courts[5].

1   *Soering v United Kingdom* (1989) A 161, paras 101–104. The applicant had not directly raised this issue: his argument under Art 3 was based upon the detention conditions on death row prior to execution. For further discussion of detention conditions on death row and Art 3, see *Poltoratskiy v Ukraine* 2003-V. See further para **4.127** below. The Canadian Supreme Court has also ruled that individuals may not be extradited to the USA without assurances that capital punishment would not be sought if convicted: *United States v Burns* 2001 SCC 7 [Canada]; and see *Judge v Canada*, Comm no 829/1998 [UN Human Rights Committee] (deportation to the United States and imposition of death sentence: violations of the ICCPR).

2   *Soering v United Kingdom* (1989) A 161, at para 103. For earlier discussion, see also 10479/83, *Kirkwood v United Kingdom* (1983) DR 37, 158 (the terms of Art 2 does not support a contention that extradition to a state without a prior binding assurance that death penalty will not be applied would result in an Art 3 violation); and 10227/82, *H v Spain* (1983) DR 37, 93 (extradition proceedings are not a 'determination' of a criminal charge in terms of Art 6: the state could only consider whether formal procedures for extradition were satisfied and not the question of guilt).

3   See also 25342/94, *Raidl v Austria* (4 September 1995) (threatened deportation to Russia, but no indication death penalty would be applied: inadmissible); *Nivette v France* (dec) 2001-VII (assurances received by the respondent state were such as to exclude the danger that the death penalty or life imprisonment without the possibility of remission would be imposed if the applicant were extradited to the USA); *Ismaili v Germany* (dec) (15 March 2001) (allegation that there is a substantial risk that the death penalty may be applied must be established; here, the country seeking extradition had indicated that the crime the applicant was accused of did not carry this penalty, an assurance which had been confirmed by the German courts: inadmissible); *Salem v Portugal* (dec) (9 May 2006) (full domestic consideration given in the context of adversarial proceedings to legal, political and diplomatic assurances given by India when seeking the extradition of a terrorist suspect that the individual would not face the death penalty if returned and convicted: since it could not be said that India was not a state based on the rule of law, it was not appropriate to reverse the findings of these courts); and *Hakizimana v Sweden* (dec) (27 March 2008) (issues under Arts 2, 3 and Prot 13 were indissociable, but failure to establish substantial grounds for believing the applicant would be exposed to a real risk of being ill-treated, arrested or killed: inadmissible).

4   *Soering v United Kingdom* (1989) A 161, at para 103; and *Bader v Sweden* 2005-XI, paras 43–49 (threatened removal to Syria where sentence of death had been passed in absentia: while in theory it would have been possible to apply for a retrial, this would have required surrender to the Syrian authorities but with no guarantee of the outcome: taken with the risk of flagrant denial of a fair trial and the justified and well-founded fear that the death sentence would be imposed resulting in considerable fear and anguish through intolerable uncertainty, removal would violate Arts 2 and 3, but no need to consider application of Prot 13). See also *Damjanovic v Federation of Bosnia and Herzegovina*, case CH/96/30 (1996) [Human Rights Chamber of Bosnia and Herzegovina] (death sentence imposed by a Bosnian military court was incompatible with Art 2 on account of Art 6 considerations: judges were able to be dismissed by the executive, there was no evidence that in practice they enjoyed any safeguards of independence, and a military court was more likely to be subjected to external pressures).

5   See eg *Jabari v Turkey* 2000-VIII, paras 38–42 (deportation to Iran of Iranian national facing a charge of adultery for which the penalty was death by stoning or flogging would have violated Art 3; the Court was not persuaded that the Turkish authorities had conducted any meaningful assessment of the applicant's claim, and also gave due weight to the UN High Commissioner for Refugees' conclusion that her fears were credible); and *N v Sweden* (20 July 2010), paras 51–62 (deportation of Afghan national who risked the death penalty if returned as she had committed adultery would constitute violation of Art 3 as women were at particular risk of ill-treatment if perceived as not conforming to ascribed gender roles; further, the applicant's husband might decide to resume their married life together against her wish in

terms of the new Shiite Personal Status Law). Other considerations exist. The imposition of a death sentence on an individual for a crime committed as a minor (under 18) is prohibited by the International Covenant on Civil and Political Rights, Art 6(5) and by the UN Convention on the Rights of the Child, Art 37(a). Saudi Arabia, Iran, Yemen and Nigeria continued to execute persons convicted of crimes committed as minors (as did the USA until 2005). Denials of consular access to detainees facing a sentence of death in the USA were addressed by the International Court of Justice in *Germany v United States of America (the 'La Grand case')* (27 June 2001) [ICJ], and in *Mexico v United States of America (the 'Avena' case)* (31 March 2004) [ICJ]. See also *The Right to Information on Consular Assistance, in the Framework of the Guarantees of the Due Process of Law* Advisory Opinion OC–16/99 [Inter-American Court of Human Rights] Series A no 16, para 136 (strictest judicial guarantees are required in capital punishment cases to prevent arbitrary infliction of death).

4.57 In the second of these judgments, *Öcalan v Turkey*, the Grand Chamber stressed the importance of fair hearing guarantees in criminal trials resulting in the imposition of a sentence of death. While the Court abstained from firmly deciding whether capital punishment in peacetime was now prohibited, it seemed to move closer to indicating that European practice could now be taken as establishing an agreement to abrogate the exception in Article 2 permitting capital punishment. In this case, the applicant had been tried and convicted in a 'state security court' and condemned to death, a sentence later commuted to life imprisonment. The Grand Chamber specifically recognised that by 2005, Council of Europe states constituted 'a zone free of capital punishment', and noted that in light of the ratification of Protocol no 6 by all bar one state, 'it could be said that capital punishment in peacetime ... [has] come to be regarded as an unacceptable form of punishment which was no longer permissible under Article 2 of the ECHR'. But the Court was still cautious, for 'the fact that there are still a large number of States who have [at the time of the judgment] yet to sign or ratify Protocol no 13 may prevent the Court from finding that it is the established practice of the Contracting States to regard the implementation of the death penalty as inhuman and degrading treatment contrary to Article 3 of the Convention'. It thus declined to rule conclusively on the question whether it could be said that the text of Article 2 could now be considered to have been amended so as to prohibit the death penalty in all circumstances[1]. In *Öcalan*, the Court did nevertheless indicate that even if Article 2 could still be construed as permitting the death penalty, the implementation of such a sentence following an unfair trial would not be acceptable as this would involve an arbitrary deprivation of life[2]. Further, the passing of such a sentence following an unfair trial would give rise to issues under Article 3 – could also be of key relevance, for this 'would generate, in circumstances where there exists a real possibility that the sentence will be enforced, a significant degree of human anguish and fear, bringing the treatment within the scope of Article 3'. In this instance, the facts were held to have amounted to inhuman treatment[3].

1   *Öcalan v Turkey* [GC] 2005-IV, at para 165.

2   *Öcalan v Turkey* [GC] 2005-IV, at para 166 (quoting with approval the Chamber judgment's observation that Art 2(1) precludes arbitrary application of the death penalty and thus 'any

'court' imposing this penalty must be independent and impartial applying 'the most rigorous standards of fairness … in the criminal proceedings both at first instance and on appeal').

3   *Öcalan v Turkey* [GC] 2005-IV, above, at paras 168–169. See also *Ilaşcu and Others v Moldova and Russia* [GC] 2004-VII, paras 414–418 (first applicant sentenced to death in Transdniestria but thereafter released: the risk of enforcement of the death penalty had been more hypothetical than real, but it was not disputed he must have suffered both on account of the death sentence imposed and of conditions of detention while under the threat of execution, and issues disposed of under Art 3).

4.58 The Grand Chamber's judgment in *Öcalan* thus confirmed that the passing of a sentence of capital punishment following an unfair trial would fall within the ambit of Article 3, and any actual execution would amount to an arbitrary deprivation of life prohibited by Article 2. In the third case, *Al-Saadoon and Mufdhi v United Kingdom*, the Court was called upon to address the question of whether international law may require the transfer of individuals to another state in conflict with a state's obligations under the Convention. The two applicants had been detained in British-run detention facilities in Iraq before being handed over to the Iraqi authorities at the ending of the UN mandate governing the presence of multinational forces in the country. In contrast to *Öcalan*, there was no suggestion of flagrantly unfair trials; nor were conditions of detention an issue as in *Soering*, for this matter had been declared inadmissible at an earlier stage for failure to exhaust domestic remedies[1]. For the Court, the well-founded fear of execution had caused intense psychological suffering throughout the course of the legal proceedings concerning the handing-over to the Iraqi officials, suffering which must have intensified after their actual physical transfer. This had constituted a violation of Article 3. The Court further revisited the question whether Article 2 had been amended through practice and near-unanimous ratification of Protocol no 13. It was now prepared to consider that the references to capital punishment in Article 2 could no longer continue 'to act as a bar to its interpreting the words "inhuman or degrading treatment or punishment" in Article 3 as including the death penalty', but in view of the finding of a violation of Article 3, it was not deemed necessary to consider whether Article 2 (or Article 1 of Protocol no 13) had also been violated. The issue remains for future clarification. The Court was also critical of the failure by the UK Government to consider whether the requirement to secure the applicants' rights could have been achieved in a manner which would still have respected Iraqi sovereignty, for no real attempt had been made by the government to negotiate with a view to preventing the risk of the death penalty, in particular, by seeking the consent of the Iraqi authorities to an alternative arrangement involving the applicants being tried by a British court, or by obtaining a binding assurance that the applicants would not be at risk of capital punishment if convicted by an Iraqi court[2]. *Al-Saadoon and Mufdhi* confirms a state is prohibited from entering into an agreement with another state in conflict with its Convention obligations, especially in a case involving the death penalty where the risk of grave and irreversible harm is particularly acute. Article 2 must now be read in conjunction with Article 3[3].

1   *Al-Saadoon and Mufdhi v United Kingdom* (dec) (30 June 2009).

2   *Al-Saadoon and Mufdhi v United Kingdom* 2010-..., paras 115–150.

3   The issue as to whether the *method* of execution can constitute a violation of Art 3 is still open. If a simulated execution is likely to be considered as resulting in an Art 3 violation, why should an actual execution involving similar levels of pre-execution stress and anxiety (even before consideration of the physical pain involved in the killing itself) escape Art 3 censure? On the other hand, the UN Convention against Torture and Other Cruel, Inhuman or Degrading Treatment or Punishment, Art 1(1) specifically excludes 'pain or suffering arising only from, inherent in or incidental to lawful sanctions' from the definition of 'torture', a position also advanced by the UK Government at the admissibility stage in *Al-Saadoon and Mufdhi v United Kingdom* (dec) (30 June 2009). Cf *Fierro v Gomez* 77 F 3d 301 (1996) [USA] (execution by lethal gas deemed unconstitutional by a federal court in the USA but the Supreme Court remanded the case back for consideration after the state in question amended its law to provide that lethal injection be administered unless the condemned requested lethal gas; on remand, the lower court held the case was moot since the prisoner had not selected to die by gassing); and *Baze v Rees* 553 US 35 (2008) [USA] (lethal injection not 'cruel and unusual punishment').

Deportation, etc involving substantial risk of death

4.59 A similar principle applies to cases where an individual alleges that, if deported, he faces a serious risk of extra-judicial killing by state agents or death at the hands of non-state actors in a situation in which the authorities are unable to provide adequate protection. In most cases, however, it will be appropriate to dispose of such applications in terms of Article 3[1]. Similarly, allegations that an individual's life expectancy would be significantly shortened if deported on account of lack of adequate health care facilitiies may exceptionally give rise to issues under Article 3 rather than Article 2[2].

1   See eg *Said v Netherlands* (dec) (5 October 2004); and *Said v Netherlands* 2005-VI, paras 46–56 (claim that the applicant's return to his home country would result in the possibility of execution for desertion from the army: forcible return to the country would result in a real risk of torture or inhuman or degrading treatment or punishment, the Art 2 complaint being indissociable from the substance of Art 3 complaint in respect of the consequences of deportation for his life, health and welfare, and expulsion would violate Art 3). See also *Ahmed v Austria* 1996-VI, paras 35–47 (serious risk of persecution if returned to Somalia: expulsion would violate Art 3); and *Elezaj and Others v Sweden* (dec) (20 September 2007) (no reason to believe there was a real and concrete risk of being killed in a blood feud in Albania, and it had not been shown that the Albanian authorities could not provide appropriate protection: inadmissible under Arts 2 and 3 as manifestly ill-founded). Similar issues have arisen in countless domestic cases concerned with asylum.

2   *D v United Kingdom*, 1997-III, para 59 (expulsion to country unable to provide adequate health care to dying individual: applicant had based complaints upon Art 3). See further para **4.137** below.

ARTICLE 3: TORTURE AND INHUMAN OR DEGRADING TREATMENT OR PUNISHMENT

Scope of the prohibition against ill-treatment

4.60 Article 3 'enshrines one of the fundamental values of the democratic societies making up the Council of Europe'[1]. The text of Article 3 is succinct; the prohibition against torture or inhuman or degrading treatment or punishment is absolute; and no derogation is permitted in time of war or other emergency[2]. The guarantee imposes upon states obligations of both a negative and positive nature: the former involving a prohibition against the infliction of ill-treatment, the latter imposing certain responsibilities to ensure the provision of an effective legal framework, to take measures to protect individuals against an identifiable risk of ill-treatment, and to carry out an effective investigation into allegations of ill-treatment (the 'procedural aspect' of Article 3)[3]. There is a clear relationship in subject-matter and interpretation with Article 2. Issues such as 'disappeared persons' and deaths in custody often involve applications seeking to rely upon both guarantees, while common approaches in interpretation are clearly evident in the case law of the Court in relation to the development of positive obligations. Further, the Court has approached evidentiary issues arising under both provisions in a similar way, placing the onus upon state authorities to furnish an adequate explanation for injuries sustained while in detention[4].

---

1   *Soering v United Kingdom* (1989) A 161 at para 88. For an example of EU standard-setting, see EU Council Regulation 1236/2005 (concerning trade in certain goods which could be used for capital punishment, torture or other cruel, inhuman or degrading treatment or punishment). See also EU Charter on Fundamental Rights, Art 4.

2   ECHR, Art 15(2).

3   See paras **4.103–4.108** below.

4   See para **4.79** below.

4.61 The prohibition of torture now forms part of customary international law[1], yet in many European states there exists what can be described as a culture of impunity, that is, one in which state officials may inflict ill-treatment without fear of sanction on account of a prevailing attitude which turns a blind eye to the practice[2]. The European Court of Human Rights has adopted a dynamic rather than a static approach to interpretation, judging state action according to generally accepted European standards[3]. Further, the Court 'takes the view that the increasingly high standard being required in the area of protection of human rights and fundamental liberties correspondingly and inevitably requires greater firmness in assessing breaches of the fundamental values of democratic societies', so that earlier classifications of acts as 'inhuman' or 'degrading' could well now justify the label 'torture'[4]. However, at the same time the Court has resisted attempts to lower the threshold test to bring more instances of state practice into Article 3 consideration. Nor can Article 3 be used to found any claim essentially of a social or economic nature[5]. Potential issues under Article 3 include the use of force during interrogation, infliction of punishment, conditions of detention, expulsion (extradition and deportation to other states), and particular discriminatory practices. In exceptional circumstances, destruction of home and possessions may also be considered to give rise to a violation of the guarantee[6].

---

1   See in particular, *Filártiga v Peña-Irala*, 630 F2d 876 (2nd Cir. 1980) [USA]. See also Universal Declaration of Human Rights, Art 5, and International Covenant on Civil and Political Rights, Art 7). For further discussion, Murdoch *The Treatment of Prisoners: European Standards* (2006), pp 113–128; Jenkins 'The European Legal Tradition against Torture and Implementation of Article 3 of the ECHR' [2007] PL 15; and Rodley with Pollard, *The Treatment of Prisoners under International Law* (3rd edn, 2009), *passim*.

2   *14th General Report*, CPT/Inf (2004) 28, para 25.

3   *Tyrer v United Kingdom* (1978) A 26, at para 31 (the Court 'cannot but be influenced by the developments and commonly accepted standards in [European] penal policy'). An attempt to extend the scope of Art 3 to include the subjection by a victim of a rape to cross-examination by the accused was eventually struck out after a friendly settlement: *JM v United Kingdom* (dec) 2000-X (*ex gratia* payment and introduction of amending legislation).

4   *Selmouni v France* [GC] 1999-V, para 101.

5   See eg *Pančenko v Latvia* (dec) (28 October 1999) (complaint concerning precarious economic and social situation arising from refusal of a residence permit declared inadmissible: the ECHR does not guarantee the right to a rent-free residence, the right to work, or the right to medical assistance or financial assistance); and *Tremblay v France* (11 September 2007), paras 24–35 (allegation by a prostitute facing demands for backdated social security contributions that she had been forced by economic necessity to continue prostitution despite her efforts to stop: no violation of Art 3 as this did not indicate she had been thereby forced to continue to work as a prostitute); but cf *Budina v Russia* (dec) 2009-... , noted at para **4.05** fn 3 above. The domestic courts have also acknowledged that the withdrawal of state support may give rise to issues under Art 3: see *R (Haggerty) v St Helen's Borough Council* [2003] EWHC 803 (Admin) (closure of private nursing home: no proof that life was at risk or that there would be Art 3 consequences, and as for Art 8, a local authority has a wide margin of discretion in balancing rights of individual with those of community); and *R (Limbuela) v Secretary of State for the Home Department* [2006] 1 AC 396.

6   *Selçuk and Asker v Turkey* 1998-II, paras 72–80; *Bilgin v Turkey* (16 November 2000), paras 100–104.

Meaning of 'victim' for the purposes of Article 3

4.62 Allegations of a violation of Article 3 may be brought by those who have been directly subjected to ill-treatment. Even failing actual infliction of any such treatment, the threat of infliction may also trigger Article 3 consideration providing it is 'sufficiently real and immediate'[1], and thus the threat of torture may be enough to constitute a violation of Article 3[2]. Further, in certain circumstances, it may also be possible to conclude that the level of mental anguish endured by a family member of a 'disappeared person' is itself sufficient to amount to a violation of Article 3, and thus such relatives will also qualify as 'victims'[3]. Since breaches of Article 3 cannot remedied exclusively by an award of compensation as state agents could continue to inflict such treatment with virtual impunity, the payment of compensation will not necessarily deprive an individual of the status of 'victim', and assessment of all measures taken by the state (including the actions of the prosecution authorities) is thus necessary to assess whether appropriate and sufficient redress has been provided[4].

1   *Campbell and Cosans v United Kingdom* (1982) A 48, at para 26.

2   *Selmouni v France* [GC] 1999-V, para 101.

3   Eg *Kurt v Turkey* 1999-III, paras 130–134 (mother of an individual who had disappeared could claim victim status); cf *Çakıcı v Turkey* [GC] 1999-IV, paras 94–99 (brother of a disappeared person not considered to be 'victim'). See further para **4.81** below.

4   *Çamdereli v Turkey* (17 July 2008), paras 26–30 (victim status upheld in light of discontinuation of criminal proceedings); and similarly, *Vladimir Romanov v Russia* (24 July 2008), paras 71–90. See also *Ciorap v Moldova (no 2)* (20 July 2010), paras 24–25 (award of €600 compensation following domestic court determination of infliction of inhuman treatment: applicant still qualified as a 'victim' as this amount was less than the minimum awarded by Court in such cases).

Application of Article 3

4.63 The application of Article 3 essentially involves two questions: first, whether the physical or mental treatment has achieved a minimum level of severity to give rise to a violation of the provision; and secondly, where this threshold test has been satisfied, whether the circumstances amount to torture, to inhuman treatment or punishment, or to degrading treatment or punishment. Both questions involve an assessment often essentially subjective in nature, for there can be an unresolved tension between recognition of the Convention as a 'living instrument' to be interpreted in a purposive manner reflecting contemporary expectations, and awareness of the historical legacy which underpinned inclusion of this guarantee at the heart of protection of physical integrity. While the guarantee is absolute in nature, practical considerations such as state interests in dealing with prisoners considered to pose particular security risks[1] or in tackling terrorism[2] can still play a part in assessment. In respect of the treatment of detainees, the impact of the Council of Europe's Committee for the Prevention of Torture ('the CPT') in discharging its mandate of enhancing the protection of detainees is now clear in the Court's jurisprudence[3]. Issues specifically relating to punishment are considered below[4].

1   Cf 8463/78, *Kröcher and Möller v Switzerland* (1981) DR 26, 24 (terrorist suspects ordered by investigating judge to be held incommunicado; legal advisers could only visit with the permission of the judge; the suspects were subjected to constant surveillance; no newspapers or radio allowed etc. The Commission accepted that the cumulative effect of security measures should also be assessed in determining whether there was an Art 3 violation, but considered that the measures had been justified on security grounds).

2   Cf *Brannigan and McBride v United Kingdom* (1993) A 258-B (sustained questioning and medical examination of suspects held incommunicado over periods of four to six days; no Art 3 issue identified by the applicants, nor any Art 3 point taken by the Commission). See too *Tomasi v France* (1992) A 241-A, at para 115: 'The requirements of the investigation and the undeniable difficulties inherent in the fight against crime, particularly with regard to terrorism, cannot result in limits being placed on the protection to be afforded in respect of the physical integrity of individuals'.

3   See paras **4.121–4.122** and **4.124** below.

4   See paras **4.112–4.117** below.

Threshold test: determining whether the minimum level of severity has been reached

4.64 The threshold question – whether the specific treatment complained of meets a minimum level of severity[1] – needs to be considered with some care, and inevitably involves a degree of subjective judgment. The issue is considered by reference to all the circumstances of the 'treatment' in question, including its duration and its physical and mental effects, as well as the sex, age and health of the victim[2]. If the suffering involved is considered excessive in the light of prevailing general standards[3] (including contemporary medical standards in the case of involuntary therapeutic treatment)[4], then this threshold test is satisfied. The lack of any evidence of a positive intention to humiliate or to debase an individual is not in itself conclusive as the absence of any such purpose does not rule out a finding of a violation of Article 3[5]. Nor need the 'treatment' be deliberate, for ill-conceived or thoughtless action on the part of state authorities can also give rise to a violation of the guarantee[6].

1   Including threatened treatment or punishment: *Campbell and Cosans v United Kingdom* (1982) A 48, para 26. Cf *M v Chief Constable, Strathclyde Police* 2003 SLT 1007 (letter sent by police to the employer of an individual facing child sex offences and working in a centre in which children would be present: the sending of the letter advising the employer of the charges did not constitute 'treatment' within the meaning of Art 3, and there was no breach of Art 6(2) as the letter only stated that he had been charged, not convicted).

2   5310/71, *Ireland v United Kingdom* (1976) YB 19, 512, para 162; *Selmouni v France* [GC] 1999-V, para 99. See also *PF and EF v United Kingdom* (dec) 2010-… (premeditated sectarian protest lasting two months and designed to intimidate young schoolchildren and their parents: minimum level of severity required to fall within the scope of Art 3 reached and thus triggering the positive obligation on the part of the police to take preventive action).

3   Cf *Tyrer v United Kingdom* (1978) A 26, paras 31 and 38 (contentions that corporal punishment was supported overwhelmingly by the local population not considered by the Court as a relevant factor). In 3344/67, *Greek case* (1969) YB 12, 186, at para 11, the Commission stressed the importance of local culture in finding that a 'certain roughness of treatment' of persons detained by state officials was tolerated and taken for granted, so 'underlin[ing] the fact that the point up to which prisoners may accept physical violence as being neither cruel nor excessive, varies between different societies and even between different sections of them'. This approach is at odds with the fundamental aim of Art 3, and is clearly now inappropriate.

4   *Herczegfalvy v Austria* (1992) A 244, paras 82–83 at para 82: 'as a general rule, a measure which is a therapeutic necessity [in terms of established principles of medicine] cannot be regarded as inhuman or degrading'.

5   *Peers v Greece* 2001-III, para 74.

6   Eg *Henaf v France* 2003-XI, paras 47–60 (elderly prisoner kept in handcuffs and shackled to a bed during hospital visit, a disproportionate response to any security consideration amounting to inhuman treatment in the light of his age and state of health, the absence of antecedents giving rise to a serious fear of a risk to security, and the prison governor's written instructions that the applicant was to be given normal supervision); *Tarariyeva v Russia* 2006-XV, paras 108–111 (unnecessary handcuffing of prisoner to a bed while he was seriously ill: violation);

Erdoğan Yağiz v Turkey (6 March 2007), paras 39–48 (handcuffing of individual with no criminal record in public and at place of work: violation); and *Taştan v Turkey* (4 March 2008), paras 27–31 (military service obligation imposed upon a 71-year-old who had been forced to undertake the same activities and physical exercises as 20-year-old recruits constituted degrading treatment).

4.65 The test has been used to rein in any tendency to appear to trivialise Article 3 by seeking to apply it to matters which arguably lack the requisite degree of seriousness at the historical heart of the article[1]. This, too, often involves an element of subjective decision-making. In *Costello-Roberts v United Kingdom*, for example, a bare majority of the European Court of Human Rights decided that the infliction of corporal punishment in a school was not serious enough to amount to a breach of Article 3, in contrast to the dissenting judgments which placed greater emphasis on consideration of the particular victim (a 'lonely and insecure 7-year-old boy') and of the circumstances surrounding the punishment (which was inflicted after a delay of three days) rather than upon any objective assessment of the treatment itself[2]. For the majority, such issues may be better addressed under Article 8's requirement of respect for private life[3]. On the other hand, the Court has shown itself prepared to reflect enhanced awareness of the impact of prolonged exposure to poor material conditions of detention, thus reversing earlier jurisprudence which insisted that treatment or punishment was to be assessed in terms of immediate impact only[4].

1   Compare eg *Raninen v Finland* 1997-VIII, paras 55–59 (handcuffing of conscientious objector while being taken to a barracks not sufficiently serious to result in an Art 3 violation) with cases such as *Selçuk and Asker v Turkey* 1998-II, paras 72–80, and *Bilgin v Turkey* (16 November 2000), paras 100–104 (premeditated destruction of applicants' homes and personal property: findings of inhuman treatment); and *Tekin v Turkey* 1998-IV, paras 48–54 (ill-treatment while detained blindfolded in cold and dark cell).

2   *Costello-Roberts v United Kingdom* (1993) A 247-C, paras 31–32 (distinguishing the facts from those in *Tyrer v United Kingdom* (1978) A 26, discussed at para 4.69 below); and joint partly dissenting opinion of Judges Ryssdal, Vilhjálmsson, Matscher and Wildhaber. Cf *R (Williamson) v Secretary of State for Education and Employment* [2005] 2 AC 241 (corporal punishment need not be administered in such a manner as to significantly impair a child's physical or moral integrity; but cf Baroness Hale's concurring opinion noting the comments of the UN Committee on the Rights of the Child).

3   *Costello-Roberts v United Kingdom* (1993) A 247-C, at para 36: 'there might be circumstances in which Article 8 could be regarded as affording in relation to disciplinary measures a protection which goes beyond that given by Article 3. [But] bearing in mind that the sending of a child to school necessarily involves some degree of interference with his or her private life, the Court considers that the treatment complained of by the applicant did not entail adverse effects for his physical or moral integrity sufficient to bring it within the scope of … Article 8'. See paras **4.88–4.92** and **6.119–6.121** below.

4   See paras **4.121–4.122** below.

Application of the threshold test by domestic courts

4.66 The German courts have determined that the tolerance of certain 'initiation rites' in the armed forces gave rise to issues arising under Article 3[1]. In another

German case, the application of security measures to a defence lawyer seeking entry to a maximum security prison and necessitating the removal of certain clothing was not considered to meet the minimum threshold for Article 3[2]. In an English case concerned with the physical restraint of children detained in secure training centres, it was observed that although there was a tendency to think of obligations under Article 3 in terms of extreme violence, deprivation or humiliation, depending on the circumstances Article 3 might be engaged by conduct that fell below that high level. Two circumstances that had been identified as imposing special obligations on the state were that the subject was dependent on the state because he had been deprived of his liberty; and that he was young or vulnerable[3]. It has been said in an English case that Article 3 requires the victim to be aware of the inhuman and degrading treatment which he or she is experiencing or at least to be in a state of physical or mental suffering[4]. However, it may be questionable whether that is correct in all circumstances[5].

1   Case 2 WD 12/00, [2001] NJW 2343, [2002] EuroCLY 865 [Germany].
2   Case Vas 567/01, [2002] NJW 694, [2002] EuroCLY 2019 [Germany].
3   *R (C (A Minor)) v Secretary of State for Justice* [2009] QB 657. See also *R (C) v Durham Constabulary* [2005] 1 WLR 1184.
4   *NHS Trust A v M* [2001] Fam 348, para 49.
5   See para **4.72** below.

4.67 The vast majority of cases on this topic in the domestic courts of the United Kingdom have concerned asylum and threatened deportation[1]. In *R (Limbuela) v Secretary of State for the Home Department* the House of Lords considered the Secretary of State's power under the Nationality, Immigration and Asylum Act 2002, s 55 to provide support to asylum seekers who had failed to apply for asylum as soon as was reasonably practicable, for the purpose of avoiding a breach of the ECHR. This category of asylum seeker was normally statutorily barred from receiving support. The House of Lords held that since the purpose of the provision was to avoid breaches of the ECHR, it was not necessary for the degree of severity required for a breach of Article 3 to have been met for the Secretary of State to exercise this power. The Secretary of State's power under s 55 and duty under the HRA 1998 arose because destitution could in certain circumstances give rise to a breach of Article 3, and to this end, the factors to consider were the age, sex, health and hygienic facilities available to the claimant as well as whether he or she had sought assistance through other means. The House of Lords did not interpret Article 3 as imposing a positive duty on the state to prevent destitution and homelessness but relied on the fact that Parliament had deliberately excluded a category of persons from a support system which was available to others[2]. On a related matter, the House of Lords has also considered the appropriate test to be applied when assessing whether evidence has been obtained by torture[3].

1   See para **4.138** below.
2   *R (Limbuela) v Secretary of State for the Home Department* [2006] 1 AC 396. 'Treatment is inhuman or degrading if, to a seriously detrimental extent, it denies the most basic needs of any

human being. As in all article 3 cases, the treatment, to be proscribed, must achieve a minimum standard of severity, and I would accept that in a context such as this, not involving the deliberate infliction of pain or suffering, the threshold is a high one. A general public duty to house the homeless or provide for the destitute cannot be spelled out of article 3. But I have no doubt that the threshold may be crossed if a late applicant with no means and no alternative sources of support, unable to support himself, is, by the deliberate action of the state, denied shelter, food or the most basic necessities of life': per Lord Bingham of Cornhill at para 7. See also *R (T) v Secretary of State Home Department* [2003] EWCA Civ 1285, *R (Q) v Secretary of State for the Home Department* [2004] QB 36 and *R (Adam) v Secretary of State for the Home Department* [2004] EWHC 354 (Admin).

3   *A v Secretary of State for the Home Department* [2006] 2 AC 221 (the rule that evidence obtained by torture was inadmissible could only be overridden by express statutory words; whether evidence had been so obtained was to be determined on the balance of probabilities; and, even if admitted, any doubt as to whether the evidence had been obtained by torture had to be borne in mind when evaluating it).

Classifying violations of Article 3: 'torture'; and 'inhuman' or 'degrading' treatment or punishment

4.68 The distinctions between 'torture', 'inhuman', and 'degrading' treatment or punishment reflect differences in the intensity of suffering as judged by contemporary standards and assessment of state purpose, but the use of the term 'torture' attaches a 'special stigma to deliberate inhuman treatment causing very serious and cruel suffering'[1]. In the early but influential *Greek case*, the Commission defined 'torture' as inhuman treatment inflicted for a specific purpose, while 'inhuman' was understood as suggesting the unjustified infliction of severe pain, and 'degrading treatment or punishment' consisted of that which grossly humiliates or that which forces an individual to act contrary to his will or conscience[2]. In the first case under Article 3 to be considered by the Court, *Ireland v United Kingdom*, this approach was merely refined. Individuals deprived of their liberty under prevention of terrorism powers in Northern Ireland had been subjected to five interrogation techniques (hooding, wall standing, exposure to continuous noise, deprivation of sleep and deprivation of food) during questioning by members of the security forces. The Commission had accepted that this ordeal had incurred 'intense physical and mental suffering' and 'acute psychiatric disturbances' such as to amount to torture. However, the Court considered that the circumstances did not display 'suffering of the particular intensity and cruelty' required for a finding of torture (defined as 'deliberate inhuman treatment causing very serious and cruel suffering'), holding instead that the treatment had amounted to inhuman treatment or punishment through the infliction of intense physical and mental suffering. The least severe form of Article 3 violation, degrading treatment or punishment, was defined as treatment 'designed to arouse in the victims feelings of fear, anguish and inferiority capable of humiliating and debasing them and possibly breaking their physical or moral resistance'[3].

1   *Ireland v United Kingdom* (1978) A 25, at para 167.

2   3321/67–3323/67 and 3344/67, *Greek Case* 1969 YB 12, 186.

3   *Ireland v United Kingdom* (1978) A 25, at para 167 (these five techniques had been 'applied in combination, with premeditation and for hours at a stretch'). Judge Fitzmaurice in a separate opinion seems to have accepted that to classify the techniques as 'torture' would be to trivialise the guarantee. Judge Zekia's opinion suggests that both an objective and a subjective test can be applied: the beating up of an 'elderly sick man' could result in torture while the same violence administered to a 'wrestler or even a young athlete' may not even result in a violation of Art 3 if considered as 'mere rough handling'. Zekia's approach itself brings with it substantial dangers in minimising the practical utility of the guarantee while ostensibly attempting to protect it, and is now out of line with the more robust approach taken to violence inflicted on detainees in *Ribitsch v Austria* (1995) A 336, discussed at para **4.79** below.

4.69 Subsequent judgments have applied this interpretation which proceeds by assessing the degree or intensity of the suffering inflicted. Consistency in jurisprudence is, however, compromised by recognition that heightened expectations may require reassessment of earlier case law: in particular, what in the past may have amounted to 'inhuman or degrading' treatment may now justify a finding of 'torture'[1]. In this area in particular, the Convention is a 'living instrument', interpreted in accordance with present-day expectations. The early judgment of *Tyrer v United Kingdom* concerned the birching of a 15-year-old youth three weeks after a juvenile court decision. The Court emphasised that the degree of humiliation must be judged according to the particular circumstances of the case: here, the fact that the birching was administered on the applicant's bare buttocks was an aggravating factor. Further, any publicity surrounding the treatment or punishment would also be of relevance in deciding whether the treatment was degrading, although the absence of publicity will not in itself prevent an Article 3 violation since 'it may well suffice that the victim is humiliated in his own eyes, even if not in the eyes of others'. In all the circumstances, the institutionalised nature of the violence taken along with the probable long-term psychological harm occasioned justified a finding of 'degrading' treatment[2].

1   *Selmouni v France* [GC] 1999-V, para 101.

2   *Tyrer v United Kingdom* (1978) A 26, paras 32–34. The case involved the Isle of Man for which the United Kingdom had assumed Convention responsibilities in terms of ECHR, Art 56.

4.70 However, heightened expectations in this area have resulted in an increased readiness to find that more serious violations of the guarantee have occurred, and judgments such as *Tyrer* and *Ireland v United Kingdom* thus require to be considered with particular care in light of the ECHR's nature of a 'living instrument'. In the first finding of torture involving an EU member state by the Court, *Selmouni v France*, the applicant had been arrested on suspicion of involvement in drug-trafficking. He had been held in police custody for some three days during which he was beaten with a baseball bat or similar implement, urinated upon and sexually assaulted. Medical examination findings were consistent with his allegations. The Court considered that this type of particularly serious and cruel physical and mental violence should now be regarded as 'torture'[1]. Similarly, in *Salman v Turkey*, the Court considered the infliction of 'falaka' (as well as a blow to the chest) during interrogation amounted to torture on account of the very serious and cruel suffering involved[2].

---

1   *Selmouni v France* [GC] 1999-V, paras 91–106; see Uildriks 'Police Torture in France' (1999) 17 NQHR 411. See also eg *Ilhan v Turkey* 2000-VI, paras 84–88 (applicant was kicked and beaten and struck at least once on the head with a rifle, resulting in severe bruising and head injuries which caused brain damage, and delay of some 36 hours before he was brought to a hospital).

2   *Salman v Turkey* [GC] 2000-VII, paras 113–116.

4.71 Subsequent cases have also stressed the importance of consideration of state motive or purpose in assessing the level of violation[1], suggesting that in relation to the definition of 'torture', the stricter test found in the United Nations Convention against Torture is appropriate[2]. In *Aksoy v Turkey* which produced the first finding by the Court of torture, the applicant had been stripped naked by police officers and then suspended by his arms which had been tied behind his back. The treatment itself had involved severe pain and subsequent temporary paralysis of both arms; its deliberate infliction had also required 'a certain amount of preparation and exertion' by state officials; its purpose appeared to be to extract information or a confession from the applicant[3]. In contrast, in *Denizci and Others v Cyprus,* the ill-treatment administered to the applicants in Cypriot police stations was classified as 'inhuman' rather than as 'torture' since it had been impossible to establish the manner in which the beatings were inflicted, and it had not been established that the aim of the officers had been to extract confessions[4]. It is often not too difficult to discern a motive for the infliction of serious ill-treatment, for example, that such treatment was motivated by a desire for reprisal[5]. The labelling of action considered as having met the threshold test under Article 3 thus proceeds principally by assessing the degree or intensity of the suffering inflicted in the light of contemporary and prevailing views. However, the Court will on occasion not distinguish between 'inhuman' and 'degrading', and merely refer to 'inhuman or degrading' treatment[6].

---

1   Cf *Akkoç v Turkey* 2000-X, at para 115 (torture may also involve a purposive element as recognised in the UN Convention against Torture, Art 1).

2   The United Nations Convention against Torture and Other Cruel, Inhuman or Degrading Treatment or Punishment, Art 1(1) imposes a four-part test: (a) the intentional infliction (b) of severe pain or suffering whether physical or mental (c) for any purpose including, for example, to obtain information, inflict punishment or intimidate him or a third person, (d) by a public official or person acting in an official capacity. See also *Dragan Dimitrijevic v Serbia and Montenegro* Case 207/02 CAT/C/33/D/207/2002 (2004) [UNCAT] (first findings of torture by UN Committee against Torture): see further Joseph 'Committee Against Torture: Recent Jurisprudence' (2006) 6HRLJ 571.

3   *Aksoy v Turkey* 1996-VI, at para 64. See also *Aydin v Turkey* 1997-VI, paras 80–86 (17-year-old Kurdish girl stripped, beaten, sprayed with cold water and subsequently raped by soldiers; the Court accepted (at para 85) that the detention had been with a view to interrogation, and thus the suffering inflicted should be seen as having been calculated to serve the same purpose); and *Sheydayev v Russia* (7 December 2006), paras 54–63 (finding of torture in light of uncontested medical report). Cf *Ireland v United Kingdom* (1976) YB 19, 512, at para 168, where the Court acknowledged that the object of the ill-treatment was 'the extraction of

confessions, the naming of others and/or information', but seemed thereafter to discount the importance of this motive.

4   *Denizci and Others v Cyprus* 2001-V, paras 383–387.

5   Eg *Vladimir Romanov v Russia* (24 July 2008), paras 58–70 (unexplained discrepancies in accounts of alleged reasons for use of violence inflicted with rubber truncheons resulting in serious physical pain, intense mental suffering and long-term damage to health had constituted torture). See also *Dedovskiy and Others v Russia* 2008-..., paras 80–86 (use of rubber truncheons in prison involving deliberate and gratuitous violence had no basis in law and had been grossly disproportionate to alleged transgressions and had been inflicted as a form of reprisal or corporal punishment: torture).

6   Eg *Akdeniz and Others v Turkey* (31 May 2001), para 98 (in respect of applicants' missing relatives); and *Selmouni v France* [GC] 1999-V, para 96 (in distinguishing 'torture' from 'inhuman and degrading' treatment). See also *Ireland v United Kingdom* (1978) A 25, at para 167, noting the existence of *one* distinction 'between "torture" and "inhuman or degrading treatment"', and that 'the first of these terms [thus attaches] a special stigma to deliberate inhuman treatment causing very serious and cruel suffering'.

4.72 The case law stresses the importance of assessing the impact of the treatment upon the particular victim. However, in certain instances this approach will not be appropriate. In *Keenan v United Kingdom,* in seeking to quantify the level of suffering a prisoner suffering from a chronic mental disorder had endured before his death, the Court observed that the issue as to whether the prison authorities had fulfilled their obligation to protect the prisoner from treatment or punishment contrary to Article 3 could be assessed without recourse to such factors: 'treatment of a mentally ill person may be incompatible with the standards imposed by Article 3 in the protection of fundamental human dignity, even though that person may not be able, or capable of, pointing to any specific ill-effects'[1].

1   *Keenan v United Kingdom* 2001-III, at para 113.

4.73 In respect of 'punishment', the level of suffering and humiliation involved must exceed 'that inevitable element of suffering or humiliation connected with a given form of legitimate treatment or punishment'[1]. Nevertheless, the infliction of punishment may certainly give rise to issues under Article 3 as with the imposition of a sentence of imprisonment grossly disproportionate to the offence, the lack of possibility of release on parole, or the failure to release from detention where there are compelling humanitarian considerations[2].

1   *Kudła v Poland* [GC] 2000-XI, at para 92.
2   See further paras **4.114–4.115** and **4.117** below.

The use of force during deprivation of liberty

4.74 The use of force against detainees by state officials will give rise to issues under Article 3. The state has particular responsibilities to protect individuals who are in its care, and disproportionate measures of security or poor conditions of detention may attract condemnation as much as the deliberate infliction of ill-treatment[1]. Case law has considered the extent of state responsibility for unauthorised behaviour of officials, the nature of the treatment which violates the guarantee, and the extent of state responsibilities for investigating allegations of ill-treatment. A state may not escape liability by asserting that the acts complained of were unauthorised or outwith the authority of an official. In the *Greek case*, the Commission established that members of the security police had inflicted torture or ill-treatment on detainees as a matter of practice. The Commission rejected the government's contention that a state could only be in breach of its obligations if the state itself had inflicted the treatment or had at an executive level shown toleration towards the challenged practices, deciding instead that state responsibility could arise in such circumstances and even where a public official was acting without express authorisation or even contrary to instructions[2]. A finding of an administrative practice of ill-treatment is also of relevance in determining whether an applicant has exhausted domestic remedies[3].

1   See eg *Henaf v France* 2003-XI, paras 47–60, noted at para 4.64, fn 6 above; and *Wiktorko v Poland* (31 March 2009), paras 44–57 (stripping naked of a female in a sobering-up centre by male staff members and immobilisation with belts for ten hours constituted degrading treatment within the meaning of Art 3). For conditions of detention, see paras **4.120–4.127** below. For domestic consideration, see eg *R (C (A Minor)) v Secretary of State for Justice* [2009] QB 657.

2   3321–3/67 and 3344/67, *Greek case* (1969) YB 12, 194. State liability thus may be engaged under Art 1 even where state officials are acting ultra vires or contrary to explicit instructions as a state is strictly liable for the conduct of its agents: *Ireland v the United Kingdom* (1978) A 25, para 159; cf International Law Commission's Draft Articles, Art 7, on the responsibility of States for internationally wrongful acts.

3   5310/71, *Ireland v United Kingdom* (1976) YB 19, 512 at 758–762 (the level of official tolerance of unauthorised ill-treatment may also be relevant in considering whether an applicant has exhausted domestic remedies, for if it is established that such tolerance existed at executive level, 'this fact alone would be a strong indication that the complainant has no possibility of obtaining redress through any national organ, including the courts').

4.75 Recourse to physical force by state officials which has not been rendered strictly necessary by a detainee's own conduct constitutes a violation of Article 3[1]. It will be easier for the authorities to justify the need to adopt physical means of restraint where an individual has resisted detention[2], but the onus is still upon the authorities to establish why impugned treatment (such as a strip-search) was necessary[3]. In *Egmez v Cyprus*, the state had accepted that the applicant had been intentionally subjected by police officers to violence at the time of his arrest and during its immediate aftermath. The Court determined that the facts disclosed a finding of 'inhuman' treatment rather than torture since the injuries had been inflicted over a short period of heightened tension at the time of arrest, no convincing evidence had been adduced to show that the ill-treatment had resulted in any long-term consequences, and it had not been shown that the officers' aim had been to extract a confession[4]. In *Rehbock v Slovenia*, a doctor had examined the applicant the day following his arrest by police officers and had diagnosed a double fracture of the jaw and facial contusions. In view of the particularly serious nature of the injury, the Court considered that it was for the state authorities to demonstrate convincingly that the use of force had not been excessive. Here, no convincing or credible arguments which would have explained or justified the degree of force used during the arrest had been furnished, and the conclusion was that the force used had been excessive and unjustified and had thus amounted to inhuman treatment[5].

1   *Ribitsch v Austria* (1995) A 336, para 38; *Tekin v Turkey* 1998-IV, para 53. The treatment must still meet a minimum level of severity: cf *Raninen v Finland* 1997-VIII, paras 55–59 (unnecessary handcuffing of detainee unlawfully deprived of liberty caused no mental or physical effects and thus there was no violation of Art 3).

2   *Berliński v Poland* (20 June 2002) paras 59–65 (use of physical force to resist legitimate actions of police officers and where in consequence the burden on the state to prove that the use of force was not excessive is less stringent).

3   See eg *Wieser v Austria* (22 February 2007), paras 39–42 (unnecessary and unjustifiable strip searching at time of arrest found to have been degrading); and *El Shennawy v France* (20 January 2011), paras 39–46 (repeated full body searches of high risk prisoner by officials wearing balaclavas up to eight times a day over a short period of time and initially recorded on video; full body searches had not only to be necessary but conducted in an appropriate manner, and in this instance had involved a degree of humiliation going beyond the level which the strip-searching of prisoners inevitably entailed).

4   *Egmez v Cyprus* 2000-XII, paras 77–79 (there was also some uncertainty concerning the gravity of the injuries caused in part by the 'retouching' of photographs submitted by the applicant). See too 15299–15300/89, *Chrysostomos and Papachrysostomou v Turkey* (1993) DR 86, 4 (use of rough treatment by police officers did not meet the minimum threshold test for Art 3 in view of the public disorder at the time the applicants were taken into custody.

5   *Rehbock v Slovenia* 2000-XII, paras 68–78; cf paras 79–81: no violation of ECHR, Art 3 during detention as opposed to at the time of arrest was established).

4.76 The use of handcuffs does not normally give rise to an Article 3 issue 'if handcuffing has been imposed in connection with a lawful detention and does not entail use of force, or public exposure, exceeding what is reasonably considered necessary' bearing in mind risks that the prisoner may abscond or cause injury or damage[1]. On the other hand, as cases such as *Henaf v France* and *Mouisel v France* illustrate, where the use of handcuffs constitutes a disproportionate response to any security risk particularly in light of the prisoner's health, the result may be a finding of a violation of Article 3[2].

1   *Mathew v Netherlands* 2005-IX, at para 180. See also *Raninen v Finland* 1997-VIII, at para 56: 'handcuffing does not normally give rise to an issue under Article 3 of the ECHR where the measure has been imposed in connection with lawful arrest or detention and does not entail use of force, or public exposure, exceeding what is reasonably considered necessary in the circumstances'.

2   *Mouisel v France* 2002-IX, para 47 (use of handcuffs while the applicant was being escorted to and from hospital where he was undergoing a session of chemotherapy); and *Henaf v France* 2003-XI, paras 47–60, noted at para **4.64**, fn 6 above. See also *Tarariyeva v Russia* 2006-XV, paras 106–111 (handcuffing of seriously ill prisoner to bed: violation); *Erdoan Yaiz v Turkey* (6 March 2007) paras 39–48 (handcuffing of individual with no criminal record in public and at place of work: violation); *Filiz Uyan v Turkey* (8 January 2009), paras 32–35 (refusal to remove handcuffs from a female prisoner serving lengthy prison sentence and taken for gynaecological examination, and presence of male guards during the consultation: violation);

and *Kashavelov v Bulgaria* (20 January 2011), paras 38–40 (systematic handcuffing of prisoner each time he was taken out of his cell, a practice applied for 13 years despite the absence of indicators of risk: violation, noting CPT standards that systematic handcuffing constituted degrading treatment).

4.77 The infliction of unwarranted physical force will be considered aggravated if it is premeditated or inflicted for a particular purpose such as to extract a confession or information[1] or when it is accompanied by unacceptable detention conditions[2]. In *Elci and Others v Turkey,* for example, defence lawyers had been detained on suspicion of being involved with a terrorist organisation on the basis of incriminating statements made against them by an individual who was standing trial for membership of this organisation. The applicants alleged they had been tortured and ill-treated while in custody through the application of techniques such as being blindfolded, subjected to continuous loud music and death threats, slapped, stripped naked, and doused with cold water. They also complained that the officers had sought to make them sign confessions by the use of undue pressure and unlawful interrogation practices. For the Court, their evidence concerning both the conditions of detention and the interrogation techniques were credible and consistent, and supported both the determination that four of the applicants had suffered physical and mental violence of a particularly serious and cruel nature such as to constitute torture, and the conclusion that four of the other applicants in addition had experienced ill-treatment of somewhat less severity but which still had amounted to inhuman treatment[3]. Non-physical methods of interrogation during detention may also give rise to concerns under Article 3[4].

1   *Aksoy v Turkey* 1996-VI, para 64.

2   *Tekin v Turkey* 1998-IV, para 53 (prisoner held blindfolded in cold, dark cell and with wounds and bruising).

3   *Elci and Others v Turkey* (13 November 2003), paras 637–647.

4   See *Magee v United Kingdom* 2000-VI, discussed at para **5.126** below; and *Gäfgen v Germany* [GC] 2010-…, discussed at para **5.125** below. Cf *Ebbinge v Netherlands* (dec) 2000-IV, and *Jager v Netherlands* (dec) (14 March 2000) (two suspects had been subjected to psychologically disorientating police interrogation methods which appeared objectionable in the context of criminal investigations but which did not support the suggestion that this had resulted in mental pain and suffering sufficient to amount to ill-treatment). Cf *Ireland v United Kingdom* (1978) A 25, discussed at para **4.68** above (but note that the conclusion that the 'five techniques' did not amount to torture is now highly suspect in light of later case law). For discussion of Art 6 concerns as to the fairness of evidence obtained through 'psychologically coercive' detention conditions, see paras **5.125** and **5.126** below.

Establishing the fact of ill-treatment

4.78 Allegations of ill-treatment must be supported by appropriate evidence[1]. This is assessed adopting the standard of proof beyond reasonable doubt, and which 'may follow from the coexistence of sufficiently strong, clear and concordant inferences or of similar unrebutted presumptions of fact'[2]. In relation to detainees, the importance of comprehensive record-keeping is thus a significant consideration in cases alleging the infliction of ill-treatment during detention, and indeed 'the absence of data recording such matters as the date, time and location of detention, the name of the detainee as well as the reasons for the detention and the name of the person effecting it, must be seen as incompatible with the very purpose of [the safeguards for persons deprived of their liberty under] Article 5'[3]. The problem of establishing sufficiency of evidence in such cases is readily acknowledged by the Court[4], and illustrated by the judgment of the Grand Chamber of the Court in *Labita v Italy*. The applicant had been detained pending trial for approximately two years and seven months on suspicion of being a member of the Mafia. He had alleged that he had been subjected to ill-treatment that had been systematically inflicted on prisoners, an allegation supported by an independent judicial report but which had not resulted in the prosecution of any official since those responsible had not been identified. The Grand Chamber of the Court decided by a majority of nine votes to eight that there was insufficient evidence to support a conclusion that the applicant had been subjected to physical and mental ill-treatment: the applicant had not produced any conclusive evidence or supplied a detailed account of the abuse to which he had allegedly been subjected, he had never suggested that he had ever been refused permission to see a doctor, and he had inexplicably taken more than a year to complain about his treatment, notwithstanding the fact that he had made several applications through his lawyers to the judicial authorities shortly after the alleged ill-treatment had diminished or ceased[5]. A strong dissenting minority opinion stresses the practical difficulties facing a prisoner who seeks to allege ill-treatment both in producing sufficient evidence to justify his complaints as well as in running the potential risk of reprisals were complaints to be lodged. In the present case, the minority considered that it had been understandable that prisoners would not have wished to have asked to be examined by doctors since medical staff had not been seen as independent. More particularly, the standard used by the majority for assessing the sufficiency of evidence was 'inadequate, possibly illogical and even unworkable'. The Court should have applied what the minority deemed a 'serious presumption' that the ill-treatment was indeed inflicted during detention, with the burden of proof of providing a satisfactory and convincing explanation being placed clearly upon the state authorities who alone could have had knowledge of events: in any event, where the domestic authorities have failed to carry out an effective investigation and to make the findings available to the Court, the standard to which the applicant must prove his case should be a lower one. If state authorities could in future 'count on the Court's refraining in cases such as the instant one from examining the allegations of ill-treatment for want of sufficient evidence, they will then have an interest in not investigating such allegations, thus depriving the applicant of proof 'beyond reasonable doubt' and limiting any state responsibility to a violation of the procedural aspect of Article 3[6], a much less serious finding than one which has established the actual infliction of ill-treatment. In any case, application of a standard of proof 'beyond all reasonable doubt' was inappropriate since the Court was not determining guilt or innocence but providing protection for individuals in custody and redress in cases of violation. This dissenting opinion appears persuasive, both in its principled reasoning and in its conclusion on the particular facts[7]. In such cases, however, application of the positive obligation arising under Article 3 – the 'procedural aspect' or 'procedural limb' of the guarantee – to carry out an effective investigation into allegations of ill-treatment may be of considerable importance[8].

1   *Klaas v Germany* (1993) A 269, para 30. See also *Ogic v Romania* (27 May 2010), paras 40–51 (application of *affirmanti incumbit probatio* – he who alleges something must prove that allegation – applies even in cases where access to information capable of corroborating or refuting allegations is held by the government alone, but the mere fact of contradictory versions cannot in itself lead to dismissal of allegations as unsubstantiated). But note *Ireland v United Kingdom* (1978) A 25, at para 160: 'In order to satisfy itself as to the existence or not in Northern Ireland of practices contrary to Article 3, the Court will not rely on the concept that the burden of proof is borne by one or other of the two Governments concerned. In the cases referred to it, the Court examines all the material before it, whether originating from the Commission, the Parties or other sources, and, if necessary, obtains material proprio motu.'

2   *Ireland v United Kingdom* (1978) A 25, para 161 (conduct of parties when evidence is being obtained may be taken into account in the assessment).

3   *Orhan v Turkey* (18 June 2002), at para 371. See also eg *Khadisov and Tsechoyev v Russia* (5 February 2009), para 148.

4   *Aksoy v Turkey* 1996-VI, at para 97: 'allegations of torture in police custody are extremely difficult for the victim to substantiate if he has been isolated from the outside world, without access to doctors, lawyers, family or friends who could provide support and assemble the necessary evidence. Furthermore, having been ill-treated in this way, an individual will often have had his capacity or will to pursue a complaint impaired'.

5   *Labita v Italy* [GC] 2000-IV, paras 113–129 (allegations of being slapped, blows, squeezing of the testicles and baton blows and of insults, unnecessary body searches, acts of humiliation such as being required to remain in handcuffs during medical examinations, intimidation and threats). Similarly (paras 130–136), the Court held that there was insufficient evidence to conclude that there had been any violation of Art 3 concerning the frequency and conditions of transfers from a prison on account of the applicant's failure to supply detailed information; however, since investigations into his allegations were slow and not sufficiently effective, the Court considered that there had been a violation of the procedural aspect of Art 3.

6   Discussed at paras **4.94** et seq below.

7   *Labita v Italy* [GC] 2000-IV, joint partly dissenting opinion, paras 1–3 (the minority considered that the matters that led the majority to establish a procedural violation of Art 3 were in themselves sufficiently clear and evident to justify finding a violation of the substantive guarantee: the suggestion that only treatment which left scars detectable on medical examination were worthy of consideration was inappropriate since (at para 2) 'there would not necessarily have been any signs left by insults, threats or acts of humiliation, by being kept handcuffed during medical examinations, or being required to run along a slippery corridor leading to the exercise yard while warders hurled insults', treatment which nevertheless could damage an individual's mental integrity; assertions concerning the psychological ill-treatment were corroborated by evidence contained in the judicial report concerning the general situation in the prison; and in any event, the respondent state had acknowledged before the Commission that the applicant had been ill-treated, describing the prison warders' conduct as 'appalling').

8   See paras **4.103–4.108** below.

4.79 The European Court of Human Rights may carry out its own investigation with a view to establishing the facts, and will make its assessment based on all the information available[1]. The isolation in which a detainee is likely to find himself and the likelihood of official denial or excuse may render this assessment a difficult one[2], but the facts may bear no reasonable interpretation other than that force has been applied by police officers or other state officials[3]. Consequently, the Court has developed the principle that where an individual alleges that he has been ill-treated while in custody, the state is under an obligation to provide a complete and sufficient explanation as to how any injuries were caused: any injury to a person in custody gives rise to a strong factual presumption which places the onus on the state to cast doubt on the allegations made by a detainee[4]. It has also endorsed proposals that detainees should have the benefit of an independent medical examination upon release from police custody[5]. This principle also extends to persons detained in a prison 'having regard to the fact that they are deprived of their liberty and remain subject to the control and responsibility of the prison administration'[6]. In *Tomasi v France*, the state was unable to provide any alternative explanation for the injuries sustained by the applicant over a period of 48 hours whilst in police custody on a charge of terrorist-related murder. The Court took this into account along with other evidence, such as the applicant's complaints when brought for judicial examination and the evidence contained in independent medical reports, in declaring itself convinced beyond reasonable doubt that the injuries had been inflicted by police officers[7]. In *Klaas v Germany*, on the other hand, the applicant's claims that injuries sustained while being detained on a drink-driving offence were the result of excessive police force were contested, and the Court was unwilling to depart from the findings of the domestic courts that it was plausible that the harm had been self-inflicted[8]. In *Ribitsch v Austria*, the state conceded that injuries had been sustained while the applicant was in police custody, but a domestic court had determined that it was not possible to establish culpable conduct on the part of any police officer. The Court accepted in principle that its role was not to substitute its own assessment of the facts for those established domestically, but neither was it formally bound by such a domestic determination. Taking into account all the circumstances of the case, the the state's explanation was incomplete and unconvincing and insufficient to establish that the injuries sustained by the applicant were caused otherwise than by ill-treatment while in custody[9].

---

1   *Cruz Varas and Others v Sweden* (1991) A 201, para 75.

2   Cf *Labita v Italy* [GC] 2000-IV, at para 125: 'the Court recognises that it may prove difficult for prisoners to obtain evidence of ill-treatment by their prison warders'.

3   *Ogic v Romania* (27 May 2010), paras 43–47 (no reasons or valid supporting documents supplied by the government whose version was uncorroborated by materials which indeed indicated beyond reasonable doubt that the conditions of detention were largely as alleged by the applicant).

4   Eg *Berktay v Turkey* (1 March 2001), para 167.

5   *Akkoç v Turkey* 2000-X, at para 118 (endorsement of the importance of independent and thorough examinations of persons on release from detention as an essential safeguard against ill-treatment of persons in custody: 'examinations must be carried out by a properly qualified doctor, without any police officer being present and the report of the examination must include not only the detail of any injuries found but the explanations given by the patient as to how they occurred and the opinion of the doctor as to whether the injuries are consistent with those explanations').

6   *Satik and Others v Turkey* (10 October 2000) at para 54; cf para 58 (when prison authorities have recourse to outside assistance in dealing with an internal incident some form of independent monitoring of the action is necessary to ensure that the force used is proportionate).

7   *Tomasi v France* (1992) A 241-A, para 115. See also *Sheydayev v Russia* (7 December 2006), paras 52–63, and *Chitayev v Russia* (18 January 2007), paras 148–160 (findings of torture in light of uncontested medical reports).

8   *Klaas v Germany* (1993) A–269, paras 30–31.

9   *Ribitsch v Austria* (1995) A 336, paras 27–40.

4.80 In establishing the facts, the Court may also take into account the conduct of the parties. In particular, the failure of a respondent government to provide active assistance by furnishing all necessary assistance without satisfactory explanation may allow inferences to be drawn[1]. The credibility of witnesses may be an issue[2].

1   Eg *Orhan v Turkey* (18 June 2002), para 287; *Medova v Russia* 2009-…, para 287.

2   Eg *Barabanshchikov v Russia* (8 January 2009), at para 44: the Court considers it extraordinary that, in the absence of any official records [and] more than four years after the applicant's arrest, the police officers were able to recollect the exact circumstances surrounding the applicant's transfer to the police station and the names of the victims who had allegedly attacked him.'

Families of 'disappeared persons'

4.81 Unacknowledged deprivation of liberty is also considered a particularly serious violation of Article 5, and a state has responsibilities to 'take effective measures to safeguard against the risk of disappearance and to conduct a prompt effective investigation into an arguable claim that a person has been taken into custody and has not been seen since'[1].The European Court of Human Rights has accepted that, in certain circumstances, it may also be possible to conclude that the level of mental anguish endured by a family member of a 'disappeared person' last known to have been in state custody is itself sufficient to amount to a violation of Article 3. However, there is no presumption or general principle that a member of a family of a 'disappeared person' is through this very fact a 'victim' of treatment falling within the scope of Article 3; rather, 'whether a family member is such a victim will depend on the existence of special factors which gives the suffering of the applicant a dimension and character distinct from the emotional distress which may be regarded as inevitably caused to relatives of a victim of a serious human rights violation'. The particular nature of the breach of the guarantee 'does not so much lie in the fact of the 'disappearance' of the family member but rather concerns the authorities' reactions and attitudes to the situation when it is brought to their attention'[2]. The nature of the breach of the guarantee thus concerns not so much the 'disappearance' of the family member but rather the reaction and attitude of state officials to the situation[3]. For example, in *Varnava and Others v Turkey*, the Grand Chamber considered that the continuing silence for more than a third of a century of the Turkish authorities as to the facts surrounding the disappearance of relatives of the applicants could only be categorised as inhuman treatment in the face of the real concerns of the applicants over the fate of their missing relatives[4].

1   *Kurt v Turkey* 1998-III, at para 124. See also *Chitayev v Russia* (18 January 2007), paras 170–173 (4-day period of unacknowledged detention).

2   *Çakıcı v Turkey* [GC] 1999-IV, paras 94–99 at para 98 (no violation established). For examples of violations of Art 3, see eg *Timurtaş v Turkey* 2000-VI, paras 91–98 at para 95 ('callous disregard' shown in relation to the disappearance of the applicant's son: relevant factors in establishing whether a family member of a 'disappeared' person qualifies as a victim of an Art 3 violation included the proximity of family tie ('a certain weight will attach to the parent–child bond'), the particular circumstances of the relationship, whether the family member witnessed any of the events, involvement in seeking information about the disappeared person, and the manner of any response from the authorities); *Taş v Turkey* (14 November 2000), paras 79–80 (at para 80: 'indifference and callousness of the authorities to the applicant's concerns (as to the fate of his son) and the acute anguish and uncertainty which he has suffered as a result and continues to suffer' were sufficient to amount to a violation of Art 3); *Cyprus v Turkey* [GC] 2001-IV, paras 156–158 (at para 157: military operations in northern Cyprus had resulted in significant loss of life, deprivation of liberty and enforced separation of families, matters still 'vivid in the minds of the relatives of persons whose fate has never been accounted for' and who 'endure the agony of not knowing whether family members were killed in the conflict or are still in detention or, if detained, have since died': violation of Art 3); *Lyanova and Aliyeva v Russia* (2 October 2009), paras 116–119 (no plausible explanation or information for eight years); *Khadzhialiyev and Others v Russia* (6 November 2008), paras 120–122 (dismemberment and decapitation of abducted relatives' bodies: profound and continuous anguish and distress caused to applicants since the body parts had still not been found and thus preventing them from burying the bodies in a proper manner: violation of Art 3); and *Sabanchiyeva and Others v Russia* (dec) (6 November 2008) (remains of deceased insurgents kept in appalling conditions: admissible under Arts 3, 8 and 9, alone and in conjunction with Arts 13 and 14).

3   See *Akpinar and Alton v Turkey* 2007-III, para 76–87 (mutilation of corpses while in the possession of security services: while the prohibition of ill-treatment is inapplicable to corpses, the presecuting of mutilated corpses to the sister and father of the deceased amounting to degrading treatment).

4   *Varnava and Others v Turkey* [GC] 2009-…, paras 200–202.

Discriminatory treatment

4.82 The ECHR, Article 14 provides general protection against discrimination in the enjoyment of Convention guarantees[1]. A state is under an obligation to carry out an effective investigation into allegations that the infliction of ill-treatment by officials was motivated by racist attitudes, and failure to investigate concrete suspicions may amount to a violation of Article 14 taken in conjunction with Article 3[2]. Further, systemic failure to address the phenomenon of domestic violence against women may also engage state responsibilities under Article 14 taken in conjunction with Article 3[3]. In certain cases, though, discriminatory treatment on the part of state official may itself amount to treatment sufficiently degrading so as to constitute a violation of Article 3. In the *East African Asians case*, British passport holders who had been forced to leave Uganda and Kenya had been denied entry to the United Kingdom. The Commission determined that denial of entry had been on account of their race or colour, institutionalised racism that had amounted to degrading treatment[4]. A similar conclusion was reached in *Cyprus v Turkey*, where the Court found that Greek Cypriots living in Turkish-controlled northern Cyprus had been subjected, because of race and religion, to state action which violated 'the very notion of respect for the human dignity of its members'. This enclaved population over a lengthy period had been - and continued to be - 'isolated, restricted in their movements, controlled and with no prospect of renewing or developing their community'. Such treatment was sufficiently debasing to qualify as degrading treatment within the meaning of Article 3[5]. In contrast, in the earlier case of *Abdulaziz, Cabales and Balkandali v United Kingdom*, no violation of Article 3 was established. Here, the treatment complained of had been taken solely to achieve goals of immigration policy, and the argument that it had been discriminatory on the ground of sex was rejected as it 'did not denote any contempt or lack of respect for the personality of the applicants and that it was not designed to, and did not, humiliate or debase'[6]. On the other hand, in the case of *Smith and Grady v United Kingdom*, the European Court of Human Rights seemed to suggest that discriminatory treatment, even in the absence of any state intention to humiliate, may still result in a violation of Article 3. Here, service personnel had been subjected to intimate questioning concerning their homosexuality before being dismissed from the armed forces. The Court considered this intrusive treatment to be of a 'particularly grave' nature, but not such as to reach the minimum level of severity required to bring it within the scope of Article 3. At the same time, the Court specifically refused to 'exclude that treatment which is grounded upon a predisposed bias on the part of a heterosexual majority against a homosexual minority ... could, in principle, fall within the scope of Article 3'[7]. The conclusion is that to be considered a violation of Article 3, discriminatory treatment must attain a level which is considered grossly humiliating[8].

---

1   See paras **3.87–3.128** above. For discussion of Art 14 taken along with Arts 2 and 3, see paras **3.102** and **4.41** above.

2   See paras **4.101–4.102** below.

3   See para **4.25** above and para **4.85** below.

4   4403/70 et al *East African Asians* (1973) DR 78, 5. The Commission's Report was only made public in 1994. See further Lester 'Thirty Years On: The East African Asians Case Revisited' [2002] PL 52. See also *97 Members of the Gidani Congregation of Jehovah's Witnesses and 4 Others v Georgia* 2007-..., paras 98–125, 129–135, and 139–142 (group attack by Orthodox believers leading to violent assaults and destruction of religious artefacts, the police being unwilling to intervene or investigate, and little attempt being made to instigate criminal proceedings: violation of Arts 3 and 9, and of Art 14 in conjunction with Arts 3 and 9). See further para **4.102** below.

5   *Cyprus v Turkey* [GC] 2001-IV, paras 305–311 at para 309: there was 'an inescapable conclusion that the interferences at issue were directed at the ... Greek-Cypriot community for the very reason that they belonged to this class of persons'.

6   *Abdulaziz, Cabales and Balkandali v United Kingdom* (1985) A 94, at para 91. See also *Çonka and Others v Belgium* (dec) (13 March 2001) (allegation by Roma due to be expelled that numbers were marked on their arms using indelible ink; explanation accepted that this was for the purpose of identification and not of humiliation: inadmissible on this issue).

7   *Smith and Grady v United Kingdom* 1999-VI, paras 118–123 at para 121.

8   Cf *Thiermann and Others v Norway* (dec) (8 July 2007) (allegations of discriminatory treatment of children born under the *Lebensborn* programme of the Nazi regime: inadmissible).

Positive obligations: (i) protection against infliction of ill-treatment through effective implementation of domestic law

4.83 Article 3 of the ECHR imposes positive obligations upon a state to ensure the effective protection of physical integrity through domestic law. These obligations also exist in respect of less serious interferences with physical and moral integrity under Article 8[1]. The provision thus has important implications for the quality of substantive law, for the discharge of responsibilities entrusted to the police and to other state agencies, for prosecution practice[2], and for the judiciary in imposing appropriate punishment[3]. In short, domestic law is expected to have in place effective criminal law provisions to deter the commission of offences against the person, backed up by law enforcement machinery for the prevention, suppression and appropriate punishment of breaches of such provisions to ensure that no person is immune from prosecution and also to act as an effective deterrence to the possibility of ill-treatment arising in other circumstances. These expectations are reinforced by the 'procedural aspect' of Article 3[4].

1   See para **6.119–6.128** below.

2   See eg *Beganović v Croatia* 2009-…, paras 75–87 (criminal proceedings against applicant's attackers time-barred on account of inactivity of the prosecuting authorities and the courts: violation of Art 3).

3   Eg *Okkali v Turkey* 2006-XII, paras 65–78 (imposition of minimal sentences upon police officers convicted of the ill-treatment of a 12-year old boy: violation of Art 3 on account of the failure of the judges to provide enhanced protection for the victim in view of his age, with the lessening of the consequences of an extremely serious and unlawful act resulting in impunity for the officers responsible); and *Valeriou and Nicolai Roşca v Moldova,* (20 October 2009), paras 72–75 (minimum sentences imposed on police officers).

4   See paras **4.94–4.108** below.

Victims of domestic violence

4.84 These positive obligations are of particular relevance in cases involving domestic violence. In a number of recent cases, the Court has considered shortcomings in substantive law and police and prosecutorial practice. For example, in *MC v Bulgaria*, domestic law still proceeded upon the requirement of physical force in the definition of rape, a situation the Court considered was out of line with modern standards in comparative and international law[1].

1   *MC v Bulgaria* 2003-XII, paras 167–187. See further paras **4.100** and **6.120** below; and Radacic 'Rape Cases in the Jurisprudence of the European Court of Human Rights: Defining Rape and Determining the Scope of the State's Obligations' [2008] EHRLR 357. See also *Bevacqua and S v Bulgaria* (12 June 2008), paras 65–83 (positive obligations arising under

Art 8 and also in certain instances under Arts 2 and 3 may include a duty to maintain and to apply in practice 'an adequate legal framework affording protection against acts of violence by private individuals'; here, certain administrative and policing measures were called for, but at the relevant time domestic law did not provide for such and the measures taken by the police and prosecuting authorities on the basis of their general powers did not prove effective to protect against domestic violence).

4.85 This positive obligation thus has important consequences for the police and prosecution authorities[1]. Responsibilities to ensure the protection of individuals at risk from domestic violence also arise under Articles 2 and 8[2]. In respect of domestic violence against women, these may also potentially engage these provisions when taken with Article 14, as indicated in *Opuz v Turkey*. In this case, the authorities had been aware of incidents of serious violence and threats made by the applicant's husband against her and her mother, but the authorities had considered the incidents to have been a 'family matter' and only one incident had resulted in a successful criminal prosecution before the applicant's mother had been killed by her husband. Repeated requests by the women for protection had been ignored. Further requests made after the husband had been convicted but released pending appeal similarly led to no effective action until the applicant had lodged a complaint with the Strasbourg Court. The Court ruled that there had been a violation of Article 2 since a lethal attack had not only been possible but even foreseeable in light of the history of violence. The response of the authorities to protecting the applicant had been manifestly inadequate: although certain proceedings had been discontinued following the withdrawal of complaints, the Court noted that the more serious the offence or the greater the risk of further offences, the more important it was that the prosecution should continue in the public interest. Crucially, too, the circumstances disclosed a violation of Article 14 taken with Articles 2 and 3 in light of international legal standards supporting the principle that the failure (even when unintentional) to protect women against domestic violence breached the women's right to equal protection of the law. The general and discriminatory judicial passivity in Turkey created a climate that was conducive to domestic violence, violence that was gender-based, and that in consequence constituted a form of discrimination against women[3].

1   Eg *MC v Bulgaria* 2003-XII, at para 185: 'the investigation of the applicant's case and, in particular, the approach taken by the investigator and the prosecutors in the case fell short of the requirements inherent in the states' positive obligations – viewed in the light of the relevant modern standards in comparative and international law – to establish and apply effectively a criminal-law system punishing all forms of rape and sexual abuse'.

2   See para **4.25** above and paras **6.119–6.121** below.

3   *Opuz v Turkey* 2009-…, paras 184–202 (consideration of the UN Convention for the Elimination of All Forms of Discrimination Against Women and the Belém do Pará Convention, of case law of the UN Commission on Human Rights, the CEDAW Committee, and the Inter-American Commission; and of reports indicating the highest number of reported victims of domestic violence in the area were women of Kurdish origin, illiterate or of a low level of education and financially dependent and research indicating police officers sought to assume the role of mediator rather than investigator and that courts mitigated sentences on the grounds of custom, tradition or honour). See also paras 132 and 149: 'the issue of domestic violence, which can take various forms ranging from physical to psychological violence or verbal abuse … is a

general problem which concerns all member States and which does not always surface since it often takes place within personal relationships or closed circuits and it is not only women who are affected; here, the conclusion was that 'the national authorities cannot be considered to have displayed due diligence' and thus had failed 'in their positive obligation to protect the right to life of the applicant's mother'.

4.86 The responsibility to provide effective protection through substantive legal provisions against the threat of violence also applies in respect of children. The use of violence by parents or others in a family setting or exercising powers *in loco parentis* gives rise to issues as to the quality of domestic law and the effectiveness of police and prosecutorial policy. In *A v United Kingdom*, the applicant, a nine-year-old boy, had been beaten repeatedly by his stepfather with a cane. This had resulted in significant bruising. An English court had accepted the defence of reasonable chastisement, and the stepfather had been acquitted. The Court accepted that the beatings were of sufficient severity as to give rise to an Article 3 issue, and that the state had failed to take adequate measures in the form of effective deterrence to protect the applicant from inhuman or degrading punishment, since the defence of 'reasonable chastisement' did not provide sufficient safeguards against abuse[1]. This case thus concerns the positive responsibilities upon states to ensure that domestic criminal law adequately protects Article 3 interests. The Commission in its report had sought to stress that the finding of a violation should not be seen as imposing any duty upon states to provide protection against any form of physical rebuke including the most mild; the Court's decision can be taken, however, as a signal to states that family and criminal law must protect with greater vigilance the rights of children.

1   *A v United Kingdom* 1998-VI, paras 20–24 (the state conceded that there had been a breach of Art 3, but requested the Court to confine itself to the facts of the case without making any general statement about corporal punishment of children: the Court (paras 25–28) decided it was not necessary in this case to consider the separate complaint under Art 8).

Domestic law

4.87 It has been held in an English case that Article 3 was breached when the prosecution decided to terminate the prosecution of a case of serious assault because the complainer, who suffered from a mental illness, was for that reason regarded as an unreliable witness. It did not follow from the medical information available to the prosecution that the complainer could not be placed before the jury as a credible witness, and by depriving the claimant of the opportunity of the proceedings running their proper course he had been caused to feel that he was a second class citizen who was beyond the protection of the law[1]. In Scots law, the extent of parental rights to inflict corporal punishment on children has now been clarified[2]. Following *A v United Kingdom*, the English Court of Appeal has also held that a jury should now be directed in detailed terms as to factors relevant to whether the chastisement in question was reasonable and moderate and that they should consider the nature and context of the defendant's behaviour, its duration, the physical and mental consequences in respect of the child, the age and personal characteristics of the child; and the reasons given by the defendant for administering the punishment[3].

1   *R (B) v Director of Public Prosecutions* [2009] 1 WLR 2072.

2   The Children and Young Persons (Scotland) Act 1937, s 12(1) provided a defence of 'moderate and reasonable chastisement', a concept which required to be interpreted in light of contemporary views on the suitability and extent of such (cf *Gray v Hawthorn* 1964 JC 69. See also the Looked After Children (Scotland) Regulations 2009, SSI 2009/210, reg 24 and Sch 6 (no child may be placed with a foster parent without written agreement from the foster parent that corporal punishment will not be administered). The Scottish Law Commission *Report on Family Law* (Scot Law Com no 135) (1992), para 2.102 recommended that the defence should not be available where a stick, belt or similar object was used, or where there was actual or a real risk of causing serious injury, or pain or discomfort lasting more than a short time. The Scottish Executive Justice Department's consultation paper, *The Physical Punishment of Children in Scotland* (1999) proposed that Scots law should make clear that physical punishment reaching the minimum level of severity for Art 3 could never be justified as 'reasonable chastisement'. The Criminal Justice (Scotland) Act 2003, s 51 reflects this approach by requiring the court to take into account the nature and context of the punishment, its duration and frequency, its physical and mental effects, and the sex, age, and state of health of the victim. However, the use of an implement, a blow to the head or the shaking of the child will not necessarily in themselves be considered unreasonable (cf s 51(3)). What is 'reasonable' seems thus to be determined by the question whether Art 3 is engaged or not. This is despite the difficulties the Court has had in applying the minimum level of severity in such cases: cf *Costello-Roberts v United Kingdom* (1993) A 247-C, discussed at para 4.65 above); and see *R v H (Assault of a Child: Reasonable Chastisement)* [2002] 1 Cr App R 7; *R (Williamson) v Secretary of State for Education and Employment* [2005] 2 AC 246 (corporal punishment need not significantly impair the physical or moral integrity of a child). Such an approach is probably in line with the current minimum requirements of the ECHR, but there is pressure to move towards a position which regards the use of any corporal punishment as unacceptable: see Parliamentary Assembly Recommendation 1666 (2004); and comments of the UN Committee on the Rights of the Child (Concluding Observations regarding consideration of the United Kingdom's second periodic report) (4 October 2002); and (Concluding Observations regarding its third and fourth periodic reports) (20 October 2008); and of the European Commissioner for Human Rights, Issue Paper 2006/1.

3   *R v H (Assault of Child: Reasonable Chastisement)* [2002] 1 Cr App R 7. The case concerned the beating of a young child with a leather belt. An acquittal on such facts might thus well raise an issue under Art 3, even if the jury had received such directions.

Positive obligations: (ii) taking of specific action to prevent ill-treatment

4.88 A failure to take reasonable steps to protect a vulnerable individual from ill-treatment in circumstances where the authorities had knowledge of the risk (or ought to have had such knowledge) will give rise to issues under Article 3[1]. This responsibility mirrors those arising under Article 2 to protect life from identifiable threats, and under Article 8 to ensure respect for private and family life[2]. It closely related to the issue whether substantive domestic law and its enforcement by relevant criminal justice agencies adequately reflect Convention expectations[3]. A range of situations may give rise to responsibilities to provide effective protection, including the adequacy of health care[4].

1 Eg *PF and EF v United* Kingdom (dec) 2010-… (premeditated sectarian protest lasting two months and designed to intimidate young schoolchildren and their parents: minimum level of severity required to fall within the scope of Art 3 reached, triggering the positive obligation on the part of the police to take preventive action; but in determining whether reasonable steps had been taken, a degree of discretion had to be accorded: here, mindful of the difficulties facing the police in a highly-charged community dispute in Northern Ireland, the applicants had not shown the police had failed to do all that could be reasonably expected of them: inadmissible).

2 See paras **4.22–4.25** above and paras **6.119–6.129** below.

3 See further paras **4.83–4.86** above.

4 See eg *Denis Vasilyev v Russia* (17 December 2009), paras 97–104 and 111–129 (significant shortcomings in the investigation of a serious assault and failures by police and hospital to provide adequate assistance to the unconscious victim: violations of Art 3 on account of the failure to protect the victim from further harm, the inadequacy of the investigation into allegations that he had been abandoned by the police, procrastination by health personnel in administering appropriate treatment which had led to serious deterioration in his condition, and inadequacy of the investigation into the alleged medical negligence).

The care of detainees

4.89 The responsibility to safeguard the well-being of individuals is most obvious in relation to persons deprived of their liberty[1]. Health care arrangements must be adequate for each detainee, and a failure to safeguard the physical integrity of a detainee by providing appropriate medical care may give rise to a violation of Article 3[2]. For example, in *McGlinchey and Others v the United Kingdom*, the family of a heroin addict who had died a week after being imprisoned claimed that not enough had been done, or done quickly enough, to treat her withdrawal symptoms. The Court found a violation of Article 3 on the grounds that there had been a failure to provide the requisite level of medical care. While there had been regular monitoring of her condition for the first six days and steps had been taken to respond to her symptoms, the serious weight loss and dehydration she had experienced as a result of a week of largely uncontrolled vomiting and inability to eat or hold down liquids had caused her distress and suffering and had posed very serious risks to her health, but although her condition was still deteriorating, she had not been examined on either of the following two days as the medical officer did not work at weekends[3]. The related issue of whether there is a positive obligation to take all reasonable steps to prevent the spread of infectious diseases (and if such a duty exists, what these reasonable steps would entail) was raised but avoided in *Khokhlich v Ukraine*[4].

1 Including *de facto* deprivation of liberty: see eg *Riad and Idiab v Belgium* 2008-…, paras 88–111 (placement of illegal aliens in airport transit zone for more than ten days without providing adequate food and hygiene: violation of Art 3).

2 Eg *VD v Romania* (16 February 2010), paras 92–99 (medical diagnoses indicated a prisoner's need for dentures, but none had been provided who was unable to pay for them himself and despite legislation making these available free of charge: degrading treatment); and *Slyusarev v Russia* 2010-…, paras 34–44 (detainee suffering from medium-severity myopia not able to use glasses for several months causing considerable distress and giving rise to feelings of insecurity and helplessness: violation).

3   *McGlinchey and Others v United Kingdom* 2003 V, paras 47–58.

4   *Khokhlich v Ukraine* (29 April 2003), paras 183–196 (not established that the applicant had
     been infected by a cell mate who had been suffering from tuberculosis, and in any case both
     prisoners had received appropriate and adequate treatment thus minimising any risk of repeat
     infection). See also *Kotsaftis v Greece* (12 June 2008), paras 51–61 (claim that infection with
     hepatitis B resulting in cirrhosis of the liver had been caused by poor conditions of detention
     not accepted given the chronic nature of the disease; but violation of Art 3 on account of failure
     to safeguard physical integrity by providing appropriate medical care, the Court deploring the
     fact the applicant while suffering from a highly infectious disease had been detained along with
     ten other prisoners in a cell measuring 24 sq m). In such cases, the Court may also make
     reference to Art 46: eg *Poghosyan v Georgia* (24 February 2009), paras 65–70 (significant
     number of cases involving lack of medical treatment in Georgian prisons for detainees suffering
     from contagious diseases revealed systemic problem calling for legislative and administrative
     measures including the screening of prisoners upon admission to be taken without delay); and
     Ghavtadze v Georgia (3 March 2009), para 106 (the prisoner should be promptly placed in
     an establishment capable concurrently of administering adequate medical treatment for hepatitis
     C and his pulmonary tuberculosis). See further Committee of Ministers Recommendation Rec
     (93) 6, Appendix, para 9. It is probably unlikely that the failure to supply condoms to
     prisoners would give rise to an issue under ECHR, Arts 3 or 8, or if it did so, that domestic
     arrangements would not be covered by a high margin of appreciation bearing in mind that any
     risk that a prisoner may attempt to carry out a sexual assault on another inmate may be better
     addressed by disciplinary measures or solitary confinement. See also Lines 'Injecting Reason:
     Prison Syringe Exchange and Article 3 of the European Convention on Human Rights' [2007]
     EHRLR 66.

4.90 The principle also applies to responding effectively to the risk of self-harm
by a detainee. The case of *Keenan v United Kingdom* involved the suicide of a
prisoner who had been suffering from a chronic mental disorder involving psychotic
episodes and feelings of paranoia and who had also been diagnosed as suffering
from a personality disorder. While in prison, and after his return from the hospital
wing to normal prison accommodation, he had displayed disturbed behaviour
involving the demonstration of suicidal tendencies, possible paranoid-type fears,
and aggressive and violent outbursts. After being subjected to segregation and
disciplinary punishment, he had killed himself. For the Court, while it was not
possible 'to distinguish with any certainty to what extent his symptoms during this
time, or indeed his death, resulted from the conditions of his detention imposed by
the authorities', such was not determinative of whether the positive obligation
arising under Article 3 to protect a prisoner, for there were situations where
'proof of the actual effect on the person may not be a major factor'. Here, the
Court was struck by the lack of medical notes concerning an identifiable suicide
risk at the time the prisoner was undergoing the foreseeable additional stresses
arising from the imposition of segregation and disciplinary punishment. This
absence was indicative of 'an inadequate concern to maintain full and detailed
records of his mental state [which undermined] the effectiveness of any monitoring
or supervision process'. On top of this, there had been no reference to a psychiatrist
for advice on future treatment or fitness for adjudication and punishment. For the
Court, 'significant defects in the medical care provided to a mentally ill person
known to be a suicide risk' together with 'the belated imposition on him in those
circumstances of a serious disciplinary punishment – seven days' segregation in

the punishment block and an additional twenty-eight days to his sentence imposed two weeks after the event and only nine days before his expected date of release' had constituted inhuman treatment[1].

---

1   *Keenan v United Kingdom* 2001-III, paras 109–116, at para 116.

4.91 The duty to ensure the care and protection of detainees extends to taking steps to protect individuals from the threat of violence at the hands of other prisoners. In *Pantea v Romania,* the applicant claimed he had been beaten by other prisoners at the instigation of prison staff and then had been made to lie underneath his bed while immobilised with handcuffs for nearly 48 hours. Thereafter, he had been held in a railway wagon crammed with other prisoners for several days while suffering from multiple fractures. No medical treatment, food or water had been provided. While not all his allegations were deemed to have been established, medical reports had attested to the number and severity of blows which had been sufficiently serious to constitute inhuman and degrading treatment. This ill-treatment had been aggravated both by the handcuffing of the applicant while he continued to share a cell with his assailants and also by the failure to provide him with necessary medical treatment. The authorities could reasonably have been expected to foresee that the applicantp:'s psychological condition had made him vulnerable, and further that his detention had been capable of exacerbating his feelings of distress and his irascibility towards his fellow-prisoners. This had rendered it necessary to keep him under closer surveillance[1].

---

1   *Pantea v Romania* 2003-VI, paras 177–196. See also *Rodić and Others v Bosnia and Herzegovina* 2008-…, paras 68–73 (integration of prisoners convicted of war crimes into general prison population not in itself inhuman or degrading but clearly entailed a serious risk to physical well-being, and inadequacy of measure had involved violation of Art 3).

Ill-treatment in the home

4.92 The obligation to take reasonable steps to protect vulnerable individuals against the risk of ill-treatment extends to situations other than in places of detention. In particular, a positive obligation exists to ensure that relevant agencies respond appropriately to threats to children in the home. The issue is distinct from (but often in practice closely related to) the extent to which domestic law and administrative arrangements adequately reflect Convention requirements[1]. In *Z and Others v United Kingdom*, the applicants were four siblings in a family which had been monitored by the social services because of concerns about their well-being. Support had been given to the family over a period of four-and-a-half years, but no steps had been taken to place the children in care, despite police and social services reports which had highlighted significant neglect and emotional abuse. Only when their mother had threatened to hit them had the children finally been placed in emergency foster care. Before the Court, the United Kingdom Government conceded that the neglect and abuse suffered by the four children had reached the threshold of inhuman and degrading treatment, and further that it had failed in its positive obligation to provide the applicants with adequate protection. The Court reiterated that Article 3 imposes a positive duty upon states to provide protection against inhuman or degrading treatment inflicted by others and involving the taking of reasonable steps to prevent ill-treatment of which the authorities had or ought to have had knowledge. While the Court acknowledged that social services often faced difficult and sensitive decisions in attempting to respect and thus preserve family life, the circumstances of the case were such as to leave no doubt as to the failure of the authorities to protect the applicants from serious and long-term neglect and abuse[2].

1   For discussion of positive obligations in respect of domestic violence, see para **4.25** above and paras **6.119–6.121** below.

2   *Z and Others v United Kingdom* [GC] 2001-V, paras 73–75. Cf *Juppala v Finland* (2 December 2008), noted at para **6.121**, fn 6 below.

Decisions of domestic courts on protection against ill-treatment

4.93 It has been accepted by domestic courts that Article 3 imposes a positive duty upon the state to protect individuals from ill-treatment at the hands of other private individuals. In a case concerned with the adequacy of the steps taken by the police to protect little girls and their parents from a hostile mob who tried to prevent them from taking their normal route on foot through a 'loyalist' area of Belfast to a Catholic primary school, the House of Lords held that the absolute obligation of the state not to inflict inhuman or degrading treatment did not extend to preventing others who were not under its direct control from inflicting such treatment, but that Article 3 did require the state to do all that could reasonably be expected to prevent the infliction by third parties of such treatment on identified individuals once the existence of that risk was known or ought to have been known to them[1]. In a number of cases the courts have protected the anonymity of persons who would otherwise be at risk of ill-treatment in breach of Article 3[2]. The UK Government was not, on the other hand, obliged under the Convention to intervene with another state whose conduct within its own territory was said to violate Article 3 requirements[3]. The English Court of Appeal has also held that a jury should now be directed in detailed terms as to factors relevant to whether any physical chastisement in question was reasonable and moderate[4].

1   *E (A Child) v Chief Constable of the Royal Ulster Constabulary* [2009] 1 AC 536. For Strasbourg consideration, see para **4.88**, fn 1 above.

2   See eg *Secretary of State for the Home Department v AP (No 2)* [2010] 1 WLR 1652; *Venables v News Group Newspapers Ltd* [2001] Fam 430; cf *A v United Kingdom* 1998-VI. Other domestic cases are noted at paras **4.32** and **4.43** above.

3   *R (Al Rawi) v Secretary of State for Foreign and Commonwealth Affairs* [2008] QB 289.

4   *R v H (Assault of Child: Reasonable Chastisement)* [2002] 1 Cr App R 7, discussed at para **4.87** above.

Positive obligations: (iii) investigating allegations of ill-treatment – the procedural aspect of Article 3

4.94 Under Article 3, there is a positive obligation on the state to carry out an effective investigation of a credible claim that an individual has been subjected to ill-treatment falling within the scope of the guarantee. The responsibility arises if it is alleged that there has been ill-treatment by the police or by other state forces, or that ill-treament has occurred at the hands of third parties. This is the so-called 'procedural aspect' or 'procedural limb' of Article 3. The result is that a violation of Article 3 may be established if any subsequent state investigation of a credible assertion that ill-treatment has taken place is deemed inadequate, even although it has not been possible to establish that any actual infliction of ill-treatment has occurred.

The procedural limb of Article 3 thus seeks to render the guarantee effective in practice[1]. To this end, the investigation must be sufficiently thorough to be capable of establishing the facts and also of leading to the identification and punishment of those responsible[2]. It is important to note, however, that 'an obligation to investigate "is not an obligation of result, but of means": not every investigation should necessarily be successful or come to a conclusion which coincides with the claimant's account of events; however, it should in principle be capable of leading to the establishment of the facts of the case and, if the allegations prove to be true, to the identification and punishment of those responsible'[3].

---

1   Art 3 is thus read in conjunction with the state's general duty under Art 1 to 'secure to everyone within their jurisdiction the rights' defined in the ECHR: *Labita v Italy* [GC] 2000-IV, para 131. There is also a procedural limb to Art 2: see paras **4.35–4.47** above. On Art 3 obligations and the interplay with other international standards and CPT standard-setting, see further Svanidze *Guidelines on International Standards on the Effective Investigation of Ill-treatment* (2010).

2   See eg *Zelilof v Greece* (24 May 2004), para 54.

3   *Barabanshchikov v Russia* (8 January 2009), at para 54.

Effective investigations and effective domestic remedies

4.95 As with this development under Article 2, this requirement is closely related to the issues of the availability of an effective domestic remedy for the purposes of Article 13 and of whether any such domestic remedies have been exhausted in terms of Article 35[1]. However, there is an important but not altogether convincing distinction to be drawn between the requirements of Article 3 and of Article 13 following the Grand Chamber's decision in *Ilhan v Turkey*. The applicant had alleged breaches of Article 3 on account both of his treatment and of the lack of an effective investigation. After finding that the applicant had been subjected to torture at the hands of the security forces, the European Court of Human Rights declined to consider the question of the lack of an investigation under Article 3 but instead considered this as more appropriate for disposal under Article 13 since a finding of actual ill-treatment under Article 3 had been established. The

Court contrasted Article 3 which is phrased in substantive terms with Article 2 which contains the requirement that the right to life be 'protected by law', and which may concern 'situations where the initiative must rest on the State for the practical reason that the victim is deceased and the circumstances of the death may be largely confined within the knowledge of state officials'. It then concluded that Article 13 of the ECHR should generally be expected to provide redress to an applicant through the provision of necessary procedural safeguards to protect an individual against ill-treatment. Thus a procedural breach of Article 3 through the failure to carry out an effective investigation would only be appropriate in circumstances where an investigation had not permitted the determination of the material facts to allow disposal of the complaint under the substantive guarantee of Article 3[2].

---

1   See eg *Mikheyev v Russia* (26 January 2006), para 121 (significant shortcomings in the investigation suggesting it was neither adequate nor sufficiently effective, thus undermining the objection that the applicant had not exhausted domestic remedies). Cf *Aksoy v Turkey* 1996-VI, paras 51–57 and 98 at para 98 (the notion of an effective remedy under Art 13 'includes the duty to carry out a thorough and effective investigation capable of leading to the identification and punishment of those responsible for any ill-treatment and permitting effective access for the complainant to the investigatory procedure'; here the Court considered that it was unreasonable to expect the applicant to have used civil, criminal and administrative remedies in light of the physical paralysis of his arms and the psychological feelings of powerlessness consequent upon the infliction of torture by police officers).

2   *Ilhen v Turkey* [GC] 2000 VII, paras 89–93 at paras 91 and 92, followed in *Büyükda v Turkey* (21 December 2000), paras 45–69. See also eg *Afanasyev v Ukraine* (5 April 2005), paras 69–70; and *Cobzaru v Romania* (26 July 2007), paras 80–84.

4.96 Subsequent cases seem difficult to reconcile with this approach[1], suggesting that whether Article 13 will also be held to have been violated seems to turn on the particular facts of each case[2]. There can thus be the apparent anomaly that inadequate investigations may indeed result in findings of violations both of Article 3 and also of Article 13 on the same grounds[3]. At the very least, an effective remedy must involve more than the mere provision of compensation[4], and to this extent the requirements of Article 13 are more extensive than those arising under Article 3[5].

---

1   Cf *Satik and Others v Turkey* (10 October 2000), paras 60–62 (the Court concluded that, in view of the absence of a plausible explanation on the part of the authorities for the injuries sustained, the applicants had been beaten and injured by state officials resulting in a violation of Art 3; moreover, in view of the investigation's serious shortcomings, there was also a violation of Art 3, but no Art 13 issue raised by applicants or identified by the Court).

2   Eg *Bati and Others v Turkey* 2004-IV, paras 126–127.

3   Eg *Assenov and Others v Bulgaria* 1998-VIII, paras 117–118 (notion of an effective remedy not only entails a thorough and effective investigation under Art 3 but also effective access to the investigatory procedure and to compensation under Art 13). See also *Kuznetsov v Ukraine* (29 April 2003), Partly Dissenting Opinion of Judge Bratza (while no substantive breach of Art 3 was found unlike in *Ilhan,* the lack of effective official investigation into the applicant's allegations of ill-treatment should have been considered under Art 13 rather than Art 3).

4   *Aksoy v Turkey* 1996-VI, para 98; and *Balogh v Hungary* (20 July 2004), at para 62: 'where

a right of such fundamental importance as the right to life or the prohibition against ill-treatment is at stake, Article 13 requires, in addition to the payment of compensation where appropriate, a thorough and effective investigation capable of leading to the identification and punishment of those responsible, including effective access for the complainant to the investigation procedure. Furthermore, in the case of a breach of Articles 2 and 3 of the Convention, which rank as the most fundamental provisions of the Convention, compensation for non-pecuniary damage flowing from the breach should in principle be part of the range of available remedies'.

5   The lack of an effective criminal investigation may have a detrimental impact upon the chance of obtaining compensation in the civil courts: see eg *Menesheva v Russia* 2006-III, para 76; and *Cobzaru v Romania* (26 July 2007), at para 83: 'While the civil courts have the capacity to make an independent assessment of fact, in practice the weight attached to a preceding criminal inquiry is so important that even the most convincing evidence to the contrary furnished by a plaintiff would often be discarded and such a remedy would prove to be only theoretical and illusory'.

Circumstances giving rise to the obligation to undertake an investigation

4.97 The duty to initiate an investigation will arise when circumstances come to the attention of the relevant authorities suggesting that ill-treatment of sufficient severity so as to fall within the scope of Article 3 has occurred. The essence is the existence of 'sufficiently clear indications that torture or ill-treatment has been used'[1], or of an 'arguable claim' of the infliction of ill-treatment giving rise to 'a reasonable suspicion'[2]. The responsibility to carry out an investigation may arise even in the absence of an express complaint when other sufficiently clear indications of such ill-treatment are evident[3], but does not do so if the allegation or indications are inherently implausible. Credible accounts of excessive use of force or of physical or psychological abuse during detention thus call for investigation[4], as do allegations that the use of physical force by police officers was not warranted in the circumstances[5] (including force leading to the destruction of homes and possessions)[6]. The obligation also extends to investigating allegations that ill-treatment has been inflicted by third parties[7]. However, the procedural aspect of Article 3 will not necessarily arise in respect of ill-treatment arising through poor conditions of detention (although if an investigation is held by the domestic authorities, it must nevertheless meet the minimum expectations of an effective investigation)[8].

1   *Bati and Others v Turkey* 2004-IV, at para 133 (reference to the UN Manual on the Effective Investigation and Documentation of Torture and Other Cruel, Inhuman or Degrading Treatment or Punishment (the 'Istanbul Protocol').

2   *Kuznetsov v Ukraine* (29 April 2003), paras 104–105; and *Preminiy v Russia* (10 February 2011), para 92. See also *Gharibashvili v Georgia* (29 July 2008), at para 64: 'the applicant's allegations made before the domestic authorities contained enough specific information – the date, place and nature of the ill-treatment, the identity of the alleged perpetrators, the causality between the alleged beatings and the asserted health problems, etc., to constitute an arguable claim in respect of which those authorities were under an obligation to conduct an effective investigation'.

3   *İlhan v Turkey* [GC] 2000-VII, para 63; and *İpek v Turkey* 2004-II, para 169 (the authorities must act of their own motion, once the matter has come to their attention). See also *Aksoy v*

Turkey 1996-VI, para 59 (visible evidence of bruising ignored by the prosecutor 'tantamount to undermining the effectiveness of any other remedies that may have existed').

4   *Maslova and Nalbandov v Russia* 2008-..., para 91.

5   *Kaya v Turkey* 1998-I, para 87; *Ay v Turkey* (22 March 2005), paras 59–60. See also *Akkum and Others* v *Turkey* 2005-II, paras 259–265 (obligation to investigate mutilation of a body on account of the anguish the multilation has caused to relatives).

6   See eg *İpek v Turkey* 2004-II, paras 202–209. A duty may also arise under Art 13 to investigate the destruction of homes and possessions: *Menteş and Others v Turkey* 1997-VIII, para 89.

7   Eg *MC v Bulgaria* 2003-XII, paras 169–187 (insufficient investigation of allegation of rape: violations of Arts 3 and 8).

8   *Ramishvili and Kokhreidze v Georgia* (27 January 2009), para 80; cf *Fedotov v Russia* (25 October 2005), paras 63, 69–70.

Allegations of ill-treatment of detainees at the hands of state officials

4.98 It may be difficult for a detainee to establish the fact of ill-treatment[1], and the obligation to carry out an effective investigation has a relationship with the responsibility upon state officials to provide a plausible explanation for injuries sustained by an individual taken into custody in good health but found to be injured at the time of release[2]. In *Assenov and Others v Bulgaria*, a 14-year-old boy had been taken to a police station after being arrested for unlawful gambling. It was not in dispute that he had been hit in the police station by his father with a strip of wood (apparently to show to the police officers that he was prepared to punish the applicant), but it was also alleged that thereafter the applicant had been beaten by police officers using truncheons. The Court accepted that in light of the time which had elapsed and the lack of any proper investigation, it could not be established that the police officers had caused the applicant's injuries. However, the perfunctory nature of inquiries into these serious allegations had not resulted in a sufficiently thorough and effective investigation, and accordingly there had been a violation of this procedural aspect of Article 3[3]. More typically, the procedural aspect of Article 3 is of relevance where it is alleged that police officers have used unwarranted force or psychological ill-treatment against a detainee in order to extract a confession or to obtain other information[4].

1   See *Aksoy v Turkey* 1996-VI, at para 97: 'allegations of torture in police custody are extremely difficult for the victim to substantiate if he has been isolated from the outside world, without access to doctors, lawyers, family or friends who could provide support and assemble the necessary evidence. Furthermore, having been ill-treated in this way, an individual will often have had his capacity or will to pursue a complaint impaired'.

2   See para **4.79** above.

3   *Assenov and Others v Bulgaria* 1998-VIII, paras 101–106. The issue of exhaustion of domestic remedies was considered at paras 82–86 (although a private prosecution against the police officers was not possible, the applicant had attempted without success to persuade the authorities to carry out a full criminal investigation; and since civil compensation cannot in itself be deemed fully to rectify a violation of Art 3, the applicant was deemed to have exhausted domestic remedies without requiring to raise any civil action). There appears to have been no discussion in this case of positive duties upon the police officers to protect the

individual from violence inflicted by his father (cf *A v United Kingdom* 1998-VI, discussed at para **4.86** above).

4   See eg *Gäfgen v Germany* [GC] 2010-..., paras 130–132 (applicant could still claim to be a 'victim', and had been threatened with torture during interrogation: violation). For discussion of *Gäfgen* and related Art 6 issues, see paras **5.125–5.126** below. For discussion, see Schriewer 'Gafgen v Germany Revisited' (2011) 53 GYIL 945 at 951 (explicit acknowledgment of unlawfulness of police action, but only modest fines imposed upon the police officers involved appears to have been condoned by the Court, noting that Judge Tulkens referred to the 'difficulty and delicacy' of sentencing in the case.

4.99 The Court's jurisprudence in this area is supplemented by (and closely related to) the standards established by the European Committee for the Prevention of Torture (the 'CPT') in seeking to combat the impunity of state officials for actions involving ill-treatment. The CPT has highlighted the particular vulnerability of detainees in police custody[1], a factor now recognised by the Court[2]. The CPT has also stressed the importance of maintaining comprehensive custody records[3], and the Court will now consider the absence of such as 'incompatible with the very purpose of Article 5'[4]. Similarly, the CPT has emphasised that the right of access to a doctor (including the right to be examined if the person detained so wishes by a doctor of his own choice[5], the importance of a medical examination in helping provide an evidentiary basis for any subsequent investigation being noted in the Court's case law[6]. Both the CPT and the Court consider that relevant authorities must carry out an investigation into the possibility that ill-treatment has occurred whenever this comes to their attention, even in the absence of a specific complaint[7].

1   See *13th General Report,* CPT/Inf (2003) 35; *14th General Report,* CPT/Inf (2004) 28, paras 25 and 31. For international standards, see the UN Manual on the Effective Investigation and Documentation of Torture and Other Cruel, Inhuman or Degrading Treatment or Punishment (the Istanbul Protocol) (referred to by the Court in *Bati and Others v Turkey* 2004-IV, para 133).

2   Eg *Cotleţ v Romania* (3 June 2003), para 71 (recognition of vulnerability of detainee held in custody with limited contacts with family or the outside world). See further paras **4.120–4.123** below.

3   *2nd General Report,* CPT/Inf (92) 3, para 40.

4   *Çiçek v Turkey* (27 February 2001), para 165 (unexplained disappearance of the applicant's two sons after their detention); see also *Shchebet v Russia* (12 June 2008), at para 63 (absence of formal detention record was a 'most serious failing' under Art 5).

5   *2nd General Report,* CPT/Inf (92) 3, para 38: 'As regards the medical examination of persons in police custody, all such examinations should be conducted out of the hearing, and preferably out of the sight, of police officers. Further, the results of every examination as well as relevant statements by the detainee and the doctor's conclusions should be formally recorded by the doctor and made available to the detainee and his lawyer.' See *Akkoç v Turkey* 2000-X, at para 118: 'the Court further endorses the comments expressed by the Commission concerning the importance of independent and thorough examinations of persons on release from detention. [The CPT] has also emphasised that proper medical examinations are an essential safeguard against ill-treatment of persons in custody. Such examinations must be carried out by a properly qualified doctor, without any police officer being present and the report of the examination must include not only the detail of any injuries found but the explanations given by the patient as to how they occurred and the opinion of the doctor as to whether the injuries

are consistent with those explanations'; and *Jasinskis v Latvia* 2010-..., paras 58–68 (death of deaf and mute detainee in sobering-up facilities in police station: failures to have him medically examined when taken into custody as required by CPT standards).

6   Eg, *Mehmet Eren* v *Turkey* (14 October 2008), para 54 (no attempts by prosecutor to obtain medical report).

7   *14th General Report*, CPT/Inf (2004) 28, para 28: 'When persons detained by law enforcement agencies are brought before prosecutorial and judicial authorities, this provides a valuable opportunity for such persons to indicate whether or not they have been ill-treated. Further, even in the absence of an express complaint, these authorities will be in a position to take action in good time if there are other indicia (eg visible injuries; a person's general appearance or demeanour) that ill-treatment might have occurred'; and *İpek v Turkey* 2004-II, para 169.

Investigations into ill-treatment inflicted by third parties

4.100 Where an individual can show that he has been the victim of ill-treatment sufficient to bring the matter within the scope of Article 3, then there is a requirement that the operation of the criminal justice system should be capable of providing appropriate redress for victims by punishing those responsible and also having a dissuasive effect capable of ensuring the effective prevention of unlawful acts. This has implications both for substantive law and for prosecution practice[1]. The consequence is that, at the very least, the relevant authorities must carry out an effective investigation with a view to considering whether criminal proceedings should be instigated against the perpetrator. In *MC v Bulgaria,* the Court considered that there had been violations both of Articles 3 and 8 in light of significant shortcomings in the investigation and determination whether to prosecute. Officials had failed to assess the credibility of conflicting evidence in a context-sensitive manner and in a way which sought to verify the facts while proceeding on the basis of the lack of any direct proof of rape in the form of violence[2]. In *Macovei and Others v Romania*, the applicants had requested the public prosecutor to bring charges of attempted murder against the perpetrators of an indisputably serious attack, but while an investigation had been carried out following these complaints, the prosecutor had insisted that the applicants abandon their original complaints and instead file allegations of less serious assault. Since at the time domestic law recognised the sole right of the prosecutor to instigate criminal proceedings, no resultant criminal investigation had been instructed, a situation resulting in a violation of the procedural aspect of the guarantee[3].

1   See paras **4.83–4.86** above.

2   *MC v Bulgaria* 2003-XII, paras 167–187. See also para **6.120** below.

3   *Macovei and Others v Romania* (21 June 2007), paras 46–57.

Allegations of discriminatory treatment

4.101 Where it is alleged that there has been a discriminatory element in the infliction of ill-treatment by state officials or in the discharge of their responsibilities in responding to the infliction of ill-treatment by third parties, there will also be an obligation to investigate whether such an allegation is substantiated. This is similar to the positive obligation which arises when it is alleged that there has been such a motive in the use of lethal force[1]. The duty to investigate whether racist or religious attitudes have played any part in the actions of state officials 'may also be seen as implicit in their responsibilities under Article 14 of the Convention to secure the fundamental value enshrined in Article 3 without discrimination'[2]. However, there must be some evidence to support an allegation that there has been discrimination. Thus in *Balogh v Hungary*, while the Court found violations of Article 3 in respect of the infliction of ill-treatment of a Roma during police interrogation and the inadequacy of the investigation, it determined that there had been no substantiation of the applicant's allegation that he had been subjected to discriminatory treatment in terms of Article 14 when taken with Article 3[3].

1   See paras **4.35–4.37** above.

2   *Bekos and Koutropoulos v Greece* 2005-XIII, paras 59–62 and at para 70 (on account of the interplay between Arts 3 and 14, whether an issue is examined 'under one of the two provisions only, with no separate issue arising under the other, or may require examination under both Articles' is a 'question to be decided in each case on its facts and depending on the nature of the allegations made').

3   *Balogh v Hungary* (20 July 2004), para 79.

4.102 The problem in such instances is clear: it is often easier to establish actual ill-treatment than it is to show that this was inflicted on account of the individual's membership of a minority group, even though it may be recognised that ingrained discriminatory attitudes are prevalent in a police service[1]. Only where there is an arguable claim or significant indicators exist that discriminatory motives may have played a part in the infliction of ill-treatment or in the investigation into the infliction of ill-treatment will the obligation to consider this matter arise. In *Cobzaru* v *Romania*, for example, the Court took explicit notice of the context of numerous anti-Roma incidents often involving public officials following the fall of the communist regime, of the public's awareness of failures to remedy instances of such violence, and of the introduction of programmes seeking to eradicate this type of discrimination. Against this background, the authorities would – or should – have known of the possibility of racist motives behind the violence and investigated whether these had played any part. However, bearing in mind the difficulty in proving racial motivation, the 'obligation to investigate possible racist overtones to a violent act is an obligation to use best endeavours and not absolute. The authorities must do what is reasonable in the circumstances to collect and secure the evidence, explore all practical means of discovering the truth and deliver fully reasoned, impartial and objective decisions, without omitting suspicious facts that may be indicative of a racially induced violence'[2]. A similar responsibility arises in respect of attacks motivated by the victim's religion[3].

1   For discussion of standard of proof, see *Bekos and Koutropoulos v Greece* 2005-XIII, para 65: 'The Court reiterates that in assessing evidence it has adopted the standard of proof "beyond reasonable doubt"; nonetheless, it has not excluded the possibility that in certain cases of alleged discrimination it may require the respondent Government to disprove an arguable allegation of discrimination and – if they fail to do so – find a violation of Article 14

of the Convention on that basis. However, where it is alleged – as here – that a violent act was motivated by racial prejudice, such an approach would amount to requiring the respondent Government to prove the absence of a particular subjective attitude on the part of the person concerned. While in the legal systems of many countries proof of the discriminatory effect of a policy or decision will dispense with the need to prove intent in respect of alleged discrimination in employment or the provision of services, that approach is difficult to transpose to a case where it is alleged that an act of violence was racially motivated.'

2   *Cobzaru* v *Romania* (26 July 2007), paras 96–101 at para 97. See also *Bekos and Koutropoulos v Greece* 2005-XIII, paras 53–55 (allegations of physical and verbal ill-treatment of Roma allegedly on grounds of race: violation of procedural requirement to carry out an investigation into racist motives).

3   *97 Members of the Gldani Congregation of Jehovah's Witnesses and Others v Georgia* 2007- …, paras 138–142 (group attack by Orthodox believers leading to violent assaults and destruction of religious artefacts, the police being unwilling to intervene or investigate, and little attempt being made to instigate criminal proceedings: violation of Art 14 in conjunction with Arts 3 and 9); and *Milanović v Serbia* (14 December 2010), paras 96–101 (attacks on Hare Krishna followers by extreme-right group: violation of Art 14 taken with Art 3).

The effectiveness of domestic investigation

4.103 Since an investigation should in principle be capable of leading to the establishment of the facts, and to the identification and punishment of those responsible if the allegations prove to be true, 'the authorities must always make a serious attempt to find out what happened and should not rely on hasty or ill-founded conclusions to close their investigation or as the basis of their decisions', and to this end, 'must take all reasonable steps available to them to secure the evidence concerning the incident'[1]. As with the procedural requirement of Article 2[2], the effectiveness of a domestic investigation is tested in accordance with five principles. First, the investigation must be carried out by a body independent of those alleged to have been implicated in the ill-treatment. Secondly, the investigation must be adequate (that is, capable of gathering evidence to determine whether police behaviour complained of was unlawful and if so, to identify and punish those responsible). Thirdly, the investigation must be carried out promptly and with reasonable expedition. Fourthly, there must be a sufficient element of public scrutiny of the investigation or its results, although the degree of public scrutiny required will be dependent upon the circumstances. Fifthly, the victim must be involved in the procedure to the extent necessary to safeguard his or her legitimate interests[3].

1   *Assenov and Others v Bulgaria* 1998 VIII, at para 102; and *Barabanshchikov* v *Russia* (8 January 2009), at para 54.

2   See paras **4.35–4.50** above for further discussion in respect of these requirements arising under Art 2.

3   Opinion of the Council of Europe Commissioner for Human Rights Concerning Independent and Effective Determination of Complaints against the Police (12 March 2009).

Independence

4.104 The test of whether the body charged with the investigation is sufficiently independent calls for examination of whether there are institutional or hierarchical connections between the investigators and the officer complained against; further, there should be actual independence in practice[1].

---

1   *Ergi v Turkey* 1998-IV, paras 83–84. See also *Kucheruk v Ukraine* 2007-X, para 157 (investigation into alleged ill-treatment in detention centre carried out by governor of pre-trial detention centre); and *Gharibashvili v Georgia* (29 July 2008), para 68 (preliminary enquiry into complaints of ill-treatment and abuses of power had been entrusted to the same division of the prosecution authority of which the alleged perpetrator was also a member).

Adequacy

4.105 An investigation should be capable of gathering evidence to determine whether unlawful behaviour has occurred, and if so, to identify and punish those responsible[1]. Perfunctory investigation[2] or even incompetence[3] is often the cause of a finding of a violation. The expectation is that all reasonable steps will be taken to secure relevant evidence and to attempt to locate and to properly interview[4] witnesses and to obtain and assess real evidence[5].

---

1   Eg *Kmetty v Hungary* (16 December 2003), para 40 (medical opinion had not addressed whether injuries had been present at arrival at police station, the officers allegedly concerned had not been interviewed; and victim had not been shown photographs of one officer allegedly involved); and *Colibaba v Moldova* (23 October 2007), paras 52–55 (request for independent medical examination rejected without plausible reasons).

2   *Maslova and Nalbandov v Russia* 2008-…, paras 92–97 (diligent and prompt reaction to identify and punish those responsible for ill-treatment had been followed by procedural errors, and in the absence of any plausible explanation, the only possible conclusion was the manifest incompetence of the prosecutor).

3   *Akkoç v Turkey* 2000-X, para 118; and *Mehmet Eren v Turkey* (6 April 2004), para 41 (collective medical examinations are superficial and cursory; and reference to CPT standards and to the Manual on the Effective Investigation and Documentation of Torture and Other Cruel, Inhuman or Degrading Treatment or Punishment (the 'Istanbul Protocol')).

4   Eg *Menteş and Others v Turkey* 1997-VIII, para 91. See also *Selçuk and Asker v Turkey* 1998-II, para 97 (officer in charge not interviewed, issue considered under Art 13)

5   Eg, *Batı and Others v Turkey* 2004-IV at para 134: '[in terms of Art 13] the authorities must take whatever reasonable steps they can to secure the evidence concerning the incident, including, inter alia, a detailed statement concerning the allegations from the alleged victim, eyewitness testimony, forensic evidence and, where appropriate, additional medical certificates apt to provide a full and accurate record of the injuries and an objective analysis of the medical findings, in particular as regards the cause of the injuries'. See also *Kucheruk v Ukraine* 2007-X, para 157 (investigation limited to establishing that prison guards had acted in accordance with regulations); *Trajkoski v FYRO Macedonia* (7 February 2008), para 48 (investigation marked by excessive formalism rather than seeking to establish facts).

Promptness and reasonable expedition

4.106 It is implicit that the investigation should meet the criteria of promptness and reasonable expedition in order to help maintain public confidence in the authorities' adherence to the rule of law and to prevent the appearance of collusion in or tolerance of unlawful acts[1]. Thus the investigation should begin as soon as possible after the matter is brought to the attention of the authorities, and thereafter be pursued expeditiously[2].

1   *Paul and Audrey Edwards v United Kingdom* 2002-II, para 72; *Indelicato v Italy* (18 October 2001), para 37.

2   See eg *Batı and Others v Turkey* 2004-IV, paras 145–147 (under Art 13: failure by courts, etc to secure prosecution and conviction before proceedings became time-barred); *Kucheruk v Ukraine* 2007-X, para 160 (investigation began 26 months after events, and proceedings still pending after five years).

Public scrutiny

4.107 It is expected that investigative procedures and decision-making should be open and transparent in order to ensure the accountability of officials, but the degree of public scrutiny required will be dependent upon the circumstances, and thus domestic arrangements must strike an appropriate balance when seeking to take into account other legitimate interests such as national security or the protection of material relevant to other investigations[1].

1   Cf *McKerr v United Kingdom* 2001-III, para 159 (in relation to Art 2).

Involvement of victim

4.108 It goes without saying that the complainant must be afforded effective access to the investigatory procedure in order to safeguard his or her legitimate interests[1]. As noted, it is expected that the national authorities hold an investigation whenever there are sufficiently clear indications that ill-treatment has occurred, rather than relying upon the individual to take the initiative in lodging a formal complaint or assuming responsibility for the investigation[2].

1   *Aksoy v Turkey* 1996-VI, para 98 (in terms of Art 13). See eg *Trajkoski v FYRO Macedonia* (7 February 2008), para 46 (unexplained delay in drawing up report, and it was not established whether the report had been communicated to the applicant).

2   *İlhan v Turkey* [GC] 2000-VII, para 63.

Decisions of domestic courts on the procedural aspect of Article 3

4.109 The procedural aspect of Article 3 was considered in *R (AM) v Secretary of State for the Home Department,* which concerned disturbances at an immigration detention centre managed by a private company on behalf of the

Home Office. A retired civil servant had been appointed to carry out an investigation. It was held by the Court of Appeal that he lacked the necessary independence, and that his remit was in any event too narrow to satisfy the requirements of Article 3, as it was focused on issues of management rather than on the protection of human rights. It was observed that the investigative obligation of the state might – depending on what facts were at issue – go beyond the ascertainment of individual fault and reach questions of system, management and institutional culture, especially in cases of death or severe physical injury while in the custody of the state[1]. In the later case of *R (P) v Secretary of State for Justice,* concerned with a prisoner in a young offenders' institution who had been transferred to hospital after repeated self-harm, it was held that the state was not obliged to conduct an inquiry in every case in which there was an arguable breach of Article 3, and that whether such an obligation arose depended on the circumstances of the case, including the availability of other means of eliciting the relevant facts. On the facts, there was no arguable breach of Article 3, since the Secretary of State's failure to transfer the claimant to hospital sooner had been based on the medical advice of an appropriately qualified doctor. Furthermore, even if there had been an arguable breach of Article 3, there would have been no obligation on the Secretary of State to conduct an inquiry since the relevant facts, including the reason why the claimant had been kept at the young offenders' institution and not transferred to hospital sooner, were known[2].

1   *R (AM) v Secretary of State for the Home Department* [2009] EWCA Civ 219.

2   *R (P) v Secretary of State for Justice* [2010] QB 317.

Particular issues arising under Article 3

Criminal process and punishment

Corporal punishment

4.110 Corporal punishment involves 'institutionalised violence', that is, a deliberate assault carried out by state authority where the individual is 'treated as an object in the power of the authorities'[1]. British law and practice were clearly out of line with a strong European consensus that judicially-sanctioned corporal punishment of juveniles was unacceptable, and thus in *Tyrer v United Kingdom* the European Court of Human Rights readily ruled that the birching of a 15-year-old boy on his bare buttocks upon the order of an Isle of Man juvenile court was 'degrading'[2]. However, cases involving the administration of corporal punishment by schoolteachers always ran the risk of appearing to trivialise the nature of Article 3[3]. In the first case before the Court to challenge this practice, *Campbell and Cosans v United Kingdom,* the Court was able to avoid giving a ruling on the Article 3 issue since on the particular facts neither child of the two applicants had been physically punished, although the Court did accept that a 'sufficiently real and immediate' threat of infliction of treatment violating the guarantee could be sufficient to breach Article 3[4]. Other applications complaining about the actual infliction of corporal punishment in schools eventually turned upon the level of violence used[5]. Corporal punishment administered by schoolteachers is now almost certainly unacceptable and undoubtedly would constitute degrading treatment prohibited by Article 3[6]. Whether such punishment when administered by parents would similarly be deemed to violate a child's rights under the guarantee is considered above in the context of discussion of a state's positive obligations to protect individuals against ill-treatment arising in a domestic context[7].

1   *Tyrer v United Kingdom* (1978) A 26, at para 33 (judicially-ordered corporal punishment).

2   *Tyrer v United Kingdom* (1978) A 26, paras 30–35.

3   Cf *Costello-Roberts v United Kingdom* (1993) A 247-C, para 32 (a seven-year-old boy 'slippered' by a headmaster was unable to show any severe or long-lasting effects, and thus no issue under Art 3; but (at para 27) state responsibility was engaged in respect of educational provision in private schools); see para **4.65** above.

4   *Campbell and Cosans v United Kingdom* (1982) A 48, paras 26 and 30. The case did result in a finding of a violation of ECHR, Prot 1, Art 2: see para **6.163** below.

5   See eg 9471/81, *Warwick v United Kingdom* (1986) DR 60, 5 (in the opinion of the Commission, heavy bruising caused to a 16-year-old girl who had been caned three times on the hand in the presence of the male deputy headmaster violated Art 3, but the Committee of Ministers subsequently failed to agree that there had been a violation); cf *Y v United Kingdom* (1992) A 247-A (friendly settlement reached by applicant and government after expression of opinion of violation by Commission).

6   For domestic discussion, see *R (Williamson) v Secretary of State for Education and Employment* [2005] 2 AC 246 (case considered in terms of Prot 1, Art 2, but see Baroness Hale's concurring opinion suggesting this matter should be determined under Arts 3 and 8 as a 'rights of the child' case). Corporal punishment was abolished in state schools and for publicly funded pupils in independent schools by the Education (Scotland) Act 1980, s 48A(1).

7   See para **4.86** above.

Juvenile justice

4.111 Article 3 cannot readily be used to challenge substantive or procedural provisions concerning juvenile justice. In the related cases of *T v United Kingdom* and *V v United Kingdom*, two ten-year-old children who had abducted and murdered an infant claimed that their prosecution in an adult court with all its attendant formality had caused psychiatric harm and a high degree of public humiliation, and further that the attribution of criminal responsibility at such a young age in English law was itself contrary to this provision. The Court ruled that there had been no Article 3 violation on either count. The intention of the state in holding the trial in an adult court had not been to humiliate or cause any suffering. An inquiry into the death of the victim involving the attendance and participation of the applicants would have had a harmful effect on any child of their age, and their suffering had not gone significantly beyond that which would have been engendered in any process. Further, although English law had one of the lowest ages of criminal responsibility in Europe, there was no common European standard and, accordingly, it could not be said that domestic law differed so disproportionately as to give rise to a violation[1].

---

1   *T v United Kingdom* [GC] (16 December 1999), paras 60–78 and 92–100; and *V v United Kingdom* [GC] 1999-IX, paras 62–80 and 93–101. These cases represented the Court's first ever consideration of the ECHR's application to child defendants. They also raised important issues under Arts 5 and 6 regarding elements of the UK's trial and sentencing procedures: see further, para **4.88** above and para **5.118** below. The age of criminal responsibility in Scotland is eight years: Criminal Procedure (Scotland) Act 1995, s 41. The Scottish Executive's Advisory Group on Youth Crime recommended that consideration be given to raising this to 12 years; see also Scottish Law Commission: Discussion Paper No 115. Cf *Notar v Romania* (friendly settlement) (20 April 2004), paras 49–53 (forcible shaving of the applicant's head, the disclosure of the applicant's identity in a television programme concerning juvenile delinquency, and a refusal to provide medical examination: friendly settlement following upon an offer to pay compensation and to take steps to instruct police officers in the implications of the presumption of innocence and more generally to improve the protection of vulnerable children).

SENTENCES OF LIFE IMPRISONMENT IMPOSED UPON MINORS

4.112 Article 3 issues may arise in respect of disproportionate sentences of imprisonment. In particular, failure to respect the process of maturation in the case of a juvenile sentenced to a period of imprisonment, which could last for the remainder of the individual's natural life, can give rise to Article 3 considerations[1]. The relative age of a young person sentenced to a lengthy period of imprisonment may thus be of relevance. In *Weeks v United Kingdom*, a 17-year-old youth who had used a starting pistol to rob a shopkeeper of 35p had been sentenced to life imprisonment. The justification for this sentence had been reconsidered at length by the English Court of Appeal and accepted as appropriate to protect the public and, indeed, additionally to help ensure the applicant's early release from prison, and the European Court of Human Rights thus accepted that the sentence did not give rise to an Article 3 issue[2].

---

1   See eg *Hussain v United Kingdom* 1996-I, para 61; and *Singh v United Kingdom* 1996-I, para 53. See further para **4.226** below.

2   *Weeks v United Kingdom* (1987) A 114, para 47. For general discussion, see van zyl Smit and Ashworth 'Disproportionate Sentences as Human Rights Violations' (2004) 67 MLR 541.

4.113 On the other hand, Article 3 does not prohibit a state from subjecting a young person convicted of a serious offence to an indeterminate sentence allowing for his continued detention where it is deemed necessary for the protection of the public, provided that release upon parole is possible. In *T v United Kingdom* and *V v United Kingdom*, the applicants further claimed that that the length of the tariff to be served by way of retribution and deterrence (set originally at 15 years before being quashed on review) amounted to inhuman and degrading treatment. However, the Court found the punitive element in their sentences to be acceptable, bearing in mind the responsibility of the state to protect the public from violent crime[1]. It is only in the most exceptional circumstances that a sentence imposed following a conviction is thus likely to give rise to a violation of Article 3.

---

1   *T v United Kingdom* [GC] (16 December 1999), paras 92–100; *V v United Kingdom* [GC] 1999-IX, paras 93–101.

Disproportionate sentences of imprisonment

4.114 Issues under Article 3 issues may arise in relation to the sentence imposed and its implementation, since a sentence disproportionate to the gravity of the offence, or one that fails to take into account other Convention concerns, may violate the guarantee. For example, in *Ülke v Turkey,* the Court determined that the applicant, a peace activist who repeatedly had been punished for refusal to serve in the military on account of his beliefs, had been subjected to treatment in violation of Article 3 on account of the 'constant alternation between prosecutions and terms of imprisonment' and the possibility that this situation could theoretically continue for the rest of his life. This had exceeded the inevitable degree of humiliation inherent in imprisonment and thus was deemed to have qualified as 'inhuman' treatment on account of the premeditated, cumulative and long term effects of the repeated convictions and incarceration, the Court noting that domestic law failed to make provision for conscientious objectors and thus was 'evidently not sufficient to provide an appropriate means of dealing with situations arising from the refusal to perform military service on account of one's beliefs'[1]. The imposition of a sentence of imprisonment may also be incompatible with Article 3 of the ECHR where the individual is severely physically disabled and where detention facilities are grossly inadequate, as occurred in *Price v United Kingdom*[2]. The severity of sanctions imposed upon an applicant may also be of relevance in assessing the proportionality of an interference with other Convention guarantees, for example, in relation to interferences with freedom of expression under Article 10[3].

---

1   *Ülke v Turkey* (24 January 2006), at paras 61 and 62.
2   *Price v United Kingdom* 2001-VII, discussed at para **4.123** below.
3   See para **7.71** below.

4.115 The principle that life imprisonment without the opportunity of parole may be disproportionate in the case of minors has now been extended to those so sentenced as adults. The key issue is whether the life sentence is indeed irreducible. In *Kafkaris v Cyprus,* the Grand Chamber was asked to consider the replacement of a scheme which had recognised eligibility for remission from a mandatory life sentence for good behaviour for murder with one which permitted release upon the recommendation or agreement of the Attorney-General. No violation of Article 3 was established in the particular case as life sentences remained both *de jure* and *de facto* reducible, nor was the Court satisfied that the anxiety caused by changes in legislation removing the expectation of release had reached the requisite level of severity to give rise to an issue under Article 3[1].

In domestic cases, it has been held that the mandatory life sentence in respect of adult murderers does not contravene Article 3[2]. Nor does a whole life sentence[3]. Nor does an indeterminate term of imprisonment for public protection[4].

1   *Kafkaris v Cyprus* [GC] 2008-..., paras 100–108. For discussion of Art 7 issues, see para **5.232** below. Cf *Léger v France* (striking out) [GC] 2009-..., paras 43–51 (continuing imprisonment of prisoner now in fortieth year of a life sentence for the abduction and manslaughter of a child despite judicial recommendation for release on parole but in light of refusal to admit responsibility for offences: complaints that the continued imprisonment was now arbitrary and discriminatory and that the lack of a possibility of early release amounted to imprisonment on 'death row': case struck out by the Grand Chamber following the applicant's death).

2   *R v Lichniak* [2003] 1 AC 903.

3   *R v Bieber* [2009] 1 WLR 223; see also *R (Wellington) v Secretary of State for the Home Department* [2009] 1 AC 335.

4   *R v Pedley* [2009] 1 WLR 2517.

INADEQUATE SENTENCES OF PUNISHMENT

4.116 While a disproportionate sentence for a criminal offence may thus give rise to an Article 3 issue, the converse may also do so if the punishment imposed following a conviction for the unwarranted use of violence amounting to ill-treatment is unduly lenient. States must ensure the protection of individuals through substantive domestic law and its effective enforcement. In consequence, it is expected that punishment is appropriate in cases where it has been established that there has been unwarranted use of force by state officials[1] or by others[2], and that it acts as an effective deterrent[3].

1   Eg *Valeriou and Nicolai Roşca v Moldova*, (20 October 2009), paras 72–75 (minimum sentences imposed on police officers). See further para **4.83** above.

2   Eg *MC v Bulgaria* 2003-XII, discussed at para **4.100** above.

3   *Okkali v Turkey* 2006-XII, noted at para **4.83**, fn 3 above.

4.117 As discussed, prison authorities must take reasonable steps to protect the health and well-being of inmates[1]. Old age in itself cannot render the detention of an elderly prisoner incompatible with Convention guarantees[2]. However, significant deterioration in a prisoner's health may make the continuing detention of an individual intolerable, although a prisoner must establish that continuing incarceration has some clear impact upon his health rather than merely alleging that a particular condition calls for some action on the part of the authorities [3]. In exceptional cases where adequate health-care is not available or provided, release on licence may be required to prevent the situation becoming unacceptable. In *Mouisel v France,* a prisoner had been diagnosed as suffering from chronic leukaemia some three years into his 15-year sentence of imprisonment, and at this stage, had been treated as a hospital in-patient every three weeks. After a subsequent report had noted that there had been a further deterioration in health and recommended permanent care in a special unit, he had merely been transferred to another prison nearer a hospital and given a cell of his own. Only after a third request for release had he been provisionally freed as his health had become incompatible with his continuing detention. The Court decided that the continued detention had 'undermined his dignity and entailed particularly acute hardship that caused suffering beyond that inevitably associated with a prison sentence and treatment for cancer', and thus the situation had amounted to a violation of Article 3[4].

1   See para **4.41** above.

2   *Papon v France (no 1)* (dec) 2001-VI. See similarly 25096/94, *Remer v Germany* (1995) DR 82, 117 (80-year-old sentenced to imprisonment for 22 months, but no allegation of ill-health on account of detention); and *Sawoniuk v United Kingdom* (dec) 2001-VI (imprisonment of 80-year-old convicted under the War Crimes Act for murder: inadmissible, as there was no prohibition in the ECHR against the detention in prison of persons who attain an advanced age). Nor can Art 5(4) be used to require the release of a detainee because of his state of health: *Kudła v Poland* [GC] 2000-XI, para 93; *Jabłoński v Poland* (21 December 2000), para 82. See further Murdoch *The Treatment of Prisoners: European Standards* (2006), pp 204–205. For CPT expectations in the case of prisoners unsuited for continued detention on the grounds of serious ill-health, see CPT/Inf (93) 12, para 70.

3   See 22564/93, *Grice v United Kingdom* (1994) DR 77, 90 (no indication that detention of a prisoner suffering from Aids had any impact upon his health); and *Gelfmann v France* (14 December 2004), paras 48–60 (continued detention of convicted prisoner with Aids: no violation).

4   *Mouisel v France*, 2002-IX, paras 45–48. See also *Farbtuhs v Latvia* (2 December 2004), paras 49–61 (prolonged detention of invalid in conditions unsuitable for his state of health); *Aleksanyan v Russia* (22 December 2008), paras 145–158 (failings in medical care – but not in availability of drugs – had entailed particularly acute hardship to a pre-trial prisoner); *Kaprykowski v Poland* (3 February 2009), paras 70–77 (prisoner suffering from severe epilepsy and forced to rely for assistance and emergency medical care on his cellmates); and *Ghavtadze v Georgia* (3 March 2009), para 96 (detainees cannot be hospitalised only when symptoms peak and before being cured sent back to prison where no treatment would be given). The situation in certain prison systems may be so bad as to call for indications of required action in the operative part of the judgment: *Dybeku v Albania* (18 December 2007), para 64 (urgent action for prisoners with health needs in respect of prison detention conditions). Cf 9044/80, *Chartier v Italy* (1982) DR 33, 41 (medical treatment provided to a long-term prisoner suffering from hereditary obesity had been sufficient, but 'particularly serious' cases may require greater sensitivity). For domestic discussion, see *R (Spinks) v Secretary of State for the Home Department* [2005] EWCA Civ 275 (terminally ill prisoner with cancer sought compassionate release under the Crime (Sentences) Act 1997, s 30 but request rejected on grounds of risk of re-offending, lack of exceptional circumstances, and that life expectancy was not particularly short: no obligation on the Minister to consult the Parole Board, and the procedural aspect of Art 3 only arose once a breach of the provision had ceased; and case distinguishable from *Mouisel v France*). See also *R (Faizovas) v Secretary of State for Justice* [2009] EWCA Civ 373; *R v Qazi* [2010] EWCA Crim 2579.

Extradition, etc carrying the risk of a disproportionate sentence

4.118 The issue of the risk of a disproportionate sentence upon conviction may also arise in the context of deportation or extradition. In *Nivette v France,* the Court was asked to rule that the return of the applicant to the United States of America where he could face imposition of a sentence of life imprisonment without the opportunity of remission of sentence would violate Article 3. In light of a binding undertaking obtained by the French authorities from the relevant prosecutor not to charge one of the special circumstances required for the death penalty or a sentence of life imprisonment without any possibility of early release, the Court rejected the application as manifestly ill-founded, but the decision does seem to support the conclusion that extradition without such an assurance to face life imprisonment would have exposed the applicant to serious risk of punishment prohibited by Article 3[1].

In the domestic case of *R (Wellington) v Secretary of State for the Home Department,* a majority of the House of Lords considered that the desirability of extradition was a factor to be taken into account in deciding whether the punishment likely to be imposed in the receiving state attained the level of severity necessary to amount to a violation of Article 3. Punishment which would be inhuman and degrading in the domestic context would therefore not necessarily be so regarded when the choice between either extraditing or allowing a fugitive offender to evade justice altogether was taken into account[2].

---

1   *Nivette v France* (dec) 2001-VII (assurances received by the respondent state were such as to exclude the danger that the death penalty or life imprisonment without the possibility of remission would be imposed if the applicant were extradited to the USA: inadmissible). See also *Léger v France* (striking out) [GC] 2009-…, noted at para **4.115**, fn 1 above.

2   *R (Wellington) v Secretary of State for the Home Department* [2009] 1 AC 335.

The treatment of detained persons

Involuntary medical treatment of patients

4.119 The treatment of mentally ill detainees in a manner grossly inappropriate to their health is liable to give rise to a finding of a violation of Article 3[1]. However, as the case of *Herczegfalvy v Austria* indicates, the involuntary therapeutic treatment of detainees in accordance with contemporary medical standards is unlikely to give rise to any issue under Article 3[2]. This principle would almost certainly apply to cases involving the forcible feeding of a prisoner or mental health patient, at least in situations where there is evidence to suggest that the individual's mental capacity is diminished[3]. In *Nevmerzhitskiy v Ukraine,* the applicant had gone on hunger strike on several occasions during a 34-month period of pre-trial detention. In concluding that the force-feeding of the applicant had constituted torture within the meaning of Article 3 in light of the lack of any proof of medical justification and the restraints and equipment used, the Court nevertheless indicated that measures such as force-feeding where these can be shown to be medically necessary in order to save life could not in principle be regarded as inhuman and degrading providing that they are accompanied by procedural guarantees protecting against arbitrariness and that the measures do not go beyond a minimum level of severity[4]. Such situations, however, can be contrasted with those in which there have been failures to provide acceptable standards of detention or treatment[5].

1   *Kucheruk v Ukraine* 2007-X, paras 130–133, 140–146, 148–152, and 157–163 (unjustified use of truncheons in the absence of any threat to other inmates or staff, placement in solitary confinement, handcuffing for seven days, and lack of adequate medical care of remand prisoner suffering from schizophrenia: violation of Art 3, and violation also of the procedural aspect on account of serious shortcomings in the investigation).

2   *Herczegfalvy v Austria* (1992) A 244, at paras 82–83: 'as a general rule, a measure which is a therapeutic necessity [in terms of established principles of medicine] cannot be regarded as inhuman or degrading'. Cf *Avci and Others v Turkey* (27 June 2006), para 34–45 (detainees chained to their beds in a casualty department in which they had been placed following a hunger strike: violation). See too 18835/91, *Grare v France* (2 December 1992) (side-effects of medication were unpleasant but not serious enough to violate Art 3). Cf *Keenan v United Kingdom* 2001-III, paras 108–115 (inadequate monitoring and lack of informed psychiatric treatment of sufficient seriousness to amount to a breach of Art 3); *Bogumil v Portugal* 2008- ..., paras 68–91 (decision to perform surgery taken by medical staff on grounds of medical necessity rather than for collecting evidence of drug-trafficking: no violation of Art 3, or of Art 8 since a fair balance had been struck between the public interest in the protection of health and the applicant's right to the protection of his physical and mental integrity). See also *Nielsen v Denmark* (1988) A 144, discussed in relation to Art 5 at para **4.152** below. For domestic application, see *NHS Trust A v M* [2001] Fam 348 (Art 3 inapplicable since patient unconscious); *R (Wilkinson) v Broadmoor Special Hospital Authority* [2002] 1 WLR 419 (administering of anti-psychotic drugs by injection: under the HRA 1998, the scrutinising of medical treatment of mental patients was crucial particularly where issues of capacity were involved, regardless of the fact that this would complicate and lengthen the course of proceedings; *R (PS) v G (Responsible Medical Officer)* [2003] EWHC 2335 (Admin); *R (JB) v Haddock* [2006] EWCA Civ 961 (administration of treatment without patient's consent and application of the *Herczegfalvy* necessity test); and *R (Munjaz) v Mersey Care NHS Trust* [2006] 2 AC 148 (seclusion of psychiatric patients in a high security hospital not in line with code of practice issued under the Mental Health Act 1983, s 118(1): the hospital had established good reason for departing from the code, and its policy should be sufficient to prevent any possible breach of Art 3 rights of a patient; further, the policy did not allow a patient to be deprived of any residual liberty and was compatible with Art 5, and sought to prevent any arbitrary interference with Art 8 rights). See also *R (B) v S (Responsible Medical Officer, Broadmoor Hospital)* [2006] 1 WLR 810 (no violation of Arts 3 or 8 rights of a patient who lacked capacity to consent to treatment shown to be a therapeutic necessity); *R (B) v Ashworth Hospital Authority* [2005] 2 AC 278 (classification of mental health patients not in itself adequate to comply with *Herczegfalvy* test, and not required in any case by the ECHR).

3   However, such a situation may conceivably also give rise to positive duties under Art 2 to protect health where there is a serious risk of death if this is ignored: cf 10565/83, *X v Germany* (9 May 1984) (force-feeding of prisoner). For discussion of Art 2 responsibilities, see paras **4.26** and **4.52** above. But see Harris O'Boyle and Warbrick *Law of the European Convention on Human Rights* (2nd edn, 2009), at p 46: 'it is submitted that a state should not be liable under Art 2 for an omission that respects the physical will and integrity of an individual who is capable of taking a decision as to matters of life and death'. See also *R (Burke) v General Medical Council* [2006] QB 273, discussed at para **4.33** above. See also *Pandjikidze and Others v Georgia* (dec) (20 June 2006) (no force-feeding of a prisoner on hunger strike, and no allegation that such action should have been taken since there was no medical imperative: inadmissible).

4   *Nevmerzhitsky v Ukraine* 2005-II, paras 93–99. See also Appendix to Committee of Ministers Recommendation Rec (98) 7 on the ethical and organisational aspects of health care in prison, paras 60–63 (responsibilities of health service in the case of refusal of treatment and hunger strike). The problem of hunger strikes has been of particular concern in Turkey: see for example CPT/Inf (2001) 31 (Part 1), paras 6–8.

5   Cf *Aerts v Belgium* 1998-V, discussed at paras 64–67 (detention conditions merely
     unsatisfactory); and 6840/74, *A v United Kingdom* (1980) DR 10, 5 (complaint concerning
     lack of appropriate regime etc in Broadmoor Hospital declared admissible). Cf *Kudla v Poland*
     [GC] 2000-XI, at para 93 (Art 3 cannot 'be interpreted as laying down a general obligation to
     release a detainee on health grounds or to place him in a civil hospital to enable him to obtain
     a particular kind of medical treatment').

Material conditions of detention

4.120 Until comparatively recently, it was difficult to use Article 3 of the ECHR
to challenge successfully general conditions of detention in prisons, possibly on
account of acceptance (at least in the case of persons convicted of an offence)
that there is always 'an inevitable element of suffering or humiliation' in the very
nature of legitimate punishment[1]. Thus failure to ameliorate living conditions which
were 'undoubtedly unpleasant or even irksome'[2] was unlikely to be deemed to
have met the minimum level of severity required for a violation of Article 3. This
was also the case as regards the material environment in other places of detention
such as mental health hospitals[3]. Specific holding conditions also escaped censure,
and security considerations or the interests of justice were readily accepted as
justifying the imposition of solitary confinement involving sensory deprivation[4].
Only extreme or excessive state action[5], or a failure to take humanitarian
measures[6] or to provide medical treatment in accordance with reasonable
professional requirements[7], or a finding of extreme physical or psychological
effects of imprisonment in an individual case caused by special holding conditions[8]
would result in a violation of the provision. Further, while dicta suggested there
was a positive duty upon states to 'maintain a continuous review of the detention
arrangements employed with a view to ensuring the health and well being of all
prisoners with due regard to the ordinary and reasonable requirements of
imprisonment'[9], the practical impact of this was rather limited. In *Assenov and
Others v Bulgaria*, for example, a 17-year-old youth had been detained for almost
11 months in a police station in conditions which even the public prosecutor
accepted as likely to be harmful to physical and mental development if prolonged,
but given the absence of any objective evidence of actual harm, the European
Court of Human Rights was unable to accept that the conditions of detention
were sufficiently severe as to violate Article 3[10]. Similarly, while it was
acknowledged that prolonged solitary confinement might be considered
undesirable, this was still to be evaluated in terms of 'the particular conditions of
its application, including its stringency, duration and purpose, as well as its effects
on the person concerned'[11].

1   *Tyrer v United Kingdom* (1978) A 26, at para 29 (in the context of discussion of infliction of
     judicially-ordered corporal punishment).

2   *Guzzardi v Italy* (1980) A 39, para 107 (detention on island involving nightly curfew, poor
     living conditions, restricted medical facilities and opportunities for religious observances, etc
     may have been 'irksome' but did not amount to a violation of Art 3).

3   Eg 6870/75, *Y v United Kingdom* (1977) DR 10, 37; *Aerts v Belgium* 1998-V; cf 6840/74, *X v United Kingdom* (1977) DR 10, 5.

4   8463/78, *Kröcher & Möller v Switzerland* (1981) DR 26, 24; 7854/77, *Bonzi v Switzerland* (1978) DR 12, 185. But cf *Castillo Petruzzi and Others v Peru [Merits]*, (30 May 1999) Series C no 52, paras 189–199 [Inter American Court of Human Rights] (isolation and lack of communication lasting over a year constituted cruel and inhuman treatment)

5   Eg *Ireland v United Kingdom* (1978) A 25, paras 167–181 (use of sensory deprivation interrogation techniques against terrorist suspects); *Tekin v Turkey* 1998-IV, paras 48–54 (the applicant had been held for two days blindfolded in a cold and dark cell and ill-treated so as to leave him with wounds and bruising, circumstances which clearly gave rise to an Art 3 violation).

6   Eg 8317/78, *McFeely v UK* (1980) DR 20, 44 (prison authorities to exercise custodial authority in such a way as to safeguard health etc of all prisoners, even those taking part in unlawful protest involving refusal to wash).

7   *Hurtado v Switzerland* (1994) A 280–A (failure to provide medical treatment until eight days after the applicant's arrest which had involved the use of force and had resulted in a fracture of a rib: the Commission accepted that this failure to safeguard the physical well-being of detainees amounted to degrading treatment, but a friendly settlement was later achieved). Cf 6870/75, *B v United Kingdom* (1981) DR 32, 5 (failure to provide any treatment while a patient in a secure mental hospital justified on account of clinical advice; the Commission concluded albeit with some reservations that the facts did not disclose a violation of Art 3); 18824/91, *Lockwood v United Kingdom* (14 October 1992) (four-month delay in seeking second medical opinion, but this had no impact upon the prisoner's health).

8   Eg *Soering v United Kingdom* (1989) A 161, discussed at para **4.130** below. Cf *Zhu v United Kingdom* (dec) (12 September 2000) (detainee held for 18 months pending deportation in prison where he alleged he was unable to communicate and suffered racial assaults; complaint declared inadmissible as the authorities had made some effort to alleviate the applicant's situation, and the behaviour of other inmates had not been sufficiently serious to give rise to an Art 3 issue).

9   10448/83, *Dhoest v Belgium* (1987) DR 55, 5 at 21; *Hurtado v Switzerland* (1994) A 280-A (the applicant had defecated in his trousers at the time of arrest and had been forced to wear soiled clothing for a day: the failure to provide clean clothes was in the opinion of the Commission 'humiliating and debasing for the applicant and therefore degrading': friendly settlement achieved).

10   *Assenov and Others v Bulgaria* 1998-VIII, paras 128–135.

11   10263/83, *R v Denmark* (1985) DR 41, 149 at 153. Cf 17525/90, *Delazarus v United Kingdom* (16 February 1993) (complaint about segregation of a prisoner from other prisoners for 14 weeks and holding conditions: declared inadmissible).

4.121 The work of the Council of Europe's Committee for the Prevention of Torture (the CPT) increasingly had the potential to prompt revisal of this jurisprudence as the CPT began to take a more demanding view of detention conditions. This more critical attitude reflected its proactive mandate to make recommendations to help prevent ill-treatment and to counteract the psychological effects of incarceration. The importance of the medical expertise available to the Committee is evident both in country reports and in the promulgation of general standards[1]. This has, in turn, led the Court to take a more robust approach to the application of Article 3, particularly where applicants have sought to rely upon CPT reports[2]. Thus in *Kudla v Poland,* the Court gave notice there was now a general expectation that state authorities will ensure that a detainee is held in conditions which are:

> 'compatible with respect for his human dignity, that the manner and method of the execution of the measure do not subject him to distress or hardship of an intensity exceeding the unavoidable level of suffering inherent in detention and that, given the practical demands of imprisonment, his health and well-being are adequately secured by, among other things, providing him with the requisite medical assistance[3].'

1   See further para **2.86** above. European Convention for the Prevention of Torture and Inhuman or Degrading Treatment or Punishment, Arts 11(2) and 10(2) respectively: CPT visits to places of detention, information received and recommendations and reports to states are confidential, but this is subject to two exceptions: first, a state may request publication of the report and any comments it may have on the report (country visit reports are now (almost) invariably published with the exception of all bar one of the reports concerning the Russian Federation); and second, if a state refuses to co-operate or to improve matters in light of CPT recommendations, a public statement may be issued (only five such public statements have been made to date, two in respect of Turkey (in 1992 and 1996), and three in respect of the Russian Federation (in 2001, 2003 and 2007)). Further, annual (or 'general') reports made to the Committee of Ministers now provide sufficient detail to provide some impressions of the care of detainees in particular states. These reports also contain general statements of expectations, statements consolidated in publication CPT/Inf/E (2002) 1 – Rev 2010. See *2nd General Report*, CPT/Inf (92) 3, paras 36–43, *6th General Report*, CPT/Inf (96) 21, paras 14–16, and *12th General Report*, CPT/Inf (2002) 15, paras 32–50 (police custody); *2nd General Report*, above, paras 44–57, *7th General Report* (CPT/Inf (97) 10, paras 12–15, and *11th General Report*, CPT/Inf (2001) 16, paras 25–33 (imprisonment); *2nd General Report*, op. cit., paras 59 and 60 (training of law-enforcement personnel); *3rd General Report* (CPT/Inf (93) 12), paras 30–77 (health care services in prisons); *7th General Report* (CPT/Inf (97) 10), paras 24–36 (foreign nationals detained under aliens legislation); *8th General Report* (CPT/Inf (98) 12), paras 25–55 (involuntary placement in psychiatric establishments); *9th General Report*, CPT/Inf (99) 12, paras 20–41 (juveniles deprived of their liberty); *10th General Report*, (CPT/Inf (2000) 13, paras 21–33 (women deprived of their liberty); *13th General Report*, CPT/Inf (2003) 35, paras 27–45 (deportation of foreign nationals by air); *16th General Report*, CPT/Inf (2006) 35, paras 36–54 (means of restraint in adult psychiatric establishments).; *19th General Report*, CPT/Inf (2009) 27, paras 75–100 (safeguards for irregular migrants deprived of their liberty); and *20th General Report*, CPT/Inf (2010) 28, paras 65–84 (use of electrical discharge weapons). In addition, the *14th General Report*, CPT/Inf (2004) 28, has a statement on 'combating impunity'. For CPT reports concerning Scotland, see CPT/Inf (96) 11 and CPT/Inf (2005)

2   See further Murdoch *The Treatment of Prisoners: European Standards* (2006), pp 46–51.

3   *Kudła v Poland* [GC] 2000-XI, paras 90–100, at para 94 (complaint of inadequate psychiatric treatment during four years spent on remand and despite a psychiatric report that continuing detention carried the likelihood of attempted suicide: no violation of Art 3 since he had received frequent psychiatric assistance even although it was accepted that his mental condition had rendered him more vulnerable than other detainees and that detention might have exacerbated his feelings of distress, anguish and fear).

4.122 The Court's task is still to consider whether the particular individual has been subjected to ill-treatment by assessing all relevant circumstances of his case. Matters such as overcrowding, hygiene, the impact of detention conditions upon a detainee's health, and access to medical care may all be relevant in any assessment. Significant threats to health in East European prisons through infectious diseases and passive smoking thus call for analysis of their direct impact upon an applicant[1]. The clear willingness on the part of the Court to refer to CPT reports both to help establish the factual background to an application and also to assist in the assessment of whether the conditions have been sufficiently serious so as to give rise to a violation of Article 3 has thus had a major impact upon jurisprudence. For example, in *Dougoz v Greece*, the Court accepted that the applicant's allegations had been corroborated by the conclusions of a CPT report on a similar institution that the detention accommodation and regime 'were quite unsuitable for a period in excess of a few days, the occupancy levels being grossly excessive and the sanitary facilities appalling'. In these circumstances, and combined with the inordinate length of the period during which the applicant had been so detained, the Court determined that there had been a breach of Article 3[2]. In *Kalashnikov v Russia*, the question of the adequacy of cellular accommodation was also assessed by reference to CPT expectations[3], and the Court now insists upon a minimum of 3 sq m per prisoner in order to satisfy Article 3[4]. At a domestic level, the adequacy of detention conditions abroad may arise in the context of deportation or extradition proceedings[5].

1   See eg *Shelley v United Kingdom* (dec) (4 January 2008) (prisoners in institutions where there was a significantly higher risk of infection of, eg, HIV could claim to be affected by the prison's health policy and thus had 'victim' status for the purposes of Art 8, but not in terms of Arts 2 and 3 unless they can show they are personally at real or immediate risk of infection). Pasive smoking now features in case law. See *Ostrovar v Moldova* (13 September 2005), paras 76–90 (poor material conditions of detention, including exposure to passive smoking although the applicant suffered from asthma: violation of Art 3); *Florea v Romania* (14 September 2010), paras 51–64 (cell shared with up to 120 other prisoners, the vast majority of whom smoked and subsequent detention in prison hospital involving exposure to passive smoking despite medical advice to avoid such: violation); and *Elefteriadis v Romania* (25 January 2011), paras 46–55 (exposure of prisoner over 6 year period to passive smoking in shared cells and on court premises leading to chronic obstructive bronchopneumopathy: violation of Art 3). In other cases the issue has been avoided: *Aparicio Benito v Spain* (dec) (13 November 2006) (non-smoking prisoner obliged to share communal areas with prisoners who smoke: issue determined under Art 8, but inadmissible as manifestly ill-founded); cf *Sakkopoulos v Greece* (15 January 2004), para 13 (allegation of detention in a cell 35 sq m with up to 10 other chain-smoking prisoners apparently not considered). For Art 2 discussion, see para **4.28**, fn 3 above.

2   *Dougoz v Greece* 2001-II, paras 44–49. See CPT/Inf (94) 20, paras 54–59.

3   *Kalashnikov v Russia* 2002-VI, at para 97 (CPT expectation of '7 m per prisoner as an approximate, desirable guideline for a detention cell … ie 56 m for 8 inmates') However, this is not entirely accurate, as this CPT reference is (a) to a 'desirable level rather than a minimum standard' in respect of (b) police cells (c) 'intended for single occupancy for stays in excess of a few hours'. The same error on the part of the Court appears to have taken place in *Mayzit v Russia* (20 January 2005). See further *Shchebet v Russia* (12 June 2008), paras 84–96 (detention exceeding a month in cell designed for holding for up to three hours: violation, with reference to CPT standards and findings); and *Ogic v Romania* (27 May 2010), paras 40–51 (exercise time in enclosed space was insufficient to compensate for the lack of cell space, regard being had to CPT materials). The Court has also made use of CPT findings of importance in deciding whether admissibility criteria have been met, as in *AB v the Netherlands* (dec) (29 January 2002) (reference to CPT findings that the relevant authorities of the Netherlands Antilles had simply ignored for more than a year court injunctions ordering the repair of serious structural shortcomings of an elementary hygienic and humanitarian nature in prison facilities in determining that the respondent government's preliminary objection of failure to exhaust

domestic remedies should be rejected in the light of the passivity of the authorities in complying with court orders).

4   *Florea v Romania* (14 September 2010), paras 51–64 at para 51 (prolonged detention of person suffering from chronic hepatitis and arterial hypertension in a cell with only 35 beds shared with up to 120 other prisoners, a space of 2 sq m: violation). See also *Mamedova v Russia* (1 June 2006) paras 61–67 (two-year detention of pre-trial detainee confined to cells with less than 2 sq m of space per prisoner for 23 hours per day, and required to use a toilet in the presence of other prisoners); and *Yakovenko v Ukraine* (25 October 2007), paras 81–102 (poor material conditions of detention involving severe overcrowding and personal space of 1.5 square metres, lack of access to appropriate medical care in respect of HIV and tuberculosis and repeated transportation between detention centres in cramped and unventilated transportation with individual compartments of 0.3 square metres: violation of Art 3).

5   See in particular *Batayav v Secretary of State for the Home Department* [2005] EWCA Civ 366 (escaped prisoner seeking asylum entitled to the protection of Art 3 on account of the Court's judgment in *Kalashnikov v Russia*). See further para **4.122** above.

4.123 Even where the minimum cellular size has been met, other factors may also suggest there has been a violation of Article 3. The applicant's health will often be a relevant factor. The impact of this more critical approach can be seen in cases such as *Price v United Kingdom* in which the applicant, a four-limb-deficient thalidomide victim suffering from kidney problems, had been committed to prison for seven days for failure to answer questions during civil proceedings for debt recovery. No steps had been taken by the judge before imposing the penalty to ascertain whether adequate detention facilities were available to cope with the applicant's severe level of disability. The first night she had been held in a police cell which had been too cold for her medical condition, and since she could not use the bed in the cell, she had been forced to sleep in her wheelchair. For the remainder of her sentence, she had been held in a prison hospital where the lack of female medical staff had meant it had been necessary for male prison officers to assist her with toileting. For the Court, the detention of 'a severely disabled person in conditions where she is dangerously cold, risks developing sores because her bed is too hard or unreachable, and is unable to go to the toilet or keep clean without the greatest of difficulty' constituted degrading treatment within the meaning of Article 3[1]. In *Peers v Greece*, a British prisoner had been held in a segregation wing where, for at least two months, he had been largely confined to a cell lacking ventilation and windows and which in consequence would at times become unbearably hot. The applicant also had been forced to use the cell's toilet in the presence of another inmate (and similarly be present when his cellmate was using the toilet). These two factors were sufficient for the Court to consider that the applicant's human dignity had been diminished. The conditions had given rise to feelings of anguish and inferiority capable of humiliating and debasing the applicant and possibly breaking his physical or moral resistance, and the failure of the authorities to take steps to improve the applicant's conditions of detention were considered to have amounted to degrading treatment[2].

1   *Price v United Kingdom* 2001-VII, paras 25–30 at para 30. Cf separate opinion of the British judge, Judge Bratza, joined by Judge Costa: 'the primary responsibility for what occurred lies not with the police or with the prison authorities ... but with the judicial authorities who committed the applicant to an immediate term of imprisonment for contempt of court'.

2   *Peers v Greece* 2001-III, paras 68–75.

Detainees subjected to particular security measures

4.124 The use of unjustified and humiliating security measures against persons deprived of their liberty may give rise to a finding of a violation of Article 3[1], as in *Ramishvili and Kokhreidze v Georgia.* Here, two accused persons of some social standing (one of whom was the host of a popular TV talk-show) had been placed during the judicial review of their pre-trial detention in a barred dock which had the appearance of a metal cage. Heavily- armed guards wearing black hood-like masks had been placed inside the courtroom, and the judicial proceedings had been broadcast on television. In the absence of any proffered justification for such stringent and humiliating measures, the Court found that there had been a violation of Article 3[2]. Here, too, the impact of CPT standards upon the Court's jurisprudence, at least by way of support to or further confirmation of its own conclusions, is apparent. In *Mouisel v France,* for example, in considering that the handcuffing of a prisoner during transportation to and from a hospital for treatment for cancer violated Article 3, the Court referred to CPT recommendations concerning the conditions of transfer and medical examination of prisoners in the light of medical ethics and respect for human dignity[3]. In *Magee v United Kingdom,* the Court accepted that detention conditions in an interrogation centre had been 'psychologically coercive', in part based upon a CPT visit report[4]. CPT reports may also assist the Court in determining the factual background to challenges to other security measures upon detainees[5].

1   See further paras **4.75 -4.76** and **4.90** above. For recent discussion see *Khider v France* (9 July 2009), paras 108–133 (conditions of detention, security measures including repeated transfers from one prison to another, prolonged periods in solitary confinement and systematic body searches: violation of Art 3); *Payet v France* (20 January 2011), paras 80–85 (repeated transfers of high-security prisoner under court orders and administrative decisions: no violation of Art 3 in respect of repeated transfers given fears of escape were not unreasonable in view of his profile, his dangerousness and his history; but violation of Art 3 in respect of detention conditions); and *El Shennawy v France* (20 January 2011), paras 39–46 repeated full body searches of high risk prisoner by officials wearing balaclavas up to eight times a day over a short period of time and initially recorded on video; full body searches had not only to be necessary but conducted in an appropriate manner, and in this instance had involved a degree of humiliation going beyond the level which the strip-searching of prisoners inevitably entailed).

2   *Ramishvili and Kokhreidze v Georgia* (27 January 2009), paras 80–88, 91–93 and 96–102. See also *Ashot Harutyunyan v Armenia* (15 June 2010), paras 126–129 (applicant accused of a non-violent crime placed in a metal cage, this being the place where defendants in criminal cases were always seated, and suggesting to the average observer that the accused was a dangerous criminal: such exposure to the public must have been humiliating while also impairing powers of concentration and mental alertness in proceedings where criminal liability was at stake).

3   *Mouisel v France* 2002-IX, para 48. See also *Kashavelov v Bulgaria* (20 January 2011), paras 38–40 (systematic handcuffing of prisoner each time he was taken out of his cell, a practice applied for 13 years despite the absence of indicators of risk: violation, noting CPT standards that systematic handcuffing constituted degrading treatment). Of course, the Court may disagree with CPT conclusions: see eg *Öcalan v Turkey* [GC] 2005-IV, paras 86–103 and 195 (despite

CPT concerns as to the applicant's social isolation, the Court accepted the applicant may seek to take advantage of improved communications, and that it would be difficult to protect his life in an ordinary prison). Cf CPT/Inf (2004) 2 (Turkey) (third visit to establish detention conditions; further criticism of lack of effective access to family and legal representatives, a situation (at paragraph 10) whose 'gravity ... is compounded by the lack of progress in implementing the recommendations previously made by the CPT as regards other forms of contact with the outside world'.

4   *Magee v United Kingdom* 2000-VI, paras 38–46 at para 43, discussed at para **5.126** below. For domestic discussion, see *A v Secretary of State for the Home Department (No 2)* [2006] 2 AC 221 (evidence is inadmissible if extracted through torture irrespective of where the torture occurred or in what circumstances). See further Grief 'The Exclusion of Foreign Torture Evidence' [2006] EHRLR 200.

5   Eg *Lorsé and Others v the Netherlands* (4 February 2003), paras 58–74 (CPT report adequately reflected the situation concerning strip-searching and other stringent security measures in an institution in the absence of challenge by the respondent state).

4.125 There is, too, now a greater willingness to examine critically the imposition of solitary confinement. In *Yurttas v Turkey,* while no actual violation of Article 3 was established on the facts, the Court noted that 'complete sensory isolation, coupled with total social isolation, can destroy the personality and constitutes a form of inhuman treatment which cannot be justified by the requirements of security or any other reason' although at the same time it acknowledged that the 'prohibition of contacts with other prisoners for security, disciplinary or protective reasons' would not in itself amount to ill-treatment contrary to Article 3, although it was unwilling to 'exclude the possibility that excessively long detention in complete isolation and in particularly difficult circumstances for the detainee constitutes treatment contrary to Article 3'[1].

1   *Yurttas v Turkey* (27 May 2004) at para 47. Cf *Ramirez Sanchez v France* [GC] 2006-IX, paras 125–150 (prolonged solitary confinement of terrorist: no violation of Art 3, taking into account the number of visits from his legal representatives).

4.126 On the other hand, the maintenance of good order is generally deemed an adequate enough ground to justify physical intrusions such as the provision of urine samples in order to control drug abuse[1], provided always that security measures are applied for appropriate purposes and not merely as routine practices or as forms of treatment designed to humiliate detainees. Thus while strip searches may sometimes be necessary, they must thus be conducted in an appropriate manner. In *Iwańczuk v Poland*, a prisoner had been ordered to undergo a body search before being allowed to exercise his right to vote. As he was undressing, he had been subjected to abusive remarks from the guards, and in light of this humiliation, had refused to remove any further clothing. In consequence, he had been denied the right to vote. For the Court, this constituted degrading treatment within the meaning of Article 3 as a body search had not been shown to have been justified[2]. Subsequently, in *Van der Ven v the Netherlands*, the Court deemed the combination of routine strip-searching with the imposition of other stringent security measures that had been criticised earlier by the CPT to have amounted to inhuman or degrading treatment. While detention in a high security prison is not in itself incompatible with the Convention, detention conditions must be compatible with respect for human dignity and not create distress or hardship of an intensity exceeding the unavoidable level of suffering inherent in detention. One of the features which had been hardest for the applicant to endure had been the weekly routine of a strip search for some three and a half years, a measure applied in the absence of convincing security needs and in addition to all the other strict security measures imposed[3].

---

1   20872/92, *AB v Switzerland* (1995) DR 80, 66; 21132/93, *Peters v Netherlands* (1994) DR 77, 75; 34199/96, *Galloway v United Kingdom* (9 September 1998).

2   *Iwańczuk v Poland* (15 November 2001), paras 50–60. See also *Valašinas v Lithuania* 2001-VII, paras 116–118 (strip-searching of prisoner in front of female officer and touching genitals: violation). Cf *Wiktorko v Poland* (31 March 2009), paras 46–57 (stripping naked of a female in a sobering-up centre by male staff members and immobilisation with belts for ten hours constituted degrading treatment within the meaning of Art 3).

3   *Van der Ven v the Netherlands* 2003-II, paras 46–63. See also *Frérot v France* 2007-VII, paras 35–48 (full body searches not based on convincing security needs but on presumption of concealment: violation).

4.127 In a number of cases, the Court has examined the detention of death row inmates held in European prisons. The Court has been able to avoid ruling conclusively that detention on death row *per se* is prohibited, even although it has accepted that 'the fear and uncertainty as to the future generated by a sentence of death, in circumstances where there exists a real possibility that the sentence will be enforced, must give rise to a significant degree of human anguish'[1]. The continuation of the imposition of 'strict' detention regimes for prisoners sentenced to death and still facing (however remotely) the possibility of death pending the legal abolition of capital punishment, on the other hand, was condemned in *Iorgov v Bulgaria*[2]. Here, the applicant had been subjected for some three and a half years to a stringent custodial regime involving solitary confinement. The possibility of human contact had been restricted to the course of a one-hour daily walk with other prisoners, the material conditions of detention had been poor, and there had been a failure to provide proper medical care. For the Court, this had involved suffering exceeding the unavoidable level inherent in detention and which had thus amounted to inhuman and degrading treatment. Similarly, the Court in *Poltoratskiy v Ukraine* found detention conditions of a prisoner sentenced to death to have constituted degrading treatment. While acknowledging that there had been substantial progress made in improving prison conditions and that the country was facing serious socioeconomic problems, the 'lack of resources cannot in principle justify prison conditions which are so poor as to reach the threshold of treatment contrary to Article 3 of the Convention', nor could they in any event explain restricted living space, no access to natural light or to outdoor exercise, little or no opportunity for activities or human contact, denial of access to a water supply, and cell walls covered with faeces[3].

---

1   *Iorgov v Bulgaria* (11 March 2004), paras 72–73 (but the applicant's situation had not been comparable to that of a person on death row as there had been no use of capital punishment during the moratorium and thus any initial fear in view of the possible resumption of executions

would have diminished with the passing of time). See also *Poltoratskiy v Ukraine* 2003-V, para 135 (the applicant had been convicted and sentenced to death at the age of 19, and for some 15 months had faced the possibility of execution until a *de facto* moratorium on executions had been introduced by the President, while three months later, the Constitutional Court had ruled the death penalty to be unconstitutional, and two months thereafter, the death penalty had been abolished by law and replaced by a sentence of life imprisonment); and similar cases *Aliev v Ukraine* (29 April 2003), para 134; and *Kuznetsov v Ukraine* (29 April 2003), para 115. For discussion of detention of juveniles, see *Güveç v Turkey* 2009-..., paras 82–98 (pre-trial detention of minor arrested on suspicion of having links to terrorist organisation, an offence carrying the death penalty, in an adult prison in breach of domestic law and international obligations, and suffering from psychological problems inadequately addressed by the authorities: finding of inhuman and degrading treatment).

2   *Iorgov v Bulgaria* (11 March 2004), paras 115–129.

3   *Poltoratskiy v Ukraine* 2003-V, paras 136–149.

Decisions of domestic courts on prison detention conditions

4.128 The practice of 'slopping out' in Scottish prisons was successfully challenged in *Napier v Scottish Ministers*. In this case, an untried prisoner was incarcerated in a multiple occupancy cell without integral sanitation and little activity regime claimed that the unhygienic conditions had exacerbated his eczema. Lord Bonomy's conclusion was that such a situation met the minimum threshold for Article 3:

> 'My consideration of the evidence of those whom I have called experienced students and examiners of prison conditions ... has led me to conclude that to detain a person along with another prisoner in a cramped, stuffy and gloomy cell which is inadequate for the occupation of two people, to confine him there together for at least 20 hours on average per day, to deny him overnight access to a toilet throughout the week and for extended periods at the weekend and to thus expose him to both elements of the slopping out process, to provide no structured activity other than daily walking exercise for one hour and one period of recreation lasting an hour and a half in a week, and to confine him to a 'dog box' [a small cell for prisoners in transit] for two hours or so each time he entered or left the prison was, in Scotland in 2001, capable of attaining the minimum level of severity necessary to constitute degrading treatment and thus to infringe Article 3.'[1]

1   *Napier v Scottish Ministers* 2005 1 SC 229. See Thomson *'Napier v The Scottish Ministers –* Implications for the Future Management of Prisoners in Scotland' 2004 SLT (News) 103; Foster 'Prison Conditions, Human Rights and Article 3 of the European Convention on Human Rights' [2005] PL 35; and Lawson and Mukherjee 'Slopping Out in Scotland: The Limits of Degradation and Respect' [2004] EHRLR 645. The court referred to CPT reports (the CPT has on several occasions criticised overcrowding, lack of integral sanitation and inadequate regime activities in British prisons: see eg *United Kingdom Report* CPT/Inf (96) 11, para 343: 'Conditions of detention in C Hall were quite unsatisfactory. The vices of overcrowding, inadequate lavatory facilities and poor regime activities were all to be found there; in addition, many of the cells were in a poor state of repair. As the CPT has already had occasion to make clear in the past, to subject prisoners to such a combination of negative elements amounts, in its view, to inhuman and degrading treatment.' For further CPT criticisms of continuing 'slopping out' in Scottish prisons, see CPT/Inf (2005) 1. For financial implications of the

judgment, see doc SE/2005/142 (Report by the Auditor General for Scotland concerning the 2004/05 Audit of The Scottish Prison Service). See also *Callison v Scottish Ministers* (25 June 2004, unreported) OH, in which the material facts in *Napier* were distinguished (the prisoner was in a single occupancy cell, only required to slop out twice per week, the periods he was able to spend out of his cell were more extensive, and while he suffered from peripheral vascular disease, the relevance of detention conditions to his health was less evident); *Martin v Northern Ireland Prison Service* [2006] NIQB 1 (sentenced prisoner held for seven months in individual cell lacking integral sanitation but allowed access for a significant part of the day to ordinary toilet facilities: toileting arrangements did not cause anxiety or psychological consequences and thus did not breach Art 3, but failed adequately to respect private life in terms of Art 8); and *Greens, Petitioner* 2011 SLT 549.

Military discipline

4.129 Similar principles apply in the context of military justice. While challenging physical exercise is recognised as an integral part of military discipline, it should not at the same time endanger the health and well-being of conscripts or undermine their dignity[1].

1   *Chamber v Russia* 2008-..., paras 43–57 (group physical exercise imposed as punishment upon conscript known to be suffering from physical health problems resulting in permanent severe disability: violation of Art 3).

Deportation or extradition to another country where there is a risk of infliction of torture or inhuman or degrading treatment

4.130 While Article 3 does not contain an explicit prohibition of refoulement, the Court has interpreted this provision in such a way as to prevent a state from deporting or extraditing an individual to another country if there is a significant risk that he will face the infliction of torture or inhuman or degrading treatment if removed, a principle applying not only where claims for refugee status have been refused but also in situations in which extradition is sought to bring an individual to trial on criminal charges, or where deportation after a sentence of imprisonment has been ordered[1]. Article 3 thus provides protection where 'substantial grounds have been shown for believing that the person concerned, if extradited, faces a real risk of being subjected to torture or to inhuman or degrading treatment or punishment in the requesting country'[2]. The leading case is *Soering v United Kingdom*, which concerned the possible extradition of the applicant to the United States to face a charge carrying the death penalty. The Court accepted the applicant's submissions that, if extradited, there was a real risk that he would be subjected to inhuman or degrading treatment in the light of his age and mental state and the lengthy time that inmates spent on death row with the consequent 'ever present and mounting anguish of awaiting execution'. Further, the Court specifically considered that the manner of imposition of the death penalty, the personal circumstances of the individual (such as his age or state of mind), or the disproportionate nature of the penalty in relation to the offence may all support challenges to extradition to face a capital charge under Article 3[3]. This principle may also apply to the threat of extradition where there is a real risk that an entirely disproportionate sentence of imprisonment may be applied[4]. The prohibition of torture or inhuman or degrading treatment is absolute, and 'accordingly, the activities of the individual in question, however undesirable or dangerous, cannot be a material consideration'[5].

1   See Mole *Asylum and the European Convention on Human Rights* (2nd edn, 2007); and Wouters International *Legal Standards for the Protection of Refoulement* (2009), pp 187–358.

2   *Soering v United Kingdom* (1989) A 161, at para 91.

3   *Soering v United Kingdom* (1989) A 161, paras 91–111 at para 111. For discussion of death penalty cases, see paras **4.54–4.58** above. See further *Jabari v Turkey* 2000-VIII, paras 38–42 (deportation to Iran of Iranian national facing a charge of adultery for which the penalty was death by stoning or flogging would have violated Art 3; the Court was not persuaded that the Turkish authorities had conducted any meaningful assessment of the applicant's claim, and also gave due weight to the UN High Commissioner for Refugees' conclusion that her fears were credible); and *N v Sweden* (20 July 2010), paras 51–62 (deportation of Afghan national who risked the death penalty if returned as she had committed adultery would constitute violation of Art 3 as women were at particular risk of ill-treatment if perceived as not conforming to ascribed gender roles; further, the applicant's husband might decide to resume their married life together against her wish in terms of the new Shiite Personal Status Law). It is not clear from *Soering* if the risk of a sentence of life imprisonment without parole passed on a person in respect of a crime committed as a minor if returned to a country which permits such a sentence would now similarly be considered as prohibited by Art 3 in light of the UN Convention on the Rights of the Child (and for discussion of disproportionate sentences, see paras **4.114– 4.115** above); and see *Einhorn v France* (dec) 2001-XI (extradition of adult after trial *in absentia*, but death penalty would not be applied, no indication that the sentence would be life without parole, and opportunity to request retrial: inadmissible). Cf views of the UN Human Rights Committee that prolonged detention on death row does not in the absence of 'further compelling circumstances' in itself constitute a violation of the International Covenant on Civil and Political Rights, Art 7: eg Communication no 683/1996, *Wanza v Trinidad and Tobago* (views of 26 March 2002).

4   *Babar Ahmad and Others v United Kingdom* (dec) (6 July 2010) (risk of life imprisonment in the USA with no possibility of parole, and a sentence of 50 years' imprisonment, sentences to be served in a high-security facility in a regime of virtual solitary confinement: admissible).

5   *Ahmed v Austria* 1996-IV, at para 41: 'The protection afforded by Article 3 is thus wider than that provided by Article 33 of the 1951 Convention relating to the Status of Refugees'. Cf van Dijk and van Hoof *Theory and Practice of the European Convention on Human Rights* (4th edn, 2006) at p 434: the norms of Art 3 and the Convention Relating to the Status of Refugees 1951 overlap 'in that if a person has a well-founded fear of being persecuted – in the sense of Article 1(A) of the Refugee Convention – in his country of origin, his forced return to this country would violate Article 3'.

4.131 In assessing the element of risk, the European Court of Human Rights will consider all available material placed before it or obtained *ex proprio motu*[1]. In certain cases, the use of interim measures under Rule of Court 39 may be appropriate to protect the situation of the applicant pending determination of the case by the Court[2]. If a case is brought to the Court in Strasbourg after a person has been expelled, the existence of the risk must be assessed primarily with reference to those facts which were known or ought to have been known to the state at the time of the expulsion, but if the applicant has not yet been expelled, the material time for assessing the risk in a given case is the time when the Court is asked to judge the case[3]. In this area, the Court may make use of credible reports from agencies and non-governmental agencies[4]. However, the applicant must always be able to substantiate the risk of ill-treatment on an individual basis[5]. In *Cruz Varas and Others v Sweden*, a family of Chilean citizens had unsuccessfully sought political asylum. Thereafter, Sweden had deported the husband back to Chile and then had commenced steps to deport the wife and son. The Court emphasised that 'the existence of the risk must be assessed primarily with reference to those facts which were known or ought to have been known ... at the time of the expulsion', although the Court could also have regard to information which becomes available after any expulsion in helping to establish or disprove whether the fears of an applicant were well founded. Here, the lack of credibility of the husband was a decisive factor in ruling that there was no violation of Article 3. There was no direct evidence that agents of the Pinochet regime had inflicted ill-treatment on him, nor was there any indication that he had been involved in clandestine political activity[6]. In consequence, each case is likely to turn upon its own facts, with careful assessment of the circumstances necessary[7].

---

1   *Cruz Varas and Others v Sweden* (1991) A 201, para 77–82.

2   Eg *Soering v United Kingdom* (1989) A 161. For discussion of application of interim measures under Rules of Court, Rule 39, see para **2.50** above.

3   *Cruz Varas and Others v Sweden* (1991) A 201, paras 45–46.

4   Eg *Abdolkhani and Karimnia v Turkey* 2009-..., paras 79–83 (removal to Iraq of Iranian nationals by the Turkish authorities in the absence of a proper legal procedure and in light of the strong possibility that they would be removed from Iraq to Iran: removal to either country would constitute a violation of Art 3, and reference to findings by UNHCR that the applicants risked arbitrary deprivation of life, detention and ill-treatment in Iran, the Court also noting reports from Amnesty International, Human Rights Watch and the UNHCR Resettlement Service about other members of the movement in question either being executed or found dead in suspicious circumstances in Iranian prisons); and *Daoudi v France* (3 December 2009), paras 65–73 (deportation to Algeria of individual suspected of links with Islamist terrorist group would violate Art 3, the Court noting reports of the UN Committee against Torture and other NGOs suggesting substantial grounds for concluding that there was a real risk of incommunicado detention and torture accompanied by a lack of adequate judicial safeguards).

5   *NA v United Kingdom* 2008-..., paras 118–147 (the deterioration in the security situation in Sri Lanka and a corresponding increase in human-rights violations did not in itself create a general risk to all Tamils returning there and assessment of the risk could only be done on an individual basis, but since there was evidence of systematic exposure to torture of persons of interest to the authorities when returning and in light of the fact the applicant had been arrested by the Sri Lankan army on several occasions and ill-treated on at least one occasion, the expulsion would violate Art 3). See also *B v Sweden* (dec) (26 October 2004) ('strong reasons to call into question the veracity of the applicant's statements and the authenticity of the documents relied on by him', and 'he has not offered sufficient and reliable explanations for the delays in submitting the documents in question or for the partly incomplete and inconsistent statements'); and *RC v Sweden* (9 March 2010), at para 50: 'owing to the special situation in which asylum seekers often find themselves, it is frequently necessary to give them the benefit of the doubt when it comes to assessing the credibility of their statements and the documents submitted in support thereof. However, when information is presented which gives strong

reasons to question the veracity of an asylum seeker's submissions, the individual must provide a satisfactory explanation for the alleged discrepancies. In principle, the applicant has to adduce evidence capable of proving that there are substantial grounds for believing that, if the measure complained of were to be implemented, he would be exposed to a real risk of being subjected to treatment contrary to Art 3. Where such evidence is adduced, it is for the Government to dispel any doubts about it.'

6   *Cruz Varas and Others v Sweden* (1991) A 201, at paras 75–84 (the Court also noted the evolution of democracy in Chile which was resulting in the voluntary return of large numbers of refugees).

7   See eg *Vilvarajah v United Kingdom* (1991) A 215, paras 107–115 (return of Tamils to Sri Lanka at time of improved situation in country: likelihood of ill-treatment by state officials was judged to be only a 'possibility' and thus there was no real risk of ill-treatment); *Ahmed v Austria* 1996-VI, paras 41–47 (violation of Art 3 established were the applicant to be returned to Somalia where his father and brother had been executed on account of assistance given to his uncle who was a leading political opponent of the regime, and forfeiture of refugee status after conviction for crime could not be a material consideration in the assessment); *HLR v France* 1997-III, paras 33–43 (an applicant arrested on drugs charges while in transit claimed that any forcible return to Columbia would pose a real risk to his life from other drug dealers on whom he had informed: the Court accepted that Art 3 could apply even where the threat emanates from private individuals rather than state agents (although a general situation of violence did not involve an Art 3 violation) but the applicant had not shown the authorities were unable to give protection; but note the dissenting opinion of Judge Pekkanen suggesting that to require an 'informer' to provide more concrete evidence of the risk of death from criminals is 'unrealistic'); *Hilal v United Kingdom* 2001-II, paras 59–68 (expulsion to Tanzania of the applicant who had been denied asylum in the UK: the applicant had previously been tortured, and his return to a country with endemic human rights problems and life-threatening detention conditions would violate Art 3); and *Iskandarov v Russia* (23 September 2010), paras 128–135 (strong indications of involvement of Russian officials in unlawful removal to Tajikistan of Tajik opposition leader: a generally clear and coherent description of the removal had been given, and in light of the poor human rights situation in the country where torture was common and officials enjoyed immunity and prison conditions were harsh, the removal constituted a violation of Art 3). Cf *Ismaili v Germany* (dec) (15 March 2001) (possibility of ill-treatment solely on the basis of political instability in the country seeking extradition insufficient: inadmissible); and *Boumediene and Others v Bosnia and Herzegovina* (dec) (18 November 2008) (failure to enforce order not to hand over suspects to US forces in BiH and thereafter to secure their return from Guantánamo Bay: inadmissible, as the state authorities had clearly demonstrated unequivocal commitment to repatriating the applicants, responsibility for any delays could not be attributed to BiH, and assurances had been obtained that the applicants would not be subjected to the death penalty, torture or inhuman or degrading treatment or punishment by the USA, the question left open whether there was jurisdiction since the transfer to US custody occurred before the entry into force of the ECHR).

4.132 Where diplomatic assurances have been given, it is still necessary to ensure that these constitute reliable guarantees of an individual's safety if deported or extradicted[1].

1   *Saadi v Italy* [GC] 2008-…, para 148 (assurances from states with longstanding problem of serious human rights violations), discussed at para **4.134** below. See also eg *Ismoilov and Others v Russia* 2008-…, para 127 (assurances from Uzbekistan Government unconvincing); *Soldatenko v Ukraine* (23 October 2008), paras 71–75 (numerous and consistent credible reports of torture and routine beatings inflicted upon criminal suspects in custody in Turkmenistan, and assurances given by the Turkmen authorities were not adequate); and *Klein v Russia* (1 April 2010), paras 55–57 (extradition request following conviction for mercenary

offences and with diplomatic assurances: extradition would constitute violation in light of reports from UNHCR and US Department of State on the situation in Columbia, the assurances being vague and insufficient). For observations of the Commissioner for Human Rights on diplomatic assurances, see CommDH (2005) 6 (visit to United Kingdom in November 2004), paras 29 and 30: 'certain inherent weakness in the practice of requesting diplomatic assurances from countries in which there is a widely acknowledged risk of torture', and assurances 'must be unequivocal and an effective monitoring mechanism be established'. For domestic consideration of diplomatic assurances, see *RB (Algeria) v Secretary of State for the Home Department* [2010] 2 AC 110.

4.133 The majority of applications have challenged threatened expulsion to non-European countries with a clear record of human rights violations, but even the law and practice of established democracies may still give rise to an Article 3 issue, and the principle is also of application where an individual is removed to an intermediary country which is bound by the ECHR[1]. In particular, national authorities may not merely assume that other states bound by EU law will treat individuals in conformity with ECHR standards, a point emphasised in *MSS v Belgium and Greece*, a case in which it was argued successfully that the Greek authorities would fail to honour their obligations if an individual were to be returned from Belgium to Greece. While the expulsion order had been issued in conformity with EU law, the transfer had knowingly exposed the applicant to detention conditions in Greece that had amounted to degrading treatment within the meaning of Article 3[2].

1   *TI v United Kingdom* (dec) 2000-III (the applicant initially but unsuccessfully had claimed asylum in Germany, then had made a similar application in Britain; at the request of the United Kingdom, Germany agreed to take responsibility for further consideration of his request following an international convention (the Dublin Convention) concerning the attribution of responsibility between member states for deciding asylum requests: inadmissible on the facts, but the Court confirmed that the removal of the applicant to Germany did not absolve the UK Government of its obligations under Art 3 to ensure that he was not subjected to inhuman or degrading treatment).

2   *MSS v Belgium and Greece* [GC] (21 January 2011), paras 362–368. See also *Stapleton v Ireland* (dec) 2010-... (argument of risk of unfair trial if extradited under European Arrest Warrant to the United Kingdom: inadmissible, the Court noting this was not a case involving non-derogable rights under Arts 2 and 3 and a risk of onward expulsion to a non-contracting state).

4.134 Judgments such as *Cruz Varas* and *Chahal v United Kingdom*[1] pose a real challenge to European state seeking to neutralise the risk posed by non-nationals who cannot, on account of the risk of ill-treatment if deported, be removed from the state's territory[2]. While acknowledging the considerable difficulties in protecting communities from the dangers of terrorism, the Grand Chamber has rejected the suggestion that a higher standard of proof of risk of ill-treatment should be required where an individual was considered to represent a serious danger to the community: it simply was not possible to weigh the risk that a person might be subjected to ill-treatment against his dangerousness to the community if he were not sent back on account of the absolute nature of the prohibition contained in Article 3. In *Saadi v Italy*, a Tunisian national who had been issued with an Italian residence permit was threatened with deportation to Tunisia upon his release from an Italian prison at the end of a sentence for dishonesty. He had also been convicted *in absentia* by a military court in Tunisia on terrorism charges and sentenced to 20 years' imprisonment. The Grand Chamber considered that there were substantial grounds for believing that there was a real risk that, if deported to Tunisia, the applicant would be subjected to treatment contrary to Article 3, given the conviction and the consistent and corroborated evidence of routine infliction of torture inflicted on persons accused of terrorism in Tunisia. Nor in this case had the Tunisian authorities provided the diplomatic assurances requested by the Italian Government. References in the *notes verbales* from the Tunisian Ministry of Foreign Affairs to domestic laws guaranteeing prisoners' rights and accession to relevant international treaties were not sufficient to ensure adequate protection for the applicant on account of reliable reports of ill-treatment manifestly contrary to the principles of the Convention. However, even if diplomatic assurances had been given, that would not have absolved the Court from the obligation to examine whether such assurances provided a sufficient guarantee that the applicant would be protected against the risk of treatment[3].

---

1   *Chahal v United Kingdom* 1996-V, discussed at para **4.197** below.

2   See, in respect of the United Kingdom, para **4.148** below.

3   *Saadi v Italy* [GC] 2008-..., paras 147–148.

Deportation or extradition to another country where there is a risk that other Convention rights may be violated

4.135 An assertion that enforced deportation or extradition will involve a risk of infliction of ill-treatment may often also allege a risk that Convention rights other than Article 3 may be violated if an individual is sent to another country. For example, issues under Article 8 may arise since the removal of a person from a country where close members of his family are living may amount to an infringement of the right to respect for family life[1], or in exceptional circumstances have such an impact upon an individual's mental health as to violate respect for private life[2]. To this end, domestic law must contain sufficient safeguards to ensure that authority to order the removal of an individual is exercised in accordance with the law and without abuse. Even in cases where it is alleged that national security is involved, 'the concepts of lawfulness and the rule of law in a democratic society require that measures affecting fundamental human rights must be subject to some form of adversarial proceedings before an independent body competent to review the reasons for the decision and relevant evidence, if need be with appropriate procedural limitations on the use of classified information'[3]. Other Convention guarantees may also be relevant. In *Soering v United Kingdom*, the Court noted that 'the right to a fair trial in criminal proceedings held such a 'prominent place in a democratic society' that it could not be excluded 'that an issue might exceptionally be raised under Article 6 by an extradition decision in circumstances where the fugitive has suffered or risks suffering a flagrant denial of a fair trial in the requesting country'[4]. The Court has also held that considerations analogous to Article 3 may apply to Article 2 and to Article 1 of Protocol no 6 where the return of an alien would place his life in danger as a result of the imposition of the death penalty or otherwise[5].

1   Cf *AM and Others v Sweden* (dec) (16 June 1999) (the family would not be split up as all would be deported together, and although the family had been in Sweden for more than four years and had adapted to life there, they had known since their arrival that they might not be permitted to remain: inadmissible under Art 8).

2   *Bensaid v United Kingdom* 2001-I, paras 32–41 (expulsion of a schizophrenic would not lead to a violation as appropriate (albeit not as favourable) health care would be available in the country to which he was to be deported).

3   *Al-Nashif v Bulgaria* (20 June 2002), paras 122–123 at para 123.

4   *Soering v United Kingdom* (1989) A 161, at para 113. See also *Einhorn v France* (dec) 2001-XI (extradition after trial *in absentia*, but death penalty would not be applied, and opportunity to request retrial: inadmissible); and *Mamatkulov and Askarov v Turkey* [GC] 2005-I, at para 91: 'although, in the light of the information available, there may have been reasons for doubting at the time that they would receive a fair trial in the state of destination, there is not sufficient evidence to show that any possible irregularities in the trial were liable to constitute a flagrant denial of justice'.

5   Eg *Bader and Kanbor v Sweden* 2005-XI, paras 43–49 (threatened removal to Syria where sentence of death had been passed in absentia; while in theory it would have been possible to apply for a retrial, this would have required surrender to the Syrian authorities but with no guarantee of the outcome: taken with the risk of flagrant denial of a fair trial, the justified and well-founded fear that the death sentence would be imposed resulting in considerable fear and anguish through intolerable uncertainty, removal would violate Arts 2 and 3, but no need to consider application of Prot 13). See further para **4.59** above.

4.136 On the other hand, the Court has not shown itself willing to extend this protection to all Convention guarantees[1]. Thus Article 9 rights are essentially matters for European states to ensure within their jurisdictions, and accordingly very limited assistance can be derived from the provision itself to assist an individual under threat of expulsion to another country where it is claimed there is a real risk that freedom of religion would be denied if returned; while the possibility that exceptionally this provision may be engaged in expulsion cases, it would be difficult to envisage circumstances which would not at the same time engage Article 3 responsibility[2].

1   See eg *F v United Kindom* (dec) (22 June 2004) (deportation of homosexual to Iran: 'on a purely pragmatic basis, it cannot be required that an expelling Contracting State only return an alien to a country which is in full and effective enforcement of all the rights and freedoms set out in the Convention').

2   *Z and T v United Kingdom* (dec) 2006-III (Pakistani Christians facing deportation to Pakistan). See also *Razaghi v Sweden* (dec) (11 March 2003): 'in so far as any alleged consequence in Iran of the applicant's conversion to Christianity attains the level of treatment prohibited by Article 3 of the Convention, it is dealt with under that provision' as expulsion 'cannot separately engage the Swedish Government's responsibility under Article 9'.

4.137 As discussed, Article 3 (itself, or read with Article 2) prevents removal where there is a real risk of loss of life at the hands of state officials or private individuals[1]. Whether the risk of ill-treatment can involve the threat of withdrawal of appropriate health care and support is less obvious. Article 3 cannot in itself support any entitlement to a minimum level of medical treatment. The ECHR is primarily concerned with civil and political rather than economic and social rights, and advances in medical science when taken with economic differences between countries mean that the level of medical treatment available will often differ considerably. Thus the guarantee cannot be read as imposing any obligation to alleviate disparities in health care through the provision of free and unlimited health care to persons who have no right to stay in a country[2]. On the other hand, where exceptionally there are compelling humanitarian considerations calling for the continuation of care, an Article 3 issue may exist where the result of the removal would result in significant hardship. In *D v United Kingdom*, the Court ruled that the deportation of a prisoner to St Kitts in the particular circumstances would have constituted a violation of the guarantee. The applicant had been in the advanced stages of AIDS, and deportation would almost certainly have resulted in acute physical and mental suffering as well as hastening his death on account of the lack of appropriate social and medical facilities in St Kitts[3]. However, submissions based upon health grounds and the likelihood that treatment in third world countries will not be adequate must be considered on their individual merits[4]. In *D v United* Kingdom, the applicant had been close to death and had no family; in contrast, in *N v United Kingdom*, medical facilities would have been available to another individual in the advanced stages of AIDS if removed to Uganda, and while the facilities there were inferior to those available in Britain with the result that her return would hasten her death, such removal would not in itself give rise to a violation of Article 3[5]. The consequence is that, in deciding whether to extradite or deport an individual, states must pay particular attention to such matters as political climate and (if relevant) medical care facilities, even if this results in lengthy detention pending determination of these matters[6]. These considerations are in addition to issues which may arise under Article 8 which guarantees respect for family life[7].

---

1   See para **4.59** above.

2   *N v United Kingdom* [GC] 2008-…, para 44.

3   *D v United Kingdom* 1997–III, paras 50–54. See too *BB v France* 1998-VI (case ultimately struck off the list; but the Commission had considered that the deportation of the applicant (who was suffering from AIDS) to the Congo would have been a violation of Art 3 because of the lack of appropriate health care). Cf *Tatete v Switzerland* (6 July 2000) (illegal immigrant suffering from AIDS sent back to the Congo: friendly settlement).

4   See for example 40900/98, *Karara v Finland* (29 May 1998) (illness of the applicant was not at an advanced stage: inadmissible; *SCC v Sweden* (dec) (15 February 2000) (refusal of residence permit for Zambian national infected by HIV declared inadmissible: treatment was available in Zambia where most of the applicant's relatives still lived); *Amegnigan v Netherlands* (dec) (25 November 2004) (rejection of asylum after diagnosis of HIV infection on the grounds that this had not reached a life-threatening stage, his reason for leaving Togo had not been on the basis of health, and he could have applied for a temporary residence permit on medical grounds:

inadmissible as the circumstances of his situation were not of such an exceptional nature as to render his expulsion proscribed by Art 3). For applications not involving HIV/AIDS patients, see 23634/94, *Tanko v Finland* (19 May 1994) DR 77, 133 (expulsion of an individual suffering from glaucoma; no indication that there was any need for an immediate operation, or that medication would not be available if deported to Ghana: inadmissible); *Bensaid v United Kingdom* 2001-I, paras 32–41 (expulsion of a schizophrenic would not lead to a violation as appropriate (albeit not as favourable) health care would be available in the country to which he was to be deported); *Abraham Lunguli v Sweden* (dec) (1 July 2003) (allegation of risk of infliction of female genital mutilation if deported: application struck out after permanent residence permit granted); and *Collins and Akaziebie v Sweden* (dec) 2007-... (failure to substantiate risk of female genital mutilation if returned to Nigeria).

5   *N v United Kingdom* [GC] 2008-...., paras 46–51. For the domestic proceedings, see *N v Secretary of State for the Home Department* [2005] 2 AC 296.

6   Cf *Chahal v United Kingdom* 1996-V, paras 73–107 (detention of Sikh activist for six years justified in terms of Art 5(1) because of Art 3 considerations (see para **4.197** below); the Court used Amnesty International reports etc in finding that return to India would result in a real risk of torture and persecution); and *Tatete v Switzerland* (dec) (18 November 1999) illegal immigrant suffering from AIDS sent back to the Congo: declared admissible): (6 July 2000) (friendly settlement). The CPT has considered the issue of appropriate procedural safeguards in such circumstances: *Seventh General Report* CPT/Inf (97) 10, paras 32–34.

7   See paras **6.67–6.70** below.

Decisions of the domestic courts on deportation or extradition where Convention guarantees may be violated

4.138 The domestic courts have given extensive consideration to the application of ECHR jurisprudence in cases involving threatened expulsion or deportation, including cases involving compulsory military service[1], poor material conditions of detention overseas[2], criminalisation or the risk of persecution on account of homosexuality[3], lack of adequate health care if returned[4], mental health[5], and allegations that an individual will face torture or ill-treatment at the hands of state officials or third parties[6]. The House of Lords in *R (Ullah) v Special Adjudicator* also left open the possibility of reliance upon Convention guarantees other than Article 3 where, if the person is deported or expelled, there is overseas 'a real risk of a flagrant violation of the very essence of the right', for example, in respect of a substantial risk to respect for family life under Articles 8 or to religious freedom under Article 9[7]. In an important case concerned with a provision which allowed asylum seekers to be returned to other EU member states where they had first claimed asylum, without their claim being investigated in the UK, the House of Lords held that EU member states were entitled to assume that other member states would adhere to their obligations under the Convention, unless the evidence showed otherwise, and that Article 3 did not impose a freestanding procedural obligation on returning member states to investigate whether there was a risk of a breach of article 3 by the receiving state, independently of whether such a risk actually existed[8].

As at the Strasbourg Court, domestic courts have accepted that Convention rights are also relevant in cases concerning extradition, but have concluded that the strong public interest in the state's observance of its obligations under extradition arrangements has the consequence that a challenge to extradition on Convention grounds is unlikely to succeed other than in exceptional circumstances[9]. In *R (Wellington) v Secretary of State for the Home Department,* a majority of the House of Lords also considered that the desirability of extradition was a factor to be taken into account in deciding whether the punishment likely to be imposed in the receiving state attained the level of severity necessary to amount to a violation of Article 3. Punishment which would be inhuman and degrading in the domestic context would therefore not necessarily be so regarded when the choice between either extraditing or allowing a fugitive offender to evade justice altogether was taken into account[10]. Regard has been had to diplomatic assurances, but they have not been accepted uncritically. It has been held that whether assurances provide a sufficient guarantee that a deportee will be protected against the risk of treatment contrary to Article 3 of the Convention is a question of fact to be decided in the light of all the evidence[11].

---

1   *Sepet v Secretary of State for the Home Department* [2003] 1 WLR 856 (return to Turkey would result in punishment for failure to enlist: held, refugee status should only be accorded where the military service would or might require individuals to commit gross human rights abuses or participate in a conflict condemned by the international community, or where the punishment would be grossly excessive or disproportionate).

2   *Batayav v Secretary of State for the Home Department* [2005] EWCA Civ 366 (escaped prisoner who had not been exposed personally to inhuman or degrading treatment in Russian prisons was entitled to the protection of Art 3 by reference to the conditions of detention in Russian prisons generally, and the immigration appeal tribunal had failed to take into account the Court's judgment in *Kalashnikov v Russia* 2002-VI (discussed at para **4.122** above) which had accepted that detainees in Russian prisons faced a consistent pattern of gross and systematic violation of human rights). The German Constitutional Court has noted that a state can demand that a receiving state should hold a prisoner in conditions compatible with relevant UN minimum standards, and that particular states are under enhanced international scrutiny: Case 2 B v R 879/03, [2004] EuGRZ 108, [2004] EuroCLY 1312 [Germany]. The fact that a state has failed to ratify the Optional Protocol to the UN Convention against Torture (and thus is unwilling to recognise the right of international inspection) may be of some relevance in such cases.

3   See *HJ (Iran) v Secretary of State for the Home Department* [2011] 1 AC 596.

4   For domestic discussion of *D v United Kingdom* 1997-III (2 May 1997), see *N v Secretary of State for the Home Department* [2005] 2 AC 296 (return of individual suffering from AIDS to Nigeria where health support not available: while prevalence of AIDS is a considerable tragedy, the present case was not a special case, and Art 3 cannot be read as requiring the provision of indefinite health care, even where removal will result in the significant shortening of the life of the individual); cf *N v United Kingdom* [GC] 2008-.... See also *ZT v Secretary of State for the Home Department* [2006] Imm AR 84 (not entitled to resist removal order to Zimbabwe on the basis that this would interrupt the medical treatment).

5   *R (Razgar) v Secretary of State for the Home Department* [2004] 2 AC 368 (if there were sufficiently strong facts to suggest that deportation would affect the mental stability of the asylum seeker, this could give rise to issues under Art 8 as opposed to Art 3); cf *R (X) v Secretary of State for the Home Dept* [2001] 1 WLR 740 (removal of illegal entrant suffering from mental illness to country where increased risk of self-harm and deterioration in mental health: no violation of Art 3).

6   See eg *R (Bagdanavicius) v Secretary of State for the Home Department* [2005] 2 AC 668 (risk
     posed by non-state actors requires additional consideration of lack of reasonable protection
     from the state); *EN (Serbia) v Secretary of State for the Home Department* [2010] QB 633 (the
     test for sufficiency of protection was not whether the home state would guarantee that
     person's safety but whether it was unable or unwilling to discharge its own duty to protect its
     own nationals).

7   *R (Ullah) v Special Adjudicator* [2004] AC 323, per Lord Steyn at paras 47 and 50. See paras
     6.78–6.85 below. For further domestic discussion, see eg *Torabi v Secretary of State for the
     Home Department* 2006 SC 567; Case 8 A 3852/03 A, [2004] NJW 1971, [2004] EuroCLY
     1339 [Germany] (assessment of risk that a requesting state may violate a deportee's Art 6
     rights was whether that state itself was bound by the ECHR as any violation could be
     addressed by complaint to the Strasburg Court).

8   *R (Nasseri) v Secretary of State for the Home Department* [2010] 1 AC 1.

9   See *Norris v Government of the United States of America (No 2)* [2010] 2 AC 487.

10   *R (Wellington) v Secretary of State for the Home Department* [2009] 1 AC 335.

11   *RB (Algeria) v Secretary of State for the Home Department* [2010] 2 AC 110. There are
     innumerable reported cases concerned with Convention rights in relation to extradition. The
     more important Scottish cases include *Kropiwnicki v Lord Advocate* 2010 JC 229 and *H v
     Lord Advocate* [2011] HCJAC 77.

ARTICLE 4: PROTECTION AGAINST SLAVERY OR SERVITUDE

Scope of Article 4

4.139 The prohibition of slavery or servitude or imposition of any requirement to
perform forced or compulsory labour found in Article 4, has attracted limited
consideration in the jurisprudence of the Commission and Court. 'Slavery' suggests
a genuine right of legal ownership over another human being reducing that person
to the status of an 'object'; 'servitude' is linked with the concept of 'slavery' and
entails 'an obligation to provide one's services that is imposed by the use of
coercion'; while 'forced or compulsory' labour suggests 'physical or mental
constraint' as well as some overriding of the person's will[1]. However, Article 4
does not prohibit obligations to provide unpaid services as part of professional
responsibilities, unless these can be considered to be unjust, oppressive or
unreasonably detrimental[2]. In *Van Der Mussele v Belgium*, the applicant had
been required to undertake representation of a client as a pupil advocate without
remuneration or even reimbursement of expenses incurred. The European Court
of Human Rights considered that this requirement fell outwith the scope of 'forced
or compulsory labour' since it was a professional obligation required for qualification
as an advocate and known to the applicant before he had voluntarily sought to
enter this profession[3]. Nor is a state precluded from insisting that eligibility for
unemployment benefits must depend upon a person making demonstrable efforts
in order to obtain and take up generally accepted employment, for such a condition
cannot be considered unreasonable or even equated with compelling a person to
perform forced or compulsory labour within the meaning of the provision[4]. Article

15 provides that a state may not derogate from its obligations under Article 4(1) (which refers to slavery and servitude) in time of emergency.

1   *Siliadin v France* 2005-VII, at paras 122, 124 and 117 respectively. Cf *Van der Mussele v Belgium* (1983) A 70 para 32 (drafters of the ECHR followed International Labour Organisation Convention no 29 concerning Forced or Compulsory Labour (1930) and the Court would thus take this into account in interpreting Art 4: here, the definition of 'forced or compulsory labour' in the Convention on Forced Labour as work or services 'extracted from any person under the menace of any penalty and for which the said person has not offered himself voluntarily' would be applied, bearing in mind that the Convention is a 'living instrument' to be interpreted in accordance with present-day requirements). See too 7641/76, *X and Y v Germany* (1978) DR 10, 224 (reference to ILO Conventions nos 29 and 105). The Slavery Convention of 1926 defines slavery as the 'status or condition of a person over whom many or all of the powers attaching to the right of ownership are exercised'; the Supplementary Convention of 1956 refers also to practices such as serfdom and debt bondage. In *Van Droogenbroeck v Belgium* (1982) A 50, at para 59 the Court observed that if a situation arose where release from detention was 'conditional on the possession of savings from pay for work done in prison ... one is not far away from an obligation in the strict sense of the term [used in the Article]'. Cf *Ould Barar v Sweden* (dec) (19 January 1999) (individual alleging he was a Mauritanian slave and would be punished by his master if returned, but no indication he had been forced to work as a slave, nor that he ran any risk of treatment contrary to Art 3: inadmissible); and *Cyprus v Turkey* [GC] 2001-IV, paras 137–141 (no evidence that missing persons were still being held in custody and in conditions amounting to slavery or servitude in respect of occupation of northern Cyprus by Turkish forces).

2   1468/62, *Iversen v Norway* (1963) YB 6, 278 (dentist required to serve in Lapland for one year as part of professional obligations to ensure provision of dental services in remote communities: inadmissible); 20781/92, *Ackerl and Others v Austria* (1994) DR 78, 116 (requirement imposed on judges to carry out work of absent colleagues without additional remuneration arose from freely accepted terms of their appointment: inadmissible); 39109/97, *Doyen v France* (1998) DR 94, 151 (requirement placed upon *avocats* to be on call one day in every 200 to assist detainees in police custody: inadmissible); and *Steindel v Germany* (dec) (14 September 2010) (statutory obligation on ophthalmologist in private practice to participate in an emergency-service scheme organised by a public body: inadmissible, the services required to be performed did not amount to 'compulsory or forced labour' as the services did not fall outwith the ambit of a physician's normal professional activities and usual work, they were remunerated, and were based upon a concept of professional and civil solidarity, nor was the burden of six days' service over a three-month period disproportionate).

3   *Mussele v Belgium* (1988) A 70, para 40.

4   *Schuitemaker v Netherlands* (dec) (4 May 2010). The Danish courts have also held that the making benefit payments conditional upon vocational training does not constitute 'forced labour': *A v Køge Kommune* UfR 2006. 67H [Denmark], [2006] EuroCLY 1687.

Trafficking in human beings

4.140 The contemporary importance of Article 4 lies in the positive obligation upon states to ensure that domestic law provides adequate protection against the exploitation of individuals through human trafficking. The phenomenon consists in 'the recruitment, transportation, transfer, harbouring or receipt of persons, by means of the threat or use of force or other forms of coercion, of abduction, of fraud, of deception, of the abuse of power of a position of vulnerability or of the giving or receiving of payments or benefits to achieve the consent of a person having control over another person, for the purpose of exploitation'[1].

The phenomenon clearly falls within the scope of Article 4, and it will not be necessary to identify whether particular treatment constitutes 'slavery', 'servitude' or 'forced and compulsory labour'[2]. Trafficking clearly undermines human dignity. As the Court observed in *Rantsev v Cyprus and Russia*:

> 'trafficking in human beings, by its very nature and aim of exploitation, is based on the exercise of powers attaching to the right of ownership. It treats human beings as commodities to be bought and sold and put to forced labour, often for little or no payment, usually in the sex industry but also elsewhere. It implies close surveillance of the activities of victims, whose movements are often circumscribed. It involves the use of violence and threats against victims, who live and work under poor conditions. It is described … as the modern form of the old worldwide slave trade.'[3]

At international and national level, co-ordinated action is now evident. In particular, both the Council of Europe[4] and the European Union[5] have taken action to tackle the issue.

---

1   Protocol to Prevent, Suppress and Punish Trafficking in Persons, especially Women and Children (Protocol to the 2000 UN Convention against Transnational Organised Crime) (the 'Palermo Protocol'). An identical interpretation is used in the Council of Europe Convention on Action against Trafficking in Human Beings (CETS 197 (2005)), Art 4. Art 3(a) of the Palermo Protocol adds that 'exploitation shall include, at a minimum, the exploitation of the prostitution of others or other forms of sexual exploitation, forced labour or services, slavery or practices similar to slavery, servitude or the removal of organs.' The consent of a victim of trafficking to the intended exploitation is irrelevant where any of the means set out in Art 3(a) have been used: Art 3(b). There are thus three elements in the definition: action, means and purpose (but note in relation to persons under 18, only action and purpose are relevant). This definition potentially encompasses a wide range of exploitation of others, including forced marriage.

2   *Rantsev v Cyprus and Russia* 2010-…, para 282.

3   *Rantsev v Cyprus and Russia* 2010-…, at para 281.

4   See Council of Europe Convention on Action against Trafficking in Human Beings (CETS 197 (2005)). The Convention entered into force in 2008, and in respect of the United Kingdom, in April 2009. As at 31 March 2011, it had been ratified by 34 states. See further para **2.87** above.

5   The Treaty of Amsterdam, Art 29 first made specific reference to the trafficking of persons and offences against children. Further measures were contained in a Council Framework Decision in 2002, and in a Council Directive in 2004 (2004/81/EC on the residence permit issued to third-country nationals who are victims of trafficking, etc). There is now an EU Anti-Trafficking Coordinator. For further details (including information on the proposed new Directive 2011/36/EU), see http://ec.europa.eu/anti-trafficking.

4.141 Many European states are now affected by trafficking, primarily of women and minors, as countries of origin, transit or destination[1]. Article 4 imposes positive obligations upon national authorities to take action to combat the phenomenon. In *Siliadin v France*, the applicant had arrived in France when 15 years old in the company of a French national who had undertaken to regularise the girl's immigration status and to arrange for her education in return for unpaid household service. Some nine months later, the applicant was 'lent' to another couple who had made the applicant work 15 hours a day, a situation which had continued for some four years until criminal proceedings had been brought against the couple. However, on appeal the couple had been acquitted with only an order for the payment of damages having been made against them. Before the Court, the applicant submitted that domestic criminal law did not afford her sufficient and effective protection as required by Article 4. The circumstances in which the applicant was held – against her will, and as a minor unlawfully present in France and afraid of being arrested by the police – led the Court to conclude that the applicant had been subjected to forced labour within the meaning of Article 4. Further, while it could not be determined that the applicant had been held in slavery in the traditional sense of that concept as the couple had not exercised a genuine right of ownership over the applicant, the vulnerability and isolation in which the applicant had found herself together with the imposition of forced labour lasting 15 hours a day and the lack of freedom of movement supported a further determination that the applicant had also been held in servitude within the meaning of the guarantee. Significantly, the Court also confirmed that Article 4 imposed a positive obligation upon states to penalise and punish via the criminal law any act aimed at maintaining a person in a situation incompatible with Article 4. Noting the opinion of the Parliamentary Assembly of the Council of Europe that thousands of individuals were trapped in 'domestic slavery', the Court considered that French legislation was inadequate as neither slavery nor servitude were as such classified as criminal offences in the criminal code, and 'in accordance with contemporary norms and trends in this field, the member States' positive obligations under Article 4 of the ECHR must be seen as requiring the penalisation and effective prosecution of any act aimed at maintaining a person in such a situation'[2].

---

1   For further discussion, see eg Johnsson (ed) *Human Trafficking and Human Security* (2009). Note that trafficking does not necessarily imply cross-border movement. See further para 2.87 above.

2   *Siliadin v France* 2005-VII, paras 64–149 at para 112 (at para 133 the Court noted that the Parliamentary Assembly had regretted in its Recommendation 1523 (2001) that 'none of the Council of Europe member states expressly [made] domestic slavery an offence in their criminal codes'). In the unreported domestic case of *Adegun v Oyedemi-Babs* (6 June 2005, Central London County Court), the claimant was awarded damages for assault, harassment and breach of contract, her former employers having brought her from Nigeria as a young girl without adult protection and having exploited her in domestic service. For domestic provisions, see eg Criminal Justice (Scotland) Act 2003, s 22; Gangmasters (Licensing) Act 2004; and Protection of Children and Prevention of Sexual Offences (Scotland) Act 2005, ss 9–12. See further Joint Committee on Human Rights, 26th report of Session 2005–06, *Human Trafficking*; Home Office and Scottish Executive *UK Action Plan on Tackling Human Trafficking* (March 2007); and Scottish Commissioner for Children and Young People *Scotland: a Safe Place for Child Traffickers?* (2011).

4.142 Where its victims are held in servitude or in forced or compulsory labour within the meaning of Article 4, the *Siliadin* case indicates that there must be an effective response from criminal justice agencies. In its second judgment in this area, *Rantsev v Cyprus and Russia,* the Court emphasised that positive obligations to prevent and to protect may arise (in the context of cross-border trafficking) both in the country of origin and also in the country of destination (and potentially also in any country of transit)[1]. Here, a young Russian woman had died in unexplained circumstances after having fallen from a window of a block of flats in Cyprus where she had gone to work on an 'artiste' visa. The death had occurred an hour after police had asked the manager of the cabaret where she had worked for three days before fleeing to collect her from a police station. An inquest had decided that she had died in an attempt to escape from the apartment in circumstances resembling an accident, but that there had been no evidence to suggest criminal liability for the death. Against the background of reports suggesting the prevalence in Cyprus of trafficking in human beings for commercial sexual exploitation and the role of the cabaret 'industry' and 'artiste' visas in facilitating such trafficking, the woman's father sought to argue that the Cypriot police had failed to protect his daughter from trafficking and to punish those responsible for her death, and also that the Russian authorities had failed to investigate his daughter's trafficking and to take steps to protect her from the risk of trafficking. The Court determined that there had been failures on the part of both national authorities: no appropriate legal and administrative framework to combat trafficking had been put in place by the Cypriot authorities and the police had failed to protect the woman even although a credible suspicion that she might have been a victim of trafficking existed, while the Russian authorities had not carried out an investigation into the recruitment with a view to identifying those responsible[2].

---

1   *Rantsev v Cyprus and Russia* 2010-…, at para 289: 'Although the Palermo Protocol is silent on the question of jurisdiction, the Anti-Trafficking Convention explicitly requires each member state to establish jurisdiction over any trafficking offence committed in its territory. Such an approach is, in the Court's view, only logical in light of the general obligation, outlined above, incumbent on all states under Article 4 of the Convention to investigate alleged trafficking offences. In addition to the obligation to conduct a domestic investigation into events occurring on their own territories, member states are also subject to a duty in cross-border trafficking cases to cooperate effectively with the relevant authorities of other states concerned in the investigation of events which occurred outside their territories.'

2   *Rantsev v Cyprus and Russia* 2010-…, paras 272–309.

Recognised exclusions

4.143 There are specific exclusions in Article 4(3)[1] from the definition of 'forced or compulsory labour' of 'any work required to be done in the ordinary course of detention' justified under Article 5[2], or of work forming part of civic obligations[3], military service (or civil service in lieu where this is recognised by a state[4]), or services in time of any emergency 'threatening the life or well-being of the community'. However, if the selection of individuals required to carry out such work is determined by discriminatory criteria, then work or labour which is otherwise in the 'normal course of affairs' could be rendered abnormal and thus unlawful[5]. In *Karlheinz Schmidt v Germany*, compulsory service as a fireman was considered to be a normal civic obligation in terms of this exclusion and, by extension, the financial levy payable in place of carrying out this service also fell to be treated as being within the scope of the paragraph. However, the European Court of Human Rights noted that these linked requirements were imposed only upon men, even though women could and did serve as volunteer firefighters; further, since there were sufficient volunteers (of both sexes) to staff the service, the reality was that no male was ever required to serve, so that payment of the financial levy was in practice effectively the only legal responsibility. In such circumstances, the Court considered that the difference of treatment on the ground of sex could not be justified and thus constituted a violation of Article 14 taken in conjunction with Article 4(3)[6]. In *Zarb Adami v Malta,* the Court considered that no valid arguments had been presented to justify the striking discrepancy between the percentage of males as opposed to females who were called upon to serve as jurors, and thus found a similar violation[7]. On the other hand, the Commission has shown less sympathy to applicants seeking to challenge exemptions on the basis of discriminatory treatment in circumstances where service or labour – as opposed to payment – is required by domestic law[8].

---

1   Cf 22956/93, *Spöttl v Austria* (1996) DR 85, 58 (para (3) is to be read as delimiting the very content of Art 4 by indicating what is excluded from 'forced or compulsory labour' rather than limiting the *exercise* of the right).

2   8500/79, *X v Switzerland* (1979) DR 18, 238. Cf European Prison Rules, Recommendation (2006) 2, rule 26 (regulating work done by convicted prisoners who may be compelled to work) and rule 100 (unconvicted prisoners may be offered work, but may not be compelled to work). Cf *Van Droogenbroeck v Belgium* (1982) A 50, paras 58–59 (applicant had been 'placed at disposal of government' as a recidivist offender following a court decision and required to carry out work; work required had not exceeded that ordinarily required in such instances).

3   Eg 9686/82, *X v Germany* (1984) DR 39, 90 (duty upon firearms licence holder to provide practical help to eradicate rabies).

4   Cf Committee of Ministers Recommendation Rec (87) 8 of the concerning military service; 10600/83, *Johansen v Norway* (1985) DR 44, 155 (Art 4(3)(b) does not require states to provide substitute civilian service for conscientious objectors). Most of the applications concerning conscientious objectors have arisen under Art 9: see para **7.23** below. However, see also (for discussion of excessive punishment in such instances) *Ülke v Turkey* (24 January 2006), discussed at para **4.114** above; and *Taştan v Turkey* (4 March 2008), paras 27–31 (military service obligation imposed upon a 71-year old who had been forced to undertake the same activities and physical exercises as 20-year-old recruits constituted degrading treatment). See also *Sepet v Secretary of State for the Home Department* [2003] 1 WLR 856 (return to Turkey would result in punishment for failure to enlist: held, refugee status should only be accorded where the military service would or might require individuals to commit gross human rights abuses or participate in a conflict condemned by the international community, or where the punishment would be grossly excessive or disproportionate).

5   *Van der Mussele v Belgium* (1983) A 70, at para 53.

6   *Karlheinz Schmidt v Germany* (1994) A 291-B, paras 22–23 and 28–29.

7   *Zarb Adami v Malta* 2006-VIII, paras 75–84.

8   Eg 2299/64, *Grandrath v Germany* (1967) YB 10, 626 (Jehovah's Witness leader of 'bible study' could be required to undertake military or civilian service although ordained clergy of Protestant and Roman Catholic churches were exempted).

Contracts of service entered into by minors

4.144 An issue in terms of Article 4 has arisen in respect of minors who had signed up for lengthy periods of service with the military forces. In *W, X, Y and Z v United Kingdom*, four serving sailors and soldiers who had entered contracts of service for nine years and who had been refused requests for discharge sought to persuade the Commission that these contractual undertakings entered into when they were aged 15 or 16 and below the age of full contractual capacity constituted 'forced or compulsory labour'. The Commission accepted that the specific exemption for military service contained in paragraph (3) could not be taken to exclude military service questions entirely from consideration under paragraph (2). However, since the applicants had entered the armed forces voluntarily and with the consent of their parents, there was no sense in which the situation they found themselves amounted to 'servitude'[1]. Paragraph (3) thus covers both voluntary and compulsory military service. Yet the decision itself appears unduly narrow and contrary to the spirit of the guarantee. There would probably now be some doubt as to whether the Commission's approach to parental consent should continue to be followed[2].

---

1   3435–38/67 *W, X, Y and Z v United Kingdom* (1968) YB 11, 562.

2   Cf Grosz, Beatson, and Duffy *Human Rights: the 1998 Act and the European Convention* (1999) at p 194: 'Even with parental consent, the practice looks highly questionable in the light of subsequent Court judgments which have emphasised the importance of showing clear consent to any waiving of rights and to developments on the rights of the child, especially the International Convention of 1989.' See now the Optional Protocol to the Convention on the Rights of the Child on the involvement of children in armed conflict (2000) requiring inter alia (Art 1) the taking of 'all feasible measures to ensure that members of their armed forces who have not attained the age of 18 years do not take a direct part in hostilities', and (Art 3) where voluntary recruitment of minors is permitted, safeguards to ensure that such recruitment is 'genuinely voluntary' and 'carried out with the informed consent of the person's parents or legal guardians'; see also comments of the UN Committee on the Rights of the Child (Concluding Observations regarding consideration of the United Kingdom's second periodic report) (4 October 2002) (approximately one-third of military recruits are below 18 and required to serve for a minimum period of four (and in some cases, six) years).

ARTICLE 5: LIBERTY AND SECURITY OF PERSON

Introduction

4.145 The essential aim of ECHR, Article 5 is to confer protection against arbitrary deprivation of liberty. In part, the substantial case law generated by Article 5 reflects the variety of systems of criminal justice and of procedural and substantive provisions throughout Europe, for police powers, criminal procedure, juvenile justice, and mental health provisions are all affected by this guarantee. Few legal systems have avoided censure, and the Strasbourg Court has upheld a number of challenges to British law and practice concerning such issues as the detention of terrorist suspects, the imposition of discretionary life sentences, release and recall of prisoners on licence, and involuntary mental health placements. The influence of ECHR case law is also evident in domestic legislation designed to ensure that domestic law and practice are in line with treaty obligations. In particular, Scots law in relation to bail has been amended so as to remove certain respects in which it failed to comply with Article 5[1]. The content of the guarantee is in any case by no means static, and Court decisions continue to emphasise the crucial importance accorded to liberty and security of person through cautious advances in established Article 5 jurisprudence. In particular, the Court has now recognised that states also have a positive obligation to protect individuals against unlawful deprivation of liberty effected by others[2].

---

1   The question of release on bail must now be considered in all cases, including murder, as required by Art 5(3): Bail and Judicial Appointments etc (Scotland) Act 2000. 'Prompt' access to a court, which is also required by Art 5(3), could still pose a problem: see para **4.203** below. Uncertainty as to whether an arrest has been effected as exemplified by cases such as *Swankie v Milne* 1973 JC 1 may cause difficulties with 'prescribed by law': see para **4.165** below.

2   *Storck v Germany* 2005-V, paras 102–107, discussed at para **4.155** below.

4.146 Article 5 provides a list of grounds for deprivation of liberty and associated procedural and substantive rights. First, paragraph (1) recognises some 15 permissible grounds for deprivation of liberty as expressed in six sub-paragraphs. These permitted grounds for deprivation of liberty are exhaustive and are to be interpreted narrowly[1]. Each is also qualified by the requirement that the detention has been 'lawful' and in accordance with a procedure prescribed by law. Secondly, paragraphs (2) to (4) confer guarantees designed to ensure a prompt and effective determination of the lawfulness of the deprivation. These provisions '[reinforce] the individual's protection against arbitrary deprivation of his or her liberty by guaranteeing a corpus of substantive rights which are intended to minimise the risks of arbitrariness by allowing the act of deprivation of liberty to be amenable to independent judicial scrutiny and by securing the accountability of the authorities for that act'[2]. Thirdly, paragraph (5) provides for an enforceable right to compensation in the event of unlawful detention or failure to accord a detainee these procedural rights. These safeguards are complemented in the case of unacknowledged deprivation of liberty by additional positive obligations on the part of the state to 'take effective measures to safeguard against the risk of disappearance and to conduct a prompt effective investigation into an arguable claim that a person has been taken into custody and has not been seen since'[3].

---

1   *Quinn v France* (1995) A 311, para 42.

2   *Kurt v Turkey* 1998-III, at para 123.

3   *Kurt v Turkey* 1998-III, at para 124; *Taş v Turkey* (14 November 2000), at para 84. See too *Cyprus v Turkey* [GC] 2001-IV, para 131. Cf *Şarli v Turkey* (22 May 2001) para 69 (where it is not established beyond reasonable doubt that state authorities were responsible for a deprivation of liberty in terms of Art 5, the responsibility for carrying out an effective investigation arises under Art 13).

Derogation in time of emergency

4.147 The ECHR, Article 15 allows a state to derogate from its obligations in time of war or other public emergency[1] 'to the extent strictly required by the exigencies of the situation, provided that such measures are not inconsistent with its other obligations under international law'[2]. Exercise of a state's right of derogation under Article 5 will be scrutinised with particular care, both as regards the question whether a state of public emergency exists, and if so, whether the actual measures in question were proportionate as 'strictly necessary'[3]. While a wide margin of appreciation is left to states, this is subject to supervision by the Court which is called upon to rule whether the authorities have gone beyond the 'extent strictly required by the exigencies' of the crisis[4]. The United Kingdom has made periodic use of Article 15 to prevent challenges arising under Article 5 to extended powers of detention under terrorism legislation[5]. A derogation made in 1988 was listed as a 'designated derogation' in the Human Rights Act 1998, Sch 3, but the United Kingdom gave notice in 2001 that this derogation would be withdrawn following upon the entry into force of the Terrorism Act 2000[6]. A further derogation was lodged at the end of this same year following upon enactment of the Anti-terrorism, Crime and Security Act 2001, which made provision for the indefinite detention of non-UK nationals suspected of involvement in terrorism[7]. This derogation was subsequently withdrawn in 2005 when these powers ceased to exist[8].

---

1   International law distinguishes between *ius ad bellum* (war undertaken for the legitimate defence of a state or action taken by the Security Council of the UN) and *ius in bello* (or armed conflict in the most general sense). The meaning of 'war' for the purposes of Art 15 was raised by the applicants in *Banković and Others v Belgium and 16 other States* (dec) [GC] 2001-XII, but avoided by the Court as the facts fell outwith the jurisdiction of the respondent parties: see further, para **3.07** above.

2   ECHR, Art 15(1). No derogation from Art 2 (except in respect of deaths resulting from lawful acts of war), Art 3, Art 4(1) and Art 7 may be made. Notification of the measures taken, the reasons for them, and when the measures have ceased to operate is to be given to the Secretary General of the Council of Europe (see eg *Aksoy v Turkey* 1996-VI, paras 31–32). See further Allain 'Derogation from the European Convention of Human Rights in the Light of "Other Obligations under International Law"' [2005] EHRLR 480; Kavanaugh 'Policing the Margins: Rights Protection and the European Court of Human Rights' [2006] EHRLR 422 at 436–442; and van Dijk, van Hoof, van Rijn and Zwaak (eds) *Theory and Practice of the European Convention on Human Rights* (4th edn, 2006) pp 1053–1075.

3   Art 15 has been invoked by Belgium, France, Greece, Ireland, the United Kingdom and Turkey, the latter two states on repeated occasions. The territorial scope of application of a derogation was considered in *Ireland v United Kingdom* (1978) A 25, paras 202–224 in which the Court accepted that the reference to 'life of the nation' could be construed as applying to a particular part of the state rather than to the whole state, and further, that recognition of a margin of appreciation on the part of national authorities was appropriate; and in *Brannigan and McBride v United Kingdom* (1993) A 258-B, paras 48–66 (derogation limited to terrorism connected 'with the affairs of Northern Ireland' upheld in view of the level of terrorist violence; but cf dissenting judgment of Judge Walsh who considered no serious effort had been made by the United Kingdom Government or Parliament to rearrange judicial procedures in such a way as to address Convention concerns when responding to security considerations). However, a derogation made in respect of a particular region cannot be relied upon elsewhere in a state's

territory even where the action challenged has been taken in relation to that emergency: *Sakik v Turkey* 1997-VII, paras 36–39. See Trechsel 'Liberty and Security of Person', in Macdonald, Matscher, and Petzold (eds) *The European System for the Protection of Human Rights* (1993), p 277 at p 281, who argues that the right of derogation under Art 5 should not extend to procedural safeguards in paras (2) to (4) on the grounds that to do otherwise would be to allow a state to deprive individuals of their liberty on arbitrary grounds and without the judicial controls necessary which provide a safeguard against ill-treatment. Yet it was precisely this removal of the right of prompt appearance before a judge in terms of para 3 which was upheld by the Court in *Brannigan and McBride*.

4   *Nuray Şen v Turkey (no 1)* (17 June 2003), at para 25. See also *Aksoy v Turkey* 1996-VI, para 83 (a power to detain for 30 days was considered unduly long and liable to result in arbitrary loss of liberty); and *Demir and Others v Turkey* 1998-VI, paras 49–58 (incommunicado detention lasting between 16 and 23 days was considered not to have been 'strictly necessary'). For earlier consideration of derogations, see 3321–3/67 and 3344/67, *Greek Case* (1969) YB 12, 186 (demonstrations did not pose an exceptional threat to the organised life of the nation and could be addressed by ordinary measures); and *Lawless v Ireland (no 3)* (1961) A 3, Law, paras 28–38 (existence of an illegal organisation posing current or imminent threat to the organisation and life of the state which could not be countered by the normal mechanisms of law enforcement).

5   The first derogation was lodged in 1957 and withdrawn only in 1984, several years after the abandonment of the policy of internment in Northern Ireland. A further derogation was lodged after the decision in *Brogan and Others v United Kingdom* (1988) A 145-B and upheld by the Court in *Brannigan and McBride v United Kingdom* (1993) A 258-B, paras 48–66. A complaint challenging the continuation of this derogation before its withdrawal in February 2001 was declared inadmissible: *Marshall v United Kingdom* (dec) (10 July 2001) (meaningful and regular review of continuing necessity for derogation: inadmissible). Cf *O'Hara v United Kingdom* 2001-X, para 46 (arrest and detention took place before the lodging of the derogation in 1988: government concession that the requirements of Art 5(3) had not been complied with).

6   See para **3.25** above. The Terrorism Act 2000 entered fully into force on 19 January 2001, and the derogation was then withdrawn. The Human Rights Act 1998 was amended accordingly with effect from 1 April 2001: Human Rights Act (Amendment) Order 2001 (SI 2001/1216). The Act was amended again with effect from 20 December 2001, by the Human Rights Act 1998 (Amendment No. 2) Order 2001 (SI 2001/4032), to reflect the derogation made in respect of the Anti-terrorism, Crime and Security Act 2001. The Act was again amended with effect from 8 April 2005, following the repeal of the relevant provisions of the 2001 Act: Human Rights Act 1998 (Amendment) Order 2005/107: Human Rights Act 1998 (Amendment) Order 2005/1071.

7   Human Rights (Designated Derogation) Order 2001 (SI 2001/3644), discussed at para **4.148** below.

8   Human Rights Act 1998 (Amendment) Order 2005 (SI 2005/1071).

4.148 In the United Kingdom and following the al-Qaeda attacks upon the USA in 2001, the Anti-terrorism, Crime and Security Act 2001 contained provisions permitting the indefinite detention of a foreign national certified by the Secretary of State as someone reasonably suspected of being an 'international terrorist' and whose continued presence in the United Kingdom was reasonably believed to constitute a threat to national security[1]. As noted above, in light of this, the United Kingdom Government lodged a further notice of derogation in terms of Article 15[2] and laid before Parliament the Human Rights (Designated Derogation) Order 2001[3]. The issues of whether a threat sufficiently serious or immediate existed to warrant derogation, and whether such measures were proportionate to any such threat, were considered in *A v Secretary of State for the Home Department*. In holding that there was indeed a public emergency threatening the life of the nation, the House of Lords nevertheless ruled that the scheme of detention was disproportionate as it could not be said to address rationally the threat to security[4]. Following this case, in which the court quashed the 2001 Order and declared the relevant provision of the 2001 Act incompatible with Convention rights, the Prevention of Terrorism Act 2005 provided for the making of control orders[5], and the Terrorism Act 2006 permitted the detention of terrorist suspects for up to 28 days[6]. The 2001 Act was also examined by the Grand Chamber in *A and Others v United Kingdom*. The wide margin of appreciation available to national authorities in determining whether there had been a public emergency necessarily implied that the Court would only be justified in arriving at a contrary conclusion if satisfied that the national courts had misinterpreted or misapplied Article 15 or the related case law, or had reached a manifestly unreasonable conclusion. Neither situation arose. Although no actual attack by al-Qaeda had taken place within the United Kingdom at the time the derogation was made, the authorities could not be criticised for fearing such an attack and could not be expected to wait for disaster to strike before taking measures. However, the Grand Chamber could not conclude that the derogating measures had been 'strictly required' as they had been disproportionate in that they discriminated unjustifiably between nationals and non-nationals. While the doctrine of 'margin of appreciation' was a tool for defining relations between domestic authorities and the Court (and thus could not have the same application to relations between different state organs at the domestic level), the careful examination of the House of Lords could not be said to have given inadequate weight to the views of the Executive or Parliament. Consideration of Article 15 was of necessity focused on the general situation and thus there was no need to examine its application on a case-by-case basis where measures had been found by the domestic courts to be generally disproportionate and discriminatory. Since the domestic courts' conclusion had turned on the absence of legislative power to detain nationals who posed a risk to national security (rather than on a rejection of the necessity to detain the applicants), it had been appropriate for the House of Lords to hold that the detention powers were not immigration measures but rather measures concerned with national security. The use of an immigration measure (where a distinction between nationals and non-nationals would be legitimate) to address a security issue had imposed a disproportionate and discriminatory burden of indefinite detention on one group of suspected terrorists. Nor had the respondent Government been able to produce evidence supporting its arguments that confining the detention scheme to non-nationals would avoid alienating the British Muslim population, or that it would be better able to respond to the terrorist threat were it able to detain its most serious source, that is, non-nationals[7].

---

1   Anti-terrorism, Crime and Security Act 2001, ss 21 and 23. This Part of the statute entered into force in December 2001, and was repealed in March 2005. During this period, 16 foreign nationals were certified and detained. An appeal lay to the Special Immigration Appeals Commission (SIAC) which reviewed the certificate at 6-monthly intervals after considering

evidence which either could be made public ('open material') or was kept confidential for reasons of national security ('closed material'). 'Open material' could be commented upon in writing and at a hearing, while 'closed material' was only disclosed to a 'special advocate' appointed by a law officer on behalf of each detainee, the special advocate being able to make submissions on behalf of a detainee during closed hearings but not having the right to have further contact with the detainee once he had seen the 'closed material'. See further para **4.237** below for discussion of Art 5(4) issues.

2   The derogation (in respect of Art 5(1)(f)) was considered necessary as certain of the individuals detained could not be deported because they risked ill-treatment in their country of origin in light of the judgment in *Chahal v United Kingdom* discussed at para **4.197** below.

3   SI 2001/3644, made pursuant to s 14 of the Human Rights Act 1998. The Order referred to the threat posed by 'foreign nationals present in the United Kingdom who are suspected of being concerned in the commission, preparation or instigation of acts of international terrorism, of being members of organisations or groups which are so concerned or of having links with members of such organisations or groups and who are a threat to the national security of the United Kingdom'. See above para **1.75**.

4   *A v Secretary of State for the Home Department* [2005] 2 AC 68. On the issue of whether the derogation satisfied Art 15, the House of Lords determined that this had been a question for the SIAC which had specific power to determine whether the derogation was compatible: see eg Lord Nicholls at para 79 (but cf Lord Hoffmann, dissenting, at paras 96–97). On whether the powers were 'to the extent strictly required by the exigencies of the situation', the court held that they were not: the indefinite detention without trial of non-UK nationals suspected of involvement in terrorism failed to address UK nationals suspected of terrorist links (and thus could not be justified under Art 14), permitted detention of individuals who posed no feasible threat to national security, and relied upon immigration law rather than criminal sanctions: see eg Lord Scott at para 155. Also note comments by Lord Rodger at para 177: 'national security can be used as a pretext for repressive measures that are really taken for other reasons'; and Baroness Hale at para 226 'unwarranted declarations of emergency are a familiar tool of tyranny'. See further Arden 'Human Rights in the Age of Terrorism' (2005) 121 LQR 604; and Tomkins 'Readings of *A v Secretary of State for the Home Department*' [2005] PL 259. For CPT consideration of the detention of individuals held under the 2001 Act, see eg CPT/Inf (2005) 10. See also Office of the Commissioner for Human Rights, Opinion 1/2002 (Comm DH (2002) 7, paras 17–19 and 33 (notification of derogation prior to enactment of measures necessitating the derogation, a sequence not consistent with the legal nature of derogations and one which undermines effective parliamentary scrutiny; and 'general appeals to an increased risk of terrorist activity post 11 September 2001 cannot, on their own, be sufficient to justify derogating from the Convention'). For wider discussion of terrorism and human rights, see eg Wilson (ed) *Human Rights in the 'War on Terror'* (2005); and Anthopoulos 'The Preventive State and the Right to Security' (2006) 18 ERevPL 773. For discussion of EU law, see Almqvist 'A Human Rights Critique of European Judicial Review: Counter-terrorism Sanctions' (2008) ICLQ 303.

5   Prevention of Terrorism Act 2005, ss 1–2. See further Joint Committee on Human Rights; 'Counter-Terrorism Policy and Human Rights': Draft Prevention of Terrorism Act 2005 (Continuation in Force of Sections 1 to 9) Order 2006', 12th Report Session 2005–06, HL 122, HC 915 (2006); Office of the Commissioner for Human Rights, Report, CommDH (2005) 6, para 22; and CPT/Inf (2006) 26 and CPT/Inf (2006) 28. For discussion, see eg Elliot 'United Kingdom: Detention without Trial and the War on Terror' (2006) 4 Int Jo Constit Law 553; Feldman 'Human Rights, Terrorism and Risk: the Roles of Politicians and Judges' [2006] PL 364; Greer 'Human Rights and the Struggle against Terrorism in the United Kingdom' [2008] EHRLR 163; Walker 'The Threat of Terrorism and the Fate of Control Orders' [2010] PL 4; and McKeever 'The Human Rights Act and Anti-Terrorism in the United Kingdom' [2010] PL 110.

6   Terrorism Act 2006, s 23.

The meaning of 'deprivation of liberty'

4.149 The focus of Article 5 is on the loss of personal freedom[1]. 'Liberty and
security of person' is best considered as a unitary concept conferring protection
against arbitrary interference with freedom of person of either a substantive or a
procedural nature by a public authority[2]. Thus the reference to 'security' cannot
be interpreted as implying any duty upon states to provide material assistance.
Indeed, within the context of Article 5, the term is largely superfluous, but protection
for 'security' in the sense of positive obligations on a state to protect physical
safety does exist within the scope of positive state obligations[3]. However, in order
to give rise to an Article 5 question, the facts must constitute a deprivation of
liberty and not merely a restriction on the freedom of movement[4]. This threshold
test, which determines the application of the guarantee, is not without difficulty.
The distinction between restriction of movement and loss of liberty has been
described as one of 'degree or intensity' rather than 'nature or substance'[5]. It
involves 'the objective element of a person's confinement in a particular restricted
space for a not negligible length of time' and 'as an additional subjective element',
the absence of 'valid [consent]'[6]. There is also some case law supporting the
view that the primary purpose of state action may be the determining factor. The
decisions and judgments on this issue do not provide clear guidance as to where
the boundary lies[7].

1   26536/95, *Boffa v San Marino* (1998) DR 92, 27. See further Trechsel *Human Rights in
     Criminal Proceedings* (2005), pp 409–411.

2   *Bozano v France* (1986) A 111, at para 54: '[Art 5] refers essentially to national law and
     establishes the need to apply its rules, but it also requires that any measure depriving the
     individual of his liberty must be compatible with the purpose of Article 5 (art. 5), namely to
     protect the individual from arbitrariness. What is at stake here is not only the "right to liberty"
     but also the "right to security of person".' See too *Cyprus v Turkey* [GC] 2001-IV, at para 226:
     'the applicant state's complaint relates to the vulnerability of what is an aged and dwindling
     population to the threat of aggression and criminality and its overall sense of insecurity.
     However, the Court considers that these are matters which fall outside the scope of Art 5 of
     the Convention and are more appropriately addressed in the context of its overall assessment
     of the living conditions of [these individuals] seen from the angle of the requirements of Art 8.'

3   'Security' thus suggests protection against arbitrary loss of liberty (see eg *Shchebet v Russia*
     (12 June 2008), at para 63 (absence of formal detention record was a 'most serious failing'
     under Art 5), and protection of the individual (see eg *Storck v Germany* 2005-V, discussed at
     para **4.155** below, and deprivation of liberty falling within the scope of Art 5 (1)(e), discussed
     at para **4.184** below). Aspects of 'security' in this latter sense are also found elsewhere in the
     ECHR in terms of positive obligations to protect individuals: see eg paras **4.22–4.31** and **4.88–
     4.92** above, and paras **6.119–6.123** and paras **7.50**, fn 2 and **7.118** below. See further Powell
     'The Right to Security of Persons in European Court of Human Rights Jurisprudence' [2007]
     EHRLR 649.

4   Restrictions on movement fall within the scope of Prot 4, Art 2: *Lavents v Latvia* (28 November
     2002), para 62. See eg 16360/90, *SF v Switzerland* (1994) DR 76, 13 (following refusal to enter

Switzerland, applicant was obliged to stay on Italian territory entirely surrounded by Swiss territory: not a 'deprivation of liberty' but mere restriction on movement). Cf *Nada v Switzerland* (question whether the applicant who lived in a 1.6sq km Italian enclave in a Swiss canton and who could not enter Switzerland on account of UN measures was deprived of his liberty: case pending before the Grand Chamber).

5   *Guzzardi v Italy* (1980) A 39, para 93 (detention on island and subjection to night curfew, restrictions on movement, limited facilities etc). But cf *Medvedyev and Others v France* [GC] 2010-…, para 74: 'while it is true that the applicants' movements prior to the boarding of [a vessel at sea] were already confined to the physical boundaries of the ship, so that there was a *de facto* restriction on their freedom to come and go, it cannot be said … that the measures taken after the ship was boarded merely placed a restriction on their freedom of movement. The crew members were placed under the control of the French special forces and confined to their cabins during the voyage [and the fact that restrictions were relaxed during the voyage] does not alter the fact that the applicants were deprived of their liberty throughout the voyage as the ship's course was imposed by the French forces.'

6   *Storck v Germany* 2005-V, at para 74.

7   See further Murdoch *The Treatment of Prisoners: European Standards* (2006) pp 73–78.

4.150 The question of the guarantee's applicability will arise most often in the exercise of powers of criminal investigation, ancillary to which are rights to detain (in order, for example, to carry out a personal search, to fingerprint, or to place a suspect in an identification parade). Whether such limited interference with liberty or movement for such specific purposes is enough to trigger the guarantees provided by Article 5 may not always have a clear answer[1]. Detention to compel the taking of a blood test may do so even although the detention is of short duration[2]; but, in contrast, instances of restriction of movement incidental to the carrying out of criminal investigations to enable police officers to carry out a search[3] or to question suspects[4] may not result in a finding of detention[5].

1   Cf Trechsel 'Right to Liberty and Security of the Person' [1980] 1 HRLJ 88, at 96: 'It is the very short arrest which raises specific problems. In point of fact, … under the legislation of several High Contracting parties there seems to exist certain forms of short-term police arrest which are hardly covered by the exceptions exhaustively listed in Article 5(1). [Such short term arrests cannot] fall outside the scope of Article 5… It is quite another question, however, whether in such cases all the specific guarantees of Article 5 apply, in particular the right to have the lawfulness of detention ascertained by a court [in terms of Article 5(4)].' However, as long as the relevant level of 'reasonable suspicion' exists, detention to question individuals suspected of having committed an offence would now be seen as an integral part of the criminal process and thus justified by Art 5(1)(c): see para **4.177** below.

2   8278/78, *X v Austria* (1979) DR 18, 154 at 156. The decision may have been influenced by the consideration that Art 5(1)(b) itself would have permitted detention of such a kind if there had been non-compliance with the lawful order of a court or if effected in order to secure the fulfilment of an obligation prescribed by law.

3   See eg *Gillan and Quinton v United Kingdom* 2010-…, at para 57 (although the time taken to stop and search the applicants did not exceed 30 minutes, during this time they were 'entirely deprived of any freedom of movement' and 'obliged to remain where they were and submit to the search and if they had refused they would have been liable to arrest, detention at a police station and criminal charges', an 'element of coercion is indicative of a deprivation of liberty'; but final determination of issue avoided in light of disposal of issue under Art 8). For domestic discussion, see *R (Gillan) v Commissioner of Police of the Metropolis* [2006] 2 AC 307 (use of 'stop and search' powers under Terrorism Act 2000, ss 44–45, was found not to amount to a

deprivation of liberty: compliance with the procedure would normally be relatively brief, and the individual not 'arrested, handcuffed, confined or removed to any different place' (at para 24)). See also 9179/80, *Hojemeister v Germany* (6 July 1981); and *Berktay v Turkey* (1 March 2001), paras 128–133 (detention of the applicant in his home during the carrying out of a police search by five police officers: deprivation of liberty established).

4   8819/79, *X v Germany* (1981) DR 24, 158 at 161 (no deprivation of liberty in the case of a ten-year-old girl who had been taken from school with two friends to a police station for two hours and kept for part of this time in an unlocked cell while police questioned her about thefts, since the object of the police action was to obtain information).

5   Cf *Baumann v France* 2001-V, para 63 (seizure of passport by police officers amounted to a restriction on the right of free movement which gave rise to an issue under Art 2 of Prot 4).

4.151 It is clear that the actual place of detention need not be a state-run institution, and house arrest may also constitute deprivation of liberty. Electronic surveillance devices which now permit the monitoring of individuals to ensure they remain at a particular location and which are imposed as an alternative to detaining them in prison on remand pending trial may thus give rise to Article 5 issues[1].

1   Relevant domestic legislation regulating electronic tagging is found in the Crime and Punishment (Scotland) Act 1997 and the Crime and Disorder Act 1998. In *Raimondo v Italy* (1994) A 281-A, para 39, the Court decided that an obligation to remain at home between 9 pm and 7 am each day did not amount to a loss of liberty. In *Giulia Manzoni v Italy* 1997-IV, the question as to the status of detention at home imposed as a preventive measure was raised, but no decision on this issue was required since the applicant was not ultimately subjected to such an order; (at para 22) the Court merely remarked that the range of preventive measures available in Italian law 'all restrict individual liberty to a greater or lesser extent'. However, in *Nikolova v Bulgaria (no 2)* (30 September 2004) para 60, the Court held that pre-trial detention which had been transformed into house arrest and had continued for some 22 months had constituted a 'deprivation of liberty'. See also *Mancini v Italy* 2001-IX, paras 16–26 (replacement of pre-trial detention by house arrest, but delay in implementing more lenient security measure: while both house arrest and imprisonment involved deprivation of liberty, 'replacing detention in prison with house arrest ... entails a change in the nature of the place of detention from a public institution to a private home' since 'detention in prison requires integration of the individual into an overall organisation, sharing of activities and resources with other inmates, and strict supervision by the authorities of the main aspects of his day-to-day life' and accordingly there had been a violation of Art 5(1)(c)). For CPT discussion, see CPT /Inf (2006) 26 (visit to persons subject to control orders restricting them to their homes).

4.152 It will be necessary, however, that an alleged deprivation of liberty is the direct result of state rather than private action and is motivated by state rather than private interests. For example, in *Nielsen v Denmark*, a 12-year-old boy had been admitted to a psychiatric hospital by his mother for treatment for neurosis. The Commission determined that the five-and-a-half-month-long detention of a boy who was not mentally ill and who was capable of appreciating the situation had amounted to a 'deprivation of liberty' but, by a bare majority, the European Court of Human Rights disagreed since the hospitalisation took place under an exercise of parental authority, and the state's role was merely to provide assistance to the mother[1]. On the other hand, in *Riera Blume and Others v Spain,* the Court held that the involvement of the police in the handing over of members of a religious sect to their families upon their release from custody, and following a judge's recommendation that the families should arrange voluntary psychiatric treatment, had been sufficient to give rise to state responsibility for a deprivation of liberty. The applicants had been taken by police officers to a hotel where for ten days they had been subjected to 'de-programming', and where police officers had questioned them in the presence of their legal representatives. These officers had thus been aware that the applicants were being held against their will (rather than being subjected to 'de-programming' on a voluntary basis as proposed by the court) and had done nothing to assist their release. The Court applied a test of whether the participation of the police had been 'so decisive that without it the deprivation of liberty would not have occurred', and held that while the 'direct and immediate' responsibility for the detention was borne by the applicants' families and an association dedicated to counteracting the influence of such sects, it was also true that without the 'active co-operation' of the police it could not have taken place. Accordingly the 'ultimate responsibility' for the deprivation of liberty lay with the national authorities[2].

1   *Nielsen v Denmark* (1988) A 144, paras 61–73 (and at para 69, the Court was 'satisfied that the mother, when taking her decision on the basis of medical advice, had as her objective the protection of [her son's] health. This is certainly a proper purpose for the exercise of parental rights.') See also (in respect to an elderly person) the 'comparable circumstances' in *HM v Switzerland* 2002-II (at para 48), noted at para 4.153, fn 5 below. In the event of a dispute as to the facts, it must also be established beyond reasonable doubt that the state authorities were responsible for a deprivation of liberty: *Şarli v Turkey* (22 May 2001), para 69.

2   *Riera Blume and Others v Spain* 1999-VII, paras 16–18, and 30–35. See also *Iskandarov v Russia* (23 September 2010), paras 143–152 (use of opaque methods by state agents to secure unlawful and unacknowledged removal to Tajikistan deeply regrettable and constituted a complete negation of the right to liberty and security of person).

4.153 Voluntary submission to detention probably does not affect the assessment[1], and it may be difficult for a respondent state to convince the Court that situations in which individuals find themselves are the consequences of personal choice rather than official action[2]. However, many cases seem to turn upon the technical or legal nature of any state intervention rather than the practical realities facing an individual. Action taken *in loco parentis* to safeguard a child's welfare may not give rise to a deprivation of liberty[3]. Nor is the placement of an elderly person in a foster home likely to amount to a deprivation of liberty if this is a responsible measure taken by the competent authorities in the applicant's own interests[4]. Similarly, exercise of police discretionary authority to protect individuals from harm may not result in a finding that there has been a 'deprivation of liberty'. In *Guenat v Switzerland,* police officers had invited an individual who had been thought to be acting abnormally to accompany them from his home to a police station. After various unsuccessful attempts to contact doctors at the clinic where the applicant had been receiving treatment, a psychiatrist had arranged for his compulsory detention in a mental health hospital. The applicant claimed that he had been arrested arbitrarily and detained for some three hours in the police station without being given any explanation for his arrest, but the majority of the Commission considered that there had been no deprivation of liberty since the police action had been prompted by humanitarian considerations, no physical force had been used, and the applicant had remained free to walk about the police station[5].

In many cases, the intensity of the state intervention appears to have been the key factor. Where there has been significant intervention by officials – as illustrated by the *Riera Blume and Others v Spain* judgment discussed above[6] and where the length of the detention and the absence of immediate physical risk seemed to be of significance – a deprivation of liberty is likely to be established. Such intervention may involve a range of actors. For example, in the *HL v United Kingdom* case, the Court determined that the applicant had been deprived of his liberty. The applicant, who was autistic and had been deemed to lack capacity to consent or to object to medical treatment, had spent a considerable time as an in-patient in an institution before being released and looked after by carers, but after incidents of self-harm had been returned to hospital. The applicant had been considered as an 'informal patient' on the grounds that he had not resisted re-admission to hospital and in consequence had not been committed under compulsory powers. However, the facts that he had been under the continuous supervision and control of health care professionals and had not been free to leave a hospital were crucial in determining that Article 5 applied[7].

1   *De Wilde, Ooms and Versyp v Belgium* (1971) A 12, para 65. But cf *Storck v Germany* 2005-V, at para 74, discussed at para 4.155 below.

2   See for domestic discussion Case (B1824/08) (2 July 2009) [2009] Ecolex 1001 [Austria] (the mere presence of police at the transfer of asylum-seekers created the impression that force would have been used and thus the transfer had constituted an act of coercive power).

3   23558/94, *ALH, ESH, DCL, BML and ME v Hungary* (1996) DR 85, 88.

4   *HM v Switzerland* 2002-II, paras 40–49 (placement of elderly pensioner in a foster home against her wishes for an unlimited period but who retained freedom of movement and social contacts with the outside world on the grounds that she was suffering from senile dementia and was being neglected by her son with whom she shared a house). Cf *Lavents v Latvia* (28 November 2002), paras 62–66 (conditions of hospitalisation were similar to that of a prison, and thus the placement had constituted a deprivation of liberty).

5   24722/94, *Guenat v Switzerland* (1995) DR 81, 130 at 134. His complaint that he had been wrongfully admitted to a psychiatric institution after a medical examination instructed by the police and without being informed of the reasons for such a measure was rejected on the ground of non-exhaustion of domestic remedies. See also *HM v Switzerland* 2002-II, paras 40–49 (an elderly pensioner had been placed in a foster home against her wishes for an unlimited period on the grounds that she was suffering from senile dementia and was being neglected by her son with whom she shared a house: this did not amount to a 'deprivation of liberty' as this was a responsible measure taken by the competent authorities in the applicant's interests on the basis of the unacceptable conditions in which she was living; moreover, the applicant had continued to enjoy freedom of movement and social contacts with the outside world).

6   At para **4.149** above.

7   *HL v United Kingdom* 2004-IX, paras 89–94.

4.154 The lack of procedural safeguards in domestic law may also be a critical factor in deciding whether Article 5 applies, for states are under a positive obligation to provide decision-making procedures for determining an individual's status along with speedy judicial review of reasons for prolonging detention. This may be of particular relevance in respect of immigration control. In *Amuur v France*, asylum seekers had been held in an airport's transit zone for 20 days under constant police surveillance. They had been technically free to return to their country of origin, which had given assurances that they would not be ill-treated. The Commission concluded that no deprivation of liberty had occurred, since the degree of physical constraint was not substantial enough: the European Court of Human Rights, on the other hand, decided that Article 5 did apply. While states had a legitimate interest in preventing unauthorised immigration, any exercise of the power to hold aliens in a transit zone could not be prolonged excessively. Here, the length of time that the applicants were held, and the lack of legal and social assistance, had amounted to a deprivation of liberty[1]. In *Shamsa v Poland* two brothers had been detained in terms of an expulsion order which was to be executed within 90 days. After some unsuccessful attempts to have them expelled, a senior police officer had deemed them to be persons whose presence on Polish territory was undesirable. This had taken place on the final day of the authorised detention, and had led to a further period of detention for five weeks by immigration authorities. A complaint that this subsequent detention was unlawful had been rejected by the domestic courts on the ground that by refusing to be expelled, the applicants had chosen of their own free will to remain at the premises of the immigration authorities. The Court considered that there had been a 'deprivation of liberty' within the meaning of Article 5, observing that the applicants had been under the permanent supervision of the immigration authorities, could not exercise freedom of movement, and had been required to remain at the disposal of the Polish authorities[2].

1   *Amuur v France* 1996-III, paras 41–49 ; and *Riad and Idiab v Belgium* 2008-…, paras 69–80 and 88–111 (placement of illegal aliens in airport transit zone for 11 and 15 days amounted to *de facto* deprivation of liberty; and finding of violation of Art 3). Cf 19066/91, *SM and MT v Austria* (1993) DR 74, 179 (no deprivation of liberty as applicants were free to leave the airport at any time). The decision in *Amuur* mirrors the approach adopted by the CPT that individuals in such circumstances are de facto being held in a 'place of detention': cf CPT/Inf (91) 10, para 89; and CPT/Inf (99) 10, para 10 (persons held in transit or international zones in Vienna and Frankfurt airports).

2   *Shamsa v Poland* (27 November 2003), paras 44–47.

4.155 The case law now makes clear that state authorities are also under a positive obligation to take steps to address deprivations of liberty of which they have notice but which are attributable to private parties. This principle is analogous to, and based upon, similar positive obligations to protect individuals' physical well-being under Articles 2, 3 and 8[1]. In *Storck v Germany* an individual who had attained her majority, who had not been placed under guardianship, and who probably had never given any consent to treatment, had been placed in a locked ward of a private psychiatric clinic at her father's request for some 20 months following various family conflicts. She had repeatedly tried to flee, and on one occasion had been brought back forcibly to the clinic by the police. The Court was satisfied the facts disclosed a deprivation of liberty for which the state was responsible, as the authorities had become actively involved in the applicant's placement in the clinic at the point when the police had compelled her return there. Of some relevance was the respondent state's failure to take steps to protect the applicant in the circumstances. In the opinion of the Court, Article 5 must 'be construed as laying down a positive obligation on the State to protect the liberty of its citizens', as any contrary conclusion would be inconsistent with related jurisprudence in the area of protection of physical integrity and 'would, moreover, leave a sizeable gap in the protection from arbitrary detention, which would be inconsistent with the importance of personal liberty in a democratic society'. In short, the authorities are required 'to take measures providing effective protection of vulnerable persons, including reasonable steps to prevent a deprivation of liberty of which the authorities have or ought to have knowledge'. It was not possible for the state to absolve itself of its responsibilities in the sphere of psychiatric treatment by delegating its obligations to private bodies or individuals, and thus it 'remained under a duty to exercise supervision and control over private psychiatric institutions' both through licensing of such institutions and regular oversight of whether confinement and medical treatment can be justified. Here, the failure of any public health officer to assess whether the applicant posed a serious threat justifying detention, and of the authorities to supervise the lawfulness of the applicant's detention throughout this period and even in the face of intervention by the police, constituted a violation of Article 5[2]. Similar principles would apply in the case of deprivation of liberty effected by agents of states that are not bound by the Convention within the territorial jurisdiction of a contracting state[3].

1   See further paras **3.26–3.30**, **4.22–4.31**, and **4.88–4.92** above, and paras **6.119–6.123** below.

2   *Storck v Germany* 2005-V, paras 89–108. The Court was also critical of the national courts for failing to interpret the provisions of civil law in terming her claim for compensation in the spirit of Article 5, but noted (at para 105) that such retrospective protection as civil damages and criminal proceedings for abduction could not provide adequate protection for vulnerable individuals. See further Campbell 'Positive Obligations under the European Convention on Human Rights: Deprivation of Liberty by Private Actors' (2006) 10 EdinLR 399.

3   For discussion of so-called 'rendition flights' involving unlawful action by the USA in Council of Europe member states with the tacit (or otherwise) knowledge of European governments, see in particular Council of Europe 'Secret Detentions and Illegal Transfers of Detainees involving Council of Europe Member States': First Report (doc AS/Jur (2006) 16), and Second Report' (Doc 11302 rev) (2007) (it had been 'factually established that secret detention centres operated by the CIA have existed for some years in Poland and Romania' and possibly elsewhere). For discussion, see Zwaak and Haeck 'Secret Detention Centres in Member States of the Council of Europe' (2006) 24 NQHR 116; Weissbrodt and Bergquist 'Extraordinary Rrendition: A Human Rights Analysis' (2006) 19 Harv HRLJ 123; and Sands 'The International Rule of Law: Extraordinary Rendition, Complicity and its Consequences' [2006] EHRLR 408. Cf *R (Abassi) v Secretary of State for Foreign and Commonwealth Affairs* [2002] EWCA Civ 1598 (lawfulness of detention of British citizen by the USA in the Guantánamo Bay detention centre: while a court could not adjudicate upon the sovereign acts of a foreign state, it could still express its opinion on whether that state was in clear breach of international law; there was no enforceable duty to intervene, diplomatically or otherwise, to protect a British citizen, but merely discretionary authority which nevertheless was reviewable if exercised (or not exercised) in a manner irrational or contrary to legitimate expectation, although a court was precluded from examining foreign policy). See further Johns 'Guantánamo Bay and the Annihilation of the Exception' (2005) 16 EJIL 613.

Domestic cases on 'deprivation of liberty'

4.156 The meaning of 'deprivation of liberty' has been considered in several domestic cases. In *Secretary of State for the Home Department v JJ*, the House of Lords considered control orders which obliged each controlled person at all times to wear an electronic tagging device, to remain within his specified residence, a one-bedroom flat, for 18 hours each day, and to permit police searches of the premises at any time. Visitors to the premises were permitted only where prior Home Office permission had been given. During the six hours when the controlled persons were permitted to leave their residences they were confined to restricted urban areas, which deliberately did not extend, except in one case, to any area where they had previously lived. Each controlled person was prohibited from meeting anyone by pre-arrangement without prior Home Office approval. The House of Lords held that the right to individual liberty in Article 5(1) connoted the physical liberty of the person, but that deprivation of liberty might take a variety of forms other than detention in prison or strict arrest: the difference between deprivation of liberty and restriction on liberty was one of degree rather than substance. It was necessary for the court to consider the concrete situation of the particular individual and to assess the impact upon him of the measures in question in the context of the life he might otherwise have been living. The judge, in taking as his starting point the detention imposed by the 18-hour curfew and considering the concrete situation in which the regime imposed on the controlled persons had placed them, had been entitled to conclude that the orders amounted to a deprivation of the controlled persons' liberty contrary to Article 5. The effect of the 18-hour curfew, coupled with the effective exclusion of social visitors, meant that the controlled persons were in practice in solitary confinement for this lengthy period every day for an indefinite duration, with very little opportunity for contact with the outside world, and with knowledge that their flats were liable to be entered and searched at any time. They were located in an unfamiliar area where they had no family, friends or contacts. The requirement to obtain prior Home Office clearance of any social meeting outside the flat in practice isolated the controlled persons during the non-curfew hours also. Their lives were wholly regulated by the Home Office, as a prisoner's would be. The judge's analogy with detention in an open prison was apt, save that the controlled persons did not enjoy the association with others and the access to entertainment facilities which a prisoner in an open prison would expect to enjoy[1].

---

1   *Secretary of State for the Home Department v JJ* [2008] 1 AC 385. The decision in *McDonald v Dickson* 2003 SCCR 311, that the appellant had not been deprived of his liberty during six days of 22-hour house arrest because he had not been subject to any physical confinement or restraint, was described as irreconcilable with Strasbourg authority. A similar conclusion was reached in *Secretary of State for the Home Department v AP* [2011] 2 AC 1, where the order subjected AP to a 16-hour curfew and required him to live 150 miles away from his family. A different conclusion was reached in *Secretary of State for the Home Department v E* [2008] 1 AC 499, where the order required E to remain in his home, where he lived with his wife and children for 12 hours each day. During the non-curfew hours there was no geographical restriction on him. He was prohibited from permitting any adult to visit his house or to meet persons outside it except by prior permission of the Home Office and his house was subject

to spot police searches. The same result was reached in *Secretary of State for the Home Department v AF* [2008] 1 AC 440, where the claimant was required to wear an electronic tagging device at all times, to remain in the flat where he was living save for 14 hours each day, and to permit police searches of the premises at any time. Adult visitors, apart from his father, were only permitted where prior Home Office authority had been given and he was prohibited from contact with specified individuals. During non-curfew hours he was restricted to a small urban area and was permitted to attend one specified mosque.

4.157 In *Austin v Police Commissioner of the Metropolis,* the House of Lords considered whether the police practice of 'kettling' amounted to a deprivation of liberty. A large group of demonstrators, some of whom were violent and disorderly, converged on Oxford Circus in central London. The police imposed a cordon around the area enclosing thousands of people. They were prevented for many hours from leaving the cordoned area. It was found that the sole purpose of the cordon was to maintain public order, that it was proportionate to that need and that those within the cordon were not deprived of their freedom of movement arbitrarily. The House of Lords noted the distinction between a restriction upon liberty of movement and deprivation of liberty. The former was governed by Article 2 of Protocol no 4, which conferred a qualified right, and had not been ratified by the United Kingdom. The latter was governed by Article 5, which conferred an unqualified right, subject to specified exceptions. The House concluded that the restriction on the claimant's liberty of movement which had resulted from being confined within the police cordon did not constitute an arbitrary deprivation of liberty, and so Article 5 was not applicable[1]. The House's approach was based upon a theory of Article 5, which it derived from the Strasbourg case law but which has not yet been adopted by the Strasbourg Court, according to which the aim and proportionality of the measure in question may be relevant to whether it is within the ambit of Article 5(1) at all.

A person who was stopped and searched by the police was not deprived of liberty[2].

1   *Austin v Police Commissioner of the Metropolis* [2009] 1 AC 564. [The case of *Austin v United Kingdom* is pending before the Grand Chamber at the time of writing.]

2   *R (Gillan) v Commissioner of Police of the Metropolis* [2006] 2 AC 307.

Grounds for deprivation of liberty under Article 5(1)

4.158 To be lawful in terms of Article 5, any detention must fall within at least one of the 15 distinct purposes provided for in the six sub-paragraphs of paragraph (1). It is possible for a particular deprivation of liberty to fall within two or more of the categories[1] or for the nature and classification of the detention subsequently to change[2]. A deprivation of liberty which cannot be deemed to fall within at least one of the sub-paragraphs may be deemed arbitrary[3].

1   Eg *X v United Kingdom* (1981) A 46, paras 36–39; and *Eriksen v Norway* 1997–III, para 76.

2   Eg 11256/84, *Egue v France* (1988) DR 57, 47 (for a deprivation to be lawful, it must at any given moment fall within one of the six categories).

3   Eg *Ichin and Others v Ukraine* 2010-…, paras 37–40 (detention in a juvenile holding facility
     of minors who were under the age of criminal responsibility fell outwith the scope of Art
     5(1)(c) as no investigative measures had been taken during detention; and it fell outwith scope
     of Art 5(1)(d) as the juvenile holding facility was an establishment for the temporary isolation
     of minors and could not be considered for 'educational supervision': and thus the deprivation
     of liberty was arbitrary).

4.159 In a domestic setting, Lord Hope of Craighead observed in *R (Wardle) v
Crown Court at Leeds*:

'As the European Court said in *W v Switzerland*[1], continued detention can be
justified in a given case only if there are specific indications of a genuine requirement
of public interest which, notwithstanding the presumption of innocence, outweighs
the rule of respect for individual liberty. To this end art 5(1) provides a right to
liberty, which is subject to six specified exceptions and to two overriding requirements.
The first requirement is that any deprivation of liberty must be in accordance with
a procedure prescribed by law. The second requirement is that it must be lawful. To
be lawful in this context, the detention must not only be lawful under domestic law.
It must satisfy the requirements of the Convention that the domestic law on which
the decision is based must be sufficiently accessible to the individual and must be
sufficiently precise to enable the individual to foresee the consequences of the
restriction[2].'

1   *W v Switzerland* (1993) A254-A.
2   *R (Wardle) v Crown Court at Leeds* [2002] 1 AC 754 at para 83.

4.160 The focus is thus upon ensuring that a particular deprivation of liberty
meets the tests imposed by Article 5, and not the underlying policy which supports
the use of detention (for example, as opposed to alternative non-custodial
disposals)[1]. In particular, imprisonment as a sanction for criminal wrongdoing or
the willingness to impose pre-trial detention as an alternative to release on bail
will not ordinarily give rise to issues under the ECHR[2]. The phenomenon of a
growing prison population is one found in most European states but cannot – at
least in the opinion of the European Committee for the Prevention of Torture – be
put down merely to increases in criminal activity[3]. There are significant distinctions
in both the rate of incarceration[4] and the rate of entry to penal institutions across
European states (in relation to the latter, for example, Scotland has a rate some
three times that of the European average)[5]. Attempts by the Committee of
Ministers at reducing the numbers of persons deprived of their liberty implicitly
recognise that such issues fall outwith the scope of Article 5[6]. Nor can Article 5
be used to challenge the conditions of detention or of treatment[7], although there is
an expectation that the grounds for the deprivation of liberty will be reflected in
the place of detention so as to prevent the suggestion of arbitrary deprivation of
liberty[8].

1   Cf *Witold Litwa v Poland* 2000-III, discussed at para **4.167** below (available alternatives for
     the disposal of an alcoholic not posing a danger to himself or to others).

2   For discussion of Art 3 considerations, see paras **4.111–4.112**, **4.114–4.115**, **4.117**, and **4.120–
     4.127** above.

3   CPT/Inf (2001) 16, at para 28: 'the fact that a State locks up so many of its citizens cannot be convincingly explained away by a high crime rate: the general outlook of members of the law enforcement agencies and the judiciary must, in part, be responsible'.

4   See Council of Europe, Annual Prison Statistics 2009 (SPACE 1), doc PC CP (2011) 3, table 1 (the mean prison population in 2009 was 144 per 100,000, (excluding San Marino) ranging from 37 (Iceland) to 621 (Russia); the rate for Scotland was 156 (England and Wales 152; Northern Ireland 81).

5   See Council of Europe, Annual Prison Statistics 2009, above, table 12.1 (the mean rate of entry to penal institutions in 2009 was 271 per 100,000 inhabitants, (excluding San Marino) ranging from 48 (Portugal) to 1471 (Cyprus); the rate for Scotland was 771 (England and Wales: 245; Northern Ireland 346)).

6   See further Murdoch *The Treatment of Prisoners: European Standards* (2006), pp 209–211. In relation to the EU, see TCE, Art III-271: 'European framework laws may establish minimum rules concerning the definition of criminal offences and sanctions in the areas of particularly serious crime with a cross-border dimension resulting from the nature or impact of such offences or from a special need to combat them on a common basis. These areas of crime are the following: terrorism, trafficking in human beings and sexual exploitation of women and children, illicit drug trafficking, illicit arms trafficking, money laundering, corruption, counterfeiting of means of payment, computer crime and organised crime.'

7   Such matters fall within the scope of Art 3: see paras **4.120–4.127** above.

8   See eg (in relation to detention of minors for educational supervision) para 4.182 below, and (in relation to detention on mental health grounds) para **4.186** below.

Ensuring that detention is 'lawful' and 'in accordance with a procedure prescribed by law'

4.161 In relation to a finding that an individual has been deprived of their liberty, the first substantive issue arising under Article 5 is whether a deprivation of liberty has been in compliance with domestic law, or in certain instances, with international law[1]. The text provides that any detention must be 'in accordance with a procedure prescribed by law', and each of the six sub-headings in paragraph 1 outlining the justifiable grounds for deprivation of liberty further provides that any arrest or detention must be 'lawful'. Article 5 thus first calls for scrutiny of compliance with domestic law, although the Court has recognised its task 'is subject to limits inherent in the logic of the European system of protection, since it is in the first place for the national authorities, notably the courts, to interpret and apply domestic law'[2]. Secondly, domestic law and procedures must themselves satisfy the expectations of the ECHR. In other words, this consideration relates

'to the quality of the law, requiring it to be compatible with the rule of law ... "Quality of the law" in this sense implies that where a national law authorises deprivation of liberty it must be sufficiently accessible, precise and foreseeable in its application, in order to avoid all risk of arbitrariness. The standard of "lawfulness" set by the Convention thus requires that all law be sufficiently precise to allow the person – if need be, with appropriate advice – to foresee, to a degree that is reasonable in the circumstances, the consequences which a given action may entail'.[3]

Thirdly, 'any deprivation of liberty must not only have been effected in conformity with the substantive and procedural rules of national law but must equally be in keeping with the very purpose of Article 5, namely to protect the individual from arbitrary detention'[4]. In particular, since deprivation of liberty is 'only justified where other, less severe measures, have been considered and found to be insufficient to safeguard the individual or public interest which might require that the person concerned be detained', the authorities must also be able to show that the loss of liberty was necessary in the particular circumstances[5].

These two requirements – 'prescribed by law' and 'lawful' – at times appear to shade into each other, and indeed, on occasion in the case law are treated as virtually indistinguishable[6], but the two tests raise distinct issues as illustrated in *Gusinskiy v Russia*. In this case, the applicant had been arrested on suspicion of fraud in terms of the criminal procedure code, which allowed detention before the laying of charges 'in exceptional circumstances'. He alleged that his arrest had been unlawful as no such exceptional circumstances existed, and in any event, his imprisonment had been prohibited in terms of an amnesty he had been awarded upon receipt of a civic award. The Court considered that while the detention had been based on a reasonable suspicion that the applicant had committed a crime, the detention had not been conducted 'in accordance with a procedure prescribed by law' as the national law had not been sufficiently accessible and precise to have avoided the risk of arbitrariness in its application, and thus it had failed the 'quality of law' requirement of Article 5. There had also been a breach of the 'lawfulness' test as, in terms of the legislation regulating the amnesty, proceedings against the applicant should have been halted[7].

---

1   *Medvedyev and Others v France* [GC] 2010-…, paras 82–103 (interception of ship flying the Cambodian flag by French authorities following information that it was carrying quantities of drugs: violation as the applicants had not been deprived of their liberty in a lawful manner, for while international law recognised certain qualifications to the principle of freedom of navigation on the high seas or when boarding by another state was provided for in specific treaties, neither instance had applied in the present case).

2   *Bozano v France* (1986) A 111, para 58. The French version of Art 5(1)(c) omits any reference to 'lawful', but in its judgment in *Guzzardi v Italy* (1980) A 39, para 102, the Court noted that this word was found in the English version, 'and the principle expressed by this adjective dominates the whole of [the paragraph]'.

3   *M v Germany* 2009-…, at para 90.

4   *Akdeniz and Others v Turkey* (31 May 2001), para 106. Here, too, there is some relationship with the right to periodic review of the continuing lawfulness of detention under Art 5(4), which must also 'comply with both the substantive and the procedural rules of the national legislation and moreover be conducted in conformity with the aim of Article 5, namely to protect the individual against arbitrariness': *Navarra v France* (1993) A 273-B, at para 26.

5   *Witold Litwa v Poland* 2000-III, at para 78; *Varbanov v Bulgaria* 2000-X, at para 46.

6   *Monnell and Morris v United Kingdom* (1987) A 115, para 50.

7   *Gusinskiy v Russia* 2004-IV, paras 52–69.

4.162 'Lawfulness' first presupposes that there is a legal basis for the deprivation of liberty in domestic law[1]. Clearly, failure by state officials to adhere to domestic law will lead to a violation of Article 5[2]. Thus in *K-F v Germany*, a delay of some

45 minutes in releasing an individual detained to allow police the opportunity of checking identity, after the maximum period of 12 hours' detention had expired, rendered the detention unlawful. The absolute nature of the permissible length of detention placed police officers under a duty to take all necessary precautions to ensure compliance with the law[3]. This situation can be contrasted with one in which there is some limited and reasonable delay on account of practical considerations before implementation of a court order to release a detained person[4], as long as a state can show that it has acted with due diligence[5]. Most obviously, deprivation of liberty without legal justification will give rise to a violation of Article 5. For example, in *Baranowski v Poland*, the prosecutor had decided to continue the applicant's detention on remand solely by reference to a practice without legal foundation which considered a request made by a prisoner for release as one which it was not necessary to determine once the indictment had been served. The applicant accordingly had been held in custody after the expiry of the period authorised by a court, and thus there had been a breach of the guarantee[6]. A more flagrant violation occurred in the case of *Assanidzé v Georgia*, in which the applicant had remained in custody some three years after his acquittal and the ordering of his immediate release by the Supreme Court[7]. However, flaws in a detention order will not necessarily render the period of detention unlawful, as long as the detention is based upon a judicial authorisation[8].

---

1   Eg *Tsirlis and Kouloumpas v Greece* 1997-III, paras 56–63 (detention of conscientious objectors in violation of settled domestic law); and *Ladent v Poland* 2008-..., paras 45–58 (ruling by appellate court that the district court had erred in determining the applicant had been evading justice and that it had failed to apply relevant domestic legislation correctly: violation as the district court's finding had been manifestly without legal foundation).

2   Including, in certain circumstances, any directly applicable EU legislation: eg 6871/75, *Caprino v United Kingdom* (1978) DR 12, 14. Customary law may also have sufficient legal force to satisfy the requirement: *Drozd and Janousek v France and Spain* (1992) A 240, para 107. Cf *Soldatenko v Ukraine* (23 October 2008), paras 112–114 (no provision made in extradition treaty for any procedure for detention).

3   *K-F v Germany* 1997-VII, paras 71–73. For domestic discussion, see *Pervez v HM Advocate* 2007 JC 89 (two periods of six-hour detention under the Criminal Justice (Scotland) Act 1995, s 14 and separated by a gap of approximately one hour: the statutory power was adequately defined, and the detentions related to different suspicions).

4   *Giulia Manzoni v Italy* 1997-IV, para 25. Cf *Quinn v France* (1995) A 311, paras 39–43 (a court had ordered the applicant to be released 'forthwith', but he remained for a further 11 hours in detention without steps being taken to implement this instruction: the Court regarded this as clearly unlawful); and *Labita v Italy* [GC] 2000-IV, paras 166–174 (detention of the applicant continued for 12 hours after his acquittal, a period only partly attributable to the need for the relevant administrative formalities to be carried out: violation of Art 5(1)).

5   Cf *Bojinov v Bulgaria* (28 October 2004), paras 32–40 (challenge to delay in the release of an individual after payment of bail, but the respondent government was unable to provide a detailed synopsis of what had occurred after the court's decision rendering it difficult to assess whether the delay was attributable to the time taken to transmit the order to the prison or to inactivity on the part of prison staff: in these circumstances, the applicant's continued detention during this period could not be shown to have been 'a first step in the execution of the order for his release' and thus had not been justified).

6   *Baranowski v Poland* 2000-III, paras 42–58.

7   *Assanidzé v Georgia* [GC] 2004-II, paras 137–150 (the responsibility of the Georgian authorities for the actions of an autonomous region was deemed to be engaged). See also *Ilaşcu and Others v Moldova and Russia* [GC] 2004-VII, paras 311–394 (detention on the basis of conviction by the court of a regime not recognised in international law); and *Lexa v Slovakia* (23 September 2008, paras 122–142 (pre-trial detention of the former director of intelligence services following the quashing of a presidential amnesty for the forcible abduction of President's son: the subsequent prosecution was not competent in domestic law as the decision to discontinue criminal proceedings had been final, and detention had been neither 'in accordance with a procedure prescribed by law' nor 'lawful'). For discussion of the holding of 'political prisoners' in Azerbaijan, see Parliamentary Assembly Resolutions 1272 (2002) and 1359 (2004); 'Cases of alleged political prisoners in Azerbaijan', Doc SG/Inf (2004) 21; and Trechsel 'The Notion of 'Political Prisoner' as Defined for the Purpose of Identifying Political Prisoners in Armenia and Azerbaijan' (2002) 23 HRLJ 293. For domestic discussion of the responsibility of the executive to intervene in unlawful detention elsewhere, see *R (Abbassi) v Secretary of State for Foreign and Commonwealth Affairs* [2002] EWCA Civ 1598 (no enforceable duty to intervene, diplomatically or otherwise, to protect a British citizen suffering at the hands of another state, but merely discretionary authority which nevertheless was reviewable if exercised (or not exercised) in a manner irrational or contrary to legitimate expectation).

8   Cf *Ječius v Lithuania* 2000-IX, paras 65–69 (regardless of the possible flaws in the wording of the order, its meaning must have been clear to the applicant). Minor clerical errors in detention orders, etc may in certain circumstances be overlooked: *Douiyeb v Netherlands* [GC] (4 August 1999), paras 39–55 (erroneous reference to statutory provision on one occasion but other references were correct: no violation).

4.163 A determination by an appellate court that a lower court erred in law does not in itself affect the lawfulness of any intervening loss of liberty, for Article 5 cannot be used by persons to challenge detention which is subsequently deemed to have been based on errors of fact or law, at least if no issue of excess of jurisdiction or bad faith arises[1]. More difficult questions can arise where a legal system distinguishes between void and voidable judicial decisions. In *Benham v United Kingdom*, English law allowed courts to enforce the payment of the community charge or 'poll tax' by imprisonment where it was established that failure to pay was because of wilful refusal or culpable neglect. The applicant had served 11 days' imprisonment before being released on bail pending his appeal. This appeal ultimately proved successful, as it was accepted that the magistrates had been mistaken in finding that culpable neglect had been established. The applicant argued that in these circumstances his deprivation of liberty had been unlawful in domestic law, since the magistrates' decision had been taken in excess of their jurisdiction. The Commission agreed that the detention had not been 'lawful' in domestic law. By a substantial majority, however, the Court ruled that no Article 5 violation had been established. The mere setting aside of a detention order on appeal could not be conclusive; instead, the distinction in domestic law between decisions within the power of a court (but which could be later held to be erroneous) and decisions that fell outwith its jurisdiction (and thus were void from the outset) was considered crucial. Had the magistrates not discharged their task in considering whether the applicant's non-payment was culpably negligent, then their decision might have fallen into the latter category, which would have rendered the detention unlawful. Here, however, the appeal court had merely decided that the evidence presented could not sustain the magistrates' decision, rather than having ruled that the magistrates had taken a fundamentally flawed decision[2].

1   See 28574/95, *Ullah v United Kingdom* (1996) DR 87, 118 (detention of an individual pending the making of a deportation order who had been held for some 18 days before being advised that he was being released since, in the opinion of the Secretary of State, the deportation decision was not in accordance with the law as full consideration had not been given to his previous applications for leave to remain; the applicant's subsequent action for damages for false imprisonment had failed in the Court of Appeal which found that his detention would have remained lawful since the conditions precedent to its lawfulness were satisfied: for the Commission, it was 'far from clear' (even despite the Secretary of State's letter) that the deportation notice was unlawful, for the lawfulness of the actual detention was not dependent upon the validity of the notice, and even although there had been procedural irregularities in the making of the order, they were not of a nature in domestic law to affect the validity of the detention; and as there had been no question as to excess of jurisdiction or bad faith, this part of the application was manifestly ill-founded). Cf *Ladent v Poland* 2008-..., paras 45–58 (ruling by appellate court that the district court had erred in determining the applicant had been evading justice and that it had failed to apply relevant domestic legislation correctly: violation as the district court's finding had been manifestly without legal foundation).

2   *Benham v United Kingdom* 1996-III, paras 35–47 and 59–77 (the imprisonment thus fell within sub-paragraph (b) since the detention was to secure the payment of a legal obligation, and accordingly, no Art 5 violation existed; however, a violation of Art 6(1) and (3)(c) taken together was established in view of the failure to provide free legal representation at the court hearing). See, too, *Perks and Others v United Kingdom* (12 October 1999), paras 64–71 at para 67 (defects 'only a fettered exercise of discretion' and thus not 'unlawful' in the sense of being beyond the court's jurisdiction).

4.164 A state must also be able to show through documentary or other means that that an apprehension and subsequent detention were in accordance with domestic procedures[1]. Unacknowledged deprivation of liberty is considered a particularly serious violation of Article 5, and the absence of administrative recording of the fact of detention is thus incompatible with the very purpose of Article 5[2]. In consequence, a state has responsibilities to 'take effective measures to safeguard against the risk of disappearance and to conduct a prompt effective investigation into an arguable claim that a person has been taken into custody and has not been seen since'[3].

1   *Elci and Others v Turkey* (13 November 2003) paras 680–682, (while the detention of a suspect required the authority of a prosecutor, none of the witnesses who appeared before the Commission delegates had accepted direct personal responsibility for the decision to detain the applicants and no clear picture emerged as to the steps taken to obtain prior authorisation for their detention; there was further a complete absence of any documentary evidence showing that a request had been made to the prosecutor).

2   *Çiçek v Turkey* (27 February 2001), para 165 (unexplained disappearance of the applicant's two sons after their detention); see also *Shchebet v Russia* (12 June 2008), at para 63 (absence of formal detention record was a 'most serious failing' under Art 5).

3   *Kurt v Turkey* 1998-III, at para 124. See also *Chitayev v Russia* (18 January 2007), paras 170–173 (4-day period of unacknowledged detention); and *Palić v Bosnia and Herzegovina* (15 February 2011), paras 63 and 71 (authorities to conduct an official investigation into an arguable claim that a person, who was last seen in their custody, subsequently disappeared in a life-threatening context, but after the identification of remains, an independent and effective

criminal investigation had taken place, and taking into account the special circumstances prevailing in BiH, no violation of Art 2).

4.165 In addition, domestic law and procedures must also satisfy the purpose of the paragraph in protecting an individual from arbitrary loss of liberty[1]. Legal rules must be 'adequately accessible' and 'formulated with sufficient precision' to permit individuals to regulate their behaviour accordingly[2]. In short, legal provisions must be sufficiently clear to allow individuals reasonably to foresee that the consequences of any behaviour could lead to application of the law[3]. This is of particular relevance when considering potentially wide concepts such as 'breach of the peace'. In *Steel and Others v United Kingdom*, protestors who had been detained for refusing to be bound over to keep the peace claimed that English law did not regulate with sufficient precision either the type of behaviour that could trigger the imposition or lead to the subsequent violation of such an order. The Court, however, accepted that recent clarification (and restriction) by the English courts of the concept of breach of the peace did satisfy this test[4].

1   *K-F v Germany* 1997-VII, para 63; *Erkalo v Netherlands* 1998-VI, para 56.

2   Cf *Steel and Others v United Kingdom* 1998-VII, at para 75; *Hashman and Harrup v United Kingdom* [GC] 2009-VIII, para 31. For domestic discussion, see Case 1P.240/2002, [2003] EuGRZ 45, [2003] EuroCLY 1484 [Germany] (prohibition on media discussion, etc of individual police officers: deprivation of liberty of journalist after photographing an officer must allow access to standing orders).

3   *Ječius v Lithuania* 2000-IX, paras 57–64 (issue whether detention whilst the applicant had been accorded access to his case file had been authorised by domestic law: effects of this law were vague enough to cause confusion amongst competent authorities and thus the detention had not been lawful). See also *Dougoz v Greece* 2001-II, paras 55–58 (opinion of a senior public prosecutor that a ministerial decision applied by analogy in the case of the applicant did not constitute a 'law' of sufficient 'quality' within the meaning of the Court's jurisprudence); and *Nasrulloyev v Russia* (11 October 2007), paras 72–78 (inconsistent interpretation of provisions applicable to detainees awaiting extradition were neither precise nor foreseeable: violation of Art 5(1)(f)).

4   *Steel and Others v United Kingdom* 1998-VII, paras 51–78. At para 55, the Court noted that English law provides that a breach of the peace is committed 'only when an individual causes harm, or appears likely to cause harm, to persons or property or acts in a manner the natural consequence of which would be to provoke others to violence'. Cf *Hashman and Harrup v United Kingdom* [GC] 1999-VIII, paras 29–41, discussed further at para **7.69** below (order by which the applicants were bound over to keep the peace and not to behave *contra bonos mores* was not 'prescribed by law' as required by ECHR, Art 10). See also *R (Laporte) v Chief Constable of Gloucestershire* [2007] 2 AC 105 (unlawful arrest of demonstrators considered in terms of Arts 10 and 11 rights).

4.166 In order to protect against arbitrariness in the application of the law, Article 5 also requires that a decision to deprive an individual of his liberty must not involve bad faith on the part of state officials[1]. Deprivation of liberty will not met the requirements of the guarantee if the real purpose behind the purported state action falls outwith the scope of paragraph (1)[2]. To this end, there is an expectation that there will be some relationship between the actual place or conditions of detention and the purported ground for loss of liberty[3].

1   Cf ECHR, Art 18 which provides that restrictions on freedoms 'shall not be applied for any purpose other than those for which they have been prescribed'. In *Bozano v France* (1986) A 111, para 60, the Court labelled the actions of the French police as a disguised form of extradition which thereby failed to be 'lawful'. In *Gusinskiy v Russia* 2004-IV, at paras 73–77, the Court found that detention had been additionally imposed for 'commercial bargaining strategies', and in consequence there had also been a violation of Art 18 in conjunction with Art 5.

2   Cf *Lukanov v Bulgaria* 1997-II, paras 40–46 (detention of former communist prime minister of Bulgaria was in reality a form of political reprisal not justified under Art 5(1)). See too *Denizci and Others v Cyprus* 2001-V, paras 323 and 392 (detention of applicants by police officers without legal authority prior to their expulsion to northern Cyprus: no lawful basis for the deprivation of liberty had been advanced by the respondent state, and thus there was a violation of Art 5).

3   See eg *Bouamar v Belgium* (1988) A 29, discussed at para 4.182 below; and *Aerts v Belgium* 1998-V, discussed at para **4.187** below.

4.167 Further, and crucially, the loss of liberty must generally be strictly justified in the particular circumstances. It is not enough in itself that the deprivation of liberty is permitted by domestic law: the particular loss of liberty must be considered necessary in the particular case to avoid the appearance of arbitrariness in the application of the law. Thus in *Witold Litwa v Poland*, while it was accepted that the detention of the applicant in a 'sobering up' centre had been in accordance with domestic procedures, the Court nevertheless found a violation of Article 5 because of considerable doubts that the applicant had been posing a danger to himself or to others, and further since no consideration had been given to other available alternatives. Detention was the most extreme of the measures available under domestic law to deal with an intoxicated person, and the police could have taken the applicant either to a public care establishment or even back to his home. In these circumstances, a violation of Article 5 was established[1].

1   *Witold Litwa v Poland* 2000-III, paras 72–80. Note Harris, O'Boyle and Warbrick *Law of the European Convention on Human Rights* (2nd ed, 2009), at p 137: 'the stricter approach (whether detention is necessary to achieve the stated aim) is taken for sub-paragraphs (b), (d), and (e). ... By contrast, no such approach is taken for Article 5(1)(f), which only requires good faith on the authorities' part....' But note *Saadi v United Kingdom* [GC] 2008-..., discussed at para 4.195 below, which suggests that in respect of sub-paragraph (f) the test of arbitrariness may focus more on whether an applicant reasonably was subjected to procedures deemed not inappropriate by the Court in light of a state's acknowledged right to control immigration.

4.168 The Court may also take into account the lawfulness of action taken by a state outwith its territory to secure the return of an individual in order to bring him before its domestic courts. It is clear that such action is not precluded, but assessment of its lawfulness is not without difficulty. In *Sánchez-Ramirez v France*, the applicant (popularly known as 'Carlos the Jackal') had been seized and handcuffed in Sudan and flown to a military air base in France, where he had been served with an arrest warrant. He claimed that his deprivation of liberty had not been lawful, and challenged the involvement of French officials in his forcible removal from Sudan. The Commission, by a majority, dismissed his application as inadmissible since action by Sudanese officials clearly fell to be excluded *ratione personae*. For the Commission, the key point was that the arrest warrant served in France clearly had been 'lawful'. The ECHR did not include any provision concerning the taking of extradition proceedings by a state, and thus it followed that even a 'disguised extradition' could not constitute a violation of France's obligations. Collaboration between the French and Sudanese authorities 'particularly in the field of the fight against terrorism, which frequently necessitates co-operation between States' thus did not raise any Article 5 issue[1]. The reasoning is perhaps unconvincing, and avoids questions which are likely to arise under other guarantees such as Article 3[2]. The Commission's approach also contrasts sharply with the Court's criticism of such instances of 'disguised extradition', at least where two contracting states are involved[3].

In the subsequent case of *Öcalan v Turkey*, the Grand Chamber had an opportunity to reconsider this issue. After unsuccessful attempts to seek political asylum in three European countries, the applicant (who was wanted by the Turkish authorities on suspicion of having committed serious crimes) had entered Kenya only to be told to leave after the authorities had discovered his identity. Arrangements had been made by the Greek embassy to fly him to a destination of his choice, and he had understood that the Netherlands was prepared to accept him. As his car had arrived at the airport, it had taken a route reserved for security personnel and the applicant had been handed over to Turkish officials who had then arrested him and had flown him directly to Turkey. The applicant sought to argue that his detention and trial should be regarded as null and void since he had been abducted by Turkish authorities rather than subjected to regular extradition procedures. The Court considered that the deprivation of liberty had been lawful. The ECHR does not preclude inter-state co-operation in criminal justice, particularly in light of increasing individual mobility, provided that any action taken does not violate Convention guarantees and proceeds upon an arrest warrant properly issued. To succeed in such a case, an applicant would require to show that 'the authorities of the State to which the applicant has been transferred have acted extra-territorially in a manner that is inconsistent with the sovereignty of the host State and therefore contrary to international law'. Here, the applicant had not shown that Turkey had failed to respect Kenyan sovereignty or to comply with international law[4].

---

1   28780/95, *Sánchez-Ramirez v France* (1996) DR 86, 155 at 162. See also 14009/88, *Reinette v France* (1989) DR 63, 189 (co-operation between authorities of a contracting state and a state which was not a Council of Europe member resulting in deprivation of liberty of the applicant in an aircraft: question of lawfulness of action judged solely by reference to actions of French officials). See also 10689/83, *Altmann v France* (1984) DR 37, 230 (extradition of Klaus Barbie from Bolivia).

2   See paras **4.130–4.135** above.

3   Cf *Bozano v France* (1986) A 111, para 60.

4   *Öcalan v Turkey* [GC] 2005-IV, paras 83–99 (but note at para 90:' the Court requires proof in the form of concordant inferences that the authorities of the State to which the applicant has been transferred have acted extra-territorially in a manner that is inconsistent with the sovereignty of the host State and therefore contrary to international law. Only then will the burden of

proving that the sovereignty of the host State and international law have been complied with shift to the respondent Government. However, the applicant is not required to adduce proof "beyond all reasonable doubt" on this point, as was suggested by the Chamber').

Decisions of the domestic courts on 'lawfulness'

4.169 The importance of ensuring that deprivation of liberty is in accordance with domestic law is illustrated by the decision of the House of Lords in *R v Governor of Brockhill Prison, ex p Evans*. The applicant's release date was calculated by the Governor on the basis of the existing case law. On her application for judicial review, the Divisional Court held that the earlier case law was erroneous, and that she had been detained in custody for 59 days after she had been entitled to be released. On her application for damages, the House of Lords held that false imprisonment was a tort of strict liability, and that the Governor was accordingly liable in damages notwithstanding that he had complied with the law as the courts had at that time declared it to be. This conclusion was observed to be consistent with Article 5: detention after the date when the applicant was entitled to be released was unlawful under domestic law, and therefore also unlawful within the meaning of Article 5[1].

1   *R (Evans) v Governor of Brockhill Prison (No 2)* [2001] 2 AC 19.

4.170 The requirement that individuals be protected from an arbitrary loss of liberty – ie that the loss of liberty be necessary in the particular circumstances – is illustrated by the English case of *R v Offen*, which concerned the statutory requirement that a life sentence be imposed on any person convicted of two serious offences unless there are exceptional circumstances relating to either of the offences or to the offender. The Court of Appeal considered that that requirement, as it had until then been interpreted by the courts, could operate in a disproportionate manner which would contravene Article 5 (and possibly Article 3 also). Construing the requirement in accordance with the Human Rights Act 1998, s 3, however, the problem disappeared:

'In our judgment, [the statutory provision] will not contravene Convention rights if courts apply the section so that it does not result in offenders being sentenced to life imprisonment when they do not constitute a significant risk to the public[1].'

The mandatory life sentence in respect of persons convicted of murder has been held not to be arbitrary[2]. The domestic courts have also considered allegations of irregularities in the lawfulness of extradition proceedings[3], and whether detention effected by British military service personnel overseas falls within the scope of the Convention[4].

1   *R v Offen* [2001] 1 WLR 253 at 277; applied in *Cochrane v HM Advocate* 2011 SCCR 63 (interpretation of legislation stipulating minimum sentence for firearms offence). See also *Kelly v United Kingdom* (dec) (24 October 2002) (life imprisonment imposed after two serious offences in terms of the Crimes (Sentences) Act 1997: friendly settlement).

2   In *R v Lichniak* [2003] 1 AC 903.

3   *R v Horseferry Road Magistrates' Court, ex p Bennett* [1994] 1 AC 42; for Scottish discussion, see *HM Advocate v Vervuren* 2002 SCCR 481 (allegation that Portuguese extradition proceedings were flawed on account of lack of effective legal assistance and interpretation: accused had not demonstrated irregularity or illegality in the Portuguese proceedings, and there had been no prima facie breach of Arts 5 or 6, per Lady Paton at para 37: 'I accept that there may be circumstances where information is placed before a Scottish Court which that court could not but regard as prima facie evidence of an irregularity or illegality meriting some further investigation before any trial should be proceeded with. Whether or not that investigation might lead to the sustaining of a plea in bar of trial would depend on the circumstances of the case. The circumstances in *R v Horseferry Magistrates' Court, ex parte Bennett* serve as an illustration of the sort of facts which a Scottish court might regard as worthy of investigation ...'.

4   *R (Al-Jedda) v Secretary of State for Defence* [2008] 1 AC 332 (since UK obligations under UN Security Council Resolutions prevailed over ECHR obligations so far as inconsistent with them, UK forces in Iraq could lawfully exercise the power to detain authorised by UN Security Council Resolutions, but must ensure that the detainee's rights under Art 5 were not infringed to any greater extent than was inherent in such detention).

Article 5(1)(a): Detention after conviction by a competent court

4.171 This provision justifies detention imposed following upon conviction of a criminal offence[1] by a court[2]. It thus covers loss of liberty after conviction but pending appeal[3], detention imposed as an alternative to the original sentence[4], and detention classified by domestic law as a disciplinary rather than a criminal matter[5]. It does not include preventive detention as such[6]. The sub-paragraph will be satisfied if the deprivation of liberty follows upon a conviction, even if the aim of the court in imposing the detention is other than retributive. In *Bizzotto v Greece*, for example, a drug addict had been sentenced to imprisonment for eight years (later reduced to six years on appeal) with an order that he be placed in an institution offering treatment for drug addiction. However, since no secure facilities offering appropriate medical facilities had been available, the applicant had been detained in an ordinary prison. Eighteen months later, he sought release on licence, claiming to have been cured of his dependency. The Commission considered that the failure to provide the treatment regime ordered by the domestic court rendered the deprivation of liberty unlawful, but the European Court of Human Rights considered that the detention fell within the scope of Article 5(1)(a) since the detention was as a consequence of his conviction for drug trafficking, rather than on account of his addiction under sub-paragraph (e), even although the humanitarian and reformative purpose behind the court's order was acknowledged[7].

1   Including certain disciplinary offences: eg *Engel v Netherlands* (1976) A 22, para 68 (military disciplinary offences). The use of imprisonment (as opposed to non-custodial disposals) falls outwith the scope of Art 5(1)(a), but may give rise in certain instances to issues under Art 3: see paras **4.111–4.112**, **4.114–4.115**, **4.117**, and **4.120–4.127** above. Additionally, an issue may also arise under Art 7: see for example *EK v Turkey* (7 February 2002) paras 51–57 (absence of clear legal basis for imposing a sentence of imprisonment, a conviction for making separatist

propaganda, and the independence and impartiality of a National Security Court: violation of Art 7). A sentence imposed following a 'flagrant denial' of justice where proceedings are manifestly contrary to Art 6 expectations will not satisfy Art 5: *Stoichkov v Bulgaria* (24 March 2005), paras 51–59, at para 56: [eg] 'criminal proceedings which have been held *in absentia* and whose reopening has been subsequently refused, without any indication that the accused has waived his or her right to be present during the trial'. See also *Ilaşcu and Others v Moldova and Russia* [GC] 2004-VII, paras 459–462 (in view of the arbitrary nature of the proceedings, none of the applicants had been convicted by a 'court' and the prison sentences imposed on them could not be regarded as 'lawful detention' ordered 'in accordance with a procedure prescribed by law').

2   A 'court' need not 'be understood as signifying a court of law of the classic kind, integrated within the judicial machinery of the country', but its members must enjoy a certain amount of stability (although perhaps only for a specified period), independence from the executive, and provide 'guarantees of judicial procedure' in the discharge of their functions. Cases have concerned convictions imposed elsewhere: see *Drozd and Janousek v France and Spain* (1992) A 240, paras 105–107 (the applicants had been convicted in Andorra but had been required to serve their sentences in either France or Spain: the Andorran court was the court which had determined the conviction for para (1)(a) purposes, even although Andorra was not a contracting state to the Convention). For domestic consideration, see *RB (Algeria) v Secretary of State for the Home Department* [2010] 2 AC 110.

3   Cf *Monnell and Morris v United Kingdom* (1987) A 115, paras 47–48 (time spent in prison awaiting disposal of appeal ordered by court not to count towards sentence; the Court ruled that this did not give rise to a violation of Art 5 since such a risk was an inherent part of the domestic appeals system and was designed to further the legitimate interest of discouraging unmeritorious appeals).

4   7994/77, *Kötalla v Netherlands* (1978) DR 14, 238 (life imprisonment imposed as an alternative to infliction of the death penalty).

5   *Engel v Netherlands* (1976) A 22, para 68. For discussion of Art 6 jurisprudence on the meaning of a 'criminal charge' see paras **5.41–5.47** below.

6   Cf *M v Germany* 2009-..., paras 92–105 (continuation of preventive detention beyond the maximum period authorised at the time of his placement not authorised by Art 5(1)(a), and neither could it be justified by Art 5(1)(e): violation).

7   *Bizzotto v Greece* 1996-V, paras 31–35. See also *Ashingdane v UK* (1985) A 93, para 44 (treatment under mental health detention under para (1)(e)); and *Bouamar v Belgium* (1988) A 129, para 50 (detention not justified under para (1)(d) since lack of proper facilities for educational supervision of minor in adult prison).

4.172 Article 5(1)(a) may also justify subsequent loss of liberty after release, but any recall to prison must result directly from the original sentence and have a sufficient causal link or connection with the original sentencing court's decision[1]. For example, in *Weeks v United Kingdom,* the applicant had been sentenced to life imprisonment for armed robbery. Thereafter, he had been released on licence but subsequently recalled. The European Court of Human Rights considered that this further loss of liberty could be brought within the sub-paragraph since there existed a requisite link between the re-detention and the original decision of the trial court to impose this sentence because of the applicant's perceived dangerousness. The recall had thus been ordered for a purpose consistent with these original aims of the trial court[2]. In earlier cases, the establishment of the requisite link did not appear to be a demanding requirement and could, for example, have included the preventive detention of a recidivist after conviction[3]. In *Stafford* *v United Kingdom,* however, the Court imposed a more stringent test of causal connection. On two occasions the applicant had been returned to prison after his release on licence following imprisonment for murder, on the first occasion when he had breached a requirement to remain within the country, and on the second, after he had been convicted of conspiracy to forge cheques for which he had been sentenced to a further period of imprisonment. After this subsequent sentence had been served, he had remained in prison despite a Parole Board recommendation that he should be released, and an acknowledgment by the Secretary of State that there was no significant risk of him committing further offences of a violent nature. For the Court, the steady erosion in domestic law of the executive's authority in respect of sentences of life imprisonment and recognition that there was no meaningful distinction between discretionary and mandatory sentences of life imprisonment now supported a finding that the applicant had served the punishment element of his original sentence. His continuing imprisonment following the second recall could only be justified on the basis of his dangerousness. Since the recall and continued imprisonment had been based upon non-violent offences, the requisite causal link could not be shown to have existed, and thus there had been a violation of Article 5[4].

---

1   *Van Droogenbroeck v Belgium* (1982) A 50, para 40.

2   *Weeks v United Kingdom* (1987) A 114, paras 42–51.

3   9167/80, *X v Austria* (1981) DR 26, 248. See too *Eriksen v Norway* 1997-III, discussed at para **4.180** below.

4   *Stafford v United Kingdom* [GC] 2002-IV, paras 78–83. See also *De Schepper v Belgium* (13 October 2009), paras 35–50 (no violation of Art 5(1)(a) in respect of the preventive detention of paedophile on social-protection grounds as the measure was not arbitrary but imposed following conviction to protect society against dangerous criminals and the authorities had not failed in their obligation to seek to provide the applicant with treatment that might have helped him regain his liberty); and *Haidn v Germany* (13 January 2011), paras 85–88 (imposition of indefinite preventive detention shortly before a period of imprisonment following conviction and following psychiatric reports suggesting the applicant posed a serious risk to others: further detention did not constitute detention 'after conviction' for the purposes of Art 5(1)(a) as there was no sufficient causal link between the original conviction and the second period of detention). For domestic discussion, see *R (West) v Parole Board* [2005] 1 WLR 350 (when a prisoner released on licence is recalled, the original sentence of the trial judge satisfies Art 5(1) not only in relation to the initial term served by the prisoner but also in relation to the licence revocation, since conditional release subject to the possibility of recall forms an integral component of the sentence passed by the court; the decision by the Parole Board to revoke a licence satisfies the requirements of Art 5(4), since the Board has the essential features of a court, provided that the review by the Board is conducted in a manner that meets the requirements of procedural fairness); in relation to the position of recalled prisoners during the extension period of an extended sentence, see *R (Sim) v Parole Board* [2004] QB 1288; see also *R (Hirst) Secretary of State for the Home Department* [2006] EWCA Civ 945 (sufficient causal connection between recall and original sentence established in light of behaviour giving rise to concern for public safety); *R (Clift) v Secretary of State for the Home Department* [2007] 1 AC 484 (although there was no requirement under the ECHR to establish an early release scheme, where provision was so made, the right to seek early release fell within the scope of Art 5, and any differential treatment would give rise to issues under Art 14 if based on considerations other than the individual merits of a case: in the first case under appeal, the difference in treatment was based upon the length of sentence, which was not a ground of distinction

prohibited by Art 14; but in respect of the other two appeals, concerning foreign prisoners liable to removal after their sentences, a declaration of incompatibility was appropriate since the Criminal Justice Act 1991 ss 46(1) and 50(2) prevented them from having their cases reviewed by the Parole Board in the same way as long-term prisoners of UK nationality); *R (Black) v Secretary of State for Justice* [2009] 1 AC 949 (recommendation for early release of prisoner serving determinate sentence does not engage Art 5(4)); and *R (James) v Secretary of State for Justice* [2010] 1 AC 553 (for a prisoner's detention under an indeterminate sentence for public protection to be justified under Art 5(1)(a) there had to be sufficient causal connection between his conviction and the deprivation of his liberty, but the causal link was not broken by the Secretary of State's failure to provide risk-reducing courses or treatment; while it might be broken by a prolonged failure to enable the prisoner to demonstrate that he was safe for release, such failure would have to be for a period of years rather than months): see further, para **4.231** below. Cf *Varey v Scottish Ministers* 2001 SC 162 (revocation of licence in terms of the Prisons (Scotland) Act 1989, s 28, which provides that the Scottish Ministers may revoke the licence of a person released on licence without consulting the Parole Board where it is in the public interest to do so before such consultation is practicable, but the case of a person so recalled shall be referred to the Parole Board following recall: the recall was affirmed by the Parole Board and thus there had been an independent review of whether the causal link between recall and original sentence existed). Other significant domestic cases include *Dunn v Parole Board* [2009] 1 WLR 728 and *R v Pedley* [2009] 1 WLR 2517 (level of risk required for imposition of sentence for public protection).

4.173 Article 5(1)(a) cannot be relied upon to seek to secure a right to early release for prisoners, but if arrangements appear to operate in a discriminatory manner, Article 14 taken in conjunction with this sub-paragraph may be of relevance. This matter is considered below[1]. Review of indeterminate sentences of imprisonment may also be required by Article 5(4), discussed below[2].

1 See para **4.231** below.
2 See paras **4.225–4.228** below.

Article 5(1)(b): non compliance with the lawful order of a court or to secure the fulfilment of a legal obligation

4.174 Article 5(1)(b) permits deprivation of liberty in two circumstances: 'for non-compliance with the lawful order of a court or in order to secure the fulfilment of any obligation prescribed by law'[1]. While there may be some overlap between these two 'limbs' of the sub-paragraph, in each case it is expected that a 'fair balance' between the importance in a democratic society of securing the fulfilment of the order or obligation and the importance of the right to liberty is achieved[2]. In respect of 'non-compliance with the lawful order of a court', the proportionality of the deprivation of liberty requires as assessment of issues such as the purpose of the court order, the feasibility of complying with it and the duration of the detention[3]. Deprivation of liberty upon refusal to be bound over to keep the public peace, as provided for in English criminal law, is a 'lawful order' or 'obligation'[4], although arguably (as with imprisonment imposed for failure to pay a fine) the distinction between sub-paragraphs (a) and (b) in such instances is a slim one[5]. Court-authorised detentions to obtain a blood test[6], or to allow compilation of a psychiatric opinion[7] or the taking of an affidavit[8] fall within the scope of the sub-paragraph, as does detention with a view to secure compliance with an order to deliver up property[9] or to pay a fine[10]. However, the particular obligation must be compatible with the ECHR. For example, deprivation of liberty may be deemed to fall within this heading when imposed for refusal to give evidence in court, as long as this obligation is not incompatible with other considerations[11].

1   This sub-paragraph should be read alongside the ECHR, Prot 4, Art 1 where ratified by a particular state even although imprisonment for debt is a practice which has largely disappeared (the United Kingdom has not ratified this protocol). This provision specifically states that 'no one shall be deprived of his liberty merely on the ground of inability to fulfil a contractual obligation'. 'Contractual obligation' covers obligations arising out of contract of all kinds including non-delivery, non-performance or non-forbearance and not just money debts, but excluded from the definition are non-contractual obligations arising from legislation in public or private law. Further, loss of liberty is not prohibited if any other factor is present in addition to the inability to fulfil a contractual obligation, as with, for example, negligence, malicious or fraudulent intent or where deprivation of liberty can be imposed as a penalty for a proved criminal offence or as a necessary preventive measure before trial for such an offence, even if criminal law recognises as an offence an act or omission which was at the same time a failure to fulfil a contractual obligation (for example, ordering of food and drink in a cafe or restaurant in the knowledge that an individual is unable to pay): see *Protocol No 4 to the European Convention on Human Rights (ETS 155 (1963)), Explanatory Report*.

2   *Gatt v Malta* 2010-..., at para 40.

3   *Gatt v Malta* 2010-..., paras 35–52 (conversion of guaranteed sum of bail following breach of conditions into detention amounting to more than five and a half years: unrealistic expectation of compliance and length of detention for a single breach of curfew disproportionate).

4   *Steel & Others v United Kingdom* 1998-VII, para 69. The length of detention of the first applicant (44 hours) was also accepted as proportionate to the aim of preventing the risk of serious physical injury in assessment of ECHR, Art 10: at para 105. See further para **7.92** below.

5   Note further that Art 5(1)(a) may authorise imprisonment for purposes not falling within the scope of a 'criminal charge' in respect of Art 6 (see *Engel and Others v Netherlands* (1976) A 22, para 69), while para (1)(b) may include detention in respect of matters considered to involve the determination of a 'criminal charge' (see *Benham v United Kingdom* 1996-III, paras 40–47: imprisonment for refusal to pay the 'poll tax' but voidable decision and no indication of bad faith: detention justified under Art 5(1)(b)). See further paras **5.44–5.49** below.

6   8278/78, *X v Austria* (1979) DR 18, 154.

7   6659/74, *X v Germany* (1975) DR 3, 92. See also *Nowicka v Poland* (3 December 2002), paras 58–65 (lengthy periods of detention to allow psychiatric examination to be carried out, and continuation of detention after examination: violation).

8   5025/71, *X v Germany* (1971) YB 14, 692.

9   Cf *Benham v United Kingdom* 1996-III, para 39 (payment of local tax).

10   6289/73, *Airey v Ireland* (1977) DR 8, 42. Presumably imprisonment following upon a sentence to pay a fine where the court at that time imposes a period of imprisonment in default would fall within Art 5(1)(a).

11   Cf *K v Austria* (1993) A 255-B (in the opinion of the Commission, the order to testify was made in violation of ECHR, Arts 6 and 10, and therefore could not justify detention under para (1)(b): case struck out after a friendly settlement). See also *Worwa v Poland*, 2003-XI, paras 80–84 (requirement to undergo a psychiatric examination imposed upon the applicant could have justified detention in terms of Art 5(1)(b) had it not been incompatible with Art 8 since

the applicant on several occasions had been ordered to undergo psychiatric examinations at brief intervals and to attend when no consultation had been arranged on the appointed day).

4.175 Detention under the second limb, in order to secure the fulfilment of a prescribed legal obligation, cannot be given too loose an interpretation as this could undermine the aim of the ECHR in protecting against arbitrary loss of liberty. Any such obligation thus must first be of a 'specific and concrete nature', as illustrated by the early case of *Lawless v Ireland*. Anti-terrorist legislation permitted individuals to be detained if they were considered to be engaging in 'activities prejudicial to the security of the state'. The applicant had been held for five months on the ground that this was necessary to secure compliance with the general duty upon citizens not to commit offences against the public peace or state security. The European Court of Human Rights considered that since no specific legal obligation was involved, the detention could not be brought within Article 5(1)(b)[1]. On the other hand, in *McVeigh, O'Neill and Evans v United Kingdom*, the Commission accepted that the duty imposed by British anti-terrorist legislation to 'submit to further examination' was a specific and concrete obligation to provide information for the purpose of permitting officials to establish status at the point of entry into the United Kingdom and not (as claimed by the applicants) in substance merely an obligation to submit to detention[2]. Secondly, the imposition of deprivation of liberty must also be a proportionate response. It may thus generally be necessary for the authorities to give an individual a prior opportunity to discharge the duty upon him. For example, while detention to ascertain an individual's identity may fall within the scope of this heading where domestic law imposes an obligation to carry an identification card and to produce this when requested[3], the prolonged detention of an individual is likely to constitute arbitrary deprivation of liberty. Thus in *Vasileva v Denmark*, the detention in a police station of an elderly bus passenger for over 13 hours after she had refused to disclose her identity to a ticket inspector during the course of a dispute as to the validity of a ticket was seen as a disproportionate response to the situation[4].

1   *Lawless v Ireland (no 3)* (1961) A 3, Law, para 9. For background to this case, see Doolan *Lawless v Ireland (1957–1961): The First Case before the European Court of Human Rights* (2001). See also Harris, O'Boyle and Warbrick *Law of the European Convention on Human Rights* (2nd ed, 2009), at p 142: '[This limb] provides a means of justifying various powers of temporary detention exercisable by the police (eg, random breath tests, road blocks, powers of stopping and searching), to enforce obligations of the criminal law to which Article 5(1)(c) would not extend'.

2   8022/77, 8025/77 and 8027/77, *McVeigh and Others v United Kingdom* (1981) DR 25, 15, paras 168–175 (and need for specific circumstances warranting detention to secure the fulfilment of the obligation before sub-paragraph (b) could be satisfied).

3   *Novotka v Slovakia* (dec) 30 September 2003 (detention of applicant for one hour following upon his refusal to show police officers his citizen's card to allow his identity to be checked: inadmissible even in the face of allegations that his identity had been confirmed by two neighbours). See also 16810/90, *Reyntjens v Belgium*, (1992) DR 73, 136 (obligation to carry an identity card and to show it to the police whenever requested does not constitute a violation of respect for private life within the meaning of Art 8, and is a sufficiently concrete and precise obligation to justify detention under Art 5(1)(b)).

4   *Vasileva v Denmark* (25 September 2003), paras 32–43 (periods during which no efforts to establish identity, and no attempt to arrange for the attendance of a doctor in view of the applicant's advanced age and to assist with communication). See also *Nowicka v Poland* (3 December 2002), paras 58–65 (two prolonged periods of arrest lasting 8 and 27 days for failing to comply with a court's order that the applicant should undergo psychiatric examination: neither period could be reconciled with the purported aim of immediate examination); and *Gatt v Malta* 2010-…, paras 35–52 (no distinction drawn between a breach of bail conditions related to the primary purpose of bail, ie appearance at trial, and other considerations of a less serious nature, eg a curfew; further, there had been no ceiling on duration of detention or assessment of proportionality). In the domestic case of *Stellato v Ministry of Justice* [2011] 2 WLR 936 it was held that the breach of a bail condition did not fall within the scope of Art 5(1)(b).

Article 5(1)(c): Arrest or detention for the purpose of bringing a suspect before the competent legal authority; or to prevent the commission of an offence or the fleeing of a criminal suspect

4.176 Three separate state interests justifying detention are covered in Article 5(1)(c): first, 'the lawful arrest or detention of a person effected for the purpose of bringing him before the competent legal authority on reasonable suspicion of having committed an offence'; secondly, 'when it is reasonably considered necessary to prevent his committing an offence'; and thirdly, when detention is considered necessary to prevent flight after the commission of any offence. These three headings are exhaustive, and this sub-paragraph cannot be used to justify detention in order to secure extradition[1], or effected solely in order to extract information about others[2]. Most attention has focused upon the first of these grounds.

1   7317/75, *Lynas v Sweden* (1976) DR 6, 141.

2   *Ireland v United Kingdom* (1978) A 25, para 196.

Detention on reasonable suspicion of having committed an offence

4.177 Article 5(1)(c) first recognises the state's right to detain a person on reasonable suspicion of having committed an offence[1], the purpose of the detention being to confirm or dispel such suspicions. Deprivation of liberty under this ground may be as the result of judicial authorisation, or effected extra-judicially by a police officer acting within the scope of his powers to arrest without a warrant. 'Reasonable suspicion' presupposes the existence of facts or information which would satisfy an objective observer that the arrested person may have committed an offence[2]. An assessment of whether the relevant standard has been achieved is called for in each instance, for what may be regarded as 'reasonable' will depend upon all the circumstances. 'There may thus be a fine line between those cases where the suspicion grounding the arrest is not sufficiently founded on objective facts and those which are'[3]. That a suspicion is honestly held is insufficient to satisfy the standard: the suspicion must be 'reasonable'[4], but need not be any higher at this stage of the investigation:

'The object of questioning during detention [under the sub-paragraph] is to further the criminal investigation by way of confirming or dispelling the concrete suspicion grounding the arrest [, and thus] facts which raise a suspicion need not be of the same level as those necessary to justify a conviction or even the bringing of a charge, which comes at the next stage of the process of criminal investigation[5].'

To fall within the scope of the sub-paragraph and prevent arbitrary deprivation of liberty, the detention must be for this purpose and not for any extraneous aim such as to exert moral pressure upon the detainee[6].

1   That is, the facts invoked must be able to be reasonably considered as constituting a crime at the time when they occurred: cf *Wloch v Poland* (19 October 2000), paras 109–117 (applicant's detention on remand was based on a suspicion that he had been involved in acts qualified as the offence of trading in children, and even although there were serious difficulties as regards interpretation of the relevant legal provision, there was nothing to suggest that reliance upon the provision was arbitrary or unreasonable: no violation of Art 5(1)). Cf *Kandzhov v Bulgaria* (6 November 2008), paras 54–62 (detention on charges of hooliganism and 'insult', but the constituent elements of the offence of hooliganism had been absent, and insult was a privately prosecutable offence and could not attract a sentence of imprisonment: in consequence, the almost four-day detention had not been 'lawful' effected 'on reasonable suspicion' of having committed an offence). For discussion of legal certainty in the definition of 'offences' see para **4.165** above.

2   *Fox, Campbell and Hartley v United Kingdom* (1990) A 182, paras 32–36, at para 32.

3   *O'Hara v United Kingdom* 2001-X, at para 41 (information provided to superior officer from four reliable informants, but only minimal information thereafter provided to the arresting officer: in the circumstances, there had been sufficient grounds for 'reasonable suspicion'. See also *Murray v United Kingdom* (1994) A 300-A, paras 61–62 (arrest on suspicion of involvement in terrorist fund-raising based on conviction of her brothers for similar offences in the USA thus implying collaboration with others in Northern Ireland, and knowledge that she had visited the USA and maintained contacts with her brothers, 'elements which were not necessarily incriminating of the applicant', but deemed sufficient for the purposes of satisfying Art 5(1)(c); and *Smirnova v Russia*, 2003-IX, paras 56–71 (repeated detention of the applicants in the course of one criminal investigation on the basis of insufficient reasons).

4   *Murray v United Kingdom* (1994) A 300-A, paras 50–69 (arrest under a provision allowing an officer to detain on the ground of a suspicion 'honestly and reasonably held': the applicant's arguments that this was insufficient to meet the standards of the sub-paragraph and that the real reason for the arrest had not been to bring her before a 'competent legal authority' but to interrogate her for the general purpose of intelligence gathering were rejected, the Court holding that there was sufficient information to provide a 'plausible and objective basis' for suspicion of involvement in offences, and that the purpose of the arrest had been 'genuinely' to bring her before a judge even although she was released without charge).

5   *Murray v United Kingdom* (1994) A 300-A, para 55. See also *Brogan and Others v United Kingdom* (1988) A 145-B at para 53 (the applicants argued that they had been held under prevention of terrorism legislation on suspicion of involvement in unspecified acts of terrorism, a contention rejected by the Court which found that detention had been with the aim of furthering police investigations 'by way of confirming or dispelling the concrete suspicions' of commission of particular offences). The principle applies equally to less serious offences: eg *K-F v Germany* 1997-VII, paras 61–62 (suspicion that applicant would abscond without paying rent).

6   *Giorgi Nikolaishvili v Georgia* 2009-..., paras 60–67 (arrest of witness on other charges designed to bring pressure upon the suspect in the murder case: while the detention was formally consistent with domestic law, it involved opaque methods liable to undermine legal

certainty, instil insecurity in persons summoned as witnesses, and further undermine public respect for and confidence in the prosecution authorities: violation of Art 5(1)(c).

4.178 This provision is thus of relevance in the initial stage of a criminal process, and must be read alongside alongside Article 5(3) entitlements to be brought promptly before a judge or other officer exercising judicial power and to trial within a reasonable time or to release pending trial[1], and Article 6 and other Convention guarantees which protect the situation of a suspect detained in police custody[2]. To ensure that deprivation of liberty is not arbitrary, the detention should cease as soon as the suspicion ceases to be 'reasonable'[3]. In other words, the fact that a person detained 'on reasonable suspicion' is not ultimately brought before a judge or is proceeded against on criminal charges does not bring the detention outwith the scope of the sub-paragraph as long as the relevant level of suspicion existed at the outset of detention[4].

1   *Lawless v Ireland (no 3)* (1961) A 3, Law, para 14.

2   See eg *İpek and Others v Turkey* (3 February 2009), paras 28–31 and 34–38 (arrest of two applicants who were minors on account of their presence in the house at the same time as the arrest of another applicant on suspicion of membership of an illegal terrorist organisation and with a view to establishing any link the two might have had with the organisation: Art 5(1)(c) not satisfied in respect of the two applicants as they had not at the time of their arrest been detained on reasonable suspicion of having committed an offence; and the detention lasting three days and nine hours before being brought before a judge further constituted a violation of Art 5(3) as they were minors and detained without any procedural safeguards such as the assistance of a lawyer). Of relevance also are provisions protecting against inhuman or degrading treatment, and fair trial considerations which may require the right of access to a legal representative during interrogation: see para **4.99** above and paras **5.204–5.205** below. For discussion of CPT standards in respect of police custody, see *Second General Report* CPT/Inf (92) 3, paras 36–43, and *Sixth General Report* CPT/Inf (96) 21, paras 14–16.

3   *Stögmüller v Austria* (1969) A 9, Law, para 4; cf *De Jong, Baljet and Van den Brink v Netherlands* (1984) A 77, at para 44: 'whether the mere persistence of suspicion suffices to warrant the prolongation of a lawfully ordered detention on remand is covered, not by [this sub paragraph] as such, but by Article 5(3), which forms a whole with Article 5(1)(c) ... to require provisional release once detention ceases to be reasonable ...'. Cf *Labita v Italy* [GC] 2000-IV, paras 155–159 (the applicant had been arrested on suspicion of being a member of the Mafia solely on the grounds of uncorroborated allegations by a former Mafioso who had decided to co-operate: while a suspect may be detained at the beginning of proceedings on the basis of statements made by *pentiti*, these statements necessarily become less relevant with the passage of time unless supported by corroboration).

4   In consequence, for the purposes of ensuring compatibility with Art 5, there is no meaningful distinction in Scottish procedure between detention for questioning (under the 'six–hour detention power') and detention following upon arrest (whether or not criminal proceedings are ultimately taken), even although detention for questioning is not part of a process which necessarily involves the detainee being brought before a competent court: the crucial issue would be the existence or otherwise of 'reasonable suspicion' at the outset of detention.

Detention to prevent the commission of crime

4.179 This purpose is interpreted restrictively. In *Lawless v Ireland*, the state argued that the phrase 'effected for the purpose of bringing him before the competent legal authority' qualified only the heading referring to reasonable suspicion of commission of an offence, with the consequence that 'when it is reasonably considered necessary to prevent his committing an offence' should be interpreted as standing alone without the need to ensure judicial supervision. The European Court of Human Rights disagreed, noting that such an argument would result in the possibility that 'anyone suspected of harbouring an intent to commit an offence could be arrested and detained for an unlimited period on the strength merely of an executive decision'[1]. The sub-paragraph cannot thus authorise 'a policy of general prevention directed against an individual or a category of individuals who ... present a danger on account of their continuing propensity to crime; it does no more than afford [states] a means of preventing a concrete and specific offence'[2]. Similarly, in *Ječius v Lithuania*, domestic law provided for detention with a view to preventing the commission of offences. The applicant had been taken into custody to prevent his involvement in three specific offences of banditism, criminal association and terrorising a person. A month later, he was again charged with murder, a charge which had earlier been dropped. The European Court of Human Rights again observed that detention under the sub-paragraph could only take place within the context of criminal proceedings for alleged past offences, and thus preventive detention of the nature applied to the applicant was incompatible with the ECHR[3].

---

1   *Lawless v Ireland (no 3)* (1961) A 3, Law, para 14.

2   *Guzzardi v Italy* (1980) A 39, at para 102. For domestic application, see Rt 1996–93-H [Norway] (use of preventive detention to detain a repeated child sex offender pending a decision to prolong the period of his preventive detention in light of the commission of offences on an earlier occasion when he had been released pending a decision on continuation of preventive detention: continuation of preventive detention held to fall both within Art 5(1)(a) and (1)(c)).

3   *Ječius v Lithuania* 2000-IX, paras 50–52.

4.180 In certain circumstances the sub-paragraph may justify in exceptional circumstances the continuing detention of an individual after the expiry of any court-authorised loss of liberty. In *Eriksen v Norway,* the applicant had developed a tendency to become aggressive after suffering brain damage, and over a period of years had been detained in prison or in mental hospitals. Shortly before the expiry of authorisation granted by a trial court to use 'security measures' to detain the appellant, the police sought and were given approval to keep him in detention for several additional weeks to allow an up-to-date medical report to be obtained. The Court accepted that this period of detention fell within the scope of both sub-paragraphs (a) and (c). The former heading applied since the extension was directly linked to the initial conviction and imposition of 'security measures' on account of the appellant's likely risk of re-offending even although the authority for these had expired. Sub-paragraph (c) also justified detention because of the applicant's previous mental history and record of assaults which had provided substantial reasons for believing he would commit further offences if released[1].

---

1   *Eriksen v Norway* 1997-III, paras 78–87. Cf *Erkalo v Netherlands* 1998-VI, paras 50–60 (failure to request an extension to a placement order had resulted in a period of unauthorised

detention). Cf *M v Germany* 2009-…, paras 92–105 (continuation of preventive detention beyond the maximum period authorised at the time of his placement was not authorised by Art 5(1)(a), and neither could it be justified by Art 5(1)(e): violation); and *Haidn v Germany* (13 January 2011), paras 89–90 (imposition of indefinite preventive detention shortly before the end of a period of imprisonment following conviction for sexual assault and following psychiatric reports suggesting the applicant posed a serious risk to others did not fall within Art 5(1)(c) as this paragraph was to be interpreted narrowly and the potential further offences were not sufficiently concrete and specific as regards the place and time of commission or the victims).

Detention to prevent a suspect from absconding

4.181 The final category of permissible detention under Article 5(1)(c) is deprivation of liberty to prevent an individual absconding after having committed an offence in order to bring him before a competent judicial authority. The danger of flight must be considered carefully in each case: such factors as the ease of leaving the jurisdiction, the possibility of a heavy sentence and the lack of domestic ties will all be relevant in assessing its likelihood and thus the 'reasonableness' of any state detention[1]. This issue is considered in greater detail in discussion of conditional release pending trial[2].

1   Cf *Wemhoff v Germany* (1978) A 7, Law, paras 13–15. But see Harris, O'Boyle and Warbrick *Law of the European Convention on Human Rights* (2nd ed, 2009), at p 147: 'the third ground of Article 5(1)(c) appears redundant since a person who is 'fleeing after having' committed an offenve can in any event be arrested under the first limb.'
2   At paras **4.210–4.213** below.

Article 5(1)(d): Detention of minors for educational supervision or for bringing minors before competent legal authorities

4.182 Article 5(1)(d) has generated little case law. Detention of minors[1] for 'educational supervision' or to bring them before a 'competent legal authority' are distinct purposes[2]. The general reference to detention of a minor 'by lawful order … for the purpose of bringing him before the competent legal authority' without further qualification as to any specific state purpose suggests approval of domestic schemes to divert minors from the ordinary criminal process[3]. In the case of a young person in public care, educational supervision 'must embrace many aspects of the exercise [by the authority] of parental rights for the benefit and protection of the person concerned', and thus the phrase cannot 'be equated rigidly with notions of classroom teaching'[4]. Deprivation of liberty for educational supervision, however, implies that the nature of the detention supports this objective in some manner. In *Bouamar v Belgium*, the applicant had been detained on numerous occasions in an adult remand prison since no suitable juvenile institution had been available. The state's argument that this was justified for 'educational supervision' was rejected because of the regime of virtual isolation in which the applicant was held, the lack of sufficiently trained staff to provide education, and the absence of any educational programme. While an interim custody measure could be adopted as a preliminary to educational supervision, any such imprisonment must be 'speedily followed by actual application of such a regime in a setting (open or closed) designed and with sufficient resources for the purpose'[5]. In *DG v Ireland*, the applicant's detention in a penal institution for some four weeks had only been ordered by a court with 'considerable reluctance'. Only thereafter had he been placed in accommodation providing appropriate therapeutic support. While the applicant had turned 17 during his loss of liberty and could no longer have been required to attend school, he had remained a 'minor' under Irish law. The Court determined that the detention in the penal institution fell outwith the scope of the sub-paragraph. Where a state decides to establish a system of educational supervision implemented through court orders to deal with juvenile delinquency, it was at the same time obliged to put in place appropriate institutional facilities to meet the security and educational demands of young people. While reiterating that 'educational supervision' must not be equated rigidly with notions of classroom teaching, the Court was not satisfied that the placement in the penal institution had involved 'educational supervision' as the applicant had not availed himself of the optional educational facilities available; moreover, the applicant's detention could not be regarded as an interim custody measure followed speedily by an educational supervisory regime as the detention was not ordered upon any specific proposal for his secure and supervised education[6].

1   The definition of 'minority' is probably one for the national legal system: 8500/79, *X v Switzerland* (1979) DR 18, 238. The CPT, however, refers to 'juveniles' and treats detainees under 18 as such: see *9th General Report* CPT/Inf (99) 12, paras 20–41.

2   *Bouamar v Belgium* (1988) A 129, para 46.

3   See the comments in *Bouamar v Belgium* (1988) A 129, at para 48. In 8500/79, *X v Switzerland* (1979) DR 18, 238, the detention of a minor for eight months in an 'observation centre' prior to disposal of criminal charges was deemed to have been imposed 'for the purpose of bringing him before the competent authority'. In *T v United Kingdom* [GC] (16 December 1999), paras 74–78, and in *V v United Kingdom* [GC] 1999-IX, paras 73–77 respectively, the Court clearly endorsed (in discussing Art 3) a welfare-based approach to juvenile justice as being in line with the UN Standard Minimum Rules for the Administration of Juvenile Justice ('The Beijing Rules') and the UN Convention on the Rights of the Child. Cf *Council of Europe Annual Penal Statistics* (Space 1) 2009, doc PC-CP (2011) 3, table 2 (in 2009, the % of the prison population who were under 18 was 1.3, and ranged between 0 (in Italy, Netherlands and Spain (Catalonia) to 8.2 (in France) (with 2.5 in England and Wales, and 2.1 in Scotland).

4   *Koniarska v United Kingdom* (dec) (12 October 2000) (complaint of a minor held in secure accommodation who had passed the school leaving age and who was suffering from mental disorder that any education offered to her was merely incidental to the real reason for her detention: inadmissible).

5   *Bouamar v Belgium* (1988) A 129, at para 50. See also *Ichin and Others v Ukraine* 2010-…, paras 38–39 (detention in a juvenile holding facility for the temporary isolation of minors could not be deemed to be for 'educational supervision').

6   *DG v Ireland* 2002-III, paras 72–85.

Decisions of domestic courts on detention for educational supervision

4.183 In domestic cases, it has been accepted that the placing of a child in secure accommodation (eg by order of a children's hearing) involves a deprivation of liberty, but that it is consistent with detention for the purpose of educational supervision within the meaning of Article 5(1)(d)[1]. In an English case, it was observed that:

'the concept of 'educational supervision' goes well beyond either normal parental control or academic lessons taught in the classroom, but, to the extent that the arrangements for the welfare of the child interfere with his liberty beyond the interference envisaged in normal parental control, and to avoid any arbitrary exercise of power by a local authority, judicial authorisation is required[2].'

1   *S v Miller (No 1)* 2001 SC 977; *Re K (A Child) (Secure Accommodation Order: Right to Liberty)* [2001] Fam 377. These cases followed *Koniarska v United Kingdom* (12 October 2000).

2   *Re K (A Child) (Secure Accommodation Order: Right to Liberty)* [2001] Fam 377 per Judge LJ at para 116: followed in *S v Miller* per Lord President Rodger of Earlsferry at para 46.

Article 5(1)(e): Detention of persons of unsound mind, vagrants, alcoholics, drug addicts, etc

4.184 'The lawful detention of persons for the prevention of the spreading of infectious diseases, of persons of unsound mind, alcoholics or drug addicts, or vagrants' justifies deprivation of liberty both on public safety grounds as well as to further the well-being of the individual who is detained[1]. Detention for the prevention of the spreading of infectious diseases has not given rise to case law under the ECHR, but there is some jurisprudence on loss of liberty of vagrants and of persons intoxicated or of unsound mind and, more recently, on detention of drug addicts.

1   *Guzzardi v Italy* (1980) A 39, at para 98.

Vagrants

4.185 The definition of 'vagrant' is primarily a matter of domestic law, as long as this reflects the generally accepted meaning of the term for the purposes of the ECHR[1]. A state may not seek to apply the label for an improper purpose[2].

1   *De Wilde, Ooms and Versyp v Belgium ('Vagrancy cases')* (1971) A 12, para 68.

2   *Guzzardi v Italy* (1980) A 39, para 98 (the fact that Art 5(1)(e) justified detention in part to protect the public could not by extension be made to apply to individuals who are considered still more dangerous).

Mental health detention

4.186 More significantly, Article 5 has proved to be an important source of procedural rights for mental health patients[1]. Recognising that judicial competence in mental welfare is limited and that medical understanding is continually developing, the European Court of Human Rights has deliberately left open the interpretation of 'unsound mind' in terms of sub-paragraph (1)(e), and instead has developed safeguards for those deprived of their liberty under this heading, requirements initially established in *Winterwerp v Netherlands*. To justify detention, first, the existence of 'unsound mind' must be reliably established on objective medical grounds; secondly, the individual's actual mental condition must justify detention[2]; and thirdly, continuing detention must be supported and justified by the continuing need for such based on the current mental condition of the patient[3]. In all circumstances, no deprivation of liberty can be considered as justified under this heading if the opinion of a medical expert has not been sought, although in cases of urgency such an opinion may be obtained after the start of the loss of liberty[4]. These requirements also apply to the re-detention of former in-patients who are recalled to hospital[5]. However, it is not necessary for a state to show that the mental illness is treatable. In *Hutchison Reid v United Kingdom*, the applicant complained that since domestic law specifically required that the mental condition warranting detention should be amenable to treatment and since psychiatrists had certified his condition was not curable, his continuing deprivation of liberty had thus been rendered unlawful. The Court disagreed, considering that there was nothing arbitrary in the decision not to release the applicant in view of the high risk that the applicant would re-offend if released. It noted that the guarantee contained no such requirement that the health condition be amenable to treatment; indeed, to the contrary, the provision permitted compulsory confinement when an individual needed control and supervision to prevent harm to himself or to others. In this case in any event, a judge had found that the applicant derived benefit from the hospital environment and that his symptoms became worse outside its supportive structure. This was deemed adequate to establish that there had continued to be a sufficient relationship between the grounds of the detention and the place and conditions of detention to satisfy the guarantee[6].

---

1   See Murdoch *The Treatment of Prisoners: European Standards* (2006), pp 283–301. For discussion of CPT standards in relation to involuntary placement in psychiatric establishments, see *8th General Report* CPT/Inf (98)12, paras 25–28.

2   That is, the assessment must be based on the current state of mental health and not solely on events taking place in the past if a significant period of time has elapsed: *Varbanov v Bulgaria* 2000-X, para 47. See also *RL and M-JD v France* (19 May 2004), paras 85–93 (applicant placed in psychiatric unit overnight after arrest: violation as the detention had no medical justification and was explicable only on the basis that the doctor had no authority to release him); and *CB v Romania* (20 April 2010), paras 48–59 (forcible confinement in psychiatric hospital for two weeks to obtain a medical opinion in order to assess mental responsibility but in the absence of consideration whether compulsorily detention was necessary: violation).

3   *Winterwerp v Netherlands* (1979) A 33, para 39. Cf *Luberti v Italy* (1984) A 75, paras 27–29; *Ashingdane v United Kingdom* (1985) A 93, paras 40–42, 48–49. See too *Magalhães Pereira*

v Portugal 2002-I, paras 40–53 (detention on the basis of a medical opinion noting that the applicant required long-term psychiatric opinion for schizophrenia; a court-instructed report obtained some seven months later indicated that the applicant's condition had stabilised, and that he could be released on condition he accepted psychiatric support and continued to take his medicine, but no action taken by the domestic court; further, there had been a two-month delay before a court considered whether the applicant's detention should continue after he was re-arrested following a seven-month period of unauthorised liberty: violation of Art 5(4), and no need to consider issues under Art 5(1)(e)). See also Committee of Ministers Recommendation Rec (2004) 10 concerning the protection of the human rights and dignity of persons with mental disorder.

4   *Varbanov v Bulgaria* 2000-X, paras 46–49 (detention ordered by a prosecutor to obtain a medical opinion to assess the need for proceedings with a view to the psychiatric internment of the applicant: the Court observed (at para 47) that in urgent cases or where a person is arrested because of his violent behaviour a medical opinion should be obtained immediately following the start of the detention; in all other instances prior consultation should be necessary and even where there is a refusal to appear for medical examination, a preliminary medical assessment on the basis of the file is required). See also *Herz v Germany* (12 June 2003), paras 43–56 (detention justified as the applicant had been considered to represent a danger to his own health and to public safety on the basis of a diagnosis obtained by telephone from a hospital doctor who had treated the applicant on earlier and recent occasions). It is crucial, however, that domestic procedures are complied with: see *Rakevich v Russia*, (28 October 2003), paras 26–35 (urgent detention had been based upon psychiatric evidence of mental illness but there had been failure to comply with domestic law requiring determination of requests for detention orders within five days of a hospital's application: violation).

5   *X v United Kingdom* (1981) A 46, paras 41–46.

6   *Hutchison Reid v United Kingdom* 2003-IV, paras 47–56.

4.187 In this context, the regime under which an individual is detained will be relevant in assessing the legality of the deprivation of liberty, since there is an expectation that the conditions of treatment reflect the justification for detention[1]. In *Morsink v the Netherlands*, the applicant had been sentenced to imprisonment on an assault charge and also at the same time ordered him to be confined to a custodial clinic on account of his poorly developed mental facilities. The confinement order had taken effect at the conclusion of his custodial sentence, but the applicant had been kept in pre-placement detention in an ordinary remand centre for some 15 months. While the Court accepted that the applicant's detention in the pre-trial facilities had been lawful under domestic law as no places had been available in custodial clinics, it considered that it was also necessary to establish whether such a detention was in conformity with Article 5's purpose in preventing arbitrary loss of liberty. The principle that deprivation of liberty of a person as a mental health patient requires to take place in an 'appropriate institution' did not imply that the applicant had to be placed immediately in such a facility at the end of the imprisonment as it was not unreasonable to commence procedures for selecting the most appropriate custodial clinic only after the confinement order had taken effect. However, any significant delay in admission to a custodial clinic would obviously affect the prospects of a treatment's success, and the delay of 15 months in admission to a custodial clinic in this case was deemed to be unacceptable[2].

1   *Ashingdane v United Kingdom* (1985) A 93, at para 44: 'in principle, the 'detention' of a person as a mental health patient will only be 'lawful' for the purposes of [Art 5(1)(e)] if effected in a hospital, clinic or other appropriate institution authorised for that purpose', although this sub-paragraph 'is not in principle concerned with suitable treatment or conditions'. See too *Aerts v Belgium* 1998-V, paras 45–50; cf *Mocarska v Poland* (6 November 2007), paras 41–49 (while it was unrealistic to expect a place would be immediately available in a psychiatric hospital, an eight-month detention pending delay in the admission to a psychiatric hospital was unacceptable); and *Haidn v Germany* (13 January 2011), paras 91–95 (imposition of indefinite preventive detention shortly before a period of imprisonment following conviction and following psychiatric reports suggesting the applicant posed a serious risk to others was not justified under Art 5(1)(e) as detention was not on the basis of mental health, and initially he had been held in an ordinary prison, rather than in a hospital, clinic or other appropriate institution).

2   *Morsink v the Netherlands* (11 May 2004), paras 61–70. See also *Brand v the Netherlands*, (11 May 2004), paras 58–67. Cf *De Schepper v Belgium* (13 October 2009), paras 35–50 (preventive detention of a paedophile on social-protection grounds justified in consequence of the obligation to seek to provide the applicant with treatment that might have helped him regain his liberty).

4.188 Domestic law must also provide sufficient protection against arbitrary deprivation of liberty. In *HL v United Kingdom,* the legal basis for the applicant's detention had been the common law doctrine of necessity. While this doctrine was still in the course of development, the Court could not be satisfied that the law had yet advanced sufficiently to prevent arbitrary application of the power to detain. The lack of any fixed procedural rules by which the detention of compliant incapacitated persons was conducted was in striking contrast to the extensive network of safeguards applicable to compulsory committal. This situation had allowed health care professionals to assume full control of the liberty and treatment of a vulnerable individual solely on the basis of their own clinical assessments without the existence of procedural safeguards which could protect individuals against misjudgments and professional lapses[1].

1   *HL v United Kingdom* 2004-IX, paras 114–124. See also *Frommelt v Liechtenstein* (dec) 2003-VII (transfer of detainee to psychiatric hospital in another state was based on the code of criminal procedure and treaty, and was not arbitrary as a psychiatrist had recommended the treatment, which had ceased as soon as the applicant's mental state improved: inadmissible).

4.189 The result of this case law is that the protection of mental health patients has been advanced significantly. All the circumstances surrounding loss of liberty will now call for careful scrutiny in each case. Procedural due diligence on the part of state officials will be essential. However, the European Court of Human Rights has accepted that any substantive determination of mental illness justifying detention calls for a certain latitude on the part of medical experts. In *Johnson v United Kingdom*, the applicant had been convicted of assault and confined to a mental hospital. Ultimately, a mental health tribunal had decided that his mental illness had ended, but that he still required a period of rehabilitation under medical supervision before it could be certain that no recall to hospital would be necessary. Accordingly, the tribunal had ordered his discharge, but made this conditional upon his residence in a suitable hostel. Implementation had been deferred until such accommodation could be found, but this had been rendered difficult on account of the lack of appropriate hostels and by problems which had arisen during a period of trial leave. In consequence, the applicant had remained for most of this time as a patient in a secure hospital, even although subsequent reviews had confirmed that he was not suffering from mental disorder. Eventually, some three-and-a-half years later, he had been given an absolute discharge. The Court clarified that a finding that deprivation of liberty on the ground of mental condition is no longer justified cannot imply a right to immediate and unconditional release. This would unacceptably fetter the exercise of expert medical opinion as to what the best interests of a patient required, particularly since the determination of a medical condition cannot be made with absolute accuracy. The Court also recognised that assessment of patients in this category must take into account the protection of the community[1]. However, in such cases it is 'of paramount importance that appropriate safeguards are in place so as to ensure that any deferral of discharge is consonant with the purposes of Article 5(1) and with the aim of the restriction in sub-paragraph (e)' and above all to ensure that any discharge 'is not unreasonably delayed'. Here, the delay was found to have resulted in a violation of Article 5[2].

---

1   Cf *Luberti v Italy* (1984) A 75, para 29.

2   *Johnson v United Kingdom* 1997-VII, paras 58–68. See also *Kolanis v United Kingdom* 2005-V, paras 67–73 (determination that the applicant should be conditionally released if treatment and supervision for her mental illness could be provided: in the absence of available treatment, her detention continued to be necessary and appropriate, and there was no requirement that a patient be discharged in such circumstances).

DECISIONS OF DOMESTIC COURTS ON MENTAL HEALTH DETENTION

4.190 Article 5(1)(e) was considered in *A v The Scottish Ministers*. The case concerned statutory applications made by three patients detained in the State Hospital, all of whom had been convicted of homicide and were suffering from a mental disorder at the time of their conviction. In their applications they sought their discharge on the basis that they were no longer requiring medical treatment: at the time when two of the applications were made, that was the only basis on which the patients could lawfully be detained. While those applications were pending, the Mental Health (Public Safety and Appeals) (Scotland) Act 1999 was passed and brought into force. It had the effect of requiring the court to refuse such applications where it was necessary, in order to protect the public from serious harm, that the patient continue to be detained in a hospital, whether for medical treatment or not. The House of Lords ruled that the continued detention of restricted patients in a hospital where this is shown to be necessary on grounds of public safety was not incompatible with Article 5(1)(e), whether or not their mental disorder was treatable. In such cases, three distinct questions require to be addressed:

(i)   whether the detention is lawful under domestic law (in terms of compliance with procedural as well as substantive rules);

(ii) whether domestic law complies with the general requirements of the Convention in terms of its being sufficiently accessible to the individual and sufficiently precise to enable the individual to foresee the consequences for himself; and

(iii) whether the detention satisfies the test of being free from arbitrariness as tested by reference to the *Winterwerp* criteria.

The House of Lords considered that all three tests had been met. In particular, in respect of the third test, 'the sheriff or the Scottish Ministers must be satisfied that the patient is suffering from a mental disorder (the first *Winterwerp* criterion) and that it is such as to make it necessary for the protection of the public that he continue to be detained in hospital (the second and third *Winterwerp* criteria). Lord Hope of Craighead added:

'The conclusion which I would draw from [Strasbourg jurisprudence] is that the question whether a person who is deprived of his liberty on the ground that he is a person of unsound mind in circumstances which meet the *Winterwerp* criteria should also receive treatment for his mental disorder as a condition of his detention is a matter for domestic law. So too is the place of his detention, so long as it is a place which is suitable for the detention of persons of unsound mind. It follows that the fact that his mental disorder is not susceptible to treatment does not mean that, in Convention terms, his continued detention in a hospital is arbitrary or disproportionate[1].'

The court's decision in respect of Article 5(4) is discussed below[2].

1   *A v The Scottish Ministers* 2002 SC (PC) 63 at 70–74.

2   At para **4.224** below.

4.191 The continued detention of a patient by reason of the non-availability of the after-care facilities necessary for the patient's care and treatment in the community, despite the exercise of all reasonable endeavours, does not violate Article 5[1]. On the other hand, since it is contrary to the ECHR to detain a patient compulsorily unless it can be shown that the patient is suffering from a mental disorder which warrants detention, a statutory test which allowed the continued detention of the patient where it could not be shown that his mental condition did *not* warrant detention (ie placing the onus on the patient to justify his discharge, rather than upon the authorities to justify his detention) was held to contravene Article 5[2].

1   *R (K) v Camden and Islington Health Authority* [2002] QB 198. A complaint to the Strasbourg Court under Art 5(1)(e) was rejected: *Kolanis v United Kingdom* 2005-V. See also *R (H) v Secretary of State for the Home Department* [2004] 2 AC 253 (a Mental Health Review Tribunal decided that an individual should be discharged upon the fulfilment of certain conditions including the availability of psychiatric supervision, but when this could not be obtained the tribunal decided not to discharge him and he remained in detention: held that there was no breach of Art 5 by virtue of the fact that the tribunal lacked the power to secure compliance with the conditions set out in its order, as the ECHR does not lay down any criteria as to the extent to which member states must provide facilities for the care of those of unsound mind in

the community, thereby avoiding the necessity for them to be detained for treatment in hospital).

2   *R (H) v Mental Health Review Tribunal, North and East London Region* [2002] QB 1. Other significant domestic cases on mental health detention include *R (A) v Secretary of State for the Home Department* [2003] 1 WLR 330; *R (Von Brandenburg) v East London and the City Mental Health NHS Trust* [2004] 2 AC 280.

Alcoholics and drug addicts

4.192 The European Court of Human Rights in *Witold Litwa v Poland* sought to clarify the extent of any power of detention of an alcoholic under the sub-paragraph. The applicant, who had been behaving offensively while drunk, had been taken to a 'sobering up' centre where he had been detained for six-and-a-half-hours. For the Court, while the normal meaning of an 'alcoholic' implied addiction to alcohol, the term was used in Article 5(1)(e) in a context which includes reference to other categories of individuals who may be deprived of their liberty both to protect public safety and for their own interests. Thus the detention of 'alcoholics' could not be restricted merely to persons medically so diagnosed, but had to include detention of individuals 'whose conduct and behaviour under the influence of alcohol pose a threat to public order or themselves', and where detention is 'for the protection of the public or their own interests, such as their health or personal safety'[1]. By clear analogy, a similar approach should apply in cases of drug abuse[2]. The decision, though, seems limited to any justification for short-term deprivation of liberty; any exercise of a power to order the detention of an individual for longer-term treatment for alcoholism or for drug dependency should certainly be justified by reference to criteria similar to the *Winterwerp* judgment (that is, any existence of dependency and treatment necessitating deprivation of liberty should be reliably established by qualified health professionals). In each instance, however, domestic law must adequately regulate the circumstances in which individuals may be detained on this ground. In *Hilda Hafsteinsdóttir v Iceland*, the applicant had been arrested and held overnight in custody on six occasions on account of intoxication, agitation and aggressive behaviour towards police officers. Although the Court accepted that the detentions were covered by the sub-paragraph as her behaviour had been under the strong influence of alcohol and could reasonably have been considered to entail a threat to public order, the quality of domestic law was considered insufficient to meet the tests of Article 5. Domestic law was not sufficiently precise as to the type of measures that the police were authorised to take in respect of a detainee, nor was the maximum authorised duration of detention specified. While internal police instructions elaborated more detailed rules on the discretion which a police officer enjoyed in ordering detention, the instructions did not permit detention in cases of mere intoxication if an alternative measure could be used. The key issues were that the exercise of discretion by the police, and the duration of the detention, had thus been governed by administrative practice rather than by a settled legal framework. The law was thus not sufficiently precise or accessible to avoid the risk of arbitrariness, and thus the applicant's deprivation of liberty had not been 'lawful'[3].

1   *Witold Litwa v Poland* 2000-III, paras 60–63.

2   See *Bizzotto v Greece* 1996-V, paras 31–35, discussed at para **4.171** above.

3   *Hilda Hafsteinsdóttir v Iceland* (8 June 2004), paras 51–56.

Detention of persons suffering from infectious diseases

4.193 Applications involving detainees suffering from an infectious disease have normally arisen in the context of challenges to the continued detention of a prisoner who is seriously ill or in relation to the provision of health care were a detainee to be removed to another country[1]. There is but limited guidance in the case law on the issue of the imposition of detention to prevent the deliberate (or at least negligent) transmission of disease, but principles of general applicability are relevant. In particular, deprivation of liberty in such instances must be shown to be strictly necessary on account of the health risk posed, and also on account of the absence of alternatives to address the risk posed. In *Enhorn v Sweden*, the applicant had been diagnosed as infected with the HIV virus after having transmitted the virus to another man through sexual contact. A medical officer had used his powers under domestic law to give instructions to the applicant on matters concerning his sexual behaviour and alcohol consumption, and the maintenance of regular consultation with a physician. Although the applicant had kept a number of appointments with his doctor, he had failed on five occasions to do so, and the medical officer in consequence had been granted judicial authority to have the applicant isolated in a hospital. However, the Court could not be satisfied that the compulsory isolation had not been a last resort to prevent the spreading of the disease since the respondent government had not provided any examples of less severe measures which might have been applied[2]. Deprivation of liberty of a person suffering from a disease which is communicable through voluntary contact with another (for example, through sexual intercourse) may be justified, but not where less onerous alternative measures to prevent the spread of the disease also exist. It is likely that similar considerations would apply in the case of an individual suffering from a disease which is highly contagious and spread through mere proximity to others.

1   See para **4.137** above.

2   *Enhorn v Sweden* 2005-I, paras 36–56. For further discussion, see Mowbray 'Compulsory Detention to Prevent the Spreading of Infectious Diseases' (2005) 5 HRLRev 387.

Article 5(1)(f): Illegal immigration, deportation and extradition

4.194 Article 5(1)(f) provides for 'the lawful arrest or detention of a person to prevent his effecting an unauthorised entry into the country or of a person against whom action is being taken with a view to deportation or extradition'. There are thus two 'limbs' to the provision. Detention must be shown to fall under either the first limb (that is, unauthorised entry) or the second (deportation or extradition)[1] and not merely to prevent flight[2] or for any other covert aim[3]. A state must be able to show that there was a legal basis for the deprivation of liberty[4] and also that it was not arbitrary[5]. Any decision to deprive an individual of their liberty must thus be taken in good faith[6]. While the ECHR does not provide any right to reside in a particular country or any guarantee against being deported or extradited[7], denial of entry to, or expulsion from, a country may give rise to other human rights considerations.

1   *Mikolenko v Estonia* (8 October 2009), paras 56–68 (while initial detention fell within the sub-paragraph, when it became clear expulsion was virtually impossible, further prolonged detention could not therefore be said to have been effected with a view to his deportation: violation of Art 5(1)(f)).

2   8081/77, *X v United Kingdom* (1977) DR 12, 207.

3   Cf *Bozano v France* (1986) A 111, paras 53–60.

4   *Soldatenko v Ukraine* (23 October 2008), paras 112–114 (lack of domestic legal provision in extradition treaty for any procedure for detention).

5   *Saadi v United Kingdom* [GC] 2008-..., para 74. See also *SD v Greece* (11 June 2009), paras 59–67 (oral request for asylum made upon arrival had not been registered but had been followed by arrest and detention pending the making of an order for deportation, but no order was ever made, and the authorities had not been able to show why release would pose a danger to public order or national security: violation of Art 5(1)(f)).

6   *Bozano v France* (1986) A 111, paras 53–60. See also *Çonka v Belgium*, 2002-I, paras 40–46 (arrest and deportation of Roma after they had been summoned to report to a police station to give information relating to their asylum applications, a strategy specifically designed to ensure compliance by the highest number of recipients: violation). See also *Nasrulloyev v Russia* (11 October 2007), paras 72–78 (inconsistent interpretation of provisions applicable to detainees awaiting extradition and which were neither precise nor foreseeable: violation of Art 5(1)(f)).

7   1983/63, *X v Netherlands* (1965) YB 8, 228 at 264; *Aslan v Malta* (dec) (3 February 2000) (immigration officers refused the applicant entry on account of visa problems; he was subsequently detained in a cell pending his return to Libya from where he had come; there had been sufficient grounds for refusing him entry and his complaint was thus inadmissible).

8   Eg under Art 3 (protection against torture etc) and Art 8 (respect for family life): see further paras **4.130–4.137** above and paras **6.67–6.70** below. The use of force to effect a removal order has been considered by the CPT: see *Seventh General Report* CPT/Inf (97) 10, para 36. See also Lambert *The Position of Aliens in Relation to the European Convention on Human Rights* (3rd edn, 2007); Mole *Asylum and the European Convention on Human Rights* (4th edn, 2007); and Council of Europe *Human Rights Protection in the Context of Accelerated Asylum Procedures: Guidelines and Explanatory Memorandum* (2009).

Preventing unauthorised entry

4.195 As far as the first 'limb' is concerned, the power to detain in order to prevent unauthorised entry must be interpreted within the context of a state's right to control the entry and residence of aliens. In consequence, the sub-paragraph permits detention not only of a person shown to be trying to evade entry restrictions but also of would-be immigrants who have applied for permission to enter, as until entry is 'authorised' it remains 'unauthorised'[1]. Four conditions must be satisfied to ensure a deprivation of liberty is not arbitrary: first, the detention must be carried out in good faith; secondly, it must be closely connected to the purpose of preventing unauthorised entry; thirdly, bearing in mind that the detainee might well have fled his home country in mortal fear, the location and conditions of the detention centre must be appropriate; and fourthly, the principle of proportionality requires that its length must not exceed that reasonably required for the purpose pursued[2]. In *Saadi v United Kingdom*, the Grand Chamber considered Britain's procedures for fast-track processing of asylum seekers as having met these tests in the case of the applicant. He had been granted temporary admission to the country, but on the fourth day – as a would-be immigrant who have applied for permission to enter and thus awaiting 'authorised' entry - had been detained for seven days in a reception centre while his application had been considered under arrangements designed to expedite the resolution of asylum applications. As the applicant's case had been considered suitable for the procedure, the government's decision to detain him to apply the fast-track procedures had been taken in good faith; detention had been closely connected to the purpose of preventing unauthorised entry; the centre had been specifically adapted to hold asylum seekers and included a full range of relevant facilities including legal assistance; and the period of seven days had not exceeded the period reasonably required to enable the speedy determination of the claim[3].

1   *Saadi v United Kingdom*[GC] 2008-..., para 65.

2   *Saadi v United Kingdom*[GC] 2008-..., para 74.

3   *Saadi v United Kingdom*[GC] 2008-..., paras 75–80.

Detention with a view to deportation, etc

4.196 In respect of the second limb, detention is permitted even although no actual decision to make an order has been taken: it is adequate merely that action is being taken 'with a view to deportation'[1]. In consequence, Strasbourg review will be restricted to 'examining whether there was a legal basis for the detention and whether the decision of the courts on the question of lawfulness could be described as arbitrary in light of the facts of the case'[2]. In practice, the key issue is likely to be whether deportation proceedings have been unduly prolonged or been of excessive duration to prevent the detention being considered arbitrary as the national authorities are expected to act with due diligence. Assessment of each case on its own facts is required. The period of detention pending determination whether to extradite in *Kolompar v Belgium* lasted 32 months, and in *Quinn v France* some 23 months. In the former instance much of the delay was attributable to repeated attempts by the applicant to seek release, and consequently no violation was established[3]; but in the latter case, the Court accepted that there had been successive delays attributable to state authorities which rendered the time taken to reach a decision excessive[4].

1   6871/75, *Caprino v United Kingdom* (1978) DR 12, 14 at 20. See van Dijk, van Hoof, van Rijn and Zwaak (eds) *Theory and Practice of the European Convention on Human Rights* (4th edn, 2006), at p 481: [the sub-paragraph] provides a lower level of protection than [Art 5(1)(c)]: all that is required under (f) is that the action is being taken with a view to deportation or

extradition. It is, therefore, immaterial whether the underlying decision can be justified under national or Convention law'.

2   9174/80, *Zamir v United Kingdom* (1983) DR 40, 42.

3   *Kolompar v Belgium* (1992) A 235-C, paras 37–43.

4   *Quinn v France* (1995) A 311, paras 44–49. See too *Amuur v France* 1996-III, at para 43: detention 'must not deprive the asylum-seeker of the right to gain effective access to the procedure for determining refugee status', discussed further, at para 4.154 above; and *Bordovskiy v Russia* (8 February 2005), paras 47–51 (challenge to quality of extradition law as too imprecise: the applicant's challenge was essentially based upon protection against too long detention pending extradition, but the period of four months was not excessively long). 'Effective access' may on occasion require the provision of free legal assistance: cf 9174/80, *Zamir v United Kingdom* (1983) DR 40, 42 (complexity of the issues and the applicant's limited command of English). For discussion of CPT standards relating to foreign nationals deprived of their liberty, see *7th General Report*, CPT/Inf (97) 10, paras 24–36.

4.197 In assessing whether the authorities have shown the necessary due diligence required by the second limb of Article 5(1)(f), the prolongation of deportation proceedings may be justifiable on account of the responsibility under Article 3 to ensure an individual is not returned to a country when there are substantial grounds for believing that deportation would carry a real risk of ill-treatment[1]. In *Chahal v United Kingdom*, a high-profile supporter of Sikh separatism had been detained for over six years pending determination of various appeals concerning the British Government's decision to return him to India. The Court considered that there had been no breach of Article 5 under this heading. It was 'neither in the interests of the individual applicant nor in the general public interest in the administration of justice that such decisions be taken hastily, without due regard to all the relevant issues and evidence'. Determination of issues of 'an extremely serious and weighty nature' called for thorough examination by state authorities, and in the circumstances, there was no corresponding lack of diligence, so that the periods of time complained of either individually or taken together could not be regarded as excessive[2]. In contrast, in *Singh v Czech Republic*, the Court considered that there had been a violation of Article 5(1)(f) on account of a lack of diligence on the part of the authorities. The applicants had been convicted of offences concerned with evading immigration controls, but had been held in detention for two and a half years at the conclusion of their sentences since it had not been possible to deport them immediately as they did not have passports. In determining that the length of duration had been excessive, the Court noted that the detention had exceeded the period of imprisonment, the offences had not been particularly serious, and the absence of passports could have been remedied by the issue of travel documents[3]. In all cases, however, the detention must be taken 'with a view to deportation', as emphasised in *A and Others v United Kingdom*. In this case, non-nationals considered to pose a threat to national security had been detained under statutory powers. Both these powers and the derogation under Article 15 lodged by the UK Government had been based upon the assumption that such individuals could not be removed or deported 'for the time being' without being put at risk of ill-treatment. The Grand Chamber concluded that where the possibility of deportation was merely kept 'under active review', this was neither sufficiently certain nor determinative to allow the deprivation of liberty to fall within the sub-paragraph[4].

1   See paras **4.130–4.137** above.

2   *Chahal v United Kingdom* 1996-V, paras 110–117. The Court did determine that any deportation to India would result in a violation of Art 3: see paras 87–107. The Art 5(4) issue is considered at para **4.238** below. For domestic discussion, see Case UfR 2001.0026 H [Denmark] (17-month detention of unidentified Algerian national for removal was not a violation of Art 5(1)(f) as the primary reason for the delay was the due to the complete lack of corroboration from the detained in establishing his identity so extradition papers could be accepted by the Algerian authorities).

3   *Singh v Czech Republic* (25 January 2005), paras 61–68. The judgment seems to avoid the issue of whether the applicants would have been readmitted to India on the basis of Czech travel documents.

4   *A and Others v United Kingdom* [GC] 2009-..., at para 167. There are many domestic cases under Art 5(1)(f). Recent examples include *M v Secretary of State for the Home Department* 2011 SLT 218 and *S v Secretary of State for the Home Department* 2011 SLT 297.

Procedural guarantees following deprivation of liberty

4.198 The remaining provisions of Article 5 provide guarantees to persons deprived of their liberty: to notification of the reasons adduced by the authorities; to the right to take proceedings to test the lawfulness of detention; and to the payment compensation where there has been a violation of the article. Additional guarantees to be brought promptly before a judge and to trial within a reasonable time or to release pending trial exist for those deprived of their liberty under Article 5(1)(c). There is some duplication here with the provisions of Article 6, but Article 5 requires there to be special diligence on the part of authorities in respect of persons who have been deprived of their liberty. Article 5's provisions are thus best considered as constituting separate and independent rights which produce their own effects[1]. These rights are in addition to other safeguards for persons deprived of their liberty[2].

1   *Stögmüller v Austria* (1969) A 9, Law, para 5

2   In particular, protection against ill-treatment under Art 3: see para **4.99** above. Evidence improperly obtained from a detainee through compulsion may also violate Art 6 guarantees: see paras **5.125–5.126** below. The CPT has also published statements of expectations concerning detainees in 'substantive' sections of its annual reports: see para **4.121** above.

Article 5(2): Prompt advising of reasons for detention

4.199 The purpose of Article 5(2) is to ensure that a detainee is adequately informed of the reasons for his detention so as to permit him to judge the lawfulness of the state action and, if he thinks fit, to take advantage of the right under Article 5(4) to challenge it. This is an 'integral part of the scheme of protection afforded by Article 5'[1]. The reference to 'arrest' in the text extends beyond the realm of the criminal law[2], and the giving of reasons applies to all of the categories provided for under Article 5(1), and not just to persons arrested or detained under Article 5(1)(c)[3]. Content, manner and time of notification are important. The legal basis for the detention together with the essential facts relevant to the lawfulness of the decision must be given in 'simple, non-technical language' that an individual can understand[4]. This does not, however, extend to a need to make the individual aware of the grounds for suspicion of involvement in an offence[5]. These requirements cannot be abridged merely because an individual is considered unable or unsuitable to receive the information; in such a case, the details must be given to a representative such as his lawyer or guardian[6]. Whether steps must be taken to ensure that a non-native language speaker understands the reason for detention is largely dependent upon the facts[7]. Further, the information must be given 'promptly'. In *Van der Leer v Netherlands*, the applicant had discovered only by accident and some ten days subsequently that she was being detained compulsorily in a hospital, a breach of Article 5(2) which was rendered all the more serious since the applicant originally had entered the hospital as a voluntary patient and thus had been unable to appreciate any factual change in her circumstances[8]. In *Saadi v United Kingdom*, an asylum seeker granted temporary admission had been detained for fast-track processing for seven days in a reception centre but had only first learnt of the real reason for his detention through his representative some 76 hours after the start of the detention. The government had sought to argue that the policy of detention in such cases had been announced in parliamentary announcements. The Grand Chamber found a breach of Article 5(2): individual notification rather than general statements of policy was necessary, and even assuming the requirement were satisfied by the giving of oral reasons to a representative, the delay in this case had been incompatible with the requirement of promptness[9]. A failure to provide information may alternatively, or in addition, raise an issue under Article 5(4) if the failure to supply information has resulted in an individual being denied a proper opportunity to challenge the legality of his detention[10]. However, as the *Çonka and Others v Belgium* case indicates, the giving of information must be assessed independently of its utility, and the fact that information is not in practice sufficient to allow applicants to lodge appeals does not mean that the requirements of paragraph 2 have not been satisfied[11].

---

1   *Fox, Campbell and Hartley v United Kingdom* (1990) A 182, at para 40.

2   *Van der Leer v Netherlands* (1990) A 170-A, paras 27–28.

3   *X v United Kingdom* (1981) A 46, para 66.

4   *Fox, Campbell and Hartley v United Kingdom* (1990) A 182, at para 40. For discussion of onus of proof, see *Abdolkhani and Karimnia v Turkey* 2009-..., paras 136–138 (conclusion drawn in the absence of a governmental reply or any document to show that the applicants had been informed: violation of Art 5(2)).

5   8022/77, 8025/77, 8027/77, *McVeigh, O'Neill and Evans v United Kingdom* (1981) DR 25, 15. In the opinion of the Commission, a person arrested upon suspicion of an offence should also be asked whether he admits or denies the allegation: 8098/77, *X v Germany* (1978) DR 16, 111 at 114. This must now be considered highly dubious in light of *Salduz v Turkey* [GC] 2008-..., discussed at para **5.204** below.

6   7215/75, *X v United Kingdom* (1980) B 41, opinion of the Commission, paras 102–108.

7   2689/65, *Delcourt v Belgium* (1967), YB10, 238 (arrest of a French-speaking individual on the
     authority of a warrant in Flemish was considered not to have breached this requirement since
     the subsequent interview had been in French and it could be assumed that the reason for the
     arrest had been known to the applicant); and *Egmez v Cyprus* 2000-XII, para 85 (detention of
     a Turkish-speaking individual who could also understand Greek on suspicion of drug trafficking
     by Greek-speaking officials who had been arrested in flagrante delicto, had expressly been
     informed of the suspicion against him on at least two occasions while in hospital, and by
     police officers who had interrogated him, one of whom spoke Turkish: Art 5(2) requirement
     satisfied).

8   *Van der Leer v Netherlands* (1990) A 170-A, paras 27–30.

9   *Saadi v United Kingdom* [GC] 2008-…, paras 84–85.

10   *X v United Kingdom* (1981) A 46, para 66.

11   *Çonka and Others v Belgium* 2002-I, paras 50–52.

4.200 However, some latitude appears evident in cases involving serious or
organised criminal activity. In *Fox, Campbell and Hartley v United Kingdom*,
the applicants had been given only minimal information as to the legal basis for
their detention, but within a few hours had been interrogated at length as to their
suspected involvement in proscribed terrorist organisations. The European Court
of Human Rights determined that in the circumstances the reasons for the detention
had thereby been brought to the notice of the applicants within the constraints of
'promptness'[1]. Similarly, in *Dikme v Turkey*, the Court considered that a threat
made to the applicant at the outset of his interrogation was in the circumstances
enough to satisfy Article 5(2), since it had contained a 'fairly precise indication'
of the suspicion of criminal activity[2]. On the other hand, the Court found a breach
of Article 5(2) in *Ireland v United Kingdom* where, following executive
instructions given to military police, detainees under anti-terrorism laws were not
informed of the grounds for deprivation of liberty but merely advised that they
were being held pursuant to the provisions of emergency legislation[3].

1   *Fox, Campbell and Hartley v United Kingdom* (1990) A 182, paras 40–42; followed in *Murray
     v United Kingdom* (1994) A 300-A, paras 71–80 (lack of any more 'probing examination'
     attributable to the applicant's refusal to refuse any further questions). See too *Kerr v United
     Kingdom* (dec) (7 December 1999) (applicant had been interviewed 39 times by police officers
     during the week that followed his arrest: it could thus be inferred that he was apprised of the
     reasons for the arrest); and *O'Hara v United Kingdom* (dec) (14 March 2000) (applicant was
     given only the most minimal of information on the reasons for his arrest but, six hours later,
     interrogation lasting four hours followed: this part of the application was rejected as manifestly
     ill-founded).

2   *Dikme v Turkey* 2000-VIII, paras 55–57 ('You belong to *Devrimci Sol* [an illegal organisation],
     and if you don't give us the information we need, you'll be leaving here feet first!').

3   *Ireland v United Kingdom* (1978) A 25, para 198.

Domestic compliance with Article 5(2)

4.201 In order to comply with Article 5(2), the Crown has since 20 May 1999
(when the relevant parts of the Scotland Act 1998 came into force) adopted a
practice of serving on the accused what is known as a 'custody statement' in

cases in which it intends to seek a remand in custody. The statement indicates the outlines of the evidence in support of the Crown case in order to inform the accused of the reasons for his arrest. Similarly, in cases in which a petition warrant is sought, the practice has been adopted of including in the petition a brief indication of the information which the Crown had received and upon which arrest and detention were sought. Challenges to these practices were unsuccessful[1].

---

1   *Vannet v Hamilton* 1999 SCCR 558; *Brown v Selfridge* 1999 SCCR 809.

Article 5(3): Pre-trial detention – (i) prompt appearance before a judge

4.202 The aim of the paragraph is to ensure that a person detained is brought before a judge or judicial officer[1] so that the lawfulness of detention can be assessed, and a determination made as to whether the individual should be released or detained in custody pending determination of guilt or innocence[2]. Article 5(3) applies only to detentions which fall within the scope of paragraph (1)(c)[3], that is, for 'the lawful arrest or detention of a person effected for the purpose of bringing him before the competent legal authority on reasonable suspicion of having committed an offence or where it is reasonably considered necessary to prevent his committing an offence or fleeing after having done so'. It thus does not apply where a person has been provisionally released[4] or is already serving a sentence of imprisonment imposed after conviction for a criminal offence[5]. The prompt involvement of a judge is also considered an important safeguard against ill-treatment while in custody[6]. Article 5(3) rights must be granted automatically, and cannot be made dependent upon a specific request by an accused person[7]. The responsibilities of the judge can be summarised as those of reviewing all the circumstances militating for or against detention, deciding whether a continuation of detention can be justified in accordance with legal criteria, recording the detailed reasons for determining that an accused should be remanded in custody awaiting trial, and ordering release if there are insufficient reasons for continuing detention[8].

---

1   See paras **4.204–4.206** below. Cf *Kenny v Howdle* 2002 SCCR 814 (appearance before an honorary sheriff without legal qualifications following apprehension after failure to appear for sentence: appellant's detention fell under Art 5(1)(b) rather than (1)(c), and Art 5(3) was not applicable).

2   *Brogan and Others v United Kingdom* (1988) A 145-B, para 58; cf *Sabeur Ben Ali v Malta* (29 June 2000), paras 28–32 at para 29 (failure to provide 'prompt, automatic review of the merits of detention); and *Stepuleac v Moldova* (6 November 2007), paras 69–74 (failure by courts to examine whether there had been a reasonable suspicion that the applicant had committed a crime when considering prosecutor's actions and requests for arrest, thus supporting the contention that the detention was for private interests).

3   *De Wilde, Ooms and Versyp v Belgium ('Vagrancy cases')* (1971) A 12, para 71.

4   8233/78, *X v United Kingdom* (1979) DR 17, 122.

5   *B v Austria* (1990) A 175, para 39.

6   Cf *Kurt v Turkey* 1998-III, at para 123: 'The requirements of Article 5(3) and (4) with their emphasis on promptitude and judicial control assume particular importance in this context. Prompt judicial intervention may lead to the detection and prevention of life-threatening

measures or serious ill-treatment which violate the fundamental guarantees contained in Articles 2 and 3 of the Convention. ... What is at stake is both the protection of the physical liberty of individuals as well as their personal security in a context which, in the absence of safeguards, could result in a subversion of the rule of law and place detainees beyond the reach of the most rudimentary forms of legal protection'.

7   *Aquilina v Malta* [GC] 1999-III, para 49.

8   Eg *TW v Malta* [GC] (29 April 1999), paras 41–44; and *Neumeister v Austria* (1968) A 8, Law, para 5: 'It is essentially on the basis of the reasons given in the decisions on the applications for release pending trial, and of the true facts mentioned by the Applicant in his appeals, that the Court is called upon to decide whether or not there has been a violation [of the guarantee]'. This principle applies also in situations where domestic law provides for a presumption in favour of relevant factors justifying the continuation of pre-trial detention since the shifting of the burden of proof to a detainee to show that the presumption does not apply 'is tantamount to overturning the rule of Article 5 of the Convention': *Ilijkov v Bulgaria* (26 July 2001), paras 84–85 at para 85.

The meaning of 'promptly'

4.203 'Promptly' suggests more latitude than is accorded by the French text's use of the word *'aussitôt'* which, literally, means 'immediately'. The Court's case-law suggests that appearance before a judge must take place within four days[1]. This, though, is subject to two provisos. First, and only in wholly exceptional cases, a period exceeding 96 hours before a detainee is released or brought before a judicial officer may be deemed justified[2], for example on account of the health of the detainee[3] or geographical considerations[4]. Secondly, since the crucial purpose of the requirement is to provide effective judicial control against arbitrary deprivation of liberty, there may in consequence be a responsibility to ensure the appearance of a detainee before a judge sooner than 96 hours in certain cases. Here, the quality of protection accorded a detainee by domestic law is of relevance[5]. In *İpek and Others v Turkey*, for example, minors had been arrested as part of investigation into terrorist offences and had been held for two days before being questioned. No assistance of a lawyer had been offered as the offences had fallen within the jurisdiction of state security courts. Only three days and nine hours after the arrests had they been brought before a judge. In emphasising that the authorities do not enjoy unrestricted power under Article 5 to arrest suspects for questioning free from effective control by domestic courts, the age of the suspect, delay in interrogating and lack of legal assistance all supported a finding that the applicant had not been brought 'promptly' before a judge[6].

1   In its reports, the Commission adopted a yardstick of four days, with any period of detention exceeding 96 hours being considered a breach of Article 5(3): see eg 11256/84, *Egue v France* (1988) DR 57, 47 (domestic law which permits detention up to four days in principle in conformity); and cf the earlier decision in 2894/66, *X v Netherlands* (1966) YB 9, 564 at 569. Early Court judgments concerned instances of clear violations: eg *McGoff v Sweden* (1984) A 83, para 27 (interval of 15 days), and the three Dutch military criminal procedures cases where applicants were held for periods between seven and 14 days before being brought before a judge where the Court considered that, 'even taking account of the exigencies of military life', such periods were in excess of what was permissible: *De Jong, Baljet and Van den Brink v*

Netherlands (1984) A 77, paras 52–53; *Van der Sluijs, Zuiderveld and Klappe v Netherlands* (1984) A 78, para 49; and *Duinhof and Duijf v Netherlands* (1984) A 79, para 41. In *Brogan and Others v United Kingdom* (1988) A 145-B, paras 61–62, there had been failures to involve any judicial official of any kind, let alone 'promptly': the shortest period of detention had lasted four days and six hours, a period which the Court indicated in any case would have been in excess of that permitted by Art 5. Cf *Sakik and Others v Turkey* 1997-VII, para 45 (in light of *Brogan and Others*, even if suspicions concerned terrorist activities, it was not possible to consider detention without judicial intervention lasting 12 and 14 days as appropriate). Following upon the Court's decision in *Brogan*, the United Kingdom Government made use of the power contained in Art 15 to derogate from its Convention obligations under para (3): see further para **4.147** above.

2   *İpek and Others v Turkey* (3 February 2009), para 36 (strict time constraint imposed for detention without judicial control amounted to a maximum of four days). See also *Taş v Turkey* (14 November 2000), para 86 (30 days' incommunicado detention authorised by the public prosecutor was incompatible with paras (3) and (4)); and *O'Hara v United Kingdom* 2001-X, at para 46 ('detention periods exceeding four days for terrorist suspects [are not] compatible with the requirement of prompt judicial control'). Several other cases have found violations of pre-trial detention by the Turkish authorities: eg *Demir and Others v Turkey* 1998-VI, paras 39–58 (23 and 16 days; not strictly required by Art 15 derogation relied upon by the state). In relation to Scottish practice, the Committee for the Prevention of Torture noted in one of its reports that 'at least in theory, a person arrested very early on a Friday morning might not be taken before a court until the following Tuesday morning, were the Monday to be a court holiday': CPT/Inf (96) 11, at para 278. Following entry into force of the Scotland Act 1998, Scottish courts sat on 26 December 2000 and 2 January 2001 (both of which were Tuesdays) so as to address this problem in part.

3   4960/71, *X v Belgium* (1972) CD 42, 49 at 55 (delay of five days acceptable in the special circumstances where the prisoner needed hospitalisation). But note *Egmez v Cyprus* 2000-XII, para 90 (judicial hearing which took place in a hospital satisfied Art 5(3) requirement).

4   *Rigopoulos v Spain* (dec) 1999–II (arrest of captain of a ship at sea two weeks' sailing from the nearest Spanish territory; delay of 16 days in bringing the suspect before a judge in all the circumstances did not constitute a violation of Art 5(3): inadmissible); and *Medvedyev and Others v France* [GC] 2010-…, paras 127–134 (interception of ship flying the Cambodian flag by French authorities, but no appearance before a judicial officer until after 15 or 16 days' deprivation of liberty: no violation as it had been materially impossible to bring the applicants physically before a judge or other legal officer any more promptly, and police custody for two days in some cases and three days in others had been justified by the needs of the investigation and for interpreters in wholly exceptional circumstances).

5   *Kandzhov v Bulgaria* (6 November 2008), paras 65–67 (detention of a minor on charges of non-violent offences for three days and 23 hours before being brought before a judge: violation of the 'promptness' requirement of Art 5(3) as the police had not involved a prosecutor for at least 24 hours and the prosecutor had ordered further detention for 72 hours without giving adequate reasons, there having been no special difficulties or exceptional circumstances which would have prevented the applicant appearing before a judge much sooner, particularly in light of the dubious legal grounds for the detention).

6   *İpek and Others v Turkey* (3 February 2009), paras 34–38.

'Judicial officer'

4.204 The provision refers to a 'judge or other officer authorised by law to exercise judicial power', and thus a certain amount of choice in the ordering of arrangements is available to domestic legal systems. The essential requirements are laid down in *Schiesser v Switzerland,* where the applicant had been detained on remand and brought before a local district attorney who had decided that he should be remanded in custody pending trial. The issue arose whether the district attorney was 'an officer authorised by law to exercise judicial power'. The European Court of Human Rights considered that arrangements for a 'judicial officer' for this purpose had to satisfy three conditions:

(i) independence of the parties (although this did not preclude an 'officer' being subordinate in some degree to other judges or 'officers' as long as they themselves enjoyed similar independence);

(ii) the requirement to follow appropriate judicial procedures in hearing the case; and

(iii) discharge of the tasks of 'reviewing the circumstances militating for or against detention, of deciding, by reference to legal criteria, whether there are reasons to justify detention and of ordering release if there are no such reasons'[1].

---

1   *Schiesser v Switzerland* (1979) A 34, para 31; see too *Assenov and Others v Bulgaria* 1998-VIII, paras 144–150 ('investigator' before whom an accused was brought lacked the power to make legally binding decisions as to detention or release and thus was not sufficiently independent); and *Moulin v France* (23 November 2010), paras 46–62 (appearance before public prosecutor after two days did not satisfy Art 5(3) as he was under authority of executive). Cf *Allen v United Kingdom* (30 March 2010), paras 50–52 (a judge does not cease to 'exercise judicial power' simply because a decision concerning bail is open to appeal).

4.205 The first criterion requires that independence of the parties must both exist and also be seen to exist because of the need to inspire and maintain public confidence in the criminal process[1]. The matter is of most relevance in continental jurisdictions with inquisitorial systems of justice, or in military justice procedures, or where the office of prosecutor is entrusted with wide responsibilities. In *Skoogström v Sweden,* for example, the Commission considered the arrangements for the Swedish public prosecutor had not fulfilled any of these requirements: first, he combined both investigatory and prosecution roles; secondly, he did not himself hear the individual; and thirdly, there were doubts as to whether his decisions were taken with reference to legal criteria[2]. In *Hood v United Kingdom,* the applicant had been arrested and brought before his commanding officer and held in detention for some four months before being tried by a court-martial. The Court ruled that the powers and position of the commanding officer (who was responsible for discipline and for determining the necessity of pre-trial detention but who could also play a central role in any subsequent prosecution) were such that he could not be regarded as independent of the parties at the relevant time; further, the Court agreed that misgivings about the commanding officer's impartiality were also objectively justified[3].

---

1   *Huber v Switzerland* (1990) A 188, para 43; *Brincat v Italy* (1992) A 249-A, paras 17–21. Cf *Ilijkov v Bulgaria* (26 July 2001), para 97 (the mere fact that a trial judge has earlier taken decisions concerning the applicant's detention on remand will not in itself justify concerns that he lacks impartiality since normally the questions addressed under Art 5 are not the same

as those arising in respect of his final judgment, and '[s]uspicion and a formal finding of guilt are not to be treated as being the same').

2   *Skoogström v Sweden* (1984) A 83 (friendly settlement at Court stage: opinion of the Commission, paras 73–83). See also *Niedbała v Poland* (4 July 2000), paras 48–57 (public prosecutors combined investigative and prosecutorial roles along with acting as guardian of the public interest: insufficient guarantees of independence).

3   *Hood v United Kingdom* [GC] 1999-I, paras 52–61. See too *Stephen Jordan v United Kingdom* (14 March 2000), paras 26–30. British law has now been amended: Armed Forces Act 1996. For earlier military justice cases, see *De Jong, Baljet and Van den Brink, v Netherlands* (1984) A 77, paras 40, 48–51; *van der Sluijs, Zuiderveld and Klappe v Netherlands* (1984) A 78, paras 43–46; and *Duinhof and Duijf v Netherlands* (1984) A 79, paras 34–42.

4.206 The second and third of the *Schiesser* criteria concern procedural and substantive requirements. The judge or 'officer' is expected to review all the circumstances of the case and decide whether continuation of detention is justified in accordance with legal criteria. This is a specific obligation which cannot be made dependent upon the accused making a request for release[1]. In *Aquilina v Malta*, the parties disputed whether the magistrate before whom the applicant appeared had enjoyed the power to order release of his own motion, but even assuming the magistrate had indeed been able to do so, the magistrate had not been able to consider all the relevant factors required by paragraph (3), for this review 'must be sufficiently wide to encompass the various circumstances militating for or against detention'[2]. Further, and crucially, the judge must also enjoy the authority to order release of the detainee, a fundamental prerequisite of Aricle 5 which recognises the importance of judicial oversight of interference with an individual's right to liberty of person[3].

1   *Aquilina v Malta* [GC] 1999-III, paras 47–55.
2   *Aquilina v Malta* [GC] 1999-III, para 49.
3   See paras **4.208–4.209** below.

Article 5(3): Pre-trial detention – (ii) trial within a reasonable time or release pending trial

4.207 The aim of the second guarantee contained in Article 5(3) is to ensure that the state does not unreasonably prolong any pre-trial detention. The text cannot be read, however, as providing states with the alternative of trial within a reasonable time or of granting provisional release[1]. 'The reasonableness of the time spent by an accused person in detention up to the beginning of his trial must be assessed in relation to the very fact of his detention. Until conviction he must be presumed innocent, and the purpose [of Article 5(3)] is essentially to require his provisional release once his continuing detention ceases to be reasonable[2]'. In respect of minors, the use of pre-trial detention should only be used as a measure of last resort, and any use of such detention must be as short as possible[3].

1   *Wemhoff v Germany* (1968) A 7, Law.

2   *Neumeister v Austria* (1968) A 8, Law.

3   *Nart v Turkey* (6 May 2008), paras 29–35 (pre-trial detention of a 17-year-old for 48 days in an adult prison: violation of Art 5 on account of international standards; further, minors must be kept apart from adults).

Power to order release

4.208 A judge or judicial officer must be able to order the conditional release of the accused pending trial with 'due expedition'[1]. In this respect, there was an issue for Scots law, which traditionally limited the right of releasing a person pending trial on murder to the Lord Advocate or to the High Court since, until the enactment of the Bail, Judicial Appointments, etc (Scotland) Act 2000, the sheriff before whom the detainee was brought had no power to order bail. The issue has been of relevance in other cases involving Britain. In *Ireland v United Kingdom*, the European Court of Human Rights remarked that, even had the applicants appeared promptly before the 'commissioners' whose task was to rule on executive detention orders, the state would still not have complied with Article 5(3) since these officials had no power to require release from custody[2]. More particularly, in *Caballero v United Kingdom*, the Government conceded that English law's prohibition of release on bail of any person charged with a designated crime where the individual had previously been imprisoned for any offence of a similar level of seriousness was a violation of Article 5(3)[3]. Subsequently, in *SBC v United Kingdom*, the Court decided to examine the matter itself without relying upon a similar governmental concession. It approved the Commission's reasoning in its report in *Caballero* that a crucial feature of the paragraph's safeguards was that of judicial control of executive interference with an individual's right to liberty of person. In order to minimise the risk of arbitrariness in pre-trial detention, the judge 'having heard the accused himself, must examine all the facts arguing for and against the existence of a genuine requirement of public interest justifying, with due regard for the presumption of innocence, a departure from the rule of respect for the accused's liberty', and this implied that a judge must have the power to order the release of an accused[4].

1   *McKay v United Kingdom* [GC] 2006-X, at para 46.
2   *Ireland v United Kingdom* (1978) A 25, para 199.
3   *Caballero v United Kingdom* [GC] 2000-II, paras 18–21.
4   *SBC v United Kingdom* (19 June 2001), paras 19–24 at para 22 (violations of Art 5(3) and (5) established).

4.209 However, as the Grand Chamber made clear in *McKay v United Kingdom*, it is not strictly necessary (although still both good practice and highly desirable) that the judicial officer before whom a detainee is brought 'promptly' for the purpose of ascertaining the lawfulness of the deprivation of liberty also has the competence to consider the issue of release on bail. In this case, the question of whether the applicant should have been released on bail only took place some 24 hours after his first appearance which had taken place before another court. In determining that the requirements of Article 5(3) had been met as the issue of release had been examined with the requisite level of due expediency, the Court noted that 'there is no reason in principle why the issues [of the lawfulness of detention, and whether to grant bail] cannot be dealt with by two judicial officers, within the requisite time-frame', particularly since 'as a matter of interpretation, it cannot be required that the examination of bail take place with any more speed than is demanded of the first automatic review [of the lawfulness of detention], which the Court has identified as being a maximum four days'[1].

1   *McKay v United Kingdom* [GC] 2006-X, paras 41–51 at para 47.

Conditional release on guarantees to appear for trial

4.210 Continued reasonable suspicion is necessary for the continuation of pre-trial detention, but it is not in itself adequate justification. While Article 5(3) does not imply any right to release on bail as such, it places an obligation upon the state to offer release on whatever terms are required to secure the presence of the accused at any subsequent trial. This is particularly so whenever the sole reason for detaining an individual on remand is the risk of his absconding[1]. In other words, an accused must be released if conditional release involving bail or other guarantees would reduce the risk of absconding[2]. Such guarantees are not restricted to the deposit of a monetary surety[3]. In calculating the requisite amount or determining the guarantees to be secured, the state authorities may take into account any relevant personal factors of the individual (for example, his means and his relationship with the person supplying security); additionally, in exceptional cases, it may be appropriate in determining the conditions for release to consider the professional environment in which the alleged offence has occurred[4]. The issue is 'the degree of confidence that is possible that the prospect of loss of the security or of action against the guarantors in case of his non-appearance at the trial will act as a sufficient deterrent to dispel any wish on his part to abscond'[5], rather than any financial amount involved in the case. To this end, the individual must co-operate by providing information on his financial means[6], but this does not necessarily absolve the state authorities from considering other relevant information which they themselves possess[7]. Bail may only be required as long as the reasons justifying detention prevail[8].

1   *Wemhoff v Germany* (1968) A 7, Law, para 15 (choice of conditions to be imposed will normally in financial cases involve the deposit of bail or monetary security).

2   *Mangouras v Spain* [GC] 2010-..., para 79.

3   10670/83, *Schmid v Austria* (1995) DR 44, 195.

4   *Mangouras v Spain* [GC] 2010-..., paras 82–93 (setting of bail at €3 million, a sum likely to exceed the applicant's own personal capacity to pay, but taking into account also the seriousness of the maritime pollution and the 'professional environment' – ie, the relationship between the applicant and the shipowner's insurers: no violation).

5   *Neumeister v Austria* (1968) A 8, Law, para 14.

6   8224/78, *Bonnechaux v Switzerland* (1979) DR 18, 100.

7   8339/78, *Schertenleib v Switzerland* (1980) DR 23, 37.

8   *Mangouras v Spain* [GC] 2010-..., para 79.

Release or 'trial within a reasonable time'

4.211 The quality of the evidence used initially to justify detention on 'reasonable suspicion' may in time become weaker and hence insufficient to sustain the loss of liberty[1]. However, the continuation of 'reasonable suspicion' will be insufficient in itself to justify the continuation of pre-trial detention. 'The persistence of a reasonable suspicion that the person arrested has committed an offence is a condition *sine qua non* for the lawfulness of the continued detention, but after a certain lapse of time it no longer suffices'[2] since the grounds for the continuing refusal of release pending trial also require to be both relevant and sufficient. In *Ječius v Lithuania,* for example, the only reasons adduced by the state for the persistence of the applicant's detention on remand on suspicion of murder and which had lasted almost 15 months had been the gravity of the offence and the strength of evidence against him. For the European Court of Human Rights, while the reasonableness of the suspicion may have initially justified the detention, it could not in itself constitute a 'relevant and sufficient' ground for the continuation of the custody for this length of time and, accordingly, there had been a violation of the guarantee[3]. Domestic courts must consequently 'examine all the circumstances arguing for or against the existence of a genuine requirement of public interest justifying, with due regard to the principle of the presumption of innocence, a departure from the rule of respect for individual liberty and set them out in their decisions on the applications for release'[4], and not simply apply a presumption that detention is justified solely on account of the gravity of the charges[5]. Relevant reasons justifying continuing detention include the danger that the accused if liberated would suppress evidence or bring pressure to bear on witnesses[6] or collude with accomplices[7] or flee to escape justice[8], or commit additional offences[9], or that his release would provoke public disorder[10] or place the accused in a position of danger from others[11]. On the other hand, his state of health is not a relevant factor under Article 5[12]. It is crucial that due regard be given to arguments for or against release. Reasons must not be 'general and abstract' or simply replicate a stereotypical formula[13]. Courts must also consider whether measures other than detention would ensure the presence of an individual at his trial[14]. Since the sufficiency of such reasons may change with time, they must be able to be challenged periodically in accordance with paragraph (4)[15].

1   Cf *Labita v Italy* [GC] 2000-IV, paras 156–161 (detention initially justified upon uncorroborated hearsay statements made by a former member of the Mafia, but no further evidence to corroborate the allegations had been uncovered during inquiries, and no account had been taken of the fact that the accusations against the applicant had been based on evidence which had become weaker rather than stronger).

2   *Ječius v Lithuania* 2000-IX, at para 93; cf *Punzelt v Czech Republic* (25 April 2000), paras 71–82 (detention pending extradition on charges of fraud and forgery: no violation on account of the refusal to release on bail).

3   *Ječius v Lithuania* 2000-IX, para 94 (the Court noted that the suspicion in any case had not been proved substantiated by the trial court which had acquitted the applicant).

4   *Tomasi v France* (1992) A 241-A, at para 84.

5   *Ilijkov v Bulgaria* (26 July 2001), paras 81–87 at para 87: 'by failing to address concrete relevant facts and by relying solely on a statutory presumption based on the gravity of the charges and which shifted to the accused the burden of proving that there was not even a hypothetical danger of absconding, re-offending or collusion, the authorities prolonged the applicant's detention on grounds which cannot be regarded as sufficient violation. See also *Kreps v Poland* (26 July 2001), paras 42–45 (reliance by the state upon the serious nature of the offences and the need to ensure proper conduct of the trial without adequate consideration of relevant factors recognised by Convention case law: violation). For domestic consideration, see *R (O) v Crown Court at Harrow* [2007] 1 AC 249 and (in relation to the Criminal Procedure (Scotland) Act 1995, s 23D) *M v Watson* 2009 SLT 1030. See also UfR 1992.877 H [Denmark] (determination by court that pre-trial detention of young person who had confessed to manslaughter should be continued after six-month period owing to the likelihood of disorder if released in light of the intensive press coverage and the severity of the crime: overturned by the Supreme Court following the *Letellier v France* and *Kemmache v France (nos 1 and 2)* judgments requiring a court to consider the specific circumstances of the case and not to assume release would provoke public disorder solely on account of the gravity of the charges).

6   *Wemhoff v Germany* (1968) A 7, Law, paras 13–14; cf *Letellier v France* (1991) A 207, paras 37–39 (any initial and genuine fear of pressure being brought to bear on witnesses would diminish with the passing of time).

7   *Ringeisen v Austria* (1971) A 13, paras 105–106; *IA v France* 1998-VII, para 109.

8   *Wemhoff v Germany* (1968) A 7, Law, paras 13–14; *Neumeister v Austria* (1968) A 8, Law, paras 9–12; *Letellier v France* (1991) A 207, paras 40–43. See also Trechsel 'Liberty and Security of Person in Macdonald, Matscher, and Petzold, eds, *The European System for the Protection of Human Rights* (1993), pp 277–344 at pp 280–281 for the suggestion that holding foreigners in detention on remand longer than nationals does not constitute discrimination within the meaning of Art 14 'insofar as it may be reasonably assumed that the danger of absconding is greater for foreigners than for nationals' and thus there is objective justification for any differentiation.

9   *Stögmüller v Austria* (1969) A 9, Law, paras 13–14; *Matznetter v Austria* (1969) A 10, Law, paras 7–9.

10 *Letellier v France* (1991) A 207, paras 47–51.

11 Eg *IA v France* 1998-VII, para 108.

12 *Kudła v Poland* [GC] 2000-XI, para 93; *Jabłoński v Poland* (21 December 2000), para 82. Cf para **4.117** above for discussion of Art 3 considerations.

13 *Smirnova v Russia* 2003 IX, paras 56–71 (violations of Art 5(1) and (3) on account of the repeated detention of the applicants in the course of a criminal investigation on the basis of insufficiently reasoned decisions; further, release must be accompanied by the return of any documentation such as an identity card which is indispensable in everyday life in the Russian Federation for the completion of even mundane tasks). See also *Giorgi Nikolaishvili v Georgia* 2009-..., paras 72–80 (pre-trial detention of witness in a murder case using standard, pre-printed reasons for remand on other unrelated charges after he attended voluntarily at a police station, and partly purportedly justified on the basis that his release might hamper the establishment of the truth in the murder case: violation of Art 5(3)).

14 *Iłowiecki v Poland* (4 October 2001), para 64. See also *Lelievre v Belgium* (8 November 2007), paras 92–108 (pre-trial detention for almost eight years before the start of a trial despite the review of continued detention on a monthly basis: while continued detention had been justified by the continuing existence of plausible reasons for suspicion, and the risk of absconding had remained throughout the proceedings, there had been a failure of the authorities to consider alternatives to continued pre-trial detention: violation of Art 5(3)).

15   See para **4.220** below.

4.212 'Trial within a reasonable time' under Article 5(3) will thus initially involve assessment of whether pre-trial detention was justified by reasons which were both relevant and sufficient, but the European Court of Human Rights in addition will consider whether the proceedings have been unduly prolonged by avoidable delay[1]. Inactivity on the part of prosecuting officials will suggest a lack of due diligence[2], but the requirement 'must not stand in the way of the efforts of the judges to clarify fully the facts in issue, to give both the defence and the prosecution all facilities for putting forward their evidence and stating their cases and to pronounce judgment only after careful reflection'[3]. The behaviour of the applicant himself may be a factor in the prolonging of pre-trial detention[4].

1   *Wemhoff v Germany* (1968) A 7, Law, para 16. The safeguard replicates to some extent the guarantee to a hearing 'within a reasonable time' under Art 6(1), but special diligence is expected where an accused is in detention: *Herczegfalvy v Austria* (1992) A 244, para 71.

2   Eg *Assenov and Others v Bulgaria* 1998-VIII, paras 151–158 (12-month period in which virtually no action was taken by investigatory authorities); and *Punzelt v Czech Republic* (25 April 2000), paras 71–82 (reasons for detention which lasted over 30 months were relevant and sufficient, but lack of due diligence on the part of the courts). For domestic discussion of delay attributable to an accused's choice of lawyer, see case Rt 1996–1366-H [Norway] (since trial within reasonable time was not possible owing to the accused's own exercise of his right to free choice of legal assistance, no violation of Art 5(3) was established, the accused being denied release pending re-trial).

3   *Wemhoff v Germany* (1968) A 7, Law, at para 17.

4   8339/78, *Schertenleib v Switzerland* (1980) DR 23, 137 at para 185–187.

4.213 The question of time held on remand is unlikely often to cause difficulty in Scots law on account of the 140-day rule[1]. In practical terms, the approach taken to determination of the 'reasonableness' of time spent in pre-trial detention in other European countries[2] continues to be a significant weakness in Strasbourg jurisprudence. It seems to reflect an unwillingness to impose upon states the basic task of making sufficient resources available to ensure effective and speedy justice. In several European countries, the high percentage of remand prisoners (in some cases, over 40 per cent of the total prison population) is not considered unreasonable[3]. Further, pre-trial detention in excess of four years can in some cases be deemed acceptable[4], and even those judgments which condemn particular lengthy detention hardly encourage optimism that this aspect of Article 5 is of utility[5], although there is now perhaps some indication of a more demanding approach, at least in ensuring that alternatives to pre-trial detention are considered in exceptional cases[6]. Still absent, though, is any suggestion of a maximum period of pre-trial detention beyond which continuing detention is likely to be unacceptable as, for example, with the 140-day rule in Scots law. There is still an unfortunate contrast between the concern expressed for the initial safeguard of a 'prompt' appearance before a judicial officer under the first part of Article 5(3), and the protracted investigations permitted thereafter. The Court's reasoning can be criticised on a number of grounds. First, if 'the justifiable length of an investigation' was 'automatically co-extensive with the justifiable length of pre-trial detention', then 'it would be possible to conceive of a case of such extreme complexity as to justify a detention of, say, ten years or more'[7]. In any case, 'complexity' here is primarily judged by reference to the efficiency and effectiveness of national law enforcement resources, while the harm which detention can occasion to the resources available to an accused for his defence does not appear to be taken into account. Secondly, the importance attached to the consideration that the period of pre-trial detention will probably be deducted from any sentence imposed on conviction (or at least taken into account) does not sit altogether happily with the presumption of innocence. Thirdly, it is still more difficult to understand why the full exercise of an applicant's rights under domestic law permitting him to seek to secure release or to refuse to co-operate with investigating or prosecuting authorities should justify even lengthier detention[8]. There is now heightened awareness as to the impact upon individuals and the prison system of the growing use of pre-trial detention, but as yet no significant change in the approach adopted by the Court[9].

---

1   On the situation where an accused is committed in respect of one offence and is later committed in respect of another offence, causing the 110-day (now 140-day) period to run afresh (*Ross v HM Advocate* 1990 SCCR 182), some assistance may be gained from *R (Wardle) v Crown Court at Leeds* [2002] 1 AC 754 which considered Art 5(3) in the context of a broadly analogous situation under English law. See also *Wardle v United Kingdom* (dec) (27 March 2003) (nine-month period of pre-trial detention justified by reasons which were relevant and sufficient; the case was complex and the evidence voluminous but the authorities had acted with due dispatch: inadmissible).

2   Continental systems may provide that execution of a sentence cannot take place until after disposal of any pending appeal, and label any detention after conviction but pending determination of appeal as a continuation of pre-trial detention. Cf *B v Austria* (1990) A 175, paras 34–40 (as the trial court had pronounced guilt, given a statement of its principal reasons, had imposed a sentence of imprisonment and also ordered continuing detention pending disposal of the appeal, this detention fell to be considered as deprivation of liberty after conviction).

3   See further Council of Europe *Penal Statistics 2009*, doc PC-CP (2010) 3, table 5 (pre-trial detention rates in 2009 per 100,000 of population (excluding Lichtenstein) range from 2 (FYRO Macedonia) to 64 (Malta); the figures for Scotland, England and Wales, and Northern Ireland were 11, 14 and 37 respectively). For further discussion, see Murdoch 'Détention préventive et « Procès dans un Délai Raisonnable » l'Article 5.3 de la Convention européenne des Droits de l'Homme et l'Effectivité de la Protection Domestique' in Flauss (ed) *Le Effectivite des Recours Internes au Service de l'Application de la Convention Europeenne des Droits de l'Homme* (2007), pp 26–69.

4   *W v Switzerland* (1993) A 254-A, paras 31–43. See too *Contrada v Italy* 1998-V, paras 54–68 (reasons for 31-month detention of senior police officer accused by Mafia informants of serious crimes considered relevant and sufficient throughout this period). See too *Van der Tang v Spain* (1995) A 321, paras 60–75 (while the Court would have welcomed 'more detailed reasoning' for the reasons for pre-trial detention, there was still an 'evident and significant risk' of absconding; and the state was also entitled to conjoin the cases of co-accused, even although the applicant's case itself did not appear particularly complex).

5   Cf *Scott v Spain* 1996-VI, paras 75–84 (pre-trial detention of fouryears and 16 days not justified: while real risk of absconding, the case was not complex and special diligence had not been observed); *Muller v France* 1997-II, paras 35–48 (four-year detention of individual who had immediately accepted guilt to allow conjoining of case with co-accused 'necessary and sufficient' reason; but some undue delay on part of state authorities in the circumstances*); IA*

v France 1998-VII (63-month detention period deemed violation of Art 5(3)); *Vaccaro v Italy* (16 November 2000), at para 44 ('the considerable duration' of the pre-trial detention 'should have been based on particularly convincing reasons'); and *Jabłoński v Poland* (21 December 2000) (detention on remand in excess of 57 months considered excessive). However, see *Belchev v Bulgaria* (8 April 2004) at para 82: 'The Court is not unmindful of the fact that the majority of length-of-detention cases decided in its judgments concern longer periods of deprivation of liberty and that against that background four months and fourteen days may be regarded as a relatively short period in detention. Article 5(3) of the Convention, however, cannot be seen as authorising pre-trial detention unconditionally provided that it lasts no longer than a certain period. Justification for any period of detention, no matter how short, must be convincingly demonstrated by the authorities. That has not happened in this case'.

6   Eg *Lelievre v Belgium* (8 November 2007), paras 97–104 (pre-trial detention for almost eight years before the start of a trial despite review of continued detention on a monthly basis: while continued detention had been justified by the continuing existence of plausible reasons for suspicion and the risk of absconding had remained throughout the proceedings, there had been a failure of the authorities to consider alternatives to continued pre-trial detention: violation). See also *Kauczor v Poland* (3 February 2009), paras 55–62 (structural problem of length of pre-trial detention: consistent and long-term efforts required in light of Art 5(3)).

7   Dissenting judgment of Judge Cremona in *Matznetter v Austria* (1969) A 10.

8   Eg 8224/78, *Bonnechaux v Switzerland* (1979) DR 18, 100 at 147.

9   See Murdoch *The Treatment of Prisoners: European Standards* (2006), pp 175–176.

DECISIONS OF DOMESTIC COURTS AND LEGISLATIVE REFORM IN RELATION TO BAIL

4.214 Scottish law and practice relating to bail underwent significant change in response to the incorporation of Article 5(3). Certain changes were made by the Bail, Judicial Appointments, etc (Scotland) Act 2000. In particular, the Act placed a duty on the sheriff or judge to consider whether to grant bail at the accused's first appearance in court without the need for an application, so as to satisfy the need for an automatic judicial review of detention; it repealed provisions which precluded the sheriff from considering bail where a person had been charged with or convicted of murder or treason, or where a person had been charged with or convicted of attempted murder, culpable homicide, rape or attempted rape and had a previous conviction for one of these offences or for murder or manslaughter; it provided that where an accused was already in custody for another matter, the court was required to consider bail for the new offence; and it enabled the accused to appeal to the High Court against the decision of a sheriff to refuse bail on first appearance or the refusal of an application made prior to committal, bringing the right of appeal of a person arrested on petition into line with that of a person charged on complaint and with that of the prosecutor.

4.215 A further change was effected by the decision of the High Court of Justiciary in *Burn, Petitioner*. The petitioner's application for bail had been opposed by the Crown on the ground that it had further inquiries to carry out which would be prejudiced by his release on bail. They did not give any further information about the inquiries. The sheriff refused bail, in accordance with the approach laid down in an earlier decision of the High Court. In the instant case, the High Court held that the previous approach did not meet the requirements of Article 5(3), as it effectively enjoined the sheriff not to consider the merits of the accused's continued detention for himself but to defer to the statement by the Crown. The court held that in future the Crown must provide sufficient general information relating to the particular case to allow the sheriff to consider the merits of their motion that the accused should be committed to prison and detained there for further examination. It is not necessary for the Crown to disclose operational details. On the other hand, where for example the Crown opposed bail on the ground of the risk that the accused would interfere with witnesses, it should be in a position to explain the basis for that fear. Where opposition to bail is based on some such ground and the relevant inquiry is completed before the date for further examination (ie within eight days), the Crown should bring the matter back before the sheriff so that he can, if so advised, order the accused's release from custody[1].

1   *Burn, Petitioner* 2000 JC 403.

4.216 The effect of Article 5 on the English law governing bail was considered with care in *R (Director of Public Prosecutions) v Havering Magistrates' Court*. The court noted that the breach of a bail condition did not in itself constitute a justification for detention under Article 5. The breach of a condition might be some evidence, even powerful evidence, of a relevant risk arising. Article 5 did not require proof of material facts by the production of evidence or subject to cross-examination of witnesses. What was necessary was that the court should come to an honest and rational opinion on the material put before it, taking proper account of the quality of that material and ensuring that the defendant had a full and fair opportunity to comment on and answer that material[1].

1   *R (Director of Public Prosecutions) v Havering Magistrates' Court* [2001] 1 WLR 805. See also in respect of interpretation of English law (Criminal Justice and Public Order Act 1994, s 25) the case of *R (O) v Crown Court at Harrow* [2007] 1 AC 249 (provisions were not incompatible with Art 5(3) as '[they serve] merely to 'remind' the courts of the risks normally posed by those to whom s 25 applies and 'will merely assist the court to adopt the proper approach' in relation to bail').

Article 5(4): Judicial determination of the lawfulness of deprivation of liberty

4.217 The inspiration for Article 5(4), which allows a detainee access to a court to challenge the lawfulness of the deprivation of liberty, is found in the remedy of *habeas corpus* in Anglo-American jurisprudence. The guarantee involves provision of review of both procedural and substantive requirements of domestic law together with the reasonableness of the suspicion justifying the continuing loss of liberty. However, 'Article 5(4) does not guarantee a right to judicial review of such a scope as to empower the court, on all aspects of the case including questions of pure expediency, to substitute its own discretion for that of the decision-making authority, although the review should be wide enough to bear on those conditions which are essential for the 'lawful' detention of a person according to Article 5(1)'[1]. Nor does it imply a right of appeal against a decision imposing or continuing detention[2], although where domestic law does indeed provide such a right of appeal, the appellate body itself must comply with the requirements of the paragraph[3]. 'Lawfulness', quite simply, has the meaning given to it under Article 5(1), and thus this is tested 'in the light not only of the requirements of domestic law, but also of the text of the ECHR, the general principles embodied therein and the aims of the restrictions permitted by Article 5(1)'[4]. All forms of deprivation of liberty are covered by the guarantee[5], for the essential purpose is to provide the individual with an effective review of the legality of his original detention and any continuing detention. Periodic review of deprivation of liberty must be available during pre-trial detention[6], and also after conviction and sentence where the sentence contains any element which is indeterminate[7]. This guarantee applies concurrently with paragraph (3) in respect of those detained on suspicion of having committed an offence or to prevent commission or flight under paragraph (1)(c)[8], but if the national authorities release the individual before it is practicable for any hearing to occur (as, for example, where there has been detention followed by immediate expulsion from a state's territory), the applicant will be deemed not to have suffered any harm under this heading and will be unable to use para (4) to challenge the legality of the original deprivation of liberty[9]. The procedures for challenge must have a judicial character and provide appropriate safeguards[10]. Once the legal justification for detention ceases, the detainee must be released without undue delay[11]. The burden of proof in proceedings challenging the continuing lawfulness of detention will lie with the authorities rather than with the detainee[12].

---

1   *E v Norway* (1990) A 181-A, at para 50.

2   *Ječius v Lithuania* 2000-IX, at para 100: 'the provision speaks of 'proceedings' and not of appeals'.

3   *Toth v Austria* (1991) A 224, para 84; *Graužinis v Lithuania* (10 October 2000), para 32.

4   *Brogan and Others v United Kingdom* (1988) A 145-B, para 65; *E v Norway* (1990) A 181-A, para 49.

5   *De Wilde, Ooms and Versyp v Belgium ('Vagrancy cases')* (1971) A 12, para 73. For recent discussion, see eg *SD v Greece* (11 June 2009), paras 72–22 (domestic law had not afforded the applicant any opportunity of obtaining a decision from the domestic courts on the lawfulness of his detention as it did not permit direct review of the lawfulness of the detention of aliens who could only be detained with a view to deportation: violation of Art 5(4)).

6   Cf *Assenov and Others v Bulgaria* 1998-VIII, paras 162–165 (domestic law only permitted remand prisoners one opportunity to challenge lawfulness of detention; lack of any further opportunity to have continuing detention (of two years) determined led to violation).

7   Where a fixed sentence of imprisonment is imposed for the purposes of punishment, the supervision required by Art 5(4) is incorporated in that court decision: *V v United Kingdom* [GC] 1999-IX, para 199. See also 32072/96, *Mansell v United Kingdom* (2 July 1997). See further para **4.218** below.These decisions were applied in relation to the recall of a prisoner released on licence in *Varey v The Scottish Ministers* 2001 SC 162, and in England, in *R (Sim) v Parole Board and Another* [2004] QB 1288.

8   *De Jong, Baljet and Van den Brink v Netherlands* (1984) A 77, para 57.

9 7376/76, *X and Y v Sweden* (1976) DR 7, 123. Art 5(4) is in general regarded as the *lex specialis* concerning complaints of unlawful deprivation of liberty, and thus where a *detained* applicant also invokes Art 13 (which requires an effective remedy to be provided in domestic law to challenge arguable breaches of the ECHR), the Court will normally declare the Art 13 issue inadmissible if it has admitted the Art 5(4) complaint for further determination: see eg *O'Hara v United Kingdom* (dec) (14 March 2000).

10 See *R (Director of Public Prosecutions) v Havering Magistrates' Court* [2001] 1 WLR 805; *R (Brooke) v Parole Board* [2008] 1 WLR 1950. In *R (D) v Secretary of State for the Home Department* [2003] 1 WLR 1315 it was held that review in accordance with Art 5(4) must be available as of right and not merely as a matter of administrative practice. The prisoner need not be present in person at the hearing, provided he is represented: *DL v HM Advocate* 2007 SCCR 472.

11 Cf *Quinn v France* (1995) A 311, paras 39–43 (a court ordered release of the applicant but this was delayed to allow the public prosecutor to be notified; the Court accepted that while some delay in executing such an instruction is understandable, the particular delay (of 11 hours) resulted in a violation of Art 5(1)).

12 *Hutchison Reid v United Kingdom* 2003-IV, paras 69–74 at para 71 (requirement upon detained patient in terms of Mental Health (Scotland) Act 1984 to show they were no longer suffering from a mental disorder requiring detention, but in light of Art 5(1)(e)'s requirement that the authorities show an individual satisfies the conditions for detention, and thus 'that it is however for the authorities to prove that an individual satisfies the conditions for compulsory detention, rather than the converse, may be regarded as implicit in the case-law': violation of Art 5(4)).

The notion of 'incorporated supervision'

4.218 The purpose of Article 5(4) is to secure judicial overview of the legality of deprivation of liberty. Where the particular detention has been ordered by a court, 'incorporated supervision' will be deemed to have taken place: that is, the responsibility for ensuring judicial scrutiny will be accepted as having been discharged by the original tribunal. The most straightforward example of 'incorporated supervision' will occur where a fixed term of imprisonment is imposed after 'conviction by a competent court' in terms of Article 5(1)(a); more complex issues may arise, however, where prisoners have been transferred between countries in terms of international agreements[1]. For incorporated supervision requirements to be satisfied, it is essential that the procedure adopted is of a judicial character which provides appropriate guarantees to the individual. In *De Wilde, Ooms and Versyp v Belgium*, the applicants had been brought before a magistrate who had placed them at the 'disposal' of the government in terms of vagrancy laws. The failure to provide a further review body having the attributes of a 'court' to allow review of the decisions of the magistrate (who was acting in an administrative capacity rather than as a judicial officer) resulted in a violation of the paragraph[2]. In *Winterwerp v Netherlands*, neither the original detention of the applicant ordered by the local mayor under mental health legislation nor the subsequent confirmation of the deprivation of liberty by the court afforded the applicant or any representative of his the opportunity to be heard, and there was thus no opportunity of testing the legality of detention[3]. In the related cases of *T v United Kingdom* and *V v United Kingdom*, the setting of the punitive 'tariff' element in an indeterminate sentence had been the responsibility of the Home Secretary rather than a task assigned to an independent tribunal and, accordingly, there had been a violation of fair hearing guarantees under Article 6. Further, on this account, it was not possible to conclude that the supervision required by Article 5(4) had been incorporated in the trial court's sentence[4].

1   See *Drozd and Janousek v France and Spain* (1992) A 240, paras 104–111; *Iribarne Pérez v France* (1995) A 325-C, paras 26–33. For domestic discussion, see *R (Giles) v Parole Board* [2003] 3 WLR 736.

2   *De Wilde, Ooms and Versyp v Belgium ('Vagrancy cases')* (1971) A 12, paras 76–80.

3   *Winterwerp v Netherlands* (1979) A 33, paras 54–61.

4   *T v United Kingdom* [GC] (16 December 1999), paras 105–121; *V v United Kingdom* [GC] 1999-IX, paras 106–122. The position of life prisoners is discussed at paras **4.225–4.228** below.

Periodic review of continuing detention

4.219 More significantly, Article 5(4) may require judicial scrutiny of the lawfulness of continuing pre-trial or post-conviction detention since the circumstances under which the original decision to detain was taken may have changed: for example, an individual may have ceased to qualify as 'dangerous' or 'of unsound mind'[1]. The form of deprivation of liberty involved will largely determine the regularity with which periodic review is required: review of pre-trial detention is called for at monthly intervals, but other forms of loss of liberty such as the committal of persons to a mental hospital may allow lengthier intervals between reviews[2]. Further, where the detention in question has followed upon conviction of a criminal offence, periodic review of continuing detention may still be called for. In the early case of *Van Droogenbroeck v Belgium*, the applicant had been sentenced to imprisonment for two years and in addition had been placed 'at the disposal of the government' for ten years as having a persistent tendency to crime. Since 'persistent tendency' and 'danger to society' were 'essentially relative concepts [which involved] monitoring the development of the offender's personality and behaviour in order to adapt his situation to favourable or unfavourable changes in his circumstances', periodic review was necessary[3]. Likewise, if a sentence of imprisonment contains an element which is indeterminate, Article 5(4) may demand periodic review to ensure that continuing detention continues to be lawful[4].

1   Cf *Soumare v France* 1998-V, para 38 (imposition of fine with imprisonment if in default; lawfulness of imprisonment was thus dependent upon applicant's solvency, a factor which could change through time, and thus periodic review of detention was required).

2   In case law, this matter strictly falls within the question as to the 'speedy' availability of review (see para **4.240** below).

3   *Van Droogenbroeck v Belgium* (1982) A 50, para 49. For domestic consideration, see *R (Giles) v Parole Board* [2004] 1 AC 1 (prisoner sentenced to extended determinate term for the protection of the public: no Art 5(4) requirement for review after punitive period expired, since detention in accordance with a lawful sentence of imprisonment for a determinate period, imposed by a judge on a prisoner for an offence of which he had been convicted, was justified

under Art 5(1) without the need for further reviews of detention under Art 5(4), which had been framed to protect persons against the arbitrary deprivation of liberty, as where decisions as to the length of detention passed from the court to the executive and there was a risk that the factors which informed the original decision would change with the passage of time).

4   See paras **4.221–4.222** and **4.225–4.228** below.

REVIEW OF PRE-TRIAL DETENTION

4.220 Review of pre-trial detention may be required at intervals of no more than one month because of the ECHR's insistence that detention on remand is to be strictly limited[1]. The review must permit consideration of both the continuing reasonableness of the suspicion which initially justified the deprivation of liberty as well as the relevancy and sufficiency of the grounds for refusal to release on bail. In *Ječius v Lithuania*, for example, although the appellate courts had noted that the lawfulness of the applicant's detention was open to question, they had failed to address his complaints and thus the applicant had been denied the opportunity of contesting the procedural and substantive conditions which had been essential for the continuing lawfulness of the pre-trial detention[2]. In relation to minors, the use of pre-trial detention should only in any event be used as a matter of last resort; where this is imposed, there is an expectation that it will be kept as short as possible[3].

1   *Bezicheri v Italy* (1989) A 164, para 21; *Assenov and Others v Bulgaria* 1998-VIII, at para 162 (review of pre-trial detention must be available 'at short intervals'); *Jabłoński v Poland* (21 December 2000), paras 91–94 at 94 (while a period of 43 days 'may prima facie appear not to be excessively long', in light of the circumstances this was considered an excessive delay).

2   *Ječius v Lithuania* 2000-IX, paras 101–102. See too *Graužinis v Lithuania* (10 October 2000), paras 53–55.

3   *Nart v Turkey* (6 May 2008), para 31 (pre-trial detention of a 17-year-old for 48 days in an adult prison: violation of Art 5).

MENTAL HEALTH DETENTION

4.221 Mental condition is perhaps the clearest example of a condition susceptible to change through time and which will thus call for periodic review at regular intervals[1]. Issues have arisen in relation to both the availability of review[2] and the nature of the safeguards available[3] in mental health cases[4], but whether the right to take proceedings exists may well depend upon careful categorisation of the deprivation of liberty. In *Silva Rocha v Portugal*, an individual who had been declared to be a danger to the public on account of a mental disorder had been placed in custody for a minimum of three years. While the trial court had concluded that the facts as established constituted aggravated homicide, it had also decided that the applicant could not be held criminally responsible for his actions and thus had ordered his placement in a psychiatric institution. Only at the end of the period of custody was he entitled under domestic law to take proceedings to test whether his mental condition required his continuing detention. For the Strasbourg

Court, the deprivation of liberty had been lawful both as a conviction within the meaning of Article 5(1)(a) and also as a 'security measure' applied to a 'person of unsound mind' in terms of paragraph (1)(e). The offence and the risk posed to others had justified the applicant's detention for at least three years, and the requirement of 'incorporated supervision' had been met at the time the detention was ordered by the trial court. It followed that only after the expiry of this period would the requirement of 'periodic review' be triggered. Earlier cases were distinguished on account of the specific findings in the present instance by the trial court of the individual's dangerousness and his likelihood of re-offending[5].

1   Cf *Megyeri v Germany* (1992) A 237-A, para 22 ('reasonable intervals' for mental health reviews not defined).

2   In 10213/82, *Gordon v United Kingdom* (1985) DR 47, 36 an individual confined to a mental hospital by a criminal court under the Mental Health (Scotland) Act 1960 challenged his return to a secure hospital after having spent a period in an ordinary mental hospital with leave privileges. Scots law did not make provision for periodic review of the need for continuing detention at the time when the application was made, a deficiency which had been condemned by the Court when it considered similar English legislation as failing to meet the requirements of Art 5(4): cf *X v United Kingdom* (1981) A 46. Accordingly, the Commission applied the Court's decision, but since Scots law was subsequently amended (by virtue of the Mental Health (Amendment) (Scotland) Act 1983) to meet the problem, the Committee of Ministers resolved that no further action was required (Resolution DH(86)9). See also *Croke v Ireland* (friendly settlement) (21 December 2000) (complaints by mental health detainee as to the absence of an independent review prior to initial detention (or immediately thereafter) and in respect of the absence of a periodic, independent and automatic review of his detention thereafter: friendly settlement achieved in light of the Irish Government's intention to secure an amendment to domestic law); and *Magalhães Pereira v Portugal* 2002-I, paras 40–51 and 54–63 (repeated attempts by an applicant, a former lawyer, to secure release on the basis of a report suggesting that he could be released on condition he accepted psychiatric support and continued to take his medicine rejected by the domestic courts on the basis that his mental illness prevented him from comprehending the abstract concept of habeas corpus: violations of Art 5(4) an account of excessive delay and lack of effective representation); *Benjamin and Wilson v United Kingdom* (26 September 2002), paras 33–38 (absence of right to bring proceedings for review of lawfulness of detention after expiry of 'tariff' period and transfer to a secure hospital: violation); and *HL v United Kingdom* 2004-IX, paras 135–142 (habeas corpus review proceedings were not wide enough to bear on those conditions which were essential for 'lawful' detention of persons of unsound of mind since it did not allow a determination of the merits of whether the mental disorder persisted; nor did other remedies at the time allow for a review satisfying the requirements of Art 5(4). For domestic discussion, see case UfR 2000.2311 V [Denmark] (individual subjected to court-authorised psychiatric treatment for periods not exceeding three months having been hospitalised four times in a period that in total did not exceed the three-month period, the necessity of hospitalisation being determined by a psychiatrist and the probation service: a subsequent request by the prosecutor for a review of the hospitalisation and for an extension of the maximum period had been made, but since the individual himself had not requested a judicial review of his hospitalisation, it did not follow from domestic law or from Art 5(4) that the hospitalisation should be reviewed, and neither could the maximum period be extended). Cf Case UfR 1995.338 Ø [Denmark] (court-authorised outpatient psychiatric treatment with hospitalisation able to be authorised by psychiatrist and probation service, but no maximum length of the outpatient psychiatric treatment had been decide by the court: failure to determine the case on its merits when judicial review had been requested by the prosecutor had been incompatible with Art 5(4)).

3   *X v United Kingdom* (1981) A 46, paras 55–62; cf *Johnson v United Kingdom* 1997-VII, paras 50–68 and 72 (issue considered under Art 5(1) rather than para (4)).

4   In *Hirst v United Kingdom (no 1)* (24 July 2001), para 41, the Court was not persuaded that it was possible to distinguish between cases of mental disorder resulting in detention on the ground of mental illness and those resulting in indeterminate imprisonment on the grounds of mental instability posing risks of dangerousness.

5   *Silva Rocha v Portugal* 1996-V, paras 26–32.

4.222 The *Silva Rocha* judgment is not without difficulty, as it seems to collapse the all-important distinction accepted in earlier decisions between the elements of retribution and protection of the public in the imposition of custodial sentences. It does confirm, however, that when a deprivation of liberty is treated as falling within both sub-paragraph 1(e) and any other additional sub-paragraph, the implications of this may modify application of the right of review of continuing detention. In *Morley v United Kingdom*, the applicant complained that his transfer back to prison from hospital on executive order and without judicial intervention had violated his right to a review of the lawfulness of his detention. He was not maintaining that the transfer from hospital back to prison breached sub-paragraph 1(e), but rather that this particular ground of detention called for a proper review of that detention in terms of paragraph 4. The applicant had been serving a sentence of life imprisonment when he had been first transferred to hospital on mental health grounds. He acknowledged that as he remained of unsound mind, his detention had fallen within sub-paragraphs 1(a) and 1(e) of Article 5. However, he argued that as he had now served the punishment part of his life sentence, his detention could now only be in a hospital or other appropriate mental health institution as his continued detention was only justifiable on the ground that he continued to pose a danger to society if released. The Court agreed that his detention fell to be considered under both sub-paragraphs. The issue was thus what significance this had for the purposes of Article 5, paragraph 4, a provision which calls not for judicial control of the legality of all aspects of the detention but rather only of the 'essential elements making up the lawfulness of that detention'. In declaring the application inadmissible as manifestly ill-founded, the Court noted that a determination by a mental health tribunal that the applicant should no longer remain in hospital would not have led to his release as he was still subject to a life sentence, and thus the applicant's situation could be distinguished from cases such as *Johnson v United Kingdom* where the authorities had been under an obligation to release the applicant within a reasonable time of the decision that detention was no longer warranted[1].

1   *Morley v United Kingdom* (dec) (6 October 2004). The *Johnson* case is discussed at para **4.189** above.

4.223 How often review is required is not clearly established by case law. In *Herzcegfalvy v Austria,* the Court considered that delays between automatic reviews of detention on the ground of mental illness of 15 months and two years were unreasonable[1]. The emerging principle sees to be that domestic arrangements must be sufficiently flexible to reflect the self-evident fact that there are significant differences in the personal circumstances of each individual detained, and where a patient is seen to be making real progress, review should be available[2].

1   *Herzcegfalvy v Austria* (1992) A 244, paras 75–78 (a period of nine months between reviews was not, however, criticised).
2   Cf *Hirst v United Kingdom (no 1)* (24 July 2001), paras 38 and 42.

Decisions of domestic courts on review of mental health detention

4.224 The effect of Article 5(4) in the context of mental health detention was considered by the House of Lords in *A v The Scottish Ministers*, the facts of which have already been discussed[1]. The applicants argued that the introduction of the overriding test of public safety enabled continued detention without any review of the lawfulness of the original ground for detention, and that the sheriff when applying the public safety test required by statute was not conducting a review but exercising the function of a primary decision maker. These arguments were rejected. Domestic law had been changed since the appellants were originally detained, and the lawfulness of the detention had to be assessed with reference to the law at the time of the assessment. It was no longer a necessary condition of the lawfulness of detention that the mental disorder should be treatable. Continued detention in a hospital was lawful if the Scottish Ministers could show that it was necessary to protect the public from serious harm, a test compatible with the *Winterwerp* tests. Application of this test could properly be described as a review[2].

1   See para **4.190** above.
2   *A v The Scottish Ministers* 2002 SC (PC) 63 at 70–74. See also *Paterson v Kent* 2007 SLT (Sh Ct) 8 (notice period to patient prior to hearing concerning treatment order was insufficient to allow effective preparation and participation, particularly with regard to arranging legal representation where – as *Megyeri v Germany* highlighted – the capacity of the individual was limited, and the proceedings involved the liberty of the patient). Other domestic decisions are cited at paras **4.90–4.191** above.

LIFE IMPRISONMENT AND DETENTION WITHOUT LIMIT OF TIME

4.225 The principle that review is required under Article 5(4) of any order to deprive an individual of his liberty that is indeterminate in nature (or contains any element of such) can arise in cases concerning sentences of life imprisonment[1]. In the United Kingdom, such a sentence is mandatory when a person aged 21 or over is convicted of murder, and can also be imposed at the discretion of the court in other cases. The corresponding sentence in the case of a person aged between 18 and 21 is one of detention for life; where a person under 18 is convicted of murder, the mandatory sentence is one of detention without limit of time. The Strasbourg case law to date has accepted that there is a justifiable difference in the treatment of mandatory and discretionary life prisoners. In the case of *Thynne, Wilson and Gunnell v United Kingdom* the Court held that, unlike mandatory life sentences, a discretionary life sentence is imposed not only because the offence is a serious one but because, in addition to the need for punishment, the accused is considered to be a danger to the public. Such sentences were therefore composed of a punitive element and a security element. Once the prisoner had served the 'tariff' or punitive part of the sentence, the justification for further detention was continuing dangerousness: something which was susceptible of change. Once the punitive element of the sentence had expired, Article 5(4) therefore required that the prisoner's continued detention should be reviewed by a court-like body at regular intervals[2]. The earlier case of *Weeks v United Kingdom* had also established that the Parole Board could not be considered to be a 'court-like body' unless it had the power to decide, rather than merely to advise Ministers. In that case a discretionary life prisoner had been released but then recalled to prison by executive order. Since any decision to recall the applicant on any ground inconsistent with the objectives of the sentence could have been a breach of Article 5(1), the Court held that the applicant was entitled to judicial scrutiny of the lawfulness of his recall[3].

1   For discussion of inderminate orders under mental health legislation, see paras **4.221–4.223** above. For discussion of Art 3 considerations in the context of sentences of life imprisonment, see paras **4.112–4.113** and **4.115** above. See also *Kafkaris v Cyprus* [GC] 2008-..., paras 118–121 and 143–152 (mandatory life sentence for murder with eligibility for remission for good behaviour replaced by scheme only permitting release on presidential constitutional powers or statutory powers: no violation of Art 5(1) as the trial court had made it plain that the sentence was life imprisonment rather than a fixed term, a situation not altered by subsequent official notification of a conditional release date; but violation of Art 7 concerning accessibility and foreseeability of domestic law (but not in respect of retroactive imposition of heavier penalty): see further para **5.232** below; and *Iorgov v Bulgaria (no 2)* (2 September 2010), paras 72–77 (life imprisonment without the possibility of commutation imposed following moratorium on death penalty, but adjustment of sentence and eventual release possible through executive pardon or commutation: no violation of Art 5(4)).

2   *Thynne, Wilson and Gunnell v United Kingdom* (1990) A 190-A, para 76; cf 21681/93 *W, H and A v United Kingdom* (16 January 1995) (applicants at liberty at time of application and thus not 'victims', therefore unable to challenge issue of revocation of life licence).

3   *Weeks v United Kingdom* (1984) A 114, paras 56–58.

4.226 In *Hussain v United Kingdom* and in *Singh v United Kingdom,* the European Court of Human Rights held that the principles set out in *Thynne, Wilson and Gunnell v United Kingdom*[1] and in *Weeks v United Kingdom*[2] applied also to persons sentenced to an indeterminate period of detention (in Scotland, detention without limit of time) for murders committed by them when they were under the age of 18. The Court considered that an indeterminate term of detention for a convicted young person, which may last as long as that person's life, can be justified only by considerations based on the need to protect the public, considerations which must of necessity take into account any developments in the young offender's personality and attitude as he or she grows older. Failure to respect the maturation process implied that young persons would be treated as having forfeited their liberty for the rest of their lives, a situation which might give rise to questions under Article 3. Against that background, that the only justifiable ground for continued detention after any punitive 'tariff' had been served was a characteristic which was susceptible to change with the passage of time, the Court held that such persons were entitled under Article 5(4) to have the grounds for their continued detention reviewed by a court at reasonable intervals[3]. In the cases of *T v United Kingdom* and *V v United Kingdom* the Court again drew a distinction between the sentencing of an adult murderer and that of a juvenile. It held that Article 6 applies to the process of setting a punishment period or tariff for a person convicted of murder aged under 18 (and, it would follow, for a discretionary life prisoner also), and that the punishment period should therefore be fixed by a court and not by the executive[4]. The Court further held that the failure to fix any new tariff, following the quashing of the original tariff fixed by the Home Secretary, meant that the applicants' entitlement to access to a tribunal for periodical review of the continuing lawfulness of their detention (as required by Article 5(4), following the *Hussain* and *Singh* judgments) had not been met[5].

1   *Thynne, Wilson and Gunnell v United Kingdom* (1990) A 190-A.

2   *Weeks v United Kingdom* (1987) A 114.

3   *Hussain v United Kingdom* 1996-I, paras 50–62, and *Singh v United Kingdom* 1996-I, 280, paras 58–70.

4   This was already the position in Scots law (unlike English law) by virtue of the Crime and Punishment (Scotland) Act 1997, s 16 which amended the Prisoners and Criminal Proceedings (Scotland) Act 1993, s 2 so as to extend the discretionary life prisoner provisions to murderers under 18 in light of the Court's decisions in *Hussain v United Kingdom* 1996-I, and *Singh v United Kingdom* 1996-I.

5   *T v United Kingdom* [GC] (16 December 1999), paras 92–100; and *V v United Kingdom* [GC] 1999-IX, paras 93–101.

4.227 However, the European Court of Human Rights long seemed unwilling to apply the same approach to mandatory life sentences, despite some comments by domestic judges that in practice the differences between a mandatory and a discretionary life sentence were narrowing. In *Wynne v United Kingdom*, the Court held that a mandatory life sentence belonged to a different category from a discretionary life sentence since it is imposed automatically as a punishment for the offence of murder irrespective of considerations about the dangerousness of the offender[1]. It followed that, in mandatory life sentences, the original trial and appeals system were deemed to satisfy the guarantee of Article 5(4), and there was no additional right to challenge the lawfulness of continued detention[2]. It became increasingly uncertain, however, whether the Court would maintain this distinction in respect of mandatory life sentences imposed upon adults, and in *Stafford v United Kingdom*, the Court signalled a change in its jurisprudence. The issue was whether the continued detention of the applicant under the original mandatory life sentence imposed on him for murder after the expiry of a fixed-term sentence imposed for fraud complied with the requirements of Article 5(1). In deciding that there was no sufficient causal connection between the possible commission of other non-violent offences and the original sentence, the Court indicated unwillingness to 'accept that a decision-making power by [the executive] to detain the applicant on the basis of perceived fears of future non-violent criminal conduct unrelated to his original murder conviction accords with the spirit of [the

ECHR], with its emphasis on the rule of law and protection from arbitrariness'. Instead, it now recognised that there were cogent reasons for departing from earlier precedents in light of the increasing similarities between discretionary life and mandatory life sentences, particularly in respect of the setting of 'tariffs' in these latter cases by the executive:

> '[W]ith the wider recognition of the need to develop and apply, in relation to mandatory life prisoners, judicial procedures reflecting standards of independence, fairness and openness, the continuing role of the [executive] in fixing the tariff and in deciding on a prisoner's release following its expiry has become increasingly difficult to reconcile with the notion of separation of powers between the executive and the judiciary, a notion which has assumed growing importance in the case-law of the Court. The Court considers that it may now be regarded as established in domestic law that there is no distinction between mandatory life prisoners, discretionary life prisoners and juvenile murderers as regards the nature of tariff-fixing. It is a sentencing exercise. The mandatory life sentence does not impose imprisonment for life as a punishment. The tariff, which reflects the individual circumstances of the offence and the offender, represents the element of punishment.'

In other words, since the continued detention of a life prisoner after expiry of the 'tariff' depended on elements of dangerousness and risk associated with the objectives of the original sentence, again elements susceptible to change through time, there should be in consequence a right to have the existence of such factors determined by a judicial body satisfying the requirements of Article 5(4)[3].

1   *Wynne v United Kingdom* (1994) A 294-A, paras 33–38.

2   This approach was reiterated by the Commission in 32875/96, *Ryan v United Kingdom*, (1 July 1998) which concerned a murderer under 21. The Commission accepted that the administrative arrangements for setting a tariff and thereafter considering release fell within the scope of the punishment imposed at the trial.

3   *Stafford v United Kingdom* [GC] 2002-IV, paras 62–90, at paras 78, 87–90. See also *Waite v United Kingdom* (10 December 2002), paras 56–60.

4.228 The key principle is that domestic arrangements for periodic review of the continuing detention of prisoners sentenced to life imprisonment must be sufficiently flexible to allow the timing of reviews to be dependent upon the particular circumstances of each individual rather than upon administrative convenience. In *Oldham v United Kingdom*, the European Court on Human Rights considered that the system of automatic review of discretionary life sentences at periods of two years or less as determined by the Secretary of State violated the requirements of Article 5(4) since this had been insufficiently adaptable to allow the applicant to seek earlier release after completion of rehabilitative work which had been required of him on his recall to prison[1]. Further, in *Hirst v United Kingdom*, the Court held that delays of 21 months and two years between reviews in a case in which the applicant had been sentenced to life imprisonment for manslaughter on the ground of diminished responsibility were unreasonable. While the Court did not want to rule on the maximum permissible period between reviews which should apply to such categories of life prisoner, established case law indicated in the case of persons detained on mental health grounds that periods between reviews of 15 months and two years had not been considered reasonable. In the applicant's case, the mental disorder had arisen not in the context of mental illness but of mental instability posing risks of dangerousness, and the Court could not accept there were grounds for accepting that the latter category was less susceptible to change over time[2].

1   *Oldham v United Kingdom* 2000-X, paras 28–37 (at para 32, the Court distinguished the Commission's report in 20488/92, *AT v United Kingdom* (29 November 1995) where a period of almost two years before review of a discretionary life sentence was considered not justified in circumstances where the Parole Board had recommended review within one year).

2   *Hirst v United Kingdom (no 1)* (24 July 2001), paras 36–44, citing *Herczegfalvy v Austria* (1992) A 244, discussed at para **4.119** above (the lack of recommendation for earlier review of the case and considerations of rehabilitation and monitoring had been insufficient to justify the delays between reviews as there had been evidence that the applicant had made progress in behaviour).

Domestic compliance with Strasbourg case law on review of sentences of life imprisonment or detention without limit of time

4.229 As a result of the decisions in *Thynne, Wilson and Gunnell* and *Weeks*, the legislation governing discretionary sentences of life imprisonment (or detention for life) in Scotland was amended by the Prisoners and Criminal Proceedings (Scotland) Act 1993, s 2. Where a court passes such a sentence, the sentencing judge has a discretion to set a 'punishment part' (the period required to be served to satisfy punishment and deterrence) when sentencing the prisoner. In determining the length of the punishment part the court considers the seriousness of the offence (and any matters associated with it), previous convictions, and the stage, if any, at which the prisoner pleaded guilty, but not his dangerousness. Once the punishment part has expired (and at two-yearly intervals thereafter), the prisoner is entitled to require the Scottish Ministers to refer his case to the Parole Board. In practice, cases are referred automatically and are reviewed more frequently if that is recommended by the Parole Board. If the Parole Board is satisfied that it is no longer necessary for the protection of the public that the prisoner should be confined, it will direct the Scottish Ministers to release him. The Scottish Ministers are bound to give effect to the Board's direction. The prisoner is released on life licence, and is liable to recall to custody if he fails to comply with the conditions of his licence. Further, as a result of the decisions in *Hussain* and *Singh*, the Crime and Punishment (Scotland) Act 1997, s 16 amended the Prisons and Criminal Proceedings (Scotland) Act 1993, s 2 so as to extend the discretionary life prisoner provisions to murderers under 18. Section 2 was further amended by the Convention Rights (Compliance) (Scotland) Act 2001. The resultant provisions are complex and have given rise to considerable difficulties of interpretation[1].

1   See eg *Ansari v HM Advocate* 2003 JC 105; *Petch v HM Advocate* 2011 SCCR 199. See also *R (Noorkoiv) v Secretary of State for the Home Office* [2002] 1 WLR 3284 (delay of up to three months in processing cases after expiry of the tariff period had been served infringed Art 5(4)); and *R (West) v Secretary of State for the Home Department* [2005] 1 WLR 350.

4.230 Under the arrangements in force before 2001[1], the Scottish Ministers had a discretionary power to release mandatory life prisoners following a recommendation of the Parole Board and after consultation with the judiciary. In practice, a non-statutory committee, the Preliminary Review Committee, met in private and considered each case after approximately four years had been served. It was chaired by a civil servant. It recommended to the Scottish Ministers the date for the first review by the Parole Board of the prisoner's suitability for release on life licence. The Scottish Ministers then decided on the timing of the first review in the light of the Committee's recommendation and representations from the prisoner. At the review, the Board focused on the question whether the risk to the public associated with the prisoner's release on life licence was acceptable. The Board made a recommendation to the Scottish Ministers. If the recommendation was in favour of release, the Scottish Ministers were required to consult the judiciary, and invite representations from the prisoner, before deciding whether to accept the recommendation. The release of such prisoners was also affected by the '20-year policy', introduced in 1984, under which prisoners convicted of certain categories of murder could expect to spend not less than 20 years in custody unless there were exceptional circumstances.

Although these procedures relating to adult mandatory life prisoners appeared to be compatible with Articles 5(4) and 6, in terms of existing Strasbourg jurisprudence, the Scottish Ministers considered that there was a risk of a domestic court taking a different view[2]. The Convention Rights (Compliance) (Scotland) Act 2001 accordingly brought the arrangements for the sentencing and release of adult mandatory life prisoners into line with those applying to discretionary life prisoners and prisoners sentenced for a murder committed before the age of 18. The 2001 Act also enhances the security of tenure of Parole Board members and ensures that the reappointment and removal of members is not at the discretion of the Scottish Government, so as to ensure that the Board satisfies the requirements of Article 6. In *Flynn v HM Advocate,* prisoners sentenced to mandatory life imprisonment prior to its entry into force sought to argue that the 2001 Act was incompatible with their Convention rights, since the effect of the legislation was to delay the earliest date when their cases would be reviewed by the Parole Board. The Privy Council considered that the transitional arrangements for such prisoners did not breach Article 5 (or when taken with Article 14), although it was appropriate that regard should be had to various matters that would not have existed at the date of sentence. However, the Committee arrived at its conclusion through contrasting reasoning, Lord Hope and Baroness Hale considering that Article 7's prohibition against the imposition of a heavier penalty than the one imposed at the time of the commission of the offence applied in such cases, while Lord Bingham, Lord Rodger and Lord Carswell disagreed, considering that the same conclusion could be arrived at through the ordinary process of interpreting the 2001 Act in a manner consistent with Convention rights[3]. In England, and following the case of *Stafford v United Kingdom,* the House of Lords determined that the determination of the 'tariff' part of a life sentence was an integral part of the sentencing process, and as such, was a matter for the judiciary rather than for the executive[4].

---

1   Ie those operating until the relevant provisions of the Convention Rights (Compliance) (Scotland) Act 2001 entered into force on 8 October 2001.

2   In *R (Anderson) v Secretary of State for the Home Department* [2003] 1 AC 837, the House of Lords issued a declaration of incompatibility in respect of English legislation permitting the executive's power to determine the minimum tariff to be served.

3   *Flynn and Others v HM Advocate* 2004 SC (PC) 1.

4   *R (Anderson) v Secretary of State for the Home Department* [2003] 1 AC 837 (declaration of incompatibility in respect of Crime (Sentences) Act 1997, s 29).

Early release of prisoners serving fixed-term sentences
4.231 As the Grand Chamber made clear in *Gerger v Turkey*, Article 5(1)(a) cannot be relied upon to seek to secure a right to early release for those sentenced to imprisonment following conviction of an offence. However, while the provision cannot be read as guaranteeing a right to automatic parole, arrangements for the release of prisoners may give rise to an issue under Article 14 when taken with this sub-paragraph if the policy affects individuals in a discriminatory manner[1]. In *Nelson v United Kingdom*, the applicant claimed that differences between Scots and English law in the release of persons sentenced to imprisonment while still minors were discriminatory. Scots law did not provide remission of sentence (as distinct from parole or release on licence) for juvenile offenders, and the applicant alleged that since there was no objective or reasonable justification for such distinctions in the domestic laws of the United Kingdom, this violated Convention guarantees. The Commission considered the application manifestly ill-founded since the ECHR did not confer a general right to question the length of any sentence. However, it acknowledged that if any aspect of sentencing policy did appear to affect individuals in a discriminatory way, there could well be an issue under Article 14 taken together with Article 5. Here, distinctions in sentencing policy based upon age reflected the state's need to ensure flexibility in treatment, and differences between the 'penal legislation of two regional jurisdictions' were not related to personal status[2]. In *Clift v United Kingdom,* on the other hand, the Court ruled that differences in early release schemes dependent upon the length of fixed-term sentences of imprisonment lacked objective justification and thus had violated of Article 14 in conjunction with Article 5. In addition to a positive recommendation from the Parole Board, prisoners serving sentences of 15 years or more required the approval of the Secretary of State for early release. In domestic proceedings, the House of Lords held that where such provision for early release is made by domestic law, the right to seek early release will consequently fall within the scope of Article 5, and any differential treatment will also give rise to issues under Article 14 if based on considerations other than upon the individual merits of a case[3]. In the Strasbourg Court, the *Gerber* case was distinguished as in that case the differences in release arrangements were on account of the gravity of types of offences rather than the position of being a prisoner serving a particular sentence. While it was acknowledged that the length of sentence had some relationship to the gravity of the offence for which the applicant was imprisoned, other factors including the trial court's assessment of the risk posed by the applicant could also have been relevant. In consequence,

differences in release arrangements based solely upon length of sentence carried the risk of arbitrary detention unless objectively justified. In the particular case, imposition of a fixed-term (rather than indeterminate) sentence of imprisonment indeed suggested the trial judge had not considered there were strong concerns for public security. The respondent state had failed to demonstrate in what manner the requirement for the approval of the Secretary of State before release for certain groups of prisoners could be justified[4]. On the other hand, the withdrawal of a scheme of eligibility for remisson of good behaviour which has the consequence of prolonging an indeterminate sentence of imprisonment is not in itself inconsistent with Article 5[5].

1   *Gerger v Turkey* [GC] (8 July 1999), para 69. See also 12118/86, *Webster v United Kingdom* (4 March 1987) (claim that parole board determinations discriminated against foreign prisoners found to be unsubstantiated, the statistics relied upon failing to reflect personal circumstances, and instructions clearly indicated nationality was not to be considered).

2   11077/84, *Nelson v United Kingdom* (1986) DR 49, 170. Cf 11653/85, *Hobgen v United Kingdom* (1986) DR 46, 231 (introduction of more stringent requirements for parole leading to disappointment on part of prisoner not a violation of Art 3). For discussion of Art 3 considerations, see paras **4.112–4.114** above.

3   *R (Clift) v Secretary of State for the Home Department* [2007] 1 AC 484 (although there was no requirement under the ECHR to establish an early release scheme, in the first case under appeal, the difference in treatment was based upon the length of sentence, which did not engage Art 14; but in respect of the other two appeals concerning foreign prisoners liable to removal after their sentences, a declaration of incompatibility was appropriate since the Criminal Justice Act 1991 ss 46(1) and 50(2) prevented these prisoners from having their cases reviewed by the Parole Board in the same way as long-term prisoners who were UK nationals). In the subsequent case of *R (Black) v Secretary of State for Justice* [2009] 1 AC 949 it was held that Art 5(4) was not engaged by a decision whether to order the early release of a prisoner serving a determinate sentence: the jurisprudence of the European Court of Human Rights drew a distinction between sentences of imprisonment for an indeterminate period, where the question of release was dependent on factors unknown at the time of the original sentence and so required periodic review by a judicial body, and sentences of imprisonment for a determinate period where the lawfulness of the detention for the purposes of Art 5(4) had been satisfied by the original sentencing procedures and where the implementation of the sentence could properly be left to the executive unless some new issue arose affecting the lawfulness of the detention. It followed that legislation which gave the Secretary of State a discretion whether to authorise the release on licence of prisoners whose release the Parole Board had recommended, after they had served more than half but less than two-thirds of a sentence of 15 years or more, did not infringe Art 5(4). In particular, the Parole Board's recommendation did not amount to a new issue affecting the lawfulness of the detention such as would break the link with the original sentencing decision and engage Art 5(4). Nor does Art 5(4) apply to the executive decision whether to release early on curfew: *Mason v Ministry of Justice* [2009] 1 WLR 509.

4   *Clift v United Kingdom* (13 July 2010), paras 55–63, 66–68, and 73–79.

5   *Kafkaris v Cyprus* [GC] 2008-..., paras 118–121 and 143–152 (mandatory life sentence for murder with eligibility for remission for good behaviour replaced by scheme only permitting release on presidential constitutional powers or statutory powers: no violation of Art 5(1) as the trial court had made it plain that the sentence was life imprisonment rather than a fixed term, a situation not altered by subsequent official notification of a conditional release date; but violation of Art 7 concerning accessibility and foreseeability of domestic law (but not in respect of retroactive imposition of heavier penalty): see further para **5.232** below.

Domestic reform of prison discipline

4.232 The deprivation of liberty (through the imposition of additional days, or loss of remission) as a punishment for breaches of prison discipline was suspended in Scotland as from June 2001 on account of concerns that these forms of punishment, imposed by a prison governor, might be at risk of successful challenge under the ECHR[1].

1   The Divisional Court had held otherwise in *R (Greenfield) v Secretary of State for the Home Department* [2001] 1 WLR 1731. For Strasbourg consideration of Art 6 issues in prison discipline cases leading to loss of remission, see para **5.48** below.

Testing the lawfulness of detention

4.233 The effectiveness of domestic procedures in providing review is assessed by considering the proceedings as a whole, since initial shortcomings may subsequently be considered to have been remedied by subsequent safeguards[1]. The Court will not rule on the general compatibility of legislation but solely on whether in an individual case there has been a violation of the provision[2]. Three general expectations exist: first, the remedy permitting review must be effective and sufficiently certain; secondly, it must be available through a 'court' enjoying independence and impartiality, able to exact procedural safeguards for the applicant, and also have the power to order the release of the individual; and thirdly, the remedy must be available 'speedily'.

1   *Winterwerp v Netherlands* (1979) A 33, para 62.
2   *Nikolova v Bulgaria* [GC] 1999-II, at para 60.

An effective and sufficiently certain remedy

4.234 Effectiveness implies the domestic remedy must be able to secure examination of both discretionary and substantive elements of the decision, not merely whether there has been an abuse of power or defect in the procedure[1]. In considering the question whether domestic law provides such a remedy, the European Court of Human Rights will thus take account not only of formal remedies but also the context in which they operate as well as the applicant's personal circumstances[3]. In *Van Droogenbroeck v Belgium*, for example, the state sought to argue that several 'remedies' were available to the applicant and thus met the requirements of Article 5(4): one was founded upon old and isolated provisions which had no bearing on the statute under consideration; two were based upon unsettled legal rules which were still evolving; a statutory appeal could only address whether detention should be terminated earlier (rather than whether it was lawful); and a final 'remedy' could not have resulted in the court ordering the release of the individual[2].

1   *E v Norway* (1990) A 181-A, para 60; cf *Ireland v United Kingdom* (1978) A 25, para 200 (remedies provided at best limited domestic judicial review); *Soumare v France* 1998-V, para

43 (unresolved issue of French law relied upon by the state); and *Nasrulloyev v Russia* (11 October 2007), paras 86–90 (review of detention proceedings only open to the prosecutor in seeking an extension of custody). For domestic consideration, see *R (James) v Secretary of State for Justice* [2010] 1 AC 553.

2 Eg *RMD v Switzerland* 1997-VI, para 47 (applicant was expecting to be transferred from one canton to another and thus was in a position of great legal uncertainty); *Sakik and Others v Turkey* 1997-VII, para 53 (no example of any detainee having successfully invoked particular provisions of domestic law: lack of precedents indicated the uncertainty of these remedies in practice); *Vodeničarov v Slovakia* (21 December 2000), paras 33–45 (possibility of consideration by constitutional court considered an insufficiently certain remedy).

3 *Van Droogenbroeck v Belgium* (1982) A 50, paras 49–56.

4.235 In relation to Scots law, there is one case which suggests an error in Strasbourg's understanding of domestic law concerning the availability of remedies to challenge detention. In *Harkin v United Kingdom* a Northern Ireland citizen who had landed at a Scottish port and subsequently had been detained under prevention of terrorism legislation claimed that British law did not provide an effective remedy to challenge the legality of detention as called for by Article 5(4). The Commission disposed of this issue by reaffirming an earlier decision that the remedy of habeas corpus was sufficient to meet Convention requirements[1] without being made aware that this English law remedy is not available in Scots law[2]. There are however other means by which detention can be challenged. There are for example numerous cases in which detention pending deportation has been challenged by way of application for judicial review[3].

1 8022/77, 8125/77 and 8027/77, *McVeigh, O'Neill and Evans v United Kingdom* (1981) DR 25, 15.

2 11539/85, *Harkin v United Kingdom* (1986) DR 48, 237. Cf *X v United Kingdom* (1981) A 46, paras 58–59 (habeas corpus remedy did not allow a court to examine the medical grounds for detention, and thus was an insufficient remedy for Art 5(4)).

3 See eg *AAS v Secretary of State for the Home Department* 2010 SC 10.

Provision of a 'court' following judicial procedures and able to order the release of a detainee

4.236 Review must be available through an independent and impartial[1] 'court' following established procedures and which can order the release of the person detained[2]. Again, what qualifies as a 'court' is interpreted widely, a matter primarily determined by the provision of appropriate judicial procedures[3]. 'Although it is not always necessary that the procedure under Article 5(4) be attended by the same guarantees as those required under Article 6 of the ECHR for criminal or civil litigation, it must have a judicial character and provide guarantees appropriate to the kind of deprivation of liberty in question'[4]. There need not be full 'equality of arms', but an individual must be accorded basic and fundamental procedural guarantees. For example, in *Sanchez Reisse v Switzerland*, the applicant had been denied the opportunity to make representations in support of his request for release pending a decision whether to extradite him. The European Court of

Human Rights considered that in the circumstances he should have been provided with the 'benefit of an adversarial procedure' which could have been discharged by permitting him to submit written comments or by allowing him to appear in person before the court[5].

1   The fact that the judge who determines the question of an accused's detention will also serve as the trial judge examining the merits of the criminal case will not of itself justify fears that he is not impartial since the questions to be considered in each case are different: *Ilijkov v Bulgaria* (26 July 2001), para 97. Cf *DN v Switzerland* [GC] 2001-III, paras 40–57 (the judge rapporteur who was the sole psychiatric expert among the judges, the only person who had interviewed the applicant, and he had previously expressed on two occasions his opinion the applicant should not be released from mental health detention: objective grounds for believing this judge lacked the necessary impartiality).

2   Cf domestic discussion of mental health cases in *R (H) v Secretary of State for Health* [2006] 1 AC 441 (admission to mental hospital of patient not competent to avail herself of statutory provision allowing for application for discharge: Mental Health Act 1983, ss 2 and 29 concerning admissions procedure and the 'next relative' provisions are not incompatible with the Convention, but can be 'read down' to comply with the freedoms protected by Art 5, and Art 5(4) does not require judicial review in every case where a patient is unable to make an application; while the courts may now be obliged to conduct a sufficient review of the merits to satisfy themselves that Art 5(1)(e) requirements have been met, they are not well equipped to do so; and note comments of Baroness Hale that there is a distinction between rights under Art 5(3) and 5(4), for while Art 5(3) guarantees an accused can have his detention brought before a court, Art 5(4) only allows a person to 'take proceedings' to question their detention, a distinction allowing a person detained under the Mental Health Act to choose whether they wish the matter to go before a court).

3   *Reinprecht v Austria* 2005-XII, at para 31.

4   *De Wilde, Ooms and Versyp v Belgium* (1971) A 12, para 78.

5   *Sanchez-Reisse v Switzerland* (1986) A 107, paras 48–51 at para 51.

4.237 The procedures required by Article 5(4) will depend upon the particular nature of the detention in issue: that is, 'the Convention requires a procedure of a judicial character with guarantees appropriate to the kind of deprivation of liberty in question'. In other words, the procedures adopted for the purposes of this paragraph need not have provided in all instances the same level of guarantee as would be required by Article 6[1]. This, though, leaves some uncertainty in the jurisprudence, but the case law does suggest increasing expectations of enhanced procedural requirements, at least in reviews of pre-trial detention, approximating to fair hearing guarantees in general[2]. There is though, no right to a legal representative of the detainee's own choice[3]. Certainly, a hearing will be required in the case of detention falling within the ambit of Article 5(1)(c)[4] (that is, a person held on detention on suspicion of committing an offence, or where detention is reasonably considered necessary to prevent the commission of an offence or the flight of an offender) and in which the principle of equality of arms between the prosecutor and the detained person is respected[5]. In these cases, the actual presence of the detainee may be necessary[6]. At the very least, there must be an opportunity to know the case to be met[7]. Indeed, the opportunity to challenge in an effective manner the statements or views put forward by the prosecutor to justify the continuation of pre-trial detention in certain instances will presuppose that the defence be given access to relevant documents. In *Lamy v Belgium,* the judge and the prosecutor had enjoyed access to a detailed investigation file, but the defence had been armed only with such information as could be gleaned from the charges. This was deemed insufficient to permit the applicant to challenge his detention effectively since 'appraisal of the need for a remand in custody and the subsequent assessment of guilt are too closely linked for access to documents to be refused in the former place when the law requires it in the latter case'[8]. As the Court put it in *Garcia Alva v Germany*, the state's legitimate goal in ensuring the efficient investigation of criminal investigations 'cannot be pursued at the expense of substantial restrictions on the rights of the defence'. In consequence, in challenging the continuing lawfulness of pre-trial detention, an accused must be accorded 'a sufficient opportunity to take cognisance of statements and other pieces of evidence underlying them, such as the results of the police and other investigations, irrespective of whether the accused is able to provide any indication as to the relevance for his defence of the pieces of evidence which he seeks to be given access to'[9]. Other categories of detainee may expect similar opportunities. In *Weeks v United Kingdom,* a recalled prisoner did not have the right of full disclosure of documents available to the Parole Board. Such did not 'allow proper participation of the individual adversely affected by the contested decision, this being one of the principal guarantees of a judicial procedure' for the purposes of Article 5[10]. In *Hussain v United Kingdom*, the applicant had only at a late stage been given sight of the reports to be considered by the Parole Board, while in *Singh v United Kingdom*, the prisoner had secured the right to see the reports which had been considered by the Parole Board only after seeking judicial review. In neither instance had there been a right to be present at the review of the case. For the Court, 'where a substantial term of imprisonment may be at stake and where characteristics pertaining to [an applicant's] personality and level of maturity are of importance in deciding on his dangerousness', an adversarial hearing with legal representation and the possibility of calling and examining witnesses was appropriate[11]. In *A and Others v United Kingdom,* procedural safeguards for review by the Special Immigration Appeals Commission of the detention of non-nationals considered to pose a danger to national security and whose removal could not be effected without exposing them to a substantial risk of ill-treatment were deemed to have been inadequate in respect of four applicants. While accepting that the commission was a fully independent court and that the device of 'special advocate' was able to review evidence not disclosed on national security grounds, the crucial question was whether allegations in material made public were sufficiently specific to to permit an effective challenge, a test not satisfied in these instances on account of either the lack of a crucial element in the evidence or because the allegations were of a general and insubstantial nature requiring the commission to rely largely on non-disclosed material[12].

---

1   *Megyeri v Germany* (1992) A 237-A, para 22.

2   See eg *Kotsaridis v Greece* (23 September 2004) (prolongation of detention on remand without public hearing); and *Ramishvili and Kokhreidze v Georgia* (27 January 2009), paras 128–136 at para 131 (oral hearings should create conditions such that verbal responses and audio-visual exchanges between the parties and the judge in a court room flow in a decent, dynamic and

undisturbed manner, and thus the judicial review of the lawfulness of the applicant's detention had therefore lacked the fundamental requisites of a fair hearing).

3   *Prehn v Germany* (dec) (24 August 2010) (right to periodic review did not entail absolute right to choose lawyer of the detainee's own choosing, refusal being on account that the lawyer did not practise in the jurisdiction while proximity of counsel to client and court facilitated proper defence and communication and kept costs down: and noted no such absolue right exists under Art 6)

4   *Kampanis v Greece* (1995) A 318-B, paras 47–59; *Włoch v Poland* (19 October 2000), para 126.

5   *Nikolova v Bulgaria* 1999-II, para 58; *Ilijkov v Bulgaria* (26 July 2001), paras 101–105. For domestic discussion, see *Roberts v Parole Board* [2005] 2 AC 738 (the Parole Board has the power to adopt a special advocate procedure and to withhold sensitive evidence from a prisoner in circumstances where evidence comes from a source who would be at risk were his identity disclosed to the prisoner, the special advocate procedure able to mitigate any unfairness to the prisoner caused by the withholding of such evidence); *R (Girling) v Parole Board* [2007] QB 783 (the decision whether or not to direct the release of a prisoner involved the discharge of a judicial function by the Parole Board, with which the Home Secretary was not entitled to interfere); and *R (Brooke) v Parole Board* [2008] 1 WLR 1950 (the Secretary of State had sought to influence the manner in which the board carried out its risk assessment, both by directions and by the use of his control over the appointment of members of the board; the Ministry's use of its funding powers was interference which exceeded what could properly be justified by the role of sponsor; and the Secretary of State's power to terminate a member's appointment if satisfied that he had failed satisfactorily to perform his duties was not compatible with the independence of members of the board).

6   That is, there may be special criteria applicable requiring an applicant's personal attendance: eg *Graužinis v Lithuania* (10 October 2000), at para 34 ('given what was at stake for the applicant, ie his liberty', in addition to factors such as the lapse of time between decisions 'and the re-assessment of the basis for the remand, the applicant's presence was required throughout the pre-trial remand hearings ... in order to be able to give satisfactory information and instructions to his counsel'). See also *Allen v United Kingdom* (30 March 2010), paras 50–52 (a judge does not cease to 'exercise judicial power' simply because a decision concerning bail is open to appeal). Cf *Reinprecht v Austria* 2005-XII, paras 31–42 (refusal to allow detainee to appear at hearing concerning prolongation of detention on remand: no violation).

7   *Lanz v Austria* (31 January 2002), paras 43–45 (non-communication of the prosecution's submissions in relation to an appeal against the refusal of a request for release from detention on remand, police supervision of a detainee's consultation with his lawyer, and non-communication of the prosecutor's submissions: violations);

8   *Lamy v Belgium* (1989) A 151, para 29. See too *Włoch v Poland* 2000-XI, paras 128–132 (restricted right of access to the court which determined the question of the lawfulness of the detention at a time when the applicant's lawyers had not been given access to the case file: violation of Art 5(4)).

9   *Garcia Alva v Germany* (13 February 2001), paras 39–43 at paras 42 and 41.

10   *Weeks v United Kingdom* (1987) A 114, para 66 (lack of disclosure of records rendered the procedures of the Parole Board defective).

11   *Hussain v United Kingdom* 1996-I, at paras 58–61; *Singh v United Kingdom* 1996-I, at paras 65–69.

12   *A and Others v United Kingdom* [GC] 2009-..., paras 212–224.

4.238 Although there is no specific right to seek legal assistance in terms of Article 5(4), in certain circumstances legal representation may be required to ensure the effectiveness of any adversarial hearing, for example if the individual is young[1]. The same principle may apply in the case of a person detained on mental health grounds[2]. It also goes without saying that a court in discharging its obligations under Article 5(4) must have available to it the information it requires to be able to come to an assessment of whether the deprivation of liberty has been lawful. This issue has arisen in the context of assertions of national security concerns. In *Chahal v United Kingdom*, the restricted procedural rights then available under British immigration law and the limited effectiveness of judicial review in cases involving issues of national security resulted in an Article 5(4) violation, the European Court of Human Rights noting that legal techniques exist in other countries which can meet national security concerns and which at the same time provide 'a substantial measure of procedural justice' to individuals[3].

1   *Bouamar v Belgium* (1988) A 129, para 60.

2   *Winterwerp v Netherlands* (1979) A 33, para 60. Cf *Magalhães Pereira v Portugal* (26 February 2002), paras 56–63 (appointment by a judge of a civil servant working in the secure hospital where the applicant was detained to serve as the applicant's representative since the lawyer appointed as his representative was not present: violation).

3   *Chahal v United Kingdom* 1996-V, paras 130–133.

4.239 The 'court' must also have the power to order release. Concerns under Article 5(4) have thus arisen in the context of British mental health law where review tribunals formerly had no authority to order the release of a patient[1]. The powers and procedures of Parole Boards have also in the past been considered wanting since they only had the power to advise Ministers[2]. Despite the introduction of new opportunities for individuals to have sight of the materials being considered at review hearings, the lack of any general power to order a prisoner's release continued to prevent these bodies from satisfying Article 5(4) requirements[3].

1   *X v United Kingdom* (1981) A 46, paras 55–62. Scots law was subsequently changed by the Mental Health (Amendment) (Scotland) Act 1999. Cf 28212/95, *Benjamin and Wilson v United Kingdom* (23 October 1997) (discretionary life sentence prisoners who had been transferred to special hospitals had no right to a review hearing: application declared admissible). See also *R (Von Brandenburg) v East London and the City Mental Health NHS Trust* [2004] 2 AC 280.

2   Eg *Weeks v United Kingdom* (1987) A 114, at paras 62–68; *Thynne, Wilson and Gunnell v United Kingdom* (1990) A 190-A, at para 80; and *von Bülow v United Kingdom* (7 October 2003), paras 23–25).

3   Following these two cases, new interim arrangements seeking to give Parole Boards strengthened powers were again challenged in *Curley v United Kingdom* (28 March 2000), paras 32–34 (detention during HM pleasure for ten years after expiry of tariff; lack of speedy review by body capable of ordering release). Cf *Ječius v Lithuania* 2000-IX, para 101 (civil proceedings brought by the applicant against the prison administration were irrelevant for the purpose of para (4) since the domestic courts were not able to order the applicant's release; in any event, the civil courts had confined themselves to the question whether formal orders existed authorising the detention rather than its underlying lawfulness). The Convention Rights (Compliance) (Scotland) Act 2001 amended the law governing parole: see paras **4.229–4.230** above.

Review which is 'speedily' available

4.240 Finally, the review must be 'speedily' available. This is tested in accordance with the particular circumstances of each case. Both access to a review procedure and the time taken to arrive at a decision are covered[1]. This is distinguishable from the right an accused person has to be brought 'promptly' before a court under Article 5(3)[2]. However, the provision guarantees no right to an appeal as such against decisions ordering or extending detention, although where a second level of jurisdiction exists for the examination of applications for release from detention, this must in principle accord to the detainee the same guarantees on appeal as at first instance[3]. Determination of this requirement is dependent on the particular circumstances of each case, and care must be taken in comparing cases or even predicting the likely response of the European Court of Human Rights. Certainly, the examination of the effectiveness of procedural review and the question of speed of review are not wholly separate[4]. In *Sanchez-Reisse v Switzerland*, the applicant's attempts to secure his release pending determination of an extradition decision took 31 and 46 days respectively to be decided, periods labelled 'unwarranted' and 'excessive' by the Court[5]. In *Sakik and Others v Turkey*, requests for release on bail pending trial took a minimum of 12 days to be considered, periods the Court considered incompatible with the guarantee[6]. In *Kadem v Malta*, a challenge to detention pending extradition took 17 days, a period also considered incompatible with the guarantee[7]. States are thus expected to organise their judicial systems in such a way as to comply with the requirements of the Convention, and domestic procedures which involve some complexity may not be relied upon by a state to justify delays in determining requests for release[8]. Nor may a state plead heavy workloads, since the Court considers that Convention obligations require states to organise their legal systems so as to comply with its requirements[9]. Delays calculated in months – rather than in weeks – appear to be in breach of the requirement of speed; but further fine tuning in clarifying whether shorter periods of delay would be acceptable is awaited[10].

---

1   Access to a review procedure involves discussion of the extent of the period between automatic reviews of detention, matters discussed above in respect to the reasonableness of the length of these periods: see paras **4.219–4.223** and **4.225–4.228** above.

2   *De Jong, Baljet and Van den Brink v Netherlands* (1984) A 77, paras 57–58

3   *Lanz v Austria* (31 January 2002), para 42.

4   Cf *Włoch v Poland* 2000-XI, paras 131–135 (initial proceedings were 'speedy' but not effective; even assuming subsequent proceedings were effective, they were not 'speedy').

5   *Sanchez-Reiss v Switzerland* (1986) A 107, at paras 59–60.

6   *Sakik and Others v Turkey* 1997-VII, para 51.

7   *Kadem v Malta* (9 January 2003) paras 41–45.

8   *M B v Switzerland* (30 November 2000), paras 27–39, and *G B v Switzerland* (30 November 2000), paras 36–43 (two-tier procedure for determining release from pre-trial detention: delays considered to violate Art 5(4)).

9   Eg *E v Norway* (1990) A 181-A, paras 63–67.

10   Cf *Koendjbiharie v Netherlands* (1990) A 185-B (four-month delay before pre-trial review completed); *E v Norway* (1990) A 181-A, (two-month period which included a five-week

delay before a hearing took place); *Erkalo v Netherlands* 1998-VI, paras 61–64, (complaint that request for release was neither determined speedily nor in accordance with domestic law was disposed of under Art 5(1) rather than para (4), but the Commission had considered that the 16-day period taken did satisfy this requirement). See too *Musiał v Poland* [GC] 1999-II, at para 44 (delay of 20 months in mental health review 'incompatible with the notion of speediness'unless there are exceptional circumstances); *Vodeničarov v Slovakia* (21 December 2000), paras 33–36 (procedure to review the lawfulness of detention in a mental hospital had been initiated by the applicant but disregarded by the national authorities when they confined him in a mental hospital: violation of Art 5(4)); and *Laidin v France (no 1)* (5 November 2002), paras 23–30 (length of time taken to decide on a request for release from psychiatric detention: violation). In *R(C) v Mental Health Review Tribunal London South and South West Region* [2002] 1 WLR 176, a practice of routinely listing applications by patients compulsorily detained under the Mental Health Act 1983 for hearing eight weeks after the application date was held to be incompatible with Art 5(4); see also the later consideration of the same issue in *R (Rayner) v Secretary of State for Justice* [2009] 1 WLR 310. In *RB (Algeria) v Secretary of State for the Home Department* [2010] 2 AC 110, a risk that a person who was deported might be held in the receiving country for up to 50 days without charge was held not to be a risk of such a flagrant breach of Art 5 as to prevent deportation. See also *Re D* [2008] 1 WLR 1499 in relation to remedies for delay in conducting proceedings to review lawfulness of detention.

Article 5(5): Enforceable right to compensation for unlawful deprivation of liberty

4.241 Persons deprived of their liberty in contravention of Article 5 must have a right to compensation. At its most straightforward, Article 5(5) requires the state to provide an enforceable claim for compensation where there has been a violation of any other provision of Article 5[1]. The right to compensation under Article 5(5) must be available in domestic courts against the state authorities responsible for the unlawful arrest or detention, although the guarantee has not been interpreted as requiring any minimum level of payment, or even that any payment should be more than merely nominal[2]. The provision complements the right under Article 41 to 'just satisfaction' for violation of the ECHR which is a matter for determination by the European Court of Human Rights. This paragraph was initially underutilised by applicants. Where the ECHR forms part of domestic law, the Court will consider the constitutional effect of incorporation to ensure that the protection afforded by Article 5(5) is available with sufficient certainty and thus is effective[3]. In the past, the United Kingdom's failure to incorporate the ECHR into domestic law resulted in the establishment of violations of this provision[4], although it was accepted that where a civil action of damages against the police for wrongful arrest and detention was available, this would constitute an enforceable right to compensation as required by the guarantee[5]. However, where the powers of the domestic courts are still limited to the issuing of declarations of incompatibility where no enforceable claim for compensation is provided by statute, a violation of this provision will also occur[6].

---

1   Cf *Benham v United Kingdom* 1996-III, para 50.

2   Just satisfaction under Art 41 will also address any violation of Art 5(5), but awards tend to be low. See eg *Steel and Others v United Kingdom* 1998-VII (three protestors each imprisoned for seven hours following peaceful exercise of freedom of expression were each awarded

£500); *Curley v United Kingdom* (28 March 2000) (the Parole Board had twice recommended the applicant's release; ten-year delay before review by a body complying with Art 5(4) requirements; the Court accepted the applicant 'must have suffered feelings of frustration, uncertainty and anxiety which cannot be compensated solely by the findings of violations', and awarded £1,500 awarded for non-pecuniary damage); *A and Others v United Kingdom* [GC] 2009-... (detention without charge under anti-terrorism legislation: non-pecuniary damages of between €1,700 and €3,500); *Allen v United Kingdom* (30 March 2010) (prosecution appeal against bail was treated by English law as a re-hearing of the application for bail, but no similar rights were available to the suspect as at first instance: non-pecuniary award of €1,000). But cf *Clift v United Kingdom* (13 July 2010) (differences in early release schemes dependent upon the length of fixed-term sentences of imprisonment: non-pecuniary award of €10,000).

3   *Ciulla v Italy* (1989) A 148, para 44.

4   Eg *Brogan and Others v United Kingdom* (1988) A 145, paras 66–67; followed in a similar case involving British anti-terrorist legislation, *Fox, Campbell and Hartley* (1990) A 182, para 46; and in *Thynne, Wilson and Gunnell v United Kingdom* (1990) A 190, para 82 concerning review of discretionary life sentences; *Hood v United Kingdom* [GC] 1999-I, para 69; and in *Stephen Jordan v United Kingdom* (14 March 2000), para 33 concerning military justice procedures. See also *R (Wright) v Secretary of State for the Home Department* [2006] EWCA Civ 67 (since the breach of Art 5 occurred before the the Human Rights Act 1998 came into force, there was no enforceable right to compensation under Art 5(5) which could be recognised by the domestic courts).

5   *Steel and Others v United Kingdom* 1998-VII, para 83.

6   See *A and Others v United Kingdom* [GC] 2009-..., para 229.

4.242 The right to compensation arises in relation to any deprivation of liberty which was unlawful in domestic law, or which (although lawful in domestic law) is found to have violated Convention guarantees. But as the Grand Chamber made clear in *NC v Italy*, the right to payment of compensation need not be specifically linked in domestic law to a prior determination that the detention was unlawful. Here, domestic law made provision for a right to compensation following an acquittal on the ground that that the alleged facts had never occurred. This was taken to satisfy the requirements of Article 5(5). This was so even though the right to compensation did not require the showing of unlawful detention since pre-trial detention could be considered 'unjust' for the purposes of Italian law independent of any consideration of lawfulness. The right to compensation in domestic law was thus indissociable from any compensation to which the applicant might have been entitled under paragraph (5)[1].

1   *NC v Italy* [GC] 2002-X, paras 52–58.

4.243 The obligation is met where an individual is able to seek such a remedy, but any resultant payment of compensation will not deprive an individual of the status of 'victim' for the purposes of considering whether any other guarantee under Article 5 has been breached[1]. The paragraph does not preclude domestic law from requiring compensation to be made available only where the 'victim' can show he has suffered either pecuniary or non-pecuniary damage, and the Court itself has increasingly reflected this principle in its own judgments on Article 41[2]. In *Wassink v Netherlands,* the applicant had been confined to a psychiatric hospital in breach of domestic procedural provisions. The Court considered that national law did provide an adequate right to compensation, but here it would have been exceptionally difficult to establish that any damage had occurred since formal compliance with national law (and thus with the ECHR) would have been most likely in any case to have led to his detention[3]. However, a merely illusory right to compensation is insufficient[4]. Article 5(5) also requires the state to refrain from imposing any hurdle which would have the effect of qualifying the clear language of the paragraph, as in *Tsirlis and Kouloumpas v Greece* where a domestic court had decided that the applicants were not entitled to compensation since their unlawful deprivation of liberty had been on account of their own gross negligence[5]. Other challenges are foreseeable. In *Benham v United Kingdom*, the applicant had challenged the immunity of magistrates from civil proceedings in English law which provided that a magistrate could be held liable in damages only if acting in excess of jurisdiction, or for action taken maliciously or without reasonable and probable cause. The issue was avoided in this case since the Court decided that no Article 5 violation had arisen[6].

---

1   10868/84, *Woukam Moudefo v France* (1987) DR 51, 62; 11256/84, *Egue v France* (1988) DR 57, 47.

2   Cf *Caballero v United Kingdom* [GC] 2000-II, at paras 30–31 (just satisfaction in several cases awarded only in respect of 'damage resulting from a deprivation of liberty that the applicant would not have suffered if he or she had had the benefit' of Art 5, and a finding of a violation could thus constitute sufficient just satisfaction in respect of any non-pecuniary damage suffered: in the present case where release on bail was not competent, an award of £1,000 was appropriate since it was accepted the applicant would have had a good chance of release on bail prior to trial). But see *Danev v Bulgaria* (2 September 2010), paras 32–37 (formalistic approach requiring proof of non-pecuniary damage suggested non-payment of compensation in cases of unlawful detention lasting a short time and not resulting in objectively perceptible deterioration in physical or psychological condition: violation). For domestic discussion, see *R (KB) v South London and South and West Region Mental Health Review Tribunal* [2004] QB 936, where a range of claims arising from delay in the consideration of the lawfulness of detention of mental health patients were assessed. The court proceeded on the basis that Art 5(5) applied even where the delay in obtaining a decision of a court did not prolong the victim's detention; that damages should not be awarded for loss of liberty where a claimant could only establish that he had lost an opportunity of having an earlier tribunal hearing as a result of delay; and that a claimant who sought damages on the basis that he would have had an earlier favourable hearing but for delay must prove on the balance of probabilities that he would have been discharged at such a hearing. See also Case UfR 1998.337 V [Denmark] (formal error in compulsory psychiatric committal order but not one which would have affected length of detention: denial of compensation upheld since no pecuniary damage could be established and the error was not of such a severity that compensation could be given non-pecuniary damage).

3   *Wassink v Netherlands* (1990) A 185-A, para 38.

4   *Sakik and Others v Turkey* 1997-VII, para 60 (no example of any litigant obtaining compensation by reliance upon domestic law, and thus no effective enjoyment of right ensured with sufficient degree of certainty). See also *Chitayev v Russia* (18 January 2007), paras 192–196 (non-functioning legal system in Chechen Republic). Awards may be low, but must not be so low as to be negligible: 28779/95 *Cumber v United Kingdom* (27 November 1996).

5   *Tsirlis and Kouloumpas v Greece* 1997-III, paras 65–66.

6   *Benham v United Kingdom* 1996-III, paras 48–50.

4.244 The right to compensation for unlawful detention must now be considered in the light of the Grand Chamber's judgment in *Göç v Turkey* in which it was accepted that domestic proceedings concerning a claim for compensation fell within the scope of Article 6 as these involved the determination of 'civil rights and obligations'. The applicant's claim for compensation for unlawful detention had been determined by the court upon the basis of a report prepared by one of its members who had decided that it was unnecessary to hear the applicant, but at a lower amount than the sum recommended and again without according the applicant a hearing. The Grand Chamber considered that the proceedings had involved a dispute over the amount of compensation payable, a matter not determined as a matter of discretion but of legal right once it had been established that the statutory conditions had been fulfilled, and further that this right was 'civil' in nature as the subject matter of the action was pecuniary. Article 6 was thus engaged, and the absence of an oral hearing had deprived the applicant of the opportunity of a fair hearing to explain orally to the court the damage which his detention had entailed in terms of distress and anxiety since these were issues which could not be dealt with properly on the basis of the case file alone[1]. It is thus clear that unless there are exceptional circumstances which could justify the determination of such claims without an oral hearing, the range of guarantees accorded by Article 6 will apply in such claims.

---

1   *Göç v Turkey* [GC] 2002-V, paras 41–52. See also *Boulois v Luxembourg*, case pending before the Grand Chamber (repeated rejections by prison board of prisoner's requests for temporary leave of absence). [In the Chamber judgment (14 December 2010), paras 56–66, the Court determined this involved a 'civil right' within the meaning of Art 6(1) as the applicant could arguably maintain entitlement to leave in view of legislative and administrative regulations and rehabilitation was vital for his right to lead a private social life and to develop his social identity].

Chapter 5

Fair administration of justice

INTRODUCTION

5.01 Procedural propriety and the prohibition of the retroactive imposition of criminal liability lie at the heart of any legal system grounded in the rule of law. The central importance of Article 6[1] is reflected in the volume and scope of challenges to the application of criminal, civil and administrative justice in European states[2]. The European Court of Human Rights has been at pains to uphold fundamental notions of fairness in the administration of justice against competing and often conflicting contemporary trends: for example, the modern administrative state may seek to promote efficiency in the delivery of public services through relaxed application of due process guarantees; reform of criminal process at domestic level may purport to achieve greater effectiveness through modification of long-held principles considered necessary to protect an accused; or an increasingly litigious society may find that enhanced awareness of civil rights and obligations giving rise to heightened expectations is not met by the allocation of additional financial and judicial resources. Study of this rich and complex resultant case law can be somewhat intimidating and initially appear less than rewarding since many of the judgments tend to reflect the peculiarities of legal systems based upon differing constitutional principles[3]; however, it must be stressed that much of the approach to interpretation has been developed in a number of leading cases which establish key tenets of general application. In some contrast, Article 7, which embodies the related principles 'that only the law can define a crime and prescribe a penalty [and] the criminal law must not be extensively construed to an accused's detriment'[4], has generated only limited jurisprudence doubtless on account of the codified nature of the criminal law in the majority of European states, although the Court has not found it difficult to accommodate legal systems based on the continuing evolution of the common law by applying the basic criterion of whether criminal liability is reasonably foreseeable[5].

---

1   *De Cubber v Belgium* (1984) A 86, para 30. For further consideration of the provision, see Trechsel with Summers *Human Rights in Criminal Proceedings* (2005) *passim*; Jackson, 'The Effect of Human Rights on Criminal Evidentiary Processes: Towards Convergence, Divergence or Realignment?' (2005) 68 MLR 737; and Summers *The European Criminal Procedural Tradition and the European Court of Human Rights* (2007), *passim*.

2   Eissen *The Length of Civil and Criminal Proceedings in the Case-Law of the European Court of Human Rights* (1996) at pp 7 and 8 suggests that in the Court's first 25 years (ie until the end of 1995) 339 of the 554 judgments delivered (ie over 60%) concerned Art 6 (and of these judgments, half concerned 'reasonable time'). A considerable percentage of the judgments delivered still involve Art 6: in 2009, for example, of the 1,625 judgments issued in which at least one violation of the Convention was established, 449 involved Art 6 and length of proceedings: *European Court of Human Rights, Annual Report 2009* (2010), p 145. The majority of these cases involve 'clone' or repetitive cases, and the Court is now applying its

'pilot-judgment' procedure: see paras **2.80–2.81** above. The continuing failure of certain states to introduce general measures following adverse judgments particularly in respect of excessive length of proceedings is having a major impact upon the Court's workload, (Italy, Greece and Poland together are responsible for over 30% of such cases) and non-enforcement of domestic judicial decisions (over 70% of such cases involve Russia and Ukraine), while the lack of an independent and impartial judiciary in Ukraine is also of considerable concern: see eg Parliamentary Assembly Committee on Legal Affairs and Human Rights *Implementation of Judgments of the European Court of Human Rights: 7th Report* doc AS/Jur(2010) 36 (2010). Opinions prepared by the Parliamentary Assembly prior to accession to the ECHR are designed to identify issues requiring reform, while the Council of Europe is also involved in a range of capacity-building activities in many new member states (including training of judges and prosecutors, promotion of judicial reform through improving efficiency, increasing professionalism and reducing corruption, and addressing problems of legal certainty through reform of appellate courts and dissemination of judgments).

3   Soyer and de Salvia 'Article 6' in Pettiti, Decaux and Imbert *La Convention Européenne des Droits de l'Homme* (1st edn, 1995), at p 241: '[the jurisprudence of the Commission and Court] est touffue, car elle s'élabore à partir d'innombrables espèces, d'autant plus variées qu'elles surgissent dans des systèmes juridiques très divers, voire dissemblables (common law, droit écrit – Etats monistes, Etats dualistes)'. For comparative discussion, see Summers *Fair Trials: The European Criminal Procedural Tradition and the European Court of Human Rights* (2007).

4   *SW v United Kingdom* (1995) A 335-B at para 35.

5   *SW v United Kingdom* (1995) A 335-B, paras 36–44, discussed at para **5.227** below.

5.02 Most challenges concerning the administration of justice raised to date by Scottish applications to Strasbourg have concerned Article 6's guarantees of a fair hearing in civil and criminal cases. The particular features of Scots law which have been scrutinised include issues as to the right of access to courts, security measures during trials, criminal appeals, bias on the part of jurors, the non-availability of legal aid in criminal cases, and certain aspects of the children's hearing system. Similarly, since the entry into force of the Scotland Act 1998, the majority of key challenges considered by the courts have founded upon aspects of Article 6[1]. This situation has been replicated since the entry into force of the Human Rights Act 1998 across the entire United Kingdom. Article 6 has also featured in extradition cases, where there has been a question whether the extradition would result in a flagrant breach of the right to a fair trial[2]. The conclusion for each domestic legal system is that the maintenance of standards of fairness in the administration of justice requires constant vigilance.

1   Craig et al *The Use of Human Rights Legislation in the Scottish Courts Scottish Executive Social Research* (2004). See further paras **1.12–1.20** above.

2   See eg *R (Al-Saadoon) v Secretary of State for Defence* [2010] QB 486 (cf *Al-Saadoon and Mufdhi v United Kingdom* 2010-…); *RB (Algeria) v Secretary of State for the Home Department* [2010] 2 AC 110; and *Allen v HM Advocate* 2010 SCCR 861.

ARTICLE 6: THE RIGHT TO A FAIR TRIAL

Introduction

5.03 The text of Article 6 is one of the most detailed of the substantive rights in the Convention. The Strasbourg authorities have sought to give Article 6(1) a purposive interpretation that furthers the principle of fairness in the administration of justice. The European Court of Human Rights has often reiterated that in a democratic society based upon the rule of law, 'the right to a fair administration of justice holds such a prominent place that a restrictive interpretation of Article 6(1) would not correspond to the aim and the purpose of that provision'[1]. Any tendency, however, to regard its sub-divisions as constituting a number of discrete guarantees has been firmly resisted by the Court: the whole provision is composed of elements 'which are distinct but stem from the same basic idea and which, taken together, make up a single right not specifically defined'[2]. Paragraph (1) thus refers to the rights to:

- 'a fair and public hearing';
- 'within a reasonable time';
- 'by an independent and impartial tribunal established by law'; and
- which pronounces its judgment publicly except in defined and narrowly construed circumstances.

Additionally, a person accused of a criminal offence acquires further minimum rights conferred by paragraphs (2) and (3), including the rights:

- to be presumed innocent until proven guilty;
- to be informed of the charge against him;
- to have adequate time and facilities to prepare his defence;
- to defend himself or have legal assistance;
- to examine (and have examined) witnesses; and
- to the free use of an interpreter.

In addition to these textual provisions, the Court will also insist that judicial proceedings are broadly adversarial in character, that legal certainty is respected in the formulation of domestic legal rules by courts, and that domestic rules of evidence applied meet a certain standard. 'In sum, the whole makes up the right to a fair hearing.'[3]

---

1   Cf *Delcourt v Belgium* (1970) A 11, at para 25.

2   The White Paper, *Rights Brought Home* (Cm 3782) originally proposed that ratification of ECHR, Prot 6 would proceed on a free vote in Parliament. Consequently, the Human Rights Bill at first did not propose to include abolition of the death penalty in its scope. However, the Government subsequently proposed an amendment to the Bill during its parliamentary stages to include this protocol, and formally ratified it in May 1999 (with entry into force on June 1999). The United Kingdom ratified Prot 13 in October 2003 (with entry into force in February 2004). Prot 13, Arts 1 and 2 are 'Convention rights' for the purposes of the Human Rights Act

1998: The Human Rights Act 1998 (Amendment) Order 2004 (SI 2004/1574). Art 1 of Prot 13 was invoked, unsuccessfully, in *Al-Saadoon v Secretary of State for Defence* [2010] QB 486.

2   *Golder v United Kingdom* (1975) A 18, at para 28.

3   *Golder v United Kingdom* (1975) A 18, at para 36.

5.04 An individual may waive his rights – or aspects of the right to a fair hearing – in certain circumstances, providing always that he does so by 'his own free will and in an unequivocal manner' and as long as no issue of public interest is involved[1]. However, a state may not reduce unilaterally the advantages attached to a waiver of certain rights inherent in the concept of fair trial as such would be contrary to the principle of legal certainty and the protection of the legitimate trust of persons engaged in judicial proceedings[2].

1   *Albert and Le Compte v Belgium* (1983) A 58, at para 35; and *Schüler-Zgraggen v Switzerland* (1993) A 263, para 58. See further paras **3.32–3.34** above and **5.156** below.

2   *Scoppola v Italy (no 2)* [GC] 2009-…, paras 132–145 (although the applicant had opted to be tried under summary procedure, he had been deprived of the most important advantage stemming from that choice under the law in force at the time – in this case, the replacement of life imprisonment with a fixed 30-year sentence – by a legislative decree so that his legitimate expectation in the likely outcome of the proceedings had been frustrated: violation).

5.05 The right under Article 6 is to 'fairness' rather than to 'justice'. The European Court of Human Rights has consistently refused to allow itself to be looked upon as a court of fourth instance and will not examine the merits of an application to consider, for example, whether a conviction has been wrongly secured[1]. In other words, the ultimate question to be determined by the Court is whether the proceedings as a whole were fair. This in consequence requires consideration of all the particular facts of each case[2], including any decision taken by an appellate court[3] and any failure on the part of state authorities to implement a court decision[4]. Thus while there may appear on the face of the facts to have been some breach of a particular element which forms part of the wider concept of a fair hearing, it will always be necessary to consider the overall impact of this on the proceedings[5]. Similarly, the mere fact that evidence has been led which was obtained in violation of domestic law or even of a Convention guarantee will not of itself render the trial unfair[6]. On the other hand, the Court has sought to interpret the guarantees in Article 6 to render them 'practical and effective as opposed to theoretical and illusory'. This may mean that, while an applicant who has been acquitted or where there has been a lack of substantive proceedings in a case cannot generally claim to be a 'victim', in certain circumstances it may still be possible to establish a violation of Article 6 where to hold otherwise would prevent examination of complaints of a violation of fair hearing guarantees[7].

1   Eg 14739/89, *Callaghan and Others v United Kingdom* (1989) DR 60, 296 (refusal to allow new evidence to be considered by a jury rather than by the Court of Appeal: Art 6(2) was not applicable to reference proceedings at appellate level, and application declared inadmissible). Contrast *Khamidov v Russia* 2007-XII, paras 165–175 at para 174 (the unreasonableness of the findings of the domestic courts was so striking that the decisions could only be described as grossly arbitrary; the standard of proof set by the courts was 'extreme and unattainable', consequently the applicant was denied the right to a fair trial).

2 *Kraska v Switzerland* (1993) A 254-B, para 30.

3 *Stanford v United Kingdom* (1994) A 282-A, para 24.

4 *Hornsby v Greece* 1997-II, paras 39–45 (failure to implement a final court decision for over five years was considered a violation of Art 6(1)).

5 Cf *Ankerl v Switzerland* 1996-V, para 38 (difference in treatment in respect of the manner in which evidence was taken from the parties' witnesses, but not one which could be taken to have placed one party at a substantial disadvantage, and thus no breach of Art 6).

6 Eg *Khan v United Kingdom* 2000-V, discussed further at para **5.127** below.

7 Eg *Minelli v Switzerland* (1983) A 62, paras 37–38 (expiry of limitation period preventing determination of guilt; but despite the lack of a conviction, the court indicated the probable guilt of the applicant: violation of Art 6(2)); *Funke v France* (1993) A 256-A, paras 39–40 (conviction for failure to supply information, but criminal proceedings in respect of initial inquiries were never initiated); *Sekanina v Austria* (1993) A 266-A, paras 22–31 (acquittal of the applicant but refusal of compensation because of suspicion of guilt contrary to the presumption of innocence); *Allenet de Ribemont v France* (1995) A 308, paras 32–37 (public comments of police officers suggestive of an accused's guilt of charges even though the proceedings on those charges were subsequently discontinued); *Quinn v Ireland* (21 December 2000), paras 43–46, and *Heaney and McGuinness v Ireland* 2000-XII, paras 43–46 (applicants had been 'charged' for the purposes of Art 6, even though in the first case the applicant had not been charged with a substantive offence; and the two applicants in the second case had not been formally charged when they were required to give information contrary to Art 6(1)).

Relationship between Article 6 and other Convention provisions

5.06 Applicants will frequently challenge both the reasons for a particular decision and the manner in which it was taken, and thus applications will often allege a violation of Article 6 at the same time as seeking to rely upon another substantive provision of the Convention. However, there may be implicit positive obligations upon a state to provide procedural protection under other Convention guarantees. In child care cases falling within the scope of Article 8, for example, the European Court of Human Rights has stressed that while this provision 'contains no explicit procedural requirements, the decision-making process leading to measures of interference must be fair and such as to afford due respect to the interests safeguarded'[1]. Under Articles 2 and 3 there are now responsibilities for ensuring that an applicant has the right to participate in an independent and public scrutiny of allegations that unlawful lethal force or unnecessary violence has been used by public officials[2]. Article 5 case law now indicates that the determination of whether there has been a 'deprivation of liberty' may involve examination of whether appropriate procedural safeguards have been accorded[3], while periodic review of the lawfulness of continuing detention under Article 5(4) implies access to a 'court' enjoying independence and impartiality and able to order the release of the individual[4]. Further, when assessing the proportionality of an interference with property rights under Article 1 of Protocol no 1, the Court will consider the degree of protection from arbitrariness that is afforded by the proceedings in a case, and in particular whether the quality of the procedures has ensured that due account has been taken of the interests of an applicant before arriving at a decision affecting property rights[5].

1   *McMichael v United Kingdom* (1995) A 307-B, at para 87; see para **6.57** below. Cf European
    Convention on the Exercise of Children's Rights (ETS 160(1996)), not yet ratified by the
    United Kingdom.

2   *McCann and Others v United Kingdom* (1995) A 324, paras 161–164 (Art 2); *Assenov v
    Bulgaria* 1998-VIII, para 102 (Art 3); see paras **4.42–4.47** and **4.103–4.108** above.

3   *Amuur v France* 1996-III, 827, paras 50–54; see para **4.157** above.

4   Eg *Hussain v United Kingdom* 1996-I, paras 58–61; see paras **4.233–4.240** above.

5   Eg *Hentrich v France* (1994) A 296-A, paras 45–49; see para **8.33** below.

Relationship with Article 13

5.07 The primary responsibility for securing ECHR guarantees falls upon member
states[1]. The subsidiary nature of the Strasbourg Court is appreciated more clearly
when Articles 1, 13 and 35(1) are considered together. Article 1 specifies that
contracting states 'shall secure to everyone within their jurisdiction the rights and
freedoms defined [in the Convention]; Article 13 provides that 'everyone whose
rights and freedoms as set forth in this Convention are violated shall have an
effective remedy before a national authority'; and Article 35(1) requires exhaustion
of domestic remedies before an application may be brought before the Court[2].
Article 1 does not require formal incorporation of the ECHR into domestic law[3].
The key provision from the perspective of an applicant is thus Article 13 which
'guarantees the availability of a remedy at a national level to enforce – and hence
to allege non-compliance with – the substance of the Convention rights and
freedoms in whatever form they may happen to be secured in the domestic legal
order'[4].

1   *Handyside v United Kingdom* (1976) A 24, para 48; *Akdivar and Others v Turkey* 1996-IV,
    para 65.

2   See further, para **2.59** above.

3   *Lithgow and Others v United Kingdom* (1986) A 102, para 205. In practice, all states have now
    in some manner 'incorporated' the Convention into domestic law.

4   *Boyle and Rice v United Kingdom* (1988) A 131, at para 52; see also *Rotaru v Romania* [GC]
    2000-V, para 67.

5.08 Detailed discussion of Article 13 – a provision of some complexity – is
outwith the scope of this work[1]. Article 13 must provide the opportunity to
challenge domestic law or practice wherever there is an 'arguable' claim that
there has been a violation of the Convention, although the provision 'cannot
reasonably be interpreted so as to require a remedy in domestic law in respect of
any supposed grievance under the Convention that an individual may have, no
matter how unmeritorious his claim may be'[2]. However, the constitutional diversity
of European legal systems is respected. The Court has accommodated concepts
such as sovereignty of parliament and, in consequence, 'Article 13 does not
guarantee a remedy allowing a contracting state's laws as such to be challenged
before a national authority on the ground of being contrary to the Convention or
equivalent domestic norms'[3]. For the purposes of Article 13, for a remedy to be

effective in domestic law it must exist with sufficient certainty[4], it must be adequate in the sense of addressing the substance of the issue raised and allowing relief to be granted[5], and it must be available to the individual[6]. In other words, the remedy must permit the individual to have his 'arguable claim' determined, and where appropriate, to obtain redress[7]. Further, the remedy must be 'effective', that is, it must be 'a remedy that is as effective as can be having regard to the restricted scope for recourse inherent in [the particular context]'[8].

---

1   See further Harris, O'Boyle and Warbrick *Law of the European Convention on Human Rights* (2nd edn, 2009), pp 557–575.

2   *Boyle and Rice v United Kingdom* (1988) A 131, at para 52. In consequence, an applicant cannot allege breach of Art 13 alone; but the Court may find a violation of Art 13 even where it has determined that there has been no breach of any other guarantee: cf *Klass and Others v Germany* (1978) A 28, paras 65–72.

3   *Leander v Sweden* (1987) A 116, at para 77.

4   Cf *Costello-Roberts v United Kingdom* (1993) A 247-C, paras 37–40 (civil action for assault was considered an effective remedy in English law to challenge corporal punishment; while the Commission had been of the opinion such a remedy would not have been effective, 'the effectiveness of a remedy ... does not depend on the certainty of a favourable outcome...').

5   Cf *Silver and Others v United Kingdom* (1981) A 61, paras 115–119.

6   Eg *Aydin v Turkey* 1997-VI, paras 104–107.

7   *Klass and Others v Germany* (1978) A 28, para 64.

8   *Klass and Others v Germany* (1978) A 28, at para 69.

5.09 An intention to furnish aggrieved parties with domestic remedies for complaints related to the ECHR lies behind the enactment of the Human Rights Act 1998 in the United Kingdom and provides the reason advanced for the exclusion of Article 13 from the list of 'Convention rights' in that legislation[1]. While Article 13 cannot thus be relied upon directly in domestic proceedings, some understanding of this guarantee may nevertheless assist in gaining an appreciation of the importance of Article 6 in the Strasbourg scheme of protection of human rights since the Court appears to be moving gradually towards an expectation that Article 13 requirements will be met through the determination by domestic courts of claims of violation of substantive Convention guarantees. There is an obvious and close relationship between the two provisions: Article 6 guarantees access to a court for the determination of disputes, while Article 13 requires states to ensure that 'everyone whose rights and freedoms as set forth in this Convention [and optional Protocols] are violated shall have an effective remedy before a national authority ...' The difficulty is that Article 6 guarantees access to a court for the determination of all 'civil rights and obligations', while Article 13 only applies to the enforcement of Convention guarantees, which may or may not also involve 'civil rights'. Certainly, Article 13 responsibilities may be secured by means other than judicial hearings, and 'although no single remedy may itself satisfy the requirements of Article 13, the aggregate of remedies provided for under domestic law may do so'[2]. Further, the Court may consider another Convention guarantee to be the *lex specialis* (rather than Article 13) in determining whether domestic law provides adequate safeguards[3]; elsewhere in the Convention, it has also shown itself unwilling to address a complaint under Article 13 if it has already examined the issue of the availability of a remedy in domestic law under another substantive provision[4]. In any case, the Court has not always been consistent in its disposal of Article 13 arguments[5]. Determination of an Article 6 point will often render discussion of any Article 13 argument unnecessary[6], but on the other hand, the court on occasion has preferred to consider Article 6 questions concerning access to a court for the purposes of vindicating substantive Convention rights under the more general Article 13 obligation of securing an effective remedy in domestic law[7].

1   *Montgomery v HM Advocate* 2001 SC (PC) 1, 16; *Brown v Stott* 2001 SC (PC) 43, 70 per Lord Hope of Craighead. See further para **1.29** above.

2   *Silver and Others v United Kingdom* (1983) A 61, at para 113. See further van Dijk, van Hoof, van Rijn and Zwaak, *Theory and Practice of the European Convention on Human Rights* (4th edn, 2006) pp 559 and 1017–1021.

3   Thus Art 5(4) rather than Art 13 will be the relevant provision to examine whether domestic law permits scrutiny of the lawfulness of detention: see para **4.219** et seq above.

4   Eg *X and Y v Netherlands* (1985) A 91, para 36 (availability of remedy considered in the context of Art 8). See too discussion of the relationship between Art 13 and Arts 2 and 3 discussed at paras **4.40** and **4.95–4.96** above.

5   Cf O'Boyle and Warbrick *Law of the European Convention on Human Rights* (1995) at p 443: 'if the general principles which [Article 13] embodies are now tolerably clear, they are not free from criticism'. See also Frowein 'Art 13 as a Growing Pillar of Convention Law' in Mahoney, Matscher, Petzold and Wildhaber (eds) *Protecting Human Rights: The European Perspective* (2000) pp 545–550.

6   *Hentrich v France* (1994) A 296-A, at para 65: the requirements of Art 13 'are less strict than, and are here absorbed by, those of Article 6 para 1'. See too, eg, *Mats Jacobsson v Sweden* (1990) A 180-A, para 38; *Pizzetti v Italy* (1993) A 257-C, para 21; *Putz v Austria* 1996-I, para 41.

7   Eg *Menteş and Others v Turkey* 1997-VIII, 2689, paras 86–88 (destruction of homes and property).

Additional Convention guarantees in the criminal process

5.10 As noted, paragraphs (2) and (3) of Article 6 are of relevance in the determination of criminal charges, while Article 7 prohibits the retroactive imposition of the criminal law or of a heavier criminal sanction than the appropriate penalty in force when the criminal act was committed, thus guaranteeing application of the maxims of *nullum crimen sine lege* and *nulla poene sine lege*. Additionally, Protocol no 7 makes provision for a right of appeal in criminal matters, for a right to compensation for wrongful conviction, and for a right not to be tried or punished again in criminal proceedings in a state where the individual has already been finally acquitted or convicted in accordance with national law. The United Kingdom has not ratified Protocol no 7[1], and it may be difficult to argue that the principle of *ne bis in idem,* which prohibits an individual from being tried twice, could apply as an aspect of the general right of fairness under Article 6[2]. However, where a state has made provision for a system of criminal appeals in domestic law, the conduct of the appellate courts will also be open to scrutiny under Article 6, irrespective of whether the state in question has ratified this optional Protocol[3].

1   As at 31 March 2011, 42 of the 47 Council of Europe states had ratified Prot 7. Although the Labour Government indicated in *Bringing Rights Home* (Cm 3782) (1997), para 4.15 that it intended to ratify Prot 7, it had not done so before losing office in 2010.

2   Cf *Maaouia v France* [GC] 2000-X, para 36 (provisions had to be construed in the light of the entire Convention system, and the terms of Prot 7, Art 1 which provided additional procedural guarantees applicable to the expulsion of aliens thus implied that Art 6 did not apply in this regard). See similarly Trechsel *Human Rights in Criminal Proceedings* (2005), p 385.

3   See *Belziuk v Poland* 1998-II, para 37. Cf *Monnell and Morris v United Kingdom* (1987) A 115, para 54 (not contested that leave to appeal proceedings formed part of the determination of a criminal charge).

Fair hearing guarantees and procedural rights for suspects under EU law

5.11 In the field of criminal law, there is now a clear attempt to apply key principles and case-law of the Strasbourg Court in strengthening the procedural rights of suspects or accused persons in criminal proceedings in EU member states[1]. This alignment with ECHR standards is at an early stage of development[2], but the impact of Article 6 jurisprudence is clear[3].

1   A 'roadmap' for strengthening procedural rights of suspects or accused persons in criminal proceedings was adopted by a Resolution of the Council (Justice and Home Affairs) on 30 November 2009 (see OJ C 295, 4.12.2009, p 1). It proposes six areas ('measures') for future action: translation and interpretation; information on rights and information about charges; legal advice and legal aid; communication with relatives, employers and consular authorities; special safeguards for vulnerable groups; and pre-trial detention.

2   See Directive 2010/64/EU (translation and interpretation); and Proposed Directive COM(2010) 392/3 (information on rights and about the charge, and access to the case file).

3   See further Pellonpää 'Article 6 of the European Convention on Human Rights and EU law' in Hartig (ed) *Trente Ans de Droit Européen des Droits de l'Homme: Études à la Mémoire de Wolfgang Strasser* pp 265–288 (2007); cf Callewaert 'The European Convention on Human Rights and European Union Law: a Long Way to Harmony' [2009] EHRLR 768.

SCOPE OF ARTICLE 6

5.12 Consideration of the scope of Article 6 is of crucial importance. Paragraph (1) provides that the bundle of rights which together constitute a fair hearing apply in the determination of 'civil rights and obligations' or of 'any criminal charge'. Each concept is recognised as having an autonomous meaning which is not dependent upon the characterisation given by the domestic legal system[1], and a substantial (but not always coherent or consistent[2]) jurisprudence has emerged. The trend has been to widen the scope of each, and particularly of 'civil rights and obligations'.

1   *König v Germany* (1978) A 27, para 89 ('civil rights'); *Engel and Others v Netherlands* (1976) A 22, paras 81–82 ('criminal charge').

2   See eg van Dijk 'The Interpretation of 'Civil Rights and Obligations' by the European Court of Human Rights – One More Step to Take', in Matscher and Petzold (eds) *Protecting Human Rights: The European Dimension* (1988) pp 131–143.

Civil rights and obligations

5.13 The first issue in discussion of fair hearings is the applicability of Article 6. Certain proceedings clearly fall within the scope of the provision. Invariably, litigation in the civil courts between two private individuals or legal persons will do so[1], but what may be less certain is whether proceedings other than those normally disposed of in the ordinary civil courts, or whether issues which fall outside the ambit of private law as traditionally understood, also involve the 'determination' of 'civil rights and obligations'. A broadening of the scope of the concept is apparent, but this has been perhaps rather more incremental than principled, and the accommodation within Article 6 of administrative proceedings and certain issues involving some element of public law has been achieved not without intellectual difficulty. Aspects of the case law have been described as 'confusing'[2] and as resulting in an 'undesirable situation' for both individuals and state authorities[3], although a more positive view is that the jurisprudence is at least 'progressive'[4] in so far as the scope of the guarantee has been gradually widened.

1   Including enforcement proceedings and other proceedings ancillary to a court decision with a view to resolving a civil dispute: *Scollo v Italy* (1995) A 315-C, para 44 and *Immobiliare Saffi v Italy* [GC] 1999-V, paras 62–63 (although domestic law labelled police assistance in enforcing a court decree as 'administrative', Art 6 rights would be merely illusory if they did not cover implementation of judicial decisions).

2   Gomien, Harris and Zwaak *Law and Practice of the European Convention on Human Rights and the European Social Charter* (1996), at p 177.

3   Van Dijk, van Hoof van Rijn and Zwaak *Theory and Practice of the European Convention on Human Rights* (4th edn, 2006), at p 404. (At pp 514–516, the authors argue for recourse to the *travaux préparatoires* to help gain clarity as to what the drafters intended, noting that an earlier version of the English text read 'rights and obligations in a suit at law').

4   Reid *A Practitioner's Guide to the European Convention on Human Rights* (3rd edn, 2007), at p 78.

5.14 In determining whether there is an issue which affects 'civil rights and obligations, four conditions must be satisfied:

(i)   there must be a genuine claim or dispute (in French, *contestation*);

(ii) this dispute must relate to a right or obligation in domestic law;

(iii) this right or obligation must be broadly civil in character; and

(iv) the outcome of the dispute must be directly decisive for the right or obligation.

Since the phrase must be given an autonomous meaning, whether these tests are satisfied rather than the status of the parties or decision-maker in domestic law is thus crucial.

The existence of a dispute or 'contestation'

5.15 The French text refers to '*contestations sur ses droits et obligations de caractère civil*', while the English version refers merely to the 'determination' of such rights. The idea of a '*contestation*' suggests the existence of a 'dispute' which has at least an arguable basis in domestic law. However, 'conformity with the spirit of the Convention requires that this word should not be construed too technically and that it should be given a substantive rather than a formal meaning'[1]. In *Le Compte, van Leuven and de Meyere v Belgium*, the Court accepted that the applicants' denial of allegations of professional misconduct and their challenge to their suspension by a professional body were sufficient to give rise to the necessary 'dispute'. 'Disputes' can thus relate not only to the actual existence of a civil right, 'but also to its scope or the manner in which it may be exercised'[2]. 'Disputes' may also concern questions of either law or fact[3], and may thus involve claims to or the assertion of rights in respect of such matters as entitlement to a pension[4], access by parents to children taken into care[5], compensation for wrongful imprisonment[6], the award of costs in civil litigation[7], and the rights to carry on trading under licence[8], to practise a profession[9], to receive compensation for culpable misconduct or other negligence on the part of state authorities[10], and to exploit land[11]. Indeed, a suggestion found in the *Moreira de Azevedo v Portugal* judgment acknowledges that the issue of 'dispute' is not likely to pose much difficulty. The applicant had intervened in a criminal prosecution against an alleged assailant as he was entitled to do, but had not expressly sought civil compensation from the wrongdoer. The Court accepted that the intervention itself was enough to constitute a 'dispute' since it gave rise to an implicit claim for compensation and thus a *contestation* could be said to have existed[12].

---

1   *Le Compte, van Leuven and de Meyere v Belgium* (1981) A 43, at para 45.

2   *Le Compte, van Leuven and de Meyere v Belgium* (1981) A 43, para 45.

3   *Benthem v Netherlands* (1985) A 97, at para 32.

4   *Deumeland v Germany* (1986) A 100, para 59; *Salerno v Italy* (1992) A 245-D, paras 15–16. Cf 39712/98, *La Parola and Others v Italy* (30 November 2000) (request for further financial assistance in respect of a disabled minor who was already in receipt of benefit on a permanent basis: proceedings were not aimed at determining a dispute but rather entitlement to the additional aid requested, and thus Art 6 was inadmissible).

5   *O v United Kingdom* (1987) A 120, paras 58–59.

6   *Baraona v Portugal* (1987) A 122, paras 38 and 41.

7   *Beer v Austria* (6 February 2001), paras 11–13.

8   *Pudas v Sweden* (1987) A 125-A, para 34; *Tre Traktörer v Sweden* (1989) A 159, para 40; *Editions Périscope v France* (1992) A 234-B, paras 37–38. Cf *Kervöelen v France* (27 March 2001), paras 27–30 (automatic expiry of a licence if no alcohol had been sold for three years:

loss of licence was thus not the result of an administrative or judicial act (as in cases such as Tre Traktörer), and in consequence, Art 6 was inapplicable).

9   *H v Belgium* (1987) A 127-B, para 43 (an advocate could expect to be readmitted after ten years' suspension: upon satisfaction of the prescribed requirements. Art 6 was applicable since the professional body had to determine whether these conditions had been satisfied); *Kraska v Switzerland* (1993) A 254-B, paras 24–27 (attempt to seek authorisation to practise again as a doctor after licence had been withdrawn).

10   *Neves e Silva v Portugal* (1989) A 153-A, para 37.

11   *Allan Jacobsson v Sweden (no 1)* (1989) A 163, paras 67–70 (prolongation of building prohibition challenged by applicants; respondent government claimed there was no 'right' to build in existence until a permit had been granted: the Court determined that in the circumstances it could be argued that the applicant had a claim to a 'right' to a permit). See also *Thery v France* (1 February 2000), paras 22–23 (the applicant's asserted right to cultivate his farmland was considered to be a subsidiary right relating to the manner in which a right of property was exercised and thus qualified as a civil right).

12   *Moreira de Azevedo v Portugal* (1990) A 189, at para 66 ('in so far as the French word 'contestation' would appear to require the existence of a dispute, if indeed it does so at all, the facts of the case show that there was one'). Cf *Hamer v France* 1996-III, paras 73–79 (no 'dispute' was established in a similar set of circumstances where French law specifically required a civil party seeking to intervene in a criminal process with a view to obtaining compensation to lodge a claim for compensation).

5.16 The 'dispute' need not necessarily involve any substantial pecuniary interest, but it at least must be genuine and of a serious nature. In *Gorou v Greece (no 2)*, the applicant had filed a criminal complaint for perjury and defamation against her superior and had applied for civil-party status in the proceedings, claiming a sum equivalent to about €3. Following the acquittal of the accused, the applicant requested the public prosecutor at the Court of Cassation to lodge an appeal on points of law. Although this request had derived from an established judicial practice, the public prosecutor had refused to do so. The Grand Chamber held that the impugned proceedings involved the right to a 'good reputation' and had an economic aspect. As to whether a 'dispute' existed, the Grand Chamber considered that it would be artificial to deny that the applicant's request to the public prosecutor arose from a real 'dispute', since the request formed an integral part of the whole of the proceedings that the applicant had joined as a civil party. Consequently, the applicant's request to the public prosecutor related to a 'dispute over a civil right' for the purposes of Article 6[1]. On the other hand, in *Van Marle v Netherlands*, the applicants had been denied registration as chartered accountants after unsuccessfully sitting a test which sought to assess professional competency. The Court considered this assessment of professional skill as 'akin to a school or university examination' and 'so far removed from the exercise of the normal judicial function that the safeguards in Article 6 cannot be taken as covering resultant disagreements' even although in domestic law the appeal board was considered to be a tribunal. On this basis, it held there was no 'dispute' within the meaning of the requirement[2].

1   *Gorou v Greece (no 2)* [GC] 2009-…, paras 27–36.

2   *Van Marle v Netherlands* (1986) A 101, paras 36–37 at para 36; but cf *Motière v France* (dec) (28 March 2000), paras 16–21 (applicant who had worked as a body builder sought a further

qualification but had been refused this by the decision of the responsible state official; while the applicant did not have a right to such a qualification she was nevertheless entitled to a lawful examination process in domestic law, a matter amenable to judicial review which the applicant had sought: the Court proceeded upon the basis that there was thus a dispute over a civil right within the meaning of Art 6(1) in considering the reasonableness of the length of proceedings).

Dispute concerning a right with an arguable basis in domestic law

5.17 As with the approach adopted in determining whether a 'dispute' exists, this requirement is considered in a manner which is in keeping with maximising the scope of the guarantee. However, Article 6 cannot be taken as requiring the recognition of any specific right in domestic law[1]. In other words, the claim must be based upon an existing right recognised by the national legal system: that is, it must be one which has at least an arguable basis in domestic law[2]. There is, though, no restriction on the type of issue which may form part of a claim, and thus the 'arguable basis' for the purposes of the test may extend to a challenge to the lawfulness or validity of legal rules[3]. The fact that a domestic court has agreed to hear an action will be sufficient to meet this test. In *Salerno v Italy*, the applicant had sought membership of a pension fund for notaries but the action had been dismissed by the domestic courts. The respondent government asserted that as the substance of his claim had already been determined, a fresh action brought by him some two years later could not be said to have been based upon any arguable claim. The European Court of Human Rights, however, considered that the domestic courts had acknowledged this fresh claim as sufficiently tenable in holding the action admissible and, accordingly, these new proceedings fell within the scope of Article 6[4].

It thus may be necessary for the Court itself to determine whether domestic law does recognise a right in domestic law[5]. In *Grădinar v Moldova*, for example, the applicant's husband had been killed before a retrial had taken place after he had been acquitted of a charge of murder of a police officer. The applicant had requested that the case be reheard so that his innocence could be established, but the retrial had resulted in a determination of guilt. The applicant then sought to challenge the absence of sufficient reasons for the conviction in proceedings in Strasbourg. Since domestic law enabled the applicant to exercise her own civil rights within the context of the criminal proceedings against her husband, the Court concluded that the proceedings had involved the determination of a 'civil right' within the meaning of Article 6, even although the Court had serious reservations about a legal system which allowed the trial and conviction of deceased persons[6].

---

1   Eg *Mihova v Italy* (dec) (30 March 2010) (inability to challenge the sentence imposed on an individual for sexual abuse of the applicant's daughter as the sentence had been imposed following a plea bargain and the applicant had not been joined to the proceedings as a civil party: inadmissible, the aim of exercising a right to 'private revenge' was not as such guaranteed by the ECHR, and the applicant had been able to bring a civil action for damages against the individual and thus had enjoyed access to a court with jurisdiction to examine her civil right to compensation).

2 Eg *Zander v Sweden* (1993) A 279-B, at para 22 (the Court 'has first to ascertain whether there was a dispute (*'contestation'*) over a 'right' which can be said, at least on arguable grounds, to be recognised under domestic law'); *Mendel v Sweden* (7 April 2009), paras 41–56 (a 'right' to be assigned to an employment scheme was not recognised under national law as the domestic authorities were not obliged to assign persons to the scheme, but the applicant's claim not to have her assignment to the scheme arbitrarily revoked on the other hand did concern a 'right' which could arguably be said to be recognised under domestic law: Art 6(1) applicable). For domestic examples, see eg *R (Kehoe) v Secretary of State for Work and Pensions* [2006] 1 AC 42 (since a mother had no right in domestic law under the Child Support Act 1991 to enforce her former husband's child maintenance liability, it followed that the 1991 Act did not limit her right of access to a court contrary to Art 6); and *M v Cook* 2003 SC 52 (statute authorised medical treatment without consent of patient; absence of statutory right of appeal against such treatment not inconsistent with Art 6, there being no dispute as to the extent of the patient's rights under domestic law).

3 *Procola v Luxembourg* (1995) A 326, para 37 (dispute whether ministerial orders fixing milk quotas made in respect of EU law could be given retrospective effect); *Süßmann v Germany*, 1996-IV, paras 38–46 (a challenge in the Federal Constitutional Court to amendments to a pension scheme for civil servants fell within the scope of Art 6). The claim must however be 'genuine and serious', see *Skorobogatykh v Russia* (dec) (8 June 2006) (prisoner's claim for non-pecuniary damages on the basis of the mere presence of HIV-infected prisoners in the same prison held not to be genuine and serious).

4 *Salerno v Italy* (1992) A 245-D, para 16. See too *Siegel v France* 2000-XII, paras 33–38 (failure to accept that Art 6 applied in respect of division of an estate carried out by notaries at the request and under the control of a court would have excluded supervision over a judicial procedure, and accordingly Art 6 applied).

5 See eg *Mennitto v Italy* [GC] 2000-X, paras 24–28 (argument by the state that the applicant's request for payment of an allowance for his disabled child involved not a right but only a legitimate interest which was protected only indirectly and as far as was consistent with the public interest: the Court held that in the circumstances the applicant could claim on arguable grounds a right to receive the full amount of the allowance, and thus it was not necessary to consider whether the autonomous concept of a right for the purposes of Art 6(1) covered only a 'personal right' or also a 'legitimate interest').

6 *Grădinar v Moldova* (8 April 2008), paras 109–117.

5.18 In consequence, if domestic law restricts the scope of a substantive right or indeed expressly or implicitly excludes a particular right, there can be no 'arguable claim', for Article 6 'does not in itself guarantee any particular content for "rights and obligations" in the substantive law of the contracting states'[1], and Article 6 cannot be employed to seek to create a right that is not so recognised[2]. Whether domestic law recognises a substantive right may thus be closely related to the question as to whether an applicant can claim to be a 'victim' for the purposes of bringing an application (as, for example, where an application is brought by an association seeking to uphold the rights of its members[3]). An applicant must thus meet domestic requirements of title and interest to sue, and cannot seek to use Article 6 to establish a 'dispute' where none is recognised by domestic law[4]. In *James and Others v United Kingdom*, tenants of property in England had been given the statutory right to convert their legal interests to those of owners. The applicants (who had held the freehold rights) had thereby been deprived of their property through the exercise of the statutory right by their former tenants, but the applicants had no remedy in domestic law to seek to challenge the transfer of property since satisfaction of the statutory conditions by the tenants had the immediate effect of changing the nature of the legal relationship. The legislation did not confer any right to challenge by appeal or review. The Court held that no Article 6 issue was in existence since there was no *contestation* over any right 'which [could] be said, at least on arguable grounds, to be recognised under domestic law'[5]. Similarly, in *Powell and Rayner v United Kingdom*, statute limited the rights of those affected by aircraft noise to seek remedies for nuisance. Again, the Court ruled that no Article 6 issue consequently arose since there was no relevant civil right in domestic law that could be enforced[6]. Further, an applicant must show that he has taken any necessary prior steps required by domestic law in order to qualify as the holder of a 'right' he seeks to enforce in the domestic courts. In *McMichael v United Kingdom*, the natural father of a child born outside marriage sought to assert that determination by a children's hearing of access rights to his child had violated his Article 6 rights. Scots law did not automatically confer parental rights upon an unmarried father, but instead required such a parent to make an application to a court for an order giving him these rights. In this particular case, the applicant had not done so, and consequently, the Court determined that the care proceedings did not involve any dispute over a civil right since he had not obtained legal recognition of his status as a father[7].

1   *H v Belgium* (1987) A 127-B, at para 40. In the domestic case of *Matthews v Ministry of Defence* [2003] 1 AC 1163 the House of Lords held that s 10 of the Crown Proceedings Act 1947 constituted a substantive limitation on the right of a serviceman to sue the Crown in tort and therefore Art 6 could not be invoked.

2   For a clear illustration of the point, see *Associazione Nazionale Reduci Dalla Prigionia dall'Internamento e dalla Guerra di Liberazione and 275 others v Germany* (dec) (4 September 2007) (an association of Italian nationals who had been subjected to forced labour during World War II had been denied compensation under a compensation scheme as the law was limited to those subjected to forced labour in a concentration camp, ghetto or similar: inadmissible, as the applicants were clearly excluded from compensation and therefore their claim had no arguable basis in law); and cf *Woś v Poland* 2006-VII, paras 68–81 (claim for compensation under a similar scheme fell within the ambit of Art 6 as the applicant met the qualifying requirements).

3   See eg *L'Erablière ASBL v Belgium* 2009-..., paras 21–30 (application by an environmental protection association for judicial review of a decision to grant planning permission to expand a landfill site: Art 6 applicable as the founders and administrators of the applicant association all resided in the region concerned).

4   Cf *Association des Amis de Saint-Raphaël et de Frejus and Others v France* (dec) (29 February 2000) (applicant association which sought to challenge the grant of building permits had not been party to domestic legal proceedings but had merely sought to defend the general interest: neither on this basis nor on other grounds was there any Art 6 dispute).

5   *James and Others v United Kingdom* (1986) A 98, at para 81. See also *Kunkova and Kunkov v Russia* (dec) (12 October 2006) (applicant's claim for damages had no basis in domestic law as the legislation in force at the relevant time did not provide for non-pecuniary damage and subsequent legislation had no retrospective effect, Art 6 not applicable); *OAO Plodovaya Kompaniya v Russia* (7 June 2007), paras 34–36 (the applicant attempted to defend a claim of corporate succession which had no basis in domestic law: no basis for the rights guaranteed by Art 6 to arise).

6   *Powell and Rayner v United Kingdom* (1990) A 172, para 36.

7   *McMichael v United Kingdom* (1995) A 307-B, para 77. See too 34308/96, *Yildrim v Austria*
     (19 October 1999) (a married father was unable to have proceedings to contest paternity
     instituted by the public prosecutor after his own action was time-barred: application declared
     inadmissible).

5.19 Purely discretionary authority conferred upon a public authority and which
is unfettered by legal rule is excluded from the scope of Article 6. In *Masson
and Van Zorn v Netherlands*, provisions of Dutch law specified that a person
acquitted of a criminal charge 'shall' have various expenses refunded to him in
certain cases, and 'may' be entitled to have other outlays reimbursed where the
court accepted that 'reasons in equity' existed for this. The Court held that 'the
grant to a public authority of such a measure of discretion indicates that no actual
right is recognised in law'[1].

1   *Masson and Van Zorn v Netherlands* (1995) A 327-A, paras 48–52 at para 51; see too
     Leutscher v Netherlands 1996-II, para 24. Cf *Georgiadis v Greece* 1997-III, paras 27–36
     (criminal procedure code established a right to compensation except where the detainee was
     intentionally or through gross negligence responsible for his detention: claims for compensation
     fell within the scope of Art 6(1)); and *Werner v Austria* 1997-VII, paras 34–36 (entitlement to
     compensation where suspicion of commission of an offence has been dispelled).

5.20 Domestic law may impose a substantive or a procedural bar to the bringing
of a civil claim. In the former case, no 'civil right' exists and thus Article 6 is
inapplicable; in the latter case, consideration of whether there has been a lack of
effective access to a court may arise. However, the distinction between a limitation
of a substantive right and a restriction upon access to court is not without difficulty.
For example, parliamentary privilege may be more appropriately considered as
involving not a substantive defence but rather as a procedural bar to the
determination of a civil claim for defamation[1]. In *Fayed v United Kingdom*, the
applicants had been prevented from bringing an action of defamation against a
government inspector whose report had labelled the applicants as dishonest. English
law considered these reports as privileged and thus conferred an immunity from
suit in respect of any action of defamation. The Court reiterated that Article 6
could not create by means of judicial interpretation a right which was not recognised
in the relevant domestic legal system. It also rejected the applicants' arguments
that an official investigatory body in discharging its functions should be open to
challenge by means of an action of defamation since such an interpretation 'would
in practice unduly hamper the effective regulation in the public interest of complex
financial and commercial activities'. However, it did try to distinguish this situation
from one in which procedural bars prevented or limited the bringing of legal action
to enforce a claim to a right with an established legal basis[2] when there may well
still be an Article 6 issue on account of restrictions on the right of access to a
court as discussed below[3].

The application of immunities may thus call for careful assessment of their
impact, for the conclusion may be that their effect is such as to defeat any claim
that a substantive right is recognised in domestic law. In *Roche v United Kingdom*,
the applicant had repeatedly sought access to his service records as part of his

claim for compensation for participation in gas tests conducted while he was in the military forces. When he had threatened to bring judicial review proceedings to challenge the refusal of a pension, the Secretary of State had issued a certificate under s 10 of the Crown Proceedings Act 1947 which had the effect of blocking any proceedings concerning events prior to 1987. The House of Lords had ruled that the Act had not intended to confer on servicemen any substantive right to claim damages against the Crown but rather had maintained the existing and absence of liability of the Crown in tort to servicemen. In other words, the provision had not removed a class of claim from the domestic courts' jurisdiction or any immunity from liability which had been previously recognised and was thus one of substantive law in delimiting the rights of servicemen to seek damages from the Crown. Accordingly, in Strasbourg, the Court concluded (by a bare majority) that the applicant had no civil 'right' recognised under domestic law which would attract the application of Article 6(1)[4]. In contrast, in *Al-Adsani v United Kingdom,* the Grand Chamber ruled that such a 'right' existed in this case. The applicant had sought to raise an action for personal damages for alleged torture against the Kuwaiti Government and a relation of the Emir of Kuwait. The action had been struck out following a determination that the State Immunity Act 1978 applied. The Court rejected the submission that the applicant's claim had no legal basis in domestic law as any substantive right had been extinguished by operation of the doctrine of state immunity since any such action could proceed to a hearing and judgment if the defendant state were to waive immunity: here, 'the grant of immunity [was] to be seen not as qualifying a substantive right but as a procedural bar on the national courts' power to determine the right'.[5]

---

1   See para **5.59** below.

2   See *A v United Kingdom* 2002-X, paras 62–89 (immunity from liability for defamatory statements made by an MP during parliamentary proceedings in terms of the Bill of Rights 1689 involved not a substantive defence to civil claims but a procedural bar to the determination by a court of any claim, and thus Art 6 was applicable; but the immunity pursued a legitimate aim and was proportionate: no violation). For earlier consideration, see 7729/76, *Agee v United Kingdom* (1977) DR 7, 164 (recognition by domestic law of parliamentary privilege attaching to statements made in the course of parliamentary proceedings resulting in no right in domestic law to raise an action against a minister who made allegedly defamatory statements, and in consequence there was no 'civil right' involved for the purposes of Art 6). See also *Cordova v Italy (no 1)* 2003-I, paras 47–66 (discontinuation of criminal proceedings on account of parliamentary immunity: violation); and *Cordova v Italy (no 2)* 2003-I, paras 58–67 (annulment of conviction for defamatory statements made by MP at electoral meeting: violation, there being no clear connection with parliamentary privilege); and *CGIL and Cofferati v Italy* (24 February 2009), paras 63–80 (civil defamation proceedings against an MP considered by domestic courts to have been covered by the MP's immunity as the opinions had been expressed in the course of his duties: violation of Art 6 since the restriction on the applicants' right of access to a court had been disproportionate, for although the interference had pursued a legitimate aim, access to justice could not be denied solely because the dispute might be of a political nature or linked to a political activity, and here the statements lacked any clear connection with parliamentary activity as they had been made outside the legislative chamber and the MP had not contributed to any debate on the subject in parliament).

3   *Fayed v United Kingdom* (1994) 294-B, paras 56–63 at para 62.

4   *Roche v United Kingdom* [GC] 2005-X, paras 116–125.

5   *Al-Adsani v United Kingdom* [GC] 2001-XI, paras 48–49; and similarly, *Fogarty v United Kingdom* [GC] 2001-XI, paras 25–28. See further para **5.60** below.

Rights and obligations which are 'civil' in nature

5.21 If the claim does not concern a right that is broadly civil in character, then no issue will arise under Article 6. In assessing whether the right is 'civil', it is important to examine the substantive nature of the issue rather than the domestic classification or the capacity in which the state or other agency is operating. In other words, the character of the right is decisive rather than the form of the proceedings. Private rights are clearly civil rights[1], but civil rights will extend to rights other than private rights since rights derived from public law and private rights which are made dependent upon authorisation by a body recognised as being of a public law nature may still be considered as 'civil' rights. In *Ringeisen v Austria,* the applicant had sought the necessary approval for a contract for the purchase of agricultural heritable property from an administrative commission. This consent had been refused, and the appellant had challenged the fairness of proceedings by alleging bias on the part of this body. In the opinion of the Commission, 'civil rights and obligations' could only apply to legal relationships between private individuals and not to relationships in which the individual is confronted with those exercising public or state authority, noting that at the time of the drafting of the Convention, planning matters were normally excluded from judicial review. However, the Court rejected such a narrow interpretation of 'civil rights and obligations' as it was not the character of the authority but the character of the right which must determine the scope of this notion. 'Civil rights and obligations' had to be interpreted to include 'all proceedings the result of which is decisive for private rights and obligations', and thus the proceedings of the administrative authority were subject to Article 6 requirements[2].

Following *Ringeisen*, a crucial question has been whether 'civil' should be treated as largely synonymous with 'private'[3], or whether (from the juxtaposition of 'criminal charge' in the text) 'civil rights' should be interpreted as including most rights of a public law nature[4]. The consequence of a narrower approach is that this is inconsistent with the aim of maximising protection for the individual and of furthering the rule of law, but an unduly wide interpretation of 'civil' may impose new and far-reaching restraints upon the exercise of administrative powers. The Court has favoured the latter approach, and it is now clear that where domestic law confers rights which can be enforced by means of a judicial remedy, these can, in principle, be regarded as civil rights within the meaning of Article 6(1)[5].

1   Cf *Zimmerman and Steiner v Switzerland* (1983) A 66, at para 22 (it was not in dispute that the rights in issue 'being personal or property rights – were private, and therefore 'civil' within the meaning' of Art 6(1)).

2   *Ringeisen v Austria* (1971) A 13, at para 94.

3   Cf *König v Germany* (1978) A 27, at para 95 (the Court did not find it necessary to determine whether 'civil rights and obligations' 'extends beyond those rights which have a private nature').

4   Van Dijk, van Hoof, van Rijn and Zwaak *Theory and Practice of the European Convention on Human Rights* (4th edn, 2006) at p 538 propose that the most appropriate solution for reducing uncertainty and thereby maximising Art 6 protection is to treat Art 6 as applicable 'to all cases in which a determination by a public authority of the legal position of a private party is at stake, regardless of whether the rights and obligations involved are of a private character'. This was the position advocated in the dissenting opinion in *Ferrazzini v Italy* [GC] 2001-VII, but effectively rejected by the majority of the Grand Chamber which (by 11 votes to 6) confirmed existing case law which excluded tax proceedings from the scope of Art 6: see further para **5.25** below.

5   See eg *Tinnelly & Sons Ltd and Others and McElduff and Others v United Kingdom* 1998-IV, para 61; *Kök v Turkey* (19 October 2006), para 37.

Admission to a profession, etc

5.22 The right to carry on a particular profession is essentially 'civil' in nature, even although such a right may be made subject in domestic law to authorisation from an administrative agency or other public body. In *König v Germany*, a medical specialist had been prevented first from operating his clinic and thereafter from practising as a doctor. Both decisions had involved the revocation of necessary authorisations by the state government, decisions which had subsequently been upheld by administrative tribunals. The Court considered that the right to operate a clinic was essentially of a private character and one which was not affected by the imposition of any state power of supervision in the interests of public health since it was a 'commercial activity carried on with a view to profit'. Nor was this assessment altered by the exercise of supervisory powers by the relevant medical professional body as the medical profession still retained its character of a traditional liberal profession, even despite the nationalisation of health services and the introduction of state regulation. What was conclusive in determining whether a right was a 'civil right' was thus not the government's claim to be acting within a sovereign or privileged capacity but instead the essential character of the right[1]. Similarly, in *Kök v Turkey*, the Court found Article 6 to be applicable to a dispute concerning the setting-aside of the authorities' refusal to authorise the applicant to practise a medical specialisation[2].

1   *König v Germany* (1978) A 27, paras 92–94. See too *Le Compte, Van Leuven and De Meyere v Belgium* (1981) A 43, paras 48–49, and *Albert and Le Compte v Belgium* (1983) A 58, para 28 (suspensions and revocations of licences to practise medicine by local medical councils had been upheld on appeal; the Court in each case applied the *König* decision, holding that the right to practise medicine involved a private relationship between a doctor and his patients normally based upon contractual obligations, and thus one which involved a civil right within the meaning of Art 6).

2   *Kök v Turkey* (19 October 2006), paras 36–37. See also *Chevrol v France* 2003-III, para 55. For discussion of the related but distinct question of assessment of knowledge, etc, see paras **5.15** above and **5.26** below.

5.23 The subsequent case law indicates that now a relatively wide but still not unrestricted scope is given to 'civil rights and obligations'. Several matters are clearly civil in nature and certainly fall within the scope of Article 6, for example, the right to occupy a house[1], or the determination of a parent's right of access to children[2]. Less obvious issues have also been accommodated within the guarantee such as grants of (or revocations or refusals to renew) licences[3] or certificates of fitness[4] which are required for the carrying on of some trade or economic activity, the award of a state subsidy for the pursuit of an economic activity[5], the right to be registered as an association[6] and to continue higher education[7], and planning determinations which have a direct impact upon an applicant's use and enjoyment of his property[8]. The right to personal reputation, so far as protected by the law of defamation, will also qualify as a civil right[9]. The principle behind these decisions seems to be that if the right is pecuniary in nature, it is likely to be considered as falling within the scope of Article 6[10] unless it clearly falls within one of the recognised exceptions which have not yet been revised by the Court.

1 Eg *Gillow v United Kingdom* (1986) A 109, para 68.

2 Eg *Olsson v Sweden (no 1)* (1988) A 130, paras 88–90.

3 Eg *Benthem v Netherlands* (1985) A 97, para 36 (refusal to grant a licence to operate a liquid petroleum gas installation); *Pudas v Sweden* (1989) A 125-A, paras 35–37 (revocation of licence to operate a taxi service on a particular route); *Tre Traktörer AB v Sweden* (1989) A 159, paras 41–43 (revocation of restaurant licence to sell alcohol); *Zander v Sweden* (1993) A 279-B, paras 26–27 (challenge to the grant of a permit for the dumping of refuse). For example, see *Catscratch Ltd v City of Glasgow Licensing Board (No 2)* 2002 SLT 503.

4 *Kingsley v United Kingdom* [GC] 2002-IV, para 34, upholding Chamber judgment (2 November 2000), paras 43–45 (revocation of certificate that an individual was a 'fit and proper person' to run a gaming establishment). See also *Kök v Turkey* (19 October 2006), paras 30–37 (dispute over the right to continue specialist medical training begun in a different country: Art 6 applicable).

5 Eg *SA 'Sotiris et Nikos Koutras ATTEE' v Greece* 2000-XII, discussed at para **5.58** below.

6 *APEH Üldözötteinek Szövetsége and Others v Hungary* 2000-X, paras 30–36 (Art 6 applicable in a case challenging the fairness of non-contentious court registration proceedings: associations could only obtain their legal existence by virtue of court registration and thus the position of an unregistered association was very different from that of a legal entity, and it was the applicant association's very capacity to become a subject of civil rights and obligations under domestic law that was at stake).

7 *Emine Araç v Turkey* 2008-..., paras 19–26.

8 Eg *Sporrong and Lönnroth v Sweden* (1982) A 52, para 79 (imposition of planning restrictions); *Allan Jacobsson v Sweden (no 1)* (1989) A 163, paras 67–71 (there was an arguable claim to a building permit upon satisfaction of the necessary conditions rather than by way of grant through unfettered administrative discretion); *Mats Jacobbson v Sweden* (1990) A 180-A, paras 29–35 (dispute over lawfulness of amendment to plan which would have the effect of annulling rights existing under the original plan); *Skärby v Sweden* (1990) A 180-B, paras 27–29 (dispute whether the applicants were covered by an exemption permitting the construction of buildings despite a prohibition order made by a commission); *Bryan v United Kingdom* (1995) A 335-A, para 31 (applicability of Art 6 to planning enforcement challenge: not contested); *O'Reilly v Ireland* (dec) (4 September 2003) (the applicants had a direct personal and private interest in the manner in which the Council's statutory duty to repair roads was exercised); and *Taşkin and Others v Turkey* 2004-X, para 133 (application for annulment of decision authorising use of toxic substance in mining involved attempt to enforce a right to protection for physical integrity, and Art 6 applicable).

9 *Tolstoy Miloslavsky v United Kingdom* (1995) A 316-B, para 58; *Loiseau v France* (dec) 2003-XII. In *Kurzac v Poland* (dec) 2000-VI the Court accepted that proceedings to have a deceased brother's conviction for anti-Soviet activities during the 1939–45 war annulled had as its aim the restoration of the reputation of the applicant's family and thus Art 6 was applicable.

10 *Procola v Luxembourg* (1995) A 326, paras 38–40 (payment of disputed additional levies under challenged ministerial orders purporting to implement EUC 'milk quota' policy could be considered as a deprivation of possessions and thus involved determination of a 'civil right'). See also *Riela v Italy* (dec) (4 September 2001) (confiscation of proceeds of crime proceedings); *Perez v France* [GC] 2004-I, paras 70–71 (civil-party complaints in criminal proceedings: Art 6 applicable); *Alatulkkila and Others v Finland* (28 July 2005), paras 47–50 (dispute over right to fish in waters owned by the applicants); and *Martinie v France* [GC] 2006-VI, paras 26–30 (proceedings leading to levying of surcharge against a state school's accountant: Art 6 applicable).

Public law issues excluded from 'civil rights and obligations'

5.24 The scope of 'civil rights and obligations' is not, though, unlimited. In particular, public law rights which do not have the necessary pecuniary base to qualify as a civil right are excluded[1]. Political rights such as the rights to stand for election and to sit in the legislature fall outwith the category of civil rights[2]. The obligation to serve in the military and the corresponding right to be exempted from military service is also clearly of a public law nature and falls outside the scope of Article 6[3]. On the other hand, the Court seems to have revised its position on whether the right to liberty can be considered as a civil right within the meaning of Article 6[4], and thus domestic proceedings seeking compensation for ill-treatment allegedly inflicted by police or other state officials involve the determination of a 'civil' right[5].

1 *SARL Du Parc d'Activités De Blotzheim et la SCI Haselaecker v France* (dec) 2003-III (proceedings concerning annulment of presidential decree amending a bilateral treaty not pecuniary in nature and was not founded on an alleged infringement of pecuniary rights). Cf *Tinnelly and Sons Ltd and McElduff and Others v United Kingdom* 1998-IV, paras 61–62 (dispute arising out of discrimination in the award of public procurement contracts concerned 'civil rights').

2 *Pierre-Bloch v France* 1997-VI, paras 50–51. See also *Refah Partisi and Others v Turkey* (dec) (3 October 2000) (right to carry on political activities); and *Guliyev v Azerbaijan* (dec) (27 May 2004) (refusal to register candidate in presidential elections).

3 *Kunkova and Kunkov v Russia* (dec) (21 October 2006).

4 In *Neumeister v Austria* (1968) A 8, at para 23, the Court considered that acceptance of such an interpretation would give 'excessively wide scope ... to the concept of 'civil rights'. In *Ireland v United Kingdom* (1978) A 25, para 235, the Court left this question open. Subsequently, in *Aerts v Belgium* 1998-V, para 59, the Court acknowledged that the right to liberty was a civil right, and thus the determination by domestic courts of the compatibility of the applicant's detention with domestic and Convention law fell within the scope of Art 6. See also *Musumeci v Italy* (dec) (17 December 2002) (placement of detainee under a strict monitoring regime: admissible) (and judgment of 11 January 2005, paras 49–52: violation); *Laidin v France (no 2)* (7 January 2003), paras 73–76 (challenge to lawfulness of proceedings resulting in detention in psychiatric hospital); *Ganci v Italy* 2003-XI, paras 22–26 at para 25 (special restrictions placed on prisoner: while these did not concern a 'criminal charge', restrictions on contact with family and those affecting pecuniary rights 'clearly fell within the sphere of personal rights and were therefore civil in nature'. See also *Boulois v Luxembourg*, case pending before the Grand Chamber, and noted at para **4.243** fn1.

5 *Aksoy v Turkey* 1996-VI, para 92. But cf *Skorobogatykh v Russia* (dec) (8 June 2006) (proceedings against prison authorities on account of the presence of HIV-infected prisoners did not involve a 'dispute' of a genuine or serious nature: inadmissible).

TAXATION, ETC

5.25 Certain matters with particular financial consequences for an individual may fail to qualify as 'civil'. In particular, determination of tax liability is considered a public law issue and does not qualify as a 'civil right'[1], a conclusion confirmed by the Grand Chamber in *Ferrazzini v Italy* in noting that the public nature of the relationship between the taxpayer and the tax authority remained predominant over any pecuniary interest in such matters[2]. However, surcharges which escape application of the designation of 'criminal charge' in domestic law may in certain circumstances fall within the scope of Article 6[3].

1   *Schouten and Meldrum v Netherlands* (1994) A 304, at para 50 (an 'obligation which is pecuniary in nature [which] derives from tax legislation or is otherwise part of normal civic duties in a democratic society' will belong 'exclusively to the realm of public law' and will thus not fall within the scope of Art 6(1)). See too *Charalambos v France* (dec) (8 February 2000), and *Bassan v France* (dec) (8 February 2000) (Art 6 was generally inapplicable to tax proceedings, and it was not enough merely to show that proceedings were of a pecuniary nature to qualify as 'civil rights and obligations': inadmissible). Cf *Hentrich v France* (1994) A 296-A, para 56 (taxation authority's decision to exercise a right of pre-emption involving an interference with property rights and based upon reasons which were too summary and general to allow the applicant to mount a reasoned challenge: violation of Art 6). This approach was followed by the Court of Appeal in *Eagerpath Ltd v Edwards* [2001] STC 26. For discussion of customs duties, see *Emesa Sugar NV v Netherlands* (dec) (13 January 2005) (Art 6 inapplicable in respect of summary injunction proceedings).

2   *Ferrazzini v Italy* [GC] 2001-VII, paras 24–31. Cf the dissenting opinion which carries an exhaustive survey of existing case law of public law issues which are considered to fall within the scope of Art 6.

3   *Jussila v Finland* [GC] 2006-XIV, discussed at para **5.49** below.

ASSESSMENT OF QUALIFICATIONS, ETC

5.26 While the Court may have reversed earlier jurisprudence that the right not to be denied education fell within the domain of public law, and thus access to education may now qualify as a 'civil' right[1], Article 6 is not applicable to proceedings which concern the evaluation of knowledge and experience in school or university examinations[2] or by professional bodies, nor is it applicable to judicial state examinations which are deemed to be 'closely related to the hard core of public-authority prerogatives'[3]. A distinction must thus be drawn between access to education or to an occupation or profession on the basis of recognised qualifications[4], and on the other hand assessment of whether an individual has the requisite knowledge or skills to be awarded a qualification.

1   *Emine Araç v Turkey* 2008-..., paras 18–26 (rejection of application for enrolment in higher education for failure to supply an identity photograph without the wearing of a veil: in light of the Turkish Constitution, the issue fell within the scope of the applicant's personal rights and was therefore civil in character). For earlier case law, see 14688/89, *Simpson v United Kingdom* (4 December 1989) (right not to be denied elementary education fell 'squarely within the domain of public law, having no private law analogy and no repercussions on private rights or obligations': inadmissible).

2   *Van Marle and Others v the Netherlands* (1986) A 101, para 36; *San Juan v France* (dec) (28 February 2002); and *Nowicky v Austria* (24 February 2005) para 34. For domestic consideration, see *R (Varma) v Duke of Kent* [2004] EWHC 1705 (Admin).

3   *Herbst v Germany* (11 January 2007), para 54.

4   See paras **5.16** and **5.22** above.

IMMIGRATION CONTROL, ETC

5.27 Decisions regarding the entry, stay and deportation of aliens are excluded from the scope of Article 6[1]. In *Maaouia v France*, the applicant had sought to have set aside a deportation order made by a criminal court. The European Court of Human Rights confirmed that this did not involve the determination of a 'civil right' for the purposes of the article even although the exclusion order would have had a major impact upon the applicant's private and family life and employment prospects. The provisions of the ECHR had to be construed in the light of the entire Convention system, and the terms of Protocol no 7 which France had ratified provided additional procedural guarantees applicable to the expulsion of aliens thus implying that Article 6 did not apply in this regard[2]. A similar approach is applied to cases in which the subject-matter of the dispute is closely related to the merits of a determination concerning immigration control[3]. However, fair hearing guarantees may still be of relevance in deportation or extradition cases. In particular, an individual may not be returned or removed to a country if he has suffered or risks suffering 'a flagrant denial of a fair trial', to Article 6 considerations[4]. Further, prosecutors or other state officials must not undermine the principle of the presumption of innocence in extradition cases[5].

1   For early discussion, see eg 3225/67, *X, Y, Z, V and W v United Kingdom* (1968) CD 25, 117 (admission of aliens); 9285/89, *X, Y and Z v United Kingdom* (1982) DR 29, 205 (expulsion of aliens); and 28979/95 and 30343/96, *Adams and Benn v United Kingdom* (1997) DR 88, 137 (questions arising under EU law concerning freedom of movement and residence within the EU are not covered by ECHR, Art 6(1)). See further Poynor '*Mamatkulov and Askurov v Turkey*: the Relevance of Article 6 to Extradition Proceedings' [2005] EHRLR 409; McBride *Access to Justice for Migrants and Asylum Seekers in Europe* (2009); and Mathisen 'On the Fairness of Proceedings for Extradition or Surrender' [2010] EHRLR 486.

2   *Maaouia v France* [GC] 2000-X, paras 35–38 (and para 39: nor did the matter constitute a 'criminal charge' merely on account that the order had been made by a criminal court following upon a conviction). Note, however, that expulsions may give rise to other issues under the ECHR which will require to be taken into account in decision-making: see in particular paras **4.54–4.59** and **4.130–4.137** above and paras **6.67–6.70** below.

3   *Panjeheighalehei v Denmark* (dec) 2009-... (compensation proceedings against the refugee board in relation to its refusal to grant the applicant asylum had been so closely connected to the subject matter of the board's decision as to be indistinguishable from proceedings determining decisions regarding the entry, stay and deportation of aliens: inadmissible); and *Dalea v France* (dec) 2010-... (inability to access or rectify personal data on the Schengen database did not concern civil rights or obligations or a criminal charge within the meaning of Art 6(1) as the procedure was closely connected to the regulation of the entry and residence of aliens: inadmissible). See also *Sergey Smirnov v Russia* (dec) (6 July 2006) (rights to nationality and to obtain a passport do not involve 'civil' rights).

4   *Soering v United Kingdom* (1989) A 161, at para 113. See further para **4.56** above.

5   *Ismoilov and Others v Russia* 2008-..., discussed at para **5.194** below.

APPLICATION TO CIVIL SERVICE EMPLOYMENT DISPUTES

5.28 A distinction had been drawn over time in the Court's case law between public service employment disputes which concerned recruitment, careers and termination of service of civil and other public servants, and those which were deemed 'purely' or 'essentially' economic such as the payment of salaries or pensions to retired civil servants or other public officials. In the latter case, disputes were treated generally as falling within the scope of Article 6[1]; in the former instance, the jurisprudence was unsatisfactory and contained a 'margin of uncertainty' calling for revision as acknowledged by the Grand Chamber in *Pellegrin v France*[2]. The applicant who had been a civil servant working overseas as a technical adviser had not had his contract of employment renewed on account of a finding of medical unfitness. He had challenged this finding in the administrative courts, but after some nine years was still awaiting a decision, and accordingly sought to argue in Strasbourg that he had been denied a determination within a reasonable time in terms of Article 6(1). The Court noted that current practice in European states was that both established civil servants (who, in France, were subject to public law rules) and officials under contract (regulated by domestic private law) frequently performed similar duties. To resolve the issue of the scope of Article 6 solely on the basis of the domestic applicability of public or private legal provisions would lead to inequality of treatment. The Court thus adopted a new criterion of functionality based upon a public servant's duties and responsibilities to determine the applicability of Article 6. The only disputes excluded from the scope of Article 6(1) were to be those complaints raised by public servants whose duties involve 'wield[ing] a portion of the State's sovereign power' where the state has 'a legitimate interest in requiring of these servants a special bond of trust and loyalty'. Clear illustrations of such office-holders, said the Court, were members of the police service and armed forces. Applying this criterion to the particular case, the Court held that Article 6 was not applicable since the applicant's post had involved considerable responsibilities in the area of public finance while exercising public law duties designed to protect the general interests of the state[3].

1   Eg *Cazenave de la Roche v France* 1998-III, paras 42–44 (award of damages to a former civil servant covered a purely economic right). Cf *Huber v France* 1998-I, paras 36–37 (decision to send a civil servant on compulsory leave of absence did not involve an Art 6 issue as this decision concerned her career and the existence of a pecuniary element in the form of a question concerning salary was not relevant). *Maillard v France* 1998-III, paras 39–41 (pecuniary element merely incidental to primary issue which concerned the applicant's career: Art 6 inapplicable).

2   Accordingly, earlier judgments cannot be relied upon: eg *Neigel v France* 1997-II (reinstatement of shorthand typist: Art 6 inapplicable); *Argento v Italy* 1997-V (recruitment and grade assignation did not involve a 'civil right').

3   *Pellegrin v France* [GC] 1999-VIII, paras 64–71 at para 65. The 'functional criterion' was based upon EU law: cf para 66 (regard was had for guidance to categorisation of activities and

posts listed by the European Commission (OJEC No C 72 of 18 March 1988) in view of the derogation from freedom of movement of workers in respect of 'employment in the public service' (EEC Treaty, Art 48(4)), a derogation interpreted restrictively by the European Court of Justice (149/79, *Commission v Belgium* [1980] ECR 3881). The 1988 Communication categorised activities according to whether or not they involved 'direct or indirect participation in the exercise of powers conferred by public law and duties designed to safeguard the general interests of the State'. For an example of an early application of the *Pellegrin* principle, see *Procaccini v Italy* (dec) (30 March 2000), paras 13–14 (employment dispute involving a school caretaker; Art 6 applicable as this role did not involve participation in the exercise of powers conferred by public law). Article 6 was not considered applicable in the resolution of a dispute concerning expatriation allowances paid to civil servants working abroad: *Martinez-Caro de la Concha Castañeda and Others v Spain* (dec) (7 March 2000) (inadmissible). See also *Stańczuk v Poland* (dec) (14 June 2001) (refusal to reinstate a former secret services agent recruited under the Communist regime: the applicant had not demonstrated that in domestic law he had an arguable claim to have the unfavourable decision reversed; further, the proceedings concerned the dismissal of a public officer working for secret services of the police and which involved the exercise of state powers conferred on the police by public law: inadmissible).

5.29 The judgment in *Pellegrin* meant that disputes between authorities and certain classes of state employees such as members of the police or armed forces were excluded from the remit of Article 6. The test was whether public sector employees participate directly in the exercise of public law powers and perform duties which are designed to safeguard state interests. Thus appeal court judges who were contending that they were entitled to a higher salary fell within this category[1], but a dispute concerning pension rights of retired judges fell within the scope of Article 6[2]. However, the Grand Chamber in *Frydlender v France* warned subsequently that this functionality test should not be applied too restrictively. Here, the applicant had been advised that he was not to have his short-term contract working abroad renewed on account of unsatisfactory performance of duties. Applying its reasoning in *Pellegrin*, the Court decided that the employment dispute in this instance did fall within the scope of Article 6. The applicant had worked for a department which was responsible to the Ministry for Economic Affairs (rather than to the Ministry of Foreign Affairs) and his duties had involved the promotion of exports of French products through giving advice and assistance to official and semi-official bodies and to individual exporters or importers. Both the nature of these duties and the relatively low level of responsibilities indicated that he had not been 'carrying out any task which could be said to entail, either directly or indirectly, duties designed to safeguard the general interests of the State'. Were the Court to hold otherwise and accept that staff in this department were by analogy or extension (and irrespective of their duties or responsibilities) to be considered as exercising public law powers, the object and purpose of Article 6 would have been compromised[3]. Further clarification of the scope of Article 6 in this area was provided in a number of subsequent cases. For example, Article 6 was held to apply to disputes relating to contracts of employment of medical staff[4] and to lawyers working as criminologists in state institutions[5].

---

1   *Kajanen and Tuomaala v Finland* (dec) (18 October 2000) (inadmissible). See also *Pitkevitch v Russia* (dec) (8 February 2001) (dispute relating to the dismissal of a judge for abuse of her office: inadmissible).

2   *Dimitrios Georgiadis v Greece* (28 March 2000), paras 20–21.

3   *Frydlender v France* [GC] 2000-VII, paras 27–41 at para 39. See also *Stojakovic v Austria* (9 November 2006), paras 36–42 (proceedings before ministerial disciplinary commission concerning the applicant's recall from post as head of a research institute and transfer to a post with a lower grade following allegations that he had made sexually harassing statements about employees, Art 6 was applicable).

4   *Sattonet v France* (2 August 2000), paras 28–30 (contract of director of medical-educational psychology centre).

5   *Castanheira Barros v Portugal* (26 October 2000), paras 26–33.

5.30 Despite these attempts to clarify the case law, there was still a realisation on the part of the Court that its jurisprudence remained unsatisfactory. In *Vilho Eskelinen and Others v Finland*, the Grand Chamber introduced a fresh approach for cases involving civil servants. The applicants were employees of the police service who sought to challenge the introduction of new rules governing their salaries and allowances. The Court noted that the application of the functional criterion as set out in *Pellegrin* could lead to 'anomalous results' and thus had to be 'further developed'. Referring to a number of cases which had been decided since *Pellegrin*, it noted not only that ascertaining the nature and status of the applicants' functions had been at times difficult but also that the category of public service in which the applicants worked was not always clearly distinguishable on the basis of their actual roles. Consequently, the Court outlined a new test. It held that in order for the respondent state to be able to rely before the Court on the applicant's status as a civil servant in excluding the protection embodied in Article 6, two conditions had to be fulfilled:

> 'Firstly, the State in its national law must have expressly excluded access to a court for the post or category of staff in question. Secondly, the exclusion must be justified on objective grounds in the State's interest. The mere fact that the applicant is in a sector or department which participates in the exercise of power conferred by public law is not in itself decisive. In order for the exclusion to be justified, it is not enough for the State to establish that the civil servant in question participates in the exercise of public power or that there exists, to use the words of the Court in the Pellegrin judgment, a "special bond of trust and loyalty" between the civil servant and the State, as employer. It is also for the State to show that the subject matter of the dispute in issue is related to the exercise of State power or that it has called into question the special bond. Thus, there can in principle be no justification for the exclusion from the guarantees of Article 6 of ordinary labour disputes, such as those relating to salaries, allowances or similar entitlements, on the basis of the special nature of relationship between the particular civil servant and the State in question. There will, in effect, be a presumption that Article 6 applies. It will be for the respondent Government to demonstrate, first, that a civil-servant applicant does not have a right of access to a court under national law and, second, that the exclusion of the rights under Article 6 for the civil servant is justified.'[1]

This test thus reduces the number of cases which can be excluded from the remit of Article 6, and has simplified (or at least brought a greater degree of certainty to) the determination of whether Article 6 applies in proceedings to which a civil servant is a party[2].

1   *Vilho Eskelinen and Others v Finland* [GC] 2007-IV, paras 50–64 at para 62.

2   See also Case Comment '*Vilho Eskelinen and Others v Finland*: The Next Step in Extending Article 6 ECHR to Disputes Concerning Civil Servants' [2007] EHRLR 441. The ruling in *Vilho Eskelinen* has been followed in a number of cases including *Dovguchits v Russia* (7 June 2007), paras 19–25 (Art 6 engaged in a case in which the applicant sued his military unit for wage arrears); *Botnari v Moldova* (19 June 2007), paras 19–21 (civil action brought by a public prosecutor against the local council on account of failure to provide housing despite the fact that a law stipulated that this should happen within one year of a prosecutor commencing employment: Art 6 applicable); *Tratar v Slovenia* (4 October 2007), para 55 (dispute concerning the employment conditions of an instructor in an army training centre: Art 6 applicable); *Olujić v Croatia* (5 February 2009), paras 31–45 (disciplinary proceedings against the President of the Supreme Court and proceedings following his constitutional complaint: Art 6(1) applicable); and *Savino and Others v Italy* (28 April 2009), paras 63–79 (possibility of obtaining a judicial remedy at national level in respect of claims against the Chamber of Deputies concerning salaries, allowances and recruitment: Art 6 applicable, and in any event exclusion of the guarantees under Art 6(1) could not be based on objective grounds linked to the interests of the state); and *Cudak v Lithuania* [GC] 2010-…, paras 39–47 (action for unfair dismissal brought by a local employee of a foreign embassy who worked as a secretary and switchboard operator: Art 6 applicable). Cf *Suküt v Turkey* (dec) 2007-X (no doubt that a dispute concerning the applicant's discharge from the army on disciplinary grounds called into question the 'special bond of trust and loyalty between the applicant and the state': Art 6 inapplicable).

DECISIONS OF THE DOMESTIC COURTS ON 'CIVIL RIGHTS AND OBLIGATIONS'

5.31 The English courts have held that applications for a sex offender order[1], an anti-social behaviour order[2], or the condemnation of goods seized by HM Customs and Excise[3], are 'civil proceedings' rather than criminal proceedings. In one such case Lord Woolf LCJ gave the following reasons for his conclusion:

'First, this is clearly a two-stage exercise: the obtaining of the order, and proceedings for breach of the order. Secondly, I rely on the fact that the process is one which is generally used for civil proceedings. Thirdly, I rely on the fact that there is no punishment properly involved here; there is, at most, a restriction on the activities of those subject to the order. Fourthly, I rely on the fact that the objective of making an order, as is clear from the statutory provisions and their historical background, is designed not to punish but to protect; it is not an order made to deprive those subject to the order of any of their normal rights. It is an order, however, which impinges on those rights, but does so for the protection of a section of the public who would otherwise be likely to be subjected to conduct of a socially disruptive nature by those subject to the order. Finally, the administrative nature of the proceedings, involving the requirement that it "appears" to the relevant authority is inconsistent with the proceedings being criminal[4].'

1   *B v Chief Constable of Avon and Somerset Constabulary* [2001] 1 WLR 340.

2   *R (McCann) v Manchester Crown Court* [2001] 1 WLR 358.

3   *Goldsmith v Customs and Excise Commissioners* [2001] 1 WLR 1673.

4   *R (McCann) v Manchester Crown Court* [2001] 1 WLR 358 at para 24.

5.32 A children's hearing determines civil rights and obligations, even if the ground of referral is the commission of an offence[1]. The absence of any penal sanction, in particular, indicates that proceedings are not to be classified as criminal[2]. Tax assessments do not normally involve civil rights and obligations[3]. In *R (Thompson) v Law Society* the Court of Appeal, following *Le Compte, van Leuven and de Meyere*, held that there was a distinction between a reprimand and a suspension of the right to practice, and only in the latter case could it be said that the right to continue was at stake so as to cross the line between a disciplinary process and a process which determined civil rights and obligations for the purposes of Article 6. Consequently, neither a reference to the Solicitors Disciplinary Tribunal nor a decision to reprimand a person amounted to a determination of his civil rights, notwithstanding that the effect of the reprimand might be to increase the cost of the solicitor's professional indemnity insurance or to vest a discretion in the Law Society which permitted it to impose conditions on the renewal of the solicitor's practising certificate[4]. That case might be contrasted with *R (G) v Governors of X School,* where a teaching assistant had been summarily dismissed on the ground of improper sexual behaviour with a pupil, and the Secretary of State had been notified of the circumstances with a view to an order being made which would prevent the person in question from working with children. It was held that Article 6 was applicable to the disciplinary proceedings before the school governors, because the outcome of those proceedings would have a substantial influence upon the outcome of the proceedings for the making of the order, and thus upon the person's ability to continue to practise his profession[5]. Following Strasbourg case law, Article 6 does not apply to an application for asylum[6]. A question which awaits authoritiative determination is whether, under the Scotland Act 1998 and the Human Rights Act 1998, Convention rights (or some of them) should themselves be regarded as 'civil rights' within the meaning of Article 6(1). It has been held at first instance in England that they do[7].

---

1   *S v Miller (No 1)* 2001 SC 977.

2   *B v Chief Constable of Avon and Somerset Constabulary* [2001] 1 WLR 340 per Lord Bingham LCJ at para 28; *R (McCann) v Manchester Crown Court* [2003] 1 AC 787; *S v Miller (No 1)* 2001 SC 977 per Lord Rodger of Earlsferry at para 22.

3   *Eagerpath Ltd v Edwards* [2001] STC 26; *Gladders v Prior* [2003] STC (SCD) 245. As to the position of objectors to a planning application, see *R (Vetterlein) v Hampshire County Council* [2002] 1 P & CR 31 and *R (Adlard) v Secretary of State for the Environment, Transport and the Regions* [2002] 1 WLR 2515. In relation to the termination of a local authority tenancy, see *R (McLellan) v Bracknell Forest BC* [2002] QB 1129.

4   *R (Thompson) v Law Society* [2004] 1 WLR 2522.

5   *R (G) v Governors of X School* [2010] 1 WLR 2218.

6   *R (MK (Iran)) v Secretary of State for the Home Department* [2010] 1 WLR 2059.

7   *Secretary of State for the Home Department v BC* [2010] 1 WLR 1542.

5.33 In relation to employment disputes concerning public officials, in *Mangera v Ministry of Defence* it was held that members of the armed forces could not rely on Article 6 in cases concerning employment, because of their status as public servants[1].

---

1   *Mangera v Ministry of Defence* [2003] EWCA Civ 801. See also *McQuade, Petitioner* 2004
       SLT 182.

SOCIAL WELFARE PROVISION AND THE APPLICABILITY OF ARTICLE 6

5.34 Jurisprudence concerning social security provision illustrates the incremental manner in which the scope of Article 6 has expanded through time. Welfare payments at first were considered essentially as matters of public law and thus were excluded from fair hearing protection under Article 6. In the 1986 case of *Feldbrugge v Netherlands*, the Court for the first time considered that social welfare benefits could fall within the definition of 'civil rights and obligations'. The case concerned a decision to stop the payment of sickness allowances to the applicant after she had been found fit to work. The Court acknowledged that there was no common European approach to the question of whether statutory health insurance schemes were to be treated as a private law right or (as in the Netherlands) as a public law matter; but in any case, the categorisation of such schemes even within a domestic legal system could vary depending upon the basis of the benefit in question. The public law features of social welfare schemes included their statutory and compulsory basis and their administration through state agencies; their private law features involved the economic and personal nature of the claims, their similarity to private schemes of insurance and their link with employment. On balance, the Court was prepared to label the case as dominated by private law concerns, and thus the case was considered to involve determination of a civil right[1]. By 1993, in *Salesi v Italy*, the Court was able to assert that the impact of its decision in *Feldbrugge*, as well as application of a general concern for equality of treatment, warranted 'taking the view that today the general rule is that Article 6(1) does apply in the field of social insurance'. While the particular case concerned welfare assistance as opposed to a scheme of insurance, the differences between these 'cannot be regarded as fundamental at the present stage of the development of social security law'. Here, again, private law features were found to predominate: the applicant had 'suffered an interference with her means of subsistence and was claiming an individual, economic right flowing from specific rules laid down in a statute' which came within the jurisdiction of the ordinary rather than administrative courts in Italy[2]. Subsequent judgments suggest that the factor whether determination of welfare entitlement is made by an administrative tribunal rather than by a non-specialised court is now of little relevance[3]. The conclusion is that with the exception of welfare benefits of a purely discretionary nature, social security entitlements will now fall to be determined as involving civil rights[4] as long as appropriate entitlement conditions are met[5].

---

1   *Feldbrugge v Netherlands* (1986) A 99, paras 29–40. Similarly, in *Deumeland v Germany*
       (1986) A 100, paras 60–74, it was considered that the payment of a supplementary pension
       to the widow of a man killed in an industrial accident involved a predominance of private law
       issues and thus Art 6 was applicable.

2   *Salesi v Italy* (1993) A 257-E, at para 19.

3   Cf *Schüler-Zgraggen v Switzerland* (1993) A 263, para 46 (the Court applied its reasoning in *Salesi* to hold Art 6(1) applicable in this case which again involved a non-contributory invalidity pension).

4   See also *Tričković v Slovenia* (12 June 2001), paras 36–41 (claim for an advance on the applicant's military pension concerned an Art 6 issue); *Mihailov v Bulgaria* (21 July 2005), para 34 (denial of disability status was directly decisive for a civil right, that is entitlement to pension and related benefits: Art 6 admissible); and *Kondrashina v Russia* (19 July 2007), para 32 (dispute as to the increase of the applicant's old-age pension entitlement involved a 'civil right'). But cf *La Parola and Others v Italy* (dec) (30 November 2000) (request for further financial assistance in respect of a disabled minor who was already in receipt of benefit on a permanent basis: proceedings were not aimed at determining a dispute but rather entitlement to the additional aid requested, and thus Art 6 was inadmissible).

5   For discussion of cases concerning social welfare entitlement involving allegations of discrimination under Art 14, see paras **3.92** and **3.105** above. For consideration of Prot 1, Art 1 issues, see para **8.10** below.

5.35 A similar approach as to whether disputes concerning contributions to social security schemes fall within Article 6 was taken in *Schouten and Meldrum v Netherlands*. The European Court of Human Rights accepted it was not sufficient merely to show that a dispute was pecuniary in nature since payments arising out of normal civic duties such as the determination of tax liability were excluded as belonging exclusively to the field of public law. However, certain additional features of social security contributory schemes including their close relationship with contracts of employment required to be taken into account. In the particular case, the Court considered that the private law features of the scheme were of greater significance than any public law elements and, accordingly, a dispute over contributions fell within the scope of the guarantee[1].

1   *Schouten and Meldrum v Netherlands* (1994) A 304, paras 49–60.

DECISIONS OF THE DOMESTIC COURTS ON SOCIAL WELFARE PROVISION AND ARTICLE 6

5.36 In *Ali v Birmingham City Council*, the Supreme Court held that Article 6 was inapplicable to the determination of a claim for accommodation under housing legislation. It was said that cases where the award of services or benefits in kind is not an individual right of which the applicant can consider himself the holder, but is dependent upon a series of evaluative judgments by the provider as to whether statutory criteria are satisfied and how the need for it ought to be met, do not give rise to 'civil rights' within the meaning of Article 6(1)[1].

1   *Ali v Birmingham City Council* [2010] 2 AC 39. The opinions clarified earlier decisions such as *R (A) v Croydon London Borough Council* [2009] 1 WLR 2557 (provision of accommodation for a child in need).

The outcome of the dispute must determine the right or obligation

5.37 The term 'determination' found in the English text requires that the outcome of the dispute must be 'directly decisive' for the civil right or obligation[1]: that is, the proceedings should result in a clear consequence for a civil right, 'mere tenuous connections or remote consequences not being sufficient to bring Article 6(1) into play'[2]. In most instances, this requirement will not cause difficulty[3]. In *Ringeisen v Austria*, the decisions of the administrative commission were judged to determine the rights between the applicant and the other party to the sale even although the tribunal's decision itself was of a public law character[4]. In *Le Compte, van Leuven and de Meyere v Belgium*, medical practitioners had been suspended pending the determination of whether the doctors had breached professional rules. The Court decided that these proceedings before disciplinary bodies clearly fell within the scope of Article 6 since their outcome directly determined whether the applicants could continue to practise[5]. But any impact on civil rights which is considered too remote will fail the test. Thus the Commission determined in *X v United Kingdom* that the consequences of a deportation order on employment or other private law rights fell outwith the scope of the article[6], and the Court in *Fayed v United Kingdom* held that the proceedings before inspectors appointed to investigate a take-over of a company had not been directly decisive of (or indeed even involved the determination of) the applicants' civil right to reputation[7]. Similarly, cases involving environmental protection claims call for careful assessment of whether the proceedings are 'directly decisive' for rights in domestic law or are too tenuous or remote to fall within the scope of the guarantee[8].

1   *Ringeisen v Austria* (1971) A 13, at para 94.

2   *Fayed v United Kingdom* (1994) A 294-B, at para 56; and *Masson and Van Zon v Netherlands* (1995) A 327-A, at para 44.

3   Cf van Dijk, van Hoof, van Rijn and Zwaak *Theory and Practice of the European Convention on Human Rights* (4th edn, 2006) at pp 521–522: 'It is sufficient that the outcome of the (claimed) judicial proceedings may be "decisive for", or may "affect", or may "relate to" the determination and/or the exercise of the right, or the determination and/or the fulfilment of the obligation, as the case may be; the effects need not be legal but may also be purely factual.'

4   *Ringeisen v Austria* (1971) A 13, para 94.

5   *Le Compte, van Leuven and de Meyere v Belgium* (1981) A 43, para 48.

6   7902/77 *X v United Kingdom* (1977) DR 9, 224.

7   *Fayed v United Kingdom* (1994) A 294-B, paras 66–68. Cf *Fayed v United Kingdom* (1994) A 294-B, paras 60–61 (discussion of the distinction between investigative and dispositive proceedings).

8   Eg *Balmer-Schafroth and Others v Switzerland* 1997-IV, paras 30–40 (inability of applicants to establish that extension of nuclear power plant licence would impose specific and imminent risk to life or health); cf *L'Erablière ASBL v Belgium* 2009-..., paras 21–30 (dismissal by the *Conseil d'État* of an application by an environmental protection association for judicial review of a decision to grant planning permission to expand a landfill site: Art 6 applicable as the action sought by the applicant association had a sufficient link to a 'right' to which it could claim to be entitled in view of the nature of the impugned measure, the fact that the aim pursued by applicant association was limited in space (a particular region of Belgium) and

substance, that the founders and administrators of the applicant association all resided in the region concerned, and the association was attempting to defend the general interest).

5.38 If the proceedings cannot have any bearing on an applicant's rights on account of a failure by the applicant to take any necessary steps to be entitled to recognition as a beneficiary of a right, these proceedings cannot be said to be able to lead to a 'determination' necessary to bring Article 6 into play[1]. The Court has not shied away from making its own assessment of whether an applicant has in fact taken such steps, but substance rather than form is important. In *Perez v France*, for instance, the Court altered its approach to the applicability of Article 6 in civil-party proceedings in holding that if 'the making of a civil party complaint amounts to the same thing as making a civil claim for indemnification, it is immaterial that the victim may have failed to lodge a formal claim for compensation'[2].

1   Cf *McMichael v United Kingdom* (1995) A 307–B, paras 76–77 (failure of an unmarried father to take steps to secure parental rights in respect of his child).

2   *Perez v France* [GC] 2004-I, para 65, overruling a series of earlier cases including *Hamer v France* 1996-III, paras 73–79).

DECISIONS OF THE DOMESTIC COURTS ON 'DETERMINATION'

5.39 The case of *R (Wright) v Secretary of State for Health* concerned legislation under which care workers could be referred to the Secretary of State for inclusion in a list of persons considered unsuitable to work with vulnerable adults. Pending the determination of the reference by a tribunal, following a lengthy procedure, the person referred could be provisionally included in the list, without at that stage being afforded a hearing. It was held by the House of Lords that the right to remain in employment or to be able to engage in a particular employment sector was a civil right within Article 6(1) of the Convention; that, since the provisional listing of a care worker could in practice result in irreparable damage to the person's employment or prospects of employment in the care sector, it amounted to a determination of a civil right within Article 6(1) notwithstanding that it was only an interim measure; and that, given the possibility of such damage, it was necessary for the procedure of provisional listing to be fair, whereas the denial of an opportunity for care workers to answer allegations before being listed made the legislation procedurally unfair and contrary to Article 6[1].

1   *R (Wright) v Secretary of State for Health* [2009] 1 AC 739.

Interim orders

5.40 Until recently, only in exceptional circumstances would Article 6 have been held applicable to interlocutory proceedings concerning the taking of interim measures (such as an interim interdict) as it was considered that such proceedings did not involve the 'determination' of a civil right or obligation[1]. However, in *Micallef v Malta*, the Grand Chamber departed from its previous case law in deciding that it was no longer justified automatically to characterise injunction proceedings as not being determinative of civil rights and obligations. The justification for this was that often such measures have the practical effect of determining the merits of a claim for a substantial period of time, for frequently both the interim and the main proceedings produce the same effect. There was also recognition that there was widespread consensus amongst member states that Article 6 guarantees were either implicitly or explicitly applied in relation to interim measures. Furthermore, it was not necessarily the case that any defect in interim proceedings would be remedied in proceedings on the merits as any prejudice suffered may have become irreversible. In consequence, the Court held that Article 6 will also apply to the taking of interim measures where the proceedings involve 'civil' proceedings within the meaning of the Convention, and where the interim measure in question can be considered (following scrutiny of its nature, object and purpose) effectively to determine the particular civil right or obligation in question, notwithstanding the length of time it is in force. Applying these principles to the facts of the case (which concerned an injunction issued against the applicant preventing her from hanging out clothes to dry over a courtyard), the Grand Chamber noted that the rights at stake in the main proceedings were of a civil character as they concerned use of property rights in accordance with domestic law. Since the purpose of the injunction was the same as that that to be contested in the main proceedings and was immediately enforceable, Article 6 was held to have been applicable to the injunction proceedings. One qualification was appropriate: while the guarantee of independence and impartiality of the tribunal is indispensable and inalienable to interim proceedings, other procedural safeguards may only apply to the extent compatible with the nature and purpose of such proceedings[2].

---

1   Art 6 was held not to apply in cases such as *APIS v Slovakia* (dec) (13 January 2000) (request for annulment of interim measure); *Starikow v Germany* (dec) (10 April 2003) (provisional grant of parental authority); *Libert v Belgium* (dec) (7 July 2004) (interim stay of execution of a judgment); *Dogmoch v Germany* (dec) 2006-XIII (order for the attachment of applicant's assets); *Dassa Foundation v Lichtenstein* (dec) (10 July 2007) (order for seizure of applicants' assets); *Saarekallas Oü v Estonia* (dec) (8 November 2007) (prohibition on disposal of applicant company's building). Article 6 on the other hand was held to be applicable in certain interim proceedings decisive for civil rights or those that disposed of the main action to a considerable degree and would have affected the legal rights of the parties for a substantial period of time unless reversed on appeal: eg *Markass Car Hire Ltd v Cyprus* (dec) (23 October 2001) (interim order to require applicant company to hand over a number of vehicles deemed to partly coincide with the main action, to have caused irreversible prejudice to the applicant's interest and to have 'drained to a substantial extent the final outcome of the proceedings of its significance'); and *Boca v Belgium* 2002-IX, paras 28–30 (summary procedures in divorce action).

2   *Micallef v Malta* [GC] 2009-..., paras 83–86.

Criminal charges

5.41 The 'determination' of a 'criminal charge' calls for application of fair hearing guarantees in terms of Article 6[1]. As with 'civil rights and obligations', the notion of a 'criminal charge' is given an autonomous interpretation[2] and one which is dependent upon a substantive rather than a formal meaning of the term[3] since 'a restrictive interpretation of Article 6(1) would not correspond to the aim and purpose of that provision'[4]. A particular legal dispute may require consideration as to whether Article 6 is applicable on account both that it gives rise to the determination of a criminal charge as well as of a civil right and obligation[5]. There are two principal issues: first, the stage at which in a criminal investigation and process a 'criminal charge' can be said to exist; and secondly, the circumstances in which a matter considered by domestic law as merely disciplinary or enforced through administrative penalty will fall nevertheless to be considered as a 'criminal charge' for the purpose of the guarantee.

---

1   The question whether there is a 'determination' is normally subsumed under discussion of the existence of a 'criminal charge', although on occasion the issues may be distinct: eg *JJ v Netherlands* 1998-II, paras 35–40 (appeal to Supreme Court against imposition of fiscal penalty which qualified as a 'criminal charge' declared inadmissible solely on account of the applicant's failure to pay the court registration fee: this gave rise to an Art 6 issue since a successful appeal would have been decisive for the determination of a criminal charge).

2   *Adolf v Austria* (1982) A 49, para 30.

3   *Deweer v Belgium* (1980) A 35, para 44.

4   *Delcourt v Belgium* (1970) A 11, at para 25.

5   Thus if in a particular instance it is considered that a matter is purely disciplinary or otherwise does not involve a 'criminal charge', the matter may still give rise to Art 6 considerations under 'civil rights': eg *Air Canada v United Kingdom* (1995) A 316-A, para 56 (application of Art 6 not disputed); *Aerts v Belgium* 1998-V, para 59 (lawfulness of detention of person of unsound mind did not give rise to determination of a criminal charge but did involve the right to liberty which was a civil right). Cf 11882/85, *C v United Kingdom* (1987) DR 54, 162 (the applicant had been employed as a janitor at a Scottish school but had been dismissed for petty theft following a hearing before a local authority educational officer and the school's headmaster; a criminal charge of theft had been dismissed in the criminal courts. While Art 6(1) did not apply in every instance of internal disciplinary proceedings in the public service, where a contract of employment (as in the present case) permits access to the civil courts and tribunals for the resolution of disputes, then such recourse may be said to have 'determined' an individual's civil rights).

The concept of a 'charge'

5.42 The first issue is of importance in identifying the stage at which rights in terms of Article 6 come into play under not only paragraph (1) but also paragraphs (2) and (3)[1]. The concept of a 'charge' is not dependent upon domestic law. In *Deweer v Belgium*, the Court considered a criminal charge to involve 'the official notification given to an individual by the competent authority of an allegation that he has committed a criminal offence', approving the Commission's test of whether the situation of the suspect has been 'substantially affected[2]. This notification can take whatever form provided for by domestic law[3] and may be constituted by arrest[4], by issue of an arrest[5] or a search[6] warrant, by official notification that a prosecution is being instigated[7], by the opening of a preliminary investigation[8], by the bringing of a private prosecution'[9], by the requirement to give evidence[10], or by other official measures carrying the implication of such an allegation and which similarly 'substantially affect the situation of the suspect'. It is thus possible for Article 6 rights to apply even although an individual has not been formally charged in domestic law with an offence[11]. Initial proceedings at the outset of a criminal process may therefore fall within the scope of Article 6, although the manner in which these guarantees apply at the investigation stage will be dependent upon the particular nature of the proceedings in question[12]. Indeed, an individual may still in certain situations qualify as a 'victim' of Article 6's procedural guarantees even although a subsequent decision is taken not to pursue criminal charges[13]. An assurance given by prosecuting authorities to an accused that he would not be prosecuted for certain offences may render subsequent criminal proceedings unfair if the authorities renege on the assurance[14]. Article 6 also applies to appellate stages in a criminal process[15].

1   Eg *Lutz v Germany* (1987) A 123, para 52.

2   *Deweer v Belgium* (1980) A 35, at para 46; see too *Eckle v Germany* (1982) A 51, para 73; *Foti and Others v Italy* (1982) A 56, para 52.

3   Eg *Corigliano v Italy* (1982) A 57, paras 34–35 (the date judicial notification was served on a suspect was the date on which there was a 'charge'); *Belilos v Switzerland* (1988) A 132, para 10 (laying of an information by police officers).

4   Eg *B v Austria* (1990) A 175, para 48.

5   Eg *Boddaert v Belgium* (1992) A 235-D, para 35.

6   Eg *Eckle v Germany* (1982) A 51, paras 73–75.

7   Eg *Mori v Italy* (1991) A 197-C, para 14 (date of formal notification); *Colacioppo v Italy* (1991) 197–D, para 13 (receipt of judicial notice of criminal proceedings).

8   Eg *Ringeisen v Austria* (1971) A 13, para 110.

9   Eg *Minelli v Switzerland* (1983) A 62, para 28 (private prosecution for defamation).

10   *O'Halloran and Francis v United Kingdom* [GC] 2007-VIII, para 35 (requirement under road traffic legislation to provide details of person driving a vehicle).

11   *Deweer v Belgium* (1980) A 35, at para 46. See also eg *Angelucci v Italy* (1991) A 196-C, para 13 (appointment of defence counsel); *Raimondo v Italy* (1994) A 281-A, para 42 (court order of confiscation of seized goods); *Quinn v Ireland* (21 December 2000), para 42, and *Heaney and McGuinness v Ireland* 2000-XII, para 42 (applicants were required to answer questions before they had been formally charged with offences; the Court considered that the making of these requirements had thus 'substantially affected' their situation); and *Aleksandr Zaichenko v Russia* (18 February 2010), paras 31–45 (admissions made prior to being charged with a criminal offence had substantially affected the applicant's situation). Cf *Padin Gestoso v Spain* (dec) 1999-II (investigative measures prior to the bringing of a criminal charge did not directly affect the situation of the applicant, and thus Art 6(1) was inapplicable at this stage).

12   See eg *John Murray v United Kingdom* 1996-I, para 62 (arrest and drawing of adverse inferences from silence under terrorism legislation).

13   *Heaney and McGuinness v Ireland* 2000-XII, paras 43–46, and *Quinn v Ireland* (21 December 2000), paras 43–46 (while in general the lack of subsequent criminal proceedings deprives an individual of status of 'victim', rights must be practical and effective and thus 'victim' status may still be recognised; and subsequent findings of violations of Art 6 even although no criminal proceedings had been initiated). See further para **5.135** below.

14   *Mustafa (Abu Hamza) v United Kingdom (no 1)* (dec) (18 January 2011).

15   See further para **5.10** above; and eg *Gast and Popp v Germany* 2000-II, paras 69–82 (lawfulness

of charges of espionage on behalf of the former German Democratic Republic considered by the Constitutional Court).

Matters excluded from Article 6

5.43 Article 6 applies to the 'determination' of a criminal charge. Matters not directly relating to such a 'determination' fall outwith the scope of the provision[1], and so Article 6 does not (at least in relation to the criminal head of Article 6) apply to forfeiture proceedings[2]. Nor does a request for a retrial involve the determination of a 'criminal charge', but rather the question whether the conditions for reopening criminal proceedings have been met[3]. Similarly, Article 6 does not generally apply under its criminal head to proceedings relating to the execution of a final criminal sentence unless the circumstances suggest that these must be regarded as an integral part of criminal proceedings[4]. Further, measures falling short of such 'official notification' do not constitute a 'charge' where these seek to prevent the commission of offences. In *R v United Kingdom*, for example, a warning under the Crime and Disorder Act 1998 was found to be 'largely preventative' and thus did not constitute a criminal charge within the meaning of Article 6(1)[5]. Extradition and deportation orders associated with a criminal process, too, are excluded. In *Maaouia v France*, the Court refused to label as 'criminal' deportation or exclusion orders made following a conviction, noting that these were considered as essentially administrative by most countries since they involved preventive measures taken within the context of immigration control[6]. Similarly in *Mamatkulov and Askarov v Turkey* the Court held that extradition proceedings did not involve the determination of a criminal charge[7]. Nor does extradition under the European arrest warrant procedure do so[8].

---

1   Eg *Montcornet de Caumont v France* (dec) 2003-VII (proceedings concerning the conditions of the application of an amnesty law to a conviction which had already become final did not concern a criminal law); and *Antoine v United Kingdom* (dec) 2003-VII (Art 6 did not apply to a hearing which, following the establishment of the applicant's unfitness to plead, involved the determination of whether he or she had carried out the act with which he had been charged).

2   *Phillips v United Kingdom* 2001-VII, discussed at para **5.47** below. But cf *Hamer v Belgium* 2007-XIII, paras 44–60 (proceedings leading to demolition of house built without permission involved determination of a criminal charge). For discussion of forfeiture consequent upon the actions of third parties, see para **5.53** below.

3   *Öcalan v Turkey* (dec) (6 July 2010).

4   Eg *Buijen v Germany* (1 April 2010), paras 40–45 (transfer proceedings under the Council of Europe Convention on the Transfer of Sentenced Persons (ETS 112 (1983)) had to be regarded as an integral part of the criminal proceedings in this instance and thus Art 6 applied since the confession to crimes specified in the arrest warrant and the waiving of the right to appeal had followed upon an assurance given by a public prosecutor that he would institute particular proceedings).

5   *R v United Kingdom* (dec) (4 January 2007). See also *Raimondo v Italy* (1994) A 281-A, para 43 (placement under police supervision was preventive measure).

6   *Maaouia v France* [GC] 2000-X, para 39.

7   *Mamatkulov and Askarov v Turkey* [GC] 2005-I, para 80: 'The Court reiterates that decisions regarding the entry, stay and deportation of aliens do not concern the determination of an

applicant's civil rights or obligations or of a criminal charge against him, within the meaning of Article 6 § 1 of the Convention'. See also *Penafiel Salgado v Spain* (dec) (16 April 2002); and *Sardinas Albo v Italy* (dec) 2004-I.

8   *Monedero Angora v Spain* (dec) 2008-....

Determining whether a charge is 'criminal'

5.44 The decision to label certain offences as 'disciplinary' or 'administrative' rather than as 'criminal' will not necessarily exclude the application of guarantees in terms of Article 6. While it is recognised that states are entitled to distinguish between the criminal law and disciplinary codes, this cannot allow states to escape their responsibilities for ensuring the fair administration of justice under Article 6 or to avoid the prohibition against retroactive imposition of sanction under Article 7[1]. In *Engel and Others v Netherlands*, the Court considered discipline sanctions imposed upon military service personnel by reference to three criteria to assess whether the proceedings fell within the scope of Article 6. First, the nature of the classification of the offence in domestic law was of relevance in any assessment: if 'criminal', this will be sufficient to bring the issue within the scope of Article 6, but if 'disciplinary' this will not be conclusive and will only provide a starting-point for further evaluation of the substance rather than form of the procedure. Secondly, the nature of the offence itself required to be assessed: a prohibition directed against a specific group such as service personnel may in principle rightly be considered as disciplinary, but it is also appropriate to take into account comparative practices applying in other European states. Thirdly, the severity of the penalty which could be imposed upon a determination of guilt was of importance: the more 'appreciably detrimental' the potential sanction, the greater the likelihood that the offence will be considered as criminal, especially if the penalty could involve not inconsiderable loss of liberty[2].

1   *Engel and Others v Netherlands* (1976) A 22, para 81. For further discussion, see Jaag, 'Verwaltungsrechtliche Sanktionen und Verfahrensgarantien der EMKR' in Donatsch, Forster and Schwarzenegger (eds) *Strafrecht, Strafprozessrecht und Menschenrechte: Festschrift für S Trechsel zum 65. Geburtstag* (2002), p 151.

2   *Engel and Others v Netherlands* (1976) A 22, paras 80–85 at para 82 (the imposition of two days' strict arrest upon a soldier for breach of military discipline was deemed insufficient to bring the matter within the category of 'criminal'); see too 7341/76, *Eggs v Switzerland* (1979) DR 15, 35 (loss of liberty through imposition of five days' strict arrest for breach of military discipline considered insufficient to establish a 'criminal' offence); and *Ezeh and Connors v United Kingdom* [GC] 2003-X, 82–84.

5.45 The Court's judgment in this early case which laid down the principles by which 'criminal charge' is to be interpreted – the *Engel* criteria – has subsequently been applied in other instances. For example, in *Öztürk v Germany*, the applicant had collided with a parked car and subsequently had been served with a notice imposing a fine and costs. After an unsuccessful appeal against this notice, he had been ordered to pay additional costs and expenses including the fees of an interpreter. His application challenged the violation of the right to a free interpreter under Article 6(3)(e), but the state responded that the case had not involved a criminal charge. The Court first noted that the ambit of the criminal law normally included 'offences that make their perpetrator liable to penalties intended, inter alia, to be deterrent and usually consisting of fines and of measures depriving the person of his liberty'. Further, the type of road traffic offence in question was classified by the overwhelming majority of European legal systems as criminal as opposed to administrative, and it was a legal rule which was directed 'not towards a given group possessing a special status – in the manner ... of disciplinary law – but towards all citizens in their capacity as road users' enforced by a sanction that was punitive. Accordingly, the imposition of the administrative penalty (even although it was relatively light) constituted the determination of a criminal charge[1]. In *Weber v Switzerland*, the applicant had been fined by a court for breaching the confidentiality of judicial proceedings in which he was a party. The Court again considered that this had involved a criminal rather than a disciplinary sanction: the legal rule prohibiting disclosure was directed against the population as a whole, and the maximum fine could in certain circumstances have been converted into a term of imprisonment[2].

---

1   *Öztürk v Germany* (1984) A 73, paras 53–54 at para 53. See too *Lauko v Slovakia* 1998-VI, paras 56–59 and *Kadubec v Slovakia* 1998-VI, paras 50–53 (applicability of Art 6 in relation to minor road traffic violations); but cf *Inocêncio v Portugal* (dec) 2001-I (a pecuniary sanction, even a substantial one, imposed for breach of planning regulations and which would not have resulted in imprisonment in default of payment could not be said to be a punitive measure of general application to all citizens: Art 6 inapplicable).

2   *Weber v Switzerland* (1990) A 177, paras 33–34. See too *Schmautzer v Austria* (1995) A 328-A, paras 27–28 (domestic law's labelling as 'administrative *offences*' to be disposed of under 'administrative *criminal* procedure' and the imposition of a fine with the alternative of imprisonment for failure to pay were sufficient to establish the offences as 'criminal').

5.46 The first of the *Engel* criterion thus is only decisive if domestic law classifies an offence as criminal. If it does not, it will thereafter be necessary to consider whether the other criteria are applicable. While the application of either the second or the third criterion may bring a case within the scope of Article 6, it may also be possible to conclude that there is a 'predominance' of aspects of a case with a 'criminal connotation: 'none of them [may be] decisive on its own, but taken together and cumulatively they [make] the "charge" in issue a "criminal" one'[1]. In respect of the second criterion, as noted in *Öztürk*, how other European states classify an offence may be important. It will also be of relevance whether there is a punitive or deterrent purpose behind the legal rule, or whether the legal rule question is directed solely at a specific group (as with members of the military, or prisoners) or is of a generally binding character[2]. It is relevant, too, whether the proceedings involve the determination of guilt, and also whether these have been instigated by a public body with powers of enforcement as in *Benham v United Kingdom*. In this case, the imprisonment of the applicant for the wilful refusal or culpable neglect to pay the community charge (or 'poll tax') was considered to involve a criminal charge despite English law's classification of the court proceedings as civil: the law was of general application, and the proceedings, which were brought by a local authority, contained a punitive element. The third criterion was also relevant in this case, for the maximum penalty (three months' imprisonment) was itself relatively severe[3]. In contrast, in *Phillips v United Kingdom,* the Court ruled that a confiscation order made under the Drug Trafficking Act 1994 following the applicant's conviction did not involve the determination of a 'criminal charge'. While refusal to pay the amount of the compensation order would have resulted in an additional two years' imprisonment, the purpose of the proceedings was neither the acquittal nor the conviction of the applicant[4].

---

1   *Bendenoun v France* (1994) A 284, at para 47.

2   *Bendenoun v France* (1994) A 284, para 47.

3   *Benham v United Kingdom* 1996-III, para 56. See too *Demicoli v Malta* (1991) A 210, paras 31–34 (failure to pay a fine could result in a maximum period of 60 days' imprisonment and thus Art 6 applied); *Garyfallou AEBE v Greece* 1997-V, paras 29–35 (fine for violation of trade regulations classified not as an administrative but as a criminal penalty); and *Malige v France* 1998-VII, paras 34–40, (sanction of deducting penalty points from a driving licence which had the possible consequence of disqualification from driving involved the determination of a criminal charge). Cf *Blokker v Netherlands* (dec) (7 November 2000) (administrative decision to require the applicant to undergo a training course at his own expense after his conviction for drink-driving under threat of loss of his driving licence should he refuse involved verification of suitability and did not involve a criminal charge); and *Gutfreund v France* 2003-VII, paras 31–47 (determination of application for legal aid, 'there being no right to which recognised in democratic law, did not involve the determination of a 'criminal charge'.

4   *Phillips v United Kingdom* 2001-VII, paras 28–36; but cf paras 37–47 (the making of the order was still covered by Art 6(1) as this followed on from the initial prosecution, and the guarantee covered the proceedings in their entirety), discussed further at para 5.190 below. For criticism see Trechsel *Human Rights in Criminal Proceedings* (2005), pp 34–35.

5.47 In practice, the third *Engel* criterion is often decisive. The nature and degree of the maximum possible severity of the sentence will be of crucial importance in assessing the application of fair hearing guarantees to offences labeled as 'disciplinary' or 'administrative' or otherwise considered not 'criminal' by domestic law[1]. In *Matyjek v Poland,* for example, the Court had to consider whether 'lustration' proceedings, designed to determine whether a person worked for or in the service of the state's security services or collaborated with them between 1944 and 1990, were to be understood as criminal in nature. The Court held that despite their classification in domestic law they possessed features which had a strong criminal connotation. Further, although neither a fine nor a prison sentence could be imposed, the proceedings could result in the person being dismissed from public office and prevented from applying for a large number of public posts for a period of ten years. The Court noted that this sanction could have a very serious impact on the person and should be regarded as having at least partly punitive and deterrent character[2].

---

1   Trechsel *Human Rights in Criminal Proceedings* (2005), p 22. See also *Matyjek v Poland* 2007-V, paras 55–56 (violation of fair hearing). Cf *Pierre-Bloch v France* 1997-VI, paras 53–61 (penalty equal to amount of unauthorised expenditure incurred by an election candidate and forfeiture of seat as an MP did not involve a criminal charge: matter was regulated by electoral

rather than by criminal law; and the measures differed in crucial respects from criminal penalties); and *Valico srl v Italy* (dec) 2006-III (imposition by administrative authorities of a fine on the applicant company for constructing a building in breach of planning permission: inadmissible). See also *Ravnsborg v Sweden* (1994) A283-B, paras 34–35 (significant that particular fine was not entered on the police register).

2   *Matyjek v Poland* (dec) 2006-VII.

Prison discipline

5.48 The *Engel* criteria have been applied to cases involving prison discipline. In *Campbell and Fell v United Kingdom*, prison disciplinary offences covered not only matters of internal discipline but also behaviour which was criminal according to domestic law and punishable by loss of remission of almost three years. The Court took into account the particularly grave character of the offences with which Campbell was charged and the substantial loss of remission (of some 570 days) in determining that Article 6 was applicable to the proceedings of the Board of Visitors[1]. In *Ezeh and Connors v United Kingdom*, the Grand Chamber confirmed that the imposition of additional days of loss of liberty by way of loss of remission involved the determination of a 'criminal charge' when this was 'appreciably detrimental'[2]. However, the Court has proved reluctant to apply Article 6 under its criminal head to the imposition of disciplinary or security measures not involving prolongation of loss of liberty[3].

1   *Campbell and Fell v United Kingdom* (1984) A 80, paras 69–73. The use of additional days and loss of remission as punishments was suspended in Scotland as from June 2001, the Scottish Prison Service having been advised that these forms of punishment might be at risk of successful challenge under the Convention. As to the fixing of the 'tariff' element of a life sentence, see paras **4.225–4.228** above.

2   *Ezeh and Connors v United Kingdom* [GC] 2003-X, paras 90–130 (and noting at para 88 that the power to impose loss of remission had now ceased in Scottish prisons). The loss of remission involved 40 days and 7 days respectively. See also *Young v United Kingdom* (16 January (16 January 2007), paras 42–45 (loss of remission of three days, and lack of independence of prison governor in adjudicating: violation of Art 6).

3   *Štitić v Croatia* (8 November 2007), paras 51–63 (imposition of short period of solitary confinement and restrictions on movement: inadmissible); and *Enea v Italy* [GC] 2009-…, paras 97–107 (placement in a high-supervision unit did not involve 'criminal charge', but ability to challenge such measures involved 'civil rights' within Art 6).

Imposition of tax surcharges

5.49 While the assessment of tax and the imposition of a surcharge fall outwith the scope of Article 6 under its civil head[1], it is now clear following the Grand Chamber's judgment in *Jussila v Finland* that these matters may in certain cases constitute the determination of a 'criminal charge', particularly in view of the nature of the offence and the deterrent and punitive role of surcharges[2]. The application of Article 6 is dependent in such cases upon four factors being present: 'the law setting out the penalties must cover all citizens in their capacity as taxpayers, the tax surcharges must be intended not as pecuniary compensation for damage but essentially as a punishment to deter reoffending; they must be imposed under a general rule, whose purpose is both deterrent and punitive; and they must be substantial'[3].

1   *Ferrazzini v Italy* [GC] 2001 VII, noted at para **5.25** above. See also *JB v Switzerland* 2001-III, discussed at para **5.135** below.

2   *Jussila v Finland* [GC] 2006-XIV, paras 29–39 (at para 38: 'The Court observes that … it may be said that the tax surcharges were imposed by general legal provisions applying to taxpayers generally. It is not persuaded by the Government's argument that VAT applies to only a limited group with a special status … The minor nature of the penalty … does not remove the matter from the scope of Article 6'). For earlier discussion, see *Janosevic v Sweden* 2002 VII. Cf *Bendenoun v France* (1994) A 284, paras 46–47 (predominance of aspects with a criminal connotation rendered the surcharge a criminal charge; but such a system of tax surcharges imposed as penalties was not inconsistent with Art 6, providing a taxpayer could challenge a decision in a court affording Art 6 guarantees).

3   *Morel v France* (dec) 2003 IX.

Decisions of domestic courts on the meaning of a 'criminal charge'

5.50 The approach outlined in the judgment in *Engel and Others v Netherlands*[1] has been applied by United Kingdom courts in a number of contexts, such as proceedings involving insane offenders[2], children's hearings[3], sex offender orders[4], anti-social behaviour orders[5], football banning orders[6], the seizure of goods by HM Customs and Excise[7] and the withdrawal of bail[8]. These decisions have emphasised in particular that the absence of any penal sanction indicates that the proceedings in question are not to be classified as criminal for the purposes of Article 6. In *McIntosh, Petitioner*, the Privy Council held that confiscation proceedings against a person previously convicted of a criminal offence did not involve the determination of a criminal charge within the meaning of Article 6[9]. In *R (McCann) v Manchester Crown Court*, the House of Lords held, applying the *Engel* criteria, that restrictions placed on an individual when an ASBO was ordered against him or her did not constitute a penalty[10]. In *Secretary of State for the Home Department v MB*, the House of Lords held that an application for permission to make a non-derogating control order under anti-terrorism legislation did not involve the determination of a criminal charge: the statutory scheme applied a procedure in which reasonable suspicion, but no assertion of criminal conduct, was raised; the controlled person was exposed to no risk of conviction or punishment; and the purpose of such an order was preventative and not punitive or retributive[11]. Penalty assessments issued by the Inland Revenue and HM Customs and Excise, on the other hand, have been held to constitute criminal charges within the meaning of Article 6[12]. A penalty scheme created under immigration legislation, which made carriers liable to a penalty for each clandestine entrant found concealed in a vehicle, was also held to be criminal for the purposes of Article 6[13]. It has been held that Article 6 is inapplicable to procedure following conviction and the deferral of sentence[14]. Nor is it applicable to the granting of a search warrant on information provided by the police[15].

1   *Engel and Others v Netherlands* (1976) A 22.

2   *R v H (Fitness to Plead)* [2003] 1 WLR 411.

3   *S v Miller (No 1)* 2001 SC 977.

4   *B v Chief Constable of Avon and Somerset Constabulary* [2001] 1 WLR 340.

5   *R (McCann) v Manchester Crown Court* [2003] 1 AC 787; cf *Lauko v Slovakia*, 1998-VI.

6   *Gough v Chief Constable of the Derbyshire Constabulary* [2002] QB 1213.

7   *Goldsmith v Customs and Excise Commissioners* [2001] 1 WLR 1673; *R (Mudie) v Kent Magistrates Court* [2003] QB 1238; *Gora v Customs and Excise Commissioners* [2004] QB 93.

8   *R (Director of Public Prosecutions) v Havering Magistrates' Court* [2001] 1 WLR 805.

9   *McIntosh, Petitioner* 2001 SC (PC) 89.

10 *R (McCann) v Manchester Crown Court* [2003] 1 AC 787; for criticism see Bakalis, 'ASBOs, "Preventative Orders" and the European Court of Human Rights' [2007] EHRLR 427.

11 *Secretary of State for the Home Department v MB* [2008] 1 AC 440.

12 *King v Walden* [2001] STC 822; *Customs and Excise Commissioners v Hall* [2001] STC 1188; *Revenue and Customs Commissioners v Khawaja* [2009] 1 WLR 398. In *R (Fleurose) v Securities and Futures Authority* Ltd [2002] IRLR 297, proceedings before the disciplinary tribunal of the Securities and Futures Authority were held not to constitute criminal proceedings for the purposes of Art 6.

13 *International Transport Roth GmbH v Secretary of State for the Home Department* [2003] QB 728.

14 *Kenny v Howdle* 2002 SCCR 814. This appears questionable.

15 *Brown v Donaldson* 2008 JC 83. As to the stage at which a person is 'charged' in criminal proceedings, see paras **5.173–5.174** below.

Contempt of court

5.51 The *Engel* criteria can also be applied in respect of determinations by a court of improper behaviour during the course of judicial proceedings. Each case must be determined on its own facts to determine whether what was at stake for the applicant is sufficiently important to warrant classifying the offence as criminal[1]. In *Ravnsborg v Sweden*, the applicant had been fined for making improper comments in written pleadings. The Court was not, however, satisfied that this exercise of judicial authority amounted to the determination of a criminal charge. Since there was room for doubt as to whether the imposition of sanctions for disturbing the good order of court proceedings was considered as criminal by Swedish law, the Court turned its attention to assessment of the nature of the offence and of the nature and degree of severity of the penalty. Noting that such a power to sanction disorderly behaviour was a common feature of European legal systems and essentially involved a determination by a judge of his own accord that a breach of good order had occurred, the Court considered that this power was closer to exercise of disciplinary authority than the imposition of a sanction for violation of the criminal law. This conclusion was clearly influenced by practical considerations: courts are required to respond to inappropriate behaviour 'even if it is neither necessary nor practicable to bring a criminal charge'.

Further, even although the fine could be converted to a term of imprisonment, this could only be done in limited circumstances and in separate proceedings, and in any case the prescribed maximum fine was not high enough to warrant the classification of 'criminal'[2]. Similarly, in *Putz v Austria*, the punishment of the applicant for unfounded accusations or offensive remarks made during a hearing and considered disruptive was not considered to fall within the scope of Article 6. The Court followed its ruling in *Ravnsborg* and considered that the nature of these sanctions was essentially disciplinary; and while the maximum fine was substantially higher in this case, a sentence of imprisonment would only arise if the fine was not paid, was limited to ten days' custody, and was subject to appeal[3]. However, there are situations where contempt of court proceedings have been deemed to fall within the scope of Article 6. In *Kyprianou v Cyprus,* the applicant had been sentenced to five days' imprisonment for contempt of court for comments made while acting as a lawyer for the accused in a murder case. In this instance, the Court found that the criminal nature of the offence of contempt of court could not be disputed[4]. Article 6 has also been held to apply in the event of action taken against a witness for failing to appear before a court[5].

---

1   See *T v Austria* 2000-XI, paras 61–67 (imposition of fine of approx £1,500 without a hearing for abuse of process – submitting a fraudulent declaration of means in support of an application for legal aid – and with the possibility of converting it into a prison term without the guarantee of a hearing: Art 6 applicable).

2   *Ravnsborg v Sweden* (1994) A 283-B, paras 31–35 (the maximum prescribed fine was approximately £500).

3   *Ravnsborg v Sweden* (1994) A 283-B, paras 33–35, at para 34 (the maximum fine was approximately £100).

4   *Kyprianou v Cyprus* [GC] 2005-XIII, para 64. See further para **5.42** above.

5   *Serves v France* 1997-VI, para 42 (applicant had been summoned to appear as a witness and fined for refusing to take the oath: Art 6 applicable). See also *Zaicevs v Latvia* 2007-IX, paras 50–53 (administrative detention of three days: Art 6 applicable).

DECISIONS OF DOMESTIC COURTS ON CONTEMPT OF COURT

5.52 Following the entry into force of the Human Rights Act 1998, procedures for dealing with contempt of court have been re-considered by domestic courts. In Scotland, a memorandum of guidance was issued by Lord Justice General Cullen on 28 March 2003[1]. Following the judgment in *Kyprianou*, that advice was amended by a Note issued on 20 February 2004[2]. In *Robertson v HM Advocate*, a Bench of five judges held that contempt of court should be treated as a crime for the purposes of Article 6. The court gave guidance on how cases of contempt should be dealt with procedurally, and did not follow the guidance earlier issued[3]. Rules of court were subsequently made to regulate the procedure to be followed in criminal cases[4].

---

1   In relation to England and Wales, see eg *Mubarak v Mubarak* [2001] 1 FLR 698; Practice Direction (Magistrates' Courts: Contempt) [2001] 1 WLR 1254.

2   See *Mayer v HM Advocate* 2005 1 JC 121.

3 *Robertson v HM Advocate* 2008 JC 146.

4 See Ch 29B of the Act of Adjournal (Criminal Procedure Rules) 1996, SI 1996/513, as amended. At the time of writing, it is anticipated that similar rules will be made during 2011 in relation to civil proceedings.

Forfeiture proceedings consequential upon criminal acts committed by a third party

5.53 Proceedings leading to the seizure of property consequential upon acts for which third parties are prosecuted will not involve a 'criminal charge'. In *AGOSI v United Kingdom*, the forfeiture of gold coins owned by the applicant company but smuggled by a third party was considered as a measure 'consequential upon' the criminal behaviour of third parties. Since the company had not been prosecuted, state action of this kind 'cannot of itself lead to the conclusion that, during the proceedings complained of, any "criminal charge", for the purposes of Article 6, could be considered as having been brought against the applicant company'[1]. Similarly, in *Air Canada v United Kingdom*, the seizure of an aircraft in which drugs had been found did not involve a criminal charge against the airline company, even although the company had only been able to recover its property by the payment of a substantial sum of money[2].

1 *AGOSI v United Kingdom* (1986) A 108, para 65.
2 *Air Canada v United Kingdom* (1995) A 316-A, paras 52–55.

ARTICLE 6: ACCESS TO A COURT

5.54 Article 6(1) guarantees practical and effective access for the determination of civil rights and criminal liability to a court or tribunal established by law which enjoys the attributes of independence and impartiality and which is able to determine all aspects of the dispute and thereafter to give a binding judgment. Article 6 does not extend to guaranteeing a right to trial by jury in states where the legal system makes use of them[1], but where a jury has formed part of the judicial process, it will be required to meet expectations of independence and impartiality[2].

1 Cf 14739/89, *Callaghan v United Kingdom* (1989) DR 60, 296 (trial by jury was not an essential aspect of a determination of a criminal charge; and thus the refusal to allow new evidence to be considered by a jury (rather than by an appeal court) did not give rise to an Art 6 issue).
2 See paras **5.81–5.82** below.

Practical and effective access to a court or tribunal

5.55 Practical and effective access implies the right to have a legal issue brought before a court or tribunal without improper or impractical difficulties. At the very least, there must be access to a judicial body[1]. States are left with a choice as to the means of facilitating access, for example, through the provision of a legal aid scheme[2]. Access to a court extends to the right to have a case determined by a judicial body[3], and also to enforcement of a court judgment which has become final since otherwise the concept of a fair hearing would cease to have any real meaning[4]. Access is not concerned solely with the conduct of proceedings already initiated. In the early case of *Golder v United Kingdom*, the refusal to allow a prisoner to contact a lawyer without the prior approval of a government minister was held to violate Article 6(1). The applicant had sought to consult a legal adviser with a view to instigating civil proceedings against a prison officer and thus exculpate himself of a charge made against him by the same officer. The Court clarified that the right to initiate legal proceedings had to be read into Article 6(1) as an inherent element having regard to its object and purpose. Were the paragraph to cover only an action already commenced in the courts, a state could 'do away with its courts, or take away their jurisdiction to determine certain classes of civil actions and entrust it to organs dependent upon the Government', a situation which would be 'indissociable from a danger of arbitrary power'[5]. However, the right of access to a court is not absolute. 'There is room, apart from the bounds delimiting the very content of any right, for limitations permitted by implication', and such regulation may 'vary in time and place according to the needs and resources of the community and of individuals'[6]. Any limitation must thus pursue an aim which is legitimate and have a reasonable relationship of proportionality between the means selected and the purpose of the restriction[7].

1   See *Khamidov v Russia* 2007-XII, paras 152–157 (temporary suspension of courts in Chechnya due to a counter-terrorism operation impaired the very essence of the applicant's right of access to a court and was clearly disproportionate). See also *Sergey Smirnov v Russia* (22 December 2009), paras 25–33 (inflexible approach of domestic courts in refusing to register legal actions on account of procedural requirement that an individual have a registered place of residence: violation); and *Boulois v Luxembourg*, case pending before the Grand Chamber (repeated rejections by prison board of requests for temporary leave of absence with no right of appeal to the administrative courts) [in its judgment (14 December 2010), paras 56–66, the Chamber determined that restrictions on the right to a court alleged by the applicant related to a set of prisoners' rights which the Council of Europe had recognised by means of the European Prison Rules].

2   *Airey v Ireland* (1979) A 32, para 26. See further para **5.69** below, and Hickman 'The "Uncertain Shadow": Throwing Light on the Right to a Court under Article 6(1) ECHR' [2004] PL 33. For discussion of legal aid in criminal cases, see paras **5.207–5.208** below.

3   *Marini v Albania* 2007-XIV, paras 118–123 (failure to give a final determination of the applicant's constitutional appeal on account of a tied vote had restricted the essence of his right of access to a court: violation of Art 6(1)).

4   Eg *Antonakopoulos, Vortsela and Antonakopoulou v Greece* (14 December 1999), paras 24–27; and *Dimitrios Georgiadis v Greece* (28 March 2000), paras 22–27.

5   *Golder v United Kingdom* (1975) A 18, paras 25–40, at para 35.

6   *Golder v United Kingdom* (1975) A 18, at para 38, citing *Belgian Linguistic case* (1968) A 6, Law, para 5. For example, the Government is not bound to grant special leave to remain in the United Kingdom in favour of any litigant in proceedings which cannot satisfactorily be conducted from abroad: *Nwokoye v Secretary of State for the Home Department* 2002 SLT 128, Ct of S.

7   *Stagno v Belgium* (7 July 2009), paras 22–35 (strict application of a statutory limitation period, which expired prior to the applicants reaching majority, limited their right of access to a court in a manner which was disproportionate to the aim of guaranteeing legal certainty and the proper administration of justice: violation). See also *Schneider v France* (dec) (30 June 2009) (the requirement to pay a fine prior to lodging an appeal in road traffic offences which concerned the entire population and were subject to frequent appeals did not inhibit access to court: inadmissible; and *Toyaksi and Others v Turkey* (dec) (20 October 2010) (imposition of small fines for vexatious applications for rectification of judgments did not violate the right of access to a court: inadmissible).

5.56 In determining domestic arrangements, a certain margin of appreciation covers domestic determination of access to a court, provided that any limitation does not 'restrict or reduce the access left to the individual in such a way or to such an extent that the very essence of the right is impaired'[1]. For example, a restriction upon access to a court in appellate proceedings such as a requirement that a litigant be represented by a qualified lawyer is not in itself contrary to Article 6[2]. It is also accepted that 'limitation periods in personal injury cases ... serve several important purposes, namely to ensure legal certainty and finality, protect potential defendants from stale claims which might be difficult to counter and prevent the injustice which might arise if courts were required to decide upon events which took place in the distant past on the basis of evidence which might have become unreliable and incomplete because of the passage of time'[3]. However, it is also expected at the same time that domestic procedures are sufficiently clear so as not to inhibit access to justice[4], and that the costs involved in bringing an action are not prohibitive[5].

The issue of access to court may also arise in relation to the determination of criminal charges. In *Kart v Turkey,* a member of parliament had sought to challenge the decision of the National Assembly to stay criminal proceedings against him until the end of his term of parliamentary office. In contrast to the approach taken by the Chamber, the Grand Chamber ruled that the delay in hearing the criminal charges had not been prejudicial to the applicant's right to a fair trial, the refusal to lift parliamentary immunity inviolability being only a temporary measure having no effect on the presumption of innocence and which merely suspended proceedings without impairing the very essence of the right of access to court[6].

1   *Ashingdane v United Kingdom* (1985) A 93, paras 55–60 at para 57. In extraordinary circumstances or states of emergency, there may be a finding that there is effectively no access to the judicial system: cf *Akdivar and Others v Turkey* 1996-IV, para 70 (discussion of exhaustion of domestic remedies).

2   *Kulikowski v Poland* 2009-..., paras 60–71.

3   *Stubbings v United Kingdom* 1996-IV, at para 51; but cf *Pérez de Rada Cavanilles v Spain* 1998-VIII, para 47 (period of three days in which application had to be made: here, no suggestion she had 'acted negligently, in view of the short period of time available to her for submitting her application': violation of right of access to court). See also *Millon v France* (dec) (30 August 2007) (neither Art 6 nor any other provision of the ECHR requires states to impose limitation periods or to fix the point at which such periods commence: inadmissible).

4   *De Geouffre de la Pradelle v France* (1994) A 253-B, discussed at para **5.67** below. See also *Lawyer Partners AS v Slovakia* 2009-..., paras 49–56 (refusal of courts to process civil actions submitted electronically despite provisions in the civil procedure code providing for

such a possibility: disproportionate limitation on the applicant's right to present its cases to a court in an effective manner, for while domestic law provided for other means of filing documents with courts, electronic lodging was entirely in keeping with the volume of cases which the applicant wished to pursue: violation).

5   See eg *Bakan v Turkey* (12 June 2007), paras 65–79 (action held inadmissible for failure to pay court fee, after legal aid was refused notwithstanding the plaintiff's lack of means: violation).

6   *Kart v Turkey* [GC] 2009-..., paras 85–114.

Restrictions on capacity to pursue civil actions or appeals on points of law

5.57 Limitations on access to a court may involve restrictions of capacity to sue. Again, providing that these restrictions meet the tests of legitimate aim and proportionality, they will be deemed not to contravene Article 6. In *Ashingdane v United Kingdom*, for example, restrictions on the rights of mental health patients to initiate legal actions were considered as necessary for preventing the undue harassment of health staff[1], while in *H v United Kingdom*, restrictions placed on the applicant as a designated vexatious litigant were accepted by the Commission as not limiting the applicant's right of access completely, and as not disproportionate to the legitimate aim of ensuring the proper administration of justice in Scotland[2]. Similarly, in *Lithgow v United Kingdom*, a statutory scheme for the collective settlement of disputes concerning compensation for industries taken into state ownership had required shareholders to have recourse solely to the relevant compensation tribunal, an arrangement deemed neither as impairing the right of access to a court, nor as inappropriate given the state's aim of avoiding multiple claims[3]. The principle also applies to the setting of fees or costs for proceedings. In *Tolstoy Miloslavsky v United Kingdom*, for example, an order requiring the applicant to pay security for costs before appellate proceedings could be instituted was upheld as pursuing the legitimate aim of protecting the other party to the action from irrecoverable costs[4]. Restrictions on the grounds on which domestic law permits review or appeal against administrative acts may also involve unwarranted restrictions on access to a court[5].

1   *Ashingdane v United Kingdom* (1985) A 93, para 58 (partial restrictions upon the right to sue the Secretary of State or the relevant health authority were considered neither to impair the essence of access to a court nor to be disproportionate: para 59).

2   11559/85, *H v United Kingdom* (1985) DR 45, 281 (restrictions imposed by virtue of the Vexatious Actions (Scotland) Act 1898).

3   *Lithgow and Others v United Kingdom* (1986) A 102, paras 195–196.

4   *Tolstoy Miloslavsky v United Kingdom* (1995) A 316-B, paras 59–67; and see *Urbanek v Austria* (9 December 2010), paras 47–67 (court fees determined by reference to value of amount in dispute rather than much lesser amount expected to be recovered: no violation of right of access to court as proceedings were not dependent on payment of fees and it was not unusual to link court fees to the disputed amount, such arrangements falling within a state's margin of appreciation). In contrast, the Court established a violation in *Garcia Manibardo v Spain* (15 February 2000), paras 36–45 (the applicant's appellate action had been ruled inadmissible by the domestic courts on account of her failure to deposit a sum of money, but

this decision had been taken at a stage before her legal aid application had been considered: this had resulted in a disproportionate interference with her right of access to a court and thus a violation of Art 6(1)); and in *Kreuz v Poland (no 1)* 2001-VI, paras 52–67 (fee required to initiate an action amounted to the average annual salary in the country: this excessive amount constituted a disproportionate restriction on the right of access to a court).

5   *Ravon and Others v France* (21 February 2008), paras 27–34 (possibility of appealing solely on points of law as regards the lawfulness of searches and seizures of property did not satisfy the requirements of Art 6(1) as it did not allow examination of the facts on which the disputed authorisation had been based: violation).

5.58 Restrictions which impair the very essence of the right of access to a court will not be compatible with Article 6. For example, in *Philis v Greece*, a limitation on legal capacity which had prevented the applicant from recovering payment of fees without direct recourse to his professional organisation was not considered justifiable[1]. Similarly in *Stankov v Bulgaria*, an order requiring a claimant in a civil action to pay court fees calculated as a percentage of any part of his claim that was disallowed was held to amount to a disproportionate restriction on the applicant's right to a court[2]. A violation was also found in *Canaea Catholic Church v Greece*, where the legal personality of the church had been called into question by its failure to comply in time with domestic law governing acquisition of legal personality and by a subsequent court decision that it had no capacity to take legal proceedings. For the Court, this injured the very substance of the right of access to a court[3]. In *SA 'Sotiris and Nikos Koutras ATTEE' v Greece*, the inadmissibility of the applicant company's application for judicial review on account of an error for which it was not responsible was considered to constitute a violation of its right to access to a court[4], while in *Khamidov v Russia,* the temporary suspension of courts in Chechnya on account of to a counter-terrorist operation was held to be clearly disproportionate and to have impaired the very essence of the applicant's right of access to a court[5].

1   *Philis v Greece* (1991) A 209, paras 59–65.

2   *Stankov v Bulgaria* 2007-VIII, paras 66–67.

3   *Canaea Catholic Church v Greece* 1997-VIII, paras 32–42. See *Ligue du Monde Islamique and Organisation Islamique Mondiale du Secours Islamique v France* (15 January 2009), paras 48–58 (domestic provision effectively preventing foreign associations which did not carry out an activity in France from obtaining legal capacity involved an actual restriction on the right of access to court that was not sufficiently foreseeable: violation).

4   *SA 'Sotiris et Nikos Koutras ATTEE' v Greece* 2000-XII, paras 17–23. See too *Annoni di Gussola and Others v France* 2000-XI, paras 48–59 (failure of applicants to comply with court order to pay designated sums resulted in refusal of appeal court to deal with legal merits of the appeal; while the obligation to execute the judgment appealed against pursued a legitimate aim, the appeal court had failed to consider the precariousness of the applicants' financial situation and had failed to give a reasoned judgment: the decision was thus disproportionate and a violation of right of access to a court). Cf *Arvanitakis v France* (dec) 2000-XII (no 'manifestly excessive consequences' in refusing to admit an appeal on points of law for failure to execute the judgment appealed against).

5   *Khamidov v Russia* 2007-XII, paras 152–157.

Rules excluding or restricting civil liability

5.59 In general, limitations on the right to sue through application of rules concerning prescription and limitation of actions will be considered as justifiable[1]. Limitations may also involve immunities such as a defence of absolute or qualified privilege. Whether such immunities are compatible with Article 6 is not without difficulty. A state's positive obligations under the ECHR may require domestic law to ensure that certain rights are recognised and enforceable in domestic law[2]. On the other hand, only a civil right with an arguable basis in domestic law will fall within the scope of Article 6. Immunity from suit which excludes a course of action by virtue of substantive provisions of domestic law (for example, in respect of an advocate's conduct of legal proceedings) is thus properly considered as an issue involving the applicability of Article 6 rather than access to a court[3]. If, on the other hand, a limitation is essentially procedural in character, then the matter is more properly one examined under Article 6 as a question of restriction of access to a court. The distinction between a substantive and procedural limitation may be a fine one, as acknowledged in *Fayed v United Kingdom*. The applicants had sought to challenge in an action of defamation statements made in a report of inspectors who had been appointed to investigate the take-over of a company. Such statements were covered by a defence of privilege in domestic law. The Court accepted that a state was entitled to determine the extent to which independent investigation into large public companies should run the inevitable 'risk of some uncompensated damage to reputation'. Attaching privilege to the reports could thus be considered a legitimate and proportionate response for furthering the supervision of public companies and to help ensure their proper conduct, although 'it may sometimes be no more than a question of legislative technique whether [such a] limitation is expressed in terms of the right or its remedy'[4]. Care is thus needed in any assessment. If the civil right sought to be asserted does not have an arguable basis in domestic law, it will not fall within the scope of Article 6[5] as was made clear by the court in *Z and Others v United Kingdom*[6]. This case concerned the compatibility with the Convention of the decision of the House of Lords in *X (Minors) v Bedfordshire County Council*[7]. The Court reiterated that Article 6 does not in itself guarantee any particular content for civil rights and obligations in national law, although other articles, such as Article 8 and Article 1 of Protocol no 1, may do so. It was not enough to bring Article 6 into play that the non-existence of a cause of action under domestic law might be described as having the same effect as an immunity, in the sense of not enabling the applicant to sue for a given category of harm. The applicants had been the victims of a breach of Article 3, and ought therefore to have had a remedy under domestic law, but that gave rise to an issue under Article 13, not Article 6[8].

---

1 Eg *Stubbings and Others v United Kingdom* 1996-IV, paras 51–57 (limitation period of six years from attaining majority for bringing an action alleging child abuse did not impair the right of access to a court). See also in relation to cases involving the striking-out of proceedings on the ground of 'immunity from suit': *Taylor v United Kingdom* (dec) (10 June 2003) (statements

made to or by investigators during a criminal investigation); and *Mond v United Kingdom* (dec) (10 June 2003) (rules pursued legitimate aims and were not disproportionate: inadmissible). Cf *De Geouffre de la Pradelle v France* (1992) A 253-B, paras 34–35 (notification of administrative action only after the expiry of the time limit for challenge), discussed at para **5.67** below. For consideration of retroactive extension of limitation periods in criminal cases, see *Coëme and Others v Belgium* 2000-VII, discussed at para **5.230** below.

2   See further paras **3.27–3.30** above.

3   The Crown's immunity from suit is thus considered as a restriction on liability imposed by substantive law: cf 10475/83, *Dyer v United Kingdom* (1984) DR 39, 246; for a domestic case, see *Matthews v Ministry of Defence* [2003] 1 AC 1163. See further para **5.20** above. For discussion of parliamentary privilege, see *CGIL and Cofferati v Italy* (24 February 2009), paras 63–80 (civil defamation proceedings against an MP considered by domestic courts to have been covered by the MP's immunity as the opinions had been expressed in the course of his duties: violation of Art 6 since the restriction on the applicants' right of access to a court had been disproportionate, for although the interference had pursued a legitimate aim, access to justice could not be denied solely because the dispute might be of a political nature or linked to a political activity, and here the statements lacked any clear connection with parliamentary activity as they had been made outside the legislative chamber and the MP had not contributed to any debate on the subject in parliament).

4   *Fayed v United Kingdom* (1994) A 294-B, paras 65–83 at paras 81 and 67 respectively.

5   See paras **5.13–5.14** above.

6   *Z and Others v United Kingdom* [GC] 2001-V, paras 91–104; see also *DP and JC v UK* (10 October 2002), paras 128–130.

7   *X (Minors) v Bedfordshire County Council* [1995] 2 AC 633.

8   See also the related case of *TP and KM v United Kingdom* [GC] 2001-V decided the same day. These two decisions of the Grand Chamber effectively overturn the judgment in *Osman v United Kingdom* 1998-VIII, paras 133–154 relating to access to court (restriction on ability to sue a chief constable for the negligent actions of his officers in failing to prevent the death of the first applicant's husband and the serious wounding of the second applicant on account of the rule in *Hill v Chief Constable of West Yorkshire* [1989] AC 53; the rule was considered by the Court not as an absolute bar to any such proceeding but as one allowing a court to assess on the basis of reasoned arguments whether the particular case was one in which the rule should be applied or not: thus the failure to allow the applicants to argue that the exclusion of liability should not be imposed was deemed a violation of Art 6).

STATE IMMUNITY

5.60 Similar principles apply to immunities applying by virtue of international law and recognised by the domestic courts as preventing the bringing of actions on this ground. In three related cases, *Al-Adsani v United Kingdom*, *Fogarty v United Kingdom*, and *McElhinney v Ireland*, the Grand Chamber upheld immunities from suit on the ground of state immunity, in each instance finding that the immunities pursued legitimate aims and were proportionate[1]. In contrast, in *Cudak v Lithuania,* the decision to decline jurisdiction to try an action for unfair dismissal brought by a local employee of a foreign embassy was held to have been disproportionate, the Grand Chamber noting the trend in international and comparative law towards limiting state immunity in respect of employment-related disputes with the exception of those concerning the recruitment (rather than the dismissal) of staff in embassies[2].

1   *Al-Adsani v United Kingdom* [GC] 2001-XI, paras 54–67 (allegations of torture carried out by agents of foreign state); *Fogarty v United Kingdom* [GC] 2001-XI, paras 34–39 (claim of sex discrimination on account of refusal of employment by a foreign embassy); and *McElhinney v Ireland* [GC] 2001-XI, paras 35–40 (acts of foreign soldiers). See also *Prince Hans-Adam II of Liechtenstein v Germany* [GC] 2001-VIII, paras 51–70 (no violation in respect of exclusion of jurisdiction of courts in respect of claims for return of property confiscated in Czechoslovakia as post-war reparations); *Markovic and Others v Italy* [GC] 2006-XIV, paras 100–116 (declinature of jurisdiction by domestic courts in action seeking damages for NATO air strike since the military action was an act of war and no right to claim reparation for damage sustained as a result of a violation of the rules of international law was recognised: no violation); and *Grosz v France* (dec) 2009-… (applicant's claim for compensation from the German State for forced labour performed during the Second World War declared by a domestic court to be inadmissible on the principle of state immunity from jurisdiction: inadmissible). See further Rozakis 'The Contribution of the European Court of Human Rights to the Development of the Law on State Immunity' in Caflisch, Callewaert, Liddell, Mahoney and Villiger (eds) *Liber Amicorum Luzius Wildhaber: Human Rights – Strasbourg Views* (2007), pp 371–386.

2   *Cudak v Lithuania* [GC] 2010-…, paras 54–75. See also the communicated cases of *Jones v United Kingdom* and *Mitchell and Others v United Kingdom* (civil proceedings in the English courts in *Jones v Kingdom of Saudi Arabia* [2007] 1 AC 270 alleging torture while in custody in Saudi Arabia and raised against the Kingdom of Saudi Arabia, the Saudi Ministry of Interior and various individuals: the House of Lords had overturned the Court of Appeal's attempt at distinguishing between immunity *ratione personae* and immunity *ratione materiae* and ruled immunity applied in all proceedings).

Decisions of domestic courts on access to a court

5.61 Article 6 requires that civil rights and obligations, and criminal charges, be determined by a court or tribunal. A fixed penalty scheme in respect of criminal charges makes no provision for determination by a court or tribunal, and may therefore give rise to an issue as to its compatibility with Article 6. In *International Transport Roth GmbH v Secretary of State for the Home Department*, a scheme under which carriers were liable to substantial fixed penalties for clandestine entrants to the UK who were concealed in their vehicles was held to be incompatible with Article 6. Simon Brown LJ stated:

> 'The hallowed principle that the punishment must fit the crime is irreconcilable with the notion of a substantial fixed penalty. It is essentially, therefore, on this account rather than because of the reversed burden of proof that I would regard the scheme as incompatible with article 6. What in particular it offends is the carrier's right to have his penalty determined by an independent tribunal. … Sentencing is, like all aspects of the criminal trial, a function that must be conducted by an independent tribunal. If, as I would hold, the determination of liability under the scheme is properly to be characterised as criminal, then this fixed penalty cannot stand unless it can be adjudged proportionate in all cases having regard to culpability involved.'[1]

Similarly the provisional listing of a care worker's name on a list of persons considered unsuitable to work with vulnerable adults, without any form of hearing, was incompatible with Article 6, since it constituted the determination of a civil right without access to a court[2].

---

1   *International Transport Roth GmbH v Secretary of State for the Home Department* [2003] QB
    728 at para 47.

2   *R (Wright) v Secretary of State for Health* [2009] 1 AC 739.

5.62 In relation to procedural matters, it has been held by the House of Lords that the dismissal of an action on the ground of irrelevancy, without hearing evidence, does not violate the right of access to a court[1]. In relation to security for costs, in *Nasser v United Bank of Kuwait,* the Court of Appeal followed *Tolstoy,* holding that an order for security for costs in relation to an appeal did not in itself violate Article 6, but observing that, for those with a real prospect of success, ease of access to appellate justice should be given greater priority than hitherto[2]. In a case concerned with a provision in the constitution of Gibraltar which guaranteed the same rights as Article 6(1) of the ECHR, the Privy Council held that to order the claimant to pay security for costs as a condition of proceeding at first instance involved a greater risk of impairing her right of access to justice than would such an order at the appeal stage, and that the court should therefore adopt a more lenient approach[3]. The need for certification that a point of law of general public importance was raised, as a precondition of an appeal to the Supreme Court in an English criminal case, was not incompatible with Article 6(1): it had a legitimate aim and was proportionate[4].

---

1   *Whaley v Lord Advocate* 2008 SC (HL) 107; *Mitchell v Glasgow City Council* 2009 SC (HL)
    21.

2   *Nasser v United Bank of Kuwait* [2002] 1 WLR 1868.

3   *Ford v Labrador* [2003] 1 WLR 2082. See also *Cachia v Faluyi* [2001] 1 WLR 1966 (whether
    action commenced by unserved writ precluding bringing of action by second writ); *Nwokoye
    v Secretary of State for the Home Department* 2002 SLT 128 (Home Secretary not bound to
    grant special leave to remain in the United Kingdom in favour of any litigant in proceedings
    which cannot satisfactorily be conducted from abroad).

4   *R v Dunn* [2011] 1 WLR 958.

5.63 In relation to prescription and limitation, it was held in *Kelly v Gilmartin's Executrix* that a person whose claim had prescribed no longer had a civil right, that Article 6 was therefore not engaged by the prescription legislation, and that, in any event, since the legislation pursued a legitimate aim and was proportionate it did not violate the right of access to a court[1]. It has also been held that the statutory bar to enforcement of consumer credit agreements which do not contain certain prescribed terms is not incompatible with Article 6(1): the legislation in question restricted the substantive rights of the creditor by rendering a regulated agreement unenforceable unless the document contained the prescribed terms, but it did not bar access to the court to determine whether or not the agreement was in fact enforceable[2].

---

1   *Kelly v Gilmartin's Executrix* 2004 SC 784.

2   *Wilson v First County Trust Ltd (No 2)* [2004] 1 AC 816.

5.64 In relation to restrictions on capacity to bring proceedings, domestic courts have repeatedly held, following *H v United Kingdom*[1], that the legislation concerned with vexatious litigants is compatible with Convention rights[2].

1 11559/85, *H v United Kingdom* (1985) DR 45, 281. See para **5.57** above.

2 See eg *Lord Advocate v Bell* 2002 SLT 527, *HM Advocate v Frost* 2007 SC 215 and *Lord Advocate v McNamara* 2009 SC 598; and, for England and Wales, *Ebert v Official Receiver* [2002] 1 WLR 320 and *Bhamjee v Forsdick* [2004] 1 WLR 88.

5.65 In relation to immunities, it has been held that Article 6 does not preclude a state from granting immunity to a foreign state as required by international law[1]. Nor is Article 6 engaged by rules of substantive law which determine the rights and liabilities that arise under civil law[2].

1 *Holland v Lampen-Wolfe* [2000] 1 WLR 1573; *Jones v Kingdom of Saudi Arabia* [2007] 1 AC 270.

2 See eg *Matthews v Ministry of Defence* [2003] 1 AC 1163 (statute exempting Crown from liability in tort for injuries suffered by members of the armed forces and substituting a system of no-fault compensation); *Re Deep Vein Thrombosis and Air Travel Group Litigation* [2003] 1 All ER 935 (claims excluded by Warsaw Convention on Carriage by Air: the point was not pursued in the subsequent appeals to the Court of Appeal and the House of Lords).

Interferences through legislative enactment

5.66 A statutory enactment influencing the outcome of a judicial determination of a dispute falling within the scope of Article 6 and which thereby deprives an applicant of his chance of success in litigation poses a challenge to respect for the rule of law. Although 'Article 6(1) cannot be interpreted as preventing any interference by the authorities with pending legal proceedings to which they are a party'[1], the introduction of legislative provisions with retrospective effect must be justified 'on compelling grounds of the general interest'[2]. It will thus always be a question on the facts whether an interference of this kind is justifiable. In *Stran Greek Refineries and Stratis Andreadis v Greece*, the applicants had been granted an enforceable arbitration award in their favour awarding them compensation against the state. The legislature had thereafter enacted a statute with the purpose of annulling the outcome of the judicial proceedings. For the Court, this legislative intervention at a time when the state was a party to litigation in such a manner as to ensure that the ultimate outcome of the proceedings would be favourable to its case had amounted to a violation of the guarantee[3]. In contrast, in *National and Provincial Building Society, Leeds Permanent Building Society and Yorkshire Building Society v United Kingdom*, legislation which had deprived the applicant societies of their opportunity of being successful in restitution proceedings against the Inland Revenue was considered not to have violated Article 6: the statute had been passed at a time when judicial review proceedings had not even been at the stage of an inter partes hearing; there had been 'even more compelling public-interest motives' than had been the case in the *Stan Greek Refineries* case, recourse to retroactive tax legislation was a feature of several legal systems, and the applicant societies must have been aware that there was a probability that the exemption from taxation upon which they had relied would be subject to parliamentary intervention[4].

1   *National and Provincial Building Society, etc v United Kingdom* 1997-VII, paras 105–113 at para 112. See also *Immobiliare Saffi v Italy* [GC] 1999-V, discussed at para **5.71** below.

2   *Agoudimos and Cefallonian Sky Shipping Co v Greece* (28 June 2001), paras 30–35 at para 30.

3   *Stran Greek Refineries and Stratis Andreadis v Greece* (1994) A 301-B, paras 44–50. See too *Papageorgiou v Greece* 1997-VI, paras 37–40; and *Anagnostopoulos and Others v Greece* 2000-XI, paras 19–21. Cf *Pressos Compania Naviera and Others v Belgium* (1995) A 332, paras 28–44 (retroactive exemption from liability for negligence and thus denial of a right of compensation was considered a violation of Prot 1, Art 1: in the circumstances, there was no need to consider any issue arising under Art 6). See further para **8.39** below).

4   *National and Provincial Building Society, Leeds Permanent Building Society and Yorkshire Building Society v United Kingdom* 1997-VII, paras 105–113 at para 112. See too *Truhli v Croatia* (28 June 2001), paras 25–28 (the applicant had been a former officer in the Yugoslav army who had unsuccessfully raised proceedings in the administrative court in respect of the reduction of his army pension; two constitutional complaints had been terminated on the basis that legislation which had come into force in the meantime had confirmed the position with regard to the pensions and had introduced new pensions provisions, and a third constitutional complaint in respect of the decisions taken by the administrative court had been dismissed on the ground that the decisions at issue were based on the relevant laws: no violation of the right of access to a court since the applicant had availed himself of the right of access to the administrative court, and the fact that the constitutional court had decided to terminate other proceedings did not restrict the exercise of this right in such a way or to such an extent that the very essence of the right was impaired).

State responsibilities in ensuring practical and effective access

5.67 The right of access must be one which is practical and effective rather than merely illusory. This implies that the legal system provides a 'sufficiently coherent and clear' indication of any decision affecting an individual's rights to allow the party concerned the opportunity of legal challenge[1]. In *De Geouffre de la Pradelle v France*, the applicant had certainly enjoyed the theoretical possibility of challenging an administrative decision affecting his property rights, but the Court considered his right of access to a court had been violated. Not only was the law on conservation areas of considerable complexity, but also the applicant had not been notified of the decision until two months after the decree had been published in the *Official Gazette* and then only when the time limit for raising an action had expired[2]. This matter is closely related to the issue of legal certainty[3].

1   *De Geouffre de la Pradelle v France* (1992) A 253-B, at para 35; see also *ID v Bulgaria* (28 April 2005), para 54 (not established that the applicant could have attained at the relevant time a judicial review of decisions against her, which were later considered as binding by the courts examining her claim for damages).

2   *De Geouffre de la Pradelle v France* (1992) A 253-B, paras 28–35. See also *Davran v Turkey* (3 November 2009), paras 31–47 (failure to serve a judgment on the applicant who was in pre-trial detention in relation to separate proceedings with the result that his appeal on points of law was declared inadmissible as the statutory time-limits had expired: violation on account of excessive restriction on the right of access to a court).

3   See paras **5.100–5.101** below.

Access to records, etc

5.68 Ensuring that access to a court is a practical and effective right can in certain circumstances require that an individual be accorded access to records held by public authorities to enable a litigant to proceed with his case. In *McGinley and Egan v United Kingdom*, former servicemen who had claimed their health problems were directly linked to their time in the armed forces had been prevented from gaining access to documents they believed would have established that they had been exposed to dangerous doses of radiation. The European Court of Human Rights accepted that the state's failure to produce such documents without good cause could have led to a violation of the right to a fair hearing, but since the applicants had inexplicably failed to use a procedure which had been available to try to obtain the evidence, there could be no finding of denial of effective access to a court or of unfairness[1].

The effect of public interest immunity certificates may thus pose problems in securing effective access to a court. In *Tinnelly and Sons Ltd and Others and McElduff and Others v United Kingdom*, a firm of contractors and a number of self-employed joiners had alleged discrimination in the allocation of contracts and employment. In each case, their complaints had been submitted to the Employment Commission which was charged with promoting equality of opportunity in Northern Ireland; but in each instance, the Commission's inquiries had been blocked by the issue of certificates by the Secretary of State to the effect that the decisions taken had involved acts 'done for the purpose of safeguarding national security or of protecting public safety or public order'. While the Court was mindful of the security concerns at stake, it could establish no reasonable relationship of proportionality between the protection of national security relied upon and the impact of the certificates on the applicants' right of access to a court. In particular, there had been no independent scrutiny of the reasons advanced for the issue of the certificates, nor any evidence as to why the applicants had been considered a security risk. The Court could not accept that such matters were inappropriate for independent judicial determination, for 'even if national security considerations are present and constitute a highly material aspect of the case', satisfactory arrangements existed in other contexts which both safeguarded national security and also provided individuals with a substantial degree of procedural justice. In short, 'the right guaranteed to an applicant under Article 6(1) of the Convention to submit a dispute to a court or tribunal in order to have a determination of questions of both fact and law cannot be displaced by the *ipse dixit* of the executive'[2].

1   *McGinley and Egan v United Kingdom* 1998-III, paras 85–90. See also *KH and Others v Slovakia* 2009-…, paras 65–69 (although the strict application of national legislation preventing the applicants' from obtaining photocopies of their medical records did not entirely bar them from bringing a civil action, it imposed a disproportionate burden on their ability to present their case to a court in an effective manner: violation of Art 6(1)).

2   *Tinnelly and Sons Ltd and Others and McElduff and Others v United Kingdom* 1998-IV, paras 72–79 at para 77.

The provision of legal aid

5.69 There is no specific mention of a right to civil legal aid in Article 6 in contrast to the reference to legal assistance for criminal defendants in paragraph (3)(d)[1]. The choice of means to ensure practical and effective access to a court is left to states, and the provision of legal aid or other state-funded assistance is one such method[2]. In certain cases, however, there is a positive obligation upon a state to provide legal aid. In *Airey v Ireland*, the Court considered the failure to provide legal aid to a woman without sufficient financial resources to instruct legal representatives to seek a judicial separation from her husband had rendered her theoretical right to a hearing ineffective. In determining there had been a violation of access to a court, the Court indicated that legal aid could only be required in cases where a litigant could not present his own case properly and effectively and where there was a reasonable prospect of success. There was no duty to supply free legal aid to every litigant seeking to enforce a 'civil right': nonetheless, the provision of free legal representation for civil matters would be necessary either where the complexity of the case made this indispensable or where domestic law makes legal representation compulsory[3]. Whether a state must ensure the provision of legal aid in a particular case 'must be determined on the basis of the particular facts and circumstances of each case and will depend, *inter alia*, upon the importance of what is at stake for the applicant in the proceedings, the complexity of the relevant law and procedure and the applicant's capacity to represent him or herself effectively'[4]. In *Munro v United Kingdom*, the Commission accepted the lack of civil legal aid in defamation proceedings in Scotland did not give rise to a violation since the protection of reputation was not as crucial an issue as matters such as regulation of personal or family relationships[5]. In *McVicar v United Kingdom*, the applicant, a journalist, had to defend himself on account of a lack of legal aid against an action of defamation raised by an athlete whom he had accused of using prohibited drugs to enhance his performance. The Court found that the applicant was a well-educated and experienced journalist, had been represented by a specialist lawyer before the start of proceedings, and should have been able to appreciate the nature of orders made by the court. Accordingly, the non-availability of legal aid had not rendered the proceedings unfair[6]. In contrast, in *Steel and Morris v United Kingdom*, members of an anti-McDonald's campaign group had been forced to defend themselves in lengthy civil court proceedings following the making of allegations that the company was involved in unethical and irresponsible practices, sold unhealthy foodstuffs, and targeted children in advertising. In this instance, Court considered that the non-availability of legal aid had resulted in unfairness. While reiterating that 'it is not incumbent on the State to seek through the use of public funds to ensure total equality of arms between the assisted person and the opposing party, as long as each side is afforded a reasonable opportunity to present his or her case under conditions that do not place him or her at a substantial disadvantage *vis-à-vis* the adversary', the Court took into account the importance of the right of freedom of expression, the financial consequences for the applicants of failing to verify each of the defamatory statements made, the particularly lengthy duration of the proceedings, and their legal complexity. The conclusion was that the lack of legal aid had deprived them of the opportunity to present their case effectively and had 'contributed to an unacceptable inequality of arms'[7].

1   See paras **5.207–5.209** below.

2   *Andronicou and Constantinou v Cyprus* 1997-VI, paras 199–201 (offer of *ex gratia* payment from the Attorney General considered adequate).

3   *Airey v Ireland* (1979) A 32, paras 24 and 26.

4   *Steel and Morris v United Kingdom* 2005-II, at para 61.

5   10594/83 *Munro v United Kingdom* (1987) DR 52, 158 at 165 (defamation claims are open to abuse and thus restrictions on availability of the action are commonly found in European legal systems; in any case, the substance of the issue had already been tested in a tribunal: no violation of Art 6). See too *Nicholas v Cyprus* (dec) (14 March 2000) (no indication that an action had been dismissed on account of the unavailability of legal aid; and the applicant could have represented himself in defamation proceedings: application was thus inadmissible).

6   *McVicar v United Kingdom* 2002-III, paras 46–62.

7   *Steel and Morris v United Kingdom* 2005-II, paras 59–72 at paras 62 and 72. See also *Kulikowski v Poland* 2009-..., paras 60–71 (refusal of a legal-aid lawyer to represent the applicant in proceedings before the Supreme Court could not be, of itself, tantamount to a denial of legal assistance which is incompatible with the state's obligations, nor does Art 6 confer an obligation on the state to ensure assistance by successive legal-aid lawyers for the purposes of pursuing legal remedies which have already been found not to offer reasonable prospects of success, but in this case, the failure by the domestic court to inform the applicant of procedural rights and time-limits after the legal-aid lawyer appointed had declined to act meant that the applicant's right of access to the Supreme Court had not been secured in a 'concrete and effective manner': violation).

DECISIONS OF DOMESTIC COURTS ON LEGAL AID IN CIVIL PROCEEDINGS

5.70 In *S v Miller (No 1)*, the Court of Session held that Article 6 in principle required legal representation in proceedings where deprivation of liberty was at stake, and might therefore require the provision of legal aid, where necessary in the interests of justice, in proceedings before a children's hearing[1]. The Convention Rights (Compliance) (Scotland) Act 2001 amended the powers of Scottish Ministers to enable the Scottish Legal Aid Board to make civil legal assistance available for certain proceedings before tribunals and other bodies where Article 6 may require the provision of legal aid to meet the requirements for a fair hearing, while other provisions concern the availability of legal aid in criminal matters[2]. Where an appellant before a VAT tribunal had been represented by an accountant, as was common in proceedings before the tribunal, his lack of awareness of the availability of legal aid did not mean that there had been a breach of Article 6[3]. It has been held that legal representation before a professional disciplinary tribunal could not be said *ab ante* to be indispensable to a fair hearing, regard being had to the possibility of a subsequent appeal to the court[4].

1   *S v Miller (No 1)* 2001 SC 977; see also *S v Miller (No 2)* 2001 SLT 1304 and *SK v Paterson*
     2010 SC 186. 'The absence of any provision whereby state-funded legal representation could
     have been made available to the appellant for the purposes of attending the children's hearing
     … if she was unable, without such representation, to participate effectively at the hearing,
     was incompatible with Articles 6, 8 (in its procedural aspect) and 14 of the Convention'.

2   See paras **5.209–5.210** below.

3   *Khan v Revenue and Customs Commissioners* [2006] STC 1167.

4   *Sutherland-Fisher v Law Society of Scotland* 2003 SC 562. See also the similar decision in
     Martin v Greater Glasgow Primary NHS Trust 2009 SC 417. Contrast *R (G) v Governors of
     X School* [2010] 1 WLR 2218, decided after the disciplinary hearing had taken place.

Enforcement of court decisions

5.71 The right of access to a court would be merely illusory if a decision of a
domestic court could remain inoperative. 'It would be inconceivable that Article 6
should describe in detail procedural guarantees afforded to litigants – proceedings
that are fair, public, and expeditious – without protecting the implementation of
judicial decisions', and thus execution of court judgments is regarded as an integral
part of a determination[1]. The principle applies to the failure of administrative
authorities to take measures necessary to comply with a final and binding court
decision[2]. However, some delay in enforcement may be acceptable on account
of competing and compelling interests. For example, in *Immobiliare Saffi v Italy*,
the European Court of Human Rights accepted that a stay of execution of a
judicial decision 'for such period as is strictly necessary' to enable a satisfactory
solution to public order problems to be found could be justified 'in exceptional
circumstances'. In this case, enforcement of an order against a tenant for
possession of his home had frequently been postponed on account of what the
state claimed was a threat of serious public disorder justifying not only refusal to
provide police assistance, but also then the introduction of a legal power conferring
the right on local prefects to intervene in the enforcement of possession orders, a
right not made subject to effective judicial review. While accepting that states
may intervene in enforcement proceedings by making use of their margin of
appreciation in controlling the use of property in exceptional circumstances, 'the
consequence of such intervention should not be that execution is prevented,
invalidated or unduly delayed or, still less, that the substance of the decision is
undermined'. Here, the legislation had the effect of annulling a court decision
since the lack of effective judicial review of the decisions of the prefect had
deprived the applicant company of its right to rely upon a favourable judicial
determination of its dispute with one of its tenants, a situation incompatible with
the rule of law[3].

1   *Hornsby v Greece* 1997-II, at para 40 (at para 41: this is of greater importance in respect of
     administrative proceedings where executive failure to comply with a judicial decision brings
     into question the concept of legality: 'the administrative authorities form one element of a
     State subject to the rule of law and their interests accordingly coincide with the need for the
     proper administration of justice'). This principle has been affirmed in a number of cases
     including in *Kutić v Croatia* 2002-II, para 25 (concerning proceedings which had been stayed

for more than six years); and *Matheus v France* (31 March 2005), paras 54–61 (refusal to assist in execution of court judgment ordering restitution of property).

2   *Hornsby v Greece* 1997-II, paras 42–45 (failure to comply with a court decision following a decision of the European Court of Justice).

3   *Immobiliare Saffi v Italy* [GC] 1999-V, paras 69–74 at para 69. See too *Antonetto v Italy* (20 July 2000), paras 27–30 (impossibility of enforcing a judgment by the *Conseil d'Etat* to demolish a building built illegally next to the applicant's property: violation of Art 6); and *G L v Italy* (3 August 2000), paras 35–41 (further discussion of the extent of a state's interests in delaying implementation of a judicial decision in exceptional cases). The withdrawal of a tax assessment following a successful appeal, and the issuing of a different assessment, does not offend against this principle: *Bennett v Customs and Excise Commissioners (No 2)* [2001] STC 137.

An independent and impartial tribunal established by law

5.72 Article 6(1) refers to 'an independent and impartial tribunal established by law'. 'Established by law' implies there is a legal basis for the very existence of the tribunal, no matter how specialised its jurisdiction[1]. It may also give rise to questions as to whether a tribunal or court's composition has been in conformity with domestic law, although such issues may in practice be subsumed by consideration of the tribunal's compatibility with Convention requirements[2]. Certainly, defects at first instance may be subsequently cured by a court with full jurisdiction to review the initial decision[3]. Much of the case law concentrates on questions of independence and impartiality. Judicial independence from the parties or the executive or legislature is determined by scrutiny of appointment and terms of office and protection against outside pressure, and impartiality denotes a lack of bias or prejudice. The principles are of general applicability to adjudicatory bodies whether constituted by professional or lay judges or involving jurors[4]. At times, however, the question of impartiality may not be readily disassociated from that of independence, and these two issues may be considered together[5]. Further, the maxim that justice must not only be done but also be seen to be done is of considerable importance[6]: the outward appearance of independence and objective impartiality will be considered necessary to help sustain public confidence in the administration of justice in democratic societies[7].

1   *Lithgow and Others* (1986) A 102, para 201. See also *Pandjikidzé and Others v Georgia* (27 October 2009), paras 103–111 (exercise by lay judges of judicial functions on the criminal division of the Supreme Court had an insufficient legal basis in domestic law: violation).

2   Cf *Piersack v Belgium* (1982) A 53, para 33 (domestic question avoided by the Court which established a lack of impartiality under Art 6). Cf *Oberschlick v Austria (no 1)* (1991) A 204, para 50 (judges disqualified by domestic law from sitting in second set of proceedings: national law recognised that their impartiality was open to doubt, and thus there was a violation of Art 6).

3   See paras **5.150–5.152** below.

4   *Holm v Sweden* (1993) A 279-A, para 30.

5   See *Ettl and Others v Austria* (1987) A 117, paras 37–41; and *Stallinger and Kuso v Austria* 1997-II, para 37 (land consolidation decisions taken by land reform boards whose members

included civil servants, but whose independence and impartiality were considered not to have been compromised); *Langborger v Sweden* (1989) A 155, paras 34–35 (specialised lay assessors adjudicating upon disputes between landlords and tenants had been nominated by and retained close links with associations having an interest in such issues: legitimate fears in the circumstances that the assessors lacked independence and impartiality); *Incal v Turkey* 1998-IV, para 71 (there were legitimate grounds for doubting the impartiality and independence of a national security court established to try cases of terrorism); *Ninn-Hansen v Denmark* (dec) 1999-V (lay judges appointed by Parliament to sit on a court of impeachment: no legitimate doubts as to independence or impartiality of judges, and application declared inadmissible); *Bochan v Ukraine* (3 May 2007), para 68; *Whitfield and Others v United Kingdom* (12 April 2005, at para 44: 'Since the concepts of structural independence and objective impartiality are closely linked, the Court will consider them together'); and *Parlov-Tkalčić v Croatia* (22 December 2009), paras 78–97 (the fact that the president of the court acting in an official capacity had previously filed a criminal complaint against the applicant had not affected the impartiality of an appeal court determining a civil action of unjustified enrichment, nor could powers vested in the court president be reasonably viewed as running counter, or having 'chilling' effects upon, the internal independence of judges).

6   *Campbell and Fell v United Kingdom* (1984) A 80, paras 80–81 (weight was to be given to prisoners' perceptions that the tribunal which also exercised supervisory responsibilities was not independent; but such perceptions were not in the circumstances sufficient to establish an actual lack of independence).

7   *Piersack v Belgium* (1982) A 53, para 30 (prosecutor who may have dealt with case subsequently sat as a judge in the same matter: impartiality open to doubt); *Sramek v Austria* (1984) A 84, para 42.

5.73 The importance of appearances was stressed in the judgment in *Kress v France* where a majority of the Grand Chamber found the procedures of the French *Conseil d'Etat* to violate the guarantee. The involvement of an independent officer whose task is to give guidance to the court – such as an *avocat général* or *procureur général* – is a common feature in many European legal systems. The applicant first challenged the lack of 'equality of arms' on as she had not been informed of the submissions of this officer (here, the 'Government Commissioner') in advance of the hearing, but since these had not been disclosed to either side, the Court considered that it could not be said that the applicant had been placed at a disadvantage; further, although she had not been able to respond orally, she had taken advantage subsequently of the opportunity to comment by means of a written memorandum before the court gave its judgment. However, the Government Commissioner had retired with the court during its deliberations. The suggestion that the Commissioner was in effect a judge was rejected as he did not have a vote, but the Grand Chamber (by a majority of ten votes to seven) was not satisfied that the arrangements had provided sufficient guarantees of impartiality. The Commissioner's public expression of the merits of the arguments submitted by both parties before he retired with the Court could legitimately be interpreted as siding with one of the parties against the other, and it was thus possible to 'imagine that a party may have a feeling of inequality if, after hearing the Commissioner make submissions unfavourable to his case at the end of the public hearing, he sees him withdraw with the judges of the trial bench to attend the deliberations held in the privacy of chambers' where he would enjoy 'if only to outward appearances, an additional opportunity to bolster his submissions in private, without fear of contradiction'. In light of the 'public's increased sensitivity to the fair administration of justice', it was considered that there were insufficient guarantees that the presence of the Commissioner during deliberations would not influence the court's outcomes[1].

---

1   *Kress v France* [GC] 2001-VI, paras 72–88 (at para 86, the Court noted that the Advocate General of the European Court of Justice does not participate in deliberations). See similarly *Martinie v France* [GC] 2006-IV, paras 53–55 (at para 53, noting that 'the mere presence of the Government Commissioner at the deliberations [of the Conseil d'Etat] be it "active" or "passive", is deemed to be a violation'. For discussion of EU issues, see Burrows and Greaves *The Advocate General and EC Law* (2007), pp 36–56. But cf *Mort v United Kingdom* (dec) 2001-IX (the practice of a clerk retiring with magistrates to provide advice in their deliberations did not give rise to any appearance of lack of impartiality as the clerk acts solely to assist the justices during deliberations: inadmissible).

A tribunal established by law

5.74 A 'tribunal' is characterised by its judicial function, that is, as a body having the power to give a binding decision[1] after determination of questions of fact and law within its competence[2] and which follows a prescribed procedure[3]. In other words, the term 'is not necessarily to be understood as signifying a court of law of the classic kind, integrated within the standard judicial machinery of the country'[4]. Its composition may include members who are not judges providing always that the appearance of independence is maintained[5]. The definition of 'tribunals' is wide enough to include regular courts as well as specialised tribunals[6], professional disciplinary bodies[7] and administrative authorities discharging non-judicial as well as judicial functions[8]. 'Established by law' reflects the principle of the rule of law. There must therefore be 'particular clarity' in rules regulating such matters as the assignment of cases to particular judges 'to ensure objectivity and transparency, and, above all, to avoid any appearance of arbitrariness'[9]. On occasion, a tribunal may be charged with additional functions which are non-judicial in nature. In such circumstances, the question will always be whether the requirements of the ECHR as to independence and impartiality have been met in a particular case, for 'neither Article 6 nor any other provision of the Convention requires States to comply with any theoretical constitutional concepts as such'[10]. In *McGonnell v United Kingdom*, the applicant challenged a decision of the Bailiff of Guernsey who combined responsibilities as a judicial officer with powers as a member of the island's executive and legislature. The Bailiff had been involved previously in the consideration of a development plan which had subsequently formed the subject of the judicial proceedings. In holding that the requirements of Article 6(1) had not been met in the particular instance, the European Court of Human Rights also noted that direct involvement in the legislative process or in the making of executive rules 'is likely to be sufficient to cast doubt on the judicial impartiality of a person subsequently called on to determine a dispute over whether reasons exist to permit a variation from the wording of the legislation or rules at issue'[11].

1   *Benthem v Netherlands* (1985) A 97, para 40 (administrative litigation division of Council of State only tendered advice; while the advice was normally followed, the division had no power to issue a binding decision). For another example of the principle, see *Fedotova v Russia* (13 April 2006), paras 38–44 (failure to comply with legal rules on participation of lay judges).

2   *Coëme and Others v Belgium* 2000-VII, paras 105–108 (trial of a government minister and four others in the Court of Cassation which had exclusive jurisdiction to try criminal charges involving ministers, but the court had no established jurisdiction to try the other co-accused who had been indicted to stand trial along with the minister on account of the connection between the charges; while it had been foreseeable that the rules on connection of trials would be applied in the light of academic opinion and domestic case law, the Court ruled that such indications could not have justified the conclusion that the rule on connection was 'established by law' within the meaning of Art 6: violation); and *Jorgic v Germany* 2007-IX, paras 64–71 (the applicant complained that the German courts were not competent to prosecute a foreigner living abroad for genocide purportedly committed in a foreign country against foreign victims: confirming that Art 6 did not guarantee a right to determine the jurisdiction of a court, the Court held that the German court's interpretation of the applicable provisions and international public law was not arbitrary and thus that Art 6 had not been violated).

3   *Belilos v Switzerland* (1988) A 132, para 64.

4   *Campbell and Fell v United Kingdom* (1984) A 80, at para 76.

5   *Belilos v Switzerland* (1988) A 132, paras 66–67 (tribunal included legally qualified civil servant from police headquarters sitting in a personal capacity, but who did not enjoy the appearance of impartiality); *Ettl and Others v Austria* (1987) A 117, paras 38–40 (civil servants were a majority on adjudicatory bodies, but this in itself did not contravene Art 6(1), noting that most legal systems contain examples of professional judges sitting alongside specialists).

6   Eg *Engel and Others v Netherlands* (1976) A 22, para 89 (military courts); *McMichael v United Kingdom* (1995) A 307-B, para 80 (children's hearings); *British-American Tobacco v Netherlands* (1995) A 331, para 77 (appeals division of Patent Office).

7   Eg *Le Compte, Van Leuven and De Meyere v Belgium* (1981) A 43, paras 57–58 (appeals council comprised of medical practitioners and judges in equal number and presided over by a judge: the method of election of medical members could not support any suggestion of bias); *Stojakovic v Austria* (9 November 2006), paras 45–50 (ministerial appeals commission concerned with civil servants' disciplinary matters was a 'tribunal').

8   Eg *Belilos v Switzerland* (1988) A 132, paras 65–66 (a police board was both an administrative authority and a judicial body). However, where members of a tribunal successively perform different and conflicting responsibilities, this will probably be sufficient to call the tribunal's impartiality into account: *Procola v Luxembourg* (1995) A 326, paras 44–45 (advisory and judicial functions discharged by members of *Conseil d'Etat*; legitimate doubts as to impartiality of several members who had ruled on the lawfulness of a regulation they had previously scrutinised in their advisory capacity).

9   *DMD Group as v Slovakia* (5 October 2010), paras 58–72 at para 66 (allocation by president of a court of a case to himself and determination of the case the same day: the reassignment had been the result of an individual decision rather than as a general administrative measure).

10 *McGonnell v United Kingdom* 2000-II, at para 51. See also *Vera Fernández-Huidobro v Spain* 2010-…, paras 118–136 (while certain procedural safeguards envisaged by Art 6(1) may not apply at the investigation stage, the requirements of the right to a fair trial in a broad sense necessarily implies that the investigating procedure should itself be impartial).

11 *McGonnell v United Kingdom* 2000-II, paras 49–58, at para 58 (issues of independence and impartiality treated together). Following *McGonnell*, the Lord Chancellor announced that he would take care not to sit in cases where to do so would violate Art 6: HL Official Report (5th series) cols 655–657 (2 March 2000). Cf *Kleyn and Others v Netherlands* [GC] 2003-VI,

paras 190–202 at para 196: 'consecutive exercise of advisory and judicial functions within one body may, in certain circumstances, raise an issue under [Art 6(1)] as regards the impartiality of the body seen from the objective viewpoint' but here the decision could not be regarded as involving 'the same case' or 'the same decision'); and *Sacilor-Lormines v France* 2006-XIII, paras 59–74 (consideration of consultative and judicial functions of the Dutch and French Conseil d'Etat in respect of the same proceedings: no violations). See further Masterman 'Determinative in the Abstract? Article 6(1) and the Separation of Powers' [2005] EHRLR 628, discussing *R (Anderson) v Secretary of State for the Home Department* [2003] 1 AC 837.

Independent and impartiality

Independence

5.75 The extent of the independence of the decision-making body from the parties to a case and from other organs of government or other external influence is determined by assessing such matters as the 'manner of appointment of its members and the duration of their terms of office, the existence of guarantees against outside pressures and the question whether the body presents an appearance of independence'[1]. Appointment of judges and tribunal members by the executive branch of government is commonplace throughout Europe, and this in itself will not cast doubt on a tribunal's independence[2]. Similarly, appointment by the legislature will not imply a lack of independence[3]. Further, 'the absence of formal recognition [of the irremovability of judges] in law does not in itself imply lack of independence provided that it is recognised in fact and that the other necessary guarantees are present'[4]. Accordingly, the length of the term of appointment will be a relevant factor in determining the extent of the independence of members of a tribunal. In *Ringeisen v Austria*, members of a regional commission had been appointed for a term of office of five years, a term which the European Court of Human Rights decided was satisfactory when considered alongside other guarantees of independence[5]. In *Campbell and Fell v United Kingdom*, a three-year term of office for members of a prison disciplinary board was considered 'admittedly short' but understandable given the unpaid nature of the task and the difficulties in finding volunteers to serve[6]. In *McMichael v United Kingdom*, the applicants argued that the manner of appointment and removal of members of the children's hearing system in Scotland was such that panel members did not enjoy sufficient independence. Members were appointed by the Secretary of State for such period as he specified, and could be removed by him with the consent of the Lord President. In practice, members were appointed initially for two years and usually thereafter for an additional five years and were removed only in exceptional circumstances. The Commission in its report had agreed with the applicants that panel members were not sufficiently independent, but the Court considered it unnecessary to arrive at any decision on this matter on account of a finding of violation of Article 6 on another ground[7].

---

1 Cf *Clarke v United Kingdom* (dec) 2005-X (challenge to independence and impartiality of judges in proceedings against the Lord Chancellor's Department: inadmissible).

2 *Belilos v Swizerland* (1988) A 132, at para 66 (appointment by the executive is not in itself sufficient 'to cast doubt on the independence and impartiality of the person concerned, especially as in many Contracting States it is the executive which appoints judges').

3 *Sramek v Austria* (1984) A 84, para 38.

4 *Campbell and Fell v United Kingdom* (1984) A 80, at para 80.

5 *Ringeisen v Austria* (1971) A 13, para 97.

6 *Campbell and Fell v United Kingdom* (1981) A 46, at para 80.

7 *McMichael v United Kingdom* (1995) A 307-B, para 78; see further para **5.107** below.

5.76 The subordination of members of the tribunal to outside influence will certainly raise issues of independence[1]. Particular difficulties have arisen with British military justice. In *Findlay and Others v United Kingdom*, applicable rules required that the convening officer in disciplinary hearings was closely linked to the prosecuting authorities, was superior in rank to the members of the court martial, and also had the power to dissolve the court martial and to refuse to confirm its decision in certain instances. In these circumstances, the European Court of Human Rights concluded a court martial could not satisfy the requirement of independence[2]. The court martial process was amended by the Armed Forces Act 1996, but the new system was the subject of further challenge in *Morris v United Kingdom*. Again the Court found a violation of Article 6, this time on the basis that there were insufficient safeguards in place to exclude the risk of outside pressure being brought to bear on the ordinary members of the court martial[3]. In contrast, in *Cooper v United Kingdom* which involved the same arrangements, the Grand Chamber unanimously decided that the submissions and material before it were such as to justify it in departing from the conclusion in *Morris*. In finding that the independence of the ordinary members was sufficiently protected, the Grand Chamber referred in particular to the existence of briefing notes which constituted a comprehensive manual which 'fully instructed ordinary members of the need to function independently of outside or inappropriate influence or instruction, and of the importance of this being seen to be done, providing practical and precise indications of how this could be achieved or undermined in a particular situation'[4].

1 Cf *Lavents v Latvia* (28 November 2002), paras 114–121 (withdrawal of judges following statements in the press by the Prime Minister and the Minister for Justice contesting their decision in respect of the applicant who was facing charges in connection with the collapse of the major bank in the country: violation); and *Salov v Ukraine* 2005-VIII, paras 80–86 (allegations of lack of sufficient guarantees against pressure from the Presidiums of regional courts upon judges: violation).

2 *Findlay and Others v United Kingdom* 1997-I, paras 73–80. See too, eg, *Coyne v United Kingdom* 1997-V, paras 56–58; *Hood v United Kingdom* [GC] 1999-I, paras 73–79; *Wilkinson and Allen v United Kingdom* (6 February 2001), paras 21–26; and *Mills v United Kingdom* (5 June 2001), paras 22–27.

3 *Morris v United Kingdom* 2002-I, paras 58–69.

4 *Cooper v United Kingdom* [GC] 2003-XII, paras 122–126, at para 122. See similarly *Grieves v United Kingdom* [GC] 2003-XII.

5.77 As indicated in *Cooper v United Kingdom*[1], Article 6 also requires that there should be no reasonable misgiving on the part of a party to proceedings that a member of the tribunal may appear to lack independence. In determining this question, 'the standpoint of the accused is important without being decisive. What is decisive is whether his doubts can be held to be objectively justified'[2]. Internal organisational issues are thus of concern, and it is not necessary to show an actual lack of independence as the appearance of lack of independence is of the essence. In *Sramek v Austria*, for example, a civil servant on a tribunal was directly subordinate to a colleague who was presenting the government's case[3], and in *Belilos v Switzerland*, the applicant had been convicted of a petty offence by a board which included a civil service lawyer who worked for the police[4].

1   *Cooper v United Kingdom* [GC] 2003-XII, para 104.

2   *Incal v Turkey* 1998-IV, at para 71 (national security courts established to try offences against the state's territorial integrity included military judges: while the independence and impartiality of the civilian judges were not in doubt, there were legitimate fears as to whether the presence of military judges could allow the courts to be unduly influenced by irrelevant considerations). For discussion of other military tribunal arrangements, see *Cyprus v Turkey* [GC] 2001-IV, paras 357–359 (legislative practice of trying civilians by military courts in northern Cyprus: violation of Art 6); *Öcalan v Turkey* [GC] 2005-IV, paras 114–115; *Ergin v Turkey (no 6)* 2006-VI, paras 50–54; and *Haci Özen v Turkey* (12 April 2007), paras 91–93 (military judge who had participated in various interlocutory decisions was replaced by a civilian judge, in accordance with an amendment enacted with a view to ensuring compliance with the Convention: the Court did not accept that the replacement of the military judge before the end of the proceedings disposed of the applicant's reasonably held concern about the trial court's independence and impartiality).

3   *Sramek v Austria* (1984) A 84, para 42.

4   *Belilos v Switzerland* (1988) A 132, paras 66–67 at para 67 (legitimate doubts as to the 'independence and organisational impartiality' of the board).

Impartiality

5.78 Impartiality is also assessed in terms of a subjective test of whether there is any actual bias or prejudice through personal conviction on the part of a member of the tribunal towards the issue or the parties[1], and further by means of an objective test of whether there exist any ascertainable facts which give rise to any legitimate doubts as to impartiality[2]. Failure to disclose the identities of the members of a tribunal is capable of casting doubt on its impartiality[3]. However, impartiality on the part of the judge is to be presumed unless there is some proof to the contrary[4]. In *Kyprianou v Cyprus*, a lawyer had been found guilty of contempt of court while representing a client in a criminal case. The applicant's complaint about the impartiality of the judges was upheld under the subjective test. The judges had not only acknowledged in their sentencing decision that they had been personally offended by the applicant's words, but they had also used emphatic language to convey their sense of indignation and shock. According to the Court, the nature of this response ran 'counter to the detached approach expected of judicial pronouncements'. The Court also drew attention to the fact that the applicant had been sentenced to five days imprisonment to be imposed immediately, and that he had only been given the option either to retract his statement or to explain it and to give reasons why he should not receive a sentence. In short, the combination of the personal involvement and the speed with which the decision was made meant that the judges had not succeeded in 'detaching themselves sufficiently from the situation' and thus could not be seen to be impartial in the sense of Article 6(1)[5].

1   *Driza v Albania* 2007-XII, paras 74–83 (the President of the Supreme Court, at whose request supervisory review proceedings had been instituted, had sat as a member of the bench that determined the proceedings: this was incompatible with the requirement of subjective impartiality since no one can be both plaintiff and judge in his own case).

2   *Hauschildt v Denmark* (1989) A 154, para 46. For further discussion, see van Dijk 'Article 6(1) of the Convention and the Concept of "Objective Impartiality"' in Mahoney, Matscher, Petzold and Wildhaber (eds) *Protecting Human Rights: The European Perspective* (2000), pp 1495–1510.

3   *Vernes v France* (20 January 2011), paras 41–44 (hearing in private by Stock Exchange Regulatory Authority whose members were not identified: violation, the applicant having been unable to satisfy himself that there had been no prejudice or links with the other party).

4   *Le Compte, Van Leuven and De Meyere v Belgium* (1981) A 43, para 58. See also *Craxi III v Italy* (dec) (14 May 2001) (the fact that a judge has ruled on similar cases in the past is not in itself enough to throw doubt on his impartiality); *Olujić v Croatia* (5 February 2009), paras 56–68 (statements of three members of the National Judicial Council, which had determined disciplinary proceedings against the applicant, while the case was pending before domestic courts raised legitimate interests as to their impartiality). But cf *Debled v Belgium* (1994) A 292-B, paras 36–37 at para 37 (professional disciplinary authority involving the participation of judges dealing with charges identical to those the judges themselves had faced 'can pose problems' under Art 6). For an example of clear lack of appearance of impartiality, see *Belukha v Ukraine* (9 November 2006), paras 52–55 (not contested that judge whose decision was upheld had demanded and accepted certain assets from the defendant company for free: violation).

5   *Kyprianou v Cyprus* [GC] 2005-XIII, paras 130–133. See also Lidell 'Reflections on Certain Aspects of the Kyprianou Judgment' in Caflisch, Callewaert, Liddell, Mahoney and Villiger (eds) *Liber Amicorum Luzius Wildhaber: Human Rights – Strasbourg Views* (2007), pp 247–262.

5.79 Each case calls for careful assessment. It is often possible to be satisfied that there is no actual 'personal conviction' in existence on the part of a member of a tribunal, but that there are still legitimate doubts as to objective impartiality. The requirements of objective impartiality were held not to have been satisfied where judges in appeal proceedings had been called upon to decide whether they had committed an error of legal interpretation[1]. However, the fact that a judge has previously considered a related case to the current proceedings is not, in itself, sufficient to establish a legitimate doubt as to his impartiality[2]. Assessment of whether legitimate doubts exist must take place in the light of the public's increased sensitivity to the importance of fair and transparent administration of justice[3].

1   *San Leonard Band Club v Malta* 2004-IX, paras 58–66.

2   *Lindon, Otchakovsky-Laurens and July v France* [GC] 2007-XI, paras 75–82 (two judges

who held the publishing of certain passages from a novel to be defamatory had also previously
held the passages to be defamatory in proceedings against the author and publisher: no violation
of Art 6(1)).

3   *Kress v France* [GC] 2001-VI, para 82, discussed at para **5.73** above.

5.80 The objective test thus involves consideration of 'whether the judge offered
guarantees sufficient to exclude any legitimate doubt in this respect'[1] and not
whether the appellant held apprehensions, however understandable[2]. Particular
judgments illustrate application of this requirement. In *Piersack v Belgium*, the
trial judge at an earlier stage had been head of the section in the public prosecutor's
office which had been responsible for the proceedings against the applicant. While
the European Court of Human Rights accepted that there had been no evidence
of actual bias, it felt that there were reasonable doubts as to the outward
appearances of impartiality[3]. Similarly, in *Kyprianou v Cyprus* the fact that in
contempt of court proceedings the same judges had taken the decision to prosecute,
tried the issues arising from the applicant's conduct, determined his guilt and
imposed the sanction meant that there was 'confusion of the roles between
complainant, witness, prosecutor and judge' which gave rise to 'objectively justified
fears as to the conformity of the proceedings with the time-honoured principle
that no one should be a judge in his or her own cause'[4]. In *Kingsley v United
Kingdom*, the Gaming Board had in earlier proceedings expressed the opinion
that the applicant was not a fit and proper person to hold a certificate approving
him to hold a management position in the industry; after holding a hearing in
private, the Board formally found this to be the case. The Grand Chamber agreed
with the applicant that these proceedings were not accompanied by the necessary
appearance of impartiality[5]. On the other hand, where a judge has ruled on a
preliminary question of whether an accused should be remanded in custody pending
trial, this in itself does not necessarily give rise to any reasonable question of
objective impartiality which would be sufficient to render the trial of the individual
unfair[6]. In *De Haan v Netherlands*, a judge had presided in a tribunal along with
two lay assessors in a case involving an objection against a decision for which he
himself had been responsible, a matter which the Court considered gave rise to
objectively justified fears as to the tribunal's impartiality[7]. However, this situation
can be contrasted with one in which an intervening higher court has set a decision
aside and remitted it back for fresh determination. Here, there is no general
requirement that a superior court is bound to send the case back to a tribunal with
a different constitution[8]. Similarly, it will always be a question whether a change
in the composition of a court during legal proceedings, or indeed the reassignment
of a case to another court[9], will give rise to a legitimate doubt as to its impartiality[10].
The requirement of impartiality applies to all bodies which may qualify as 'tribunals'
for the purposes of Article 6, and so the question of the lack of objective impartiality
may even arise in the determination of an alleged breach of parliamentary
privilege[11].

1   *Fey v Austria* (1993) A 255-A, para 28. See too *Hauschildt v Denmark* (1989) A 154, para 52
     (judges at pre-trial stage had to be satisfied of a 'particularly confirmed suspicion' of guilt;

here, circumstances did establish legitimate doubts as to objective impartiality); *Gautrin and Others v France* 1998-III, paras 57–60 at para 59 (professional tribunals had a 'worrying connection' in the context of the particular dispute with competitors of an organisation appearing before them); *Tierce and Others v San Marino* 2000-IX, paras 77–83 (the same judge had dealt with the judicial investigation and trial at first instance and the preparation of the file for the appeal hearing: in the circumstances, objective fears as to impartiality justified); *Daktaras v Lithuania* 2000-X, paras 30–38 (the President of the Criminal Division of the Supreme Court had combined the role of prosecutor, had appointed the judge rapporteur, and was to constitute the court which was to examine the case: insufficient guarantees to exclude any legitimate doubt as to the absence of inappropriate pressure on the Supreme Court led to a violation of Art 6); *Rojas Morales v Italy* (16 November 2000), paras 31–35 (charges of criminal conspiracy and international drug-trafficking: violation of Art 6 because of the lack of appearance of impartiality of the trial court); *Wettstein v Switzerland* 2000-XII, paras 43–50 (lack of impartiality of two judges in administrative proceedings in circumstances where the judges had acted either directly as lawyers, or through their office partner, against the applicant in separate proceedings); *Sigursson v Iceland* (10 April 2003), paras 37–46 (husband of judge was indebted to the bank party to proceedings: violation); *Pescador Valero v Spain* 2003-VII, paras 21–29 (judge employed as an associate professor participated in proceedings involving the university: violation); *Tocono and Profesorii Prometeişti v Moldova* (26 June 2007), paras 28–33 (Supreme Court judge's son had been expelled from a school run by one of the parties: violation); *Dubus SA v France* (11 June 2009) (doubts regarding the Banking Commission's independence and impartiality had been objectively justified because of the lack of any clear distinction between the functions of prosecution, investigation and adjudication in the exercise of its judicial power: violation); and *Micallef v Malta* [GC] 2009-…, paras 100–104 (close family ties between the opposing party's advocate and the presiding judge sufficed to conclude that the composition of the court was not such as to guarantee its impartiality and failed to meet the objective test in this respect: violation Art 6(1)). Cf *Salaman v United Kingdom* (dec) (15 June 2000) (trial judge and an appeal court judge had not disclosed the fact of their membership of the freemasons in a case where one of the parties was also a freemason: membership of the freemasons was not in itself enough to cast doubt over impartiality, and the applicant had not provided any further evidence to substantiate his fears: inadmissible); *Lie and Bernstein v Norway* (dec) (16 December 1999) (application challenging the determination of a judge on the question of compensation for the length of criminal proceedings in which he had sat as a trial judge declared inadmissible as there were no legitimate grounds for fearing the judge had any preconceived ideas when dealing with the subsequent claim to compensation); *Lindon, Otchakovsky-Laurens and July v France* [GC] 2007-XI, paras 75–82 (no violation of the impartiality requirement despite the fact that two of the appeal court judges who ruled that certain passages from a novel which had been published in a newspaper were defamatory had already found the passages to be defamatory in earlier proceedings against the author and publisher); and *Procedo Capital Corporation v Norway* 2009-…, paras 56–72 (continuation of proceedings after the withdrawal of one judge had been ordered had not been capable of giving rise to legitimate doubts as to impartiality of the court as a whole, for any misgivings that the withdrawn judge had exerted influence on other members of the court had been adequately addressed).

2   *Nortier v Netherlands* (1993) A 267, para 33.

3   *Piersack v Belgium* (1982) A 53, paras 30–31; see too *Oberschlick v Austria (no 1)* (1991) A 204, para 50 (breach of rule prohibiting any judge who had dealt with a matter in initial proceedings from hearing the case on appeal; disposal of appeal thus was by a court whose impartiality was specifically recognised as open to doubt); and similarly, *Castillo Algar v Spain* 1998-VIII, paras 43–51. Cf *Pabla KY v Finland* 2004-V, paras 31–35 (judge was also member of the legislature: no violation, the Court noting at para 32 that 'there is no objection per se to expert lay members participating in the decision-making in a court … [There are] many examples of tribunals in which professional judges sit alongside specialists in a particular sphere whose knowledge is desirable and even essential in settling the disputes').

4   *Kyprianou v Cyprus* [GC] 2005-XIII, paras 124–128.

5   *Kingsley v United Kingdom* [GC] 2002-IV, paras 32–34, upholding the Chamber judgment (7 November 2000), paras 49–50.

6   *Sainte-Marie v France* (1992) A 253-A, paras 32–34; *Garrido Guerrero v Spain* (dec) 2000-III (a judge had earlier taken part in confirmation of an indictment purely as a procedural matter and thus there were no legitimate doubts as to his impartiality); *Ilijkov v Bulgaria* (26 July 2001), para 97; and *Ekeberg and Others v Norway* (31 July 2007), paras 31–50 (the judge in ordering the continued detention on remand had, according to the criminal procedure code, to be satisfied that there was a 'particularly confirmed suspicion' that the accused had committed the crime, violation). See also *Nešták v Slovakia* (27 February 2007), paras 99–101 (the court responsible for determining the applicant's appeal had previously decided on issues concerning his detention and had made statements in a decision – which had been preceded by deliberations in camera to which the prosecutor, but not the applicant, was privy – implying that the applicant had committed the offence in question before the trial was concluded; in such circumstances the statements and the context in which they were made gave rise to legitimate and objectively justified misgivings about the impartiality of that tribunal).

7   *De Haan v Netherlands* 1997-IV, paras 50–55.

8   *Thomann v Switzerland* 1996-III, paras 32–37 (the imposition of any such requirement would slow down the administration of justice).

9   *Bochan v Ukraine* (3 May 2007), paras 67–85 (after the courts of two levels of jurisdiction had made, for the second time, findings contrary to those of the Supreme Court, the latter had transferred the applicant's case to the courts in a different jurisdiction without issuing a procedural decision in this respect: the circumstances of the reassignment combined with the insufficient reasoning had violated Art 6(1).

10 See eg *Academy Trading Ltd and Others v Greece* (4 April 2000), paras 43–47 (the retirement of a judge had required a fresh hearing to be held in which two judges who had taken part in earlier deliberations took part again; however (by four votes to three) the Court considered that the applicants had not established any illegality or radical departure from normal court practice sufficient to establish a want of impartiality); and *Moiseyev v Russia* (9 October 2008), paras 172–185 (eleven judicial replacements during the applicant's trial which were not circumscribed by any procedural safeguards and for nine of which no reasons had been provided: objective justification for doubts as to the independence and impartiality of the trial court).

11 *Demicoli v Malta* (1991) A 210, paras 39–41 (punishment of editor of periodical by House of Representatives which included the two MPs who had been criticised and subsequently raised the matter of breach of privilege: objective impartiality open to doubt).

Issues relating to juries

5.81 Where a jury forms part of an adjudicatory tribunal, similar considerations of independence and impartiality apply[1]. The handful of judgments of the European Court of Human Rights in this area concentrate upon whether there were legitimate doubts as to a jury's objective impartiality rather than the existence of actual bias on the part of a juror or jurors, but the outcomes have not always been consistent. The existence of safeguards is of considerable relevance. In the Scottish case of *Pullar v United Kingdom*, no violation of Article 6 was established. After a guilty verdict had been returned, it transpired that one of the members of the jury had been an employee of the principal prosecution witness and had personally known another of the witnesses. The Court (by five votes to four) disagreed with the Commission's assessment and held that there had been no violation of the requirement of objective impartiality. The particular juror at the centre of the dispute had been merely a junior employee, had been facing redundancy, and had no personal knowledge of the issues in the case. Of some importance for the majority of the Court were the safeguards offered by the system of jury trial in Scotland including the random method of selection of jurors and the nature of the charge by the presiding judge to the jury which reminded its members that they were to consider in a dispassionate manner the evidence presented[2]. In *Szypusz v United Kingdom*, the jury in a criminal trial had been left alone to review video footage with an investigating officer charged with operating the video equipment. Noting that the trial judge had emphasised to the jurors that the officer was only to operate the equipment, that there was to be no communication for any other purpose and that the defence counsel had consented to the viewing in the manner proposed, the Court held there had been sufficient safeguards in place to exclude any objectively justified or legitimate doubts as to the impartiality of the jury[3]. In *Mustafa (Abu Hamza) v United Kingdom (no 1)*, the applicant had been charged with soliciting to murder and stirring up racial hatred. He had argued that widespread media attention had been such as to negate the chances of a fair trial, and further, that the delay in holding the trial had destroyed his opportunity to defend himself as the intervening terrorist attacks of 11 September 2001 had rendered it impossible to give an explanation of the context in which his public speeches had been made. These arguments had not succeeded in the domestic courts. In Strasbourg, the two issues of pre-trial publicity and delay were considered together. In declaring the application inadmissible as manifestly ill-founded, the Court noted that the applicant's complaint related to the adverse publicity surrounding the applicant. This was a matter concerning the jury's objective impartiality, not its subjective impartiality. While accepting that a virulent media campaign could in certain circumstances undermine the fairness of a trial by influencing public opinion (and thus the jury) in a case, a number of factors would ensure the fairness of proceedings in the majority of cases: these included the nature of the trial process, the trial judge's responsibilities in directing the jury, and the powers of domestic courts to prevent adverse media reporting (and if necessary to stay proceedings on grounds of an abuse of process). These factors, taken together in the present case with the careful directions given to the jury and repeated warnings given to the media by the trial judge, had excluded any objectively justified or legitimate doubts as to the jury's impartiality[4].

1   *Gregory v United Kingdom* 1997-I, para 43. However, there is no specific right to trial by jury under the Convention, nor can one be implied even in states whose legal systems make use of juries: cf 14739/89, *Callaghan v United Kingdom* (1989) DR 60, 296 (trial by jury was not an essential aspect of a determination of a criminal charge; and thus the refusal to allow new evidence to be considered by a jury (rather than by an appeal court) did not give rise to an Art 6 issue).

2   *Pullar v United Kingdom* 1996-III, paras 36–41. See also *Ekeberg and Others v Norway* (31 July 2007), paras 48–49 (after the first four days of a trial, the court was informed that a juror had given the police a witness statement that related to the case and she was ordered to withdraw from further participation: no violation of Art 6 as her presence on the jury was

limited to and terminated after a relatively early phase of the trial, and there was no indication that she had influenced the jury before she was discharged).

3   *Szypusz v United Kingdom* (21 September 2010), paras 82–90.

4   *Mustafa (Abu Hamza) v United Kingdom (no 1)* (dec) (18 January 2011). Cf 8403/78, *Jespers v Belgium* (1980) DR 22, 100 (virulent press campaign may adversely affect the fairness of a trial and thus invoke state responsibility, particularly if sparked off by a state authority). Reid *A Practitioner's Guide to the European Convention on Human Rights* (3rd edn, 2007), p 143 notes that no finding of unfair trial based on prejudicial pre-trial publicity has yet been established, but that probably 'it would take more than close media interest in a case and it would be likely that the fact[s] that the jurors took oaths, and would be warned to discount news coverage, would be regarded as offsetting prejudice'. See further paras **7.102–7.103** below. Additional security measures which can be shown to have been necessary in the circumstances will not be considered to have unduly influenced a jury as to the dangerousness of the accused: 11837/85, *Auguste v France* (1990) DR 69,104.

5.82 However, a more critical approach may be called for in dealing with allegations of juror bias[1]. Objective impartiality was in question in *Holm v Sweden*, where a majority of the jurors hearing a libel case had been active members of a political party which in the past had directly owned and still indirectly controlled the publishing company defending the action. The Court considered that the court's independence and impartiality were open to doubt[2]. A similar conclusion as to the existence of a legitimate doubt as to impartiality was reached in *Remli v Fance*, where a juror had been overheard to say 'what's more, I'm a racist' and the trial court had refused to take any formal note of this event or any remedial action since the statement had been made outwith the courtroom[3]. Both cases appear to subsume the question of possible subjective bias into that of objective appearance of impartiality. In *Sander v United Kingdom*, a juror had passed a note to the judge towards the end of a trial expressing concerns that the jury was likely to determine the matter on the basis of racial prejudice. The judge had reminded the jury that they had taken an oath, and invited any juror who felt unable to try the case fairly to advise him. The judge then had received a letter signed by all members of the jury refuting the allegations of racial bias, and a second letter from a juror apologising for any racist statements he may have made which had resulted in the suggestion of prejudice. The jury thereafter had found the applicant guilty but had returned a verdict of not guilty in respect of another co-defendant from an Asian background. The Court did not accept that there had been any breach of the jury's subjective impartiality. While it was clear from the initial note to the trial judge and from the letter of apology written by a juror that at least one juror had made racist jokes, this could not be taken as establishing actual bias. On the other hand, there were legitimate grounds for believing that objective impartiality was in question. English law protected the secrecy of jury deliberations, and thus it had not been possible for the judge to question jurors as to the nature and content of the racist statements. The letter from the jury had to be considered alongside the admission from the individual juror of having made racist statements, the judge's admonition to the jury was considered unlikely to have changed a juror's racist attitudes and, accordingly, the jury's objective impartiality had been open to doubt[4].

In the earlier case of *Gregory v United Kingdom*, the trial judge had been passed a note reading 'Jury showing racial overtones. 1 member to be excused'. There had been no admission on the part of any juror of the making of racist remarks, and the allegation was vague. The trial judge had dealt with the matter by reminding them of their oath and instructing them to disregard any prejudice, and the Court accepted that this approach was sufficient to deal with any question of perceived bias[5]. This judgment places far greater reliance upon the power of the judge to address questions of prejudice by simple admonition. It is not easy to reconcile this judgment with *Saunder v United Kingdom*[6].

1 For discussion of pre-trial media coverage and statements made by public officials in advance of a trial, see paras **5.194** and **7.102–7.103** below.

2 *Holm v Sweden* (1993) A 279-A, paras 32–33.

3 *Remli v France* 1996-II, paras 46–48.

4 *Sander v United Kingdom* 2000-V, paras 29–35. See further Daly and Pattenden 'Racial Bias and the English Criminal Trial Jury' (2005) 64 CLJ 679.

5 *Gregory v United Kingdom* 1997-I, paras 43–50.

6 In *Saunder v United Kingdom* (9 May 2000), para 34, the Court attempted to distinguish *Gregory* on the facts, but did so rather unconvincingly (and see the dissenting judgment of Judge Bratza: the facts of *Gregory* 'bear a strong similarity to those in the present case'). The English courts have ruled that a misdirection to a jury does not necessarily result in a breach of Art 6: *R v Francom* [2001] 1 Cr App R 237.

Decisions of domestic courts on independence and impartiality

5.83 Although domestic law in the United Kingdom has for centuries contained a variety of principles designed to ensure the independence and impartiality of courts and tribunals, the effect given to Article 6 by the Scotland Act 1998 and the Human Rights Act 1998 has resulted in a large number of challenges based on the Convention and in some significant changes to existing institutions and practices.

INDEPENDENCE

5.84 The first Scottish case to raise this issue was *Starrs v Ruxton*, which concerned a temporary sheriff appointed under the Sheriff Courts (Scotland) Act 1971, s 11(2). Such a sheriff was appointed by the Executive for a year at a time, and the appointment was subject to recall by the Executive at any time and for any reason. The appointment could also be effectively recalled by the Executive's not allocating any work to the temporary sheriff. It had become recognised that the normal route to appointment as a permanent sheriff was by way of appointment as a temporary sheriff (which was normally, but not invariably, renewed annually). The court held that the absence of any security of tenure was fatal to the compatibility of the system of temporary sheriffs with Article 6. Following the decision in *Starrs v Ruxton*, the Bail, Judicial Appointments, etc (Scotland) Act 2000 abolished the office of temporary sheriff and replaced it with the office of part-time sheriff (with security of tenure). The 2000 Act also reformed the system of appointment and removal of Justices of the Peace, prevented politically nominated justices from performing court duties, and prevented local authorities from bringing prosecutions in the District Court (where the legal assessor advising the justices was at that time an employee of the local authority). These changes were all designed to ensure that the District Court fulfilled the Article 6 requirement of independence and impartiality.[1]

---

1   *Starrs v Ruxton* 2000 JC 208. The decision did not apply to determinations which were made by temporary sheriffs before the HRA 1998 came into force: *Dickson v HM Advocate* 2008 JC 181. The separation of the judiciary from the other arms of government was also considered, in the context of the island of Sark, in *R (Barclay) v Lord Chancellor* [2010] 1 AC 464.

5.85 The use of temporary judges of the Court of Session was challenged in *Clancy v Caird*, but without success. Appointment as a temporary judge was for a term of three years and carried security of tenure within that period. They were deployed as required by the Lord President. Although the appointment was part-time, the common law rules on declinature of jurisdiction, together with the judicial oath, adequately guaranteed against any conflict of interest. In these circumstances, the temporary judge constituted an independent and impartial tribunal. In addition, the court held that the pursuer had waived his right to an independent and impartial tribunal (*esto* the temporary judge did not constitute such a tribunal) by failing to object at the outset of the case. In that connection, Lord Coulsfield observed:

> 'It is, I think, not irrelevant to bear in mind what sort of litigation this is. It is, in every possible respect, a private dispute between private parties ... It is the sort of dispute which parties might well have agreed to dispose of by arbitration or by summary procedure or by commercial procedure. In these circumstances, in my opinion, the pursuer must be held to have passed from any objection to the disposal of the case by a temporary judge when he failed to raise any objection to the allocation of the temporary judge to hear the case or, at latest, to object at the start of the proof.'[1]

---

1   *Clancy v Caird* 2000 SC 441. For English discussion, see *Locabail (UK) Ltd v Bayfield Properties Ltd* [2000] QB 451.

5.86 The use of temporary judges of the High Court of Justiciary was challenged in *Kearney v HM Advocate*, again without success. The judge was appointed by the Scottish Ministers to act as a judge on such occasions as the Lord Justice General might direct, the term of appointment being one of three years. Although the appointment had been made by the Scottish Ministers (who included the Lord Advocate), the trial was compatible with the right to an independent and impartial tribunal, there being nothing in the judge's conduct giving rise to a suspicion that he lacked the qualities of independence and impartiality; the process of appointment was not initiated by the Lord Advocate (unlike the situation in *Starrs v Ruxton*); and the manner and nature of the judge's appointment and his security of tenure did not suggest his freedom to discharge his judicial functions had been comprised[1].

---

1   *Kearney v HM Advocate* 2006 SC (PC) 1.

5.87 The implications of *Starrs v Ruxton* were again explored in *Millar v Dickson*[1], which concerned a number of appeals by persons who had been convicted or sentenced in proceedings before temporary sheriffs, no objection having been taken to the proceedings at any earlier stage. It was held by the High Court of Justiciary that the objection came too late, and that the complainers had tacitly waived their right to an independent and impartial tribunal. That decision was reversed by the Judicial Committee of the Privy Council in a judgment which strongly endorsed the importance of judicial independence. In *Clark v Kelly*, the question was raised whether a trial before the District Court amounted to a fair and public hearing by an independent and impartial tribunal. It was argued that the clerk of court was a member of the court and did not have the security of tenure required by Article 6(1), and that the practice whereby the clerk retired with the justices to advise them on points of law was in breach of the accused's right to a public hearing. The court, however, held that the clerk was not a member of the District Court, and under reference to *Delcourt v Belgium*[1] and *Borgers v Belgium*[3], that private communication between an impartial legal adviser and the justices was not incompatible with Article 6(1). The court emphasised the importance of the justices raising in open court any matter upon which the parties might reasonably wish to comment[4]. This issue was referred to the Privy Council which determined that while the clerk formed part of the court for the purposes of Article 6, but that a number of features (including the professional obligations of the clerk and the restriction of his responsibilities to the provision of legal advice) supported the conclusion that a fair minded and informed observer would consider the court to be independent and impartial[5].

---

1   *Millar v Dickson* 2002 SC (PC) 30.

2   *Delcourt v Belgium* (1970) A 11.

3   *Borgers v Belgium* (1991) A 214.

4   *Clark v Kelly* 2001 JC 16.

5   *Clark v Kelly* 2003 SC (PC) 77, applying *Mort v United Kingdom* (dec) 2001-IX (magistrates' clerk acts solely to assist the justices during deliberations: inadmissible). Note comments by Lord Hope of Craighead at para 69: 'Any advice which the clerk gives to the justice in private on matters of law, practice or procedure should be regarded by them as provisional until the substance of that advice has been repeated in open court and an opportunity has been given to the parties to comment on it. The clerk should then state in open court whether that advice is confirmed or is varied, and if it is varied in what respect, before the justice decides to act upon it.' See also *Robbie the Pict v Wylie* 2007 JC 101 (challenge to the independence and impartiality of district court determining a road traffic case since its clerk was an employee of the local authority responsible for setting the speed restriction: held, in his capacity as clerk of the court, the clerk was not an employee of the local authority but rather employed by it to perform statutory functions under the District Courts (Scotland) Act 1975).

5.88 The issue has also been considered by the English courts. For example, in *R (Chief Constable of the Lancashire Constabulary) v Crown Court at Preston* the composition of the Crown Court when hearing an appeal from licensing justices was at issue. The requirement that two justices for the petty sessions area where the relevant premises are situated be included meant, in practice, that the appeal panel in the Crown Court included two members who belonged to the same licensing committee as the justices who made the decision appealed against. Members of the licensing committee sitting in the Crown Court were expected to pass objective judgment on their colleagues who were members of the same committee which made the first instance decision. In view of the danger that members of the committee sitting in the Crown Court on appeal from a first instance decision of licensing justices may incline, unconsciously, to conform with their colleagues, the arrangements could not be said to be compatible with the principles of Article 6(1)[1].

---

1   *R (Chief Constable of the Lancashire Constabulary) v Crown Court at Preston* [2002] 1 WLR 1332.

IMPARTIALITY

5.89 The High Court of Justiciary has been held to be an impartial tribunal when reviewing the compatibility with the ECHR of its own Acts of Adjournal[1]. The impartiality of a judge, forming part of an appeal court, was successfully challenged in *Hoekstra v HM Advocate (No 2)* on the basis of a newspaper article which the judge had written, in which he was strongly critical of the Convention in general and Article 8 in particular. The article was published shortly after the issue of an opinion by the court, over which he had presided, in an appeal based on Article 8. The court (differently composed) upheld the challenge. It stressed that, in reaching that conclusion, it attached particular importance to the tone of the language and the impression which the author deliberately gave that his hostility to the operation of the Convention as part of Scots law was both long-standing and deep-seated; and that the position would have been very different if all that he had done was to publish, say, an article in a legal journal drawing attention, in moderate language, to what he perceived to be the drawbacks of incorporation. Judges were entitled to criticise (or to welcome) developments in the law; but what they could not do with impunity was to publish either criticism or praise of such a nature or in such language as to give rise to a legitimate apprehension that, when called upon in the course of their judicial duties to apply that particular branch of the law, they would not be able to do so impartially.[2] In *Lawal v Northern Spirit Ltd*, the House of Lords confirmed that the appropriate test was '… whether a fair minded and informed observer, having considered the given facts, would conclude that there was a real possibility that the tribunal was biased'[3]. In *Davidson v Scottish Ministers (No 2)*, this test was applied by the House of Lords which concluded that the fact that a judge before being appointed to this office had made statements about the effect of a statute in the course of debates in Parliament while serving as Lord Advocate had given rise to such an appearance of bias[4]. In contrast, in *Gillies v Secretary of State for Work and Pensions*, the House of Lords did not consider that a fair-minded and informed observer would have considered that a medical member of a tribunal determining an appeal against disability who also undertook work for an agency providing reports as an independent expert adviser for the Benefits Agency could be considered to have been biased against benefits claimants (and indeed, the medical member's experience of report-preparation was likely to have benefited the tribunal when evaluating the evidence contained in reports prepared by other medical experts)[5].

---

1   *Dickson v HM Advocate* 2001 JC 203.

2   *Hoekstra v HM Advocate (No 2)* 2000 JC 391. For another example of a case where a judge might be thought to lack impartiality, see *In re Medicaments and Related Classes of Goods (No 2)* [2001] 1 WLR 700. Changes have been introduced in Scotland, and in England and Wales, to the procedures for dealing with contempt of court, with Art 6 in mind: see para **5.52** above.

3   *Lawal v Northern Spirit Ltd* [2003] ICR 586 (real possibility of bias where counsel appeared before an Employment Appeal Tribunal which included one or two lay members with whom he had previously sat as a part time judge). For other statements of general principle, see *Porter v Magill* [2002] 2 AC 357; and *Helow v Secretary of State for the Home Department* 2009 SC (HL) 1.

4   *Davidson v Scottish Ministers (No 2)* 2005 1 SC (HL) 7. There have been numerous other cases concerned with allegations of bias made against judges. Amongst the more significant are *R (DPP) v Acton Youth Court* [2001] 1 WLR 1828 (judge can conduct trial after making preliminary ruling in favour of Crown); *Umair v Umair* 2002 SC 153 (judge can decide whether to grant leave to appeal against his own decision); *Haney v HM Advocate (No 1)* 2003 JC 43 (judge had been advocate depute at time of pre-trial publicity but not personally involved in appellants' case: no objective justification for any suspicion of bias); *Robbie the Pict v HM Advocate* 2003 JC 78 (a judge's having considered a previous similar case did not preclude his participation in unrelated matters of a like nature, his judicial oath ensuring impartiality; and his membership of an unobjectionable private society was not in itself of any significance); *Mellors, Petitioner* 2002 SCCR 1007 (member of court had been Lord Advocate when criminal proceedings initiated by procurator fiscal but had no personal involvement); *Bryceland, Petitioner* 2006 SCCR 291 (judge who refused bail prior to trial subsequently sat on appeal against conviction: no appearance of bias); contrast *Rimmer, Petitioner* 2002 SCCR 1 (judge had previous involvement in case as Lord Advocate); *Brown v Scottish Ministers* 2003 SLT 1002 (danger of appearance of bias if judge who had refused bail were to hear application for judicial review, where same material relied on); and *R v Dunn* [2011] 1 WLR 958 (Court of Appeal can decide whether a point of law of general public importance is raised, as precondition of appeal to Supreme Court in criminal case). In relation to proceedings for contempt of court, see para **5.52** above.

5   *Gillies v Secretary of State for Work and Pensions* 2006 SC (HL) 71.

JURIES

5.90 A number of cases in the Scottish courts have concerned the impartiality of juries. In *Montgomery v HM Advocate*[1], the issue concerned the prejudicial effect of pre-trial publicity. The Judicial Committee held that the question was not confined to the residual effect of the publicity on the minds of each of the jurors but that account must also be taken of the part which the trial judge would play; and that, on the facts of the case, the directions which the judge might be expected to give to the jury would be sufficient to remove any legitimate doubt that might exist prior to trial about the objective impartiality of the jury. The Judicial Committee also made it clear that the right of the accused to a fair trial by an independent and impartial tribunal was unqualified. The disclosure to a jury that an accused has previously been charged with a criminal offence[2], or has previously been convicted of an offence[3], has been held not to contravene Article 6(1). The fact that a defence witness, who was a convicted prisoner, was handcuffed while giving evidence has also been held not to contravene Article 6(1)[4]. In a case concerned with the contamination of the public water supply of Edinburgh, and its consequent interruption for a period of time, it was held that an Edinburgh jury would constitute an impartial tribunal: only part of the Edinburgh area had been affected; the addresses of jurors were disclosed; three years had passed since the events in question; and the standard procedures and directions would provide sufficient safeguards[5]. On the other hand, where a juror failed to disclose personal knowledge of dishonest conduct on the part of the accused, and that knowledge came to light after the verdict had been reached, in a case in which the credibility of the accused was of critical importance, it was held that objectively justified and legitimate doubts as to the impartiality of the jury could not be excluded[6]. The balloting of a jury of 15 from a panel of 22 has been held to lack the appearance of fairness[7].

1   *Montgomery v HM Advocate* 2001 SC (PC) 1. The same issue was also discussed in *HM Advocate v Fraser* 2000 SCCR 412; *Sinclair v HM Advocate* 2008 SCCR 1; *Coia v HM Advocate* 2009 SCCR 1; *Beggs v HM Advocate* 2010 SCCR 681; and *Transco v HM Advocate (No 2)* 2005 1 JC 44 (contention that trial by jury would be incompatible with the company's rights under Art 6(1)). See further para **5.148** below.

2   *Boyd v HM Advocate* 2001 JC 53.

3   *Andrew v HM Advocate* 2000 SLT 402. See also *Moir v HM Advocate* 2005 1 JC 102; *DS v HM Advocate* 2007 SC (PC) 1 (possibility of disclosure of previous convictions, where evidence led of previous sexual history of complainer, was not incompatible with Art 6).

4   *Trotter v HM Advocate* 2000 SCCR 968.

5   *Crummock (Scotland) Ltd v HM Advocate* 2000 JC 408.

6   *McLean v HM Advocate* 2001 SCCR 526; see also *McTeer v HMA* 2003 JC 66 (the verdict was quashed on the basis that the appellant knew the foreman of the jury and had previously assaulted his son in a manner similar to the charge on which he was being tried).

7   *Brown v HM Advocate* 2006 JC 159.

5.91 The Human Rights Act 1998 has not resulted in a relaxation of the common law principles which impose strict limitations upon the circumstances inquiry can be made into the deliberations of juries. This matter was considered by the House of Lords in the conjoined appeals *Connor* and *Mirza*[1]. Following the verdict in *Mirza* a member of the jury had sent a letter to defence counsel alleging that other members of the jury had demonstrated racist sentiments towards the appellant. Similarly in *Connor* the judge received, after the trial, a letter from a member of the jury expressing concern at the nature of the deliberations. The Court of Appeal refused to investigate the allegations concerning the jury deliberations. This approach was confirmed by the House of Lords, notwithstanding a strongly expressed dissenting speech by Lord Steyn. A similar approach has been followed in Scotland[2].

1   *R v Mirza* [2004] 1 AC 1118; see further K Quinn, 'Jury Bias and the European Convention on Human Rights: A Well-Kept Secret' (2004) Crim LR 998.

2   See eg *Clow v HM Advocate* 2007 SCCR 201; *Casey v HM Advocate* 2010 JC 197.

'Tribunals' other than the ordinary courts

5.92 Independence and impartiality have also been considered in a number of cases concerned with bodies other than the ordinary courts. The leading cases have concerned planning law, disciplinary tribunals and children's hearings. In relation to planning law, in the English case of *R (Alconbury Developments Ltd) v Secretary of State for the Environment, Transport and the Regions* it was held that, although a planning application involved the determination of 'civil rights' within the meaning of Article 6, and the Secretary of State was not an independent and impartial tribunal, nevertheless decisions taken by him were not incompatible with Article 6 provided they were subject to review by an independent and impartial tribunal which had as full jurisdiction as the nature of the decision required. In so far as the decision involved questions of administrative policy, it was not necessary for the reviewing body to redetermine the merits of the decision[1]. The power of the court to review, by way of judicial review, the legality of the decision and the procedures followed was sufficient to ensure compliance with Article 6[2].

1   *R (Alconbury Developments Ltd) v Secretary of State for the Environment, Transport and the Regions* [2003] 2 AC 295; followed in the Scottish case of *County Properties Ltd v Scottish Ministers* 2002 SC 79. See also *R (Kathro) v Rhondda Cynon Taff County Borough Council* [2002] Env LR 15 (planning authority determining own application).

2   See also *R (Aggregate Industries UK Limited) v English Nature* [2003] Env LR 3.

5.93 The independence and impartiality of a disciplinary tribunal came under scrutiny in *Tehrani v United Kingdom Central Council for Nursing, Midwifery and Health Visiting*, which concerned disciplinary proceedings against a registered nurse. The body regulating the nursing profession had a committee which considered complaints about nurses and instituted disciplinary proceedings, and another committee which heard and decided those proceedings. The same individuals served from time to time on both committees, but not in respect of the same case. There was a right of appeal to the Court of Session. It was held that the disciplinary proceedings could lead to a determination of civil rights and obligations within the meaning of Article 6(1), having regard to decisions of the European Court of Human Rights concerning disciplinary proceedings, since they could result in the person's losing the status of a registered nurse and in consequence being prevented, in practice if not in law, from pursuing a career as a nurse in the United Kingdom. It was not, however, necessary that the disciplinary committee be an independent and impartial tribunal, if the requirements of Article 6(1) were met by the right of appeal to the Court of Session. Construing the statutory right of appeal so as to be compatible with Convention rights (as required by the Human Rights Act 1998, s 3), it was held that the right of appeal required to be viewed as unrestricted, and as allowing a complete re-hearing of any case in which the disciplinary committee had decided that the nurse's name should be removed from the register. Considered as a whole, the disciplinary proceedings therefore met the requirements of Article 6(1)[1]. A similar approach was adopted by the Privy Council in *Preiss v General Dental Council*. Disciplinary charges brought on behalf of the General Dental Council were determined by its Professional Conduct Committee. That Committee had a preponderance of members of the Council, and was chaired by the president of the Council, who had also acted as preliminary screener. It was held that the Committee was not an independent and impartial tribunal within the meaning of Article 6. Compliance with the Convention was however secured by the right of appeal (on fact as well as law) to the Privy Council itself[2]. There have been numerous other cases concerned with a variety of other professional disciplinary tribunals[3].

1   *Tehrani v United Kingdom Central Council for Nursing, Midwifery and Health Visiting* 2001 SC 581.

2   *Preiss v General Dental Council* [2001] 1 WLR 1926. Contrast *R (Nicolaides) v General Medical Council* [2001] EWHC Admin 625, where the claimant was only reprimanded and Art 6 was held not to be engaged.

3   See eg *McMahon v Council of the Law Society of Scotland* 2002 SC 475; *Harris v Appeal Committee of the Institute of Chartered Accountants of Scotland* 2005 SLT 487; *Robson v Council of the Law Society of Scotland* 2005 1 SC 125 and 2008 SC 218; *Salsbury v Law Society* [2009] 1 WLR 1286.

5.94 The independence of the children's hearing was challenged unsuccessfully in *S v Miller*. Noting that the members of the hearing were unpaid lay people appointed and trained with the aim of providing assistance to children, the court held that the fact that they did not enjoy the kind of security of tenure associated with judges of courts of the classic kind did not mean that they were not independent. There was no evidence that they had ever been influenced by the executive or that they lacked independence of judgment. They could not be removed without the consent of an independent judge, and in practice no member had been removed except on account of a refusal to take part in training.[1]

1   *S v Miller (No 1)* 2001 SC 977. See also *C v Miller* 2003 SLT 1379.

5.95 A permanent president of a court-martial does not lack the independence and impartiality required by Article 6(1)[1]. It has been held that employment tribunals, as constituted in 1999, could not be regarded as an independent and impartial tribunal in cases involving the Secretary of State for Trade and Industry, but that subsequent administrative changes have secured their independence and impartiality[2].

1   *R v Spear* [2003] 1 AC 734.

2   *Scanfuture UK Ltd v Secretary of State for Trade and Industry* [2001] ICR 1096. In relation to immigration adjudicators, see *R (Husain) v Asylum Support Adjudicator* [2001] EWHC Admin 852 and *Singh v Secretary of State for the Home Department* 2004 SC 416.

LEGISLATIVE REFORMS

5.96 Certain reforms were effected by the Convention Rights (Compliance) (Scotland) Act 2001 in order to ensure compliance with Article 6(1) in the sentencing of life prisoners. The punitive part of a mandatory life sentence was thenceforth fixed by the court, and release was decided on by the Parole Board for Scotland. The constitution of the Parole Board was reformed so as to ensure its independence and impartiality. Reforms to the Lyon Court were also effected to ensure its independence and impartiality. Much more extensive reforms of the tribunal system, so as to make UK tribunals part of the judiciary rather than part of the executive, were effected by the Tribunals, Courts and Enforcement Act 2007.

ARTICLE 6: WHAT CONSTITUTES A FAIR HEARING?

5.97 Of paramount importance in the jurisprudence of Article 6 is the overarching and all-pervading notion of 'fairness'. In applying this assessment, the European Court of Human Rights will consider the proceedings as a whole, so that account will be taken of relevant appellate hearings[1] with allowance being made for the possibility that a defect at first instance may be cured at a subsequent stage[2]. The ultimate question is whether the proceedings as a whole were fair[3]. This allows the Court to consider a range of issues which are not specifically mentioned in the text of Article 6[4], including the extent to which domestic law is interpreted by appellate courts in such a way as to ensure legal certainty[5].

1   *Delcourt v Belgium* (1970) A 11, para 25; *Monnell and Morris v United Kingdom* (1987) A 115, para 54; *Ekbatani v Sweden* (1988) A 134, para 24; *Belziuk v Poland* 1998-II, para 37. Cf 12002/86, *Grant v United Kingdom* (1988) DR 55, 218 (during appeal proceedings, the applicant's counsel had sensed that the High Court of Justiciary was coming round to the opinion that the trial court's sentence of six years' imprisonment was too light and accordingly had attempted to abandon the appeal but was not given permission to do so; the sentence was thereafter increased to ten years' imprisonment. In declaring the application inadmissible as manifestly ill-founded, the Commission considered that the proceedings had to be looked at as a whole, and it was inevitable that an appeal court must form an 'initial inclination or view' from the appeal papers and other materials from the trial court before the opening of the appeal hearing. Furthermore, the court had benefited from hearing submissions on the sentence. Scots law did permit an individual to abandon his appeal, but in this case the motion to seek authority to do so had been made after the start of the hearing).

2   Eg *De Cubber v Belgium* (1984) A 86, para 33 (the trial judge had been the investigating judge and thus could be supposed to have formed a view as to the applicant's guilt or innocence, but the appeal court had not quashed the conviction on this particular ground: the Court noted that the opportunity for the subsequent curing of defects was the justification for the requirement that an applicant exhaust domestic remedies in terms of Art 35(1)). See further paras **5.150– 5.152** below.

3   That is, 'what the proper administration of justice required': *Vaudelle v France* 2001-I, paras 57–66 (conviction and imprisonment *in absentia* of the applicant who had been placed under supervisory guardianship on account of deterioration of his mental facilities without the national authorities having taken additional steps to try to examine him and summoning him to appear: violation).

4   A range of issues has been examined: see eg *Gillow v United Kingdom* (1986) A 109, paras 70–71 (no unfairness disclosed through the failure to make available a tape recording of a hearing); *Barberà, Messegue and Jabardo v Spain* (1988) A 146, paras 76–89 (brevity of trial on serious charges and failure to adduce crucial evidence); *Colak v Germany* (1988) A 147, paras 31–32 (assurance given by the president of the court to the defence before the court had deliberated did not constitute unfairness); *Stanford v United Kingdom* (1984) A 282-A, paras 24–31 (applicant's difficulties in hearing the court proceedings did not give rise to a situation of unfairness as the applicant was represented by skilled counsel); *Kraska v Switzerland* (1993) A 254-B, paras 28–33 (allegation that a judge gave his opinion without an adequate knowledge of the case not established); *Kremzow v Austria* (1993) A 268-B, para 72 (practice of circulating a draft judgment in advance amongst judges which did not bind them did not indicate any unfairness); *Sawoniuk v United Kingdom* (dec) 2001-VI (conviction of applicant for murder committed during the 1939–45 war: the Convention does not impose any time-limit in respect of war crime prosecutions, and there was no suggestion that the criminal proceedings were unfair: inadmissible); and *Mustafa (Abu Hamza) v United Kingdom (no 1)* (dec) (18 January 2011) (no assurance that the applicant would not be prosecuted in the present case had been given, nor could the decisions to deprive the applicant of his citizenship and to accede to his extradition be taken to have amounted to such an assurance of non-prosecution: inadmissible as manifestly ill-founded).

5   *Beian v Romania (no 1)* 2007-XIII, paras 25–38 (contradiction in the case law of the Court of Cassation was contrary to the principle of legal certainty and undermining public confidence in the judicial system, and here had effectively deprived the applicant of any possibility of qualifying for rights prescribed by law: violation of Art 6(1)); and *Iordan Iordanov and Others v Bulgaria* (2 July 2009), paras 47–53 (profound and persistent differences in the Supreme Administrative Court's interpretation of domestic law had effectively deprived the applicants of legal certainty, one of the essential guarantees of a fair hearing: violation of Art 6(1)). See further paras **5.100–5.101** below.

5.98 The requirements inherent in the concept of a 'fair hearing' in the determination of civil rights and obligations are perhaps less demanding than in the determination of criminal charges on account of the presence of additional detailed guarantees provided by paragraphs (2) and (3) which apply in criminal cases. 'Thus, although these provisions have a certain relevance outside the strict confines of criminal law[1]..., the Contracting States have greater latitude when dealing with civil cases concerning civil rights and obligations than they have when dealing with criminal cases'[2]. However, 'fairness' is a standard both broader than and transcendent of the collective minimum rights for criminal defendants contained in paragraphs (2) and (3), which in any case merely 'represent specific applications of the general principle of a fair trial'[3]. In *Philips v the United Kingdom,* for example, the Court observed that, in addition to being specifically mentioned in Article 6(2), a person's right in a criminal case to be presumed innocent and to require the prosecution to bear the onus of proving the allegations forms part of the general notion of a fair hearing under Article 6(1)[4]. In consequence, the application of a single and generalised standard of fairness has resulted in some lack of clarity in the jurisprudence. Additional considerations determining the assessment of the fairness of a criminal trial are, in short, best considered as specific applications of the general requirement to ensure a fair hearing under the first paragraph, particularly since these subsequent provisions are themselves non-exhaustive and constituent elements of a fair criminal process[5]. In consequence, the Court will normally consider the application of paragraphs

(2) and (3) in conjunction with the disposal of any paragraph (1) question. Where the difficulty lies is in the Court's somewhat unsatisfactory tendency to neglect to examine complaints under paragraph (3) if a violation of the general fairness requirement in paragraph (1) has already been established. Arguably, the effect of this approach has been gradually to diminish the clarity and coherence with which the distinction between the specific individual guarantees can be drawn: while it is clear that certain minimum rights are being protected, one cannot be sure exactly of which paragraph a failure to observe those rights will fall foul.

1   *Albert and Le Compte v Belgium* (1983) A 58, para 39.

2   *Dombo Beheer BV v Netherlands* (1993) A 274, at para 32.

3   *Pakelli v Germany* (1983) A 64, at para 42.

4   *Phillips v United Kingdom* 2001-VII, at para 40, discussed at para **5.190** below. See also *Grayson and Barnham v United Kingdom* 2008-..., paras 37–50 (the rights of defence were protected by safeguards built into the system and that the judge had a discretion not to apply the assumption if he considered that applying it would give rise to a serious risk of injustice: no violation).

5   *Deweer v Belgium* (1980) A 35, para 56; see Trechsel *Human Rights in Criminal Proceedings* (2005), pp 86–87.

5.99 Four main constituent elements of a fair hearing emerge as being of particular importance: legal certainty; proceedings which are adversarial in character; fair rules of evidence; and the issuing of a reasoned judgment.

Legal certainty

5.100 The requirement for legal certainty is found throughout the Convention[1], and is also recognised as an inherent aspect of a fair hearing in terms of Article 6. The existence of contradictory case law is contrary to the principle of legal certainty and undermines public confidence in the judicial system[2]. Issues of legal certainty may also arise in respect of access to a court[3]. Where there are 'profound and persistent differences' in judicial interpretation of domestic law, this may also be sufficient to allow the conclusion to be drawn that that individuals have been thereby deprived of the possibility of a fair determination of their rights[4]. However, the requirement of legal certainty to ensure the protection of litigants' expectations cannot be taken as preventing the development of the common law or the provision of settled guidance in statutory interpretation[5]. For example, in *Schwarzkopf and Taussik v Czech Republic,* the applicants had brought an action under a 1991 statute for recovery of property that had originally belonged to Jewish members of their family who had suffered persecution during the Second World War. The applicants' claims had been dismissed in 2000 by the Supreme Court which had given a narrow interpretation to the legislation. Subsequently, however, the Supreme Court had settled on a more open interpretation. The Court found that although domestic interpretation of the 1991 Act had not been settled at the time that the applicants' claims had been dismissed, the legislation had introduced measures to promote coherency, and it was to be expected that harmonising the case law would take time. The fact that the decision adopted in respect of the applicants at the material time had not yet reflected this more open approach was not sufficient to conclude that the principle of legal certainty had been violated[6].

1   See further paras **3.62–3.72** above. For discussion of legal certainty in criminal cases in relation to Art 7, see paras **5.225–5.237** below.

2   *Beian v Romania* 2007-XIII, paras 29–40.

3   Eg *De Geouffre de la Pradelle v France* (1992) A 253-B. See further para **5.67** above.

4   *Beian v Romania (no 1)* 2007-XIII, at para 38; see also *Iordan Iordanov and Others v Bulgaria* (2 July 2009), paras 47–53 (divergent decisions of supreme administrative court on statutory interpretation).

5   *Unédic v France* (18 December 2008), paras 71–78.

6   *Schwarzkopf and Taussik v Czech Republic* (dec) (2 December 2008).

5.101 The principle of legal certainty also requires that where domestic courts have finally determined an issue, their ruling should not be called into question. In other words,

> 'Legal certainty presupposes respect for the principle of *res judicata* ... that is the principle of the finality of judgments. This principle underlines that no party is entitled to seek a review of a final and binding judgment merely for the purpose of obtaining a rehearing and a fresh determination of the case. Higher courts' power of review should be exercised to correct judicial errors and miscarriages of justice, but not to carry out a fresh examination ... A departure from that principle is justified only when made necessary by circumstances of a substantial and compelling character[1]'.

This point is illustrated by *Brumarescu v Romania*. Here, the applicant had brought proceedings seeking a declaration that the nationalisation of his parents' house was null and void. A first instance court had ruled in favour of the applicant, and as no appeal had been lodged, the judgment had become final and the house had been returned to him. Subsequently, the procurator-general had lodged a successful application in the Supreme Court requesting that the judgment be quashed on the grounds that the first instance court had exceeded its jurisdiction in examining the lawfulness of the nationalisation. Since this official had power under the Code of Civil Procedure to apply for a final judgment to be quashed and since the exercise of this power was not subject to a time-limit, judgments were liable to challenge indefinitely. Such a situation had infringed the principle of legal certainty and thereby the applicant's right to a fair hearing[2].

It may be easier to support a contention that 'circumstances of a substantial and compelling character' arise where an individual has been convicted of a criminal offence. The Court has recognised that the quashing of a final judgment by way of supervisory review procedure is indeed justified where there have been serious deficiencies in a criminal trial, and in such instances, exercise of the power to overturn a conviction is likely to achieve a proper balance between the competing interests of finality and justice[3]. However, such a balance may also arise in other contexts. In *OOO Link Oil SPB v Russia*, the Court addressed the compatibility with Article 6 of a new supervisory review procedure in commercial proceedings which limited the grounds for review, imposed short time-limits, and restricted those who could apply for supervisory review. Since the enforcement proceedings in the instant case had been lawfully stayed pending the supervisory review, and as the binding and enforceable decision was not liable to challenge indefinitely but only once on restricted grounds and within a limited time-frame, the procedure in the current case could not be said to have been incompatible with the principle of legal certainty[4].

1   *Ryabykh v Russia* 2003-IX, at para 52.

2   *Brumrescu v Romania* [GC] 1999-VII, paras 56–62. See for other examples of violations, *Sovtransavto Holding v Ukraine* 2002-VII (quashing of judicial decisions as a result of supervisory review proceeding lodged by the President of the Supreme Arbitration Tribunal); *Ryabykh v Russia* 2003-IX (supervisory review proceedings lodged by the president of a regional court infringed the principle of legal certainty and the applicant's right to a court); and *Driza v Albania* 2007-XII, paras 63–71 (quashing of a final judgment as a result of supervisory review proceedings instituted at the request of the President of the Supreme Court).

3   *Lenskaya v Russia* (29 January 2009), at para 44.

4   *OOO Link Oil SPB v Russia* (dec) (25 June 2009).

DOMESTIC CASES ON LEGAL CERTAINTY

5.102 Domestic cases in which issues of legal certainty have arisen have generally considered such issues under Article 7 of the Convention. Article 6 was, however, considered in *R (Robinson) v Secretary of State for Justice,* which concerned legislation in England and Wales removing the right of a prisoner recalled to prison while on licence to be released after serving three-quarters of his sentence. It was held that the provisions governing early release did not form part of the sentence imposed by the court, but were rather part of the arrangements for the administration of that sentence. The change in the provisions did not interfere with the sentence and was therefore not contrary to Article 6[1].

1   *R (Robinson) v Secretary of State for Justice* [2010] 1 WLR 2380.

Proceedings which are adversarial in character

5.103 An adversarial hearing is a vital characteristic in both criminal and civil proceedings. Efforts are made throughout the ECHR to limit the inquisitorial functions of tribunals and courts in favour of an approach which permits challenge, contradiction and counter-evidence[1]. The right to an adversarial hearing ought to translate into 'the opportunity for the parties ... to have knowledge of and comment on all evidence adduced or observations filed ... with a view to influencing the court's decision'[2]. In the majority of instances, this right is most effectively secured by a public hearing in the presence of all parties, with provision for each party to participate and contribute on an equal footing. Where the nature of proceedings does not allow for this optimum, however, the European Court of Human Rights will assess the extent to which a fair balance between the rights of the parties and the requirements of justice has been struck. Infringements of the right to adversarial proceedings may not result exclusively from imbalances that favour one party unfairly over the other; they can also occur when both parties are denied knowledge of or opportunity to comment on a piece of evidence before the court. In *Krcmár v Czech Republic*, a violation was established where the constitutional court had failed to disclose pivotal documentary evidence to either party in a case concerning nationalisation of a family company under the communist regime. The applicants, who were asserting a civil right to restitution, had thus been denied the chance to comment on documents which undoubtedly had influenced the court's decision[3].

1   See eg paras **6.52** and **8.33** below. This statement is of particular validity in the context of deprivation of liberty of a criminal suspect: see paras **4.236–4.238** above.

2   *Vermeulen v Belgium* 1996-I, at para 33.

3   *Krčmář v Czech Republic* (3 March 2000), paras 41–46. See too *Kamasinski v Austria* (1989) A 168, paras 87–93. Cf *Kress v France* [GC] 2001-VI, discussed at para **5.73** above.

'Equality of arms'

5.104 Adversarial proceedings are closely related to the notion of 'equality of arms'[1]. 'Equality of arms' requires that 'each party must be afforded a reasonable opportunity to present his case – including his evidence – under conditions which do not place him at a substantial disadvantage vis-à-vis his opponent'[2]. This is only one aspect of the wider concept of a fair civil or criminal trial and thus must be considered in terms of the overall fairness of the proceedings[3] with the result that certain differences in the procedural situation of parties which are not deemed prejudicial may be overlooked[4].

1   Cf *Belziuk v Poland*, 1998-II, paras 37–39 at para 37 ('the principle of equality of arms is only one feature of the wider concept of a fair trial, which also includes the fundamental right that criminal proceedings should be adversarial'; here, the principle of equality of arms and the right to adversarial proceedings both required that the applicant should have been allowed to attend the hearing and to contest the prosecutor's submissions). See further Wasek-Wiaderek *The Principle of Equality of Arms in Criminal Procedure under Article 6 of the European Convention on Human Rights and its Function in Criminal Justice of Selected European Countries: A Comparative View* (2000); Trechsel *Human Rights in Criminal Proceedings* (2005), pp 94–102; Summers *Fair Trials: The European Criminal Procedural Tradition and the European Court of Human Rights* (2007), pp 103–110.

2   *Bönisch v Austria* (1985) A 92, paras 29–35 (defence expert witness to be accorded the same facilities as one appointed by the prosecution); *Dombo Beheer BV v Netherlands* (1993) A 274, at para 33; *Hentrich v France* (1994) A 296-A, at para 56; and *Stran Greek Refineries and Stratis Andreadis v Greece* (1994) A 301-B, at para 46. See too *Reinhardt and Slimane-Kaïd v France* 1998-II, paras 105–107 (communication of the report and draft judgment of the judge *rapporteur* to the *advocat général* but not to the appellant prior to a hearing: violation of Art 6); *Beer v Austria* (6 February 2001), paras 17–21 (non-communication of appeal against an order relating to costs: violation of Art 6); and *Eroğlu Aksoy v Turkey* (31 October 2006), paras 24–31 (inability to obtain access to defence ministry's case-file which had formed the basis for a judgment upholding a civil servant's dismissal from the army: violation).

3   *Ruiz-Mateos v Spain* (1993) A 262, para 63.

4   *Kremzow v Austria* (1993) A 268-B, para 75 (differences in time limits for submitting pleadings and for responding were not deemed material); *Ankerl v Switzerland*, 1996-V, para 38 (evidence of one party was not able to be taken on oath, but she was still able to address the court and give evidence; in consequence, there was no breach of Art 6). Cf *Dombo Beheer v Netherlands* (1993) A 274, dissenting judgment of Judge Martens joined by Judge Pettiti: 'in relation to litigation concerning civil rights and obligations, the concept of "equality of arms" can only have a formal meaning: both parties should have an equal opportunity to bring their case before the court and to present their arguments and their evidence'. It cannot imply substantive implications requiring adaptation of substantive rules of procedure and evidence 'in order to guarantee both parties substantively equal chances of success'; and *Varnima Corporation International SA v Greece* (28 May 2009), paras 28–35 (application of different periods of limitation to parties enjoying an equivalent status in proceedings concerning a claim of breach of contract against the state had contravened the principle of equality of arms as the parties had enjoyed an equivalent status in the proceedings and the difference in treatment was not sufficiently justified by the general interest).

DOMESTIC CASES ON EQUALITY OF ARMS

5.105 The Judicial Committee of the Privy Council followed this approach in *Buchanan v McLean,* where it was argued that restrictions imposed upon the fees and outlays payable to the defence solicitors, under legal aid arrangements, produced an inequality of arms which was incompatible with a fair trial. The argument was rejected on the particular facts, although the Judicial Committee warned that there might be a breach of Article 6 in other circumstances. In the instant case, however, it had not been shown that the effect of the arrangements on the performance of their duties by the appellants' solicitors was such that the proceedings as a whole would be unfair. It was in addition far from clear that the prosecution would enjoy any advantage:

> 'At first sight there is bound to be some measure of inequality of arms as between the prosecutor, who has all the resources of the state at his disposal, and an accused who has to make do with the services that are available by way of criminal legal aid. But in *M v United Kingdom*[1] the Commission recognised that financial restraints may be necessary to ensure the most cost effective use of the funds available for legal aid. It can be assumed that, as the procurator fiscal service is funded by public money, there are pressures on that side also to ensure cost effectiveness. What has to be demonstrated is that the prosecutor in this case will enjoy some particular advantage that is not available to the defence or that would otherwise be unfair'.[2]

It has also been pointed out in a domestic case that, while equality of arms requires that each party must be afforded a reasonable opportunity to present his case under conditions which do not place him at a substantial disadvantage vis-à-vis his opponent, the word 'opportunity' is to be emphasised: a party who fails to prepare adequately for a hearing, having had a reasonable opportunity to do so, cannot complain of a breach of Article 6[3].

1   9728/82, *M v United Kingdom* (1983) DR 36, 155.

2   *Buchanan v McLean* 2002 SC (PC) 1 at para 40 per Lord Hope of Craighead. This decision was followed in *Vickers v Buchanan* 2002 SCCR 637.

3   *Thomson Pettie Tube Products Ltd v Hogg* (4 May 2001, unreported), Ct of S.

Knowledge of the case to be met

5.106 'Equality of arms' may call for positive steps on the part of judicial or other state authorities to ensure that parties have a proper knowledge of the case to be met. This will normally involve disclosure of evidence to allow the opportunity to respond effectively. In *Kerojärvi v Finland*, the court had not sought to have made available to the unrepresented appellant either relevant files or a legal opinion relating to an insurance claim. For the European Court of Human Rights, the procedure followed by the domestic tribunal had not been such as to allow the applicant's proper participation[1]. In *McMichael v United Kingdom*, the fairness of the Scottish system of children's hearings was found wanting on the lack of equality of arms. An infant had been made subject to compulsory measures of care on the grounds that lack of parental care was 'likely to cause him unnecessary suffering or seriously to impair his health or development'[2]. Both the children's hearing which took the decision and the sheriff court which reviewed the disposal had sight of social reports, but these reports had been withheld from the parents who had only been made aware of the general substance of their contents. The Court considered that there had been a violation of Article 6(1)'s guarantee of a fair hearing through the failure to disclose vital documents to the parents which in consequence had meant that their ability to participate in the hearing and to assess prospects of success in an appeal had been unduly restricted[3]. This issue is closely related in certain cases to the issue of ensuring practical and effective access to a court for the resolution of disputes[4].

1   *Kerojärvi v Finland* (1995) A 322, paras 40–43. See also *KS v Finland* (31 May 2001), paras 21–24, and *KP v Finland* (31 May 2001), paras 25–28 (failure to disclose opinions on the merits of the applicants' claims for social welfare entitlement: violation of Art 6(1) in each instance); and *FR v Switzerland* (28 June 2001), paras 34–41 (failure to disclose opinion of tribunal before proceedings in Federal Insurance Court).

2   In terms of the Social Work (Scotland) Act 1968, s 32(c). See also *S v Miller (No 1)* 2001 SC 977.

3   *McMichael v United Kingdom* (1995) A 307-B, paras 80–84. For further discussion of Scots practice, see Hallett and Murray 'Children's Rights and the Scottish Children's Hearing System' (1999) 7 Int Jo Children's Rights 31.

4   See eg *Tinnelly and Sons Ltd and Others and McElduff and Others v United Kingdom* 1998-IV, discussed at para **5.68** above.

DISCLOSURE OF EVIDENCE

5.107 Within the context of a criminal case, the application of this principle is more rigorous since paragraphs (2) and (3) impose additional safeguards[1]. It requires that 'both prosecution and defence must be given the opportunity to have knowledge of and comment on the observations filed and the evidence adduced by the other party'. However domestic law seeks to secure this end, 'it should ensure that the other party will be aware that observations have been filed and will get a real opportunity to comment thereon'[2]. The principle is thus that the prosecuting and investigating authorities must disclose material in their possession (or to which they could gain access) which may assist the accused in exculpating himself or in mitigating sentence as well as material which may assist in undermining the credibility of prosecution witnesses[3].

1   *Dombo Beheer BV v Netherlands* (1993) A 274, paras 32–33.

2   *Brandstetter v Austria* (1991) A 211, at para 67; *Lobo Machado v Portugal* 1996-I, 195, para 31; *Belziuk v Poland* 1998-II, 558, para 37.

3   8403/78, *Jespers v Belgium* (1981) DR 27, 100, at para 58; *Edwards v United Kingdom* (1992) A 247-B, Commission opinion, para 50.

5.108 Where evidence has been withheld on public interest grounds, the European Court of Human Rights will not consider whether non-disclosure was strictly necessary as this is generally a matter for domestic courts, but rather will 'ascertain whether the decision-making procedure applied in each case complied, as far as possible, with the requirements of adversarial proceedings and equality of arms and incorporated adequate safeguards to protect the interests of the accused'[1]. In each instance, however, the proceedings as a whole have to be assessed. In *Edwards v United Kingdom*, the police had not disclosed to the defence that one of the victims had failed to identify the applicant from a police photograph album after having made a statement that she thought she would be able to recognise her assailant, nor that fingerprints had been found at the scene of the crime. The Court confirmed that there is a duty upon the prosecutor to make available all material evidence whether or not favourable to an accused, and that the failure to provide this can render the proceedings defective. The referral of the case by the Home Secretary to the Court of Appeal when these failures had come to light had, however, remedied these defects in the present case[2]. In contrast, the Court considered there had been a violation of Article 6 in the case of *Rowe and Davis v United Kingdom*. The applicants and a co-defendant had been convicted of murder, robbery and assault primarily on the evidence of four accessories. During the trial, the defence had sought to allege that three of these witnesses had deliberately lied in order to exculpate themselves, and that two had been influenced by a substantial sum of reward money offered by the police. The prosecutor had refused to disclose to the defence whether any of the witnesses had claimed a reward or had been paid, and the trial court had declined to order disclosure after being shown certain documents by the prosecutor. The Court held that entitlement to disclosure of relevant evidence could never be an absolute right since competing interests (such as national security, the need to protect witnesses at risk of reprisals, and safeguarding police investigation methods) had to be weighed against the rights of an accused: indeed 'in some cases it may be necessary to withhold certain evidence from the defence so as to preserve the fundamental rights of another individual or to safeguard an important public interest'. In each case, however, 'only such measures restricting the rights of the defence which are strictly necessary' were permissible. Here, determination of the need to conceal information had been made by the prosecution itself without judicial intervention. Nor had the review by the Court of Appeal of the undisclosed evidence in ex parte hearings with the benefit of submissions from the Crown but in the absence of the defence cured the defect: the appeal court had been left to rely for an understanding of the material's possible relevance on transcripts of the trial hearings and on the account of the issues given by prosecuting counsel. The conclusion was that the trial had been unfair[3]. Each case requires careful consideration. In *Botmeh and Alami v United Kingdom*, the applicants had found out only after being convicted at first instance that the intelligence services had withheld information from the police. Following the Home Secretary's issuing of a public-interest immunity certificate, the appeal court had viewed the material *ex parte* and had ordered that the applicants be provided with a summary of the undisclosed evidence, but had refused to order full disclosure on the grounds that there was no reason to believe that the applicants' convictions were unsafe. In holding that Article 6 had not been violated, the Court stressed that the appeal court had enjoyed the opportunity to view the evidence and to consider its impact on the safety of the applicants' conviction[4].

1   *Rowe and Davis v United Kingdom* [GC] 2000-II, at para 62. See also *Mirilashvili v Russia* 2008-..., paras 200–209 (decision of a court not to disclose material obtained by wiretapping was not accompanied by adequate procedural guarantees and was not sufficiently justified, and while the material had been examined by the presiding judge *ex parte*, the decision was based on the type of material at issue rather than upon analysis of its content and the court had not analysed whether the material would have been of any assistance to the defence or whether disclosure would have arguably harmed an identifiable public interest).

2   *Edwards v United Kingdom* (1992) A 247–B, paras 33–39; see also *IJL, GMR* and *AKP v United Kingdom* 2000-IX, paras 114–118 (no violation as the material was disclosed before the appeal hearing, the defence had the chance to challenge it and the appeal court considered the issue in detail)

3   *Rowe and Davis v United Kingdom* [GC] 2000-II, paras 59–67 at para 61 (the Court considered the matter in terms of para (1)'s guarantees of fair process, finding it unnecessary to consider whether paras (3)(b) and (3)(d) were of relevance). See also the related cases of *Fitt v United Kingdom* [GC] 2000-II, and *Jasper v United Kingdom* [GC] (16 February 2000); and the case of *Atlan v United Kingdom* (19 June 2001), para 44–46 at para 44 (the prosecution had repeatedly denied the existence of evidence stemming from an informant, despite the fact that the applicants' defence was that they had been falsely implicated by an undercover officer, and after conviction but before the appeal the prosecution confirmed that an informant had indeed been involved: the 'repeated denials by the prosecution at first instance of the existence of further undisclosed relevant material, and their failure to inform the trial judge of the true position, were not consistent with the requirements of Article 6(1)'. For domestic consideration, see *R v H* [2004] 2 AC 134.

4   *Botmeh and Alami v United Kingdom* (7 June 2007), paras 36–45.

DECISIONS OF DOMESTIC COURTS ON DISCLOSURE AND RECOVERY OF EVIDENCE, AND 'CLOSED MATERIAL'

5.109 The right of the defence in criminal proceedings to recover material in the possession of the Crown has been considered in the light of Article 6 in several recent Scottish cases. In *McLeod v HM Advocate*, decided prior to the incorporation of the Convention into Scots law but after consideration of Convention jurisprudence, a bench of five judges held that Scottish criminal procedure proceeded on the basis that the Crown had a duty to disclose to the defence information in their possession which would tend to exculpate the accused. Where an accused sought an order for the production or recovery of documents, he required to explain the basis on which he sought the order, and the court only granted such orders when satisfied that the particular documents would be likely to be of material assistance to the proper preparation or presentation of the defence[1]. In *Maan, Petitioner*, it was held that the Crown's duty of disclosure extends not only to information which bears directly on the guilt or innocence of the accused, but also to information which would tend to undermine the credibility of a Crown witness[2].

---

1   *McLeod v HM Advocate* 1998 JC 67. This test was not met in *Hoekstra v HM Advocate (No 4)* 2001 JC 131.

2   *Maan, Petitioner* 2001 SCCR 172. In this case it was also said: 'The court must consider on the one hand the public interest in securing for the accused a fair trial, and on the other hand the public interest put forward as justifying non-disclosure ... It is ... for the court to decide whether the former interest outweighs the latter.' This, with respect, appears (if understood literally) to be incorrect. Although the accused's right to disclosure is not absolute, it is nevertheless necessary to ensure that he receives a fair trial (see *Rowe and Davis v United Kingdom* [GC] 2000-II, para 61). The right to a fair trial is not something to be balanced against other considerations: *R v Forbes* [2001] 1 AC 473, para 24; *R v A (No 2)* [2002] 1 AC 45, para 38. Similarly *DS v HM Advocate* 2007 SC (PC) 1 at para 17 per Lord Hope of Craighead (amongst other authorities).

5.110 Matters were taken further in subsequent cases. In *Holland v HM Advocate*, it was held that information about the previous convictions of any witnesses to be led at the trial would be likely to be of material assistance to the proper preparation or presentation of the defence, and under Article 6(1) the defence was accordingly entitled to have that information disclosed along with information about any outstanding criminal charges faced by the witnesses of which the Crown were aware[1]. In *Sinclair v HM Advocate*, a trial was held to have been unfair by reason of the Crown's failure to disclose a statement made by a witness to the police, which had been in the Crown's possession. It was observed that the police statements of all the witnesses who were to be called at the trial were to be regarded as containing material evidence either for or against the accused, and the Crown were accordingly under an obligation, in terms of Article 6(1), to disclose their statements to the defence[2]. In *McDonald v HM Advocate,* however, where the defence had lodged petitions for the recovery 'all material in the possession or under the control of the Lord Advocate which ought to have been (and ought to be) disclosed in terms of her obligation under Article 6(1)', the Judicial Committee emphasised the limits to the Crown's duty of disclosure. Lord Rodger of Earlsferry observed that the representatives of the Crown were under no duty to comb through all the material in their possession to look out for anything which might assist the defence and so should be disclosed:

rather they must disclose disclosable material of which they became aware, or to which their attention was drawn, while diligently carrying out their core duties of preparing and prosecuting the case. Furthermore, while a failure by the Crown to disclose material might be incompatible with Article 6(1), it by no means necessarily followed that the accused had not had a fair trial in terms of Article 6[3]. In *HM Advocate v Murtagh*, the question arose whether the disclosure of witnesses' convictions and outstanding charges was compatible with their Article 8 rights. The Privy Council held that a rule that the entire criminal history of a witness had to be disclosed would go beyond what was necessary for the protection of the accused's right to a fair trial and would not be justifiable under Article 8(2), but a rule which required only such parts of the history to be disclosed as were material could be justified under Article 8(2). Accordingly, the accused's right to a fair trial required the disclosure only of such previous convictions and outstanding charges as materially weakened the Crown's case or materially strengthened the case for the defence. The Privy Council further held that Article 6(1) also required the disclosure of warnings by the procurator fiscal or measures offered and accepted as alternatives to prosecution, but only if they materially weakened the case for the Crown or materially strengthened the case for the defence[4]. In *McInnes v HM Advocate,* it was held that the question which the appeal court must ask itself, in a case of non-disclosure, is whether after taking full account of all the circumstances of the trial, including the non-disclosure in breach of the appellant's Convention right, there was a real possibility that the jury would have arrived at a different verdict if the withheld material had been disclosed to the defence[5].

The information which requires to be disclosed is not confined to information concerning the records of witnesses. It includes, for example, information as to the identities of witnesses[6], or as to the evidence which they are able to give[7].

---

1   *Holland v HM Advocate* 2005 1 SC (PC) 3. See also *Scott v HM Advocate* 2008 SCCR 110.

2   *Sinclair v HM Advocate* 2005 1 SC (PC) 28.

3   *McDonald v HM Advocate* 2010 SC (PC) 1.

4   *HM Advocate v Murtagh* 2010 SC (PC) 39.

5   *McInnes v HM Advocate* 2010 SC (UKSC) 28. See also *Allison v HM Advocate* 2010 SC (UKSC) 19. There are numerous examples of the application of the *McInnes* test.

6   See eg *Dyer v Von* 2008 SCCR 265.

7   See eg *Fraser v HM Advocate* 2011 SLT 515.

5.111 The courts have also had to consider the use of 'closed material' which, on public interest grounds, is not disclosed to the party against whom the proceedings have been taken, but may be disclosed to a 'special advocate' who is appointed to represent that party but cannot consult with the party after he has seen the material in question. In *R v H*, the House of Lords issued guidance, in the light of the relevant Strasbourg case law, on how applications for the non-disclosure of material on public interest grounds should be dealt with in an ordinary criminal trial. It was made clear that non-disclosure could only be permitted where it would not render the trial process unfair to the defendant. It was accepted that the appointment of a special advocate might be a necessary part of that procedure[1]. The issue was considered by the House of Lords in a different context in *Secretary of State for the Home Department v MB*, where two suspected terrorists who were subject to control orders challenged the use by the court of closed material in the hearings in which those orders were confirmed. The proceedings were classified as civil in character for the purposes of Article 6: there was no assertion of criminal conduct, only a foundation of suspicion; no identification of any specific criminal offence was provided for; the order made was preventative in purpose, not punitive or retributive; and the obligations imposed must be no more restrictive than were judged necessary to achieve the preventative object of the order. It was, however, accepted that under the civil limb of Article 6(1) a person against whom such an order was proposed was entitled to procedural protection commensurate with the gravity of the potential consequences. In that regard, although differing views were expressed by their Lordships, it was accepted that there could be cases in which the non-disclosure of material would not render the proceedings unfair (eg where the controlee received an adequate summary of the material in question, or that material was not relied on). The requirements of procedural fairness under domestic law or under the Convention would not however be met if the controlee were denied such knowledge of what was said against him as was necessary to enable him, with or without a special advocate, effectively to challenge or rebut the case against him. The court's task was to ascertain whether, looking at the process as a whole, a procedure had been used which involved significant injustice to the controlee. The statutory provisions by which material might be withheld from the controlee were therefore to be read down under section 3 of the Human Rights Act 1998 so as to take effect only where it was consistent with fairness for them to do so. On the facts of the cases before the House, the appellants had not had a fair hearing[2].

The matter was re-considered by the House of Lords, following the judgment of the Grand Chamber in *A and Others v United Kingdom*[3], in *Secretary of State for the Home Department v AF (No 3)*. It was then held that the controlee must be given sufficient information about the allegations against him to enable him to give effective instructions in relation to those allegations. Provided that this requirement was satisfied there could be a fair trial notwithstanding that the controlee was not provided with the detail or the sources of the evidence forming the basis of the allegations. Where, however, the open material consisted purely of general assertions and the case against the controlee was based solely or to a decisive degree on closed materials, the requirements of a fair trial would not be satisfied, however cogent the case based on the closed materials might be[4].

---

1   *R v H* [2004] 2 AC 134.

2   *Secretary of State for the Home Department v MB* [2008] 1 AC 440. See also *R (Roberts) v Parole Board* [2005] 2 AC 738, a case concerned with release on licence, where the issue was considered in the light of the procedural requirements of Art 5(4); and *RB (Algeria) v Secretary of State for the Home Department* [2010] 2 AC 110, a deportation case where Art 6 was held not to be engaged, but the issue was considered in the light of the procedural requirements of Art 3, and MB was distinguished.

3   *A and Others v United Kingdom* [GC] 2009-…, discussed at para **4.237** above.

4   *Secretary of State for the Home Department v AF* (No 3) [2010] 2 AC 269.

5.112 The decision in *AF (No 3)* was applied by the Court of Appeal, in relation to the use of closed material in civil proceedings, in *Bank Mellat v HM Treasury*. The case concerned a direction made by the Treasury which prohibited all persons operating in the financial sector in the United Kingdom from entering into or participating in any transaction or business relationship with the claimant, a major Iranian commercial bank. The bank's application to set aside the decision was met by open and closed evidence and argument from the defendant. According to the open evidence, the purpose of the direction was to hamper Iran's nuclear and ballistic missile programmes by shutting the bank out from the United Kingdom financial sector, it being believed that the bank was supporting and facilitating those programmes and funding nuclear-related companies. More detailed evidence was available on a closed basis. The bank contended that the defendant's open case was insufficient to enable it to give proper instructions to its legal representatives or to a special advocate. On a preliminary issue to determine the standard of disclosure of evidence required, that the claimant had to be provided with information which was sufficient to enable it not merely to deny what was said against it but actually to refute, in so far as that was possible, the defendant's case. What constituted sufficient information therefore depended on the facts of the particular case, including the issues between the parties, the contents of the statements of case, the nature and import of the evidence in question, and the state of knowledge of the party seeking the information[1].

Similar issues to those arising in relation to 'closed material' can also arise in relation to the use of anonymous witnesses. These issues are discussed below[2].

1   *Bank Mellat v HM Treasury* [2010] 3 WLR 1090.
2   See para **5.221** below.

Intervention by law officers

5.113 The right to equality of arms extends to the opportunity for the parties to a case 'to have knowledge of and comment on all evidence adduced or observations filed, even by an independent member of the national legal service, with a view to influencing the court's decision'[1]. This principle holds for cases in which it is maintained that, at a criminal appeal hearing, the prosecutor is present in his capacity as guardian of the public interest but where it is clear that his intervention seeks to have a conviction upheld and where his role in reality is thus that of a prosecuting authority[2]. Similarly, it applies where a law officer is present to assist the court in the determination of a civil matter but his task in reality is that of assisting the defending party to an action. For example, in *APEH Uldozotteinek Szovetsege, Ivanyi, Roth and Szerdahelyi v Hungary*, both the public prosecutor's office and the Attorney General had intervened in non-contentious civil proceedings involving an application to register the applicant association, but the domestic court had not advised the association of these facts. For the Court, the intervention by the public prosecutor may well have had a repercussion on the outcome of the case, and while it was not possible to assess the impact if any of the submissions made by the Attorney General, 'the principle of equality of arms does not depend on further, quantifiable unfairness flowing from a procedural inequality' since 'it is a matter for the parties to assess whether a submission deserves a reaction and it is inadmissible for one party to make submissions to a court without the knowledge of the other and on which the latter has no opportunity to comment'[3]. In contrast, in *Kress v France*, the Court found no violation on the facts of the case. The applicant had raised an action of damages in the administrative courts against a hospital authority, and had ultimately appealed on points of law to the *Conseil d'Etat*. She had not been informed of the submissions of the Government Commissioner in advance, and had been unable to respond to these orally at the hearing but had subsequently submitted a memorandum to the court before it gave judgment. The Court noted that the submissions had not been communicated to either side or even to the judges in advance of the hearing, and thus there had been no violation of the principle of equality of arms since the applicant had not been placed at a disadvantage vis-à-vis her opponent. Further, litigants were afforded sufficient safeguards by the court's procedures, for while the applicant had not had the opportunity to reply during the hearing to the submissions, she had made use of the opportunity to respond in writing in a memorandum[4].

---

1   *Vermeulen v Belgium* 1996-I, at para 33.

2   *Van Orshoven v Belgium* 1997-III, paras 37–38; see too *Voisine v France* (8 February 2000), paras 25–26 (failure to communicate the submissions of the *avocat général* to the applicant).

3   *APEH Üldözötteinek Szövetsége and Others v Hungary* 2000-X, paras 40–44 at para 42.

4   *Kress v France* [GC] 2001-VI, paras 72–76 (but there was a violation of the requirement of independence and impartiality through the participation of the Commissioner in the court's deliberations, even although the Commissioner was acknowledged to be objective and did not have a vote: see further para **5.73** above).

The right of attendance at a court hearing

5.114 It goes without saying that an adversarial hearing is most likely to be secured where the parties are accorded a right of attendance at an oral hearing. There is an obvious link with the guarantee of a right to a public hearing, a provision which is designed to protect litigants against the secret administration of justice and maintain public confidence in the judicial system[1]. However, just as the right of a public hearing is not an absolute right, so too the right of attendance at an oral hearing is determined according to the extent to which fairness dictates that attendance would be considered necessary. This is assessed by factors such as the nature of the hearing, its meaning in the context of the proceedings as a whole, and the importance of what is at stake for the parties[1].

---

1   See paras **5.154–5.157** below. See also *Augusto v France* 2007-I, paras 50–53 (failure to communicate opinion of court's medical expert to the applicant, violation); and *Ferreira Alves v Portugal (no 3)* (21 June 2007), paras 33–43 (failure to communicate to the applicant documents sent by the prosecutor and the court of first instance to the appeal court: violation).

2   Cf *Allan Jacobsson v Sweden (no 2)* 1998-I, paras 47–49 (applicant's submissions to the
    Supreme Administrative Court were not of such a nature as to require an oral hearing to allow
    their proper determination).

CRIMINAL TRIALS

5.115 The matter is of particular importance in a criminal process where the
right conferred by Article 6(3)(c) on an accused to defend himself in person is
also in play[1]. While there is no requirement that an individual should be present at
all stages of criminal proceedings, it is of the utmost importance that an accused
should be able to attend in person at his trial[2], although a trial in the absence of an
accused is not in principle incompatible with Article 6, providing always that an
individual can obtain a fresh determination of the merits of the charge as regards
both facts and law[3]. However, 'the personal attendance of the defendant does
not necessarily take on the same significance for an appeal or nullity hearing as it
does for a trial hearing'[4]. The right of attendance is essentially considered by the
effect absence will have on the fairness of proceedings and in particular the
consequent inability of the court to assess directly the evidence of the accused.
In determining whether Article 6 will require a public hearing and the attendance
of the individual, 'regard must be had in assessing this question, inter alia, to the
special features of the proceedings involved and the manner in which the defence's
interests were presented and protected before the appellate court, particularly in
the light of the issues to be decided by it, and their importance for the appellant'[5].
In *Belziuk v Poland*, the applicant, who had been sentenced to three years'
imprisonment, had sought to contest his conviction and to adduce evidence in
support of his case, but he had not been allowed to be present at the appeal
hearing, even although he had elected not to be legally represented. The European
Court of Human Rights considered that a fair hearing required a direct assessment
of the evidence given by the applicant in person thus allowing the opportunity
both to challenge the submissions of the public prosecutor and also to present
evidence in support of his appeal. The absence of counsel was not material since
under paragraphs (1) and (3)(c) taken together an individual had the right to be
present at his appeal and to defend himself in person[6].

Where an appellate court is called upon to examine factual issues and points of
law and carry out an overall determination of guilt or innocence, it is thus vital that
an accused can give evidence in person to allow the court to assess directly the
evidence. In *Tierce and Others v San Marino*, the domestic appeal courts had
jurisdiction to decide factual issues as well as points of law without a hearing in
public, and where an appeal court considered that further investigations were
necessary, an investigative hearing could be held before the judicial officer
responsible for investigations on appeal. In this case, the appellate court had been
called upon to examine the entire issue of the guilt or innocence of the applicants
as well as to determine points of law. The appellate court had revised the legal
characterisation of the first applicant's conduct as involving fraud rather than
misappropriation without directly assessing evidence adduced by the applicant in
person, even although the requisite element of intent differed. Similarly, in relation

to the second and third applicants, the court had established requisite intent, again without taking direct evidence. The Court determined that in these circumstances the appellate court should have permitted the applicants to give direct evidence in person, and thus there had been a violation of Article 6(1) in each case[7]. If a doubt arises, the burden of establishing that the applicant was in fact summoned to appear at the hearing lies with the government, and in the event that the summons has been sent too late[8] or not at all[9], there will be a violation of Article 6(1).

---

1   See paras **5.210–5.214** below.

2   *Poitrimol v France* (1993) A 277-A, para 34; cf *Pelladoah v Netherlands* (1994) A 297-B, paras 37–41; *Stefanelli v San Marino* 2000-II, paras 19–22 (trial judge sentenced the applicant to four-and-a-half years' imprisonment but without holding a public hearing or even seeing the accused: violation of Art 6(1)); see Trechsel *Human Rights in Criminal Proceedings* (2005), pp 252–256.

3   *Poitrimol v France* (1993) A 277-A, para 31; and see also *Medenica v Switzerland* 2001-VI, paras 53–60 (the applicant had been prevented from attending his trial by a judicial decision preventing him leaving the USA: no violation).

4   *Kremzow v Austria* (1993) A 268-B, paras 58–63 at para 58 (the applicant was legally represented in appellate proceedings considering pleas of nullity and appeals against sentence, and he was able to make submissions through his counsel: no breach of para (1) or of (3)(c)).

5   *Kremzow v Austria* (1993) A 268-B, paras 58–59 at para 59. See also *Helmers v Sweden* (1991) A 212-A, paras 31–32; *Belziuk v Poland* 1998-II, para 37.

6   *Belziuk v Poland* 1998-II, paras 37–38. See too *Botten v Norway* 1996-I, para 52; and *Csikós v Hungary* 2006-XIV, at para 21 (increase in sentence imposed by appeal court sitting in camera and without the presence of the applicant or legal representative: violation, the Court noting that, unlike in *Belziuk*, the prosecutor and the applicant were both absent, but while no equality of arms issue thus arose, 'the applicant's sentence should not have been increased, as a matter of fair trial, without him or his lawyer being present').

7   *Tierce and Others v San Marino* 2000-IX, paras 92–102.

8   *Ziliberberg v Moldova* (1 February 2005), paras 7–36.

9   *Gutu v Moldova* (7 June 2007), paras 51–54.

DOMESTIC CASES ON THE RIGHT OF ATTENDANCE AT A COURT HEARING

5.116 In *R (Hammond) v Secretary of State for the Home Department*, the House of Lords considered a provision which excluded the possibility of an oral hearing when a life prisoner's minimum term of imprisonment was being fixed by the court. It was held that the provision had to be read as being subject to an implied condition that the judge had discretion to order an oral hearing where it was required in the interests of fairness, in order to comply with the prisoner's rights under Article 6(1)[1]. The case of *R v Ukpabio* concerned an application, by a defendant who was mentally ill, to give evidence and participate in his trial by video link. It was held that, having regard to a defendant's right to appear before a court which was protected by the common law and by Article 6, there could be circumstances in which it would be appropriate that a defendant on his own application should not be present in court for all or part of a trial, provided that his participation in the trial could be adequately secured by video link or in some other way[2].

1   *R (Hammond) v Secretary of State for the Home Department* [2006] 1 AC 603.

2   *R v Ukpabio* [2008] 1 WLR 728.

The right to participate effectively in proceedings

5.117 Fairness implies the opportunity of effective participation, a notion which itself is bound up with discussion of effective access to a court through the provision of legal aid[1], of knowledge of the case to be met[2], and of the right to interpretation facilities[3]. 'Equality of arms' at the most basic presupposes the right of each side to call its own witnesses, including expert witnesses[4]. In *Dombo Beheer v Netherlands*, for example, the applicant company had sought to establish the basis of an oral agreement between it and a bank arrived at during a meeting at which only the apparent owner of the company and a bank representative had been present. However, it had been denied the opportunity to call its own representative as the domestic courts had identified the apparent owner with the company itself, and the applicant company had thus been placed at a substantial disadvantage in comparison with the bank[5].

1   See paras **5.67–5.69** above and (in relation to criminal trials) paras **5.212–5.204** below.

2   See paras **5.106–5.108** above.

3   See para **5.223** below (in relation to criminal trials).

4   *Bönisch v Austria* (1985) A 92, paras 32–35.

5   *Dombo Beheer v Netherlands* (1993) A 274, paras 34–35.

5.118 The manner in which a hearing is held may also be indicative of unfairness. In *Makhfi v France*, where the proceedings had lasted 15 hours and where the applicant's counsel gave his address at 5am, the Court held that the requirements of a fair trial had not been met[1]. The question has also arisen in respect of juvenile justice. In the related cases of *T v United Kingdom* and *V v United Kingdom*, the Court was asked for the first time to consider the position of children as accused persons. The two applicants who had been 11 years old at the time of their trial for the murder of an infant for which they were convicted argued that the formality and ritual of the adult criminal court had prevented their effective participation. The Court considered that the trial must have seemed at times both incomprehensible and intimidating, and it was not sufficient in the circumstances for the purposes of Article 6(1) that the applicants had been represented by skilled and experienced counsel. Indeed, certain of the steps taken to modify the courtroom for the accused (for example, by raising the height of the dock) had resulted in a heightening of their sense of discomfort. There was also evidence that the accused had been suffering from post-traumatic stress disorder. The complaints that they had found the trial sufficiently distressing and had not been able to discuss their defence meaningfully with their legal representatives were accepted by the Court which held that the applicants had been denied a fair hearing[2]. In *SC v United Kingdom*, the Court ruled that the trial of an 11-year-old boy with a low intellectual level had not been fair, in particular as it had been necessary to persuade the jury that he was so intellectually impaired that he was unable even to understand whether he was guilty, medical evidence merely indicating that on balance he probably did have sufficient intelligence to understand that what he had done was wrong. It did not follow in the opinion of the Court that he had been capable of participating effectively in his trial. When a decision is taken to deal with a child 'who risks not being able to participate effectively because of his young age and limited intellectual capacity, by way of criminal proceedings rather than some other form of disposal directed primarily at determining the child's best interests and those of the community, it is essential that he be tried in a specialist tribunal which is able to give full consideration to, and make proper allowance for, the handicaps under which he labours, and adapt its procedure accordingly'. This had not been done in the present case[3].

---

1   *Makhfi v France* (19 October 2004), paras 32–42.

2   *T v United Kingdom* [GC] (16 December 1999), paras 83–89; and *V v United Kingdom* [GC] 1999-IX, paras 85–91.

3   *SC v United Kingdom* 2004-IV, paras 32–37 at para 35.

Domestic court decisions on effective participation

5.119 Article 6 is not necessarily breached where a court refuses to adjourn a hearing in order to enable one party to obtain legal representation, the other parties being legally represented. The Court of Appeal so held in a case concerned with care proceedings, where an adjournment to enable the parents to obtain fresh representation (following the withdrawal of their counsel) would have resulted in delay which would have been incompatible with the rights of the children[1]. In *R v O'Hare* the defendant failed on numerous occasions to appear for trial and was subsequently convicted in his absence and without representation. His conviction in absentia was held to be fair as he was deemed to have waived his right to participate by choosing not to be present and failing to instruct his lawyers adequately in order that they could represent him. Further, the appellant was provided with the opportunity to explain himself before the Court of Appeal where he was represented[2].

---

1   *Re B and T (Care Proceedings: Legal Representation)* [2001] 1 FLR 485. As to disabled litigants, see *R (King) v Isleworth Crown Court* [2001] EWHC Admin 22.

2   *R v O'Hare* [2006] EWCA Crim 471; see also Taylor 'Trial: Defendant Voluntarily Absenting Himself from Trial – Representatives Withdrawing from Trial' [2006] Crim LR 950. See also *R v Smith* [2006] EWCA Crim 2307.

Fair rules of evidence

5.120 Rules of evidence are essentially matters for domestic regulation[1]. The Court will not question the national courts' interpretation of domestic law unless there has been a flagrant non-observance or arbitrariness in the application of the relevant provisions[2]. 'The question which must be answered is whether the proceedings as a whole, including the way in which the evidence was obtained, were fair. This involves an examination of the unlawfulness in question and, where the violation of another Convention right is concerned, the nature of the violation found'[3]. In other words, the central concern of Article 6 is the fairness of proceedings, and thus the question whether evidence has been properly assessed during proceedings is only of concern in relation to the wider question 'whether evidence for and against the accused has been presented in such a manner ... as to comply with the demands of a fair trial'[4]. The European Court of Human Rights thus 'is not called upon to rule in general whether it is permissible to exclude the evidence of a person in civil proceedings to which he is a party', far less to examine the 'law of evidence in civil procedure *in abstracto*'; under Article 6, the Court's task is limited to considering whether the proceedings in their entirety were 'fair', but this may involve examination of the method in which evidence was obtained[5] and subsequently admitted in proceedings[6], including the use of evidence from anonymous witnesses or witnesses who are not called to give evidence[7]. Evidentiary issues can thus have some bearing on the fairness of proceedings, although the Court's approach to such questions is often rather pragmatic.

---

1   Eg 13274/87, *TS and FS v Italy* (1990) DR 66, 164 (Art 6 does not require examination of the compatibility of questioning with domestic law). See also *Sara Lind Eggertsdóttir v Iceland* 2007-VIII, para 44 (a decision to appoint an expert, be it with or without the parties' consent, is a matter that normally falls within the national court's discretion under Art 6(1) in assessing the admissibility and relevance of evidence).

2   See eg *Société Colas Est and Others v France*, 2002-III, para 43; *Lavents v Latvia* (28 November 2002), para 114; *Laudon v Germany* (26 April 2007), para 56 (the applicant complained about the findings of facts, the assessment of evidence and the application of national law by the domestic courts, but the Court held that there was no evidence of arbitrariness and therefore the complaint was manifestly ill-founded).

3   *Gäfgen v Germany* [GC] 2010-..., paras 162–163 at para 163.

4   8876/80 *X v Belgium* (1980) DR 23, 233. There is, of course, considerable variation in the regulation of proof in European legal systems, differences not solely attributable to the distinction between accusatorial and inquisitorial systems of justice (cf the approaches adopted by Scots and English law on admissibility of irregularly-obtained evidence). See further Harding, Fennell, Jörg and Swart *Criminal Justice in Europe* (1995); Jackson, 'The Effect of Human Rights on Criminal Evidentiary Processes: Towards Convergence, Divergence or Realignment?' (2005) 68 MLR 737.

5   Eg *Barbera, Messegué and Jabardo v Spain* (1988) A 146, para 68; *Delta v France* (1990) A 191-A, para 35; *Ferrantelli and Santangelo v Italy* 1996-III, para 48; *Magee v United Kingdom* 2000-VI, discussed at para **5.126** below.

5   *Dombo Beheer BV v Netherlands* (1993) A 274, para 31.

6   See paras **5.215–5.222** below (in relation to criminal trials).

DOMESTIC COURT DECISIONS ON FAIR RULES OF EVIDENCE

5.121 Domestic cases concerning the ECHR have included a number of cases relating to the law of evidence. Cases concerning disclosure and the use of 'closed material' have been considered above[1]. Cases concerning hearsay evidence[2] and evidence given anonymously[3] are considered below. Cases concerning irregularly obtained evidence[4], evidence obtained by torture[5], and self-incrimination[6] are considered in the next sections. There have also been cases concerned with whether children or cohabitees should be required to give evidence[7], and cases concerned with identification evidence[8]. Generally, the domestic courts have adopted the same approach as the European Court of Human Rights, namely treating evidence as essentially a matter for regulation by domestic law, subject to the requirement of Article 6 of the Convention that the proceedings in their entirety must be fair. This has implications for the timing of any challenge. In *HM Advocate v Robb*, for example, the court observed:

> 'It is when and only when the court has determined the admissibility of the evidence, and when, if appropriate, the trial judge has directed the jury on the use of the evidence that any question of the fairness of the trial can be considered.'[9]

This is not however an absolute rule[10].

1 See paras **5.109–5.112** above.

2 Para **5.217** below.

3 Para **5.221** below.

4 Paras **5.127** and **6.101** below.

5 Para **5.142** below.

6 Paras **5.138–5.140** and **5.142** below.

7 See *In re W (Children) (Family Proceedings: Evidence)* [2010] 1 WLR 701 (whether Art 6 required that child give evidence in family proceedings where stepfather accused of sexual abuse); *R v Pearce* [2002] 1 WLR 1553 (Art 8 not breached on account that cohabitee and child were compellable witnesses in criminal proceedings).

8 See eg *R v Forbes* [2001] 1 AC 473 (failure to hold identification parade, in breach of code of practice); *Holland v HM Advocate* 2005 1 SC (PC) 3 (dock identification); *Britz v HM Advocate* 2007 JC 75 (breach of guidelines for conduct of identification parades); *Scott v HM Advocate* 2008 SCCR 110 (alleged impropriety in conduct of identification parade, and dock identification); *Hanif v HM Advocate* 2009 JC 191 (dock identification).

9 *HM Advocate v Robb* 2000 JC 127 at 132. Similarly *Rose v HM Advocate* 2003 SCCR 569 (destruction of evidence prior to trial); *HM Advocate v G* 2010 SCCR 146 (credibility and reliability of witnesses).

10 See eg *R v A (No 2)* [2002] 1 AC 45; *N v HM Advocate* 2003 JC 140.

The admissibility of irregularly obtained evidence

5.122 The admissibility of evidence improperly obtained is in principle a matter for domestic tribunals[1]. The outcome is that, even where the European Court of Human Rights has established that the state has obtained evidence in violation of domestic law or of a guarantee under the ECHR and has led this evidence in a criminal trial, this will not in itself render the proceedings unfair. In each case, in assessing whether the rights of the defence have been respected, regard will be had to a number of factors including whether the applicant was given the opportunity of challenging the authenticity of the evidence and of opposing its use, whether the admissions made by the applicant were made voluntarily (that is, there is no evidence of entrapment or of the applicant being under inducements to make admissions), and whether the circumstances in which the evidence was obtained cast doubt on its reliability or accuracy[2]. In particular, 'the quality of the evidence must be taken into consideration, as must the circumstances in which it was obtained and whether these circumstances cast doubts on its reliability or accuracy', for 'while no problem of fairness necessarily arises where the evidence obtained was unsupported by other material, it may be noted that where the evidence is very strong and there is no risk of its being unreliable, the need for supporting evidence is correspondingly weaker'[3]. The question whether the evidence in question was or was not decisive for the outcome of the proceedings will thus be of considerable relevance.

1   *Schenk v Switzerland* (1988) A 140, para 46. See further Ormerod 'ECHR and the Exclusion of Evidence: Trial Remedies for Article 8 Breaches' [2003] Crim LR 61; and Omerod and Mckay 'Telephone Intercepts and their Admissibility' [2004] Crim LR 15.

2   Eg *Khan v United Kingdom* 2000-V, paras 36–37; and *Allan v United Kingdom* 2002-IX, para 43.

3   *Gäfgen v Germany* [GC] 2010-..., at para 164.

Evidence obtained in violation of Article 8

5.123 In assessing whether the use of evidence obtained in violation of Article 8 has rendered the trial unfair in terms of Article 6, the Court will examine 'all the circumstances of the case, including, respect for the applicant's defence rights and the quality and importance of the evidence in question'[1]. In *Schenk v Switzerland*, for example, the applicant had been convicted of incitement to murder his wife partly on the basis of a recording of a conversation made with him but taped without his knowledge or consent. He complained that the use of unlawfully obtained evidence had rendered his trial unfair. The Court did not 'exclude as a matter of principle and in the abstract that unlawfully obtained evidence ... may be admissible', but its task centred upon an assessment of the fairness of the trial. In this case, the rights of the defence had not been disregarded: the applicant had sought unsuccessfully to challenge the authenticity of the recording and also its use in evidence; further, the conviction had not been solely based upon the recordings. In the circumstances, the Court considered that the trial had not been unfair[2].

1   *Gäfgen v Germany* [GC] 2010-..., at para 165.

2   *Schenk v Switzerland* (1988) A 140, paras 46–47 at para 46. Cf *Lüdi v Switzerland* (1992) A 238, paras 38–40 (in terms of Art 8, telephone intercept deemed necessary in a democratic

society, and use of an undercover agent did not involve 'private life'). See also *Bykov v Russia* [GC] 2009-…, paras 94–105 (assessment of admissibility and reliability of irregularly-obtained intercept evidence by the domestic courts and availability of other corroborating evidence: no violation).

5.124 Several judgments have involved the use of intercept evidence in the English courts. In *Khan v United Kingdom*, the applicant had been one of a number of visitors to the house of an individual who was being investigated for drugs trafficking and in which the police had installed a listening device. At one point in a conversation which was being recorded, the applicant had admitted dealing in drugs. During his trial, the applicant had sought to challenge the admissibility of the evidence obtained through the surveillance, but after the judge had considered the question of admissibility and had declined to exercise his powers to exclude this, the applicant had pled guilty to an alternative charge. Although the Court accepted there had been a violation of the applicant's Article 8 rights, it did not find that there had been an unfair trial within the meaning of Article 6. On this point, the Court attached considerable weight to the fact that, were the admission of evidence to have given rise to substantive unfairness, the national courts would have had discretion to exclude it[1]. In *Allan v United Kingdom*, the applicant complained that he had been convicted on the basis both of evidence obtained from audio and video bugging devices which had been placed in a police cell and in the visiting area of a police station, and also upon the basis of the testimony of a police informant who had been placed in his cell for the sole purpose of eliciting information about the alleged crime. Relying on the principles set out in *Khan*, the Court held that the use of the evidence obtained by video and audio recordings did not conflict with the requirements of fairness guaranteed by Article 6: the statements made by the applicant could not be said to have been involuntary, and the applicant had been accorded at each stage of the proceedings the opportunity to challenge the reliability of the evidence. On the other hand, the use of the evidence obtained from the informant who had been placed in the prison cell 'for the specific purpose of eliciting from the applicant information implicating him in the offences of which he was suspected' was not compatible with the right to a fair trial. Unlike in *Khan*, the admissions allegedly made to the informant had not been 'spontaneous and unprompted statements volunteered by the applicant, but were induced by persistent questioning' of the informant[2].

1   *Khan v United Kingdom* 2000-V, paras 36–40; in the *Schenk* case (1988) A 140, para 53, the Court had considered it unnecessary to rule on this matter. See also *Elahi v United Kingdom* (20 June 2006), para 15; and *PG and JH v United Kingdom* 2001-IX, paras 79–81. For discussion of Art 8, see para **6.93** below.

2   *Allan v United Kingdom* 2002-IX, paras 46–48 and 52–53; see further para **5.138** below.

Evidence obtained through ill-treatment

5.125 The Court has taken a more resolute stance with regard to evidence obtained under ill-treatment, indicating that evidence obtained in breach of Article 3 will generally violate the right to a fair trial[1]. Crucially, it has eschewed any reference to a 'sole and decisive-type' test, holding instead that an issue may arise under Article 6 in respect of evidence obtained in violation of Article 3, even if the admission of the evidence was not decisive in securing the applicant's conviction[2]. In short, 'the use of such evidence, secured as a result of a violation of one of the core and absolute rights guaranteed by the Convention, always raises serious issues as to the fairness of the proceedings'[3]. The importance of Article 3 as 'one of the most fundamental values of democratic societies' is such that 'even in the most difficult circumstances, such as the fight against terrorism and organised crime, the Convention prohibits in absolute terms torture and inhuman or degrading treatment or punishment, irrespective of the victim's conduct'[4]. In *Harutyunyan v Armenia*, for example, the applicant and two witnesses had been forced to make statements as a result of torture and intimidation. In finding that there had been a violation of Article 6, the Court observed that 'incriminating evidence – whether in the form of a confession or real evidence – obtained as a result of acts of violence or brutality or other forms of treatment which can be characterised as torture should never be relied on as proof of the victim's guilt, irrespective of its probative value. Any other conclusion would only serve to legitimate indirectly the sort of morally reprehensible conduct which the authors of Article 3 of the Convention sought to proscribe or, in other words, to "afford brutality the cloak of law"'[5]. Furthermore, for the purposes of Article 3, ill-treatment by state authorities inflicted for a particular purpose such as to extract a confession or information is treated as an aggravated violation of the guarantee[6].

The rationale for the right to silence and the right not to incriminate oneself includes protection of an accused against improper compulsion with a view to minimising the risk of a miscarriage of justice[7]. However, assessment of whether such a risk has arisen is not without difficulty. In *Gäfgen v Germany,* police had obtained evidence from the applicant by methods of interrogation which had amounted to ill-treatment within the meaning of Article 3. The ill-treatment had been deemed necessary by the police in order to attempt to save the life of a child who, unknown to the police, had already been murdered by the applicant. The applicant had thereafter confessed to the police, and had taken officers to the spot where he had hidden the victim's body. Subsequently, the applicant had repeated his confession to a prosecutor. Before the Strasbourg Court, he sought to argue that the impugned real evidence had been decisive in (rather than merely accessory to) securing his conviction as the self-incriminating evidence obtained as a result of his extracted confession had been wholly necessary for the conviction for murder. The Court disagreed. Two matters called for scrutiny: first, consideration of the extent to which the applicant had enjoyed an opportunity to challenge the authenticity and the use of the evidence was necessary; and secondly, the Court required to assess the quality of the evidence and the circumstances in which the evidence was obtained to evaluate its reliability or accuracy, for 'while no problem of fairness necessarily arises where the evidence obtained was unsupported by other material, it may be noted that where the evidence is very strong and there is no risk of its being unreliable, the need for supporting evidence is correspondingly weaker'. In this instance, the Grand Chamber held that, in light of the second confession, the failure of the domestic courts to exclude the evidence obtained following the ill-treatment had not had a bearing on the overall fairness of the trial[8].

1 In *Jalloh v Germany* [GC] 2006-IX, para 107 the Court stated that 'the general question whether the use of evidence obtained by an act qualified as inhuman and degrading treatment automatically renders a trial unfair' could be 'left open'. In *Hacı Özen v Turkey* (12 April 2007), para 101, however, the Court seemed to interpret *Jalloh* broadly stating that it had 'already held that the use of evidence obtained in violation of Article 3 in criminal proceedings infringed the fairness of such proceedings even if the evidence was not decisive in securing the conviction'. See also *Harutyunyan v Armenia* 2007-VIII, paras 58–67 (reliance on statements by the accused and witnesses who had been tortured: violation). See further Pattenden 'Admissibility in Criminal Proceedings of Third Party and Real Evidence Obtained by Methods Prohibited by UNCAT' (2006) 10 Int Journal of Evidence and Proof 1; Duff, Farmer, Marshall and Tadros *Trial on Trial 3: Towards a Normative Theory of the Criminal Trial* (2007), pp 102–110.

2 Eg *Içöz v Turkey* (dec) (9 January 2003); *Koç v Turkey* (dec) (23 September 2003); *Jalloh v Germany* [GC] 2006-IX, para 99; *Söylemez v Turkey* (21 September 2006); *Örs and Others v Turkey* (20 June 2006); *Levinca v Moldova* (16 December 2008), paras101–105; *Haci Özen v Turkey* (12 April 2007), para 101; *Harutyunyan v Armenia* 2007-VIII, para 63. Cf *Latimer v United Kingdom* (dec) (31 May 2005) (allegations that self-incriminating statements had been made while held in an environment designed to be coercive: inadmissible).

3 *Gäfgen v Germany* [GC] 2010-…, at para 165.

4 *Jalloh v Germany* [GC] 2006-IX, para 99 (the administration of emetics to retrieve evidence, which could have been retrieved using less intrusive methods, subjected the applicant to a grave interference with his physical and mental integrity against his will and thereby violated both Art 3 and Art 6).

5 *Harutyunyan v Armenia* 2007-VIII, para 63: the quotation stems from the US Supreme Court judgment in *Rochin v California* (342 US 165 (1952)). *Göçmen v Turkey* (17 October 2006), paras 67–76 (evidence obtained in absence of lawyer and in breach of Art 3).

6 *Aksoy v Turkey* 1996-VI, para 64; see further para **4.71** above.

7 Eg *John Murray v United Kingdom* 1996-I, discussed at para **5.144** below. For further discussion, see *Quinn v Ireland* (21 December 2000), para 40; and *Heaney and McGuinness v Ireland* 2000-XII, para 40; see also *Allan v United Kingdom* 2002-IX, paras 52–53.

8 *Gäfgen v Germany* [GC] 2010-…, paras 162–188 at para 164.

5.126 Domestic determination that a confession has been given voluntarily rather than under compulsion is not conclusive. In *Magee v United Kingdom*, the applicant had been held incommunicado in a Northern Ireland holding centre and interviewed for extended periods on five occasions by police officers operating in relays before he confessed his part in the planning of a terrorist attack. His initial request for access to a solicitor had been refused. He complained that he had been kept in virtual solitary confinement in a coercive environment and prevailed upon to incriminate himself. In part, his submissions relied upon the opinion of the European Committee for the Prevention of Torture (the CPT) that the detention conditions in the holding centre were unacceptable[1]. The domestic court had found that the applicant had not been ill-treated and that the confession had been voluntary, and the incriminating statements had formed the basis of the prosecution case against him. The Court concluded that denial of access to a lawyer for over 48 hours and in a situation where the rights of the defence had been irretrievably prejudiced was incompatible with the rights of the accused under paragraphs (1) and (3)(c) of Article 6. For the Court, 'the austerity of the conditions of his detention and his exclusion from outside contact were intended to be psychologically coercive and conducive to breaking down any resolve he may have manifested at the beginning of his detention to remain silent'. In such circumstances, the applicant 'as a matter of procedural fairness, should have been given access to a solicitor at the initial stages of the interrogation as a counterweight to the intimidating atmosphere specifically devised to sap his will and make him confide in his interrogators'[2].

---

1   Cf *Report to the United Kingdom Government,* CPT/Inf (94) 17, at para 109: 'Even in the absence of overt acts of ill-treatment, there is no doubt that a stay in a holding centre may be – and is perhaps designed to be – a most disagreeable experience. The material conditions of detention are poor ... and important qualifications are, or at least can be, placed upon certain fundamental rights of persons detained by the police (in particular, the possibilities for contact with the outside world are severely limited throughout the whole period of detention and various restrictions can be placed on the right of access to a lawyer). To this must be added the intensive and potentially prolonged character of the interrogation process. The cumulative effect of these factors is to place persons detained at the holding centres under a considerable degree of psychological pressure. The CPT must state, in this connection, that to impose upon a detainee such a degree of pressure as to break his will would amount, in its opinion, to inhuman treatment.'

2   *Magee v United Kingdom* 2000-VI, paras 38–46 at para 43.

Domestic court decisions on the admissibility of irregularly obtained evidence

5.127 United Kingdom courts dealing with questions of admissibility of evidence which is said to have been obtained in contravention of rights in terms of the ECHR have applied the *Schenk v Switzerland*[1] and *Khan v United Kingdom*[2] judgments. In *R v P*, for example, Lord Hobhouse of Woodborough said:

'The critical question is the fairness of the trial. Questions of the admissibility of evidence are not governed by Article 8. The fair use of intercept evidence at a trial is not a breach of Article 6 even if the evidence was unlawfully obtained ... The defendant is not entitled to have the unlawfully obtained evidence excluded simply because it has been so obtained. What he is entitled to is an opportunity to challenge its use and admission in evidence and a judicial assessment of the effect of its admission upon the fairness of the trial.'[3]

Domestic cases concerned with the admissibility in criminal proceedings of evidence obtained in violation of Article 8 are discussed below[4].

---

1   *Schenk v Switzerland* (1988) A 140.

2   *Khan v United Kingdom* 2000-V.

3   *R v P* [2002] 1 AC 146, HL. See also *Attorney General's Reference (No 3 of 1999)* [2001] 2 AC 91, especially per Lord Cooke of Thorndon; *R v Loveridge* [2001] 2 Cr App R 29. Cf *HM Advocate v McLean* 2000 SCCR 987; and *A v Secretary of State for the Home Department (No 2)* [2006] 2 AC 221 (evidence is inadmissible if extracted through torture irrespective of where

the torture occurred or in what circumstances). See further para **5.142** below; and Grief 'The Exclusion of Foreign Torture Evidence' [2006] EHRLR 200.

4   See para **6.101** below.

Incitement to criminal activity

5.128 Since the admissibility of evidence is primarily a matter for regulation by domestic law, the Court will not in the context of Article 6 examine whether evidence was obtained unlawfully but rather whether any unlawfully-obtained evidence resulted in an unfair trial. A crucial distinction exists between the investigation of criminal behaviour and its incitement. While recognising the need to use undercover agents, informers and covert practices in tackling organised crime and corruption (including corruption in the judicial sphere), the Court has stressed that the risk of police incitement entailed by such techniques requires that their use must be kept within clear limits. Certainly, 'the Convention does not preclude reliance, at the preliminary investigation stage and where the nature of the offence may warrant it, on sources such as anonymous informants'. However, 'the subsequent use of such sources by the trial court to found a conviction is a different matter and is acceptable only if adequate and sufficient safeguards against abuse are in place, in particular a clear and foreseeable procedure for authorising, implementing and supervising the investigative measures in question'. Moreover, 'while the use of undercover agents may be tolerated provided that it is subject to clear restrictions and safeguards, the public interest cannot justify the use of evidence obtained as a result of police incitement, as to do so would expose the accused to the risk of being definitively deprived of a fair trial from the outset'[1]. Where the Court has found sufficient grounds to establish entrapment solely on the basis of the substantive test of incitement, as a general rule it will also examine whether the applicant was able to raise the issue of incitement effectively in the domestic proceedings, and thereby assess the manner in which the domestic court dealt with any such plea[2].

1   *Ramanauskas v Lithuania* [GC] 2008-..., at paras 53–54.

2   *Bannikova v Russia* (4 November 2010), paras 33–79 (notwithstanding that the substantive test of incitement was inconclusive, the applicant's plea of incitement had been adequately addressed by the domestic courts which had taken the necessary steps to reveal the truth and to eradicate doubts as to whether she had committed the offence as a result of incitement: no violation of Art 6(1)).

5.129 The use of evidence obtained as a result of police incitement exposes an accused person 'to the risk of being definitively deprived of a fair trial from the outset'. Police incitement occurs 'where the officers involved – whether members of the security forces or persons acting on their instructions – do not confine themselves to investigating criminal activity in an essentially passive manner, but exert such an influence on the subject as to incite the commission of an offence that would otherwise not have been committed, in order to make it possible to establish the offence, that is, to provide evidence and institute a prosecution'[1]. In *Teixeira de Castro v Portugal*, two plain-clothes police officers acting as undercover agents had approached the applicant during a drug trafficking operation and had asked him to supply heroin. The applicant's name had been supplied to the officers. He had been arrested when he had handed over sachets of the drug. Relying on Article 6, he complained that he had not had a fair trial in that he had been incited to commit an offence by plain-clothes police officers who had acted on their own initiative as *agents provocateurs* and without judicial supervision. For the Court, the behaviour of the officers had gone beyond what was acceptable of undercover agents 'because they instigated the offence and there is nothing to suggest that without their intervention it would have been committed' and so, 'right from the outset, the applicant was definitively deprived of a fair trial'. Although recognising that the rise in organised crime called for appropriate measures, the fair administration of justice could not be 'sacrificed for the sake of expedience' since the public interest could not be used to justify the admission of evidence obtained through police incitement[2]. The use of undercover agents must thus be restricted and accompanied by appropriate safeguards. In *Ramanauskas v Lithuania*, a prosecutor had been convicted of bribery for agreeing to ensure the acquittal of a third party in return for money after having been approached several times by an individual who it later transpired had been an officer from a special anti-corruption police unit. The Grand Chamber considered there had been a violation of the right to a fair trial since there had been no indication that the offence would have been committed without such an intervention, noting also that the domestic courts had taken no steps to carry out a proper examination of the applicant's allegations of incitement[3].

1   *Ramanauskas v Lithuania* [GC] 2008-…, at paras 54–55.

2   *Teixeira de Castro v Portugal* 1998-IV, paras 34–39 at paras 36 and 39.

3   *Ramanauskas v Lithuania* [GC] 2008-…, paras 62–74 (and at para 50, noting that the Council of Europe's Criminal Law Convention on Corruption (ETS 173(1999)), Art 23 requires states to adopt measures permitting the use of special investigative techniques).

5.130 Each case must thus be determined on its own facts. In contrast, in the earlier case of *Lüdi v Switzerland* which the Court distinguished in *Teixeira de Castro*[1], the Court did not find any suggestion of unfairness when the applicant had been convicted on evidence obtained by an undercover police officer during the course of a preliminary investigation under judicial authority[2]. Similarly, in *Miliniene v Lithuania,* no violation was established. Here, a judge had been convicted of corruption following a conversation between her and a private individual who had secretly recorded the discussion. The individual had then approached the police. While noting that the police had 'influenced' events (through approval to offer financial inducements and by supplying technical equipment to record conversations), the role of the police was deemed not 'to have been abusive, given their obligation to verify criminal complaints and the importance of thwarting the corrosive effect of judicial corruption on the rule of law in a democratic society'. Further, the determinative factor had been the conduct of the individual and the judge, and on balance, 'the police may be said to have "joined" the criminal activity rather than to have initiated it'[3].

1　*Teixeira de Castro v Portugal* 1998-IV, para 37. See also *Vanyan v Russia* (15 December 2005), paras 45–50; *Khudobin v Russia* 2006-XII, paras 133–13; and *V v Finland* (24 April 2007), paras 69–72.

2　*Lüdi v Switzerland* (1992) A 238, paras 40–41 and 44–50 (violation established because of refusal to call the undercover agent as a witness). See also *Eurofinacom v France* (dec) 2004-VII (investigations more akin to 'infiltration' than 'instigation': inadmissible).

4　*Milinienë v Lithuania* (24 June 2008), paras 35–41 at para 38 (and also distinguishing *Ramanauskas v Lithuania* on the ground that the applicant had enjoyed a full opportunity to challenge the authenticity and accuracy of the evidence against her).

5.131 The Court has also had to consider cases where applicants have alleged that they were unable to prove the involvement of *agents provocateurs* as the relevant evidence had been withheld from them. In *Edwards and Lewis v United Kingdom,* evidence concerning the involvement of undercover police officers and informants had been withheld from the defence on the grounds of public interest immunity, and the defence therefore had been unable to argue the case on entrapment in full. In finding a violation of Article 6, the Court held that the procedure employed to determine the issues of disclosure of evidence and entrapment failed to comply with 'the requirements to provide adversarial proceedings and equality of arms' or to incorporate adequate safeguards to protect the interests of the accused[1].

1　*Edwards and Lewis v United Kingdom* (22 July 2003), paras 57–59 – the case was initially referred to the Grand Chamber but the Government subsequently declared that it was happy for the GC to endorse the findings of the judgment of the Chamber: *Edwards and Lewis v United Kingdom* [GC] 2004-X, para 47.

Domestic court decisions on incitement to criminal activity

5.132 It was noted in the leading English case of *R v Looseley* that it is clear from the judgments of the European Court of Human Rights, including in particular *Teixeira de Castro v Portugal,*[1] that the right guaranteed by Article 6(1) is not confined to a fair determination of the question of guilt. It is also a right not to be tried at all in circumstances in which this would amount to an abuse of state power, such as where the offence has been committed as a result of entrapment by agents of the state.[2] The same approach was followed in a recent Scottish case on entrapment, *Jones v HM Advocate*[3]. Although the United Kingdom technique for authorising and supervising police undercover operations is different from the judicial supervision in continental countries, to which the European Court referred in *Teixeira de Castro,* the purpose is the same, namely to remove the risk of extortion, corruption or abuse of power by policemen operating without proper supervision.

1　*Teixeira de Castro v Portugal* 1998-IV.

2   *R v Looseley* [2001] 1 WLR 2060. See also *Nottingham City Council v Amin* [2000] 1 WLR 1071.

3   *Jones v HM Advocate* 2010 JC 255.

The right to remain silent and the right not to incriminate oneself

5.133 While the text of Article 6 does not specifically mention either the right to remain silent when being questioned by the police or the privilege against self-incrimination, these are 'generally recognised international standards which lie at the heart of the notion of a fair procedure under Article 6'[1] and which are based upon the assumption that the prosecution proves its case without recourse to methods involving coercion or oppression[2]. In particular, the right not to incriminate oneself is closely linked with the presumption of innocence under paragraph (2)[3] and concerns respect for 'the will of an accused person to remain silent' rather than use of compulsory powers to obtain real evidence, that is 'material ... which ha[s] an existence independent of the will of the suspect, such as inter alia documents acquired pursuant to a warrant, breath, blood and urine samples and bodily tissue for the purposes of DNA testing'[4]. Interferences with the right to remain silent or the right against self-incrimination are likely to take the form of either imposition of penalties for failing to answer questions, or the application of evidentiary rules allowing adverse inferences to be drawn from silence or the direct or indirect use of statements obtained under compulsion. No Article 6 issue arises, however, if the coercion against a person 'charged' with an offence within the meaning of Article 6[5] falls short of a direct attempt to make an individual incriminate himself[6].

1   *John Murray v United Kingdom* 1996-I, at para 45. Cf International Covenant on Civil and Political Rights, Art 14(3)(g). See further Berger 'Self-incrimination and the European Court of Human Rights: Procedural Issues in the Enforcement of the Right to Silence' [2007] EHRLR 514.

2   *Saunders v United Kingdom*, 1996-IV, para 68.

3   Cf *Saunders v United Kingdom* 1996-IV, para 68 (right against self-incrimination is closely linked to the presumption of innocence). Thus the use in evidence of documents delivered up under compulsion, but not containing statements made under compulsion, does not contravene Art 6: *Attorney General's Reference (No 7 of 2000)* [2001] 1 WLR 1879. For an overview of the various reasons provided to justify the principle see Trechsel *Human Rights in Criminal Proceedings* (2005), pp 347–349.

4   *Saunders v United Kingdom* 1996-IV, at para 69. See too *Tirado Ortiz and Lozano Martin v Spain* (dec) 1999-V. The right not to incriminate oneself applies also to witnesses who are regarded as co-suspects: cf *Lucà v Italy* 2001-II, 33.

5   See para **5.42** above.

6   *Serves v France* 1997-VI, paras 46–47 (sanction imposed for refusal to take an oath was designed to ensure that statements were truthful rather than to force a witness to give evidence which was potentially self-incriminating).

5.134 It will always be a question on the facts whether statements have been given voluntarily or under compulsion. In *Kamasinski v Austria*, the appellant complained that questions put to him by the presiding judge had resulted in the shifting of the burden of proof from the prosecution onto the defence through exercise of the power to put questions. However, the European Court of Human Rights considered that the law provided merely an option which an accused could decide to make use of in his own interest and did not impose an obligation to answer any question put, and thus there was no suggestion that the presumption of innocence had been undermined[1]. The matter is also illustrated by the Court's determination in *Staines v United Kingdom* that the application was inadmissible under Article 6(1) and (2). A chartered accountant had been convicted of illegal share-dealing practices after advising her father to buy shares in a company the subject of a take-over bid. The advice had been given after social contact with another accountant who had been considered to be a 'connected person' in possession of unpublished and price-sensitive information. She had been interviewed several years after the share purchase by Department of Trade and Industry inspectors and had confirmed that no improper information had been disclosed to her. Thereafter, she had been summoned to a formal interview during which she was under a legal duty to answer questions on oath, but she had adhered to her earlier voluntary statements. In time, she was prosecuted and found guilty. The Court confirmed that the right not to incriminate oneself protected an individual from being convicted on the ground of statements or evidence given by means of oppression or coercion and against the will of the accused. Here, however, the applicant had already given unsolicited and voluntary statements, had been consistent at all times in the account she had given, and far from challenging the prosecution's reliance on the statements given on oath to the inspectors had attempted to found upon them to establish an unwavering line of defence[2]. In contrast, in *Aleksandr Zaichenko v Russia*, the applicant had only been informed of his right to remain silent after he had already made a self-incriminating statement even although it had been incumbent on the police to inform the applicant of the privilege against self-incrimination and his right to remain silent. In this instance, the Court held that the detriment the applicant suffered had not been remedied at the trial, and found that Article 6(1) had been violated[3].

1   *Kamasinski v Austria* (1989) A 168, paras 94–95.
2   *Staines v United Kingdom* (dec) 2000-V.
3   *Aleksandr Zaichenko v Russia* (18 February 2010), paras 55–60.

Imposition of sanctions for failure to answer questions or to provide incriminating evidence

5.135 The imposition of a penalty on a person 'charged' with a criminal offence within the meaning of Article 6 for refusal to answer questions or to hand over real evidence which is incriminating may violate the protection against the right to remain silent. In *Funke v France*, customs officers had instigated proceedings against the applicant in an attempt to obtain incriminating documents which they believed existed since the authorities were unable or unwilling to obtain these documents by other means. The proceedings had resulted in a conviction and the imposition of a fine and a penalty for each additional day that the documents were not disclosed. The European Court of Human Rights considered that the guarantee against self-incrimination under paragraph (1) had been breached, and that there was thus no need to consider the issue of the presumption of innocence under paragraph (2)[1]. In the related cases of *Heaney and McGuinness v Ireland* and *Quinn v Ireland*, the Court again confirmed that the imposition of sanctions for failing to answer questions could violate Article 6. The applicants had been arrested on suspicion of serious criminal charges and required under domestic law to answer questions put to them. Their refusal had led to each being convicted and sentenced to imprisonment for six months. The Court rejected the state's argument that the domestic law in question was a proportionate response to the threat to public order posed by terrorism, considering that such concerns 'cannot justify a provision which extinguishes the very essence of the applicants' rights to silence and against self-incrimination'[2]. Likewise in *Shannon v United Kingdom*, the Court noted that 'the security context – the special problems of investigating crime in Northern Ireland' could not 'any more than in *Heaney and McGuiness*' justify the infringement of the applicant's right to silence. In this case the applicant had not complied with the requirement that he attend an interview and give information to financial investigators exercising their powers under the Proceeds of Crime (Northern Ireland) Order 1996. His subsequent prosecution and conviction for failing to attend was held by the Court to be incompatible with the applicant's right not to incriminate himself[3]. Similarly, in *JB v Switzerland,* the Court held that the obligation to submit documents to the tax authorities in the context of tax proceedings had violated Article 6. The applicant had admitted that he had made investments without properly declaring the income, but had refused to submit documents requested by the tax authorities which had imposed substantial disciplinary fines. For the Court, although the proceedings were not expressly classified as constituting either supplementary tax proceedings or tax evasion proceedings, they had served both purposes since throughout the proceedings the tax authorities could have imposed a fine for the criminal offence of tax evasion. This offence involved the determination of a 'criminal charge' for the purposes of Article 6, and thus the authorities had been attempting to compel the applicant to submit documents which could have contained information constituting tax evasion[4].

1   *Funke v France* (1993) A 256-A, para 44. For domestic consideration, see para **5.141** below
2   *Heaney and McGuinness v Ireland* 2000-XII, paras 53–59 at para 58, and *Quinn v Ireland* (21 December 2000), paras 53–60, at para 59 (violation of paras (1) and (2) on account of the close relationship with the presumption of innocence).
3   *Shannon v United Kingdom* (4 October 2005), paras 38–41.
4   *JB v Switzerland* 2001-III, paras 63–71.

5.136 Cases involving powers under UK statutes to require a suspect to provide answers to questions put to him in complex fraud cases have also been considered by the European Court of Human Rights. In *Saunders v United Kingdom*, inspectors had been appointed by the Secretary of State for Trade and Industry to investigate the acquisition of a company by another of which the applicant had been chief executive following allegations of unlawful share support. The inspectors could require individuals to answer the questions put to them, and failure to do so could lead to a determination of contempt of court and the imposition of a fine or a prison sentence of up to two years[1]. The respondent government had argued that only statements made which were self-incriminating could fall within the privilege against self-incrimination, a submission rejected by the Court on the ground that any testimony obtained under compulsion had the potential of being subsequently deployed in criminal proceedings by the prosecution, even if only to seek to undermine the credibility of an accused. Such a situation could be especially harmful where credibility is assessed by a jury. Indeed, in the instant case, extensive use had been made of the transcript by the prosecution. This suggested that the transcripts of answers had been of assistance in establishing the applicant's dishonesty. Without deeming it necessary to determine whether the right not to incriminate oneself is absolute or subject to justification in certain circumstances, the Court in ruling that there had been an infringement of the right not to incriminate oneself also confirmed that the general requirements of fairness contained in Article 6 are applicable in all types of criminal offences 'without distinction from the most simple to the most complex'[2].

1   In terms of the Companies Act 1985, ss 434 and 436.
2   *Saunders v United Kingdom* 1996-IV, paras 69–76 at para 74. See too the related case of *IJL and Others v United Kingdom* 2000-IX, paras 82–83. See further Riley '*Saunders* and the Power to Obtain Information in Community and UK Competition Law' (2000) 25 ELRev 575. Other recent cases include *DC, HS and AD v United Kingdom* (dec) (14 September 1999); and *WGS and MLS v United Kingdom* (23 November 1999). See also *Weh v Austria* (8 April 2004), paras 39–57 (penalty imposed on account of failure by registered owner of vehicle to disclose the name of the person who had driven his car: no violation, the case not concerning criminal proceedings conducted against him).

5.137 The judgment in the case of *O'Halloran and Francis v United Kingdom* seems, however, to mark something of a shift in the Court's jurisprudence. Both applications concerned the requirement under s 172 of the Road Traffic Act 1988 to provide details of who was driving a vehicle. The applicants were the registered keepers of vehicles caught on speed cameras exceeding (in both instances, considerably) the speed limit. One applicant had sought to exclude the answer given in response to the notice of intention to prosecute; the other had refused to reveal who was driving the vehicle at the material time. The argument that the application of any form of direct compulsion to require an accused person to make incriminatory statements against his will violated the privilege against self incrimination was not accepted: instead, the Court considered it was necessary to 'focus on the nature and degree of compulsion used to obtain evidence, the existence of any relevant safeguards in the procedure, and the use to which any material so obtained was put'. In finding that the right to remain silent and the privilege against self incrimination had not been violated, the Court sought to distinguish the second applicant's case from earlier jurisprudence. While the compulsion was of a direct nature and both the compulsion and the underlying offence were criminal in nature, the obligation to disclose information flowed from the fact that all those 'who own or drive motor cars know that by doing so they subject themselves to a regulatory regime' and therefore must accept certain responsibilities and obligations. Further, the Court was influenced by the fact that the applicant had only had to provide information 'as to the identity of the driver', which was 'markedly more restricted than in previous cases', and by Lord Bingham's characterisation in domestic proceedings of the penalty for declining to answer as 'moderate and non-custodial'. Finally, the Court referred to the existence of relevant safeguards, namely the defence available to the keeper of the vehicle if he could show that 'he did not know and could not with reasonable diligence have known who the driver of the vehicle was'. The conclusion was that there had been no violation of Article 6. The offence was 'not one of strict liability', and 'the risk of unreliable admissions' was therefore 'negligent'[1]. This judgment is not without its critics. In a dissenting judgment, Judge Pavlovschi agreed with the applicants that their right to silence had been violated and noted that it was 'perfectly obvious that for an individual to state that he was the driver of a car which was speeding illegally' was 'tantamount to a confession that he was in breach of the speed regulations'. This dissenting opinion also considered that the degree of compulsion could only be seen to be being 'disproportionately high' in view of the fact that the punishment laid down for a failure to disclose the information was equal to the punishment laid down for the criminal offence'. The judgment seems to mark the introduction of 'public interest considerations', previously rejected in the Court's jurisprudence, as relevant factors in the determination of whether the privilege against self incrimination has been violated[2].

1   *O'Halloran and Francis v United Kingdom* [GC] 2007-VIII, paras 53–63 at 53 and 57, relying on the comments of Lord Bingham in *Brown v Stott*, 2001 SC (PC) 43. See also *Lückhof and Spanner v Austria* (10 January 2008), paras 47–59; but cf *Krumpholz v Austria* (18 March 2010), paras 30–43 (conviction for speeding only on account of refusal to disclose the identity of the person who had been driving: violation of Art 6).

2   *O'Halloran and Francis v United Kingdom* [GC] 2007-VIII. See also Judge Myjer, dissenting, para 6–7. Both dissenting judges had been prosecutors before their appointment to the Court. On the implications of this judgment see Ashworth 'Human Rights: Article 6(1) – Privilege Against Self Incrimination' [2007] Crim LR 897 at 900: 'Rather than recognising a limited exception to the privilege against self-incrimination, based on an emerging European consensus and on an assessment that the exception would not be too damaging to the privilege overall, it has followed the *Jalloh* judgment in suggesting that a wider range of factors should be considered in deciding whether a particular instance of self incrimination constitutes a violation of the privilege. ... the fear is that, having stepped away from (and indeed ignored) key points from its previous judgment in *Saunders*, it will come to regard this and other Art 6 rights as capable of being traded off against the public interest'.

Use of statements obtained through deception, etc

5.138 The Court has also had to consider other stratagems employed to obtain evidence. In *Allan v United Kingdom*, the applicant, who was suspected of involvement in a murder committed during a robbery, complained that the placing of a police informant in his cell for the specific purpose of eliciting from him information implicating him in the offences of which he was suspected violated Article 6. In finding that there had been a violation of fair hearing guarantees, the Court reiterated that the right to silence 'serves in principle to protect the freedom of a suspected person to choose whether to speak or to remain silent when questioned by the police'. Thus 'such freedom of choice is effectively undermined in a case in which, the suspect having elected to remain silent during questioning, the authorities use subterfuge to elicit, from the suspect, confessions or other statements of an incriminatory nature, which they were unable to obtain during such questioning and where the confessions or statements thereby obtained are adduced in evidence at trial'. In this case the Court was influenced in particular by the fact that the informant had been coached by the police and instructed to 'push for what you can', and therefore the informant could only be seen as an agent of the state who was *de facto* charged with interrogating the applicant[1].

1   *Allan v United Kingdom* 2002-IX, paras 45–53, at paras 50 and 52.

Domestic court decisions on the use of statements obtained under compulsion

5.139 The implications of the judgment in *Saunders v United Kingdom*[1] were considered by the domestic courts in *Brown v Stott*, which concerned a requirement made of a motorist to give information to the police as to the identity of the driver of her car at a time when the driver was alleged to have committed an offence, non-compliance with the requirement being itself a criminal offence. The accused was suspected of driving her car while under the influence of drink, and was required to give the police information as to who had been driving the car at the material time. She replied that she was. She then gave a positive breath test, and was charged. The High Court of Justiciary held that for evidence to be led of her reply would contravene the protection against self-incrimination provided by Article 6(1). The court noted that it was accepted that to compel the accused to go into the witness box and admit that she had been driving the car at the material time would infringe Article 6(1). To compel her to make the admission prior to the trial, and allow the admission to be led in evidence, would allow that protection to be circumvented. The Privy Council however took a different view and reversed the decision of the High Court of Justiciary, holding that the rule against self-incrimination was not absolute and that the public interest justified the requirement in question[2]. The European Court subsequently agreed with the Privy Council[3].

1   *Saunders v United Kingdom* 1996-IV, discussed at para **5.136** above.

2   *Brown v Stott* 2001 SC (PC) 43.

3   *O'Halloran and Francis v United Kingdom* [GC] 2007-VIII, discussed at paras **5.137** and **5.145** above.

5.140 The wider implications of *Brown v Stott* were made clear by the House of Lords in the subsequent case of *R v Forbes*:

'Reference was made in argument to the right to a fair trial guaranteed by article 6 of the ECHR. That is an absolute right. But, as the Judicial Committee of the Privy

Council has very recently held in *Stott v Brown*, the subsidiary rights comprised within that article are not absolute, and it is always necessary to consider all the facts and the whole history of the proceedings in a particular case to judge whether a defendant's right to a fair trial has been infringed or not[1].'

---

1   *R v Forbes* [2001] 1 AC 473, para 24. See also *Attorney General's Reference (No 7 of 2000)* [2001] 1 WLR 1879 (use in criminal proceedings of documentary evidence delivered to official receiver under compulsion); and *R v Dimsey* [2002] 1 AC 509 (prosecution for failure to declare benefits to tax authorities and to respond truthfully to questioning).

5.141 The question whether a person may refuse to answer questions put to him under statutory powers by bodies other than the police, on the ground that he may incriminate himself, has also been considered in a number of cases. In *R v Hertfordshire County Council, ex parte Green Environmental Industries Ltd*, the question was whether a person who had unlawfully deposited waste without a licence could refuse to provide information about his activities which had been requested pursuant to a statutory power by a local waste regulation authority on the ground that his answers might incriminate him or lead to the discovery of evidence which might be used against him in a criminal prosecution. The House of Lords decided that he could not. It observed that the information was required not only with a view to possible prosecution, but also for reasons of public health, including the risks to the health of people who had handled the waste in question. It was also noted that, under English law, the judge at any subsequent trial could exclude evidence of the answers given to the questions on the ground that having regard to the circumstances in which the evidence was obtained, its admission would have an unduly adverse effect on the fairness of the trial[1].

---

1   *R v Hertfordshire County Council, ex parte Green Environmental Industries Ltd* [2000] 2 AC 412. The speech of Lord Hoffmann contains a discussion of the Funke judgment: see para **5.134** above. The decision has been followed in other contexts: see eg *R (Bright) v Central Criminal Court* [2001] 1 WLR 662 (production order sought by police against journalists: the opinion of Judge LJ contains a powerful account of the protection of civil liberties under the common law); *Liquidator of Tay Square Properties Ltd, Noter* 2005 SLT 468 (examination on oath under insolvency legislation); and *Child Maintenance Enforcement Commission v Forrest* [2010] 2 FLR 1805 (request for information under child support legislation).

5.142 In domestic cases concerned with the admission of evidence obtained under compulsion, it has been established (applying long-established principles of English common law, and an early UK statute applying the same principles to Scotland) that evidence obtained by torture cannot lawfully be admitted against a party to proceedings in a United Kingdom court[1]. On the other hand, the recovery of real evidence such as breath or urine specimens under statutory powers does not interfere with the right not to incriminate oneself and does not prejudice the right to a fair trial[2]. The use in criminal proceedings of incriminating statements made under compulsion in civil proceedings may also be incompatible with Article 6. In a case where the question concerned the admissibility in criminal proceedings of financial information which the accused had been required to disclose for the purposes of earlier matrimonial proceedings, and which suggested that he had been involved in tax evasion, the Court of Appeal stated:

> 'The essential principle to be derived from their Lordships' decision [in *Brown v Stott*] is that a restriction of an accused person's right not to incriminate himself will not infringe his right to a fair trial provided that the compulsion under which the information is obtained is of a moderate nature and the use of the evidence obtained by it represents a proportionate response to a pressing social need. ... It is therefore necessary to consider the nature of the compulsion applied, the nature of the evidence obtained by means of it and the social need which the admission of such evidence at a subsequent trial is intended to meet.
>
> A wilful refusal to comply with an order for disclosure will amount to a contempt of court which may attract the not insignificant sanction of imprisonment. The nature of the compulsion that may be applied to enforce compliance with the obligation to disclose information that is of an incriminating nature is therefore severe. The social purpose for which the Crown seeks to adduce the evidence in criminal proceedings is the suppression of tax evasion. No doubt the protection of the public revenue is an important social objective, but the question is whether the admission of evidence obtained from the accused under threat of imprisonment is a reasonable and proportionate response to that social need. In our view it is not. This is an unusual case in as much as the Crown accepts that without the admissions made by K it has insufficient evidence to maintain a case against him. In many cases information obtained by way of disclosure in ancillary relief proceedings will provide leads that enable the Crown to obtain evidence from other sources that is sufficient to support a prosecution and in such cases there will be no need to rely on evidence obtained from the accused himself. That has not been possible in this case, but even so, we do not think that the need to punish and deter tax evasion is sufficient to justify such an infringement of the right of the accused not to incriminate himself.'[3]

---

1   *A v Secretary of State for the Home Department (No 2)* [2006] 2 AC 221.

2   *Brown v Gallacher* 2002 SCCR 943.

3   *R v K* [2010] QB 343 at paras 41–42 per Moore-Bick LJ.

Use of statements in civil proceedings

5.143 The use of statements obtained under compulsory powers may also give rise to an issue of fairness under Article 6 in civil proceedings[1]. This matter was considered by the Court of Appeal in a case concerned with disqualification proceedings, where it was observed:

> 'The issue of fair trial is one that must be considered in the round, having regard to all relevant factors. The relevant factors include (but are not limited to): (i) that disqualification proceedings are not criminal proceedings, and are primarily for the protection of the public, but do nevertheless often involve serious allegations and almost always carry a degree of stigma for anyone who is disqualified; (ii) that there are degrees of coercion involved in different investigative procedures available in corporate insolvency, and these differences may be reflected in different degrees of prejudice involved in the admission, in disqualification proceedings, of statements obtained by such procedures; and (iii) that in this field as in most other fields, it is

generally best for issues of fairness or unfairness to be decided by the trial judge, either at a pre-trial review or in the course of the trial.'[2]

1   Cf *DC, HS and AD v United Kingdom* (dec) (14 September 1999) and *WGS and MSLS v United Kingdom* (dec) (23 November 1999).

2   *Official Receiver v Stern* [2000] 1 WLR 2230 at 2258 per Henry LJ. See also *R (Fleurose) v Securities and Futures Authority Ltd* [2002] IRLR 297. The recovery of documents under compulsion does not violate Art 6: see eg *Office of Fair Trading v X* [2004] ICR 105.

The drawing of adverse inferences from silence

5.144 The right to remain silent and the privilege against self-incrimination may be compromised by the drawing of adverse inferences from the refusal to answer questions. In *John Murray v United Kingdom*, the question facing the European Court of Human Rights was whether such inferences were compatible with Article 6. While the right to remain silent was a generally recognised international standard, it was not clear whether it was an absolute right in the sense that its exercise could not be taken into account in the assessment of evidence at trial stage. The Court considered that it was 'self-evident that it is incompatible with the immunities under consideration to base a conviction solely or mainly on the accused's silence or on a refusal to answer questions or to give evidence himself'. However, it was 'equally obvious that these immunities cannot and should not prevent that the accused's silence, in situations which clearly call for an explanation from him, be taken into account in assessing the persuasiveness of the evidence adduced by the prosecution'. In deciding whether Article 6 was indeed infringed by the drawing of adverse inferences from an accused's silence, it was in any case necessary to consider 'all the circumstances of the case, having particular regard to the situations where inferences may be drawn, the weight attached to them by the national courts in their assessment of the evidence and the degree of compulsion inherent in the situation'. Here, the applicant was able to remain silent and he remained a non-compellable witness, his refusal to answer did not constitute a criminal offence or contempt of court, and a conviction could not be based solely upon exercise of the right to silence. While denial of access to a solicitor had implications for the rights of the defence, there had been no indication that the applicant had not appreciated the significance of the warning that inferences could be drawn from his silence prior to access to his solicitor, and thus there had been no unfairness or infringement of the presumption of innocence[1].

1   *John Murray v United Kingdom* 1996-I, paras 44–58 at para 47. See also *Averill v United Kingdom* 2000-VI; *Quinn v Ireland* (21 December 2000), para 40; *Heaney and McGuinness v Ireland* 2000-XII, para 40; cf *Serves v France* (dec) 2000-V (reports drafted for military administrative disciplinary charges and subsequently used in criminal proceedings were not the only evidence used in the trial; nor had the applicant alleged he had been unable to cross-examine the officer who had compiled the reports: and thus the application was inadmissible).

5.145 The particular facts of each case must therefore be considered with some care. In *Condron and Others v United Kingdom*, the Court concluded that there had been a denial of a fair hearing. The applicants had been suspected of drug-trafficking following a police surveillance team having observed them passing certain items to other individuals. During an interview with police, the applicants had refused to answer questions on the advice of their solicitor who considered that they were not fit to do so as they were suffering from drug withdrawal symptoms. This explanation was put to the jury which was also given an option of whether to draw an adverse inference from the applicants' failure to explain what had been taking place. Although the appeal court had criticised the trial judge's direction to the jury, it had nevertheless considered the convictions to be safe. The Court reiterated that particular caution is required before an accused's silence can be invoked against him since basing a conviction wholly or mainly upon an accused person's refusal to answer a question would be incompatible with the Convention. Here, the applicants had advanced an explanation for their refusal to answer questions. The charge to the jury had left the jury free to draw an adverse inference were it to have been satisfied that the explanation was plausible rather than instructing it to refuse to draw any such inference in such a situation. Since juries did not give reasons for their decisions, it was impossible to ascertain what weight had been given to the refusal to answer questions, and accordingly there had been a violation of paragraph (1)[1].

A similar violation was found in *Telfner v Austria*. Here, the applicant had been convicted of a driving offence in circumstances where it was open to the accused to have given a contrary version of events without having to inculpate another person. The victim of the accident had identified the registration number but not the driver of a car registered in the name of the applicant's mother but regularly driven by other members of the family. Police officers had observed the applicant driving the car in the past and thus considered him as the main driver of the car and as the suspect; additionally, suspicion had fallen upon him on account of his absence from home when police had called to make inquiries. The applicant had pled not guilty to the charge of causing injury by negligent driving, stating only that he had not been the driver but he had declined to give any further evidence. Neither his mother nor his sister had testified, and the victim had again confirmed his inability to identify the driver. For the Court, the case was not one which involved the operation of legal presumptions. It again clarified that it is acceptable in terms of Article 6(2) to draw inferences from silence, but only 'where the courts freely evaluate the evidence before them, provided that the evidence adduced is such that the only common-sense inference to be drawn from the accused's silence is that he had no answer to the case against him'. Here, and unlike the situation in the *John Murray* case, the trial court had relied upon two uncorroborated elements of evidence which could not be taken to have constituted 'a case against the applicant which would have called for an explanation from his part'. The conclusion was thus that 'in requiring the applicant to provide an explanation although they had not been able to establish a convincing prima facie case against him, the courts shifted the burden of proof from the prosecution to the defence'. In consequence, there has been a violation of the presumption of innocence[2].

In contrast, in *O'Halloran and Francis v United Kingdom*, the Court determined that there had been no violation of Article 6. In this case the vehicle of the first applicant had been caught on a speed camera exceeding the speed limit. He had been informed that he was required to state who was driving the vehicle at the material time and that failure to do so constituted a criminal offence. Unlike the second applicant, he had confirmed that he had been driving the vehicle at the relevant time, but subsequently and unsuccessfully had sought to have this evidence excluded on the basis that his confirmation was induced by the threat of criminal sanctions resulting in failure to respect the privilege against self incrimination. The Court held that as the identity of the driver was only one element of the offence of speeding, and as there was no question of a conviction arising in the underlying proceedings in respect solely of the information obtained as a result of the provisions in question, the applicant's 'right to remain silent and their privilege against self incrimination had not been destroyed'[3].

1   *Condron and Others v United Kingdom* 2000-V, paras 63–68. See further Jennings, Ashworth and Emmerson 'Silence and Safety: The Impact of Human Rights Law' [2000] Crim LR 879. The Court came to the same conclusion in *Beckles v United Kingdom* (8 October 2002), paras 57–66, (the manner in which the trial judge in his direction left the jury with the option of drawing an adverse inference from his silence during police questioning violated the applicant's right to a fair hearing).

2   *Telfner v Austria* (20 March 2001), paras 15–20 at paras 17 and 18. The Court additionally considered that speculation that the applicant had been under the influence of alcohol at the time of the offence, while not directly relevant to establishing guilt, contributed 'to the impression that the courts had a preconceived view of the applicant's guilt' (at para 19). For discussion of the presumption of innocence and the burden of proof, see paras **5.109–5.110** below.

3   *O'Halloran and Francis v United Kingdom* [GC] 2007-VIII, paras 60–63. See further para **5.137**, above; see also the earlier cases of *Weh v Austria* (8 April 2004) and *Rieg v Austria* (24 March 2005).

The right to a reasoned judgment

5.146 In general, Article 6 obliges courts to give reasons for their judgment[1]. The giving of reasons is generally implicit in the concept of a fair trial: reasons inform the parties of the basis of the decision and enable them to exercise any right of appeal available to them, and also enable the public to understand the rationale for judicial decisions[2]. The giving of reasons can thus be regarded as being implied in certain of the express requirements of Article 6, such as 'a fair and public hearing', the public pronouncement of judgment, and the provision of adequate facilities for the preparation of the defence in criminal cases. At the same time, states enjoy considerable freedom in the choice of the appropriate means to ensure that their judicial systems comply with the requirements of Article 6[3]. Thus the extent of the duty to give reasons varies according to the nature of the issue in question:

'It is moreover necessary to take into account, inter alia, the diversity of the submissions that a litigant may bring before the courts and the differences existing in the Contracting States with regard to statutory provisions, customary rules, legal opinion and the presentation and drafting of judgments. That is why the question whether a court has failed to fulfil the obligation to state reasons, deriving from Article 6 of the Convention, can only be determined in the light of the circumstances of the case.'[4]

The right to a reasoned judgment imposes on domestic courts a duty, in principle, to examine and address the arguments and evidence put forward by the parties to a case[5]. A reasoned judgment does not have to deal with every matter raised, provided it indicates the grounds on which the decision is based with sufficient clarity[6]. The reasons given must be valid in law[7], and must not appear arbitrary or unreasonable[8]. The reasons must be available in time to enable any right of appeal to be exercised[9].

1   *Hadjianastassiou v Greece* (1992) A 252-A, para 33. See also *Gorou v Greece (no 2)* [GC] 2009-..., paras 37–42 (extension of duty to a prosecutor in rejecting the request of a civil party to criminal proceedings: summary response of the prosecutor had given sufficient reasons for his discretionary decision).

2   Eg *Baucher v France* (24 July 2007) paras 48–52 (no reasons had been given for the criminal court's judgment before the expiry of the time-limit for the appeal as a result, the applicant's right to due process had been infringed). On the various reasons underpinning the right to a reasoned judgment, see Trechsel *Human Rights in Criminal Proceedings* (2005), pp 102–106.

3   *Hadjianastassiou v Greece* (1992) A 252, para 33.

4   *Ruiz Torija v Spain* (1994) A 303-A, para 29; *Hiro Balani v Spain* (1994) A 303-B.

5   *Quadrelli v Italy* (11 January 2000), para 34; *Ruiz Torija v Spain* (1994) A 303-A, para 19.

6   *Van der Hurk v Netherlands* (1994) A 288, para 61; *Georgiadis v Greece* 1997-III, para 43; *Helle v Finland* 1997-VIII, para 55; *Higgins and Others v France* 1998-I, para 42.

7   *De Moor v Belgium* (1994) A 292-A, paras 54–55.

8   *Khamidov v Russia* 2007-XII, paras 170–175 (the unreasonableness of the domestic courts' conclusion was so striking and palpable that it could be regarded as grossly arbitrary and set an extreme and unattainable standard of proof for the applicant so that his compensation claim could not, in any event, have had even the slightest prospect of success, depriving the applicant of a fair hearing: violation).

9   *Hadjianastassiou v Greece* (1992) A 252-A, paras 35–37; cf *Zoon v Netherlands* 2000-XII, paras 36–51. See too *Saric v Denmark* (dec) (2 February 1999) (failure of juries to give reasons is not incompatible with Art 6). Note also *CG v United Kingdom* (dec) (19 December 2001) (national appellate courts are well-placed to determine whether the handlung of trials by jury by trial judges were unfair); and *Snooks and Drowse v United Kingdom* (dec) (8 October 2002) (convictions for drug-related offences in the Jersey courts which consisted of a judge of law (the deputy bailiff) and two judges of fact (the jurats): in the first application, the deputy bailiff gave his summing-up to the jurats in public, while it was done in private in the latter case; in both instances, the deputy bailiff retired with the jurats when the latter were to reach their verdicts, for which no reasons were given: inadmissible, the issues of unfairness having been examined on appeal).

Determinations by juries

5.147 The principle that reasons should be given for a judgment may also apply in certain instances to jury trials. Until recently, the case law suggested that such a duty did not extend to determinations made by juries. For example, the Commission ruled inadmissible a complaint about the failure of the Belgian assize court to issue reasons, observing that the requirement that reasons be given must accommodate the particular nature of the procedure in jury trials where the jury is not required, or is not able, to give reasons for their verdict. In this instance, though, the Commission also observed that the jury's decision was not susceptible to appeal on the facts[1]. The Court has also held that the Convention does not require jurors to give reasons for their decision and that Article 6 does not preclude an accused from being tried by a lay jury even where reasons are not given for the verdict[2]. However, the suggestion that a person convicted of an offence by a jury must be able to understand the verdict was not entirely absent in the case law. In the case of *R v Belgium*, for example, the Commission considered that although the jury had provided no reasons for its verdict, the questions put to the jury by the president of the trial court had formed a framework for the decision and thus had compensated sufficiently for the brevity of the jury's response[3].

The matter has been revisited recently by the Grand Chamber in *Taxquet v Belgium*. This judgment indicates that the accused must be able to understand the verdict that has been given since this constitutes a vital safeguard against arbitrariness. Here, the Court considered that in the context of a factually and legally complex case, neither the indictment nor the questions put to the jury by the president of the trial court had contained sufficient information as to the jury's findings concerning the applicant's involvement in the commission of the offences of which he was accused. Moreover, the Belgian system made no provision for an ordinary appeal against the judgment. In consequence, the applicant had not been afforded sufficient safeguards enabling him to understand why he was found guilty, and accordingly the proceedings had not been fair[4]. However, it is clear that the *Taxquet* judgment is confined to situations in which in which there is no satisfactory procedural 'framework' to provide sufficient safeguards for an individual to understand why he was found guilty by a jury. In its admissibility decision in *Judge v United Kingdom*, the Court considered that arrangements in Scots law more than adequately met Convention expectations:

> 'in Scotland the jury's verdict is not returned in isolation but is given in a framework which includes addresses by the prosecution and the defence as well as the presiding judge's charge to the jury. Scots law also ensures there is a clear demarcation between the respective roles of the judge and jury: it is the duty of the judge to ensure the proceedings are conducted fairly and to explain the law as it applies in the case to the jury; it is the duty of the jury to accept those directions and to determine all questions of fact. In addition, although the jury are "masters of the facts" it is the duty of the presiding judge to accede to a submission of no case to answer if he or she is satisfied that the evidence led by the prosecution is insufficient in law to justify the accused's conviction.'

In this case, the Court also noted that the manner in which an indictment had been framed (by specifying the factual basis for each count of the alleged conduct) meant that it had been clear to the applicant that the jury had accepted the evidence of the complainers. Further, and again in contrast to the situation in *Taxquet*, rights of appeal in Scotland were deemed sufficient to remedy any improper jury verdict[5].

1   15957/90, *R v Belgium* (1992) DR 72, 195. In a case concerned with the Contempt of Court
     Act 1981, s 8, the Commission accepted the necessity, in general, of preventing disclosure of
     the deliberations of a jury in a criminal trial: 24770/94, *Associated Newspapers Ltd v United
     Kingdom* (30 November 1994).

2   *Saric v Denmark* (dec) (2 February 1999).

3   15957/90, *R v Belgium* (1992) DR 72, 195.

4   *Taxquet v Belgium* [GC] 2010-..., paras 83–100.

5   *Judge v United Kingdom* (dec) (8 February 2011).

Domestic court decisions on the duty to give reasons

5.148 The duty under Article 6 to give reasons has been discussed in several cases before United Kingdom courts[1]. Several Scottish cases have concerned the implications of this aspect of Article 6 for civil jury trials. The contention that the Human Rights Act 1998 precluded the allowance of a jury trial was rejected[2]. The contention that the Human Rights Act 1998 required the court to introduce a new test for the allowance of a new trial on the ground that the damages were excessive – intervening when the court considered the damages to be in excess of what a judge would have awarded, rather than (as under existing law) when the damages were in excess of what any reasonable jury could award – was also rejected[3]. In a further case, it was argued that, in the particular circumstances of the case, the inability of the jury to give reasons for any award for loss of earnings would prevent the defenders from exercising a right of appeal. The argument was rejected, the court holding that the approach taken to the determination of a motion for a new trial, when the amount of damages was called into question, did not require detailed reasons to be given by a jury before the right to such a new trial could be exercised[4]. The argument that criminal jury trials are incompatible with the requirement that reasons be provided for a verdict has also been considered, and rejected, in a number of cases[5].

In an English case where a conviction was quashed as a result of a failure by the Crown to disclose confidential material, it was held that there was no duty to give detailed reasons, by reference to the confidential material, for the court's decision[6].

1   See eg *Stefan v General Medical Council* [1999] 1 WLR 1293; *Flannery v Halifax Estate
     Agencies Ltd* [2001] 1 WLR 377; *English v Emery Reimbold & Strick Ltd* [2002] 1 WLR 2409.

2   See eg *Gunn v Newman* 2001 SC 525; *Heasman v JM Taylor & Partners* 2002 SC 326.

3   *McLeod v British Railways Board* 2001 SC 534.

4   *Sandison v Graham Begg Ltd* 2001 SC 821. The form of the issue – the questions which the
     jury is required to answer - should reflect the matters in dispute. The jury :'s verdict,
     answering the questions put to it, when taken with the terms of the presiding judge's charge
     and the evidence before the jury, should enable any motion for a new trial to be fully considered.

5   Eg *Transco v HMA (No 2)* 2005 1 JC 44; *Beggs v HM Advocate* 2010 SCCR 681. See now
     Judge v United Kingdom (dec) (8 February 2011), discussed at para **5.147** above.

6   *R v Doubtfire* [2001] 2 Cr App R 13.

ARTICLE 6: REMEDYING DEFECTS AT FIRST INSTANCE

5.149 Article 6 does not guarantee a right to an appeal[1], but where a state has made provision for a system of appeals in domestic law, the provision will be applicable in accordance with the principle that the fairness of the proceedings as a whole must be assessed[2]. Further, in terms of Article 35, an applicant is expected to exhaust domestic remedies before bringing an application to the Strasbourg Court, and this will normally involve making use of channels of appeal and review accorded by domestic law[3]. In consequence, there will be no violation of Article 6 where a reviewing court has corrected the defect, for example by providing the necessary guarantees of independence and impartiality[4]. However, if the proceedings concern the determination of a serious criminal charge, however, then the requirements of Article 6 must in general be met at first instance[5]. Issues such as effective access to appeal courts through the provision of legal aid[6] and the extent of the right to a public hearing and to participate in the hearing[7] are thus of some relevance in appeal proceedings.

1   ECHR, Prot 7, Art 2 provides for a right of appeal in criminal matters, but the UK has not ratified this protocol.

2   Eg *Belziuk v Poland* 1998-II, at para 37: 'criminal proceedings form an entity and the protection afforded by Article 6 does not cease with the decision at first instance. A State is required to ensure also before courts of appeal that persons amenable to the law shall enjoy before these courts the fundamental guarantees contained in this Article'.

3   See para **2.59** above.

4   See paras **5.75–5.80** above. For recent discussion, see *Vera Fernández-Huidobro v Spain* 2010-..., paras 118–136 (lack of impartiality during investigation remedied by new investigation by a judge from a different court).

5   *Findlay v United Kingdom* 1997-I, 263, para 79. Contrast *Öztürk v Germany* (1984) A 73, para 56; *Lutz v Germany* (1987) A 123, para 57. Even in criminal proceedings concerning serious charges, however, certain defects at first instance can be remedied by subsequent procedure on appeal: see eg *Edwards v United Kingdom* (1992) A 247-B; followed in *R v Craven* [2001] 2 Cr App R 12.

6   Cf paras **5.208–5.210** below (in relation to criminal proceedings).

7   See para **5.154** below.

Curing defects through review of administrative decision-making by a court with 'full jurisdiction'

5.150 Whether it is accepted that a defect which has arisen at first instance has been cured subsequently depends on the powers of the reviewing court. For this to have occurred, the court or tribunal hearing the case must be able to deal with all aspects of the dispute, including questions of fact and of law[1]. Stated simply, 'the concept of "full jurisdiction" involves that the reviewing court not only considers the complaint but has the ability to quash the impugned decision and to remit the case for a new decision by an impartial body' if the review court does not itself then take the decision[2]. In determining the 'sufficiency of review', regard will be had to various factors, including the subject-matter of the decision appealed against, the manner in which that decision was arrived at, and the content of the dispute including the desired and actual grounds of appeal[3]. If a professional body which itself does not comply with the requirements of a fair trial is itself subject to appeal on all relevant aspects of the case, then Article 6 will be deemed to have been satisfied[4]. However, if an appeal court is more properly a court exercising judicial review of the legality rather than of the merits, for example where review is limited to consideration of whether a public authority has acted unlawfully, unreasonably or unfairly, this is unlikely to be adequate to cure any earlier defects[5]. In *W v United Kingdom*, while the Court accepted that judicial review of wardship proceedings had allowed the domestic courts to consider the issue of access by a parent to his child who had been taken into public care, such proceedings could only examine the lawfulness of the decision rather than its merits. Since no tribunal was able to determine this latter matter, a violation of Article 6's requirement of access to a court was established[6]. Similarly, in *Kingsley v United Kingdom*, the Court considered that the scope of judicial review had been insufficient to cure its finding that the Gaming Board had not been an impartial tribunal in determining to revoke the applicant's certificate that he was a 'fit and proper person' to run a casino. It was 'generally inherent in the notion of judicial review that, if a ground of challenge is upheld, the reviewing court has power to quash the impugned decision, and that either the decision will then be taken by the review court, or the case will be remitted for a fresh decision by the same or a different body'. However, neither the High Court nor the Court of Appeal in disposing of the application for review based on allegations of illegality, irrationality (or *Wednesbury* unreasonableness) or procedural impropriety had the power to remit the case for a fresh decision by the Board or by another independent tribunal, and thus there had been a violation of Article 6[7].

---

1   *Le Compte, van Leuven and de Meyere v Belgium* (1981) A 43, para 51.

2   *Kingsley v United Kingdom* (7 November 2000) at para 58, upheld by the Grand Chamber in *Kingsley v United Kingdom* [GC] 2002-IV, paras 32–34.

3   *Tsfayo v United Kingdom* (14 November 2006), para 43 (the Housing Benefit and Council Tax Benefit Review Board, which was charged with determining the applicant's claim, was not independent and impartial; as the applicant's claim was refused as she had been found not to be a credible witness and as the High Court did not have jurisdiction to rehear the evidence or substitute its own views as to the applicant's credibility, there was never the possibility that the central issue would be determined by a tribunal that was independent of one of the parties to the dispute – violation of Art 6). Cf *Bryan v United Kingdom* (1995) A 335-A, discussed at para 5.151 below.

4   Cf *Albert and Le Compte v Belgium* (1983) A 58, para 36 (lack of public hearing not subsequently remedied by public character of Court of Cassation hearing as this court did not take cognisance of the merits of the case).

5   Eg *O v United Kingdom* (1987) A 120, para 63 (review of decision to take a child into public care). Cf *Oerlemans v Netherlands* (1991) A 219, paras 56–57 (civil courts able to carry out a full review of all administrative acts, and thus met the requirements of Art 6(1)); *Fischer v Austria* (1995) A 312, paras 29 and 33 (constitutional court had limited competence in

considering whether an administrative decision was in conformity with the Constitution and thus did not have the requisite jurisdiction; but the administrative court so qualified as it could consider all points made by the applicant without declining jurisdiction); 28530/95, *X v United Kingdom* (19 January 1998) (determination by the Secretary of State that the applicant was not a fit and proper person to be chief executive of an insurance company); 29419/95, *Stefan v United Kingdom* (9 December 1997) (proceedings before the General Medical Council to establish whether or not the applicant was mentally ill and thus unfit to practise as a doctor); 31503/96, *Wickramsinghe v United Kingdom* (9 December 1997) (disciplinary proceedings before the GMC).

6   *W v United Kingdom* (1987) A 121, paras 79–82.

7   *Kingsley v United Kingdom* [GC] 2002-IV, para 33, confirming the Chamber judgment of *Kingsley v United Kingdom* (7 November 2000), paras 51–59 (at para 53: the subject matter of the decision appealed against was 'a classic exercise of administrative discretion', and thus the Court did not agree with the applicant that the benefit of a full court hearing on both the facts and the law in initially determining the revocation of his certificate had been required: the panel had been advised by officials who were experts in the gaming industry even if the members taking the decision lacked this expertise, and the procedure had thus been an appropriate one).

Review of planning decisions

5.151 In cases involving planning law where full review of the facts may not be available, somewhat different expectations apply. Limited judicial control of administrative decision-making is a common feature found in most European legal systems[1], and while in the past it was clear that judicial review would not have been deemed to have cured any initial defects in fair hearing guarantees[2], *Bryan v United Kingdom* seemed to signal a modification of case law. The applicant had sought to challenge a planning inspector's findings of fact (rather than of law) in the High Court. A planning inspector had dismissed the applicant's appeal after an inquiry into an enforcement notice requiring the demolition of two buildings had been served by the Secretary of State. It was accepted that the inspector who was a civil servant in the department headed by the Secretary of State had not been sufficiently independent to qualify as an independent adjudicator, and in consequence the Court turned to the issue of whether the scope of judicial review was sufficient to provide the necessary control by a judicial body and thus cure the defect of lack of independence. While the appeal had been restricted to matters of law, the Court noted that the inspector's decision could also have been quashed on legal grounds which were related closely to factual matters such as the perverse or irrational drawing of inferences from facts, or a determination that findings of fact were not supported by the evidence. Further, the procedure before the inspector had provided considerable procedural safeguards, and in any case the applicant had not sought to challenge the primary facts established. For the Court, the conclusion was that questions both of fact as well as of law could have been adequately addressed by judicial review in this instance[3].

1   *Bryan v United Kingdom* (1995) A 335-A, para 47.

2   Eg *Sporrong and Lönnroth v Sweden* (1982) A 52, para 86 (admissibility of application for judicial review did not involve a full review of the issues, and thus this remedy did not satisfy Art 6(1)).

---

3   *Bryan v United Kingdom* (1995) A 335-A, paras 39–47 (the inspector's decision that there had
     been a breach of planning controls involved some fact-finding, namely that the buildings which
     Mr Bryan had erected had the appearance of residential houses rather than agricultural barns;
     however, the inspector was also called upon to exercise his discretion on a wide range of policy
     matters involving development in a green belt and conservation area, and it was these policy
     judgments, rather than the findings of primary fact, which Mr Bryan challenged in the High
     Court: consequently the extent of the High Court's review was sufficient).

5.152 The Grand Chamber confirmed this approach in the related cases of
Chapman v United Kingdom and *Jane Smith v United Kingdom*. The applicants
were gypsies by birth. They had bought land on which they intended to live in
order to maintain their traditional Roma lifestyle and culture. They complained
that enforcement measures taken against them for contravening planning
regulations violated Convention rights including respect for family life and the
protection of property; in addition, they alleged that their right to a fair trial under
Article 6 had been violated since the decisions to uphold enforcement proceedings
and to refuse planning permission had been made by inspectors employed by the
Secretary of State rather than by an independent and impartial tribunal. As in the
Bryan case, no appeal was possible against the inspector's decision to a court of
law because the challenged issues were of fact and not of law. The argument of
the applicants was essentially that *Bryan* had been decided on its particular facts,
and the review by the High Court could neither examine whether the planning
inspector had given adequate weight to the needs of the gypsy family in pursuing
their lifestyle nor the proportionality of a measure interfering with their rights.
The Court again considered that the scope of judicial review of decisions taken
after a public procedure before an inspector had 'enabled a decision to be
challenged on the basis that it was perverse, irrational, had no basis on the evidence
or had been made with reference to irrelevant factors or without regard to relevant
factors'. This had thus been sufficient to comply with Article 6[1].

---

1   *Chapman v United Kingdom* [GC] 2001-I, paras 122–125 at para 124; *Jane Smith v United
     Kingdom* [GC] (18 January 2001), paras 133–134 at para 133.

Domestic court decisions on the remedying of defects at first instance

5.153 In domestic case law, there has been considerable discussion of the extent
to which defects at first instance can be remedied by an appeal or by an application
for judicial review. In *R (Wright) v Secretary of State for Health*, Baroness
Hale of Richmond summarised the position:

'It is a well-known principle that decisions which determine civil rights and
obligations may be made by the administrative authorities, provided that there is
then access to an independent and impartial tribunal which exercises "full
jurisdiction": *Bryan v United Kingdom*[1], applied domestically in *R (Alconbury
Developments Ltd) v Secretary of State for the Environment, Transport and the
Regions*[2] and *Runa Begum v Tower Hamlets London Borough Council (First
Secretary of State intervening)*[3]. What amounts to "full jurisdiction" varies
according to the nature of the decision being made. It does not always require

access to a court or tribunal even for the determination of disputed issues of fact. Much depends upon the subject matter of the decision and the quality of the initial decision-making process. If there is a "classic exercise of administrative discretion", even though determinative of civil rights and obligations, and there are a number of safeguards to ensure that the procedure is in fact both fair and impartial, then judicial review may be adequate to supply the necessary access to a court, even if there is no jurisdiction to examine the factual merits of the case.'[4]

In relation to rights of appeal, it was observed in *Millar v Dickson* that the remedy of appeal to a higher court was an imperfect safeguard: many aspects of a decision taken at first instance, such as decisions on the credibility of witnesses or the exercise of judgement in matters which are at the discretion of the presiding judge, were incapable of being reviewed effectively on appeal[5]. It was also observed in the same case that the impartiality of the tribunal in criminal cases was not a matter which could be cured by the existence of a right of appeal[6]. As explained earlier, there has been a development in the nature of the review undertaken by courts hearing appeals from professional disciplinary bodies which do not themselves fulfil Article 6 requirements of independence and impartiality, in order to ensure that any shortfall from the perspective of Article 6 is remedied on appeal[7]. The possibility of an appeal remedying a defect at first instance has also been considered in relation to the enforcement of a foreign judgment[8]. It has been noted that Article 6 does not require a right of appeal[9].

In relation to judicial review, it has been noted that the Strasbourg jurisprudence establishes that where the initial decision as to civil rights is taken by a person or persons who cannot be described as 'an independent and impartial tribunal', the fact that the decision is subject to judicial review can satisfy Article 6. In that regard, emphasis has been placed upon the amplitude of modern judicial review[10]. In some cases, the procedure followed on judicial review has reflected the need to meet Article 6 requirements, for example by permitting oral examination of witnesses[11]. In other cases, it has been suggested that judicial review may have to encompass a proportionality review in order to meet Convention requirements. In other cases again, emphasis has been placed upon the limited extent to which the decision in question turned upon the resolution of factual issues[12].

---

1   *Bryan v United Kingdom*, See para **5.151** above.

2   *R (Alconbury Developments Ltd) v Secretary of State for the Environment, Transport and the Regions* [2003] 2 AC 295.

3   *Runa Begum v Tower Hamlets London Borough Council (First Secretary of State intervening)* [2003] 2 AC 430.

4   *R (Wright) v Secretary of State for Health* [2009] 1 AC 739 at para 23.

5   *Millar v Dickson* 2002 SC (PC) 30 at para 52 per Lord Hope of Craighead.

6   *Millar v Dickson* 2002 SC (PC) 30 at para 81 per Lord Clyde.

7   See para **5.93** above.

8   *SA Marie Brizzard et Roger International v William Grant & Sons Ltd (No 2)* 2002 SLT 1365.

9   See eg *R (Langley) v Crown Court at Preston* [2009] 1 WLR 1612 (variation of ASBO); *RB (Algeria) v Secretary of State for the Home Department* [2010] 2 AC 110 (deportation proceedings).

10 See eg *R (Q) v Secretary of State for the Home Department* [2004] QB 36 (refusal of asylum support).

11 See eg *R (Wilkinson) v Broadmoor Special Hospital Authority* [2002] 1 WLR 419 (compulsory medical treatment).

12 See eg *Runa Begum v Tower Hamlets London Borough Council* [2003] 2 AC 430 (whether accommodation offered by housing authority 'suitable'). See also *Ali v Birmingham City Council* [2010] 2 AC 39.

ARTICLE 6: PUBLIC HEARING AND JUDGMENT PRONOUNCED IN OPEN COURT

5.154 Article 6(1) makes provision for a public hearing and further requires that 'judgment shall be pronounced publicly'. These aspects of a fair trial initially appear the least complex. There is detailed provision for the exclusion of the press and the public from all or part of a trial for three specific purposes: for the protection of collective interests (that is 'in the interests of morals, public order or national security in a democratic society'); or of individual concerns (that is 'where the interests of juveniles or the protection of the private life of the parties so require'); or of the integrity of the particular proceedings (that is, 'to the extent strictly necessary in the opinion of the court in special circumstances where publicity would prejudice the interests of justice').

The requirements of public hearing and public judgment should not be read too literally as they are interpreted in accordance with the purposes of the guarantees and there is thus some flexibility in their application. Here, the Court has identified two principal goals: the protection of litigants against the secret administration of justice; and the maintenance of public confidence in the judicial system. 'By rendering the administration of justice visible, publicity contributes to the achievement of the aim of Article 6(1), namely a fair trial, the guarantee of which is one of the fundamental principles of any democratic society'[1]. A 'public hearing' principally applies to proceedings at first instance[2] rather than to the summary disposal of 'screening' decisions[3] or hearings at appeal stage where other considerations such as securing the expeditious disposal of court business come into play[4]. The lack of a public hearing at second or third instance will normally be considered acceptable where the proceedings concern questions of law or leave to appeal[5] and where such questions can be considered without oral hearing through written pleadings[6]. Indeed, a public hearing may not be required where an appellate court can additionally reconsider questions of fact[7], but where an appeal court is called upon to make a full assessment of an individual's guilt, fairness will require direct assessment of the individual's own evidence given in person[8]. Further, since the requirement of public pronouncement of judgment is to permit public scrutiny of the administration of justice, this may be achieved through other means as long as the principle of public access to judgments is secured[9], for example, through the deposit of the full text of any appellate decision in the court registry[10]. More obviously, the authorities are required to ensure that the location of the hearing is such as to ensure free access to the public[11].

1   *Axen v Germany* (1983) A 72, at para 25. As regards the special considerations which apply to proceedings involving children, see eg *V v United Kingdom* [GC] 1999-IX. For subsequent consideration, see *Martinie v France* [GC] 2006-IV, paras 39–44 (inability to request a public hearing concerning surcharge imposed by court of audit: violation); *Stojakovic v Austria* (9 November 2006), paras 45–55 (lack of oral hearing in proceedings concerning recall from post and transfer to a post with a lower grade for disciplinary reasons: violation); and *Jussila v Finland* [GC] 2006-XIV, paras 40–49 (imposition of tax surcharge without oral hearing: no violation in view of the minor sum of money and ample opportunity to comment in writing). For a critique of the importance of public justice, see Duff, Farmer, Marshall and Tadros *The Trial on Trial 3: Towards a Normative Theory of the Trial* (2008), pp 259–285.

2   And to other closely-related proceedings such as proceedings for compensation for detention following upon an acquittal where such proceedings are recognised by domestic law: eg *Szücs v Austria* 1997-VII, paras 44–48; *Werner v Austria* 1997-VII, paras 48–51; cf *Lamanna v Austria* (10 July 2001), paras 29–32 (public pronouncement of appellate court decision on compensation for detention remedied the lack of public hearing at first instance). See also *Miller v Sweden* (8 February 2005), paras 28–37 (violation of Art 6 on account of lack of oral hearing in disability benefit entitlement proceedings).

3   *Bulut v Austria* 1996-II, paras 40–42.

4   *Ekbatani v Sweden* (1988) A 134, para 31; *KDB v Netherlands* 1998-II, para 39.

5   Cf *Helmers v Sweden* (1991) A 212-A, paras 36–39 (circumstances of appellate proceedings requiring presence of applicant in person to help determine questions of law, also taking into account seriousness of what was at stake (professional reputation and career)); *Elsholz v Germany* [GC] 2000-VIII, paras 62–66 (lack of psychological expert evidence and failure by the Regional Court to conduct a further hearing when the applicant's appeal raised questions of fact and law which could not adequately be resolved on the basis of the written submissions alone: violation of Art 6(1)).

6   *Sutter v Switzerland* (1984) A 74, para 30 (military appeal court).

7   *Jan-Åke Andersson v Sweden* (1991) A 212-B, paras 27 and 29 (no questions of fact or of law which could not have been resolved from the case file, and thus no requirement of a public hearing).

8   Eg *Ekbatani v Sweden* (1988) A 134, para 32 (absence of full rehearing in public constituted a violation of Art 6); *Muttilainen v Finland* (22 May 2007) (the appeal court had examined the case as to both the facts and the law and had assessed the applicant's guilt or innocence: as the crucial question concerned the credibility of the statements of the persons involved, the refusal to hold an oral hearing violated Art 6). On the Court's tendency to link the accused's right to be present and the right to a public trial, as in *Stefanelli v San Marino* 2000-II, see Trechsel *Human Rights in Criminal Proceedings* (2005), p 129; and Summers, *Fair Trials: The European Criminal Procedural Tradition and the European Court of Human Rights* (2007), p 116.

9   Cf *Szücs v Austria* 1997-VII, para 42; and *Werner v Austria* 1997-VII, para 45.

10   *Pretto and Others v Italy* (1983) A 71, at para 27 (principle applies 'at any rate as regards cassation proceedings'); but see *Moser v Austria* (21 September 2006), para 103 ('in the present case, in which dispensing with a public hearing was not justified in the circumstances, the above means of rendering the decisions public, namely giving persons who establish a legal interest in the case access to the file and publishing decisions of special interest, mostly of the appellate courts or the Supreme Court, did not suffice to comply with the requirements of Article 6 (1)'). See also *Blücher v Czech Republic* (11 January 2005), paras 59–61 (lack of public hearing before the constitutional court: no violation); and *Sejdovic v Italy* [GC] 2006-II, paras 81–106 (conviction *in absentia* of an applicant not to be found and declared a runaway and not having been informed of the proceedings: violation).

11 *Hummatov v Azerbaijan* (29 November 2007), paras 140–152 (failure to provide public transportation and information to the public at a trial in a remote prison: violation). See also the cases cited by Trechsel *Human Rights in Criminal Proceedings* (2005), at p 127.

5.155 Limitations on public hearing or pronouncement of judgment must properly satisfy one or more of these permissible grounds such as reasons of public order and security[1] or protection of professional confidence and privacy[2]. When a trial is held in a secure location or arrangements are such as to present a serious obstacle to its public character, the authorities are under an obligation to take compensatory measures in order to ensure that the public and the media are duly informed about the place of the hearing and are granted effective access[3]. Reading out only the operative provisions of a judgment in open court when the availability of a copy of the full judgment is restricted to the parties and other participants to the proceedings cannot achieve the object of ensuring public scrutiny of the judiciary[4]. Each case calls for careful assessment of the facts. In *B and P v United Kingdom*, the applicants had each instituted proceedings seeking custody of their sons and had asked in each case for a public hearing and public delivery of the judgments. Each of these requests had been refused, and the applicants had further been prohibited from disclosing any documents used in the proceedings. For the Court, the exclusion of the press and public in cases involving custody upon divorce or separation were prime examples where private hearings might be justified to protect the privacy of the child and of parties to the proceedings. Further, in such hearings it was crucial that parents and others felt able to express themselves candidly on highly personal issues without fear of public curiosity or comment to allow the court to gain as full and accurate a picture as possible of the merits of the range of options open to it. Nor was the Court prepared to accept that the absence of public delivery of the judgment had violated Article 6, since any individual who had been able to establish an interest in child residence cases could consult or obtain a copy of the full text of orders and judgments made at first instance. Further, appellate court decisions in cases of special interest were routinely published to allow scrutiny of the disposal of such proceedings[5]. In contrast, in *Moser v Austria*, which concerned the transfer of custody of the applicant's son to a youth welfare office, the Court came to a different conclusion. Unlike in *B and P*, the dispute was not between two individual parties but rather between an individual and the state. In view of this 'the reasons for excluding a case from public scrutiny' must be the subject of 'careful examination'. This had not occurred in the case at issue as domestic law provided for a blanket exception to the public hearing requirement in such cases, thereby excluding judicial consideration of the possibility of a public hearing even if requested by one of the parties[6]. A similar conclusion was reached in *Olujić v Croatia* in which the Court held that exclusion of the public from disciplinary proceedings against the President of the Supreme Court before the National Judicial Council could not be justified as necessary to protect the applicant's dignity since the applicant himself had requested that the proceedings be held in public, nor could it be deemed necessary to uphold the dignity of the judiciary in view of the general interest in ensuring that the proceedings be susceptible to public scrutiny on account of allegations that the case had been politically motivated[7].

1   *Campbell and Fell v United Kingdom* (1984) A 80, paras 87–88 (prison disciplinary hearings); *Moiseyev v Russia* (dec) (9 December 2004) (holding a trial *in camera*, the trial involving a prosecution for disclosing state secrets to a foreign intelligence agent: inadmissible, as this was justified on grounds of national security as necessary to prevent further disclosure of sensitive information); and *Skorobogatykh v Russia* (dec) (8 June 2006) (legal inability of prisoner to attend hearings in civil proceedings against prison authorities: inadmissible). But cf *Riepan v Austria* 2000-XII, paras 27–34 (criminal trial involving charges of dangerous menace took place in the prison where the applicant was serving an 18-year prison sentence for murder and burglary: violation of Art 6(1); and not remedied by subsequent proceedings: paras 35–41).

2   This suggests that appropriate scrutiny is required of any reason advanced: cf *Le Compte, Van Leuven and De Meyere v Belgium* (1981) A 43, para 59 (professional disciplinary body was not considering medical treatment of patients, and thus no question of professional secrecy or protection of private life arose); *Diennet v France* (1995) A 325-A, paras 33–35 (disciplinary proceedings only concerned a doctor's method of consultation by correspondence and there had been no suggestion that professional confidence would be breached); and *Vernes v France* (20 January 2011), paras 30–32 (hearing in private by Stock Exchange Regulatory Authority whose members were not identified: the possible reluctance of financial sector professionals to have their management scrutinised was not a sufficient reason, public scrutiny being a necessary condition for transparency and protection of an individual's rights: violation).

3   *Hummatov v Azerbaijan* (29 November 2007), paras 140–152 (failure to adopt adequate compensatory measures to counterbalance the detrimental effect which the holding of the applicant's trial in a closed area of a prison had on its public character: violation).

4   *Ryakib Biryukov v Russia* 2008-…, paras 38–46.

5   *B and P v United Kingdom* 2001-III, paras 35–49 (para 52: in the circumstances, there was no need to examine the complaints under Art 10).

6   *Moser v Austria* (21 September 2006), paras 96–97.

7   *Olujić v Croatia* (5 February 2009), paras 56–76.

5.156 The requirement of a public hearing applies with equal measure to administrative tribunals determining civil rights[1], to disciplinary tribunals considering criminal charges[2], and also, as the Court made clear in *Scarth v United Kingdom*, to arbitration proceedings for the recovery of debt[3]. However, the absence of a public hearing may be remedied on appeal[4]. Generally, a litigant need not show he has suffered actual prejudice since an interference in this area will be sufficient to qualify him as a 'victim'[5], but an individual involved in proceedings (including relevant professional disciplinary hearings) may waive his entitlement to a public hearing by 'his own free will and in an unequivocal manner'[6] providing always that the case does not raise an issue of public interest[7]. A waiver may be made by implication, for example, by failing expressly to request an oral hearing where the practice of a court or tribunal is not to hear the parties unless such a request is made[8].

1   *Ringeisen v Austria* (1971) A 13, para 98. See too *Stallinger and Kuso v Austria* 1997-II, paras 50–51 (practice of administrative court not to hear the parties unless a party requested a hearing; here, the applicants had expressly requested an oral hearing which had been refused on the grounds that such was unlikely to clarify the case further: violation of right to a public

hearing); and *Martinie v France* [GC] 2006-VI, paras 39–44 (absence of public hearing before the Court of Audit: violation).

2   That is, within the meaning of Art 6(1): *Engel and Others v Netherlands* (1976) A 22, para 89. See paras **5.44–5.49** above. In *Findlay v United Kingdom* 1997-I, para 80, the Court decided it was not necessary to consider the lack of public hearings in courts-martial on account of a finding that the tribunal had lacked independence and impartiality.

3   *Scarth v United Kingdom* (22 July 1999), paras 28–29 (application for hearing in public refused by the arbiter who conducted the hearing in private).See for domestic discussion *Bundesgericht* (5A-201/2008) (6 October 2008) [2009] EuGRZ 238 (fairness and impartiality requirements also apply to private arbitration tribunals) [Switzerland].

4   Defects at first instance (in particular, during disciplinary hearings held by professional bodies) may, on the other hand, be remedied where the superior court has full power to review all the issues, including questions of sanction: *Diennet v France* (1995) A 325-A, para 33; *Helle v Finland* 1997-VIII, paras 45–48. See also *Lamanna v Austria* (10 July 2001), paras 29–32 (public pronouncement of appellate court decision on compensation for detention remedied the lack of public hearing at first instance). Cf *Gautrin and Others v France* 1998-III, 1009, paras 39–43 (the fact that the applicants would have had a public hearing had they appealed to the *Conseil d' Etat* from the decisions of the regional and national councils of the professional body which was precluded from holding public hearings was irrelevant: here, there had been no issue involving professional secrecy or the protection of private life, and there was a violation of Art 6); *Riepan v Austria* 2000-XII, paras 35–41 (criminal trial which took place in a prison was not remedied by subsequent proceedings); and *Malhous v Czech Republic* [GC] (12 July 2001), paras 55–63 (land tribunal proceedings held in private were not remedied by review courts).

5   *Engel and Others v Netherlands* (1976) A 22, para 89.

6   *Albert and Le Compte v Belgium* (1983) A 58, at para 35; *H v Belgium* (1987) A 127-B, para 54; *Pauger v Austria* 1997-III, paras 58–62 (the applicant, a professor of public law, was considered to have waived unequivocally his right to a public hearing before the constitutional court); *Rolf Gustafson v Sweden* 1997-IV, para 47 (failure to request hearing before a board led to the reasonable conclusion the applicant had waived this right). Cf *Deweer v Belgium* (1980) A 35, paras 48–54 (waiver of criminal hearing through payment of administrative fine deemed 'tainted by restraint'); *Werner v Austria* 1997-VII, para 48 (applicant could not be criticised for failing to request a public hearing where such an application would have had no prospect of success). and *Hermi v Italy* [GC] 2006-XII, paras 68–103 (applicant had requested that his case be dealt with by way of summary proceedings held in private).

7   *Schüler-Zgraggen v Switzerland* (1993) A 263, para 58. Cf *Pauger v Austria* 1997-III, paras 62–63 (principle of equality between widows and widowers as regards pension entitlement had already been decided by the constitutional court, and thus the present case raised no issue of public interest warranting a public hearing).

8   *Zumtobel v Austria* (1993) A 268-A, para 34 ('dispute' raised no questions of public interest); and *Hermi v Italy* [GC] 2006-XII, paras 77–81 (specific request for summary procedure so that the public was excluded from his trial). Cf *Fischer v Austria* (1995) A 312, para 44 (express request made for oral hearing at first instance court but refused on the ground this would not be likely to help to clarify the merits of the case: breach of 'public hearing' requirement in the circumstances). A presumption in favour of a 'tacit waiver' does not apply in criminal cases: Trechsel *Human Rights in Criminal Proceedings* (2005), p 125.

Decisions of domestic courts on the right to a 'public hearing'

5.157 The domestic courts have had to deal with a small number of cases concerned with the 'public hearing' requirement. It is clear that Article 6 does not require that every step in proceedings must be conducted in public. For example, the statutory requirement that a trial judge furnish a written report to the appeal court is not incompatible with Article 6[1]. Nor is the practice of continuing diets by means of a written minute[2]. In *Hoekstra v HM Advocate (No 1)*, it was held that a site visit by a jury to view productions (three tonnes of cannabis resin, and two vessels) which were too large to be produced in court, under the supervision of an officer of the court, and the accused being present (although unable to be present with every juror throughout their tour of the vessel), did not infringe the principle of a public hearing. The evidence, the submissions and the judge's directions to the jury had all been heard in public. The fact that, for practical reasons, the circumstances under which the jury had viewed objects too large to be produced in the courtroom had not involved the public or the accused being present with every juror throughout did not involve an infringement of the principle that there should be public scrutiny of the administration of justice[3]. In *Clark v Kelly*, a challenge to justices of the District Court receiving legal advice in private from their clerk failed[4].

It is to be noted that the common law principle of open justice, although not absolute, may be stricter than Article 6: there may be a public interest in court proceedings being held in public even when the parties would be content for them to be held in private[5].

1   *Megrahi, Petitioner* 2002 JC 38.

2   *Degnan v HM Advocate* 2001 SCCR 810.

3   *Hoekstra v HM Advocate* 2002 SCCR 135.

4   *Clark v Kelly* 2003 SC (PC) 77. See also *Chalmers v Griffiths* 2005 1 JC 158 (advice given to Justice by clerk not disclosed).

5   See eg *Scott v Scott* [1913] AC 417; *A-G v Leveller Magazine Ltd* [1979] AC 440; *R (Mohamed) v Secretary of State for Foreign and Commonwealth Affairs* (No 2) [2011] QB 218; cf *In re Times Newspapers Ltd* [2009] 1 WLR 1015. See also cases on the anonymisation of parties to proceedings, noted in para **6.136**, fn3 below.

ARTICLE 6: JUDICIAL DETERMINATION WITHIN A 'REASONABLE TIME'

5.158 Justice delayed is justice denied. The reasonableness of the length of civil or criminal proceedings has given rise to substantial case law[1], but comparatively little of it concerning the United Kingdom[2]. The proceedings are considered as a whole, including (if relevant) appellate and constitutional proceedings. Two key questions arise: first, calculation of the period of time to be taken into account; and secondly, consideration of whether this period is 'reasonable'. This latter issue requires assessment of the complexity of the factual or legal issues raised, the conduct of the applicant, and the conduct of the domestic authorities as assessed in light of what was at stake for the individual[3].

1   The issue has been a longstanding one. See Eissen *The Length of Civil and Criminal Proceedings in the Case-Law of the European Court of Human Rights* (1996), p 8 ('reasonable time' was considered in 165 of the 554 judgments (ie some 30%) delivered by the Court in its first 25 years). (This part of the chapter draws upon this work written by the former Registrar of the Court.) For general discussion, see Edel *The Length of Civil and Criminal Proceedings in the Case-law of the European Court of Human Rights* (2nd edn, 2007). State action to address systemic problems in domestic legal systems is often inadequate. Italy has long been a particular source of cases challenging excessive length of domestic proceedings together with the associated issue of lack of an effective remedy under Art 13. Domestic reforms (the 'Pinto law') prompted by earlier and repeated findings of violations are now in turn giving rise to further challenges: see *Scordino v Italy (no 1)* [GC] 2006-V, paras 173–227 at para 176 (noting it had adopted more than 1,000 judgments against Italy since 1999 in civil length-of-proceedings cases, the Court observed that awards of 'just satisfaction' under Art 41 at higher levels were designed 'to encourage States to find their own, universally accessible, solution to the problem and [also] allowed applicants to avoid being penalised for the lack of domestic remedies'. See also *Simaldone v Italy* 2009-..., paras 76–85 (despite holding that the amount awarded under the Pinto Act in compensation for the excessive length of proceedings was deficient and that the length of the Pinto proceedings had been excessive, the Court considered that these factors were insufficient to cast doubt on the effectiveness of the Pinto remedy, observing that where a compensatory remedy had been introduced, a wider margin of appreciation had to be left to the state to allow it to organise that remedy in a manner coherent with its own legal system and traditions); and *Daddi v Italy* (dec) (2 June 2009) (no reason at present to doubt the effectiveness of 'Pinto law' remedies). See further Wolf 'Trial Within a Reasonable Time: The Recent Reforms of the Italian Justice System in Response to the Conflict with Article 6(1) of the European Convention on Human Rights' (2003) 9 EPL 189.

2   Violations of 'reasonable time' have been established in *H v United Kingdom* (1987) A 120, paras 70–86 (2 years and 7 months in seeking access to a child); *Darnell v United Kingdom* (1993) A 272, para 21 (some 9 years before final decision regarding unfair dismissal in employment tribunals); 21437/93, *Dougan v United Kingdom* 1997 SCCR 56 (11 years between accused's failure to appear for trial and execution of non-appearance warrant); *Robins v United Kingdom* 1997-V, paras 30–35 (more than 4 years for relatively straightforward dispute over costs to be determined); *S v United Kingdom* (21 September 2000) paras 25–30, discussed at para **5.162** and **5.165** below; *Davies v United Kingdom* (16 July 2002) para 39 (state responsible for the greater part of the delay in proceedings under s 6 of the Company Directors Disqualification Act 1986 which lasted 4 years and 5 months); *Somjee v United Kingdom* (15 October 2002) (proceedings before an employment tribunal which lasted almost 9 years); *Foley v United Kingdom* (22 October 2002) (proceedings lasting more than 14 years and 9 months); *Jordan v United Kingdom (no 2)* (10 December 2002 (court martial proceedings which lasted 4 years, 7 months and 15 days); *Mitchell and Holloway v United Kingdom* (17 December 2002) (10 years and 4 months between the beginning of the substantive proceedings and the end of enforcement proceedings); *Obasa v United Kingdom* (16 January 2003) (7 years, 4 months delay between initiation of proceedings before an employment tribunal and rejection of leave to appeal at the House of Lords); *Easterbrook v United Kingdom* (12 June 2003) ('unacceptable' 9 year period of delay in fixing the applicant's tariff following his murder conviction); *Mellors v United Kingdom* (17 July 2003) (criminal proceedings lasted more than 3 years and 8 months, with theappeal taking more than 3 years to be determined); *Price and Lowe v United Kingdom* (29 July 2003) (proceedings lasted more than 12 years); *Eastaway v United Kingdom* (20 July 2004) (almost 9 years); *Henworth v United Kingdom* (2 November 2004) (6 years in criminal proceedings involving a re-trial); *King v United Kingdom* (16 November 2004) (more than 13 years in proceedings involving tax assessments); *Massey v United Kingdom* (16 November 2004) (criminal proceedings lasting more than 4 years and 9

months); *Crowther v United Kingdom* (1 February 2005) (confiscation proceedings lasted 8 years, 5 months); *Yetkinsekerci v United Kingdom* (20 October 2005) (criminal proceedings lasted 3 and a half years, of which the appeal proceedings took up almost 3 years); *Blake v United Kingdom* (26 September 2006) (9 years and 10 months in dispute over publication); *Crompton v United Kingdom* (27 October 2009) (11 years to determine dispute over dismissal from a military post); and *Richard Anderson v United Kingdom* (9 February 2010) (proceedings in the Scottish courts lasting 6 years and 8 months but which turned on the veracity of allegations of fraud and did not involve novel points of law). The *Richard Anderson* judgment resulted in changes to practice in the Court of Session, in order to ensure that cases were not delayed by prolonged periods of inactivity on the part of the parties.

3   *Zimmerman and Steiner v Switzerland* (1983) A 66, para 24.

5.159 The issue of reasonableness in criminal proceedings is also relevant in terms of Article 5(3)'s guarantee of 'trial within a reasonable time or to release pending trial'. In certain cases lengthy pre-trial detention may give rise to violations of both Article 5 and Article 6. There is thus some overlap in the content of each consideration. However, the focus in the first instance is upon the relevancy and sufficiency of the reasons justifying continuing detention and any lack of due diligence on the part of the prosecutor, while the latter guarantee requires consideration of such matters as complexity of the case and conduct of the accused as well as that of the prosecutor. The crucial distinction is in the latitude given to the prosecutor. In *IA v France*, for example, pre-trial detention lasting some 63 months was found to violate Article 5(3), but the length of the criminal proceedings themselves which had amounted to some 81 months did not breach Article 6(1)'s guarantee of reasonableness on account of the complex factual issues[1].

1   *IA v France* 1998-VII, paras 99–112, 116–122; see further paras **4.211–4.213** above.

Calculation of the period

Start of the period

5.160 In criminal matters, calculation of the period normally begins with the point at which a person is charged with an offence[1]. However, as discussed above, the concept of 'charge' is given an autonomous meaning under the ECHR rather than any formal definition found in domestic legal systems[2], and denotes the 'official notification given to an individual by the competent authority of an allegation that he has committed a criminal offence'[3]. Invariably the start of this period will take place before the first court appearance and may be constituted by interview[4], arrest[5], by issue of an arrest[6] or a search[7] warrant, by official notification that a prosecution is being investigated[8], by the opening of a preliminary investigation[9], or by other official measures carrying the implication of a similar allegation and which similarly 'substantially affect the situation of the suspect'[10]. The reasonableness of the time taken for the 'determination' of any criminal charge thus clearly applies to pre-trial proceedings as much as it does to the period after the first appearance for trial. For example, in *Angelucci v Italy*, the period which fell to be considered began with the appointment of defence counsel, and ended more than eight years later with the pronouncement that there was no case to answer or alternatively (a few days later) when the time limit for an appeal against this decision had expired[11].

1 Or in some cases, from the date of the state's acceptance of the right of individual petition if this is later, although assessment of the 'reasonableness' of the time will take account of the state of proceedings at this date: eg *Foti and Others v Italy* (1982) A 56, para 53.

2 See paras **5.42–5.43** above

3 *Deweer v Belgium* (1980) A 35, paras 42 and 44 (concept has to be understood within the meaning of the Convention; the Court has to look behind formalities and consider the realities of the procedure).

4 *Howarth v United Kingdom* (21 September 2000), para 20 (interview by officers of the Serious Fraud Office in connection with allegations of market rigging, theft and false accounting).

5 Eg *B v Austria* (1990) A 175, para 48.

6 Eg *Boddaert v Belgium* (1992) A 235-D, para 35. Cf *Etcheveste and Bidart v France* (21 March 2002), paras 82–93 (the applicants fled following the issuing of arrest warrants and were only arrested several years later; the start of the period was not the date on which the arrest warrants were issued but the date on which the applicants were charged and committed for trial).

7 *Eckle v Germany* (1982) A 51, para 75.

8 Eg *Mori v Italy* (1991) A 197-C, para 14 (date of formal notification); *Colacioppo v Italy* (1991) 197-D, para 13 (receipt of judicial notice of criminal proceedings).

9 *Ringeisen v Austria* (1971) A 13, para 110. See too *ILJ and Others v United Kingdom* 2000-IX, paras 130–132 (the period to be considered for assessing the reasonableness of the length of the proceedings ran from the dates when the first and second applicants were charged and the third applicant was arrested).

10 *Deweer v Belgium* (1980) A 35, at para 46; *Eckle v Germany* (1982) A 51, para 73. See also *Angelucci v Italy* (1991) A 196-C, para 13 (appointment of defence counsel); *Raimondo v Italy* (1994) A 281-A, para 42 (court order of confiscation of seized goods); *Löffler v Austria (no 1)* (3 October 2000), para 19 (starting-point to be taken as date when criminal proceedings were re-opened (following earlier investigations which had resulted in a conviction) as only after that time was the applicant again someone charged with a criminal offence). Cf *Reinhardt and Slimane-Kaïd v France* 1998-II, para 93 (first applicant had been taken into custody in connection with investigations concerning the second applicant; and in consequence neither this measure nor a search of her home to obtain evidence against the second applicant was an 'official notification' to her that a criminal offence had been alleged).

11 *Angelucci v Italy* (1991) A 196-C, paras 13 and 15.

5.161 As far as the determination of civil rights and obligations is concerned, calculation of the period of 'reasonable time' normally begins from the time an action is instituted in a court or tribunal[1]. In most cases, this will involve the date of institution of proceedings in a local court[2] or specialised court or tribunal[3] of first instance, unless a higher court has exclusive jurisdiction to hear the matter[4]. In certain circumstances, however, the period may begin at an earlier stage as with the application for interim relief[5], the making of a confiscation order[6], the submission of a preliminary claim for compensation[7], or the lodging of an objection[8] or request to a public authority[9]. The key issue is the point at which a 'dispute' can be said to exist. In *Lithgow and Others v United Kingdom*, negotiations between various companies subject to nationalisation and the Department of

Industry had sought to agree the amount of compensation payable to shareholders. At this stage, only one company had instituted proceedings before a statutory arbitration tribunal, although at any point the negotiations seeking to achieve common agreement could have been broken off and the matters referred to the tribunal. The Court considered that the period for calculating the 'reasonable time' requirement only ran from the point when formal reference was made to the tribunal[10].

1   *Erkner and Hofauer v Austria* (1987) A 117, para 64. In certain cases, however, this will be from the date of the state's acceptance of the right of individual petition if later, although in assessing the issue of 'reasonableness', the stage of the proceedings at this date will be taken into account: eg *Pretto and Others v Italy* (1983) A 71, para 30.

2   Eg *Guincho v Portugal* (1984) A 81, para 29.

3   Eg *Buchholz v Germany* (1981) A 42, para 48 (commencement of action in Labour Court).

4   Eg *Zimmerman and Steiner v Switzerland* (1983) A 66, paras 25–32 (administrative appeal against decision of assessment commission determined by federal supreme court).

5   Eg *Cesarini v Italy* (1992) A 245-B, para 16 (request for emergency order).

6   Eg *Raimondo v Italy* (1994) A 281-A, para 42.

7   Eg *Vallée v France* (1994) A 289-A, para 33 (compensation for infected blood transfusions).

8   Eg *König v Germany* (1978) A 27, para 98 (objection to withdrawal of authority to practise as a doctor); *Van Vlimmeren and van Ilveerenbeck v Netherlands* (26 September 2000), paras 34–36 (period for calculation of reasonableness of time taken to determine a claim for compensation for flood damage began when the applicants had informed the relevant commission that they held it responsible).

9   Eg *Olsson v Sweden (no 2)* (1992) A 250, para 101 (submission of request to council for termination of state care of applicant's children).

10   *Lithgow and Others v United Kingdom* (1986) A 102, para 199. Cf *H v France* (1989) A 162-A, para 49 (question as to whether preliminary legal aid procedure should be included was avoided given the total length (seven-and-a-half years) of the civil proceedings); *Blake v United Kingdom* (26 September 2006), para 40 (Treasury Solicitor's letters to a publisher about the applicant's alleged breaches were not sufficient to mark the beginning of a dispute to be determined between the applicant and the Government).

End of the period

5.162 The entirety of the duration of the proceedings including any appeal stage is assessed: that is, the period 'extends right up to the decision which disposes of the dispute'[1]. In criminal cases, the aim of this aspect of Article 6 is to ensure persons accused of an offence 'do not have to lie under a charge for too long and that the charge is determined', and consequently it is necessary to consider all stages of a criminal process[2] including any proceedings before an appeal court which can determine the merits of a prosecution[3]. In *Howarth v United Kingdom*, the applicant had been convicted of theft and conspiracy to defraud and had been sentenced to community service. He had lodged a notice of appeal against conviction, and the Attorney General had also made a reference to the English Court of Appeal for a review of the applicant's sentence. Some two years after the conviction and after he had completed the community service order, the applicant's appeal against conviction had been dismissed but the Attorney General's reference had resulted in the imposition of a sentence of imprisonment of 20 months. The Court determined that the proceedings were only concluded with the determination of the reference, and thus the period to be considered for the purposes of Article 6 was just over four years[4].

---

1   *Erkner and Hofauer v Austria* (1987) A 117, at para 65. Proceedings will thus generally end with an acquittal or conviction or termination by the trial judge; or additionally, through notification of a decision by the prosecutor not to proceed (*Slezevicius v Lithuania* (13 November 2001), para 27) or finding by a court of unfitness to stand trial by reason of psychiatric condition (*Antoine v United Kingdom* (dec) 2003-VII) even though in these latter instances a theoretical possibility that proceedings could be taken on these charges exists. In *Withey v United Kingdom* (dec) 2003-X, the Court considered that an order leaving charges on the file also terminated the proceedings since the prosecutor would require court consideration of the fairness of reopening proceedings when an excessive period of time had elapsed.

2   *Wemhoff v Germany* (1968) A 7, at para 18.

3   *Neumeister v Austria* (1968) A 8, para 19.

4   *Howarth v United Kingdom* (21 September 2000), para 20.

5.163 In civil matters, the period will terminate when a judgment becomes final, either at first instance level[1] or after the time for lodging an appeal has expired[2], or after an appeal court has refused leave to appeal[3], or final disposal by a supreme court[4] or a constitutional court[5]. Disposal of the question of costs also forms part of the proceedings[6]. To engage the state's responsibility under this aspect of Article 6(1), it is not necessary that such a stage has been reached in domestic proceedings: proceedings which are still pending may give rise to a violation of 'reasonable time'[7]. Proceedings not related to the final determination of the decision (as, for example, an application for the reopening of a case which is more properly regarded as a fresh set of proceedings[8]) are disregarded. The proceedings may also be deemed to have ended at a stage earlier than a final judicial determination on the merits, for example, where the parties secure a friendly settlement[9] or when proceedings are otherwise discontinued[10]. However, it may also continue beyond the date any court decision is secured to include the length of enforcement proceedings when any 'dispute' can only be said to be finally settled at this stage. In *Silva Pontes v Portugal*, for example, a court had upheld the applicant's claim for damages for injuries arising out of a road accident, but in accordance with domestic law had reserved for the subsequent enforcement proceedings the question of the transport costs incurred to enable hospital treatment after the accident. The Court considered that these subsequent enforcement proceedings were not simply to secure the payment of a civil award but also to determine the amount of damages due, and accordingly this stage in the proceedings also fell to be calculated since the right to damages could only have been finally resolved at this stage[11]. In *Scollo v Italy*, the applicant had sought the assistance of a bailiff in enforcing an eviction notice to eject a tenant from property. The bailiff had in turn on numerous occasions but without success requested police assistance. The Court considered the period to be assessed for the purposes of Article 6 ended on the day that the tenant left of his own accord, the additional delay on the part of the police authorities being included in the calculation[12]. Similarly, in *Dimitrios Georgiadis v Greece*, the failure of the authorities to comply with an enforceable court decision concerning the amount of a supplementary pension due to a retired judge was considered a violation of Article 6, the Court noting that the execution of a judgment was an integral part of a 'hearing' within the meaning of the guarantee without which the concepts of a fair hearing and of the rule of law would cease to have any meaning[13].

1   Eg *Milasi v Italy* (1987) A 119, para 14 (date of judgment by court).

2   Eg *Ridi v Italy* (1992) A 229-B, para 14.

3   Eg *H v United Kingdom* (1987) A 120, para 70 (refusal of appeal committee to grant leave to appeal to the House of Lords).

4   Eg *Zimmerman and Steiner v Switzerland* (1983) A 66, para 23.

5   Eg *Deumeland v Germany* (1986) A 100, para 77 (reversing earlier approach in *Buchholz v Germany* (1981) A 42); *Gast and Popp v Germany* 2000-II, paras 69–82 (lawfulness of charges of espionage on behalf of the former German Democratic Republic considered by the Constitutional Court).

6   *Robins v United Kingdom* 1997-V, para 30 (period of 50 months from the determination of the substantive dispute to the dismissal by the Court of Appeal of an appeal against the judgment on costs).

7   Eg *Erkner and Hofauer v Austria* (1987) A 117, para 65 (period under consideration already exceeded sixteen-and-a-half years: violation). In certain circumstances, the issue of length of proceedings will be subsumed under consideration of the general right to a court: eg *Immobiliare Saffi v Italy* [GC] 1999-V, para 75.

8   *Deumeland v Germany* (1986) A 100, para 77.

9   Eg *Caleffi v Italy* (1991) A 206-B, para 16.

10 Eg *Mori v Italy* (1991) A 197-C, para 14 (court decision that an offence was time-barred).

11 *Silva Pontes v Portugal* (1994) A 286-A, paras 33–36.

12 *Scollo v Italy* (1995) A 315-C, para 44.

13 *Dimitrios Georgiadis v Greece* (28 March 2000), paras 22–27.

Determining the 'reasonableness' of the period

5.164 Each case is considered on its own merits by reference to 'the complexity of the factual or legal issues raised by the case, to the conduct of the applicants and the competent authorities and to what was at stake for the former', but only delay which is the responsibility of the state will be calculated[1]. In other words, consideration of whether the guarantee has been breached will be dependent upon careful consideration of the particular facts, rather than simple calculation of the period of time. However, in certain situations where there is inordinate delay which on the face of it exceeds what appears 'reasonable time', the state will be expected to provide an explanation and adequate justification for this[2]. Inadequate resources (as in low staffing levels) will not be accepted as an excuse: in *Zimmerman and Steiner v Switzerland*, administrative proceedings which had dragged on for three and a half years were considered to have breached the guarantee since no adequate steps had been taken to deal with a backlog that was clearly foreseeable[3]. Similarly in *Blake v United Kingdom*, the Court concluded that the delay at issue before the House of Lords derived, to a large extent, from 'the failure by the State to take adequate steps to advance the proceedings and, more generally, to organise its system in such a way as to meet its Convention obligations'[4]. There is, though, no overall trend which can be drawn from the reported case law: 'there is the risk that the Court will sometimes be regarded as over-indulgent and sometimes as too severe'[5]. The Court is required to reach an overall assessment of whether particular proceedings were concluded within a 'reasonable time', taking into account the issue at stake and any delay attributable to the applicant rather than to the state authorities[6]. Even if the overall length of the proceedings appears reasonable, a lack of special diligence on the part of the authorities might nevertheless give rise to a violation of the reasonable time requirement[7]. The existence of significant delay between the commission of the alleged offences and prosecution does not of itself render criminal proceedings unfair[8]. Failure to adhere to limits laid down in domestic law does not in itself result in a finding of unreasonable time[9], although this may indicate that the proceedings were unreasonably lengthy[10]. Accordingly, the case law can give at best an indication of the type of case which has arisen and the approach adopted by the Court: a period of delay similar to that in the *Zimmerman and Steiner* case can just as readily be considered not to give rise to any violation in the particular circumstances[11].

---

1   *Zimmerman and Steiner v Switzerland* (1983) A 66, at para 24; see also *Guincho v Portugal* (1984) A 81 para 40 (the steps taken by the authorities were regarded as 'insufficient and belated').

2   Eg *Eckle v Germany* (1982) A 51, para 80 (proceedings lasting 17 years and 10 years); *Corigliano v Italy* (1982) A 57, para 47 (two periods of delay of 13 and 14 months where absence of preliminary investigation measures).

3   *Zimmerman and Steiner v Switzerland* (1983) A 66, at para 29 (temporary backlog will not engage state liability provided remedial action reflecting the urgency and importance of the matter for the individual is taken with requisite promptness; however, if the problem of resources becomes prolonged 'and becomes a matter of structural organisation, such methods are no longer sufficient and the State will not be able to postpone further the adoption of effective measures'). After a welter of cases each finding violations of 'reasonable time' requirement, Italy eventually notified the Committee of Ministers that it was appointing an additional 4,700 judges, and the state also carried out reform of civil procedure: cf *Ciricosta and Viola v Italy* (1995) A 337-A, para 31; for subsequent developments, see para **5.158**, fn 1 above. See too *Pammel v Germany* 1997-IV, paras 68–73 at para 69 (the 'chronic overload' which had affected the German Constitutional Court for some 20 years could not justify excessively long proceedings; however a 'temporary backlog' of business will not entail a violation of Art 6 if appropriate remedial action is taken). Cf *Süßmann v Germany* 1996-IV, para 60 (implications of German reunification treaty resulting in the dismissal of some 300,000 former GDR civil servants had resulted in significant increase in the court's workload).

4   *Blake v United Kingdom* (26 September 2006), para 45.

5   Eissen *The Length of Civil and Criminal Proceedings in the Case-Law of the European Court of Human Rights* (1996), at p 40.

6   Eg *Duclos v France* 1996-VI, at para 86 ('while the applicant's conduct was not beyond reproach, most of the delays were due to the conduct of the administrative and judicial authorities': a period of eight years and eight months taken to determine payment of a life

annuity for applicant who was disabled and unemployed 'cannot be regarded as reasonable'). In a series of cases involving Greece the Court has also examined the effect of withdrawal of labour by striking lawyers: eg *Papageorgiou v Greece* 1997-VI, paras 44–49 at para 48 (the Court was 'not unaware' of the complications which prolonged strikes can have; such events are not the responsibility of a state, but efforts subsequently made to reduce any resultant delays are to be considered in the assessment of reasonable time).

7   *Matwiejczuk v Poland* (2 December 2003) at para 86: 'The Court recalls its finding that the domestic authorities did not display "special diligence" in the conduct of the criminal proceedings against the applicant. In this connection, it notes that although the overall length of the proceedings may not seem excessive, the period of eighteen months without a hearing in a criminal case shows the lack of diligence required in such cases'.

8   *Stapleton v Ireland* (dec) 2010-... (transfer to the United Kingdom under a European Arrest Warrant in respect of fraud offences allegedly committed over 20 years beforehand did not disclose substantial grounds for believing that there was a real risk that the applicant would be exposed to a flagrant denial of his right to a fair trial in view of the United Kingdom's observance of the Convention and the existence of various domestic remedies: inadmissible).

9   Eg *Wiesinger v Austria* (1991) A 213, para 60; *G v Italy* (1992) A 228-F, para 17 (but cf the position in respect of a person detained under Art 5: see para **4.165** above).

10   Eg *B v Austria* (1990) A 175 (33-month delay in publication of the written judgment to be published, although the criminal procedure code required that the judgment be published within 14 days). See also Trechsel *Human Rights in Criminal Proceedings* (2005), p 147.

11   Eg *Pretto and Others v Italy* (1981) A 71, para 37 (three years and six months (on top of two years before recognition of right of individual petition) in civil proceedings considered reasonable).

Complexity of the case

5.165 The nature of the proceedings may help determine what constitutes a 'reasonable time'. The case may give rise to complexity in the establishment of the facts (where, for example, there are a significant number of witnesses[1] or a substantial amount of evidence[2], or on account of the complexity or nature of any charges[3]) or of the law (including difficulties with statutory interpretation[4] or EU or international law[5]). In *IJL and Others v United Kingdom*, the applicants who had been convicted for offences arising out of the take-over of the Distillers Group by Guinness challenged the reasonableness of the length of the proceedings. The Court considered the period to be assessed was around four-and-a-half years, but in view of the complexity of the case and the conduct of the parties, the Court concluded that the criminal charges against the applicants had been determined within a reasonable time[6]. Similarly, in *CP and Others v France*, criminal proceedings lasting some eight years and involving 18 accused were considered to have involved considerable complexity on account of the scale of the fraudulent activity. The investigating magistrate had pursued his responsibilities with energy, and in the circumstances, the Court again held that there had been no violation of the guarantee[7]. In contrast, in the case of *Howarth v United Kingdom* considered above, while the Court accepted that the combination of the appeals of the applicant and co-defendants and the Attorney General's reference had 'rendered the proceedings more complex than they would otherwise have been', by the time the first instance proceedings had ended the transcripts of the trial had been available and the issues had been aired. Nor had the Attorney General's reference been regarded by the appeal court as having given rise to any particular difficulty. There were thus no convincing reasons for the delay of two years in determining the appeal, and there was a violation of Article 6[8].

1   Eg *König v Germany* (1978) A 27, paras 102–105 (significant number of witnesses with difficulties in tracing several who had changed their names or addresses: but reasonable time still exceeded).

2   Eg *Neumeister v Austria* (1968) A 8, para 21 (case record exceeded 10,000 pages plus large number of other documents).

3   Eg *Boddaert v Belgium* (1992) A 235-D, para 38 (separate investigations into two serious but interdependent crimes: no violation); *Dobbertin v France* (1993) A 256-D, at para 42 (sensitive nature of offences relating to national security could not 'on their own justify the total length of the proceedings': violation).

4   Eg *Pretto and Others v Italy* (1983) A 71, para 32 (application of recent statute of some complexity: no violation).

5   Eg *Beaumartin v France* (1994) A 296-B, paras 32–33 (wording and interpretation of bilateral treaty: violation because of lengthy periods of inactivity); *Pafitis and Others v Greece* 1998-I, paras 94–95 at 95: (reference to the European Court of Justice took two-and-a-half years to be answered; but to take this period which could appear relatively long into account 'would adversely affect the system instituted by [TFEU, Art 267] and work against the aim pursued in substance in that Article'). Delays in the disposal of work by the CJEU have been addressed, and a new 'fast track' procedure has been introduced. The average length of time taken for an Art 267 preliminary ruling to be given is now 15 months: *European Court of Justice Annual Report* 2010 (2011), p 96

6   *IJL and Others v United Kingdom* 2000-IX, paras 133–138.

7   *CP and Others v France* (1 August 2000), paras 26–35. See also *Pedersen and Baadsgaard v Denmark* [GC] 2004-XI, paras 48–51 (criminal proceedings lasting over five years and nine months: no violation on account of the complexity and behaviour of the applicants).

8   *Howarth v United Kingdom* (21 September 2000), paras 25–30 at para 26 (at para 28: the fact the applicant had completed his non-custodial sentence was 'not strictly relevant to the Court's consideration of the reasonableness of the length of the proceedings'), the case further discussed at para **5.162** above. See also *Yetkinsekerci v United Kingdom* (20 October 2005), paras 21–22.

5.166 Despite early dicta to the effect that the complexity of domestic procedures should not be considered an exculpatory factor[1], the Court is prepared to recognise that uncertainty in jurisdictional matters can help explain some delay. This may also excuse an applicant from not using procedures which ultimately would likely prove to be inappropriate. In *Allenet de Ribemont v France*, the complexities of French law in allocating jurisdiction between the administrative courts and the ordinary civil courts were accepted as a factor to be taken into account in explaining part of the reasons for the length of proceedings involving the applicant's action for compensation[2]. Similarly, in *Katte Klitsche de la Grange v Italy* where an important issue had arisen in proceedings concerning environmental and planning law and which potentially had considerable repercussions for domestic law, the Court accepted that this factor was of relevance in considering the question of reasonableness[3].

1   *König v Germany* (1978) A 27, at para 100 ('eminently praiseworthy concern' to enforce individual rights, but should such measures 'result in a procedural maze, it is for the State alone to draw the conclusions and, if need be, to simplify the system').

2   *Allenet de Ribemont v France* (1995) A 308, para 46.

3   *Katte Klitsche de la Grange v Italy* (1994) A 293-B, paras 57–62. See, too, *Süßmann v Germany* 1996-IV, para 56 and *Gast and Popp v Germany* 2000-II, para 75 (constitutional court is entitled to prioritise cases rather than deal with cases in chronological order).

Conduct of the parties

5.167 Since it is the state which is liable to be held responsible for undue delay in the determination of civil obligations or criminal charges under Article 6(1), only delays attributable to it in some way are relevant in the assessment of whether the 'reasonable time' requirement has been breached[1]. State responsibility can arise where the state itself is a party to a civil action or where the state is involved as the prosecuting authority[2]. In such cases, delays on the part of public officials in the submission of evidence[3], refusal to hand over vital evidence to a litigant[4], or failure either to secure the services of official translators[5] or to separate proceedings to help expedite their conclusion[6] will be considered relevant factors in the assessment. On the other hand, delays which cannot be attributable to the state include an accused's disappearance[7] or refusal to appoint a defence lawyer[8] in criminal cases, and in civil matters the initiating of an action in the wrong forum[9], the lodging of numerous and lengthy submissions[10] or delay in responding to observations or submissions by the other party[11] or caused by attempts to obtain funding for legal representation[12].

1   In exceptional circumstances, the political situation in a state may excuse state responsibility for delay: eg *Acquaviva v France* (1995) A 333-A, para 57 (departure of witnesses from Corsica for personal safety and consequent need to transfer jurisdiction to another court). Cf *Moreira de Azevedo v Portugal* (1990) A 189, para 74 (recognition of implementation of reforms of legal system after ending of dictatorship, but no indication in the case that acceleration of progress in the criminal proceedings had been achieved).

2   *Buchholz v Germany* (1981) A 42, para 49.

3   Eg *H v United Kingdom* (1987) A 120, paras 73–77.

4   Eg *Allenet de Ribemont v France* (1995) A 308, para 64.

5   Eg *Mansur v Turkey* (1995) A 319-B, para 64.

6   Cf *Kemmache v France (nos 1 and 2)* (1991) A 218, paras 66–67.

7   Eg *Girolami v Italy* (1991) A 196-E, para 13 (period of 14 months when the accused had absconded disregarded from the assessment).

8   Eg *Corigliano v Italy* (1982) A 57, paras 41–43 (at para 42: 'Article 6 does not require the person concerned actively to co-operate with the judicial authorities').

9   *Allenet de Ribemont v France* (1995) A 308, paras 52 and 53 (delay of two years and seven months for determination of jurisdiction by administrative court disregarded); cf *Paccione v Italy* (1995) A 315-A, para 20 (procedural defect should have resulted in immediate determination by court rather than result in needless investigation).

10 Eg *Stoidis v Greece* (17 May 2001), paras 18 and 20 at para 18 (issue rendered complex by the applicant's invoking of 65 grounds of appeal in 'numerous and voluminous' submissions).

11 Eg *Phocas v France* 1996-II, para 72.

12 *Blake v United Kingdom* (26 September 2006), para 44.

Conduct of the judicial authorities in respect of the importance of the issue at stake

5.168 Additionally, state responsibility can be engaged where courts or tribunals fail to deal expeditiously with a civil case involving private parties[1]. Delays attributable to the private parties to an action can still thus involve violation of the guarantee: even where the conduct of a civil action is in the hands of the parties to the action, this will not 'dispense the courts from ensuring the expeditious trial of the action'[2]. The matter is of considerable relevance where the subject matter in a civil case is of particular importance to a party. In *A and Others v Denmark*, the applicants had sought damages after contracting AIDS. They were deemed by the Court responsible 'to a significant extent' for the protracting of the civil proceedings through having sought substantial numbers of adjournments and having delayed agreement on the appointment of experts. However, the readiness of the domestic court to grant each adjournment request and its failure to use its power to give directions to speed up the action in a case in which clearly exceptional diligence was required on account of the applicants' reduced life expectancy resulted in a violation of Article 6(1)[3]. In *Bock v Germany*, the Court criticised the prolongation of an action of divorce which had been attributable to the court's 'excessive amount of activity' in focusing upon the petitioner's mental health rather than disposing of any issue of capacity at the earliest moment. The 'abnormal' length of the proceedings which had lasted over nine years was considered unreasonable, 'regard being had to the particular diligence required in cases concerning civil status and capacity'[4]. Particular diligence has also been held to attach to cases involving social welfare claims[5], parental rights in relation to custody and access to children in care[6], compensation cases involving road traffic accidents[7], claims for payment for professional services[8] and even constitutional questions which could have major social and economic implications[9]. Preventing unnecessary loss of liberty will also require that proceedings are expedited. In *Henworth v United Kingdom*, the Court stressed that the facts that the applicant was in custody and that the Crown had elected to retry him for a second time placed a responsibility upon the relevant authorities to proceed with particular diligence, and thus 'it was incumbent on the authorities to ensure that any delay was kept to an absolute minimum'[10].

1   Eg *Styranowski v Poland* 1998-VIII, para 56 (two periods of inactivity on the part of the judicial authorities amounting to 15 months: in the circumstances, violation of Art 6).

2   *Guincho v Portugal* (1984) A 81, at para 32.

3   *A and Others v Denmark* 1996-I, paras 74–81 at para 74. See also *Van Vlimmeren and van Ilverenbeek v Netherlands* (26 September 2000), paras 33–37 at para 33 (violation of Art 6 in respect of compensation proceedings in relation to a land consolidation project: noted that 'even if proceedings are dealt with as expeditiously as possible once they get under way, a reasonable time may still have been exceeded if an individual was unable for a considerable time

to put his claims before a tribunal without sufficiently weighty and pertinent reasons for that delay'); and *Svetlana Orlova v Russia* (30 July 2009), paras 44–52 (repeated remittals of the case for fresh examination at first instance by either the appeal courts or supervisory review procedure had contributed to excessive length of proceedings: violation).

4   *Bock v Germany* (1989) A 150, at paras 47–49.

5   Eg *Deumeland v Germany* (1986) A 100, para 90 (11-year delay in determination of widow's supplementary pension: violation); cf *Süßmann v Germany* 1996-IV, para 61 (reduction in supplementary pension rights determined after some three years and five months did not result in a violation as the matter was not one of urgency); and *Maltzan and Others,* (dec) [GC] 2005-V (consideration by constitutional court of expropriations during the communist regime in GDR: inadmissible, the court's 'role as guardian of the Constitution makes it particularly necessary for [it] sometimes to take into account considerations other than the mere chronological order in which cases are entered on the list … [and] while Article 6 requires that judicial proceedings be expeditious, it also lays emphasis on the more general principle of the proper administration of justice').

6   Eg *H v United Kingdom* (1987) A 120, para 85 (two years and seven months to determine access to child in care: violation).

7   *Silva Pontes v Portugal* (1994) A 286-A, paras 37–42 (11 years to determine compensation claim arising out of a road traffic accident: special diligence was appropriate).

8   *Doustaly v France* 1998-II, paras 46–48 (fees amounted to more than 30% of an architect's annual turnover).

9   *Ruiz-Mateos v Spain* (1993) A 262, para 52 (compatibility of nationalisation legislation with the constitution).

10   *Henworth v United Kingdom* (2 November 2004), para 29.

5.169 In criminal proceedings, 'mitigation of sentence and discontinuation of prosecution granted on account of the excessive length of proceedings do not in principle deprive the individual concerned of his status as a victim' of a violation of Article 6, but such a rule 'is subject to an exception when the national authorities have acknowledged either expressly or in substance, and then afforded redress for, the breach of the Convention'[1], for example 'by reducing the sentence in an express and measurable manner'[1].

1   *Eckle v Germany* (1982) A 51, at para 66.

2   *Beck v Norway* (26 June 2001), at para 27; *Pietiläinen v Finland* (5 November 2002), para 44.

Domestic court decisions on a hearing within a 'reasonable time'

INTRODUCTION

5.170 Since the ECHR was given domestic legal effect in Scotland, cases concerned with the right to have a judicial determination within a 'reasonable time' have formed the largest category of cases to come before the Scottish courts, reflecting experience in Strasbourg. The first case of this kind, *HM Advocate v Little*[1], demonstrated the significance of Article 6(1) when compared with the traditional Scottish approach[2] to the effect of delay. The accused was charged with sexual offences against three children, allegedly committed between 1978 and 1989. He was charged by the police in January 1988 with offences against two of the children. In April 1988 the Crown decided to take no further proceedings. In November 1997 he was charged by the police with offences against the third child, and he appeared on petition in respect of those offences in March 1998. In February 1999 he was indicted in respect of the offences against all three children. He challenged the proceedings in respect of the charges concerning the first two children, both at common law and under Article 6(1). The common law challenge was unsuccessful. In relation to Article 6(1), it was agreed that the appropriate starting-point was the date when the accused was charged by the police, even though under Scottish procedure that was not a charge by the authority competent to commence or proceed with court proceedings[3]. It was also agreed that each case would depend on its own facts and circumstances, and that, in assessing the reasonableness of the time, factors which were relevant included the complexity of the proceedings, the accused's conduct and the conduct of the authorities. The delay of 11 years from being charged by the police to being indicted was one which called for satisfactory explanation by the Crown. The explanation given was that further information had come to light in 1997 which provided support for the earlier allegations and warranted a re-assessment of whether it was in the public interest that proceedings be instituted. This was not regarded by the court as a satisfactory explanation, since its acceptance would mean that the Crown could keep open the question of possible proceedings for a period of many years, defeating the purpose of this part of Article 6[4]. The court also rejected the argument that the accused had to show specific prejudice, beyond the prejudice inherent in the infringement of the right. Although the court was referred to Strasbourg authorities indicating that a person whose trial was unreasonably delayed could not claim to be the victim of a violation if the breach of Article 6 was acknowledged by the national authorities and redressed (eg by a reduction in sentence)[5], it upheld a plea in bar of trial in respect of the charges in question[6]. There was no fully developed argument as to whether it was necessary to have regard to the public interest in the prosecution of crime, or to the Convention rights of others[7].

---

1   *HM Advocate v Little* 1999 SCCR 625.

2   See *McFadyen v Annan* 1992 SCCR 186.

3   Consistently with 21437/93, *Dougan v United Kingdom* (11 January 1995), 1997 SCCR 56.

4   Ie to avoid that a person charged should remain too long in a state of uncertainty about his fate: *Stögmüller v Austria* (1969) A 9, Law, para 5.

5   Indeed, in *Beck v Norway* (26 June 2001), para 27 the Court held that there had been no violation of Art 6 where the national court had acknowledged the delay in the proceedings and had afforded adequate redress by way of a reduction in sentence.

6   *HM Advocate v Little* 1999 SCCR 625.

7   As 'historical' child sex abuse cases form a category which is particularly prone to lengthy delay, for a variety of reasons (eg the difficulty of obtaining sufficient evidence for proceedings to be considered to be in the public interest; and the change in public attitudes since the 1960s and 1970s), it is necessary to bear in mind in this context the positive obligation under Art 3 to ensure that the criminal law protects the rights of children (see para **4.86** above; and para

6.121 below, for discussion of positive duties under Art 8), as well as the rights of the accused under Art 6. Cf *HM Advocate v S* 2003 SCCR 551.

5.171 The first case of this kind to be considered by the High Court on appeal was *McNab v HM Advocate*, in which a person who had previously pled guilty to a charge of attempted murder, and been sentenced to a long term of imprisonment, was charged with murder following the victim's death. A period of 11 months elapsed before the accused was indicted for murder (the starting-point being taken as the date when the accused was officially informed that she was to be prosecuted for murder). The plea in bar of trial was repelled. As in *HM Advocate v Little*, the court held that the accused did not require to show that prejudice had been or was likely to be suffered in consequence of the delay. How long was more than 'a reasonable time' was a matter which had to be assessed in each instance according to the particular circumstances. There was no universally applicable norm. A number of factors might be relevant and there was not an exhaustive list. The court observed that it was necessary to take into account not only the need to avoid delay in the particular case, but also what was required in order to meet the needs of other cases, and that it was unrealistic to expect all cases to progress towards trial at the same speed. The fact that the accused was serving a long sentence of imprisonment and had pled guilty to the earlier charge also narrowed what was at stake for her. The period which had elapsed was not prima facie unreasonable, and the Crown did not require further to explain or justify it[1].

---

1   *McNab v HM Advocate* 2000 JC 80.

5.172 Subsequent cases have followed the approach established in those early authorities to determining whether there has been an unreasonable delay, and have clarified some points, including the calculation of time and the appropriate remedy where there has been an unreasonable delay.

DOMESTIC CASES ON CALCULATION OF THE PERIOD

5.173 The starting point of the period in criminal cases was considered in the Scottish case of *Reilly v HM Advocate*, where it was said, following *Eckle,* to be the date when the accused person received official notification of the allegation. That was taken, on the facts, to be the date on which the accused was interviewed by the police[1]. In *Unterschutz v HM Advocate,* where the appellant had been interviewed under caution by officials of the Inland Revenue, it was emphasised, again following *Eckle,* that the official notification had to be given by a competent authority: that is to say, an authority which was an integral part of the criminal justice system[2]. The Inland Revenue did not meet that requirement. In the subsequent Scottish case of *Burns v HM Advocate*[3], it was common ground before the Privy Council that the approach to be followed was encapsulated in the following passages from the speech of Lord Bingham of Cornhill in *Attorney General's Reference (No 2 of 2001)*[4]:

'As a general rule, the relevant period will begin at the earliest time at which a person is officially alerted to the likelihood of criminal proceedings against him. This formulation gives effect to the Strasbourg jurisprudence but may (it is hoped) prove easier to apply in this country. In applying it, regard must be had to the purposes of the reasonable time requirement: to ensure that criminal proceedings, once initiated, are prosecuted without undue delay; and to preserve defendants from the trauma of awaiting trial for inordinate periods. The Court of Appeal correctly held ([2001] 1 WLR 1869 at p 1872, para 10 of its judgment) that the period will ordinarily begin when a defendant is formally charged or served with a summons, but it wisely forbore (pp 1872–1873, paras 11–13) to lay down any inflexible rule.

The interviewing of a person for purposes of a regulatory inquiry in England and Wales will not meet the test laid down above: *Fayed v United Kingdom* (1994) 18 EHRR 393, 427–428, para 61; *IJL, GMR and AKP v United Kingdom* (2000) 33 EHRR 225, 258–259, para 131. Nor, ordinarily, will time begin to run until after a suspect has been interviewed under caution, since Code C made under section 66 of the Police and Criminal Evidence Act 1984 generally requires the charging process to be set in train once an interviewing officer considers that there is sufficient evidence to prosecute a detained person and that there is sufficient evidence for a prosecution to succeed. In *Howarth v United Kingdom* (2000) 31 EHRR 861 the European Court held that the period had begun with the first police interview of the defendant, but only 4 1/2 months separated that interview from the charge and attention was largely focused (p 865, para 20) on the passage of time between sentence and final determination of a reference by the Attorney General under section 36 of the Criminal Justice Act 1988. Arrest will not ordinarily mark the beginning of the period. An official indication that a person will be reported with a view to prosecution may, depending on all the circumstances, do so.'

In *Burns,* time was taken as running from a date when the appellant had been arrested, interviewed under caution and informed that the police officers would recommend that proceedings be taken against him.

1   *Reilly v HM Advocate* 2000 JC 632.

2   *Unterschutz v HM Advocate* 2003 JC 70.

3   *Burns v HM Advocate* 2010 SC (PC) 26 at para 15.

4   *Attorney General's Reference (No 2 of 2001)* [2004] 2 AC 72 at paras 27–28.

5.174 A number of other Scottish cases illustrate how time has been calculated in the context of particular facts. In *McLean v HM Advocate*, it was held that investigations and other actions of social work authorities (in another case concerned with offences against a child), prior to any criminal charge, have no bearing on the assessment of time under Article 6(1)[1]. In *Baillie v HM Advocate*, the appellant had voluntarily attended the local police station with his solicitor. The reporting officer explained to the appellant and his solicitor that the police were in the very early stages of their inquiries and were not in a position to put questions to him. After conferring with his solicitor, the appellant declined the opportunity afforded to him to have his comments recorded on tape under caution but stated that he was prepared to co-operate fully with the police when they were in a position to interview him fully and to put questions to him. In the event no such interview ever took place and the next stage in the proceedings only occurred several years later when a warrant for the applicant's arrest was issued. The appeal court held that the initial attendance of the appellant at the police station could not be understood as meaning that the appellant was 'charged' with a criminal offence for the purposes of Article 6[2]. In *Burns v HM Advocate*, it was held that, where a person had been arrested in England and subsequently placed on petition in Scotland, time ran from the date of his arrest in England. It was observed that it was the United Kingdom, not Scotland, which was party to the ECHR, and the guarantees in Article 6 had to be fulfilled by the UK as a whole[3].

1   *McLean v HM Advocate* 2000 JC 140.

2   *Baillie v HM Advocate* 2007 SCCR 1. In *HM Advocate v Shell UK Ltd* 2003 SCCR 598 it was held that correspondence from the Health and Safety Executive could not be taken as the starting point for the calculation of the relevant period.

3   *Burns v HM Advocate* 2010 SC (PC) 26. See also *HM Advocate v P* 2007 SCCR 370 (an allegation concerning a criminal offence in relation to a specific complainer made during questioning by English police officers at the request of a Scottish police force can amount to a charge in the sense of the Convention and thus set the reasonable time period running).

DOMESTIC CASES ON DETERMINING THE 'REASONABLENESS' OF THE PERIOD

5.175 The most authoritative discussion of the approach to be adopted when determining whether there has been a breach of the reasonable time guarantee is to be found in *Dyer v Watson*[1], a decision of the Privy Council. Lord Bingham of Cornhill began by pointing out that Scots criminal law was distinctive, in a European context, in its inclusion of stringent rules designed to avoid delay. The Convention was designed to achieve a common measure of protection, and had to be applied in Scotland in the same way as in other jurisdictions[2]. Lord Bingham also observed that the interest of the accused in having the charge determined without delay was not the only relevant interest:

'The reasonable detention provision and the reasonable time requirement confer important rights on the individual, and they should not be watered down or weakened. But the individual does not enjoy these rights in a vacuum. He is a member of society and other members of society also have interests deserving of respect. ... While, for the reasons already given, it is important that suspects awaiting trial should not be detained longer than reasonably necessary, and proceedings (including any appeal) should be determined with reasonable expedition, there is also an important countervailing public interest in the bringing to trial of those reasonably suspected of committing crimes and, if they are convicted, in their reasonably suspected of committing crimes and, if they are convicted, in their being appropriately sentenced. If the effectiveness and credibility of the administration of justice are jeopardised by excessive delay in bringing defendants to trial, they are liable to be jeopardised also where those thought to be guilty of crime are seen to escape what appear to be their just deserts.'[3]

Lord Bingham continued:

'In any case in which it is said that the reasonable time requirement (to which I will
henceforward confine myself) has been or will be violated, the first step is to consider
the period of time which has elapsed. Unless that period is one which, on its face
and without more, gives grounds for real concern it is almost certainly unnecessary
to go further, since the Convention is directed not to departures from the ideal but
to infringements of basic human rights. The threshold of proving a breach of the
reasonable time requirement is a high one, not easily crossed. But if the period
which has elapsed is one which, on its face and without more, gives ground for real
concern, two consequences follow. First, it is necessary for the court to look into
the detailed facts and circumstances of the particular case. The Strasbourg case law
shows very clearly that the outcome is closely dependent on the facts of each case.
Secondly, it is necessary for the contracting state to explain and justify any lapse of
time which appears to be excessive.

The court has identified three areas as calling for particular inquiry. The first of
these is the complexity of the case. It is recognised, realistically enough, that the
more complex a case, the greater the number of witnesses, the heavier the burden of
documentation, the longer the time which must necessarily be taken to prepare it
adequately for trial and for any appellate hearing. But with any case, however
complex, there comes a time when the passage of time becomes excessive and
unacceptable.

The second matter to which the court has routinely paid regard is the conduct of
the defendant. In almost any fair and developed legal system it is possible for a
recalcitrant defendant to cause delay by making spurious applications and
challenges, changing legal advisers, absenting himself, exploiting procedural
technicalities, and so on. A defendant cannot properly complain of delay of which
he is the author. But procedural time-wasting on his part does not entitle the
prosecuting authorities themselves to waste time unnecessarily and excessively.

The third matter routinely and carefully considered by the court is the manner in
which the case has been dealt with by the administrative and judicial authorities. It
is plain that contracting states cannot blame unacceptable delays on a general want
of prosecutors or judges or courthouses or on chronic under-funding of the legal
system. It is, generally speaking, incumbent on contracting states so to organise
their legal systems as to ensure that the reasonable time requirement is honoured.
But nothing in the Convention jurisprudence requires courts to shut their eyes to
the practical realities of litigious life even in a reasonably well-organised legal system.
Thus it is not objectionable for a prosecutor to deal with cases according to what he
reasonably regards as their priority, so as to achieve an orderly dispatch of business.
It must be accepted that a prosecutor cannot ordinarily devote his whole time and
attention to a single case. Courts are entitled to draw up their lists of cases for trial
some time in advance. It may be necessary to await the availability of a judge
possessing a special expertise, or the availability of a courthouse with special
facilities or security. Plans may be disrupted by unexpected illness. The pressure on
a court may be increased by a sudden and unforeseen surge of business. There is
no general obligation on a prosecutor … to show that he has acted "with all due
diligence and expedition". But a marked lack of expedition, if unjustified, will point
towards a breach of the reasonable time requirement, and the authorities make clear
that while, for purposes of the reasonable time requirement, time runs from the date

when the defendant is charged, the passage of any considerable period of time before charge may call for greater than normal expedition thereafter.'[4]

Applying that approach to the facts, a period of 20 months between the charging of police officers with perjury and the date of their trial, during which period the officers were not in custody, did not on its face cause concern. On the other hand, a period of 28 months between charge and trial, where the accused was a child of 13 at the time of the charge, gave ground for real concern[5]. No attempt had been made to treat the case with the urgency which it deserved, and the reasonable time requirement had been breached.

1   *Dyer v Watson* 2002 SC (PC) 89. In the light of this decision, some earlier (and subsequent) decisions must be regarded as questionable at best. Examples include *HM Advocate v Hynd* 2000 SCCR 644; and *Haggart v Spiers* 2003 SCCR 514.

2   This point had been made earlier in *HM Advocate v McGlinchey* 2000 JC 564 at 572 per Lord Justice-General Rodger:

   'If in applying the Convention a court were simply to concentrate on the standards to be expected in its own domestic system, then this would lead to article 6(1) of the Convention being applied differently in different Contracting States ... More particularly, such an approach could have the apparently perverse result that a breach of the Convention would be established more readily in a Contracting State where proceedings were generally relatively fast than in a Contracting State where proceedings generally moved more slowly ... we are applying the international standard which is set by the Convention.'

3   *Dyer v Watson* 2002 SC (PC) 89 at para 51.

4   *Dyer v Watson* 2002 SC (PC) 89, at paras 52–55.

5   The need for expedition in cases involving children had earlier been emphasised in *HM Advocate v P* 2001 SCCR 210, and *Kane v HM Advocate* 2001 SCCR 621. See also *Smith v Angiolini* 2002 SCCR 806; and *Haston v HM Advocate* 2003 SCCR 740.

5.176 As is apparent from *Dyer v Watson,* a period of unexplained inactivity on the part of the prosecuting authorities does not in itself mean that there has been a breach of the reasonable time guarantee: it is also necessary to consider whether the overall period is excessive. This point has been made in a number of other cases[1]. At the same time, if the overall period is such as to give real cause for concern, it will be important to consider whether there have been unexplained periods of inactivity[2].

1   See eg *Clark v HM Advocate* 2004 SCCR 92. Equally, delay occasioned by error on the part of the Crown does not in itself mean that there has been a breach of the reasonable time guarantee: cf *Simpson v Thompson* 2007 SCCR 503.

2   See eg *HM Advocate v Morton* 2003 SCCR 305; *HM Advocate v Hannigan* 2003 SCCR 594; *Cunningham v Ralph* 2004 SCCR 549. In the European Court of Human Rights, 'the question is whether there were any unexplained delays or periods of inactivity. Only in exceptional circumstances, and especially when they have not contributed to a considerable prolongation of the proceedings, will a case with such delay be regarded as acceptable': Trechsel *Human Rights in Criminal Proceedings* (2005), at p 146, and in particular the references in fn 83. See eg *Mellors v United Kingdom* 2003 SCCR 370. In summary proceedings, a period of three years between charge and the completion of an appeal against conviction does not give rise to real concern: *McLarnon v McLeod* 2004 SCCR 397.

5.177 In *Robb v HM Advocate* (concerned with the sexual abuse of children), the court observed:

'If at the beginning of the relevant period there is a clear insufficiency of evidence, or if the competent authorities reasonably then consider that to be the position, the passage of time thereafter, with no further proceedings being taken, will often be unsurprising ... And while the provision in Article 6(1) is designed to avoid a person remaining too long in a state of uncertainty about his fate, it does not seem to us to be unreasonable to keep the file open for review, when serious allegations have been made. A lapse of time in unchanging circumstances may not be "attributable" to the State or entail unreasonable delay on the part of the State.'[1]

1   *Robb v HM Advocate* 2000 JC 368. The point is illustrated by *HM Advocate v P* 2007 SCCR 370, where a period of 11 years between the allegation being made and the subsequent trial was held not to involve an unreasonable delay, corroborative evidence not having emerged until nine years had passed.

5.178 It was made clear in *Docherty v HM Advocate* that a shortage of resources is not necessarily an adequate explanation for delay[1]. Equally, however, the fact that greater expedition could be achieved through the deployment of more resources does not in itself demonstrate any unreasonable delay:

'In general, and subject to questions of prioritisation between particular cases, timescales reflect available resources, and any claim that a case or cases are not coming to trial within a reasonable time, on the basis that greater resources would result in better timescales, would need averments (as opposed to simple assertions or assumptions) indicating that the existing timescales produced a period of time between charge and trial which was not reasonable.'[2]

The court has also observed:

'Part at least of the *raison d'être* of the venerable system of public prosecution in Scotland is indeed that independent, legally qualified, prosecutors should examine police reports and should identify, discuss and resolve concerns about the case before deciding whether to embark upon serious proceedings ... These procedures take time. But it is time which is, generally at least, well spent in the interests of justice and in the interests of securing a fair trial. Attempts by the courts to second-guess the procurator fiscal and to say that he or she had been unduly cautious, had pursued an unnecessarily detailed line of enquiry or had exaggerated the difficulties of some course of action, could only have a chilling effect on the work of conscientious procurators fiscal. It would be wrong to apply the Convention in such a way as to bring that about.'[3]

1   *Docherty v HM Advocate* 2000 JC 307. See also *O'Brien v HM Advocate* 2001 SCCR 542.
2   *Gibson v HM Advocate* 2001 JC 125 at para 14; similarly *Mitchell v HM Advocate* 2001 SCCR 110; *HM Advocate v Wright* 2001 SCCR 509.
3   *Valentine v HM Advocate* 2002 JC 58 at para 14.

5.179 In relation to prioritisation, the court has emphasised the importance of prejudice to the accused:

'In deciding upon priorities, a wide discretion is inevitable. Almost every case will have some feature which can be said to point to this being given priority. But all such features must be weighed in what will be quite imprecise but practical processes of 'prioritisation'. That implies no unreasonableness. We would add one specific comment. While prejudice is not an essential element in breach of Article 6(1), it is in our opinion obvious that if the passage of time is likely to be prejudicial to the accused in a given case, that will weigh heavily in favour of giving that case priority over others where such prejudice is not regarded as likely. In this respect absence of prejudice is very relevant to the issue of reasonableness.'[1]

It has been accepted that financial prejudice to the accused may be relevant to an assessment of the reasonableness of the period in question[2].

1   *Gibson v HM Advocate* 2001 JC 125 at para 15.
2   *Hansen v HM Advocate* 2005 SCCR 293.

5.180 Other criminal cases illustrate particular circumstances, for example a delay occasioned by the scientific complexity of the case[1]; the preparation of a complex case of fraud[2] or embezzlement[3]; the need for samples to be analysed at a forensic laboratory[4], or other difficulties of investigation[5]; the need to obtain the co-operation of a non-compellable witness[6]; the need for expedition in cases involving children[7]; and difficulties in obtaining representation[8].

1   *Crummock (Scotland) Ltd v HM Advocate* 2000 JC 408.
2   *Docherty v HM Advocate* 2000 JC 307.
3   *Reilly v HM Advocate* 2000 JC 632.
4   *Farrell v HM Advocate* 2005 SCCR 411.
5   *Gibson v HM Advocate* 2001 JC 125.
6   *Morrison v HM Advocate* 2002 SLT 795.
7   See para **5.175** fn 5 above.
8   *Hoekstra v HM Advocate* 2002 SCCR 135.

Domestic cases on remedy

5.181 Scottish cases proceeded for several years on the basis that the elapse of an unreasonable time in criminal proceedings prior to trial automatically entailed the consequence that the prosecution must be discontinued. That approach was capable of having unfortunate effects, since no regard could be paid to the public interest in the trial of accused persons or to the interest of victims of crime. The decisions proceeded on the basis that s 57(2) of the Scotland Act 1998 prevented the Crown from continuing with a prosecution after a reasonable time had elapsed. This approach was rejected at first instance and by the Appeal Court in *HM Advocate v R,* in which the accused was charged with various offences of indecent behaviour towards young girls, and it was conceded that an unreasonable time had elapsed. By a majority, however, the Privy Council confirmed that in the event that the trial had not been carried out within a reasonable time, the court was obliged to dismiss the charges[1]. The position was different in England and Wales[2], and it was also different in Scotland where the delay had occurred after conviction[3]. In England, it had been held by the House of Lords in *Attorney General's Reference (No 2 of 2001)* that it would be appropriate to stay or dismiss the proceedings only if either a fair hearing was no longer possible or it would be, for any compelling reason, unfair to try the defendant. Lord Bingham of Cornhill stated:

> 'The appropriate remedy will depend on the nature of the breach and all the circumstances, including particularly the stage of the proceedings at which the breach is established. If the breach is established before the hearing, the appropriate remedy may be a public acknowledgement of the breach, action to expedite the hearing to the greatest extent practicable and perhaps, if the defendant is in custody, his release on bail. It will not be appropriate to stay or dismiss the proceedings unless (a) there can no longer be a fair hearing or (b) it would otherwise be unfair to try the defendant. The public interest in the final determination of criminal charges requires that such a charge should not be stayed or dismissed if any lesser remedy will be just and proportionate in all the circumstances. The prosecutor and the court do not act incompatibly with the defendant's Convention right in continuing to prosecute or entertain proceedings after a breach is established in a case where neither of conditions (a) or (b) is met, since the breach consists in the delay which has accrued and not in the prospective hearing. If the breach of the reasonable time requirement is established retrospectively, after there has been a hearing, the appropriate remedy may be a public acknowledgement of the breach, a reduction in the penalty imposed on a convicted defendant or the payment of compensation to an acquitted defendant. Unless (a) the hearing was unfair or (b) it was unfair to try the defendant at all, it will not be appropriate to quash any conviction. Again, in any case where neither of conditions (a) or (b) applies, the prosecutor and the court do not act incompatibly with the defendant's Convention right in prosecuting or entertaining the proceedings but only in failing to procure a hearing within a reasonable time.'[4]

1   *HM Advocate v R* 2003 SC (PC) 21.

2   *Attorney General's Reference (No 2 of 2001)* [2004] 2 AC 72.

3   *Mills v HM Advocate (No 2)* 2003 SC (PC) 1, where post-conviction delay was remedied by a reduction in sentence.

4   *Attorney General's Reference (No 2 of 2001)* [2004] 2 AC 72 at para 24.

5.182 The conflict between the approaches adopted by the Privy Council and the House of Lords was resolved in *Spiers v Ruddy*, where *Attorney General's Reference (No 2 of 2001)* was followed and *HM Advocate v R* was departed from. Lord Bingham of Cornhill stated, in relation to a situation where there has been (or may have been) such delay in the conduct of proceedings as to breach a party's right to trial within a reasonable time but where the fairness of the trial has not been or will not be compromised:

> 'Such delay does not give rise to a continuing breach which cannot be cured save by a discontinuation of proceedings. It gives rise to a breach which can be cured, even where it cannot be prevented, by expedition, reduction of sentence or

compensation, provided always that the breach, where it occurs, is publicly acknowledged and addressed. The European Court does not prescribe what remedy will be effective in any given case, regarding this as, in the first instance, a matter for the national court. The Board, given its restricted role in deciding devolution issues, should be similarly reticent. It is for the Scottish courts, if and when they find a breach of the reasonable time provision, to award such redress as they consider appropriate in the light of the Strasbourg jurisprudence.'[1]

---

1   *Spiers v Ruddy* 2009 SC (PC) 1 at para 16.

5.183 The approach to be adopted where an unreasonable time has elapsed after conviction, during the appeal process, has been considered in a number of cases. In *Mills v HM Advocate*, there had been a delay in the appeal process, which the Appeal Court held to constitute a breach of the reasonable time guarantee. It reduced the sentence (of eight and a half years) by nine months. On appeal to the Privy Council, a contention that the conviction should have been quashed was rejected. The reduction in sentence was held to be an appropriate and sufficient remedy[1]. It was noted that other remedies available might include monetary compensation or an acknowledgment of the breach[2]. A reduction in sentence has also been allowed in some subsequent cases[3], but not where a minimum sentence was specified by legislation[4]. Where an appellant in Scottish criminal proceedings seeks to maintain that the reasonable time guarantee has been breached and that a remedy should be afforded to him by the criminal court, he should do so by focusing that contention in a ground of appeal. Where the remedy sought is a reduction in sentence, that will be a ground of appeal against sentence[5].

---

1   *Mills v HM Advocate* 2003 SC (PC) 1.

2   In two unreported cases, where the appellant had been on interim liberation during part of the appeal process and had only a short time remaining to serve, the court declined to grant a warrant for his imprisonment, in the light of the delay that had occurred and the short time remaining to serve: *Shepherd v Procurator Fiscal, Dornoch*, 17 March 2011, unreported, HCJ; *Cairns v HM Advocate*, 18 March 2011, unreported, HCJ.

3   See *Gillespie v HM Advocate* 2003 SCCR 82; *Miller v Director of Public Prosecutions* [2005] RTR 3.

4   *Myles v Director of Public Prosecutions* [2005] RTR 1.

5   *Beggs, Applicant* 2011 SCCR 347.

DOMESTIC CASES ON DELAY IN CIVIL PROCEEDINGS

5.184 Article 6(1) has also been invoked in respect of delays in civil proceedings. Some of the cases have involved central government. In *Lafarge Redland Aggregates Ltd v Scottish Ministers*, it was held that a delay in determining a called-in planning application contravened Article 6(1)[1]. In *Scottish Ministers v Doig*, delay was considered in relation to an application for an order for the recovery of the proceeds of crime[2]. In *Re Abermeadow Ltd* delay was considered in relation to proceedings for the disqualification of a company director[3]. In *King* *v Walden*, delay was considered in relation to penalty proceedings under revenue law[4]. A number of other cases have involved local authorities. In *Dundee City Council v GK*, delay was considered in relation to an application for an order freeing a child for adoption[5]. In *Bibi, Petitioner* delay was considered in relation to the recovery of the cost of emergency repairs to a building[6]. Delay in relation to proceedings before professional disciplinary proceedings has been considered in a number of cases[7]. In actions between private parties, the court has an inherent power of dismissal if there has been such a delay in proceedings that the court cannot be satisfied that a just determination of the dispute remains possible[8].

1   *Lafarge Redland Aggregates Ltd v The Scottish Ministers* 2001 SC 298.

2   *Scottish Ministers v Doig* 2007 SLT 313. Cf *R (Lloyd) v Bow Street Magistrates' Court* [2004] 1 Cr App R 11 (delay in institution of committal proceedings in default of patment of sum due under confiscation order); *R (Minshall) v Marylebone Magistrates' Court* [2010] 1 WLR 590 (delay in enforcement of confiscation order).

3   *Re Abermeadow Ltd* [2000] 2 BCLC 824.

4   *King v Walden* [2001] STC 822. Delay in the determination of an appeal against an assessment was considered in *Bennett v Customs and Excise Commissioners (No 2)* [2001] STC 137.

5   *Dundee City Council v GK* 2006 SC 326.

6   *Bibi, Petitioner* 2007 SLT 173.

7   See *Council of the Law Society of Scotland v Hall* 2002 SC 620; *Council of the Law Society of Scotland v McPherson* 2002 SC 628; *Gray v Nursing and Midwifery Council* 2010 SC 75.

8   *Hepburn v Royal Alexandra Hospital NHS Trust* 2011 SC 20.

ARTICLE 6: ADDITIONAL GUARANTEES APPLYING TO CRIMINAL PROCEEDINGS

5.185 Persons facing a 'criminal charge' enjoy additional guarantees under Article 6(2) and (3)[1]. In *Lutz v Germany*, the Court confirmed that the notion of 'criminal charge' in paragraph (1) and the phrases 'charged with a criminal offence' found in paragraphs (2) and (3) indicate that 'the three paragraphs of Article 6 [refer] to identical situations'[2]. The consequences of this were clarified in *Deweer v Belgium* in which the Court noted that these two latter paragraphs 'represent specific applications of the general principle stated in paragraph 1, [since] the presumption of innocence embodied in paragraph 2 and the various rights of which a non-exhaustive list appears in paragraph 3 ("minimum rights", "*notamment*") are constituent elements, amongst others, of the notion of a fair trial in criminal proceedings'[3].

1   For the definition of 'criminal charge' see paras **5.41–5.42** above. For general discussion on the responsibilities of the public prosecutor under the ECHR, see Nørgaard, 'Human Rights and the Prosecutor' in Donatsch, Forster and Schwarzenegger (eds) *Strafrecht, Strafprozessrecht und Menschenrechte: Festschrift für S Trechsel zum 65. Geburtstag* (2002), pp 47–54. See further McBride *Human Rights and Criminal Procedure: the Case Law of the European Court of Human Rights* (2009).

2   *Lutz v Germany* (1987) A 123, at para 52.

3   *Deweer v Belgium* (1980) A 35, at para 56.

5.186 It is important to emphasise that these additional provisions must be read in the context of Article 6 as a whole, that is, they are to be construed in the light of paragraph (1)'s general notion of a fair trial[1]. The ultimate question will always be whether the proceedings as a whole achieved the necessary degree of fairness required by Article 6[2]. Not only is this consistent with the Court's approach under issues arising exclusively under paragraph (1), it also acknowledges that there is in practice considerable overlap between the particular elements of a fair trial guaranteed in these additional paragraphs. Indeed, an applicant may well seek to rely upon two or more specific textual provisions which cannot be examined as if they were discrete guarantees. For example, in *Daud v Portugal*, the applicant had complained that he had been denied a fair trial because of inadequate legal assistance, the shortcomings of his officially assigned lawyers, the refusal of his application for a judicial investigation and of his application to submit evidence, and the poor quality of the interpreting during the proceedings. He sought to rely upon Article 6(1) and (3)(c) and (e). At the outset of its assessment, the Court indicated it would examine these complaints successively under paragraph 3(c) and (e) but 'without isolating that paragraph from the common core to which it belongs'[3]. While this approach emphasises that Article 6 is comprised of elements 'which are distinct but stem from the same basic idea and which, taken together, make up a single right not specifically defined'[4] and thus the guarantee must be considered as a whole, it does so at some expense of coherency in jurisprudence. Often the Court will spend less effort than it ought to on clarifying the exact parameters of these latter provisions. It also can lead to the situation where the Court establishes that there has been a lack of compliance with a particular aspect of Article 6, but that the proceedings as a whole were still fair and thus there has been no breach of the guarantee[5].

---

1   17265/90, *Baragiola v Switzerland* (1993) DR 75, 76.

2   In any case, these principles of fairness are also applicable in the determination of civil rights and obligations: matters such as adequate time and facilities for the preparation of a case, the availability of legal aid, and the right to examine and to cross-examine witnesses all are accommodated in paragraph (1)'s concerns of fairness and effective access to a court: see paras **5.55–5.68** and **5.106–5.18** above.

3   *Daud v Portugal* 1998-II, at para 33.

4   *Golder v United Kingdom* (1975) A 18, at para 28.

5   As, for example, in *Edwards v United Kingdom* (1992) A 247–B, para 33 (the applicant alleged that the failure of the police to disclose relevant evidence to the defence meant that he had been denied the opportunity to examine police witnesses and thus had not been on an equal footing with the prosecution as required by para (3)(d); the Court held that in the circumstances of the case it was unnecessary to examine the relevance of this specific sub-paragraph to the case as the allegations amounted to a complaint that the proceedings had been unfair).

Article 6(2): the presumption of innocence

5.187 Article 6(2) provides that 'everyone charged with a criminal offence shall be presumed innocent until proved guilty according to law'. Whether a person is 'charged' with a criminal offence is determined by general considerations as to whether there exists a 'criminal offence' for the purposes of paragraph (1)[1]. In straightforward terms, it requires at least that 'when carrying out their duties, the members of a court should not start with the preconceived idea that the accused has committed the offence charged; the burden of proof is on the prosecution, and any doubt should benefit the accused'[2]. The presumption of innocence will be violated if a judicial decision concerning a person charged with a criminal offence reflects an opinion that an accused is guilty before guilt has been proven according to law. It suffices, in the absence of a formal finding, that there is some reasoning suggesting that the court or the official in question regards the accused as guilty. In *Garykci v Poland*, for example, Article 6(2) was held to be violated by the appeal court's statement in its decision extending the applicant's detention that the applicant had committed the offence with which he had been charged[3]. However, the presumption of innocence relates primarily to the establishment of proof of guilt and not to issues of punishment following upon a determination of guilt[4]. Failure to observe the presumption of innocence may be remedied by a higher court subsequently correcting the defect[5]. The European Court of Human Rights has also read into this principle a prohibition against imposing criminal liability in respect of acts committed by a deceased person, as 'inheritance of the guilt of the dead is not compatible with the standards of criminal justice in a society governed by the rule of law'[6].

---

1   *Lutz v Germany* (1987) A 123, para 52; see further para **5.42** above. For discussion, see Tadros and Tierney 'The Presumption of Innocence and the Human Rights Act' (2004) 67 MLR 402; and Jebens 'The Scope of the Presumption of Innocence in Article 6(2) of the Convention – Especially in its Reputation-Related Aspects', in Caflisch, Callewaert, Liddell, Mahoney and Villiger (eds) *Liber Amicorum Luzius Wildhaber: Human Rights – Strasbourg Views* (2007), pp 207–227.

2   *Barberà Messegué and Jabardo v Spain* (1988) A 146, at para 77.

3   *Garycki v Poland* (6 February 2007), paras 71–73 (it was immaterial that the applicant had later been found guilty as the Court's statement amounted to a pronouncement of the applicant's guilt before he had been proved guilty according to law); see also *Matijaševiç v Serbia* 2006-X, paras 47–51 (reason for pre-trial detention was said to be accused's guilt); and *Nešák v Slovakia* (27 February 2007), at para 89 ('a fundamental distinction must be made between a statement that someone is merely suspected of having committed a crime and a clear judicial declaration, in the absence of a final conviction, that an individual has committed the crime'.)

4   *Engel v Netherlands* (1976) A 22, para 90; *Phillips v United Kingdom* 2001-VII, para 35; cf *Bernard v France* 1998-II, paras 37–41 (a psychiatric examination to establish whether the applicant suffered a psychological disorder which could help explain his behaviour and which thus proceeded upon the hypothesis that the applicant had committed the offences did not in the circumstances violate the presumption of innocence); and *Garycki v Poland* (6 February 2007), para 68 ('once an accused has been found guilty, in principle, [the presumption of innocence] ceases to apply in respect of any allegations made during the subsequent sentencing procedure'.

5   *Adolf v Austria* (1982) A 49, paras 39–40 (a lower court's judgment could have been read as suggesting the applicant was guilty of an offence but one which did not call for punishment; but this judgment had to be read alongside that of the supreme court which clarified that the applicant had been cleared of any guilt).

6   *A P, M P and T P v Switzerland* 1997-V, paras 44–48 at para 48; and *E L, R L and J O-L v Switzerland* 1997-V, paras 49–53 (the applicants had been subjected to criminal sanction for tax evasion allegedly committed by the applicants' deceased husbands or fathers).

The burden of proof

5.188 Rules of strict liability which place the burden of proof on the accused through the operation of presumptions of fact or law may give rise to considerations under Article 6(2), but only in exceptional cases will the application of such rules amount to an incompatibility. In principle, domestic law may penalise the occurrence of an objective fact irrespective of criminal negligence or intent. In *Salabiaku v France*, the applicant had been found in possession of drugs by customs officers as he was entering the country. French law provided that the mere fact of possession of goods unlawfully imported would result in the establishment of criminal liability. In finding there was no violation, the Court confirmed that the paragraph clearly did not preclude the application of such rules of strict liability. It was for states to determine the content of the criminal law and the constituent elements of any defined offence unless this had an impact upon one of the substantive guarantees under the Convention. However, presumptions of fact or law required to be confined within appropriate and reasonable limits, for otherwise 'the national legislature would be free to strip the trial court of any genuine power of assessment and deprive the presumption of innocence of its substance, if the words "according to law" were construed exclusively with reference to domestic law'. In this case, the domestic courts had assessed the question of guilt on the basis of evidence presented rather than merely having relied upon the presumption. Further, the presumption based upon the fact of possession had not been subsequently rebutted by any evidence which would have helped the applicant avoid its application. In consequence, there was no violation of the guarantee[1]. Presumptions which are rebuttable (for example, by allowing an accused to establish error or necessity) and are accompanied by an assessment of all the evidence presented before a court establishes guilt will thus be deemed to have been applied in a manner consistent with the guarantee[2].

---

1 *Salabiaku v France* (1988) A 141-A, paras 28–30 at para 28; see also *Radio France and Others v France* 2004-II, para 24; *Vos v France* (dec) (5 December 2006); *Västberga Taxi Aktiebolag and Vulic v Sweden* (23 July 2008), para 112; *Janosevic v Sweden* 2002-VII, paras 96–110; *Blum v Austria* (3 February 2005), para 27; and *Müller v Austria* (5 October 2006), para 34.

2 *Pham Hoang v France* (1992) A 243, paras 34–36. See too 26280/95, *Bates v United Kingdom* (16 January 1996), 28846/95, *Foster v United Kingdom* (16 January 1996); and 26279/95, *Brock v United Kingdom* (16 January 1996), cited in Reid *A Practitioner's Guide to the European Convention on Human Rights* (3rd edn, 2007) p 173 (no violation of the presumption where owners of certain dogs are required to overcome a rebuttable presumption that the dogs were of a breed or class deemed dangerous).

Confiscation orders under drug trafficking legislation

5.189 Article 6(2) has been considered by the domestic courts in a series of cases concerned with applications for confiscation of the proceeds of drugs trafficking, culminating in the decision of the Privy Council in *HM Advocate v McIntosh*[1]. Such an application can be made following a conviction of a drug trafficking offence. If such an application is made, the court is required to assess the value of the proceeds of the accused's drug trafficking. In doing so, it can assume that any property acquired by him during the six years prior to his being indicted, or any expenditure by him during that period, was financed by drug trafficking, unless that assumption is shown to be incorrect. The statutory scheme thus enables the court to assume that the accused's involvement in drug trafficking has been more extensive than the offence of which he has been convicted, unless the accused establishes a legitimate explanation of his financial affairs. In *HM Advocate v McSalley*, for example, the accused had been convicted on the basis that he had acted as a custodian of drugs for one day for a payment of £100; but the proceeds of his drug trafficking, calculated on the basis of the foregoing assumptions, were assessed at almost £20,000[2]. In *HM Advocate v McIntosh*, the High Court decided that a person against whom a confiscation order was sought was 'charged with a criminal offence' within the meaning of Article 6(2), and that the statutory assumptions were inconsistent with the presumption of innocence guaranteed by that provision. The Privy Council, on the other hand, held that Article 6(2) had no application (essentially because the accused was not 'charged with a criminal offence' during the confiscation proceedings but was, instead, faced with a sentencing procedure in respect of the offence of which he had previously been convicted), and that the statutory assumptions were in any event compatible with Article 6(2), being a proportionate means of achieving the legitimate aim of punishing and deterring drug trafficking[3].

---

1   *HM Advocate v McIntosh (No 1)* 2001 SC (PC) 89. For discussion of the presumption of innocence in Scots law, see Summers 'Presumption of Innocence' 2001 JR 37.

2   *HM Advocate v McSalley* 2000 JC 485; similarly *HM Advocate v Urquhart* 2002 SCCR 300; *HM Advocate v Bowie* 2004 SCCR 105.

3   *HM Advocate v McIntosh (No 1)* 2001 SC (PC) 89. See also *R v Benjafield* [2003] 1 AC 1099; and, following the Strasbourg judgments discussed in para **5.190** below, *R v Briggs-Price* [2009] 1 AC 1026.

5.190 Subsequently, in *Phillips v United Kingdom*, the European Court of Human Rights was able to rule upon the compatibility of confiscation orders made under the Drug Trafficking Act 1994 with the presumption of innocence under Article 6(2). The applicant had been sentenced to imprisonment in connection with the importation of a large quantity of cannabis. At a subsequent confiscation hearing, the judge had concluded that property acquired by the applicant had been met out of payments received in connection with drug trafficking, and had made a confiscation order to the extent of £100,000. Under the legislation, the confiscation procedure following a conviction for drug-trafficking offences initially placed the onus on the prosecution to establish on the balance of probabilities that specific sums of money had been spent or received during the six years period preceding the offence, but then the burden passed to the accused to rebut on the balance of probabilities the presumption that these receipts or expenditures derived from the proceeds of drug trafficking. The United Kingdom Government sought to argue that Article 6(2) did not apply as the confiscation order was to be considered as a penalty imposed upon the conviction for drug trafficking rather than as involving the determination of a 'criminal charge'; the applicant sought to rely upon Lord Prosser's analysis in *HM Advocate v McIntosh*[1] in the High Court. The Court first sought to consider whether the applicant had indeed been 'charged with a criminal offence' in terms of paragraph (1). Applying its standard criteria[2], the Court first noted that domestic law did not classify the proceedings as criminal. When next considering the type and severity of the penalty and the nature of the proceedings, the Court observed that refusal to pay the amount of the compensation order could result in an additional two years' imprisonment. However, the purpose of the proceedings was neither the acquittal nor the conviction of the applicant. While Article 6(2) certainly governed criminal proceedings in their entirety, 'the right to be presumed innocent [under this guarantee] arises only in connection with the particular offence "charged"'. Thus once an accused person has been proved guilty of an offence, the paragraph 'can have no application in relation to allegations made about the accused's character and conduct as part of the sentencing process, unless such accusations are of such a nature and degree as to amount to the bringing of a new "charge" within the autonomous Convention meaning [of the term]'. Article 6(2) was thus inapplicable. Nor was the reversal of the burden of proof in confiscation proceedings following a conviction for a drug trafficking offence incompatible with Article 6[3].

In *Geerings v Netherlands*, however, the Court came to a different conclusion. In this case the appeal court had ruled 'by accepting a conjectural extrapolation based on a mixture of fact and estimate contained in a police report' that the applicant had obtained unlawful benefit from the crimes in question even though he had never been shown to have been 'in possession of any assets for whose provenance he could not give an adequate explanation'. In distinguishing the case from *Phillips*, the Court stated that '"confiscation" following on from a conviction … is a measure … inappropriate to assets which are not known to have been in the possession of the person affected, the more so if the measure concerned relates to a criminal act of which the person affected has not actually been found guilty. If it is not found beyond a reasonable doubt that the person affected has actually committed the crime, and if it cannot be established as fact that any advantage, illegal or otherwise, was actually obtained, such a measure can only be based on a presumption of guilt'. In view of the fact that the confiscation order related to crimes of which the applicant had been acquitted, Article 6(2) had been violated[4].

---

1 *HM Advocate v McIntosh (No 1)* 2001 JC 78, reversed by 2001 SC (PC) 89.

2 See para **5.42** above.

3 *Phillips v United Kingdom* 2001-VII, paras 28–36; and paras 37–47 (Art 6(1) was, however, applicable, but there had been no denial of the right of a fair hearing since the statutory assumptions had not been applied in order to determine guilt but to assess the proper amount at which the confiscation order should be assessed; and the assessment had been carried out by a court following judicial procedures and involving prior disclosure of the case to be met, a public hearing etc). See also *Grayson and Barnham v the United Kingdom* 2008-…, paras 37–50 (the rights of defence were protected by safeguards built into the system and that the judge had a discretion not to apply the assumption if he considered that applying it would give rise

to a serious risk of injustice: no violation). For consideration of other domestic practices, see eg *Van Offeren v Netherlands* (5 July 2005).

4   *Geerings v Netherlands* 2007-III, paras 47–48. This judgment was considered in the domestic cases of *R v Briggs-Price* [2009] 1 AC 1026. Article 6(2) has been held to have no application to civil recovery proceedings: *Scottish Ministers v Doig* 2009 SC 474; and *Serious Organised Crimes Agency v Gale* [2010] 1 WLR 2881. An appeal in the latter case was heard by the Supreme Court in May 2011.

Domestic court decisions concerning the presumption of innocence

5.191 In addition to the cases concerned with confiscation orders, Article 6(2) has also been considered by domestic courts in a number of criminal cases concerning statutory provisions which place upon the accused the burden of proving a statutory defence. Such cases have concerned a variety of provisions, including offences under anti-terrorism legislation[1], the Misuse of Drugs Act 1971, s 28[2], road traffic offences[3], offences relating to the possession of knives in public places without good reason[4] and offences under insolvency law[5]. The courts have followed the approach taken by the European Court of Human Rights, examining whether the placing of the burden of proof on the accused has an objective justification and is not disproportionate. In the context of penalty assessments issued by the Inland Revenue, it has been held that statutory provisions as to the effect of earlier commissioners' decisions do not violate Article 6(2)[6]. Issues have also been raised in relation to offences of strict liability. In *R v G,* the appellant was a boy of 15 who had had consensual sexual intercourse with a girl of 12. He sought to challenge his conviction on a charge of rape on the basis that the fact that the offence was one of strict liability was incompatible with Article 6(2). The argument was rejected by the House of Lords: while the provision at issue created an offence of strict liability, it could not be characterised as reversing the burden of proof. Since the prosecution retained the burden of proving the commission of the offence, there was no violation of Article 6(2). Their Lordships approved an observation in the Court of Appeal that, so far as Article 6 is concerned, the fairness of the provisions of the substantive law of the contracting states is not a matter for investigation. The content and interpretation of domestic substantive law is not engaged by Article 6[7].

Article 6(2) was held not to be violated when the police notified a person's employer that he had been charged with an offence[8]. Nor was it violated when the Financial Services Authority published information about a person charged with fraud which was intended to warn potential investors[9]. Nor was it violated by legislation providing compensation to some (but not all) persons whose convictions were quashed[10].

1   *R v Director of Public Prosecutions, ex p Kebilene* [2000] 2 AC 326; *Sheldrake v Director of Public Prosecutions* [2005] 1 AC 264.

2   *R v Lambert* [2002] 2 AC 545. See also *Goldsmith v Customs and Excise Commissioners* [2001] 1 WLR 1673 (burden of establishing whether imported goods required for non-commercial purpose); *R v Charles* [2010] 1 WLR 644 (burden of establishing reasonable excuse for breach of ASBO).

3   *Sheldrake v Director of Public Prosecutions* [2005] 1 AC 264. See also *Parker v Director of Public Prosecutions* [2001] 165 JP 213 (irrebutable presumption under Road Traffic Offenders Act 1988, s 15).

4   *L (A Juvenile) v Director of Public Prosecutions* [2003] QB 137 (burden of establishing good reason or lawful authority for the possession of a blade or pointed article in a public place); *R v Matthews* [2004] QB 690 (burden of establishing good reason or lawful authority for the possession of a blade or pointed article in a public place); and *Donnelly v HM Advocate* 2009 SCCR 512 (burden of establishing good reason or lawful authority for the possession of a blade or pointed article in a public place).

5   *R v Carass* [2002] 1 WLR 1714; *Attorney General's Reference (No 1 of 2004)* [2004] 1 WLR 2111 (questions of onus arising in connection with a variety of statutory offences relating to insolvency, evictions, suicide pacts and witness intimidation); and *R (Griffin) v Richmond Magistrates' Court* [2008] 1 WLR 1525.

6   *King v Walden* [2001] STC 822.

7   *R v G* [2009] 1 AC 92 (sexual intercourse with girl under 13 constituted rape); *Watson v King* 2009 SCCR 323 (man accused of having sexual intercourse with girl under 16 had no defence of reasonable belief that she was over 16). See also *Barnfather v Islington Education Authority* [2003] 1 WLR 2318 (offence of failing to ensure that child attended school regularly: strict liability, but no breach of Art 6(2)).

8   *M v Chief Constable, Strathclyde Police* 2003 SLT 1007.

9   *Coia v HM Advocate* 2009 SCCR 1.

10   *R (Adams) v Secretary of State for Justice* [2011] 2 WLR 1180.

5.192 Article 6(2) has also been considered in connection with civil recovery proceedings. These are proceedings for the recovery of property obtained through unlawful conduct. Unlike confiscation proceedings, the powers are exercisable regardless of any criminal proceedings, and can be exercised following an acquittal. Although unlawful conduct is criminal, the proceedings are not criminal proceedings in domestic law, and have been held to be civil proceedings for the purposes of Article 6. Nevertheless, it has been accepted that Article 6(2) may apply, and be infringed, in the course of proceedings which are not criminal in nature but which follow an acquittal in criminal proceedings. In particular, Article 6(2) would apply if the later proceedings can be said to be sufficiently linked (in particular by law and practice) as to be the consequence, and to some extent a concomitant, of the criminal proceedings in which the person was acquitted, and would be infringed in the later proceedings if it can be said that the court casts doubt on the soundness of the earlier acquittal. On the facts of the cases in question, it has been held that civil proceedings brought following acquittals did not violate Article 6(2)°:[1].

1   *Scottish Ministers v Doig* 2009 SC 474; *Serious Organised Crimes Agency v Gale* [2010] 1 WLR 2881. An appeal in the latter case was heard by the Supreme Court in May 2011.

Orders made after a determination of innocence

5.193 The presumption of innocence may be called into question by a judicial order after a prosecution has been discontinued or where an accused has been acquitted where the order 'amounts in substance to a determination of the accused's guilt'[1]. This may occur through, for example, the rejection of a claim for compensation for detention where this decision can be seen 'as a consequence, and to some extent, the concomitant of the decision on [criminal liability]'[2]. There should be no qualitative difference between an acquittal for lack of evidence and an acquittal resulting from a finding that the person's innocence was beyond doubt[3]. In *Minelli v Switzerland,* a private prosecution for defamation based upon the publication of a newspaper article had been declared extinguished on account of limitation. However, the court had ordered the accused to bear certain court costs and to pay compensation to private prosecutors in respect of their expenses. The European Court of Human Rights considered that the domestic assize court which had determined that the publication 'would very probably have led to the conviction' of the applicant had thus treated the allegations of the private prosecutors as having been proved even although these comments had been couched in cautious terms. Such an appraisal was one which was 'incompatible with respect for the presumption of innocence'[4]. The presumption of innocence is thus violated where there is a judicial determination which reflects an opinion of guilt without either a finding of guilt or even the opportunity to present a defence[5]. Statements made by English judges in dealing with requests for costs after the acquittals of defendants have resulted in similar findings of violations of paragraph (2) on this ground in several applications[6]. The Court seems to have developed this line of jurisprudence further in *Capeau v Belgium* in which the proceedings against the applicant had been discontinued without a final acquittal. The applicant was refused compensation as he had failed to comply with a law which required that he adduce evidence establishing his innocence. Although in earlier cases such as *Minelli* and *Lutz* the Court had suggested that the mere 'state of suspicion' following the discontinuation of criminal proceedings did not impact on the presumption of innocence, in *Capeau* it held that 'requiring a person to establish his or her innocence, which suggests the court regards that person as guilty, is unreasonable and discloses an infringement of the presumption of innocence'[7].

1   *Lutz v Germany* (1987) A 123, at para 60; *Englert v Germany* (1987) A 123, paras 37–40; and *Nölkenbockhoff v Germany* (1987) A 123, paras 35–40. Cf *Ringvold v Norway* 2003-II, paras 36–42 (damages awarded in civil proceedings against person previously acquitted of criminal offence: no violation of Art 6, as Art 6 was inapplicable). See also *Poncelet v Belgium* (30 March 2010), paras 45–62 (by setting aside the criminal court's correct judgment that the applicant's right to be presumed innocent had been breached and holding that the prosecution had become time-barred, the court of appeal had invalidated the effects of the finding of a breach of the right to be presumed innocent and had crystallised the feeling that only the limitation period had prevented the applicant's conviction: violation of Art 6(2)); and *Tendam v Spain* (13 July 2010), paras 35–41 (dismissal of the applicant's claim for compensation for his pre-trial detention on the basis that he had been acquitted on appeal for lack of sufficient evidence cast doubt on the applicant's innocence: violation of Art 6(2)). In Scots law, is an acquittal on a verdict of 'not proven' a determination of a 'state of suspicion' without an actual finding of guilt (cf *Lutz* at para 62)? The suggestion can be rebutted in three ways: the verdict is historically antecedent to the development of a 'not guilty' verdict (which was a more resounding affirmation of innocence); it has no consequences which could be said to 'amount in substance to a determination of guilt' (as with a refusal to allow expenses as in *Lutz*); and it provides an effective means of ensuring that 'any doubt should benefit the accused' (cf *Barberà, Messegué and Jabardo v Spain* (1988) A 146). On the other hand, in the public perception the verdict probably on occasion carries with it a 'state of suspicion'.

2 *Sekanina v Austria* (1993) A 266-A, paras 22–31 at para 22 (domestic law recognised a right to compensation for pre-trial detention following the acquittal of the applicant; the court determining this issue relied heavily upon the trial court's case file and rejected the claim; thereby, it cast doubt on the applicant's innocence and the decision of the trial court and this gave rise to a violation of para (2)). See also *Asan Rushiti v Austria* (21 March 2000), paras 27–32 (there had been no new assessment of guilt; but the court in determining the question of compensation had voiced certain suspicions after an acquittal had been earlier recorded, a matter considered incompatible with the presumption of innocence); *Baars v Netherlands* (28 October 2003), paras 25–32 (refusal to pay costs and compensation after discontinuing of proceedings on basis of probable guilt: violation); *Y v Norway* 2003-II (comments made in separate civil proceedings which were inconsistent with the acquittal in the criminal proceedings: violation); *Del Latte v Netherlands* (9 November 2004), paras 30–34 (comments reflected applicant's guilt despite acquittal); and *Puig Panella v Spain* (25 April 2005), paras 50–59 (setting-aside of prison sentence for lack of evidence required absolute certainty of innocence).

3 *Vassilios Stavropoulos v Greece* (27 September 2007), paras 33–41 (explicit reliance to the detriment of the applicant by administrative court that in related criminal proceedings the applicant had been acquitted on the basis of the principle that any reasonable doubt must benefit the accused: violation).

4 *Minelli v Switzerland* (1983) A 62, paras 37 and 38 at para 37.

5 See also *Panteleyenko v Ukraine* (29 June 2006), para 70 (rejection of the applicant's compensation claim for unlawful criminal prosecution with reference to the fact that the criminal proceedings against him had been discontinued on non-exonerating grounds violated Art 6(2)).

6 22401/93, *D F v United Kingdom* (24 October 1995); 22613/93, *Moody v United Kingdom* (16 January 1996); and 22614/93, *Lochrie v United Kingdom* (18 January 1996); and cited by Reid *A Practitioner's Guide to the European Convention on Human Rights* (3rd edn, 2007) p 175.

7 *Capeau v Belgium* 2005-I, paras 22–26. See also the domestic cases considered in para **5.192** above.

Statements made by other public officials

5.194 The obligation to respect the presumption of innocence also applies to other public officials. In *Allenet de Ribemont v France*, two senior police officers during a press conference had referred to the applicant who had just been arrested as one of the instigators of a murder. While acknowledging that Article 6(2) cannot prevent the public being informed of the progress of criminal investigations, the Court confirmed that it does require the relevant authorities to act 'with all the discretion and circumspection necessary if the presumption of innocence is to be respected'. The statement in this case had been a clear declaration that the applicant was guilty. This had both encouraged public belief in the applicant's guilt and also tainted the objective assessment of the relevant facts, and thus resulted in a finding of violation of paragraph (2)[1]. Statements to the media by public officials must thus not undermine the presumption of innocence nor render a trial unfair[2].

The issue has also arisen in relation to statements made by prosecutors in the context of judicial proceedings. In *Ismoilov and Others v Russia*, the deputy prosecutor-general had ordered the extradition of the applicants to Uzbekistan to face criminal prosecution on the ground that that they had 'committed' acts of terrorism and other criminal offences in that country. While the extradition proceedings had not concerned a determination of a criminal charge within the meaning of Article 6, the link between the extradition proceedings and the criminal proceedings in Uzbekistan justified the extension of the scope of the application of Article 6(2) to the extradition proceedings themselves. In this instance, the extradition decision had not been limited to describing a 'state of suspicion' against the applicants, but rather had amounted to a declaration by the prosecutor of the applicants' guilt which could have encouraged the belief that the applicants were guilty and thus could have prejudged the assessment of the facts by the competent judicial authority in Uzbekistan[3]. In contrast, the Court held in *Daktaras v Lithuania* that paragraph (2) had not been breached since not only the actual words used by a public official but also the context in which the statement was made have to be considered. Here, the prosecutor had asserted that the applicant's guilt had been 'proved' in the course of a reasoned decision at a preliminary stage of proceedings in rejecting the applicant's request to discontinue the prosecution, and not, as in the *Allenet de Ribemont* case, in a context independent of the criminal proceedings themselves. While the Court considered the term 'proved' had been unfortunate, the reference had not been to whether the applicant's guilt had been established by the evidence, but to the question whether the case file had disclosed sufficient evidence of the applicant's guilt to justify proceeding to trial[4].

---

1   *Allenet de Ribemont v France* (1995) A 308, paras 35–41 at para 38. See also *Samoil and Cionca v Romania* (4 March 2008), paras 99–101 (presentation of remand prisoners in prison garments at court hearing of application for release and following refusal of a judge to allow civilian clothing: violation of Art 6(2) as the refusal was against the law, unjustified and likely to confirm the public's impression that the applicants were guilty when taken along with statements made by other officials). But cf *Mustafa (Abu Hamza) v United Kingdom (no 1)* (dec) (18 January 2011) (announcement by government minister of intention to deprive the applicant of his citizenship for promoting anti-Western sentiment and violence through preaching had not involved clear declaration as to the applicant's guilt as an allegation that conduct rendered an individual's presence undesirable did not imply the same conduct constituted a criminal offence: inadmissible as manifestly ill-founded).

2   See also *Samoil and Cionca v Romania* (4 March 2008), paras 91–101 (statements to journalists by police chief that the applicants were 'guilty of serious misconduct' and subsequently by the prosecutor that they had attempted to influence and had threatened witnesses: violation of Art 6(2) as both comments amounted to declarations of guilt able to prejudice judicial assessment of the facts). See further paras **5.80–5.82** above and para **7.103** below.

3   *Ismoilov and Others v Russia* 2008-…, paras 160–170 (violation of Art 6(2)).

4   *Daktaras v Lithuania* 2000-X, paras 40–45. See too *Adolf v Austria* (1982) A 49, paras 36–41; and *YB and Others v Turkey* (28 October 2004), paras 43–51 (statements made by police officers concerning suspects and their photographing by the media: violation). Cf *Zollmann v United Kingdom* (dec) 2003-XII (statement by MP in the House of Commons that the applicants were guilty of breaching a UN embargo and of having bribed Namibian officials: inadmissible, the applicants not having been charged with any offence in the UK); and *Arrigo and Vella v Malta* (dec) (10 May 2005) (statement by Prime Minister to press regarding criminal investigation into possible offences committed by senior judges: inadmissible). See also *Ansvarshavende Redaktør B v A* [2003] UfR 624H, [2003] EuroCLY 1147 [Denmark] (defamation action raised by individual after discontinuation of police investigation against newspaper for publication of statement that there was conclusive incriminating evidence: need to read Art 10 in the context of presumption of innocence under Art 6(2)); and *X v X* [2003] NJ

413, [2003] EuroCLY 1149 [Netherlands] (repetition of allegations after charges dropped was actionable wrong). See also the domestic cases considered in para **5.191** above.

The drawing of inferences from exercise of the right of silence

5.195 This matter is discussed above[1].

1   See para **5.144–5.145** above.

Article 6(3)(a) notification of the accusation

5.196 Article 6(3) makes provision for five additional guarantees which are specifically stated to be the minimum rights of an accused person in a criminal process leading to the determination of criminal charges. These are best considered as specific aspects of a fair hearing[1]. First, sub-paragraph (a) provides that everyone charged with a criminal offence is to be 'informed promptly, in a language which he understands and in detail, of the nature and cause of the accusation against him'. Article 6(3)(a) is given a straightforward and non-technical meaning. This provision to some extent replicates the requirement under Article 5(2) that a detained person must be 'informed promptly, in a language which he understands, of the reasons for his arrest and of any charge against him', but the focus of each provision is different[2]. Since Article 6(3)(a) is designed to ensure an accused is 'provided with sufficient information as is necessary to understand fully the extent of the charges against him with a view to preparing an adequate defence', the adequacy of this information is assessed by reference to not only paragraph (1)'s more general right to a fair hearing, but also to paragraph (3)(b)'s guarantee of adequate time and facilities for the preparation of the defence[3]. The requirement normally is satisfied by giving the accused details of the offences, victim, locus and relevant dates[4]. No particular formalities are prescribed, but since the purpose is to enable the accused to prepare his defence, the details provided must be sufficient to achieve this goal[5]. The information required may be given verbally[6]. A mere clerical error which does not affect the substance of the notification of the components of the charge[7], or failure to specify an aggravating circumstance which is implicit in the factual basis of the charge[8], will not result in a breach of the obligation. Particular care must be taken in the event that an offence is re-qualified, especially if the indictment has not been amended in advance, to ensure that the applicants are afforded the possibility of exercising their defence rights on that issue in a practical and effective manner and in good time[9].

1   *F C B v Italy* (1991) A 208-B, para 29. The guarantees are also applicable in respect of disciplinary offences falling within the scope of 'criminal charge': *Albert and Le Compte v Belgium* (1983) A 58, para 39. See paras **5.44–5.49** above. 'Charged' is given an autonomous meaning which refers not to a formal but a material situation; but a person is certainly 'charged' once committed for trial: 10889/84, *C v Italy* (1988) DR 56, 40.

2   See paras **4.199–4.200** above. The purpose of Art 5(2) is to allow the lawfulness of the deprivation of liberty to be tested; that of Art 6(1)(a) to permit preparation of the defence case.

3   *Mattoccia v Italy* 2000-IX, at para 60.

4   *Brozicek v Italy* (1989) A 167, para 42.

5   Cf 14723/89, *Erdogan v Turkey* (1992) DR 73, 81 (information in arrest warrant sufficient in the circumstances; non-service of indictment attributable to the applicant).

6   8361/78, *X v Netherlands* (1981) DR 27, 37; but see *Sipavicius v Lithuania* (21 February 2002), para 27: 'Particulars of an offence play a crucial role in the criminal process, in that it is from the moment of their service that the suspect is formally put on written notice of the factual and legal basis of the charge against him'.

7   *Gea Catalán v Spain* (1995) A 309, paras 28–29.

8   *De Salvador Torres v Spain* 1996-V, paras 30–32 (embezzlement of public funds aggravated by nature of the accused's position as a public official which he had never sought to dispute).

9   *Campbell and Fell v United Kingdom* (1984) A 80, para 96; *Miraux v France* (26 September 2006), paras 31–38 (applicant charged with attempted rape and sexual assault but convicted of rape and aggravated sexual assault, violation).

5.197 There may be a certain level of responsibility upon an accused to take advantage of any opportunity to seek further clarification of a charge. In *Campbell and Fell v United Kingdom*, a prisoner who had been charged with the prison disciplinary offence of 'mutiny' claimed that the offence was of such complexity that he had not been able to understand what it involved. The Court rejected this contention, pointing out that the prisoner could have sought clarification but had failed to do this, on one occasion indeed refusing to attend a hearing where this information could have been made available[1]. On the other hand, a violation of this provision was established in *Mattoccia v Italy*. The applicant had been accused of the rape of an 11-year-old handicapped girl, but no specification of the charge other than it had occurred 'in Rome, in November 1985' had been provided even by the stage of the service of the indictment and at a time when the prosecuting authorities had obtained more precise details of the date and locus. The state had sought to argue that an earlier request for access to the case file could have provided the applicant with the necessary information, but in the view of the Court, the requirement of sub-paragraph (a) 'rests entirely on the prosecuting authorities and cannot be complied with passively by making information available without bringing this to the attention of the defence'. While it was recognised that cases of rape raise particularly sensitive issues and more so where the victim is young or mentally handicapped, in the present instance the applicant had faced exceptional levels of difficulty in preparing his defence. This had resulted in a violation of his rights[2].

1   *IH and Others v Austria* (20 April 2006), para 38

2   *Mattoccia v Italy* 2000-IX, paras 58–72 at para 65 (violation of paras (3)(a) and (3)(b) taken together with para (1)).

5.198 The requirement to provide information in a language which the accused understands will be of concern where the authorities cannot establish that an individual has sufficient understanding of the language normally used in official communications[1]. It is up to the state to take any necessary action rather than for the accused to seek assistance. While the sub-paragraph does not specify that relevant information concerning the charge should be in writing or even translated into written form and thus cannot imply a right to have court files translated[2]. However, the indictment is of such central importance in a criminal process that an accused who is not provided with a translated copy of this document is liable to be considered as having been placed at a disadvantage[3].

1   *Brozicek v Italy* (1989) A 167, para 41 (applicant was not of Italian origin and did not reside in Italy, and had difficulty understanding the contents of official communications sent in Italian).

2   6185/73, *X v Austria* (1975) DR 2, 68.

3   Cf *Kamasinski v Austria* (1989) A 168, para 79–80 (the charges were relatively straightforward as regards the facts and the law; the indictment was six pages long; the applicant had been questioned on the charges at length and with the assistance of interpreters: no violation). See further para **5.223** below for discussion of the right to an interpreter.

Domestic court decisions on notification of the accusation

5.199 Article 6(3)(a) has been invoked without success in a number of Scottish cases concerned with the width of a charge in relation to the date of the offence[1], the locus[2], the details of the conduct said to constitute the offence[3], and the possibility of an alternative verdict[4]. In *McLean v HM Advocate*, for example, the accused was indicted in 1999 on a charge that he had assaulted a child 'between 1 November 1994 and 27 November 1994'. Details were given of the nature and location of the assault, but the Crown was unaware of the precise date. The court held that sufficient information had been given:

'The amount of detail which is required may vary with the nature of the allegation ... there will be many cases in which the Crown cannot know the precise date on which a crime was committed.'[5]

The difficulties involved where the accused requires the assistance of a translator were considered in *Ucak v HM Advocate*[6].

1   *McLean v HM Advocate* 2000 JC 140; *Stewart v HM Advocate* 2005 SCCR 635.

2   *Aitken v Spencer* 2005 SCCR 721.

3   *Jones v Carnegie* 2004 JC 136 (accused charged with breach of the peace in that he conducted himself in a disorderly manner: he had list of Crown witnesses whom he could have precognosed, and he could have raised issue before sheriff if prejudiced by absence of greater specification).

4   *McMaster v HM Advocate* 2001 SCCR 517 (conviction of lesser offence than was charged).

5   2000 JC 140.

6   *Ucak v HM Advocate* 1998 SCCR 517. See further para **5.224** below.

Article 6(3)(b): adequate time and facilities for the preparation of the defence

5.200 Article 6(a) and (b) are clearly inter-dependent, for the right to have adequate time and facilities to prepare the defence presupposes that an accused has been accorded sufficient information as to 'the nature and cause of the accusation against him' as required by sub-paragraph (a)[1]. The Court has succinctly restated the requirements of this second sub-paragraph:

'The Court recalls that Article 6(3)(b) guarantees the accused "adequate time and facilities for the preparation of his defence" and therefore implies that the substantive defence activity on his behalf may comprise everything which is "necessary" to prepare the main trial. The accused must have the opportunity to organise his defence in an appropriate way and without restriction as to the possibility to put all relevant defence arguments before the trial court and thus to influence the outcome of the proceedings. Furthermore, the facilities which everyone charged with a criminal offence should enjoy include the opportunity to acquaint himself for the purposes of preparing his defence with the results of investigations carried out throughout the proceedings. The issue of adequacy of time and facilities afforded to an accused must be assessed in the light of the circumstances of each particular case.'[2]

The aim of the provision is to ensure that an accused 'is afforded a reasonable opportunity to present his defence in conditions that do not place him at a disadvantage vis-à-vis his opponent'[3]. Whether adequate time has been accorded is a matter for assessment at each stage of the proceedings[4], taking into account all the circumstances and features of a case[5]. Positive measures may thus be called for. For example, a court may find it necessary to postpone or adjourn the hearing[6] if this is required to allow an accused proper time to instruct his legal representative[7]. However, the right of an accused to consult with his legal representative may be subject to necessary limitation[8], and cannot imply the right to unrestricted consultation[9]. The sub-paragraph may require the taking of other forms of action by the authorities on behalf of the accused, unless these are unlikely to serve any useful purpose in the preparation of the defence case[10]. More particularly, the authorities must allow access to the case file or to information which could be of assistance in the preparation of the defence[11]. Thus in *Jespers v Belgium*, the Commission took the view that the sub-paragraph implied the right of the accused to acquaint himself with the results of any investigations carried out[12]. Similarly in *Dowsett v United Kingdom*, the right to adequate time and facilities was held to be violated as evidence acknowledged to be relevant and material was not made available to the accused's counsel in time for use in the appeal[13].

---

1   10857/84, *Bricmont v Belgium* (1986) DR 48, 106; 14723/89, *Erdogan v Turkey* (1992) DR 73, 81; *Mattoccia v Italy* 2000-IX, discussed at para **5.197** above; *Sadak and Others v Turkey* (8 April 2004), para 50.

2   *Galstyan v Armenia* (15 November 2007), at para 84.

3   *Bulut v Austria* 1996-II, at para 47.

4   7628/76, *X v Belgium* (1977) DR 9, 169; 7909/74, *X and Y v Austria* (1978) DR 15, 160.

5   Eg *Vacher v France* 1996-VI, paras 27–30 (appeal dismissed in a shorter than average period which may have taken the applicant by surprise; placing the onus on the applicant to find out when a prescribed period of time ran was incompatible with the diligence states must show in ensuring that Art 6 rights are effective). See also *Öcalan v Turkey* [GC] 2005-IV, paras 130–148 (refusal to allow access to a lawyer for almost seven days, restrictions on the length and

frequency of consultations, and lack of confidential consultation and of access to file: violation); and *Miraux v France* (26 September 2006), paras 31–38 (attempted rape charge reclassified to rape following a court hearing: violation). Cf *Zoon v Netherlands* 2000-XII; and *Melin v France* (1993) A 261-A (the applicant was held to be to blame for the fact that he had been unable to present a memorandum: for criticism see Trechsel *Human Rights in Criminal Proceedings* (2005), p 214); *Twalib v Greece* 1998-IV, paras 40–43 (court-appointed lawyer who replaced the applicant's counsel who had not appeared at first instance proceedings had been afforded very little time to prepare the defence in a case of some seriousness, but on appeal, his lawyer had not attempted to suggest the conviction was unsafe); *Dallos v Hungary* 2001-II, paras 47–53 (initial conviction of aggravated embezzlement was reclassified on appeal as aggravated fraud; while this impaired the applicant's opportunity to defend himself in respect of this latter charge, the appellate court had reviewed all aspects of the case with the power to have acquitted the applicant and the applicant had enjoyed the opportunity to put forward his defence to the reformulated charge: no violation of Art 6(3)(a) and (b)); and *Le Pen v France* (dec) (10 May 2001) (conviction of the applicant for assault was reclassified by the appeal court as one of assault of a person vested with public authority: inadmissible).

6   *Goddi v Italy* (1984) A 76, para 31.

7   *Campbell and Fell v United Kingdom* (1984) A 80, paras 98–99 (a prisoner was advised of the charges against him five days before the disciplinary board was due to sit; the Court considered that in all the circumstances he had been given adequate time to prepare his defence, noting that in any case he did not request an adjournment).

8   Cf 8339/78, *Schertenleib v Switzerland* (1979) DR 17, 180 (the applicant was detained in solitary confinement but able to consult his lawyer frequently and without impediment: no violation; but observed that the sub-paragraph cannot be interpreted as giving an unrestricted right of access); 11219/84, *Kurup v Denmark* (1985) DR 42, 287 (prohibition on defence counsel from discussing with the applicant statements of witnesses who were interviewed outwith his presence to protect their anonymity).

9   7854/77, *Bonzi v Switzerland* (1978) DR 12, 185 (applicant held in solitary confinement but still able to consult his lawyer: no violation).

10   *Bricmont v Belgium* (1989) A 158, paras 91–93 (neither an audit of accounts nor the making available of a production would have been of use in the trial; and thus no violation of Art 6(1) and (3)(b) taken together). See also 11396/85, *Ross v United Kingdom* (1986) DR 50, 179 (request by a prisoner preparing his appeal before the High Court of Justiciary for specified legal textbooks, statutes and case reports but which were not readily available: there were practical limits to the steps the prison authorities could reasonably have been expected to take, and in the circumstances of the case there had been no apparent violation of Art 6: the application was manifestly ill-founded). Cf 11058/84, *F v United Kingdom* (1986) DR 47, 230 (seizure and examination of files and tape recordings an accused had prepared as part of his defence but which ultimately were not relied upon by the prosecutor: no violation).

11   However, the right is not unrestricted: 7412/76, *Haase v Germany* (1977) DR 11, 78 (allegations of espionage involving disclosure of some 80,000 pages of reports of a technical nature; certain restrictions on access to the case file for national security purposes were considered appropriate); *Kamasinski v Austria* (1989) A 168, paras 87–99 (domestic law restricted access to the case file to an accused's legal representative, a restriction not incompatible with the sub-paragraph). Cf *Foucher v France* 1997-II, paras 31–38 at para 35 (applicant had chosen to represent himself as he was entitled to do; consequently, the reasoning in *Kamasinski* did not apply and the applicant ought to have been allowed access to his case file: violation of Art 6(3)(b) taken with para (1)).

12   8403/78 *Jespers v Belgium* (1981) DR 27, 100.

13   *Dowsett v United Kingdom* 2003-VII, para 50.

Domestic court decisions on preparation of the defence

5.201 The High Court of Justiciary has considered whether the Crown infringed the rights of the defence under Article 6(3) (b) and (c) by citing as a witness an expert who had been instructed on behalf of the defence, communications between the expert and the defence and material prepared for the purposes of the defence being treated as confidential under domestic law[1]. A challenge to the transfer of a prisoner from one prison to another, on the ground that it would interfere with the preparation of his defence, was rejected on the merits[2].

1   *Wales v HM Advocate* 2001 SCCR 633.

2   *Beggs v HM Advocate* 2004 SLT 755.

Article 6(3)(c): legal representation and assistance

5.202 Article 6(3)(c) applies to proceedings involving the determination of a criminal charge within the sense of Article 6(1)[1], and provides an accused person with three inter-related rights: 'to defend himself in person'; to defend himself 'through legal assistance of his own choosing'; and 'if he has not sufficient means to pay for legal assistance, to be given it free when the interests of justice so require'[2]. When read alongside sub-paragraph (d) which provides for the right to examine witnesses, it also implies a right for an accused person to be present at his trial[3]. The right of legal representation, however, cannot be made conditional upon an accused's attendance at his trial[4]. These rights must be practical and effective and not merely illusory or theoretical[5]. The majority of cases have concerned the second and third aspects of the provision, since without the services of a legal practitioner an accused person will not be able to make 'a useful contribution to the examination of the legal issues arising'[6]. A provision in domestic law requiring that a litigant be assisted by counsel at all stages of legal proceedings is not in itself incompatible with the Convention, and to this extent, an accused may not be able to waive his right to representation[7]. 'Assistance' implies that a legal representative has had the opportunity of adequate time and facilities to prepare the case for the defence, and there is thus a clear link between this sub-paragraph and sub-paragraph (b)[8]. It goes without saying that an accused's right to communicate with his legal representative out of earshot of any other party is a fundamental aspect of a fair trial, and the grounds advanced for any restriction on this right will be scrutinised with particular vigilance[9].

1   *Ezeh and Connors v United Kingdom* [GC] 2003-X, paras 82–130 (the refusal to allow the applicants legal representation in prison disciplinary proceedings was found to violate the sub-paragraph). See also *Whitfield and Others v United Kingdom* (12 April 2005), para 48; and *Young v United Kingdom* (16 January 2007), paras 39 and 44.

2   Cf *Pakelli v Italy* (1983) A 64, para 31.

3   *Botten v Norway* 1996-I, paras 48–53 (the Supreme Court overturned an acquittal and imposed a sentence in the absence of the applicant; the court to some extent had required to assess the facts and the applicant's personality and character without the benefit of his presence, matters which could not as a matter of fair trial have been considered properly: violation); *Zana v*

Turkey 1997-VII, paras 68–73 (security court had convicted and sentenced the applicant to 12 months' imprisonment in his absence and without requesting his attendance: taking into account what was at stake for the applicant, the court was unable to give judgment without benefit of assessment of the applicant's evidence given in person: violation).

4   *Krombach v France* 2001-II, paras 84–91.

5   *Artico v Italy* (1980) A 37, para 33; cf *Goddi v Italy* (1984) A 76, paras 27–30 (accused was in prison and not brought before the court; his lawyer did not attend the hearing; and a court-appointed lawyer had not had the opportunity of acquainting himself with the case or taking instructions: thus there had been no 'practical and effective' defence).

6   *Pakelli v Italy* (1983) A 64, at para 38. See too *Van Pelt v France* (23 May 2000), paras 62–70 (refusal to allow the legal representation of an accused who was absent from the trial amounted to a violation of Arts 6(1) and (3)(c): the impossibility for the applicant's lawyers to make submissions on the merits of the case contravened the right of every accused to be effectively represented by a lawyer which was a fundamental feature of the right to a fair trial, and a right an accused did not forfeit merely by not being present at the hearing). A similar provision applies to proceedings before the European Court of Human Rights: see Rules of Court, Rule 36(3) (applicants must be legally represented at hearings unless exceptional leave is given to an applicant to present his case subject 'if necessary, to bein g assisted by an advocate or other approved representative'.

7   *Croissant v Germany* (1992) A 237-B, paras 27–32; and *Melin v France* (1993) A 261-A, paras 24–25 (applicant had practised as a lawyer, and in the circumstances, he was under a responsibility to show due diligence in the preparation of his case). Cf *Foucher v France* 1997-II, para 35. See also *Prosecutor v Milosevic* (4 April 2003) [ICTY] (in adversarial rather than inquisitorial systems, it is for the accused to determine whether to have legal representation). See further paras **3.32–3.34** above.

8   *Campbell and Fell v United Kingdom* (1984) A 80, para 99.

9   *S v Switzerland* (1991) A 220, para 48 (the authorities feared that there was a risk of collusion between the applicant's court-appointed lawyer and other defence counsel: but such collaboration with a view to co-ordinating a common defence strategy is not out of the ordinary; and at no time was it suggested the lawyer had breached his professional code of ethics or the law). See also *Öcalan v Turkey* [GC] 2005-IV, paras 130–148 (refusal to allow access to a lawyer for almost seven days, restrictions on the length and frequency of consultations, and lack of confidential consultation and of access to file: violation); *Zagaria v Italy* (27 November 2007), paras 32–36 (interception and transcription of telephone conversation between the applicant and his lawyer during a hearing by videoconference: violation of Art 6(3)(c) and Art 6(1) taken together); and *Sakhnovskiy v Russia* [GC] 2010-..., paras 99–109 (confidential communication via video link limited to 15 minutes forcing the newly-appointed legal aid counsel to plead the applicant's case on the basis of submissions prepared by another lawyer: violation of Art 6(3)(c)).

5.203 Restrictions on the right of access to legal assistance to particular aspects of the proceedings will not in themselves be deemed incompatible with the guarantee if these can be reconciled with the interests of justice[1]. On the other hand, access to a legal adviser during detention by the police is now generally required at the time of interrogation, as the case of *Salduz v Turkey* indicates[2]. The principle in this line of cases is that the possibility of 'irretrievable prejudice' to an accused through failure to accord access to legal representation must be avoided.

1   Eg *Engel and Others v Netherlands* (1976) A 22, para 91 (legal representation restricted to discussion of the legal issues in dispute; and since the applicants were not incapable of

furnishing explanations on the simple facts of the case, there was no violation of the sub-paragraph).

2   *Salduz v Turkey* [GC] 2008-..., discussed at para **5.204** below.

Access to legal representation during investigation

5.204 The avoidance of 'irretrievable prejudice' to an accused's rights is most likely to require access to legal representation during the period when a suspect is questioned. The possibility of such prejudice is obvious where inferences may be drawn from an individual's silence or refusal to answer questions[1]. In *Averill v United Kingdom*, for example, the Court held that the denial of access to a solicitor during the first 24 hours of detention failed to comply with the requirements of the sub-paragraph when taken in conjunction with paragraph (1). The applicant had been held and interrogated under caution on suspicion of involvement in terrorist-related murders in Northern Ireland. Failure to allow access to legal assistance during this period had compromised his rights on account of the 'fundamental dilemma' facing such a detainee in such circumstances: a decision to remain silent could allow inferences to be drawn against him at a trial, but answering questions could also have prejudiced his defence without the risk of such inferences being removed in all instances. As a matter of fairness, the possibility of irretrievable prejudice to the rights of an accused through the existence of this dilemma meant that the applicant should have been guaranteed access to his solicitor before his interrogation began[2].

An important recent development has been an insistence that access to legal representation should be available more generally at the outset of any interviewing of a suspect[3]. In *Salduz v Turkey*, the conviction of a minor for aiding and abetting an illegal organisation had been largely based upon a statement given during police questioning without having had access to a lawyer. The Grand Chamber considered that in order to ensure fair hearing rights were 'practical and effective', Article 6(1) requires that 'as a rule, access to a lawyer should be provided as from the first interrogation of a suspect by the police, unless it is demonstrated in the light of the particular circumstances of each case that there are compelling reasons to restrict this right'. Further, 'even where compelling reasons may exceptionally justify denial of access to a lawyer, such restriction – whatever its justification – must not unduly prejudice the rights of the accused'. While it is possible for an individual to waive his rights under Article 6 either expressly or tacitly, provided waiver is 'established in an unequivocal manner and [...] attended by minimum safeguards commensurate to its importance', the making of incriminating statements during police interrogation but without access to a lawyer, which are subsequently used to secure a conviction, will 'in principle' irretrievably prejudice the rights of the defence. In this case, the applicant had been affected by the restrictions on access to a lawyer in that his statement to the police had formed the basis for the conviction. Neither the assistance provided subsequently by a lawyer nor the adversarial nature of the ensuing proceedings could have remedied the situation in the opinion of the Court[4].

The reasoning in *Salduz* was subsequently applied in *Panovits v Cyprus*. Here, the pre-trial questioning of a minor in the absence of his guardian and without being sufficiently informed of his right to receive legal representation was held to have violated his rights of defence under Article 6(3)(c) in conjunction with Article 6(1). The confession had been treated as voluntary and thus admissible as evidence, and although it was not the sole evidence on which the applicant had been convicted, it had constituted a significant element. For the Court, 'the passive approach adopted by the authorities in the present circumstances was clearly not sufficient to fulfil their positive obligation to furnish the applicant with the necessary information enabling him to access legal representation'. While he had been cautioned before being interviewed, 'it was unlikely that a mere caution in the words provided for in the domestic law would be enough to enable him to sufficiently comprehend the nature of his rights'. Nor had subsequent proceedings remedied the nature of the detriment suffered at pre-trial stage. The conclusion was that there had been a violation of Article 6(3)(c) in conjunction with Article 6(1), while the subsequent use at the trial stage of the applicant's confession was also considered to have given rise to a separate violation of Article 6(1)[5]. In contrast, in *Aleksandr Zaichenko v Russia*, the absence of legal representation at the time the applicant made self-incriminating statements following a roadside check of his vehicle had disclosed 'no significant curtailment of the applicant's freedom of action, which could be sufficient for activating a requirement for legal assistance already at this stage of the proceedings'. He had neither been formally arrested nor interrogated while in police custody, but had made the statements at the time of the inspection of the vehicle and in public before two witnesses[6].

---

1   *John Murray v United Kingdom* 1996-I, para 62.

2   *Averill v United Kingdom* 2000-VI, paras 55–61 at para 59. See too *Magee v United Kingdom* 2000-VI, paras 38–46 (use of statements obtained from a suspect in a coercive environment and without providing him with the benefit of legal assistance: violation of para (1) when taken with (3)(c). A further complaint of discrimination under Art 14 on the grounds that individuals arrested under prevention of terrorism legislation applying elsewhere in the UK were entitled to immediate access to a solicitor was dismissed since differences in treatment fell to be explained in terms of geographical location and not personal characteristics: paras 47–51).

3   Cf Committee for the Prevention of Torture *CPT Standards*, CPT/Inf/E (2002) 1 - Rev 2010, p 6 citing *2nd General Report*, CPT/Inf (92) 3, para 36: fundamental safeguards against ill-treatment during detention involved providing from the very outset of deprivation of liberty the rights to have the fact of detention notified to a third party, of access to a lawyer, and the right to request a medical examination by a doctor of his choice.

4   *Salduz v Turkey* [GC] 2008-..., paras 50–63, at paras 55 and 59 (violation of Art 1 in conjunction with Art 6(3)(c)). For discussion of waiver of the right to legal representation, see *Yoldaş v Turkey* (23 February 2010), paras 49–55 (voluntary and unequivocal waiving of the right to assistance of a lawyer while in police custody and after having been repeatedly informed of the right; moreover, the domestic court had excluded certain offences from the case file after the applicant subsequently denied some of the charges on the ground that they were based solely on the applicant's testimony in police custody: no violation).

5   *Panovits v Cyprus* 2008-..., paras 64–77, at paras 72 and 74, and paras 84–86 (and at paras 94–101, a further violation of the trial court's handling of prolonged confrontation between it and the applicant's defence lawyer was established, the lawyer having himself been the applicant in *Kyprianou v Cyprus* [GC] 2005-XIII, discussed at paras **5.78** and **5.80** above.

6   *Aleksandr Zaichenko v Russia* (18 February 2010), paras 46–51 at para 47 (*Salduz* distinguished as the applicant was not formally arrested nor interrogated in police custody: no violation).

5.205 The right to an oral hearing before a trial judge is implicit within the context of Article 6(1), for inherent in the notion of a fair trial is the accused's right to attend a first instance hearing[1], and provided this has occurred, there may be justification in certain cases for not holding an appeal hearing in public[2]. In *Cooke v Austria*, for example, the Court considered that the applicant's appeal based upon a plea of nullity had not required his presence before the supreme court. However, the refusal to allow him to attend the hearing of his appeal against sentence had given rise to a violation of Article 6(1) and (3)(c) as the supreme court had been called upon to consider whether the sentence should be reduced or increased, an issue that could not have been determined without allowing the court to gain a proper appreciation of the character of the applicant, thus rendering it essential that he should have been given the chance to attend and to participate[3].

1   See paras **5.114–5.118** above.

2   *Tierce and Others v San Marino* 2000-IX, para 95.

3   *Cooke v Austria* (8 February 2000), paras 40–44. See too *Pobornikoff v Austria* (3 October 2000), paras 24–33; and *Kari-Pekka Pietiläinen v Finland* (22 September 2009) (discontinuance of criminal appeal proceedings owing to the applicant's absence notwithstanding that he was legally represented at the hearing: violation of Art 6(1) in conjunction with Art 6(3)(c)). Cf *Prinz v Austria* (8 February 2000), paras 34–46 (no violation through the court's refusal to allow a legally-represented appellant to attend a hearing considering a plea of nullity which only involved issues of law and thus did not require his presence where he was legally represented).

Domestic court decisions on legal representation during investigation

5.206 In *Cadder v HM Advocate*, the Supreme Court held, overruling a number of earlier decisions of the High Court of Justiciary[1], that Article 6(3)(c), read in conjunction with Article 6(1), required that a detainee should have access to advice from a lawyer before he was subjected to police questioning unless, in the particular circumstances of the case, there were compelling reasons to restrict that right. The Convention therefore precluded, as a general rule, the admission in evidence of any incriminating answers obtained by the police from a detainee who was subjected to questioning without access to legal advice[2]. The decision resulted in emergency legislation[3]. The implications of the *Cadder* decision are being worked out in a number of subsequent cases[4].

1   *Paton v Ritchie* 2000 JC 271; *Dickson v HM Advocate* 2001 JC 203; *HM Advocate v McLean* 2010 SLT 73.

2   *Cadder v HM Advocate* 2010 SCCR 951.

3   Criminal Procedure (Legal Assistance, Detention and Appeals) (Scotland) Act 2010.

4   Other domestic cases concerning Art 6(3)(c) are discussed at paras 5.116, 5.118 and 5.201 above, and paras **5.209–5.210** and **5.212–5.214** below.

Provision of free legal assistance

5.207 The right to legal assistance or aid is normally dependent upon two conditions: inability to pay for the services of counsel; and the existence of factors suggesting that the interests of justice require the provision of legal aid[1]. As discussed, the provision of legal assistance is of relevance from the point at which a suspect is questioned. The obligation to provide legal assistance may also extend to the appeal stage. Despite the wording of the second aspect of the provision (which refers to the right of an accused to be represented by a legal representative 'of his own choosing'), where free legal aid is made available this is subject to limitation: thus in appointing counsel, the wishes of the accused should certainly be taken into account, but these can be overridden where there are relevant and sufficient reasons for doing so[2]. The issue of determination of the financial circumstances of an accused person has not given rise to much consideration[3]. On the other hand, significantly more discussion has taken place of whether free representation is required in the 'interests of justice' in particular cases. The principle is that the state must ensure that the accused has a 'realistic chance to defend him- or herself throughout the whole trial'[4]. Factors of relevance in determining whether the 'interests of justice' require the provision of free legal assistance include the seriousness of the offence and of the likely penalty if convicted[5], and at appeal stage, the likelihood of success[6]. Application of any pre-determined and unofficial policy may violate the guarantee. In *McDermitt v United Kingdom*, a stipendiary magistrate in Glasgow had rejected an application for legal aid in a criminal case involving a breach of the peace and assault of a police officer on the ground that as a matter of personal policy the magistrate considered that the 'interests of justice' could not be deemed to apply to charges of breach of the peace or of resisting arrest by a police officer. In this case, the matter was disposed of by way of friendly settlement in the form of an ex gratia payment by the government and acceptance that the application for legal aid had not been appropriately dealt with by the magistrate[7]. In *Perks and Others v United Kingdom*, the lack of legal aid in proceedings in English courts relating to the non-payment of the community charge was considered a violation of Article 6(1) taken with (3)(c). It was clear that the applicants had lacked sufficient financial means to pay for legal representation, and having regard to the complexity of the law and the potential severity of the penalty for non-payment (which had indeed involved imprisonment), the interests of justice had required that the applicants should have benefited from free legal representation[8]. The personal characteristics of the accused are also of relevance in determining whether the interests of justice require that legal aid should be provided. Particular care must be taken in this regard in relation to minors, persons with mental disabilities[8], and foreigners unfamiliar with the language and nature of the legal system[9].

1   *Quaranta v Switzerland* (1991) A 205, para 27.

2   *Croissant v Germany* (1992) A 237-B, para 29; 8295/78, *X v United Kingdom* (1978) DR 15, 242.

3   Eg *Pakelli v Italy* (1983) A 64, at para 34 (it was impossible in practice for the Court to

determine whether the accused had insufficient means to pay for his lawyer at the time of his trial: while there were factors indicating he was indigent, these were not sufficient to prove this beyond reasonable doubt; but taking into account his offer to the domestic court to show his lack of financial means and 'in the absence of clear indications to the contrary, they lead the Court to regard the first of the two conditions ... as satisfied').

4   *RD v Poland* (18 February 2001), para 49.

5   *Quaranta v Italy* (1991) A 205, at para 33 (the imposition of a sentence of more than 18 months' imprisonment was 'not a legal impossibility'; the maximum statutory penalty was three years' imprisonment; and even though the applicant was only sentenced to six months' imprisonment, 'free legal assistance should have been afforded by reason of the mere fact that so much was at stake'). The Court has since held that 'where deprivation of liberty is at stake, the interests of justice in principle call for legal representation': *Lloyd and Others v United Kingdom* (1 March 2005), para 134; for criticism see Trechsel *Human Rights in Criminal Proceedings* (2005), pp 273–275.

6   Although the complexity of appeal proceedings may militate in favour of the need for counsel: *Boner v United Kingdom* (1994) A 300-B, para 41. See para **5.208** below.

7   11711/85 *McDermitt v United Kingdom* (1987) DR 52, 244.

8   *Perks and Others v United Kingdom* (12 October 1999), paras 75–76, following *Benham v United Kingdom* 1996-III, paras 57–64 (severity of penalty faced by the applicant and the complexity of the law required that legal aid should have been made available). See also *Lloyd and Others v United Kingdom* (1 March 2005), para 134; *Beet and Others v United Kingdom* (1 March 2005), paras 38–40.

9   *Twalib v Greece* 1998-IV, para 53: 'the preparation of a notice of appeal must also be considered to require legal skills and experience and in particular knowledge of the grounds on which an appeal can be brought. It is noteworthy that the applicant, of foreign origin and unfamiliar with the Greek language and legal system, was unable to indicate any grounds of appeal in his written notice of appeal and that this failure resulted in his appeal being declared inadmissible ... In these circumstances, the Court considers that the interests of justice required that the applicant be granted free legal assistance in connection with his intended appeal to the Court of Cassation'. See also Trechsel *Human Rights in Criminal Proceedings* (2005), p 276.

Appellate proceedings

5.208 Certain judgments have considered the question of the provision of legal aid during appellate proceedings. In *Monnell and Morris v United Kingdom*, no legal aid had been available at the appeal stage. In rejecting the complaint, the European Court of Human Rights noted that each applicant had enjoyed free legal representation both in relation to the trial and also following conviction when they had been advised whether there existed any arguable grounds for appeal. The 'interests of justice' could not be 'taken to require an automatic grant of legal aid whenever a convicted person, with no objective likelihood of success, wishes to appeal after having received a fair trial at first instance in accordance with Article 6'[1].

The right of access to the criminal appeal court traditionally recognised by Scots law did result in a tension between an 'open door' policy and the principle of 'equality of arms' where legal aid had been refused. In three cases, the Court seemed to view an appellant's rights in Scotland as more illusory than real. Where a convicted person's grounds of appeal were considered as having no likelihood of success, no legal aid was made available; and in any case, the code of professional ethics of the Faculty of Advocates prohibited an advocate acting on an appellant's behalf in such circumstances. However, a convicted but unrepresented appellant was still entitled to address the court, and thus a situation could arise where the appeal court became convinced during proceedings that the case did indeed raise some legal issue of difficulty. In *Granger v United Kingdom*, the applicant had given statements to the police in connection with serious charges of wilful fire-raising and murder in which he had named the persons he believed responsible. At the trial he had denied having made any such statements, and had subsequently been convicted of perjury. He had been granted legal aid to cover the preparation, trial, and initial appeal stages of his case, but further legal aid for representation at the appeal hearing had been refused by a legal aid committee which had received counsel's opinion that there were no reasonable prospects of success[2]. The applicant decided to present his own appeal and read out a statement presented by his solicitor who had continued to give him advice but who had been precluded from appearing since he had no rights of audience. The appeal court then had decided that it could not dispose of the appeal without first obtaining a transcript of parts of the evidence, and had adjourned the hearing. The appeal failed. In Strasbourg, the Court considered that there had been a violation of paragraph (3)(c) taken together with paragraph (1). A matter of some complexity calling for an adjournment had arisen during the appeal, and legal aid at least for the adjourned hearing should have been made available since the applicant had not been in a position to oppose the arguments advanced by the Crown or even fully to comprehend the prepared address he had read out. In short, the appeal court had not had the benefit of 'expert legal argument from both sides on a complex issue'[3]. A subsequent practice direction made by the Lord Justice-General recommended the appeal court to adjourn in such cases to allow the review of the refusal of legal aid[4]. This allowed the disposal by the Commission of several other pending applications from Scotland[5]. Thereafter, statute provided that legal aid should be granted if an individual had established 'substantial grounds' for any criminal appeal and it was 'reasonable in the particular circumstances' that it should be awarded[6]. However, these reforms were also found wanting in the related cases of *Boner v United Kingdom*[7] and *Maxwell v United Kingdom*[8]. In each, the factual situation which had arisen in *Granger* was distinguished in that the legal issues had not been particularly complex, but the crucial matter was still the inability of each applicant who had been denied legal aid at the appeal stage to make an effective contribution to the proceedings. During Boner's trial, a prospective prosecution witness had entered the courtroom and spoken to a co-accused. The trial judge exercised his discretion to permit the witness to give evidence[9], but after his conviction, Boner had sought to have this discretion reviewed on appeal. In the second case, Maxwell's appeal had concerned his instructions to his representatives and the reliability and sufficiency of evidence. In neither instance had counsel concluded that there was any reasonable prospect of success and thus neither appellant had been legally represented. The Court again found a breach of Article 6(3)(c) in both applications. The Court attached importance to the severity of the penalty imposed by the trial courts (imprisonment for eight years and five years respectively) and 'the limited capacity of an unrepresented appellant to present a legal argument', leading to the finding that the interests of justice again had required the provision of legal aid in each case[10].

---

1   *Monnell and Morris v United Kingdom* (1987) A 115, at para 67, applying *Benham v United Kingdom* 1996-III, paras 57–64 (severity of likely penalty and complexity of the legal issues both required that the applicant be accorded legal aid).

2   In terms of the Legal Aid (Scotland) Act 1967, s 1(7).

3   *Granger v United Kingdom* (1990) A 174, paras 42–48 at para 47. (The Commission had been of the opinion that paragraph (3)(c) alone had been violated, and that no separate issue had arisen under para (1).)

4   In such circumstances, legal aid would in practice be awarded: cf *Boner v United Kingdom* (1994) A 300-B, paras 30–1; *Maxwell v United Kingdom* (1994) A 300-C, paras 27–28.

5   Eg 14778/89, *Higgins v United Kingdom* (1992) DR 73, 95.

6   By virtue of the Legal Aid (Scotland) Act 1986, s 25(2).

7   *Boner v United Kingdom* (1994) A 300-B.

8   *Maxwell v United Kingdom* (1994) A 300-C.

9   In terms of the Criminal Justice (Scotland) Act 1975, s 140.

10   *Boner v United Kingdom* (1994) A 300-B, paras 40–44; *Maxwell v United Kingdom* (1994) A 300-C, paras 37–41. The judgments are probably best appreciated as examples of the application of the principle of equality of arms: see para **5.104** above. The 'open door' policy relied to a large extent (as the Court at least noted) upon the principle that 'counsel cannot properly occupy the time of the court in advancing arguments which he knows to be without foundation'. The judgments do not address this point. The concurring opinion of the British judge, Sir John Freeland, perhaps further confuses the issues by seeming to read the text of Art 6's reference to the 'interests of justice' as if this reads as the 'appearance of injustice'. Leave to appeal in such instances is now required by the Criminal Procedure (Scotland) Act 1995, s 107. See too *Pham Hoang v France* (1995) A 243, paras 40–41 (the applicant had been acquitted at first instance but convicted on appeal and subsequently had sought to challenge the compatibility of the customs code with the Convention, but the refusal of legal aid taken with his lack of legal training had resulted in his inability to develop and present complex legal arguments: violation of Art 6); and *Biba v Greece* (26 September 2000), paras 26–31 (the applicant had been convicted of murder and sentenced to life imprisonment but had been denied access to the appeal court on account that legal aid was not available and he had been unable to pay for legal representation: violation of Art 6(1) and (3)(c)).

Domestic court decisions on free legal assistance and legislative reforms

5.209 The Scottish courts have considered issues relating to legal aid and Article 6(3)(c) in a number of cases. In *Shaw, Petitioner*, dealing with the withdrawal of a legal aid certificate, the court held that an order withdrawing legal aid should be made only where, by reason of specified conduct of the accused, it would be unreasonable for the solicitor to continue to act on his behalf, and the order would be a proportional response to the accused's conduct when measured against any potential effects on his right to a fair trial[1]. In *Buchanan v McLean*, the court considered a scheme under which a fixed sum of £500 was payable as legal aid for all work done in respect of a summary prosecution up to the first 30 minutes of any trial. It was argued that the system placed the solicitor in a situation which was in conflict with the client's interest, as the solicitor would maximise his remuneration by minimising the outlays devoted to the case (for example, by advising the client to plead guilty), and could find himself unable economically to prepare the case fully. It was also argued that there was an inequality of arms and an appearance of disadvantage to an accused. It was accepted that, in the instant case, the solicitor had done and would continue to do all that was necessary for the accused's defence, in accordance with the relevant professional codes. The court accepted that there might be cases in which the client would be affected in such a way that a breach of Article 6(3)(b) or (c) would occur. The court did not, however, accept that such a breach was inevitable in every case, or in the instant case. The court accepted that the fixed payment would not be sufficient to meet outlays and remuneration in the instant case, but that did not deprive the accused of a fair trial given his solicitor's willingness to prepare the case fully despite the lack of remuneration[2].

---

1   *Shaw, Petitioner* 1998 SCCR 672.

2   *Buchanan v McLean* 2002 SC (PC) 1. See also *Vickers v Buchanan* 2002 SCCR 637.

5.210 Following the decision of the High Court of Justiciary in *Buchanan v McLean*[1], cases predictably occurred in which solicitors refused to represent accused persons on the basis that the fixed fees available were inadequate, and in at least one of which a plea in bar was consequently upheld[2]. The Scottish Executive responded to that development, and to the decision in *Buchanan v McLean*, by proposing amendments to the legal aid system. Under the Convention Rights (Compliance) (Scotland) Act 2001 the Scottish Legal Aid Board was given a discretion to exempt cases from the fixed payment scheme where an accused would be deprived of the right to a fair trial as a result of the solicitor being paid under the scheme. The Board was also empowered to employ solicitors to represent accused persons who would otherwise be unrepresented. In addition, the Act enabled measures to be taken to extend the availability of legal aid in proceedings before tribunals[3].

---

1   *Buchanan v McLean* 2000 SCCR 682.

2   *McLeod v Glendinning* (February 2001, unreported), Sh Ct; and *Buchanan v McLean* 2002 SC (PC) 1 eg per Lord Hobhouse of Woodborough at para 78).

3   This enabled the Scottish Ministers to address the legal aid issue discussed in *S v Miller (No 1)* 2001 SC 977.

The effectiveness of legal representation

5.211 Several cases have considered the effectiveness of the legal representation provided by the state. The appointment of more than one legal representative at different stages of a criminal process is not in itself incompatible with Article 6, but the implications of this should be considered with some care[1]. The fact that a lawyer has been nominated to represent an accused does not in itself ensure effective assistance since the legal representative nominated may be unwilling or unable to act. In these cases, there will be a positive duty upon the state to replace the nominated lawyer 'or cause him to fulfil his responsibilities'[2]. This responsibility may also extend to the taking of appropriate action by the courts[3]. The issue may require detailed examination of the particular circumstances of each case. Minor shortcomings in representation will rarely be judged prejudicial. In *Kamasinski v Austria*, the European Court of Human Rights conceded that some of the applicant's complaints had some substance (his defence could perhaps have been conducted in another way, and his lawyer had to some extent acted contrary to what the applicant considered to be in his own best interests), but could not be satisfied that the circumstances of his legal representation during the trial had indicated a failure to provide effective legal assistance[4]. In contrast, the situation in *Daud v Portugal* was such as to lead to a violation of the sub-paragraph when read with paragraph (1). The first officially assigned lawyer had not taken any action on the applicant's behalf because of illness, and the applicant was only told of the appointment of his second lawyer three days before the beginning of his trial. This period was considered inadequate to have allowed the lawyer to have mastered the complex file, to have visited the applicant in prison, and to have prepared his defence. The state had also been aware of 'a manifest shortcoming' on the part of the first lawyer and of the applicant's difficulties in securing a practical and effective defence. It was also clear that the trial court should have been aware that the applicant had not had any proper legal assistance, and thus ought to have adjourned the trial on its own initiative. The Court reiterated that assigning counsel to an individual does not in itself discharge state obligations, although a state cannot be deemed responsible for every shortcoming of a legal aid lawyer on account of the legal profession's independence which implied that 'the conduct of the defence is essentially a matter between the defendant and his counsel'. Only where the lack of 'effective representation is manifest or sufficiently brought to their attention in some other way' would state responsibility be engaged[5]. This was held to be the case in *Kemal Kahraman and Ali Kahraman v Turkey* where two lawyers, despite having been appointed on the request of a criminal court to assist the applicants, had failed to attend any of the six hearings held at that court. In finding that Article 6(3)(c) had been violated, the Court noting that the criminal court 'must have been aware of the lawyers' failure to fulfil their obligations' but that no measures had been taken 'to ensure that the lawyers comply with their duties'[6]. Although the majority of cases considered have concerned state-appointed legal aid lawyers, the Court has left open the possibility for a state to be held liable for the ineffectiveness of privately financed counsel[7].

1   *Croissant v Germany* (1992) A 237-B, para 27.

2   *Artico v Italy* (1980) A 37 paras 33–36 at para 33 (no effective assistance from a nominated lawyer; state inactivity despite attempts by the accused to remedy the situation resulted in a breach of the requirement). This does not mean an individual has unlimited choice in selecting legal representation: 7572/76 etc, *Ensslin v Germany* (1978) DR 14, 64.

3   *Alimena v Italy* (1991) A 195-D, paras 18–20 (disposal of an appeal by the court without the presence of the applicant's lawyer).

4   *Kamasinski v Austria* (1989) A 168, paras 63–71. Cf *Milone v Italy* (dec) (23 March 1999)
     (non-representation of the applicant in appellate proceedings owing to his lawyer being on
     strike: a state cannot be held responsible for a failure on the part of a lawyer chosen by the
     applicant, and application declared inadmissible); *Rutkowski v Poland* (dec) 2000-XI (refusal
     of a court-appointed lawyer to lodge an appeal after having studied the case file and considered
     there were no grounds: application declared inadmissible, but observed that the authorities
     could not remain passive where an issue concerning legal assistance has been brought to their
     attention); and *Franquesa Freixas v Spain* (dec) 2000-XI (the lawyer assigned to the applicant
     (who was himself a lawyer) had not been a specialist in criminal law; but the applicant had not
     furnished any plausible evidence that the lawyer had been incompetent: inadmissible as
     manifestly ill-founded).

5   *Daud v Portugal* 1998-II, paras 37–43 at para 38. See too *Kamasinski v Austria* (1989) A 168,
     para 65; *Imbrioscia v Switzerland* (1993) A 275, paras 38–44; *Stanford v United Kingdom*
     (1994) A 282-A, paras 27–32; and *Sannino v Italy* 2006-VI, para 49 (the lawyer chosen by the
     applicant withdrew from the case, but the lawyer appointed by the court to represent the
     applicant was not informed of his appointment and did not appear, which led to the applicant
     being represented at each hearing by a different replacement lawyer: violation of Art 6(3)(c)).

6   *Kemal Kahrman and Ali Kahraman v Turkey* (26 April 2007), paras 35–37 at para 36.

7   *Sannino v Italy* 2006-VI, at para 49: 'a State cannot be held responsible for every shortcoming
     on the part of a lawyer appointed for legal aid purposes or chosen by the accused. It follows
     from the independence of the legal profession from the State that the conduct of the defence is
     essentially a matter between the defendant and his counsel, whether counsel be appointed
     under a legal-aid scheme or be privately financed'. The Court relied upon *Cuscani v United
     Kingdom* (24 September 2002), para 39 despite the fact that this case concerned Art 6(3)(e)
     and not 6(3)(c), but in which the trial judge was cast in the role of the 'ultimate guardian of the
     fairness of the proceedings'.

Domestic decisions on effectiveness of legal representation

5.212 In *Anderson v HM Advocate*, it was held that defective representation
had the potential to compromise the right to a fair trial. Since *Anderson*, there
have been a number of appeals brought on the basis of ineffective representation[1].
In *AJE v HM Advocate*, the appellant alleged that although he had provided his
legal representatives with material which concerned medical evidence which the
Crown intended to rely on at trial, this had not been used by his counsel. In view
of this he alleged that his defence had not been prepared and presented in
accordance with his wishes[2]. In allowing the appeal, the court held that an accused
person was not only entitled to the presentation of his defence at his trial, but also
to the due preparation of that defence in advance of trial, and that there were
circumstances in which the court could hold that the conduct of the defence at
the trial was such as to deny the accused a fair trial. In the case at issue, senior
counsel had decided that certain relevant and significant lines of defence urged
on him by the appellant should not be pursued and consequently imperilled the
whole defence on the strategy of bringing out contradictions and inconsistencies
in the evidence and prior statements of the complainers. Although cases such as
Anderson and *AJE* made it clear that in order to succeed in an appeal on the
basis of ineffective representation it was necessary to prove that the conduct of
the defence had resulted in a miscarriage of justice, they nevertheless provided a

clear basis for challenging the fairness of the trial on the basis of ineffective representation. In *Grant v HM Advocate*, it was made clear that there were strict criteria for granting leave to appeal on the grounds of defective representation. Lord Justice Clerk Gill observed that 'many of the increasing number of *Anderson* appeals are based on allegations of breach of instructions that rest on the say-so of the appellant himself ... In my view this court should not countenance the granting of leave in such cases'. Instead the court ruled that an *Anderson* ground of appeal ought not to be put forward unless (1) it set out a prima facie case that on the information available to trial counsel the defence was not properly put before the court, and that in consequence there was a miscarriage of justice; (2) it specified that allegation on all material points; and (3) there was objective support for the allegation[3].

1   *Anderson v HM Advocate* 1996 JC 29.

2   *AJE v HM Advocate* 2002 JC 215.

3   *Grant v HM Advocate* 2006 JC 205; see also Shiels 'Case Comment: *Grant v HM Advocate*' 2006 SLT (News) 131; Strachan, 'Is *Anderson* Finally Dead?' 2006 SLT (News) 203. There are numerous subsequent Scottish cases concerned with defective representation. There is an analogous line of authority in England and Wales: see eg *R (Adams) v Secretary of State for Justice* [2010] QB 460.

Domestic decisions on other aspects of Article 6(3)(c)

5.213 A legislative provision which prohibited a person accused of a sexual offence from representing himself, and provided for the appointment of a solicitor by the court where the accused failed to instruct a solicitor of his own choice, was held to be compatible with Article 6(3)(c)[1]. The inability of a lay person to represent an accused did not involve any violation of Article 6(3)(c)[2]. It has been held that it was not a violation of Article 6(3)(c) for the prosecution to rely on the evidence of an interpreter, who had interpreted during the procedures followed at the police station and also, subsequently, at a consultation between the accused and his solicitor, where the evidence was to relate solely to the procedure followed at the police station[3].

1   *McCarthy v HM Advocate* 2008 SCCR 902.

2   *Robbie the Pict v HM Advocate* 2002 SCCR 213.

3   *R (Bozkurt) v Thames Magistrates' Court* [2002] RTR 15. This decision might be contrasted with *Wales v HM Advocate* 2001 SCCR 633, discussed at para **5.201** above.

5.214 There have also been a number of domestic cases concerned with conflicts of interest affecting the legal representatives of accused persons. In *Hoekstra v HM Advocate*[1], for example, it was held that the counsel formerly instructed on behalf of the appellants should not have attempted to represent the Crown at a procedural hearing relating to their appeal, but that his misjudgment had not deprived the appellants of their right to a fair trial. In *James v HM Advocate*, on the other hand, it was held that the accused had not received a fair trial by reason of an undisclosed conflict of interest on the part of his solicitor[2].

1   *Hoekstra v HM Advocate* 2002 SCCR 135. See also *R (Haase) v District Judge Nuttall* [2009] QB 550 (no right under Art 6 to an independent and impartial prosecutor).
2   *James v HM Advocate* 2006 SCCR 170.

Article 6(3)(d): the right to call and to cross-examine witnesses

5.215 Article 6(3)(d) provides that everyone charged with a criminal offence has the rights 'to examine or have examined witnesses against him and to obtain the attendance and examination of witnesses on his behalf under the same conditions as witnesses against him'. The matter is closely related to the requirement that proceedings be adversarial in nature[1]. While the text refers specifically to 'witnesses', the term is to be afforded an autonomous interpretation[2]: general fairness considerations require that experts be treated in a similar fashion[3]. Although the sub-paragraph contains two distinct rights, the right to cross-examine witnesses on the one hand and the right to call witnesses on the other, the latter guarantee has been restrictively interpreted and is of considerably less practical relevance than the former[4]. The Court has held that it does not entail 'the attendance and examination of every witness on the accused's behalf' as 'its essential aim, as is indicated by the words "under the same conditions" is a full "equality of arms" in the matter', and thus domestic courts may properly assess the question of the relevance of any proposed evidence within the confines of ensuring a fair trial[5].

1   See para **5.104** above.
2   Eg *Kostovski v Netherlands* (1989) A 166, para 40; *Perna v Italy* [GC] 2003-V, para 29
3   *Bönisch v Austria* (1985) A 92, para 29 (complaints under para (3)(d) considered under the general requirements of para (1); an expert witness allegedly independent was more akin to an expert witness for the prosecution; there had been no opportunity for the defence to obtain their own expert, and consequently there was a violation of para (1)).
4   For rare examples of a case in which a violation was found in relation to the right to call witnesses see *Vidal v Belgium* (1992) A 235-B; and *Borisova v Bulgaria* (21 December 2006), para 47 (the applicant was not allowed to call any witnesses in her defence even though she stated on several occasions that she wanted to do so and that they could refute the prosecution's evidence). See also Trechsel *Human Rights in Criminal Proceedings* (2005), pp 322–323.
5   *Engel and Others v Netherlands* (1976) A 22, at para 91. See also *Kamasinski v Austria* (1989) A 168, para 91 (absence of witnesses at a trial raised no Art 6 issue as the conviction was not based upon their evidence); *Perna v Italy* [GC] 2003-V, paras 29–32 (failure to allow a journalist facing a criminal charge of defamation of the public prosecutor to cross-examine the complainant, but no indication as to what additional information would have been obtained in the particular case, and no violation of Art 6(1) taken with (3)(d)); and *Orhan Çaçan v Turkey* (23 March 2010), paras 31–43 (inability to challenge incriminating statements which were retracted but nonetheless relied upon by the domestic court in convicting the applicant: violation of Art 6(1) in conjunction with Art 6(3)(d)).

Cross-examination of witnesses

5.216 The right to cross examine witnesses has been the subject of a considerable number of applications. In essence, the rights of an accused must include 'an adequate and proper opportunity to challenge and question a witness against him, either at the time the witness was making his statement or at some later stage of the proceedings'[1]. At the very least, an accused must have a real opportunity to cross-examine key witnesses against him[2]. Special arrangements for the taking of evidence from family members[3] or from high-ranking officials[4] are not precluded as long as there is the opportunity to challenge such evidence in an adversarial manner. Similarly, while evidence in a criminal trial must in principle be produced at a public hearing in the accused's presence to allow it to be challenged through adversarial proceedings, the use of statements obtained at earlier stages of a criminal process (for example, during police inquiries or at judicial examination) is not inconsistent with the provision provided the rights of the defence have been respected[5]. Crucially, the Court has held that, '[i]n particular, the rights of the defence are restricted to an extent that is incompatible with the requirements of Article 6 if the conviction is based solely or in a decisive manner, on the depositions of a witness whom the accused has had no opportunity to examine or have examined either during the investigation or at trial'[6]. This means that there will be no violation of Article 6(3)(d) in the event that the evidence of the witness, who the accused was unable to confront, was not the sole or decisive basis for the conviction[7]. Thus the Court did not find a breach of the provision in *Artner v Austria*. It had not been possible to secure the attendance of the victim at the hearing, but her written statements had been read out before the trial court and had been corroborated by other evidence, and in these circumstances it was not possible to conclude that the rights of the defence had been infringed to such an extent that there had been a violation of a fair trial[8]. Where however the accused has not had the opportunity to cross examine a witness whose testimony is deemed to be the sole or decisive basis for the conviction, there will be a violation of Article 6(3)(d)[9]. The domestic authorities are required to make reasonable efforts to ensure the attendance and examination of the witness and their failure to do so will result in a violation of the applicant's right to confrontation[10].

---

1   *Kostovski v Netherlands* (1989) A 166, at para 41. Cf *Popov v Russia* (13 July 2006), paras 175–189 (refusal to hear defence witnesses despite previous rulings to do so: violation).

2   *AM v Italy* 1999-IX, paras 24–28 (conviction based exclusively on statements taken in the USA before the trial: violation of Art 6(1) taken along with Art 6(3)(d)). Cf *CG v United Kingdom* (19 December 2001), paras 35–43 (while there was substance in criticisms of the trial judge in persistently interrupting the applicant's defence counsel, the trial as a whole had not been rendered unfair).

3   *Unterpertinger v Austria* (1986) A 110, paras 30–31.

4   *Bricmont v Belgium* (1989) A 158, paras 77–89.

5   *Kostovski v Netherlands* (1989) A 166, para 41; cf para 43 (importance of courts being able to observe the demeanour of witnesses in order to help determine reliability of evidence); *Saïdi v France* (1993) A 261-C, paras 43–44 (pre-trial statements constituted the sole basis of the applicant's conviction, but at no stage was the applicant able to examine the witnesses who had made the statements; and accordingly there had been a breach of paras (1) and (3)(d)); 35253/97, *Verdam v Netherlands* (31 August 1999) (statements made by rape victims to police officers were used in evidence at the subsequent trial; despite the absence of these witnesses at the trial, one witness had been examined by the accused's lawyer, and the conviction was corroborated by other evidence: application declared inadmissible). Provision

for challenge at pre-trail confrontation hearings rather than during actual trials are found in several domestic legal systems: for a survey, see, eg, Harding, Fennell, Jörg and Swart *Criminal Justice in Europe* (1995) However, it is not immediately clear whether the right to have the assistance of counsel at this stage is implied: cf *Isgrò v Italy* (1991) A 194-A, para 36 (absence of both prosecutor and accused's representative at pre-trial confrontation: no violation); for criticism, see Summers *Fair Trials: The European Criminal Procedural Tradition and the European Court of Human Rights* (2007), pp 148–155.

6   *Van Mechelen and Others v Netherlands*, 1997-III.

7   For a contrasting approach to the regulation of witness evidence, see the US Supreme Court decision in *Crawford v Washington* 124 S Ct 1354 (2004).

8   Eg *WS v Poland* (19 June 2007), paras 53–64.

9   Eg *Pello v Estonia* (12 April 2007), para 35; *Sadak and Others v Turkey* 2001-VIII, para 67; *Taal v Estonia* (22 November 2005); *Mild and Virtanen v Finland* (26 July 2005). However, *impossibilium nulla est obligatio*: provided that the authorities cannot be accused of a lack of diligence in their efforts to award the defendant an opportunity to examine the witnesses in question, the witnesses' unavailability as such does not make it necessary to discontinue the prosecution: see eg *Artner v Austria* A 242-A, para 21; and *Haas v Germany* (dec) (17 November 2005).

10   *Artner v Austria* (1992) A 242-A, paras 19–24. But cf dissenting judgment of Judge Vilhjálmsson: '… it is not always possible to apply strictly the important rule set out in [Art 6(3)(d)], despite the fact that it is stated in this very same paragraph that the rights set out therein are minimum rights. Unfortunately, the interpretation of this rule takes our Court into forbidden territory so to say, ie the assessment of evidence, which should be the reserved domain of the national courts.' See also *Al-Khawaja and Tahery v United Kingdom*, case pending before the Grand Chamber (inability to cross-examine witnesses whose statements had constituted decisive elements in securing convictions, warnings having been given to the jury as to the dangers of relying on written statements without having had the opportunity to see the witness or hear a cross-examination) [violation established in Chamber judgment (20 January 2009), paras 34–48].

Domestic court decisions on the right to call and to cross-examine witnesses

5.217 The domestic courts have had to consider Article 6(3)(d) in a number of cases. Cases concerned with the protection of vulnerable witnesses[1] and the admission of evidence or questioning as to the character or sexual history of complainers in cases concerned with sexual offences[2] are discussed below. Many other cases have considered hearsay evidence[3]. The Scottish courts have applied the 'sole or decisive' test developed by the Strasbourg court. The point was perhaps most fully considered in *Campbell v HM Advocate*, where the court stated:

'Most of the situations in which it has been held by the [Strasbourg] Court that there had been a violation of Art 6(1) and (3)(d) could not arise in Scotland. Against the requirement for corroboration of all crucial facts, a conviction could not be based solely on the evidence of a single witness, whether in primary or in secondary form. Violations of the Convention right have been established where the principal witness against the accused has not been made available for questioning or, in circumstances where there have been a number of principal witnesses, where none of them has been made so available. No case was cited to us in which a violation was held to have occurred in circumstances where the accused had had an opportunity to question or have questioned the complainer or other direct or central witness and other supporting evidence was in statement form. 'To a decisive extent', as used in the European authorities, appears to be concerned with the significance of the evidence as a matter of weight. It is not concerned with any rule that a conviction cannot be based on a single source of evidence. The fact that the hearsay is required to meet the rule about corroboration does not of itself render that hearsay 'decisive' in the European sense.

In these circumstances we are not persuaded that in every case in which hearsay evidence is a necessary ingredient of the Crown's corroborated proof there will be a violation of Art 6(1) and (3)(d). It will, however, be necessary for the trial judge to address, in the context of the whole evidence in the case, the significance of any hearsay evidence relied on by the Crown and to take appropriate action to ensure that the accused's entitlement to a fair trial is not violated thereby. Where in a jury trial the verdict is left to the jury's determination, the judge will require to give to the jury, as the factual decision-makers, appropriate directions as to how they should approach the hearsay evidence. Such directions are necessary to protect the accused against the disadvantage which may arise from the absence of an opportunity to cross-examine in person the maker of a statement, the truth or reliability of which is in issue at the trial. The extent, if any, to which the credibility of the maker of the statement has been effectively tested by the adducing of evidence under sec 259(4) of the [Criminal Procedure (Scotland)] Act [1995] will also require to be taken into account. The guidance by Lord Justice-Clerk Gill in *Nulty v HM Advocate*[4] (para 37) should be borne in mind – though failure to adhere to his Lordship's exact words will not in every case lead to a miscarriage of justice.'[5]

In England, where the absence of a requirement for corroboration means that hearsay evidence may be the sole evidence against an accused, the Supreme Court has challenged the aptness of the 'sole or decisive' test[6].

---

1   Para **5.221** below.

2   Para **5.222** below.

3   See for example, in relation to Scotland, the cases of *McKenna v HM Advocate* 2000 JC 291, *Daly v HM Advocate* 2003 SCCR 393, *McKenna v HM Advocate (No 2)* 2003 SCCR 399, *HM Advocate v M* 2003 SCCR 632, *Humphrey v HM Advocate* 2008 JC 362 and *Allison v HM Advocate* 2009 SCCR 387, amongst many others, in addition to those cited below.

4   *Nulty v HM Advocate* 2003 JC 140.

5   *Campbell v HM Advocate* 2004 JC 1.

6   *R v Horncastle* [2010] 2 AC 373. The court declined to follow the Chamber judgment in *Al-Khawaja and Tahery v United Kingdom* (20 January 2009) [case now pending before the Grand Chamber]. See also *Grant v The Queen* [2009] 1 AC 1.

Protection of vulnerable witnesses

5.218 The European Court of Human Rights has accepted that special arrangements may be appropriate in certain cases to protect vulnerable witnesses, for example by withholding their identity or by screening them while they are giving evidence in court. However, such measures taken on the ground of expediency cannot be allowed to interfere with the fundamental right to a fair trial[1]. The matter is generally considered in terms of the fairness of the admissibility of evidence. Over the course of time, the Court has elaborated its approach. In *Kostovski v Netherlands,* convictions had been based upon statements made to the police and to the examining magistrate by witnesses who had wished to remain anonymous in order to protect their identity. The defence had only been given the opportunity to submit written questions to one of the witnesses indirectly through the examining magistrate. For the Court, 'if the defence is unaware of the identity of the person it seeks to question, it may be deprived of the very particulars enabling it to demonstrate that he or she is prejudiced, hostile or unreliable', a situation giving rise to obvious dangers. Further, the absence of the witnesses had precluded the trial courts from observing their demeanour under questioning, and while the courts had observed caution in evaluating their statements, 'this can scarcely be regarded as a proper substitute for direct observation'. While Article 6 did not preclude reliance on information given by anonymous witnesses at the investigation stage, 'the subsequent use of anonymous statements as sufficient evidence to found a conviction, as in the present case, is a different matter' which had involved limitations on defence rights irreconcilable with fair trial guarantees, even taking into account the need to respond to the threat imposed by organised crime[2]. In *Lüdi v Switzerland*, statements had been given by an undercover police officer whose actual identity was not known to the applicant, but whom he had met on five occasions. The state had sought to argue that the need to protect the undercover agent's anonymity was vital in order to continue with the infiltration of drug-dealers, but the Court considered that the legitimate interest in protecting the identity of a police officer engaged in such investigations could have been met in a manner which was also consistent with respect for the interests of the defence. Here, neither the investigating judge nor the trial courts had been willing to hear the officer as a witness or to carry out a confrontation to allow his statements to be contrasted with the applicant's assertions, nor had the defence enjoyed even the opportunity to question the officer to attempt to cast doubt on his credibility, and thus there had been a violation of the guarantee[3].

1   *Kostovski v Netherlands* (1989) A 166, para 44. See also Committee of Ministers Recommendation R (97) 13.

2   *Kostovski v Netherlands* (1989) A 166, paras 38–45 at paras 42–44; see too *Windisch v Austria* (1990) A 186, paras 25–32.

3   *Lüdi v Switzerland* (1992) A 238, paras 44–50 (violation of para (3)(d) in conjunction with para (1)). This case was distinguished in *Teixeira de Castro v Portugal* 1998-IV, para 37 discussed at para **5.129** above (undercover police officers had incited the commission of an offence leading to a violation of Art 6(1): in *Lüdi*, the police officer had been sworn in, the investigating judge had been aware of his mission and a preliminary investigation had been opened).

5.219 In *Doorson v Netherlands*, the Court sought to provide a comprehensive statement of its approach. Again, the issue concerned the protection of witnesses in the prosecution of an individual suspected of drug dealing. The Court first reiterated that the use of anonymous witness statements was not in itself incompatible with the Convention since the protection of a witness's rights to life, liberty of the person, and respect for private and family life all were relevant considerations. Accordingly states 'should organise their criminal proceedings in such a way that those interests are not unjustifiably imperilled' by balancing the interests of the defence with those of witnesses required to testify. A decision to protect the anonymity of a witness had to be justified by reasons which were both relevant and also sufficient in each case to ensure that the interests of a witness properly outweighed those of the accused. Further, 'handicaps under which the defence laboured' must be 'sufficiently counterbalanced by the procedures followed by the judicial authorities', for example by allowing counsel to ask whatever questions were deemed appropriate other than those which could result in the identification of the witness. Finally, any evidence obtained from witnesses 'under conditions in which the rights of the defence cannot be secured to the extent normally required by the Convention' must be treated with particular care, and thus a conviction should not be based solely or even to a decisive extent upon evidence from anonymous witnesses. Here, the Court was satisfied that 'counterbalancing' procedures had been in place, and it was sufficiently clear that the trial court had not based its conviction of the applicant solely or to a decisive extent on the evidence of the two anonymous witnesses[1].

---

1   *Doorson v Netherlands* 1996-II, paras 67–76 at paras 70, 72 and 76 (circumstances justifying the retention of anonymity of two witnesses considered as appropriate, and their evidence had been treated with the necessary caution and circumspection).

5.220 However, careful balancing is required. In *Van Mechelen and Others v Netherlands*, the Court held that there had been a violation of Article 6 since the defence had not only been unaware of the identity of the police officers but had also been prevented from observing their demeanour while under direct questioning and thus from testing their reliability. The state had not been able to explain to the Court's satisfaction why such extreme limitations on the rights of an accused had been required, and there had been a failure to counterbalance the handicaps under which the defence laboured in presenting its case. Further, the Court considered that the position of a police officer in such situations 'is to some extent different from that of a disinterested witness or a victim' on account of his close link with the prosecution, and consequently the use of an anonymous police witness 'should be resorted to only in exceptional circumstances'[1]. The Court's jurisprudence also highlights the importance of the domestic court's assessment of the need for the witness to remain anonymous. In *Visser v Netherlands*, the Court criticised the domestic authorities for failing to assess 'the reasonableness of the personal fear of the witness either as this had existed when the witness was heard by the police or when he or she was heard by the investigating judge nearly six years later'[2]. As the domestic court had failed to clearly establish that there had been a need for anonymity, the Court held that the anonymity could not be justified and that there was no need to examine further whether the procedures in place could have 'counterbalanced' the difficulties faced by the defence[3]. The Court has found a violation of this provision in a number of cases involving the sexual abuse of children, in which the authorities had failed to allow the defence to test the reliability of the witness[4]. However, this right may be waived. For example, in *B v Finland*, the applicant was held to have waived his confrontation rights by failing to avail himself of the possibility to put questions to the witness during the pre-trial investigation[5].

1   *Van Mechelen and Others v Netherlands* 1997-III, paras 56–65 at para 56.

2   *Visser v Netherlands* (14 February 2002), para 47.

3   See also *Krasniki v Czech Republic* (28 February 2006) ('[n]either did the Regional Court carry out such an examination into the seriousness and substantiation of the reasons for granting anonymity to the witness when it approved the judgment of the District Court which had decided to use the anonymous witnesses in evidence against the applicant').

4   Eg *WS v Poland* (19 June 2007), paras 61–63; and *Bocos-Cuesta v Netherlands* (10 November 2005), paras 64–74.

5   *B v Finland* (24 April 2007), paras 44–45; *SN v Sweden* 2002-V; and *Klimentyev v Russia* (16 November 2006) (the applicant and his lawyer both stately expressly that they had no objections to beginning or concluding the examination of the case in the absence of the witness).

Domestic court decisions on the protection of vulnerable witnesses

5.221 These cases were considered by the High Court of Justiciary in *HM Advocate v Smith*, which concerned an application by the Crown prior to a trial to allow undercover police officers to give evidence without revealing their true identities (other than to the trial judge, if required) and while concealed from the public and the press (but not the accused, their lawyers or the jury) by screens. The officers had been involved in a drug trafficking investigation, and it was maintained that their safety and their effectiveness in future operations would be jeopardised if these precautions were not taken. The court granted the application. In practice, it is not uncommon for evidence to be given by undercover police officers whose true identities are not revealed to the accused. In such cases, it is unnecessary for the accused to know the true identities of the officers in order to receive a fair trial: their identities have no bearing on their evidence[1]. In *R v Davis*, on the other hand, it was held that the concealment of the identify of witnesses had been inconsistent with the right to a fair trial: the effect of the protective measures imposed had been to prevent defence counsel from investigating the witnesses or pursuing in cross-examination any effective challenge to the decisive evidence they had given, with the consequence that he had been hampered in the conduct of the defendant's case in a manner and to an extent which rendered the trial unfair[2].

1   *HM Advocate v Smith* 2000 SCCR 910. See also *R (Al Fawwaz) v Governor of Brixton Prison* [2002] 1 AC 556.

2   *R v Davis* [2008] 1 AC 1128. The decision was followed by the enactment of emergency legislation: see the Criminal Evidence (Witness Anonymity Act) 2008.

Domestic cases on the character or sexual history of complainers in sexual offences

5.222 Article 6 has been considered in relation to the leading of evidence, in a rape trial, as to the complainer's character and previous sexual history. In England and Wales, a statutory provision excluding all evidence of a previous sexual relationship between the complainant and the defendant had to be interpreted, in accordance with s 3 of the Human Rights Act 1998, as permitting the admission of such evidence where it was so relevant to the issue of consent that to exclude it would endanger the fairness of the trial under Article 6[1]. In Scotland, where the legislation allowed such evidence to be admitted where it was relevant to guilt and its probative value was significant and likely to outweigh any risk of prejudice to the proper administration of justice, the provisions were held to be compatible with Article 6[2]. That conclusion was subsequently endorsed by the European Court of Human Rights[3].

---

1   *R v A (No 2)* [2002] 1 AC 45.

2   *Moir v HM Advocate* 2005 1 JC 102; see also *DS v HM Advocate* 2007 SC (PC) 1.

3   *Judge v United Kingdom* (dec) (8 February 2011), discussed at para **5.147** above. See also Council of Europe *Procedural Protective Measures for Witnesses* (2006).

Article 6(3)(e): free assistance of an interpreter

5.223 Article 6(3)(e) provides that an accused has the right to have the 'free assistance of an interpreter if he cannot understand or speak the language used in court'. The provision is given a common-sense and straightforward interpretation. It requires the provision of an interpreter to allow the translation of documents and the interpretation of statements necessary for a fair trial[1], but does not require a written translation of every document in the process since the assistance required is that only necessary to allow the accused 'to have knowledge of the case against him and to defend himself, notably by being able to put before the court his version of events'[2]. This, too, may require the state authorities to ensure the quality of interpretation provided is adequate to achieve this goal: a state does not discharge its obligations merely by appointing and paying for an interpreter[3]. 'Free' is unqualified. In *Luedicke, Belkacem and Koç v Germany*, the Court declined to read into the provision any suggestion that an accused could be made to bear the costs of interpretation if convicted since this would amount to 'limiting in time the benefit of the Article' depriving it of much of its effect 'for it would leave in existence the disadvantages that an accused who does not understand or speak the language used in court suffers as compared with an accused who is familiar with that language', a disadvantage the provision sought to attenuate[4]. In *Cuscani v United Kingdom*, the Court underlined the importance of the guarantee by finding a violation of the provision, even though the accused's senior counsel had quite clearly waived the right to an interpreter. In spite of his client's lack of proficiency in English, his counsel had told the judge that, in the absence of the interpreter, he would 'make do and mend' and the case proceeded accordingly. The Court was unconvinced that the accused's right to a fair trial had been guaranteed and, in finding a violation of Article 6(1) and Article 6(3)(e), held that the 'ultimate guardian of the fairness of the proceedings was the trial judge who had been clearly apprised of the real difficulties which the absence of interpretation might create for the applicant'[5].

1   *Luedicke, Belkacem and Koç v Germany* (1978) A 29, para 48. See also para **5.198** above.

2   *Kamasinski v Austria* (1989) A 168, para 74.

3   *Kamasinski v Austria* (1989) A 168, para 74. See also *Diallo v Sweden* (dec) (5 January 2010) (absence of an authorised interpreter during initial questioning by a customs officer who had a command of the applicant's language, and involvement of authorised interpreter during subsequent pre-trial proceedings: no appearance of unfairness).

4   *Luedicke, Belkacem and Koç v Germany* (1978) A 29, paras 42–48. See too *Öztürk v Germany* (1984) A 73, paras 57–58; and *Husain v Italy* (dec) 2005-II.

5   *Cuscani v United Kingdom* (24 September 2002), paras 38–40.

Domestic court decisions on the free assistance of an interpreter

5.224 The scope of the right to an interpreter was considered in the case of *Erkurt v Higson* which concerned the role of an interpreter at an intermediate diet, at which the accused had chosen to plead not guilty. Although an interpreter had been provided by the court, he had neither been sworn in nor had he translated anything other the date of the trial when advised by the clerk of court. In finding that the accused had not been denied a fair trial, the appeal court held that it was necessary to 'make a clear distinction between the function of an interpreter present in court at an intermediate diet such as the one in this case, where it is anticipated that only formalities are to be carried through, and an interpreter sworn faithfully to translate evidence at a trial diet'. It did however note that the need for an interpreter could also arise in a situation 'where an accused is pleading guilty and a detailed Crown narrative of the circumstances of the offence is given'[1].

1   *Erkurt v Higson* 2004 JC 23. The difficulties involved where the accused requires the assistance of a translator were also considered in ! *Ucak v HM Advocate* 1998 JC 283.

ARTICLE 7: 'NO PUNISHMENT WITHOUT LAW': THE PROHIBITION AGAINST RETROACTIVE CRIMINAL OFFENCES OR PENALTIES

Introduction

5.225 Article 7 embodies certain fundamental aspects of the rule of law and provides additional safeguards against arbitrariness in the criminal process through the prohibition of retroactive imposition of criminal liability or penalty[1]. Paragraph

(1) of the provision provides first that 'no one shall be held guilty of any criminal offence on account of any act or omission which did not constitute a criminal offence under national or international law at the time when it was committed', and secondly, that no heavier penalty may be imposed 'than the one that was applicable at the time the criminal offence was committed'. The nature and purpose of Article 7 was succinctly stated by the Court in *Kokkinakis v Greece*: it not only prohibits retrospective application of the criminal law to the disadvantage of an accused, but more generally 'embodies ... the principle that only the law can define a crime and prescribe a penalty (*nullum crimen, nulla poene sine lege*) and the principle that the criminal law must not be extensively construed to an accused's detriment, for instance by analogy'[2]. Paragraph (2) seeks to protect the prosecution of crimes recognised as criminal in accordance with the general principles of law 'recognised by civilised nations'[3]. No derogation from this provision is permissible in time of war or other national emergency in terms of Article 15[4].

---

1   For discussion, see Barreto 'La Jurisprudence de la nouvelle Cour europeénne des Droits de l'Homme sur l'Article 7 de la Convention europeéne des Droits de l'Homme' in Donatsch, Forster and Schwarzenegger (eds) *Strafrecht, Strafprozessrecht und Menschenrechte: Festschrift für S Trechsel zum 65. Geburtstage:* (2002), pp 3–16; and Murphy 'The Principle of Legality in Criminal Law under the European Convention on Human Rights' [2010] EHRLR 192.

2   *Kokkinakis v Greece* (1993) A 260–A, at para 52. An example of an extensive construction of a legal rule by analogy and which violated Art 7 is found in *Başkaya and Okçuolu v Turkey* [GC] 1999-IV, para 42 (imprisonment of publisher under a provision of domestic law relating only to editors). For a domestic example, see *Smith v Donnelly* 2001 JC 65.

3   See para **5.237** below.

4   See paras **3.23** and **4.147** above.

Retroactive application of criminal offences

5.226 The retroactive application of the criminal law is prohibited by Article 7 which thus reflects the importance attached by the ECHR to the general principle that domestic law must be adequately accessible[1]. Within the context of the criminal code, an individual must be able to know 'from the wording of the relevant provision and, if need be, with the assistance of the courts' interpretation of it, what acts and omissions will make him liable'[2]. The prohibition extends to criminal liability imposed both by statute and by development of the common law. However, absolute legal certainty is by no means required on account of the very nature of a court's responsibilities in interpreting the law: the test is one of reasonable foreseeability as determined by the quality of the law in question, even where this requires an individual to take appropriate legal advice[3].

---

1   Cf the requirements of 'lawful', etc under Art 5, and of 'prescribed by law' or 'in accordance with law' under Arts 8–11. See paras **3.62–3.71** and **4.161–4.168** above and paras **6.49,7.31**, **7.69** and **8.22–8.25** below. See *Achour v France* [GC] 2006-IV, paras 41–43: 'When speaking of "law" Article 7 alludes to the very same concept as that to which the Convention refers elsewhere when using that term, a concept which comprises statute law as well as case-law and implies qualitative requirements, including those of accessibility and foreseeability'.

2   *Kokkinakis v Greece* (1993) A 260-A, at para 52. See too 8710/79, *X Ltd and Y v United Kingdom* (1982) DR 28, 77 (domestic courts may clarify but not change the constituent elements of a common law crime to the detriment of an accused).

3   *Cantoni v France* 1996-V, paras 29–36 (the manager of a supermarket ought to have appreciated that he ran the risk of prosecution for the unlawful sale of medicinal products, and consequently there was no violation of Art 7). See too 8141/78, *X v Austria* (1978) DR 16, 141 (the degree of precision must be assessed by reference of the particular technical knowledge of the individuals to whom the law is addressed). But see *Pessino v France* (10 October 2006), where the Court held that there had been a violation of Art 7 even though the applicant was a professional and able to engage the services of lawyers (the Court of Cassation's departure from precedent was difficult or even impossible for the applicant to foresee).

Development of the criminal law

5.227 Article 7 does not preclude the further development of the criminal law, particularly when the law seeks to reflect ECHR expectations that domestic law will provide adequate protection against threats to physical integrity[1]. There is an 'inevitable element of judicial interpretation' inherent in any legal rule on account of the need for elucidation of any doubtful issue and for the law's adaptation to new and changing circumstances: indeed, in European legal systems 'the progressive development of the criminal law through judicial law-making is a well entrenched and necessary part of legal tradition'[2]. The point is well illustrated by two related applications in which the removal by the English criminal courts of an immunity which protected an accused in certain circumstances against a criminal charge of rape was considered. In *SW v United Kingdom* and in *CR v United Kingdom*, the applicants had sought during their trials to rely upon a common law principle that a husband could not be found guilty of the rape of his wife. According to the applicants, a series of recent court decisions had indeed affirmed this general principle, but in each of their trials the English courts had revised the principle so as to lead to the conviction of the applicants for rape and attempted rape respectively. The Court was not convinced, however, that in either case the requirements of Article 7 had been breached. Providing always that 'the resultant development is consistent with the essence of the offence and could reasonably be foreseen', the gradual clarification and development of rules of criminal liability through judicial interpretation was thus not inconsistent with Article 7. Here, domestic law on marital rape had developed in such a way as to have resulted in the removal of the immunity as a reasonably foreseeable event; in any case, the abandonment of the principle was entirely consistent with the Convention's concern for the protection of human dignity[2].

1   See *G v France* (1995) A 325-B, paras 24–27 (consistent case law on the notions of 'violence' and 'abuse of authority'; further, retrospective legislation operated in favour of the applicant: no violation of Art 7(1)). For further discussion of positive obligations, see paras **4.83–4.86** above, and **6.120–6.121** below.

2   *SW v United Kingdom* (1995) A 335-B, paras 34–47 at para 36; *C v United Kingdom* (1995) A 335-C, paras 32–44 at para 34.

3   *SW v United Kingdom* (1995) A 335-B, at para 36; *CR v United Kingdom* (1995) A 335-C, at para 34.

5.228 This concern to uphold core fundamental rights concerning physical integrity is also apparent in other cases involving loss of life. However, it is in every case necessary to assess whether the applicable law at the relevant time made provision for the punishment of the conduct in question. This is made clear in the related cases of *Streletz, Kessler and Krenz v Germany* and *K-HW v Germany*. In the first case, the applicants had been senior government ministers in East Germany who had been directly responsible for a 'shoot to kill' policy to deal with those seeking to escape to the west, while the applicant in the second case had been an East German border guard who had shot dead an East German citizen in 1972. Each of the applicants had subsequently been convicted after reunification of the two German states of intentional homicide under relevant provisions of East Germany's criminal code. The Court considered that the domestic law applying at the time of the commission of the offences had been defined with sufficient accessibility and foreseeability, and while there had been a broad divide between legal provision and official practice, the first three applicants themselves had largely been responsible for this situation. Further, the Court felt compelled to consider applicable rules of international law dealing with protection of the right to life and of freedom of movement. These principles – particularly the pre-eminence of the right to life – justified a strict interpretation by the German Federal courts of the legal provisions in force in the former communist state. Nor could even a private soldier such as the applicant in the second case show total and blind obedience to official orders which had been in clear violation of both East German law and international legal norms. Accordingly, no violation of Article 7 was established[1].

---

1   *Streletz, Kessler and Krenz v Germany* [GC] 2001-II, paras 49–107, and *K-HW v Germany* [GC] 2000-II, paras 44–113 (at para 106 in each judgment the Court noted that the offences could also have given rise to issues under international legal rules on crimes against humanity, but found it unnecessary to consider this point further). For discussion, see Rytter 'No Punishment without Guilt: The Case Concerning German Prosecution of a Former GDR Border Guard' (2003) 21 NQHR 39. See too *Glässner v Germany* (dec) 2001-VII (application of these principles in respect of the conviction of a former East German public prosecutor in respect of his submissions seeking a sentence which was particularly harsh in respect of a dissident: inadmissible). See also *Baumgarten v Germany* [2004] EuGRZ 143, [2004] EuroCLY 1345 [UN Human Rights Committee] (conviction for homicide of persons seeking to flee GDR).

Decisions of the domestic courts on retroactive application of criminal offences

5.229 The domestic case of *Interfact Ltd v Liverpool City Council* concerned defendants who had been convicted of offences relating to pornography, contrary to a 1984 Act of Parliament. It subsequently emerged in 2009 that the Act of Parliament was unenforceable, as the Government had failed to comply with an EU directive which required such legislation to be notified to the EU Commission. Notification was then effected, following which identical legislation was brought into force, but without retrospective effect. Leave to appeal out of time was sought by the defendants on the basis that their convictions were incompatible inter alia with Article 7. Leave was refused. The 1984 Act was valid and in force, notwithstanding that domestic courts would have been obliged under the European Communities Act 1972 to disapply it if the failure to comply with the notification requirement had been known about. The conduct prohibited by the 1984 Act was clearly defined. In any event, the case law of the European Court of Human Rights did not require contracting states to undo all the consequences of a national law which was later held to be incompatible with the Convention, but acknowledged that the principle of legal certainty dispensed with any such need[1].

Scottish courts have considered this aspect of Article 7 in relation to the common law offence of breach of the peace, which was argued (unsuccessfully) to be so widely defined as to offend against legal certainty[2]. The judicial development of the law of rape, so as to remove the supposed necessity that force be employed, was also held to be compatible with Article 7[3]. A similar conclusion was reached by the English courts in respect of the scope of the defence of reasonable chastisement, in *R v H*[4].

---

1   *Interfact Ltd v Liverpool City Council* [2011] 2 WLR 396.

2   See *Smith v Donnelly* 2001 JC 65 and *Jones v Carnegie* 2004 JC 136. Cf *Custers and Others v Denmark* (3 May 2007), paras 95–96 (the applicants, who were Greenpeace protesters, could have foreseen that the area that they had entered was not 'freely accessible' within the meaning of the criminal code).

3   *HM Advocate v PH* 2002 SCCR 927. See also *Matthew v Aitken* 2004 SCCR 515 (whether condition in fishing licence lacking in specification). Other issues considered in relation to Article 7 have included corporate manslaughter *(Transco plc v HM Advocate (No 1)* 2004 JC 29) and public indecency *(Webster v Dominick* 2005 1 JC 65).

4   *R v H* [2002] 1 Cr App R 7.

Extension of periods in which prosecutions may be brought

5.230 The retroactive application of provisions extending the time in which a prosecution can be raised was considered in *Coëme and Others v Belgium.* In this case, two of the applicants had been found guilty of forgery and uttering forgeries, offences classified as crimes *(crimes)* in domestic law but which had been treated in the prosecution as less serious offences *(délits)* on account of extenuating circumstances. Determination of whether the offences had been time-barred had been accordingly considered by the domestic courts having regard to the limitation period for these less serious indictable offences, a period which had been extended by the retrospective application of a statute which had allowed for the extension of this period. For the Court, this situation did not give rise to a violation of Article 7. Domestic law followed the general principle that procedural rules apply immediately to proceedings that are under way, save where expressly provided to the contrary, and treated laws modifying rules on limitation as legislation on matters of jurisdiction and procedure rather than affecting the criminal nature of the behaviour when it took place[1].

1   *Coëme and Others v Belgium* 2000-VII, paras 145–151.

Retroactive imposition of a heavier criminal penalty

5.231 The second aspect of Article 7(1) is a prohibition on the retroactive imposition of a heavier penalty than the one applying at the time of the act or omission[1]. For the Court, the concept of a 'penalty' has to be given an autonomous Convention meaning to render Article 7 an effective guarantee: in consequence, it may be necessary to go behind appearances to examine the substance of a measure[2]. The guarantee only applies to proceedings which lead to a conviction or the imposition of a criminal penalty, and will thus not apply to decisions affecting rules of evidence[3], storage of DNA[4], bankruptcy proceedings[5], or extradition[6]. Similarly, a requirement to register under the Sex Offenders Act 1997 in respect of offences committed before the statute came into force did not constitute a 'penalty' for the purposes of Article 7, for while the registration followed upon a conviction for a criminal offence, the essential nature of the requirement was preventative rather than punitive[7]. On the other hand, the scope of the provision will include an increase in the length of imprisonment which may be imposed for default in the payment of a fine[8], the retroactive extension of a period of deprivation of liberty[9], and the retroactive imposition of a harsher sentence through the replacement of a period of imprisonment with deportation accompanied by a lengthy prohibition on re-entering a country[10].

1   *Ecer and Zeyrek v Turkey* 2001-II, paras 29–36 (the applicants were sentenced in terms of a statute which had increased the maximum penalty in respect of terrorist offences but in relation to an offence carried out before the legislation came into effect; the Court rejected the state's contention that the offence had been a continuing one and the reference in the indictment to the period before the entry into force of the statute had referred only to the commencement of the offence on account of the lack of a clear finding to this effect by the trial court: violation).

2   *Welch v United Kingdom* (1995) A 307-A, para 27.

3   6683/74, *X v United Kingdom* (1975) DR 3, 95.

4   *Van der Velden v Netherlands* (dec) 2006-XV.

5   8988/80, *X v Belgium* (1981) DR 24, 198.

6   7512/76, *X v Netherlands* (1976) DR 6, 184.

7   *Ibbotson v United Kingdom* (dec) (21 October 1998). This approach was followed, in relation to football banning orders, in *Gough v Chief Constable of Derbyshire* [2002] QB 459. See also *Gardel v France* 2009-…, paras 34–47 (registration on national sex-offenders register for a period of 30 years commencing on the date of completion of prison sentence: inadmissible).

8   *Jamil v France* (1995) A 317-B, paras 30–36 (four-month period of imprisonment upon default increased to two years; violation of Art 7(1)).

9   *M v Germany* 2009-…, paras 177–137 (extension of the applicant's preventative detention beyond the maximum period authorised at the time of his placement had amounted to the imposition of an additional penalty imposed retroactively).

10   *Gurguchiani v Spain* 2009-…, paras 32–44 (deportation and ten year exclusion in lieu of a sentence of 18 months' imprisonment).

5.232 Careful assessment of the nature of particular measures is required. The provision only applies to the imposition of a 'penalty'. Remission of a sentence or a change in a regime for early release does not form part of the 'penalty' for the purposes of Article 7[1]. In *Kafkaris v Cyprus,* the applicant complained of amendments to prison regulations issued under prison disciplinary law which had altered the definition of mandatory 'life imprisonment' and which had effectively increased the applicant's sentence from a fixed term to an indefinite term lasting for the remainder of his life. This was as a result of the removal of life prisoners from the categories of prisoners enjoying the possibility of remission of sentences. For the Grand Chamber, the first issue was what the 'penalty' of life imprisonment actually entailed at the material time. Even although the trial court had indicated when passing sentence that 'life imprisonment' should be for the remainder of the applicant's life, relevant executive and administrative authorities had clearly assumed that this would be tantamount to a maximum period of 20 years' imprisonment. This factor thus permitted the Court to conclude that there had been a violation of Article 7 as regards the quality of the law applicable at the material time. Domestic law had not been 'formulated with sufficient precision as to enable the applicant to discern, even with appropriate advice, to a degree that was reasonable in the circumstances, the scope of the penalty of life imprisonment and the manner of its execution'. However, and crucially, the Grand Chamber did not find that the retrospective imposition of a heavier penalty had occurred. The essence of the challenge had centred upon the execution of the sentence as opposed to the 'penalty' imposed by the trial court. Certainly, changes in prison legislation and in conditions of release had indeed rendered the imprisonment 'effectively harsher'. However, these amendments could not be 'construed as imposing a heavier "penalty" than that imposed by the trial court on account of the changes in the prison law since in view of substantive criminal law it could not be maintained that the penalty of a life sentence could clearly be taken to have amounted to twenty years' imprisonment'. There had thus been 'no element of retrospective imposition of a heavier penalty'[2].

---

1   11653/85, *Hogben v United Kingdom* (1986) DR 46, 231. See also 26293/95, *Hosein v United Kingdom* (28 February 1996); and *Szabó v Sweden* (dec) (27 June 2006) (transfer of a prisoner under the Convention on the Transfer of Sentenced Persons ((1982) ETS 112) and resulting in a longer *de facto* term of imprisonment: inadmissible).

2   *Kafkaris v Cyprus* [GC] 2008-..., paras 143–152, at paras 150 and 151, noting at para 151 that 'issues relating to release policies, the manner of their implementation and the reasoning behind them fall within the power of [states] in determining their own criminal policy'.

5.233 Where there are differences between the criminal law in force at the time of the commission of the offence and subsequent criminal laws enacted before a final judgment is rendered, domestic courts are required to apply the law whose provisions are the more favourable to the individual. Article 7 thus guarantees 'not only the principle of non-retrospectiveness of more stringent criminal laws but also, and implicitly, the principle of retrospectiveness of the more lenient criminal law', a principle 'embodied in the rule that where there are differences between the criminal law in force at the time of the commission of the offence and subsequent criminal laws enacted before a final judgment is rendered, the courts must apply the law whose provisions are most favourable to the [accused]'[1].

However, Article 7 does not prohibit the imposition of a heavier sentence on appeal[2], providing always that the sentence was available to a trial court at the time of conviction. Careful assessment of domestic law is necessary. In *Achour v France,* the appeal court had relied on new legislation concerning repeat offenders to increase the applicant's eight year prison sentence to one of 12 years. The applicant sought to argue that the appeal court had retrospectively applied the harsher provisions of the new legislation. In finding a violation of Article 7, the Chamber held that the relevant provision of the new Criminal Code 'should not have been applied retrospectively and that in the second set of proceedings the applicant should have been tried as a first offender and not as a recidivist', as his original conviction pre-dated the new legislation. In contrast, the Grand Chamber considered that the application of the law had been foreseeable since the commission of another offence before the termination of the statutory period carried the risk of conviction as a recidivist, a situation that had been consistent in domestic law for the past century. In its opinion, the applicant should have been able 'to foresee the legal consequences of his actions and to adopt his conduct accordingly[3].'

---

1   *Scoppola v Italy (no 2)* [GC] 2009-..., paras 108–109 at para 109 (reversing the Commission in the case of 7900/77, *X v Germany* (1978) DR 13, 70), and at para 108: 'it is consistent with the principle of the rule of law ... to expect a trial court to apply to each punishable act the penalty which the legislator considers proportionate. Inflicting a heavier penalty for the sole reason that it was prescribed at the time of the commission of the offence would mean applying to the defendant's detriment the rules governing the succession of criminal laws in time. In addition, it would amount to disregarding any legislative change favourable to the accused which might have come in before the conviction and continuing to impose penalties which the State – and the community it represents – now consider excessive'.

2   Cf *Howarth v United Kingdom* (21 September 2000), paras 28 and 31, at para 28: (the fact that the applicant had completed his non-custodial sentence was 'not strictly relevant to the Court's consideration of the reasonableness of the length of the proceedings' for the purposes of Art 6; nor did the facts disclose any violation of Art 3).

3   *Achour v France* [GC] 2006-IV, para 44–46 at para 53 (Chamber judgment (10 November 2004), paras 46–51).

Decisions of the domestic courts on retroactive imposition of a heavier penalty

5.234 The imposition of automatic life sentences for a second serious offence under English legislation enacted in 1997 was challenged in *R v Offen* as being incompatible with Article 7 where the first offence pre-dated the 1997 legislation. The court however held that the life sentence was imposed in respect of the second offence alone: the offender was not being sentenced again, or having his sentence increased, for the earlier offence[1]. In *Flynn v HM Advocate*, the Privy Council interpreted legislation requiring the retrospective fixing of punishment parts for life prisoners as allowing account to be taken of events that had occurred since they were originally sentenced, thereby avoiding an effective increase in their sentences[2]. In *R (Uttley) v Secretary of State for the Home Department*, the application to a prisoner of early release arrangements which were in force at the time of his conviction but not at the time when the offences were committed was held by the House of Lords to be compatible with Article 7: in considering whether the applicant's rights under Article 7 had been infringed, the proper comparison was between the sentence which the court had imposed for the offences (12 years) and the penalty which could have been imposed for those offences at the time when they were committed (life imprisonment). As was noted, this has a bearing on the correctness of certain of the views expressed in *Flynn* as to the applicability of Article 7 in that case[3]. This approach was followed by the High Court of Justiciary in *Wilson v Harvie,* a case concerning an increase in the sentencing powers available to a sheriff in summary proceedings (but no increase in the sentence which the court could have imposed for the offence, albeit in proceedings on indictment)[4].

The application of orders of a preventive nature to persons previously convicted of criminal offences has been held not engage Article 7, on the basis that the order does not amount to a penalty[5]. A similar conclusion was reached in relation to civil recovery proceedings[6].

---

1   *R v Offen* [2001] 1 WLR 253.

2   *Flynn v HM Advocate (No 1)* 2004 SC (PC) 1. In *McIlvanny v United Kingdom* (dec) (6 March 2007), the European Court of Human Rights declared a complaint relating to an identical case inadmissible on the basis that: 'Insofar as the applicant complains under Art 7 that the courts imposed a longer punishment part than the executive did, the Court notes that at the time at which the applicant's offence was committed the maximum sentence of life was applicable: it cannot, therefore, be said, that the High Court retrospectively increased this sentence'.

3   *R (Uttley) v Secretary of State for the Home Department* [2004] 1 WLR 2278.

4   *Wilson v Harvie* 2010 JC 105.

5   See eg *Gough v Chief Constable of Derbyshire* [2002] QB 459 (football banning orders) (the point was not pursued on the further appeal, reported at [2002] QB 1213); *Boyle v HM Advocate* 2007 SCCR 286 (notification requirements imposed on sex offenders).

6   *McGuffie v Scottish Ministers* 2006 SLT 1166 (recovery of property obtained through unlawful conduct). This might be contrasted with *Togher v Revenue and Customs Commissioners* [2008] QB 476, which concerned the consequences of a failure to pay the amount specified in a confiscation order. At the time of the offences, service of the default period of imprisonment had the effect of discharging the pecuniary obligation. The applicant served the default period of imprisonment but, under the legislation then in force, the sum due under the confiscation order remained payable. This was held to be incompatible with Art 7.

Confiscation orders under the drugs trafficking legislation

5.235 Particular issues have arisen in relation to the Drug Trafficking Offences Acts in the United Kingdom in regard to confiscation orders applying to the proceeds of crimes which took place before the statute entered into force[1]. In *Welch v United Kingdom*, the applicant had been sentenced to 22 years' imprisonment for drug trafficking in respect of offences occurring before the entry into force of the 1986 legislation. In addition, the court had imposed a confiscation order under the statute requiring the payment of some £67,000. In default of payment, he would have been liable to a consecutive sentence of two years' imprisonment. The applicant argued that the confiscation order was in the nature of a penalty: an order could only be made following upon a criminal conviction, and by confiscating the proceeds (as opposed to the profits) of drug dealing, the order went beyond the notions of reparation and prevention, and the order took into account the degree of the accused's culpability. In response, the Government submitted that an order sought to deprive only the profits of drug trafficking and to remove the value of the proceeds from possible future use in the drugs trade, and in consequence, the order was essentially a confiscatory and preventive measure. The Commission had agreed with these submissions from the state, but only by a decision of seven votes to seven with a casting vote being decisive in ruling that there had been no violation of Article 7. For the Court, the starting-point was whether the measure had been imposed following a criminal conviction. However, other factors were also of relevance in any assessment, including 'the nature and purpose of the measure in question; its characterisation under national law; the procedures involved in the making and implementation of the measure; and its severity'. In the present case, the conclusion was that the confiscation order was indeed a 'penalty' within the meaning of Article 7. The imposition of a confiscation order was not only dependent upon the establishment of a criminal conviction, but the legislative background of the 1986 Act also suggested that the statute's purposes were not only preventive in nature but also contained punitive elements. In particular, there was ' a strong indication of ... a regime of punishment' because of the 'sweeping statutory assumptions ... that all property passing through the offender's hands over a six-year period is the fruit of drug trafficking unless he can prove otherwise'. Further, 'the fact that the confiscation order is directed to the proceeds involved in drug dealing and is not limited to actual enrichment or profit; the discretion of the trial judge, in fixing the amount of the order, to take into consideration the degree of culpability of the accused; and the possibility of imprisonment in default of payment by the offender' all pointed to the conclusion that the retroactive application of the legislation in the particular case violated Article 7[2].

1   See further Bell 'The ECHR and the Proceeds of Crime Legislation' [2000] Crim LR 783. For discussion of dismissals of challenges based upon Art 6(2) by the Privy Council in *HM Advocate v McIntosh (No 1)* 2001 SC (PC) 89 (reversing the earlier decision of the High Court of Justiciary) and subsequently by the Court in *Phillips v United Kingdom* 2001-VII, discussed at para 5.190 above.

2   *Welch v United Kingdom* (1995) A 307-A, paras 26–36 at paras 28 and 33. See also *Yildirim v Italy* (dec) 2003-IV (confiscation of vehicle).

5.236 In *Welch*, the Court also sought to stress that the judgment 'did not call into question in any respect the powers of confiscation conferred on the courts as a weapon in the fight against the scourge of drug trafficking'[1]. The Commission had the opportunity to reiterate this in declaring a subsequent application inadmissible. In *Taylor v United Kingdom*, the appellant had been convicted in

1986 of drug trafficking in respect of offences committed between 1974 and 1979, and again in 1994 in respect of offences committed between 1990 and 1993. On the latter occasion, the trial court had also made a confiscation order for more than £15 million under the 1986 Act, relying on the applicant's own admission that he had benefited from drug trafficking during the period between 1974 and 1979, and on the evidence tendered during the proceedings in respect of the second period between 1990 and 1993. The applicant sought to challenge the confiscation order but only in so far as it concerned this earlier period. Following *Welch*, the Commission accepted that the confiscation order constituted a 'penalty' for the purposes of Article 7, but it did not consider there had been any retroactive application of the law in relation to the confiscation order made in respect of the earlier period. As regards the period between 1974 and 1979, the applicant would had been aware only when committing offences during 1990 and 1993 that he would have been liable to a confiscation order since the 1986 Act had been in force for some time. The 1986 legislative provisions linked the power to make a confiscation order to the accused's having 'benefited' from criminal drug trafficking, rather than to his conviction, and thus there had been no retroactive application of the law[2].

---

1   *Welch v United Kingdom* (1995) A 307-A, at para 36.

2   31209/96, *Taylor v United Kingdom* (10 September 1997): 'according to the Act a person may be considered to have 'benefited' from drug trafficking without having been convicted, while a person who has been convicted is not necessarily considered to have benefited. Following this logic, the Crown Court, in order to make the confiscation order, did not rely on the applicant's previous conviction but on his own admission that he had 'benefited' from drug trafficking between 1974 and 1979'. See too *Elton v United Kingdom* (dec) (11 September 1997) (complaints that a confiscation order violated Art 6(2) as well as Art 7 declared inadmissible).

Crimes against humanity

5.237 The prosecution of crimes against humanity is specifically protected by paragraph (2) of Article 7. 'Crimes against humanity' includes war crimes and genocide, offences regarded as criminal in accordance with the general principles of law 'recognised by civilised nations', a phrase wider than customary international law or legal obligations based upon international treaty[1]. Similar considerations apply as in the case of other criminal laws and penalties. It is necessary to examine the applicable law at the relevant time the acts were committed, although absolute certainty in the law is not necessary. Careful assessment is required of the state of the development of an area of law whose content today is still of some uncertainty. In *Jorgic v Germany,* the applicant was a national of Bosnia and Herzegovina of Serb origin who had ben convicted in Germany of genocide. He complained that, as the first person to have been convicted of this crime in the German courts, it had not been foreseeable that these courts would have interpreted the notion of genocide so broadly (to include 'intent to destroy') as to encompass his conduct. In this case, the Court found that that at the material time several scholars and international authorities had already suggested 'genocide' be construed in the manner that the German courts had done, even although other bodies (such as the International Criminal Tribunal for the Former Yugoslavia) had not done so. In consequence, 'the applicant, if need be with the assistance of a lawyer, could reasonably have foreseen that he risked being charged with and convicted of genocide for the acts he had committed in 1992'[2]. In *Kononov v Latvia*, the applicant had been convicted of war crimes committed during an attack carried out as a member of a Soviet commando unit during the Second World War. He sought to argue that the acts of which he had been convicted had not constituted an offence under either domestic or international law at the time of their commission. The charges had been brought under an article of the 1961 Criminal Code which referred to 'relevant legal conventions' in defining those acts that could be categorised as war crimes. The Grand Chamber found that the conviction had been based on international rather than domestic law, and thus the lack of reference to such offences in domestic legislation at that time was not decisive. However, in the opinion of the Court it was also possible to conclude that, by 1944, international laws and customs of war were themselves sufficiently settled so as to allow for the punishment of individuals for such crimes, and thus there had been a sufficiently clear legal basis for the conviction and punishment as the applicant's acts at the time of commission had constituted offences defined with sufficient accessibility and foreseeability by the laws and customs of war[3].

The state of development of international law was also of key relevance in another Grand Chamber judgment, *Korbely v Hungary*, in which a violation of Article 7 was established. The applicant had been charged with offences allegedly committed while an army officer during the 1956 Budapest uprising. He had sought unsuccessfully to argue that the actions had amounted to homicide (and thus that their prosecution was now statute-barred) rather than crimes against humanity. While the act in question had constituted an offence defined with sufficient accessibility at the time it was committed, the Court was not satisfied it had been foreseeable that the act would have been classified as a crime against humanity as this notion was understood in 1956: while murder within the meaning of common Article 3 of the Geneva Conventions could have provided a basis for such a conviction, other elements derived not from common Article 3 but from the international-law elements inherent in the notion of crime against humanity at that time also had to be present for that classification to apply. Because the domestic courts had not examined whether these additional criteria had been applicable, it was open to question whether the constituent elements of a crime against humanity had been met[4].

---

1   Cf *Streletz, Kessler and Krenz v Germany* [GC] 2001-II, paras 90–105, and *K-HW v Germany* [GC] 2001-II, paras 92–105 (international law may be of relevance in assessing whether, at the time of commission, acts were defined with sufficient accessibility and foreseeability). See also 268/57, *X v Belgium* (1957) YB 1, 239 at 240–241; and *Naletilić v Croatia* (dec) 2000-V (applicant facing charges of crimes against humanity and breaches of the Geneva Conventions before the International Criminal Tribunal for Former Yugoslavia: application under ECHR, Art 7 was inadmissible for, even if it applied, it would have done so under para (2) rather than para (1)). British law makes provision for the trial and punishment of such offences in statutes such as the Genocide Act 1969, the Criminal Justice Act 1988, s 134 (in respect of acts of

torture), and the War Crimes Act 1991 (crimes committed in German-occupied territories during the 1939–45 war).

2   *Jorgic v Germany* 2007-IX, paras 100–116. See also *Kolk and Kislyiy v Estonia* (dec) 2006-I (no prescription period in respect of crimes against humanity: inadmissible); and *Van Anraat v Netherlands* (dec) 2010-... (given that a norm of customary international law which prohibited the use of mustard gas as a weapon of war in international conflict was in existence at the time, the conviction for supplying Iraqi authorities with chemical substances used to produce poisonous gas was reasonably foreseeable: inadmissible).

3   *Kononov v Latvia* [GC] 2010-..., paras 196–223.

4   *Korbely v Hungary* [GC] 2008-..., paras 74–95.

Chapter 6

Private and family life; and education

INTRODUCTION

6.01 Family life lies at the heart of the protection accorded by Articles 8 and 12[1]. Article 12 guarantees the right to marry and to found a family, while Article 8(1) provides that 'everyone has the right to respect for his private and family life, his home and his correspondence'. Additionally, Article 2 of Protocol no 1 requires that the religious and philosophical convictions of parents are taken into account in the provision of education by the state. These articles reflect commonplace values found in domestic legal systems across Europe. The scope of each guarantee, however, varies. Article 12's focus is upon the traditional or nuclear family unit. As such, it is of limited application. Article 2 of Protocol no 1 calls for respect for parents' religious and philosophical convictions in the provision of education, and here the guarantee is conferred upon the holders of parental rights irrespective of marital status. In contrast, Article 8 protection extends far beyond the family as a traditionally understood legal entity. Its central concern is protection for the home and the determination of family relationships. These guarantees are buttressed by other ECHR concerns such as fair hearings in determination of family law disputes[2] and protection for the physical integrity of family members[3]. The provisions also concern development of personality. Most obviously, Article 2 of Protocol no 1 provides for access to education, while the scope of Article 8 further extends to determination of personal relationships and complements other safeguards for an individual's moral and physical integrity[4]. None of these rights is, however, immune from a state's right to take measures derogating from its obligations in time of emergency in terms of Article 15[5].

---

1   ECHR, Prot 7, Art 5 also provides for equality of rights and responsibilities between spouses, but the United Kingdom has not ratified this protocol.

2   In particular, fair hearing considerations can often arise in discussion of Art 8 concerns as to child care determinations: see further para **6.57** below.

3   Under Art 2, near relations of a deceased may enforce obligations upon a state as 'victims', while deportation or extradition may also give rise to Art 3 considerations: see paras **4.06** and **4.130–4.134** above. A further link between Arts 3 and 8 is clear in the protection of physical integrity in situations falling short of violation of Art 3: see paras **6.119–6.121** below. Article 5 issues may also arise in respect of the exercise of parental decision-making (cf *Nielsen v Denmark* (1988) A 144, discussed at para **4.152**, above) or detention for the educational supervision of a child: see para **4.182** above.

4   In particular, Arts 3 and 5 are concerned with physical integrity, while Art 9 protects freedom of thought and conscience and Art 11 the right of association. See paras **4.88–4.93** and **4.155** above and paras **7.13–7.15** and **7.125** below.

5   See further paras **3.23–3.25** above.

ARTICLE 12: THE RIGHTS TO MARRY AND TO FOUND A FAMILY

6.02 Article 12 provides two separate but related rights: to marry; and to found a family. The second aspect is not a condition of the first and the inability to conceive or parent a child, does not remove the right to marry. Neither right is absolute for in each case the right is specifically subject to regulation by domestic legal systems, but always providing domestic law does not unduly impair the very essence of the rights[1]. There has been comparatively little use made of this provision. Strasbourg interpretation has lacked the creativity displayed elsewhere in this area, although certain recent judgments exhibit a willingness to extend the scope of the guarantee, particularly where there appears to be an emerging European consensus upon an issue[2]. The right to marry is further restricted to the 'formation of marital relations not their dissolution', and Article 12 does not imply any right to divorce[3]. Article 12 relates to the right to found a family, but the circumstances in which interferences with family life between parents and an existing child may be justified fall to be determined under Article 8[4].

1   *Christine Goodwin v United Kingdom* [GC] 2002-VI, paras 98 and 99.

2   See eg *Christine Goodwin v United Kingdom* [GC] 2002-VI, at para 103 (revising the line of case law in judgments such as *Rees v United Kingdom* (1986) A 106): the fact that fewer countries permit the marriage of transsexuals than recognise the change of gender itself does not support the suggestion that the matter should be entirely left to a state's margin of appreciation as such 'would be tantamount to finding that the range of options open ... included an effective bar on any exercise of the right to marry'; and while the state may determine whether conditions for legal recognition as a transsexual have been established, there is 'no justification for barring the transsexual from enjoying the right to marry under any circumstances'.

3   *Johnston v Ireland* (1986) A 112, at paras 52 and 54: 'in a society adhering to the principle of monogamy, [a restriction on divorce cannot] be regarded as injuring the substance of the right guaranteed by Article 12'. But see *Ostrowski v Poland* (dec) (15 December 2009) (refusal by the domestic courts to grant a divorce opposed by the wife as the applicant was solely at fault for the breakdown of the marriage: communicated under Arts 8 and 14, but ultimately struck out after the death of the applicant). See also *Airey v Ireland* (1979) A 32, para 24 (lack of legal aid to allow applicant to pursue judicial separation denied her any effective means of access to a court required by Art 6). Cf *Pellegrini v Italy* 2001-VIII, paras 40–48 (breach of fairness requirements under Art 6 in proceedings before a Vatican ecclesiastical court lacking impartiality and which had annulled the applicant's marriage on the basis of consanguinity).

4   *P, C, and S v United Kingdom* 2002-VI, para 142.

The right to marry

6.03 Article 12 of the ECHR most obviously enshrines the traditional concept of marriage as being between a man and a woman, but irrespective of whether gender determination derives from attribution at birth or from recognition of gender re-assignment[1]. The right to marry is subject to substantive and procedural domestic regulation. Domestic formalities and issues of legal capacity must be complied with[2]. In general, Article 12 cannot be used to extend domestic rules on capacity to contract marriage[3] or to require that effect should be given to marriages contracted elsewhere if based upon principles of capacity not recognised by domestic law[4], always assuming that the law is applied in a non-discriminatory manner[5].

An assessment of the purpose and effect of any legal rule which restricts marriage may be necessary. For example, in *B and L v United Kingdom*, a father-in-law and daughter-in-law had been legally prohibited from marrying each other until both their former spouses died or unless they obtained a private Act of Parliament. While it was accepted that this prohibition sought to protect the integrity of the family, it was also clear that the bar was not absolute. This allowed the Court to determine that since 'the inconsistency between the stated aims of the incapacity and the waiver applied in some cases undermines the rationality and logic of the measure', domestic law violated Article 12[6]. Further, the very essence of the guarantee must be protected, and thus a policy prohibiting convicted prisoners serving lengthy sentences of imprisonment from marrying violates the provision[7].There is, too, some suggestion that changing social mores should be recognised in domestic law. For example, in *Christine Goodwin v United Kingdom,* denial of the right to transsexuals to marry a person of the sex opposite to their re-assigned gender was held to violate Article 12, the Court now no longer accepting that it could still be assumed that the phrase 'men and women' must refer to determination of gender purely in biological criteria. This was the consequence of a determination in the same case that the denial of legal recognition to the change of gender of a post-operative transsexual violated Article 8[8].

---

1   *Parry v United Kingdom* (dec) 2006-XV (failure to make allowance for a small number of transsexuals in subsisting marriages in introducing a gender recognition procedure: inadmissible).

2   7114/75, *Hamer v United Kingdom* (1979) DR 24, 5, para 62 (domestic law may determine formalities (such as notice and publicity) and contractual issues determined on grounds of public interest (such as capacity, consent, prohibited degrees of consanguinity)); cf 22404/93, *Senine Vadbolski and Demonet v France* (1994) DR 79, 79 (failure to comply with domestic formalities to obtain a declaration of facts by repute in lieu of a birth certificate which the applicant could not obtain but required for marriage: inadmissible).

3   11579/85, *Khan v United Kingdom* (1986) DR 48, 253 (Muslim couple of 21 and 14 married in accordance with Islamic law; male convicted for having sexual relations with under-age girl: application manifestly ill-founded). Cf 14501/89, *A and A v Netherlands* (1992) DR 72, 118 (no violation of Art 8 in respect of failure to allow child of polygamous marriage to join his father and his second wife); and see in respect of Art 8, *Şerife Yiit v Turkey* [GC] 2010-... paras 99–103 (only civil marriages were recognised by domestic law, but there was no obligation on the state to recognise religious marriage and it was not unreasonable for Turkey to afford protection only to civil marriage).

4   2991–92/66, *Alam and Khan; and Singh v United Kingdom* (1967) CD 24, 116 (friendly settlement). While this case appears to suggest that states are under no obligation to recognise polygamous marriages, the issues were considered under Art 8 rather than Art 12. For domestic consideration, see *Wilkinson v Kitzinger* [2006] HRLR 36, discussed at para **6.06** below.

5   Cf *Selim v Cyprus* (friendly settlement) 2002-VI (friendly settlement following introduction of domestic law extending possibility of civil marriage between Muslims). For domestic discussion, see *R (Baiai) v Secretary of State for the Home Department* [2009] 1 AC 287, discussed at para **6.06** below.

6   *B and L v United Kingdom* (13 September 2005), paras 34–41 at para 40. Cf 11089/84, *Lindsay v United Kingdom* (1986) DR 49, 181 (taxation arrangements did not interfere with the right to marry); and 31401/96, *Sanders v France* (1996) DR 87, 160 (rules designed to preclude marriages of convenience not per se contrary to Art 12).

7   7114/75, *Hamer v United Kingdom* (1979) DR 24, 5 (five-year sentence of imprisonment); 8186/78, *Draper v United Kingdom* (1980) DR 24, 72 (life imprisonment). See also *Frasik v Poland* 2010-..., paras 88–100 (complete discretion left to authorities in determining a detainee's request for leave to marry in prison; while Art 12 does not require the introduction of separate laws or rules on marriage of prisoners, the arbitrary exercise of the decision-making power by a judge and the failure to strike a fair balance of proportionality between competing interests impaired the very essence of the applicant's right to marry). For domestic consideration, see *R (Crown Prosecution Service) v Registrar-General of Births, Deaths and Marriages* [2003] QB 122, discussed at para **6.06** below.

8   *Christine Goodwin v United Kingdom* [GC] 2002-VI, paras 97–104.

Same-sex relationships

6.04 Article 12 does not require the recognition of a right to marry where the partners are of the same sex, but nevertheless the guarantee may be applicable where domestic law does make such provision. In *Schalk and Kopf v Austria*, the applicants who were in a homosexual relationship had been denied permission to marry, the domestic courts considering that the wording of the provision was geared to the possibility of parenthood and thus did not extend to same-sex relationships. However, the Court considered that the reference to 'men and women' in Article 12 need not prevent same-sex marriage falling within the scope of the guarantee, for while only six member states of the Council of Europe at the time of the judgment recognised this, the exclusion of the reference in the corresponding provision of the Charter of Fundamental Rights of the European Union granting the right to marry allowed the drawing of the conclusion that the right to marry need not in all circumstances be limited to marriage between two persons of the opposite sex. Nevertheless, no obligation to amend domestic law could be implied: the Charter itself left the decision whether or not to allow same-sex marriages to domestic regulation, while in respect of the Convention, it was accepted that national authorities are best placed to assess the need for such recognition, given that the concept of marriage has deep-rooted social and cultural connotations differing largely from one society to another[1].

1   *Schalk and Kopf v Austria* 2010-..., paras 54–64 and 87–110 (by a majority of 4–3) (a cohabiting same-sex couple living in a stable partnership fell within the notion of 'family life' and were in a relevantly similar situation to a similarly-situated different-sex couple as regards the need for legal recognition of their relationship, but the Convention was to be read as a whole and since no obligation to recognise marriage arose under Art 12, similarly no obligation to recognise same-sex civil partnerships could be derived from Art 14 taken in conjunction with Art 8 as this area was still one of evolving rights with no established consensus where states enjoyed a margin of appreciation even despite the emerging tendency to provide recognition).

Remarriage

6.05 Restrictions placed upon individuals seeking to remarry where divorce is recognised may also be challenged, even although Article 12 does not require recognition of the right to divorce. In *F v Switzerland*, a temporary restriction lasting three years had prohibited the applicant from marrying again following his third divorce. The European Court of Human Rights acknowledged that while a state has a legitimate interest in seeking to protect the stability of the institution of marriage, the temporary prohibition in question was disproportionate. It could not be said to protect the interests of any future spouse, nor did the prohibition encourage measured reflection on the part of the applicant, 'a person of full age in possession of his mental facilities'[1].

---

1   *F v Switzerland* (1987) A 128, at paras 30–40. The Court noted (at para 33) that Switzerland alone retained such a provision requiring delay before marriage and was thus in an 'isolated position', but was not on this account by itself willing to find a violation of Art 12, especially since the issue of matrimony was 'so closely bound up with the cultural and historic traditions of each society and its deep-rooted ideas about the family'. This sentiment could equally apply to the approach taken in *Johnston v Ireland* (1986) A 112 which involved a prohibition on divorce, although in *F v Switzerland* (at para 38) the Court distinguished the situation of these two applicants 'since what was at issue in [*Johnston*] was the right of a man who was still married to have his marriage dissolved. If national legislation allows divorce, which is not a requirement of the Convention, Article 12 secures for divorced persons the right to remarry without unreasonable restrictions'.

Domestic consideration of the right to marry

6.06 The right to marry under Article 12 has been considered in a number of domestic cases. In *R (Crown Prosecution Service) v Registrar General of Births, Deaths and Marriages,* it was held that a prisoner awaiting trial for murder could not be prevented from marrying a prosecution witness notwithstanding that the witness would cease to be compellable upon marriage: neither the prisoner nor the witness was to be denied the right to marry that had long been recognised by domestic law and was also enshrined in Article 12[1]. In *Bellinger v Bellinger,* on the other hand, it was held that a purported marriage entered into between a man and a transsexual person who had been correctly registered as female at birth was invalid: the domestic legislation which required the parties to a marriage to have been of different genders at birth could not be construed compatibly with Articles 8 and 12, as applied by the European Court of Human Rights in the case of *Christine Goodwin v United Kingdom*[2]. A declaration of incompatibility was accordingly granted[3]. In *Wilkinson v Kitzinger,* the issue was whether a same-sex marriage entered into in British Columbia (where such a marriage was valid), between two women domiciled in England, should be recognised under English private international law. Reliance was placed on Articles 8, 12 and 14. It was held that the rule of private international law required that the parties to a marriage must have had the capacity to marry each other in England. Two persons of the same sex did not have that capacity. The Convention rights relied upon did not alter the position: Article 8 did not require the recognition of same sex marriages, Article 12 had no application, and the difference in treatment was justifiable under Article 14[4].

The most significant domestic case is possibly *R (Baiai) v Secretary of State for the Home Department*, which concerned a statutory requirement that persons who required leave to enter or remain in the UK, and who wished to marry otherwise than in accordance with the rites of the Church of England, must obtain the Secretary of State's approval to marry, on payment of a fee. Under the Secretary of State's policy, such approval was only granted if the person had leave to enter or remain for more than six months, or to have exceptionally compelling compassionate grounds. The object of the legislation was to avoid the abuse of immigration rights by marriages of convenience. The House of Lords held that the scheme violated Article 12. Although it was possible, consistently with Article 12, to require those subject to immigration control to give notice of a proposed marriage, to enable the authorities to investigate whether it was a marriage of convenience, and to withhold permission where that appeared to be so, the policy had no relevance to the genuineness of a marriage, and prevented the exercise of the right to marry even where the marriage might be genuine. The fee was also fixed at such a high level that it might impair the essence of the right to marry. A decision of the lower court that the exemption of Church of England marriages was also objectionable under Articles 12 and 14, since there was no evidence that such marriages were more likely to be genuine than other marriages, was not challenged on appeal[5]. This scheme was considered subsequently by the Strasbourg Court which found violations of Article 12, of Article 14 when taken with Article 12, and of Article 14 with Article 9[6].

1   *R (Crown Prosecution Service) v Registrar General of Births, Deaths and Marriages* [2003] QB 1222.

2   *Christine Goodwin v United Kingdom* [GC] 2002-VI, discussed at para **6.03** above.

3   *Bellinger v Bellinger* [2003] 2 AC 467. See also *Bellinger v United Kingdom* (dec) (11 July 2006) (case struck out following proposal to change domestic law).

4   *Wilkinson v Kitzinger* [2006] HRLR 36.

5   *R (Baiai) v Secretary of State for the Home Department* [2009] 1 AC 287.

6   *O'Donoghue and Others v United Kingdom* 2010-…, paras 82–92 (requirement for persons subject to immigration control to submit an application for a certificate of approval before being permitted to marry where unwilling or unable to do so in the Church of England, while not inherently objectionable, gave rise to grave concerns: the grant was not based solely on the genuineness of the proposed marriage, there was a blanket ban on foreign nationals with either insufficient or no leave to remain, and the level of fee could impair the essence of the right to marry if an individual had insufficient resources); for Art 14 discussion, see para **3.122** above.

Founding a family

6.07 The associated right of a married couple to found a family (including by means of adoption)[1] is likewise subject to compliance with applicable rules of domestic law. However, Article 12 cannot support a claim that the legal effects of marriage should also apply to relationships and situations comparable with marriage[2], although discrimination in the enjoyment of Convention rights on the basis of birth or status may give rise to a question under Article 14[3]. Nor does the right entail a general right of procreation[4].

---

1   The right to choose the circumstances in which a mother gives birth falls within the scope of Art 8: *Ternovszky v Hungary* (14 December 2010), para 22. But note *Schwizgebel v Switzerland* 2010-…, paras 70–99 (refusal to allow a 47-year-old unmarried mother permission to adopt: while the matter fell within the scope of Art 8, there had been no violation of Art 14 in conjunction with Art 8, the setting of minimum and maximum ages for adoption falling within the scope of a state's margin of appreciation). See also 8896/80, *X v Netherlands* (1981) DR 24, 176 (complaint based on an inability to meet substantive domestic law provisions declared inadmissible); cf 6482/74, *X v Belgium and Netherlands* (1976) DR 7, 75 and 31924/96, *Di Lazarro v Italy* (1997) DR 90, 134 (right to found a family by means of adoption implies the existence of a couple, and thus cannot include adoption by an unmarried person). For domestic consideration, see *Briody v St Helen's and Knowsley Area Health Authority* [2002] QB 856, discussed at para **6.09** below.

2   *Marckx v Belgium* (1979) A 31, para 67; and see *Schalk and Kopf v Austria* 2010-…, discussed at para **6.04** above.

3   See paras **3.102–3.128** above and paras **6.142–6.144** below.

4   *Šijakova and Others v Former Yugoslav Republic of Macedonia* (dec) (6 March 2003) (applicants' children joined monastic order imposing celibacy: inadmissible, as 'the right to have grandchildren or the right to procreation is not covered by Art 12 or any other Article of the Convention'. Cf *Evans v United Kingdom* [GC] 2007-IV, discussed further below at para **6.54** (refusal by former husband to allow frozen embryos to be implanted into former partner: issue disposed of under ECHR, Art 8, the applicant not invoking Art 12). For discussion of abortion, see para **4.51** above.

Prisoners' rights

6.08 The issue of founding a family has been of some concern to married prisoners in the handful of European countries (as in the United Kingdom) where prisoners are not permitted conjugal visits. Neither the Commission nor the Court had been sympathetic to applications raising this matter[1]. In a recent judgment, however, the Court has confirmed that 'the right of a couple to conceive a child and to make use of medically assisted procreation for that end comes within the ambit of Article 8 as such a such a choice is clearly an expression of private and family life'[2]. In *Dickson v United Kingdom*, the Grand Chamber (arriving at a conclusion differing from the Chamber) determined that the refusal to provide facilities for artificial insemination to a life prisoner and his wife did give rise to an issue under Article 8 and held that there had been no proper assessment been made of the competing public and private interests involved, but having found that there had been a violation of Article 8, that no separate issue arose under Article 12[3]. This case law helps clarify that the right to marry under Article 12 must be considered independently of any right to consummate the marriage, or thereby to found a family.

1   Cf 6564/74, *X v United Kingdom* (1975) DR 2, 105 (complaint by long-term prisoner of a denial of conjugal rights: the situation a prisoner finds himself in 'falls under his own responsibility' and thus the application was declared manifestly ill founded); 7114/75, *Hamer v United Kingdom* (1979) DR 24, 5 (parties must decide if they wish to marry in circumstances where cohabitation is not possible); and 32094/96 and 32568/96, *ELH and PBH v United Kingdom* (1997) DR 91, 61 (refusal to authorise conjugal visits for prisoners amounted to an interference with Art 8 rights, but was considered necessary for the prevention of crime or disorder). Cf *Kalashnikov v Russia* (dec) 2001-XI '[in relation to Art 8] the Court notes with interest the reform movements in several European countries to improve prison conditions by facilitating such visits. It considers however that the refusal of conjugal visits may for the present time be regarded as justified for the prevention of disorder and crime'. Such decisions focus upon the rights of prisoners, rather than the rights of spouses of prisoners. In certain applications involving the United Kingdom, friendly settlements have been secured: eg 17142/90, *GS and RS v United Kingdom* (10 July 1991); and 20004/92, *RJ and WJ v United Kingdom* (7 May 1993) (the Government accepted that facilities for artificial insemination treatment would be made available). For domestic consideration, see *R (Mellor) v Secretary of State for the Home Department* [2002] QB 13, discussed at para **6.09** below. Most European countries (in particular, those of central and east Europe) permit conjugal visits, a practice welcomed by the European Committee for the Prevention of Torture as of importance in safeguarding relationships with spouses as long as such visits take place in conditions which respect human dignity: cf *Irish Report*, CPT/Inf (95) 14, para 161.

2   *SH and Others v Austria* (1 April 2010), at para 60 [note that this case was pending before the Grand Chamber at the time of writing].

3   *Dickson v United Kingdom* [GC] 2007-XIII, paras 77–86. See also *Boso v Italy* (dec) 2002-VII – inability to challenge wife's decision to terminate pregnancy did not give rise to a violation of Art 8, and since this part of the application was manifestly ill-founded, it followed that the same conclusion was appropriate in respect of Art 12.

Domestic consideration of the right to found a family

6.09 The right to found a family under Article 12 was considered in *R (Mellor) v Secretary of State for the Home Department,* where the question was whether the policy of allowing prisoners access to artificial insemination facilities only in exceptional circumstances was compatible with Article 12. It was held that it was: one of the purposes of imprisonment was to punish the criminal by depriving him of certain rights and pleasures, including the enjoyment of family life, the exercise of conjugal rights and the right to found a family[1].

The right to found a family was also considered in *Briody v St Helen's and Knowsley Area Health Authority,* in the context of a claim for damages brought by a woman who had, through the defendants' negligence, been deprived while a teenager of the opportunity to bear children. Almost 30 years later, she sought to recover the cost of having a child born by a surrogate mother, using donor eggs and her partner's sperm. Rejecting the claim, Hale LJ observed that the right to marry and to found a family 'is quite different from having a right to be supplied with a child (or a spouse)'[2].

1   *R (Mellor) v Secretary of State for the Home Department* [2002] QB 13.

2   *Briody v St Helen's and Knowsley Area Health Authority* [2002] QB 856, 867.

ARTICLE 8: RESPECT FOR PRIVATE AND FAMILY LIFE, HOME AND CORRESPONDENCE

The scope of Article 8

6.10 Article 8[1] requires respect for private life, family life, home and correspondence. These concepts are closely related and are given an 'autonomous' interpretation consistent with maximising the scope of the guarantee, and there is considerable interplay between these related notions which are, on occasion, indistinguishable[2]. The case law is predominantly dynamic in character, and while in the past Article 8 jurisprudence may have perhaps appeared to have lacked much underlying principle, more recent case law helps underline the fundamental values the guarantee seeks to protect. The focus is upon protection of family relationships and the moral and physical integrity of the individual, including development of personality, choice of lifestyle and establishment of relationships[3]. The provision may not only involve the negative duty upon a state to refrain from arbitrary interference with an individual's rights, but also impose a positive duty to adopt specific measures designed to secure respect for these guarantees[4]. Until recently, Article 8 interpretation was somewhat underdeveloped if not somewhat lacking in coherence and consistency[5]. Jurisprudence concentrates upon a number of disparate areas such as sexual orientation, child care, state surveillance, prisoners' correspondence and deportation, with more recent extension to such areas as privacy and environmental protection.

1　For a survey of Art 8 case law, see eg Sudre (ed) *Le Droit au Respect de la Vie Privée au Sens de La Convention Europeenne des Droits de l'Homme* (2005).

2　See eg *Klass and Others v Germany* (1978) A 28, para 41 (telephone conversations are covered by notions of 'private life' and 'correspondence', and possibly also by 'home'); *Stjerna v Finland* (1994) A 299-B, para 37 (use of name involves identification with a family and thus concerns private and family life); *López Ostra v Spain* (1994) A 303-C, para 51 (pollution could affect enjoyment of home in such a way as to affect private and family life); and *Pannullo and Forte v France* 2001-X, paras 31–40 (14 month delay in returning child's body to parents: violation of right to private and family life).

3　In consequence, the scope of Art 8 is broad enough to encompass even the choice of family names: *Burghartz v Switzerland* (1994) A 280-B, para 24; *Guillot v France* 1996-V, paras 23–27. See also *GMB and KM v Switzerland* (dec) (27 September 2001) (administrative refusal to recognise child as having mother's surname when family name of spouses is that of the father: inadmissible); *Bulgakov v Ukraine* (11 September 2007), paras 42–54 (complaint concerning use of Ukrainian names of a Russian citizen in passports: no violation); *Daróczy v Hungary* (1 July 2008), paras 28–35 (imposition of change of name from that used for the past 50 years when new identity card issues: violation); *Güzel Erdagöz v Turkey* (21 October 2008), paras 47–57 (refusal to rectify the spelling of the applicant's first name in official records because it reflected a regional pronunciation not recognised by the dictionary of the Turkish language: violation); and *Kemal Taşkýn and Others v Turkey* (2 February 2010), paras 64–72 (refusal to allow the applicants to officially spell their names with letters outwith the official Turkish alphabet did not amount to a violation of Art 8 since the interference was proportionate: the interference was aimed at protecting the rights of others, and the Turkish spelling of names would not result in any ridiculous meanings nor cause inconvenience or an obstacle to identification, the Court noting that states are generally free to determine usage of official languages in official documents).

4　　Eg *Marckx v Belgium* (1979) A 31, para 31 (existence of legal safeguards which allow integration 'from the moment of birth' of a child into his family); *Airey v Ireland* (1979) A 32, paras 32–33 (effective access to a court for action of judicial separation); *Stubbings v United Kingdom* 1996-IV, paras 64–65 (effective deterrence of child sex abuse through protection provided by civil and criminal law). See further para **6.121** below. For domestic examples, see eg *Venables v News Group Newspapers Ltd* [2001] Fam 430.

5　　Cf opinion of Judge Wildhaber in *Stjerna v Finland* (1994) A 299-B, discussed by Warbrick 'The Structure of Article 8' [1998] EHRLR 32.

6.11 Treatment of this article is best considered in three parts: discussion of the scope or application of the guarantee; discussion of what constitutes an 'interference'; and examination of those circumstances where a state interference will be deemed justified. It will also be necessary to examine the circumstances in which positive obligations arise on the part of public authorities. The Court has also confirmed the existence of a 'procedural aspect' of the provision[1].

1　　Eg *HM v Turkey* (8 August 2006), paras 25–30 (lack of investigation into allegedly unlawful search of the applicant's home in the face of denial of responsibility by any authority: violation of the procedural aspect of Art 8 to carry out an effective investigation).

6.12 Much case law in this area concerns the response of public authorities to disputes between family members, and thus often involves scrutiny of determinations by domestic courts. There is limited competence for an international tribunal to review such conclusions taken at national level. However, although

> 'the [Strasbourg] Court is not in theory required to settle disputes of a purely private nature, ... in exercising the European supervision incumbent on it, it cannot remain passive where a national court's interpretation of a legal act, be it a testamentary disposition, a private contract, a public document, a statutory provision or an administrative practice appears unreasonable, arbitrary or ... blatantly inconsistent with the prohibition of discrimination ... and more broadly with the principles underlying the Convention[1]'.

Similarly, in respect of other disputes between private parties (as between an employer and an employee), the Court will examine the extent to which domestic determinations have properly reflected Convention requirements in ensuring respect for private and family life[2].

1　　*Pla and Puncernau v Andorra* 2004-VIII, at para 59.

2　　See eg *Obst v Germany* 2010-...; and *Schüth v Germany* 2010-..., discussed at para **7.28** below.

'Family life'

6.13 'Family life' is interpreted widely, and is not confined to marriage-based relationships. The key question is whether *de facto* 'family' ties exist in a particular instance[1], but even in the absence of 'family life', a relationship (for example, as between an applicant and his fiancée) may alternatively fall within the scope of the notion of 'private life'[2]. Further, 'family life does not consist only of social, moral or cultural relations, for example in the sphere of children's education; it also comprises interests of a pecuniary nature' on account of maintenance obligations imposed by domestic law, and thus such issues as intestate succession and voluntary dispositions between near relatives can be 'intimately connected with family life'[3].

---

1 *Lebbink v Netherlands* 2004-IV, para 35.

2 *Hofmann v Germany* (dec) (23 February 2010).

3 *Hofmann v Germany* (dec) (23 February 2010) (Art 8 was inapplicable in a claim for damages for causing death against a surgeon who carried out an operation on the applicant's fiancée as such an action did not concern any existing family ties between the applicant and his late fiancée but rather a relationship between the applicant and the respondent surgeon which was not one which raised issues of family or private life). See also *Velcea and Mazăre v Romania* 2009-..., paras 125–134 (failure of the domestic courts in a claim to disinherit a murderer who had not been convicted of murder by a final court ruling as he had committed suicide: following a person's death, the unlawfulness of his or her actions cannot remain without effect, and there had thus been an unjustified interference with the 'family life' of the family of the person murdered). However, Art 8 does not support a claim to be recognised as the heir of a deceased person for inheritance purposes: *Haas v Netherlands* 2004-I, para 43.

Determining the existence of 'family life'

6.14 In contrast with Article 12, where the right to found a family is largely restricted to the traditional notion of a 'nuclear' family, recognition of the existence of 'family life' under Article 8 has been interpreted more creatively in line with changing social attitudes in Europe. In the determination of whether 'family life' exists, it will be necessary to consider all the circumstances of the case, including the intentions of the individuals involved and the stability of their relationships (for example, whether the couple live together, the length of their relationship and whether they have had children together). The key requirement will normally be cohabitation or the existence of other factors indicating that a 'relationship has sufficient constancy to create de facto 'family ties'[1]. Thus 'the question of the existence or non-existence of "family life" is essentially a question of fact depending upon the existence of close personal ties'[2] and is not determined solely by domestic legal status. Certainly, a lawful and genuine marriage involving cohabitation between two persons of the opposite sex will fall within the scope of the article. However, a relationship outwith marriage may also qualify as a 'family'[3], and the scope of Article 8 may also further extend to situations in which a full family life has not yet been established as long as there is a genuine intention to cohabit and to lead a normal family life[4]. It certainly now applies to stable single-sex relationships, even although as yet Article 8 does not require legal recognition of such[5]. The actual circumstances surrounding any relationship are thus of the essence. Further, since near relatives can play a vital role in families, 'family life' may also extend to ties between relatives such as grandparents and children[6], siblings[7], foster parents[8] and, in certain circumstances, between an uncle and a nephew[9].

1   *Keegan v Ireland* (1994) A 290, para 36; *Kroon and Others v Netherlands* (1994) A 297-C, para 30. Cf 14501/89, *A and A v Netherlands* (1992) DR 72, 118 (recognition of 'family life' in polygamous marriage where there had been frequent contact between father and son); *X, Y and Z v United Kingdom* 1997-II, paras 36 and 37 (the Court recognised that there were *de facto* family ties between a transsexual, his partner of the same biological sex and a child born to the latter by artificial insemination). See also paras 99–103 (applicant denied the benefit of the pension and social security of her deceased partner because their marriage was a religious one, rather than a civil one, and only civil marriages were recognised by law: no violation, as there was no obligation on the state to recognise religious marriage and it was not unreasonable for Turkey to afford protection only to civil marriage). Cf *Korelc v Slovenia* (dec) (12 May 2009) (inability of applicant to cohabiting in an economic relationship rather than as part of a long-lasting life community to inherit tenancy from deceased cohabitant: inadmissible).

2   11468/85, *K v United Kingdom* (1986) DR 50, 199 at 207. See also *Elli Poluhas Dödsbo v Sweden* 2006-I, para 24 (not necessary to determine whether refusal to transfer remains of applicant's deceased husband involved 'family life' or 'private life').

3   *Johnston and Others v Ireland* (1986) A 112, para 56 (15 years' cohabitation, but each party legally unable to divorce and thus remarry).

4   *Abdulaziz, Cabales and Balkandali v United Kingdom* (1985) A 94, paras 62–63. Cf 15817/89, *Wakefield v United Kingdom* (1990) DR 66, 251 (prisoner requested transfer to prison in Scotland to be near his fiancée; the relationship between the applicant and his fiancée did not fall within the scope of family life envisaged by Art 8).

5   *Schalk and Kopf v Austria* 2010-…, paras 96–110 discussed at para **6.04** above. See also 16106/90, *B v United Kingdom* (1990) DR 64, 278 (homosexual relationships fall within the meaning of private life for the purposes of Art 8).

6   *Marckx v Belgium* (1979) A 31, para 45 (ties with near relatives covered since 'such relatives may play a considerable part in family life'); *Bronda v Italy* 1998-IV, para 51. Cf *Hokkanen v Finland* (1994) A 299-A, para 45 (a child was brought up by grandparents while its father was in prison; that there were sufficient links to establish a 'family life' since the father retained legal powers over the child and had continuously sought access; but the question of grandparents' interests in 'family life' appears not to have been argued by the respondent government).

7   *Moustaquim v Belgium* (1991) A 193, para 36.

8   *Moretti and Benedetti v Italy* 2010-…, paras 44–52 and 60–71 (19-month relationship between foster parents and an infant constituted 'family life'; and violation of Art 8 on account of the authorities' failure to examine properly the foster parents' adoption request before making the child available for adoption).

9   *Boyle v United Kingdom* (1994) A 282-B (refusal of a local authority to allow applicant access to his nephew with whom he had formed close bonds before the child was removed from its mother on suspicion of child abuse: the Commission found that the bonds supported 'family life', but friendly settlement thereafter achieved). Cf *Negrepontis-Giannisis v Greece* (question whether it is contrary to protection of family life to prevent a monk from adopting his nephew on grounds of public policy: communicated). See also *R v Governor of Wakefield Prison, ex p Banks* [2002] 1 FCR 445; and *Michalak v Wandsworth London Borough Council* [2003] 1 WLR 617, discussed at para **6.20** below.

PARENTS AND CHILDREN

6.15 Ties between a parent and a child clearly fall within the scope of Article 8 which thus encompasses a broad range of decisions, including the very decision as to how a mother gives birth[1]. Other Convention provisions also cover decisions taken by a parent on behalf of a child, including those in respect of education[2], health care[3] and discipline, but always having regard to other countervailing rights of the child[4]. More particularly, a decision to take a child into care or to allocate custody to one parent upon divorce or separation will give rise to an Article 8 issue. 'The mutual enjoyment by parent and child of each other's company constitutes a fundamental element of family life'[5], irrespective of the legal nature of the union existing between the biological parents. The existence of family life between a parent and child is again determined by the actual circumstances of each case, but there appears to be a stronger presumption in favour of the existence of such ties. Biological kinship alone is insufficient to attract Article 8 protection in the absence of any further legal or factual elements indicating the existence of a close personal relationship between parent and child[6], and in any event is not a necessary prerequisite as for the purposes of Article 8 a 'family life' between a child and an adult who is not the biological parent[7] of the child may be established where one parent is a step-parent or through legal or social ties involving adoption[8] or fostering[9]. On the other hand, it must be possible to take proceedings to challenge and thereby rebut any legal presumption of paternity[10].

1   *Ternovszky v Hungary* (14 December 2010), paras 23–27 (legislation dissuading health professionals from providing assistance for giving birth at home lacked the requisite degree of 'foreseeability' and thus was not 'in accordance with the law': violation).

2   See paras **6.161–6.165** below (in respect of Prot 1, Art 2).

3   *Nielsen v Denmark* (1988) A 144, para 61 (the hospitalisation by a mother of a child who was not mentally ill in a psychiatric ward was not a 'deprivation of liberty' for the purposes of Art 5: see para **4.152** above).

4   For example, in terms of Art 3's prohibition of degrading treatment: eg *A v United Kingdom* 1998-VI, discussed at para **4.86** above. The European Convention on the Exercise of Children's Rights (ETS 160 (1996)) entered into force in 2000, but has not yet been ratified by the United Kingdom. It provides a number of procedural measures to allow children to exercise their rights more effectively, in particular in family legal proceedings. Courts (and any person appointed to act on behalf of a child) have responsibilities in facilitating the exercise of rights by children (such as the right to be informed and the right to express their views either themselves or through other persons or bodies).

5   *Olsson v Sweden (no 1)* (1988) A 130 at para 59.

6   *Lebbink v Netherlands* 2004-IV, paras 35–37 (no recognition of daughter or cohabitation with her and her mother, but the child had been born out of a genuine relationship and the applicant had acted as his daughter's auxiliary guardian and had visited and discussed health problems, and the decision of the courts to declare a request for access inadmissible on the ground that there was no family life with the mother constituted a violation of Art 8 since biological kinship and social ties had been enough to attract Art 8 protection). See also *Phinikaridou v Cyprus* 2007-XIV, paras 50–67 (time bar on children born out of wedlock seeking judicial recognition of their parentage: violation).

7   Cf 16944/90, *Maassen v Netherlands* (1993) DR 74, 120 (the Commission refused to consider that the donation of sperm for the purpose of enabling a woman to take advantage of artificial insemination to become pregnant gave the donor any Art 8 rights; actual contact between donor and child were insufficient in the particular case to establish family life). See, too, *X, Y and Z v United Kingdom* 1997-II, discussed at para **6.22** below.

8   9993/82, *X v France* (1992) DR 31, 241 (judicial decision withdrawing applicant's parental authority in respect of her adopted son: the relations between adoptive parents and an adopted child are as a rule family relations protected by Art 8). See also *Pini and Bertani v Romania* 2004-V, paras 144–148 (applicability of Art 8 to the situation of adoptive parents of abandoned

children living in a children's home in another country and granted judicial authorisation to adopt, but in light of the failure of the home to hand over the children: while the applicants did not have de facto family relationships with their adopted children as there had been no cohabitation, there was a relationship protected by Art 8 in light of final judicial determinations ending rights and obligations existing between the children and their progenitors despite the absence of minors' consent to adoption); and *Wagner and JMWL v Luxembourg* 2007-VII, para 117 (refusal to give effect to adoption decision of the Peruvian courts since Luxembourg law did not recognise adoption by a single person: de facto, the applicant had behaved as the mother of the child, and Art 8 was applicable).

9   8257/78, *X v Switzerland* (1978) DR 13, 248 (complaint by the applicant that the court's decision to grant custody of her foster child to the parents was an interference with her private and family life, but it was not necessary to consider whether interference amounted to family life, as the separation undoubtedly affected her private life).

10   *Mizzi v Malta* 2006-I, paras 75–91 (inability to rebut presumption despite claims based upon biological evidence). See also *Paulik v Slovakia* 2006-XI, paras 41–47 and 51–59 (violation of Art 8 and of Art 14 in conjunction with Art 8 in regard to impossibility of challenging judicial determination of paternity); and *Tavli v Turkey* (9 November 2006), paras 31–35 (refusal to accept DNA testing as ground for reopening of paternity case: violation). Cf *ILV v Romania* (dec) (24 August 2010) (refusal to order mother and child to undergo DNA tests to establish scientific evidence of paternity where a court had already determined this issue: inadmissible, for while Art 8 was applicable in cases where an individual sought to determine whether he was the father of a child, it was necessary to balance his interest with the child's interests and those in maintaining the integrity of the legal system).

6.16 The tie between a parent and a child is not dependent upon the continuing cohabitation of its parents. Any child born of a union recognised as constituting a 'family' is '*ipso jure* part of that relationship', and thus

> 'from the moment of the child's birth and by the very fact of it, there exists between him and his parent a bond amounting to "family life", even if the parents are not then living together[1].'

1   *Berrehab v Netherlands* (1988) A 138, at para 21. See also *Emonet and Others v Switzerland* 2007-XIV, paras 70–88 (stipulation in domestic law that adoption of an adult even by her mother's partner would have the effect of terminating the legal effects of the mother-daughter relationship: violation); *Iordache v Romania* (14 October 2008), paras 57–69 (automatic ban on exercise of parental rights following sentence of 20 years' imprisonment without assessment of the child's interests or the applicant's alleged unfitness: violation); and *Clemeno and Others v Italy* (21 October 2008), paras 48–61 (severing of all links with father even after his acquittal of charges of sexual assault, and no attempt help the biological family to reconstitute the family: violation). Cf *Re G (Children)* [2006] 1 WLR 2305 (weight to be given to biological link in determining custody issues when a same-sex partnership breaks down: biological link was to be considered a significant factor).

CHILDREN BORN OUTSIDE MARRIAGE

6.17 The determination of the legal relationship between a child born out of wedlock and its natural father concerns an aspect of the child's 'private life'[1]. The status of illegitimacy has largely ceased throughout Europe to carry legal disabilities, and Article 14 provides that 'birth or other status' may not be used as a ground for discrimination in the provision of rights under the Convention[2]. This provision taken along with Article 8 has resulted in the successful challenge of national laws which discriminate on this ground, and now 'very weighty reasons' would have to be advanced before any such difference of treatment could be regarded as compatible[3]. In the early case of *Marckx v Belgium*, domestic law required an unmarried mother to follow certain legal procedures in order to establish a legal bond with her child; further, the rights of inheritance on intestacy of a recognised illegitimate child were less than those of a child born within marriage. The European Court of Human Rights noted that the text of Article 8 did not distinguish between family units constituted through marriage and those outside wedlock, and considered that to imply any such interpretation would both be inconsistent with the general principle that Convention guarantees apply to 'everyone', as well as contrary to Article 14's prohibition of any discrimination in the enjoyment of Convention rights on grounds including 'birth'[4].

---

1   *Mikulić v Croatia* 2002-I, paras 50–55 (private life may embrace aspects of an individual's physical and social identity, and no reason of principle for excluding such from the notion of 'private life')

2   See eg *Zaunegger v Germany* 2009-…, paras 44–65 (legal provision that a mother would have sole custody of a child born out of wedlock unless the parents marry or she provides consent that there will be joint custody with the father: violation of Art 14 taken with Art 8 as the applicant was treated differently from married and divorced fathers in the requirement for consent). For discussion of Art 14, see paras **3.113–3.114** above. See also European Convention on the Legal Status of Children born out of Wedlock (ETS 85(1975)). The language of the UN Convention on the Rights of the Child is arguably tighter: Art 2 provides that states must ensure that rights under the treaty are made available to each child 'without discrimination of any kind irrespective of the child's or his parent's or other legal guardian's race, colour, ... birth or other status'.

3   *Brauer v Germany* 2009-…, paras 34–46 at 40 (applicant had lived in former East Germany barred from inheriting from estate of deceased father who had lived in West Germany on account of illegitimate status: violation of Art 14 when taken with Art 8).

4   *Marckx v Belgium* (1979) A 31, paras 28–65 (various violations of Art 8 taken alone, of Art 8 taken in conjunction with Art 14, of Art 14 taken in conjunction with Art 8, and of Art 14 taken in conjunction with Prot 1, Art 1). The Court noted (at para 52) that while inheritance rights are normally exercised only upon death when 'family life' undergoes a fundamental change, 'this does not mean that no issue concerning such rights may arise before death: the distribution of the estate may be settled ... by the making of a will or of a gift on account of a future inheritance [and] therefore represents a feature of family life that cannot be disregarded'.

PARENTAL RIGHTS

6.18 The ECHR does not require that a father must enjoy equality of treatment with the mother of a child. The lack of any common European consensus on parental rights has allowed the Commission and the European Court of Human Rights to decline to insist that domestic law treats unmarried fathers and mothers equally[1]. In *McMichael v United Kingdom*, the Court upheld the distinction in Scots law between the automatic conferment of parental rights on a married father and the requirement placed upon an unmarried father to take some form of positive step to acquire these rights (such as through an application to a court) as being a proportionate response in achieving the legitimate aim of distinguishing between fathers who had some justifiable claim and those whose status lacked sufficient merit[2]. While Article 5 of Protocol no 7 specifically provides that 'spouses shall enjoy equality of rights and responsibilities', by implication, where a state has not ratified this protocol certain differences in treatment are not incompatible with the Convention[3]. In *Petrovic v Austria*, a father had his claim for parental leave allowance rejected by an employment office since at that time only mothers could qualify. While agreeing with the Commission that payment of social welfare assistance by the state was made with a view to promoting family life, the Court did not accept that the discrimination violated Article 14 when taken with Article 8. Of crucial importance was the lack of any common European standard in determining whether social security provision for parental leave should be paid to fathers. Although most states were moving gradually towards according a high priority to equality of the sexes, there was still no uniformity in this aspect of welfare provision. Accordingly, the state was entitled to a wider margin of appreciation in its assessment of whether there was a need for a difference of treatment between mothers and fathers[4].

1   The weaker standing of an unmarried father was found elsewhere in Europe: eg 9639/82, *B, R and J v Germany* (1984) DR 36, 130 (differences in treatment could be justified; no practical effect on children; the weaker position of the father was mainly a consequence of a choice on the part of the unmarried parents; and the father's disadvantage was proportionate to the aim of the regulation which was to protect the child).

2   *McMichael v United Kingdom* (1995) A 307-B, para 98.

3   The United Kingdom has not ratified this protocol, and it is thus not a 'Convention right' for the purposes of the Human Rights Act 1998.

4   *Petrovic v Austria* 1998-II, paras 22–43 (the Commission had considered by a majority of 25 to 5, that there had been a violation. For the two dissenting judges on the Court, the lack of any standard European norm 'was not conclusive'; and while states were not under a duty in terms of Art 8 to pay any such allowance, if they chose to do so it would not be appropriate to do this in a discriminatory manner).

ENDING OF 'FAMILY LIFE'

6.19 While a broad interpretation is given to the notion of 'family life', it is important to note that 'family life' ties are not indefinite. Subsequent events will break the bond between a child and its parent or other adult in a family relationship through any intervening loss of contact considered substantial enough to break these ties[1]. Most obviously, the loss of dependency upon the parent through maturation of the young person will bring 'family life' to an end[2], although the mere fact that a child is taken into care will not do so[3], nor will a parent's failure to contribute to the costs of a child's upbringing and care[4]. The consequence is that 'family life' must be construed in a manner consistent with Strasbourg interpretation, not domestic law. Thus a parent who does not enjoy parental rights in domestic law may still be able to rely upon Article 8 guarantees. In *Keegan v Ireland*, an unmarried father had sought court approval to be recognised as his child's guardian after the child had been placed for adoption shortly after her birth but without his knowledge.

The European Court of Human Rights accepted that the adoption process was an interference with the father's rights under Article 8[5]. Conversely, a parent who is still recognised by domestic law as enjoying parental rights may not be able to satisfy the tests for enjoyment of Article 8 guarantees where the link between the parent and the child has become tenuous[6]. However, the existence or otherwise of 'family life' is not necessarily conclusive, as an issue may still be deemed to fall within the scope of Article 8 if it involves 'private life'[7].

1 Cf *Berrehab v Netherlands* (1988) A 138, para 21 (frequency, regularity and length of contact with daughter after ending of cohabitation with child's mother such as to maintain ties of 'family life'); *Gül v Switzerland* 1996-I, paras 32–43 (refusal by the state to allow a child to join his father who had left his home country when the child was three months old in circumstances suggesting the father had never attempted to develop a family life; further, a 'family life' could have been established in Turkey in any case); and *Kearns v France* (10 January 2008), paras 76–92 (two-month period to reverse the giving up of child by its mother: no violation in respect of the time-limit for withdrawing consent, the best interests of the child being paramount and in the absence of consensus in the field of adoption in Europe, policy seeking to integrate a child into its new family as soon as possible was not disproportionate).

2 Cf *JT v United Kingdom (striking out)* (30 March 2000) (failure to allow the applicant, who had been detained for some time as a psychiatric patient, to have her mother replaced as her 'nearest relative' by a social worker in view of the difficult relationship she had with her mother: friendly settlement whereby the UK Government indicated that domestic legislation would be amended to provide the detainee with the power to apply to court to have the 'nearest relative' replaced where the patient reasonably objected to a certain person acting in that capacity, and to exclude certain persons from acting as 'nearest relative').

3 *Eriksson v Sweden* (1989) A 156, para 58.

4 *Kroon v Netherlands* (1994) A 297-C, para 30.

5 *Keegan v Ireland* (1994) A 290, paras 46–55. See also *McMichael v United Kingdom* (1995) A 307-B, paras 86–90, discussed at para **6.57** below.

6 Eg *Söderbäck v Sweden* 1998-VII, discussed at para **6.63**, fn 2 below. Additional issues may arise where a parent seeks to resist a requirement to return a child abducted from abroad under the Child Abduction and Custody Act 1985 on account of possible incompatibility with ECHR: see Karsten 'Atypical Families and the Human Rights Act' [1999] EHRLR 195 at 201. Cf 22920/93, *MB v United Kingdom* (1994) DR 77, 108 (a person who is not the guardian or legal representative of a child cannot bring a complaint under Art 8 on behalf of that child).

7 *Shofman v Russia* (24 November 2005), paras 36–54 (challenge to presumed paternity of a child born in wedlock by husband involves 'private life', the issue as to whether determination of a father's legal relations with a putative child fall within 'family life' left open). See also *Znamenskaya v Russia* (2 June 2005), paras 23–27 (inability of mother to register uncontested paternity of stillborn child as stillborn children could not acquire civil rights: 'private life' was involved as the mother had undoubtedly developed a strong bond with the embryo).

DOMESTIC DECISIONS ON THE SCOPE OF 'FAMILY LIFE'

6.20 The Convention concept of family life has been considered in numerous cases before domestic courts. An illuminating general observation was made by Sedley LJ in *Re F (Adult: Court's Jurisdiction)*:

'The family life for which article 8 requires respect is not a proprietary right vested in either parent or child: it is as much an interest of society as of individual family members, and its principal purpose, at least where there are children, must be the safety and welfare of the child. It needs to be remembered that the tabulated right is not to family life as such but to respect for it. The purpose, in my view, is to assure within proper limits the entitlement of individuals to the benefit of what is benign and positive in family life. It is not to allow other individuals, however closely related and well-intentioned, to create or perpetuate situations which jeopardise their welfare.'[1]

It has been noted that that the existence of family life for the purposes of Article 8 is essentially a question of fact that depends upon the real existence in practice of close personal ties. A relationship which was based upon an adoption which contravened international conventions and was not recognised in the UK was therefore not necessarily incompatible with the existence of family life within the meaning of Article 8[2]. It has been observed that grandparents have a right to respect for family life, but that whether the right extends to the potential relationship between a natural father and a child born outside marriage appears to depend on the circumstances, including the nature of the relationship between the natural parents and the demonstrable interest in and commitment by the natural father to the child both before and after the birth. It was noted that even a potential relationship may not be outside the protection of Article 8[3]. In a case concerned with restrictions upon prison visits, it was held that whether the relationship between an uncle and his nephew amounts to family life depends upon the circumstances of the particular case: in the case of a young nephew born after his uncle had begun to serve his sentence, and who had seen his uncle only during a few short visits, there was held to be no family life[4]. It has been accepted that the family life of adult siblings living together is capable of engaging Article 8[5]. Another case concerned the consequences of a mistake made in the course of fertility treatment of two couples, where the sperm of one woman's husband was used to fertilise the eggs of the other woman. It was held that neither the biological father nor his wife had a sufficiently close relationship with the resultant twins to assert Article 8 rights. The partner of the child's mother could however assert Article 8 rights on account of his close relationship with the twins, whom he regarded as his own children[6]. It has been noted that the family life that exists between two persons ends when one of them dies[7].The question has been raised whether the natural parents of an adopted child retain any Article 8 rights[8].

In a case decided in 2005, the House of Lords considered that in the then state of Strasbourg jurisprudence, homosexual relationships did not fall within the scope of the right to respect for family life protected by Article 8[9].

1   *Re F (Adult: Court's Jurisdiction)* [2001] Fam 38 at pp 57–58.

2   *Singh (Pawandeep) v Entry Officer, New Delhi* [2005] QB 608.

3   *C v XYZ County Council* [2008] Fam 54 at paras 53–54 per Lawrence Collins LJ.

4   *R (Banks) v Governor of Wakefield Prison* [2001] EWHC Admin 917.

5   *Senthuran v Secretary of State for the Home Department* [2004] 4 All ER 365.

6   *L Teaching Hospitals NHS Trust v A* [2003] 1 FLR 1091.

7   *Michalak v Wandsworth London Borough Council* [2003] 1 WLR 617.

8   *In re J (A Child) (Adopted Child: Contact)* [2011] Fam 31.

9   *M v Secretary of State for Work and Pensions* [2006] 2 AC 91.

Positive obligations

6.21 The duty to secure 'respect' for family life can also involve positive obligations upon domestic authorities. Employment courts and tribunals must therefore examine whether dismissal on the grounds of incompatibility of private and family life with a contract of employment has properly balanced an employee's Article 8 rights with the interests of the employer[1]. In child custody cases, the overriding principle is that public authorities are expected to act in a manner which facilitates contact between parents and siblings[2]. When a child has been placed in care, Article 8 may also require a state to help the individual construct a personal or family identity through allowing access to records concerning his upbringing[3]. Domestic courts have held that there can also be positive obligations to provide welfare support where necessary to enable family life to continue[4].

1   *Obst v Germany* 2010-…; and *Schüth v Germany* 2010-…, discussed at para **7.28** below. See also *Özpinar v Turkey* (19 October 2010), paras 67–79 (complaints - leading to her dismissal - about a judge's repeated lateness for work, unsuitable clothing and make-up, and close relationship with a lawyer whose clients allegedly benefited from favourable decisions: certain aspects of the complaints had involved 'private life' although a judge's ethical duties may encroach upon her private life when her conduct tarnishes the image or reputation of the judiciary; and violation established as the proceedings had failed to provide adequate protection against arbitrariness).

2   *Mustafa and Armagan Akin v Turkey* (6 April 2010), paras21–30 (award of custody of one child to one parent and its sibling to the other parent, with provision only for exchange of the children between the parents at certain times and thus effectively preventing the children from spending time with each other, and either parent from spending time with both of their children at once: violation of Art 8 on account of failure to comply with positive obligations to act with a view to maintaining and developing the applicants' family ties, the Court also noting the lack of reasoning justifying the separation of the children particularly since neither parent had requested such an arrangement). But cf *RR v Romania (no 1)* (10 November 2009), paras 144–181 (Art 8 construed in the light of the Hague Convention: no positive obligation exists under Art 8 upon domestic authorities to ensure the return of a child where the parent concerned does not have a right of custody but merely a right of access; further, relevant decisions had been taken after adversarial proceedings).

3   *Gaskin v United Kingdom* (1989) A 160, paras 36–37.

4   *Anufrijeva v Southwark London Borough Council* [2004] QB 1124, discussed at para **6.86** below.

Widening the scope of Article 8 protection in respect of the 'family'

6.22 Article 8 jurisprudence in respect of recognition of 'family life', while recognising a wide range of family relationships, is perhaps still rather more cautious than some domestic legal systems in which a more liberal attitude in the regulation of family and private life is obvious. For example, in *X, Y and Z v United Kingdom*, the state had refused to register a transsexual as the father of a child born to his partner by artificial insemination of the donor. The Court accepted that there were *de facto* family ties linking the three applicants and thus domestic law had to ensure the integration of the child into the family from as early a stage in the child's life as was practicable. However, the lack of any common European standard on the issue of parental rights for transsexuals meant that states had a wide margin of appreciation in regulating this area in which general state interests (including protection of the integrity of domestic family law) outweighed any individual interest[1], while in *Fretté v France*, the lack of a common European approach to the question of the right of a homosexual to adopt was the crucial factor for the majority of the Court in determining that the refusal to provide the necessary prior authorisation did not involve a violation of Article 8[2]. While *Fretté* was subsequently reversed by the Grand Chamber in *EB v France*[3], the Court still takes a less progressive stance in this area, especially where there is considerable variation amongst states in domestic approaches[4]. The practical effect of all of this (as illustrated by cases such as *Petrovic v Austria*) is the recognition of a wider margin of appreciation on the part of state authorities and a corresponding reticence to extend the scope of Article 8 obligations.

1   *X, Y and Z v United Kingdom* 1997-II, paras 38–52 (at para 50 the Court observed that the first applicant was 'not prevented in any way from acting as [the child's] father in the social sense').

2   *Fretté v France* 2002-I, discussed at para **6.144** below.

3   *EB v France* [GC] 2008-….

4   See eg *Schwizgebel v Switzerland* 2010-…, paras 82–99 (refusal to allow a 47-year-old unmarried mother permission to adopt: the setting of minimum and maximum ages for adoption falls within the scope of a state's margin of appreciation).

6.23 Just as Article 12 has not been recognised as supporting any right of homosexuals to marry, so Article 8 is also more cautious than some domestic legal systems which take a more liberal attitude in the regulation of family and private life[1]. On the other hand, where the Court is satisfied that there has been a clearly-identifiable trend in European states in relation to a matter, it is more likely to recognise an enhanced responsibility of states. For example, in *Christine Goodwin v United Kingdom,* evidence of the increased social acceptance and legal recognition of the new sexual identity of post-operative transsexuals in European practice permitted the Court to review its existing jurisprudence in this field, holding also (in respect of Article 12) that denial of the right to transsexuals to marry a person of the sex opposite to their re-assigned gender was now contrary to this guarantee, too[2].

1   *Schalk and Kopf v Austria* 2010-…, discussed at para **6.04** above.

2   *Christine Goodwin v United Kingdom* [GC] 2002-VI, discussed at para **6.145** below.

'Home'

6.24 'Home' is closely related to both 'family life' and 'private life'[1]. The facts must support the establishment of a 'home', and this is determined by factors such as nature and length of residence, and intention[2]. However, the mere intention to establish a home in the future is insufficient[3]. A wide range of accommodation may constitute 'home', including a prison cell[4] and possibly even a camping van[5]. Even if the home has been established unlawfully in terms of domestic law, there may still be a 'home' deserving state respect in terms of Article 8. In *Buckley v United Kingdom*, the applicant had purchased land and had then occupied a caravan on this property with her children but in contravention of planning controls. The facts of the case, including length of residence, absence of any intention to move elsewhere and integration of her eldest children into the local school, allowed the Court to categorise the issue of failure to provide retrospective planning consents as one concerning the right to respect for 'home'[6]. The concept of 'home' is thus given an interpretation consistent with maximising the scope of the Article. For example, in *Gillow v United Kingdom*, the applicants had lived on Guernsey for some four years during which period they had bought a house. During an absence from the island for almost 19 years, they had retained ownership of the house and maintained an intention to return to Guernsey. The European Court of Human Rights considered that in these circumstances there were sufficient continuing links with the house to allow it to be considered their 'home'[7].

---

1   And ECHR, Prot 1, Art 1: eg *Depalle v France* [GC] 2010-..., paras 80–96 (decision to demolish homes considered under Prot 1, Art 1, and no separate issue arose under Art 8). See further Buyse 'Strings Attached: the Concept of "Home" in The Case Law of the European Court of Human Rights' [2006] EHRLR 294; and Kenna 'Housing Rights: Positive Duties and Enforceable Rights at the European Court of Human Rights' [2008] EHRLR 193. Cf *López Ostra v Spain* (1994) A 303-C, at para 51 (severe environmental pollution may prevent enjoyment of homes in such a way as to affect private and family life); and *Giacomelli v Italy* 2006-XII, paras 78–98 (delay in requiring environmental impact study, and failure to enforce court decisions suspending operation of plant emitting toxic pollutants: violation).

2   Eg *Menteş and Others v Turkey* 1997-VIII, para 73 (occupation of a house for significant periods annually was sufficient to establish an Art 8 interest); *Prokopovich v Russia* 2004-XI, paras 36–39 (sufficient and continuing links with the flat belonging to the applicant—'s late partner to allow it to constitute a 'home' for the purposes of Art 8).

3   *Loizidou v Turkey* 1996-VI, para 66.

4   *Brânduşe v Romania* 2009-..., paras 64–67 (complaint went beyond conditions of detention and concerned the applicant's only 'living space').

5   12474/86, *Kanthak v Germany* (1988) DR 58, 94 (the question whether the applicant's camping car could be considered a 'home' was left unresolved). See also *Hartung v France* (dec) (3 November 2009) (doubted whether a dressing room used on a temporary basis could constitute a 'home' for the purposes of Art 8, but even if it could do so, an identity check carried out within it was a justified interference with privacy as it was prescribed by law, pursued a legitimate aim, and the checking of identity papers was not disproportionate: inadmissible as manifestly ill-founded); and *Chelu v Romania* (12 January 2010), paras 43–46 (a laundry room not the exclusive property of the applicant nor where the applicant lived could not be regarded as a 'home' within the meaning of Art 8).

6   *Buckley v United Kingdom* 1996-IV, para 54. Cf *Varey v United Kingdom* (friendly settlement) [GC] (21 December 2000) (friendly settlement in relation to complaint that planning enforcement measures taken in respect of the applicants' occupation of land which they had bought in order to maintain their traditional gypsy lifestyle and culture violated Art 8).

7   *Gillow v United Kingdom* (1986) A 109, para 46.

6.25 Further, 'home' may extend beyond the domestic sphere to business premises. The case of *Niemietz v Germany* involved a court-authorised search of a lawyer's office. In deciding that in certain circumstances business premises could fall within the scope of 'home', the Court remarked that any precise distinction between office and home would often be difficult to draw 'since activities which are related to a profession or business may well be conducted from a person's private residence and activities which are not so related may well be carried on in an office or commercial premises'[1]. It is also possible for a company to claim protection under Article 8 for its offices and premises[2].

1   *Niemietz v Germany* (1992) A 251-B, paras 30–31. This judgment mirrors the approach adopted by the UN Human Rights Committee in the interpretation given to the International Covenant on Civil and Political Rights, Art 17: see General Comment 16(32), ORGenAss, 40th Session, Supplement No 40 (A/40/40) (1985): 'the term "home" ... is to be understood to indicate the place where a person resides or carries out his usual occupation'. 'Home' cannot, though, extend to buildings for livestock: *Leveau and Fillon v France* (dec) 2005-X.

2   *Stés Colas Est and Others v France* (16 April 2002), paras 40–50 (searches of offices of applicant companies: Art 8 could apply in certain circumstances to a company's right to respect for its principal office, local offices and commercial premises). Cf Cases 46/87 and 227/88, *Hoechst AG v Commission* [1989] ECR 2859 (ECJ decided that commercial premises were not encompassed by 'home' within the meaning of Art 8).

6.26 Respect for 'home' may give rise to questions including termination of a tenancy[1], physical intrusion into a home[2] to carry out a search[3], the taking of planning and control decisions[4], environmental nuisances which have a substantial impact upon enjoyment of the property[5], and possibly also non-physical intrusion through telephone tapping[6]. However, the concept does not include questions relating to rights or obligations arising from a lease[7] or compulsory purchase[8] or other matters which more properly fall within the scope of Article 1 of Protocol no 1 which protects property rights[9]. Further, 'home' does not extend to protection of activities of an essentially public nature[10].

1   *Blečić v Croatia* (29 July 2004), paras 66–71 (termination of special protected tenancy of a flat on account of unjustified absence: no violation, but the case was ultimately declared inadmissible before the Grand Chamber: see *Blečić v Croatia* [GC] 2006-III). See also *Ćosić v Croatia* (15 January 2009), paras 18–23 (domestic law contained no procedural safeguards for assessing the fairness of a decision to evict the applicant: violation); *Zehentner v Austria* 2009- ..., paras 53–65, and 70–74 (eviction from home without the opportunity to participate properly in proceedings which lacked effective safeguards to assess the proportionality of the decision in light of the lack of mental capacity: violation).

2   12474/86, *Kanthak v Germany* (1988) DR 58, 94.

3   Eg *Murray v United Kingdom* (1994) A 300-A, paras 84–86 (entry and search by military personnel); *Chappell v United Kingdom* (1989) A 152-A, para 51 (*Anton Piller* orders); and

Imakayeva v Russia 2006-XIII, paras 183–189 (search and seizure in absence of authorisations or safeguards: violation).

4   Eg *Buckley v United Kingdom* 1996-IV, para 54; *Menteş v Turkey* 1997-VIII, para 73 (destruction of homes by security forces constituted a 'particularly grave interference').

5   Eg *Powell and Rayner v United Kingdom* (1990) A 172, para 40 (airport noise).

6   *Klass v Germany* (1978) A 28, para 41 (point raised but not decided).

7   *Langborger v Sweden* (1989) A 155, paras 38–39 (power to negotiate rent conferred on tenants' association).

8   10825/84, *Howard v United Kingdom* (1987) DR 52, 198 (compulsory purchase order for the applicant's house was justified by Art 8(2) as being necessary for the protection of the rights of others who would benefit from the development).

9   See para **8.08** below.

10 *Friend and Others v United Kingdom* (dec) (24 November 2009) (challenge to the Protection of Wild Mammals (Scotland) Act and the Hunting Act 2004 declared inadmissible, the Court noting that the ban did not restrict employment or create difficulties in earning a living, and rejecting the argument that the laws prevented hunting with dogs in the applicants' homes as the definition of 'home' could not be extended as far as land upon which the owner permitted sport).

6.27 The guarantee is essentially a civil and not an economic right, and thus cannot be interpreted as requiring states to provide a 'home' for every family[1]. Certainly, though, a person who is at risk of losing his home must be able to have the proportionality of the measure determined by an independent tribunal, even if the right of occupation has come to an end. In *McCann v United Kingdom*, the applicant had been evicted from the matrimonial home after the breakdown of his marriage following proceedings seeking a possession order. His wife had obtained an order requiring him to leave, and thereafter a housing officer had persuaded her to sign a common law notice to quit after the applicant had moved back into the house following her rehousing. Judicial review proceedings had upheld the lawfulness of the notice to quit even though it had been signed without an understanding of its consequences. For the Court, while the proceedings had been in accordance with the law and had pursued legitimate aims, these had bypassed the complex statutory scheme which would have accorded the applicant as a secure tenant the opportunity of having his personal circumstances examined, nor had the common-law proceedings provided any opportunity for an independent tribunal to examine the proportionality of the notice to quit or of the repossession. The conclusion was that the test of 'necessary in a democratic society' had not been satisfied[2].

1   *Velosa Barreto v Portugal* (1995) A 334, para 24 (a landlord had sought recovery of possession of a rented house; the Court accepted that legislation sought to protect tenants and had a tendency to promote the economic well-being of the country and thus had a legitimate aim; the landlord had failed to show that he had any need of the property and the state was under no obligation to give a landlord the right to recover possession of a rented house on request and in any circumstances). See also *Ward v United Kingdom* (dec) (9 November 2004) (refusal to relocate gypsy site following report indicating location was prejudicial to health: inadmissible as the applicant had voluntarily moved onto the site, had taken no steps to find another official site, and no exceptional circumstances allowing the derivation of a right to be provided with alternative housing).

2   *McCann v United Kingdom* 2008-..., paras 46–55.

Domestic court decisions on respect for the home

6.28 Domestic law in England and Wales, where almost all the cases have so far arisen, has encountered serious difficulties in relation to Article 8 in the context of proceedings for the recovery of possession of property owned by local authorities which is being occupied unlawfully. A major cause of the difficulty is the meaning of 'home' in Article 8. A person may have a home for the purposes of Article 8 without having any proprietary right, and may indeed have a right to respect for his home even if his occupation is unlawful[1]. The existence of a home is identified with 'efficient and continuing link' in terms of the social and psychological attachment or bond that develops with one's accommodation and neighbourhood, rather than simply with the concept of a roof over one's head. As the Strasbourg Court held in *Connors v United Kingdom*[2], the concept of a home is 'concerned with identity, self-determination, physical and moral identity, maintenance of relationships with others and a settled and secure home and a place in the community'. The concept is thus more philosophical than proprietorial. By its nature, it is difficult to reconcile with domestic property law, which places importance on certainty and clear legal norms. A further problem has been the number of applications for possession orders, and the summary procedure under which they are obtained, which gave rise to concern about the practical implications of inquiring into Article 8 issues, if prolonged and expensive proceedings were to ensue.

1   See eg *Buckley v United Kingdom* 1996-IV, para 54.
2   *Connors v United Kingdom* (27 May 2004), para 82.

6.29 In the case of *Harrow London Borough Council v Qazi*, the House of Lords held by a majority of 3 to 2 that a landlord's contractual and proprietary right to possession could not be defeated by a defence based on Article 8[1]. Soon aterwards, however, the jurisprudence of the Strasbourg Court started to develop rapidly, notably in the judgment of the First Section in *Connors v United Kingdom*[2]. In *Kay and Others v Lambeth London Borough Council*, the House of Lords considered the matter again in the light of *Connors* and affirmed *Qazi* by a majority of 4 to 3[3]. Later, in *McCann v United Kingdom,* the Fourth Section of the Strasbourg Court held, on similar facts to those of *Qazi,* that Article 8 imposed an obligation on the state to apply Article 8(2) to the individual facts of each case. It remarked that, as the minority of the House of Lords in *Kay* observed, it would be only in very exceptional cases that an applicant would succeed in presenting an arguable case which would require the court to examine the Article 8 issue[4]. The House of Lords returned to the matter in *Doherty v Birmingham City Council,* and adhered to the decision of the majority in *Kay,* with some additional guidance[5]. The losing parties in *Kay* were then successful in Strasbourg, initially before the Fourth Section[6]. The impasse was finally resolved in *Manchester City Council v Pinnock,* where the Supreme Court held that, if domestic law was to be compatible with Article 8, a court which was asked to make an order for possession of a person's home at the suit of a local authority had to have the power to assess the proportionality of making the order in the light of Article 8 and, in making that assessment, to resolve any relevant dispute of fact. The court observed that in virtually every case where a residential occupier has no contractual or statutory protection, and the local authority is entitled to possession as a matter of domestic law, there will be a very strong case for saying that making an order for possession would be proportionate. However, the court added, in some cases there may be factors which would tell the other way. The court also emphasised that its judgment had no bearing on cases where the person seeking the order for possession was a private landowner[7]. The implications of the *Pinnock* case were considered in greater detail in the subsequent case of *Hounslow London Borough v Powell*[8].

1 *Harrow London Borough Council v Qazi* [2004] 1 AC 983.

2 *Connors v United Kingdom* (27 May 2004).

3 *Kay v Lambeth London Borough Council* [2006] 2 AC 465.

4 *McCann v United Kingdom* 2008-....

5 *Doherty v Birmingham City Council* [2009] 1 AC 367.

6 *Kay and Others v United Kingdom* (21 September 2010).

7 *Manchester City Council v Pinnock* [2010] 3 WLR 1441.

8 *Hounslow London Borough v Powell* [2011] 2 WLR 287. In relation to tenants on caravan sites, see also *R (Smith) v Barking and Dagenham LBC* [2003] EWCA Civ 385; and in relation to trespassing travellers, see *R (Casey) v Crawley Borough Council* [2006] EWHC 301 (Admin).

6.30 The implications of Article 8 for homelessness legislation have been considered in a number of cases. In a case concerned with a gypsy who faced homelessness as a result of eviction from an illegal caravan site, it was held that she was not entitled to be housed by the local authority on a caravan site: the authority's decision that the bricks and mortar accommodation offered to the appellant was suitable for her occupation did not violate her rights under Article 8 taken with Article 14[1]. Legislation requiring a dependent child to be disregarded in assessing priority need, if the child was subject to immigration control, was on the other hand incompatible with Article 8 taken with Article 14[2]. The question whether illegal immigrants are entitled to be provided with accommodation has also been considered in a number of cases[3].

1 *Codona v Mid-Bedfordshire District Council* [2005] HLR 1.

2 *R (Morris) v Westminster City Council* [2006] 1 WLR 505.

3 See para **6.86** below.

6.31 Article 8 has also been considered in relation to compulsory purchase[1] and planning issues. In *Lough and others v First Secretary of State,* which concerned a challenge to a planning decision permitting a development which would interfere with the amenity of local residents, it was held that Article 8 created no absolute right to amenities currently enjoyed, and its role, though important, had to be seen in the context of competing rights, including rights of other landowners and of the community as a whole. By referring to the protection of the rights and freedoms of others, Article 8 acknowledged a landowner's right to make beneficial use of his land, subject amongst other matters to appropriate planning control. The provisions of the Convention should inform the decision maker's approach to material considerations in a planning matter, and the concept of proportionality and the need to strike a balance was inherent in that approach[2]. Several other cases have concerned travelling people who had established homes in breach of planning law[3], or had applied for planning permission[4]. The inability to recover expenses in respect of a planning inquiry has been held not to infringe Article 8 or Article 1 of Protocol no 1[5]. Article 8 has also been considered in cases concerned with other environmental issues[6].

1   See *Pascoe v First Secretary of State* [2007] 1 WLR 885; *Smith v Secretary of State for Trade and Industry* [2008] 1 WLR 394.

2   *Lough and others v First Secretary of State* [2004] 1 WLR 2557. See also *R (Vetterlein) v Hampshire County Council* [2002] 1 P & CR 31.

3   See eg *Davis v Tonbridge and Malling Borough Council* [2004] EWCA Civ 194; *R (Coates) v South Buckinghamshire District Council* [2004] EWCA Civ 1378; *Chichester District Council v First Secretary of State* [2005] 1 WLR 279.

4   See eg *Clarke v Secretary of State for the Environment, Transport and the Regions* [2002] EWCA Civ 819 (review of planning application lodged by Roma: need to take into account Arts 8 and 14).

5   *Cannell v Scottish Ministers* 2003 SC 404.

6   See para **6.129** below.

6.32 Article 8 has also been considered in relation to a number of other issues affecting the home, including covert surveillance[1], searches of premises[2] and the rights of persons detained in a high security hospital[3]. In relation to confiscation orders, has been held that Article 8 rights are not engaged at the stage when the court is determining the offender's realisable assets, but that they may be engaged if the confiscation order is not met and the court is asked to make an order for the sale of the family home. The court will then have to consider whether or not it would be proportionate to make the order in the circumstances of the case[4].

1   See para **6.99** below.

2   See para **6.110** below.

3   *R (N) v Secretary of State for Health* [2009] EWCA Civ 795 (ban on smoking inside Rampton Hospital: Art 8 not engaged); *L v Board of State Hospital* 2011 SLT 233 (ban on patients at State Hospital receiving food parcels from visitors or ordering food from outside sources: Art 8 engaged, and restrictions required to be justified).

4   *R v Ahmed* [2005] 1 WLR 122.

'Private life'

6.33 'Private life' is 'a broad term not susceptible to exhaustive definition' and covers the physical and psychological or moral integrity of a person[1]. Thus Article

8 'can sometimes embrace aspects of an individual's physical and social identity ... [and] protects a right to personal development, and the right to establish and develop relationships with other human beings and the outside world'. In consequence, 'the notion of personal autonomy is an important principle underlying the interpretation of its guarantees'[2], and to this end 'private life' includes 'the right to live privately, away from unwanted attention' thus securing 'to the individual a sphere within which he or she can freely pursue the development and fulfilment of his or her personality'[3]. In short, the scope of 'private life' is wide[4].

1   *Gunnarsson v Iceland* (dec) (20 October 2005) (application alleging failure to protect honour and reputation: while professional reputation as such had not hitherto been recognised as falling within the scope of Art 8 (cf International Covenant on Civil and Political Rights, Art 17) although such issues could be taken into account in a complaint, but even assuming that the matter in the applicant's case fell within the scope of Art 8, the domestic courts could reasonably have concluded that the interests in protecting freedom of speech had been preponderant: inadmissible). Cf 27436/95 and 28406/95, *Stewart-Brady v United Kingdom* (1997) DR 90, 45 (a state need not provide legal aid for actions of defamation for harm to reputation).

2   *Pretty v United Kingdom* 2002–III, at para 61.

3   *Smirnova v Russia* 2003-IX, para 95.

4   See further Marshall 'A Right to Personal Autonomy at the European Court of Human Rights' [2008] EHRLR 337.

6.34 The concept can thus accommodate a broad range of issues, including the quality of private life as affected by the amenities of his home[1], educational provision[2], infliction of corporal[3] and other forms of punishment or treatment falling short of violations of Article 3[4], telephone tapping and electronic surveillance[5], release of images by the police to the media[6], data collection[7], personal identity[8] and autonomy (including suicide)[9] including use of family names[10] and registration of ethnic origin[11], access to information on personal identity[12] or state security records[13], arbitrary denial of citizenship[14] or of recognition of professional qualification[15], deprivation of documentation necessary for everyday transactions[16], legal determination of personal status[17], forcible medical examination[18], involuntary medical treatment[19], imposition of liability on account of ill-health[20], excessive delay in providing medical treatment[21], the preservation of stability in mental health[22], recognition of transsexualism[23], and the criminalisation of homosexual conduct[24].

1   *Powell and Rayner v United Kingdom* (1990) A 172, para 40.

2   *Belgian Linguistic case* (1968) A 6, Law, para 7.

3   *Costello-Roberts v United Kingdom* (1993) A 247-C, para 36.

4   Cf *Raninen v Finland* 1997-VIII, paras 63–64 (the applicant had been handcuffed when he was taken from prison to a military hospital: while the Court did not exclude the possibility that Art 8 could be regarded as affording protection in relation to conditions during detention which do not meet the level of severity required by Art 3, in this case, however, there was not sufficient evidence to warrant a finding that there had been a breach of Art 8).

5   Eg *Klass and Others v Germany* (1978) A 28, para 41; *Peck v United Kingdom* 2003-I, paras 57–63; *Khan v United Kingdom* 2000-V, para 25. Surveillance by private parties also engages Art 8: *Köpke v Germany* (dec) (5 October 2010) (covert video surveillance instructed by employer and carried out by detective agency of employee and her workplace).

6   *Khuzhin and Others v Russia* (23 October 2008), paras 115–118 (photographs taken from the criminal case files and shown during a broadcast in which prosecutors discussed the case of the accused: the removal of the photograph and its transmission to a journalist had constituted an interference with private life).

7   Eg *Lingens v Austria* (1986) A 103, paras 37–47.

8   For discussion of the relationship between 'private' and 'family' life in respect of paternity issues, see **6.19** above.

9   *Pretty v United Kingdom* 2002-III, discussed at para **4.53** above; and see at para 61: 'Although no previous case has established as such any right to self-determination as being contained in Art 8 of the Convention, the Court considers that the notion of personal autonomy is an important principle underlying the interpretation of its guarantees'. See also *Haas v Switzerland* (dec) (20th May 2010) (refusal to supply medication to be used for suicide: admissible).

10   *Stjerna v Finland* (1994) A 299-B.

11   *Ciubotaru v Moldova* (27 April 2010), paras 49–59 (failure to secure effective respect for private life through preventing the applicant from changing the recording of his ethnic origin notwithstanding the fact that there was objectively verifiable evidence supporting such a change).

12   *Gaskin v United Kingdom* (1989) A 160, paras 36–37 (personal file containing history and development of child who had been in foster care).

13   *Haralambie v Romania* (27 October 2009), paras 84–96 (procedure for gaining access to personal files held by Securitae and other former security services during Romania's communist period was ineffective and inaccessible: violation).

14   *Karassev v Finland* (dec) 1999-II (while the Convention did not guarantee the right to the citizenship of a particular state, in certain cases arbitrary denial of citizenship could give rise to an Art 8 issue).

15   *Bigaeva v Greece* (28 May 2009), paras 22–25 and 30–36 (legally-settled non-national who had undertaken undergraduate and postgraduate legal studies in law in Greece with a view to practising in and integrating into that country had been prevented from taking the bar exam on account of her nationality: Art 8 applied because the restriction represented an halt to years of personal and academic endeavour and a will to integrate into Greek society and work in accordance with her qualifications).

16   *Smirnova v Russia* 2003-IX, paras 95–100 (seizure of 'internal passport' resulting in a number of everyday inconveniences as well as for more crucial needs such as finding employment or receiving medical care).

17   18643/91, *Benes v Austria* (1992) DR 72, 271 (annulment of marriage was an interference in the circumstances with respect for private life); and *Shtukaturov v Russia* 2008-…, paras 90–96 (proceedings resulting in an individual suffering from mental illness being deprived of his capacity taken without his knowledge and which he could not challenge constituted a very serious interference with his private life as he had become fully dependent on his official guardian in almost all areas of his life for an indefinite period).

18   *Matter v Slovakia* (5 July 1999), para 64; *YF v Turkey* 2003-IX, paras 41–43 (compulsory gynaecological examination carried out on detainee following allegation of ill-treatment by police officers).

19   *Peters v Netherlands* (1994) DR 77, 75; *Glass v United Kingdom* 2004-II, para 83 (proposed treatment in the absence of authorisation by a court resulted in a breach of Art 8).

20   *Glor v Switzerland* 2009-…, paras 52–56 (Art 8 was applicable in respect of an obligation imposed upon an individual to pay an exemption tax on account of a finding that he was unfit for military service as the liability arose from illness, a fact independent of the person's will).

21   32647/96, *Passannante v Italy* (1998) DR 94, 91 (where a state has assumed responsibilities for health care, an excessive delay which is likely to have an impact on a patient's health may

give rise to an Art 8 issue; but, on the facts of the case, there was no evidence of any such impact: inadmissible).

22   *Bensaid v United Kingdom* 2001-I, at para 47 ('the preservation of mental stability is in [the context of identity and personal development, and the right to establish and develop relationships with other human beings and the outside world] an indispensable precondition to effective enjoyment of the right to respect for private life').

23   Eg *Christine Goodwin v United Kingdom* [GC] 2002-VI, paras 81–85.

24   Eg *Dudgeon v United Kingdom* (1983) A 45.

6.35 Nor was the Court in *Niemietz v Germany* willing to restrict 'private life' to 'an "inner circle" in which the individual may live his own personal life as he chooses and to exclude therefrom entirely the outside world not encompassed within that circle'. In this case, the Court accepted that the concept of private life 'must also comprise to a certain degree the right to establish and develop relationships with other human beings'. Thus Article 8 could not be assumed 'to exclude activities of a professional or business nature since it is, after all, in the course of their working lives that the majority of people have a significant, if not the greatest, opportunity of developing relationships with the outside world'[1]. Restrictions imposed upon individuals preventing access to various spheres of employment in the private sector may also in certain circumstances give rise to issues falling within the notion of 'private life'[2]. 'Private life' may also include an individual's wishes concerning the disposal of his remains after death[3].

1   *Niemietz v Germany* (1992) A 251-B, at para 29. Cf 23953/94, *Reiss v Austria* (1995) DR 82, 51 (public showing of obscene videos in a bar: the extent to which business premises are covered by Art 8 protection depends on the nature of the premises and the activities carried out, and here the conviction of the applicant did not involve an interference with Art 8 rights).

2   *Sidabras and Džiautas v Lithuania* 2004-VIII, paras 51–62 (wide-ranging restrictions introduced almost a decade after the re-establishment of Lithuanian independence and barring former KGB officers in Lithuania from access to various spheres of employment in the private sector: violation of Art 14 in conjunction with Art 8). See also *Turek v Slovakia* 2006-II, paras 110–117 (restrictions on the ability of civil servant to challenge in the context of judicial proceedings his registration as alleged former collaborator in light of confidentiality of files dating back to the communist era: violation); and *Bigaeva v Greece* (28 May 2009), paras 30–36 (non-national prevented from taking the bar exam on account of her nationality: allowing her to commence pupillage when it was clear that on completion she would not be entitled to sit for the Bar examinations showed a lack of consistency and respect towards the applicant personally and professionally and constituted unlawful interference with her private life). In the domestic case of *R (Pamplin) v Law Society* [2001] EWHC Admin 300, Art 8 was held to have no application to the disclosure by the police to the Law Society of a transcript of a police interview concerning the applicant's activities as a solicitor's clerk.

3   *Elli Poluhas Dödsbo v Sweden* 2006-I, para 24 (not necessary in the circumstances to determine whether refusal to transfer remains of applicant's deceased husband involved 'family life' or 'private life'). See also *Hadri-Vionnet v Switzerland* 2008-..., paras 53–62 (burial of a still-born child in a communal grave without the attendance or consent of the mother who had been entitled to attend her child's burial, to have the body transported in a suitable vehicle, and possibly to have a ceremony: violation as there had been no legal basis for the interference with private and family life, even although there had been no bad faith, the Court noting that in a sphere as private and sensitive as the death of a close relative, a particularly high degree of diligence and care is required).

6.36 Such judgments illustrate the dynamic interpretation given to 'private life' under Article 8 and one which includes but is significantly wider than 'privacy' as traditionally understood in Anglo-American jurisprudence. There are however certain limits to the extent to which 'private life' may be stretched. For example, it probably does not cover regulation of personal appearance[1]. It is also unlikely to extend to activities involving significant numbers of individuals, or possibly to activities which degrade or debase rather than help promote self-identity and worth[2].

1   *Tiğ v Turkey* (dec) (24 May 2005) (university decree prohibiting having a beard: inadmissible, even accepting physical appearance was an aspect of private life).

2   Eg *Laskey, Jaggard and Brown v United Kingdom* 1997–I, discussed at para **6.141** below.

Positive obligations

6.37 Certain positive obligations arise in relation to 'private life'. For example, there is now a responsibility to ensure that domestic law adequately protects respect for private life from unwarranted interference by the media in relation to protection of privacy and also reputation[1]. Domestic law and national authorities must also ensure the effective protection of physical and psychological integrity, an obligation complementing responsibilities arising under Articles 2 and 3[2], and thus states must ensure that the criminal law imposes adequate sanctions enforced by criminal justice agencies to deter certain behaviour or acts[3]. This development is of particular significance in respect of domestic violence and violations of the physical or moral integrity of young people. In *KU v Finland,* for example, the failure of the authorities to force an internet service provider to disclose the identity of the person who placed an advertisement of a sexual nature on the internet under the name of the applicant, a 12 year old boy, without his knowledge and which had resulted in his being targeted by paedophiles was held to have constituted a violation of Article 8, the Court considering that the possibility of obtaining damages from the service provider was not a sufficient remedy and that it was inappropriate to accord precedence to confidentiality over the physical and moral welfare of children given the potential threat to the applicant's physical and mental welfare and his vulnerable age[4]. In other cases, the positive obligation to protect aspects of private life may be discharged through the availability of adequate civil compensation, for example, in relation to invasions of privacy or unwarranted attacks on reputation or honour[5]. There is also an expectation that surveillance instructed by private parties is adequately regulated by law in light of the need for 'increased vigilance in protecting private life which is necessary to contend with new communication technologies which make it possible to store and reproduce personal data'[6].

1   See paras **6.130–6.132** below.

2   See paras **4.22–4.25** and **4.88–4.92** above.

3   *Sandra Janković v Croatia* (5 March 2009), paras 44–59 (the applicant, who had been

assaulted by other individuals, had no effective criminal law protection due to the defective manner in which the domestic authorities implemented their provisions: violation).

4   *KU v Finland* 2008-..., paras 40–51.

5   Cf *Armonienë v Lithuania* (25 November 2008), at para 46 (limits for compensation for non-pecuniary damage for intrusions into private life 'must not be such as to deprive the individual of his or her privacy and thereby empty the right of its effective content').

6   *Köpke v Germany* (dec) (5 October 2010) (covert video surveillance instructed by employer and carried out by detective agency of employee and her workplace: Art 8 was engaged, although 'covert video surveillance at the workplace following substantiated suspicions of theft does not concern a person's private life to an extent which is comparable to the affection of essential aspects of private life by grave acts in respect of which the Court has considered protection by legislative provisions indispensable'

Domestic decisions on respect for private life

6.38 The domestic courts have considered the Article 8 guarantee in respect of private life in a number of different contexts. Those which have arisen most frequently – such as covert surveillance[1], search powers[2], access to and disclosure of personal data[3], medical treatment[4], intrusions into private life by the media[5], the protection of reputation[6], and sexuality[7] – are discussed in detail below. Detailed consideration was given to the scope of the guarantee in relation to anti-hunting legislation. It was held that the legislation did not engage Article 8: the prohibition was directed solely at activities which were of a public nature and lay outside the private sphere of a person's existence which was protected by Article 8. Nor could the protection afforded to the cultural lifestyle of national or ethnic minorities be converted into the protection of all minority activities[8]. In *R (Wright) v Secretary of State for Health* the House of Lords treated Article 8 as being potentially engaged by the loss of an employment, where there was a sufficiently serious impact upon personal relationships[9]. In *R (Purdy) v Director of Public Prosecutions*, Article 8 was held to be engaged, and violated, by a lack of clarity as to the policy which would be followed by the DPP in deciding whether to prosecute the husband of a woman who was terminally ill, in the event that he were to be complicit in her assisted suicide[10]. Other matters considered have included the withdrawal of nutrition and hydration from patients[11], random breath tests[12], the conditions which may be attached to a probation order[13], the conditions for qualifying for disability living allowance[14], the grant of welfare assistance to destitute unlawful immigrants[15], and the right to choose what one eats and drinks[16].

1   See paras **6.99–6.102** below.

2   See para **6.110** below.

3   See paras **6.116–6.118** below.

4   See para **6.124** below.

5   See paras **6.134–6.136** below.

6   See para **6.138** below.

7   See para **6.147** below.

8   *R (Countryside Alliance) v A-G* [2008] 1 AC 719; *Whaley v Lord Advocate* 2008 SC (HL) 107.

There were suggestions in *Countryside Alliance* that the right to participate in leisure activities of a less public nature (such as mountaineering, playing music or ice skating) was protected by Art 8.

9   *R (Wright) v Secretary of State for Health* [2009] 1 AC 739. One might wonder how far this approach might extend: cf *R (Countryside Alliance) v A-G* [2007] QB 305 at para 103 per Sir Anthony Clarke MR See also *Security Industry Authority v Stewart* [2009] 1 WLR 466 (refusal of licence to work as a door supervisor: any interference with Art 8 rights justified as a proportionate response to the need to regulate the industry in the public interest).

10   *R (Purdy) v Director of Public Prosecutions* [2010] 1 AC 345. The House of Lords departed from its earlier decision in *R (Pretty) v Director of Public Prosecutions* [2002] 1 AC 800 in the light of the judgment of the European Court of Human Rights in *Pretty v United Kingdom* (2002)-III.

11   *NHS Trust A v M* [2001] Fam 348; *R (Burke) v General Medical Council* [2006] QB 273.

12   *Miller v Bell* 2004 SCCR 534.

13   *Reid v Napier* 2002 SLT 1229.

14   *M's Guardian v Advocate General for Scotland* 2010 SLT 621.

15   *R (Clue) v Birmingham City Council* [2011] 1 WLR 99.

16   *L v Board of State Hospital* 2011 SLT 233.

'Correspondence'

6.39 The scope of respect for 'correspondence' is obviously related closely to both 'private life' and 'family life'[1]. The actual content of the communication is irrelevant, and business or non-private 'correspondence' also falls within the guarantee[2]. Thus where the challenge is to an interference with expression contained in correspondence, the *lex specialis* governing the application is Article 8, rather than Article 10[3]. The term covers communication by means of letter, telegram[4] and telephone conversations[5], and use of email. It may also involve the seizure of magazines[6]. The scope of positive obligations in respect of 'correspondence' is perhaps less obvious. It may extend, for example, to facilitating communication by prisoners by providing necessary material resources[7]. The scope of 'respect for correspondence' is in practice unlikely to cause difficulty. Domestic cases concerned with respect for correspondence are considered below[8].

1   Cf *Funke v France* (1993) A 256-A, para 48 (house search and seizures conceded by state to have involved private life; found by Commission additionally to have involved respect for home; and also respect for correspondence by the Court). Receiving unwanted or offensive communications amounts to an interference with right to respect for private life: *Muscio v Italy* (dec) (13 November 2007) (receipt of unsolicited pornographic email: inadmissible, as connecting to the internet effectively deprives individuals of their privacy and stopping 'spam' was not technically surmountable).

2   *A v France* (1993) A 277-B, paras 36–37 (police tapping of conversations relating to serious crimes); *Halford v United Kingdom* 1997-III, paras 43–52 (interception of conversations of senior police officer relating both to police work and to merely private matters); *Kopp v Switzerland* 1998-II, para 50 (interception of telephone calls made to and from a law firm).

3   Eg *Campbell v United Kingdom* (1992) A 233, discussed further at para **6.51** below.

4   21482/93, *Christie v United Kingdom* (1994) DR 78, 119 (applicant's telexes were routinely intercepted; this was held to be an interference with the guarantees of Art 8); *Messina v Italy* (1993) A 257-H, para 30.

5   Telephone conversations may also be covered by the notion of 'private life': *Klass and Others v Germany* (1978) A 28, para 41. Additionally, telephone calls between family members will also be covered by the notion of 'family life': *Margareta and Roger Andersson v Sweden* (1992) A 226-A, para 72.

6   7308/75, *X v United Kingdom* (1978) DR 16, 32 (seizure of pornographic magazine).

7   *Gagiu v Romania* (24 February 2009), paras 88–92 (failure to provide a prisoner with stamps for the purpose of correspondence with the Court, having had to sell his food to other detainees in order to buy stamps: violation).

8   See paras **6.100** and **6.152** below.

Determining whether there has been an 'interference'

6.40 The duty imposed by Article 8(1) upon states to ensure 'respect' for private and family life, home and correspondence can involve both negative and positive duties: that is, the provision imposes obligations not only to refrain from taking state action which interferes with the guarantee, but also in certain circumstances the duty to take positive action to ensure domestic law encourages or ensures effective 'respect' in the conduct of private and family life relationships and activities. Normally, the question whether a state by its action has failed to refrain from interfering[1] with an individual's rights is a straightforward one. In respect of private life, there will be an interference when state action has a direct impact upon an individual's rights as, for example, with the storage and release of information concerning an individual's private life[2]. Similarly, there will be an interference with the right to respect for 'home' through state action such as house searches by state officials[3], by authorising activity which has a direct impact on enjoyment of the amenities of a home[4] or through inaction and the continuing failure of public authorities and the legal system to respond appropriately to breaches of individuals' rights[5]. Delays in determining issues involving parental rights may also result in an interference with respect for 'family life'[6]. Impeding the initiation of correspondence (as for example by requiring that a prisoner obtain official permission before contacting a solicitor[7]), delaying a communication (for example, through opening and reading mail[8]), or intercepting a conversation (for example, by telephone tapping[9]) clearly give rise to Article 8 issues, as will the release to a third party of information gathered for a legitimate purpose[10]. Interception by itself will constitute an 'interference', and the question of whether there has been any subsequent use of recordings is not a relevant consideration in this assessment[11].

1   The Court makes use of the notion of 'interference' found in the opening words of para 2 in order to discuss whether any para 1 issue has arisen.

2   *Leander v Sweden* (1987) A 116, para 48.

3   Eg *Funke v France* (1993) A 256-A, para 48; *Murray v United Kingdom* (1994) A 300-A, paras 84–86.

4   *Powell and Rayner v United Kingdom* (1990) A 172, para 40 (noise of aircraft when using Heathrow Airport); *López Ostra v Spain* (1994) A 303-C, para 51 (severe pollution from waste treatment plant close to applicant's home

5   *Moldovan and Others v Romania (no 2)* 2005-VII, paras 93–101 (continuing and serious violation of Art 8 rights involving perpetuation of insecurity affecting Roma villagers forced to sleep in livestock premises after the destruction of their homes by a mob which included state officials).

6   *H v United Kingdom* (1987) A 120 paras 89–90 (delays in determining whether a child born to father with history of drug abuse and violent behaviour and mother recently discharged from mental hospital should be freed for adoption. For domestic discussion, see *Re D (A Child) (Intractable Contact Dispute: Publicity)* [2004] 1 FLR 1226 (defects in procedures in the court system in cases involving parental contact and residence disputes).

7   *Golder v United Kingdom* (1975) A 18, para 43.

8   *Silver and Others v United Kingdom* (1983) A 61, paras 83–84; *Campbell v United Kingdom* (1992) A 233, para 32.

9   *Malone v United Kingdom* (1984) A 82, para 64. However, the use of electronic 'bugging devices' in private homes is more likely to fall within respect for private life and home life: cf 12175/86, *Hewitt and Harman v United Kingdom* (1989) DR 67, 88 (applicants subject to telephone and mail intercepts by government surveillance agents; it was not contested that this constituted an interference with the applicants' Art 8 rights); and 20271/92 *Redgrave v United Kingdom* (1 September 1993) (the applicant, who was a well-known actress and a member of the Marxist party, discovered an electronic listening device in her house).

10   *Malone v United Kingdom* (1984) A 82 para 84 (release of information to the police on calls made on a telephone line, collated to ensure a telephone subscriber is correctly billed).

11   *Kopp v Switzerland* 1998-II, paras 51–53 (recorded conversations not disclosed to the prosecutor and subsequently destroyed).

DOMESTIC CASES ON 'INTERFERENCE'

6.41 The question whether there has been an interference with Article 8 rights has been considered in a large number of domestic cases, many of which are considered below in the context of their particular subject matter. One case of interest which is not discussed below is *Whitefield v General Medical Council*, in which the Privy Council held that the imposition on a doctor of conditions requiring him to abstain from alcohol was not an interference with the right to respect for private life under Article 8(1): the appellant was not prevented from going to his local public house or engaging in his social life while drinking non-alcoholic drinks[1].

1   *Whitefield v General Medical Council* [2003] IRLR 39.

'Victim' status

6.42 Some jurisprudence indicates that an individual can indeed be a 'victim' of an interference even where there has been no actual or obvious application of state action. The mere existence of certain legal provisions (for example, those which render certain forms of homosexual conduct criminal[1]) may also be sufficient without the necessity of establishing application of the legal powers: the 'chilling effect' upon an individual's behaviour may in itself constitute an interference with respect for private life. A similar approach may in certain circumstances be taken in regard to covert surveillance which by its very nature is hidden or not obvious. For example, the very existence of legislation authorising telephone tapping which thus creates the 'menace of surveillance' may in certain circumstances amount to an 'interference'[2] where the applicant is a member of a class reasonably likely to be subjected to surveillance measures[3].

1   Eg *SL v Austria* (dec) (22 November 2001). See further para **6.140** below.

2   Eg *Klass and Others v Germany* (1978) A 28, at para 41.

3   Cf *Malone v United Kingdom* (1984) A 82, para 64; and 12015/86, *Hilton v United Kingdom* (1988) DR 57, 108 (collection of data on the applicant's private life for a security check for an appointment to a post in the broadcasting services: the Commission determined that someone who shows a reasonable likelihood that the authorities have collected and retained data on his or her private life may claim to be a victim of Art 8).

Interferences involving positive obligations

6.43 In addition to this essentially negative requirement to refrain from action impinging upon Article 8 rights, and as discussed above, a state may be under a positive obligation to ensure that domestic law adequately reflects the guarantee's requirements. This normally entails the taking of measures to ensure that an individual's rights are effectively protected, even in the sphere of non-state activities. A failure to provide adequate legal safeguards to ensure implementation of human rights guarantees or an inability or unwillingness to enforce any such safeguard in the context of private law may thus violate Convention guarantees[1]. Legal rules which permit discriminatory treatment of illegitimate children[2] or make it impossible for a mother to deny the husband's paternity of her child[3] or fail to provide a natural father with an opportunity to be consulted before his child is placed for adoption[4], or allow the surveillance of individuals by other private parties without adequate legal safeguards[5] are examples of such failings. Similar concerns will apply to a state's responsibility to enforce the decisions of a court which seek to protect Article 8 rights[7].

1   In the United Kingdom, the issue is frequently referred to in language referring to the 'horizontality' of rights (see eg, Wade 'Horizons of Horizontality' (2001) 116 LQR 217; however, on the continent (and in most legal writing on the ECHR), the expression of *Drittwirkung* (or 'third party applicability') is used: see eg van Dijk, van Hoof, van Rijn and Zwaak (eds) *Theory and Practice of the European Convention on Human Rights* (4th edn, 2006) pp 28–32. See further Clapham *Human Rights Obligations of Non-State Actors* (2005).

2   *Marckx v Belgium* (1979) A 31, para 31.

3   *Kroon and Others v Netherlands* (1994) A 297-C, para 36 (domestic law prevented recognition of a child by its natural father without a denial of paternity by the applicant's former husband who was untraceable; positive obligation to allow a family to establish legal family ties as soon as possible).

4   *Keegan v Ireland* (1994) A 290, at para 51 ('secret placement of [a] child for adoption without the applicant's knowledge or consent' in circumstances where it was accepted 'family life' existed).

5   *Hokkanen v Finland* (1994) A 299-A, paras 60–62 (non-enforcement of access and custody rights against the grandparents of child).

6   Cf *Verliere v Switzerland* (dec) 2001-VII, discussed at para **6.90** below.

6.44 Further, the state may be under an obligation to ensure that such rights can be effectively enforced through the provision of legal representation. In *Airey v Ireland*, the appellant had been unable to institute proceedings to enable her to obtain a judicial separation since legal aid was not available for such actions. The European Court of Human Rights ruled that the state was under an obligation to ensure that parties to a marriage were accorded the right to relieve themselves of the legal duty to cohabit when appropriate, and that this right must be 'effectively accessible' through ensuring proper access to a court by the provision of legal aid[1]. Judgments such as *Airey* thus suggest that there may be a duty to provide adequate resources to ensure the effective enjoyment of Article 8 rights, but determination of the allocation of limited public resources is not readily within judicial competence, and inevitably involves recognition of a wide margin of appreciation on the part of the authorities[2].

1   *Airey v Ireland* (1979) A 32, para 32; cf *Johnston v Ireland* (1986) A 112, paras 51–58 (the Convention is to be read as a whole; and thus there was no positive duty to ensure the availability of divorce when the article was read alongside Art 12).

2   Eg *Pentiacova and Others v Moldova* (dec) 2005-I (complaints that patients suffering from chronic renal failure forced to meet own costs for necessary treatment not provided by the state: inadmissible, as applicants had enjoyed access to standard health care).

6.45 There may even now be a positive obligation (in the form of a 'procedural aspect' of the guarantee akin to that arising under Articles 2 and 3) to carry out an effective investigation into allegations of irregular interferences of Article 8 rights by public officials, and thus any shortcomings in this respect will involve an 'interference'[1].

1   *HM v Turkey* (8 August 2006), paras 26–30 (lack of investigation into allegedly unlawful search of the applicant's home in the face of denial of responsibility by any authority: violation of the procedural aspect of Art 8 to carry out an effective investigation).

6.46 In determining whether a positive obligation arises, 'regard must be had to a fair balance that has to be struck between the general interest of the community and the interests of the individual, the search for which balance is inherent in the whole of the Convention'[1]. Positive obligations may indeed arise in areas in which Article 8 may be perceived to compete with another basic right. For example, in relation to freedom of expression, an obligation now exists to ensure that domestic law adequately protects the private life of individuals by upholding their honour or reputation[2] or providing protection for their images in certain cases[3]. However, where a positive obligation is held to exist, the choice of means as to how best to meet these obligations will be a matter for the state[4]. This assessment is affected by the extent to which an emerging international consensus on an issue is obvious[5], but with the important caveat that while states are increasingly intervening in the private lives of individuals in the light of changing societal expectations, the sphere of state intervention and the notion of private life do not always coincide. The Court has noted that it is appropriate to take into account the boundary between the rights guaranteed by the Convention and the social rights guaranteed by the European Social Charter in determining the extent of the positive duty to ensure 'respect' for private life under Article 8[6].

1   *Rees v United Kingdom* (1986) A 106, at para 37.

2   *Pfeifer v Austria*, 2007-XII, para 35. See further para **6.133** below.

3   *Von Hannover v Germany* 2004–VI, discussed at paras **6.131–6.132** below.

4   *X and Y v Netherlands* (1985) A 91, para 24.

5   Eg *Christine Goodwin v United Kingdom* 2002-VI discussed further at para **6.145** below. Cf the earlier case of *Sheffield and Horsham v United Kingdom* 1998-V, paras 55–58 (no consensus amongst European states on question of registering change of sex).

6   *Zehnalová and Zehnal v Czech Republic* (dec) 2002-V.

6.47 Whether a positive obligation can be assumed to exist under Article 8 is thus not without difficulty. It is always necessary not to lose sight of the essential core of each concept. 'Private life' concerns an individual's physical and psychological integrity and the development of personality through relations with others, and so may involve positive obligations on the part of state authorities[1]. Thus the Court was not prepared in *Botta v Italy* to extend the scope of Article 8 to claims which concern 'interpersonal relations of such broad and indeterminate scope that there can be no conceivable direct link' between the measures sought by an applicant and his private life[2]. In any case, the Court has subsequently recognised that 'the boundaries between the State's positive and negative obligations ... do not lend themselves to precise definition' and, indeed, it has accepted that the principles that underlie an assessment of whether there has been a violation of the guarantee are similar[3]. In consequence, the labelling of state obligations as positive or negative may have at the end of the day little practical importance, and the starting-point for any assessment of an Article 8 question will often be the purpose of the guarantee in seeking to provide protection against arbitrary state decision-making or an interference that otherwise cannot be shown to have been 'necessary in a democratic society'.

1   Eg *Stubbings v United Kingdom* 1996-IV, paras 64–65 (effective deterrence of child sex abuse through protection provided by civil and criminal law): discussed at para **6.121** below.

2   *Botta v Italy* 1998-I, paras 27–35 at para 35 (physically disabled applicant sought to gain access to beach facilities while on holiday at a place distant from his normal home). See also *Zehnalová and Zehnal v Czech Republic* (dec) 2002-V (lack of access for the disabled to buildings open to the public: inadmissible as it had not been shown that there had been a direct and immediate link between the absence of measures and private or family life, for Art 8 could not be applicable each time there was difficulty in accessing buildings, but only in the exceptional cases in which lack of access interfered with personal development through the right to

establish and maintain relations); and *Mołka v Poland* (dec) 2006-IV (failure to provide assistance to a severely physically disabled person: not ruled out that positive obligations under Art 8 could be engaged, but in the circumstances the complaint concerned one isolated incident: inadmissible).

3   *Keegan v Ireland* (1994) A 290, at para 49. See also *Hatton and Others v United Kingdom* [GC] 2003-VIII (noise disturbances caused by private operators, but state responsibility in environmental issues may also arise through the failure to regulate private industry in an appropriate manner).

Assessing whether an 'interference' is justified

6.48 In terms of Article 8(2), any interference with respect for private or family life or home or correspondence must be 'in accordance with the law', have a legitimate aim, and be 'necessary in a democratic society'. These three requirements are replicated in other provisions of the Convention[1]. The onus is upon the state to satisfy the Court that the interference satisfied these three tests.

1   See paras **3.62–3.82** above.

'In accordance with the law'

6.49 The first issue calls for scrutiny of both the extent to which state activity is covered by domestic legal rules, and also the quality of these rules themselves. Strasbourg supervision of compliance with domestic legislation is limited: the initial responsibility for securing the interpretation of such law rests with the national courts[1]. The interference must have some legal basis in domestic law[2]. Further, the law must be adequately accessible and possess sufficient clarity. Absolute certainty and clarity are not essential, however, since 'many laws are inevitably couched in terms which, to a greater or lesser extent, are vague and whose interpretation and application are questions of practice'[3], and, as long as there is reasonable foreseeability of the consequences of any action, the requirement will be satisfied[4]. Finally, the law itself must conform to the notion of the rule of law in that there must be some safeguard against arbitrariness in its application[5], and domestic law which confers too wide or untrammelled authority will be found wanting[6]. In relation to the United Kingdom, this aspect of paragraph (2) has been of particular importance in cases involving interception of communications where domestic law has failed to provide sufficient regulation of state activities[7]. Use of covert surveillance techniques continues to pose questions as to the adequacy of legal guarantees against arbitrary interference with Article 8 rights[8].

1   *Chappell v United Kingdom* (1989) A 152-A, paras 52–57.

2   Eg *Eriksson v Sweden* (1989) A 156, para 65 (restrictions on access to children did not have the requisite basis in domestic law); *Sciacca v Italy* 2005-I, paras 23–25 (release of photograph of detainee to the press not regulated by 'law' within the meaning of the Convention but merely by custom); and *Sari and Çolak v Turkey* 2006-V, para 37 (incommunicado police detention for more than a week: while it had not been established that the applicants had been denied the

right to contact their families, there had been no legislative framework protecting against a violation of Art 8). See also *MAK and RK v United Kingdom* (23 March 2010), paras 64–80 (medical examination of a child suspected of having been a victim of child abuse initially without parental consent or a court order as required by domestic law and practice: the only possible justification for the decision to proceed with the examination and tests was urgency, but the facts did not suggest any such need; the interference was not in accordance with domestic law; and further violation on account of the lack of legal basis for a decision to prevent the father from visiting his daughter on the night of her admission to hospital).

3   Eg *Olsson v Sweden (no 1)* (1988) A 130, at para 62 (circumstances in which a child may require to be taken into care 'are so variable that it would scarcely be possible to formulate a law to cover every eventuality').

4   In *Silver and Others v United Kingdom* (1983) A 61, paras 85–90, the Court considered that Prison Rules which admittedly did not have the force of law could still be taken into account for the purpose of considering whether the test of foreseeability was satisfied.

5   *Malone v United Kingdom* (1984) A 82, paras 67–68.

6   But in certain cases the failure to adhere to domestic law (as opposed to shortcomings in the quality of the law) can lead somewhat confusingly to a determination that the interference was not 'necessary in a democratic society': see eg *Wieser and Bicos Beteiligungen GMBH v Austria* 2007-IV, paras 56–68 (failure by police to comply with procedural safeguards in place to protect against abuse of powers to search a lawyer's electronic files: violation as the search and seizure of electronic data was disproportionate to the legitimate aim pursued). Cf *Van Vondel v Netherlands* (25 October 2007), paras 47–55 (assistance given by police to a civilian to record conversations with the applicant for the purposes of an officially commissioned fact-finding inquiry: violation on account of lack of procedural safeguards in domestic law, and thus not 'in accordance with the law').

7   *Malone v United Kingdom* (1984) A 82, paras 69–80 (no legal regulation for issue of warrants authorising interceptions); *Halford v United Kingdom* 1997-III, para 51 (no legal regulation of interception of domestic calls on internal communications systems operated by public authorities); *Vetter v France* (31 May 2005), paras 21–27 (use of listening devices in private premises not adequately authorised).

8   Cf *Khan v United Kingdom* 2000-V, paras 26–28 (failure to provide statutory framework for use by police of electronic 'bugging' device).

Legitimate aim

6.50 In contrast, the second requirement, that an interference must meet the test of 'legitimate aim', will seldom pose a problem. Invariably, any interference can be brought under one of the listed aims of Article 8(2): that is, national security, public safety, national economic well-being, prevention of disorder or crime, protection of health, protection of morals, or protection of the rights of others. Only in exceptional cases will it be difficult for a state to show that one or more of the prescribed interests will not be applicable[1].

1   Rare examples involve release of images of accused persons by the police: *Khuzhin and Others v Russia* (23 October 2008), paras 115–118 (photographs taken from the criminal case files and shown during a broadcast in which prosecutors discussed the case of the accused: the removal of the photograph and its transmission to a journalist had constituted an interference with private life: there had been no justification advanced by the respondent government for the interference, and even assuming there was a lawful basis for granting the press access to the

case-file, no legitimate aim was discernible); and *Toma v Romania* (24 February 2009), paras 89–93 (photographing and filming of arrested detainee by journalists leading to the publication of a photograph and reference to him as a 'drug trafficker': no legitimate aim discernible, even if a legal basis for the interference could be found: violation). See also *Juhnke v Turkey* (13 May 2008), paras 74–82 (gynaecological examination of remand prisoner without free and informed consent: violation, as the examination had been purely discretionary and not in accordance with the law, and even if protection against a potential false accusation by her of sexual assault could have constituted a legitimate aim, the examination had not been proportionate).

'Necessary in a democratic society'

6.51 The real complexity lies in the determination of the third requirement: whether any interference is 'necessary in a democratic society'. The phrase suggests some 'pressing social need'[1]; requires the reasons for any interference to be both 'relevant' and 'sufficient'; and involves a test of proportionality in assessing whether the relationship between the action taken and the aim of the intervention is acceptable[2]. The recognition of a margin of appreciation confers a certain amount of discretion on state authorities, but the European Court of Human Rights will still expect domestic decision-makers to show that they have addressed this test[3]. Some consideration of contemporary European standards, too, may be relevant to this assessment, since it will be easier to condemn any interference as not being 'necessary in a democratic society' where domestic law or practice is out of line with standards generally applied elsewhere in Europe[4]. Where there has been a particularly grave interference with Article 8 rights, however, the Court's approach to the assessment of necessity is likely to be peremptory. In *Menteş and Others v Turkey*, for example, where the Court accepted that Turkish security forces had destroyed the applicants' homes and expelled them from their village, the Court simply noted that these measures were 'devoid of justification' in establishing a violation of the provision[5].

1   *Dudgeon v United Kingdom* (1983) A 45, at paras 51 and 53.

2   Eg *Olsson v Sweden (no 2)* (1992) A 250, paras 87–91; cf *MAK and RK v United Kingdom* (23 March 2010), paras 64–74 (while initially there had been relevant and sufficient reasons for action on the basis a child may have been a victim of child abuse, the delay in referral to a specialist had prolonged the interference so as to constitute a violation of Art 8).

3   See paras **3.134–3.140** above.

4   Eg *Dudgeon v United Kingdom* (1981) A 45, para 60 (the majority of other European states had decriminalised homosexual behaviour).

5   *Menteş and Others v Turkey* 1997-VIII, paras 70–73 at para 73.

Procedural safeguards in decision-making

6.52 Assessment of whether an interference was 'necessary in a democratic society' may also call for scrutiny of whether the decision-making process giving rise to the interference has been fair and has afforded due respect to the rights protected by this guarantee, even although there is no specific textual reference to procedural propriety[1]. The approach taken by Strasbourg is that due process requirements help protect against arbitrary decision-making by public authorities in such issues as surveillance or interception of communications[2], search of premises[3], eviction from a home[4], and even access to a therapeutic abortion[5]. At the same time, the Court is also accorded an opportunity to examine whether at domestic level there has been a convincing explanation of the proportionality of any interference. This permits the Strasbourg Court more readily to recognise whether domestic determination has exceeded any 'margin of appreciation' available. Some care in this area is appropriate as the distinction in jurisprudence between the absence of safeguards in domestic law (thus conferring too wide a discretion upon decision-makers and permitting arbitrary interference with rights) and the failure to adhere to any prescribed safeguards or to accord an applicant the chance to have his representations considered (and thus potentially failing the test of 'necessary in a democratic society') is not always clearly drawn[6]. This insistence upon procedural propriety is of particular importance in child care cases where there is acceptance of limited international judicial competence in reviewing domestic decisions but one offset by a corresponding high level of insistence that proceedings are open and fair[7].

1   *W v United Kingdom* (1987) A 121, para 63; *McMichael v United Kingdom* (1995) 307-B, para 87.

2   See para **6.96** below; and *The Association for European Integration and Human Rights and Ekimdzhiev v Bulgaria* (28 June 2007), paras 58–62 (since all users of the postal and telecommunications services potentially could be subjected to surveillance, a legal person such as an association could also establish 'victim' status for the purposes of Art 8).

3   See para **6.108** below.

4   *Connors v United Kingdom* (27 May 2004), paras 85–90 (summary eviction of family from local authority gypsy site rescinded on account of nuisance: the need for a statutory scheme permitting summary eviction had not been sufficiently demonstrated and thus the eviction had not been attended by the requisite procedural safeguards: violation).

5   *Tysiąc v Poland* 2007-IV, para 115; and *A, B and C v Ireland* [GC] 2010-…, discussed at para **6.55** below.

6   See *Wieser and Bicos Beteiligungen GMBH v Austria* 2007-IV.

7   See paras **6.57–6.58** below.

Particular substantive issues arising under Article 8

Family life issues: child birth, child custody and access; state assumption of care; and deportation

6.53 Article 8 provides safeguards against arbitrary interference by the state in the development and maintenance of family relationships[1]. While Article 12 specifically guarantees the rights to marry and to found a family[2], aspects of contraception and pregnancy may arise in respect of Article 8[3]. The provision is also of relevance in respect of attempts by a natural father to have legal recognition for his child[4], and by a child to seek to obtain information about her natural parents[5]. More obviously, decisions concerning the regulation of custody or access of children upon divorce or separation or the removal of children from their parents[6] and issues of health care[7] fall within the scope of the guarantee.

1 As noted, 'family life' is given a broad interpretation, and can include relationships between grandparents and grandchildren and *de facto* family arrangements: see paras **6.02–6.09** above. A relatively wide approach is taken to standing as 'victim' in this area: see eg 23715/94, *SP, DP, & AT v United Kingdom* (20 May 1996) (the legal representative of children may bring an application where no other appropriate representative exists or is available); and *P, C and S v United Kingdom* 2002-VI (natural parent may bring a case in order to protect a child's rights even if no longer enjoys parental rights in domestic law).

2 See para **6.02–6.09** above.

3 *Dickson v United Kingdom* [GC] 2007-XIII, discussed at para **6.08** above (refusal to provide facilities for artificial insemination to a prisoner and his wife considered neither arbitrary nor unreasonable in terms of Art 8, and thus the interference did not constitute a violation of Art 12); and *SH and Others v Austria* (1 April 2010), paras 74–85 and 88–94 (ban on using sperm and ova donation for in vitro fertilisation constituted a violation of Art 14 in conjunction with Art 8 in view of the differences between both procedures: there was no uniform approach to medically assisted procreation and no obligation under Art 8 to permit this, but once the decision to do so had been taken, the legal framework must be coherent, a responsibility not achieved by the difference in treatment between in vitro fertilisation with the use of ova and that with the use of sperm from donors) [case referred to the Grand Chamber in October 2010]. For discussion of abortion, see para **4.51** above.

4 *Yousef v Netherlands* 2002-VIII, paras 67–75 (refusal to allow natural father to recognise child where the biological paternity was not in dispute and the applicant had lived with the mother and daughter for a certain period and had continued to have contacts with the daughter after the mother's death: no violation, as he continued to have access to his daughter, and domestic courts had not failed to take the applicant's rights sufficiently into account in determining the best interests of the child, nor determined this in an arbitrary manner). Cf *Shofman v Russia* (24 November 2005), paras 48–75 (inflexible application of time-bar concerning disclaimed presumed paternity even although the applicant had not suspected the child was not his until two years after the birth: violation)

5 See eg *Odièvre v France* [GC] 2003-III, paras 40–49 (applicant abandoned at birth only able to obtain non-identifying information about her natural family: since the circumstances in which the child was born formed part of her private life, Art 8 was applicable, but both the child and her mother had Art 8 rights and a woman's interest in remaining anonymous also having to be recognised; anonymous births raised the issue of the protection of third parties such as adoptive parents, and domestic law sought to strike an appropriate balance and to ensure sufficient proportion between the competing interests, and there was no violation of Art 8 or of Art 14 taken together with Art 8 in respect of inheritance rights). See also *Mikulić v Croatia* 2002-I, paras 56–66 (absence of compulsion of an alleged father to undergo a DNA test can in principle be considered compatible with Art 8, but the interests of the person seeking to establish paternity must nevertheless be secured, while the principle of proportionality requires that alternative means be provided to enable the speedy determination of such claims: violation, as no such means were available to the applicant and the procedure available did not strike a fair balance between her right to have uncertainty as to personal identity eliminated without unnecessary delay); and *Jäggi v Switzerland* 2006-X, paras 33–44 (refusal to authorise a DNA test of the remains of a putative biological father who had admitted before his death having had sexual relations with the applicant's mother but had refused to submit to medical tests: violation).

6 Cf 24875/94, *Logan v United Kingdom* (1996) DR 86, 74 (regulations relate to maintenance payments of absent parents and so the legislation does not by its nature affect family life); and

20357/92, *Whiteside v United Kingdom* (1994) DR 76, 80 (refusal of the court to grant injunction against the husband in a case of alleged domestic violence: inadmissible on account of failure to exhaust domestic remedies, but the Commission noted that there could exist a positive duty to protect against persistent and distressing harassment).

7   Cf *Re C (Immunisation: Parental Rights)* [2003] 2 FLR 1095, noted at para **6.124** below.

Contraception, etc

6.54 A range of contraception and pregnancy issues will fall within the scope of Article 8, including the right of a couple to conceive a child and to make use of medically assisted procreation[1] and sterilisation[2]. Such cases can involve difficult assessments of proportionality. In *Evans v United Kingdom*, the applicant had undergone *in vitro* fertilisation treatment with the support of her partner before the surgical removal of her ovaries. Following the break-up of their relationship and her former partner's withdrawal of consent for the continued storage of the embryos and their implantation, the applicant had sought to prevent a clinic from destroying the embryos as it required to do so in light of domestic law. For the Grand Chamber, the right to respect for the decision to become a parent in the genetic sense fell within the scope of Article 8. Here, however, the applicant was not complaining that she was being prevented from becoming a mother since domestic law did not preclude her from adopting a child or even giving birth to a child originally created *in vitro* from donated gametes. Rather she was seeking to challenge the prohibition of using the embryos she and her former partner had created together and thus from having a child to whom she was genetically related, but if she were to be permitted to use the embryos, her former partner would be forced to become a father. The case thus involved an irreconcilable conflict between the Article 8 rights of two private individuals in the context of legislation seeking to serve a number of other public interest concerns including the principle of the primacy of consent and the promotion of legal clarity and certainty. In determining that the legislative provisions of the Human Fertilisation and Embryology Act 1990 could be deemed to strike a fair balance between the competing public and private interests involved, the Grand Chamber noted the lack of European consensus, the fact that the domestic rules were clear, and the rules had been brought to the attention of the applicant at the time of treatment. The applicant's right to respect for the decision to become a parent in the genetic sense could not thus be accorded greater weight than the right of her former partner to respect for his decision not to have a genetically-related child with the applicant[3].

1   *SH and Others v Austria* (1 April 2010), para 60.

2   *VC v Slovakia* (dec) (16 June 2009) (sterilisation of a Roma woman allegedly without her full and informed consent: admissible under arts 3, 8, 12, 13 and 14).

3   *Evans v United Kingdom* [GC] 2007-IV, paras 83–92.

6.55 Restrictions on the availability of abortion also fall within the scope of 'private life'[1]. In *A, B and C v Ireland*, the Court was called upon to examine the compatibility of Irish law, which restricted the ability of a woman to obtain an abortion to life-threatening situations, with the Convention. The Grand Chamber reiterated that while Article 8 cannot in itself be interpreted as conferring a right to abortion, the prohibition of abortion falls within the scope of right to respect for physical and psychological integrity as protected by the guarantee. The interference had pursued the legitimate aim of protecting public morals as understood in Ireland, and it had also been prescribed by law. Assessment of whether there had been a 'pressing social need' for the interference was covered by a wide margin of appreciation in light of the absence of European consensus on when life began since the right of the foetus and mother were inextricably linked. Each of the applicants had become pregnant unintentionally and had decided to have an abortion. However, the personal circumstances of the first and second applicants differed from those of the third applicant. In the former cases, the Court accepted that a fair balance had been struck between the rights of the mothers and their foetuses, taking into account their rights to travel abroad to obtain an abortion and the availability of appropriate pre- and post-abortion medical care in Ireland. In contrast, a violation was established in respect of the third applicant who had been in remission from a rare form of cancer and who had believed that the pregnancy would cause a relapse. The establishment of any such risk to her life clearly concerned essential aspects of her right to respect for her private life, but in this instance there had been a lack of appropriate means for establishing whether her condition was indeed sufficiently life-threatening so as to permit a lawful abortion, for neither a medical consultation (in light of the risk of criminal prosecution and imprisonment facing medical professionals) nor recourse to litigation (involving recourse to the courts) constituted effective and accessible procedures allowing access to a lawful abortion[2].

1   See further para **4.51** above.

2   *A, B and C v Ireland* [GC] 2010-..., paras 212–268 (and at paras 216 and 244–246: interference examined under negative obligations in respect of the first two applicants, and under the positive obligation for the third applicant). See also *RR v Poland* (refusal of genetic test to ascertain if the applicant qualified for an abortion: application communicated).

Decisions concerning child custody and access

6.56 Significant numbers of cases concern the compatibility of domestic determinations involving custody of children[1]. Invariably, assessment will focus upon the questions whether the decision-making process has been fair, and whether the reasons for an interference with family life have been relevant and sufficient. A wide margin of appreciation is accorded to domestic decision-makers in determining which parent should have custody or whether a child should be placed in care. The fundamental principle is that a positive obligation exists on the part of authorities to act with a view to maintaining and developing family ties[2]. Authorities are also required to act with due expediency as the passage of time can have irremediable consequences on parent-child relationships[3]. At the same time, the authorities are also required to protect the physical and psychological integrity of a child[4], and the Court has recognised that mistaken judgments or assessments by professionals do not *per se* render child-care measures incompatible with the requirements of Article 8 as these individuals cannot be held liable every time a genuine and reasonably-held concern about the safety of children proves wrong[5].

1   For other relevant standards, see European Convention on Recognition and Enforcement of Decisions concerning Custody of Children and on Restoration of Custody of Children (ETS 105 (1980)); and the European Convention on Contact concerning Children (CETS 192 (2003)).

2   Eg *Mustafa and Armagan Akin v Turkey* (6 April 2010), paras 19–30 (award of custody of one child to one parent and its sibling to the other parent, with provision only for exchange of the children between the parents at certain times and thus effectively preventing the children from spending time with each other and either parent from spending time with both of their children at once: violation of Art 8 on account of failure to comply with positive obligations to facilitate contacts, the Court also noting the lack of reasoning justifying the separation of the children particularly since neither parent had requested such an arrangement maintain and develop family ties).

3   Eg *Stochlak v Poland* (22 September 2009), paras 60–67 (failure to make sufficient efforts to enforce the applicant's right to have his child returned from its mother: proceedings relating to the granting of parental responsibility called for urgency as the passage of time could have irremediable consequences for the relationship between a parent and a child); *Eberhard and M v Slovenia* (1 December 2009), paras 132–143 (failure to ensure that a father could enforce his right of access to his child: violation of Art 8 on account of a failure to take steps taken to reunite parents with their children in light of the obligations on the national authorities to facilitate such a reunion and to take all necessary steps to execute access decisions).

4   Eg *Kurochkin v Ukraine* (20 May 2010), paras 43–60 (annulment of adoption order following divorce and placing of child into care on the grounds that the applicant had failed to demonstrate he could secure the child's normal development, but the child nevertheless continued to live with the applicant and the applicant became the child's appointed guardian: violation, as there had been insufficient reasons for annulment of the adoption order and no careful assessment of the annulment's impact upon the child had taken place).

5   *RK and AK v United Kingdom* (30 September 2008), paras 32–40 (child placed in temporary care on account of fears of non-accidental injury until it was confirmed she suffered from a rare condition: no violation). See also *D and Others v United Kingdom* (dec) (12 February 2008) (placing of child's name on an 'at risk' register was an administrative step which had not had had any direct effect on the mother's enjoyment of her right to respect for her family or private life, and even assuming she had to be a victim of an interference under Art 8, such was necessary for the protection of her son's rights: inadmissible); and *MAK and RK v United Kingdom* (23 March 2010), paras 64–74 (while at the outset of the case there had been relevant and sufficient reasons for suspecting abuse, delay in consulting a specialist had prolonged the interference and rendered the response disproportionate to the legitimate aim of protecting the child from harm).

PROCEDURAL PROPRIETY IN CHILD CARE CASES

6.57 The insistence upon procedural propriety in child care cases reflects acceptance of limited international judicial competence in a sensitive and difficult area but also recognition that such decisions can have significant impact upon children and their parents. The Court is thus concerned to ensure that fair decision-making procedures ensuring due 'respect' has been given to family life considerations have prevented arbitrary interference with Article 8 rights[1]. In other words, it is vital that procedures ascertain and give due consideration to all material views[2]. This requirement complements any applicable Article 6 interests[3]. In *McMichael v United Kingdom*, for example, the Court reiterated that failure to accord the parents of a child subject to care proceedings taken through the Scottish system of children's hearings could also give rise to an Article 8 issue[4]. In short, procedures in child care or custody cases must allow adequate involvement by parents in the decision-making process; further, these must be carried out with sufficient expedition so as to avoid undue delay to prevent *de facto* determination of child care questions through the establishment of new ties with any foster parents or other carers[5].

1   See eg *Sahin v Germany* [GC] 2003-VIII, paras 83–95 (refusal of access to child: while reasons were relevant, their sufficiency could only be determined by assessing whether the decision-making process as a whole had provided the applicant with the requisite protection of his interests: no violation of Art 8). See similarly *Sommerfeld v Germany* [GC] 2003-VIII, paras 62–75. The European Convention on the Exercise of Children's Rights (ETS 160 (1996)) (not yet signed or ratified by the United Kingdom) seeks to provide procedural measures to allow children to exercise their rights more effectively, in particular, in family legal proceedings.

2   See eg *W v United Kingdom* (1987) A 121, paras 62–70 (natural parents could not be excluded from deliberations in determining whether a child should be taken into care). See also *Venema v Netherlands* 2002-X, paras 88–99 (provisional care order without opportunity accorded to parents to contest: violation); *Covezzi and Morselli v Italy* (9 May 2003), paras 101–139 (no violation in respect of emergency removal of the children, the failure to hear the parents before taking the decision to remove their children, the prolonged break in relations between the applicants and their children, and the placing of children in separate accommodation; violation in respect of inability to influence procedural hearings and unwarranted delays); *Haase v Germany* 2004-III, paras 96–105 (provisional withdrawal of parental rights without hearing the parents or children on the basis of expert report unsupported by relevant and sufficient reasons and lack of sufficient involvement in the decision-making process, while the manner in which the measure was implemented involving the removing the children the following day from their respective schools or from home went beyond the exigencies of the situation: violation); *C v Finland* (9 May 2006), para 67 (reversal of lower court decision on determination of custody predominately upon basis of expressed preferences of children without according the father the chance to be heard: violation); *Hunt v Ukraine* (7 December 2006), paras 49–60 (prohibition on entry to country after proceedings commenced leading to deprivation of parental rights without fair hearing: violation); and *X v Croatia* (17 July 2008), paras 44–55 (daughter of mother suffering from paranoid schizophrenia put up for adoption without the mother having been given an opportunity to express her views about the potential adoption: violation as the mother had not been sufficiently involved in the decision-making process).

3   Cf *McMichael v United Kingdom* (1995) A 307-B, para 87 and 91 (different nature of interests protected by Arts 6 and 8 discussed: here, the repercussions on 'a fundamental element of the family life' of the applicant was such as to warrant an examination of Art 8, while in respect of the mother, these two articles provided parallel safeguards). See too *Elsholz v Germany* [GC] 2000-VIII, paras 48–53 (a domestic court had concluded that a child's development would be endangered if he had to take up contacts with the applicant (his father) contrary to his mother's will, but had arrived at this conclusion without having ordered an independent psychological report and in the absence of sufficient involvement of the applicant in the decision-making process: violation of Art 8). Art 6, however, only applies where there is a civil right or obligation recognised by domestic law or where parental interests are sufficiently vital so as to require domestic law to allow access to a court: 11468/85, *K v United Kingdom* (1986) DR 50 199; (1988) DR 56, 138 (child removed from natural father and placed with foster parents by the local authority: friendly settlement); *Paulsen-Medalen and Svensson v Sweden*

1998-I, para 42 (delay of some 30 months in determining appeal by mother against taking children into care: violation of Art 6(1)).

4   *McMichael v United Kingdom* (1995) 307-B, paras 87–93 (an unmarried father did not enjoy automatic parental rights in Scots law and thus had no standing in proceedings under Art 6; and in light of the state's concession that children's hearing and sheriff court proceedings were unfair in the context of Art 6, the Court also found violations of Art 8).

5   *H v United Kingdom* (1987) A 120, paras 89–90. For similar cases involving the taking of children into care, see *O v United Kingdom* (1987) A 120; *W, B and R v United Kingdom* (1987) A 121; and *Keegan v Ireland* (1994) A 290. Cf *Bronda v Italy* 1998-IV, paras 61–63 (substantial judicial delays etc could 'appear incomprehensible and unacceptable' in a sensitive case in which 'the passage of time may have irreversible effects on the child's mental equilibrium, since she is forced to live in a state of uncertainty'; but the Court was ultimately satisfied that the decisions taken were based on both relevant and sufficient reasons).

6.58 The provision of adequate decision-making procedures may also imply a positive obligation to make information held by public authorities available to parents to allow them to participate effectively. In *TP and KM v United Kingdom*, the failure to determine promptly the question of whether to disclose to a mother the contents of an interview with a young child which had led to the child being taken into care was considered a violation of Article 8. During the interview, the child had alleged she had been sexually assaulted, and had identified the perpetrator as someone no longer living with her mother. A doctor and social worker had proceeded upon the basis that the alleged abuser was the mother's boyfriend then living in the home, and had instigated action which resulted in the child being taken into care. A request for access to the video had been opposed. Her solicitors eventually obtained a transcript of the interview in which it was clear that her daughter had exonerated her mother's current boyfriend. Although it accepted that the initial care measure had been justified, the Court concluded that the subsequent procedures had failed to protect the Article 8 interests of both the mother and her daughter. In the opinion of the Court, resolution of the issue whether to disclose the video of the interview and its transcript should have been determined promptly to allow the mother 'an effective opportunity' to challenge the allegations that her daughter could not return safely to her care. While a parent could not enjoy an absolute right to access to all information held by a local authority in these circumstances, 'the potential importance of the contents of such interviews renders it necessary for careful consideration to be given to whether they should be disclosed to the parents'. However, since a local authority could not be regarded as able to determine such a question in an objective way, the authority's failure to submit the issue to the court for determination had deprived her of 'an adequate involvement in the decision-making process concerning the care of her daughter and thereby of the requisite protection of their interests'[1].

1   *TP and KM v United Kingdom* [GC] 2001-V, paras 78–83 at paras 81 and 83 (at para 82: 'the positive obligation on the Contracting State to protect the interests of the family requires that this material be made available to the parent concerned, even in the absence of any request by the parent'). See also *Tsourlakis v Greece* (15 October 2009), paras 37–45 (inability of applicant to consult a child welfare society report in domestic proceedings concerning the custody of his child: violation on account of refusal to allow the contents of the report to be

disclosed after the conclusion of the proceedings as the authorities had failed to demonstrate that compelling reasons existed for not disclosing to the individual concerned a report that contained personal information which affected him directly).

RELEVANCY AND SUFFICIENCY OF REASONS FOR AN INTERFERENCE

6.59 Certain considerations suggest caution on the part of the European Court of Human Rights when faced with applications alleging violation of Article 8 on account of determinations affecting children. Since national authorities have the advantage of having direct contact with the relevant parties in determining the crucial issue of what is in the best interests of the child, it is not appropriate for the Strasbourg Court to substitute its judgment for that of domestic decision-makers[1]. Further, views as to when it is appropriate to place a child in care can vary considerably in Europe and depend upon such factors 'as traditions relating to the role of the family and to State intervention in family affairs and the availability of resources for public measures'[2]. There can also be some tension between the positive obligation to take action to protect the physical and moral well-being of children[3], and that requiring states to facilitate 'family life' contacts. The result is that in most cases a wide margin of appreciation is accorded to domestic decision-makers in determining custody questions or whether a child should be taken into care, but a state must still show that the reasons for an interference with family life have been both relevant and sufficient, and that less onerous alternatives had been considered[4].

1   Cf *Tiemann v France and Germany* (dec) (27 April 2000) (decision of courts in Germany to order the return of the children of the applicant to their mother who was living in France; and refusal of the French courts to order the return of the children to Germany: applications declared inadmissible). Respect for family life may, however, give greater weight to parental decision-making than the rights of a child: cf *Nielsen v Denmark* (1988) A 144, discussed at para **4.152** above (placement by a mother of her 12-year-old son, who was not mentally ill, in psychiatric hospital).

2   *Johansen v Norway* 1996-III, at para 54.

3   See paras **6.119–6.121** below. See *AD and OD v United Kingdom* (16 March 2010), paras 80–94 (while certain mistaken judgments by a local authority with the view to protecting a child had not amount to a violation of Art 8, the failure to conduct a risk assessment of the child had done so); and *MAK and RK v United Kingdom* (23 March 2010), paras 64–80 (refusal to allow a parent to visit a child in hospital: while the interference had the legitimate aim of protecting the child's rights, the delay in consulting a specialist on the child's injuries which had led to an allegation of abuse and restriction of visitation rights had been disproportionate).

4   Eg *Saviny v Ukraine* (18 December 2008), paras 53–61 (taking into care of four of seven children of a blind couple but without adequate procedural safeguards and placing of the children in different institutions: violation of Art 8, as while relevant reasons had been adduced, these were not sufficient, and the authorities had not sufficiently explored the effectiveness of less far-reaching alternatives).

6.60 Some examination of case law illustrates the Court's approach. In the leading case of *Olsson v Sweden (no 1)*, a married couple had challenged the decision by the local authority to place their three children in separate foster homes at considerable distances away from the parents, the procedure involved, and the refusal to terminate the care arrangements. The placements had followed several case conferences (with the parents having been present at one of these sessions); later, the parents had also learnt that their access rights had been restricted. The Court confirmed that Strasbourg review was not confined to merely determining whether the decision-makers had exercised their discretion 'reasonably, carefully and in good faith', but extended to consideration of whether the reasons adduced were both relevant and sufficient. A minority of the Court (following a majority of the Commission) considered that the state had not shown that the reasons adduced could support the interference. The majority of the Court, however, was prepared to accept that the domestic court had given reasons which were both relevant (such as the parents' inability to provide a satisfactory home environment, the children's social and educational retardation, and the lack of success of other preventive measures) and in all the circumstances also sufficient after taking into account the substantial investigations that had taken place into the family background. Similarly, there had been relevant and sufficient reasons for holding that the care arrangements should not have been terminated. However, the manner in which the care decision had been implemented did give rise to a violation of Article 8 since it had involved the placement of the three children in separate homes and at some distance from the parents. While there was nothing to suggest that the public authority had acted other than in good faith, the measures taken were not consistent with its ultimate goal of reintegrating the children into the family unit[1]. This case does suggest that some scrutiny of any stated reasons for a care decision is appropriate, at least to ensure that the measures selected can be shown to be in line with the purported aim of state intervention.

1   *Olsson v Sweden (no 1)* (1988) A 130, paras 66–83. See too *Margareta and Roger Andersson v Sweden* (1992) A 226, at para 96 (prohibition of contact by correspondence and telephone by parents with children taken into care were relevant, 'but do not sufficiently show that it was necessary to deprive the applicants of almost every means of maintaining contact with each other for a period of approximately one and a half years. Indeed, it is questionable whether the measures were compatible with the aim of reuniting the applicants').

6.61 However, it is not always clear that the reasons for domestic determinations are scrutinised rigorously, and other cases suggest less demanding standards of review. The failure to enforce custody orders was considered rather unconvincingly in *Hokkanen v Finland* where a child's grandparents had proven reluctant to hand over a child who had been in their care for several years to its father. The Court declined to consider whether Article 8 could require forcible measures to be used, merely commenting that in certain circumstances preparatory measures may be required to secure the co-operation of all parties to such a dispute. In any case, it noted that 'the interests as well as the rights and freedoms of all concerned must be taken into account, and more particularly the best interests of the child and his or her rights under Article 8'. Ultimately, the crucial element in this instance was that the authorities had 'taken all necessary steps to facilitate reunion as can reasonably be demanded in the special circumstances of each case[1].'

1   *Hokkanen v Finland* (1994) A 299-A, at para 58 (violation established in respect of one period of time taking into account the limited steps to reunite the father with his child). See too *Bronda v Italy*, 1998-IV, paras 52–63 (failure to return a child to its original family contrary to an appeal court decision considered not to violate Art 8; reasons for allowing a child to remain with foster parents were both relevant and sufficient, the court attaching special weight to the overriding interest of the child); *Nuutinen v Finland* 2000-VIII, paras 129–138 (in the continuous re-assessment of the child's best interests the national authorities could have reasonably formulated a recommendation that the access rights should be revoked until the child had reached a more mature age; and having regard to the margin of appreciation afforded to the state, and the authorities had taken all necessary steps with a view to enforcing the access rights as could reasonably be demanded in the very difficult conflict at hand: no violation of Art 8); *Scozzari and Giunta v Italy* [GC] 2000-VIII, paras 148–151, 169–183, 201–216 and 221–227 (complaints of infringements of Art 8 in that the applicant's parental rights had been suspended, her children had been taken into care, the authorities had delayed before finally allowing her to see the children, too few contact visits had been organised and the authorities had placed the children in a home: certain violations of Art 8 established, but not in respect of the second applicant's complaint concerning the discounting of the possibility of her being given the care of her grandsons and delay in organising contact with them).

6.62 There are several qualifications, however. First, the European Court of Human Rights will wish to examine carefully any domestic decision which has been influenced by a factor based upon discriminatory treatment and which thus may violate Article 14 when taken together with Article 8[1].

1   Eg *Salgueiro da Silva Mouta v Portugal* 1999-IX, discussed at para **6.144** below; *Hoffman v Austria* (1993) A 255-C, paras 32–36 (decision on child custody heavily influenced by consideration that mother was a Jehovah's Witness: the Court considered that this discrimination had no objective or reasonable justification). See also *Cosac v Romania* (dec) (12 January 2010) (refusal by the domestic courts to grant a father custody of his daughter on account of his membership of a religious sect: communicated). Determinations based upon illegitimacy are inherently suspect: see eg *Sahin v Germany* [GC] 2003-VIII, paras 85–95 (violation of Art 14 in conjunction with Art 8 as application of legal provisions providing for different standards applying to parents not having custody of children born in wedlock and fathers of children born out of wedlock had led to unjustified difference of treatment, the Court distinguishing this case on the facts from *Elsholz v Germany* [GC] 2000-VIII, discussed at para **6.57**, fn 3 above); *Sommerfeld v Germany* [GC] 2003-VIII, paras 88–98; and *Zaunegger v Germany* 2009-…, paras 57–65 (legal provision that a mother would have sole custody of a child born out of wedlock unless the parents marry or she provides consent that there will be joint custody with the father: violation of Art 14 taken with Art 8 as the applicant was treated differently from married and divorced fathers in the requirement for consent).

6.63 Secondly, the removal of a child from a parent should in principle be seen as a temporary measure, and the ultimate aim must be to establish the reunion between parent and child[1]. Thus the Court will apply a stricter scrutiny of the justifications advanced for restrictions on parental rights of access[2] and the removal of children from their parents[3].

1   Eg *Gnahoré v France* 2000-IX, at para 59: 'the interest of the child dictates that family ties may only be severed in very exceptional circumstances and that everything must be done to preserve personal relations and, if and when appropriate, to "rebuild" the family'.

2   *Johansen v Norway* 1996-III, paras 64–84 (order made to take applicant's daughter into public care; complaint concerned the deprivation of her parental rights, the termination of her

access to her daughter, the excessive length of the proceedings and their lack of fairness; only violation concerned lack of access and termination of parental rights which had not been supported by relevant and sufficient reasons). See also *Söderbäck v Sweden* 1998-VII, paras 22–35 (an adoption order had the effect of cutting all legal ties between the applicant and his daughter who had enjoyed only infrequent and limited contact; there were *de facto* family ties between the mother, the adoptive father and the daughter which had been in existence for over five years; and thus, given the adoption order's formalisation of these ties, it could not be said that any adverse effects on the applicant's relationships with the child had been disproportionate); *E P v Italy* (16 November 1999), paras 62–70 (absolute and irreversible ending of relationship between mother and daughter on the basis of the mother's pathological behaviour towards her child was based upon factual inaccuracies and without sufficiently rigorous analysis of the situation by the authorities: violation of Art 8). Cf *Kleuver v Norway* (dec) (30 April 2002) (inability of mother who had given birth in detention on remand to keep her baby with her in prison: inadmissible on the facts as she had sent the baby to its grandmother for three months and had enjoyed time with her child daily, and she had been fully aware of her pregnancy when she committed the criminal offence; and *Pini and Bertani v Romania* 2004-V, paras 149–150 (no violation of positive obligations to secure rights of adoptive parents of abandoned children in the face of the failure of the home to hand over the children, particular importance being attached to the best interests of the child which could take priority over those of the parents). It is suggested that the 'best interests of the child' principle thus demands a case-by-case approach rather than application of any rigid administrative policy.

3   *Wallová and Walla v Czech Republic* (26 October 2006), paras 67–97 (sole ground for taking children into care had been inadequacy of family's housing, an unduly drastic measure, particularly when the authorities had power to help the family improve their accommodation: violation).

6.64 Thirdly, unduly harsh or oppressive interferences will be subject to particular scrutiny. There are certainly limits to what will be recognised as acceptable in scrutinising the relevancy and sufficiency of reasons. In *K and T v Finland*, for example, a Chamber had accepted that there had been a violation of the provision. The application had been brought by a mother and her cohabiting partner, the father of the youngest of the mother's three children. The mother had been diagnosed on several occasions as suffering from schizophrenia, and various care measures (both emergency and 'normal') had been taken which restricted the access of the parents to the children. Most of the administrative proceedings had not involved oral hearings. The Chamber considered that the reasons given and the methods used were arbitrary: the applicants had not even been given the opportunity of beginning a family life with a new-born daughter who had been placed in care immediately, and a care order concerning a son had been taken on the basis of purported risks none of which had been relevant since he was already in a safe home environment. It found a further violation of Article 8 in respect of the state's failure to consider with any seriousness the question of termination of the care orders despite some suggested improvement in the position of the mother[1]. The judgment was accepted for referral to the Grand Chamber which in consequence reheard the case. However, it approached the matter by considering the emergency care order separately from the normal care order since the two orders were of different natures and had involved different decision-making processes. Unanimously, the Grand Chamber held that the taking of the 'normal' care orders in each case had been in accordance with Article 8 since the applicants had been properly involved in the proceedings and it had been reasonable to conclude that care measures were in the best interests of the children. The Grand Chamber also found that there had been a violation of the state's responsibilities to take proper steps to try to reunite the family. However, by a majority, the Court ruled that the state had not shown that there had been 'extraordinarily compelling reasons' for the taking of the new-born baby into care at the time of its birth. Such a measure was 'extremely harsh', and the 'shock and disarray felt by even a perfectly healthy mother are easy to imagine'. Less draconian measures to deal with the situation had existed, but the state could not show that these had been considered[2].

---

1   *K and T v Finland* (27 April 2000), paras 143–146, 155–164.

2   *K and T v Finland* [GC] 2001-VII, paras 164–170, 173–174, 177–179, 192–194 (on the other hand, a majority of the Court did accept that the emergency care order in respect of an older child had been justified: this would not have had as great an impact; the child was already physically separated from his family; and the applicants' lack of participation in the process was understandable so as not to add to the stress facing the applicants at the time of the birth of another child). See also *Nolan and K v Russia* (12 February 2009), paras 83–89 (refusal without advance notice or reason to allow a single parent to re-enter his country of residence so as to allow him to rejoin his infant child, the only subsequent but unsubstantiated justification put forward being national security: violation on account of manifest failure to assess the impact on the child's welfare).

HAGUE CONVENTION ON CIVIL ASPECTS OF INTERNATIONAL CHILD ABDUCTION

6.65 Fourthly, Article 8 must be construed in the light of the Hague Convention on Civil Aspects of International Child Abduction of 1980[1]. In *Ignaccolo-Zenide v Romania*, the failure of the domestic authorities to enforce a court order granted by the Romanian courts in favour of the applicant to allow her to be reunited with her two children who had been taken by their father from the USA to Romania was held to have violated the guarantee. The Court reiterated that the article imposed positive obligations inherent in an effective 'respect' for family life which included the right for parents to have measures taken by the state with a view to reuniting them with their children. However, this obligation could not be absolute, on account both of the need for preparation before the reunion with a child who has been living for any length of time with the other parent and also of the limited scope for the use of coercion. The key question was whether the national authorities had taken all reasonable steps in the particular circumstances of the case to facilitate the enforcement of the court order, bearing in mind the need to take into account the paramount interests of the child and his own rights under Article 8. Here, initial steps to enforce the order had been taken promptly but then had been followed by minimal efforts; no proper preparation had been made for the children's return (for example, by arranging meetings of child psychiatrists and psychologists); and the authorities had not implemented the measures set out in the Hague Convention, Article 7 to secure the children's return to the applicant. In these circumstances, a violation of Article 8 was established[2].

1   For domestic discussion of the Hague Convention, see *BRB v FLM* (24 October 2003, unreported) OH (return to USA of child taken by his mother to Scotland); and *S v B (Abduction: Human Rights)* [2005] 2 FLR 878 (Hague Convention, even when interpreted in accordance with Art 8, places paramount importance upon the rights of the abducted child over those of the mother and any other of her children).

2   *Ignaccolo-Zenide v Romania* 2000-I, paras 101–113. See also *Sylvester v Austria* (24 April 2003), paras 54–72 (decisions quashing an order requiring return of children based upon on the lapse of time, but delays in authorities' response: in such cases, swiftness of implementation is vital as the passage of time can have irremedial consequences, and while non-enforcement of a final return order may exceptionally be based on a change of relevant facts under the Hague Convention, the change cannot be attributable to a state's failure to take all measures that could reasonably be expected, and violation established); *Iglesias Gil and AUI v Spain* 2003-V, paras 47–63 (inadequate measures taken by the authorities to enforce court decisions in respect of her son who had been taken abroad by her ex-husband, including determination that the removal did not constitute a ground for issuing an international arrest warrant against the father: violation); *Paradis v Germany* (dec) (15 May 2003) (illegal return of children to Germany and determination based upon the Hague Convention that children should be returned to Canada was not arbitrary: inadmissible); *Bianchi v Switzerland* (22 June 2006), paras 91–100 (while the authorities had taken a number of measures to trace a child and its mother, their attitude had been somewhat lax and passive despite the particularly clear and rigorous wording of the Hague Convention: violation); *Mattenklott v Germany* (dec) (11 December 2006) (relevant and sufficient reasons for order to return a child to the USA: inadmissible); and *Carlson v Switzerland* 2008-…, paras 70–82 (incorrect finding that the abduction of a child by its mother did not contravene the Hague Convention on the Civil Aspects of International Child Abduction: violation).

6.66 In subsequent cases, the Court has expressed its strong support for the philosophy underlying the Convention:

'Inspired by a desire to protect children, regarded as the first victims of the trauma caused by their removal or retention, that instrument seeks to deter the proliferation of international child abductions. It is therefore a matter, once the conditions for the application of the Hague Convention have been met, of restoring as soon as possible the *status quo ante* in order to avoid the legal consolidation of *de facto* situations that were brought about wrongfully, and of leaving the issues of custody and parental authority to be determined by the courts that have jurisdiction in the place of the child's habitual residence, in accordance with Article 19 of the Hague Convention'[1].

This principle is of general application, for even when a state is not a party to the Hague Convention, a similar positive obligation to take all necessary measures to ensure the reunion of parents with their children will arise[2]. However, no positive obligation exists under the Hague Convention upon domestic authorities to ensure the return of a child where the parent concerned does not have a right of custody but merely a right of access, although Article 8 construed in light of the Hague Convention does require the authorities to take measures to uphold such access[3]. Again, authorities must act promptly to ensure that the risk of harm to the relationship between parent and child is reduced[4].

1   *Maumousseau and Washington v France* 2007-…, at para 69.

2   *Bajrami v Albania* 2006-XIV, paras 65–69 (no remedy providing practical or effective protection to prevent or punish child abduction: violation).

3   *RR v Romania (no 1)* (10 November 2009), paras 148–181.

4   *Macready v Czech Republic* (22 April 2010), paras 60–68.

IMMIGRATION, DEPORTATION AND EXTRADITION

6.67 Article 8 cannot in itself be used to found a right to live as a family unit in any particular country since international law recognises a state's right to control the entry of aliens into its territory and their residence[1]. States thus have the power to expel an alien convicted of criminal offences in pursuance of their task of maintaining public order, irrespective of the length of time an alien has lived in the country[2]. Immigration issues therefore fall outside the scope of ECHR protection unless a related consideration under a Convention guarantee arises, for example, where there is a real risk of ill-treatment were an individual to be removed to another country[3]. In respect of Article 8, the guarantee will only be applicable where it can be shown that there is a sufficiently established family life in existence[4]. Thus such matters as the threatened or actual removal of an individual, or the failure of the immigration authorities to admit a near relative of an immigrant, will only fall within the scope of the provision where an individual can be shown to have dominant and long-established family roots and relationships such as to constitute 'family life'. Failing the establishment of 'family life', Article 8 may then only be of relevance in certain cases where it can be shown that deportation or extradition would have an adverse impact upon the maintenance of an individual's health where there are sufficiently adverse effects on physical and moral integrity such as to fall within the scope of the protection of 'private life'[5].

1   *Abdulaziz, Cabales and Balkandali v United Kingdom* (1985) A 94, para 67. For other Council of Europe standards, see Committee of Ministers Recommendation Rec (2000)15 concerning the security of long-term migrants; and Committee of Ministers Recommendation Rec (2002)4 on the legal status of persons admitted for family reunification. For relevant EU provisions regulating the right of nationals of non-EU states to family reunification, see Directive 2003/86/EC, considered in Case 540/03 *European Parliament v Council of the European Union* [2006] 3 ECR-I 5769, Directive 2004/83/EC on refugees, considered in Case C-465/07 *Elgafaji v Staatssecretaris van Justitie* [2009] ECR I-921, and Directive 2008/115/EC; for rights of EU nationals, see Directive 2004/38/EC (on the right of citizens of the Union and their family members to move and reside freely). For domestic discussion, see paras **6.78–6.83** below. For further discussion, see Lambert *The Position of Aliens in Relation to the European Convention on Human Rights* (3rd edn, 2007); Mole *Asylum and the European Convention on Human Rights* (4th edn, 2007).

2   *Üner v Netherlands* [GC] 2006-XII, para 55.

3   See in relation to Arts 2 and 3, paras **4.59** and **4.130–4.134** above; in relation to Art 6, see para **4.135** and **5.02** above; and in respect of Art 9, para **7.10** below.

4   *El Boujaïdi v France* 1997-VI, para 33 (question whether 'family life' has been established to be determined in the light of the position when an exclusion order becomes final). See also *Gül v Switzerland* 1996-I, paras 38–43 (no duty upon state to admit applicant's son since there

were no obstacles to developing a family life in the country where the son was living and had been brought up); *Ahmut v Netherlands* 1996-VI, paras 67–73 (a father had arranged for his son to be schooled abroad, often visited his son abroad, and had dual nationality: the Court determined that a fair balance had been struck between the applicants' interests and the public interest in controlling immigration).

5   *Maslov v Austria* [GC] 2008-..., at para 63: '[As Art 8] also protects the right to establish and develop relationships with other human beings and the outside world and can sometimes embrace aspects of an individual's social identity, it must be accepted that the totality of social ties between settled migrants and the community in which they are living constitutes part of the concept of "private life" within the meaning of Article 8. Regardless of the existence or otherwise of a "family life", the expulsion of a settled migrant therefore constitutes an interference with his or her right to respect for private life. It will depend on the circumstances of the particular case whether it is appropriate for the Court to focus on the "family life" rather than the "private life" aspect.' See also *Bensaid v United Kingdom* 2001-I, paras 46–49; and for domestic discussion, *R (Razgar) v Secretary of State for the Home Department* [2004] 2 AC 368 (if there were sufficiently strong facts to suggest that deportation would affect the mental stability of the asylum seeker, this could give rise to issues under Art 8).

6.68 Whether 'family life' can be shown to have been established is thus dependent upon the particular facts of each case. This will involve consideration of a wider range of circumstances, such as whether the person's near relatives also reside in the state, his language, education and upbringing, length of residence, and the extent of his existing links with the country to which the state intends to expel him[1].

1   Eg *Moustaquim v Belgium* (1991) A 193; and *Beldjoudi v France* (1992) A 234-A, paras 67–76 (marriage and subsequent establishment of matrimonial home in France for 20 years had established 'family life', despite lengthy periods of enforced separation of spouses through imprisonment). Cf *Maslov v Austria* [GC] 2008-..., at para 75: 'for a settled migrant who has lawfully spent all or the major part of his or her childhood and youth in the host country very serious reasons are required to justify expulsion. This is all the more so where the person concerned committed the offences underlying the expulsion measure as a juvenile.'

6.69 Where a deportation or extradition would give rise to issues under Article 8 on account of an interference with 'family life', it must be shown that the interference is 'in accordance with the law', that it is for a prescribed aim, and that it is 'necessary in a democratic society'. This latter test permits scrutiny of the proportionality of the threatened or actual removal in light of the reasons adduced by the authorities[1], but always recognising that they enjoy a certain margin of appreciation in such determinations[2].

1   *Üner v Netherlands* [GC] 2006-XII, paras 54–55 and 57–58.

2   *Slivenko v Latvia* [GC] 2003-X, para 113.

6.70 In *Maslov v Austria,* the Grand Chamber summarised the criteria to be adopted when determining whether an expulsion measure may be deemed proportionate:

- the nature and seriousness of the offence committed by the applicant;

- the length of the applicant's stay in the country from which he or she is to be expelled;

- the time elapsed since the offence was committed and the applicant's conduct during that period;

- the nationalities of the various persons concerned;

- the applicant's family situation, such as the length of the marriage, and other factors expressing the effectiveness of a couple's family life;

- whether the spouse knew about the offence at the time when he or she entered into a family relationship;

- whether there are children of the marriage, and if so, their age;

- the seriousness of the difficulties which the spouse is likely to encounter in the country to which the applicant is to be expelled[1];

- the best interests and well-being of the children, in particular the seriousness of the difficulties which any children of the applicant are likely to encounter in the country to which the applicant is to be expelled; and

- the solidity of social, cultural and family ties with the host country and with the country of destination[2].

Further, the removal of two groups of aliens will call for particular scrutiny: first, aliens who have spent most (if not all) of their childhood in the host country where they were brought up and educated[3]; and secondly, young adults who have not yet founded a family of their own[4]. There is extensive case law examining whether particular removals have met these tests[5].

1   *Boultif v Switzerland* 2001-IX, para 40.

2   *Maslov v Austria* [GC] 2008-..., para 55.

3   *Maslov v Austria* [GC] 2008-..., at para 75: 'For a settled migrant who has lawfully spent all or the major part of his or her childhood and youth in the host country very serious reasons are required to justify expulsion. This is all the more so where the person concerned committed the offences underlying the expulsion measure as a juvenile'.

4   *Maslov v Austria* [GC] 2008-..., paras 71–76: (the relevant criteria in such a case are the age of the person concerned; the nature and seriousness of the offence; the length of the stay in the country from which he is to be expelled; the time elapsed since the offence was committed and conduct during that period; and the solidity of social, cultural and family ties with the host country and with the country of destination).

5   See eg *Cruz Varas and Others v Sweden* (1991) A 201, para 88 (no evidence to show that the applicants could not establish a family life in their home country); *Nasri v France* (1995) A 320-B, paras 43–46 (deportation of deaf and dumb applicant of limited education whose parents and nine siblings lived in France had been ordered after his conviction for gang rape; the deportation would violate Art 8); *Dalia v France* 1998-I, para 45 (the permanent exclusion of a woman who had joined her mother and seven siblings in France and who subsequently gave birth to a child in the country gave rise to an Art 8 issue; but the order imposed after a conviction for drug-trafficking was considered justified); *Baghli v France* 1999-VIII, paras 45–49 (expulsion of an Algerian national convicted of drug-trafficking who had arrived in France at the age of two, who had lived most of his life there, and whose close family were resident there, but who had not taken French nationality and who had retained some links with the country of birth: no violation of Art 8 in view of the serious breach of public order his

behaviour had occasioned); *Boultif v Switzerland* 2001-IX, paras 39–56 (expulsion of the applicant who had entered the country with a tourist visa, married a Swiss national, and been sentenced to a two-year prison sentence for robbery and other offences: since it was practically impossible for him to live with his family outside Switzerland and he presented only a comparatively limited danger to public order, the interference with respect for family life was not proportionate and thus constituted a violation of Art 8); *Slivenko v Latvia* [GC] 2003-X, paras 117–121 (expulsion of family of Russian military officer from Latvia where they since birth had developed the network of personal, social and economic relations: while a treaty and implementing measures providing for this could be accepted as for the protection of national security in light of Latvia's history, here specific circumstances concerning the public interest in removal did not outweigh the applicant's interests in staying, and violation established); *Najafi v Sweden* (dec) (6 July 2004) (deportation to Iran following conviction for an aggravated narcotics offence following three previous criminal offences: inadmissible, even although expulsion would have serious implications for his family life as implications for family life had to be balanced against public safety and the prevention of disorder and crime); *Rodrigues da Silva and Hoogkamer v Netherlands* 2006-I, para 44 (refusal to allow mother to remain in the country: violation since she could have reasonably have expected to have been allowed to remain, and expulsion would have had far-reaching consequences upon family life); *Üner v Netherlands* [GC] 2006-XII, paras 64–67 (withdrawal of residency permit and imposition of exclusion order for ten years following convictions for violent offences: applicant's children were very young and thus of an adaptable age, and even although the applicant's social and cultural ties with the country of his nationality were limited, he would be able to return to the country); *Gulijev v Lithuania* (16 December 2008), paras 43–47 (foreign national's deportation on the basis of a secret report which stipulated that he was a threat to national security and public order and following a conviction for theft from Lithuania and prohibition on re-entry where he had lived since 1989 and had a wife and children and strong social and cultural ties: violation); *Omojudi v United Kingdom* (24 November 2009), paras 43–47 (deportation order following conviction for sexual assault a criminal offence had been disproportionate in view of the relatively mild nature of the offence, the extremely strong family ties with the UK, and the difficulties the applicant and his family would face if returned to the country of origin, the Court considering that the only relevant offence that could be considered for the purposes of proportionality was that committed after he had been granted indefinite leave to remain since the authorities must have been fully aware of his offending history); and *Mutlag v Germany* (25 March 2010), paras 54–63 (deportation of a foreign national responsible for serious and violent offences from Germany where he was born, grew up and had permanent residence did not violate Art 8).

DECISIONS OF THE DOMESTIC COURTS ON FAMILY LIFE ISSUES

Pregnancy and related issues
6.71 Issues relating to Article 8 in the context of pregnancy and childbirth have been considered by domestic courts in a number of cases. In *Blood and Tarbuck v Secretary of State for Health*[1] a declaration of incompatibility was granted of consent in respect of s 28(6)(b) of the Human Fertilisation and Embryology Act 1990, to the extent that it did not allow a deceased father's name to be given on the birth certificate of a child who had been conceived after the father's death, using gametes which had been stored. The non-availability of damages for the birth of a healthy child[2] was held not to be incompatible with Article 8[3]. In a case where embryos had been created by in vitro fertilisation using the gametes of the claimant and her partner, following which they had separated, legislation which entitled her partner to withdraw his consent to the use of the embryos was held to

be an interference with the claimant's Article 8 right to respect for her private life, but was justified under Article 8(2)[4]. Another case concerned the consequences of a mistake made in the course of fertility treatment of two couples, where the sperm of one woman's husband was used to fertilise the eggs of the other woman. It was held that neither the biological father nor his wife had a sufficiently close relationship with the resultant twins to assert Article 8 rights. The partner of the child's mother could however assert Article 8 rights on account of his close relationship with the twins, whom he regarded as his own children[5]. It has been held that children born by artificial insemination by donor are entitled under Article 8 to establish details of their paternal identity, as an aspect of respect for their private life[6]. The Article 8 rights of a mother of girls aged 12 and 15 have been held not to be infringed by a policy of giving contraceptive advice to persons under 16 without parental knowledge[7].

1   *Blood and Tarbuck v Secretary of State for Health*, 28 February 2003, Sullivan J, unreported.

2   *McFarlane v Tayside Health Board* 2000 SC (HL) 1.

3   *Greenfield v Irwin* [2001] 1 WLR 1279.

4   *Evans v Amicus Healthcare Ltd* [2005] Fam 1.

5   *L Teaching Hospitals NHS Trust v A* [2003] 1 FLR 1091.

6   *R (Rose) v Secretary of State for Health* [2002] 2 FLR 962.

7   *R (Axon) v Secretary of State for Health* [2006] QB 539.

Child care proceedings

6.72 There have been a number of important cases in which domestic courts have considered Article 8 in relation to state assumption of responsibility for the care of children. The earliest such case is *Re S (Minors) (Care Order: Implementation of Care Plan)*, which concerned the compatibility with Article 8 of the statutory provisions in force in England and Wales. The House of Lords accepted that the manner in which a local authority discharged its responsibilities to a child in its care might violate the rights of the child or his parents under the article. An intervention in the life of a child which was justified at the outset might cease to be justifiable under Article 8(2), if for example it kept the child away from his family for purposes which were not being realised. Further, the local authority's decision making process must be conducted fairly and so as to afford due respect to the interests protected by Article 8. The procedural provisions of the legislation were, however, found to be compatible with Article 8. The contention that the legislation failed to provide an adequate remedy if a local authority failed to discharge its responsibilities properly, with the consequence that the rights of the child or his parents under Article 8 were violated, did not itself infer any violation of Article 8: failure by the state to provide an effective remedy for a violation of Article 8 was not itself a violation of Article 8[1].

Another important decision was that in *Principal Reporter v K*, which concerned the rights of an unmarried father to participate in proceedings before a children's hearing. The child had lived with both parents until their relationship broke down, and had then continued to have regular contact with the father. The father was however excluded from proceedings before the children's hearing and related proceedings before the sheriff, which were concerned with allegations made against him, and which resulted in an order prohibiting contact between the father and the child. He was excluded because he was not a 'parent enjoying parental rights and responsibilities' or 'a person in whom [such rights] are ... vested' or 'a person who ordinarily ... has charge of, or control over the child', and so did not fall within the definitions of a 'relevant person' within the meaning of the relevant legislation. The Supreme Court held that the father had established a family life with the child, and that the decision of the children's hearing to prohibit contact between the father and the child constituted interference by a public authority with the right to respect for that family life. In order for that interference to be proportionate, procedural safeguards had to be in place so that a parent or other person whose family life with the child was at risk in the proceedings was given a proper opportunity to participate in the decision-making process. In the absence of such an opportunity, the Article 8 rights of both the father and the child had been violated. The court further held that the incompatibility of the definition of 'relevant person' with Article 8 could be cured by applying the interpretative remedy provided by s 3 of the HRA 1998, and that the appropriate remedy was to insert into the definition the words 'or who appears to have established family life with the child with which the decision of the children's hearing may interfere'[2].

A variety of other aspects of child care proceedings have been considered in the light of Article 8, including the application of the law of defamation.[3]

---

1   *Re S (Minors) (Care Order: Implementation of Care Plan)* [2002] 2 AC 291. There would be a breach of Art 13, but that article is not a Convention right as defined in the HRA 1998.

2   *Principal Reporter v K* 2011 SLT 271.

3   *W v Westminster City Council* [2005] 1 FLR 816. The legislation governing local authorities' powers and duties in relation to child protection in England and Wales has been found to be compatible with Art 8 in so far as it required a balance to be struck between the principle of non-intervention in family life and the need to protect the child: *Re S (Sexual Abuse Allegations: Local Authority Response)* [2001] 2 FLR 776.

Residence and contact orders

6.73 In *White v White,* it was said that the structure of Scots law complies with the requirements of Article 8 since it respects family life and contains provisions enshrined in legislation for balancing the competing interests of the various members of the family. In particular, in making regard for the child's welfare the paramount consideration, s 11(7) (a) of the Children (Scotland) Act 1995, which governs the circumstances in which an order (including a contact order) may be made in relation to parental responsibilities and rights, is in conformity with the approach laid down by the Strasbourg Court[1].

---

1   *White v White* 2001 SC 689. A similar conclusion was reached, in respect of the corresponding English legislation, in *Payne v Payne* [2001] Fam 473, which concerned the removal of a child from the jurisdiction, allegedly in breach of the non-custodial parent's rights under Art 8. The paramountcy of the interests of the child, under Art 8(2), was also affirmed in *Re L (A Child) (Contact: Domestic violence)* [2001] Fam 260.

6.74 There have been a number of cases concerning contact between prisoners and their children. In cases concerned with visits by children to prisoners, the English courts have usually found that decisions which comply with the guidance and procedures issued by the Secretary of State will also comply with Article 8(2), and have quashed decisions in which the guidance and procedures have not been followed[1]. The guidance in question required careful consideration to be given to the particular circumstances of individual cases. The rigid application of a policy that female prisoners should be separated from their children when the children reached the age of 18 months was successfully challenged in a case where the mother had a relatively short time remaining to serve and there was no acceptable alternative to her continuing to care for the child. The Court of Appeal observed that the case concerned the rights of the child as much as those of the mother. It also made important observations about the implications of Article 8 for the sentencing of women caring for children[2].

1   See eg *Westwater v Secretary of State for Justice* [2010] EWHC 2403 (Admin); *X v Secretary of State for Justice* [2010] EWHC 2507 (Admin).

2   *R (P) v Secretary of State for the Home Department* [2001] 1 WLR 2002. A different conclusion was reached in the same case in relation to another claimant who had a much longer term to serve. See also *R (D) v Secretary of State for the Home Department* [2003] EWHC 155 (Admin) (the decision-maker must consider the baby's right to respect for his family life before a young baby can be separated from his mother in prison and determine whether the interference with such right is proportionate).

Adoption

6.75 One of the more significant decisions under the HRA 1998 is *Re G (Adoption: Married Couple)*, which concerned the question whether a prohibition on adoption by unmarried couples, imposed by a statutory instrument in force in Northern Ireland, was compatible with the Convention rights arising under Article 8 read with Article 14. The House of Lords held that it was not, even if the issue were to be regarded by the Strasbourg Court as falling within the margin of appreciation of national authorities: the margin of appreciation available to member states in delicate areas of social policy was not automatically appropriated by the legislature[1].

1   *Re G (Adoption: Married Couple)* [2009] 1 AC 173. See also *T, Petitioner* 1997 SLT 724 (sexual orientation only one factor to be taken into account in an adoption case).

6.76 The courts have also considered the compatibility with Article 8 of the Scottish legislation under which an order freeing a child for adoption has the effect of permanently depriving the natural parents of the right to apply to the court for an order for parental rights or responsibilities. The legislation was held to be compatible with Article 8[1]. The case of *C v XYZ County Council* concerned the question whether Article 8 required that the father of a baby (who did not know of her existence), and the parents of the mother, should be informed of the mother's request that the baby should be placed for adoption. The court held that there was no such requirement: the father had no family life with the child, and non-disclosure to the grandparents was justifiable under Article 8(2) if it was in the best interests of the child[2]. Article 8 has also been mentioned in a number of cases concerned with other issues arising in relation to adoption, including whether a child should be declared free for adoption on the ground that parental agreement to the making of an adoption order is being withheld unreasonably[3], and whether an adoption order should be made in favour of one natural parent with the effect of excluding the other[4]. The Convention has not, however, played an important part in the court's consideration of such cases, since they have proceeded on the basis that the domestic legislation, if applied correctly, is consistent with the requirements of Article 8. The private life aspect of Article 8 was also raised in *R (Gunn-Russo) v Nugent Care Society*, where the claimant succeeded in judicial review proceedings to obtain disclosure of records held by the voluntary adoption agency that handled her adoption. She succeeded because the policy of the first defendants (the successors to the agency) was applied without due consideration to the facts of her case. Her claim against the Secretary of State for failure to fulfil a positive obligation under Articles 8 and 14 to make available an appeal procedure against the decision of bodies such as the first defendant was unsuccessful[5].

1   *Dundee City Council v GK* 2006 SC 326.

2   *C v XYZ County Council* [2008] Fam 54. It has however been held that natural fathers should normally be informed of adoption proceedings, even if they do not have statutory 'parental responsibility' (in which event they would be entitled to notice of the proceedings as of right), if the factual relationship between the father and the child constitutes family life within the meaning of Art 8: *Re H (A Child) (Adoption: Consultation of Unmarried Fathers)* [2001] 1 FLR 646. See also *City of Edinburgh Council v G* 2002 SC 440 (unmarried father had no parental rights or responsibilities, but had continued to have contact with child since the parents separated, and been heard at hearing of application for freeing order: father entitled to appeal against order). Cf *Principal Reporter v K* [2011] 1 WLR 18, discussed at para **6.72** above.

3   See eg *East Lothian Council v A* 2002 SC 106; *West Lothian Council v McG* 2002 SC 411.

4   *Re B (A Minor) (Adoption: Natural Parent)* [2002] 1 WLR 258.

5   *R (Gunn-Russo) v Nugent Care Society* [2002] 1 FLR 1.

Child maintenance

6.77 The system of child maintenance established under the Child Support Act 1991 has been considered in a number of cases and has been held to be compatible with Article 8 and Article 1 of Protocol no 1[1].

1   See eg *R (Denson) v Child Support Agency* [2002] 1 FLR 938; *R (Plumb) v Secretary of State for Work and Pensions* [2002] EWHC 1125; *R (Qazi) v Secretary of State for Work and Pensions* [2004] EWHC 1331 (Admin).

Immigration, deportation and extradition

6.78 Any removal or deportation of an alien may engage Convention rights under domestic law because of its potential effects either (a) within the jurisdiction or (b) abroad. The distinction can be important with regard to the degree of risk of such effects which needs to be shown before the domestic court will act to restrain removal[1]. Article 1 of the Convention 'cannot be read as justifying a general principle to the effect that a Contracting State may not surrender an individual unless satisfied that the conditions awaiting him in the country of destination are in full accord with each of the safeguards of the Convention'[2].

1   See *R (Ullah) v Special Adjudicator* [2004] 2 AC 323, paras 9, 24 and 50; *EM (Lebanon) v Secretary of State for the Home Department* [2009] AC 1198; and *RB (Algeria) v Secretary of State for the Home Department* [2010] 2 AC 110.

2   This was said in a minority judgment in *Mamatkulov and Askarov v Turkey* [GC] 2005-I and applied to Art 8 in *EM (Lebanon) v Secretary of State for the Home Department* [2009] 1 AC 1198 at para 34 per Lord Bingham of Cornhill.

6.79 Articles 2 and 3 of the Convention raise particular issues in relation to removal, which are discussed in chapter 4[1]. As to other Convention articles, the potential effects of removal may be felt either *within* the jurisdiction or, after removal, abroad. Conduct or a situation which would be unacceptable if it occurred domestically does not automatically entitle a person to resist removal if it would only take place abroad. Thus, a person relying on Article 8 in the latter situation must establish 'at least a real risk of a flagrant violation of the very essence of the right'[2].

1   See paras **4.54–4.59** and **4.130–4.137** above.

2   *R (Ullah) v Special Adjudicator* [2004] 2 AC 323 at para 50 per Lord Steyn.

6.80 This test in respect of risks abroad ('a real risk of a flagrant violation of the very essence of the right') was satisfied in *EM (Lebanon) v Secretary of State for the Home Department*. There, a mother had separated from her husband shortly after birth of their son in the Lebanon, and under Lebanese law the husband would have been entitled to automatic custody (with only occasional, supervised visits by the mother), as soon as the son reached the age of seven. Before that age, the mother went into hiding and fled the Lebanon. When she arrived in the United Kingdom her child was eight, and by the time of the House of Lords decision he was twelve and had had no contact with the father or his family since birth. Her claim for asylum failed (on the grounds that there was no risk of 'persecution'), but she relied successfully upon Article 8 to resist removal to the Lebanon with her son, on the ground that the effect of her return there would be to destroy the family life which she had established with her son. Lord Hope of Craighead noted[1] that the European Court of Human Rights (agreeing with the British courts) had applied a similar approach in 'healthcare' cases. Only in 'very exceptional cases', where the effects of removal would be flagrant (as where the person was critically ill and close to death), would removal be precluded on the grounds of a difference in the medical facilities or treatment that would be received abroad[2]. In *RB (Algeria) v Secretary of State for the Home Department*, the same test of flagrancy was applied by the House of Lords when rejecting a claim to resist deportation to Jordan, on the ground that the claimant would be tried and was likely to be found guilty there in a manner which would infringe his rights to fair trial and liberty under Articles 5 and 6[3].

1   *EM (Lebanon) v Secretary of State for the Home Department* [2009] AC 1198, at para 17.

2   *EM (Lebanon) v Secretary of State for the Home Department* [2009] AC 1198. For an example of this type of case, see *ZT v Secretary of State for the Home Department* [2006] Imm AR 84 (removal of Aids sufferer to Zimbabwe challenged on the basis that this would interrupt the medical treatment she was receiving: did not meet the high threshold for Art 3, and her position was insufficiently exceptional to come within Art 8).

3   *RB (Algeria) v Secretary of State for the Home Department* [2010] 2 AC 110.

6.81 The position regarding risks which would be suffered within the jurisdiction as a result of removal is different. The flagrancy test does not apply. The court has to weigh the competing considerations justifying removal against those militating against removal - the latter frequently being considerations arising under Article 8(1) and (2). It has to reach a proportionate decision, striking that 'fair balance between the rights of the individual and the interests of the community which is inherent in the whole of the Convention'[1]. In *Huang v Secretary of State for the Home Department,* the House of Lords rejected the Home Secretary's submission that the courts should pay considerable deference to his decision 'save in an exceptional case'. It was for the court to apply a test of proportionality, not of exceptionality, even though the House's expectation was that it would only be in a very small minority of cases that claimants not covered by the immigration rules and supplementary directions could still resist removal under Article 8[2]. A very large number of cases have now arisen in which domestic courts have considered whether an individual has established private or family life in the United Kingdom, and if so, whether removal is incompatible with Article 8[3].

1   *R (Razgar) v Secretary of State for the Home Department* [2004] 2 AC 368 at para 20 per Lord Bingham of Cornhill.

2   *Huang v Secretary of State for the Home Department* [2007] 2 AC 167 at para 20.

3   Other recent cases at House of Lords or Supreme Court level include *Chikwamba v Secretary of State for the Home Department* [2008] 1 WLR 1420; *Beoku-Betts v Secretary of State for the Home Department* [2009] AC 115; *EB (Kosovo) v Secretary of State for the Home Department* [2009] AC 1159; *AS (Somalia) v Secretary of State for the Home Department* [2009] 1 WLR 1385; and *ZH v Secretary of State for the Home Department* [2011] 2 WLR 148 (weight to be given to children's best interests). There are many more cases at the level of the Inner House and the Court of Appeal.

6.82 The proportionality exercise can be particularly difficult in the case of an alien who has become 'virtually a national'[1] of the country from which he or she is to be deported, but whose deportation the Home Secretary deems to be conducive to the public good. Relevant factors include on the one hand the nature and seriousness of any offence committed, viewed in the light of the person's previous record and the likelihood of any future offending, and on the other the length of stay and degree of integration in the United Kingdom, including the effect on any established family life and any children here. The relevant considerations were reviewed in *JO (Uganda) v Secretary of State for the Home Department*[2] and *KB (Trinidad and Tobago) v Secretary of State for the Home Department*[3]. In the former case, the Court of Appeal summarised the principles:

'20. As to private life, it is emphasised at para 59 of the *Üner* judgment[4] that settled immigrants will have ties with the community that constitute part of the concept of private life, which must therefore be considered even if the applicant has no family life in the host country ...

24. ... in considering the position of family members in deportation cases as well as in removal cases the material question is not whether there is an "insuperable obstacle" to their following the applicant to the country of removal but whether they "cannot reasonably be expected" to follow him there.

26. Concentration on whether family members can reasonably be expected to relocate with the applicant ensures that the seriousness of the difficulties which they are likely to encounter in the country to which the applicant is to be deported (the relevant criterion in the Strasbourg case-law) is properly assessed as a whole and is taken duly into account, together with all other relevant matters, in determining the proportionality of deportation...

27. ... [E]ven if the difficulties do make it unreasonable to expect family members to join the applicant in the country to which he is to be deported, that will not necessarily be a decisive feature in the overall assessment of proportionality. ...

28. I have concentrated so far on deportation. Cases of ordinary administrative removal of persons unlawfully present in the country operate within the same legal framework and ... require essentially the same approach. ...

29. There is, however, one material difference between the two types of case, in that they generally involve the pursuit of different legitimate aims: in deportation cases it is the prevention of disorder or crime, in ordinary removal cases it is the maintenance of effective immigration control. The difference in aim is potentially important because the factors in favour of expulsion are in my view capable of carrying greater weight in a deportation case than in a case of ordinary removal ...

30. Where the person to be removed is a person unlawfully present in this country who has also committed criminal offences, the decision to remove him may pursue a double aim, namely the prevention of disorder or crime as well as the maintenance of effective immigration control ...'[5]

---

1 A phrase taken from the dissenting judgment of Judges Costa and Tulkens in *Baghli v France* 1999-VIII.

2 *JO (Uganda) v Secretary of State for the Home Department* [2010] 1 WLR 1607.

3 *KB (Trinidad and Tobago) v Secretary of State for the Home Department* [2010] 1 WLR 1630.

4 *Üner v Netherlands* [GC] 2006-XII.

5 *JO (Uganda) v Secretary of State for the Home Department* [2010] 1 WLR 1607 at paras 20–30 per Richards LJ.

6.83 Similar issues can arise in relation to entry to the United Kingdom. There is a large body of case law concerned with the the implications of Article 8 in the context of applications for entry clearances and other controls over immigration[1].

1   See eg *Singh (Pawandeep) v Entry Officer, New Delhi* [2005] QB 608, discussed at para **6.20**
     above; and *A (Afghanistan) v Secretary of State for the Home Department* [2009] EWCA Civ
     825.

6.84 Generally speaking, similar principles are capable of applying to extradition
(whether of United Kingdom citizens or aliens), but extradition by its very nature
introduces a powerful extra consideration: that of justice and comity. Extradition
conduces to the general international good, by ensuring that those properly
suspected of serious crime are tried and, where appropriate, convicted, sentenced
and imprisoned. 'The public interest in extraditing a person to be tried for an
alleged crime is of a different order from the public interest in deporting or removing
from this country an alien who has been convicted of a crime and who has served
his sentence for it, or whose presence here is for some other reason not
acceptable'[1]. There are very few reported cases where the potential effect of
extradition on Article 8 rights within the jurisdiction has operated as a bar to
extradition[2].

1   *Norris v Government of the United States of America* [2010] 2 AC 487 at para 15 per Lord
     Phillips of Worth Matravers. For a Scottish example, see *H v Lord Advocate* [2011] HCJAC
     77.

2   The only reported exceptions as at the end of 2010 were *W v Provincial Court of Katowice*
     [2008] All ER (D) 273, which recorded that extradition of the appellant's wife was refused on
     Art 8 grounds in the court below; and *Jansons v Latvia* [2009] EWHC 1845 (Admin).

6.85 In *Norris v Government of the United States of America*, reliance was
placed on Article 8 with reference to the disruption to family and private life that
extradition would cause within the United Kingdom jurisdiction. Mr Norris was a
United Kingdom citizen, whose extradition was requested by the USA for trial
there on serious charges of obstructing the course of justice. He submitted that
the courts below had erred in looking for 'striking and unusual facts' and effectively
adopting a test of exceptionality as a condition of any stay on extradition. The
Supreme Court disagreed:

   'The reality is that only if some quite exceptionally compelling feature, or combination
   of features, is present that interference with family life consequent upon extradition
   will be other than proportionate to the objective that extradition serves. That, no
   doubt, is what the Commission had in mind in *Launder*[1] when it stated that it was
   only in exceptional circumstances that extradition would be an unjustified or
   disproportionate interference with the right to respect for family life. I can see no
   reason why the District Judge should not, when considering a challenge to
   extradition founded on article 8, explain his rejection of such a challenge, where
   appropriate, by remarking that there was nothing out of the ordinary or exceptional
   in the consequences that extradition would have for the family life of the person
   resisting extradition. "Exceptional circumstances" is a phrase that says little about
   the nature of the circumstances. Instead of saying that interference with article 8
   rights can only outweigh the importance of extradition in exceptional circumstances
   it is more accurate and more helpful, to say that the consequences of interference
   with article 8 rights must be exceptionally serious before this can outweigh the

importance of extradition. A judge should not be criticised if, as part of his process of reasoning, he considers how, if at all, the nature and extent of the impact of extradition on family life would differ from the normal consequences of extradition.'[2]

The Supreme Court in *Norris* also examined, without enthusiasm, the argument (not infrequently raised) that the possibility of prosecution in the requested state should weigh against extradition, saying:

'is it of relevance when considering proportionality that a prosecution for the extradition offence might be brought in the requested jurisdiction? ... [T]he Strasbourg Court gave a positive answer to this question in *Soering*[3]. There has recently been a spate of cases in which the extraditee has argued that he ought to be prosecuted in this jurisdiction ... In each one the argument was rejected.

Extradition proceedings should not become the occasion for a debate about the most convenient forum for criminal proceedings. Rarely, if ever, on an issue of proportionality, could the possibility of bringing criminal proceedings in this jurisdiction be capable of tipping the scales against extradition in accordance with this country's treaty obligations. Unless the judge reaches the conclusion that the scales are finely balanced he should not enter into an enquiry as to the possibility of prosecution in this country.'[4]

---

1   27279/95, *Launder v United Kingdom* (8 December 1997).

2   *Norris v Government of the United States of America* [2010] 2 AC 487 at para 56 per Lord Phillips of Worth Matravers.

3   *Soering v United Kingdom* (1981) A 161.

4   *Norris v Government of the United States of America* [2010] 2 AC 487, at paras 66–67 per Lord Phillips.

6.86 The treatment of immigrants within the United Kingdom may also raise issues under Article 8. In *R (Q) v Secretary of State for the Home Department*, it was held that the denial of wefare support was capable of engaging Article 8, so as to require justification under Article 8(2), if it impacted sufficiently on the asylum seeker's private and family life, which extended to the individual's physical and mental integrity and autonomy[1]. In *Anufrijeva v Southwark London Borough Council* it was said that Article 8 was capable of imposing on a state a positive obligation to provide support, but that it was hard to conceive of a situation in which the predicament of an individual would be such that Article 8 required him to be provided with welfare support, where his predicament was not sufficiently severe to engage Article 3. Article 8 might be more readily engaged where a family unit was involved. Where the welfare of children was at stake, Article 8 might require the provision of welfare support in a manner which enabled family life to continue[2]. In *R (Morris) v Westminster City Council* a provision in housing legislation which required a dependent child who was subject to immigration control to be disregarded when deciding whether a person had a priority need for accommodation was held to violate Article 8 taken with Article 14[3].

---

1   *R (Q) v Secretary of State for the Home Department* [2004] QB 36.

2   *Anufrijeva v Southwark London Borough Council* [2004] QB 1124. See also *R (Kimani) v*

Lambeth London Borough Council [2004] 1 WLR 272 ('a state owes no duty under the Convention to provide support to foreign nationals who are in a position freely to return home'); *R (Grant) v Lambeth London Borough* [2005] 1 WLR 1781 ('the local authority ... could enable the claimant and her children to maintain their rights under article 8 of the Convention and avoid destitution by making arrangements for (1) them to travel to her homeland, and (2) their accommodation for a short time until the travel arrangements to take effect'); and *R (Clue) v Birmingham City Council* [2011] 1 WLR 99 ('a local authority which is faced with an application for assistance pending the determination of an arguable application for leave to remain on Convention grounds, should not refuse assistance if that would have the effect of requiring the person to leave the UK thereby forfeiting his claim': *Kimani* and *Grant* distinguished).

3   *R (Morris) v Westminster City Council* [2006] 1 WLR 505.

Anti-terrorism measures

6.87 Measures taken under anti-terrorism legislation to control the movements and whereabouts of persons suspected of terrorism have raised issues under Article 8, of both a procedural[1] and a substantive[2] nature.

1   See eg *Secretary of State for the Home Department v AP (No 2)* [2010] 1 WLR 1652 (prohibition of identification of suspected terrorist); *BX v Secretary of State for the Home Department* [2010] 1 WLR 2463 (right to make representations).

2   See eg *Secretary of State for the Home Department v AP* [2011] 2 AC 1 (person required to live 150 miles from London, where his family life was established; relationship between consideration of Art 8 and Art 5).

Private life issues: surveillance and searches; and protection of personal data

COVERT SURVEILLANCE

6.88 A range of techniques used in the prevention or investigation of crime such as data-gathering[1], the interception of communications[2], the use of electronic listening devices[3], the monitoring of emails[4] and the use of GPS tracking devices[5] involve interferences with Article 8 rights. In light of the difficulties in establishing whether surveillance measures have been applied in practice, an applicant need merely establish that he is a member of a class reasonably likely to have his communications intercepted to qualify as a 'victim' for the purposes of Article 8[6].

1   Eg 9702/82, *X v United Kingdom* (1983) DR 30, 239 (data gathering by means of compulsory census involved an 'interference', but was justified in terms of para (2)); *Leander v Sweden* (1987) A 116, para 48 (secret police file containing details of applicant's private life); 12015/86, *Hilton v United Kingdom* (1988) DR 57, 108 (collection of data for security check); and *Amann v Switzerland* [GC] 2000-II, paras 65–67 (storage of cards concerning details of applicant's private life). Cf 25099/94, *Martin v Switzerland* (1995) DR 81,136 (archiving of police register for 50 years may not involve an interference).

2   Eg *Malone v United Kingdom* (1984) A 82, para 64 (telephone tapping); 21482/93, *Christie v United Kingdom* (1994) DR 78, 119 (interception of telexes); and *Lambert v France* 1998-V, para 21 (interception of communications on a telephone line belonging to another person). See also *R v P* [2001] 2 WLR 463.

3   Eg *Khan v United Kingdom* 2000-V, para 25 (evidence obtained by tape-recording of conversations); *PG and JH v United Kingdom* 2001-IX, paras 37 and 42 (visual surveillance, covert listening device, and obtaining details of telephone calls).

4   *Copland v United Kingdom* 2007-IV, paras 41–42 (reasonable expectation as regards the privacy of telephone calls and email and internet usage: Art 8 engaged).

5   *Uzun v Germany* 2010-..., paras 49–53 (surveillance via GPS tracking device).

6   *Klass and Others v Germany* (1978) A 28, para 33. See further para **2.67** above. Cf *Halford v United Kingdom* 1997-III, paras 47–48 and 56–60 (the Court found it established that there was a reasonable likelihood that calls from her office telephone had been intercepted, but not that there had been any interception of calls made from her home telephone);; 12015/86, *Hilton v United Kingdom* (1988) DR 57, 108 (no reasonable likelihood that security services had retained personal information).

INTERFERENCES

6.89 The mere existence of legislation permitting monitoring entails a surveillance threat and so constitutes an interference with the rights of all those to whom it may be applied[1]. In *Kennedy v United Kingdom,* the applicant had complained to the Investigatory Powers Tribunal alleging his communications had been intercepted, but after examining the complaints in private, the tribunal had made no determination in his favour and thus the applicant had been unsure whether no interception had taken place, or that any interception had indeed been lawful. The question whether there had been an 'interference' in such cases was to be considered not only in light of the risk of secret surveillance measures being applied in a particular case but also taking into account the availability of domestic remedies. Where (as in the United Kingdom) there was no possibility of challenging the alleged application of secret surveillance measures, the existence of widespread suspicion and concern that secret surveillance powers were being abused could not be considered as unjustified. While the applicant had failed to demonstrate a reasonable likelihood that there had been actual interception, it could not be excluded that secret surveillance measures had indeed been applied to him as he had been at risk of being subjected to such measures, and thus it was appropriate to conclude there had been an 'interference'[2]. In such cases, it is immaterial that the information gathered or the purpose of the surveillance does not relate to 'private life' but rather to the public interest in investigating crime[3] or in ensuring the proper discharge of public office[4]. An interference will still have taken place even if no subsequent use is ever made of the data obtained[5]. In relation to intelligence-gathering by means of visual observation in public places, however, Article 8 is only engaged if the state action goes beyond mere observation and involves the active monitoring of individuals[6]. Further, since data-gathering may often occur for legitimate reasons associated with service provision, the essential purpose of data-gathering may help determine the question of whether there has been any interference with Article 8 rights[7].

1   *Klass and Others v Germany* (1978) A 28, para 41. See also *Liberty and Others v United Kingdom* 2008-..., paras 64–70.

2   *Kennedy v United Kingdom* 2010-..., paras 118–129.

3   *A v France* (1993) A 277-B, para 36–37 (monitoring of murder suspect).

4   Eg *Halford v United Kingdom* 1997-III, paras 44–52 (interception of calls made by a senior police officer on internal communications system).

5   *Kopp v Switzerland* 1998-II, paras 51–53.

6   *Peck v United Kingdom* 2003-I, paras 57–63, discussed below at para 6.98; *Murray v United Kingdom* (1994) A 300-A, para 88 (photographs taken during arrests and search of home: the Court seems to have accepted as implicit that the retention of the photographs involved an interference with Art 8). See also *Friedl v Austria* (1995) A 305-B Commission report, paras 49–52 (police photographing of demonstrators without tracing the identity of participants was not an Art 8 violation: friendly settlement after notification of introduction of independent administrative tribunals to deal with complaints of police photography); 28122/95, *Hutcheon v United Kingdom* (27 November 1996) (75 ft-high security tower build beside applicant's home did not constitute an Art 8 violation since the applicant had not shown she was under surveillance and, in any case, visual surveillance was within normal police duties); and 32200–32201/96, *Herbecq and Association 'Ligue des Droits de l'Homme' v Belgium* (1998) DR 92, 92 (surveillance without recording of public places involved surveillance of public conduct, and did not give rise to an Art 8 issue).

7   *Malone v United Kingdom* (1984) A 82, para 84 (Art 8 issue where information gathered for a legitimate purpose such as telephone service delivery is disclosed to a third party for another reason). See also *PG and JH v United Kingdom* 2001-IX, at para 42: 'metering, which does not *per se* offend against Article 8 if, for example, done by the telephone company for billing purposes, is by its very nature to be distinguished from the interception of communications which may be undesirable and illegitimate in a democratic society unless justified'.

POSITIVE OBLIGATIONS

6.90 Certain positive obligations exist in this area. In relation to personal files held by public authorities, individuals must have recourse to an 'effective and accessible procedure' for obtaining access to 'all relevant and appropriate information' held[1]. There is also a responsibility to publish data where there is a known risk to public health[2]. While there is some authority for the proposition that surveillance by non-state actors does not engage state responsibility[3], a positive obligation may nevertheless exist to ensure effective respect for private life through application of domestic law in regard to surveillance carried out by private individuals or bodies. For example in *Verliere v Switzerland*, the applicant complained of surveillance measures carried out by private detectives. Following a road accident, the applicant had lodged a claim for compensation alleging that she was suffering the after-effects of injuries, but her insurers had doubts about the genuineness of her claim, and had instructed private detectives to investigate. Swiss law, though, recognised both civil and criminal remedies to protect privacy, and the applicant had sought to make use of these processes. The domestic courts had sought to analyse carefully the competing interests of the applicant and of the insurance company, and had decided that the latter's obligation to verify the justification for the claim outweighed those of the applicant. In considering that the domestic courts had thus discharged the positive obligation inherent in ensuring effective respect for private life, the Court declared the application inadmissible[4]. In *Köpke v Germany*, covert video surveillance in the workplace was found to engage positive obligations arising under Article 8 to ensure that domestic law adequately regulates such activities. Here, an employer had instructed a private detective agency to investigate a supermarket employee suspected of theft. The video material thereafter had been examined by others working for the employer and used in domestic proceedings. The Court was satisfied that this had concerned the applicant's 'private life', although such covert surveillance 'at the workplace following substantiated suspicions of theft does not concern a person's private life to an extent which is comparable to the affection of essential aspects of private life by grave acts in respect of which the Court has considered protection by legislative provisions indispensable'. In ruling the application inadmissible, the Court found that the interference had been adequately regulated by case law and that the measure had been proportionate, but observed that 'the competing interests concerned might well be given a different weight in the future, having regard to the extent to which intrusions into private life are made possible by new, more and more sophisticated technologies'[5]. The obligation to ensure that the media respect the private life of an individual (including matters of reputation and honour) is considered below[6].

1   See eg *Gaskin v United Kingdom,* para 49, discussed at para **6.115** below; and *Haralambie v Romania* (27 October 2009), paras 86–97 at para 97 (procedure for gaining access to personal files held by former security services during Romania's communist period was ineffective and inaccessible).

2   See eg *Roche v United Kingdom* [GC] 2005-X, para 167, discussed at para **6.128** below.

3   *Steel and Morris v United Kingdom* (dec) (22 October 2002) (hiring of private investigators by multinational company to discover who was responsible for a publication they considered defamatory: inadmissible, as it was not clear how the state could be held responsible for a private company making use of private investigators, and the investigations were not carried out on private property but in places to which the public had free access).

4   *Verliere v Switzerland* (dec) 2001-VII. For domestic discussion, see *Martin v McGuiness* 2003 SLT 1424, discussed at para **6.99** below; but cf Case 8 Ob 108/5 y [2006] JBl 447 [Austria], [2006] EuroCLY 1744 (covert video surveillance by private party with a view to instigate legal proceedings through service of writ: while goal was legitimate, the means of surveillance had not been the least restrictive means of achieving this).

5   *Köpke v Germany* (dec) (5 October 2010) (the surveillance involved 'considerable intrusion into the employee's private life' as this 'entail[ed] a recorded and reproducible documentation of a person's conduct at his or her workplace, which the employee, being obliged under the employment contract to perform the work in that place, cannot evade.'

6   See paras **6.130–6.133** below.

ASSESSING WHETHER AN INTERFERENCE IS JUSTIFIED – LEGITIMATE AIM

6.91 The justification advanced by a state for measures of surveillance will inevitably involve national security, public safety, or for the prevention of disorder or crime[1].

1   *Klass and Others v Germany* (1978) A 28, paras 46–48.

6.92 The initial focus of the case law is likely to be in determining whether the interference is 'in accordance with the law'. Most obviously, an unauthorised interception, which takes place without legal basis, will constitute a violation of Article 8[1]. Further, the law must also provide sufficient legal regulation to protect against arbitrary interference: that is, the law must also meet the tests of accessibility and foreseeability[2], and legal rules which leave the authorities with too much latitude will fail this test[3]. However, 'in assessing whether the criterion of foreseeability is satisfied, account may be taken also of instructions or administrative practices which do not have the status of substantive law, in so far as those concerned are made sufficiently aware of their contents'[4]. In *Malone v United Kingdom*, the European Court of Human Rights found that the scope and manner of exercise of powers to intercept communications were not prescribed with sufficient certainty, and reiterated that 'in accordance with law' not only referred to the existence of domestic law but also to its quality, which had to be compatible with the notion of the rule of law. Domestic law must thus determine with sufficient clarity both the scope and manner of exercise of any discretionary authority conferred[5].

1 *A v France* (1993) A 277-B, paras 38–39 (unauthorised interception); *Foxley v United Kingdom* (20 June 2000), para 35 (interception of mail after expiry of order). See also *MM v Netherlands* (8 April 2003), paras 44–46 (recording of telephone conversation by one party with the assistance of the police but in the absence of preliminary judicial investigation and an order by an investigating judge as required by legislation: violation).

2 *Leander v Sweden* (1987) A 116, at para 51.

3 *Lambert v France* 1998-V, paras 23–28. See also *Bykov v Russia* [GC] 2009-..., paras 72–83 (use of covert recording of conversation by police without any adequate safeguards against abuse: inconsistent with the requirements of lawfulness).

4 *Petra v Romania* 1998-VII, para 37; *Rotaru v Romania* [GC] 2000-V, paras 55–63 (complaint that the Romanian intelligence service held a file containing information on the applicant's private life and that it was impossible to refute the untrue information that he had been a member of an extremist political organisation: domestic law did not define the kind of information that could be recorded, the categories of people against whom or the circumstances in which surveillance measures could be taken, the procedure to be followed, or limits on the age of information held or the length of time for which it could be kept; and, accordingly, domestic law did not indicate with reasonable clarity the scope and manner of exercise of the relevant discretion); and *The Association for European Integration and Human Rights and Ekimdzhiev v Bulgaria* (28 June 2007), paras 71–94 (no possibility of review of implementation of surveillance measures, control solely entrusted to the Ministry of Internal Affairs: violation).

5 *Malone v United Kingdom* (1984) A 82 at paras 67–68. This decision resulted in the enactment of the Interception of Communications Act 1985. See too *Valenzuela Contreras v Spain* 1998-V, paras 49–61; and *Iordachi and Others v Moldova* (10 February 2009), paras 41–54 (lack of domestic safeguards against abuse of the ability to intercept communications, the law failing the foreseeability requirement as it lacked clarity and detail in respect of subject-matter and subject). See also *Köpke v Germany* (dec) (5 October 2010), discussed at para **6.90** above.

6.93 The legal situation in Britain, on a number of occasions, has been judged as failing to meet these standards. The legislation introduced following *Malone* itself has been found wanting in this respect[1]. Other practices have also been condemned. In *Halford v United Kingdom*, the Court found that domestic law failed to regulate the monitoring or interception of calls made on an internal telecommunications system in the workplace[2]. In *Khan v United Kingdom*, the use of electronic covert listening devices by English police forces, regulated only by Home Office guidelines which were neither binding nor publicly accessible, were found not to fulfil the demands of Article 8[3], while in *Perry v United Kingdom,* the covert videoing of the applicant on his arrival at a police station had not been 'in accordance with law' as the police had failed to comply with the procedures set out in a code of practice, the Court observing that while the normal use of security cameras in premises such as police stations where they serve a legitimate and foreseeable purpose does not in itself raise an issue under Article 8, the situation is otherwise where their use goes beyond the normal or expected use of security cameras as when police officers seek to obtain clear footage of an individual to show to witnesses and where there is no expectation that a suspect is being filmed for identification[4].

1   *Liberty and Others v United Kingdom* 2008-…, paras 64–70 (interception of communications of British and Irish civil liberties organisations over a seven-year period: 1985 legislation conferred a virtually unlimited discretion to intercept any communications between the UK and an external receiver, warrants covered very broad classes of communications, and gave wide discretion to decide which communications from those physically captured should be listened to or read: violation as domestic law was of insufficient clarity to protect against abuse of power). But cf *Kennedy v United Kingdom* 2010-…, paras 118–129 (in contrast with *Liberty and Others,* here the issue was internal communications, warrants were required to specify the interception subject clearly, and the indiscriminate capturing of vast amounts of communications was forbidden: no violation as it was not reasonable to require any further clarification of the categories of persons liable to have their communications intercepted).

2   *Halford v United Kingdom* 1997-III; and see also *Copland v United Kingdom* 2007-IV, paras 41–49 (monitoring of telephone, email and internet usage of public sector employee in order to assess whether facilities were being used excessively for personal purposes: in the absence of any warning that such monitoring was taking place, there was a reasonable expectation of the privacy of telephone calls and of email and internet usage: violation, as there was no domestic regulation of such monitoring).

3   *Khan v United Kingdom* 2000-V, paras 26–28 (the Court noted that the Police Act 1997 now provides a statutory framework for such practices). See too 27237/95, *Govell v United Kingdom* (14 January 1998) (drilling of hole into living room wall and installation of surveillance devices; the Commission noted the lack of any statutory framework to regulate the use of covert listening devices, and that Home Office Guidelines were neither legally binding nor publicly accessible, nor did the system of investigation of complaints by the Police Complaints Authority 'meet the requisite standards of independence needed to constitute sufficient protection against the abuse of authority'); and *Heglas v Czech Republic* (1 March 2007), paras 62–76 (lack of legal basis for listing of telephone calls made and use of listening devices).

4   *Perry v United Kingdom* 2003-IX, paras 44–49.

'Necessary in a democratic society'

6.94 Determination of whether surveillance, data-gathering or interception of communications is 'necessary in a democratic society' requires at the outset consideration of the sufficiency of domestic safeguards to protect against arbitrary application of powers. This issue appears to overlap with examination of the quality of domestic law required in considering whether the interference has been 'in accordance with the law', but the focus here is distinct: the necessity for an interference is best determined by domestic authorities, and the Court will thus focus upon whether there were 'adequate and effective guarantees against abuse'[1] in each case. The basis for this approach is twofold: first, a wide margin of appreciation covers application of surveillance which aims to protect national security or to prevent or investigate criminal activity; and second, the article cannot require state disclosure that the surveillance has been ordered or carried out since this would defeat the very purpose of the measure[3]. Assessment of the existence and effectiveness of safeguards prohibiting misuse will thus allow the Court to ensure that domestic decision-makers have addressed the existence of a pressing social need[2]. In other words, the Court's assessment of the relevancy and sufficiency of the reasons for any interception or monitoring will normally be subsumed by examination as to the quality of these safeguards. Thus the Court will be concerned to ensure that domestic decision-makers have taken into account circumstances such as:

the nature, scope and duration of the possible measures, the grounds required for ordering such measures, the authorities competent to permit, carry out and supervise such measures, and the kind of remedy provided by the national law[4].

1 See eg *Kennedy v United Kingdom* 2010-…, paras 155–170 (surveillance had been carried out on the basis of the Regulation of Investigatory Powers Act 2000 as supplemented by the Interception of Communications Code of Practice, and the lawfulness of the interference was closely related to the question whether the 'necessity' test had been complied with in respect of the RIPA regime).

2 *Klass and Others v Germany* (1978) A 28, at para 58 (failure to inform a person subjected to surveillance cannot be incompatible with Art 8 since 'it is this very fact which ensures the efficacy of the "interference"').

3 *Leander v Sweden* (1987) A 116, paras 59–60.

4 *Klass and Others v Germany* (1978) A 28, at para 50.

6.95 As with the question whether domestic law is sufficiently precise to satisfy the foreseeability requirement required by the 'in accordance with the law' test, determination of whether domestic law and procedure afford adequate safeguards against abuse must be judged by reference to the degree of intrusiveness. While rather strict standards apply to certain forms of surveillance such as surveillance by telecommunications, these requirements are less demanding where the measures are less invasive as in the case of surveillance of movements in public places[1].

1 *Uzun v Germany* 2010-…, paras 49–53, 64–74, and 77–81 (conviction on terrorist charges based upon evidence obtained through surveillance including GPS evidence linking the location of a car to the locus of an attack: the GPS surveillance had affected the applicant only when he was travelling in an accomplice's car, and there had not been comprehensive surveillance).

Safeguards

6.96 Supervisory control of the exercise of executive action is in principle most appropriately discharged by judicial officers[1], although other arrangements which provide independent and 'effective and continuous control' of surveillance are acceptable[2]. Sufficient safeguards against arbitrariness were found to have existed in *Leander v Sweden*[3] which concerned the collection of personal data. However, in the related cases of *Kruslin v France* and *Huvig v France*, safeguards against arbitrariness in the use of telephone tapping were considered wanting[4]. In *Kennedy v United Kingdom,* the Court examined British arrangements at some length, and concluded that these provided adequate protection[5].

---

1   Eg 10439–10441/83, *Mersch v Luxembourg* (1985) DR 43, 34. See also *Greuter v Netherlands* (dec) (19 March 2002) (effective supervision of telephone interception should normally be carried out by the judiciary, at least in the last resort, since judicial control affords the best guarantees of independence, impartiality and a proper procedure); and *Weber and Saravia v Germany* (dec) 2006-XI (adequate procedures for supervision and monitoring of telecommunications: inadmissible).

2   *Klass and Others v Germany* (1978) A 28, at para 56 (Parliamentary Board and a commission both of which were independent of those carrying out the surveillance and able to give objective rulings on measures ordered by the relevant government minister); 21482/93, *Christie v United Kingdom* (1994) DR 78, 119 (British arrangements (an independent tribunal subject to scrutiny by a commissioner holding high judicial office) contained in the Interception of Communications Act 1985 were considered acceptable).

3   *Leander v Sweden* (1987) A 116, paras 54–56 (scope of discretion to make entries in police register was limited by law (entries required to satisfy the test of necessity for attainment of specific objectives) and detailed provision of conditions had to be satisfied before information could be communicated).

4   *Kruslin v France* (1990) A 176-A, paras 34–36, and *Huvig v France* (1990) A 176-B, paras 33–34 (categories of persons liable to interception not defined; no limits on duration of intercepts; no specification of procedure for reports; procedure for transmitting reports intact unspecified). See also *Kopp v Switzerland* 1998-II (interception of calls made to a lawyer without adequate safeguards for client confidentiality; and failure to determine with sufficient certainty the scope, etc of interceptions); *Prado Bugallo v Spain* (18 February 2003), paras 30–33 (adequacy of domestic law); *Doerga v Netherlands* (27 April 2004), paras 43–54 (interception of prisoner's telephone conversations and retention of records on court order despite internal prison regulations requiring the immediate erasure: violation); and *Vetter v France* (31 May 2005), paras 21–27 (use of listening devices in private premises inadequately authorised). Cf *Coban v Spain* (dec) (25 September 2006) ('law' was the legislative enactment as judicially interpreted, and rules permitting interception of telephones were sufficiently precise: inadmissible); and *Marchiani v France* (dec) 2008-… (adequate domestic procedural safeguards in the case of interception of communications of an MEP: inadmissible).

5   *Kennedy v United Kingdom* 2010-…, paras 155–170 (no violation: the Regulation of Investigatory Powers Act 2000 clearly stipulated when an interception warrant would expire and the conditions for renewal; cancellation or renewal of interception warrants was systematically supervised by the Secretary of State; the overall duration of measures depended on the complexity and duration of the investigation, a matter not unreasonable to leave to the discretion of the domestic authorities providing safeguards existed; the procedure for examining, using and storing data limited the scope of the authorities' discretion to intercept and listen to private communications; any captured data unnecessary for any of the authorised purposes had to be destroyed; domestic law strictly limited the number of persons to whom intercept material could be disclosed; there was a strict procedure for security vetting as well as

requirements for the appropriate level of security clearance and for communication of only so much data as the individual needed to know; material was to be destroyed as soon as there were no longer any grounds for its retention, the necessity for such was periodically reviewed; and the supervision of the whole regime was adequate and in particular, the Interception of Communications Commissioner scrutinised any errors which had occurred in the operation of the legislation and he was independent of the executive and the legislature and a person who held or had held high judicial office and he had effective access to details of surveillance activities undertaken, while publication of the Investigatory Powers Tribunal's legal rulings further enhanced scrutiny over secret surveillance activities).

Relevancy and sufficiency of reasons

6.97 A state must also be able to show that there are relevant and sufficient reasons for an interference, and that the measures taken have been proportionate. In exceptional cases, highly intrusive surveillance may be necessary[1]. In *Van der Tang v Netherlands*, the applicant had been subjected to permanent video observation for a period of about four and a half months whilst held in a remand centre on charges of having killed a well-known politician. The surveillance had been deemed appropriate given the reaction of society to the charges faced, and also had minimised any risk of suicide by (or other harm to) the prisoner. In declaring the application inadmissible, the Court considered that while the lack of privacy may have caused distress, it had not been sufficiently established that such a measure had in fact subjected the applicant to mental suffering of a level of severity such as to constitute inhuman or degrading treatment within the meaning of Article 3[2]. On the other hand, it will be difficult for a state to justify why the interception of communications with a legal adviser. In *Foxley v United Kingdom*, a postal packet re-direction order made under the English Insolvency Act 1986 in favour of the trustee in bankruptcy had led to the opening, reading and copying of correspondence from the applicant's legal advisers. The European Court of Human Rights could not be persuaded that there was any pressing social need for this, bearing in mind the principles of confidentiality and professional privilege attaching to relations between a lawyer and his client[3].

1   *Uzun v Germany* 2010-..., paras 49–53, 64–74, and 77–81 (GPS surveillance ordered only after less intrusive methods of investigation had proved insufficient, had been in place only for a relatively short period, and the investigation had concerned very serious crimes: no violation).

2   *Van der Tang v Netherlands* (dec) (1 June 2004).

3   *Foxley v United Kingdom* (20 June 2000), paras 43–46, citing *Campbell v United Kingdom* (1992) A 233, discussed at para 6.149 below. The principle also applies to correspondence with the Strasbourg Court: *Petra v Romania* 1998-VII, paras 35–36. Cf *Valle v Finland* (7 December 2000) (complaints of applicant subject to compulsory psychiatric care that restrictions on visits and telephone calls were unlawful, and (in terms of Art 13) that there was no effective remedy in domestic law to challenge restrictions on telephone calls from his lawyer: friendly settlement achieved).

6.98 Careful scrutiny of the reasons advanced by a state for an interference may be required to ensure the reasons are indeed proportionate and relevant[1]. In *Peck v United Kingdom,* the applicant had been unaware that he was being filmed by a closed circuit television as he had attempted to commit suicide in a deserted public street, but the filming had allowed the police to render medical assistance. Subsequently, the local had released still photographs and video footage of the immediate aftermath of the incident authority in an attempt to portray the advantages of CCTV. This material had appeared in newspapers and on television, and had allowed the applicant to be identified. The domestic courts had ruled that a local authority had the lawful authority to distribute the video footage[2]. For the Strasbourg Court, however, while the monitoring by means of photographic equipment of the actions of an individual in a public place would not in itself amount to an interference with private life, the recording of data in a systematic or permanent manner could well do so. Here, the incident had been seen to an extent which far exceeded any exposure to a passer-by or to security observation, and had been to a degree surpassing what the applicant could reasonably have foreseen. The disclosure thus involved a serious interference with the right to respect for his private life, and in the circumstances had also constituted a violation of Article 8 as there had not been relevant and sufficient reasons to justify the direct disclosure of material without obtaining the applicant's consent or masking his identity[3].

1   And in certain cases, whether a legitimate aim exists: see *Toma v Romania* (24 February 2009), paras 92–93 (photographing and filming of arrested detainee by journalists leading to the publication of a photograph and reference to him as a 'drug trafficker': no legitimate aim discernible, even if a legal basis for the interference could be found: violation).

2   *R (Peck) v Brentwood Council* [1998] EMLR 697. Subsequent complaints to the Broadcasting Standards Commission and to the Independent Television Commission had been upheld, but a third complaint to the Press Complaints Commission had been rejected because the events had taken place in a public street open to public view.

3   *Peck v United Kingdom* 2003-I, paras 76–87. The statutory basis for CCTV installation appears minimal: the Criminal Justice and Public Order Act 1994, s 163 merely provides that local authorities may establish CCTV systems in consultation with chief constables, and planning control requirements were largely removed by the Town and Country Planning (General Permitted Development) (Scotland) Amendment Order 1996, SI 1996/1266. However, as *Peck* makes clear, the issue is not so much the installation as the recording of data (the applicant's complaint concerned not the monitoring of the incident by CCTV, but rather the disclosure to the media of recorded data). See further Wadham 'Remedies for Unlawful CCTV Surveillance' (2000) 150 NLJ 1173 and 1236. The Data Protection Act 1998 now requires registration of CCTV systems and compliance with the principles of data protection; before this Act came into force, prohibition of misuse of CCTV relied primarily upon a voluntary code of practice (BS 7958). See further Edwards, 'Switching off the Surveillance Society?' in Nouwt et al (eds) *Reasonable Expectations of Privacy?* (2005) pp 91–114. Cf Case 1 S 377/02, [2004] NJW 1473, [2004] EuroCLY 1332 [Germany] (legislation permitting CCTV installation had to be clear and unambiguous, and the authorities had to show the necessity of installation and the absence of alternative means of surveillance); *Anklagemyndigheden v T* [2005] UfR 2979V, [2005] EuroCLY 1709 [Denmark] (prohibition of publication on the internet of private CCTV images allowing identification of individuals upheld); and Case 2765/2005), [2006] EuroCLY 1705 [Greece] (continued use of CCTV in public places initially installed for security purposes could no longer be considered justified and hindered social and political activities).

DOMESTIC CONSIDERATION OF COVERT SURVEILLANCE

Interferences

6.99 It has been held that there was no interference with Article 8 rights where police officers maintained observations for several hours, from another building on the same street, on the entrance to a block of flats where a suspected drug dealer lived, and stopped some of the people leaving the block to question them about why they had gone there. The court concluded that there had been no intrusion into the 'inner circle' of the accused's private life[1]. On the other hand, the taking and retention by the police of photographs which officers had taken (overtly) in the street of an employee of an association which campaigned against the arms trade, after he had left a meeting of a company with an involvement in the arms trade (there having been no disturbance at the meeting, and the employee having never been arrested or convicted of any offence), was held to be a breach of Article 8. Although the mere taking of a photograph in the public street was not in itself an interference with the right protected by Article 8(1), the circumstances in which the photograph was taken, or the use to which the photograph was to be put, might result in such an interference. On the facts, although the taking and retention of the photographs had been in accordance with the law and had a legitimate aim, their continued retention was disproportionate[2].

Similar issues have also been considered in connection with the activities of private investigators employed in connection with a civil claim for damages for personal injuries[3], and in relation to employment disputes[4].

---

1   *Connor v HM Advocate* 2002 JC 255. Similarly *Gilchrist v HM Advocate* 2005 1 JC 34.

2   *R (Wood) v Commissioner of Police of the Metropolis* [2010] 1 WLR 123.

3   *Martin v McGuiness* 2003 SLT 1424 (surveillance instructed by private investigators considered reasonable and proportionate; the video surveillance of the pursuer took place from public areas).

4   *McGowan v Scottish Water* [2005] IRLR 167; cf *Amwell View School Governors v Dogherty* [2007] ICR 135.

Justification under Article 8(2)

6.100 In a case concerned with the monitoring of a telephone conversation made by a prisoner, in accordance with the relevant legislation, as a result of which an attempt to smuggle drugs into the prison had been detected, it was held that the interference with respect for private life was justified in accordance with Article 8(2). The prisoner had notice that any telephone call which he made from the prison telephone might be monitored, listened to and tape recorded, and the caller was notified by a recorded message that the call originated from the prison. The legislation was readily accessible, and there was no suggestion that the monitoring or recording of the telephone call was secret or covert[1]. The subsequent case of *Potter v Scottish Ministers* concerned the compatibility with Article 8 of the practice of having telephone calls from prisoners preceded by the recorded message. While the Lord Ordinary had concluded that this practice was incompatible with Article 8, the Inner House held that he had erred in failing to take into account the need to avoid infringement of the Article 8 rights of the recipients of the calls, and the relevance in that respect of the arrangements for the monitoring or recording of such calls[2]. In a case concerned with the covert surveillance of legal or medical consultations held with detainees held in police custody or in prison, the House of Lords held that covert directed surveillance under the existing code of practice infringed Article 8 rights and was therefore unlawful, and that, in order to comply with Article 8, such surveillance required to be subject to an enhanced level of authorisation[3]. The retention by the police of photographs of a person, after any reasonable need for them had passed, was disproportionate and unjustied under Article 8(2)[4].

---

1   *Dudley v HM Advocate* 2003 JC 53. See also *Porter v HM Advocate* 2005 1 JC 141 (where, however, no reliance was placed on Art 8).

2   *Potter v Scottish Ministers* 2007 SLT 1019.

3   *McE v Prison Service of Northern Ireland* [2009] 1 AC 908.

4   *R (Wood) v Commissioner of Police of the Metropolis* [2010] 1 WLR 123.

The admissibility of evidence

6.101 In a case in which a tracking device had been placed unlawfully on a vessel suspected of being used for drug-smuggling, in order to identify the area in which the vessel was located and commence observations as she approached the point at which the transfer of cargo was to be made, it was held by the High Court that the breach of Article 8 did not render evidence about the vessel's subsequent movements inadmissible either under the common law (applying the test in *Lawrie v Muir*[1]) or by virtue of Article 6. The use of the device had not played such a central part in the prosecution as to render the later observations tainted and inadmissible under the common law. Essentially the same issues arose under Article 6: the fairness of the proceedings had not been affected by the introduction of that evidence. The court observed that if the illegality had consisted or resulted in the recording of conversations, a very strong argument might have been presented that any such evidence was inadmissible[2]. In *McGibbon v HM Advocate*, however, where conversations were recorded, the court, again under reference to *Lawrie v Muir*, upheld the decision of the sheriff to admit the evidence despite the infringement of Article 8, in the overall context of compliance with Article 6 and the basic requirement for 'fairness'[3]. That approach was followed in *Henderson v HM Advocate,* where a person convicted of extortion appealed on the basis that evidence had been led of threatening phone calls which he had made, which had been recorded by means of a tape recorder fitted to the victims'' telephone. They had agreed to the recording of the calls, but it was not established that the necessary authorisation had been obtained under the Regulation of Investigatory Powers Act[4].

A similar approach was adopted by the House of Lords in *R v P,* a case concerned with the admissibility of evidence of intercepts made in a foreign country of calls made by or to a citizen of that country using a mobile telephone network in that country. The evidence in question was of conversations between that person and the appellants, most of the calls being made when one or both of the parties to the conversation were in the UK. The interceptions had been authorised in the foreign country where they were made. The House held that no breach of Article 8 had been shown, and that the criteria to be applied in determining whether a person would have a fair hearing within Article 6 of the Convention were the same as those to be applied under domestic law. Where secrecy was not required in the public interest, it was 'necessary in a democratic society' within Article 8(2) for all relevant and probative evidence, including intercept evidence obtained abroad, to be admissible to assist in the apprehension and conviction of criminals and ensure that their trial was fair[5]. A similar approach has been followed in relation to covert video recordings[6].

These cases might be contrasted with *HM Advocate v Higgins,* where the accused were placed by the police in adjacent cells in the police station after they had been arrested but before they had been charged. The police then stationed officers outside the cells with instructions to listen to and write down any conversations between the accused, which they did. No authorisation was obtained under the Regulation of Investigatory Powers (Scotland) Act 2000. Evidence of the conversations was held to be inadmissible, since what had occurred had been deliberately devised as a trap, in the hope that the accused would incriminate themselves, and the admission of the evidence would render the proceedings unfair[7].

---

1   *Lawrie v Muir* 1950 JC 19.

2   *Hoekstra v HM Advocate* 2002 SCCR 135.

3   *McGibbon v HM Advocate* 2004 JC 60.

4   *Henderson v HM Advocate* 2005 1 JC 301.

5   *R v P* [2002] 1 AC 146.

6   See eg *R v Loveridge* [2001] 2 Cr App R 29; *R v Button* [2005] EWCA Crim 516.

7   *HM Advocate v Higgins* 2006 SCCR 305.

6.102 In order to secure compliance with Article 8, the use of covert investigation techniques in Scotland was put on a statutory footing by the Regulation of Investigatory Powers (Scotland) Act 2000. That Act applies to the Scottish police and the National Criminal Intelligence Service. The use by Scottish police of some other techniques (interference with property and wireless telegraphy) was already covered by the Police Act 1997. UK public authorities which operate in Scotland, such as HM Customs and Excise and the Security Service, are regulated by the Regulation of Investigatory Powers Act 2000. The Intelligence Services Act 1994 and the Police Act 1997 also apply to UK public authorities operating in Scotland. The focus of the Regulation of Investigatory Powers (Scotland) Act 2000 is on 'directed surveillance', 'intrusive surveillance' and the conduct and use of covert human intelligence sources. 'Directed surveillance' is surveillance which is covert and which is undertaken in relation to a specific investigation in order to obtain information about, or identify, a particular person or to determine who is involved in a matter under investigation. 'Intrusive surveillance' is surveillance which is covert and carried out in relation to anything taking place on residential premises or in any private vehicle. This type of surveillance may take place by means either of a person or device located inside a residential premises or a private vehicle, or by means of a device placed outside which provides a product of equivalent quality and detail to the product which would be obtained from a device located inside. The use of 'covert human intelligence sources' covers the use of informants, agents and undercover officers. Less intrusive forms of surveillance where there is a general awareness on the part of the public that surveillance is taking place, such as CCTV for crime prevention, public order or traffic management purposes, are excluded from the authorisation process.[1]

1   For discussion, see Benjamin 'Interception of Internet Communications and the Right to Privacy: An Evaluation of some Provisions of the Regulation of Investigatory Powers Act against the Jurisprudence of the European Court of Human Rights' [2007] EHRLR 637. For Strasbourg consideration, see *Kennedy v United Kingdom* 2010-... noted at para **6.96** above. The Regulation of Investigatory Powers (Scotland) Act 2000, s 65(2) exempts the police and the security and intelligence agencies from challenge in a court of law and instead requires complaints to be dealt with by a tribunal. In relation to CCTV, see para **6.98** above.

Private life issues: search powers

Intrusive searches of the person

6.103 Searches of the person, including intimate searches, may fall within the scope of Article 8 where these involve a degree of coercion, for a voluntary submission to a search (for example, as in an airport) will not constitute an 'interference'[1]. Similar considerations apply as with surveillance and data-gathering, discussed above, in assessing whether an interference can be justified. Any interference must be for a legitimate aim, 'in accordance with the law', and 'necessary in a democratic society'[2].

1   *Gillan and Quinton v United Kingdom* 2010-..., paras 61–66 (application of search powers under the Terrorism Act 2000, ss 44–47: allowing individuals to be stopped anywhere and at any time and without notice or choice as to whether to submit were to a search could not be compared to searches of travellers at airports or of visitors to public buildings as these involved consenting to a search by choosing to travel or to visit).

2   See eg *Juhnke v Turkey* (13 May 2008), paras 74–82 (gynaecological examination of remand prisoner without free and informed consent: violation, as the examination had been purely discretionary and not in accordance with the law, and even if protection against a potential false accusation by her of sexual assault could have constituted a legitimate aim, the examination had not been proportionate).

6.104 Domestic law must meet Strasbourg expectations in relation to the quality of domestic law. In *Gillan and Quinton v United Kingdom,* two individuals attempting to attend a protest against an arms fair had been searched by police. The statute permitted senior police officers if they considered it 'expedient for the prevention of acts of terrorism' to authorise uniformed police officers to stop and search people and vehicles, even in the absence of any reasonable suspicion of wrongdoing. The Court readily found that the use of coercive powers to require an individual to submit to a detailed search amounted to a clear interference with the right to respect for private life, the Court considering that the element of humiliation and embarrassment involved in the public nature of a search having in certain cases the potential to compound the seriousness of the interference. While application of the stop and search powers had a basis in statute combined with the relevant Code of Practice, the quality of the provisions was found not to have offered adequate protection against arbitrary interference and was defective on two counts. First, the authorisation of the power to stop and search if police officers considered it 'expedient' as opposed to 'necessary' to prevent acts of terrorism meant that there was no requirement for any assessment of the proportionality of the authority, and various devices designed to control or review authorisations were either inadequate or never exercised in practice. Secondly, the powers of individual police officers were of very broad scope and did not require any showing of reasonable suspicion and employed merely on a 'hunch' or 'professional intuition', the sole proviso being that the purpose of the search was to look for articles which could be used in connection with terrorism, a category of considerable breadth which could cover many articles commonly carried in the streets. The conclusion was thus that such widely-framed powers could be misused, not only against demonstrators and protestors, but also against (as suggested by statistics) ethnic minorities. They were thus insufficiently circumscribed and not subject to adequate legal safeguards against abuse to meet the test of 'in accordance with the law'[1].

The necessity of any intrusive search will depend upon the particular facts of the case[2]. In particular, to satisfy the test of 'necessary in a democratic society', searches must be carried out in accordance with prescribed procedures. For example, in *Wainwright v United Kingdom*, the Court determined that the strip-searching of a remand prisoner's mother and disabled brother in a manner which disregarded prescribed procedures and safeguards designed to protect the dignity of those being searched had violated the provision[3].

---

1   *Gillan and Quinton v United Kingdom* 2010-..., paras 76–87.

2   See eg *Madsen v Denmark* (dec) (7 November 2002) (mandatory drug test for crew member of ferry: inadmissible, even assuming the obligation to submit to a urine test was an interference by a public authority within the meaning of Art 8, the obligation imposed by collective agreement (the Danish labour model) rather than legislation provided sufficient legal basis, the aims were legitimate, and it was essential for the safety of a ferry); and *Bogumil v Portugal* 2008-..., paras 89–91 (surgery performed on drug-trafficker without his prior consent to remove swallowed drugs: no violation, the interference having been in accordance with the law and carried out to protect his health, and a fair balance had been struck between the public interest in the protection of health and the applicant's right to the protection of his physical and mental integrity).

3   *Wainwright v United Kingdom* 2006-X, paras 41–49 (visible examination of the mother's sexual organs and anus, and the physical examination of the brother's penis).

TAKING AND RETENTION OF FINGERPRINTS AND DNA SAMPLES

6.105 The taking and retention of fingerprints and DNA samples without consent will involve an interference with respect for private life. Fingerprints contain unique information about the individual and their retention cannot be considered as neutral or insignificant, while cellular samples hold significant amounts of personal information and DNA profiles provide a means of identifying genetic relationships and permit inferences concerning ethnic origin to be drawn[1]. While the quality of the law and its capacity to protect against arbitrary application of powers may be of relevance, the key issue in determining whether an interference can be justified is likely to be its proportionality. In *Van der Velden v Netherlands*, the Court declared inadmissible a complaint by an individual who had been convicted and sentenced to a period of imprisonment. Domestic law authorised the taking of a sample of cellular material from convicted prisoners serving sentences of over four years, the period of retention of the DNA profile determined by the nature of the conviction and the length of sentence imposed. In accepting that the interference served the legitimate aims of the prevention of crime and the protection of the rights and freedoms of others (even although DNA had played no role in the investigation and trial of the particular offences), the Court further considered that such an obligation imposed on all persons convicted of offences of a certain seriousness to undergo DNA testing could not be deemed unreasonable in light of the substantial contribution to law enforcement which DNA profiling now makes, a benefit which additionally could be deemed to extend to individuals such as the applicant in allowing the rapid elimination of possible suspects in investigations involving DNA samples[2].

1   *S and Marper v United Kingdom* [GC] 2008-..., paras 68–86.
2   *Van der Velden v Netherlands* (dec) 2006-XV.

6.106 English law, on the other hand, permitted the taking and retention of DNA samples from a wide range of individuals[1]. In *S and Marper v United Kingdom*, the Grand Chamber was called upon to consider the taking of fingerprints and DNA samples from two applicants who were suspected, but never convicted, of crimes. The data were to be retained without limit of time. One of the applicants had been an 11-year-old minor when the data had been taken. It was readily accepted that the retention of the data pursued the legitimate aim of the prevention of crime by assisting in the identification of future offenders (and that the extension of the database had indeed contributed to the detection and prevention of crime). The Court avoided determining the question whether the interferences had been 'in accordance with the law', the Court did at least doubt whether the statutory provision was adequately precise in respect of the conditions and arrangements for the storing and use of the information, noting that clear and detailed rules on the scope and application of such measures and minimum safeguards in such cases were essential. The principal failing was in respect of the proportionality of the measures. It could not be concluded in the case of the two applicants who had merely been suspected but never convicted of certain criminal offences that the retention of their fingerprints, cellular samples and DNA profiles could be justified. The consensus in other European law and practice (as in Scotland) required retention of data to be proportionate in relation to the purpose of collection, and also limited in time. What was so striking about English law was the blanket and indiscriminate nature of the power of retention, irrespective of the nature or gravity of the offence or of the age of the suspect. Further, there was only limited opportunity for a person acquitted to have his data removed or the material destroyed. There was a real risk of stigmatisation, for persons who had not been convicted of any offence (and who were in any event entitled to the presumption of innocence) were treated in the same way as those convicted of crimes. Indeed, in respect of young persons, the retention of such data could be particularly harmful in view of the importance of their future development and integration into society[2].

---

1 Police and Criminal Evidence Act 1976, s 64(1A). Cf *Under the Microscope: Thematic Inspection Report on Scientific and Technical Support,* report of HM Inspector of Constabulary for England and Wales (2000), para 2.23 (English police forces are holding DNA samples taken from suspects found not guilty or where the prosecution is discontinued without legal authority; it is estimated that in the lifetime of the National DNA database, as many as 50,000 samples may be being held when they should have been removed). See also *Report of the Data Protection Commissioner* (HC Paper 575 (2000)) at para 2.23 (proposals for increased data-matching as part of the national fraud initiative 'may well contravene the Human Rights Act ... because of lack of safeguards for individuals'); and Roberts and Taylor 'Privacy and the DNA Database' [2005] EHRLR 373. In Scotland, retention of samples taken from people who are not subsequently convicted of an offence is generally prohibited by the Criminal Procedure (Scotland) Act 1995, s 18. There are however exceptions in relation to persons suspected of certain categories of offence even if not convicted, under ss 18A–18F of the 1995 Act as amended by the Criminal Justice and Licensing (Scotland) Act 2010.

2 *S and Marper v United Kingdom* [GC] 2008-..., paras 95–99 and 105–126 (at para 112, the Court noting that 'any State claiming a pioneer role in the development of new technologies bears special responsibility for striking the right balance in this regard' in response to arguments advanced by the government that England and Wales were in the vanguard of scientific and technological innovation). For the domestic proceedings, see *R (S) v Chief Constable of South Yorkshire Police* [2004] 1 WLR 2196, in which the House of Lords held that the retention of fingerprints and samples of non-convicted persons did not constitute an interference with Art 8, and that even if it were to do so, this was justified under Art 8(2), observing that there was no clear approach in Strasbourg jurisprudence on the retention of data.

Search of premises

6.107 The search of homes and other premises falling within the scope of Article 8[1] is likely to be undertaken in order to obtain evidence, and thus the aim of such measures will invariably be for the purpose of the prevention or detection of crime. Consideration of whether any interference by means of a search of a person or of premises meets the requirements of Article 8 will therefore invariably focus upon whether the interference was 'in accordance with the law' and 'necessary in a democratic society. When it is alleged that a search has taken place but the authorities have denied any responsibility for it, the authorities are under a positive obligation to carry out an effective investigation of the circumstances, as in such circumstances Article 8 also has a 'procedural aspect'[2].

1 Including business premises in certain circumstances: *Niemietz v Germany* (1992) A 251-B, paras 29–33, discussed at para 6.25 above. Cf 12474/86, *Kanthak v Germany* (1988) DR 58, 94 (question whether the applicant's camping car could be considered a 'home' was left unresolved). See also *X v Société Cathnet-Science* EurCLY 1750 [France] (inspection of computer hard drive by employer in absence of employee violated Art 8, such a search only justifiable in the most exceptional circumstances).

2 *HM v Turkey* (8 August 2006), paras 25–30 (lack of investigation into allegedly unlawful search of the applicant's home in the face of denial of responsibility by any authority: violation of the procedural aspect of Art 8 to carry out an effective investigation).

6.108 To meet the test of 'in accordance with the law', a search must be carried out in accordance with domestic legal requirements[1]. As is the case with surveillance, the test of 'necessary in a democratic society' calls for consideration of the extent to which relevant domestic legislation and practice provide adequate and effective safeguards against abuse of powers. This will often determine the issues of the relevancy and sufficiency of reasons advanced by the state for the search and whether the search was proportionate[2]. The question of whether domestic law provided adequate safeguards calls for careful assessment of each case. In *Funke v France*, customs officers had searched the appellant's house and had removed certain documents. The appellant argued that the search was not properly prescribed by domestic law, but the Court declined to address this question as it was able to dispose of the matter on the basis of lack of effective protection against abuse of search powers. Here, customs officers had exclusive competence in assessing crucial matters such as the length and scale of any customs inquiry. When this was considered along with the lack of any requirement of a judicial warrant for a search, the Court was of the opinion that domestic law was 'too lax and full of loopholes' for the interference to have been strictly proportionate to the legitimate aim of protecting the economic well-being of the country[3]. In contrast, in *Camenzind v Switzerland* the Court accepted that relevant Swiss law at the relevant time did provide effective safeguards. The case involved a search in order to seize an unauthorised cordless telephone that the applicant had admitted having used. Relevant safeguards included the authorisation of searches by warrant which could only be issued by a limited number of designated and senior officers on carefully prescribed grounds, and the requirement that searches were carried out by specially trained officials with the presence of a public officer at the premises to ensure that the search was properly conducted[4].

1 See eg *Panteleyenko v Ukraine* (29 June 2006), paras 47–53 (search of lawyer's office in disregard of safeguards requiring warrant to be served on the occupier, the authorities having had knowledge of his whereabouts: violation as 'not in accordance with the law'); and *Imakayeva v Russia* 2006-XIII, paras 186–189 (absence of authorisations or safeguards concerning search of home: violation).

2 *Camenzind v Switzerland* 1997-VIII, para 45. See further para **6.94** above. See also *Niemietz v Germany* (1992) A 251-B, para 37; *Van Rossem v Belgium* (9 December 2004), paras 45–51 (delegation of power of investigating judge to issue search warrants to criminal investigation

officers permitting them to conduct immediate searches and seizure of any items and documents which they would consider of use: violation on account on the failure to indicate in the warrant the nature of the evidence sought); and *André and Other v France* (24 July 2008), paras 36–49 (search of lawyers' offices by tax inspectors investigating one of the applicants' client companies but carried out without any special procedural guarantees for the searching of legal offices: searches and seizures at a lawyer's office interfered with professional privilege at the heart of the relationship of confidence and if permitted required to be accompanied by special guarantees, but here the warrants were worded in broad terms and issued only in the hope of finding evidence of tax evasion). See also *Chappell v United Kingdom* (1989) A 152-A, paras 52–61 (conditions for English 'Anton Piller' order were laid down with sufficient precision to sastisfy 'in accordance with the law', and in the present case had also been sufficiently limited in scope with sufficient safeguards to meet the 'necessary in a democratic society' test).

3   *Funke v France* (1993) A 256-A, paras 53–59 at para 57. See too *Crémieux v France* (1993) A 256-B, paras 38–40; and *Miailhe v France (no 1)* (1993) A 256-C, paras 36–39. As to tax investigations, see *Tamosius v United Kingdom* (dec) 2002-VIII (warrant to search tax lawyer's premises issued in *ex parte* proceedings: inadmissible, as there may be good reason not to give forewarning of a search, judicial scrutiny was an important safeguard, there had been sufficient indication of the purpose of the search to enable the applicant to assess whether the investigation team had acted unlawfully, and the a prohibition on the removal of documents covered by legal professional privilege provided a concrete safeguard against interference with professional secrecy). For a domestic example, see *R (Banque Internationale à Luxembourg) v Inland Revenue Commissioners* [2000] STC 708.

4   *Camenzind v Switzerland* 1997-VIII, paras 41–47.

6.109 The method of carrying out a search must also be proportionate[1]. In *McLeod v United Kingdom*, police officers had secured entry to a house to assist the applicant's former husband and his solicitor to remove certain items of property following a court order requiring the applicant to hand over the property. The former husband honestly but mistakenly believed that agreement to collect the items had been reached, but the police officers had failed to check the terms of the court order when advising the applicant's mother (the applicant herself not being present initially) that their action was based upon a judicial instruction. The domestic courts had accepted that the police officers had behaved properly, since they had believed that there was a real and imminent risk of a breach of the peace. While accepting that the power of the police to enter private premises without a warrant to deal with or prevent a breach of the peace was defined with sufficient precision and was clearly for the legitimate aim of preventing disorder or crime, the European Court of Human Rights found that that the means employed by the police officers had been disproportionate. Scrutiny of the court order would have shown that the property was to be handed over rather than collected, and further, that the applicant still had some days left in which to do so. In any event, the appellant's absence when the police arrived should have suggested there was then minimal risk of disorder[2]. In *Keegan v United Kingdom,* the Court determined that there had been a violation of Article 8 on account of the failure by the police to carry out adequate verification of the current occupants of a house several months previously vacated by a relative of a person suspected of involvement in armed crimes. Although the Court was willing to accept that there had been relevant reasons for the search, it could not accept that the reasons had in this instance been sufficient given the failure to take proper precautions prior to carrying out the search. Nor was it relevant that the police had not acted out of malice in light of the importance of protecting individuals against abuse of power[3].

1   Eg *Murray v United Kingdom* (1994) A 300-A, paras 90–94 (entry into and search of a family home by army personnel in order to arrest the first applicant who was suspected of involvement in terrorist activities had been accompanied by the confinement of other members of her family in another room for a short period; the manner of the search was judged proportionate in view of the threat posed to democratic society by organised terrorism); *Buck v Germany* 2005-IV, paras 42–53 (search of residential and business premises following refusal of the applicant, the owner of a company, to give evidence against his son in connection with traffic offence allegedly committed by his son while driving a company car: while domestic law was adequate and effective in protecting against abuse of authority, in the particular circumstances the search had been disproportionate and not limited to what was indispensable for the case, and violation of Art 8); and *Kucera v Slovakia* (17 July 2007), paras 116–124 (early morning raid of home by armed and masked police officers to advise of charges and to escort the applicant to an investigator: violation of Art 8 as raid was disproportionate and carried an inherent risk of abuse of authority and violation of human dignity).

2   *McLeod v United Kingdom* 1998-VII, paras 38–58.

3   *Keegan v United Kingdom* 2006-X, paras 29–36.

Domestic cases on search powers

6.110 There have been numerous domestic cases in which Article 8 has been considered in relation to powers of search. The use of stop and search powers under anti-terrorism legislation was considered in *R (Gillan) v Commissioner of Police of the Metropolis*. It was held that any intrusion on private life was not sufficiently serious to amount to a breach of Article 8(1) to respect for private life, or alternatively that a proper exercise of the power to stop and search was proportionate within Article 8(2) as being necessary in a democratic society to counter the danger of terrorism[1]. The Strasbourg Court, however, subsequently held that the powers of stop and search were neither sufficiently circumscribed nor subject to adequate legal safeguards against abuse, and were not, therefore, 'in accordance with the law' within the meaning of Article 8 of the Convention[2].

The power of the Office of Fair Trading to obtain by *ex parte* application to the court a warrant authorising it to enter business premises, search for documents and require answers to questions about them, in support of an investigation into suspected anti-competitive practices, was accepted in *Office of Fair Trading v X*. The court concluded that the grant of such a warrant was compatible with both Article 6 and Article 8[3]. A similar conclusion was reached in a Scottish case concerned with an *ex parte* application for the transfer to the USA, in accordance with legislation concerned with mutual legal assistance, of evidence recovered during a search of premises carried out under warrant[4].

The procedure for obtaining a search warrant under s 23 of the Misuse of Drugs Act 1971 has been held to be in conformity with Article 8[5].

1   *R (Gillan) v Commissioner of Police of the Metropolis* [2006] 2 AC 307.

2   *Gillan and Quinton v United Kingdom* 2010-…, discussed at para **6.104** above.

3   *Office of Fair Trading v X* [2004] ICR 105. The judgment contains a consideration of ECJ and ECHR case law and may be of wider relevance, eg to issues arising in relation to the Administration of Justice (Scotland) Act 1972, s 1. Procedure under s 1, as laid down in Ch 64 of the Rules of the Court of Session 1994 (SI 1994/1443), was reformed with effect from 2 October 2000 by Act of Sederunt (Rules of the Court of Session Amendment No 4) (Applications under s 1 of the Administration of Justice (Scotland) Act 1972) (SSI 2000/319) so as to ensure compliance with Art 8.

4   *Calder v Frame* 2007 JC 4.

5   *Birse v Mitchell* 2000 JC 503. In relation to searches without a warrant, see *Hoekstra v HM Advocate* 2002 SCCR 135, discussed at para 6.101 above; and *Gillies v Ralph* 2009 JC 25. In relation to production orders under s 31 of the Crminal Law (Consolidation) (Scotland) Act 1995, see *HM Advocate v Bowie* 2004 SCCR 105.

Private life issues: protection of personal data

Access to and disclosure of personal data

6.111 The disclosure of personal data without the express consent of the individual concerned may give rise to Article 8 considerations[1]. Whether disclosure (or a requirement to do so) of personal records to other parties can be considered justified depends upon the situation in question[2], but in each case must be for a legitimate aim, 'in accordance with the law', and 'necessary in a democratic society'. There may indeed be a positive duty upon the authorities to make available information held by them to the data subjects, and thus an Article 8 issue may arise in respect of a refusal to grant an individual access to his personal records. Even if information is in the public arena, data may fall within the scope of 'private life' if this is systematically collected and stored in files[4]. In this area, there is a recognised need for 'increased vigilance in protecting private life which is necessary to contend with new communication technologies which make it possible to store and reproduce personal data', and the Court's greater sensitivity in ensuring that interferences are adequately regulated by domestic law and are proportionate is now obvious[5].

1   EU law also provides safeguards in this area: in particular, see Directive 95/46/EC, implemented in the UK by virtue of the Data Protection Act 1998.

2   Cf *Wypych v Poland* (dec) (25 October 2005) (obligation on an elected politician to declare assets and income serves the legitimate public interest in ensuring transparency in political life: inadmissible).

3   See eg *Peck v United Kingdom* 2003-I, discussed at para **6.9**8 above.

4   *Cemalettin Canli v Turkey* (18 November 2008), para 34 (in keeping with the Convention for the Protection of Individuals with regard to the Automatic Processing of Personal Data (ETS 108 (1981)).

5   *Köpke v Germany* (dec) (5 October 2010) (covert video surveillance instructed by employer and carried out by detective agency of employee and her workplace, and subsequent processing and examination of the video material by others working for the employer and by the courts: Art 8 engaged, but not to an extent which is comparable to the affection of essential aspects of private life by grave acts in respect of which the Court has considered protection by legislative provisions indispensable).

Disclosure of personal records

6.112 Data held by public authorities may cover many aspects of an individual's 'private life'. Disclosure can take place in a wide range of circumstances: for example, the police may provide the media with personal details of a suspect[1], or personal details may be disclosed during the course of legal proceedings[2]. Where information on an individual is collated, there is a responsibility to ensure the data is accurate[3]. Where such information is disclosed, the release of the information must be for a legitimate aim, be prescribed by law[4], and also meet the test of 'necessary in a democratic society' (that is, the reasons must be relevant and sufficient and the disclosure must not be disproportionate to the end to be achieved).

1   *Sciacca v Italy* 2005-I, paras 22–32 (release of photograph of detainee to the press and subsequent publication of the photograph in newspapers).

2   *Craxi v Italy (no 2)* (17 July 2003), paras 60–76 (transcripts of telephone conversations intercepted in the context of criminal proceedings of former Prime Minister read out during a criminal trial and subsequently released into the public domain: violation as some of the conversations published in the press were of a strictly private nature and had little or no connection with the criminal charges and had been made available without appropriate safeguards, state responsibility being engaged since the source was a court registry; further, the court had failed to follow required procedures before allowing the transcripts to be read out); cf *NN and TA v Belgium* (13 May 2008), paras 43–52 (love letters exchanged between a husband and a third party added to case file by wife during divorce proceedings: no violation, as domestic law sufficiently regulated what could be lodged in process, the publicity the case had given rise to stemmed mainly from attempts to prevent production, and the documents had not been rendered public as there was restricted access to the case file).

3   *Cemalettin Canli v Turkey* (18 November 2008), paras 33–44 (inaccurate police record-keeping of information insofar as outcome of proceedings was not recorded).

4   *Sciacca v Italy* 2005-I, paras 22–32 (release of photograph press not regulated by 'law' within the meaning of the Convention but merely by custom: violation).

6.113 Medical records in particular are likely to contain highly sensitive information about an individual, and ensuring respect for the confidentiality of these records is considered to be crucial in order to maintain public confidence in the health services[1]. This aspect of Article 8 essentially protects the patient or client, although justification for the confidentiality of records may well also involve the protection of professional advisers and other third parties[2]. Where personal records have been disclosed, the questions which will arise will relate not only to whether this has been 'in accordance with the law'[3] but also as to the relevance and sufficiency of the reasons for the disclosure, including the extent to which the disclosure was 'subjected to important limitations and accompanied by effective and adequate safeguards against abuse'[4]. These issues will be of particular importance in instances where disclosure of personal information has been made in accordance with regulations or upon the order of a court during the course of legal proceedings[5]. Assessment will normally focus upon whether there were relevant and sufficient grounds for the disclosure[6], or whether disclosure could indeed have been avoided. The ability of any member of the public to obtain a copy of a court judgment was one decisive factor in determining that there had been a breach of Article 8 in the case of *LL v France*. In this case, a judge had quoted extracts from a confidential medical report in his judgment concerning the applicant's divorce, but the judge could have reached the same conclusion without having had recourse to the report. The Court determined that the interference with private life had not been justified in view of the crucial importance of protecting private life[7].

1   *MS v Sweden* 1997–IV, paras 35 and 41. See also *Biriuk v Lithiuania* (25 November 2008), paras 41–47 (crucial that domestic law safeguarded patient confidentiality by discouraging disclosures, especially in view of the negative impact of disclosures on the willingness of others to take voluntary tests for HIV and seek appropriate treatment). See too Committee of Ministers Recommendation Rec (97) 5 on the protection of medical data. The *MS* judgment was distinguished in *De Keyser Ltd v Wilson* [2001] IRLR 324, which concerned references to a litigant's private life in the opposing party's letter of instruction to their medical expert. See also *Szuluk v United Kingdom* 2009-…, paras 43–55 (monitoring of prisoner's correspondence with his medical adviser, a neuro-radiology specialist, in the absence of evidence of actual or likely abuse of the confidentiality of his communications or of any high-risk status as a prisoner: violation).

2   *I v Finland* (17 July 2008), paras 35–49 (no system of protection of confidentiality against any unauthorised access allowing medical records of an HIV-positive nurse to have been read at any time by her colleagues: violation). Cf *Gaskin v United Kingdom* (1989) A 160, para 49.

3   *Panteleyenko v Ukraine* (29 June 2006), paras 59–62 (confidential psychiatric information obtained by prosecutor from a hospital and disclosed in a public court hearing: violation as 'not in accordance with the law' since the information had been obtained outwith prescribed limitations).

4   *Z v Finland* 1997-I, para 103 (disclosure of applicant's infection with HIV from confidential medical records, in proceedings where applicant's husband was prosecuted for attempting manslaughter of another by deliberately subjecting her to risk of HIV infection and limited period of confidentiality of ten years: violation).

5   See eg *CC v Spain* 2009-…, paras 26–41 (publication of the applicant's identity in a case file during proceedings for the purpose of giving the other party access to the applicant's medical record regarding his HIV positive status despite the power to protect anonymity on the grounds of public policy: violation).

6   See eg *Szuluk v United Kingdom* 2009-…, paras 43–55 (monitoring of correspondence of a prisoner not considered high risk with his specialist medical adviser in the absence of evidence of actual or likely abuse of the confidentiality of the communications: violation).

7   *LL v France* 2006-XI, paras 27–34.

6.114 Where disclosure can be justified, there will be an expectation that dissemination of the information will be restricted to the extent strictly necessary to achieve the purpose in question. In *MS v Sweden*, a state clinic had disclosed the applicant's health records, including information that she had undergone an abortion, to the social insurance office which was dealing with her claim for compensation for an alleged injury sustained while at work. The European Court of Human Rights accepted that Article 8 applied as it could not be inferred that the applicant, in initiating the claim for compensation, had waived her right to confidentiality. The assessment of whether the disclosure of the records had been necessary had been left to the state authorities without allowing the applicant the opportunity to be consulted or informed beforehand. It was accepted that this interference was in accordance with domestic law and had the legitimate aim of determining whether public funds should compensate her for the alleged injury, and could be said to be in the interests of the 'economic well-being of the country'. However, the applicant challenged the disclosure of the abortion and the absence of her participation in the determination that disclosure of this information was 'necessary in a democratic society'. The Court accepted that the state had a genuine need to transmit medical records from one public authority to another to allow it to verify whether the applicant met the tests required for compensation, and that this information had indeed been relevant to the determination of the claim. Further, and crucially, the information disclosed was itself subject to protection ensuring it remained confidential. Not only clinical staff but also the social insurance officers who received the data were under duties enforceable by sanction to treat the information as confidential. Accordingly there had been no breach of Article 8[1].

1   *MS v Sweden* 1997-IV, paras 31–44.

Access to personal records

6.115 An Article 8 issue may arise in respect of a refusal to grant an individual access to his personal records held by public authorities. The general principle is that the authorities have a duty to provide individuals with an 'effective and accessible procedure' for obtaining access to 'all relevant and appropriate information'[1] held by them. Where public authorities hold personal records, there is an obligation to ensure that the records are accurate[2]. Access to personal data is of particular importance in certain circumstances. In *Gaskin v United Kingdom*, the applicant had been taken into care as a six-month-old child following his mother's death and had been cared for by a succession of foster parents. After attaining majority, he had attempted to gain access to his case papers which contained various reports written by his doctors, teachers, social workers, and probation officers. This access had been denied on the basis that the effective conduct of a child care system justified the treating of such reports as confidential except where the express consent of the contributor to disclosure had been given. The European Court of Human Rights accepted that 'confidentiality of public records is of importance for receiving objective and reliable information' and that this could also be necessary to protect third parties who contributed information. However, the state was also under an obligation to ensure that the applicant's right to receive 'the information necessary to know and to understand their childhood' was properly considered when the consent of a contributor to disclosure was not available. This could be achieved through, for example, the involvement of an independent authority which could make an assessment of the competing interests between state and individual[3].

1   See eg *KH and Others v Slovakia* 2009-..., paras 44–58 (legislation providing that medical records were owned by the hospital and which thus effectively prevented former patients from making copies of their medical records: violation of the positive obligation to make available to the data subject copies of his data files); and *Haralambie v Romania* (27 October 2009), paras 84–96 (procedure for gaining access to personal files held by Securitae and other

former security services during Romania's communist period was ineffective and inaccessible: violation).

2   *Cemalettin Canli v Turkey* (18 November 2008), paras 33–44 (inaccurate police record-keeping in respect of outcomes of proceedings and subsequently forwarded to other authorities: violation).

3   *Gaskin v United Kingdom* (1989) A 160, at paras 42–49. See also *MG v United Kingdom* (24 September 2002), paras 23–32 (denial of access to personal records including specific information as to whether the applicant had been on the 'risk register' and whether his father had ever been investigated or convicted for crimes against children: violation, for while he had a strong interest in obtaining the documents, there was no statutory right of access to the records or any clear indication by way of a binding circular or legislation of the grounds on which he could request access or appeal). Cf *Leander v Sweden* (1987) A 116, which the Court distinguished in *Gaskin*; and *Menéndez Garcia v Spain* (dec) (5 May 2009) (refusal by the domestic authorities to have the applicant's late father recognised as the illegitimate child of another man, also deceased: the interest in knowing one's identity varied depending on the degree of kinship in the ascending line and the weight of the interest diminished as the degree of kinship became more distant: inadmissible as manifestly ill-founded).

DOMESTIC CONSIDERATION OF ACCESS TO AND DISCLOSURE OF PERSONAL DATA

6.116 Domestic courts have recognised the bearing of Article 8 upon the disclosure of personal data in a variety of contexts. It has been accepted in criminal proceedings in England and Wales that the disclosure to the defence of a witness's medical or other personal records should not be ordered without allowing the person in question an opportunity to make representations[1]. Equally, Article 8 may be infringed if the nearest relative of a mental patient is informed or consulted against the wishes of the patient[2]. The compulsory recovery of confidential business documents for the purposes of a criminal investigation also engages Article 8 rights, but is likely to be justified under Article 8(2) where the disclosure is necessary for the prevention of crime[3]. In the case of *R (Robertson) v Wakefield Metropolitan District Council* it was held that the practice of selling the the data contained in the electoral register to commercial concerns without affording an individual elector a right of objection was a disproportionate way in which to give effect to the legitimate objective of retaining a commercially available register, and breached the individual's right to respect for private life under Article 8[4]. When a person who had been charged with sexual offences against young girls subsequently obtained employment at a children's centre, the disclosure of the charge by the police to his employers, in confidence, was justified under Article 8(2)[5]. A similar conclusion was reached in a case concerned with a school assistant, employed to supervise children, whose employers were notified, in an enhanced criminal record certificate, of her own child's inclusion on the child protection register on the ground of neglect due to her lack of ability adequately to care for and supervise him, of her refusal to co-operate with social services, and of her child's subsequent criminal activities, conviction and sentence[6].

The retention by the police of photographs of a person who had not committed any offence, and was not suspected of having any involvement in the commission of any offence, has been held (in particular circumstances) to be a violation of

Article 8[7]. The retention on the police national computer of details of old minor convictions (as distinct from their disclosure) was held not to engage Article 8[8].

1   *R (B) v Stafford Combined Court* [2007] 1 WLR 1524. The Scottish procedures governing the recovery of medical and other records for use in legal proceedings are capable of meeting the issues identified in this case and the Strasbourg cases. A difficulty under Art 8 could, however, arise where the documents concern a person who is neither a party nor the person in possession of the documents, as in the case of a witness in criminal proceedings. In such a situation, 'respect' for that person's private life is likely to require that he be given intimation of the application for the recovery of the documents.

2   *R (E) v Bristol City Council* [2005] EWHC 74 (Admin). See also *R (M) v Secretary of State for Health* [2003] EWHC 1094 (Admin).

3   *R (Hafner) v City of Westminster Magistrates' Court* [2009] 1 WLR 1005. See also *R (Prudential plc) v Special Commissioner of Income Tax* [2011] 2 WLR 50 (requirement to disclose documents containing advice on points of law given by accountants did not infringe Art 8 taken together with Art 14).

4   *R (Robertson) v Wakefield Metropolitan District Council* [2002] QB 1052.

5   *M v Chief Constable of Strathclyde* 2003 SLT 1007.

6   *R (L) v Commissioner of Police of the Metropolis* [2010] 1 AC 410.

7   *R (Wood) v Commissioner of Police of the Metropolis* [2010] 1 WLR 123.

8   *Chief Constable of Humberside Police v Information Commissioner* [2010] 1 WLR 1136.

6.117 Cases concerned with the registration of sex offenders can also be considered under this head. In *R (F (A Child)) v Secretary of State for the Home Department*, legislation imposing notification requirements for an indefinite period upon persons convicted of sexual offences, without any procedure for reviewing the need for the requirements in respect of individual offenders, was held to be a disproportionate interference with the right to respect for private and family life, and therefore incompatible with Article 8[1].

1   *R (F (A Child)) v Secretary of State for the Home Department* [2011] 1 AC 331. The corresponding Scottish case of *A v Scottish Ministers* (reported at first instance at 2008 SLT 412) was resolved by agreement after the Scottish Ministers introduced amending legislation: see the Sexual Offences Act 2003 (Remedial) (Scotland) Order 2010, SSI 2010/370.

6.118 Article 8 issues have also been considered in relation to access to personal data. Matters considered have included a person's access to data concerning their paternity[1] and adoption[2].

1   *R (Rose) v Secretary of State for Health* [2002] 2 FLR 962, discussed at para **6.70** above.

2   *R (Gunn-Russo) v Nugent Care Society* [2002] 1 FLR 1, discussed at para **6.75** above.

Private life issues: protection of physical and psychological integrity

General considerations

6.119 Article 8 provides additional protection for the physical and psychological integrity of an individual through a responsibility to ensure effective respect for private life[1]. While certain of these positive obligations complement the protection available under Article 3 (in that circumstances that do not meet the threshold test for inhuman and degrading treatment or punishment may nevertheless fall within the scope of respect for private life[2]), Article 8 also extends the responsibility upon state authorities to the protection of reputation and honour as well as of certain aspects of a person's privacy from unwarranted intrusion. In particular cases, the positive obligation will also involve a requirement to have in place criminal law sanctions which are effectively enforced through adequate investigation and prosecution of offences. In addition, the Court has also considered a number of cases in which the authorities' failure to address severe environmental pollution has been held to constitute a failure to respect the home and family life, obligations which again complement responsibilities arising under other Convention provisions[3].

These obligations to ensure 'respect' for Article 8 interests thus extend to a range of public service provision, and thereby may engage the responsibilities of officials such as police officers[4], medical staff[5] and immigration services[6]. It can also involve consideration of whether there is effective regulation of private sector provision, for example, in the areas of health[7] and education[8].

---

1   *Botta v Italy* 1998-I, para 32; *A, B and C v Ireland* [GC] 2010-…, para 212.

2   See paras.4.28, 4.51, 4.53 and 4.83 above.

3   See para 4.28 above.

4   *Storck v Germany* 2005-V, paras 151–155, discussed further at para **4.155** above (unlawful confinement to private clinic, with state responsibility engaged both on account of police action in returning her to the clinic, the failure of the courts to interpret domestic law in a manner compatible with Art 8, and the lack of effective control over private psychiatric institutions).

5   Eg *YF v Turkey* 2003-IX, paras 41–43.

6   See further para **6.67–6.70** above. But note that threatened deportation or extradition may not readily engage Art 8: *Fashkami v United Kingdom* (dec) (22 June 2004) (threatened expulsion of homosexual to Iran, the applicant claiming a risk of extra-judicial execution and ill-treatment: inadmissible under Arts 2 and 3 since it had not been established that there were substantial grounds for believing he would face such treatment, and inadmissible under Art 8 since such compelling considerations requiring states to ensure fundamental rights under Arts 2 and 3 do not automatically apply under other ECHR provisions). This decision can be contrasted with the approach adopted in domestic case-law: see paras **6.78–6.85** above. See also the decision, based on the Geneva Convention on Refugees, in *HJ (Iran) v Secretary of State for the Home Department* [2011] 1 AC 596.

7   *Costello-Roberts v United Kingdom* (1993) A 247-C, at para 36 (corporal punishment of a young school pupil in a private had not attained the minimum level of severity required under Art 3; while Art 8 in certain situations could afford some additional protection for the physical integrity of an individual, here, taking into account that the schooling of a child 'necessarily involves some degree of interference with his or her private life', no violation of Art 8 established, the Court noting at paras 27–28 that a state remains responsible for a breach of Convention guarantees committed in the course of the provision of education in a private school since the assumption of responsibilities in the field of regulation of education is sufficient to establish liability in certain circumstances).

8   *Storck v Germany* 2005-V, paras 151–155, discussed further at para **4.155** above (unlawful confinement to private clinic, with state responsibility engaged both on account of police action in returning her to the clinic, the failure of the courts to interpret domestic law in a

manner compatible with Art 8, and the lack of effective control over private psychiatric institutions).

Responsive and effective criminal justice

6.120 Article 8 may impose positive obligations upon a state to adopt measures or to take action to further 'respect' for Article 8 concerns. These may extend to the taking of measures to protect an individual against threats of domestic violence[1], including in certain cases the provision of criminal law sanctions. In *MC v Bulgaria,* the Court considered that state's positive obligations under Articles 3 and 8 required both the penalisation and the effective prosecution of all non-consensual sexual acts in line with modern standards in comparative and international law. In particular, substantive law regulating rape should not now require an element of physical resistance by the victim. Here, there had been significant shortcomings in the investigation and determination whether to prosecute in that officials had failed to assess the credibility of conflicting evidence in a context-sensitive manner and in a way which sought to verify the facts while proceeding on the basis of the lack of any direct proof of rape in the form of violence. This had elevated the apparent lack of resistance to the status of the defining element of the offence rather than focusing upon the issue of lack of consent thus resulting in a violation of both provisions[2]. Persistent threats giving rise to a well-founded fear of violence will be sufficient to give rise to this obligation to protect an individual, even in the absence of actual physical violence[3].

1   Cf *Whiteside v United Kingdom* (1994) DR 76, 80 (refusal of the court to grant injunction against the husband in a case of alleged domestic violence: inadmissible on account of failure to exhaust domestic remedies, but the Commission noted there could exist a positive duty to protect against persistent and distressing harassment).

2   *MC v Bulgaria* 2003-XII, paras 167–187. See further Choudhry and Herring 'Domestic Violence and the Human Rights Act 1998: a New Means of Legal Intervention?' [2006] PL 752; and Londono 'Positive Obligations, Criminal Procedure and Rape Cases' [2007] EHRLR 158.

3   *Hajduová v Slovakia* (30 November 2010), paras 45–52 (failure to order detention of husband for psychiatric treatment and in the light of history of violence).

6.121 The effective deterrence and punishment of certain behaviour through the provision of an adequate response by criminal justice agencies will also apply to behaviour harmful to other vulnerable individuals such as children. In *X and Y v Netherlands,* a mentally handicapped 16-year-old girl had been sexually assaulted while resident in a home. The girl's father had complained to the police on her behalf, but the public prosecutor had decided not to institute proceedings since domestic law required such complaints to be made by the alleged victim. The Court ruled that the lack of proceedings in the criminal courts failed to provide the appellant with sufficient protection since the opportunity available to the victim to raise a civil action would have been insufficient on its own to vindicate Article 8 requirements in light of the 'fundamental values and essential aspects of private life' involved in the particular case[1]. Whether adequate protection in this manner has been provided is a question to be determined on the particular facts of the case[2]. In *Stubbings v United Kingdom*, victims of child sex abuse had found themselves prevented by a limitation statute from raising civil actions against the perpetrators. In finding that Article 8 had not been violated, the Court noted the provision did not require the provision of unlimited civil remedies, at least not where the criminal law also provided protection and where there was sufficient evidence for a prosecution[3]. The discharge of positive obligations under Article 8 to protect vulnerable individuals may itself give rise to other considerations under this guarantee. For example, while the registration of sex offenders will generally be considered to be justifiable[4], such a measure would require to be accompanied by adequate safeguards to ensure that any legitimate disclosure of this information to third parties is not abused[5]. Here, though, some recognition of practical realities is apparent, for 'the seriousness of child abuse as a social problem requires that persons who act in good faith, in what they believe are the best interests of the child, should not be influenced by fear of being prosecuted or sued when deciding whether and when their doubts should be communicated to health care professionals or social services'[6].

1   *X and Y v Netherlands* (1985) A 91, at paras 23–27 (the Court decided it was not necessary to consider the application of Art 3; nor whether Art 14 was relevant).

2   Cf *Osman v United Kingdom* 1998-VIII, paras 128–130 (not established that the police knew or ought to have known at the time that an individual represented a real and immediate risk; nor was there any evidence implicating the individual in attacks on the family home).

3   *Stubbings v United Kingdom* 1996-IV, paras 58–67. Cf *August v United Kingdom* (dec) (21 January 2003) (denial of criminal injuries compensation to applicant who, as a minor in care, had engaged in sexual acts for payment with an adult as he had contributed to the incident: inadmissible, the case being significantly different from *X and Y v Netherlands* as the adult concerned had been sentenced to a substantial term of imprisonment and domestic law did not condone the behaviour and Art 8 does not in any event include the right to compensation, while the failure to equate sexual offences against children with crimes of violence in all circumstances did not deprive the applicant of protection of his physical and moral integrity). See also *KU v Finland* 2008-…, (inability to discover identity on account of confidentiality of telecommunications of person placing defamatory advertisement on the internet and purporting to come from a minor seeking an intimate relationship), discussed at para **6.37** above.

4   Eg *Gardel v France* 2009-…, paras 57–71 (placing of the name of the applicant on a national judicial register of sexual offenders for 30 years on account of criminal convictions involved an interference with Art 8, but was prescribed by law and had the legitimate aims of protecting public order and the prevention of crime, while the retention period involved had involved an appropriate balance as it was not disproportionate to the database's aim of protecting the public).

5   In particular, to protect the physical safety of individuals: see eg *Shanaghan v United Kingdom* 2001-III, discussed at para **4.38** above.

6   *Juppala v Finland* (2 December 2008), paras 34–46 (convicted of criminal defamation for reporting her suspicions that her grandson was being abused by his father to a doctor: violation of Art 10 guarantee of freedom of expression).

Health care

6.122 Medical treatment imposed without consent will certainly involve an interference with private life[1], and thus Article 8 requires that a patient is appropriately involved in the choice of medical care provided to them[2], informed consent presupposing access of information enabling individuals to assess the health risks to which they are exposed[3]. In consequence, if a foreseeable risk materialises without a patient having been duly informed in advance, liability under Article 8 may arise. To this end, appropriate regulations must be in place to ensure respect for patients' physical integrity in light of the serious consequences which may arise from medical procedures[4]. However, Article 8 does not generally give rise to any positive obligation to pursue any particular preventive health policy as matters of health care policy are covered by a margin of appreciation on the part of domestic authorities (although such an obligation to eradicate or prevent the spread of a particular disease or infection may arise under Articles 2 or 3)[5].

1   *YF v Turkey* 2003-IX, paras 41–43 (compulsory gynaecological examination carried out on detainee following her allegation of ill-treatment by police officers and carried out at the insistence of the police who had wished to protect themselves against possible allegations of rape: violation as not 'in accordance with the law', although accepted that medical examination of detainees can provide a significant safeguard against false accusations of sexual ill-treatment).

2   *Pretty v United Kingdom* 2002-III, para 63, discussed at para **4.53** above.

3   *Roche v United Kingdom* [GC] 2005-X, para 155, discussed at para **6.128** below.

4   *Trocellier v France* (dec) 2006-XIV (unforeseen complications: inadmissible).

5   *Shelley v United Kingdom* (dec) (4 January 2008) (challenge by a prisoner of a decision not to implement a needle-exchange programme in prisons: inadmissible, the Court noting that some preventive steps to reduce drug use in prisons had been taken). But see *L v Lithuania* 2007-..., paras 57–60 (inability of a transsexual who had undergone partial gender-reassignment surgery to complete gender reassignment surgery and officially change gender in documents: violation on account of the limited legislative gap in gender-reassignment surgery leaving the applicant in a situation of distressing uncertainty, even although the budgetary burden would not be unduly heavy).

6.123 The obligation to ensure protection for physical or psychological integrity in the provision of health care may also impose a responsibility to ensure the availability of an effective and independent system to investigate the cause of unforeseen harmful effects of medical treatment[1], an obligation mirroring the 'procedural aspects' of Articles 2 and 3[2].

1   *Trocellier v France* (dec) 2006-XIV. See also *Codarcea v Romania* (2 June 2009), paras 101–109 (formal rather than substantive access to legal proceedings allowing redress against a negligent doctor and thus no effective system in place to ensure monetary damages for injuries caused: violation).

2   See paras **4.35–4.47** and **4.94–4.108** above.

Domestic consideration of protection of physical and psychological integrity and health care

6.124 The implications of Article 8 in the context of health care have been considered by domestic courts in a number of cases. Those relating to contraception, pregnancy and related issues have been discussed above[1]. Other cases have included cases concerning treatment against the will of the patient[2], treatment of children against the will of their parents[3], the withdrawal of life-prolonging treatment from patients who were unable to give informed consent[4], the denial of life-prolonging treatment to competent patients who wished to receive it[5], assisted suicide[6], the seclusion of a mentally disordered patient[7], and the designation of the 'nearest relative' of a person detained under mental health legislation[8]. Other cases relevant to the protection of physical and psychological integrity have concerned anonymity orders[9].

---

1   See para **6.71** above.

2   See eg *R (Wilkinson) v Broadmoor Special Hospital Authority* [2002] 1 WLR 419 (administering of anti-psychotic drugs by injection); *M v Cook* 2003 SC 52; and *R (B) v S* [2006] 1 WLR 810. See also *R (N) v M* [2003] 1 WLR 562 (Art 3).

3   *Re C (Immunisation: Parental Rights)* [2003] 2 FLR 1095.

4   See eg *NHS Trust A v M* [2001] Fam 348; *W Healthcare NHS Trust v H* [2005] 1 WLR 834.

5   See eg *R (Burke) v General Medical Council* [2006] QB 273.

6   *R (Purdy) v Director of Public Prosecutions* [2010] 1 AC 345, departing from *R (Pretty) v Director of Public Prosecutions* [2002] 1 AC 800.

7   *R (Munjaz) v Mersey Care NHS Trust* [2006] 2 AC 148.

8   *R (M) v Secretary of State for Health* [2003] EWHC 1094 (inability of detainees to challenge the appointment of a 'nearest relative' declared incompatible with the right to respect for private life in Art 8).

9   See eg *Venables v News Group Newspapers Ltd* [2001] Fam 430; *X (A Woman formerly known as Mary Bell) v O'Brien* [2003] EMLR 37 (lifetime protection for the identity of a person convicted of a notorious crime, and her daughter, from media disclosure granted after balancing the press's right of freedom of expression under Art 10 with Art 8 rights); *Secretary of State for the Home Department v AP (No 2)* [2010] 1 WLR 1652 (anonymity of a successful appellant against a control order continued).

Environmental, etc protection

6.125 Environmental concerns have now been accommodated within Article 8's requirement of effective respect for private and family life and home[1]. Such issues may also arise under related guarantees[2]. The Court, however, is reluctant to acknowledge any special status of 'environmental human rights'; rather, it approaches such questions by assessing whether a fair balance has been achieved and whether the decision-making process has accorded due weight to the interests of affected individuals on a case-by-case basis[3]. In consequence, real threats to 'private and family life' or to 'home' requiring a positive obligation on the part of state authorities to take effective action may not only involve environmental pollution (including noise pollution[4]), but also harassment, victimisation or vandalism[5].

---

1   Including nomadic lifestyles: cf 9278/81 and 9415/81, *G and E v Norway* (1983) DR 35, 30 (flooding of area traditionally used by Sana reindeer herders gave rise to Art 8 issue, but justified by para (2)); and imprisonment: *Brânduşe v Romania* 2009-..., paras 64–76 (Art 8 found to be applicable in a complaint by a prisoner that he was forced to endure the stench of a refuse tip, the complaint going beyond merely detention conditions: violation on account of significant levels of nuisance caused by offensive smells). Cf *Ward v United Kingdom* (dec) (9 November 2004) (refusal to relocate gypsy site following report indicating location was prejudicial to health: inadmissible as the applicant had voluntarily moved onto the site, had taken no steps to find another official site, and no exceptional circumstances allowing the derivation of a right to be provided with alternative housing). For international texts, see Council of Europe *Human Rights and the Environment* (2002).

2   *Hatton and Others v United Kingdom* [GC] 2003-VIII.

3   Potentially fatal risks can give rise to Art 2 issues (see paras **4.28–4.30** above); environmental concerns may have an impact upon property considerations under Prot 1, Art 1 (eg *Fredin v Sweden (no 1)* (1990) A 192); and fair hearing requirements may exist in determination of environmental and planning questions under Art 6 (eg *Bryan v United Kingdom* (1995) A 335-A, discussed at para **5.151** above).

4   *Moreno Gómez v Spain* 2004-X, paras 58–62 (repeated failure of authorities to enforce anti-noise regulations to deal with noise nuisance from discotheques: violation). For examples of applications declared inadmissible, see *Furlepa v Poland* (dec) (18 March 2008) (car repair garage built illegally in a residential area); *Fägerskiöld v Sweden* (dec) 2008-... (alleged noise disturbance from wind turbine); *Borysiewicz v Poland* (1 July 2008) (allegation that noise emanating from a tailor's shop had affected the applicant's health and family life, but no evidence to show that the noise had reached the minimum level of severity in order to engage Art 8); *Galev and Others v Bulgaria* (dec) (29 September 2009) (opening of a dental surgery in a residential block of flats did not cause the minimum level of severity required to constitute an interference with the private lives of the other residents, the assessment considering whether the detriment complained of was negligible in comparison to the environmental hazards inherent to life in every modern city); and *Deés v Hungary* (9 November 2010), paras 18–24 (noise, pollution and vibration occasioned by heavy traffic and directly attributable to the introduction of motorway tolls by a private party involved a direct and serious nuisance which the state had failed to address adequately: violation). For general discussion, see McManus 'Noise Pollution and Human Rights' [2005] EHRLR 575.

5   Cf *Osman v United Kingdom* 1998-VIII, paras 128–130 (the facts did not support any finding that the police had failed to take appropriate steps in all the circumstances); and 20357/92, *Whiteside v United Kingdom* (1994) DR 76, 80 (positive obligations on a state may extend to providing protection against persistent harassment).

6.126 The complaint must meet a certain level of threat to the home or family life, either on account of its seriousness or persistency, for Article 8 does not contain any explicit right to a clean and quiet environment[1] or any general right against industrial or commercial development[2]. At the outset, it must therefore be shown that the complaints amount to allegations of serious harm which has a direct impact upon the applicant or his family[3]. Thus where it is possible to conclude that an individual's health has deteriorated on account of prolonged exposure to pollutants to a degree sufficient to bring the matter within the scope of Article 8, the failure of the authorities to take action to regulate private industry will engage state responsibility[4]. Two cases illustrate the Court's approach. In *López Ostra v Spain*, the Court accepted that the failure to take steps to address the significant levels of pollution generated by a treatment plant situated only a few metres from the applicant's home was a violation of Article 8 which required the state to take steps to ensure the effective protection of the applicant's right to respect for her private and family life. The plant's operation had had a marked effect on the health of the applicant, and indeed the pollution had required the evacuation of local residents from their homes for a lengthy period[5]. In *Fadeyeva v Russia*, the Court was able to conclude that the authorities had been aware of continuing environmental hazards and had been able to take measures to reduce or prevent these, but had not done so. While it accepted that there was a wide margin of appreciation in respect of environmental practices, in this case a fair balance between the economic welfare of the region and the applicant's effective right to the enjoyment of her home and private life had not been struck[6].

1   *Greenpeace EV and Others v Germany* (dec) (12 May 2009) certain measures to curb emissions from diesel vehicles had been taken, and the choice of means as to how to deal with environmental issues fell within the state's margin of appreciation: inadmissible).

2   *Kyrtatos v Greece* 2003-VI, paras 51–55 (absence of convincing evidence that damage to natural habitat for protected species had affected applicants' rights). See also 7407/76, *X and Y v Germany* (1976) DR 5, 161 (no right to nature preservation contained in the Convention, and application by environmental group seeking to prevent use of marshland manifestly ill-founded).

3   *Taşkin and Others v Turkey* (10 November 2004), paras 111–114 (applicability of Art 8 where dangerous effects of an activity to which individuals are likely to be exposed has been determined through an environmental impact assessment procedure in such a way as to establish a sufficiently close link with private and family life).

4   *Fadeyeva v Russia* 2005-IV, paras 83–88 (presumption that pollutants had been potentially harmful based upon submission of documentation showing pollutants had exceeded domestic norms, the failure of the respondent state to produce other documentation (allowing the Court to conclude that the emissions had been worse than it appeared) and acceptance by domestic courts that the applicant had a right to be resettled).

5   *López Ostra v Spain* (1994) A 303-C, paras 50–58. See further Sands 'Human Rights, Environment and the *López Ostra* Case' [1996] EHRLR 597.

6   *Fadeyeva v Russia* 2005-IV, paras 128–134. See also *Giacomelli v Italy* 2006-XII, paras 76–98 (delay in requiring environmental impact study, and failure to enforce court decisions suspending operation of plant emitting toxic pollutants: violation).

6.127 The ultimate question in determining whether an interference has been 'necessary in a democratic society' calls for consideration of the type of policy or decision involved, the extent to which the views of individuals are taken into account and the procedural safeguards available[1]. However, while the decision-making process in complex issues of environmental and economic policy must of necessity involve appropriate investigations and studies, it does not follow that a decision can only be taken if 'comprehensive and measurable data ... in relation to each and every aspect of the matter'[2] exist. In any event, the choice of means for dealing with a nuisance falls within a state's margin of appreciation[3]. The risk is of inappropriate intervention in policy-determinations, and caution on the part of judicial bodies is called for. In *Hatton and Others v United Kingdom*, for example, the Grand Chamber (in arriving at a different conclusion to the Chamber) considered that a fair balance had been achieved between individual and state interests when an increase in night flights at Heathrow airport had been authorised on economic grounds, measures having been taken to try to keep noise disturbance at an acceptable level and the applicants having the possibility of moving elsewhere without financial loss[4].

---

1   *Taşkin and Others v Turkey* 2004-X, at para 118: 'whilst Art 8 contains no explicit procedural requirements, the decision-making process leading to measures of interference must be fair and such as to afford due respect for the interests of the individual as safeguarded by Art 8. It is therefore necessary to consider all the procedural aspects, including the type of policy or decision involved, the extent to which the views of individuals were taken into account throughout the decision-making process, and the procedural safeguards available'. See eg *Ttar v Romania* 2009-..., paras 89–125 (failure by the state to act in accordance with its obligation to carry out a risk assessment of a hazardous industrial process and to inform properly the public: violation). See also *Di Sarno v Italy* (allegations of detrimental impact upon health and welfare through the failure over 15-year period to uplift and dispose of rubbish properly: communicated).

2   *Hatton and Others v United Kingdom* [GC] 2003-VIII, at para 128.

3   *Powell and Rayner v United Kingdom* (1990) A 172, paras 41–44 (decision to deal with the nuisance of aircraft noise by means of regulation rather than by civil action for nuisance). See too 7889/77, *Arondelle v United Kingdom* (1982) DR 26, 5 (friendly settlement) and 9310/81, *Baggs v United Kingdom* (1987) DR 52, 59 (friendly settlement).

4   *Hatton and Others v United Kingdom* [GC] 2003-VIII, paras 128–130 at para 128 (the situation had been constantly monitored the situation, a series of investigations and studies had preceded the scheme, and the applicants had enjoyed access to a consultation exercise: no violation). The Chamber judgment (2 October 2001), at para 106 had considered there had been no 'serious attempt to evaluate the extent or impact of the interferences with the applicants' sleep patterns, and generally in the absence of a prior specific and complete study with the aim of finding the least onerous solution as regards human rights, it is not possible to agree that in weighing the interferences against the economic interest of the country – which itself had not been quantified – the Government struck the right balance'. See also *Taşkin and Others v Turkey* 2004-X, paras 115–126 (failure to enforce decision that the use of sodium cyanide in mining was impermissible as this presented dangers for the local ecosystem and for human health and safety: violation as the applicants had been deprived of procedural safeguards, and new authorisations had no legal foundation).

6.128 In this area, there is also a positive duty upon the state to make available any necessary or essential information to allow those affected by a clear and obvious environmental hazard to assess the risk of continuing to live in a particular locality. In *Guerra and Others v Italy*, a fertiliser plant with a history of accidents which had resulted in the hospitalisation of many residents had eventually been subject to inspection and inquiry. However, local townspeople, who would have been most vulnerable in the event of a further accident at the factory, had not been provided with information until after a significant delay. The Court considered that there had been a failure on the part of the authorities to secure the applicants' rights under Article 8[1]. This principle also applies where the exposure has occurred in the past. In *Roche v United Kingdom,* the Grand Chamber considered that the state had failed in its positive obligation to provide the applicant with 'an effective and accessible procedure' allowing him access to all relevant and appropriate information to permit an assessment of the risks associated with his participation in toxic chemical and biological tests while serving as a soldier, stressing that Article 8 imposes 'an obligation of disclosure not requiring the individual to litigate to obtain it'[2].

1   *Guerra and Others v Italy* 1998-I, paras 57–60.

2   *Roche v United Kingdom* [GC] 2005–X, paras 155–169 at para 162. Cf *McGinley and Egan v United Kingdom* 1998-III, paras 98–103 (no violation of Art 8 in light of access to documentation through legal proceedings), discussed at para 5.68 above.

DOMESTIC CONSIDERATION OF ENVIRONMENTAL PROTECTION

6.129 Article 8 has been considered in a number of domestic cases concerned with environmental issues. In *Marcic v Thames Water Utilities Ltd,* for example, the House of Lords accepted that Article 8 and Article 1 of Protocol no 1 were engaged by the repeated flooding of the claimant's home due to inadequate sewerage, but held that the relevant statutory scheme was compatible with the Convention rights, since it enabled a fair balance between the competing interests of the individual and the community to be struck by an independent regulator whose decisions were subject to judicial review[1]. On the other hand, since Article 8 imposes no obligation upon the state to provide a home, there is no breach of Article 8 merely by virtue of the fact that local authority housing is affected by dampness and condensation[2]. The basis on which a financial award should be made by way of just satisfaction for a violation of Article 8 in a case of loss amenity, and the relationship between such an award and common law damages for nuisance, has been considered[3].

1   *Marcic v Thames Water Utilities Ltd* [2004] 2 AC 42. See also *Arscott v The Coal Authority* [2005] Env. L.R. 6 (defence in nuisance of a land owner who took steps to prevent flood waters coming into his land, with consequence that they flooded another's land, did not contravene Art 8 or Prot 1, Art 1).

2   *Lee v Leeds City Council* [2002] 1 WLR 1488. See also *Furness v Environment Agency* [2002] Env LR 26 (risk to health and property caused by an incineration facility was not substantial enough to involve interference with Art 8).

3   *Dobson v Thames Water Utilities Ltd* [2009] 3 All ER 319. See also *Dennis v Ministry of Defence* [2003] Env LR 34 (nuisance caused by military jets involved interference with rights under Art 8 and Prot 1, Art 1, but a claim for nuisance would be a sufficient remedy); and *Andrews v Reading Borough Council (No 2)* [2005] EWHC 256 (QB) (failure of authority to consider taking any steps to mitigate the extra noise created by the traffic scheme and refusal to pay any compensation constituted a violation of Art 8). In relation to domestic consideration of Art 8 in relation to planning issues, see para **6.31** above.

Intrusions into private life by the media

6.130 Underlying the Court's jurisprudence on respect for private life is the value of personal autonomy. The 'right to establish and develop relationships with other human beings and the outside world'[1] free from unwanted attention in order to secure 'to the individual a sphere within which he or she can freely pursue the development and fulfilment of his or her personality'[2] readily explains the Court's increasing emphasis upon the state's obligation to ensure appropriate regulation of the activities of private parties, particularly of the media, in respect of privacy. However, the question of privacy and press intrusion cannot be considered in isolation from the consideration of freedom of expression under Article 10 which includes the freedom 'to receive and impart information and ideas without interference by public authority'. Under Article 10, there is a presumption in favour of freedom of speech as a means to the enhancement of democracy and development of the person: 'pluralism, tolerance and broadmindedness' are crucial to the maintenance of democratic society. Differing levels of protection of speech are thus justified, depending upon the issue at stake[3]. Political expression and debate on matters of public concern call for the highest safeguards, and this can imply reduced protection for the personal privacy of those in the political arena who have voluntarily placed themselves in a public position of accountability[4]. At the same time, the exercise of freedom carries with it responsibilities. More recent jurisprudence emphasises the positive obligation upon states to ensure that aspects of an individual's private life are adequately protected. For example, where there has been an abuse of press freedom (such as the disclosure of matters of patient confidentiality in an article which does not contribute to any debate of general interest to society), it is necessary that domestic law adequately redresses the damage suffered by the victim and thereby helps deter the recurrence of such abuses in future[5]. Balancing respect for private life with freedom of expression is thus likely to involve consideration of how best to maintain the media's role in contributing to the democratic accountability of political figures with the need to reflect other fundamental Convention values.

1   *Bensaid v United Kingdom* 2001-I, para 47.

2   *Smirnova v Russia* 2003-IX, at para 95.

3   See paras **7.75–7.76** below.

4   Eg *Lingens v Austria* (1986) A 103, at paras 42–44 (publication of articles criticising the Austrian Chancellor's fitness for office had resulted in a successful private defamation action, a form of censure likely to inhibit political discussion and debate and thus had been 'liable to hamper the press in performing its task as purveyor of information and public watchdog'; further, 'the limits of acceptable criticism are ... wider as regards a politician as such than as regards a private individual' since a politician 'inevitably and knowingly lays himself open to close scrutiny of his every word and deed', and accordingly, while protection of reputation is a recognised ground for state interference and will extend to protection of the reputation of politicians, 'in such cases the requirements of such protection have to be weighed in relation to the interests of open discussion of political issues'). In *Fayed v United Kingdom* (1994) A 294-B, at para 75, the Court extended this to businessmen actively involved in the affairs of major public companies who also 'inevitably and knowingly lay themselves open to close scrutiny of all their acts' not only by the media but also by inspectors and other institutions representing the public interest. It would be difficult to extend this principle further to include media or sports celebrities whose private lives are unlikely to involve questions of democratic accountability. See further paras **7.81–7.84** below.

5   *Biriuk v Lithiuania* (25 November 2008), paras 41–47 at para 46 ('outrageous' abuse of press freedom via disclosure of HIV status having a negative impact on the willingness of others to

take voluntary tests for HIV and seek appropriate treatment, the fact that the applicants had lived in a village increasing the possibility of public humiliation and exclusion from social life: violation on account of the significant limitations on the amount of damages the courts could award).

6.131 Intrusions of privacy by the media purportedly justified as being in the public interest now require to be subjected to more rigorous scrutiny[1]. In *Von Hannover v Germany,* the daughter of Prince Rainier of Monaco complained of the refusal of the domestic courts to prevent the publication in the tabloid press of a series of photographs taken without her knowledge and showing her going about her daily business. The domestic courts had decided that she qualified as a 'figure of contemporary society *par excellence*', and further, that there was a public interest in knowing how a princess behaved outside her representative functions unless the 'criterion of spatial isolation' applied (that is, where it was objectively apparent that an individual had retired to a 'secluded place' in order to be able to behave in a manner unconstrained by being in public). For the Court, this approach by the domestic courts to the determination of privacy claims was defective, the criterion being too vague to apply and too difficult to prove in any subsequent challenge. Here, the publication of photographs showing the applicant engaged in purely private activities fell within the scope of 'private life' as there had been a legitimate expectation of privacy. Further, a state's obligation to ensure that domestic law provided adequate protection for private life extended to upholding the right to control the use of one's image. It could not be reasonably asserted that the publication had contributed to any debate of general interest to society: the publication had concerned images rather than ideas, and the sole purpose had been to satisfy the curiosity of readers regarding the private life of the applicant who, while being a member of a royal family, did not discharge any official function on behalf of Monaco and therefore was not a public figure within the sense of the Convention. In reaffirming that Article 8 also covers the psychological integrity of an individual and the development of relations with others (and so included interaction with others even in a public place), the Court also took note that the applicant was suffering harassment from photographers on a daily basis. In its opinion, there was now a necessity for increased vigilance in protecting private life in view of new communication technologies which make possible the dissemination of photographs of individuals to a broad section of the public. While it was mindful of the important role the press played in a democracy and indeed acknowledged that the publication of photographs also fell within the scope of freedom of expression under Article 10, the Court stressed that this was an aspect of expression where the protection of the rights of individuals assumed a particular importance[2].

---

1 Providing always that Art 8 is engaged: see eg *Pipi v Turkey* (dec) (12 May 2009) (publication of photographs already in the public domain and which did not concern details of the applicant's private life: inadmissible). For examples of private life and free expression balancing by the Court, see eg *Krone Verlag GmbH v Austria* (26 February 2002), paras 29–39 (injunction on publication of photograph of politician: violation, the Court noting (at para 37) that what matters is whether a politician has entered the public arena, not how well known an individual is); *Plon v France* 2004-IV, paras 42–43 (suppression of book containing medical information

on the late President Mitterand: while such a measure could have been justified shortly after his death to protect the deceased's family, in time this would cease to meet any pressing social need given that the public interest in discussing the history of the President's period in office would take precedence over the right to medical confidentiality); *Karhuvaara and Iltalehti v Finland* 2004-X, paras 43–55 (conviction for publication of material infringing privacy of an MP in publishing articles on a criminal trial concerning the drunken and disorderly behaviour of the MP's husband: violation); and *Österreichischer Rundfunk v Austria* (7 December 2006), paras 59–73 (there may be good reasons to prohibit the publication of a picture of a convicted person after his release on parole, but when weighing the individual's interest not to have his physical appearance disclosed against the public's interest in the publication of his picture, it was appropriate to consider the degree of notoriety of the person concerned, the lapse of time since the conviction and the release, the nature of the crime, the connection between the photograph and the textual report: here, the domestic courts had attached great weight to the long lapse of time since a well-known neo-Nazi politician had been convicted but had paid no particular attention to the fact that only a few weeks had elapsed since his release, nor to his notoriety nor the political nature of the crime, and the injunction applied only to the public service broadcaster: violation of Art 10). Cf *Société Prisma Presse v France* (dec) (1 July 2003) (court order to a publisher to issue a press communiqué concerning finding by court that a magazine article whose sole purpose was to satisfy the curiosity of a sector of the public of the intimacy of a well-known singer and his wife had thereby intruded into their private life: domestic law was adequately foreseeable, and such a measure may constitute appropriate compensation); *Leempoel and SA Ed Ciné Revue v Belgium* (9 November 2006), paras 69–85 (withdrawal of sale of magazine disclosing documents protected as confidential in the context of a parliamentary inquiry and which may have prejudiced defence rights and interfered with respect for private life: no violation); and *Hachette Filipacchi Associés v France* 2007-…, paras 45–62 (order to publish statement imposed by domestic court following the publication of a photograph of a murdered state official shortly after his assassination and considered an intolerable interference with the private lives of the deceased's family: no violation). For earlier case law, see eg 6959/75, *Brüggeman and Scheuten v Germany* (1977) DR 10, 100 at 115 (no expectation of privacy where an individual by his own actions brings 'his private life into contact with public life'); and 28851–28852/95, *Spencer v United Kingdom* (1998) DR 92, 56 (publication of photograph of celebrity taken with telephoto lens while she was walking in the grounds of private clinic: action for breach of confidence now sufficiently certain in domestic law, and the applicants could have been expected to utilise this and thus a failure to exhaust domestic remedies); and 20683/92, *N v Portugal* (20 February 1995) cited by Naismith in 'Photographs, Privacy and Freedom of Expression' [1996] EHRLR 150 at p 156 (conviction of a magazine publisher for defamation and invasion of privacy involving the publication of photographs of a businessman involved in sexual activities with a number of women was accepted as proportionate for protection of the rights of individuals for the purposes of Art 10).

2   *Von Hannover v Germany* 2004-VI, paras 56–80 (at para 42, referring to Parliamentary Assembly Resolution 1165(1998)). See further Hedigen 'The Princess, the Press and Privacy: Observations on Caroline von Hannover v Germany' in Caflisch, Callewaert, Liddell, Mahoney and Villiger (eds) *Liber Amicorum Luzius Wildhaber: Human Rights – Strasbourg Views* (2007), pp 193–205 (at p 204, the author suggests that 'a film star or football icon must accept that a certain measure of their privacy has been inevitably lost in their quest for the life blood of publicity'). Further consideration is pending: see *Von Hannover v Germany (no 2)* (refusal by domestic courts to grant injunctions restraining publication of further publication of photographs of Princess Caroline Von Hannover taking part in private activities on the basis that the media's rights outweighed Art 8 rights: relinquishment of jurisdiction to the Grand Chamber).

6.132 Particular care must be exercised by the media when the interference with 'private life' involves children and young persons. The right to control a minor's image is exercisable by his parents[1]. More crucially, the special position of minors in criminal justice calls for the protection of their privacy at criminal trials[2].

---

1   *Reklos and Davourlis v Greece* 2009-..., paras 41–43 (professional photographer allowed by hospital to enter a sterile environment to which only doctors and nurses had access to take photos of a new born baby without the prior consent of the parents: violation, as the prior consent of the parents was essential to determine the circumstances in which it would be used).

2   *T v United Kingdom* [GC] (16 December 1999), paras 75 and 85, citing the UN Convention on the Rights of the Child (1989), Art 40(2)(b). See also para **5.155** above.

Reputation, etc

6.133 A recent development has been the recognition of both reputation[1] and honour[2] as interests protected by Article 8[3], and thus as giving rise to positive obligations to guarantee effective respect for private life by legislative, executive and judicial authorities[4]. However, 'in order for Article 8 to come into play, the attack on personal honour and reputation must attain a certain level of gravity and in a manner causing prejudice to personal enjoyment of the right to respect for private life'[5]. In consequence, there is also a positive obligation upon the state to protect honour and reputation from attacks by others, a matter of particular concern in respect of unwarranted media intrusion, and to this end, the Court will examine the extent to which the state has put in place a legal framework protecting these interests. This assessment often calls for a careful examination of whether a proper balance has been achieved between freedom of expression and Article 8 interests[6]. In *A v Norway,* for example, a newspaper in reporting upon the rape and murder of two girls had disclosed details of the applicant's criminal convictions, had published details of his employment and residence (although he was not named specifically) along with somewhat grainy photographs, and had suggested he was 'probably the most interesting of several convicted persons' being interviewed by the police. The result was that the applicant had found himself unable to continue working and had been forced to leave his home at a time when he was being rehabilitated following upon his recent release from prison. While accepting that the articles were defamatory inasmuch as they left the impression that the applicant was suspected of the murders, the domestic court had determined that publication had been justified by the applicant's own statements protesting his innocence to the media and also both by the public interest in view of the balanced coverage and the clear statement by the police that no one was in fact under suspicion at the time. For the Court, the issue was whether the state had fulfilled its positive obligation to protect the applicant's honour and reputation. He had been persecuted by journalists, the newspaper articles had allowed him to be identified, and the publication had conveyed the impression that there was a factual basis for the suspicion. Publication had been particularly harmful to his moral and psychological integrity and had gravely damaged his reputation and honour. While the press had the right to deliver and the public had the right to receive information on such a serious matter, this could not justify such defamatory allegations and the harm it caused: 'there was not in the Court's view a reasonable relationship of proportionality between the interests relied on by the domestic courts in safeguarding [the newspaper's] freedom of expression and those of the applicant in having his honour, reputation and privacy protected'[7].

---

1   *White v Sweden* (19 September 2006), para 26; and *Pfeifer v Austria* 2007-XII, para 35. Cf *Gunnarsson v Iceland* (dec) (20 October 2005) (application alleging failure to protect honour and reputation: even assuming that the matter in the applicant's case fell within the scope of Art 8, the domestic courts could reasonably have concluded that the interests in protecting freedom of speech on a political matter had been preponderant: inadmissible, noting that 'to date, in no case brought under Article 8 … has the Court ruled that this provision embodies a right to protection of reputation and honour as such, albeit that these are interests that may be taken into account in the determination of a complaint about a State's failure to ensure "the right to respect for ... private ... life"'). Cf also 27436/95 and 28406/95, *Stewart-Brady v United Kingdom* (1997) DR 90, 45 (a state need not provide legal aid for actions of defamation for harm to reputation). See further Spielmann and Cariolou 'The Right to Protection of Reputation under the European Convention on Human Rights' in Katuoka (ed) *Law in the Changing Europe: Liber Amicorum Pranas Kuris* (2008), pp 410–424.

2   *Sanchez Cardenas v Norway* (4 October 2007), para 38.

3   *Taliadorou and Stylianou v Cyprus* 2008-…, paras 45–55 (reversal of award of damages to police officers wrongly accused of torture without adequate explanation: violation).

4   A distinction thus can be drawn between two notions of personal integrity: aspects of an individual's personal identity (as in *Von Hannover*) and psychological integrity (reputation): see *Karakó v Hungary* (28 April 2009), para 23 (reputation has been deemed an independent right only sporadically and only when factual allegations had been of such a seriously offensive nature that their publication had had an inevitable direct effect on the applicant's private life).

5   *A v Norway* (9 April 2009), at para 64, and citing Committee of Ministers Recommendation Rec (2003) 13 on the provision of information through the media in relation to criminal proceedings, Appendix, Principle 8 – Protection of privacy in the context of on-going criminal proceedings. See also *Sidabras and Džiautas v Lithuania* 2004-VIII, para 49; and *Karakó v Hungary* (28 April 2009), paras 17–29 (dismissal of criminal libel proceedings against a political opponent dismissed on the grounds that the statements involved value judgments made during a political campaign: allegation that reputation had been harmed was not sustainable).

6   See eg *Pipi v Turkey* (dec) (12 May 2009) (publication of information which affected the reputation of the applicant but which did not concern purely personal details of the applicant's life or was the result of an intolerable or ongoing intrusion into private life: inadmissible as the domestic court had not overstepped its margin of appreciation in attributing less weight to Art 8 concerns of the applicant in balancing these with the freedoms of the media under Art 10); and *Polanco Torres and Movilla Polanco v Spain* (21 September 2010), paras 44–54 (article suggesting wife of senior judge had been involved in improper commercial dealings: no violation, the article being of considerable public interest and the journalist having taken measures to check veracity).

7   *A v Norway* (9 April 2009), paras 67–75 at para 74. See also *Petrina v Romania* (14 October 2008), paras 34–52 (satirical magazine alleged that a politician had been part of the Securitate during the communist regime in Romania, but a claim for damages had been unsuccessful on account of the absence of intent: the media had overstepped acceptable bounds as the accusations had directly concerned the applicant in his personal rather than professional capacity, and reality had been misrepresented without any factual basis).

6.134 The law relating to privacy and breach of confidence is perhaps the clearest example of an area where the common law has gained a new vigour and momentum from the introduction of human rights norms: partly because of the need to follow general principles in a way that is somewhat analogous to the doctrine of precedent, although less rigidly structured, and partly because of the need to adapt those principles creatively to local conditions. It has been said on various occasions, on high authority, that there is no freestanding cause of action for infringement of privacy[1]; but the Article 8 right has provided the impetus for the development of a number of discrete rights which provide protection in relation to the same interests. As Lord Hoffmann said in the leading case of *Campbell v MGN Ltd*:

> 'What human rights law has done is to identify private information as something worth protecting as an aspect of human autonomy and dignity. And this recognition has raised inescapably the question of why it should be worth protecting against the state but not against a private person ... I can see no logical ground for saying that a person should have less protection against a private individual than he would have against the state for the publication of private information for which there is no justification.'[2]

---

1   See eg *Kaye v Robertson* [1990] FSR 62; and *Wainwright v Home Office* [2004] 2 AC 406; cf *Wainwright v United Kingdom* 2006-X, discussed at para **6.104** above.

2   *Campbell v MGN Ltd* [2004] 2 AC 457.

6.135 Prior to the HRA 1998, the principal basis for protecting privacy, in the absence of contract, had been the equitable principles whereby a duty of confidence could be enforced. It was generally necessary to be able to demonstrate a pre-existing relationship giving rise to a duty of confidence. Such a duty was owed, for example, by long term sexual partners to one another, such that the courts could restrain a breach[1]. Such a relationship would, however, ordinarily be difficult to establish in a case where privacy was infringed out of the blue by paparazzi or a tabloid scoop. Under the influence of the Convention and the HRA 1998, however, as was explained by Lord Nicholls of Birkenhead in *Campbell v MGN Ltd*, the duty of confidence can be regarded as having evolved into a duty not to misuse private information[2]. As to the ambit of what is private, Lord Nicholls said in the same case:

> 'Essentially the touchstone of private life is whether in respect of the disclosed facts the person in question had a reasonable expectation of privacy.'[3]

Lord Hoffmann explained the implications in another important passage in the same case:

> 'The result of these developments has been a shift in the centre of gravity of the action for breach of confidence when it is used as a remedy for the unjustified publication of personal information. It recognises that the incremental changes to which I have referred do not merely extend the duties arising traditionally from a

relationship of trust and confidence to a wider range of people. As Sedley LJ observed in a perceptive passage in his judgment in *Douglas v Hello! Ltd*[4], the new approach takes a different view of the underlying value which the law protects. Instead of the cause of action being based upon the duty of good faith applicable to confidential personal information and trade secrets alike, it focuses upon the protection of human autonomy and dignity—the right to control the dissemination of information about one's private life and the right to the esteem and respect of other people.

These changes have implications for the future development of the law. They must influence the approach of the courts to the kind of information which is regarded as entitled to protection, the extent and form of publication which attracts a remedy and the circumstances in which publication can be justified.'[5]

1   *Stephens v Avery* [1988] 1 Ch 449. The equitable duty of confidence was also recognised in Scots law, although less fully developed: see eg *Lord Advocate v Scotsman Publications Ltd* 1989 SC (HL) 22. Other types of infringement of privacy can be prevented under other principles of the common law, as developed in the light of the HRA 1998. An example is harassment: see eg *Howlett v Holding* [2006] EWHC 41 (QB) (defendant flew banners behind his aircraft over the area where the claimant lived, referring to her in derogatory terms, and dropped leaflets with a similar content into the area from the plane: violation of Art 8 rights); cf *Ward v Scotrail Railways Ltd* 1999 SC 255 (sexual harassment at work).

2   *Campbell v MGN Ltd* [2004] 2 AC 457 at para 14.

3   *Campbell v MGN Ltd* [2004] 2 AC 457 at para 21.

4   *Douglas v Hello! Ltd* [2001] QB 967, 1001. In *Douglas*, photographs of a wedding were considered confidential information, with the consequence that a publisher who had purchased exclusive rights to the photographs could enforce the duty of confidentiality against third parties.

5   *Campbell v MGN Ltd* [2004] 2 AC 457 at paras 51–52.

6.136 There is a need to reconcile the imperatives of Article 8 with the right to freedom of expression of Article 10. This involves a balancing process, carried out by judges according to the facts before them. This was made clear in *Campbell v MGN Ltd*, which concerned a famous model who was photographed emerging from a drug treatment clinic[1], and in the later case of *Re (S) (A Child) (Identification: Restrictions on Publication)*, which concerned the very different question whether a judge in care proceedings could restrain press reporting of the murder trial of the child's mother, who was charged with the murder of his brother[2]. As a result of these cases, an approach has been established which requires the court first to decide whether the relevant information is such that the person has 'a reasonable expectation of privacy' in respect of it. If so, the court must balance the competing Convention rights according to the individual circumstances of the case[3]. It has become clear that the answer cannot therefore depend on generalities, eg that the claimant is a 'public figure' or a 'role model', or has sought publicity in the past and is therefore to be regarded as fair game for the media. It has also become apparent that the weight to be attached to the right of free expression may depend on an assessment of the worth of what is intended to be published. In *Campbell*, for example, Baroness Hale of Ricmond observed that the political and social life of the community, and the intellectual, artistic or personal development of individuals, were not obviously assisted by poring over the intimate details of a fashion model's private life. Equally, it may be that publication of part of the information in question may be justified, but that there are other parts whose publication would not be justified. In the *Campbell* case, for example, Lord Hoffmann referred to:

'cases in which (for example) there is a public interest in the disclosure of the existence of a sexual relationship (say, between a politician and someone whom she has appointed to public office), but the addition of salacious details or intimate photographs is disproportionate and unacceptable. The latter, even if accompanying a legitimate disclosure of the sexual relationship, would be too obtrusive and demeaning.'[4]

The answer in each case is likely to turn on considerations of proportionality, as Lord Hoffmann explained in the *Campbell* case:

'How are they [the freedom of the press and the common law right of the individual to protect personal information] to be reconciled in a particular case? There is in my view no question of automatic priority. Nor is there a presumption in favour of one rather than the other. The question is rather the extent to which it is necessary to qualify the one right in order to protect the underlying value which is protected by the other. And the extent of the qualification must be proportionate to the need.'[5]

In *Re S (A Child)*, the earlier authorities were analysed as supporting four propositions:

'First, neither article has as such precedence over the other. Secondly, where the values under the two articles are in conflict, an intense focus on the comparative importance of the specific rights being claimed in the individual case is necessary. Thirdly, the justifications for interfering with or restricting each right must be taken into account. Finally, the proportionality test must be applied to each.'[6]

---

1   *Campbell v MGN Ltd* [2004] 2 AC 457.

2   *Re (S) (A Child) (Identification: Restrictions on Publication)* [2005] 1 AC 593.

3   Related cases include *Venables v News Group Newspapers Ltd* [2001] Fam 430; *X (A Woman formerly known as Mary Bell) v O'Brien* [2003] EMLR 37 (lifetime protection for the identity of a person convicted of a notorious crime, and her daughter, from media disclosure granted after balancing the press's right of freedom of expression under Art 10 with Art 8 rights); *R (Stanley) v Metropolitan Police Commissioner* [2005] EMLR 3 (publication by the police and a local authority of details of anti-social behaviour orders obtained against youths in the form of posters, an article in a tenants' newsletter and a posting on the authority's website did not violate the youths' rights under Art 8, since publication was justified under Art 8(2)); *Carr v News Group Newspapers Ltd* [2005] EWHC 971 (continuation of injunction against media disclosure of new identity and whereabouts of person convicted of notorious crime); *Re Trinity Mirror plc* [2008] QB 770 (order preventing identitification of person convicted of child pornography offences: order discharged); *Re British Broadcasting Corporation* [2010] 1 AC 145 (order preventing identification of defendant in television programme suggesting consideration of retrials of acquitted defendants: order discharged); *Re Guardian News and Media Ltd* [2010] 2 AC 697 (orders preventing identification of suspected terrorists: orders discharged); *Secretary of State for the Home Department v AP (No 2)* [2010] 1 WLR 1652 (anonymity of a successful appellant against a control order continued); *Independent News*

and Media Ltd and others v A [2010] 1 WLR 2262 (media seeking authorisation to attend Court of Protection hearing concerning well-known musician with view to court later granting permission to report the proceedings: authorisation granted); and *Donald v Ntuli* [2011] 1 WLR 294 (whether 'super-injunction', ie prohibition on disclosure of the existence of the proceedings, was justified; and whether anonymisation of parties justified).

4   *Re (S) (A Child) (Identification: Restrictions on Publication)* [2005] 1 AC 593, at para 60. See also *Donald v Ntuli* [2011] 1 WLR 294.

5   *Re (S) (A Child) (Identification: Restrictions on Publication)* [2005] 1 AC 593, at para 55.

6   *Re (S) (A Child) (Identification: Restrictions on Publication)* [2005] 1 AC 593, at para 17 per Lord Steyn.

6.137 This area of the law remains in a state of evolution[1]. The implications of the *Von Hannover v Germany* judgment, in particular, remain to be fully considered within the United Kingdom[2]. Its fullest consideration to date was in *R (Wood) v Commissioner of Police of the Metropolis,* where Laws LJ (with whose opinion on this issue the other members of the Court of Appeal agreed) observed that the mere taking of someone's photograph in a public street had been consistently held to be no interference with privacy. The snapping of the shutter of itself breached no rights, unless something more was added. The real vice in the *Von Hannover* case (and in the domestic cases of *Campbell*[3] and *Murray*[4]) was the fact or threat of publication in the media, and not just the snapping of the shutter. Laws LJ added:

> 'I would certainly acknowledge that the circumstances in which a photograph is taken in a public place may of themselves turn the event into one in which article 8 is not merely engaged but grossly violated. The act of taking the picture, or more likely pictures, may be intrusive or even violent, conducted by means of hot pursuit, face-to-face confrontation, pushing, shoving, bright lights, barging into the affected person's home. The subject of the photographers' interest—in the case I am contemplating, there will usually be a bevy of picture-takers—may be seriously harassed and perhaps assaulted. He or she may certainly feel frightened and distressed. Conduct of this kind is simply brutal. It may well attract other remedies, civil or criminal, under our domestic law. It would plainly violate article 8(1), and I can see no public interest justification for it under article 8(2).'

Laws LJ concluded that the bare act of taking pictures, by whoever done, was not of itself capable of engaging Article 8(1) unless there were aggravating circumstances. On the facts of the case, Article 8(1) was engaged:

> 'The Metropolitan Police, visibly and with no obvious cause, chose to take and keep photographs of an individual going about his lawful business in the streets of London. This action is a good deal more than the snapping of the shutter. The police are a state authority. And as I have said, the claimant could not and did not know why they were doing it and what use they might make of the pictures.

> In these circumstances I would hold that article 8 is engaged. On the particular facts the police action, unexplained at the time it happened and carrying as it did the implication that the images would be kept and used, is a sufficient intrusion by the state into the individual's own space, his integrity, as to amount to a prima facie

violation of article 8(1). It attains a sufficient level of seriousness and in the circumstances the claimant enjoyed a reasonable expectation that his privacy would not be thus invaded. ' [5]

---

1   Early cases under the HRA 1998, such as *A v B plc* [2001] 1 WLR 2341 and *Theakston v MGN Ltd* [2002] EMLR 22, should be treated with caution. Recent appellate cases include *McKennitt v Ash* [2008] QB 73 (book disclosing details of musician's private life, written by former friend); *Browne v Associated Newspapers Ltd* [2008] QB 103 (information concerning personal life and business activities of CEO of BP disclosed by former sexual partner); *Wales v Associated Newspapers Ltd* [2008] Ch 57 (confidential journal of Prince of Wales); and *Donald v Ntuli* [2011] 1 WLR 294 (information concerning relationship between pop star and former girlfriend). For discussion, see Tugendhat and Christie (eds) *The Law of Privacy and the Media* (2006).

2   See para **6.131** above. In relation to celebrity photographs, see *Campbell v MGN Ltd* [2004] 2 AC 457; *John v Associated Newspapers Ltd* [2006] EMLR 27 (no expectation of privacy when shopping); and *Murray v Express Newspapers Ltd* [2009] Ch 481. It appears that the Press Complaints Commission is interpreting Clause 3 (Privacy) and its Code of Practice in a manner which reflects the *von Hannover* judgment: see eg *Elle Macpherson (Hello!) Adjudication* (29 January 2007). Protection against the taking and publication of photographs without consent is considerably more advanced elsewhere in Europe: see eg Case 945/05–6, [2006] EuroCLY 1743 [Portugal] (publication of photograph had no connection with professional activities of well-known professional photographer, and legal protection accorded to home and surroundings); Case 959/2004, [2004] NV 52/1590, [2005] EuroCLY 1708 [Greece] (taking photograph or making an artistic reproduction of an individual without consent amounted to violation of personality); but cf *S v Societé P* [2002] Dalloz Jur 1380, [2002] EuroCLY 2013 [France] (right of newspaper to publish photograph without consent of person charged with an offence). French law (Art 9, Code Civil) enshrines 'le droit à son image' as a category of aspects of personality which are protected, and thus a French newspaper could not claim that publishing photographs with a story was merely 'peripheral'. The *von Hannover* judgment was applied in *Rudolph v Qvortrup* (431/2008) (10 June 2010) (HR) [2010] UFR 2010 H [Denmark] (publication of photographs of pregnant media personality while bathing topless at a deserted beach). See further Delaney and Murphy 'Towards Common Principles Relating to the Protection of Privacy Rights? An Analysis of Recent Developments in England and France and before the European Court of Human Rights' [2007] EHRLR 568.

3   *Campbell v MGN Ltd* [2004] 2 AC 457.

4   *Murray v Express Newspapers Ltd* [2009] Ch 481.

5   *R (Wood) v Commissioner of Police of the Metropolis* [2010] 1 WLR 123 at paras 34 and 45–46 per Laws LJ.

6.138 In relation to the protection of reputation, the domestic law of defamation has evolved a set of criteria – such as justification, fair comment and qualified privilege – for achieving a fair balance between competing rights and interests. This body of law appears to remain largely compliant with modern Strasbourg jurisprudence, at least in its essentials[1]. It is to be noted that, in domestic law, a claim brought in defamation is intrinsically different in character from one brought for misuse of private information[2]. In a privacy claim, truth does not provide a defence: the wrong consists in intrusion into personal areas of a person's life. For the same reason, damages for loss of reputation are inappropriate in a privacy claim. It is also likely to be easier to obtain an interim remedy on privacy grounds, since in most cases of tabloid gossip it will be easier to decide whether the pursuer is likely to succeed at trial, as required by s 12(3) of the HRA 1998[3].

1 See eg *Nicol v Caledonian Newspapers Ltd* 2002 SC 493 (qualified privilege); *Westcott v Westcott* [2009] QB 407 (absolute privilege).

2 They may however be combined, as in *Applause Store Productions Ltd v Raphael* [2008] EWHC 1781 (QB).

3 See eg *Terry v Persons Unknown* [2010] EMLR 16; cf *X v British Broadcasting Corporation* 2005 SLT 796. As to s 12(3), see para **1.102** above.

Private life issues: sexuality

6.139 Sexuality concerns a most intimate aspect of private life. Thus any interference in this area such as the imposition of a sanction in respect of homosexual behaviour will call for the most searching scrutiny of the reasons advanced for this[1]. Further, the justification for any 'pressing social need' for discriminatory treatment based upon sexual orientation is likely to pose particular difficulties for a state under Article 14[2]. Here most clearly is an illustration of the Convention as a 'living instrument'. Advances in European social attitudes are of considerable relevance, and some of the earliest case law must certainly now be disregarded[3]. In this area, too, are applications of the hallmarks of pluralism, tolerance and broadmindedness as the keystones of European democratic society[4]. Even when claims concern respect for family life (as opposed to private life) there is recent indication of a more progressive jurisprudence[5].

1 See further Hale 'Homosexual Rights' [2004] CFLQ 125.

2 See further paras **3.115–3.118** above.

3 Eg 7215/75, *X v the United Kingdom* (1978) DR 19, 66 (age of homosexual consent fixed at 21 justified as being necessary for the protection of the rights of others); 17279/90, *W Z v Austria* (13 May 1992) (prohibition of males over the age of 19 from engaging in homosexual acts with a person of the same sex who was under that age compatible with the Convention): reports cited and now doubted in 25186/94, *Sutherland v United Kingdom* (1 July 1997) (report of the Commission, paras 59–60). See also *Sutherland v United Kingdom* (striking out) [GC] (22 March 2001),

4 *Lustig-Prean and Beckett v United Kingdom* (27 September 1999), para 80. See also *Alekseyev v Russia* 2010-..., paras 68–88 (refusals to permit 'gay pride' parades following receipt of petitions opposing the marches: violation of Art 11 on account of decision-making based upon the basis of prevailing moral values of the majority and in the absence of measures to assess public safety risks or of the prosecution of those making threats of violence, the purpose of the parades being to promote respect for human rights and tolerance).

5 See eg *EB v France* [GC] 2008-..., discussed at para **6.144** below; and *Kozak v Poland* (2 March 2010), paras 95–99 (refusal to recognise the right of a homosexual to succeed to the tenancy of his partner's flat following his partner's death: the Court had to take into account developments in modern society, and in light of the narrow margin of appreciation in cases involving a difference in treatment based on sexuality, it found a violation of Art 14 in conjunction with Art 8). But note the caution highlighted in paras **6.04** and **6.22** above. For domestic discussion, see *Ghaidan v Godin-Mendoza* [2004] 2 AC 557 (same-sex partner of a deceased statutory tenant is entitled to the same rights of succession as a heterosexual partner under the Rent Act 1977 as 'a person who was living with [the deceased] as his husband or wife' as there is no rational ground for any discriminatory treatment); see also the earlier case before the Human Rights Act entered into force of *Fitzpatrick v Sterling Housing Association Ltd* [2001] 1 AC 27 (same-sex partner was entitled to succeed to an assured tenancy).

Criminalisation of homosexuality

6.140 The effect of criminally sanctioning homosexual acts reinforces the misapprehension and general prejudice of the public and increases the anxiety and guilt feelings of homosexuals. In consequence, to qualify as a 'victim' for the purposes of Article 34, it is merely necessary to show that an individual runs a risk of being directly affected by such legislation, for example, by requiring to reveal sexual identity even although no prosecution is likely or even legally possible[1]. Many of the leading cases have challenged British law. In *Dudgeon v United Kingdom*, the European Court of Human Rights examined Northern Ireland legislation which treated homosexual behaviour between consenting adult males as a criminal offence. While the applicant had not actually faced prosecution, the Court accepted that the existence of this law was enough to constitute an interference with his Article 8 rights on account of the continuous and direct effect it had on his private life. Further, the state could not show sufficient indication of a pressing social need for such legislation either on account of risk of harm to any vulnerable section of the community or in order to protect public morals. The fact that members of the public could be 'shocked, offended or disturbed' could not by itself justify the prosecution of private homosexual acts[2]. Subsequently, in *ADT v United Kingdom*, the Court extended this approach to criminal laws which penalised homosexual activities in private involving more than two individuals. The applicant had been convicted of gross indecency after video tapes showing the applicant and four others engaging in consensual homosexual acts not involving any physical harm had been seized by the police. The Court considered that the circumstances did not justify any state interference on the grounds of protection of health or morals. Taking into account the restricted number of participants, as well as the fact that the videos were for personal consumption and would not enter the public domain, the activities were considered genuinely 'private'. In short, there were insufficient reasons both for the existence of the English legislation criminalising homosexual acts between men in private, and more particularly, for the present prosecution and conviction[3]. In light of this decision, the Convention Rights (Compliance) (Scotland) Act 2001 repealed the relevant section of the equivalent Scottish statute[4].

1   *SL v Austria* (dec) (22 November 2001) (prohibition of homosexual acts involving an adult male and a minor between 14 and 18 even although only the adult could be prosecuted). See also *SL v Austria* 2003-I, paras 35–46 (violation of Art 14 in conjunction with Art 8); and *L and V v Austria* 2003-I, paras 43–54.

2   *Dudgeon v United Kingdom* (1981) A 45, paras 41 and 60 at para 60. It is not entirely clear the extent to which an applicant must show that he falls within a class of person who is liable to prosecution under such legislation to qualify as a 'victim'. See for earlier discussion *Sutherland v United Kingdom* [GC] (22 March 2001), report of the Commission, paras 34–37; and 10389/83, *Johnson v United Kingdom* (1986) DR 47, 72 (violation of respect for private life requires that domestic law continuously and directly affects his private life). See also *Norris v Ireland* (1988) A 142, para 46; *Modinos v Cyprus* (1993) A 259, para 25.

3   *ADT v United Kingdom* 2000-IX, paras 37–39; see Davenport 'None of the Law's Business' (2000) 150 NLJ 1233.

4   Ie the Criminal Law (Consolidation) (Scotland) Act 1995, s 13(2)(a).

6.141 However, the notion of 'private life' in the area of sexual practices 'cannot be stretched indefinitely', as illustrated by *Laskey, Jaggard and Brown v United Kingdom*. The applicants sought to challenge their convictions for assault in respect of consensual sado-masochistic acts involving over 40 other homosexual men over a ten-year period. The Court observed that Article 8 did not extend to every form of sexual activity carried out behind closed doors, and questioned whether the organisation and scope of the activities could be said to have taken them outwith the character of 'private life'. Without deciding this point, it distinguished other cases which had concerned only private sexual behaviour from the present application which involved 'significant injury or degree of wounding which could not be characterised as trifling or transient'. Taking into account the serious nature of the harm inflicted, the Court considered that both relevant and sufficient reasons had been established for the prosecution and conviction of the applicants, and that these measures were proportionate to the aim of protecting health[1]. That the applicants and other participants were all homosexual males was thus of incidental relevance; and this case is best considered as an illustration of the principle that the scope of Article 8 in the area of private life is not unlimited[2].

1   *Laskey, Jaggard and Brown v United Kingdom* 1997-I, paras 36–51 at 45. The Court specifically stated (at para 51) that it did not consider it necessary to consider the issue in respect of protection of morals, but this finding, however, 'should not be understood as calling into question the prerogative of the State on moral grounds to seek to deter acts of the kind in question'. See also *KA and AD v Belgium* (17 February 2005), paras 78–88 (conviction for sado-masochistic practices in which ending of consent of the 'victim' had not been respected and suspended sentences of imprisonment and fines: no violation, the practices not having taken place in conditions in which safeguards were permitted, and the sentences not being disproportionate).

2   Cf *Laskey, Jaggard and Brown v United Kingdom* 1997-I, concurring opinion of Judge Pettiti: 'The concept of private life cannot be stretched indefinitely' and 'the fact that the behaviour concerned takes place on private premises does not suffice to ensure complete immunity and impunity. ... The protection of private life means the protection of a person's intimacy and dignity, not the protection of his baseness or the promotion of criminal immoralism'. See also *Pay v United Kingdom* (dec) (16 September 2008) (dismissal of probation officer who worked with sex offenders following discovery that he had engaged in sadomasochistic performances in a private members' club both live and on the internet: inadmissible, without the need to determine whether 'private life' was engaged as performances were broadcast over the internet although anonymised, as employees owe a duty of loyalty, reserve and discretion, particularly in view of the sensitive nature of the applicant's employment and his refusal to curb even those aspects of private life most likely to enter into the public domain).

Discrimination

6.142 Other cases have considered the impact of discriminatory policies against homosexuals. Such policies can give rise to questions under Article 8 alone, or this guarantee taken along with Article 14's general prohibition of discrimination[1]. Inequalities in treatment based upon sexual orientation are subject to particular scrutiny[2]. Thus differences in the ages of consent as between heterosexuals and homosexuals were considered a violation of Article 8 taken along with Article 14 by the Commission in *Sutherland v United Kingdom*. British law prohibited homosexual acts between males over the age of 16 but under the age of 18 years, while the minimum age for heterosexual activity was 16. The Commission could find no objective and reasonable justification for the distinction, even after attaching some weight to recent deliberations by the British Parliament which had considered the reasoning that certain young men between the ages of 16 and 18 did not yet have a settled sexual orientation and thus required protection. However, Parliament had also discussed current medical findings which now suggest that sexual orientation is already fixed in both sexes by the age of 16, and thus the Commission could not accept arguments that the law required to protect young men over this age. In considering Parliament's conclusion that society was entitled to indicate disapproval of homosexual conduct by displaying its preference for children to 'follow a heterosexual way of life', the Commission applied the Court's dictum in *Dudgeon v United Kingdom*[3] that preference for a heterosexual lifestyle could not constitute an objective or reasonable justification[4]. Following this report, amending legislation was introduced which equalised the age of consent for homosexual acts, and thus the Court subsequently struck out the case[5].

1   For Art 14, see paras **3.115–3.118** above.

2   See further Besnard 'La Cour européenne des Droits de l'Homme et les Discriminations fondées sur le Sexe et l'Orientation sexuelle' in *Les Droits Sociaux et la CEDH: Actes du Colloque du Concours Habeas Corpus* (2010), pp 39–46; Brayson 'Gendered Rights on the European Stage: do Marginalized Groups find a "Voice" in the European Court of Human Rights?' (2010) 16 EPL 437; Commissioner for Human Rights *Discrimination on Grounds of Sexual Orientation and Gender Identity in Europe* (2011). See also EU Council Directive 2000/78/EC of 27 November 2000, establishing a general framework for equal treatment in employment and occupation by prohibiting discrimination in employment and vocational training on grounds of religion or belief, disability, age and sexual orientation.

3   *Dudgeon v United Kingdom* (1981) A 45.

4   *Sutherland v United Kingdom* [GC] (22 March 2001), report of the Commission, of 1 July 1997, paras 55–66.

5   *Sutherland v United Kingdom* [GC] (22 March 2001), paras 16–21. Domestic law was amended by virtue of the Sexual Offences (Amendment) Act 2000.

6.143 Changing societal attitudes in Britain, however, had little impact in its armed forces. In *Lustig-Prean and Beckett v United Kingdom*, the Ministry of Defence's absolute policy of excluding homosexuals from the armed forces was challenged by applicants who complained that the investigations into their homosexuality and leading to their subsequent discharge from the Royal Navy had violated Article 8. The English Court of Appeal had confirmed this policy to be lawful in terms of both domestic and applicable European Union law. In Strasbourg, the Court accepted that the purpose of the investigations and the policy of dismissal had been to ensure the operational effectiveness of the armed forces, matters covered by the aims of 'interests of national security' and 'prevention of disorder'. However, the Court could find no convincing or weighty reasons for the exceptionally intrusive character of the investigations which had continued well after the applicants had confirmed their sexual orientation. The state had further attempted to justify the policy of instant discharge irrespective of an individual's conduct or service record on the ground that the presence of open or suspected homosexuals in the armed forces would have had a substantial and negative effect on morale, citing an internal survey in support. The Court, however, was not persuaded of the reliability or validity of the report whose conclusions were based solely upon predisposed bias against a minority of service personnel of homosexual orientation. This could not amount to sufficient justification, given the lack of any concrete evidence to substantiate any alleged damage to morale or operational effectiveness[1].

1   *Lustig-Prean and Beckett v United Kingdom* (27 September 1999), paras 80–105. The Court declined to consider the Art 14 issue (at para 108), noting that this matter 'amounts in effect to the same complaint, albeit seen from a different angle'.

6.144 A similar distrust of decision-making on the grounds of sexuality is also obvious in cases involving the determination of many family law issues. For example, in *Salgueiro da Silva Mouta v Portugal*, the refusal to grant custody of the daughter of a marriage to the father, who was by then living in a homosexual relationship, on the ground that such an environment could not be a healthy one in which to raise a child, was considered a violation of Article 8 taken together with Article 14[1]. It is also now clear following *EB v France* that denying an unmarried homosexual man the necessary prior approval before he can adopt a child solely on the basis of his sexuality is incompatible with the Convention. This will be so even although there is not necessarily any pre-existing family link between an individual and a child[2]. Similar principles now apply in respect of the legal regulation of rights of succession arising upon the death of one partner in a homosexual relationship[3].

1   *Salgueiro da Silva Mouta v Portugal* 1999-IX, paras 21–36. It is thus doubtful whether the dicta in *T, Petitioner* 1997 SLT 724 at 734 concerning Arts 8 and 14 reflect the current interpretation of the Convention.

2   *EB v France* [GC] 2008-…, paras 80–98 (refusal to allow a woman living in a lesbian relationship to adopt: requirement of paternal referent ran the risk of rendering ineffective the right of single persons to apply for authorisation and may have permitted arbitrary refusal or a pretext for rejecting the application on grounds of homosexuality) This judgment by a majority of 10 to 7, effectively overrules *Fretté v France* 2002-I, paras 37–43 (refusal of prior approval on 'choice of lifestyle' upheld by a majority of 4 to 3, the majority stressing the lack of a common European consensus, the minority considering that while the Convention did not contain a right to adopt as such, as France had made such a provision, the state was under a duty to ensure that 'no unwarranted discrimination' was made, particularly as 'all the countries of the Council of Europe are engaged in a determined attempt to counter all forms of prejudice and discrimination'). The sentiment of the majority in *Fretté* was perhaps an obvious aberration, but not to the sizeable minority in *EB*.

3   See *PB and JS v Austria* (22 July 2010), paras 25–44 (homosexual partner excluded from insurance cover programme as a dependent as a dependent could only be a related person or an unrelated person of the opposite sex: violation of Art 14 taken with Art 8); and *Kozack v Poland* (2 March 2010), paras 93–99 (denial of succession to the tenancy of a deceased partner's flat, the Court accepting that while the state was pursuing the legitimate aim of the protection of traditional families, it had to take into account developments in modern society).

Recognition of transsexuals

6.145 The European Court of Human Rights for long proved reluctant to recognise any positive duty to recognise an individual's change of sexual identity[1]. Repeated challenges by post-operative transsexuals to official refusal to alter or otherwise amend information recorded on an individual's birth certificate so as to help protect private life concerns generally failed, inevitably on the ground that any detriment suffered by an applicant was not sufficient to outweigh the recognition of a wide margin of appreciation on the part of states on account of the 'complex scientific, legal, moral and social issues' involved[2] unless the particular facts of the case allowed the Court to accept that these concerns had reached a particular degree of seriousness[3]. This was in some contrast to the Court's treatment of issues involving homosexuality, and despite an increasingly obvious trend elsewhere towards legal recognition of gender re-assignment. This area of jurisprudence was clearly one awaiting revision. In *Christine Goodwin v United Kingdom,* in deciding that there was now indeed a positive obligation on states to alter the register of births or to issue modified birth certificates, the Grand Chamber noted the clear and continuing international trend in favour of increased social acceptance and the legal recognition of the new sexual identity of post-operative transsexuals. 'The stress and alienation arising from a discordance between the position in society assumed by a post-operative transsexual and the status imposed by law which refuses to recognise the change of gender' in light of the existence of 'a conflict between social reality and law arises which places the transsexual in an anomalous position, in which he or she may experience feelings of vulnerability, humiliation and anxiety' were of some importance. It was also relevant that medical operations were state financed through the National Health Service, making it somewhat illogical for the state to refuse to recognise their legal implications[4].

---

1   See further Council of Europe *Transsexualism in Europe* (2000).

2   See *Rees v United Kingdom* (1986) A 106, para 37; *Cossey v United Kingdom* (1990) A 184, paras 32–42; *Stubbings v United Kingdom* 1996-IV, paras 63–67; *X, Y and Z v United Kingdom* 1997-II, paras 41–52, and *Sheffield and Horsham v United Kingdom* 1998-V, paras 49–61. For the autobiography of an applicant in one of the leading cases, see Cossey *My Story* (1991).See also *Bellinger v Bellinger* [2003] 2 AC 467 (post-operative male-to-female transsexual is to continue to be treated as a biological male for the purposes of marriage, but declaration of incompatibility made in respect of s 11(c) of the Matrimonial Causes Act 1973 as incompatible with Arts 8 & 12); and *Bellinger v United Kingdom* (dec) (11 July 2006) (case struck out in light of change to domestic law).

3   *B v France* (1992) A 232-C, paras 48–62 (differences in English and French law and practice were specifically discussed (at paras 49–51), thus justifying the distinguishing (but not the overruling) of earlier decisions involving the United Kingdom).

4   *Christine Goodwin v United Kingdom* [GC] 2002-VI, paras 74–93 at para 77; and see also the related case of *I v United Kingdom* [GC] (11 July 2002).

6.146 Following this judgment, the British Parliament enacted the Gender Recognition Act 2004. This permitted the issue of a full 'gender recognition certificate' necessary for the issue of a new birth certificate to persons who were single. Married applicants, on the other hand, could only obtain an interim certificate permitting its use as grounds for a divorce, but following a divorce, an applicant thereafter could apply to have the certificate translated into a full certificate. In the related cases of *R and F v United Kingdom* and *Parry v United Kingdom*, two husbands who had undergone gender reassignment surgery lodged complaints (along with their wives) that they would be forced to divorce in order to obtain proper recognition of their new gender status. The husband in *R and F* considered a civil partnership as being qualitatively different to a marriage; in the *Parry* case, the couple involved claimed to have deep religious convictions concerning the sanctity of marriage. The Court declared the cases inadmissible since it considered that the effects of the system had not been shown to be disproportionate. The question under Article 8 was whether the state had discharged its positive obligation to ensure the rights of the applicant husbands through the particular means chosen to give effective legal recognition to gender re-assignment. In deciding that a fair balance had been struck in the circumstances, the Court noted that the requirement for divorce in order to obtain full recognition was consequent upon domestic law's insistence that only persons of the opposite gender could marry: were the applicant couples to divorce, they could then enter into a civil partnership which would allow them to continue their relationships in the context of a legal status akin (if not identical) to marriage[1].

---

1   See also the similar case of *IA v United Kingdom* (dec) (28 November 2006). See also *Van Kück v Germany* 2003-VII, paras 73–85 (refusal to order private insurance company to reimburse costs of gender re-assignment surgery: violation of positive obligations, the burden of proving the necessity of treatment relating to a most intimate matter being disproportionate and courts having reached the conclusion that the applicant had deliberately caused the condition of transsexuality on the basis of general assumptions as to male and female behaviour rather than medical evidence); and *Grant v United Kingdom* 2006-VII, paras 40–43 (male to female post-operative transsexual denied recognition of status and payment of retirement pension at age applicable to other women: violation).

DECISIONS OF THE DOMESTIC COURTS ON SEXUALITY

6.147 A number of domestic cases concerned with the implications of Article 8 in the context of sexuality have already been noted[1]. It has been held in a Northern Irish case that legislation prohibiting sodomy between consenting adults was incompatible with Article 8[2]. On the other hand, the prosecution for rape of a 15-year-old boy who had had sexual intercourse with a 12-year-old girl was not incompatible with Article 8[3]. In relation to legislation restricting the scope for cross-examination of witnesses on their sexual history, it has been observed that 'a legal system which allows wide-ranging cross-examination about the sexual history of a complainant, clearly aimed at prejudicing the jury against her, while prohibiting any attack upon the sexual history of the accused person, might one day be held to be incompatible with the effective deterrence required by Article 8'[4]. A number of cases have concerned the dismissal of employees following their commission of sexual offences. In *X v Y*, it was accepted that Article 8 may be relevant to the determination of an unfair dismissal claim, even in a case concerned with a private employer. Article 8 was, however, held not to be engaged on the facts, since the sexual conduct in question had occurred in a public place[5].

1   See eg the discussion of *Ghaidan v Godin-Mendoza* [2004] 2 AC 557, and *Bellinger v Bellinger* [2003] 2 AC 467 at paras 6.139, and **6.06** and **6.145** above, respectively. In relation to discrimination on grounds related to sexual orientation and transsexualism, see paras **3.119** and **3.120** above, respectively.

2   *Re McR's Application for Judicial Review* [2002] NIQB 58.

3   *R v G* [2009] 1 AC 92. See also *Watson v King* 2009 SCCR 323, where a challenge to a prosecution for having sex with a girl aged under 16, based on Art 6, was equally unsuccessful.

4   *DS v HM Advocate* 2007 SC (PC) 1 at para 95 per Baroness Hale of Richmond. See also *Judge v United Kingdom* (dec) (8 February 2011).

5   *X v Y* [2004] ICR 1634. Cf *Pay v United Kingdom* (dec) (16 September 2008).

Prisoners' rights

Family life

6.148 Article 8 has been interpreted as requiring prison authorities to assist prisoners to maintain effective contact with their close relatives and friends[1], but always having regard to the 'ordinary and reasonable requirements of imprisonment and to the resultant degree of discretion' which must be accorded to the national authorities in regulating contact in order to maintain security and good order[2]. The notion of implied limitations on prisoners' rights through loss of liberty which influenced early Commission decisions and reports has long been rejected[3]. Thus an automatic ban on exercising parental rights as a direct consequence of imprisonment for an offence wholly unrelated to questions of parental responsibility and where there had been no allegation concerning a lack of care on the applicant's part or ill-treatment of his children represents 'a moral reprimand aimed at punishing the convicted person rather than a child-protection measure'[4]. However, Article 8 has been of reduced utility where a prisoner has sought increased visiting rights[5] or location in a prison closer to his home[6]. In *Boyle and Rice v United Kingdom*, for example, the Court considered that an annual visit entitlement which totalled 12 visits of one hour each did not violated the guarantee, nor that the particular circumstances in which one of the applicants had been refused compassionate leave supported any such claim[7], although a prisoner can only be denied permission to attend the funeral of a parent where there are compelling reasons for refusing this and no alternative solution such as escorted leave can be found[8]. Nor does a prisoner have an absolute right to be accorded artificial insemination facilities[9].

1   See eg *Ferla v Poland* (20 May 2008), paras 42–49 (strict restrictions placed upon visits from a remand prisoner's wife on account of the possibility of calling her as a prosecution witness could have been initially justifiable, but their continued application had not been so, the authorities not having considered any alternative means: violation); *Gülmez v Turkey* (20 May 2008), paras 45–55 (restrictions on family visits on account of disciplinary proceedings for almost 12 months: violation); and *Petrov v Bulgaria* (22 May 2008), paras 39–45 (a prisoner was prevented from contacting his partner by telephone as only married prisoners could do

so: violation of Art 14 taken with Art 8); and *Moiseyev v Russia* (9 October 2008), paras 246–259 (restrictions on family visits to a remand prisoner not prescribed by law in light of the unfettered discretion of the investigator to determine family visits without defining the circumstances in which they could be refused to visit him: violation). For general discussion of prisoners' rights under the Convention, see Murdoch *The Treatment of Prisoners: European Standards* (2006), pp 237–248.

2   *Boyle and Rice v United Kingdom* (1988) A 131, at para 74. Interferences must be prescribed by law: *Poltoratskiy v Ukraine* 2003-V, paras 153–162 (restrictions on visits and correspondence were at the material time governed by an instruction which was an internal and unpublished document not accessible to the public, and thus the interferences were not 'in accordance with the law').

3   *Golder v United Kingdom* (1975) A 18, at para 44. See also *Lind v Russia* (6 December 2007), paras 92–99 (remand prisoner restricted to a one minute conversation in a language his father had difficulty understanding when bidding farewell to his father who was about to die through euthanasia: violation, as the request for release should have been examined with particular attention and scrutiny in light of the exceptional circumstances of the case and the strong humanitarian considerations involved).

4   *Sabou and Pircalab v Romania* (28 September 2004), paras 46–49 at para 48.

5   Eg 9054/80, *X v United Kingdom* (1982) DR 30, 113 (restrictions on visits with persons campaigning about prison medical treatment did not violate Art 8).

6   Eg 14462/88, *Ballantyne v United Kingdom* (12 April 1991) (decision to place applicant in Peterhead prison several hundred miles distant from his family rather than in a local prison; Art 8 did not confer a general right on prisoners to choose the place of their detention, and in any case the applicant's move to a prison offering a more secure regime was as a consequence of his behaviour; separation from family is an inevitable consequence of imprisonment: inadmissible); 23241/94, *Hacisüleymanoglu v Italy* (1994) DR 79, 121 (the European Convention on Transfer of Sentenced Prisoners does not require a state to transfer a prisoner; and the distance between a prisoner and his family is an inevitable consequence of detention); 15817/89, *Wakefield v United Kingdom* (1990) DR 66, 251 (engagement did not constitute 'family life' but did involve 'private life'; and the conditions imposed on the visits by a prisoner temporarily transferred to a Scottish prison with his fianceé were considered justified); and *Selmani v Switzerland* (dec) 2001-VII (deportation of a prisoner's wife and children did not give rise to an Art 8 issue: while separation and distance from families are inevitable consequences of detention, where exceptionally the detention of a prisoner at a distance from his family which renders any visit highly difficult if not impossible may constitute an interference with family life, the lack of means to travel could not be taken into account for practical reasons. Here, in any case, the prisoner was serving a short sentence and communication through writing and telephone was possible).

7   *Boyle and Rice v United Kingdom* (1988) A 131, paras 74–82.

8   *Płoski v Poland* (12 November 2002), paras 35–39.

9   Eg *Dickson v United Kingdom* [GC] 2007-XIII, para 81, discussed at para **6.08** above.

Censorship of prisoners' correspondence

6.149 The guarantee has proved to be of most use in challenging censorship of prisoners' mail where Court judgments have led to the progressive reduction of the ability of state authorities to interfere with prisoners' correspondence to the extent strictly necessary to meet state interests[1]. The issue has been of particular relevance in respect of communications with legal advisers. In *Campbell v United Kingdom*, correspondence with a solicitor which related to various civil and criminal matters and with the European Commission on Human Rights had been interfered with by the Scottish prison authorities on the ground that the only way to establish whether correspondence contained prohibited material was to read it. The Court considered that while the state could justify the interferences as falling within the legitimate state aim of preventing disorder or crime, the necessity of the particular interferences had not been established. 'The fact that the opportunity to write and to receive letters is sometimes the prisoner's only link to the outside world' could not be overlooked; further, consultation with a lawyer required to take place under circumstances 'which favour full and uninhibited discussion'. Only when state authorities had reasonable cause to believe that a letter from a legal representative 'contains an illicit enclosure which the normal means of detection have failed to disclose' should a letter be opened – but not read. Any such action had also to be accompanied by 'suitable guarantees' such as opening the letter in the presence of the prisoner[2]. A similar principle of proportionality applies in regard to other correspondence: while 'some measure of control is not of itself incompatible with the Convention ... the resulting interference must not exceed what is required by the legitimate aim pursued'[3].

1   In particular, in *Golder v United Kingdom* (1975) A 18; *Silver and Others v United Kingdom* (1983) A 61; *Campbell and Fell v United Kingdom* (1984) A 80; *Boyle and Rice v United Kingdom* (1988) A 131; *Schönenberger and Durmaz v Switzerland* (1988) A 137. The Scottish case of *McCallum v United Kingdom* (1990) A 183, paras 10–31, involved a challenge to the stopping of letters written to the applicant's solicitor, his Member of Parliament, a journalist, an academic, and a public prosecutor. The state conceded – as in *Boyle and Rice* – that these interferences constituted breaches of Art 8. See too 10621/83, *McComb v United Kingdom* (1986) DR 50, 81 (friendly settlement involving the introduction of new prison standing orders narrowing the power of the authorities to censor correspondence with a legal adviser: but these standing orders were subsequently found wanting in the later case of *Campbell v United Kingdom* (1992) A 233)); *Peers v Greece* 2001-I, paras 81–84 at 84 (risk of drugs being contained in a letter from the Secretariat of the European Commission on Human Rights was 'so negligible that it must be discounted': violation); *Cotleţ v Romania* (3 June 2003) paras 56–65. Cf *Christi v Portugal* (dec) (2 October 2003) (prohibition of communicating in Urdu with family members in Pakistan for security reasons: inadmissible as the prisoner had rejected an offer to find and bear the costs of a translator).

2   *Campbell v United Kingdom* (1992) A 233, paras 44–53 at para 48.

3   *Pfeifer and Plankl v Austria* (1992) A 227, paras 46–48 at 46 (deletion of jokes about prison staff which were considered insulting). See too 8231/78, *T v United Kingdom* (1982) DR 28, 5 (blanket prohibition on communication of artistic or scientific material not justified); *Calogero Diana v Italy* 1996-V; *Domenichini v Italy* 1996-V, paras 32–33 (too much latitude left to the authorities in deciding the scope and manner of the exercise of their discretion in censoring mail). For further discussion, see *Demirtepe v France* 1999-IX; *Messina v Italy (no 2)* 2000-X; *Rinzivillo v Italy* (21 December 2000); *Doerga v Netherlands* (27 April 2004), paras 43–54 (interception of prisoner's telephone conversations and retention of records on court order despite internal prison regulations requiring the immediate erasure: violation); *Petrov v Bulgaria* (22 May 2008), paras 39–45 (systematic monitoring of all of a prisoner's correspondence: violation); and *Szuluk v United Kingdom* 2009-..., paras 43–55 (monitoring of non-high risk prisoner's correspondence with his medical adviser but no actual or likely abuse of the confidentiality of his communications: violation). For discussion of interference with the correspondence of mental health patients, see *Herczegfalvy v Austria* (1992) A 244, paras 88–91 (forwarding of letters to a patient's guardian to decide whether the letters should be sent on had no legal basis: violation).

Other aspects of imprisonment

6.150 The Court has proved reluctant to become involved in matters of internal prison administration, preferring instead to recognise a high degree of discretion to deal with such matters on the part of prison authorities. Similarly, the maintenance of internal security may be readily accepted as justification for intrusions into private life, such as the imposition of solitary confinement[1], strip searches or drug testing[2], providing always that prescribed procedures are followed[3]. Other aspects of prisoners' rights have been discussed above[4].

1   8317/78, *McFeely v United Kingdom* 20 DR 44, para 82.

2   21780/93, *TV v Finland* DR 76, 140 (disclosure of prisoner's HIV status to prison staff was an interference with respect for his private life; but justified as necessary, and no evidence of any wider disclosure); 21132/93 *Peters v Netherlands* (1994) DR 77, 75; and 20872/92, *A B v Switzerland* (1995) DR 80, 66 (compulsory medical intervention, in this case urine tests undergone by prisoners, constitutes an interference with respect for private life; but is justified as necessary for the prevention of crime and disorder); and *Matter v Slovakia* (5 July 1999), paras 64–72 (forcible examination of mental health detainee justified on the grounds of his own interests).

3   Cf *Wainwright v United Kingdom* 2006-X, paras 45–49 (strip-searching of a remand prisoner's mother and disabled brother by means of visible examination of the mother's sexual organs and anus and the physical examination of the brother's penis but in disregard of prescribed procedures: violation).

4   See eg paras **6.08** (marry and found a family), **6.125** (environmental protection), and **6.97** above (covert surveillance).

Standard-setting by the European Committee for the Prevention of Torture

6.151 The Committee for the Prevention of Torture and Inhuman or Degrading Treatment or Punishment (the CPT)[1] has had some impact upon prison policy in Council of Europe member states. Its starting-point is that the maintenance of contact between a prisoner and his family and close friends is not only a fundamental human right but is also of crucial importance in helping ensure that the prisoner's eventual re-integration into his family and community will be effective. Thus limitations on visits, written correspondence or telephone conversations should be based solely upon security concerns of an appreciable nature or resource considerations, and the aim should be the promotion of contact. The Committee's recommendations to states stress that there should be some flexibility as regards the application of rules on visits and telephone contacts where a prisoner is located some distance from his family and where in consequence it is difficult for regular visits to take place. Such prisoners, for example, should be permitted to accumulate visiting time entitlement, and enjoy enhanced telephone contact. Letters sent by inmates should not be immediately recognisable as having been sent from a prison, visiting accommodation should also be appropriate to facilitate communication and, where families live some distance from a prison, some flexibility in visiting arrangements should be possible[2]. The CPT has also been prepared to consider specific problems facing non-nationals, and has encouraged states to utilise the

European Convention on the Transfer of Sentenced Persons to permit the remainder of sentences to be served in home institutions.

1   See para **2.86** above.

2   *Second General Report*, CPT/Inf (92) 3, paras 51–52; see further Murdoch *The Treatment of Prisoners: European Standards* (2006) pp 330–331.

DOMESTIC DECISIONS ON PRISONERS' RIGHTS UNDER ARTICLE 8

6.152 Domestic cases concerned with prisoners' Article 8 rights in relation to contact with their children[1], visits from other persons[2], and telephone calls[3] have been considered above. In relation to correspondence, it was held in *R (Daly) v Secretary of State for the Home Department* that a practice of searching prisoners' legally privileged correspondence in their absence, in order to check that nothing had been written on it or concealed within it which might endanger prison security, was both unlawful under the common law and a violation of Article 8[4]. In *R (Ponting) v Governor of HM Prison Whitemoor*, it was held to be justifiable under Article 8(2) to impose restrictions upon a prisoner's use of a computer[5]. Rules permitting the physical restraint of young offenders for the purpose of good order and discipline were held to violate Article 8 in a case where the Secretary of State was unable to establish that such restrant was necessary for that purpose[6].

1   See para **6.74** above.

2   See para **6.20** above.

3   See para **6.100** above.

4   *R (Daly) v Secretary of State for the Home Department* [2001] 2 AC 532.

5   *R (Ponting) v Governor of HM Prison Whitemoor* [2002] EWCA Civ 224.

6   *R (C (A Minor)) v Secretary of State for Justice* [2009] QB 657.

ARTICLE 2 OF PROTOCOL NO 1: THE RIGHT TO EDUCATION

Introduction

6.153 In providing for a child's right to education, Article 2 of Protocol no 1 of the ECHR recognises the duty upon a state to respect parents' religious and philosophical convictions in exercising its powers and responsibilities in this area. 'It is in the discharge of a natural duty towards their children – parents being primarily responsible for the "education and teaching" of their children – that parents may require the State to respect their religious and philosophical convictions', and thus this right 'corresponds to a responsibility closely linked to the enjoyment and the exercise of the right to education'[1]. There is an obvious link between the provision of education and respect for private and family life under Article 8, and also with guarantees of freedom of thought, conscience and religion under Article 9 and of freedom of expression under Article 10[2]. The general prohibition of discrimination in the enjoyment of Convention rights in terms of Article 14 can also give rise to considerations of equal treatment in the provision of education[3]. The overall thrust of the jurisprudence, though, suggests that Strasbourg takes a rather cautious approach to interpretation of this guarantee, reflecting the Court's awareness of limited judicial competence in an aspect of Convention protection which transgresses upon social and cultural human rights rather than one that is firmly located within the sphere of civil and political rights[4].

1   *Kjeldsen, Busk Madsen and Pedersen v Denmark* (1976) A 23, at para 52.

2   *Kjeldsen, Busk Madsen and Pedersen v Denmark* (1976) A 23, at para 52 (provision to be read alongside Arts 8–10 and thus curriculum matters are in principle for the state); *Belgian Linguistic case* (1968) A 6, at para 7: (state educational measures which affect Art 8 rights in an unjustifiable manner, eg 'by separating parents from their children in an arbitrary way' are open to challenge).

3   Cf *Kjeldsen, Busk Madsen and Pedersen v Denmark* (1976) A 23, para 56 (provision of sex education is not similar to religious instruction and was consistent with Art 14's requirements).

4   For recent illustration of this point, see *Lautsi v Italy* [GC] (18 March 2011), paras 63–77 (the presence of crucifixes in state-run school classrooms did not exceed the state's margin of appreciation in determining how to ensure education in conformity with the religious and philosophical convictions of parents). See further Landau 'Reflections on the Right to Education: the European Perspective' in Kohen (ed) *Promoting Justice, Human Rights and Conflict Resolution through International Law: Liber Amicorum Lucius Caflisch* (2007), pp 281–305.

The right to education

6.154 Article 2 of Protocol no 1 first provides that 'no person shall be denied the right to education'. This sentence dominates the article: any interpretation given to the right of parents to have philosophical convictions taken into account must not conflict with the primary right to education enjoyed by the child[1]. In essence, the right to education involves a right of access to educational facilities existing at a given time[2]. However, this right may be made subject to restrictions[3], and the responsibilities of states in determining the nature of provision is respected as long as regulation does not injure the very substance of the guarantee[4]. In other words, providing there is no 'denial of the substance of the right at issue' and that the right to access to educational facilities is a real rather than an illusory one[5], the provision cannot support a claim to be educated in a particular language[6] or in a particular country[7] or to be educated in a private school[8]. Nor can it support a claim of a private school to receive state funding[9] or to be exempted from ordinary planning controls[10], although the guarantee does protect the right to establish and to run private schools subject to state regulation to ensure the quality of education[11]. Nor does a requirement that students should belong to an association interfere with their right to education[12]. The guarantee also extends to official recognition of completed studies in order to be able to derive profit from the education received[13], although any such recognition of studies completed abroad may be subject to an examination in terms of domestic regulation[14].

1   *Campbell and Cosans v United Kingdom* (1982) A 48, para 36; *Martins Casimiro and Cerveira*

Ferreira v Luxembourg (dec) (27 April 1999) (a refusal to grant a general exemption from attending school on Saturdays on religious grounds to the sons of the applicants, Seventh Day Adventists, could be regarded as an interference with the manifestation of belief, but no general dispensation could be recognised which would adversely affect a child's right to education which prevailed over the parents' rights to have their religious convictions taken into account: the application was deemed inadmissible); and *Konrad v Germany* (dec) 2006-XIII (denial of right of home education to Christian parents: inadmissible as parents may not refuse the right of education to children on the basis of their convictions).

2   *Belgian Linguistic case* (1968) A 6, Law, para 4. Cf *Coster v United Kingdom* [GC] (18 January 2001), para 137; *Lee v United Kingdom* [GC] (18 January 2001), para 125; and *Jane Smith v United Kingdom* [GC] (18 January 2001), para 129 (complaints that enforcement of planning controls had effectively deprived the applicants' children and grandchildren of the right to education: no violation on account of the applicants having failed to substantiate their allegations). In respect of a child deprived of his liberty for educational supervision, the nature of the detention conditions must support this purpose to justify application of Art 5(1)(d): *Bouamar v Belgium* (1988) A 129, discussed at para **4.182** above.

3   *Köse and Others v Turkey* (dec) 2006-II (foreseeable prohibition on wearing of headscarf had been proportionate in view of constitutional principle of secularism and state's obligations to impart knowledge in an objective, critical and pluralist manner: inadmissible). Restrictions must also be in accordance with domestic law: *Timishev v Russia* 2005-XII, paras 63–67 (children's access to education was made conditional on the registration of their parent's place of residence in violation of domestic law: violation).

4   *Campbell and Cosans v United Kingdom* (1982) A 48, paras 40–41 (suspension of pupil for an academic year pending acceptance by parents that he should be punished in a manner contrary to their convictions was not reasonable and in any case fell outwith the state's power of regulation: violation of the child's right to education in terms of the first sentence, and of respect for parents' convictions in terms of the second sentence). The assumption of state responsibilities in the field of regulation of education is sufficient to establish liability in certain circumstances in respect of private educational institutions: cf *Costello-Roberts v United Kingdom* (1993) A 247-C, paras 27–28.

5   *Cyprus v Turkey* [GC] 2001-IV, paras 277–280 at paras 277 and 278 (children of Greek Cypriot parents living in an enclave in Turkish-occupied northern Cyprus wishing to continue their education in the Greek language beyond primary school had been required to transfer to secondary schools in the southern part of the island; while confirming that Prot 1, Art 2 'does not specify the language in which education must be conducted in order that the right to education be respected', the Court ruled that there had been a violation of the right to education in this case. The key point was that no appropriate secondary school facilities were available: while secondary schooling was available either in Turkish- or in English-language schools and thus there had been no denial of education in the strict sense, these options were unrealistic. The authorities had assumed responsibility for Greek-language primary schooling, and thus 'the failure ... to make continuing provision for it at the secondary-school level must be considered in effect to be a denial of the substance of the right at issue': violation of Prot 1, Art 2). See also *Catan and Others v Moldova and Russia* (dec) (15 June 2010) (closing of schools in 'Moldavian Republic of Transdniestra' for failing to use Cyrillic script: admissible).

6   *Belgian Linguistic case* (1968) A 6, Law, para 6.

7   *R (Holub) v Secretary of State for the Home Dept* [2001] 1 WLR 1359.

8   14688/89, *Simpson v United Kingdom* (1989) DR 64, 188 (no requirement that a disabled child should be educated in a private school with the state paying the fees where a place was available in a state school with special facilities for handicapped pupils).

9   6853/74, 40 *Mothers v Sweden* (1977) DR 9, 27; 23419/94, *Verein Gemeinsam Lernen v Austria* (1995) DR 82, 41.

10   20490/92, *Iskon and Others v United Kingdom* (1994) DR 76, 90.

11 11533/85, *Jordebo Foundation of Christian Schools and Jordebo v Sweden* (1987) DR 51, 125.

12 6094/73, *Association X v Sweden* (1977) DR 9, 5 (a students' association was not considered a trade union for the purposes of Art 11).

13 *Belgian Linguistic case* (1968) A 6, Law, para 4.

14 7864/77, *X v Belgium* (1978) DR 16, 82; 11655/85, *Glazewska v Sweden* (1985) DR 45, 300 (no requirement to recognise professional status acquired abroad). See further Convention on the Recognition of Qualifications concerning Higher Education in the European Region (ETS 165 (1997)).

6.155 The imposition of disciplinary measures resulting in exclusion from education is not necessarily incompatible with the guarantee, providing a fair balance has been struck. This requires consideration of a number of relevant factors, including

'... the procedural safeguards in place to challenge the exclusion and to avoid arbitrariness; the duration of the exclusion; the extent of the co-operation shown by the pupil or his parents with respect to attempts to re-integrate him; the efforts of the school authorities to minimise the effects of exclusion and, in particular, the adequacy of alternative education provided by the school during the period of exclusion; and the extent to which the rights of any third parties were engaged.'[1]

1 *Ali v United Kingdom* (11 January 2011), paras 55–64 at para 58 (temporary exclusion of pupil from school in accordance with domestic law and during criminal investigation into a fire at a school with the offer of alternative educational provision: no violation, the failure of the parents to attend a meeting about the pupil's reintegration or otherwise contact the school in time to prevent expulsion). See also 14524/89, *Yanasik v Turkey* (1993) DR 74, 14 (expulsion from a military academy); and 24515/94, *Sulak v Turkey* (1996) DR 84-A, 98 (expulsion from university for cheating in examinations).

DOMESTIC CONSIDERATION OF THE RIGHT TO EDUCATION

6.156 The right to education under Article 2 of Protocol no 1 has been considered in a number of domestic cases. The case of *A v Head Teacher and Governors of Lord Grey School* concerned a pupil who had been excluded from school. While excluded, the pupil had been regularly provided with school work and was offered a place at a pupil referral unit which was rejected. The House of Lords rejected the submission that there was a breach of this provision on the ground that an alternative package of education was on offer and not taken up. Lord Bingham of Cornhill stated, in relation to Article 2 of Protocol no 1:

'It was intended to guarantee fair and non-discriminatory access to that system by those within the jurisdiction of the respective states. The fundamental importance of education in a modern democratic state was recognised to require no less. But the guarantee is, in comparison with most other Convention guarantees, a weak one, and deliberately so. There is no right to education of a particular kind or quality, other than that prevailing in the state. There is no Convention guarantee of compliance with domestic law. There is no Convention guarantee of education at or by a particular institution. There is no Convention objection to the expulsion of a pupil from an educational institution on disciplinary grounds, unless (in the ordinary way) there is no alternative source of state education open to the pupil'. [1]

1   *A v Head Teacher and Governors of Lord Grey School* [2006] 2 AC 363, at para 24. Similarly *Dove v Scottish Ministers* 2002 SC 257 (restoration of a self-governing school to the control of the local education authority did not violate Art 14 in conjunction with Prot 1, Art 2: the right to education was a right to such educational institutions as the state may provide, and to be able to make effective use of that access, and the change of status did not fall within the ambit of the provision).

6.157 In *A v Essex County Council*, damages were sought on behalf of a severely disabled child with special educational needs, on the basis that the 18 months taken by the local authority to provide a suitable residential placement for him (at a cost of over £200,000 per annum) had infringed his Convention right to education. During that time, he had been provided with limited educational activities at home. The Supreme Court held, by a narrow majority, that the fact that it had taken the local authority 18 months to secure a placement at a suitable school did not amount to a denial of the claimant's right to education. Article 2 of Protocol no 1 did not impose a positive obligation on contracting states to provide effective education for children who had special educational needs. The right was to effective access without discrimination to the educational facilities which the state provided. In so far as a state's system of education made provision for children with special needs, Article 2 of Protocol no 1 guaranteed fair and non-discriminatory access for those children to the special facilities that were available. But if the facilities were limited, so that immediate access could not be provided, the right of access must have regard to that limitation. Thus the right of access to education conferred on the claimant by Article 2 of Protocol no 1 had to have regard to the limited resources actually available to deal with his special needs. These caused the delay in catering for his special needs. In these circumstances that delay did not constitute a denial of his right to education. There was, however, an arguable case that his right to education had been violated on the basis that more educational assistance could have been provided during the period while a placement was awaited[1].

1   *A v Essex County Council* [2011] 1 AC 280.

6.158 In *R (Holub) v Secretary of State for the Home Department* it was held that the deportation of a family, with the consequence that the child would be educated in Poland rather than in the United Kingdom, would not infringe the child's right to education[1].

1   *R (Holub) v Secretary of State for the Home Department* [2001] 1 WLR 1359.

Higher education

6.159 It is now clear that the provision also applies to higher education and not just to elementary education[1]. In *Leyla Şahin v Turkey*, the Grand Chamber considered whether there had been an interference with the applicant's right to education in terms of Article 2 of Protocol no 1 on account of the refusal to allow her to attend classes and sit examinations at university in light of her failure to adhere to a regulation prohibiting the wearing of an Islamic headscarf. By analogy with the reasoning applying to disposal of the application under Article 9, the Court also accepted that the refusal had been foreseeable, that it had pursued legitimate aims, and that the interference had been proportionate. The measures in question had in no way hindered the performance of religious observances by students, and indeed the university authorities judiciously had sought a means of avoiding having to turn away students wearing the headscarf while simultaneously protecting the rights of others and the interests of the education system[2].

1   Eg *Irfan Temel and others v Turkey* (3 March 2009), paras 38–47 (suspension of university students for petitioning for optional Kurdish language classes: suspension was a clearly disproportionate interference on the right to education as the request did not express views at a level of extremity that could lead to polarisation, nor had the students resorted to violence). For earlier case law, see eg 5962/72, *X v United Kingdom* (1975) DR 2, 50; 7671/76, *15 Foreign Students v United Kingdom* (1977) DR 9, 185; 14524/89, *Yanasik v Turkey* (1993) DR 74, 14; and 24515/94, *Sulak v Turkey* (1996) DR 84, 98. The line taken in this jurisprudence was doubted by certain commentators: cf van Dijk and van Hoof *Theory and Practice of the European Convention on Human Rights* (3rd edn, 1998) at p 644: the Commission's position that Prot 1, Art 2 is concerned primarily with elementary education 'is corroborated neither by the text of Article 2 nor by the Court's case-law'.

2   *Leyla Şahin v Turkey* [GC] 2005-XI, paras 157–162, discussed at para **7.34** below.

6.160 There is, though, some jurisprudence which supports the proposition that limiting entry to higher studies to those candidates who have attained a sufficient level of achievement to undertake such studies successfully does not constitute a violation[1]. On the other hand, assessment processes must minimise the risk of arbitrariness so as to meet expectations of lawfulness. In *Mürsel Eren v Turkey*, a student's complaint as to the annulment of the results of his university admissions examination was successfully upheld. The domestic courts had upheld a decision to annul the results upon a recommendation of an academic council which had considered that his excellent grades could not be explained in light of his poor performance at other diets. For the Court, this decision had been untenable on the facts, the legal basis for the exercise of the discretion was unclear, and in any event the grant of such a broad discretion could well produce legal uncertainty incompatible with the rule of law[2].

1   11655/85, *Glazewska v Sweden* (1985) DR 45, 300. See also 8844/80, *X v United Kingdom* (1980) DR 23, 228 (failure to allow a student with a poor first year performance and attendance to continue with studies: inadmissible).

2   *Mürsel Eren v Turkey* 2006-II, paras 46–51.

Provision of education in conformity with parents' religious and philosophical convictions

6.161 The second sentence of Article 2 of Protocol no 1 provides that 'in the exercise of any functions which it assumes in relation to education and to teaching, the State shall respect the right of parents to ensure such education and teaching in conformity with their own religious and philosophical convictions'. The right to respect for religious and philosophical convictions belongs to the parents of a child and not to the child itself[1] or to any school or religious association[2]. The fact that a child has been taken into care does not extinguish parental rights in this area[3], although a mother whose child has been adopted by another person no longer enjoys rights in this regard[4]. As noted, parental interests are considered to be secondary to the child's basic right to education[5], and parents may not refuse the right of education of a child on the basis of their convictions[6].

1   *Erikkson v Sweden* (1989) A 156, para 93. See further Levinet 'La Conciliation du Droit à l'Instruction de l'Enfant et l'Obligation de Respecter les Convictions Religieuses des Parents' (2011) 87 RTDH 481.

2   Cf 11533/85, *Jordebo Foundation of Christian Schools and Jordebo v Sweden* (1987) DR 51, 125 (the parents of pupils in a private school which was refused permission to provide the higher stage of compulsory education qualified as 'victims', but not the school itself).

3   *Olsson v Sweden (no 1)* (1988) A 130, para 95 (but 'no serious indication' that atheist parents were concerned that children were being given a religious upbringing); 10554/83, *Aminoff v Sweden* (1985) DR 43, 120 (decision to remove a child from its adoptive mother; subsequent complaint by the mother that the child's education is contrary to her wishes declared admissible); cf 10723/83, *Widén v Sweden* (1986) DR 48, 93 (decision to remove two children from their mother; in consequence, mother unable to place them in a private religious school: friendly settlement).

4   7626/76, *X v United Kingdom* (1977) DR 11, 160.

5   See para **6.153** above. Cf 10233/83, *Family H v United Kingdom* (1984) DR 37, 105 (a state may require parents who have chosen to educate their children at home to co-operate in the assessment of their children's educational standards).

6   *Konrad v Germany* (dec) 2006-XIII (denial of right of home education to Christian parents who objected to private or state schooling on account of sex education, study of fairytales, and inter-pupil violence: inadmissible).

6.162 'Education' suggests 'the whole process whereby, in any society, adults endeavour to transmit their beliefs, culture and other values to the young', while 'teaching or instruction refers in particular to the transmission of knowledge and to intellectual development'[1]. 'Respect' suggests more than mere acknowledgment or even that a parent's views have been taken into account, but rather 'implies some positive obligation on the part of the State'[2]. The matter may arise in regard to the content and implementation of curriculum, but will not extend to the provision of a specific form of teaching through, for example, the placement of a child in a particular school[3]. 'Philosophical convictions' suggests views 'as are worthy of respect in a "democratic society" ... and are not incompatible with human dignity' and which also 'attain a certain level of cogency, seriousness, cohesion and importance'. These include settled beliefs which refer to 'a weighty and substantial aspect of human life and behaviour'. However, linguistic preferences are not 'philosophical convictions' since this would distort the ordinary meaning of the term[4]. Nor has the House of Lords accepted that a parent may claim that a statutory prohibition on the use of corporal punishment in schools is a violation of his religious convictions[5].

1   *Campbell and Cosans v United Kingdom* (1982) A 48, at para 33.

2   *Campbell and Cosans v United Kingdom* (1982) A 48, at para 37; *Valsamis v Greece* 1996-VI, at para 27. For domestic application, see *R (K) v Newham London Borough Council* [2002] EWHC Admin 405 (inability of Muslim parent to indicate whether religious convictions played a part in selection of single-sex school for daughter).

3   14135/88, *PD and LD v United Kingdom* (1989) DR 62, 292 (attempt to have child removed from special needs schooling: inadmissible); and 13887/88, *Graeme v United Kingdom* (1990) DR 64, 158 (placement of disabled children in special schools against the wishes of the parents: inadmissible); and 25212/94, *Klerks v Netherlands* (1995) DR 82, 129 (respect for parents' convictions does not require the admission of a severely handicapped child to an ordinary school). See too 10228/82 and 10229/82, *W & DM v United Kingdom* and *M & HI v United Kingdom* (1984) DR 37, 96 (state education provision included both single-sex grammar schools and mixed-sex comprehensive schools; parents sought to assert that the failure to place their children in the former type of school on account of a shortage of places violated their philosophical convictions: application declared inadmissible). Cf *R (K) v Newham London Borough Council* [2002] EWHC 405 (Admin) (when considering the admission of a child to a particular school, the religious convictions of the parent – here, that his daughter be educated in a single-sex school – must be given due weight).

4   *Belgian Linguistic case* (1968) A 6, Law, para 6; cf *Cyprus v Turkey* [GC] 2001-IV, at para 278 (the authorities were aware that Greek Cypriot parents living in an enclave in northern Cyprus wished their children's education 'to be completed through the medium of the Greek language', and while this education was available in the southern part of the island, it could not be maintained that this possibility 'suffice[d] to fulfil the obligation laid down in Article 2 of Protocol No 1, having regard to the impact of that option on family life').

5   *R (Williamson) v Secretary of State for Education and Employment* [2005] 2 AC 246 (the right is restricted to parents, not teachers, and the interference is justified in terms of the protection of children), discussed at para **7.47** below.

6.163 In each instance, the European Court of Human Rights must first determine whether parents are entitled to rely upon the provision to secure respect for their philosophical and religious convictions, and then consider whether the state has indeed respected these convictions[1]. The outcome of such an assessment is not always obvious. For example, in *Valsamis v Greece* and in *Efstratiou v Greece*, pupils who were Jehovah's Witnesses had been punished for failing to attend parades commemorating the country's national day. The parents of the pupils had sought exemptions from the requirement to take part in the parades on account of their belief that such events were incompatible with their firmly held pacifism. The Court accepted that Jehovah's Witnesses enjoyed the status of a 'known religion', and thus parents were entitled to rely upon the right to respect for these convictions. While the Court expressed surprise 'that pupils can be required on pain of suspension from school – even if only for a day – to parade outside the school precincts on a holiday', it considered that the nature of these parades (even taking into account the involvement of military personnel) contained nothing which could offend the applicants' pacifist convictions[2]. On the other hand, 'the imposition of disciplinary penalties is an integral part of the process whereby a school seeks to achieve the object for which it was established, including the development and moulding of the character and mental powers of its pupils'[3], and thus the use of corporal punishment may not simply be dismissed as a matter merely of internal administration. In *Campbell and Cosans v United Kingdom*, parents of pupils in Scottish schools had objected to the practice of administering the belt or tawse. The Court accepted that the applicants' views met the test of 'philosophical convictions' in that they related to a 'weighty and substantial aspect of human life and behaviour, namely the integrity of the person', and thus the state's failure to respect these convictions had violated the guarantee[4].

1   *Valsamis v Greece* 1996-VI, para 26.

2   *Valsamis v Greece* 1996-VI, paras 26–33 at para 31; *Efstratiou v Greece* 1996-VI, paras 27–34 at para 32 (public celebration of democracy and human rights not vitiated by presence of military; similarly, no violation of Art 9).

3   *Valsamis v Greece* 1996-VI, at para 29.

4   *Campbell and Cosans v United Kingdom* (1982) A 48, paras 33–37 at para 36. Corporal punishment was ultimately prohibited in state schools, and in relation to pupils in state assisted places at independent schools, by the Education (Scotland) Act 1980, s 48A as amended by the Education Act 1993, s 294.

DETERMINATION OF CURRICULUM

6.164 Curriculum setting and planning are matters which fall within the competence of the domestic authorities. Here, judicial expertise is limited[1], and consequently the recognition of a margin of appreciation is appropriate. In *Kjeldsen, Busk Madsen and Pedersen v Denmark*, parents objected to the provision of sex education to their children. In a crucial part of the judgment which encapsulates the manner in which conflicting interests of the state, of pupils and of their parents are expected to be resolved, the Court drew a distinction between the imparting of knowledge even of a directly or indirectly religious or philosophical nature, and teaching which sought to inculcate a particular value or philosophy which did not respect the views of a parent. The Court clarified that the provision does not 'permit parents to object to the integration of such teaching or education in the school curriculum, for otherwise all institutionalised teaching would run the risk of proving impracticable' since most school subjects involved 'some philosophical complexion or implications'. However, a school has to ensure that the education provided by way of teaching or instruction conveyed information and knowledge 'in an objective, critical and pluralistic manner'. The key guarantee is against the state pursuing an 'aim of indoctrination that might be considered as not respecting parents' religious and philosophical convictions', this being 'the limit that must not be exceeded'[2]. In short, providing indoctrination is avoided, decisions on such issues as the place accorded to religion are covered by a margin of appreciation on the part of national authorities. As the Grand Chamber emphasised in *Lautsi and Others v Italy*, arrangements in education and teaching may indeed reflect historical tradition and dominant religious adherence. The requirement for the presence of crucifixes in classrooms, for example, while conferring upon the majority religion in Italy a 'preponderant visibility', cannot in itself denote a process of indoctrination as a crucifix is an essentially passive symbol whose influence cannot be deemed comparable to that of didactic speech or participation in religious activities, particularly as the curriculum did not include any compulsory teaching about Christianity and as there were clear attempts to provide an understanding of other faiths and promote tolerance of others' beliefs[3].

1   *Kjeldsen, Busk Madsen and Pedersen v Denmark* (1976) A 23, para 53.
2   *Kjeldsen, Busk Madsen and Pedersen v Denmark* (1976) A 23, at para 53. See also 17187/90, *Bernard v Luxembourg* (1993) DR 75, 57 (requirement to attend moral and social education in the absence of any allegation of indoctrination did not give rise to an interference with Art 9 rights); *Köse and Others v Turkey* (dec) 2006-II (foreseeable prohibition on wearing of headscarf had been proportionate in view of constitutional principle of secularism and state's obligations to impart knowledge in an objective, critical and pluralist manner: inadmissible) and *Appel-Irrgang and Others v Germany* (dec) 2009-… (compulsory ethics classes of a secular nature in schools contrary to religious beliefs of parents: inadmissible as the state's margin of appreciation had not been exceeded.) Cf *Konrad v Germany* (dec) (11 September 2006) (denial of right of home education to Christian parents who objected to private or state schooling on account of sex education, study of fairytales, and inter-pupil violence: inadmissible as parents may not refuse the right of education to children on the basis of their convictions, and the state's assumption that schooling helped integrate children into society and gain social experience was compatible with the promotion of pluralism and fell within a state's margin of appreciation).
3   *Lautsi v Italy* [GC] 2011-…, paras 62–77 at para 71 (no violation of Prot 1, Art 2, and no separate issue arose under Art 9, Prot 1 Art 2 being the *lex specialis* in this area). The judgment reversed the approach taken by the Chamber (3 November 2009).

6.165 It is nevertheless necessary that care be taken in ensuring that curricular provision meets the minimum expectations of the guarantee. This may require careful assessment. In *Folgerø and Others v Norway*, the Grand Chamber by a bare majority ruled that the introduction of new arrangements for the teaching of religion and philosophy in primary schools had failed to respect the rights of parents. The new curriculum required a greater emphasis to be placed upon knowledge of the Christian religion, although other faiths were also to be covered in classes. The rights of parents to withdraw their children from classes was also to be restricted: in the past, a parent could withdraw his child from lessons in Christianity. For the majority of the Court, the emphasis upon knowledge about Christianity was not in itself objectionable in light of the importance that Christianity had played in the country's history and tradition. However, the curriculum's purported aim of helping provide a Christian and moral upbringing, albeit in co-operation with the home, suggested that the distinctions between Christianity and other faiths and religions were not only quantitative but also qualitative. This in turn called into question the curriculum's stated aims of addressing sectarianism and promoting pluralism and understanding. In these circumstances, the state had to ensure that parental convictions were adequately protected. The majority of the Court could not be satisfied that these arrangements were sufficient to meet the requirements of Article 2 of Protocol no 1. Not only would parents need to be informed in advance as to lesson plans to allow them to identify and to notify which aspects of teaching would be incompatible with their beliefs, but the requirement that any request for withdrawal from teaching was to be supported by reasonable grounds also carried the risk that parents would be forced to disclose their own religious and philosophical convictions to an unacceptable extent. Further, schools were to be given authority to respond to requests for withdrawal from teaching by withdrawing the child merely from the activity rather than from the classroom. All of this thus supported the conclusion that the arrangements were highly complex and likely to deter parents from making use of requests for exemption[1].

---

1   *Folgerø and Others v Norway* [GC] 2007-VIII, paras 85–102. The dissenting minority (the Court split 9 votes to 8) considered that the curriculum conveyed knowledge 'in an objective, critical and pluralistic manner' and 'could not be said to have pursued an aim of indoctrination'. See also *Hasan and Eylem Zengin v Turkey* 2007-XI, paras 58–77 (religious culture and ethics syllabus failed to meet the criteria of objectivity and pluralism and restricted possibility of exemption from instruction: violation).

United Kingdom reservation

6.166 The United Kingdom's obligations under this provision are subject to a reservation made at the time of ratification and protected by the Human Rights Act 1998 to the effect that this particular obligation applies only in so far as 'it is compatible with the provision of efficient instruction and training, and the avoidance of unreasonable public expenditure'[1]. Certainly, a state is not required to provide a financial subsidy to a particular form of education to meet its obligations: rather, the duty is to 'respect' such convictions in the provision of any existing form of education[2]. In *X and Y v United Kingdom*, the applicants complained that the state did not help fund a Rudolf Steiner school which provided their children with education in accordance with their commitment to the 'anthroposophical movement'. The complaint was rejected as manifestly ill-founded even without the need to consider the reservation: in the opinion of the Commission, Article 2 of Protocol no 1 could not be interpreted as obliging a state to establish or to support any educational establishment serving any particular set of religious beliefs or convictions. In any case, adequate 'respect' had been given through the grant of charitable status to the school and also by the decision to extend an assisted places scheme to it[3].

---

1   The reservation appears in the Human Rights Act 1998, Sch 3, as given effect to by s 1(2). The reservation was referred to in 14135/88, *PD and LD v United Kingdom* (1989) DR 62, 292. See also 29046/95 *McIntyre v United Kingdom* (21 October 1998) (failure to install a lift in a school: inadmissible). For domestic consideration, see *Buchan v West Lothian Council* 2001 SLT 1452 (decision to close a primary school fell within the scope of the reservation); and *R (R) v Leeds City Council* [2005] EWHC 2495 (Admin) (refusal to provide free transport from claimants' home to the nearest Jewish school some 45 miles away, although transport to other faith school outside the administrative area up to six miles distant was provided: there was no proper comparator and thus no discriminatory treatment; Art 8 was neither engaged nor

infringed, since the claimants were attending the school of their choice; Art 9 was not engaged since the claimants were attending the faith schools; and even if Prot 1, Art 2 were engaged, the refusal would fall within the terms of the United Kingdom's reservation).

2   10476/83, *W & KL v Sweden* (1985) DR 45, 143.

3   9461/81 *X and Y v United Kingdom* (1982) DR 31, 210.

Discrimination

6.167 Article 14 when taken together with Article 2 of Protocol no 1 prohibits discriminatory treatment not pursuing a legitimate aim or which is disproportionate[1]. These articles cannot, however, be read as implying any right for a child to be educated in a particular language, or for parents to insist that education is provided using their language of choice[2]. Furthermore, determination of the curriculum or of how best to respond to children who have specific educational needs is covered by a wide margin of appreciation[3]. In respect of education, Article 14 prohibits the imposition of any discriminatory treatment which has 'as its basis or reason a personal characteristic ('status') by which persons or groups are distinguishable from each other'[4], and which falls within the scope of Article 2 of Protocol no 1[5]. Where arrangements involve the application of discriminatory criteria, the onus lies on the state to show that the policy or practice is objectively justified, appropriate and necessary. The placement of Roma children in 'special' schools, for example, has been found to constitute a violation of Convention guarantees where the state was not able to satisfy the Court that the selection of pupils did not involve racial or ethnic considerations[6]. The state must also be able to show that safeguards are in place if a specific ethnic group requiring special protection is the subject of the measures in question. In *Oršuš and Others v Croatia*, Roma children had been placed into Roma-only classes since this had been considered necessary to address their alleged poor knowledge of the Croatian language. However, the tests that had been applied to the children had not been designed specifically to assess linguistic performance, nor had the children been given any special language classes. Further, other children with a poor grasp of the language had not been placed in separate classes, and although the children had spent a substantial period of their education in Roma-only classes, there had been no transparent procedure for the monitoring of the scheme. In the opinion of the Grand Chamber, the high drop-out rate amongst Roma pupils required implementation of positive measures to raise awareness of the importance of education among the Roma population and to assist Roma children who needed help in following the school curriculum[7]. The segregation of children thus gives rise to issues under Article 14 taken in conjunction with Article 2 of Protocol no 1. There is also an argument that discrimination in arrangements for the funding of educational provision may also raise similar concerns: for example, in relation to the Scottish system of publicly-funded denominational education, refusal to accord Muslim parents these facilities in communities in which there is a demand for this may be difficult to justify under the Convention where similar demands from parents of other faiths have been accommodated[8].

1   See paras **3.87–3.128** above.

2   *Belgian Linguistic case* (1968) A 6, Law, para 11.

3   But see *DH and Others v Czech Republic* [GC] 2007-XII, at para 206: ' whenever discretion capable of interfering with the enjoyment of a Convention right is conferred on national authorities, the procedural safeguards available to the individual will be especially material in determining whether the respondent State has, when fixing the regulatory framework, remained within its margin of appreciation.'

4   *Kjeldsen, Busk Madsen and Pedersen v Denmark* (1976) A 23, at para 56. Cf *Folgerø and Others v Norway* [GC] 2007-VIII, discussed above at para **6.165** (in view of finding of violation of Prot 1, Art 2, it was not necessary to examine the complaint under Art 14 in conjunction with Arts 8 and 9 or Prot 1, Art 2). For discussion of 'status', see para **3.94** above.

5   It has been held that it is not discriminatory for a mature student to be denied a student loan: *Douglas v North Tyneside Metropolitan Borough Council* [2004] 1 WLR 2363. Differences of treatment in the funding arrangements of students attending Scottish universities based upon residence status should escape censure since the guarantee cannot imply the requirement to provide any particular financial support. In any case, even if Prot 1, Art 2 were engaged, there would presumably be an arguable case that any difference in treatment pursued a legitimate aim and was not disproportionate: cf *R (Mitchell) v Coventry University* [2001] ELR 594 (no violation of Art 14 taken in conjunction with Prot 1, Art 2 in respect of a requirement to pay overseas university fees, any discrimination being reasonably justified). Nor does the fact that the children will arrive late if sent to a different school amount to discrimination in the field of the provision of education: *R (Khundakji) v Cardiff CC Admissions Appeal Panel* [2003] EWHC 436 (Admin).

6   *DH and Others v Czech Republic* [GC] 2007-XII, discussed at paras **3.98** and **3.104** above.

7   *Oršuš and Others v Croatia* [GC] 2010-..., paras 180–186 (majority of 9 to 8), and note also paras 156–179 (passivity and lack of objections of parents in respect of the placements was explicable as the parents were themselves members of a disadvantaged community and often poorly educated, and thus had not been capable of weighing up all the aspects of the situation and the consequences of giving their consent; in any event, no waiver of the right not to be subjected to racial discrimination can be recognised as this would be counter to an important public interest). Cf the Chamber judgment of 17 July 2008 in which the Court held, unanimously, that there had been no violation. See also *Sampanis and Others v Greece* (5 June 2008), paras 84–97 (children of Roma origin denied access to a school until they had been transferred to a segregated classroom in the annex of the school: violation of Art 14 taken with Prot 1, Art 2).

8   Cf Murdoch 'Religion, Education and the Law' (1989) 34 JLSS 258 at 261; but see *R (SB) v Governors of Denbigh High School* [2007] 1 AC 100, discussed at para **7.45** below (the right to education under Art 2 of Prot 1 did not confer a right to attend any particular school, and the right was infringed only if the claimant was denied access to the general educational provision available from the system as a whole: since the claimant's failure to attend school was the result of her unwillingness to comply with a rule to which the school was entitled to adhere and she could have found another school which allowed her to wear the jilbab if she had notified the local education authority in time of her requirements, the claimant had not been denied access to the general education system and there had been no infringement of her right to education); see also *R (R) v Leeds City Council* [2005] EWHC 2495 (Admin) (refusal to provide free transport from claimants' home to the nearest Jewish school some 45 miles away, although transport to other faith school outside the administrative area up to six miles distant was provided: there was no proper comparator and thus no discriminatory treatment; Art 8 was neither engaged nor infringed, since the claimants were attending the school of their choice; Art 9 was not engaged since the claimants were attending the faith schools; and even if Prot 1, Art 2 were engaged, the refusal would fall within the terms of the United Kingdom's reservation).

Chapter 7

Civil and political liberties: thought, expression, assembly and association; and free elections

INTRODUCTION

7.01 Articles 9, 10 and 11 of the ECHR guarantee freedom of thought, conscience and religion, expression, assembly and association. The guarantees are closely linked, in terms of both substantive content[1] and textual formulation[2]. These provisions are crucial for the protection of collective political freedom and the development of individual identity as shaped through personal attitudes and beliefs. Article 3 of Protocol no 1 further guarantees the holding of free elections at reasonable intervals by secret ballot. Policy issues shape much of the jurisprudence, for the European Court of Human Rights has been at pains to highlight the particular importance of these rights in maintaining democratic discussion[3], accountability[4], pluralism and tolerance[5]. None of these guarantees is absolute, for a state may interfere with each right, providing always that this is done in accordance with domestic law and is 'necessary in a democratic society' for the achievement of prescribed interests[6]. The duties upon a state go beyond merely refraining from interfering with the rights of individuals, for each guarantee can require positive action on the part of the state to ensure that the right is an effective right[7]. In this area most of the jurisprudence has arisen under Article 10, with Articles 9 and 11 generating much less in the way of case law. Article 3 of Protocol no 1 is probably more of symbolic than practical use since the variety of different voting systems and constitutional arrangements amongst European states justifies a wide margin of appreciation[8].

---

1   Cf *Young, James and Webster v United Kingdom* (1981) A 44, at para 57: 'the protection of personal opinion afforded by Articles 9 and 10 in the shape of freedom of thought, conscience and religion and of freedom of expression is also one of the purposes of freedom of association as guaranteed by Article 11'.

2   That is, paragraph (1) of each article makes provision for the general right, while paragraph (2) recognises certain state interests which may justify interference with individual freedoms.

3   Eg *Barfod v Denmark* (1989) A 149, para 29: importance of 'not discouraging members of the public, for fear of criminal or other sanctions, from voicing their opinions on issues of public concern'.

4   Eg *Lingens v Austria* (1986) A 103, at paras 41 and 42: 'it is 'incumbent [upon the press] to impart information and ideas on political issues, [and] freedom of the press affords the public one of the best means of discovering and forming an opinion of the ideas and attitudes of political leaders'.

5   Cf *Handyside v United Kingdom* (1976) A 24, at para 49 (expression was crucial for promotion of 'pluralism, toleration and broadmindedness').

6   For discussion of the general limitations in Arts 8–11, see paras **3.62–3.66** and **3.73–3.82** above.

7   The notion of positive obligations was first apparent under Art 11 and was then developed further under Arts 9 and 10: cf *Plattform 'Ärzte für das Leben' v Austria* (1988) A 139, discussed at para **7.118** below; *Otto-Preminger-Institut v Austria* (1994) A 295-A, discussed at paras **7.24** and **7.108** below; and *Özgür Gündem v Turkey* 2000-III discussed at para **7.50**, fn 2 below. Prot 1, Art 3 is largely secured through positive state action: *Mathieu-Mohin and Clerfayt v Belgium* (1987) A 113, discussed at para **7.136** below.

8   Cf *Mathieu-Mohin and Clerfayt v Belgium* (1987) A 113, para 54. For discussion of 'margin of appreciation', see paras **3.134–3.141** above.

7.02 These guarantees are also subject to other provisions restricting their protection. A state may take measures derogating from its obligations in time of emergency, in terms of Article 15[1]. Further, Article 16 provides that 'nothing in Articles 10, 11 and 14 shall be regarded as preventing the High Contracting Parties from imposing restrictions on the political activity of aliens'[2]. Finally, Article 17 restrains use of the Convention by those seeking to use it in a manner that is 'aimed at the destruction of any of the rights and freedoms', for example, through the use of racist speech or Holocaust denial[3].

1   See further paras **3.23–3.24** and **4.147–4.148** above.

2   Cf *Piermont v France* (1995) A 314, paras 62–64 (possession of EU citizenship by the German applicant who was also a Member of the European Parliament did not allow Art 16 to be raised against her by the respondent state in respect of violation of her Art 10 rights when expelled from a French overseas territory represented in the European Parliament). Article 16 was considered in *R (Farrakhan) v Secretary of State for the Home Department* [2002] QB 1391 and in *R (Barclay) v Lord Chancellor* [2010] 1 AC 464.

3   See further paras **3.31** above and **7.99** below.

7.03 Since the ECHR is to be read as a whole[1], the substantive content of each guarantee may be influenced by competing considerations[2]. In any case, factual circumstances may give rise to simultaneous challenges under two or more of these guarantees, although the European Court of Human Rights will invariably either determine the *lex specialis* at the outset[3], or dispose of an application under only one article when it considers that the merits of the application can be addressed adequately in this way[4].

1   *Belgian Linguistic case* (1968) A 6, at para 1.

2   Eg *Kjeldsen, Busk Madsen and Pedersen v Denmark* (1976) A 23, paras 52 and 53 (parental interests in education under Prot 1, Art 2 to be interpreted in a way consistent with Arts 8, 9 and 10); *Otto-Preminger-Institut v Austria* (1994) A 295-A, para 56 (permissible restrictions on expression under Art 10 read alongside promotion of religious tolerance under Art 9); *News Verlags and GmbH & CoKG v Austria* 2000-I, para 56 (restrictions on prejudicial pre-trial publicity under Art 10(2) consistent with accused's rights under Art 6(1) and (2)).

3   See eg *Women on Waves and Others v Portugal* 2009-…, para 28 (prohibition on entry into territorial waters of ship engaged in protest had affected the substance of the ideas and information intended to be imparted, and issue examined under Art 10 rather than Art 11).

4   Eg *Young James and Webster v United Kingdom* (1981) A 44, para 66 (disposal under Art 11 rather than in terms of Arts 9 or 10); *Kokkinakis v Greece* (1993) A 260-A, para 54

(dissemination of religious beliefs considered under Art 9 rather than Art 10); *Steel and Others v United Kingdom* 1998-VII, para 113 (various protests both peaceful and non-peaceful considered under Art 10 rather than Art 11); *Feldek v Slovakia* 2001-VIII, para 92 (Art 10); *Refah Partisi (the Welfare Party) and Others v Turkey* [GC] 2003-II, para 137 (Art 11); and *Jehovah's Witnesses of Moscow v Russia* 2010-..., paras 106–160 and 170–182 (violation of Art 9 in the light of Art 11; and violation of Art 11 in the light of Art 9).The impact of religious or philosophical convictions upon employment may give rise to issues better determined under Art 10: see paras **7.26–7.28** below. Issues which concern the right of access to a court for the determination of a religious community's civil rights fall to be considered under Art 6: eg *Canea Catholic Church v Greece* 1997-VIII, paras 40–42.

7.04 The Human Rights Act 1998 makes specific provision for freedom of expression (s 12) and for the freedom of thought, conscience and religion of religious organisations (s 13). These provisions are the results of amendments made during the parliamentary passage of the legislation, and require to be taken into account in any relevant domestic proceeding. They may, however, have little practical impact[1].

1   See paras **1.100–1.104** above. The issue of how a court would consider a case involving the balancing of freedom of expression with respect for religious belief where the Human Rights Act 1998, ss 12 and 13 are themselves in issue seems not to have been considered, but would in any case most likely be resolved by reference to existing Strasbourg case law: cf *Otto-Preminger Institut v Austria* (1994) A 295-A, discussed at paras **7.24** and **7.108** below.

ARTICLE 9: FREEDOM OF THOUGHT, CONSCIENCE AND RELIGION

The scope of protection accorded 'freedom of thought, conscience and religion' under Article 9

7.05 Article 9 is of potentially wide scope[1]. Not only does it seek to protect that 'true religious pluralism'[2] which is a hallmark of a democratic society and for religious worship and practice,[3] 'but it is also a precious asset for atheists, agnostics, sceptics and the unconcerned'[4]. The guarantee is not absolute, for paragraph (2) confirms that the state may interfere with the manifestation of belief. However, a close reading of the text suggests that the right to hold and to change religious and other convictions – the so-called *forum internum* – is an absolute right[5] since permitted interferences are restricted to 'external' manifestations of thought, conscience or religious belief. Until comparatively recently, however, case law was rather under-developed: Article 9 did not produce much in the way of jurisprudence, probably on account of the high level of acceptance of religious toleration found in most west European states, but attempts (often in east European legal systems) to restrict or otherwise hinder the growth of religious faiths considered alien have now resulted in a growing body of judgments[6]. Two particular groups of cases dominate judicial consideration: interferences with individual exercise of belief; and the failure of state organs to retain neutrality by favouring particular faiths over others.

1   See Evans *Freedom of Religion* (2005); and for discussion of domestic law, Uitz *Freedom of Religion in European Constitutional and International Case Law* (2007); and Martinez-Torrón and Durham (eds) *Religion and the Secular State: National Reports* (2010). For an international perspective, see Iliopoulos-Strangas (ed) *Constitution and Religion* (2005).

2   *Manoussakis and Others v Greece* 1996-IV, at para 44.

3   Cf *Kokkinakis v Greece* (1993) A 260-A, at para 31: 'bearing witness in words and deeds is bound up with the existence of religious convictions'.

4   *Kokkinakis v Greece* (1993) A 260-A, para 31. See too *Re Crawley Green Road Cemetery, Luton* [2001] Fam 308.

5   Discussed at paras **7.13–7.15** below.

6   Violations of Art 9 have been found in 30 judgments between 1959 and 2009 (8 have concerned Greece, with Bulgaria and Russia each with 4, Latvia, Moldova and Ukraine each with 3, and Austria, Georgia, San Marino, Switzerland and Turkey each with 1): European Court *Annual Report 2009* (2010), pp 150–151. The first such judgment establishing a violation of Art 9 – *Kokkinakis v Greece* – was delivered in 1993.

7.06 Article 9 in essence involves an individual's rights to hold philosophical or religious convictions, to change these beliefs, and to manifest these individually or in common with others[1]. A range of issues may thus arise under Article 9, including the imposition of religious oaths[2] or a requirement to attend religious ceremonies[3], the wearing of religious clothing in public[4], registration of religious faith in identity documents[5] and refusal to allow resident aliens to enter a country on account of belief[6], as well as restrictions on proselytism[7]. At the same time, a significant number of judgments concern collective manifestation of belief, for example, restrictions on the establishment of places of worship[8], refusal to register religious groups[9], undue interference in disputes between adherents[10], and even restrictions on freedom of movement preventing members of a community from gathering to worship[11].

1   *Kokkinakis v Greece* (1993) A 260-A, para 31.

2   *Buscarini and Others v San Marino* [GC] 1999-I, para 34.

3   Cf *Valsamis v Greece* 1996-VI, paras 21–37 (no interference with Art 9 rights).

4   *Ahmet Arslan and Others v Turkey* 2010-…, paras 44–52 (conviction for wearing religious clothing in public: violation). See further para **7.34** below.

5   *Sinan Işık v Turkey* 2010-…, paras 37–53 (identity cards carried a 'religion' data field but which could be left blank: violation, as a decision to have a card with the religion field left blank inevitably carried specific connotations).

6   *Nolan and K v Russia* (12 February 2009), paras 61–75 (exclusion of resident alien on account of activities as a member of the Unification Church: violation).

7   *Kokkinakis v Greece* (1993) A 260-A, paras 31–33, discussed at para **7.33** below.

8   *Manoussakis and Others v Greece* 1996-IV, paras 36–53, discussed at para **7.42** below.

9   See para **7.38–7.39** below.

10 See para **7.42–7.43** below.

11 *Cyprus v Turkey* [GC] 2001-IV, para 242–246.

7.07 On the other hand, the scope of the provision does not extend to such issues as the non-availability of divorce[1], allegations of discriminatory treatment in the application of tax regulations[2], or deprivation of a religious organisation's material resources[3] as such matters either do not involve 'manifestations' or interferences with manifestations of belief. Nor can the guarantee imply any right of a taxpayer to demand that the state allocates his payments to particular purposes[4], or allows the use of any particular language in exercising freedom of thought.[5] Disposal of human remains in accordance with religious wishes does not probably involve freedom of thought, conscience or religion but rather may give rise to respect for private and family life under Article 8[6] (although there is some domestic authority to the contrary[7]). However, if a state goes beyond its core obligations under Article 9 and creates additional rights falling within the wider ambit of freedom of religion or conscience, such rights are then protected by Article 14 in conjunction with Article 9 against discriminatory application of domestic law[8].

At a domestic level, the House of Lords has held that Article 9 was not engaged by a ban on hunting with hounds: 'The current jurisprudence does not support the proposition that a person's belief in his right to engage in an activity which he carries on for pleasure or recreation, however fervent or passionate, can be equated with beliefs of the kind that are protected by art 9'[9].

1   *Johnston and Others v Ireland* (1986) A 112, paras 62–63 (issues considered under Arts 8, 12 and 14).

2   *Darby v Sweden* (1990) A 187, paras 28–35 (application disposed of under Prot 1, Art 1 taken with Art 14; the Court considered that the establishment of a particular church in a state did not give rise to any Art 9 issue if membership is voluntary (para 35)).

3   *Holy Monasteries v Greece* (1994) A 301-A, paras 86–87 (matters considered under Prot 1, Art 1 since the complaint did not concern 'objects intended for the celebration of divine worship').

4   10358/83, *C v United Kingdom* (1983) DR 37, 142 (a Quaker opposed the use of any tax paid by him for military purposes; the Commission noted Art 9 could not always guarantee the right to behave in the public sphere (eg refusing to pay tax) in a manner dictated by belief); and *Alujer Fernández and Caballero García v Spain* (dec) 2001-VI (the impossibility for members of a church to earmark part of their income tax for the support of their church as was possible for members of the Roman Catholic Church did not give rise to a violation of Art 9 taken with Art 14: the state had a certain margin of appreciation in such a matter on which there was no common European practice).

5   2333/64, *Inhabitants of Leeuw-St Pierre v Belgium* (1968) YB 11, 228.

6   8741/79, *X v Germany* (1981) DR 24, 137 (but matter can fall within the scope of Art 8). Cf *Sabanchiyeva and Others v Russia* (dec) (6 November 2008) (refusal to return bodies of alleged terrorists killed by law-enforcement personnel: admissible under Arts 3, 8 and 9, taken alone and in conjunction with Arts 13 and 14). See further para **6.35**, fn 3 above.

7   *Re Durrington Cemetery* [2001] Fam 33 (interment in accordance with Jewish law); *Re Crawley Green Road Cemetery, Luton* [2001] Fam 308 (interment of humanist in unconsecrated ground).

8   *Savez Crkava 'Riječ Žlvota' and Others v Croatia* (9 December 2010), paras 55–59 and 85–93 (unequal allocation of criteria for rights to have religious marriages recognised as equal to those of civil marriages and to allow religious education in public schools: violation of Art 14 in conjunction with Art 9, for while these rights could not be derived from the ECHR, discriminatory measures were inappropriate).

9   *Whaley v Lord Advocate* 2008 SC (HL) 107 at para 18 per Lord Hope of Craighead.

'Thought, conscience and religion' and 'belief'

7.08 The phrase 'thought, conscience and religion' and the term 'belief' suggest a potentially wide scope for Article 9, but in practice a somewhat narrower approach to interpretation of certain of these concepts has been adopted. A 'consciousness' of belonging to a minority group (and in consequence, the aim of seeking to protect a group's cultural identity) does not give rise to an Article 9 issue[1]. 'Belief' in any event is much more than mere opinion, and in order to attract Article 9 protection, beliefs must 'attain a certain level of cogency, seriousness, cohesion and importance' and also be such as to be considered compatible with respect for human dignity. In other words, the belief must relate to a 'weighty and substantial aspect of human life and behaviour' and also be such as to be deemed worthy of protection in European democratic society[2]. Not all line-drawing is straightforward. Belief in assisted suicide does not qualify as a religious or philosophical belief since this is rather a commitment to the principle of personal autonomy more appropriate for discussion under Article 8[3]. Language preferences[4] or disposal of human remains after death[5] do not involve 'beliefs' within the meaning of the provision. On the other hand, pacifism[6], atheism[7] and veganism[8] are value-systems clearly encompassed by Article 9 as is a political ideology such as communism[9] (although interferences with thought and conscience in respect of political beliefs will often be treated as giving rise to issues arising within the scope of Article 10's guarantee of freedom of expression or the right of association under Article 11)[10].

---

1   *Sidiropoulos and Others v Greece* 1998-IV, para 41.

2   *Campbell and Cosans v United Kingdom* (1982) A 48, at para 36 (re Prot 1 Art 2). See too 19459/92, *FP v Germany* (29 March 1993) (Art 9 'is essentially destined to protect religions, or theories on philosophical or ideological universal values'); and *Refah Partisi (the Welfare Party) and Others v Turkey* [GC] 2003-II, discussed at para **7.130** below (prohibition on a political party which sought to introduce Islamic law contrary to the state's secular constitution upheld, in part since the values of such a legal system were contrary to those of the Convention).

3   *Pretty v United Kingdom* 2002-III, para 82. See also *Whaley v Lord Advocate* 2008 SC (HL) 107 (Art 9 not engaged by interference with hunting).

4   *Belgian Linguistic case* (1968) A 6, Law, para 6.

5   See para **7.07**, fns 6 and 7 above.

6   7050/75, *Arrowsmith v United Kingdom* (1978) DR 19, 5.

7   10491/83, *Angelini v Sweden* (1986), DR 51, 41.

8   18187/91, *W v United Kingdom* (10 February 1993).

9   16311/90–6313/90, *Hazar, Hazar and Acik v Turkey* (1991) DR 72, 200 (offence of belonging to the Communist Party: admissible under ECHR, Art 9). Cf Harris, O'Boyle and Warbrick *Law of the European Convention on Human Rights* (1st edn, 1995) at p 357: 'the line between a philosophy and a political programme may yet be hard to draw'.

10   Eg *Vogt v Germany* (1995) A 323.

7.09 As far as 'religion' is concerned, what may be considered mainstream religions[1] and minority variants of such faiths[2] are readily accepted as falling within the scope of the provision. However, the textual formulation of 'religion or belief' (or 'religion or beliefs') provides considerable scope to avoid determining what is meant by a 'religion'[3]. 'It is clearly not the Court's task to decide *in abstracto* whether or not a body of beliefs and related practices may be considered a "religion"', and where there is no European consensus on the religious nature of a body such as Scientology, the Court 'being sensitive to the subsidiary nature of its role' may instead simply rely on the position of domestic authorities[4]. Where there is a doubt, an applicant may be expected to establish that a particular 'religion' does indeed exist[5]. Religious movements of recent origin may qualify[6].

1   20490/92, *ISKON and 8 others v United Kingdom* (1994) DR 76, 90.

2   Eg *Cha'are Shalom Ve Tsedek v France* [GC] 2000-VII. See further Gunn 'The Complexity of Religion and the Definition of "Religion" in International Law' 16 Harv Hum Rts Jo 189 (2003).

3   Cf Harris, O'Boyle and Warbrick *Law of the European Convention on Human Rights* (2nd edn, 2009) at p 426: '... any definition of "religion" would need to be flexible enough to to satisfy a broad cross-section of world faiths, as well as sufficiently precise for practical application in specific cases. Such a balance would be practically impossible to strike ...'.

4   See eg *Church of Scientology Moscow v Russia* (5 April 2007), para 64; and *Kimlya and Others v Russia* 2009-..., paras 79–81 (domestic recognition of 'religious' nature of activities, and thus Art 8 applied). Cf 7805/77, *X and Church of Scientology v Sweden* (1979) DR 16, 68.

5   7291/75, *X v United Kingdom* (1977) DR 11, 55 (question whether the Wicca movement qualified left open); and see also 12587/86, *Chappell v United Kingdom* (1987) DR 53, 24, noted above.

6   Eg 8652/79, *X v Austria* (1981) DR 26, 89 (the Moon Sect); 8188/77, *Omkarananda and the Divine Light Zentrum v United Kingdom* (1981) DR 25, 105; cf 12587/86, *Chappell v United Kingdom* (1987) DR 53, 241(question whether Druidism could be classified as a 'religion' avoided).

Deportation, etc and Article 9

7.10 The protection accorded by Article 9 is essentially a matter for European states to ensure within their jurisdictions, and accordingly very limited assistance can be derived from the provision itself when an individual is under threat of expulsion to another country where it is claimed there is a real risk that freedom of religion would be denied if returned or expelled[1]. However, the domestic courts have accepted that, in exceptional cases, a substantial risk to an individual's respect for religious belief if deported may render his removal incompatible with Convention rights.[2]

1   *Z and T v United Kingdom* (dec) 2006-III (Pakistani Christians facing deportation to Pakistan: while the Court would not rule out the possibility that exceptionally Art 9 may be engaged in expulsion cases, it was difficult to envisage such circumstances which in any event would not engage Art 3 responsibility). See too *Al-Nashif and Others v Bulgaria* (20 June 2002) (deportation on account of having taught Islamic religion without proper authorisation: in view of finding that deportation would constitute a violation of Art 8, no need to consider Art 9)

2   *R (Ullah) v Secretary of State for the Home Department* [2004] 2 AC 323.

Relationship with other ECHR guarantees

7.11 The provision covers individual thought, conscience and religion, and collective manifestation of that opinion or belief with others. Consequently, the concerns it raises are closely allied to other ECHR guarantees and in particular to protection of expression, peaceful assembly, and respect for religious and philosophical convictions of parents in the provision of state education for their children under Articles 10 and 11 and Article 2 of Protocol no 1 respectively[1]. The guarantee is also buttressed by Article 14's prohibition of discrimination on the grounds inter alia of religious and political opinion[2]. Thus if it is ultimately determined that Article 9 is not applicable, it will nevertheless be necessary to consider whether the issue in question can be considered under another provision of the ECHR, either alone or in conjunction with Article 14. The deprivation of a religious organisation's material resources, for example, has been held not to fall within the scope of Article 9, but rather to give rise to issues under the protection of property in terms of Article 1 of Protocol no 1[3]. Similarly, refusal to grant an individual an exemption from the payment of a church tax on the ground of non-registration may be better considered in terms of the right to property taken in conjunction with the prohibition on discrimination in the enjoyment of ECHR guarantees rather than as a matter of conscience or religion[4]. The refusal to recognise marriage with an underage girl as permitted by Islamic law was deemed not to involve an interference with manifestation of belief falling within the scope of Article 9 but rather as a matter concerning the right to marry under Article 12[5]. Freedom of conscience issues may also arise under Article 3's prohibition of inhuman or degrading treatment or punishment[6], and under the protection of liberty and security of the person under Article 5[7].

---

1 See eg *Lombardi Vallauri v Italy* 2009-..., paras 43–56 (refusal to renew teaching post at a denominational university as views were considered incompatible with Catholic religious doctrine: violation of Art 10); *Masaev v Moldova* (12 May 2009), at para 26 (recognition of power 'to put in place a requirement for the registration of religious denominations in a manner compatible with Articles 9 and 11 of the Convention'); and *Lautsi v Italy* [GC] 2011-..., paras 59–78 (passive display of Crucifix on wall of state school did not restrict the rights of parents to have their children educated in conformity with their religious beliefs and the right of children to form their own opinions on religion: no violation of Prot 1, Art 2), discussed at para **6.164** above.

2 Eg *Thlimmenos v Greece* [GC] 2000-IV, discussed at para **7.12** below. See further paras **3.121–3.123** above.

3 *The Holy Monasteries v Greece* (1994) 301-A, paras 74–75 (Prot 1, Art 1), and cf paras 86–88 (no breach of Art 9). But cf *Association of Jehovah's Witnesses v France* (dec) (21 September 2010) (refusal to grant association of Jehovah's Witnesses tax exemption available to religious organisations following classification as a 'sect' and resulting in €45 million tax liability: admissible under Art 9).

4 *Darby v Sweden* (1990) A 187, paras 30–34.

5 11579/85, *Khan v United Kingdom* (1986) DR 48, 253.

6 *Ülke v Turkey* (24 January 2006), discussed at para **4.114** above.

7 See eg *Tsirlis and Kouloumpas v Greece* 1997-III, paras 56–63 (refusal of authorities to exempt ministers of certain religions from military service contrary to domestic law: issue

considered under Art 5); *Riera Blume and Others v Spain* 1999-VII, paras 25–35 (holding of sect members on the order of a judge to allow their 'de-programming': not in accordance with domestic law, and thus violation of Art 5), discussed at para **4.152** above.

Religious discrimination

7.12 Discriminatory treatment based upon religious beliefs may give rise to questions under Article 9 or this provision taken along with Article 14[1]. The potential scope of the corresponding protection can be wide, as the Court made clear in its judgment in *Savez Crkava 'Rijeè Žlvota' and Others v Croatia*. Reformed churches complained that they were unable – in contrast to other religions – to have religious marriages conducted in accordance with their rites recognised as equal to those of civil marriages, or to be permitted to offer religious education in public schools. Although the Convention could not be interpreted so as to impose an obligation to have the effects of religious marriages recognised as equal to those of civil marriages, the Court accepted that the celebration of a religious marriage as it amounts to observance of a religious rite did constitute a manifestation of religion. Similarly, while the right to manifest religion in teaching could not be taken to extend to an obligation to allow religious education in public schools, such teaching when permitted did constitute a 'manifestation' of belief. In consequence, the Court held that when a state goes beyond its core obligations under Article 9 and creates additional rights falling within the wider ambit of freedom of religion or conscience, Article 14 of would also apply 'to those additional rights, falling within the wider ambit of any Convention Article'[2].

Discriminatory treatment may also involve indirect discrimination. In *Thlimmenos v Greece,* the refusal to allow an individual to be admitted as a chartered accountant on account of a criminal conviction from refusal to wear military uniform on account of his religious beliefs as a Jehovah's Witness was found to have violated Article 14 when taken with Article 9. The Court noted that access to a profession was not as such covered by the ECHR, but treated the complaint as one of discrimination on the basis of the exercise of freedom of religion. Although states could legitimately exclude certain classes of offenders from various professions, the particular conviction in question could not suggest dishonesty or moral turpitude. The treatment of the applicant therefore did not have a legitimate aim, and was in the nature of a disproportionate sanction (additional to the substantial period of imprisonment he had already served)[3].

1   Eg *Hoffman v Austria* (1993) A 255-C, discussed at para **3.122** above. See also *Religionsgemeinschaft der Zeugen Jehovas and Others v Austria* (31 January 2008), paras 64–99 (differences in application of eligibility criteria for registration as a religious society: violations of Art 9 and of Art 14 taken with 9).

2   *Savez Crkava 'Riječ Žlvota' and Others v Croatia* (9 December 2010), paras 55–58.

3   *Thlimmenos v Greece* [GC] 2000-IV, paras 39–49 (consideration of issue under Art 9 alone not necessary in view of the finding of violation). Cf *CR v Switzerland* (dec) (14 October 1999) (withdrawal of licence permitting applicant to run a private security agency on account of his connections with a sect whose beliefs were considered potentially destabilising for public

order declared inadmissible); and see also *Association Solidarité des Français v France* (dec) (16 June 2009), paras 77–82 and 87–99 (ban on the distributing of meals primarily consisting of pork to underprivileged persons: inadmissible, as the ban was necessary and proportionate to the legitimate aim pursued: prohibition considered in terms of Arts 9 and 11, but inadmissible in light of the clearly discriminatory aims of the applicant association, the affront to the dignity of vulnerable persons and the considerable risk of public disorder in view of the controversy surrounding the handouts).

The **forum internum**

7.13 Protection of personal thought, conscience and belief at the outset involves the rights to hold and to change beliefs, the area often referred to as the *forum internum*[1]. These rights appear to be absolute rights, for paragraph 2 provides that only the 'freedom to manifest one's religion or beliefs' may be limited by domestic law in particular circumstances and thus the clear implication is that freedom of thought, conscience and religion *not* involving an 'external' manifestation of belief cannot be subject to state interference[2]. Certainly, it must be possible for an individual to leave a religious faith or community[3]. Similarly, domestic law may not impose an obligation to provide support to a religious organisation by means of taxation without recognising the right of an individual to leave the church and thus to obtain an exemption from the requirement[4].

1   22838/93, *Van den Dungen v Netherlands* (1995) DR 80, 147; and 23380/94, *CJ, JJ and EJ v Poland* (1996) DR 84, 46 (Art 9 primarily protects personal beliefs and faiths, that is, the area often referred to as the *forum internum*, and acts intimately related to these beliefs). Harris, O'Boyle and Warbrick *Law of the European Convention on Human Rights* (2nd edn, 2009), at p 428 note that the distinction between 'internal' and external' dimensions of Art 9 is not a clear one.

2   ECHR, Art 15 allows for derogation in time of public emergency etc, but it is difficult to see how a state could in practice 'take measures' to interfere with the holding of convictions. Cf *Riera Blume and Others v Spain* 1999-VII, paras 31–35 (unlawful deprivation of liberty of individuals in order to attempt to "de-programme" beliefs acquired when members of a sect, but a finding of a violation of Art 5 meant that it was unnecessary to consider Art 9). This appears to be the sole instance of obstruction of the rights to hold and to change personal convictions found in the jurisprudence. Note also the right of parents to have their philosophical convictions respected in the education of their children, discussed at paras **6.161–6.165** above.

3   *Darby v Sweden* (1980) A 187, opinion of Commission, para 45.

4   *Darby v Sweden* (1980) A 187, paras 30–34 (violation of Art 14 taken with Prot 1, Art 1. However, this principle does not extend to general legal obligations falling exclusively in the public sphere, and thus taxpayers may not demand that their payments are not allocated to particular purposes: 10358/83, *C v the United Kingdom* (1983) DR 37, 142.

7.14 While there is no explicit reference in the text to the prohibition of indoctrination or coercion to hold or to adopt a religion or belief, Article 9 issues may also arise in situations in which individuals are required to act against their conscience or beliefs. Protection of the *forum internum* thus is inextricably linked to the negative aspect of freedom to manifest one's beliefs: that is, the individual's right not to be obliged to manifest religious beliefs and not to be obliged to act in such a way as to enable conclusions to be drawn regarding whether an individual holds – or does not hold – such beliefs[1]. In *Buscarini and Others v San Marino*, for example, two individuals who had been elected to parliament had been required to take a religious oath on the Bible as a condition of their appointment to office. The respondent government sought to argue that the form of words used ('I swear on the Holy Gospels ever to be faithful to and obey the Constitution of the Republic ...') was essentially of historical and social rather than religious significance. In agreeing with the Commission that it 'would be contradictory to make the exercise of a mandate intended to represent different views of society within Parliament subject to a prior declaration of commitment to a particular set of beliefs', the Court determined that the imposition of the requirement could not be deemed to be 'necessary in a democratic society'[2].

---

1   *Alexandridis v Greece* 2008-..., paras 35–41 (requirement for solemn declaration instead of oath involved an obligation to reveal in part religious beliefs, the procedure reflecting a presumption that lawyers were Orthodox Christians: the fact that the applicant had had to reveal to the court that he was not such constituted an interference with the freedom not to have to manifest his religious beliefs); and 869*Dimitras and Others v Greece* (3 June 2010), paras 79–88 (requirement to disclose that an individual was not an Orthodox Christian and in certain cases was Jewish or an atheist to avoid having to take a religious oath in criminal proceedings: violation).

2   *Buscarini and Others v San Marino* [GC] 1999-I, paras 34–41 at para 39.

7.15 Forcing an individual to disclose his beliefs thus undermines protection of the *forum internum* and constitutes an interference with Article 9 rights[1]. However, in a limited set of circumstances where a compelling justification such a requirement can be advanced, for example where an individual is seeking himself to take advantage of a special privilege made available in domestic law on the grounds of belief, there is unlikely to be a violation of the guarantee. This situation may arise in respect of requests for exemption from military service or in the context of employment. In *Kosteski v 'The Former Yugoslav Republic of Macedonia'*, a case concerning the penalisation of the applicant for failing to attend his place of work on the day of a religious holiday, the Court observed that 'while the notion of the State sitting in judgment on the state of a citizen's inner and personal beliefs is abhorrent and may smack unhappily of past infamous persecutions', it had not been inappropriate for the authorities to seek to ascertain whether the applicant properly could take advantage of legislation providing that Muslims could take holiday on particular days. In employment cases where unauthorised absences could be treated as disciplinary matters and an employee then seeks to rely on a particular exemption on the basis of belief 'it is not oppressive or in fundamental conflict with freedom of conscience to require some level of substantiation when that claim concerns a privilege or entitlement not commonly available and, if that substantiation is not forthcoming, to reach a negative conclusion'[2]. The qualification 'privilege or entitlement not commonly available' suggests a restricted application of this principle. While a state may seek to ascertain the values and beliefs held by candidates for public employment on the grounds that they hold views incompatible with their office[3], the failure to appoint to a post on the ground of belief may be difficult to justify as an interference with freedom of expression[4]. Nor can education authorities probe too far into the beliefs of parents who seek to have their philosophical convictions taken into account in the provision of education for their children[5].

1   See also *Sinan Işık v Turkey* 2010-…, paras 37–53 (identity cards carried a 'religion' data field but which could be left blank: violation, as a decision to have a card with the religion field left blank inevitably carried specific connotations). The question of questions relating to religious belief in censuses is discussed in Harris, O'Boyle and Warbrick *Law of the European Convention on Human Rights* (2nd ed, 2009), at p 429, noting that while the requirement to complete a census form can be justified under Art 8, the same is unlikely to be the case under Art 9: 'The state may… neither dictate nor demand to know what an individual believes… Perhaps the explanation for this positive affirmation of freedom of thought, conscience and religion is that there are unlikely to be good reasons why the state should need such information, but there are undoubtedly many bad ones ….' For international standards, see Human Rights Committee, General Comment 22, Article 18, CCPR/C/21/Rev.1/Add (1993): 'Article 18 [of the ICCPR] distinguishes the freedom of thought, conscience, religion or belief from the freedom to manifest religion or belief. It does not permit any limitations whatsoever on the freedom of thought and conscience or on the freedom to have or adopt a religion or belief of one's choice. These freedoms are protected unconditionally, as is the right of everyone to hold opinions without interference….. In accordance with articles 18.2 and 17, no one can be compelled to reveal his thoughts or adherence to a religion or belief.

2   *Kosteski v 'The Former Yugoslav Republic of Macedonia'* (13 April 2006), paras 37–40 at para 39. See also 10410/83, *N v Sweden* (1984) DR 40, 203; and 20972/92, *Raninen v Finland* (7 March 1996).

3   *Vogt v Germany* (1995) A 323, paras 41–68 (disposal under Arts 10 and 11).

4   See further paras **7.65** and **7.88–7.89** below. See also *Lombardi Vallauri v Italy* 2009-…, paras 43–56 (university lecturer refused a teaching post at a denominational university on account of incompatible views with religious doctrine: violation of Art 10 on account of the failure to explain how the applicant's views were liable to affect the interests of the university); but cf *Schüth v Germany* 2010-…,discussed at para **7.28** below.

5   *Folgerø and Others v Norway* [GC] 2007-VIII, para 98, discussed at para **6.165** above (requirement upon parents to disclose beliefs to education authorities may be contrary to Arts 8 and 9); and *Hasan and Eylem Zengin v Turkey* 2007-XI, at para 73: 'the fact that parents must make a prior declaration to schools stating that they belong to the Christian or Jewish religion in order for their children to be exempted from the classes in question may also raise a problem under Article 9'.

Manifestations of religion or belief

7.16 Protection of thought, conscience and belief also covers 'manifestations' of religion or belief, that is, the right includes the 'freedom, either alone or in community with others and in public or private, to manifest his religion or belief in worship, teaching, practice and observance'. As discussed above, there is also a negative aspect of the freedom to manifest one's beliefs, that is, the rights not to be obliged to manifest religious beliefs and not to be obliged to act in such a way as to enable conclusions to be drawn regarding whether an individual does or does not hold such beliefs[1]. However, care is needed in determining whether the facts support a conclusion that a 'manifestation' of belief has occurred, for as the Commission clarified in *Arrowsmith v United Kingdom,* this term 'does not cover each act which is motivated or influenced by a religion or a belief'. In this case, the applicant had been convicted for distributing leaflets to soldiers which were critical of government policy in Ulster. The Commission accepted that any public declaration which proclaimed the idea of pacifism and urged acceptance of a commitment to the belief in non-violence would fall to be considered as a 'normal and recognised manifestation of pacifist belief'. However, the leaflets in question did not so qualify as they focused not upon the promotion of non-violent means for dealing with political issues (matters that would have attracted Article 9 protection) but rather with British policy in Northern Ireland, and thus the distribution of leaflets which failed to express the authors' own pacifist values could not be a 'manifestation' of a belief for the purposes of Article 9. A crucial distinction thus exists between actions merely motivated by belief (in this case, the distribution of the leaflets) and actual 'manifestations'[2].

1   *Alexandridis v Greece* 2008-..., para 38.

2   7050/75, *Arrowsmith v United Kingdom* (1978) DR 19, 5 (the distribution of leaflets was admissible under Art 10). See too 22838/93, *Van der Dungen v Netherlands* (1995) DR 80, 147 (distribution of anti-abortion material outside a clinic did not involve expression of the applicant's religious beliefs); and *Zaoui v Switzerland* (dec) (18 January 2001) (publication of political propaganda on behalf of an Islamic group resulting in the confiscation of means of communication: activities did not concern the expression of a religious belief, and thus inadmissible under Art 9).

7.17 The text of paragraph 2 suggests that 'manifestations' may only relate to 'religion or beliefs' rather than to the exercise of freedom of thought and conscience (and thus that interferences with the *forum internum* cannot be justified)[1]. Disposing of claims that a particular action is a 'manifestation' of an individual's religious belief runs the risk of requiring the Court to assess the acceptability of individual beliefs and values or of determining matters of religious dogma, matters of dubious competence for judges. Certainly, matters such as proselytism[2], general participation in the life of a religious community[3], following a diet dictated by religion[4] or slaughtering animals in accordance with religious prescriptions[5] have been readily recognised as qualifying as 'manifestations'. It appears less easy to satisfy the test of 'manifestation' when the claims appear not to be grounded in mainstream religious observation[6]. Thus cases involving the physical chastisement of children on religious grounds[7], the placing of advertisements of a commercial nature concerning religious objects[8], and the refusal of pharmacists to sell contraceptives[9] will not so qualify as a 'manifestation'. Focusing upon majority practice rather than upon individual interpretation of religious teachings may not be entirely appropriate, particularly if this requires intrusive scrutiny of individual belief. Some retreat from – or at least, relaxation of – the *Arrowsmith* approach is now evident: for example, it is now accepted that the wearing of conspicuous signs of religious beliefs in schools should be considered as a restriction on the freedom to manifest religious faith[10].

1   *Kokkinakis v Greece* (1993) A 260-A, at para 33: 'Unlike the second paragraphs of Articles 8, 10 and 11 which cover all the rights mentioned in the first paragraphs of those Articles, that of

Article 9 refers only to "freedom to manifest one's religion or belief". In so doing, it recognises that in democratic societies, in which several religions coexist within one and the same population, it may be necessary to place restrictions on this freedom in order to reconcile the interests of the various groups and ensure that everyone's beliefs are respected'. See also *R (Pretty) v Director of Public Prosecutions* [2002] 1 AC 800 (assisted suicide).

2   *Kokkinakis v Greece* (1993) A 260-A. See too *Al-Nashif and Others v Bulgaria* (20 June 2002) (deportation on account of having taught Islamic religion without proper authorisation: in view of finding that deportation would constitute a violation of Art 8, no need to consider Art 9).

3   *Hasan and Chaush v Bulgaria* [GC] 2000-XI, paras 60–65 (Art 9 to be interpreted in light of Art 11).

4   Cf 13669/88, *DS and ES v United Kingdom* (1990) DR 65, 245 (restriction on ability of Orthodox Jews to obtain 'kosher' meat; failure to exhaust domestic remedies and thus inadmissible).

5   *Cha'are Shalom Ve Tsedek v France* [GC] 2000-VII, para 74, discussed at para **7.25** below.

6   See also *Valsamis v Greece* 1996-VI, paras 37–38; and *Efstratiou v Greece* 1996-VI, paras 38–39, discussed at para **7.25** below.

7   Eg 8811/79, *Seven Individuals v Sweden* (1982) DR 29, 104 (prohibition of parental chastisement of children even where practice is based upon religious beliefs not a breach of Art 9). See also *R (Williamson) v Secretary of State for Education and Employment* [2005] 2 AC 246.

8   7805/77, *X and the Church of Scientology v Sweden* (1979) DR 16, 68, para 4 (distinction drawn between 'informational' advertisements which may fall within Art 9, and those which seek to sell goods for profit which do not).

9   *Pichon and Sajous v France* (dec) 2001-X.

10   *Aktas v France* (dec) (30 June 2009) (expulsion from school for refusing to remove various religious symbols). See further para **7.34** below.

The collective aspect of Article 9

7.18 As the text of paragraph (1) makes clear, a 'manifestation' of belief may take place 'either alone or in community with others' and both in the private and public spheres. Worship with others may be the most obvious form of collective manifestation of religious belief, and restrictions placed upon access to places of worship or upon adherents' ability to take part in services or observances thus will give rise to Article 9 issues[1]. States, too, may seek to place restrictions upon organisational recognition, for example, by denying registration where domestic law requires such in order to allow a religious community to take advantage of privileges in domestic law. As a believer's right to freedom of religion includes the expectation that his religious community will be able to function free from arbitrary state intervention, so a failure by the state to remain neutral in exercising powers of registration of a religious community will involve an interference with freedom to manifest belief[2]. In this area, then, Article 9 needs to be interpreted in light of the protection accorded by Article 11. Further, since a religious community must be guaranteed access to court to safeguard its interests, Article 6 may also be of crucial importance, for 'one of the means of exercising the right to manifest one's religion, especially for a religious community, in its collective dimension, is the possibility of ensuring judicial protection of the community, its members and its assets, so that Article 9 must be seen not only in the light of Article 11, but also in the light of Article 6'[3].

1   *Cyprus v Turkey* [GC] 2001-IV, paras 241–247 (restrictions on movement including access to places of worship curtailed ability to observe religious beliefs). Cf *Barankevich v Russia* (26 July 2007), paras 28–35 (refusal to allow minority church group to hold worship in a park: violation of Art 11 interpreted in the light of Art 9).

2   *Hasan and Chaush v Bulgaria* [GC] 2000-XI, para 82 (favouring of one faction in a leadership dispute between rivals for the post of Chief Mufti of Muslims living in the country). See further para **7.39** below.

3   *Metropolitan Church of Bessarabia v Moldova* 2001-XII, at para 118.

7.19 Whenever individual and collective aspects of Article 9 conflict, it will generally be appropriate to consider that the collective rather than the individual manifestation of belief should prevail, for the reason that 'a church is an organised religious community based on identical or at least substantially similar views', and thus a religious community 'itself is protected in its rights to manifest its religion, to organise and carry out worship, teaching, practice and observance, and it is free to act out and enforce uniformity in these matters'. In consequence, it will be difficult for a member of the clergy to maintain that he has the right to manifest his own individual beliefs in a manner contrary to the standard practice of his church[1]. For the purposes of Article 9, though, it is crucial that the challenge involves action taken by a state rather than by an ecclesiastical body. Thus where a dispute involves a matter such as use of the liturgy, state responsibility will not be engaged since such involves a challenge to a matter of internal church administration taken by a body that is not a governmental agency[2]. This is so even when the religious body involved is recognised by domestic law as enjoying the particular status of an established church[3].

1   8160/78, *X v United Kingdom* (1981) DR 22, 27. See also 11045/84, *Knudsen v Norway* (1985) DR 42, 247.

2   24019/94, *Finska Fösamlingen I Stockholm and Hautaniemi v Sweden* (1996) DR 85, 94 (Lutheran Church and its parishes were non-governmental organisations, and thus decisions of the Church Assembly concerning freedom of religion did not engage state responsibility under Art 9); but see too *Pellegrini v Italy* 2001-VIII, paras 40–48 (breach of fairness requirements under Art 6 in proceedings before a Vatican ecclesiastical court lacking impartiality, the domestic courts having given effect to the determination).

3   7374/76, *X v Denmark* (1976) DR 5, 158.

'Victim' status and religious organisations

7.20 The collective aspect of Article 9 is further acknowledged by recognition that a church or other religious organisation may qualify as a 'victim' within the meaning of Article 34 for the purpose of satisfying admissibility criteria on the basis that it is acting on behalf of its members[1]. However, recognition of representative status will not extend to a commercial body[2], and recognition of representative status in respect of an association appears only to extend to religious belief and not to allegations of interference with thought or conscience[3].

1   See eg 7805/77, *X and Church of Scientology v Sweden* (1979) DR 16, 68 (Church in lodging an application under Art 9 does so in a representative capacity on behalf of its members); but a church or legal person cannot claim to be victim of freedom of conscience: 11921/86, *Verein Kontakt-Information-Therapie and Hagen v Austria* (1988) DR 57, 81. In *Canea Catholic Church v Greece* 1997-VIII, paras 44–47 the Court found a violation of Art 6(1) taken alone and with Art 14 (legal capacity of Greek Catholic Church to take legal proceedings was restricted, and thus the very substance of 'right to a court' was impaired; further, no formalities or restrictions were imposed on the Orthodox Church or the Jewish community, and there was no objective or reasonable justification for such a difference of treatment). Cf 34614/96, *Scientology Kirche Deutschland v Germany* (1997) DR 89, 163 (only the members of an association and not the association itself could claim to be a 'victim' of Art 8's guarantee of respect for private life).

2   20471/92, *Kustannus Oy Vapaa Ajattelija Ab, Vapaa-Ajattelijain Liitto – Fritänkarnas Förbund ry and Sundström v Finland* (1996), DR 85, 29.

3   11921/86, *Verein 'Kontakt-Information-Therapie' and Hagen v Austria* (1988) DR 57, 81. See also *Féderation Chrétienne des Temoins de Jehovah v France* (dec) (6 November 2001) (inclusion of Jehovah's Witnesses in a list of sects considered dangerous by a parliamentary commission and which allegedly triggered a policy of repression: issue avoided as the applicant association was not a 'victim' for the purposes of Art 34).

Positive obligations

7.21 The duty upon the state to refrain from interfering with thought, conscience or religious belief may extend in certain circumstances to the taking of action to provide protection to help ensure respect for these rights. In deciding generally whether or not a positive obligation arises, the Strasbourg Court will seek to 'have regard to the fair balance that has to be struck between the general interest of the community and the competing private interests of the individual, or individuals, concerned'[1]. It goes without saying that the authorities must respond diligently to violent acts directed against adherents of a religious group[2]. Religious adherents should be permitted to practise their faith in accordance with dietary requirements, although any positive obligation within this area may be limited to ensuring there is reasonable access to the foodstuff, rather than access to facilities for the ritual preparation of meat[3]. The state will also be expected to recognise the religious needs of those deprived of their liberty by ensuring the provision of religious observances[4] and respect for religious practices unless these are considered inconsistent with the maintenance of good order[5].

1   33490/96 and 34055/96, *Dubowska and Skup v Poland* (1997) DR 89, 156.

2   *97 Members of the Gidani Congregation of Jehovah's Witnesses and 4 Others v Georgia* (3 May 2007), paras 98–125, 129–135, and 139–142 (group attack by Orthodox believers leading to violent assaults and destruction of religious artefacts, the police being unwilling to intervene or investigate, and little attempt being made to instigate criminal proceedings: violation of Arts 3 and 9, and of Art 14 in conjunction with Arts 3 and 9 since the authorities had allowed the perpetrators of the attacks to stir up religious hatred in the media, no justification for such discriminatory treatment having been advanced).

3   *Cha'are Shalom Ve Tsedek v France* [GC] 2000-VII, para 76 (exception permitting ritual slaughter of animals was an example of the discharge of a positive obligation under Art 9).

4   Cf *Guzzardi v Italy* (1980) A 39, para 110 (applicant had not specifically requested provision of services, and consequently no issue in terms of Art 9 arose). For discussion of diet for prisoners, see para **7.35** below.

5   Cf 6886/75, *X v United Kingdom* (1976) DR 5, 100 (prisoner sought access to martial arts book as part of his religious beliefs: refusal justified under Art 9(2) by the security threat posed).

7.22 The fundamental principle in this regard is the duty to ensure that religious liberty exists within a spirit of pluralism and mutual tolerance[1]. For example, it may be necessary for the authorities to help resolve internal dispute within religious communities, but as the case of *The Supreme Holy Council of The Muslim Community v Bulgaria* makes clear, the nature of such an intervention must be considered carefully. Here, the respondent government had attempted to address long-standing and continuing divisions caused by conflicts of a political and personal nature within the Muslim religious community. The question was essentially whether the resultant change of religious leadership had been the result of undue state pressure rather than the outcome of a decision freely arrived at by the community. While agreeing that that states have a duty to try to help resolve tensions between groups, caution was required 'in this particularly delicate area'. The Court concluded that the authorities had actively sought the reunification of the divided community by taking steps to compel the imposition of a single leadership against the will of one of the two rival leaderships, action that had gone beyond 'neutral mediation' and thus had involved an interference with Article 9 rights[2].

1   *Kokkinakis v Greece* (1993) A 260-A, para 33.

2   *Supreme Holy Council of the Muslim Community v Bulgaria* (16 December 2004), paras 81–99.

7.23 The extent of any positive obligation to recognise exemptions from generally applicable civic or legal obligations[1] is not always obvious, for the Court has not drawn a clear distinction between the *obligation* to take steps, and approval of state action which has been taken at domestic level with the aim of advancing protection for belief[2]. In other words, there appears to be an important difference between Strasbourg Court approbation of domestic measures taken with a view to promote belief, and cases in which the failure to take steps to protect belief is determined to have involved an interference. Whether action is mandatory or merely permissive will always depend on the circumstances. In light of Article 4, which makes specific provision for 'service of a military character', Article 9 cannot probably in itself imply any right of recognition of conscientious objection to compulsory military service[3] although any discriminatory or disproportionate treatment[4] or sanctions imposed for failure to serve in the military[5] may give rise to issues under other provisions of the ECHR.

1   Cf *Martins Casimiro and Cerveira Ferreira v Luxembourg* (dec) (27 April 1999) (a refusal to grant a general exemption from attending school on Saturdays on religious grounds to the sons

of the applicants, Seventh Day Adventists, could be regarded as an interference with the manifestation of belief, but no general dispensation could be recognised which would adversely affect a child's right to education which prevailed over the parents' rights to have their religious convictions taken into account: application deemed inadmissible); and the related cases of *Valsamis v Greece* and *Efstratiou v Greece* 1996-VI, paras 37–38, and 1996-VI, paras 38–39, discussed at para **7.25** below.

2   See eg *Otto-Preminger-Institut v Austria* (1994) A 295-A, discussed at para **7.24** below; and *Cha'are Shalom Ve Tsedek v France* [GC] 2000-VII, discussed at para **7.25** below.

3   7705/76, *X v Germany* (1977) DR 9, 196 (no right to be exempted from compulsory civilian service where the state recognises this as an alternative to military service). However, by 2000, only three Council of Europe states (Albania, FYRO Macedonia, and Turkey) with military service did not recognise alternative civilian service: see Council of Europe 'Report of the Committee on Legal Affairs and Human Rights on the Exercise of the Right of Conscientious Objection to Military Service', doc 8809, 13 July 2000. It is not clear whether the Court in future would read into Art 9 a right to recognition of alternative civilian service in a clear case where an individual otherwise would be compelled to act contrary to fundamental religious beliefs. The issue was raised but avoided in *Stefanov v Bulgaria* (3 May 2001), paras 14–16 (prison sentence imposed on Jehovah's Witness for his refusal to undertake military service; the Constitution provided that substitute civilian service should be regulated by statute, but no such law had been enacted: friendly settlement providing that all convictions of citizens for failing to undertake military service would be quashed where citizens had been willing to undertake civilian service); but note that the case of *Bayatyan v Armenia* 2009-…, paras 55–66 (conviction for refusing to perform military service on grounds of conscience did not violate Art 9) has been referred to the Grand Chamber. See also 17086/90, *Autio v Finland* (1991) DR 72, 245 (lengthier period of service prescribed for civilian service as opposed to military service falls within a state's margin of appreciation: inadmissible). See further para **4.143** above. For domestic discussion, see *Sepet v Secretary of State for the Home Department* [2003] 1 WLR 856 (conscientious objection); *Khan v Royal Air Force Summary Appeal Court* [2004] EWHC 2230 (Admin) (no interference with Art 9 rights of a reservist member of the armed forces claiming status of a conscientious objector until he had informed the services of his belief).

4   See in particular *Thlimmenos v Greece* [GC] 2000-IV, discussed at para **7.12** above. See also 10600/83, *Johansen v Norway* (1985) DR 44, 155 (limited exemptions of certain ministers of religion from military service: no breach of Art 9 taken together with Art 14); 10410/83, *N v Sweden* (1984) DR 40, 203 (question whether exemptions from military service were operated in a discriminatory manner: no violation).

5   Eg *Ülke v Turkey* (24 January 2006), paras 61 and 62, discussed at para **4.114** above; and *Tsirlis and Kouloumpas v Greece* 1997-III, discussed at para **4.243** above.

7.24 The obligation to encourage mutual tolerance and understanding may justify protection of the sensibilities of adherents of particular faiths by preventing or punishing the display of insulting or offensive material which could discourage adherents from practising or professing their faith through ridicule. Achieving an appropriate balance between the freedom to express controversial ideas which may appear offensive, and protection for thought, conscience and religion is not always a straightforward one, as illustrated by *Otto-Preminger-Institut v Austria*. Here, the authorities had seized and ordered the forfeiture of a film which ridiculed the beliefs of Roman Catholics. In interpreting Article 10's guarantee of freedom of expression, the European Court of Human Rights accepted that those who manifest their religious convictions 'must tolerate and accept the denial by others of their religious beliefs and even the propagation by others of doctrines hostile to their faith'. However, the Court also considered that national authorities could deem it necessary to take action to protect believers against 'provocative portrayals of objects of religious veneration' where such constitute 'malicious violation of the spirit of tolerance, which must also be a feature of democratic society'[1]. Similarly, in *Wingrove v United Kingdom*, the Court rejected a complaint brought under Article 10 concerning the refusal of the British Board of Film Classification to license a video considered blasphemous, an interference which was deemed justified as for the protection of the rights of Christians[2]. In both these cases, the Court stressed that objection was taken to the manner in which the opinions had been expressed rather than to the content of the opinions themselves[3].

---

1   *Otto-Preminger-Institut v Austria* (1994) A 295-A, at para 47. Cf 33490/96 and 34055/96, *Dubowska and Skup v Poland* (1997) DR 89, 156 (criminal investigations were instituted into the display of a picture causing offence to religious sensitivities, but the conclusion that no offence had been committed did not involve a failure to protect the applicants' rights under Art 9); and *Vereinigung Bildender Künstler v Austria* 2007-II, discussed at para **7.113** below.

2   *Wingrove v United Kingdom* 1996-V, paras 57–65. Cf the approach of the Commission in 17439/90, *Choudhury v United Kingdom* (5 March 1991) (failure to extend protection of the law of blasphemy in England to other religions including the Muslim faith did not directly interfere with the applicant's freedom to manifest his belief: inadmissible).

3   *Otto-Preminger-Institut v Austria* (1994) A 295-A, para 56; *Wingrove v United Kingdom* 1996-V, para 60. See too 8710/79, *X Ltd and Y v United Kingdom* (1982) DR 28, 77 (protection accorded by English law of blasphemy justified as 'necessary in a democratic society': no violation of Art 10). See further para **7.108** below. For discussion of domestic provisions, see Goodall 'Incitement to Religious Hatred: All Talk and No Substance?' (2007) 70 MLR 89.

Interferences

7.25 The facts must support a finding that there has been an 'interference' with rights in terms of Article 9. This issue is not always as clear as determining whether there has been an interference with freedom of expression under Article 10[1], even where a complaint has been motivated by deep and sincere conviction. In the related cases of *Valsamis v Greece* and *Efstratiou v Greece*, pupils who were Jehovah's Witnesses had been punished for failing to attend parades commemorating the country's national day because of their belief that such events were incompatible with their firmly-held pacifism. The Court considered that the nature of these parades (even taking into account the involvement of military personnel) contained nothing which could offend the applicants' pacifist convictions[2]. The judgment seems unconvincing: the dissenting judges could discern no ground for holding that participation in a public event designed to show solidarity with symbolism which was anathema to personal religious belief could be 'necessary in a democratic society'[3]. In *Cha'are Shalom Ve Tsedek v France*, a religious body sought to challenge a refusal by the authorities to grant the necessary permission to allow it to perform the slaughter of animals for consumption in accordance with its ultra-orthodox beliefs. Another Jewish organisation had received approval for the slaughter of animals according to its own rites which differed only marginally from those of the applicant association. Further, meat prepared in a manner consistent with the applicant association's beliefs was also available from other suppliers in a neighbouring country. On these grounds, the Court determined that there had been no interference since it had not been made impossible for the association's adherents to obtain meat slaughtered in a manner considered appropriate[4]. The issue of *accessibility* to such meat rather than the grant of authority to carry out ritual slaughter was treated as crucial, but the case also suggests that there are limits to the state's responsibilities to respect cultural pluralism without explaining the grounds for this or where these limits lie.

---

1   See para **7.65** below. Cf *Cyprus v Turkey* [GC] 2001-IV, paras 245–246 at para 245: (restrictions placed on the freedom of movement of Greek Cypriots in northern Turkey 'considerably curtailed their ability to observe their religious beliefs, in particular their access to places of worship outside their villages and their participation in other aspects of religious life': violation of Art 9).

2   *Valsamis v Greece and Efstratiou v Greece* 1996-VI, paras 37–38; and 1996-VI, paras 38–39 (public celebration of democracy and human rights not vitiated by presence of military; similarly, no violation of Prot 1, Art 2).

3   Cf the dissenting opinion of the Commission President, Trechsel, who considered that the issue was more appropriate for consideration under Art 11.

4   *Cha'are Shalom Ve Tsedek v France* [GC] 2000-VII, paras 73–85. The Court also noted that, even if there had been an interference, this would have pursued the aim of protection of public health and order and would not have been considered disproportionate. The judgment of the majority of the Court (12 to 5) differs sharply from the majority of the Commission (14 to 3) which had been of the opinion that there had been a violation of Art 9 taken along with Art 14. The Court on this point considered that the difference of treatment was limited in scope and also met the test of proportionality, and no Art 14 question arose (at paras 86–88).

Employment and belief

7.26 The Court has been for long reluctant to recognise any positive obligation on the part of the state to ensure that employers take steps to facilitate the manifestation of belief, for example, by organising the discharge of responsibilities to allow an individual to worship at a particular time or in a particular manner. The justification for such an approach was the contractual nature of employment and the voluntary acceptance of restrictions[1]. In other words, the assumption was that an employee who leaves his employment will thereby be able to follow whatever observances felt necessary. Thus employees have a duty to observe the rules governing their working hours, and dismissal for failing to attend work on account of religious observances does not give rise to an issue falling within the scope of Article 9[2]. Indeed, in respect of certain public sector employment, 'in order to perform its role as the neutral and impartial organiser of the exercise of religious beliefs, the State may decide to impose on its serving or future civil servants, who will be required to wield a portion of its sovereign power, the duty to refrain from taking part' in the activities of religious movements[3]. A member of the clergy of an established church is expected not only to discharge religious but also secular duties, and cannot complain if the latter conflict with his personal beliefs, for his right to relinquish his office will constitute the ultimate guarantee of his freedom of conscience[4]. In short, unless there are special features accepted as being of particular weight, incompatibility between contractual or other duties and personal belief or principle will not normally give rise to an issue under Article 9, and thus action taken as a result of the deliberate non-observance of contractual duties is unlikely to constitute an interference with an individual's rights[5]. Where a right or privilege based upon belief is further conferred in the course of employment, an employee who seeks to rely upon this may reasonably be expected to show that he so qualifies[6].

1   *Kalaç v Turkey* 1997-IV, paras 28–31 (a member of the armed forces had voluntarily accepted restrictions upon his ability to manifest his beliefs when joining up on the grounds of the exigencies of military life, but in any event, it had not been shown that the applicant had been prevented from fulfilling his religious observations). See also *Kurtulmuş v Turkey* (dec) (24 January 2006) (university professor refused authorisation to wear a headscarf). This issue may also arise under Art 10: eg 12242/86, *Rommelfanger v Germany* (1989) DR 62, 151 (dismissal of a doctor employed in a Roman Catholic hospital for expressing views on abortion not in conformity with the Church's teaching: inadmissible). Note though EU Council Directive 2000/78/EC of 27 November 2000 establishing a general framework for equal treatment in employment and occupation by prohibiting discrimination in employment and vocational training on grounds of religion or belief, disability, age and sexual orientation. The Equality Act 2010 applies to discrimination on grounds of religion or belief. However, Sch 9 permits discrimination on grounds of religion or belief if possessing a particular religion or belief is an occupational requirement and the application of the requirement is a proportionate means of achieving a legitimate aim (in accordance with Art 4.2 of the Directive). See further para **7.44** below. See generally Vickers *Religious Freedom, Religious Discrimination and the Workplace* (2008).

2   24949/94, *Kotinnen v Finland* (1996) DR 87, 68. See also 29107/95, *Stedman v United Kingdom* (1997) DR 89, 104. See also *Jehovah's Witnesses of Moscow v Russia* 2010-…, paras 170–182 (refusal to re-register a religious association and its dissolution in part on account of perceived restrictions imposed by belief upon adherents despite assurances that they determined for themselves their place of employment: violation, the Court noting also that voluntary work or part-time employment or missionary activities were not contrary to the ECHR).

3   *Refah Partisi (the Welfare Party) and Others v Turkey* [GC] 2003-II, at para 94.

4   11045/84, *Knudsen v Norway* (1985) DR 42, 247.

5   *Cserjés v Hungary* (dec) (5 April 2001) (disciplinary remand imposed upon a judge who had withdrawn from a case as he had felt himself biased: no interference with Art 9. See also *Buscarini and Others v San Marino* [GC] 1999-I, paras 34–41, noted at para **7.14** above, but cf *McGuiness v United Kingdom* (dec) 1999-V (elected representatives required to take an oath of allegiance to the monarch; application declared inadmissible under Art 10 since the oath could be viewed simply as an affirmation of loyalty to the UK's constitutional principles). For further examples, see 8160/78, *X v United Kingdom* (1981) DR 22, 27 (refusal of rearrangement of teacher's timetable to allow him to attend the mosque not a violation as he had previously accepted an offer of employment without making any such request; but the Commission considered that in certain circumstances dismissal could raise an issue under Art 9); and 29107/95, *Stedman v United Kingdom* (1997) DR 89, 104 (employee who was a Christian dismissed because of refusal to work on Sundays: the Commission considered that dismissal was because of refusal to work certain hours rather than her religious beliefs).

6   *Kosteski v 'The Former Yugoslav Republic of Macedonia'* (13 April 2006), discussed at para **7.15** above.

7.27 In this area, too, there has been some suggestion of a revision of existing jurisprudence. Thus restrictions on access to employment[1] or termination of employment on account of a policy of discriminatory treatment against a particular religion may well in itself constitute an unjustifiable interference with Article 9. In *Ivanova v Bulgaria*, the applicant's dismissal from a non-teaching role in a school on account of her membership of an Evangelical Christian group that had been denied state registration and that had carried on its activities clandestinely and in the face of continuing official and media harassment was held to have involved a violation of the guarantee. Significant pressure had been placed on the applicant to resign, but ultimately she had been dismissed on the ostensible ground of not meeting the requirements for her post as a result of the school's claimed need that the post-holder should hold a university degree. The Court, however, concluded that the real reason for the dismissal was the application of a policy of intolerance towards members of this evangelical group, and found a violation of the guarantee[2].

1   *Thlimmenos v Greece* [GC] 2000-IV, discussed at para **7.12** above.
2   *Ivanova v Bulgaria* 2007-..., paras 81–86. See also 11045/84, *Knudsen v Norway* (1984) DR 42, 247; and (in respect of Art 10) *Vogt v Germany* (1995) A 323, paras 44 and 65.

7.28 Where an individual is dismissed from employment with a religious organisation on the grounds of incompatibility of practice with professed beliefs of the church, careful assessment is needed as to whether state authorities have discharged the positive obligation to ensure that employee's rights to respect for private and family life under Article 8 have been properly safeguarded, for while the autonomy of religious communities is protected against undue state interference under Article 9 read in the light of Article 11's protection for freedom of assembly and association, domestic courts and tribunals must nevertheless ensure that the grounds for dismissal take appropriate account of Convention expectations. This is of particular relevance when an employee who has been dismissed by a religious organisation has limited opportunities of finding new employment. The related cases of *Obst v Germany* and *Schüth v Germany* illustrate this point. In *Obst*, the European director of public relations for the Mormon church had lost his job for self-confessed adultery; in *Schüth*, the organist and choirmaster of a Roman Catholic parish had been dismissed after it became known that he and his new partner were expecting a child following his separation from his wife. In *Obst*, the Court agreed with the domestic employment court's ruling that the dismissal based upon the appellant's own decision to confess his infidelity could be viewed as a necessary measure aimed at preserving the church's credibility as he should have been aware of the contractual importance of marital fidelity for his employer and thus of the incompatibility of the extra-marital relationship in light of the enhanced obligations of loyalty that this particular post entailed. Here, the domestic courts had also considered the feasibility of a less severe sanction and the degree of likelihood that the appellant would find other employment. In *Schüth*, in contrast, the Court found a violation of Article 8. In its opinion, the employment courts had not properly balanced the interests of the church as employer with the applicant's right to respect for his private and family life. No mention of his de facto family life had been made, and the courts had simply reproduced the opinion of the church that its credibility would have been undermined had no dismissal taken place, even although the domestic courts had also accepted that this post was not one in which serious misconduct was entirely incompatible with continuation of employment (as would have been the case of employees whose responsibilities involved counselling or religious teaching). While the contract of employment had limited the applicant's right to respect for private life to a certain degree as it had entailed a duty of loyalty towards the church, such a contract could not be seen as implying an unequivocal undertaking to live a life of abstinence in the event of separation or divorce. Further, in this instance the applicant's chances of finding alternative employment were considered to be limited[1].

---

1   *Obst v Germany* 2010-..., paras 39–53; and *Schüth v Germany* 2010-..., paras 53–75. See also *Siebenhaar v Germany* (3 February 2011), paras 36–48 (contract as kindergarten assistant for the Protestant Church made clear that incompatible religious activities would also be incompatible with employment: no violation of Art 9). Cf *Lombardi Vallauri v Italy* 2009-..., noted at para **7.15**, fn 4 above. For discussion, see Grabenwarter 'Kirchliches Arbeitsrecht und EMKR' in Hohmann-Dennhardt, Masuch and Villiger (eds) *Festschrift für Renate Jaeger* (2011), pp 639–652.

Assessing whether an interference with a 'manifestation' of religion or belief meets the requirements of paragraph (2)

7.29 Article 9(2) provides that the state may only interfere with a 'manifestation' of thought, conscience or belief. As with related guarantees under the ECHR, the state must establish that any interference with the guarantee has a legitimate aim, is 'prescribed by law', and is 'necessary in a democratic society'.

Legitimate aim

7.30 The identification of a particular state interest for the interference (restricted under the paragraph to the protection of public safety, public order, health and morals and the rights and freedoms of others) is a matter for the respondent state; but this is hardly an onerous task. Thus in *Serif v Greece*, a conviction for the offence of having usurped the functions of a minister of a 'known religion' was accepted as an interference which had pursued the legitimate aim of protecting public order[1], while in *Kokkinakis v Greece* the aim of the prohibition of proselytism was the protection of the rights and freedoms of others[2], and in *Metropolitan Church of Bessarabia and Others v Moldova*, the refusal to register a religious community was accepted as having been for the interests of public order and public safety[3].

---

1   *Serif v Greece* 1999-IX, paras 49–54. 'Public' order' may also encompass the general functioning of the labour market: *El Majjaoui and Stichting Touba Moskee v Netherlands* (dec) (14 February 2006) (prospective imam from outside the EU refused work permit: admissible).

2   *Kokkinakis v Greece* (1993) A 260-A, para 44.

3   *Metropolitan Church of Bessarabia and Others v Moldova* 2001-XII, at paras 111–113.
    Unlike Arts 8, 10 and 11, national security is not recognised as a legitimate aim in this
    guarantee.

'Prescribed by law'

7.31 The lawfulness of any interference, in contrast, calls for more detailed scrutiny
by the Court. Again, the crucial requirement is the absence of arbitrary application
of domestic law. Each case calls for careful analysis. In *Kokkinakis v Greece,*
the applicant sought to argue that the definition of 'proselytism' was insufficiently
defined in domestic law thus rendering it both possible for any kind of religious
conversation or communication to be caught by the prohibition, and also impossible
for any individual to regulate his conduct accordingly. The Court, noting that it is
inevitable that the wording of many statutes will not attain absolute precision,
agreed with the respondent government that the existence of a body of settled
and published national case-law which supplemented the statutory provision was
sufficient in this case to meet the requirements of the test of 'prescribed by
law'[1]. On the other hand, in *Hasan and Chaush v Bulgaria*, the test was not
satisfied. In this case, a governmental agency had favoured one faction to another
in a dispute over the appointment of a religious leader, but deficiencies in substantive
criteria and in procedural safeguards had meant that the interference was
considered to have been arbitrary as it had been 'based on legal provisions which
allowed an unfettered discretion to the executive and did not meet the required
standards of clarity and foreseeability'[2].

1   *Kokkinakis v Greece* (1983) A 260-A, paras 37–41. See also *Larissis and Others v Greece*
    1998-I, paras 40–42. In any event, the Strasbourg Court may avoid having to give a firm
    answer to whether an interference is 'prescribed by law' if it is satisfied that the interference
    has not been 'necessary in a democratic society': eg *Supreme Holy Council of the Muslim
    Community v Bulgaria* (16 December 2004), para 90. Where the interference with Art 9 rights
    has involved the imposition of a criminal sanction, an applicant may well additionally allege a
    violation of Art 7, which enshrines the principle of *nullum crimen, nulla poena sine lege*. In
    such instances, the Strasbourg Court is likely to address the issues raised under Arts 7 and 9
    by using a similar approach: see for example *Kokkinakis v Greece* (1993) A 260-A paras 32–
    35; and *Larissis and Others v Greece* 1998-I, paras 39–45.

2   *Hasan and Chaush v Bulgaria* [GC] 2000-XI, paras 84–89 at para 85. See also *Kuznetsov and
    Others v Russia* (11 January, 2007), paras 69–75 (termination of religious meeting by the
    chairwoman of regional 'Human Rights Commission' and police acting without authority:
    violation). Cf *Tsirlis and Kouloumpas v Greece* 1997-III, paras 56–63 (detention following
    unlawful refusal to excuse certain ministers of religion from military service; issue determined
    under Art 5).

'Necessary in a democratic society'

7.32 The crucial question in most instances is likely to be whether an interference
with Article 9 rights can be shown to have been 'necessary in a democratic

society'. As with Articles 8, 10 and 11, the interference complained of must correspond to a pressing social need, be prescribed by law, and be proportionate to the legitimate aim pursued[1]. Again, the onus is upon the respondent state to show that this test has been met. It is in turn the task of the Court to ascertain whether measures taken at national level and amounting to an interference with Article 9 rights are justified in principle and also proportionate, but there may often be difficulty in determining this as the Court may not be best placed to review domestic determinations. In consequence, it may recognise a certain 'margin of appreciation' on the part of national decision-makers. This has the consequence in practice of modifying the strictness of the scrutiny applied by the Court to the assessment of the quality of reasons adduced for an interference with Article 9 rights. Certainly, the quality of reasons adduced for an interference must support the requisite test which requires 'very strict scrutiny'[2].

1   See further paras **3.69–3.82** above.
2   *Manoussakis and Others v Greece* 1996-IV, at para 44.

Particular issues of freedom of religion: manifestation of belief

Individual 'manifestation': proselytism

7.33 Manifestation of belief through 'teaching' includes the right to proselytise by attempting to persuade others to convert to another religion. Two cases indicate that states may in certain instances take steps to prohibit the right of individuals to try to persuade others of the validity of their beliefs, even although this right is often categorised by adherents as an essential sacred duty; but in each instance it must be shown that the interference with the right to proselytise was necessary in the particular circumstances. In *Kokkinakis v Greece*, a Jehovah's Witness had been sentenced to imprisonment for proselytism which was specifically prohibited by the Greek Constitution and by statute. The European Court of Human Rights accepted that the right to try to convince others to convert to another faith was included within the scope of the guarantee, 'failing which ... "freedom to change [one's] religion or belief", enshrined in Article 9, would be likely to remain a dead letter'[1]. While accepting that the prohibition was prescribed by law and had the legitimate aim of protecting the rights of others, the Court, however, could not accept that the interference could be justified as necessary in a democratic society. A distinction had to be drawn between 'bearing Christian witness' or evangelicalism and 'improper proselytism' involving undue influence or even force, especially upon weak and vulnerable members of society. The former was accepted by Christians as part of the Church's mission; the latter was incompatible with respect for belief and opinion. The failure of the domestic courts to specify the reasons for the conviction meant that the state could not show that there had been a pressing social need for the conviction, and thus the sentence had not been proportionate to the aim of the protection of others[2]. In contrast, in *Larissis v Greece*, the conviction of senior officers who were members of the Pentecostal faith for the proselytism of three airmen under their command was deemed not to be a breach of Article 9 in light of the crucial nature of military hierarchical structures which the Court accepted could potentially involve a risk of harassment of a subordinate where the latter sought to withdraw from a conversation initiated by a superior officer. Here, the Court accepted respondent government's arguments that the senior officers had abused their influence, and that their convictions had been justified by the need to protect the prestige and effective operation of the armed forces and to protect individual soldiers from ideological coercion[3].

1   *Kokkinakis v Greece* (1993) A–260A, para 31.

2   *Kokkinakis v Greece* (1993) A–260A, paras 31–50. The Court in its judgment (para 48) made use of a report of the World Council of Churches. Cf Naismith 'Religion and the European Convention on Human Rights' (2001) HR & UK P 8, at 13 who warns against too ready use of the concept of abuse since there would 'be a real danger of the right to communicate one's beliefs under Article 9 being restricted in a manner inconsistent with the liberal interpretation ... given to the more general right of freedom of expression guaranteed by Article 10 of the Convention'). But see Parliamentary Assembly Recommendation 1412 (1999) on the illegal activities of sects and calling for domestic action against 'illegal practices carried out in the name of groups of a religious, esoteric or spiritual nature', and to provide and exchange information on such sects.

3   *Larissis v Greece* 1998-I, paras 40–61 (conviction of senior officers for proselytism of three airmen under their command held not to be a breach of Art 9; but there was a violation in respect of conviction for proselytism of civilians even where it was argued that this had involved the improper exploitation of individuals suffering from personal and psychological difficulties as it was of 'decisive significance' that these civilians had not been subjected to pressures and constraints of the same kind as the airmen at the time the applicants had sought to convert them).

Individual 'manifestation': dress codes

7.34 Restrictions on the wearing of items of clothing or other conspicuous signs of religious belief will now be accepted as involving interferences with Article 9 rights[1]. In consequence, assessment of the reasons advanced for any prohibition will call for judicial consideration, but the Court is likely to recognise a certain 'margin of appreciation' on the part of state authorities, particularly where the justification advanced by the state is public safety[2] or the need to prevent certain fundamentalist religious movements from exerting pressure on others belonging to another religion or who do not practise their religion[3]. In *Leyla Şahin v Turkey,* the complaint concerned a prohibition on the wearing of the Islamic headscarf at university. The Grand Chamber proceeded on the basis that there had been an interference with the applicant's right to manifest her religion, and the crucial question was whether the interference had been 'necessary in a democratic society'. By a majority, the Court ruled that the interference in issue had been both justified in principle and proportionate to the aims pursued:

'Where questions concerning the relationship between State and religions are at stake, on which opinion in a democratic society may reasonably differ widely, the role of the national decision-making body must be given special importance. This will notably be the case when it comes to regulating the wearing of religious symbols in educational institutions, especially ... in view of the diversity of the approaches taken by national authorities on the issue. It is not possible to discern throughout Europe a uniform conception of the significance of religion in society and the meaning or impact of the public expression of a religious belief will differ according to time and context. Rules in this sphere will consequently vary from one country to another according to national traditions and the requirements imposed by the need to protect the rights and freedoms of others and to maintain public order. Accordingly, the choice of the extent and form such regulations should take must inevitably be left up to a point to the State concerned, as it will depend on the domestic context concerned.'

In this case, the principles of secularism and equality at the heart of the Turkish Constitution were clearly crucial. The national constitutional court had determined that freedom to manifest one's religion could be restricted in order to defend the role played by secularism as the guarantor of democratic values in the state: secularism was the meeting point of liberty and equality, necessarily entailed freedom of religion and conscience, and prevented state authorities from manifesting a preference for a particular religion or belief by emphasising the state's role as one of impartial arbiter. The Grand Chamber appears also to have been influenced by the emphasis on the protection of the rights of women in the Turkish constitution, a value also consistent with the key principle of gender equality underlying the ECHR. The Court further considered that any examination of the question of the prohibition upon wearing the Islamic headscarf had to take into consideration the impact which such a symbol may have on those who chose not to wear it if presented or perceived as a compulsory religious duty, particularly in a country where the majority of the population adhered to the Islamic faith. Of some importance, too, was the fact that practising Muslim students in Turkish universities remained free to manifest their religion in accordance with habitual forms of Muslim observance within the limits imposed[4].

---

1   *Aktas v France* (dec) (30 June 2009).

2   Eg *Phull v France* (dec) 2005-I (requirement to remove turban during airport security screening: inadmissible).

3   See *Dahlab v Switzerland* (dec) 2001-V (refusal to allow a teacher of a class of small children to wear the Islamic headscarf was deemed justified in view of the 'powerful external symbol' which wearing a headscarf represented: not only could the wearing of this item be seen as having some kind of proselytising effect since it appeared to be imposed on women by a religious precept that was hard to reconcile with the principle of gender equality, but also this could not easily be reconciled with the message of tolerance, respect for others and equality and non-discrimination that all teachers in a democratic society should convey to their pupils).

4   *Leyla Şahin v Turkey* [GC] 2005-XI, paras 104–162 at para 109 (and by analogy with the reasoning applying to disposal of the application under Art 9, there had been no violation of Prot 1, Art 2 in respect of refusal to allow access to lectures and examinations). See also 16278/90, *Karaduman v Turkey* (1993) DR 74, 93 (requirement that official photograph could not show a graduate wearing an Islamic headscarf, but only bare-headed); *Köse and Others v Turkey* (dec) 2006-II (prohibition on wearing headscarf within limits of religiously-oriented school, a general measure imposed upon all students irrespective of belief: inadmissible);

Kurtulmuş v Turkey (dec) (24 January 2006) (university professor refused authorisation to wear a headscarf); *Dogru v France* 2008-..., paras 47–78 (exclusion of female pupils from state schools for refusing to remove religious attire during physical education and sports lessons: no violation); and *Aktas v France* (dec) (30 June 2009) (expulsion from schooling for refusing to remove various religious symbols – Muslim headscarves, and the Sikh keski or under-turban – during lessons: inadmissible, as the interference could be considered proportionate to legitimate aim of protecting the rights and freedoms of others and public order, the expulsion not being on account of any objection to religious convictions as such and the ban also sought to protect the constitutional principle of secularity, an aim in keeping with the values underlying the ECHR and Art 9 case law). For commentary, see Knights 'Religious Symbols in the School: Freedom of Religion, Minorities and Education' [2005] EHRLR 499; Gilbert 'Redefining Manifestation of belief in *Leyla Sahin v Turkey*' [2006] EHRLR 308; Gallala 'The Islamic Headscarf: An Example of Insurmountable Conflict between Shari'a and the Fundamental Principles of Europe' (2006) 12 ELJ 593; McGoldrick *Human Rights and Religion: The Islamic Headscarf Debate in Europe* (2006); Nathwany 'Islamic Headscarves and Human Rights: A Critical Analysis of the Relevant Case Law of the European Court of Human Rights' (2007) 25 NQHR 221; and Sandberg 'Is Nothing Sacred? Clashing Symbols in a Secular World' [2007] PL 488. For domestic consideration, see *R (SB) v Governors of Denbigh High School* [2007] 1 AC 100, discussed at para **7.45** below (no interference with Art 9 rights). For other domestic discussion, see *Tamarante v French Community of Belgium* (2 September 2005), [2006] EuroCLY 1696 [Belgium] (refusal to suspend prohibition of headscarf in schools since no irreparable harm shown); Cases 2 BvR 1436/02 and 1657/05 [German Constitutional Court]; and *Re Association United Sikhs* (6 March 2006), [2006] EuroCLY 1693 [France] (legitimate reasons for requiring driving licence photographs not to feature any headgear).

Individual 'manifestation': prisoners and religious belief

7.35 Prison authorities will be expected to recognise the religious needs of those deprived of their liberty by allowing inmates to take part in religious observances. Thus where religion or belief dictates a particular diet, this should be respected by the authorities[1]. Further, adequate provision should be made to allow detainees to take part in religious worship or to permit them access to spiritual guidance. In the related cases of *Poltoratskiy v Ukraine* and *Kuznetsov v Ukraine*, prisoners on death row complained that they had not been allowed visits from a priest or to take part in religious services available to other prisoners. The applicants succeeded in these cases on the ground that the interferences based upon a prison instruction had not been 'prescribed by law'[2]. However, the maintenance of good order and security in prison may justify interferences with the rights of prisoners. Article 9 cannot, for example, be used to require recognition of a special status for prisoners who claim that wearing prison uniform and being forced to work violate their beliefs[3]. Further, in responding to such order and security interests, a rather wide margin of appreciation is recognised on the part of the authorities: the need to be able to identify prisoners may warrant the refusal to allow a prisoner to grow a beard, while security considerations may justify denial of the supply of materials to a prisoner, even in cases where it can be established that access to such items is indispensable for the proper exercise of a religious faith[4].

---

1   *Jakóbski v Poland* 2010-..., paras 42–55 (refusal to provide a practising Buddhist with a meat-free diet in prison constituted a violation of Art 9 as adherence to a vegetarian diet was motivated or inspired by a religion and was not unreasonable or unduly burdensome). See also

5947/72, *X v the United Kingdom* (1976) DR 5, 8. See in particular European Prison Rules, Recommendation Rec (2006) 2, Rules 29(2)–(3) (cited in *Jakóbski*): prison regimes to be 'organised so far as is practicable to allow prisoners to practise their religion and follow their beliefs, to attend services or meetings led by approved representatives of such religion or beliefs, to receive visits in private from such representatives of their religion or beliefs and to have in their possession books or literature relating to their religion or beliefs'. However, 'prisoners may not be compelled to practise a religion or belief, to attend religious services or meetings, to take part in religious practices or to accept a visit from a representative of any religion or belief.'

2   *Poltoratskiy v Ukraine* 2003-V, paras 163–171; and *Kuznetsov v Ukraine* (29 April 2003), paras 143–151. For domestic discussion, see Case 2P.245/2002, [2003] EuGRZ 743, [2004] EuroCLY 1326 [Switzerland] (visit from priest could constitute access to worship where restrictions were necessary for safety and order; and a prisoner could not refuse to work on Saturdays, the Orthodox day of rest, as the strict accommodation of all faiths could lead to organisational chaos).

3   8317/78, *McFeely and Others v United Kingdom* (1980) DR 20, 44.

4   1753/63, *X v Austria* (1965) CD 16, 20 (prayer chain); 6886/75, *X v United Kingdom* (1976) DR 5, 100 (book on martial arts).

Particular issues of freedom of religion: state neutrality

7.36 The duty upon state authorities in a pluralist democratic society to remain neutral towards religions, faiths and beliefs implies at the outset that assessment of the legitimacy of religious beliefs or the ways in which those beliefs are expressed is incompatible with Article 9[1].Cases challenging intervention in matters of internal dispute between members of a religious community also illustrate the interplay between freedom of religion and freedom of association. Article 9 when interpreted in the light of Article 11 'encompasses the expectation that [such a] community will be allowed to function peacefully, free from arbitrary State intervention'[2].

1   *Hasan and Chaush v Bulgaria* [GC] 2000-XI, para 78; *Hasan and Eylem Zengin v Turkey* 2007-XI, para 54. See also *Ivanova v Bulgaria* 2007-IV, discussed at para **7.27** above.

2   *Supreme Holy Council of the Muslim Community v Bulgaria* (16 December 2004), at para 73 (attempts at placing a divided religious community under unified leadership). See also *Holy Synod of the Bulgarian Orthodox Church (Metropolitan Inokentiy) and Others v Bulgaria* (22 January 2009), paras 122–160; and *Miroļubovs and Others v Latvia* (15 September 2009), paras 82–96 (issue decided under Art 9 only).

State neutrality: interfering in internal disputes between adherents of a religious community

7.37 The expectation that religious or faith communities may function free from arbitrary intervention by the authorities at the outset implies that 'State measures favouring a particular leader or group in a divided religious community or seeking to compel the community, or part of it, to place itself under a single leadership against its will would constitute an infringement of the freedom of religion'[1]. The taking of measures by state authorities to ensure that religious communities remain or are brought under a unified leadership will thus be difficult to justify if challenged, even where the action is purportedly taken in the interests of public order or ensuring effective spiritual leadership. In *Serif v Greece,* the applicant had been elected as a mufti, a Muslim religious leader, and had begun to exercise the functions of that office. However, he had not secured the requisite state authority to do so, and criminal proceedings were brought against him for having usurped the functions of a minister of a 'known religion' with a view to protecting the authority of another mufti who had secured the necessary official recognition. The Court accepted that the resultant conviction had pursued the legitimate aim of protecting public order. However, it was not persuaded that there had been any pressing social need for the conviction. There had been no instance of local disturbance, and the respondent government's suggestion that the dispute could even have resulted in inter-state diplomatic difficulty had never been anything other than a remote possibility. In any case, the function of the state in such instances was to promote pluralism rather than to seek to eliminate it[2]. In short, since tension is the unavoidable consequence of pluralism, it should never be necessary in a democracy to seek to place a religious community under a unified leadership by favouring a particular leader over others[3].

1   *Supreme Holy Council of the Muslim Community v Bulgaria* (16 December 2004), at para 76.

2   *Serif v Greece* 1999-IX, paras 49–54.

3   *Agga v Greece (no 2)* (17 October 2002), paras 56–61 at para 60.

State neutrality: official recognition

7.38 Article 11 protects the right of individuals to form an association for the purpose of furthering collective action in a field of mutual interest. When Article 9's guarantees for the collective manifestation of belief are considered in conjunction with Article 11's protection for freedom of association, the consequence is a high degree of concern for the right to establish religious associations: 'seen in that perspective, the right of believers to freedom of religion, which includes the right to manifest one's religion in community with others, encompasses the expectation that believers will be allowed to associate freely, without arbitrary state intervention'. This is particularly so since 'the autonomous existence of religious communities is indispensable for pluralism in a democratic society and is thus an issue at the very heart of the protection which Article 9 affords'[1]. This interplay between the two guarantees of freedom of religion and freedom of association is thus of considerable significance in resolving questions concerning refusal to confer official recognition upon religious groups; when these provisions are read alongside the prohibition of discrimination in the enjoyment of Convention guarantees as provided for by Article 14, the requirement for state neutrality is obvious. State registration may be necessary in order to take advantage of privileges such as exemption from taxation or recognition of charitable status which in domestic law may be dependent upon prior registration or state recognition.

Arrangements which favour particular religious communities do not, in principle, contravene the requirements of the ECHR 'providing there is an objective and reasonable justification for the difference in treatment and that similar agreements may be entered into by other Churches wishing to do so'[2]. In consequence, when domestic law also requires official recognition in order to obtain the legal personality necessary to allow a religious body to function effectively, mere state tolerance of a religious community is unlikely to suffice[3].

1   *Metropolitan Church of Bessarabia and Others v Moldova* 2001-XII, at para 118.

2   *Alujer Fernández and Caballero García v Spain* (dec) 2001-VI.

3   *Metropolitan Church of Bessarabia and Others v Moldova* 2001-XII, para 129. Cf Framework Convention for the Protection of National Minorities, Art 8: recognition that 'every person belonging to a national minority has the right to manifest his or her religion or belief and to establish religious institutions, organisations and associations'.

7.39 While the imposition of a requirement of state registration is not in itself incompatible with freedom of thought, conscience and religion, a state must be careful to maintain a position of strict neutrality and be able to demonstrate it has proper grounds for refusing recognition, and also that the process for registration guards against unfettered discretion and avoid arbitrary decision-making[1]. While the state is 'entitled to verify whether a movement or association carries on, ostensibly in pursuit of religious aims, activities which are harmful to the population'[2], it may not appear to be assessing the comparative legitimacy of different beliefs[3]. Even where a state seeks to rely upon national security and territorial integrity as justification for refusal to register a community, rigorous assessment of such claims is required. Vague speculation is inadequate. In *Metropolitan Church of Bessarabia and Others v Moldova*, the applicants had been prohibited from gathering together for religious purposes and had not been able to secure legal protection for the church's assets against harassment. The respondent government sought to argue that registration in the particular circumstances of this case could lead to the destabilisation of both the Orthodox Church and indeed of society as a whole since the matter concerned a dispute between Russian and Romanian patriarchates; further, it was suggested that recognition could have had an adverse impact upon the very territorial integrity and independence of the state. By taking the view that the applicant church was not a new denomination, and by deciding that recognition should depend on the will of another ecclesiastical authority that had previously been recognised, the Court considered that the duty of neutrality and impartiality had not been discharged. Nor was the Court satisfied in the absence of any evidence to the contrary either that the church was (as the respondent government submitted) engaged in political activities contrary to Moldovan public policy or to its own stated religious aims, or that state recognition might constitute a danger to national security and territorial integrity[4].

1   *Supreme Holy Council of the Muslim Community v Bulgaria* (16 December 2004), para 33.

2   *Manoussakis and Others v Greece* 1996-IV, para 40.

3   *Hasan and Chaush v Bulgaria* [GC] 2000-XI, paras 84–89 at para 78.

4   *Metropolitan Church of Bessarabia and Others v Moldova* 2001-XII, paras 101–142. See also
     Pentidis and Others v Greece 1997-III, para 46.

7.40 A refusal to register a religious community may also carry with it the
consequence that the community is thereby precluded from enforcing its interests
in the courts. Churches may also hold property, and any interference with these
rights is in principle liable to give rise to questions falling within the scope of
Article 1 of Protocol no 1[1]. In *Canea Catholic Church v Greece,* for example,
a decision of the domestic courts to refuse to recognise the applicant church as
having the necessary legal personality was successfully challenged, the Court
considering that the effect of such a decision was to prevent the church now and
in the future from having any dispute relating to property determined by the
domestic courts[2].

1   *The Holy Monasteries v Greece* A 301-A, paras 54–66.
2   *Canae Catholic Church v Greece* 1997-VIII, paras 40–42. See also *Jehovah's Witnesses of
     Moscow v Russia* 2010-…, paras 170–182 (refusal to re-register a religious association and its
     dissolution without relevant and sufficient grounds as many court findings had not been
     substantiated and were not grounded on an acceptable assessment of the relevant facts: violation
     of Art 11 in the light of Art 9). Cf *Moscow Branch of the Salvation Army v Russia* 2006-XI,
     paras 81–98; and *Church of Scientology Moscow v Russia* (5 April 2007), paras 94–98 (violations
     of Art 11 read in conjunction with Art 9).

7.41 Domestic law must also provide a right of access to court for the
determination of a community's civil rights and obligations in terms of Article 6.
In the *Metropolitan Church of Bessarabia and Others v Moldova* case, the
Court further noted that Article 9 had to be read in the light of Article 6 and the
guarantees of access to fair judicial proceedings to protect a religious community,
its members and its assets. The government's assertion that it had shown tolerance
towards the church and its members could not be a substitute for actual recognition,
since recognition alone had been capable in domestic law of conferring rights on
those concerned to defend themselves against acts of intimidation. The refusal to
recognise the church had thus resulted in such consequences for the applicants'
rights under Article 9 that could not be regarded as necessary in a democratic
society[1].

1   *Metropolitan Church of Bessarabia and Others v Moldova* 2001-XII, para 118.

State neutrality: controls upon places of worship, etc

7.42 State regulation can also involve measures such as restrictions upon the
entry of religious leaders[1] and the imposition and enforcement of planning controls[2].
Care is necessary to ensure that the legitimate considerations which underpin the
rationale for immigration controls or planning consent are not used for ulterior
purposes. For example, in *Manoussakis and Others v Greece,* domestic law
had required religious organisations to obtain formal approval for the use of
premises for worship. Jehovah's Witnesses had sought unsuccessfully to obtain

such permission, and thereafter had been convicted of operating an unauthorised place of worship. The Court accepted that national authorities had the right to take measures designed to determine whether activities undertaken by a religious association were potentially harmful to others, but this could not allow the state to determine the legitimacy of either the beliefs or the means of expressing such beliefs. In this instance, the context in which the application arose was also of relevance, for the Court noted the tendency 'to impose rigid, or indeed prohibitive, conditions on practice of religious beliefs by certain non-Orthodox movements, in particular Jehovah's Witnesses'. In this case, it was also of some significance that authorisation for the place of worship was still awaited at the time of the judgment, authorisation that was to come not only from state officials but also from the local bishop. The Court concluded that that the applicants' convictions could not be said to have been a proportionate response[3].

1   See *El Majjaoui and Stichting Touba Moskee v Netherlands* (dec) (14 February 2006) (prospective imam from outside the EU refused work permit: admissible), but stuck out after relinquishment to the Grand Chamber following the issue of a permit (20 December 2007); and *Nolan and K v Russia* (12 February 2009), paras 61–79 (refusal to allow Unification Church missionary and his son re-entry on secret orders of security service: violation of Art 9, and not necessary to consider issue under Art 14 taken with Art 9).

2   Including restrictions on access to places considered significant: 12587/86, *Chappell v United Kingdom* (1987) DR 53, 241. Cf 24875/94, *Logan v United Kingdom* (1996) DR 86, 74. For domestic discussion, see *X v Syndicat des Copropriétaires les Jardins de Gorbella* (8 June 2006), [2006] EuroCLY 1750 [France] (construction of temporary place of worship contrary to co-owners' regulations not justified by purpose of construction).

3   *Manoussakis and Others v Greece* 1996-IV, paras 44–53. See too 28626/95, *Christian Association of Jehovah's Witnesses v Bulgaria* (1997) DR 90, 77 (suspension of the association's registration followed by arrests, dispersal of meetings held in public and private locations and confiscation of religious materials declared admissible under Arts 6, 9–11 and 14), and (9 March 1998) (friendly settlement ultimately achieved); *Institute of French Priests and Others v Turkey* (friendly settlement) (14 December 2000) (decision by the Turkish courts to register a plot of land belonging to the Institute in the name of state bodies on the ground that the Institute was no longer eligible for treatment as a religious body as it had let part of its property for various sporting activities: friendly settlement secured after a life tenancy in favour of the priests representing the Institute was conferred).

7.43 Such situations, however, must be contrasted with those in which an applicant is seeking to modify the outcome of planning decisions taken in a objective and neutral manner. In *Vergos v Greece*, the applicant had been refused permission to build a prayer-house for the community on a plot of land which he owned on the basis that the land-use plan did not permit the construction of such buildings, and further that in any event he was the only member of his religious community in the town. The planning authorities had accordingly concluded there had been no social need justifying modification of the plan so as to permit the building of a prayer-house. In determining that this interference was 'necessary in a democratic society', the Court accepted that the criterion applied by the domestic authorities when weighing the applicant's freedom to manifest his religion against the public interest in rational planning control could not be considered arbitrary. Having regard to a state's margin of appreciation in matters of town and country planning, the public interest should not be made to yield precedence to the need to worship of a single adherent of a religious community when there was a prayer-house in a neighbouring town which met the community's needs in the region[1].

1   *Vergos v Greece* (24 June 2004), paras 36–43. The recent constitutional amendment in Switzerland prohibiting the building of minarets is the subject of a pending application: see *Ouardiri v Switzerland*.

Decisions of the domestic courts on Article 9

The statutory framework

7.44 The UK has two distinct statutory frameworks under which issues about religious freedom have come before the courts. First, under the Human Rights Act 1998, public authorities (including the courts) have a duty not to act in a way which is incompatible with the Convention rights[1], including the rights described in Article 9[2]. Some attempt is made by the HRA 1998 to give particular weight to freedom of thought, conscience and religion in any domestic determination of an issue under Article 9. The HRA 1998, s 13(1) provides that 'if a court's determination of any question arising under this Act might affect the exercise by a religious organisation (itself or its members collectively) of the ECHR right to freedom of thought, conscience and religion, it must have particular regard to the importance of that right'[3]. The extent to which churches (including established churches) are bound by ECHR requirements is not entirely clear in existing jurisprudence[4].

Secondly, under the Equality Act 2010 it is unlawful for anyone, whether in the private or public sector, to discriminate on grounds of religion or belief in conducting certain activities. The obligation not to discriminate on these grounds was introduced in the field of employment and training in 2003, in implementation of a European directive[5], and was extended by the Equality Act 2006 to the provision of goods, facilities, services, accommodation and education, in anticipation of a currently proposed European directive[6]. Both sets of provisions are now consolidated in the 2010 Act. The definition of discrimination covers both direct discrimination (treating someone less favourably because of their religion or belief than one treats or would treat others), for which there is no justification defence; and indirect discrimination (imposing a provision, criterion or practice which puts a person of the claimant's religion at a disadvantage) which cannot be justified as a proportionate means of achieving a legitimate aim[7]. The same facts could give rise to claims under both the HRA 1998 and the anti-discrimination legislation. Any court or tribunal hearing an anti-discrimination claim has also to act compatibly with the Convention rights. The converse, however, is not true, as the exercise of judicial functions is excluded from the scope of the 2006 Act.

In addition to the ECHR and the European directive, there are other international instruments of various kinds which may be relevant to legal questions concerning religion[8]. These do not form part of the domestic law of the UK, but may be taken into account in certain circumstances (eg as an aid to the interpretation of Convention rights or of EU law).

1   HRA 1998, s 6(1). See para **1.59** above.

2   As in the Strasbourg case law, ECHR, Arts 10 (freedom of expression), 11 (freedom of assembly), 12 (right to marry) and Prot 1, Art 2 (children to be educated in accordance with their parents' religious and philosophical convictions) may also raise issues of religious freedom. Discrimination in the enjoyment of any of the Convention rights is also prohibited by Art 14. For example, exempting marriages to be performed after Anglican preliminary formalities from the requirement imposed on persons subject to immigration control to obtain Home Office approval for their marriage was held incompatibly discriminatory in *R (Baiai) v Secretary of State for the Home Department* [2009] 1 AC 287. But (with the possible exception of the right to marry) these are all qualified rights, interference with which may be justified as a proportionate means of achieving a legitimate aim.

3   See para **1.104** above. See further Thorp 'The Human Rights Bill: Churches and Religious Organisations', House of Commons Research paper 98/26 (1998); Cumper 'The Protection of Religious Rights under Section 13 of the Human Rights Act 1998' [2000] PL 254.

4   See *Aston Cantlow and Wilmcote with Billesley Parochial Church Council v Wallbank* [2004] 1 AC 546. See further Naismith 'Religion and the European Convention on Human Rights' (2001) HR & UK P, 8 at 19, discussing 21283/93, *Tyler v United Kingdom* (1994) DR 77, 81 (dismissal of a clergyman after determination by an ecclesiastical court of the Church of England that he had been guilty of adultery: no finding of violation of Art 6 requirement of independence in the circumstances). In *Percy v Church of Scotland Board of National Mission* 2006 SC (HL) 1, the issue of whether a sex discrimination claim brought against the Church by a former minister fell within the exclusive jurisdiction of Church courts was disposed of by reference to the Church of Scotland Act 1921 and the Sex Discrimination Act 1975.

5   Directive 2000/78/EC, implemented in the UK by the Employment Equality (Religion or Belief) Regulations 2003, SI 2003/1660.

6   The proposed Council directive on implementing the principle of equal treatment between persons irrespective of religion or belief, disability, age or sexual orientation was published as COM (2008) 426 of 2 July 2008.

7   Most religious discrimination cases at appellate level have been unsuccessful. An exception is *Saini v All Saints Haque Centre* [2009] IRLR 74, which concerned the harassment of a Hindu employee by Ravidassi employers. There have been many more cases in the first instance Employment Tribunals. There was, however, an early House of Lords case which held Sikhs included within the race discrimination legislation: *Mandla v Dowell Lee* [1983] 2 AC 548. Jews were also held to be a racial group: *Seide v Gillette Industries Ltd* [1980] IRLR 427; cf *R (E) v Governing Body of JFS* [2010] 2 AC 728. Muslims were not: *Nyazi v Rymans*, 10 May 1998, unreported. Nor were Rastafarians: *Crown Suppliers v Dawkins* [1993] ICR 517.

8   Eg the UN Declaration on the Elimination of all Forms of Religious Intolerance, the UN Declaration on the Elimination of all Forms of Intolerance and of Discrimination Based on Religion or Belief, and the UN Declaration on the Rights of Persons Belonging to National or Ethnic, Religious and Linguistic Minorities. International instruments whose primary focus is not religious may also have a bearing on religious questions: examples would include the UN Standard Minimum Rules for the Treatment of Prisoners and the UN Convention on the Rights of the Child. The Charter of Fundamental Rights of the European Union has a particular relevance to the interpretation of EU law: see paras **2.16–2.24** above.

The case law

<small>CASES CONCERNED WITH RELIGIOUS DRESS AND SYMBOLS</small>

7.45 The issue of religious dress has raised repeated and difficult questions for the courts in the UK in recent years. These questions have come to the court in the form of individual complaints to be considered on their individual facts. *R (SB) v Governors of Denbigh High School* concerned a Muslim schoolgirl who on reaching puberty wanted to wear the jilbab (a long shapeless black dress) when the school uniform allowed only the shalwar kameez (trousers and a tunic) together with the hijab (headscarf) if wanted. Was the school rule compatible with her right to manifest her religion? The school's uniform policy was intended to promote a sense of communal identity and to protect Muslim girls from coming under pressure to wear the jilbab even if they did not wish to do so. The school maintained that some Muslim girls at the school feared being pressured into wearing the jilbab, which they associated with an extremist group. The school defended its policy by relying on the judgment of the European Court of Human Rights in *Leyla Şahin v Turkey,* where the Strasbourg Court deferred to the judgment of the Turkish authorities as to the threat that even a permission to use Islamic dress posed to freedom of conscience and religion[1]. In the *SB* case, this line of thought, concerned with intimidatory pressures for conformity with the religious beliefs of others, is reflected in the speeches in the House of Lords. The Law Lords did not venture into whether the Islamic rule requiring that members of both sexes dress modestly did indeed require her to wear the jilbab (a question which had been discussed in the Court of Appeal). The majority held that this was not an interference at all, because her parents had chosen the school knowing its uniform policy, which had been carefully worked out with members of the local communities, and she could have moved to a school with a different policy. The minority thought that there was an interference. All five held that it was justified as being necessary for the protection of the rights and freedoms of others. The House recognised that it was for the court to make its own evaluation of the justification advanced, rather than to assess what the decision-maker had done on judicial review principles[2]. Nevertheless, the majority were prepared to leave a wide margin of discretion to the school. Lord Bingham, for example, said that:

> 'It would in my opinion be irresponsible of any court, lacking the expertise, background and detailed knowledge of the head teacher, staff and governors, to overrule their judgment on a matter as sensitive as this'.[3]

Lady Hale's view was that the school's policy deserved closer scrutiny than that, but that in all the circumstances it was 'a thoughtful and proportionate response to reconciling the complexities of the situation':

> '[The school's] task is to help all of their pupils achieve their full potential. This includes growing up to play whatever part they choose in the society in which they are living. The school's task is also to promote the ability of people of diverse races, religions and cultures to live together in harmony. Fostering a sense of community and cohesion within the school is an important part of that. A uniform dress code

can play its role in smoothing over ethnic, religious and social divisions. But it does more than that. Like it or not, this is a society committed, in principle and in law, to equal freedom for men and women to choose how they will lead their lives within the law.'[4]

The approach adopted in *SB* has been applied in other school uniform cases[5].

1   *Leyla Şahin v Turkey* [GC] 2005-XI, discussed at para **7.34** above.

2   *R (SB) v Governors of Denbigh High School* [2007] 1 AC 100.

3   *R (SB) v Governors of Denbigh High School* [2007] 1 AC 100 at para 34.

4   *Leyla Şahin v Turkey* [GC] 2005-XI, para 97.

5   *R (X) v Y School* [2008] 1 All ER 249 (refusal to allow a pupil to wear a niqab – face veil – no interference because she could have gone to another school and in any event justified); *R (Playfoot) v Millais School Governing Body* [2007] EWHC 1698 (Admin) (refusal to allow girl to wear purity ring as symbol of her Christian faith and belief in chastity before marriage: Art 9 not engaged).

7.46 It may be that there are differences between the approach to the issue of religious dress and symbols in human rights and anti-discrimination cases[1]. In *Mandla v Dowell Lee*, a discrimination case under the Race Relations Act 1976, the headmaster of a private school was held not justified in refusing to admit a Sikh pupil unless he agreed to remove his turban and cut his hair. The headmaster's belief that allowing him to retain his hair and turban would accentuate religious and social distinctions which the school wished to minimise was not enough[2]. *Azmi v Kirklees Metropolitan Borough Council* was a more recent discrimination case in which a Muslim teaching assistant was suspended for refusing to comply with her employer's instruction not to wear a face veil in the classroom as it hindered her communication with the children. The EAT upheld a finding that this was neither direct nor indirect discrimination on the ground of religious belief. As to direct discrimination, the correct comparator was another woman who insisted on covering her face for some other reason. The employer would have suspended her too. Nor was there any indirect discrimination because, although the rule did put persons of her belief at a particular disadvantage, it was objectively justified. Her communication with the pupils was indeed impaired when she was wearing the veil, and various other methods of resolving the problem had been considered and rejected for good reasons[3]. Difficulties in communication have also led to guidance to judges in England and Wales that they have a discretion to require advocates to remove the niqab in court if to do so is in the interests of justice. The case of *Eweida v British Airways plc* concerned a Christian member of check-in staff who was not permitted to wear a crucifix over her uniform. Staff were permitted to wear any item under their uniform, but could wear religious items over their uniform only if wearing the item was a requirement of their religion. Her claim of religious discrimination was unsuccessful in the absence of evidence that this was a religious requirement rather than a personal choice, or that any other Christian staff at BA had suffered a disproportionate impact[4].

These and other[5] cases may indicate the adoption of a more stringent approach under anti-discrimination law than under the ECHR. Under anti-discrimination law the burden of proof lies on the respondent to establish that there has been no breach of the prohibition of discrimination, once facts have been proved from which the court could conclude, in the absence of a reasonable alternative explanation, that a breach had occurred. Had Mrs Amzi's case been brought under the Human Rights Act, she would not have faced the comparator problem, because an interference with her right to manifest her religion would have had to be justified even if the employer would have treated other people in exactly the same way. But, on the majority approach in *SB*, the employers' reasons for the rule might have received less rigorous scrutiny. She would have borne the entire burden of proof. She would also have faced the argument that there was no interference with her religious rights because she had voluntarily chosen the work. The Strasbourg 'free to resign' approach has been said to be 'difficult to square with the supposed fundamental character of the [Article 9] rights'[6].

1   See *R (E) v Governing Body of JFS* [2010] 2 AC 728.

2   *Mandla v Dowell Lee* [1983] 2 AC 548. The main point in the case, however, was that Sikhs were recognised as a distinct ethnic group under the Race Relations Act 1976, as Jews had been in much earlier cases, thus strengthening calls for the introduction of legislation to combat discrimination against members of other religions.

3   *Azmi v Kirklees Metropolitan Borough Council* [2007] ICR 1154.

4   *Eweida v British Airways plc* [2010] EWCA Civ 80.

5   In *R (Watkins-Singh) v Governing Body of Aberdare Girls' High School* [2008] EWHC 1865 (Admin), it was held indirectly discriminatory on grounds of race and religion to refuse to allow a Sikh girl to wear her Kara (bangle) to school. She believed that she was required by her religion to wear the Kara, and it was unobtrusive compared with the niqab and jilbab. There was no Art 9 claim.

6   *Copsey v WBB Devon Clays* [2005] ICR 1789, where a claim for unfair dismissal for refusing to work on Sundays failed, on one view because the applicant was free to resign, and in the majority view because the employer had compelling economic reasons for changing its working practices and had done everything it reasonably could to accommodate the applicant's wish.

OTHER DOMESTIC CASES

7.47 Other domestic cases concerned with Article 9 have raised a wide variety of issues. In *R (Williamson) v Secretary of State for Education and Employment*, parents and teachers in a number of small independent Christian schools complained that the statutory ban on corporal punishment in schools was an interference with their right under Article 9 to manifest their religious beliefs 'in worship, teaching, practice or observance'. They took literally biblical texts which are usually summarised as 'spare the rod and spoil the child'. One judge in the Court of Appeal concentrated on whether this qualified for protection as a religious belief at all and concluded that it did not. The other two concentrated on whether there was an interference with that belief and concluded that there was not, because the parents were still permitted to punish their own children. The House of Lords concentrated on justification and held the ban justified in the interests, not only of these children, but of children generally[1].

Several cases have concerned employees who have complained that they were required to perform acts which were incompatible with their religious convictions.

One such case was *London Borough of Islington v Ladele*, which concerned a Christian registrar who refused to carry out the registration of civil partnerships between same sex couples. She claimed that disciplinary proceedings taken against her were direct discrimination, and that requiring her to register civil partnerships was unjustified indirect discrimination, all on the ground of her religious beliefs. She also founded on Article 9 of the ECHR. The Court of Appeal held that she was not the victim of direct discrimination, since the actions of the local authority had resulted from the claimant's refusal to officiate at civil partnerships and were not directed or motivated by her religious beliefs. Nor was she the victim of indirect discrimination: her own behaviour constituted unlawful discrimination on the ground of sexual orientation, and the local authority was not only entitled but obliged to insist on her performing her duties as a registrar without discrimination. The interference with her beliefs was justified under Article 9(2): respect for her religious views relating to marriage should not be permitted to override the local authority's concern to ensure that its registrars accorded equal respect towards the homosexual community as towards the heterosexual community[2].

The case of *R (Suryananda) v Welsh Ministers* concerned the slaughter of the temple bullock belonging to a Hindu community, to them a particularly sacrilegious act. The animal's slaughter was held to be justified in pursuance of a national policy of slaughtering all cattle which gave a positive reaction to the test for bovine tuberculosis, even though the animal in question appeared to be perfectly healthy, would never enter the food chain and was kept separate from other animals[3].

In *Gallagher v Church of Jesus Christ of Latter Day Saints*, it was held that withholding a tax exemption from a Mormon temple (which was not open to the public) because it was not a place of 'public religious worship' did not fall within the ambit of Article 9: the absence of exemption from tax was not based upon religion but upon the fact that no benefit was provided to the general public, and the liability to tax did not prevent Mormons from manifesting their religion[4].

Other cases have concerned such matters as assisted suicide[5], anti-abortion activism[6], conscientious objection to military service[7], anti-hunting legislation[8], interment[9] and cremation[10].

1   *R (Williamson) v Secretary of State for Education and Employment* [2005] 2 AC 246.

2   *London Borough of Islington v Ladele [*2010] 1 WLR 955. See also *Copsey v WBB Devon Clays* [2005] ICR 1789 (claim for unfair dismissal for refusing to work on Sundays failed, on one view because he was free to resign, and in the majority view because the employer had compelling economic reasons for changing its working practices and had done everything it reasonably could to accommodate the applicant's wishes); *McClintock v Department for Constitutional Affairs* [2008] IRLR 29 (a magistrate was not entitled to be excused from hearing adoption cases in which he might be obliged to place a child with a homosexual couple even if this was contrary to his religious or philosophical beliefs); and *McFarlane v Relate Avon Ltd* [2010] IRLR 872 (a counsellor unwilling to give psychosexual counselling to same-sex couples). For cases involving conscientious objection and military service, see para **7.23** above.

3   *R (Suryananda) v Welsh Ministers* [2007] EWCA Civ 893 (bovine tuberculosis could not be diagnosed until after the animal was dead).

4   *Gallagher v Church of Jesus Christ of Latter Day Saints* [2008] 1 WLR 1852.

5   *R (Pretty) v Director of Public Prosecutions* [2002] 1 AC 800 (a person is not entitled to manifest their belief in assisted suicide by committing it).

6   *Connolly v Director of Public Prosecutions* [2008] 1 WLR 276.

7   *Khan v Royal Air Force Summary Appeal Court* [2004] EWHC 2230 (Admin).

8   *Whaley v Lord Advocate* 2008 SC (HL) 107 (Art 9 not engaged).

9   *Re Durrington Cemetery* [2001] Fam 33 (interment in accordance with Jewish law); *Re Crawley Green Road Cemetery, Luton* [2001] Fam 308 (interment of humanist in unconsecrated ground).

10 *Ghai v Newcastle City Council* [2011] QB 591 (refusal of local authority to dedicate land for funeral pyres conforming to traditional Hindu beliefs, on basis that such pyres were prohibited by legislation: held by the Court of Appeal that Hindu beliefs could be accommodated within the terms of the legislation. Article 9 arguments did not require to be decided).

ARTICLE 10: FREEDOM OF EXPRESSION

The scope of 'freedom of expression' under Article 10

7.48 Article 10 seeks to protect freedom of expression[1]. The text specifically provides that the freedom 'to hold opinions and to receive and impart information and ideas without interference by public authority' is included. The article has generated a substantial amount of case law. There is no one judicial approach; rather, the European Court of Human Rights will be influenced in particular by the particular type of speech issue at stake[2]. The justification for free speech is drawn both from its importance in a pluralist society and also as a means of self-fulfilment[3]: the presumption is that expression acts as a tool for the enhancement of democracy as well as for individual personal development. One central aim is the furtherance of 'pluralism, tolerance and broadmindedness without which there is no "democratic society"', and thus ideas or information which 'offend, shock or disturb the State or any sector of the population' are as much covered as those 'favourably received or regarded as inoffensive or as a matter of indifference'[4]. As well as political speech, Article 10 covers artistic expression 'which affords the opportunity to take part in the public exchange of cultural, political and social information and ideas of all kinds'[5], and commercial information and advertisements[6].

1   See further Council of Europe *Freedom of Expression in Europe: Case-law concerning Article 10 of the European Convention on Human Rights* (2006); Ferreres Comella 'Freedom of Expression in Political Contexts: Some Reflections on the Case Law of the European Court of Human Rights' in Sadurski (ed) *Political Rights under Stress in 21st Century Europe* (2006), pp 84–119; and Verpeaux *Europeans and their Rights – Freedom of Expression* (2010). Between 1959 and 2009, the Court established 392 violations of Art 10, 182 of which concerned Turkey; other states with high numbers of adverse judgments are Austria (32), France (19), Moldova and Russia (16 each), Poland (13), and the United Kingdom (10): European Court *Annual Report 2009* (2010), pp 150–151.

2   Cf Mahoney 'Universality versus Subsidiarity in the Strasbourg Case Law on Free Speech' [1997] EHRLR 364; Lester of Herne Hill 'Universality versus Subsidiarity: A Reply' [1998] EHRLR 73.

3   The classic justification for freedom of expression is found in Mill *On Liberty* (1848). See,

further Schauer *Freedom of Speech: A Philosophical Inquiry* (1982), pp 50–52; and Barendt *Freedom of Speech* (2nd edn, 2005) pp 1–38.

4   *Handyside v United Kingdom* (1976) A 24, para 49. It follows under Prot 1, Art 2 that the state may determine school curricular issues and impart factual information concerning religious or philosophical matters, provided always it does so in an 'objective, critical and pluralistic manner': *Kjeldsen, Busk Madsen and Pedersen v Denmark* (1976) A 23, para 53.

5   *Müller and Others v Switzerland* (1988) A 133, para 27.

6   *Markt intern Verlag GmbH and Klaus Beerman v Germany* (1989) A 165, para 35 (statements published in a specialised bulletin critical of a mail-order firm); *Groppera Radio AG and Others v Switzerland* (1990) A 173, para 55 (light music and commercials retransmitted by cable originating in another country); cf *Casado Coca v Spain* (1994) A 285-A, paras 54–55 (ban on professional advertising by lawyers).

7.49 The right to freedom of expression also includes the choice of the form in which ideas are conveyed. The scope of the guarantee thus covers a broad range of means of expression[1] including symbolic protest activities[2]. The context forum Article 10 also protects freedom to receive information[3], and thus its scope extend to questions concerning access to means of communication[4] including the reception and transmission of broadcasts[5].

1   See eg 11674/85, *Stevens v United Kingdom* (1986) DR 46, 245 at para 2 (expression 'may include the right for a person to express his ideas through the way he dresses'); *Steel and Others v United Kingdom* 1998-VII, para 92 (protests against a grouse shoot and the extension of a motorway respectively involving physical impediment involved expression of opinion); *Hashman and Harrup v United Kingdom* [GC] 1999–VIII, para 28 (noise disruption by hunt saboteurs constituted expression of opinion); and *Von Hannover v Germany* 2004-VI, para 59 (freedom of expression 'also extends to the publication of photos ... The present case does not concern the dissemination of "ideas", but of images containing very personal or even intimate "information" about an individual'). However, where the challenge is to an interference with expression through interference with correspondence, the *lex specialis* governing the application is Art 8 rather than Art 10: see para **6.39** above. For a domestic example, see *Mayor of London v Hall* [2011] 1 WLR 504 (expression of views in form of setting up camp on square opposite Parliament in breach of byelaws within the scope of Arts 10 and 11).

2   *Thoma v Luxembourg* 2001-III, para 45; and see *Women on Waves and Others v Portugal* 2009-..., paras 28–44 (refusal to allow entry of vessel chartered to support a campaign for the decriminalisation of abortion into territorial waters: violation, the Court noting that the choice of the vessel for the events planned by the associations had been crucially important and in line with other activities in other European states).

3   For discussion of the right to freedom of information, see Cohen-Jonathan 'Transparence, Démocracie et Effectivité des Droits Fondamentaux dans la Convention Européenne des Droits de l'Homme' in Mahoney, Matscher, Petzold and Wildhaber (eds) *Protecting Human Rights: The European Perspective* (2000) pp 245–263. Cf *Cyprus v Turkey* [GC] 2001-IV, para 252 (vetting of school books ostensibly sought to identify material which could harm inter-communal relations, but the reality was that a significant number of books were subjected to unilateral censorship which 'far exceeded the limits of confidence-building methods and amounted to a denial of the right to freedom of information').

4   Eg 8317/78, *McFeely v United Kingdom* (1980) DR 20, 44 (restrictions imposed on prisoners as to means of communication (no access to television, radio etc) justified for prevention of disorder); and *Zaoui v Switzerland* (dec) (18 January 2001) (confiscation of fax machine and preventing access to the Internet constituted interferences, but were justified on security and public order grounds). Article 10 does not guarantee a right to access to broadcasting facilities:

25060/94, *Haider v Austria* (1995) DR 83, 66 (complaint by applicant that the reporting of news events concerning him did not meet the requirements of plurality, information and objectivity as required by Art 10: application declared inadmissible); *Murphy v Ireland* 2003-IX (discussed at para **7.109** below). See also *R (Ponting) v Governor of HM Prison Whitemoor* [2002] EWCA Civ 224 (there was no infringement of Arts 6 or 8 when a prisoner suffering from dyslexia was denied unrestricted access to IT facilities, the restrictions on use being proportionate to meet security concerns).

5   *Autronic AG v Switzerland* (1990) 178, at para 47: 'Article 10 applies not only to the content of information but also to the means of transmission or reception since any restriction imposed on the means necessarily interferes with the right to receive and impart information' (refusal by state to permit reception of satellite transmissions from another state: violation of Art 10). Cf 10462/83, *B v Germany* (1984) DR 37, 155 (Art 10 does not guarantee a right to install an antenna for an amateur radio station); 17713/91, *Schindewolf v Germany* (2 September 1991) (removal of unauthorised aerial on planning grounds: inadmissible); and *Faccio v Italy* (dec) (31 March 2009) (the licence fee is a tax intended for funding the public broadcasting service, and action taken to collect this is not incompatible with Art 10).

Positive obligations

7.50 Under Article 10, certain positive obligations to protect freedom of expression may arise[1]. For example, public authorities may be obliged to take steps to safeguard the right of freedom of expression by providing protection against unlawful acts by others designed to restrict or inhibit free speech[2], or even by securing the enactment of appropriate legislation to reflect Convention expectations[3]. Thus, for example, if domestic law places the onus on a defender in defamation proceedings of proving the truth of challenged statements, the state must ensure that civil proceedings contain sufficient procedural safeguards to protect the general interest in promoting the free circulation of information and ideas, a responsibility which may even extend to making available legal aid for defenders in particular cases[4].

1   Other initiatives of the Council of Europe have also sought to stress the responsibilities of the state in ensuring equality of access to the media for minority groups and in encouraging journalistic independence and pluralism: see eg Committee of Ministers Recommendations Rec (99) 1 on measures to promote media pluralism; Rec (2006) 3 on the UNESCO Convention on the protection and promotion of the diversity of cultural expressions; and Rec (2007) on media pluralism and diversity of media content.

2   *Özgür Gündem v Turkey* 2000-III, paras 41–46 (deliberate and concerted attacks upon journalists, distributors etc associated with the newspaper; no action taken by the state despite requests by the newspaper: the Court reiterated key importance of free expression and held the state had failed to comply with its positive duty to protect the newspaper). Cf the related cases of *Yaşa v Turkey* 1998-VI, paras 118–120 (attacks on newsagents considered under Arts 2 and 13); *Tekin v Turkey* 1998-IV, (detention and ill-treatment of journalists etc: not established that loss of liberty was because of the applicant's occupation, and consequently no violation of Art 10); and *Dink v Turkey* 2010-..., paras 66–75 and 102–139 (failure to protect life of journalist who had commented on identity of Turkish citizens of Armenian extraction: violation of Arts 2 and 10).

3   *VgT Verein gegen Tierfabriken v Switzerland* 2001-VI, para 45 (refusal of a television company to broadcast the applicant association's commercial on the ground that it was prohibited from 'political advertising'); but cf para 46: 'the Court does not consider it desirable, let alone necessary, to elaborate a general theory concerning the extent to which the Convention guarantees

should be extended to relations between private individuals *inter se*'. This case was applied by the German domestic courts in Case 2A.303/2004, [2005] EuGRZ 719 [Germany] (prohibition on broadcasting political advertisements: item in question was not per se political but sought to highlight inconsistencies in interpretation of regulations); and by the Swiss courts in (2F.6/ 2009) (4 November 2009) [2010] EuGRZ 79 [Switzerland].

4   *Steel and Morris v United Kingdom* 2005-II, discussed at para **7.83** below.

7.51 Positive obligations may also apply to cases where the relations between an employer and an employee are governed by rules of private rather than public law. In *Fuentes Bobo v Spain*, a television producer had been dismissed after making comments which had been considered critical of the management of the state broadcasting company. The European Court of Human Rights rejected the state's contentions that it could not be held responsible for the applicant's dismissal since the television station was a private law undertaking, and clarified that in certain cases there could be a positive obligation on the state to ensure that freedom of expression was properly respected in such circumstances. Here, the severity of the penalty imposed could not be supported by any pressing social need and consequently there had been a violation of the guarantee[1].

1   *Fuentes Bobo v Spain* (29 February 2000), paras 44–50.

7.52 While the state's positive obligations do not extend to ensuring that there is an unfettered right for the private citizen or any organisation to have access to the media in order to put forward opinions, in certain exceptional circumstances a positive obligation may nevertheless arise to require the press to publish retractions or apologies or even judgments in defamation cases, even although privately-owned media should in principle remain free to exercise editorial discretion in deciding whether to publish material submitted by private individuals[1].

1   *Melnychuk v Ukraine* (dec) 2005-IX. Cf *Société Prisma Presse v France* (dec) (1 July 2003) (court order to issue a press communiqué concerning finding by court that a magazine article, whose sole purpose was to satisfy the curiosity of a sector of the public about the intimacy of a well-known singer and his wife, had thereby intruded into their private life: domestic law was adequately foreseeable, and such a measure may constitute appropriate compensation)

7.53 Article 10, on the other hand, does not go as far as to establish any general duty to establish a public forum to allow for the expression of individual opinion. In *Appleby and Others v United Kingdom*, protestors opposed to a proposed local development had been prohibited from setting up a stand at the entrance to a shopping mall built by a public corporation and subsequently sold to a private company. In determining that the respondent state had no direct responsibility for the restrictions imposed, the Court thereafter considered whether there had been any failure in any positive obligation to protect the applicants' freedom of expression from interference by the private owner of the shopping mall. Here, the owner's right of property was also of relevance. 'While it is true that demographic, social, economic and technological developments are changing the ways in which people move around and come into contact with each other', the Court was not convinced that 'this requires the automatic creation of rights of entry to private property, or even, necessarily, to all publicly owned property'. Article 10 thus 'does not bestow any freedom of forum for the exercise of that right', although it was not possible to exclude that a positive obligation to regulate property rights could arise where a bar on access to property had the effect of preventing any effective exercise of freedom of expression or destroying the essence of the right. Here, the protestors had not been effectively prevented from communicating their views by other means, and in consequence, the court did not find that the provision had been violated[1].

1   *Appleby and Others v United Kingdom* 2003-VI, paras 41–50 at para 47. Cf *Women on Waves and Others v Portugal* 2009-…, paras 28–44 (refusal to allow entry of vessel chartered to support a campaign for the decriminalisation of abortion into territorial waters: the choice of the vessel for the events planned by the associations had been crucially important in this case and in line with other activities in other European states). See also the domestic case of *Mayor of London v Hall* [2011] 1 WLR 504 (occupation of public land opposite Parliament, in breach of byelaws and of property law: Arts 10 and 11 engaged).

Access to information

7.54 Despite the textual reference to the right 'to receive and impart information and ideas', Article 10 does not confer any general right to freedom of information or access to personal information held by state authorities, but merely prevents any governmental restriction on receiving information that others wish or may be willing to impart[1]. Restraints placed upon the publication of information properly considered confidential or received in confidence may thus be deemed justifiable, although even the disclosure of confidential material may be justified when the public interest is sufficiently compelling[2]. However, unwarranted obstacles designed to hinder access to information of public interest and which may discourage those working in the media or related fields from performing a 'public watchdog' role and thereby affect their ability to provide accurate and reliable information to others may give rise to a violation of the guarantee[3]. Additionally, in certain circumstances the ECHR may impose positive responsibilities upon the state to make available information held by it, for example in respect of protection of life under Article 2[4] or where this concerns respect for private or family life under Article 8[5].

1   *Leander v Sweden* (1987) A 116, para 74 (prohibition on national security grounds on gaining access to personal information on applicant held by state authorities: no violation of Art 10); *Open Door and Dublin Well Woman v Ireland* (1992) A 246-A, para 55; (access to information on abortion facilities); *Guerra and Others v Italy* 1998-I, para 53 (question whether there was a positive duty upon a state to publish a report on a serious environmental hazard: the Commission considered such was an essential method of protecting health and well-being, but the Court reiterated its position that Art 10 could not require any positive duty 'to collect and disseminate information of its own motion'); and *Albayrak v Turkey* 2008-…, paras 40–49 (sanctions imposed upon a judge for having read a newspaper and having watched television both of which were pro-Kurdish: violation). For domestic consideration of freedom to receive information, see eg *BBC, Petitioners (No 2)* 2000 JC 521 (Art 10 not engaged by absence of ability to broadcast trial proceedings), *R (Wagstaff) v Secretary of State for Health* [2001] 1

WLR 292 (holding of inquiry in private into deaths of patients of Dr Harold Shipman); and *R (Persey) v Secretary of State for the Environment* [2003] QB 794 (no duty to hold public inquiry into outbreak of foot and mouth disease).

2   *Leempoel and SA Ed Ciné Revue v Belgium* (9 November 2006), paras 69–85 (withdrawal of sale of magazine disclosing documents protected as confidential in the context of a parliamentary inquiry and which may have prejudiced defence rights and interfered with respect for private life: no violation). See also *Dammann v Switzerland* (25 April 2006), paras 50–58 (information relating to previous convictions of private individuals obtained by journalist from administrator in prosecutor's office, but information not subsequently published: the information was not sought through deception and could have been obtained by other means since it was already in the public domain and was not 'information received in confidence', was obtained as part of an investigation into a matter of public interest, and no damage had been done to the individuals' interests: conviction of journalist constituted violation of Art 10); *Radio Twist SA v Slovakia* 2006-XV, paras 56–65 sanctions following the publication of private conversations between Ministers on matters of public concern obtained unlawfully but without any suggestion the information was untrue: violation); and *Stoll v Switzerland* [GC] 2007-..., paras 108–162 (conviction for publication of confidential report by ambassador on negotiation strategies concerning compensation to be paid by Swiss banks to relatives of Holocaust victims: no violation, taking into account the 'truncated and reductive form' in which articles were published was likely to mislead, the manner in which information is obtained is of relevance, and the relatively modest fine imposed).

3   *Társaság a Szabadságjogokért v Hungary* 2009-..., paras 35–39 (refusal to allow a human rights NGO access to case-file concerning a pending constitutional case: the constitutional court's monopoly of information amounting to a form of censorship, and in view of the nature of the NGO's activities involving human-rights litigation and the fact that an application for abstract review of constitutionality of a law undoubtedly constituted a matter of public interest, refusal of access constituted a violation of Art 10).

4   Eg *McGinley and Egan v United Kingdom* 1998-III paras 85–90; and *Öneryildiz v Turkey* [GC] 2004-XII, paras 97–118, discussed at paras **3.29** and **4.21** above.

5   Eg *Gaskin v United Kingdom* (1989) A 160, paras 42–49; *TP and KM v United Kingdom* [GC] 2001-V, paras 78–83. See paras **6.115** and **6.58** respectively above.

The media and freedom of expression

7.55 Protection of the media is considered a vital feature of a democracy[1]. '[A]lthough the press must not overstep the bounds required, for example, to provide protection against threats of violence, disorder or crime, its duty is nevertheless to impart – in a manner consistent with its obligations and responsibilities – information and ideas on all matters of public interest, including divisive ones'[2]. Journalists thus act as a conduit for information and thereby have a vital role in contributing to public discussion and debate and in acting in a 'watchdog' role through investigative journalism. This justifies a high level of protection for the media[3] (and for non-governmental organisations fulfilling a similar 'watchdog' role)[4], but it carries with it certain responsibilities for journalists, in particular, to act in good faith[5] and to verify in advance factual statements that are potentially defamatory where this does not involve 'an unreasonable, if not impossible task'[6], although 'the press should normally be entitled, when contributing to public debate on matters of legitimate concern, to rely on the contents of official reports without having to undertake independent research'[7]. Further, competing considerations such as the responsibility to respect private life under Article 8 may justify (and possibly require as a matter of positive obligation) restrictions on expression on the ground of protection of individual privacy[8].

1   Eg *Goodwin v United Kingdom* 1996-II, at para 39 ('protection of journalistic sources is one of the basic conditions for press freedom'); *Thoma v Luxembourg* 2001-III, at para 64 (there had to be 'particularly cogent reasons' for punishing a journalist for assisting in the dissemination of statements made by another person since this would seriously hamper the contribution of the press to discussion of matters of public interest)'; and *Wojtas-Kaleta v Poland* (16 July 2009), paras 44–53 (protection for statements made by a journalist critical of his employer, a state public broadcaster). For domestic recognition of the importance of a free press, see eg *McCartan Turkington Breen v Times Newspapers Ltd* [2001] 2 AC 277 per Lord Bingham at 290–291.

2   *Ürper and Others v Turkey* (20 October 2009), at para 36.

3   For the purposes of Art 10, 'victims' of interference with the guarantee can include newspaper companies, journalists and editors but not trade union associations: 11553/85 and 11658/85, *Hodgson and Others v United Kingdom* (1987) DR 51, 136 (National Union of Journalists could not be a 'victim' for the purposes of the application); and 15404/89, *Purcell and Others v Ireland* (1991) DR 70, 262 (even although unions considered themselves guardians of collective interests of their members, their rights were not affected by the challenged measures, and thus they were not 'victims'). In 25798/94, *BBC v United Kingdom* (1996) DR 84, 129 and again in 34324/96, *BBC Scotland, McDonald, Rodgers and Donald v United Kingdom* (23 October 1997), the Commission left open the question of whether a state public service broadcaster could qualify as a 'victim', but in *Österreichischer Rundfunk v Austria* (7 December 2006), paras 50–53, the Court considered the Austrian Broadcasting Corporation could qualify as a non-governmental organisation in light of its editorial and journalistic independence, ability to set its own programme fees, and lack of governmental control. The point was conceded in *Mackay and BBC Scotland v United Kingdom* (7 December 2010). Other Council of Europe initiatives in this area stress the importance of a free press and of co-operation in broadcasting: see eg European Convention on Transfrontier Television (ETS 132 (1989)) and amending Protocol (ETS 171 (1998)); and Committee of Ministers Recommendations Rec (94) 13 to member States on measures to promote media transparency; Rec (96) 10 on the guarantee of the independence of public service broadcasting; Rec (99) 1 on measures to promote media pluralism; Rec (2000) 23 on the independence and functions of regulatory authorities for the broadcasting sector; Rec (2007) 15 on measures concerning media coverage of election campaigns; and Rec (2008) 6 on measures to promote the respect for freedom of expression and information with regard to Internet filters. See also Parliamentary Assembly Resolution 1535 (2007) on threats to the lives and freedom of expression of journalists. The maintenance of pluralism, protection for journalists and regulation of 'hate speech' are all of current concern in Europe. See further Council of Europe *Guarding the Watchdog – The Council of Europe and the Media Media* (2003); and Komorek 'Is Media Pluralism a Human Right?: The European Court of Human Rights, the Council of Europe and the Issue of Media Pluralism' [2009] EHRLR 395. For examples of threats to domestic media freedom, see *Manole and Others v Moldova* (dec) (26 September 2006) (alleged censorship imposed upon sole national public broadcaster: admissible); and *Kommersant Moldovy v Moldova* (9 January 2007), paras 29–39 (closure of newspaper allegedly for endangering territorial integrity and national security without detailed reasoning: violation).

4   Eg *Vides Aizsardzîbas Klubs v Latvia* (27 May 2004), para 42 (statutory authorisation for voluntary associations to give views and to issue requests), discussed at para **7.73** below; *Steel and Morris v United Kingdom* 2005-II, para 95 (strong public interest in allowing small and informal campaign groups outside the mainstream to contribute to the public debate by

disseminating information and ideas on matters of general public interest), discussed at para **7.83** below; and *Társaság a Szabadságjogokért* 2009-…, para 27 (human rights NGO).

5   See eg *Katamadze v Georgia* (dec) (14 February 2006) (conviction for publication of offensive comments constituting gratuitous personal attack upon fellow-journalists: inadmissible).

6   Cf *Thorgeir Thorgeirson v Iceland* (1992) A 239, at para 65 (newspaper articles reported numerous allegations of police brutality made by others and sought an independent inquiry; conviction of journalist was in part based upon his failure to justify the allegations which had not been established as without foundation). See further para **7.76** below.

7   *Bladet Tromsø and Stensaas v Norway* [GC] 1999-III, at para 68; *Colombani and Others v France* 2002-V, para 65.

8   See eg *Cumpănă and Mazăre v Romania* [GC] 2004-XI, para 113, noted at para **7.71**, fn 6 below.

7.56 Particular weight is accorded to media attempts to promote discussion and debate on matters of legitimate public concern. This may require allowing access to events in order to allow for the proper discharge of these functions[1]. However, journalists are expected to discharge their responsibilities to act in good faith and ascertain the veracity of factual statements[2]. In *Lingens v Austria*, the applicant had been punished for publishing articles in a newspaper criticising the head of state's fitness for office. The Court considered that such sanctions operated as a form of censure which would be likely to inhibit future political discussion and debate and thus were 'liable to hamper the press in performing its task as purveyor of information and public watchdog' since 'freedom of the press ... affords the public one of the best means of discovering and forming an opinion of the ideas and attitudes of political leaders'[3]. This sentiment shapes much of the application of Article 10. In *Castells v Spain*, a Member of Parliament had been convicted for criticising in the press the government's apparent failure to investigate terrorist activities (the responsibility for which he had attributed to the government) without having been allowed to try to prove the allegations by way of defence in court. The importance of a free press was again emphasised in aiding democratic communication between the electorate and those chosen as its representatives: 'it gives politicians the opportunity to reflect and comment on the preoccupations of public opinion; it thus enables everyone to participate in the free political debate which is at the very core of the concept of a democratic society'[4]. In such circumstances, 'the dominant position which the Government occupies makes it necessary for it to display restraint in resorting to criminal proceedings, particularly where other means are available for replying to the unjustified attacks and criticisms of its adversaries or the media'[5]. Similar concerns apply to the perceived role of the media in scrutinising the administration of justice[6]. It is thus crucial that domestic law does not unduly deter the media from 'fulfilling their role of alerting the public to apparent or suspected misuse of public power', a risk which undoubtedly exists where investigative journalists are liable 'as one of the standard sanctions imposable for unjustified attacks on the reputation of private individuals' to be sentenced to imprisonment or being prohibited as acting as journalists[7].

1   *Gsell v Switzerland* (8 October 2009), paras 50–62 (blanket nature of police ban had prevented journalists from gaining access to allow reporting on the proceedings of the World Economic Forum: violation).

2   The level of responsibility may depend on the gravity of any allegations: see *Radio France and Others v France* 2004-II, paras 34–39 (requirement upon a journalist of being able to show highest caution and particular moderation in respect of serious accusation of active role in deportation of Jews to concentration camps). See also *Radio Twist SA v Slovakia* 2006-XV, paras 54–65 (sanctions following the publication of private conversations between Ministers on matters of public concern obtained unlawfully but without any suggestion the information was untrue: violation); and *Europapress Holding doo v Croatia* (22 October 2009), paras 54–74 (publication in bad faith concerning serious allegations concerning a government minister: no violation). For discussion, see Bismuth 'Le Développement de Standards Professionnels pour les Journalistes dans la Jurisprudence de la Cour Européenne des Droits de l'Homme' (2010) 21 RTDH 39.

3   *Lingens v Austria* (1986) A 103, at para 42.

4   *Castells v Spain* (1992) A 236, at para 43. See, too, *Oberschlick v Austria (no 1)* (1991) A 204, paras 57–63 (conviction of applicant for criminal libel).

5   *Castells v Spain* (1992) A 236, at para 6, noting that the government may react nevertheless 'appropriately and without excess' to unfounded defamatory accusations. See also *Fatullayev v Azerbaijan* (22 April 2010), paras 115–131 (conviction of editor for articles calling into question official version of events and for terrorist offence of inciting ethnic hostility by criticising government policy and sentences of imprisonment for 30 months and eight and a half years respectively: no justification for imposition of prison sentence in relation to the first conviction, while the second interference had been grossly disproportionate as the article had been hypothetical and discursive in nature).

6   Eg *Prager and Oberschlick v Austria* (1995) A 313, para 34; see further para **7.105** below.

7   *Cumpănă and Mazăre v Romania* [GC] 2004-XI, para 113 (sanctions of seven months' imprisonment and prohibition from working as journalists for one year for publishing an article and cartoon suggesting that there had been irregularities in the allocation of a contract by a local authority).

Protection for journalistic sources

7.57 This underlying policy also implies recognition of the importance of protection for journalists' sources which is acknowledged as a fundamental prerequisite for a free press. Careful examination is required of any interference with such sources, in particular, to ensure the reasons are both relevant and sufficient. In *Goodwin v United Kingdom*, a court had made a disclosure order against a journalist which required him to disclose the identity of the source who had supplied unsolicited information on the company's financial activities. The journalist had refused to comply with the order and had been fined. It was accepted that this interference pursued a legitimate aim, but the applicant alleged that any compulsion to disclose sources had to be limited to the most exceptional circumstances where there were vital public or individual interests at stake to satisfy the test of pressing social need. In light of the injunction prohibiting any publication of the information, the Court considered whether the disclosure order could have served any additional purposes. While there were undoubtedly relevant reasons for the order (such as identifying any disloyal employee), it was not possible to say that the reasons were sufficient, and a violation of Article 10 was established[1]. Nor is it decisive if it is concluded that the source of the information has acted in bad faith. In *Financial Times Ltd and Others v United Kingdom*, a disclosure order had been made which was liable to lead to the identification of the source of information relating to a possible takeover bid of a company. The order had been made on the basis that the interest in identifying the source of a deliberate leak of confidential and false information, with serious consequences for the integrity of the share market, outweighed the public interest in protecting the source of the leak. While the disclosure order had not been enforced, it remained capable of being so (no matter how remote a possibility) and thus had constituted an interference with freedom of expression. In holding that there had been a violation of Article 10, the Court assessed the purpose of the leak, the authenticity of the leaked document, the interests of the company in identifying the source and bringing proceedings, and the effect of the disclosure order. It also noted that the conduct of the source could never be decisive in determining whether a disclosure order ought to be made but merely operated as one (albeit important) factor, and also that domestic courts should be slow to assume bad faith in the absence of compelling evidence. In considering the effect of the disclosure order, the Court concluded that no crucial distinction could be made between disclosure that would directly result and disclosure that might result in the identification of the source: a 'chilling effect' arose whenever journalists were seen to assist in the identification of anonymous sources[2]. However, where a criminal trial is involved and the liberty of an individual may be at stake, the pressing social need for disclosure of sources may be more readily justified[3].

1   *Goodwin v United Kingdom* 1996-II, paras 36–46. See also *Ernst and Others v Belgium* (15 July 2003), paras 99–105 (search of premises of a television company and of two newspapers and confiscation of journalists' data in the context of a criminal investigation into disclosure of confidential information by legal service officials not shown to have been proportionate to the achievement of legitimate aims bearing in mind the interest of democratic societies in ensuring and maintaining freedom of the press); and *Voskuil v Netherlands* (22 November 2007), paras 63–74 (detention following refusal to disclose source for article concerning criminal investigation into arms trafficking).

2   *Financial Times Ltd and Others v United Kingdoms*: 2009-…, paras 59–73. For the domestic proceedings, see *Interbrew SA v Financial Times* [2002] 2 Lloyd's Rep 229, noted at para **7.60**, fn 1 below.

3   25798/94, *BBC v United Kingdom* (1996) DR 84, 129 (requirement to disclose material which had been filmed during riots, for the purposes of evidence in a criminal trial, did not violate Art 10). But cf *Nordisk Film & TV A/S v Denmark* (dec) 2005-XIII (order to hand over to the police limited unedited footage taken by undercover journalist and involving a suspected paedophile: inadmissible, as the persons involved were unaware they were talking to a journalist or that they were being recorded and were not freely assisting the press to inform the public about matters of public interest; and while a compulsory hand over of research material may have a chilling effect on the exercise of journalistic freedom of expression and thus engage Art 10, the degree of protection to be applied in such a situation does not reach the same level as the right to keep sources confidential).

7.58 Similar principles apply in respect of actual searches undertaken with a view to discover the source of journalists' information. In *Roemen and Schmit v Luxembourg,* following the publication of a newspaper article suggesting that a government minister had committed fraud, the home and office of a journalist had been searched with a view to establishing the civil servant who had provided him with this confidential information. While the Court was satisfied that the reasons for the search had been relevant, the same could not be said for their sufficiency, since other measures could well have enabled the authorities to obtain this information[1].

---

1   *Roemen and Schmit v Luxembourg* 2003-IV, paras 47–60. See also *Tillack v Belgium* 2007-XIII, paras 56–68 (insufficient reasons advanced for searches and seizures at a journalist's home and place of work: violation).

7.59 To this end, before any order may be made for the search or seizure of material that may identify journalists' sources, domestic law must make provision for a review by an independent and impartial body to determine whether the public interest should override protection of journalistic sources in the particular case. The preventive nature of the review thus requires it to be available prior to the handing over of any relevant material in order to prevent unnecessary access; further, the review body not only must be able to weigh up the potential risks and respective interests prior to any disclosure by reference to clear criteria, but also have the power to refuse disclosure or to make limited or qualified orders to protect a journalist's sources. In arriving at its determination, the body must specifically consider whether less intrusive measures would suffice[1].

---

1   *Sanoma Uitgevers BV v Netherlands* [GC] 2010-...., paras 84–101 (order made by prosecutor to surrender photographs obtained following assurances that participants' identities would not be disclosed and following threats to detain journalists, to search premises and to seize computers: interference not prescribed by law, the ex post facto review available through the courts being insufficient).

DECISIONS OF THE DOMESTIC COURTS ON PROTECTION OF JOURNALISTS' SOURCES

7.60 These judgments of the European Court of Human Rights were considered by the House of Lords in *Ashworth Hospital Authority v MGN Ltd*. The case concerned the disclosure to the press of medical records held by Ashworth Hospital relating to one of the 'Moors murderers'. The starting-point was a presumption against ordering disclosure of the identity of a journalist's source:

'The fact is that information which should be placed in the public domain is frequently made available to the press by individuals who would lack the courage to provide the information if they thought there was a risk of their identity being disclosed. The fact that journalists' sources can be reasonably confident that their identity will not be disclosed makes a significant contribution to the ability of the press to perform their role in society of making information available to the public. It is for this reason that it is well established now that the courts will normally protect journalists' sources from identification.'

However, neither the Contempt of Court Act 1981 nor Article 10 was absolute. In determining that the disclosure ordered had been necessary and proportionate, the House of Lords took into account the importance of preserving the confidentiality of patients' medical records, the particular difficulties involved in caring for patients detained in high security accommodation, and the need to dispel suspicion and to deter similar wrongdoing in the future[1].

---

1 *Ashworth Hospital Authority v MGN Ltd* [2002] 1 WLR 2033, at paras 61–66 per Lord Woolf CJ. See also *Kelly v British Broadcasting Corporation* [2001] Fam 59 (broadcasting of interview with child who was a ward of court); and *Interbrew SA v Financial Times* [2002] 2 Lloyd's Rep 229 (relief on grounds of breach of confidence was refused as the claimant had failed to particularise the details of the confidential information disclosed to the defendants, although the interests of the claimant in removing the continuing threat to its confidentiality was so important that it overrode the public interest in protecting journalistic sources). Cf *Financial Times Ltd and Others v United Kingdom* 2009-…, discussed at para **7.57** above.

7.61 In the subsequent proceedings in *Mersey Care NHS Trust v Ackroyd,* in which an order was sought compelling the person who had acted as an intermediary between the source and the newspaper (and whose identity had been disclosed by the newspaper as a result of the earlier proceedings) to disclose the name of the source, the Court of Appeal determined that a hearing was necessary to determine whether there remained a pressing social need for the disclosure of the source[1]. The judge who then considered that matter at first instance concluded that it was not possible to establish convincingly that there remained any such pressing social need some six years after the leak, it having also been established that the source had not been paid and that the intermediary had believed that he was acting in the public interest to prevent the mistreatment of the detained patient. This decision was upheld by the Court of Appeal[2].

---

1 *Mersey Care NHS Trust v Ackroyd* [2003] EWCA Civ 663.

2 *Mersey Care NHS Trust v Ackroyd (No 2)* [2007] EWCA Civ 101.

Licensing of broadcasting, cinemas etc

7.62 Article 10(1) additionally provides that states are not to be prevented 'from requiring the licensing of broadcasting, television or cinema enterprises'. This permits states to regulate the technical aspects of broadcasting rather than the actual content of broadcasts themselves, although the object or purpose and the exercise of the power to license must be in accordance with the overall context of the guarantee of freedom of expression[1]. However, the grant or refusal of a licence may also take into account such matters as 'the nature and objectives of a proposed station, its potential audience at national, regional or local level, the rights and needs of a specific audience and the obligations deriving from international legal instruments', and thus a refusal to grant a licence 'may lead to interferences whose aims will be legitimate under the third sentence of paragraph 1, even though they may not correspond to any of the aims set out in paragraph 2'[2]. In *Informationsverein Lentia and Others v Austria*, the Court accepted that a state broadcasting monopoly which protected public service broadcasting and which satisfied quality and balance concerns through the operation of state supervision could meet the requirements of paragraph (1). However, since a licensing determination could also involve other factors such as 'the nature and objectives of a proposed station, its potential audience at national, regional or local level, the rights and needs of a specific audience and the obligations deriving from international legal instruments', further consideration of the acceptability of any refusal to allow commercial broadcasting was required in terms of the general principles applying under paragraph (2). The Court in this particular case was not persuaded that there was any pressing social need for the continuation of any such restriction, nor that this was proportionate to the state aim of preventing the establishment of a private broadcasting monopoly[3].

1   *Groppera Radio AG and Others v Switzerland* (1990) A 173, para 61. Cf 8266/78, *X v United Kingdom* (1978) DR 16, 190 (prosecution for advertising broadcasts of a pirate radio station: inadmissible); 8962/80, *X and Y v Belgium* (1982) DR 28, 112 (prosecution for unlawful use of CB radio: inadmissible). For domestic discussion see *R (Pro Life Alliance) v BBC* [2004] 1 AC 185, discussed at para **7.78** below, and *R (Animal Defenders International) v Secretary of State for Culture, Media and Sport* [2008] AC 1312, discussed at para **7.79** below. See further Lewis and Cumper 'Balancing Freedom of Political Expression against Equality of Political Opportunity' [2009] PL 89.

2   *Demuth v Switzerland* 2002-IX, para 33.

3   *Informationsverein Lentia and Others v Austria* (1993) A 276, paras 32–43 at para 32. See too *Telesystem Tirol Kabeltelevision v Austria* 1997-III (refusal to allow company to broadcast cable television programmes on account of state monopoly: friendly settlement and case struck off the list); *Radio ABC v Austria* 1997-VI, paras 30–38; *Tele 1 Privatfernsehgesellschaft v Austria* (21 September 2000), para 35 (refusal to grant radio operating licence violation of Art 10 following *Informationsverein Lentia* case and after consideration of subsequent domestic legislative proceedings); and *Demuth v Switzerland* 2002-IX, paras 40–50 (refusal to grant broadcast licence on account of requirement of cultural and linguistic pluralism fell within the state's margin of appreciation: no violation). The ECHR case law was considered by the Judicial Committee of the Privy Council in *Benjamin v Minister of Information and Broadcasting* [2001] 1 WLR 1040; in *Cable and Wireless (Dominica) Ltd v Marpin Telecoms and Broadcasting* [2001] 1 WLR 1123; and in *Observer Publications Ltd v Matthew* [2001] UKPC 11.

7.63 Restrictions on the content of broadcasts will thus require to satisfy the general tests applied under paragraph (2), and in particular, to be shown to have been 'necessary in a democratic society'. For example, in *VgT Verein gegen Tierfabriken v Switzerland*, a television advertisement prepared by an animal protection society denouncing the industrial rearing of pigs and encouraging people to eat less meat had been rejected by a broadcasting authority because of domestic law which prohibited the broadcasting of advertisements of a political nature. While the European Court of Human Rights accepted that the prohibition pursued a legitimate aim in preventing financially strong groups from obtaining an advantage in politics, it found that the limitation of the prohibition solely to radio and television broadcasts was not particularly pressing, and that the primary aim of the advertisement had been to participate in an ongoing general debate on animal protection. Accordingly, it had not been shown that the interference with free speech had been relevant and sufficient[1]. On the other hand, the Court has often noted that broadcasting involves a means of communication which has 'a more immediate, invasive and powerful impact' than the press, and accordingly is a medium in which it may be easier to justify restrictions on expression[2].

1   *VgT Verein gegen Tierfabriken v Switzerland* 2001-VI, paras 35–79. See also *Verein gegen Tierfabriken Schweiz (VgT) v Switzerland (no 2)* [GC] 2009-…, paras 78–98 (fresh violation on account of failure of positive obligation to implement judgment and to authorise the broadcasting of the commercial, the courts having taken the place of the applicant association in judging whether the debate in question was still a matter of public interest).Cf 15404/89, *Purcell and Others v Ireland* (1991) DR 70, 262 (prohibition on broadcasting of interviews with members of a political party: inadmissible); 18714/91, *Brind and Others v United Kingdom* (1994) DR 77, 42 (prohibition on broadcasting spoken comments by supporters of organisations linked with Sinn Fein: inadmissible). The House of Lords declined to follow *VGT* in *R (Animal Defenders International) v Secretary of State for Culture, Media and Sport* [2008] 1 AC 1312, discussed at para **7.79** below.

2   Eg *Murphy v Ireland* 2003–IX, discussed at para **7.109** below.

DOMESTIC CASES ON LICENSING

7.64 In *Belfast City Council v Miss Behavin' Ltd* the House was willing to assume, without deciding, that the concept of freedom of expression in Article 10(1) was wide enough to cover the use of premises to sell pornography, and that in an appropriate case it might be necessary to restrict this use of premises in order to protect health or morals, as envisaged in Article 10(2)[1].

1   *Belfast City Council v Miss Behavin' Ltd* [2007] 1 WLR 1420. See also *In re St Peter and St Paul's Church* [2007] Fam 67 (grant of faculty for installation of mobile phone mast on church, subject to condition requiring precautions to prevent children from accessing pornography).

Establishing whether there has been an 'interference'

7.65 The guarantee protects both the content of the message sought to be communicated and the manner and form in which it is made. Neither the type of information in question nor the category of individual seeking to exercise freedom of expression is relevant in the assessment of whether there has been any state interference[1]. In the language of Article 10(2), 'interferences' can involve 'formalities, conditions, restrictions or penalties'. In practical terms, these can take the form of seizure and confiscation of a publication[2] or film[3]; grant of an injunction (temporary or permanent) restraining publication of a newspaper article[4] or the right to make comment in the press[5]; the issue of a disclosure order (even if there is only a remote possibility of its enforcement)[6], refusal to grant a video a certificate permitting distribution[7] or to allow re-transmission of television signals[8]; the vetting of school books before distribution[9]; the imposition of disciplinary[10] or criminal sanctions following publication[11] or for refusal to reveal information sources[12]; the making of a civil award of damages against an author[13]; dismissal from (rather than refusal of access to) public employment because of political sympathies[14] or refusal to re-appoint to a post on account of expression of opinions[15]; and even expulsion from a territory for participation in a protest[16] or refusal to allow entry into a country[17].

1 Cf *Hadjianastassiou v Greece* (1992) A 252, para 39 (freedom of expression applies to servicemen; and information relating to military issues is also protected).

2 Eg *Handyside v United Kingdom* (1976) A 24 (seizure of English translation of *Little Red Schoolbook*).

3 *Otto-Preminger-Institut v Austria* (1994) A 295-A (prohibition of screening of film).

4 Eg *Sunday Times v United Kingdom (no 1)* (1979) A 30; and *Sunday Times v United Kingdom (no 2)* (1991) A 217 (restraints against publication of articles on testing of thalidomide and of extracts from unauthorised memoirs of secret service agent).

5 *Barthold v Germany* (1985) A 90 (prohibition on veterinary surgeon who operated an emergency hours service from making critical comment in local press about lack of such facilities on account of professional code of ethics and unfair competition statute); cf *Houdart and Vincent v France* (dec) 2006-X (reprimand and minor penalties imposed upon journalists who were also qualified doctors for article published in breach of medical ethics code: inadmissible).

6 *Financial Times Ltd and Others v United Kingdom* 2009-..., para 56.

7 *Wingrove v United Kingdom* 1996-V (refusal to grant a certificate by British Board of Film Classification on the grounds that the work was blasphemous).

8 Eg *Groppera Radio AG v Switzerland* (1990) A 173; *Autronic AG v Switzerland* (1990) A 178. As to the televising of a trial, or the use of encrypted television signals, see *BBC, Petitioners (No 2)* 2000 JC 521.

9 *Cyprus v Turkey* [GC] 2001-IV, para 252.

10 Where the disciplinary body can reasonably be held to be a 'public authority' through its recognition by domestic law and responsibilities towards protection of the public: eg as in *Le Compte, Van Leuven and De Meyere v Belgium* (1981) A 43, para 64 (sanctions imposed by medical professional bodies); and *Casado Coca v Spain* (1994) A 285-A, para 38 (action taken by Bar Council).

11 Eg *Castells v Spain* (1992) A 236; *Jersild v Denmark* (1994) A 298 (television journalist convicted for assisting in dissemination of racist statements).

12 *Goodwin v United Kingdom* 1996-II (disclosure order made against journalist to reveal sources for information).

13 Eg *Tolstoy Miloslavsky v United Kingdom* (1995) A 316-B (award of £1.5 million, three times the amount of the previous highest award, and made by a jury without 'adequate or effective safeguards ... against a disproportionately large award' (at para 51)). See too *Independent News and Media and Independent Newspapers (Ireland) Ltd v Ireland* 2005-V, paras 119–124 (damages in favour of a leading politician assessed by a jury at IEP 300,000, the highest amount ever awarded in the state, but it had not been shown that there were inadequate or ineffective safeguards against disproportionate awards by juries: no violation). For domestic consideration of the bearing of Art 10 on awards of damages for defamation, see *Jameel v Wall Street Journal Europe Sprl* [2007] 1 AC 359.

14 *Vogt v Germany* (1995) A 323 (dismissal of civil servant for communist sympathies), distinguished in *Otto v Germany* (dec) (24 November 2005) (refusal of promotion of civil servant on account of right-wing political activities: inadmissible, the applicant not being threatened with loss of livelihood by not receiving further promotion). See also *Glasenapp v Germany* (1986) A 104, and *Kosiek v Germany* (1986) A 105 (failure to grant tenure to probationary civil servants because of membership of extremist political party not considered interference with Art 10). A case involving the *failure* to exercise expression is *Petersen v Germany* (dec) 2001-XII (dismissal of university professor on account of lack of professional qualifications and subsequent failure to publish: inadmissible).

15 *Wille v Liechtenstein* [GC] 1999-VII, paras 36–51 (refusal by the sovereign to re-appoint the applicant who was president of the administrative court after he had given an academic lecture which sought to explore whether the sovereign was subject to the jurisdiction of the constitutional

court). It is not, however, clear whether failure merely to promote an individual inter alia on the basis of his opinions would similarly constitute an interference: 12242/86, *Rommelfanger v Germany* (1989) DR 62, 151 (dismissal of a doctor employed in a Roman Catholic hospital for expressing views on abortion not in conformity with the Church's teaching: inadmissible); and cf *Fuentes Bobo v Spain* (29 February 2000), discussed at para **7.51** above.

16   *Piermont v France* (1995) A 314. However, Art 10 cannot imply protection against deportation for a journalist who is not a national of the state involved: 7729/76, *Agee v United Kingdom* (1977) DR 7, 164.

17   *Cox v Turkey* (20 May 2010), paras 38–45 (refusal to allow re-entry of non-national university academic for having made statements in the course of teaching referring to the 'massacre' of Kurds by the Turkish authorities: violation, for while the right to enter a country was not guaranteed by the ECHR as such, the grounds for the refusal had been on account of expression, but it was impossible to conclude that the applicant's views had been deemed harmful to national security).

Decisions of domestic courts on 'interferences'

7.66 There are numerous cases in which domestic courts have considered whether restrictions on freedom of expression have involved interferences with Article 10 rights. A few examples may be given of different types of situation in which the question has arisen. Others are discussed elsewhere in this chapter. A number of cases have concerned the question whether inquiries should be held in public or in private: differing views have been expressed as to the bearing of Article 10 upon the question[1]. In the case of *Ashdown v Telegraph Group Ltd*, it was accepted that the law of copyright was capable of restricting the right to freedom of expression, so as to engage Article 10, in circumstances in which it was important that ideas and information (which are not in themselves protected by copyright) should be conveyed using the form of words devised by a particular author[2]. An obsolete statutory provision dating from 1848, which made it a criminal offence to advocate the abolition of the monarchy, did not constitute an interference with freedom of expression: there was no plausible argument that the existence of the 1848 provision on the statute book had a 'chilling effect' on journalists or anyone else, and s 3 of the HRA 1998 made it plain in any event that the 1848 provision could not be used to mount a successful prosecution[3]. Nor did a ban on hunting with dogs interfere with the expression of beliefs about hunting[4]. Nor does damage to reputation constitute an interference with freedom of expression, notwithstanding that it may affect the credibility of what is said[5].

There have also been a number of cases in which the question has been raised whether particular restrictions on the distribution of pornography constitute 'interferences' within the meaning of Article 10(2). The courts have not discussed the question in detail, proceeding on the basis that if there was any interference it was one which, on the facts, could readily be justified[6]. There have in addition been a number of cases concerned with political demonstrations and other forms of protest. These are discussed below[7].

1   Contrast *R (Wagstaff) v Secretary of State for Health* [2001] 1 WLR 292 (a private inquiry into the deaths of the patients of Harold Shipman was incompatible with Art 10) and *Persey v*

Secretary of State for the Environment, Food and Rural Affairs [2002] EWHC 371 (a closed inquiry into an epidemic of foot and mouth disease did not involve an interference with Art 10). Similarly, in *BBC, Petitioners (No 2)* 2000 JC 521 the refusal of facilities to televise a criminal trial was held not to raise any issue under Art 10.

2   *Ashdown v Telegraph Group Ltd* [2002] Ch 149.

3   *R (Rusbridger) v A-G* [2004] 1 AC 357.

4   *Whaley v Lord Advocate* 2008 SC (HL) 107.

5   *R (Matthias Rath BV) v Advertising Standards Authority Ltd* [2001] HRLR 22.

6   See eg *Belfast City Council v Miss Behavin' Ltd* [2007] 1 WLR 1420; and *In re St Peter and St Paul's Church* [2007] Fam 67, discussed at para **7.64** above.

7   See para **7.124** below.

Assessing whether an interference meets the requirements of Article 10(2)

7.67 A determination that there has been an 'interference' by a public authority of a right which falls within the scope of Article 10 will trigger consideration of whether such an interference is nevertheless justified under paragraph (2). This determination calls in turn for scrutiny of three separate issues: first, whether the interference falls within one of the prescribed state interests; secondly, whether it is 'prescribed by law'; and thirdly, whether the interference in any case was 'necessary in a democratic society'.

Legitimate aim

7.68 The first issue will rarely, if ever, pose difficulty since normally it will be possible for the state to rely upon one of the aims listed. These state aims comprise competing state or public interests (protection of national security, territorial integrity, public safety, prevention of disorder[1] or crime, protection of health or morals[2], and maintenance of the authority and impartiality of the judiciary), and private or individual interests (including protection of the reputation or rights of others[3], the prevention of disclosure of information received in confidence, and even the safeguarding of the interests of foreign producers[4]).

1   Including prevention of disorder 'within the confines of a special social group': *Engel and Others v Netherlands* (1976) A 22, para 98 and *Vereinigung Demokratischer Soldaten Österreichs and Gubi v Austria* (1994) A 302, para 32 (maintenance of military discipline); to protect the right of peaceful assembly and procession: *Chorherr v Austria* (1993) A 266-B (conviction for breach of the peace during a military ceremony); and maintenance of international telecommunications order: *Groppera Radio AG and Others v Switzerland* (1990) A 173, paras 69–70 (international co-operation on usage of limited radio frequencies).

2   Including protection of the morals of the young: *Handyside v United Kingdom* (1976) A 24, para 52.

3   Including commercial reputation: *Markt Intern Verlag GmbH and Klaus Beermann* (1989) A 165, para 31.

4   *Willem v France* (16 July 2009), paras 28–42 (conviction of mayor for calling for boycott of Israeli produce: the aim of the interference was the protection of the rights of Israeli producers).

Prescribed by law

7.69 An interference must also be 'prescribed by law', that is, the law must be adequately accessible and the interference reasonably foreseeable[1] even although statutory language or common-law concepts (such as 'obscene') may lack precise legal definition[2]. The law must minimise the risk of arbitrariness in its application. In *Hashman and Harrup v United Kingdom*, English law on binding over to keep the peace was found wanting on this head. Hunt saboteurs had been found by a court not to have committed a breach of the peace but nevertheless had been bound over to keep the public peace by being required to pay a surety. The nature of breach of the peace and of behaviour considered *contra bones mores* in English law had been considered in an earlier case concerning Article 5[3], but in that instance there had been an actual finding of breach of the peace and the binding-over order had been imposed as a sanction. In the present case, the European Court of Human Rights considered that the order was entirely prospective in effect, and that in consequence it was not possible to consider that the applicants knew what behaviour was being prohibited. Accordingly, there was a violation of Article 10 as the interference had not been 'prescribed by law'[4]. In *Gawęda v Poland*, there was a similar conclusion in a case involving the refusal of requests for registration of the title of a periodical on the basis that the suggested titles were 'in conflict with reality', an ambiguous provision which failed to provide a clear indication of the circumstances in which restraints were permissible, the Court considering that previous interpretations of the provision had not provided a basis for the approach adopted by the courts in the present case. While the guarantee does not prohibit the imposition of prior restraints on publications, the Court reiterated that domestic law must be adequately foreseeable. Here, a requirement that the title of a magazine embody truthful information would at least require a specific legislative provision to this effect, the Court indeed doubting that such a measure could in any case be appropriate since a periodical's title is not a statement as such but merely a device to identify the periodical on the market[5].

---

1   'Prescribed by law' is discussed further at paras **3.62–3.72** above.

2   See for example *Wingrove v United Kingdom* 1996-V, para 42 (law of blasphemy); and *Tammer v Estonia* 2001-I, para 38 (although the relevant provision of the criminal code was worded in rather general terms, it still satisfied the test of 'prescribed by law').

3   *Steel and Others v United Kingdom* 1998-VII, paras 70–75 and 94 (orders to be bound over to keep the peace and be of good behaviour met the test of 'lawfulness' since the elements of breach of the peace were adequately defined by English law): see para **4.165** above.

4   *Hashman and Harrup v United Kingdom* [GC] 1999-VIII, paras 35–41. See also *Karademirci and Others v Turkey* 2005-I, paras 33–43 (statutory requirement of prior authorisation for 'publishing or distributing leaflets, written statements and similar publications' formed basis of conviction for reading aloud a press statement: violation of Art 10 as the applicants could not reasonably have foreseen that the public reading and distribution of a press statement which was of a materially different nature could be considered as an action which fell within the scope of the statute); and *Blake v United Kingdom* (dec) 2005-XII (order made for account of profits in respect of publication written by a former agent of the security services convicted

of passing secrets to the Soviets: such an order was a reasonably foreseeable development of the common law on breach of contract, and inadmissible).

5   *Gawęda v Poland* 2002-II, paras 36–50. For domestic discussion of 'prescribed by law', see eg *R (Gillan) v Commissioner of Police of the Metropolis* [2006] 2 AC 307 (contrast *Gillan and Quinton v United Kingdom* (12 January 2010), discussed at para **6.14** above; *R (Laporte) v Chief Constable of Gloucestershire Constabulary* [2007] 2 AC 105, discussed at para **7.94** below, *R (Matthias Rath BV) v Advertising Standards Authority Ltd* [2001] HRLR 22, and *Interfact Ltd v Liverpool City Council* [2011] 2 WLR 396 (discussed at paras **3.72** and **5.229** above).

'Necessary in a democratic society'

7.70 It is the 'necessary in a democratic society' test which is likely to be at the heart of any issue in terms of Article 10. The balancing of interests in speech with competing public or private interests provides much of the substantive case law associated with the article. The test to be applied under paragraph (2) is, in principle, a demanding one. The exceptions 'must be narrowly interpreted and the necessity for any restrictions must be convincingly established[1]'. The interference complained of must correspond to a pressing social need', be proportionate to the legitimate aim pursued, and be justified by relevant and sufficient reasons[2]. 'Pressing social need' suggests a compelling reason rather than one which is merely "'admissible", "ordinary", "useful", "reasonable" or "desirable"'; but the test is not as high as 'indispensable'[3]. Further, the interference must be proportionate to the legitimate aim pursued, and this requires consideration of the relationship between the means selected and the stated aim. Finally, the reasons advanced by the state for the interference must be considered first in terms of their relevancy and then their sufficiency in the particular case. Prior restraints affecting the media, in particular, call for the closest scrutiny: news is a 'perishable commodity' and even the shortest of delays in authorising publication may significantly diminish its interest[4]. The European Court of Human Rights will require to satisfy itself that domestic decision-makers 'applied standards which were in conformity with the principles embodied in Article 10 and, moreover, that they based their decisions on an acceptable assessment of the relevant facts'[5]. To this end, the Court will scrutinise with particular care the reasoning adopted by domestic courts in justifying an interference with freedom of expression[6], and while the reasons for interfering with freedom of expression may be relevant and sufficient, there may still be no 'pressing social need' for the interference[7].

1   *Vogt v Germany* (1995) A 323, para 52.

2   *Sunday Times v United Kingdom (no 1)* (1979) A 30, para 62.

3   *Handyside v United Kingdom* (1976) A 24, para 48.

4   *Sunday Times v United Kingdom (no 2)* (1991) A 217, at para 51. See also *Obukhova v Russia* (8 January 2009), paras 19–29 (overly-broad interlocutory injunction restricting a journalist's ability to report on an incident involving a judge: violation); and *Ürper and Others v Turkey* (20 October 2009), paras 37–45 at para 44 (suspension of newspapers by domestic courts 'largely overstepped the narrow margin of appreciation afforded to them and unjustifiably

restricted the essential role of the press as a public watchdog', while the 'practice of banning the future publication of entire periodicals ... went beyond any notion of "necessary" restraint in a democratic society and, instead, amounted to censorship'.

5   *Vogt v Germany* (1995) A 323, para 52.

6   Eg *Selistö v Finland* (16 November 2004), paras 56–70 (conviction of journalist for defamation of surgeon: violation).

7   Eg *Éditions Plon v France* 2004-IV, paras 44–57 (relevant and sufficient reasons for prohibiting of book containing medical information on the late President Mitterand, but in time the pressing social need for such no longer existed given that the public interest in discussing the history of the President's time in office was taking precedence over the right to medical confidentiality).

7.71 The outcome is that the level of protection ultimately accorded depends upon the particular circumstances, including 'the nature of the restriction in question, the degree of interference, the nature of the type of opinions or information involved, the societal or political context of the case, the persons involved, the type of medium involved, the public involved'[1]. It is appropriate that there is a high level of protection for journalists and for non-governmental organisations fulfilling a 'watchdog' role or otherwise contributing to public debate by disseminating information and ideas[2], for as will be discussed, certain categories of individuals (and legal persons) must expect scrutiny[3]. Judgments, too, will reflect the underlying aims and values of the Convention: political expression which contributes to democratic discussion will attract the highest safeguards, while there will be a wide margin of appreciation recognised on the part of state authorities in cases involving less worthy expression such as obscenity or blasphemy. The variety of factors, underlying values, and practical concerns render the jurisprudence a rich if at times complex one[4]. In particular, the nature and severity of the penalties imposed will be factors to be taken into account when assessing the proportionality of an interference[5], and the Court will 'exercise the utmost caution where the measures taken or sanctions imposed by the national authorities are such as to dissuade the press from taking part in the discussion of matters of legitimate public concern'[6].

1   Voorhoof 'Guaranteeing the Freedom and Independence of the Media', in Council of Europe, *Media and Democracy* (1998) pp 35–59 at p 53.

2   See paras **7.55–7.56** above.

3   See paras **7.82–7.83** below.

4   Including the extent of the publication: see eg *IA v Turkey* 2005-VIII, para 5 (publication of theological and philosophical views upon religion 'in a novelistic style' in a book with a print run of 2,000). Further, it may be possible to identify two or more legitimate state aims for a particular interference with speech: eg *Observer and Guardian Newspapers v United Kingdom* (1991) A 216, para 56 (injunctions prohibiting publication justified both as necessary for the maintenance of the authority of the judiciary (in the sense of protection of litigants' rights) and also national security); and *Castells v Spain* (1992) A 236, para 39 (penalty imposed for criticism of government fell both under prevention of disorder and protection of reputation of others).

5   See eg *Ceylan v Turkey* [GC] 1999-IV, para 37; *Tammer v Estonia* 2001-I, para 69; *Skałka v Poland* (27 May 2003), paras 41–42. Cf *IA v Turkey* 2005-VIII, para 32 (insignificant fine, and

publication not seized by the authorities); and *Dąbrowski v Poland* (19 December 2006), paras 36–37 (conviction of journalist for defamation of politician: while penalty was comparatively light, the conviction was disproportionate and could deter press freedom).

6   *Cumpn and Mazăre v Romania* [GC] 2004-XI, paras 111–122 at paras 115 and 118 (imposition of seven months' imprisonment and prohibition from working as journalists for publishing an article and cartoon suggesting that there had been irregularities in the allocation of a contract by a local authority: such 'undoubtedly very severe' sanctions would have a chilling effect upon press freedom and were in the circumstances entirely unjustified, and in particular, loss of liberty was only appropriate 'where other fundamental rights have been seriously impaired, as, for example, in the case of hate speech or incitement to violence', while the prohibition from working as journalists 'could not in any circumstances have been justified by the mere risk of the applicants' reoffending').

'Duties and responsibilities'

7.72 Article 10(2) specifically acknowledges that the exercise of freedom of expression 'carries with it duties and responsibilities'. This is of particular importance in respect of four aspects of Article 10 jurisprudence. First, there is an obligation 'to avoid as far as possible expressions that are gratuitously offensive to others and thus an infringement of their rights, and which therefore do not contribute to any form of public debate capable of furthering progress in human affairs', a responsibility of particular relevance in the context of discussion of religious opinions and beliefs[1]. Secondly, political leaders have a duty to defend democracy and its principles, for example, by showing a certain neutrality and exercising discretion when acting on behalf of the community to avoid acting in a discriminatory manner[2] or stirring up intolerance or tensions between sections of the community[3]. Thirdly, employees owe an obligation of discretion and constraint to their employer and thus this justifies certain restrictions on freedom of expression[4], a matter of particular relevance to certain categories of public officials[5]. Fourthly, those seeking to rely upon freedom of expression must take care to ensure that there is an adequate factual basis for opinions and assertions, a responsibility of particular relevance to journalists and, in certain instances, to authors and their publishers[6].

1   *Otto-Preminger-Institut v Austria* (1994) A 295-A, at para 49. See further para **7.108** below.

2   *Willem v France* (16 July 2009), paras 28–42 (conviction of mayor for calling on municipal authorities to engage in a boycott of Israeli produce, an act of positive discrimination: no violation, for while an interference with the freedom of expression of a mayor required particular vigilance, the conviction had been for inciting a discriminatory act rather than for voicing political opinions).

3   *Féret v Belgium* 2009-..., paras 66–82 (MP and president of extremist right-wing party convicted for incitement to racial hatred during electoral campaign: no violation, as insults, ridicule or defamation aimed at specific population groups or incitement to discrimination constituted irresponsible use of freedom of expression undermining people's dignity or even their safety and called for a proper response from the authorities).

4   *Wojtas-Kaleta v Poland* (16 July 2009), paras 44–53 (but this responsibility does not apply with equal force to journalists as it is in the nature of their function to impart information and ideas).

5   See paras **7.88–7.89** (civil servants and local government officials), **7.91** (military), and **7.104–7.105** (judiciary) below.

6   See paras **7.73**, **7.84** and **7.87** below.

Facts and value judgments

7.73 The Court has drawn a distinction between facts (whose existence can be proved or disproved) and value judgments (which are not susceptible to proof and thus are worthy of enhanced protection)[1], providing always that the factual basis for such judgments are 'substantially correct' and made in good faith[2]. There is thus an onus upon journalists to ascertain the veracity of facts, although journalists are at least entitled to rely upon official reports for their material[3]. The distinction between fact and value judgment may not always be clear-cut[4]. Certain judgments help illustrate the Court's approach. In *Vides Aizsardzÿbas Klubs v Latvia,* an environmental protection association's resolution had contained allegations that the chairman of a district council had signed illegal documents facilitating unlawful construction work on a stretch of coastline. While subsequent checks had indeed detected some irregularities, the chairman had succeeded in obtaining compensation from the association in legal proceedings. For the Court, the resolution had sought to highlight local government malpractice, a sensitive matter of public interest, and thus one which had contributed to transparency in the actions of public authorities. The description of the chairman's behaviour as 'illegal' had been a value judgment the truthfulness of which could not be proven, and in any event the association had demonstrated the truth of the factual allegations for which it had been criticised. Accordingly, there had been a violation of Article 10[5]. In *Karman v Russia,* the applicant had been convicted of criminal defamation for calling an anti-Semitic political activist a 'neo-fascist', the domestic courts having considered that such a designation could only be applied to an individual who was in fact a member of a neo-fascist party. The Strasbourg Court, on the other hand, considered that the term 'neo-fascist' was to be regarded as a value-judgment rather than a statement of fact and should be understood in the sense of describing a general political affiliation with the ideology of racial distinctions and anti-Semitism. The standards applied by the Russian courts were not compatible with the principles embodied in Article 10 since they did not adduce 'sufficient' reasons justifying the interference at issue. In reiterating that a requirement to prove the truth of a value judgment was impossible to fulfil and in itself infringed freedom of opinion, the Court again emphasised that a value judgment without any factual basis to support it would not attract protection. Here, however, the applicant had offered the courts documentary evidence to support his opinion but this material had been refused[6].

In *Pedersen and Baadsgaard v Denmark,* on the other hand, a bare majority of the Grand Chamber considered that Article 10 had not been violated in a case in which two television producers had been convicted of criminal defamation for suggesting that a senior police officer had suppressed evidence in a case in which an individual had been convicted of murder. While this individual subsequently had been granted a re-trial and had been acquitted, the applicants had not been convicted for highlighting legitimate matters of public interest in the criminal investigation but rather for specific allegations against a named police officer. In reiterating that special grounds are required before the media can be deemed to have been excused their obligation to verify factual statements that are defamatory of a private individual, the Court considered that in this case the comment had not been limited to discussion of the evidence and to value judgments about the conduct of police officers, but instead had involved, albeit indirectly, an allegation of fact susceptible of proof but without any attempt to provide justification for the allegations. Nor could the sentences imposed be considered disproportionate or excessive, nor such as to have a chilling effect on freedom of expression[7].

---

1   Thus in *Lingens v Austria* (1986) A 103, at para 46 the Court was critical of domestic law which placed the onus of proving the truthfulness of the offending comments upon the accused, but since the expression complained of essentially concerned value judgments, the Court noted that the requirement to prove the truthfulness of the allegations 'is impossible of fulfilment and it infringes freedom of opinion itself, which is a fundamental part of the right secured by Article 10'. See too *Thorgeir Thorgeirson v Iceland* (1992) A 239, para 65 (domestic law requiring the accused to prove the truthfulness of his allegations of police brutality, an 'unreasonable, if not impossible task'). Cf *Schwabe v Austria* (1992) A 242-B, para 34 (defamation conviction for comment made about politician; the Court found a breach of Art 10, as the applicant could not have been considered to have exceeded the limits of freedom of expression).

2   See *Nilsen and Johnsen v Norway* [GC] 1999-VIII, paras 43–53 (five statements concerning police violence: three could not be said to have exceeded the limits of permissible criticism and were unsupported by sufficient reasons, but statements of deliberate lying were allegations of fact susceptible to proof and which had no factual basis); *Feldek v Slovakia* 2001-VII, paras 85–90 (value judgment concerning a minister's background in a fascist organisation); and *Radio France and Others v France* 2004-II, paras 37–39 (journalist not able to show highest caution and particular moderation had been exercised in respect of serious accusation of active role in deportation of Jews to concentration camps).

3   *Bladet Tromsø and Stensaas v Norway* [GC] 1999-III, paras 63–73 (reliance upon report on seal-hunting); and *Colombani and Others v France* 2002-V, paras 59–70 (conviction for defamation of king of Morocco but assertions based upon a European Commission report on drug-trafficking: journalists may rely upon an official report and had no duty to investigate the facts upon which the report was based, and violation of Art 10). See also *Radio Twist AS v Slovakia* 2006-XV, paras 56–65 (unlawfully obtained tape recording of conversation between two Ministers concerning management of state resources, but not established that the recording was untrue or distorted: imposition of requirement to broadcast apology and fine was a disproportionate response).

4   *Unabhängige Initiative Informationsvielfalt v Austria* 2002-I, paras 41–49 (domestic courts' labelling of statement about racist agitation as statement of fact was inappropriate as the statement was properly a value-judgment). See also *Jerusalem v Austria* 2001-II, at paras 42–43 ('the requirement to prove the truth of a value judgment is impossible to fulfil and infringes freedom of opinion ... [but] even where a statement amounts to a value judgment, the proportionality of an interference may depend on whether there exists a sufficient factual basis for the impugned statement, since even a value judgment without any factual basis to support it may be excessive'); *Perna v Italy* [GC] 2003-V, paras 47–48 (defamation proceedings in relation to a statement concerning a public prosecutor's alleged abuse of position ('when he entered the State Legal Service he swore a threefold oath of obedience – to God, to the Law and to [the Communist Party]' and allegations concerning the prosecutor's intention of gaining control of all prosecutors' offices): at no time had the applicant attempted to prove the truth

of these allegations and thus the conviction for defamation and the sentence had not been disproportionate); *Ukrainian Media Group v Ukraine* (29 March 2005), paras 59–62 (domestic law on defamation made no distinction between value judgments and statements of fact, in that it referred uniformly to 'statements' and proceeded from an assumption that any statement was amenable to proof in civil proceedings, standards that were not compatible with the principles embodied in Art 10); and *Keller v Hungary* (dec), (4 April 2006) (conviction of MP for accusing a Minister of neglecting his duties for personal reasons connected with his father's loyalties with a Nazi movement, a factual statement for which no proof had been given: inadmissible). The distinction between facts and value judgments is also drawn in domestic legal systems in the UK. For a suggestion that the approach adopted by the English courts is open to challenge, see Young 'Fact, Opinion and the Human Rights Act 1998: Does English Law need to Modify its Definition of Statements of Opinion?' (2000) OJLS 89.

5   *Vides Aizsardzîbas Klubs v Latvia* (27 May 2004), paras 41–49, the Court noting (at para 43) that 'in certain situations, it may prove to be difficult to draw a precise line between the two notions'.

6   *Karman v Russia* (14 December 2006), paras 31–43. See also *Bodrožić and Vujin v Serbia* (23 June 2009), paras 49–59 (conviction for references to a prominent historian as 'an idiot' and 'a fascist': while the words had been harsh and offensive, they had been a reaction to a provocative interview given in the context of a free debate on an issue of general interest likely to provoke a strong response and the words could only have been interpreted as value judgments and therefore as opinions not susceptible of proof); and *Karsai v Hungary* 2009-…, paras 29–38 (civil sanctions for defamation imposed upon historian for an article criticising the right wing press's comments in favour of the erection of a commemorative statue of a former prime minister who had been a Nazi collaborator: violation, as there had been considerable public interest in the article, and the sanctions imposed were capable of producing a chilling effect on expression).

7   *Pedersen and Baadsgaard v Denmark* [GC] 2004-XI, paras 71–95.

Determining 'necessity' where there has been prior publication

7.74 Where information has already entered the public domain through prior publication, it may be difficult to establish either that the reasons for interference are sufficient or that the measures taken are proportionate. In *Weber v Switzerland*, a journalist had been convicted for disclosing information relating to a pending judicial procedure at a press conference in violation of domestic law which sought to protect the confidentiality of judicial investigations. Much of this information had already been disclosed at an earlier press conference, and in the circumstances the European Court of Human Rights determined that the necessity of protecting the confidentiality of the information no longer existed[1]. In *Observer and Guardian Newspapers v United Kingdom* which concerned attempts to prevent the publication of extracts from the 'Spycatcher' memoirs by a former member of the UK security service, the Court accepted there had been relevant grounds for an interference both to protect national security and to prevent prejudice to the Government's position as a litigant. However, the Court drew a distinction between the period from the initial granting of temporary injunctions against newspapers until the time when much of the information became available through publication abroad, and the period after such publication which had involved worldwide dissemination of the book's content. In the first period, the Court accepted that the grounds for restraining publication were also sufficient; but in the second period (and after publication of the book in the USA) this was no longer the case[2]. In *Vereniging Weekblad 'Bluf! v Netherlands*, a magazine containing the results of a confidential survey had been seized and withdrawn from sale, but only after significant numbers of the publication had already been sold. On this ground, the Court held that the seizure was disproportionate[3]. In *Éditions Plon v France*, despite an injunction prohibiting distribution of a book containing medical information on the late President Mitterand, a substantial number of copies of the book had been sold and its contents had also been published on the internet and discussed in the media thus rendering any further need to preserve medical confidentiality no longer a pressing one[4].

---

1   *Weber v Switzerland* (1990) A 177, paras 51 and 52. See also 10038/82, *Harman v United Kingdom* (1984) DR 38, 53, and (1986) DR 46, 57 (finding of contempt of court made against solicitor for allowing journalist to have sight of documents which had been read out in open court: friendly settlement ultimately achieved with change of domestic law to preclude the publication of any document disclosed in court proceedings from being considered a contempt of court).

2   *Observer and Guardian Newspapers v United Kingdom* (1991) A 216, paras 62–68. See, similarly, *Sunday Times v United Kingdom (no 2)* (1991) A 217, paras 50–55. For discussion, see Oliver 'Spycatcher Case: Confidence, Copyright and Contempt' in Shetreet (ed) *Free Speech and National Security* (1991).

3   *Vereniging Weekblad 'Bluf! v Netherlands* (1995) A 306-A, paras 40–46 (at para 45, the Court acknowledged that while the withdrawal of the magazine was no longer justified, 'it would have been quite possible, however, to prosecute the offenders'). Cf *Gawęda v Poland* 2002-II, paras 36–50 (refusal of registration of a periodical on the basis that the suggested titles were 'in conflict with reality': Art 10 does not prohibit the imposition of prior restraints on publications, but domestic law must be adequately foreseeable, and a requirement that the title of a magazine embody truthful information required specific legislative provision to this end).

4   *Éditions Plon v France* 2004-IV, paras 53–55.

Determining whether an interference is 'necessary in a democratic society': particular issues

Participation in public debate

7.75 The highest level of protection under Article 10 attaches to expression which contributes to the maintenance and furtherance of public debate or the enhancement of democratic accountability. The necessity 'in a democratic society' for an interference with discussion on matters of general public concern will call for sensitive assessment. The Court has generally refused to draw any distinction between the narrower idea of 'political discussion' and 'discussion of other matters of public concern', preferring a wide approach to determination of what helps constitute a healthy 'democratic society'[1]. Only the most compelling reasons will outweigh free speech in this area, even when such expression is considered harmful to the protection of individual reputation. In short, 'there is little scope under

[Article 10(2)] for restrictions on political speech or on debate on questions of public interest'[2].

---

1   *Thorgeir Thorgeirson v Iceland* (1992) A 239, at para 64. See further Spielmann and Cariolou 'The Right to Protection of Reputation under the European Convention on Human Rights' in Katuoka (ed) *Law in the Changing Europe: Liber Amicorum Pranas Kuris* (2008), pp 410–424.

2   *Feldek v Slovakia* 2001-VIII, para 74.

FREE SPEECH AND ELECTED REPRESENTATIVES

7.76 Special protection is thus accorded to expression associated with the exercise of democracy or discussion of constitutional issues[1]. Free speech is of particular importance for Members of Parliament, local councillors, political parties and their activists since 'they represent their electorate, draw attention to their preoccupations and defend their interests'. In consequence, an interference with the rights under Article 10 of a politician calls for 'the closest scrutiny'[2]. However, there are two caveats. First, political leaders have particular responsibilities in helping uphold democratic values, and are expected to avoid acting in a discriminatory manner or inciting intolerance[3]. Secondly, there may be a fine line between political expression which is considered worthy of protection, and that which seeks to undermine democracy and thus is deemed incompatible with the Convention because of Article 17, which prohibits the abuse of Convention rights[4]. Such considerations may have had some part to play in the disposal of applications challenging restrictions on broadcasts with members of political parties considered to have links with terrorist organisations[5], although the Court will still review a conviction for the crime of 'hate speech' to ensure the interference with expression can be justified[6].

---

1   Cf *Thorgeir Thorgeirson v Iceland* (1992) A 239, para 64 (there is 'no warrant' in Art 10 jurisprudence for distinguishing 'between political discussion and discussion of other matters of concern'). See too *Wille v Liechtenstein* [GC] 1999-VII, paras 67–70 (refusal by the sovereign to re-appoint the applicant who was president of the administrative court after he had given an academic lecture which sought to explore whether the sovereign was subject to the jurisdiction of the constitutional court: while a judge had to show particular restraint in the expression of views, the opinions he had stated were tenable and had been expressed in an appropriate way and accordingly the interference was not 'necessary in a democratic society'). For further discussion, see Mowbray 'The Role of the European Court of Human Rights in the Promotion of Democracy' [1999] PL 703; and Fenwick and Phillipson 'Public Protest, the Human Rights Act and Judicial Responses to Political Expression' [2000] PL 627.

2   *Incal v Turkey* 1998-IV, para 46. See also See also *Salov v Ukraine* 2005-VIII, paras 111–117 (conviction, imprisonment and loss of practising licence of legal representative of presidential candidate for dissemination of false information claiming a fellow candidate and present incumbent was dead: the limited circulation of the information which he himself doubted and the severity of the penalties were disproportionate and constituted a violation of Art 10); *Malisiewicz-Gsior v Poland* (6 April 2006), paras 63–70 (conviction of parliamentary candidate for making defamatory allegations suggesting abuse of power by the deputy Speaker of Parliament: violation); and *Mamère v France* 2006-XIII, paras 18–30 (conviction of a politician speaking in his capacity as an elected representative committed to ecological issues: the

authorities' margin of appreciation in deciding on the necessity of the conviction had been particularly limited). Similar protection is justified for journalists and for non-governmental organisations contributing to pubic debate: see paras **7.55–7.56** above.

3   Eg *Willem v France* (16 July 2009), paras 37–38; and *Féret v Belgium* 2009-…, paras 72–77.

4   See para **7.99** below.

5   15404/89, *Purcell and Others v Ireland* (1991) DR 70, 262 (prohibition on broadcasting of interviews with members of a political party: inadmissible); 18714/91, *Brind and Others v United Kingdom* (1994) DR 77, 42 (prohibition on broadcasting spoken comments by supporters of organisations linked with Sinn Fein: inadmissible). See too *McGuiness v United Kingdom* (dec) 1999-V (elected representatives required to take an oath of allegiance to the monarch; application declared inadmissible under Art 10 since the oath could be viewed simply as an affirmation of loyalty to the UK's constitutional principles). This decision can be contrasted with *Buscarini and Others v San Marino* [GC] 1999-I, paras 34–41 at para 39 (interferences with Art 9 rights where applicants who were elected to parliament were required to take a religious oath on the Bible as a condition of sitting, making the 'exercise of a mandate intended to represent different views of society within Parliament subject to a prior declaration of commitment to a particular set of beliefs' which could not be considered appropriate).

6   *Gündüz v Turkey* 2003-XI, paras 42–53, discussed at para **7.100** below; and *IA v Turkey* 2005-VIII.

ELECTION CAMPAIGNS

7.77 Issues under Article 10 may arise in respect of regulation of electoral campaigns. Free speech and free elections 'together form the bedrock of any democratic system' and Article 10 and Article 3 of Protocol no 1 'are interrelated and operate to reinforce each other', although the two provisions may come into conflict with each other at election time when it may be appropriate to place certain restrictions on free speech[1]. In *Bowman v United Kingdom*, the applicant challenged the prohibition found in the Representation of the People Act 1983 against the incurring of unauthorised expenditure of more than £5 with a view to promoting the return of a particular candidate in a parliamentary election. As the director of an anti-abortion pressure group, she had arranged for the distribution of leaflets in individual constituencies outlining the views of each of the candidates on this subject. The European Court of Human Rights considered that the restriction on expression had pursued the legitimate aim of protecting the rights of electoral candidates, but found the means selected disproportionate in the light of the lack of restraints at national or regional campaign level[2]. However, the determination of access to broadcast facilities is covered by a margin of appreciation on the part of state authorities, and it has proved difficult for applicants to use the Convention to challenge domestic arrangements[3].

1   *Bowman v United Kingdom* 1998-I, paras 41–43 at para 42.

2   *Bowman v United Kingdom* 1998-I, paras 45–47.

3   Eg 4750/71, *M v United Kingdom* (1972) CD 40, 29 (refusal of BBC to give broadcasting time to a political party declared inadmissible); 24744/94, *Huggett v United Kingdom* (1995) DR 82, 98 (rules determining allocation of broadcasting time were not arbitrary: inadmissible). See also Committee of Ministers Recommendation Rec (2007)15 on measures concerning media coverage of election campaigns.

DECISIONS OF DOMESTIC COURTS ON EXPRESSION RELATING TO POLITICAL MATTERS

7.78 In *R (ProLife Alliance) v British Broadcasting Corporation*, a political party opposed to abortion challenged the refusal of broadcasters to transmit a party election broadcast which included several minutes primarily devoted to images of aborted foetuses. The refusal was based upon the broadcasters' statutory obligation not to broadcast material which offended against good taste and decency or was likely to be offensive to public feeling. The challenge was unsuccessful: the decision to refuse to transmit shocking or offensive material was justifiable under Article 10(2). It was observed that there was no human right to broadcast on television, and that many political parties did not qualify for party election broadcasts. The right conferred by Article 10, in that context, was a right not to have one's access to public media denied on discriminatory, arbitrary or unreasonable grounds. The condition as to taste and decency was not discriminatory or unreasonable[1].

The case of *R (Gaunt) v Office of Communications* concerned a 'shock jock' (ie a radio broadcaster known for his outspoken and aggressive style of presentation) who, in the course of an interview with a local authority councillor which was broadcast live, called the councillor, among other things, 'a Nazi', 'a health Nazi' and 'you ignorant pig'. Following complaints from members of the public, the regulatory authority Ofcom found that the radio station had breached the relevant code of practice. Ofcom rejected representations from the claimant that this finding involved disproportionate interference with his freedom of expression under Article 10. His claim for judicial review was dismissed. It was accepted that, since the subject matter of the interview was political and controversial, the interviewee was an elected politician who would expect to receive and tolerate a rough ride, and the words complained of were expressions of opinion rather than statements of fact, the claimant's freedom of expression had to be accorded a high degree of protection and was capable of extending to offensive expression. It did not however extend to gratuitously offensive insults or abuse which had no contextual content or justification, such as the broadcast complained of. In the circumstances, Ofcom's finding did not materially interfere with the claimant's Article 10 right to freedom of expression[2].

---

1   *R (ProLife Alliance) v British Broadcasting Corporation* [2004] 1 AC 185, at paras 58–73 per Lord Hoffmann

2   *R (Gaunt) v Office of Communications* [2011] 1 WLR 663.

7.79 In *R (Animal Defenders International) v Secretary of State for Culture, Media and Sport*, the House of Lords held that a statutory ban on political advertising was compatible with Article 10, being prescribed by law, having the legitimate aim of protecting the democratic rights of others, and being proportionate: in essence, the ban was necessary to achieve a level playing field in public discussion of political issues, undistorted as far as possible by the financial resources of those involved[1].

1   R *(Animal Defenders International) v Secretary of State for Culture, Media and Sport* [2008] 1 AC 1312.

7.80 In the case of *Ashdown v Telegraph Group Ltd*, which concerned the unauthorised publication of an extract from a politician's private diary following which proceedings were brought by the politician for breach of copyright, it was said that in most circumstances the principle of freedom of expression would be sufficiently protected if there was a right to publish information and ideas set out in another's literary work, without copying the very words which that person had employed to convey the information or express the idea. In such circumstances it would normally be necessary in a democratic society that the author of the work should have his property in his own creation protected. There would, however, be occasions when it was in the public interest not merely that information should be published, but that the public should be told the very words used by a person, notwithstanding that the author enjoyed copyright in them. In circumstances where the right of freedom of expression came into conflict with the protection afforded by the Copyright, Designs and Patents Act 1988, the court was bound in so far as possible, to apply the Act in a manner that accommodated the right of freedom of expression[1]. Usually this might be done by declining to grant an injunction, ie allowing the newspaper to copy the exact words, but indemnifying the author for any loss or accounting to him for any profit. In the rare case where it was in the public interest that the words should be copied without any sanction, this could be permitted under the statutory 'public interest' exception. There have in addition been a number of cases concerned with political demonstrations and other forms of protest. These are discussed below[2].

1   *Ashdown v Telegraph Group Ltd* [2002] Ch 149. See also Case 4 Ob 127/01, [2002] GRUR Int 341, [2002] EuroCLY 2006 [Austria] (right of individual claiming to have been subjected to sustained newspaper attack to reproduce articles on internet homepage irrespective of copyright claims by the newspaper).

2   See para **7.124** below.

POLITICAL DEBATE AND PERSONAL REPUTATION

7.81 In assessing the justification for an interference with free speech where the expression concerns discussion of public affairs, the status of both the applicant as well as that of the party whose reputation is under threat will be of direct relevance. The 'watchdog' role of the media and of related organisations may often be crucial, but the exercise of freedom of expression also carries with it duties and responsibilities[1]. In *Lingens v Austria*, a journalist had been punished for publishing articles criticising the Chancellor of Austria as 'immoral' or 'undignified' for his protection of former Nazis. The European Court of Human Rights considered that these criticisms could have been said to have been well founded, and had been made in good faith. The particular role of the press in helping the public come to an assessment of their leaders was acknowledged as of critical importance; further 'the limits of acceptable criticism are ... wider as regards a politician as such than as regards a private individual' since a politician 'inevitably and knowingly lays himself open to close scrutiny of his every word and deed'. Accordingly, while protection of the reputation of individuals is a recognised ground for state interference under Article 10(2) and extends to protection of the reputation of politicians, 'in such cases the requirements of such protection have to be weighed in relation to the interests of open discussion of issues'[2].

1 See para **7.55** above.

2 *Lingens v Austria* (1986) A 103, at para 42. Note *Krone Verlag GmbH v Austria* (26 February 2002), paras 35–39 (injunction on publication of photograph of politician: violation, the Court noting (at para 37) that what matters is whether a politician has entered the public arena, not how well known an individual is). See too *Lopes Gomes da Silva v Portugal* 2000-X, paras 31–37 (prosecution for criminal libel concerning a candidate for election considered disproportionate: violation of Art 10); *Ukrainian Media Group v Ukraine* (29 March 2005), paras 66–70 (criticism of politicians in strong, polemical and sarcastic language had been value judgments used in the context of political rhetoric and which were not susceptible of proof: thus the reasons put forward to justify the conviction could not be regarded as 'sufficient'); and *Dąbrowski v Poland* (19 December 2006), paras 33–38 (conviction of journalist for referring to 'mayor-burglar' after politician's conviction: while penalty was comparatively light, the conviction was disproportionate and could deter press freedom). Cf *Demicoli v Malta* (1991) A 210, paras 39–41 (satirical newspaper attack upon MPs punished under parliamentary privilege rules: matter considered under Art 6 with violation established because of procedural impropriety).

DISCUSSION OF POLITICIANS AND OTHER PUBLIC FIGURES

7.82 The need for, and expectation of, greater public exposure of politicians has been stressed in subsequent cases. In *Castells v Spain*, the European Court of Human Rights went as far as to suggest that the boundaries of acceptable criticism had to be wider as regards a member of the executive (rather than a parliamentarian or other politician) since the maintenance of democracy required close scrutiny. In this case, an elected senator had been convicted of the offence of insulting the government through the publication of an article critical of the situation in the Basque region; the fact that the applicant was an elected Member of Parliament was of considerable relevance in determining that there had been a breach of Article 10[1]. Greater latitude is thus appropriate for those charged with (or who take it upon themselves) to enter political life, and even virulent language which may be considered seditious may require protection. In *Incal v Turkey*, the applicant was a member of the executive committee of a political party who had been punished for distributing leaflets considered separatist propaganda seeking to incite insurrection. The penalties imposed involved imprisonment for six-and-a-half months, debarment from entering the civil service, and restrictions upon further political activities. While mindful of the problems posed by terrorism, the Court considered the 'radical' nature of the penalties disproportionate bearing in mind that the authorities under domestic law could have required changes to be made in the leaflet before publication. Restraint on the part of prosecutors was called for in such cases[2].

1   *Castells v Spain* (1992) A 236, paras 42 and 46. Cf *Piermont v France* (1995) A 314, para 76: 'a person opposed to official ideas and positions must be able to find a place in the political arena' (expulsion of a German MEP from a French overseas territory after participation in a demonstration). *Castells* was distinguisheded in the domestic case of *Quinan v Donnelly* 2005 1 JC 729.

2   *Incal v Turkey* 1998-IV, paras 46–58. See too further cases decided by the Grand Chamber on 8 July 1999 involving the punishment of 'separatist' expression claimed by the state as incitement to violence or insurrection: *Ceylan v Turkey* [GC] 1999-IV (trade union leader); *Arslan v Turkey* [GC] (8 July 1999) (author); and *Gerger v Turkey* [GC] (8 July 1999) (journalist); each held to be violations of Art 10. Cf the cases decided the same day of *Sürek v Turkey (no 1)* [GC] 1999-IV; and *Sürek v Turkey (no 3)* [GC] (no violation of Art 10 established).

7.83 The assumption that politicians lay themselves open to enhanced scrutiny has subsequently been extended to other categories of individuals. In *Fayed v United Kingdom*, the Court applied this approach to businessmen actively involved in the affairs of major public companies who thus also 'inevitably and knowingly lay themselves open to close scrutiny of all their acts' not only by the media but also by inspectors and other institutions representing the public interest[1]. In *Jerusalem v Austria*, the extension was to private individuals and associations when they enter the arena of public debate[2]; in *Haguenauer v France* to university professors acting in their personal capacity[3]; and in *Steel and Morris v United Kingdom*, to large corporate bodies on account of their commercial activities. In *Steel and Morris*, members of an anti-McDonald's campaign group had been forced to defend themselves in lengthy civil court proceedings after alleging that the company was involved in unethical and irresponsible practices, sold unhealthy foodstuffs, and targeted children in advertising. In noting that there was both a strong public interest in allowing small and informal campaign groups outside the mainstream to contribute to the public debate and also that large powerful corporations laid themselves open to enhanced scrutiny, the Court nevertheless confirmed that companies had the right to protect their commercial reputations and that such campaign groups were expected to act in good faith and ascertain the veracity of factual statements. However, if domestic law placed the onus on a defendant in libel proceedings of proving the truth of defamatory statements as had occurred in this case, the state was under an obligation to provide a measure of procedural fairness and equality of arms to protect the general interest in promoting the free circulation of information and ideas. Here, the lack of legal aid to allow individuals to defend themselves in defamation proceedings had led to a failure to ensure procedural fairness in the proceedings, and had constituted both a violation of Article 6 and thereby also of Article 10[4].

1   *Fayed v United Kingdom* (1994) A 294-B, para 75 (discussing enforcement of the right to a good reputation under Art 6). See also *Verlagsgruppe News Gmbh v Austria* (no 2) (14 December 2006), paras 36–44 (prohibition on publishing photographs of business magnate in context of reports concerning tax evasion: violation).

2   *Jerusalem v Austria* 2001-II, paras 38–39.

3 *Haguenauer v France* 22 April 2010), paras 42–55 (local government representative convicted for response to comments made by professor in respect of discussion of the Holocaust).

4 *Steel and Morris v United Kingdom* 2005-II, paras 95–98. Cf *McVicar v United Kingdom* 2002-III, paras 74–82 (non-availability of legal aid to defend defamation action brought by well-known athlete: no interference with right of expression as costs order and injunction were not disproportionate).

7.84 As noted, language which is provocative may still attract protection[1]. Sanctions imposed in relation to offensive speech directed against public figures such as politicians and high-profile businessmen will not necessarily be easier to justify as interferences with free expression than more moderately worded criticism. Certainly, a politician 'who expresses himself [in such a manner as to shock] exposes himself to a strong reaction on the part of journalists and the public' and thus should expect strong comment in return[2]. In other words 'a degree of exaggeration should be tolerated in a heated and continuing public debate of affairs of general concern, where on both sides professional reputations are at stake'[3]. On the other hand, journalists are expected to act in good faith, factual statements must be verifiable, and value judgments have at least some factual basis[4]. The importance attached to promotion of open debate thus implies that statements attacked on the basis that they are defamatory may require to be considered in their wider context[5] and with considerable care[6] to ensure that Convention expectations are met. Strasbourg jurisprudence may point to possible difficulties with certain substantive rules of defamation in Scots and English law[7].

1 Eg *Bodrožić and Vujin v Serbia* (23 June 2009), paras 49–59 (harsh and offensive language in context of article concerning a prominent historian had been a reaction to a provocative interview on an issue of general interest likely to provoke a strong response, the offending words interpreted as value judgments and therefore as opinions not susceptible of proof: violation). Cf *Bodrožić and Vvujin v Serbia* (23 June 2009), paras 28–41 (conviction for comparing an adult man to a blonde woman did not involve an attack on the integrity and dignity of men, and the article concerning a reputed local lawyer had been somewhat mocking but as a whole was not a gratuitous personal insult: violation).

2 *Oberschlick v Austria (no 1)* (1991) A 204, para 61 (private prosecution for defamation against applicant who alleged that racist comments made by politician were similar to those made by the Nazis); *Oberschlick v Austria (no 2)* 1997-IV, paras 29–35 (conviction of journalist for insulting the leader of the right-wing Austrian Freedom Party by calling him 'an idiot' in an article after he had made a speech glorifying the Austrians who had fought in the 1939–45 war: the politician had clearly intended being provocative, the article had provided an objective assessment of the speech, and the insult was not a gratuitous personal attack); and *Feldek v Slovakia* 2001-VIII, paras 77–90 (use of harsh language concerning a minister's background but made in good faith and with the aim of protecting the development of democracy in a newly-established state emerging from totalitarian rule: violation). Cf *Constantinescu v Romania* 2000-VIII, paras 66–78 (trade union leader could have voiced criticism of previous leadership without having used the offensive description of 'receivers of stolen property').

3 *Nilsen and Johnsen v Norway* [GC] 1999-VIII, para 52. See also *Vitrenko and Others v Ukraine* (dec) (16 December 2008) (warning given to a politician for calling her opponent a thief in a live debate, the opponent being also granted a right to reply: inadmissible).

4 See para **7.55** above.

5 Cf *Bladet Tromsø and Stensaas v Norway* [GC] 1999-III, paras 61–73 (relevant reasons for award of damages against a journalist for defamation of seal-hunters (protection of the reputation

of the hunters), but the reasons were not sufficient to outweigh public interest in public debate on issue of concern: impugned statements were part of a series of articles which involved a wide range of opinions and which sought to encourage proper public debate); *Bergens Tidende and Others v Norway* 2000-IV, paras 51–60 (defamation award of approximately £375,000 in favour of a cosmetic surgeon held a violation of Art 10; correct accounts of treatment were accurately recorded in a balanced article and thus the reasons for interference were not sufficient); *Marônek v Slovakia* 2001-III, paras 54–60 (award of damages for defamation equivalent to 25 times the average monthly salary against the applicant who had written an open letter in a newspaper complaining about his failure to gain possession of a state-owned flat allocated to him and the behaviour of the occupants of the property; the letter urged others with a similar problem to take joint action since he considered that resolution of the issue was a matter of public concern and also crucial for strengthening the rule of law in a new democracy: the statements did not appear excessive, most of the events on which he had relied had already been made public, and the reasons invoked by the domestic courts did not justify the relatively high damages awarded and thus there was no reasonable relationship of proportionality between the measures applied by the domestic courts and the legitimate aim pursued); and *Colombani and Others v France* 2002-V, paras 59–70 (conviction for defamation of king of Morocco based upon assertions contained in European Commission report: journalists may rely upon an official report and had no duty to investigate the facts upon which the report was based).

6   Eg *Nilsen and Johnsen v Norway* [GC] 1999-VIII, paras 43–53 (five statements made by the applicants who were police officers about findings of police violence by an academic researcher were considered defamatory: the Court considered that three of the statements could not be said to have exceeded the limits of permissible criticism for the purposes of Art 10 and the findings of defamation had not been supported by sufficient reasons nor were they proportionate to the aim of protecting the academic's reputation; but statements of deliberate lying were allegations of fact susceptible to proof and which had no factual basis).

7   For domestic discussion see *Reynolds v Times Newspapers* [2001] 2 AC 127 and *Jameel v Wall Street Journal Europe* [2007] 1 AC 359. See also *Branson v Bower (No 1)* [2001] EWCA Civ 791; *Berezovsky v Forbes* [2001] EMLR 1030; *Loutchansky v Times Newspapers Ltd* [2002] QB 321; *Culhane v Morris* [2006] 1 WLR 2880; and *Warren v Random House Group Ltd* [2009] QB 600.

CRITICISM OF CIVIL SERVANTS, ETC

7.85 On the other hand, the European Court of Human Rights has been more reluctant to extend the latitude of protection accorded public debate to expression unduly critical of civil servants or other public officials who cannot be taken to have 'knowingly la[in] themselves open to close scrutiny' unlike politicians. Thus it is open for a state to punish 'offensive and abusive verbal attacks' against civil servants or public officials since these individuals 'must enjoy public confidence in conditions free of undue perturbation if they are to be successful in performing their tasks'[1]. Robust (if not insulting) expression directed against public officials such as police officers, prosecutors or judges[2] who cannot readily engage in political debate or public response thus will more readily justify state interference to protect their reputation and rights, particularly in the absence of substantiated or corroborated evidence[3] or good faith, since the media should be able to discharge their function of contributing to political debate and accountability without exceeding generally acceptable standards[4].

1 *Janowski v Poland* [GC] 1999-I, paras 31–35 at para 33 (punishment for intervening out of civic concern in a street incident in which municipal guards were called 'dumb' and 'oafish': the majority of the Court considered that even accepting law enforcement officers were trained how to respond to abusive language, the insults had taken place in a public place in front of others and while the officers were carrying out their duties and thus sufficient grounds existed for the conviction).

2 Eg *Schöpfer v Switzerland* 1998-III, paras 28–34 (disciplinary penalties imposed by the Bar on a lawyer following criticism of judges at a press conference held not a violation of Art 10). For further discussion of attacks upon the judiciary, see paras **7.104–7.105** below. See also *Thorgeir Thorgeirson v Iceland* (1992) A 239, paras 63–69 (strongly worded allegations of police brutality: onus on accused to establish veracity of allegations considered unreasonable and a violation of Art 10).

3 *Perna v Italy* [GC] 2003-V, paras 47–48 (serious and factual allegations concerning a public prosecutor but unsupported by evidence or corroboration). Cf *Nikula v Finland* 2002-II, paras 47–56 (defamation proceedings raised by prosecutor against defence lawyer for remarks made in courtroom: while a lawyer's right of expression was not unlimited, there must be increased protection for criticism of a prosecutor by an accused); and *Steur v Netherlands* (28 October 2003), paras 41–46 (disciplinary action in respect of accusation of civil servant's unacceptable pressure brought to bear upon a lawyer's client: violation, the accusation being confined to the courtroom, and based on fact, and such action could have had a 'chilling effect' upon exercise of professional duties).

4 Cf Art 10(2) which specifically acknowledges that the exercise of free speech carries with it certain duties and responsibilities. In *Lingens v Austria* (1986) A 103, para 46, the Court accepted that there had been no absence of good faith on the part of the applicant. Cf *Castells v Spain* (1992) A 236, paras 47–48 (the applicant had been unable to plead truth or good faith by means of defence in the domestic criminal court).

7.86 The context in which statements considered defamatory of public officials are made requires to be considered with sensitivity. In *Thoma v Luxembourg*, a journalist had been ordered to pay nominal damages and costs to some 60 Forestry Commission officials who had raised an action of defamation in respect of remarks made during a radio programme. The journalist had quoted from a newspaper article written by another journalist suggesting that Forestry Commission officials were corruptible, but when doing so had clearly indicated that he was quoting the strongly worded comments of another individual. The domestic court had considered that by failing to distance himself formally from the quote he had thus endorsed the views put forward and had also led listeners to believe that the allegations were true. For the Strasbourg Court, there had to be 'particularly cogent reasons' for punishing a journalist for helping disseminate statements made by others since otherwise this would seriously hamper the contribution of the press to discussion of matters of public interest. The topic discussed in the programme concerned a matter of general interest which had been widely debated in the local media. While it was reasonable to accept that the journalist had adopted to some extent the content of the quotation in issue, the determination that he had not acted without malice, essentially on account of his failure to distance himself systematically from the views of the other journalist, could not constitute 'particularly cogent reasons' capable of justifying the interference with free speech. Such a general requirement upon journalists was not reconcilable with the media's role of providing information on current events, opinions and ideas, and thus there had been a violation of Article 10[1].

1   *Thoma v Luxembourg* 2001-I, paras 50–66 at para 64 ('particularly cogent reasons' required, but the Court accepted that even though the journalist had not identified any individual by name, the comparatively small size of Luxembourg and the limited number of Commission staff meant that the officials concerned had been easily identifiable to listeners). The implications of this judgment for the 'repetition rule' of defamation law in the UK was considered in *Mark v Associated Newspapers Ltd* [2002] EMLR 38 (defamation laws which prevent dissemination of statements made by others do not interfere with press freedom if the repetition is truly defamatory, but a newspaper which does not go beyond responsible reporting of a contentious matter is protected by *Reynolds* privilege). See also *Jersild v Denmark*, discussed at para **7.99** below ('punishment of a journalist for assisting in the dissemination of statements made by another person ... would seriously hamper the contribution of the press to discussion of matters of public interest and should not be envisaged unless there are particularly strong reasons for doing so').

DISCUSSION OF HISTORICAL EVENTS

7.87 These principles also apply to contemporary discussion or expression of opinion in relation to contentious historical events[1]. In certain cases where there is an attempt to deny the existence of crimes against humanity, Article 17 may be of relevance[2]. Article 10 requires that there must be evidence to support facts susceptible of proof, and some factual basis to support any value judgments. In *Chauvy and Others v France,* the author and publisher of a book suggesting that leading members of the French Resistance had committed acts of betrayal had subsequently been convicted of criminal libel. In accepting that the quest for historical truth was an integral aspect of the rights protected by Article 10, the Court nevertheless accepted that the author had failed to comply with essential rules of historical method in making particularly serious insinuations[3]. Further, any penalty imposed must not be overtly restrictive of freedom of expression. For example, in civil cases for defamation, disproportionate awards of damages are impermissible. In *Tolstoy Miloslavsky v United Kingdom,* the question arose whether the amount of damages awarded for defamation – £1.5 million – was disproportionate to the legitimate aim of protecting the reputation or rights of a person in respect of actions performed by him in his capacity as a public officer at the end of the 1939–45 war. While the European Court of Human Rights considered that the failure to prescribe any maximum amount of compensation a jury could make did not in itself render the interference one which was not 'prescribed by law', the Court nevertheless considered that the size of the particular award together with the lack of adequate and effective safeguards against a disproportionately large award had resulted in a violation of Article 10[4].

1   Including assessment of events or personalities of recent significance: see *Éditions Plon v France* 2004-IV, paras 51–55 (suppression of book containing medical information on the late President Mitterand: while such a measure could have been justified shortly after his death to protect the deceased's family, in time this ceased to meet any pressing social need given that the public interest in discussing the history of the President's time in office was taking

precedence over the right to medical confidentiality). See also *Giniewski v France* 2006-I, para 43–56 (article seeking to explore links between a papal encyclical and the Holocaust: violation of Art 10, the article constituting a non-offensive way to an issue of contemporary discussion); and *Cox v Turkey* (20 May 2010), paras 38–45 (refusal to allow re-entry of non-national university academic for having made statements in the course of teaching referring to the 933 'massacre' of Kurds by the Turkish authorities, a matter still of considerable contemporary controversy in Turkey).

2   See further para **7.99** below. See also *Garaudy v France* (dec) 2003-IX (denial of Holocaust 'undermines the values on which the fight against racism and anti-Semitism are based' and such expression falls within the scope of Art 17); but cf *Lehideux and Isorni v France* 1998-VII, paras 50–58 (supporters of the Pétain regime who took out an advertisement in a newspaper were convicted of defending war crimes and collaboration: the Court considered that the statements did not fall within clearly established historical facts such as the holocaust, denial or rejection of which would have removed the statements from Art 10 protection in light of Art 17, and affirmed that speech striking at the Convention's underlying values would not attract protection, but in this case the criminal convictions were considered disproportionate and thus a violation of Art 10, and accordingly, it was unnecessary to consider Art 17).

3   *Chauvy and Others v France* 2004-VI, paras 69–80; and *Radio France and Others v France* 2004-II, paras 34–41 (conviction of journalists for criminal libel of an individual accusing him of active role in deportation of Jews and order to broadcast details of the conviction: no violation, the journalist not being able to show that the required highest caution and particular moderation in respect of the extreme gravity of the suggestions broadcast throughout the country).

4   *Tolstoy Miloslavsky v United Kingdom* (1995) A 316-B, paras 46–51. See also *Steel and Morris v United Kingdom* 2005-II, paras 96–98 (the damages awarded, even if no steps had yet been taken to enforce them, had been disproportionate as they had not borne a reasonable relationship of proportionality to the injury to reputation suffered); cf *Chauvy and Others v France* 2004-VI, paras 78–80 (the courts had not prohibited publication of the book or ordered its destruction).

Expression and public sector employment, etc

7.88 While restrictions on access to the civil service or public office upon grounds of qualification or fitness for office based on belief or expression generally fall outwith the scope of Convention guarantees[1], freedom of expression protection applies to civil servants and other public sector employees[2], police officers[3] and service personnel[4], and journalists employed by public broadcasters[5] since to decide to the contrary would leave substantial numbers of citizens without protection and significant areas of activity immune from commentary and press scrutiny. However, certain additional considerations are of importance in assessing interferences in this area. Employees owe an obligation of discretion and constraint to their employer, and thus this justifies certain restrictions on freedom of expression unless the nature of the employment is to impart information and ideas as is the case with journalists[6]. Further, when the aim of restricting expression on the part of public sector officials is national security[7] or the protection of democratic institutions[8], a wide margin of appreciation on the part of domestic authorities will be recognised.

1   For discussion of Art 9 and employment, see paras **7.26–7.28** above. See also *Glasenapp v Germany* (1986) A 104, paras 50–53; *Kosiek v Germany* (1986) A 105, paras 36–39 (conditions

of appointment of civil servants involved an obligation to uphold democratic constitutional values, conditions deemed not to have been satisfied in respect of the applicants who were members of extremist political parties); and *Volkmer v Germany* (dec) (22 November 2001) and *Petersen v Germany* (dec) 2001-XII (dismissal of civil servants on account of collaboration with GDR regime: inadmissible under Art 10). Cf *Leander v Sweden* (1987) A 116, paras 71–73 (access sought to confidential files concerning the applicant which had been used by military authorities to determine that he was not qualified for a particular post: the Court considered that the essence of the challenge was to the assessment of relevant information by the authorities to ensure the applicant was qualified for the post, and accordingly there had been no violation of his freedom to express opinions); and *Erdel v Germany* (dec) 2007-II (revocation of call-up of reserve army officer on account of membership of extreme right-wing political party: inadmissible, the revocation not amounting to a loss of livelihood or of rank, but only ineligibility for future training).

2   Cf 11389/85, *Morrissens v Belgium* (1988) DR 56, 127 (suspension of teacher after attacking superiors on television considered justified as necessary for the protection of reputation and rights of others).

3   Cf *Rekvényi v Hungary* [GC] 1999-III, paras 46–50.

4   Eg *Hadjianastassiou v Greece* (1992) A 252, para 39 (freedom of expression applies to servicemen; and information relating to military issues also protected).

5   *Wojtas-Kaleta v Poland* (16 July 2009), paras 44–53 (public service television journalist sanctioned for criticising programming policy: violation, the combined professional and trade-union roles of the applicant being relevant to the assessment, and a public broadcaster's programming policy was also an issue of public interest and concern allowing of little scope for restrictions on debate).

6   *Wojtas-Kaleta v Poland* (16 July 2009), para 46. But note the protection accorded 'whistleblowers' in certain situations: *Marchenko v Ukraine* (19 February 2009), paras 43–54 (suspended prison sentence imposed upon a public servant for accusing his superior of misbehaviour and for requesting an official investigation: violation of Art 10).

7   *Zana v Turkey* 1997-VII, discussed at para **7.93** below.

8   Eg *Vogt v Germany* (1995) A 323, at para 51: 'the civil service is the guarantor of the Constitution and democracy'; but distinguished in *Otto v Germany* (dec) (24 November 2005) (refusal of promotion rather than dismissal of civil servant on account of political activities: inadmissible); cf *Ahmed and Others v United Kingdom* 1998-VI, para 52 (protection of the rights of council members and electorate through effective local political democracy); and *Seurot v France* (dec) (18 May 2004) (dismissal of teacher for publication of racist article in school newspaper: inadmissible, the views expressed being incompatible with the duties of a teacher expected to play a key role in education for democratic citizenship).

7.89 Restrictions on expression by public-sector employees purportedly to meet long-term state interests are required to satisfy the test of 'pressing social need'. Further, the reasons for any interference must be relevant and sufficient, and the relationship between means and ends must be proportionate. In *Vogt v Germany*, a teacher had been dismissed from her post because of political activities deemed incompatible with a duty of political loyalty to the constitutional order of the state. While accepting the historical background to the imposition of the obligation, the European Court of Human Rights considered that the post did not carry any particular security risk, nor was there any evidence that the applicant had sought to indoctrinate her pupils or even had made any anti-constitutional statements outside school. Accordingly, the conclusion was that the real ground for dismissal had been her active membership of the Communist Party, including her candidature in public elections, and while the reasons advanced by the state were relevant, they were not 'sufficient to establish convincingly that it was necessary in a democratic society to dismiss her'[1]. Assessment may be more difficult when the state argues that restrictions on free expression are needed to protect democratic institutions. In *Ahmed and Others v United Kingdom*, a majority of the Court accepted such a justification in respect of the imposition of a requirement of political neutrality, which included limitations on expression, on some 12,000 senior local authority officials. The Court did not accept the applicants' argument that there had to be a clear threat to the stability of the state before the protection of effective democracy could be invoked as a justification for limitations on rights under Article 10, but preferred to recognise that a state could take steps to safeguard democratic institutions when it considered this was justified. While the Commission had been of the opinion that the state had shown no pressing need for the restrictions, the majority of the Court accepted that the conclusions of a committee set up to consider how best to maintain the political neutrality of officials with a view to protecting local democracy were sufficient to establish a need for regulation. Further, the means selected were sufficiently proportionate since they had made use of a focused and function-based approach which sought to avoid partisan commentary[2].

1   *Vogt v Germany* (1995) A 323, paras 57–61 at para 60. Cf *Kern v Germany* (dec) (29 May 2007) (dismissal of civil servant responsible for press release apparently supporting terrorist attack on World Trade Center and Pentagon: inadmissible).

2   *Ahmed and Others v United Kingdom* 1998-VI, paras 57–65 (challenges to regulations made in terms of the Housing and Local Government Act 1989).

DECISIONS OF DOMESTIC COURTS ON PUBLIC SECTOR EMPLOYEES

7.90 In *R v Shayler*, the defendant was a former member of the security service who had disclosed documents relating to security or intelligence matters to a national newspaper. He was prosecuted under the Official Secrets Act 1989. The House of Lords noted that the ban imposed by the Act on the disclosure of information by former members of the security service was not absolute but was confined to disclosure without lawful authority, and that there were safeguards built into the Act to ensure that unlawfulness and irregularity could be reported to those who could take effective action, that the power to withhold authorisation was not abused and that proper disclosures were not stifled. In those circumstances, and in view of the special position of members of the security and intelligence services and the highly confidential nature of information which came into their possession, the interference with their right to freedom of expression prescribed by the 1989 Act was not greater than was required to achieve the legitimate object of acting in the interests of national security. Accordingly, the restrictions imposed by the 1989 Act came within Article 10(2) as a justified interference with the right to freedom of expression guaranteed by Article 10[1].

1   *R v Shayler* [2003] 1 AC 247. See also *A-G v Punch Ltd* [2003] 1 AC 1046, discussed at para **7.106** below.

MILITARY SERVICE

7.91 Military order may also justify restrictions on expression where a real threat to military discipline exists. In *Engel and Others v Netherlands*, conscript soldiers had been punished for distribution of pamphlets to other soldiers. The Court indicated that it would take into account such factors as the general nature of military life and the corresponding responsibilities of armed force personnel, and in the circumstances of the case concluded that there had been 'well-founded reasons for considering that [the applicants] had attempted to undermine military discipline'[1]. On the other hand, there will be a more critical assessment of any state justification for restriction of opinions of military personnel where these concern general service conditions and do not pose an immediate threat to good order. In *Vereinigung Demokratischer Soldaten Österreichs and Gubi v Austria*, the Court rejected allegations that the applicants' periodical represented a threat to military effectiveness. While the tenor of the complaints voiced was often polemical, the publication could not be said to have 'overstepped the bounds of what is permissible in the context of a mere discussion of ideas, which must be tolerated in the army of a democratic State'[2]. Further, circulation of military or security information which is considered no longer sensitive or which has entered the public domain will be difficult to restrict since justification of censorship or imposition of post-publication sanction is unlikely to be considered necessary to achieve the aim of protecting state security[3].

---

1   *Engel and Others v Netherlands* (1976) A 22, para 101 (the Court noted that the applicants had not been denied their freedom of expression, merely that they had been punished for their 'abusive exercise' of this right). Cf *Erdel v Germany* (dec) 2007-II (revocation of call-up of reserve army officer on account of membership of extreme right-wing political party: inadmissible, the revocation not amounting to a loss of livelihood or of rank, but only ineligibility for future training).

2   *Vereinigung Demokratischer Soldaten Österreichs and Gubi v Austria* (1994) A 302, para 38. See too *Grigoiades v Greece* 1997-VII, paras 46–47 (letter containing intemperate remarks, but made in the context of a general criticism of the army as an institution and not disseminated to a wider audience: this was considered to have had only an insignificant impact on military discipline, and thus prosecution and the conviction were not necessary in a democratic society).

3   Eg *Vereiniging Weekblad Bluf! v Netherlands* (1995) A 306-A, discussed at para **7.74** above.

Maintenance of public order and safety

7.92 The maintenance of public order and public safety may justify restrictions on expression, provided always that the tests of necessity and proportionality can be met. In *Steel and Others v United Kingdom*, the first two applicants had been involved in hunt sabotage and disruption of road construction work respectively and had been detained pending appearance before a court for 44 and 17 hours in each case; the final three applicants had taken part in a peaceful protest against the sale of military equipment by distributing leaflets in a conference centre which had led to their detention for seven hours. The European Court of Human Rights considered each case on its own merits. In respect of the first two protestors, the

Court accepted that there had been a continuing risk of disorder inherent in each of the protest activities and thus their arrest and detention by police officers could not be said to have been disproportionate. However, the measures taken against the remaining three applicants were considered disproportionate because of the entirely peaceful nature of their protest[1]. Assertions that restrictions are necessary on this ground must therefore be supported, and further take into account the positive obligation upon authorities to protect protestors from counter-demonstrators[2].

1   *Steel and Others v United Kingdom* 1998-VII, paras 102–111. See also *Chorherr v Austria* (1993) A 266-B, paras 31–33 (arrest of counter-demonstrator at military parade justified to protect the public peace: non-violation of Art 10); *Medya Fm Reha Radyo Ve letiim Hizmetleri A v Turkey* (dec) (14 November 2006) (limited suspension of right to broadcast consequent upon repeated broadcasts of programmes deemed to be contrary to principles of national unity and territorial integrity and likely to incite violence, hatred and racial discrimination: inadmissible). Cf *Piermont v France* (1995) A 314, paras 76–86 (expulsion of MEP from French overseas territory following her participation in a demonstration not justified).

2   See para **7.50** above.

7.93 Greater latitude may be shown by the Court in considering interferences with expression that can be justified by a state on the grounds of current national security concerns. In *Zana v Turkey*, a former mayor had been prosecuted for statements published in a newspaper indicating his support for an illegal terrorist liberation movement. Since the statements had been made at a time of serious disturbances in south-east Turkey, it was accepted that the prosecution had sought to maintain national security and public safety. In determining the necessity for the interference, the statement could not be considered in isolation but had to be assessed against the background of terrorist attacks carried out on civilians. The interview, which was carried in a major national newspaper, thus had to be regarded as likely to exacerbate an already explosive situation, and in consequence the penalty imposed could reasonably have been regarded as supported by a pressing social need. Further, the reasons adduced by the Turkish state were relevant and sufficient, and the actual penalty imposed was also deemed proportionate to the legitimate aims pursued[1]. In contrast, in *Yasar Kemal Gökçeli v Turkey*, the Court determined a collection of articles advocating a peaceful resolution to the political situation concerning the Kurdish minority in Turkey could not have been taken to have incited support for terrorism, even when a distinctly aggressive and virulent note had been obvious in the text[2].

1   *Zana v Turkey* 1997-VII, paras 55–62 (factual situation distinguished in *Incal v Turkey* 1998-IV, discussed at para **7.82** above). See also *Sürek v Turkey (no 1)* [GC] 1999-IV (use of emotive language likely to lead to violence against named individuals: no violation); *Falakaolu and Saygili v Turkey* (23 January 2007), paras 28–37 (conviction for newspaper publication of declaration of a terrorist group: no violation); and *Gül and Others v Turkey* (8 June 2010), paras 34–45 (imprisonment of peaceful demonstrators for shouting slogans in support of an illegal organisation: violation as there had been no indication that there had been a clear and imminent danger to national security or public order). For other examples, see *Hogefeld v Germany* (dec) (20 January 2000) (the applicant was allowed only one interview with a journalist during her trial on terrorist offences and on condition she did not refer to her

organisation or her trial; these restrictions were considered a reasonable response to the pressing social need to ensure she did not encourage sympathisers to carry on with the campaign of terrorism, and the application was considered inadmissible); and *Osmani and Others v Former Yugoslav Republic of Macedonia* (dec) 2001-X (conviction for statements fomenting inter-ethnic tensions: inadmissible). For domestic consideration outside the UK, see *Stoll v Statthalteramt des Bezirks Zürich* [2001] EuGRZ 416, [2002] EurCLY 2012 [Switzerland].

2   *Gökçeli v Turkey* (4 March 2003), paras 31–40 (violation of Art 10).

DOMESTIC CASES ON MAINTENANCE OF PUBLIC ORDER AND SAFETY

7.94 In *R (Laporte) v Chief Constable of Gloucestershire Constabulary,* the claimant was a passenger on one of a number of coaches travelling from London to a protest demonstration at an air base in Gloucestershire. The defendant chief constable instructed police officers to intercept the coaches. The police then escorted the coaches back to London. The claimant asserted that the defendant's actions preventing her from demonstrating at the air base and forcibly returning her to London constituted unlawful interference with the exercise of her rights of freedom of expression and assembly protected by Articles 10 and 11. The House of Lords upheld her claim, holding that, since there had been no indication of any imminent breach of the peace when the coaches were intercepted, and since the defendant had not considered that such a breach was then likely to occur, the action taken in preventing the claimant from continuing to the demonstration had been an interference with her right to demonstrate at a lawful assembly which was not prescribed by domestic law. Furthermore, the police action had in any event been premature and indiscriminate and represented a disproportionate restriction on the claimant's rights under Articles 10 and 11[1].

1   *R (Laporte) v Chief Constable of Gloucestershire Constabulary* [2007] 2 AC 105.

7.95 The use of stop and search powers under anti-terrorism legislation was considered in *R (Gillan) v Commissioner of Police of the Metropolis*, where a student who had been stopped and searched on his way to take part in a demonstration, and a journalist who had been stopped and searched while in the area to film the demonstration, sought judicial review of their treatment. It was accepted that the exercise of stop and search powers might infringe Article 10 rights, but only if the powers were misused. On the facts, it was held that they had not been[1]. On a subsequent application to the Strasbourg Court, a violation of Article 8 was found, and the Court did not need to consider the complaint under Article 10[2]. The prosecution and conviction for breach of the peace of a protester who disrupted proceedings in the Scottish Parliament was held to be an interference with her Convention rights under Articles 10 and 11, but one which was prescribed by law and necessary for the prevention of disorder[3]. A similar conclusion was been reached in a case concerned with a protest by a member of the Scottish Parliament who blocked traffic on a public road and refused to move[4].

1   *R (Gillan) v Commissioner of Police of the Metropolis* [2006] 2 AC 307.

2   *Gillan and Quinton v United Kingdom* (12 January 2010), discussed at para **6.104** above.

3   *Jones v Carnegie* 2004 JC 136.

4   Eg *Quinan v Donnelly* 2005 1 JC 279. See also *Hutchinson v Director of Public Prosecutions* (9 October 2000, unreported), QBD (anti-nuclear protester cut fencing at Aldermaston in order to be prosecuted and use the trial as a means of publicising her views: no breach of Art 10 in her prosecution and conviction); *Silverton v Gravett* (19 October 2001, unreported) QBD (harassment of furriers by animal rights activists: injunctions not in breach of Art 10); *R (Farrakhan) v Secretary of State for the Home Department* [2002] QB 1391 (refusal of entry to Islamic extremist on ground that his presence in the UK would threaten public order had struck a proportionate balance between the aim of prevention of disorder and freedom of expression under Art 10). For a domestic example where personal safety outweighed freedom of expression, see *Venables v News Group Newspapers Ltd* [2001] Fam 430.

PRISON DISCIPLINE AND FREE SPEECH

7.96 The reference to the rights 'to hold opinions and to receive and impart information and ideas without interference by public authority' in the text of the Article requires to be interpreted in a manner consistent with the proper maintenance of good order and security within a prison[1]. Thus the right of a prisoner to seek to have his opinions made known or to have information held by him publicised more widely must also take into account other considerations, including the protection of the rights of others[2].

1   For early discussion, see 8317/78, *McFeely v United Kingdom* (1980) DR 20, 44 (restrictions upon access to television, radio, etc justified for prevention of disorder); and for discussion of access to religious material, 5442/72, *X v United Kingdom* (1974) DR 1, 41. The focus of the Revised European Prison Rules (2006), rule 24, para 10 is upon the *receiving* rather than the imparting of ideas, etc.

2   See eg *Nilsen v United Kingdom* (dec) (9 March 2010) (serial killer prevented from publishing autobiography containing accounts of killings and the disposal of the bodies of the victims on account of the impact on families and surviving victims: inadmissible, some level of control over prisoners' communication being part of the ordinary and reasonable requirements of imprisonment and the domestic courts had properly balanced competing interests in considering the prison standing order which did not impose a blanket restriction). See also *R (A) v Secretary of State for the Home Department* [2004] HRLR 12 (monitoring of journalists' interviews with suspected terrorists detained under the Anti-Terrorism, Crime and Security Act 2001 did not breach Art 10: the restrictions imposed fell within para 2 as the individuals were suspected of being terrorists who threatened national security); and *R (Ponting) v Governor of HM Prison Whitemoor* [2002] EWCA Civ 224, discussed at para **7.49** above, fn 4.

'Balancing' competing interests: protection for private and family life

7.97 Article 8 requires respect for private life. In particular, the Court has made it clear in cases such as *von Hannover v Germany*[1] that there is a positive obligation upon states to ensure that domestic law provides adequate protection against intrusions upon private life by non-state parties, particularly by the media. Further, the Court has now accepted that reputation and honour are interests which are protected by Article 8, giving rise to positive obligations to ensure that domestic law secures respect for private life[2]. The implications for UK law, which has never recognised such a right to privacy, are considered elsewhere[3].

1   *Von Hannover v Germany* 2004-VI, discussed at para **6.131** above.
2   *A v Norway* (9 April 2009), discussed at para **6.133** above.
3   See paras **6.134–61.38** above.

7.98 The guarantees of a fair hearing under Article 6 include a requirement that judicial proceedings are held in public and that 'judgment shall be pronounced publicly', but the media and the public may be excluded from all or part of a trial inter alia when 'the protection of the private life of the parties so require'. This matter is considered above[1].

1   At paras **5.154–5.157** above.

'Balancing' competing interests: racially offensive, etc speech

7.99 Where expression attacks those values of 'pluralism, tolerance and broadmindedness' which underlie Article 10, assessment of whether Article 17 comes into play is necessary. This provision prohibits the abuse of any Convention right which could undermine other guarantees, an issue which will arise in the consideration of 'hate speech'[1]. In other words, Article 10 may not be applied in a manner inconsistent with the intention of Article 17. For example, and most obviously from the case law, denial or revision of the Holocaust involves expression removed from the protection of Article 10 on this account[2]. However, a sensitive assessment of intent and outcome will always be necessary. In *Jersild v Denmark*, a television journalist had been fined for having aided and abetted the dissemination of racially offensive statements. The television programme had featured interviews with young people who had expressed racist views on immigrant groups as part of a programme seeking to expose the existence of racism in Danish society. The European Court of Human Rights accepted that the medium of communication was of relevance in determining the extent of a journalist's duties or responsibilities, and that audiovisual media such as television 'have often a much more immediate and powerful effect than the print media'. However, in all the circumstances, the Court accepted that the broadcast had neither the purpose nor the unintended outcome of dissemination of racist views, and thus the conviction was not justified by Article 10(2)[3].

1   12194/86, *Kühnen v Germany* (1988) DR 56, 205 (prosecution for publishing material promoting fascism: conviction 'necessary in a democratic society'); 32307/96, *Schimanek v Austria* (1 February 2000) (applicant involved in activities inspired by National Socialism, a totalitarian doctrine 'incompatible with democracy and human rights' whose adherents 'undoubtedly pursue aims of the kind referred to in Article 17', and the conviction was thus justified by Art 10(2) as read together with Art 17). Cf *Giniewski v France* 2006-I, para 43–56 (prosecution for publication of article seeking to explore links between a papal encyclical and the Holocaust: violation of Art 10, the article constituting a non-offensive way to an issue of contemporary discussion). See also *Lehideux and Isorni v France* 1998-VII, paras 50–58 (supporters of the Pétain regime who took out an advertisement in a newspaper were convicted of defending war crimes and collaboration: the Court considered that the statements did not fall within clearly established historical facts such as the holocaust, denial or rejection of which

would have removed the statements from Art 10 protection in light of Art 17, and affirmed that speech striking at the Convention's underlying values would not attract protection, but in this case the criminal convictions were considered disproportionate and thus a violation of Art 10, and accordingly, it was unnecessary to consider Art 17).

2   *Chauvy and Others v France* 2004-VI, para 69. See also 36773/97, *Nachtmann v Austria* (9 September 1998) (punishment for denial of Holocaust; the Court reiterated that Art 10 could not be invoked in a sense incompatible with Art 17); and *Garaudy v France* (dec) 2003-IX (denial of Holocaust 'undermines the values on which the fight against racism and anti-Semitism are based' and such expression falls within the scope of Art 17, and convictions for incitement to racial hatred and for racially defamatory statements were justified under Art 10(2)); and *Norwood v United Kingdom* (dec) (16 November 2004) (display by BNP organiser of anti-Islamic poster featuring photograph of the 2001 terrorist attack on New York: inadmissible). See further Jaconelli 'Defences to Speech Crimes' [2007] EHRLR 27; and Belavusau 'A *Dernier Cri* from Strasbourg: an Ever Formidable Challenge of Hate Speech' (2010) 16 EPL 373. For international standards, see Weber *Handbook on Hate Speech* (2009)

3   *Jersild v Denmark* (1994) A 298, paras 25–36. The Court also took account of the state's obligations under the UN Convention on the Elimination of All Forms of Racial Discrimination in assessing whether the conviction was justified (paras 30–31). For domestic discussion, see 1 BvR 2266/04 (20 February 2009) [2009] EuGRZ 269 [Germany] (prohibition of animal welfare campaign placing suffering of Jewish victims of Nazi persecution on same level as farmed animals could be taken as belittling the plight of Jews: prohibition upheld).

7.100 Journalism which seeks to expose rather than to promote extremism and intolerance will thus fall within the scope of Article 10 protection as will that which seeks to examine and explore these topics in a pluralist manner. In such circumstances, no recourse to Article 17 will be necessary. As *Jersild* illustrates, careful assessment is necessary. In *Gündüz v Turkey*, the applicant had taken part in a television programme which aimed to present the views of the radical Islamic sect of which he was the leader. During the programme, he had expressed his opinions on a range of subjects including religious costumes, religion, and secularism and democracy in Turkey. Subsequently, he had been convicted by a state security court for having incited hatred and hostility, and had been sentenced to two years' imprisonment. For the Court, while the programme's focus upon the role of religion in a democratic society had concerned an issue of general interest in respect of which the restrictions on freedom of expression were to be interpreted strictly, it was not satisfied that the applicant had made comments which could be construed as a call to violence or as 'hate speech' based on religious intolerance. While pejorative language had been used, this had occurred during the course of an animated but balanced public discussion live on television, and although statements which aimed to propagate, incite or justify hatred based on intolerance did not attract the protection of Article 10, the applicant had merely expressed support for sharia law without calling for the use of violence to bring about its introduction[1].

1   *Gündüz v Turkey* 2003-XI, paras 42–53.

DECISIONS OF DOMESTIC COURTS ON RACIALLY OFFENSIVE, ETC SPEECH

7.101 The English courts have refused to strike out an action brought against a newspaper for statutory harassment, the newspaper's argument being that if the statute were interpreted consistently with Article 10, no action would lie in the circumstances complained of. The Court of Appeal held that the plaintiff had pleaded an arguable case that the *Sun* had harassed her by publishing racist criticism of her which was foreseeably likely to stimulate a racist reaction on the part of its readers and cause her distress[1].

More widely, it has been recognised that the 'rights of others' protected by Article 10(2) include a right not to receive grossly offensive or indecent material sent for the purpose of causing distress and anxiety[2].

1   *Thomas v News Group Newspapers Ltd* [2002] EMLR 4.

2   *Connolly v Director of Public Prosecutions* [2008] 1 WLR 276 (photographs of aborted foetuses sent by anti-abortion campaigner to pharmacists selling 'morning after' pill: conviction under Malicious Communications Act 1988 not incompatible with Art 10).

'Balancing' competing interests: interference with the administration of justice

7.102 Article 10(2) specifically identifies maintenance of the 'authority and impartiality of the judiciary' as a legitimate aim which may justify interference with expression. Insertion of this particular interest in Article 10 appears to have been at the insistence of the United Kingdom, which was concerned to ensure that British contempt of court law was protected[1]. The balance to be achieved is between on the one hand protection of public discussion of matters of legitimate interest in a democracy, and on the other prevention of interference in a particular court proceeding or of undermining faith in the administration of justice more generally. There are thus two principal concerns: protection of the integrity of any particular court proceeding, and protection of the legal system in the longer term. Different considerations apply to each. It may be easier to determine whether an interference corresponds to a 'pressing social need' and is proportionate to the aim of protecting the rights of litigants or of an accused in a particular trial, than it is in cases where the general authority of the court system is called into question. An important element in this area is the 'watchdog' role of the media in scrutinising the administration of justice[2].

1   In *Sunday Times v United Kingdom (no 1)* (1979) A 30, para 60, the Court noted that, even assuming that the drafters of the Convention had added maintaining the 'authority and impartiality of the judiciary' specifically to provide for the continuation of British contempt of court law, this would not have resulted in the transposition of contempt law as it stood at the time of ratification since the phrase had to be read as an autonomous concept in which the 'necessity' of any interference would have to be assessed on a case-by-case basis. The Contempt of Court Act 1981 was enacted in response to a finding of a violation of Art 10 in this case.

2   Cf *P4 Radio Hele Norge v Norway* (dec) 2003-VI (refusal to authorise broadcast of a high-profile murder trial: inadmissible, as there was no common approach amongst European states on this matter, and broadcasting could increase the existing pressure on participants and possibly influence their behaviour and thus affect the administration of justice; in any event, live broadcasting cannot replace physical attendance by the public, a crucial means for ensuring transparency and public scrutiny of the judiciary); and *Dumas v France* (15 July 2010), paras

40–52 (conviction of former president of constitutional court for defamation in respect of publication of details of a high-profile trial: violation).

PREJUDICING THE OUTCOME OF COURT PROCEEDINGS

7.103 The Convention calls for a balance between the press's rights and responsibilities under Article 10 and the interests of litigants or accused under Article 6[1]. Restrictions on prejudicial pre-trial publicity will be consistent with an accused's rights to a fair hearing under Article 6(1) and to the presumption of innocence under Article 6(2)[2]. There is, however, both recognition of the watchdog role of the media in the administration of justice in helping ensure a fair trial[3] as well as acceptance that a judicial proceeding may attract legitimate public and press discussion, particularly where a public figure is involved and in which case the limits of acceptable comment will be wider[4]. In *Worm v Austria*, the applicant had been punished for publishing an article calculated to interfere with the trial of a former Finance Minister and Vice-Chancellor of Austria. The Court accepted that the reasons for the conviction were relevant: the conviction did not impinge upon the applicant's right to provide information in an objective manner about the trial of a political figure, and the article instead had concerned an unfavourable assessment of evidence presented at the trial including a clear statement of opinion on the accused's guilt. The reasons adduced to justify interference were also sufficient: the domestic courts had taken into account the impugned article in its entirety, and it was not possible to conclude that the article was incapable of warranting the domestic court's conclusion as to its potential for influencing the outcome of the trial. Nor was the sanction imposed disproportionate, given the amount of the fine imposed and the fact that the publishing firm was made jointly and severally liable for payment along with the applicant[5]. Similarly, the Commission in *BBC Scotland, McDonald, Rodgers and Donald v United Kingdom* accepted that use of the *nobile officium* by the High Court of Justiciary to prevent the screening of a documentary concerning allegations of brutality against prisoners was justified to protect the rights of three prison officers who were shortly to stand trial on charges of assaulting prisoners, even although the programme would not have featured any of the accused[6]. In contrast, in *News Verlags GmbH & CoKG v Austria*, the Court did not consider that a prohibition order made on the application of an accused person preventing the publishing of any report containing his photograph was justified. The court order had been directed against the applicant company alone, and other publishers had remained free of any restraint. While the Court acknowledged that the prohibition of prejudicial pre-trial publicity was a relevant reason for prohibiting any such publication, the reasons could not be considered sufficient in the particular case, nor was there any reasonable relationship of proportionality with the legitimate aim of protecting the rights of the accused person[7].

1   Cf 11553/85 and 11685/85, *Hodgson and Others v United Kingdom* (1987) DR 51, 136 (restrictions on televised reporting of court proceedings: inadmissible). See further Committee of Ministers Recommendation Rec (2003) 13 on the provision of information through the media in relation to criminal proceedings.

2   *News Verlags GmbH & CoKG v Austria* 2000-I, para 56.

3   *Axen v Germany* (1983) A 72, para 25.

4   *Worm v Austria* 1997-V, para 50. See too *Du Roy and Malaurie v France* 2000-X, paras 28–37 (absolute and general ban on publication of reports on pending criminal proceedings involving political figures but not instigated by the public prosecutor: the measure was disproportionate and thus a violation of Art 10); and *Furuholmen v Norway* (dec) (18 March 2010) (sanction imposed upon defence counsel for disclosing to the press evidence ruled inadmissible and before the jury had returned its verdict: inadmissible as the disclosure had been aimed at influencing the jury, the freedom to criticise the proceedings had related only to excluded evidence and before the jury's verdict, and the fine had not been severe).

5   *Worm v Austria* 1997-V, paras 52–59 at para 52.

6   34324/96 *BBC Scotland, McDonald, Rodgers and Donald v United Kingdom* (23 October 1997). In this case the Contempt of Court Act 1981 did not apply as the broadcast had not been made, but the High Court applied the Act's test and held that there was more than a minimal risk of prejudice to the fairness of the trial. Transmission was delayed until after the trial by means of an order made under the court's discretionary and inherent power, even although the last recorded use of the *nobile officium* in this way had been a century or so ago. The Commission considered the reasoning adduced by the High Court in *Muir v BBC* 1996 SCCR 584 and concluded that the interference was both 'prescribed by law' and 'necessary in a democratic society'. The Commission again raised but avoided answering the question whether the BBC as a public broadcaster properly qualified as a 'victim'; but cf *Österreichischer Rundfunk v Austria* (7 December 2006), paras 46–53, (Austrian Broadcasting Corporation could qualify as a non-governmental organisation in light of its editorial and journalistic independence, ability to set its own programme fees, and lack of governmental control).

7   *News Verlags v Austria* (11 January 2000), paras 55–60. At para 58, the Court indicated that any prohibition of a suspect's photograph would itself require to be justified on a case-by-case basis. See too *Weber v Switzerland* (1990) A 177, paras 47–52 (press conference organised by the applicant did not prejudice the fairness of judicial proceedings against him since most of the information had already been disclosed and the proceedings were almost complete); *Dupuis and Others v France* 2007-VII, paras 39–49 (use and reproductivity of material from a pending criminal investigation: no violation); and *Ormanni v Italy* (17 July 2007), paras 68–78 (conviction of journalist for interview with an accused in which comments were made suggesting impropriety on the part of public prosecutor: violation, as the article was not a gratuitous personal attack and had addressed issues of public interest).

PROTECTING THE INTEGRITY OF THE ADMINISTRATION OF JUSTICE

7.104 The European Court of Human Rights takes a more searching approach in cases involving interferences with expression purportedly justified by the need to protect the integrity of the courts. In the early case of *Sunday Times v United Kingdom (no 1)*, the Court had noted that the 'authority and impartiality of the judiciary' particularly covered 'the notion that the courts are, and are accepted by the public at large as being, the proper forum for the ascertainment of legal rights and obligations and the settlement of disputes relative thereto; further that the public at large have respect for and confidence in the courts' capacity to fulfil that function'[1]. However, judges must themselves expect some level of scrutiny while at the same time it is recognised that they must of necessity show restraint in expressing their opinions[2]. Sanctions imposed for criticism of judges through the application of contempt of court laws or other criminal penalty thus can give rise to difficult questions in determining their proportionality. It is recognised that 'journalistic freedom also covers possible recourse to a degree of exaggeration, or even provocation'[3], and also that the limits of acceptable criticism of a judge involved in political activities are wider than is otherwise the case[4]. Furthermore, the public interest in the subject matter of the judicial proceedings may warrant greater latitude. In *De Haes and Gijsels v Belgium*, for example, two journalists who had criticised named judges and the Advocate General for cowardice and for political bias in their disposal of a case involving sexual abuse of children had subsequently been convicted of criminal defamation. The Court reiterated that in a state based upon the rule of law, the judiciary required protection against destructive and unfounded criticism, especially since judges themselves were precluded from answering back. Here, though, the Court decided that there had been a violation of Article 10 in the particular facts of the case since the 'severely critical' opinions expressed in a 'polemical and even aggressive tone' could be justified as 'proportionate to the stir and indignation caused by the matters alleged'[5].

1   *Sunday Times v United Kingdom (no 1)* (1979) A 30, para 55. See also 14132/88, *Channel 4 Television v United Kingdom* (1989) DR 61, 285. For a domestic example, see *Harris v Harris* [2001] 2 FLR 895.

2   *Wille v Liechtenstein* [GC] 1999-VII, para 64 (at para 67: the lecture given by a judge concerned constitutional issues which by their very nature were political, but this in itself was not a reason for sanctioning the judge whose comments in any case were shared by many). Cf *Harabin v Slovakia* (dec) 2004-VI (action taken upon publication of critical report by the Executive suggesting an article written by the President of the Supreme Court was indicative of his desire to strengthen his own personal powers and was indicative of his untrustworthiness: inadmissible as measures taken in regard to fitness of members of the judiciary fell outwith the scope of the Convention). The maintenance of the authority of the judiciary may also justify interference with the freedom of expression of judges: *Pitkevich v Russia* (8 February 2001) (dec) (district court judge who was a member of an evangelical sect had been dismissed for allegedly having proselytised during judicial hearings: inadmissible).

3   *De Haes and Gijsels v Belgium* 1997-I, at para 46.

4   *Hrico v Slovakia* (20 July 2004), paras 40–50; cf *Wille v Liechtenstein* [GC] 1999-VII, noted at fn 2 above.

5   *De Haes and Gijsels v Belgium* 1997-I, paras 37–49 at paras 46 and 48. See also *Amihalachioaie v Moldova* 2004-III, paras 32–40 (fine imposed on president of bar association for comments reported in a newspaper, but the comments concerned a matter of public interest and were not disrespectful: violation); *Kobenter and Standard Verlags GmbH v Austria* (2 November 2006), paras 30–33 (reasons for conviction of journalist fulfilling 'watchdog' role for criticism of court's judgment as in line with 'medieval witch trials', a value judgment albeit expressed in a provocative manner but based on facts, were neither relevant nor sufficient: violation of Art 10); and *Obukhova v Russia* (8 January 2009), paras 19–29 (overly-broad interlocutory injunction restricting a journalist's ability to report on an incident involving a judge: violation).

7.105 Bad faith or insulting language may remove or reduce Article 10 protection for such expression[1], although a clear distinction between criticism and insult is required[2]. In *Prager and Oberschlick v Austria*, the Court decided that harsh criticisms of a judge's personal integrity fell outwith Article 10 protection since these had not been made in good faith and had violated principles of professional ethics, even although the Court recognised that the role of the media in both reporting and commenting on the administration of justice was of fundamental importance in a democratic society[3]. A similar conclusion was reached in *Barfod v Denmark* where the applicant had been fined for publishing an article suggesting that two lay judges had been motivated by bias in determining his tax case in favour of the government which was also the 'employer' of the judges. The Court rejected the applicant's assertions that the criticism should be seen as part of wider political debate as to judicial impartiality, accepting the state's arguments that the article had been a direct attack unsupported by evidence upon two judges which had been likely to lower their esteem in public opinion[4]. In *Kyprianou v Cyprus*, remarks perceived to be discourteous (if not also possibly insulting) made by counsel during the course of a hearing had led to a finding of contempt of court and the imposition of a sanction of imprisonment for five days. In this case, in finding that there had been a violation of Article 10, the Grand Chamber considered that the disproportionately severe penalty imposed without procedural fairness could have a 'chilling effect' on the performance of the duties of defence lawyers[5]. Similar principles apply to attacks upon the dignity of a court made in the course of proceedings by an accused[6].

1   Applications considered inadmissible on this point include 30339/96, *Bossi v Germany* (15 April 1997) (written appeal pleadings included references to the trial judge's lack of moral fibre and incompetence); 26602/95, *WR v Austria* (30 June 1997) (judicial opinion labelled 'ridiculous' by a lawyer); 26601/95, *Leiningen-Westerburg v Germany* (1997) DR 88, 85 (judge referred to fellow members of the judiciary variously as 'whores' or 'turds', and suggested that they were open to bribery).

2   *Skałka v Poland* (27 May 2003), paras 36–43 (letter written by prisoner referring to a judge using the terms 'irresponsible clowns' and 'cretin': while the terms were derogatory, the sentence of eight months' imprisonment was disproportionate).

3   *Prager and Oberschlick v Austria* (1995) A 313, paras 34–38. See too *Schöpfer v Switzerland* 1998-III, paras 28–34 (disciplinary penalties imposed by the bar on a lawyer following criticism of judges at a press conference held not to be a violation of Art 10: it was legitimate to expect lawyers to help maintain public confidence in administration of justice).

4   *Barfod v Denmark* (1989) A 149, paras 34–35.

5   *Kyprianou v Cyprus* [GC] 2005–XIII, paras 176–183 (use of a word which in Greek could have referred either to a love letter or to a note).

6   *Saday v Turkey* (30 June 2006), paras 33–37 (contempt of court of an accused representing himself before a national security court and resulting in the imposition of the maximum penalty of six months' imprisonment including two months' solitary confinement: while it could have been deemed necessary to impose a penalty, imposition of the maximum permitted penalty was disproportionate, and a violation of Art 10).

DECISIONS OF DOMESTIC COURTS ON INTERFERENCES WITH THE ADMINISTRATION OF JUSTICE

7.106 The domestic courts have had to decide a number of cases concerned with interferences with freedom of expression designed to protect the administration of justice. The case of *A-G v Punch Ltd* concerned interlocutory injunctions obtained by the Attorney General against S, a former MI5 officer, and a newspaper publisher. The injunctions restrained the publication of information obtained from

S relating to the security service, pending the trial of an action for alleged breach of confidence by S. It was maintained by the Attorney that the disclosures by S would endanger national security. The purpose of the injunctions was to preserve the rights of the parties pending a final determination of the issues. The editor and publishers of a magazine, knowing the terms of the injunctions, published an article by S which included information restrained by the injunctions. The House of Lords held that a contempt of court had been established. The restraint on freedom of expression was necessary in order to protect national security pending a trial of the issues, and the magazine's conduct had interfered with the administration of justice[1]. The case of *Anwar, Respondent* on the other hand was concerned with statements made to the press by a solicitor following his client's conviction. It was held that no contempt of court had been committed. The court observed that, while the importance of the right of freedom of expression enshrined in Article 10(1) could hardly be over-emphasised, it was equally plain that that right had its limits. Certain of those limits were to be found in the law of contempt of court, where the purpose to be served was the maintenance of the authority and impartiality of the judiciary[2].

---

1   *A-G v Punch Ltd* [2003] 1 AC 1046. Lord Nicholls of Birkenhead remarked at para 29 that 'in principle the public has a right to know of incompetence in the Security Service as in any other government department. Here, as elsewhere where questions arise about the freedom of expression, the law has to strike a balance. On the one hand, there is the need to protect the nation's security. On the other hand, there is a need to ensure that the activities of the Security Service are not screened unnecessarily from the healthy light of publicity. In striking this balance the seriousness of the risk to national security and the foreseeable gravity of the consequences if disclosure occurs, and the seriousness of the alleged incompetence and errors sought to be disclosed, are among the matters to be taken into account'.

2   *Anwar, Respondent* 2008 JC 409.

7.107 In relation to pre-trial publicity, Scottish cases on contempt of court since 1998 have shown a change in attitude on the part of the court, with a much greater emphasis being placed on the freedom of press, and the adoption of a robust attitude to the likelihood of juries being influenced by press reporting. The court has made it clear that it will be only in exceptional circumstances that prejudicial pre-trial publicity will prevent an accused from receiving a fair trial before a jury, as required by Article 6; and, equally, it will only be in unusual circumstances that publicity will 'create a substantial risk that the course of justice will be seriously impeded or prejudiced', as required by the Contempt of Court Act 1981, s 2(2). Both the change in attitude (as a result of the enactment of the 1981 Act, and thus as a result of Article 10, which the 1981 Act was intended to implement), and the link between the test under s 2 of the 1981 Act and the question whether a jury would be likely to be significantly influenced by the publication in question, were made clear in *Cox and Griffiths, Petitioners*[1] and subsequent cases[2].

---

1   *Cox and Griffiths, Petitioners* 1998 JC 267.

2   Eg *HM Advocate v Scottish Media Newspapers Ltd* 1999 SCCR 599; *Galbraith v HM Advocate* 2000 SCCR 935; *Montgomery v HM Advocate* 2001 SC (PC) 1; *BBC, Petitioners* 2002 JC 27.

See also *R (Telegraph Group) v Sherwood* [2001] 1 WLR 1983; *Re X (Disclosure of Information)* [2001] 2 FLR 440 (disclosure to press of affidavit evidence in matrimonial proceedings: no contempt); *Clibbery v Allan* [2001] 2 FLR 819 (disclosure of evidence conveyed in chambers: no injunction). See also *Ansvarshavende Redaktør B v A* UfR 2003.624H, [2003] EuroCLY 1147 [Denmark] (defamation action raised by individual after discontinuation of police investigation against newspaper for publication of statement that there was conclusive incriminating evidence: need to read Art 10 in the context of presumption of innocence under Art 6(2)); and *X v X* [2003] NJ 413, [2003] EuroCLY 1149 [Netherlands] (repetition of allegations after charges dropped was actionable wrong).

'Balancing' competing interests: attacks on religious belief

7.108 Particular issues may arise where the exercise of freedom of expression is perceived to overlap with aspects of thought, conscience and belief arising under Article 9. Artistic expression which challenges religious belief in a manner considered offensive may also justify state interference, for freedom of expression carries with it certain responsibilities to exercise this right in an acceptable manner. In *Otto-Preminger-Institut v Austria*, a seizure order had been made against a film on the ground that it ridiculed particular beliefs of the Roman Catholic Church. While accepting that those who manifest their religious convictions 'must tolerate and accept the denial by others of their religious beliefs and even the propagation by others of doctrines hostile to their faith', the European Court of Human Rights considered that national authorities could consider it necessary to take action to protect believers against 'provocative portrayals of objects of religious veneration' where such constitute 'malicious violation of the spirit of tolerance, which must also be a feature of democratic society'[1]. A similar approach was adopted in *Wingrove v United Kingdom*, where the refusal of the British Board of Film Classification to grant a distribution certificate for a video was challenged. The Court accepted that the English law on blasphemy contained adequate safeguards to protect against arbitrary decision-making, and that the decision by the Board in the particular case had not been unreasonable[2]. The distinction between offensive speech and that which is merely unpopular may be difficult to draw. A sustained campaign of harassment by private individuals or organisations may engage state responsibility[3], but on the other hand it is legitimate that individuals are free to criticise religious groups, particularly if the criticism concerns the potentially harmful nature of their activities, and when made in a political forum in which issues of public interest are expected to be debated openly[4]. Furthermore, it is possible to be strongly critical of office-holders within a religious body without denigrating the content of the faith itself[5]. Measured discussion of historical opinion on a matter of public interest free from malicious attack on religious belief similarly attracts protection under Article 10[6].

1 *Otto-Preminger-Institut v Austria* (1994) A 295-A, at para 47.

2 *Wingrove v United Kingdom* 1996-V, paras 57–65 (the Court viewed the film). See also *IA v Turkey* (13 September 2005), paras 21–32 (prosecution for blasphemy for publication of work examining philosophical and theological issues: no violation). See Heinze 'Viewpoint Absolutism and Hate Speech' (2006) 69 MLR 543; Jaconelli 'Defences to Speech Crimes' [2007] EHRLR 27; Martinez-Torron 'Freedom of Expression versus Freedom of Religion in

the European Court of Human Rights' in Sajo (ed) *Censorial Sensitivities: Free Speech and Religion in a Fundamentalist World* (2007), pp 233–269; Temperman 'Blasphemy, Defamation of Religions and Human Rights Law' (2008) 26 NQHR 517; and Tulkens 'Conflicts between Fundamental Rights: Contrasting Views on Articles 9 and 10 of the ECHR' in Venice Commission *Science and Technique of Democracy 47: Blasphemy, Insult and Hatred: Finding Answers in a Democratic Society* (2010), pp 121–131. See also Parliamentary Assembly Resolution Res 1510 (2006), prompted by the controversy surrounding the publication in Denmark of cartoons featuring the Prophet Mohammed (on which, see Boyle 'The Danish Cartoons' (2006) 24 NQHR 185; Nathwani 'Religious Cartoons and Human Rights: a Critical Legal Analysis of the Case Law of the European Court of Human Rights on the Protection of Religious Feelings and its Implications in the Danish Affair concerning Cartoons of the Prophet Muhammad' [2008] EHRLR 488; and Cram 'The Danish Cartoons, Offensive Expression, and Democratic Legitimacy' in Hare and Weinstein (eds) *Extreme Speech and Democracy* (2009), pp 311–330).

3   8282/78, *Church of Scientology v Sweden* (1980) DR 21, 109.

4   *Jerusalem v Austria* 2001-II, paras 38–47. See also *Aydin Tatlav v Turkey* (2 May 2006), paras 21–31 (strong criticism of religion, but not an abusive attack on the Muslim faith).

5   *Klein v Slovakia* (31 October 2006), paras 45–55 (conviction of journalist for defamation of a Catholic archbishop, the highest representative of the Roman Catholic Church in Slovakia, and thereby also for having disparaged a group of citizens for their Catholic faith through publication of an article critical of the archbishop's attempts to prevent the distribution of a film on the grounds of its blasphemous nature and strong imagery of sexual connotation and allusions to the archbishop's alleged co-operation with the former communist regime: violation of Art 10 since the strongly-worded pejorative opinion published in a weekly with rather limited circulation and which the archbishop had pardoned had related exclusively to the archbishop and had not unduly interfered with the right of believers to express and exercise their religion, nor had it denigrated the content of their religious faith).

6   *Giniewski v France* 2006-I, paras 43–56 (conviction for defamation of Christians, and particularly Roman Catholics, for publication of article critical of a papal encyclical and the Roman Catholic Church's role in the Holocaust: violation, as the article was written by a journalist and historian and concerned a matter of indisputable public interest, and did not seek to attack religious belief as such but confined itself to addressing a Pope's position).

7.109 As far as religious expression is concerned, this is likely to be considered in terms of Article 10 unless it involves a clear 'manifestation' of belief[1]. The refusal to allow the broadcast of a religious advertisement on the radio was challenged by the applicant in *Murphy v Ireland* under both Article 9 and Article 10 but disposed of by the Court under the latter guarantee as the interference primarily concerned the regulation of the applicant's means of expression and not manifestation of religious belief. Here, a wide margin of appreciation was again appropriate since national authorities were better placed than an international court to decide when action may be necessary to regulate freedom of expression in relation to matters liable to offend intimate personal convictions 'since what is likely to cause substantial offence to persons of a particular religious persuasion will vary significantly from time to time and from place to place, especially in an era characterised by an ever growing array of faiths and denominations'. In consequence, the Court accepted that the authorities had been justified in determining that the particular religious sensitivities in Irish society were such that the broadcasting of any religious advertising could be considered offensive: domestic courts had noted that religion had been a divisive issue in society, that

Irish people holding religious beliefs tended to belong to one particular church, and that religious advertising from a different church might be considered offensive and open to the interpretation of proselytism. There had thus been highly 'relevant reasons' for the interference, particularly since the prohibition concerned broadcasting, a means of communication which has 'a more immediate, invasive and powerful impact' than the press. In any event, the applicant could still have advertised via local and national newspapers and retained the same right as any other citizen to participate in programmes on religious matters, public meetings and other assemblies[2]. This judgment hardly promotes the notion of pluralism and broadmindedness, and resentment on the part of television viewers is hardly the most compelling ground for interference with free speech. On the other hand, an international judicial forum should be particularly careful to refrain from interfering with domestic determinations on particularly sensitive issues.

---

1   Eg *Bowman v United Kingdom* 1998-I, paras 35–47 (restrictions on the amount of expenditure that can be incurred at election time were challenged successfully by an anti-abortionist as a disproportionate restriction of freedom of expression); 7805/77, *X and Church of Scientology v Sweden* (1979) DR 16, p 68 (expression essentially of a commercial nature may be restricted on the grounds that this is necessary for the protection of the public from misleading claims).

2   *Murphy v Ireland* 2003-IX, paras 73–82. See further Geddis 'You Can't Say "God" on Radio: Freedom of Expression, Religious Advertising and the Broadcast Media after *Murphy v Ireland*' [2004] EHRLR 181.

Commercial speech

7.110 Expression concerning information essentially of a commercial nature also falls within the ambit of protection of Article 10[1], and both individuals and companies can claim to be 'victims' of interferences with freedom of expression[2]. However, unless such expression can be shown to serve the 'public interest' rather than commercial interest, it will receive reduced protection. The distinction between 'commercial' and other expression deemed worthy of enhanced protection is thus not entirely clear. In *Barthold v Germany,* a veterinary surgeon had been prohibited by competition law and professional conduct rules from making comments about the lack of after-hours care for animals. The applicant himself operated a clinic, and colleagues alleged that he had been using his concerns about the inadequate emergency service to gain unfair publicity. Here, though, the European Court of Human Rights held that any publicity was secondary to the principal content of the article and the nature of the issue being put to the public at large, and as such, the restrictions on his speech were disproportionate and there had been a violation of Article 10[3]. Where the public interest in open debate is less obvious, the Court has proved to be more restrictive in its application of the guarantee. It has accepted that a number of factors may justify restrictions[4] or even prohibitions[5] on speech which properly can be considered as purely commercial in so far as it seeks to advance economic interests. In this area, a certain margin of appreciation is 'essential in commercial matters, and in particular, in an area as complex and fluctuating as that of unfair competition' where issues of business confidentiality, protection of consumers, and fairness to enterprises can all be of relevance[6]. Nevertheless, the sufficiency of such reasons[7], as well as the proportionality of the measures to the aim sought to be achieved[8], will still require to be established by the state.

1   *Markt Intern Verlag GmbH and Klaus Beerman v Germany* (1989) A 165, para 26; *Krone Verlag GmbH v Austria (no 3)* 2003-XII, para 31. For domestic discussion, see *R (Matthias Rath BV) v Advertising Standards Authority Ltd* [2001] HRLR 22 (advertising); *R (Smithkline Beecham plc) v Advertising Standards Authority Ltd* [2001] EMLR 23 (advertising); and *Levi Strauss v Tesco Stores* [2002] 3 CMLR 11 (trademark).

2   *Autronic AG v Switzerland* (1990) A 178, para 47; *Hertel v Switzerland* 1998-VI, paras 31 and 46–51 (unfair competition laws prevented expression of opinion that microwave-cooked food was dangerous to health; violation of Art 10 established). Cf *Hertel v Switzerland* (dec) 2002-I (applicant was prohibited from making statements as to the dangers of microwaves without referring to current differences of opinion, a minor limitation of his rights which was not unreasonable: inadmissible); and *Murphy v Ireland* 2003-IX, para 70–82, discussed at para **7.109** above (advertisement concerned religious rather than commercial material and thus called for enhanced scrutiny of the necessity of the interference with Art 10).

3   *Barthold v Germany* (1985) A 90, paras 55–58. At para 42, the Court rejected any attempt to distinguish clearly between factual data and 'elements which go more to manner of presentation than to substance' and which may thus have an advertising or 'publicity-like effect'. See too *Colman v United Kingdom* (1993) A 258-D (General Medical Council (GMC) restrictions on advertising by medical practices: the case was struck off the list following the achievement of a friendly settlement involving revision of the GMC's rules on advertising restrictions); *Casado Coca v Spain* (1994) A 285-A, paras 50–56 (disciplinary action against lawyer who had advertised his professional services not considered a violation); and *Stambuk v Germany* (17 October 2002), paras 43–54 (disciplinary action against ophthalmologist featured in article claiming a 100% success rate in treatment: violation). Cf Case V 56/00, [2002] EuGRZ 619, [2003] EuroCLY 1482 [Austria] (distribution of more than factual information could result in a lowering of esteem in the eyes of the public, and could therefore be prohibited).

4   Cf *Open Door Counselling and Dublin Well Women v Ireland* (1992) A 246 (restraints upon counselling agencies from providing pregnant women with information on available abortion facilities abroad were considered: the Court noted that the corporate applicants were engaged in the counselling of pregnant women in the course of which counsellors neither advocated nor encouraged abortion but confined themselves to an explanation of the available options and thus these restraints were disproportionate).

5   See *Hachette Filipacchi Presse Automobile and Dupuy v France* (5 March 2009), paras 53–64 (convictions for illegally advertising tobacco pursued a pressing social need and had been proportionate: no violation). For domestic discussion, see *R (British American Tobacco v Secretary of State* [2004] EWHC 2493 (Admin) (regulations governing tobacco advertising were made with the legitimate aim of deterring smoking and fell to be judged in the context of the social goal of the protection of health: although there were areas in which the court had to be particularly wary of imposing its own value judgments upon a legislative scheme, the regulations in question were not a disproportionate restriction of commercial free speech).

6   *Markt Intern Verlag GmbH and Klaus Beermann v Germany* (1989) A 165, paras 33–37 (prohibition on publisher and editor of specialist commercial bulletin from repeating information).

7   Thus in *Groppera Radio AG and Others v Switzerland* (1990) A 173, the Court (at para 73) listed and approved the factors advanced by the state in justifying restrictions on the company's rights to retransmit broadcasts from Italy. However, in *Autronic AG v Switzerland* (1990) A 178, paras 61–63, the Court was not persuaded that the state's refusal to allow retransmission without consent of the broadcaster of uncoded broadcast signals from a satellite was justified, primarily on account of an international convention specifically permitting such.

8   Eg *Jacubowski v Germany* (1994) A 291-A, paras 26–30 (prohibition on journalist from circulating material critical of former employer considered proportionate: applicant retained right to defend himself elsewhere); and *Krone Verlag GmbH v Austria (no 3)* 2003-XII, paras 28–35 (even although no penalty had been imposed, the prohibition on comparing newspapers by price without indicating quality of coverage had far-reaching consequences as regards future advertising involving price comparisons and thus the injunction had been over-broad).

'Artistic' speech and the maintenance of public morality

7.111 Artistic expression clearly falls within the ambit of Article 10[1], but where state authorities claim that interference is necessary for the protection of morals, the European Court of Human Rights may recognise that there is a wide margin of appreciation on the part of the state, and appears to defer readily to national decision-making on account of the difficulty in giving effect to the term 'morals'. As the Court held in the early case of *Handyside v United Kingdom*, there is no uniform European approach to the protection of public morality since views on morality vary 'from time to time and from place to place, especially in our era which is characterised by a rapid and far-reaching evolution of opinion on the subject'. More particularly, the Strasbourg authorities have recognised that their competence in such questions is limited. 'By reason of their direct and continuous contact with the vital forces of their countries', national authorities are better placed to determine whether a matter is necessary to achieve a particular state aim. In consequence, where there has been an interference with artistic expression, at least in relation to material considered indecent or obscene and which has no obvious social benefit, supervision is limited to consideration of whether the state has advanced reasons for any interference which are relevant and sufficient[2], and of whether any penalty was disproportionate[3], but these tests may not be demanding in practice.

1   Cf *Müller v Switzerland* (1988) A 133, para 43.

2   *Handyside v United Kingdom* (1976) A 24, paras 48–50 at para 48. For domestic examples of freedom of expression being balanced against considerations relating to morality, see *Belfast City Council v Miss Behavin' Ltd* [2007] 1 WLR 1420 and *In re St Peter and St Paul's Church* [2007] Fam 67, discussed at para **7.64** above; cf *R (ProLife Alliance) v British Broadcasting Corporation* [2004] 1 AC 185, discussed at para **7.78** above.

7.112 'Relevant' reasons for interferences may thus include evidence of public opinion on a particular matter of morality[1], while an assessment of the 'sufficiency' of such reasons to justify an interference is likely in such cases to be limited to a cursory examination of whether the state can show that a domestic decision-maker had a reasonable basis for considering that the interference was necessary for the protection of morals[2]. Thus in the *Handyside* case, the Court noted that the offending publication, *The Little Red Schoolbook*, could have been interpreted by young people 'as an encouragement to indulge in precocious activities harmful for them or even to commit certain criminal offences', and thus domestic courts 'were entitled, in the exercise of their discretion, to think that [the work] would have pernicious effects on the morals of many children and adolescents who would read it'[3]. In *Müller and Others v Switzerland*, the Court accepted (after having inspected the works of art in question) that it was not unreasonable for the domestic courts to have considered paintings displayed in a public exhibition as 'liable grossly to offend the sense of sexual propriety of persons of ordinary sensitivity'. The imposition of a criminal penalty for publishing obscenity and the confiscation of the paintings thus did not involve a breach of the guarantee[4]. The deference shown to decision-making by national authorities in such instances can at times seem difficult to reconcile with the Court's stated intention of promoting 'pluralism, toleration and broadmindedness'[5].

1   Eg 31211/96, *Hoare v United Kingdom* (2 July 1997) (30 months' imprisonment for distribution of obscene video cassettes to a restricted circle of customers outwith the video certification scheme, and where no artistic merit was claimed for the works, considered proportionate to the legitimate aim pursued).

2   Cf *Open Door and Dublin Well Woman v Ireland* (1992) A 246-A, para 63 (domestic anti-abortion laws based upon 'profound moral values' as indicated by referendum result); *Otto-Preminger-Institut v Austria* (1994) A 295-A, para 56 (Roman Catholic religion was the faith of the 'overwhelming majority' of population in particular locality). Such factors may, though, not be relevant in other Convention guarantees where local public opinion conflicts with prevailing values in the member states: eg *Tyrer v United Kingdom* (1978) A 26, para 31 (birching supported by local population); *Dudgeon v United Kingdom* (1981) A 45, paras 57–61 (majority of Northern Irish were against legalisation of homosexuality); and *Alekseyev v Russia* 2010-…, paras 71–88 (prohibition of 'gay pride' parades on account of moral values of the majority although the purpose of the parades was to promote respect for human rights and tolerance).

3   *Handyside v United Kingdom* (1976) A 24, at para 52.

4   *Müller and Others v Switzerland* (1988) A 133, paras 36–43 at para 36. The question of accessibility to the offending material may be relevant in such circumstances. In *Handyside v United Kingdom* (1976) A 24, the publication had been specifically targeted at young people, while in *Müller v Switzerland*, the paintings had been displayed in an art gallery which was open to members of the public without payment. On the other hand, in *Otto-Preminger-Institut v Austria* (1994) A 295-A, the film in question was to be screened to paying adults at a late hour of the day. Cf *Scherer v Switzerland* (1994) A 287 (screening of pornographic video in private club; nature of the establishment was not apparent to passers-by, but customers knew about it through advertisements placed in specialist magazines etc; domestic court distinguished factual circumstances from *Müller* in that no unwilling adult or young person had been confronted with the film, but nevertheless still considered punishment was appropriate: the Commission was of the opinion there had been a violation of Art 10, but the Court struck the case off its list after the applicant's death). See also *Perrin v United Kingdom* (dec) 2005-XI (conviction for publication of obscene material on the internet: inadmissible); *SB and DB v Belgium* (dec) (15 June 2006) (complaints concerning prohibition of advertising for sexual services: inadmissible); and *Palusinski v Poland* (dec) 2006-XIV (conviction of publisher of book inciting drug-taking: inadmissible).

5   For a defence of this approach, see Mahoney 'Universality versus Subsidiarity in the Strasbourg Case Law on Free Speech' [1997] EHRLR 364; for a response, see Lester of Herne Hill 'Universality versus Subsidiarity: A Reply' [1998] EHRLR 73.

7.113 The practical consequence for artistic expression was that it was accorded little in the way of protection under Article 10. However, some recent revision of case law appears to have taken place in relation to certain forms of artistic expression. It is now expressly recognised that those who create or distribute such works contribute to the exchange of ideas and opinions which is essential for a democratic society, and thus national authorities must not encroach unduly on their freedom of expression[1]. First, a work which forms part of Europe's literary heritage should be available to all[2]. Secondly, as the Court noted in *Vereinigung Bildender Künstler v Austria*, artistic work which also seeks to convey social commentary (as with caricature or satire) calls for careful scrutiny[3]. Thirdly, works of fiction seeking to examine issues of current historical or political controversy may call for similar levels of protection to that accorded to discussion of matters of contemporary interest, although the Court remains sensitive to the need for care in this area[4]. In particular, if it is expected in respect of non-fiction that evidence exists to support facts susceptible of proof and that there should be some factual basis to support value judgments, those who write or distribute works of fiction purporting to be based upon historical reality may similarly be considered to have certain duties and responsibilities. In *Lindon, Otchakovsky-Laurens and July v France,* the author and publishers of a novel recounting the trial of a *Front National* militant for a racially-motivated murder had been found guilty of criminal defamation. The book had been based on actual events and sought to raise questions about the responsibility of Le Pen, the chairman of the *Front National*, for murders committed by its far-right militants. The text had likened the chairman to the leader of 'a gang of killers' and had asserted that a murder committed by a fictional character had been 'advocated' by him; subsequently Le Pen had been described as a 'vampire who thrives on the bitterness of his electorate, but sometimes also on their blood'. The Grand Chamber found no violation of Article 10. The virulent content of the offending passages and the actual naming of the *Front National* and its chairman had not been subjected to basic verification of their factual basis, and while the distinction between facts and value-judgments was not generally relevant when dealing with extracts from a novel, such a distinction was pertinent when a work is not simply one of pure fiction but introduces real characters or facts. The conclusion that there had been no violation had also taken into account that individuals taking part in a public debate on a matter of general concern are permitted to have recourse to a degree of exaggeration or even provocation, or to make somewhat immoderate statements, and that the limits of acceptable criticism are wider as regards politicians or their parties. Here, though, the minimum degree of moderation and propriety had been overstepped, particularly since the passages were such as to stir up violence and hatred, going beyond what was tolerable in political debate, even in respect of a figure who occupied an extremist position in the political spectrum[5].

1   *Lindon, Otchakovsky-Laurens and July v France* [GC] 2007-XI, para 47 (in respect of novels).

2   *Akdaş v Turkey* (16 February 2010), paras 24–32 (conviction of editor for publishing erotic literary work in translation: violation, there having been no pressing social need, and the interference had been disproportionate as speakers of a certain language cannot be denied access to a work which forms part of European literary heritage).

3   *Vereinigung Bildender Künstler v Austria* 2007-II, paras 26–39 (at para 8: the painting in question 'showed a collage of various public figures, such as Mother Teresa, the Austrian

cardinal Hermann Groer and the former head of the Austrian Freedom Party (FPÖ) Mr Jörg Haider, in sexual positions', and depicted a former general secretary of the FPÖ 'gripping the ejaculating penis of Mr Haider while at the same time being touched by two other FPÖ politicians and ejaculating on Mother Teresa'); and at para 33: 'satire is a form of artistic expression and social commentary and, by its inherent features of exaggeration and distortion of reality, naturally aims to provoke and agitate').

4   *Alinak v Turkey* (29 March 2005), paras 39–47, at para 41: 'graphic details are given of fictional ill-treatment and atrocities committed against villagers, which no doubt creates in the mind of the reader a powerful hostility' and 'taken literally, certain passages might be construed as inciting readers to hatred, revolt and the use of violence', but 'the medium used by the applicant was a novel, a form of artistic expression that appeals to a relatively narrow public', and the seizure was disproportionate).

5   *Lindon & Otchakovsky-Laurens and July v France* [GC] 2007-XI, paras 47–60.

ARTICLE 11: ASSEMBLY AND ASSOCIATION

The scope of Article 11

7.114 Article 11 protects the rights of peaceful assembly and of association with others[1]. These two interrelated rights are fundamental aspects of political life, and have a direct importance for political parties as well as other non-governmental associations and organisations whether national, regional or local. Their importance, though, is not confined to furthering democratic institutions, as they are also relevant for community life in general[2]. These rights also have a close relationship with other Convention concerns such as the manifestation of religious and philosophical convictions and freedom of expression, concerns which must be taken into account in the application of Article 11[3]. In particular, 'the protection of opinions and the freedom to express them is one of the objectives of the freedoms of assembly and association'[4], and Article 10 protects not only the content but also the means of expression[5]. Article 11 also has certain implications for aspects of employment law, such as the right to join trade unions which is specifically recognised in paragraph (1), although this provision may be of more limited utility than some commentators would wish[6].

1   Between 1959 and 2009, the Court established 98 violations of Art 11. The vast majority have concerned Turkey (39), followed by Bulgaria (8), Armenia, Moldova and Russia (6 each) and Azerbaijan and Greece (5 each). The United Kingdom had 3 adverse judgments during this period: European Court *Annual Report 2009* (2010), pp 150–151.

2   Eg *The Gypsy Council and Others v United Kingdom* (dec) (14 May 2002) (the relocation of horse fair fell within the scope of Art 11).

3   For cases in which Art 9 was interpreted in the light of Art 11, see eg *Metropolitan Church of Bessarabia and Others v Moldova* 2001-XII, at para 118, discussed at para **7.39** above; *Young, James and Webster v United Kingdom* (1981) A 44, para 57, discussed at para **7.126** below; *Moscow Branch of the Salvation Army v Russia* 2006-XI, paras 76–98 (violation of Art 11 read in conjunction with Art 9 on account of bad faith decision-making entirely devoid of factual basis, including a determination that the Salvation Army was a paramilitary organisation); *Barankevich v Russia* (26 July 2007), paras 28–35 (refusal to allow minority church group to hold worship in a park: violation of Art 11 interpreted in the light of Art 9); *Association*

Solidarité des Français v France (dec) (16 June 2009) (ban on the distributing of meals primarily consisting of pork to underprivileged persons: inadmissible, as the ban was necessary and proportionate to the legitimate aim pursued, the prohibition considered in terms of Arts 9 and 11, but inadmissible in light of the clearly discriminatory aims of the applicant association, the affront to the dignity of vulnerable persons and the considerable risk of public disorder in view of the controversy surrounding the handouts); and *Jehovah's Witnesses of Moscow v Russia* 2010-..., paras 106–160 and 170–182 (refusal to re-register a religious association and its dissolution without relevant and sufficient grounds as many court findings had not been substantiated and were not grounded on an acceptable assessment of the relevant facts: violation of Art 9 in the light of Art 11; and violation of Art 11 in the light of Art 9).For cases in which the Court has considered Art 11 in the light of Art 10, see eg *Socialist Party of Turkey and Others v Turkey* 1998-III, para 41; *Bukta and Others v Hungary*, 2007-IX, para 41 (spontaneous protest against prime minister); and *Galstyan v Armenia* (15 November 2007); paras 95–96 at para 96 (Art 10 was the *lex generalis* and Art 11 a *lex specialis*, but Art 11 had to be interpreted in accordance with Art 10 as 'the protection of personal opinions, secured by art 10, is one of the objectives of freedom of peaceful assembly as enshrined in art 11'). Cf *Steel and Others v United Kingdom* 1998-VII, para 113 (peaceful protest considered under Art 10 rather than Art 11); *Hashman and Harrup v United Kingdom* [GC] 1999-VIII, para 24 (complaint under Art 11 not pursued before the Court, and merits considered under Art 10).

4   *Öztürk v Turkey* [GC] 1999-VI, para 49.

5   *United Communist Party of Turkey and Others v Turkey* 1998-I, para 42.

6   Note that the European Social Charter seeks to protect employment rights which are of the nature of economic and social rights: see para **2.92** above.

7.115 The format of Article 11 follows that of Articles 8, 9 and 10: that is, paragraph (1) first recognises the freedoms of peaceful assembly and association, and paragraph (2) thereafter permits interferences on the grounds of listed state interests where prescribed by law and 'necessary in a democratic society'[1]. The legitimate interests recognised include national security, public safety, the prevention of disorder or crime, and the individual aims of protection of health or morals or the rights and freedoms of others. It will invariably be possible to bring any interference under one of these heads, and satisfying the test of 'prescribed by law' has not often proved to be a matter of difficulty[2]. In this area, the critical question again has concerned scrutiny of the necessity of an interference which must correspond to a pressing social need, be proportionate to the legitimate aim pursued, and be justified by relevant and sufficient reasons. Article 11(2) makes specific provision for state restrictions on the exercise of these rights by 'members of the armed forces, of the police or the administration of the state', an issue considered below in respect of the withdrawal of recognition of trade union membership[3].

1   See further paras **3.62–3.66** and **3.73–3.82** above.

2   Note *NF v Italy* 2001-IX, paras 26–34 (the applicant, a judge, was a former freemason who was reprimanded after his resignation from his lodge during the course of disciplinary proceedings for having undermined the prestige of the judiciary in terms of a directive read in conjunction with an earlier decree; however, the terms of the directive had not been sufficiently clear to allow even a judge trained in the law to realise that a magistrate joining an official masonic lodge could face disciplinary action: the sanction was thus not 'forseeable' and thus not 'prescribed by law', and the interference involved a violation of Art 11); and similarly *Maestri v Italy* [GC] 2004-I, paras 34–42 (violation: not foreseeable that freemasonry membership could result in

disciplinary sanction). See also *Djavit An v Turkey* 2003-III, paras 63–69 (respondent government was unable to refer to any regulations concerning the issue of permits to cross the 'green line' between Northern and Southern Cyprus: violation of Art 11.

3   See paras **7.132–7.133** below.

Peaceful assembly

Scope of the right to peaceful assembly

7.116 An 'assembly'[1] can take the form of either a meeting or a procession, and can take place either on private property or in a public space[2]. Article 11 applies irrespective of whether the assembly is unlawful in terms of domestic law, although the qualification of 'peaceful' indicates that any meeting seeking to provoke violence or occasioning disorder falls outwith the scope of the guarantee[3], the intentions of the organisers being of relevance[4]. The right is one enjoyed not only by the participants in but also by the organisers of a demonstration, including any association or corporate body[5]. Aliens unlawfully in a country also have the right to take part in protest[6]. While the right is essentially concerned with participation for democratic or related purposes and thus purely social gatherings are excluded from the scope of the guarantee[7], the range of associations covered by Article 11 is potentially of wide scope:

'While in the context of Article 11 the Court has often referred to the essential role played by political parties in ensuring pluralism and democracy, associations formed for other purposes are also important to the proper functioning of democracy. For pluralism is also built on genuine recognition of, and respect for, diversity and the dynamics of cultural traditions, ethnic and cultural identities, religious beliefs and artistic, literary and socio-economic ideas and concepts. The harmonious interaction of persons and groups with varied identities is essential for achieving social cohesion. It is only natural that, where a civil society functions in a healthy manner, the participation of citizens in the democratic process is to a large extent achieved through belonging to associations in which they may integrate with each other and pursue common objectives collectively'[8].

1   See further Mead 'The Right to Peaceful Protest under the European Convention on Human Rights – a Content Study of Strasbourg Case Law' [2007] EHRLR 345.

2   8191/78, *Rassemblement Jurassien v Switzerland* (1979) DR 17, 93; and 8440/78, *Christians against Racism and Fascism v United Kingdom* (1980) DR 21, 138.

3   8440/78, *Christians against Racism and Fascism v United Kingdom* (1980) DR 21, 138.

4   *The Gypsy Council and Others v United Kingdom* (dec) (14 May 2002) (relocation of horse fair to another venue on account of serious disruption to the life of the community: inadmissible). See also *Barraco v France* 2009-..., paras 41–49 (conviction for taking part in a motorway blockade as a demonstration: no violation).

5   *Djavit An v Turkey* 2003-III, para 56. See also 8440/78, *Christians against Racism and Fascism v United Kingdom* (1980) DR 21, 138 (those rights being guaranteed to persons organising as well as participating in a demonstration).

6   *Cisse and Others v France* 2002-II, paras 47–54 (action taken on health and sanitation

grounds against occupation by illegal immigrants of church but not at the request of the church authorities: no violation).

7   See 33689/96, *Anderson and Others v United Kingdom* (1997) DR 91, 79 (exclusion of applicants from a shopping centre because of misconduct did not give rise to an Art 11 issue in the absence of any history of their having used the centre for any assembly or association: the guarantee is not intended to protect assembly for purely social purposes); and *Friend and Others v United Kingdom* (24 November 2009) (statutory bans on hunting wild mammals with dogs: inadmissible). The same conclusion had been reached by the House of Lords: *R (Countryside Alliance) v A-G* [2008] 1 AC 719 per Lord Hope of Craighead and Baroness Hale of Richmond; *Whaley v Lord Advocate* 2008 SC (HL) 107.

8   *Bączkowski and Others v Poland* 2007-VI, at para 62; (and at paras 67–68, refusals to give authorisation 'could have had a chilling effect on the applicants and other participants in the assemblies. It could also have discouraged other persons from participating in the assemblies on the grounds that they did not have official authorisation and that, therefore, no official protection against possible hostile counter-demonstrators would be ensured by the authorities' and thus at the time of the holding of the assemblies the applicants were negatively affected by the refusals to authorise them). See also *Gypsy Council and Others v United Kingdom* (dec) (14 May 2002) (horse fair was of significant cultural and social importance to the gypsy community, and thus covered by Art 11, but the question whether the applicants were 'victims' left open); and *Alekseyev v Russia* 2010-..., paras 71–88 ('gay pride' parades prohibited on account of moral values of the majority although the purpose of the parades was to promote respect for human rights and tolerance).

Interferences

7.117 There will be an 'interference' with this right where an assembly or procession is prohibited[1] or relocated[2] or where there is a sanction imposed for the exercise of the right[3]. However, the mere fact that an assembly or procession requires prior approval does not itself constitute an interference[4], although sanctions imposed for having knowingly disregarded the requirements of domestic law under which an organiser of a planned public meeting is required to give prior notice to the authorities will do so[5].

1   13079/87, *G v Germany* (1989) DR 60, 256 (obstruction of a road by way of protest does not constitute a violent demonstration); and 8440/78, *Christians against Racism and Fascism v United Kingdom* (1980) DR 21, 138 (peaceful nature of assembly cannot be lost by violent nature of any counter-demonstration). The suggestion is thus that restrictions placed on an assembly inherently (or intended to be) not of a peaceful nature need not be scrutinised for compliance with para (2): van Dijk, van Hoof, van Rijn and Zwaak (eds) *Theory and Practice of the European Convention on Human Rights* (4th edn, 2006) p 821. However, as the authors note, 'a peacefully organised demonstration that runs the risk of resulting in disorder by developments beyond the control of the organisers ... does not for that reason fall outside the scope of Article 11'.

2   *Stankov and The United Macedonian Organisation Ilinden v Bulgaria* 2001–IX, para 78 (arguments of the government that the applicant organisation had sought to use violence for political ends, and posed a threat to national security and territorial integrity, rejected after examination of evidence produced by the parties).

3   13079/87, *G v Germany* (1989) DR 60, 256.

4   8191/78, *Rassemblement Jurassien v Switzerland* (1979) DR 17, 93. See too 25522/94, *Rai and Others v United Kingdom* (1995) DR 81, 146 (prohibition on meetings in Trafalgar Square

not a violation: the policy was not designed to discriminate between different organisations but instead to prevent disorder, and the applicants could have met elsewhere); and *Rai and Evans v United Kingdom* (dec) 2009-.... But cf an apparently stricter line on choice of forum by protestors in *Öllinger v Austria* 2006-IX, paras 34–51 (prohibition of entirely peaceful demonstration commemorating Jews murdered by the SS at the same time and location as a permitted assembly of an association commemorating SS soldiers, the coincidence in time and place being an essential feature of the planned assembly: violation). See further Mead 'Strasbourg Discovers the Right to Counter-demonstrate – a Note on Öllinger v Austria' [2007] EHRLR 133.

5   *Skiba v Poland* (dec) (7 July 2009).

Positive obligations

7.118 The guarantee can require positive action on the part of the state. 'Genuine, effective freedom of peaceful assembly' cannot be secured simply by a duty upon the state itself not to interfere, but must entail positive state assistance to those seeking to meet and to protest through protection against those opposed to the expression of the particular opinion, since 'in a democracy the right to counter-demonstrate cannot extend to inhibiting the exercise of the right to demonstrate'[1]. In *Plattform 'Ärzte für das Leben' v Austria*, the European Court of Human Rights considered an application from an association of doctors campaigning against abortion legislation who had their protest disrupted by groups opposed to their views and complained that the police had given them insufficient protection. The Court held that Article 11 imposed a duty upon public authorities to take such reasonable measures as were appropriate in order to allow a lawful demonstration to take place peacefully, although the state had a wide discretion in its choice of methods and there could not be an absolute guarantee of protection for participants against those opposed to the expression of such views[2]. Further, when it is not clear where responsibility lies for any interference with freedom of assembly or association, there is a duty upon the competent authorities to undertake an effective investigation[3]. The obligation on the state to ensure the effective enjoyment of Article 11 rights may also include an obligation to intervene in relationships between private parties, for example, to ensure that the negative aspect of the guarantee – the right *not* to associate – is respected[4], but does not extend to requiring the owners of private property to facilitate assemblies on their premises[5].

1   *Plattform 'Ärzte für das Leben' v Austria* (1988) A 139, para 32. See also *Ouranio Toxo and Others v Greece* 2005-X, paras 36–44; and *Bzkowski and Others v Poland* 2007-..., paras 61–73 (positive obligation of particular importance in respect of groups with unpopular views or minorities); and *Barankevich v Russia* (26 July 2007), paras 28–35 (refusal to allow minority church group to hold worship in a park: violation of Art 11 interpreted in the light of Art 9). Cf *Öllinger v Austria* 2006-IX, noted at para **7.117**, fn 4 above.

2   *Plattform 'Ärzte für das Leben' v Austria* (1988) A 139, paras 32 and 34 (no violation established in the circumstances). See also *Stankov and the United Macedonian Organisation Ilinden v Bulgaria* 2001–IX, at para 107: 'if every probability of tension and heated exchange between opposing groups during a demonstration were to warrant its prohibition, society would be faced with being deprived of the opportunity of hearing differing views on any question which offends the sensitivity of the majority opinion. ... The national authorities must display

particular vigilance to ensure that national public opinion is not protected at the expense of the assertion of minority views, no matter how unpopular they may be.'

3 *Ouranio Toxo and Others v Greece* 2005-X, paras 38–44 (prior incitement by local authorities to participate in counter-demonstration, passivity of the police in protecting a demonstration, and no subsequent investigation until complaint lodged: violation).

4 *Young, James and Webster v United Kingdom* (1981) A 44, para 45, discussed at para **7.126** below.

5 33689/96, *Anderson and Others v United Kingdom* (1997) DR 91, 795; cf *Appleby and Others v United Kingdom* 2003-VI, paras 41–50 and 52 (issue disposed of under Art 10), discussed at para **7.53** above.

Decisions of the domestic courts on interferences

7.119 Like the Strasbourg Court, domestic courts have held that Article 11 does not guarantee a right to assemble for purely social purposes[1]. In the case of *R (Gillan) v Metropolitan Police Commissioner* the House of Lords found that police stop and search powers under the Terrorism Act 2000 did not constitute an interference with Arts 10 and 11, and that they were in any event justified under Arts 10(2) and 11(2)[2]. The Strasbourg Court subsequently found that there was a violation of Article 8, and did not require to consider the complaint under Articles 10 and 11[3]. Other domestic cases concerning interferences with Article 11 rights are discussed below[4].

1 *R (Countryside Alliance) A-G* [2008] AC 719 per Lord Hope of Craighead and Baroness Hale of Richmond; *Whaley v Lord Advocate* 2008 SC (HL) 107.

2 *R (Gillan) v Metropolitan Police Commissioner* [2006] 2 AC 307.

3 *Gillan and Quinton v United Kingdom* (12 January 2010), discussed at para **6.104** above.

4 See para **7.124** below.

Assessing whether an interference meets the requirements of Article 11(2)

7.120 Under Article 11(2), any interference must be prescribed by law, seek to achieve one of the prescribed legitimate interests, and meet the 'necessary in a democratic society' test. The 'legitimate aim' advanced by the government in such cases is likely to be the prevention of disorder, and this is unlikely to pose any difficulty. The test of 'prescribed by law' assesses the extent to which domestic law adequately regulates interferences[1]. It is the determination of whether the interference was 'necessary in a democratic society' that most of the case law is concerned with. While recognising a margin of appreciation on the part of state authorities, the European Court of Human Rights will scrutinise interferences with political protest with some care, particularly on account of the close relationship with Article 10' guarantees of freedom of expression, for 'if every probability of tension and heated exchange between opposing groups during a demonstration were to warrant its prohibition, society would be faced with being deprived of the opportunity of hearing differing views on any question which offends the sensitivity of the majority opinion'. In consequence, the authorities 'must display particular vigilance to ensure that national public opinion is not protected at the expense of the assertion of minority views, no matter how unpopular they may be'[2]. The questions of whether the interference was proportionate to its purported aim and whether the reasons adduced to justify it were 'relevant and sufficient' therefore require the authorities to show that they have based their decisions on an acceptable assessment of the relevant facts[3].

1   See eg *Mkrtchyan v Armenia* (11 January 2007), paras 38–45 (uncertainty over law regulating demonstrations); and *Bązkowski and Others v Poland* 2007-VI, paras 69–73 (determinations by domestic courts that the interference was not 'lawful'). The Court may on occasion decide to address solely the 'necessity' question and thereby avoid determining whether an interference has been 'prescribed by law': see eg *Christian Democratic People's Party v Moldova* 2006-II, paras 71–78 (temporary prohibition on a political party on grounds considered unjustifiable, including lack of prior authorisation for meetings as required by a statute initially considered unclear, but in any event failure to seek prior approval could not justify prohibition: violation).

2   *Stankov and the United Macedonian Organisation Ilinden v Bulgaria* 2001-IX, at para 107. See also *Freedom and Democracy Party (ÖZDEP) v Turkey* [GC] 1999-VIII, para 37.

3   *Gerger v Turkey* [GC] (8 July 1999), para 46.

Notification requirements

7.121 'Blanket' prohibitions are inherently suspect, and call for close scrutiny. In *Christians against Racism and Fascism v United Kingdom*, the Commission considered a blanket prohibition order which had been imposed on all forms of procession. The question of proportionality was tackled by considering first whether the security and public order reasons justified the prohibition, and then whether the same ends could have been achieved by less onerous alternatives. In the circumstances, the order was considered to have been reasonable[1]. However, a requirement to seek authorisation for an assembly in advance is not in itself incompatible with Article 11, 'if only in order that the authorities may be in a position to ensure the peaceful nature of a meeting' and thus to protect the public as the demonstrations may be likely to annoy or to give offence; further, it is expected that organisers of demonstrations, 'as actors in the democratic process, should respect the rules governing that process by complying with the regulations in force'[2]. On the other hand, notice periods that do not allow for relatively spontaneous protest may be considered unreasonable[3].

1   8440/78 *Christians against Racism and Fascism v United Kingdom* (1980) DR 21, 138. For another example of restrictions upon religious gatherings, see *Barankevich v Russia* (26 July 2007), paras 28–35 (religious service of evangelical Christian group prohibited as likely to lead to discontent: violation). Protest promoting tolerance calls for particular protection: *Alekseyev v Russia* 2010-..., paras 71–88 (repeated refusals to permit 'gay pride' parades on public order grounds following receipt of petitions opposing the marches and the making of statements by local officials indicating no such parade would ever be permitted: violation of Art 11 on account of decisions based upon the basis of prevailing moral values of the majority and in the absence of measures to assess public safety risks or of the prosecution of those making threats of violence, the purpose of the parades being to promote respect for human rights).

2   *Rai and Evans v United Kingdom* (dec) 2009-... (conviction for staging an unauthorised demonstration in Whitehall, a 'designated area' requiring prior authorisation in terms of the

Serious Organised Crime and Police Act 2005: inadmissible, as the interference was proportionate). See also *Selvanayagam v United Kingdom* (dec) (12 December 2002) (breach of injunction against animal rights' protestor involved in peaceful protests: inadmissible under Arts 10 and 11 as applicant had breached a properly obtained restraining order instead of challenging the order through appellate proceedings); *Ziliberberg v Moldova* (dec) (4 May 2004) (requirement to obtain authorisation for a demonstration not incompatible with Art 11 and the sanction imposed was strictly for this and and at the lower end of the range of penalties: inadmissible); and *Oya Ataman v Turkey* 2006-XIV, para 37), discussed at para **7.122** below; cf 25522/94, *Rai and Others v United Kingdom*, (6 April 1995), DR 81-A, 146). See also the domestic cases of *Blum v Director of Public Prosecutions* [2006] EWHC 3209 (Admin) and *Mayor of London v Hall* [2011] 1 WLR 504, discussed at para **7.124** below.

3   *Bukta and Others v Hungary* 2007-IX, paras 33–39 (three days' notice required of a demonstration in a case where protestors only had one day's notice of a political event – the visit of the prime minister – provoking the demonstration: violation). Cf *Rai and Evans v United Kingdom* (dec) 2009-… (demonstration concerned an ongoing event, the British involvement in Iraq, and notification time-limits had not been an obstacle to assembly).

The policing of demonstrations

7.122 Action taken by the authorities in respect of a protest (whether previously authorised or not) must be proportionate, and excessive use of force will fail this test. In *Oya Ataman v Turkey,* for example, an entirely peaceful human rights protest involving some 50 people in a park had been broken up by police on the ground that the demonstration was unlawful as prior notification had not been given. The Court, in deciding that the response had been disproportionate, reiterated that the authorities must show a certain degree of tolerance towards peaceful gatherings[1]. As well as this 'tolerance', authorities must also take practical steps to ensure that its demonstrations pass off peacefully by protecting protestors from counter-demonstrators[2].

1   *Oya Ataman v Turkey* 2006-XIV, paras 33–44. See also *Bukta and Others v Hungary* 2007-IX, paras 31–39 (dispersal of assembly called at short notice notice and in absence of due notice to the authorities; violation, since dispersal solely upon this ground in the circumstances was a disproportionate response); *Balçýk and Others* (29 November 2007), paras 45–54 at para 52: 'where demonstrators do not engage in acts of violence, it is important for the public authorities to show a certain degree of tolerance towards peaceful gatherings'. See also *Samüt Karabulut v Turkey* (27 January 2009), paras 31–44 (use of excessive force against a peaceful demonstration by a human rights organisation: violation of Art 11, and in respect of force used during apprehension, of Art 3). Cf *Cisse and Others v France* 2002-II, paras 47–54 (action taken on health and sanitation grounds against occupation by illegal immigrants of church but not at the request of the church authorities: no violation); *Çiloğlu and Others v Turkey* (6 March 2007) (police action to break up sit-in on public highway which had taken place weekly for three years: no violation, the protest clearly regularly disrupted traffic, and the protestors had achieved their goal of alerting the public to their grievance); and *Rai and Evans v United Kingdom* (dec) 2009-… (demonstration ended in a 'reasonable and calm manner' by police).

2   *Plattform "Ärzte für das Leben" v Austria* (1988) A 139, discussed at para **7.118** above.

Sanctions

7.123 The imposition of sanctions for taking part in a protest can call for scrutiny of their proportionality, particularly if these involve criminal sanctions[1]. In *Ezelin v France*, an office-bearer of an association of lawyers had taken part in a duly authorised protest during which offensive comments had been directed by other participants at the police and also made about the judiciary. He had been disciplined for having neither disassociated himself from the disorder nor having expressed disapproval. For the Court, although the sanctions imposed were minimal, they were considered disproportionate since the applicant had not committed any blameworthy act, the Court observing that even lawyers should not be discouraged 'for fear of disciplinary sanctions, from making clear their beliefs'[2].

---

1   See eg *Rai and Evans v United Kingdom* (dec) 2009-... (opportunity had been given to disband without the imposition of any sanction, and the sanctions actually imposed were not severe: inadmissible).

2   *Ezelin v France* (1991) A 202, paras 37–41, 51–53 at para 52.

Decisions of the domestic courts on whether interferences with assembly meet the requirements of Article 11(2)

7.124 The impact of the Human Rights Act upon the exercise of discretionary powers at common law to take action to deal with an apprehended breach of the public peace was considered in the case of *R (Laporte) v Chief Constable of Gloucestershire Constabulary*. In this case, protestors heading in coaches to a demonstration at a military base had been stopped by police officers and forcibly escorted back to London. The House of Lords held that the actions of the police had not been authorised by domestic law, and that the interference therefore failed to meet the test of 'prescribed by law'; further, the action had in any event been disproportionate, for while it might have been reasonable to have considered that some of the protestors might have intended to cause damage, less onerous alternatives had been available to the police to deal with any such threat[1]. The case is perhaps the clearest example of the courts' willingness to insist that any interference with democratic protest is subjected to tests of necessity and proportionality. The prosecution and conviction, on a charge of breach of the peace, of a protester who obstructed a public road was on the other hand consistent with Article 11(2)[2].

The prosecution and conviction of persons who took part in a demonstration in Parliament Square and Whitehall without the necessary statutory authorisation (which cannot be withheld, but may be granted subject to conditions) was upheld in the case of *Blum v Director of Public Prosecutions*[3]. In *Mayor of London v Hall*, it was accepted that the defendants' desire to express their views in Parliament Square in the form of their exclusive long-term occupation of part of the square as a camp, in breach of the applicable byelaws and in breach of property rights, fell within the scope of Articles 10 and 11. The byelaws, which envisaged demonstrations, speeches, camping, placards and the like being permitted in Parliament Square, subject to the mayor's consent, did not violate Article 11. The removal of the defendants' camp, after they had occupied the area in question for over two months, was justified for the protection of the rights and freedoms of others (including others who wanted to demonstrate in the same area, and members of the public who wanted to visit the area in question for other purposes), the protection of health (since the camp had no running water or toilet facilities) and the prevention of crime (since there was evidence of criminal damage). On the other hand, an individual demonstrator who had separately pitched a tent on a very small area of the square, and in whose case there was no suggestion of interference with the rights of other members of the public or of criminal damage, was held to be in a different position, and to require separate consideration[4].

1   *R (Laporte) v Chief Constable of Gloucestershire Constabulary* [2007] 2 AC 105. Earlier case law did not as clearly reflect the application of such principles: see eg *Silverton v Gravett* (19 October 2001, unreported) QBD (the prohibitions on harassment imposed by legislation and common law constituted a justifiable restriction on animal rights activists under Arts 10 and 11). Cf *R (Gillan) v Metropolitan Police Commissioner* [2006] 2 AC 307 where police stop and search powers under the Terrorism Act 2000 were held to meet the test of legal certainty as required by Arts 10(2) and 11(2). The Strasbourg Court subsequently held that there had been a breach of Art 8: *Gillan and Quinton v United Kingdom* (12 January 2010), discussed at para **6.104** above.

2   *Jones v Carnegie* 2004 JC 136. Cf Case B 1034/03, [2005] EuGRZ 337, [2005] EuroCLY 247 [Austria] (blanket ban on Nazi organisations and assemblies seeking to proclaim national socialism could be justified).

3   *Blum v Director of Public Prosecutions* [2006] EWHC 3209 (Admin). The Strasbourg Court rejected a subsequent complaint in respect of the same circumstances as being manifestly ill-founded: *Rai and Evans v United Kingdom* (dec) 2009.

4   *Mayor of London v Hall* [2011] 1 WLR 504.

Freedom of association

7.125 Freedom of association[1] involves a general right or liberty of individuals 'to join without interference by the state in association in order to attain various ends'[2] (including social and cultural ends[3]), and thus an 'association' is a more formal or organised concept than an 'assembly'[4]. Both the importance of freedom of association and its wide scope were highlighted in *Bączkowski and Others v Poland* thus:

'While in the context of Article 11 the Court has often referred to the essential role played by political parties in ensuring pluralism and democracy, associations formed for other purposes are also important to the proper functioning of democracy. For pluralism is also built on genuine recognition of, and respect for, diversity and the dynamics of cultural traditions, ethnic and cultural identities, religious beliefs and artistic, literary and socio-economic ideas and concepts. The harmonious interaction of persons and groups with varied identities is essential for achieving social cohesion. It is only natural that, where a civil society functions in a healthy manner, the participation of citizens in the democratic process is to a large extent achieved through belonging to associations in which they may integrate with each other and pursue common objectives collectively.'[5]

The scope of the freedom does not, however, extend to any right merely to be in the company of others[6], let alone to insist upon the right to join an association against the association's wishes[7]. More crucially, it does not apply to institutions with a public law nature which pursue public interests. In *Le Compte, Van Leuven and De Meyere v Belgium*, for example, a statutory body charged with the professional regulation of medical practitioners through administrative, disciplinary and rule-making means was considered not to be an 'association' covered by Article 11[8].

---

1   'Association' is given an autonomous meaning, and the domestic legal system's classification has only relative value and constitutes no more than a starting-point: *Chassagnou and Others v France* [GC] 1999-III, paras 99–102.

2   6094/73, *Association X v Sweden* (1978) DR 9, 5.

3   See eg *Grande Oriente d'Italia de Palazzo Giustiniani v Italy (no 1)* 2001-VIII (freemasons); *Sidiropoulos and Others v Greece* 1998-IV (cultural association known as 'Home of Macedonian Civilisation'); and *Koretskyy and Others v Ukraine* (3 April 2008) (environmental group). For discussion of trade unions, see para **7.132** below.

4   Gomien, Harris and Zwaak *Law and Practice of the European Convention on Human Rights and the European Social Charter* (1996) p 304.

5   *Bączkowski and Others v Poland* 2007-VI, at para 62.

6   Cf 8317/78, *McFeely v United Kingdom* (1980) DR 20, 44 (prisoner held in solitary confinement could not rely upon application of Art 11 to claim to 'association'). For domestic consideration, see *Re Section Française de l'Observatoire International des Prisons* [2005] EurCLY 1704 [France] (right of access by MPs to prisons was for protecting human dignity of prisoners, not for holding political meetings with prisoners).

7   10550/83, *Cheall v United Kingdom* (1985) DR 42, 178 (the right to join a trade union could not be interpreted as conferring a general right to join the union of one's choice irrespective of the rules of the union). This judgment was followed in *Royal Society for the Prevention of Cruelty to Animals v Attorney General* [2002] 1 WLR 448.

8   *Le Compte, Van Leuven and De Meyere v Belgium* (1981) A 43, paras 64–65 (establishment of the professional body did not prevent doctors from joining other associations, and thus the obligation to be subject to the body in no way limited Art 11 rights); *Bota v Romania* (dec) (12 October 2004) ('Union of Romanian Lawyers' was a public law association pursuing aims serving the public good, and thus not an association covered by Art 11). Cf *Sigurður A Sigurjónsson v Iceland* (1993) A 264, paras 31–37 (taxicab drivers' association considered predominantly a private law organisation: compulsion to join the association against the applicant's wishes gave rise to an Art 11 issue).

Interferences with the freedom of association

7.126 Article 11 in respect of the right of association has both a positive and a negative aspect: protection for associations and their members; and protection against compulsion to join an association. The positive aspect was considered briefly in *Vogt v Germany*, where a teacher had been dismissed from her post because of her failure to disassociate herself from a political party, membership of which was considered incompatible with her office as a civil servant. This was considered to be an interference with Article 11(1)[1]. The negative aspect was at issue in *Young, James and Webster v United Kingdom*, where three employees of British Rail had been dismissed after the introduction of an obligation to join a trade union. The European Court of Human Rights accepted that even assuming that the negative aspect of Article 11 does not carry as much weight as the positive right to associate, the threat of dismissal and consequent loss of livelihood were serious interferences which went to the very heart of the essence of the guarantee, particularly since the compulsion also gave rise to considerations under Articles 9 and 10[2]. Article 11 thus protects individuals against any abuse of a trade union's dominant position in the workplace[3].

1   *Vogt v Germany* (1995) A 323, para 64 (matter ultimately disposed of under Art 10: see para **7.89** above). See too 11002/84, *Van der Heijden v Netherlands* (1985) DR 41, 264 (termination of employment on account of membership of a political party was considered justified for the protection of the rights of others since the party concerned had views contrary to the welfare of immigrants which the employer sought to promote).

2   *Young, James and Webster v United Kingdom* (1981) A 44, paras 55 and 57 (but (at para 55) compulsion to join a trade union 'may not always be contrary to the Convention'). See too *Sibson v United Kingdom* (1993) A 258-A, paras 28–30 (applicant had no objection to trade union membership on the grounds of any conviction, no closed shop agreement was in place, and dismissal was not inevitable; no violation established); and *Sigurður A Sigurjónsson v Iceland* (1993) A 264, noted at para **7.125** fn 7 above.

3   15533/89, *Englund and Others v Sweden* (1994) DR 77, 10.

Recognition of legal personality

7.127 There may also be an interference with the right of association through failure to recognise legal personality or refusal to grant registration[1]. This may call into question a state's commitment to the promotion of pluralist views and democratic debate. In *Sidiropoulos and Others v Greece*, some 50 individuals living in northern Greece had sought to establish a cultural association called 'Home of Macedonian Civilisation' which the domestic courts had refused to register for several reasons including the prevention of disorder and protection of the state's cultural identity. This refusal gave rise to an issue in terms of Article 11[2]. In particular, only in the most exceptional case is it permissible to refuse registration to a political party[3]. Similar principles apply in respect of religious associations[4].

1   *Sidiropoulos and Others v Greece* 1998-IV, para 40: 'that citizens should be able to form a legal entity in order to act collectively in a field of mutual interest is one of the most important aspects of the right to freedom of association, without which that right would be deprived of any meaning'. See also *Partidul Comunistilor (Nepeceristi) et Ungureanu v Romania* 2005-I, paras 54–55 (refusal to register a party whose programme distanced itself from abuses of former Communist Party, advocated democracy and contained no suggestion of violence to achieve political aims: violation); and *Koretskyy and Others v Ukraine* (3 April 2008), paras 43–58 (refusal to register environmental group as articles of association were not in conformity with 'the legislation of Ukraine': violation, as domestic law allowed too broad an interpretation

and thus the interference was not 'prescribed by law'). For discussion of refusal to register religious groups, see para **7.38** above; and *Moscow Branch of the Salvation Army v Russia* 2006-XI. However, refusal of registration because of the association's name being considered misleading will not result in a violation: *Apeh Üldözötteinek Szövetsege, Ivanyi, Róth and Szerdaheli v Hungary* 2000-X, paras 30–44 (association refused registration in the name of 'Alliance of [National Tax Authority's] Persecutees' as this was considered defamatory and to prevent any impression that the association was linked to the tax authority: case considered under Art 6). See also *Gorzelik and Others v Poland* [GC] 2004-I, paras 97–106 (refusal to register 'Union of People of Silesian Nationality' unless name and memorandum of association changed to omit references to Silesian 'nationality' had not restricted freedom of association *per se*, and authorities had been entitled to refuse to create a legal entity which would have enjoyed special status under electoral law as the contested interference met a 'pressing social need' and was not disproportionate).

2   *Sidiropoulos and Others v Greece* 1998-IV, para 31 (interference was a disproportionate response to the legitimate aim of protecting national security and prevention of disorder). But compare decisions of the Commission which appear to take a less liberal approach: 8652/79, *X v Austria* (1981) DR 26, 89 (the dissolution by the state of two organisations intended to provide support for the 'Moon' sect (or 'Moonies') was not a violation of ECHR, Art 11); 9905/82, *A Association and H v Austria* (1984) DR 36, 187 (prohibition of meeting supporting reunification with Germany necessary for national security given the state's international obligations to respect neutrality); and 23892/94, *ACREP v Portugal* (1995) DR 83, 57 (association seeking to promote Portuguese monarchy and constitutional order of 1838 dissolved by judicial decision: inadmissible in view of the state's margin of appreciation in determining whether this was necessary to prevent disorder).

3   *Linkov v Czech Republic* (7 December 2006), paras 39–45, at paras 34–46 (refusal to register Liberal Party as one of its goals – to break 'the legal continuity with totalitarian regimes' – was considered unconstitutional as seeking to destroy the democratic foundations of the state: violation, as the party had not sought to justify the use of violence, its registration had been refused even before it had undertaken any activities, and indeed the legislature had declared that communism was fundamentally undemocratic). Cf *Kalifatstaat v Germany* (dec) (11 December 2006) (prohibition of association seeking to establish an Islamic state based on sharia law: inadmissible).

4   *Jehovah's Witnesses of Moscow v Russia* 2010-…, paras 170–182 (refusal to re-register a religious association which had existed for many years without breach of any relevant domestic law or regulation: the reasons for refusing re-registration had to be particularly weighty and compelling, but not only were the grounds invoked for refusing re-registration without lawful basis, the authorities had failed to act in good faith and had neglected their duty of neutrality and impartiality towards the religious association: violation of Art 11 in the light of Art 9).

Status of 'victim'

7.128 An association itself can claim to be the victim of a violation of Article 11 in its own right. In *Grande Oriente d'Italia de Palazzo Giustiniani v Italy*, an association of a number of Italian masonic lodges challenged the adoption of a law requiring candidates for public office to declare that they were not freemasons. The Court accepted that the association was protected by Article 11, and since the measure could well have resulted in a loss of membership and prestige, there had been an 'interference'[1]. However, the article cannot be taken as requiring an association to be given title and interest to sue in a legal action at domestic level where otherwise it would not be recognised as having standing[2].

1   *Grande Oriente d'Italia de Palazzo Giustiniani v Italy (no 1)* 2001-VIII, paras 15–16. This
     decision seems to suggest that a low threshold test is required to establish 'victim' status for
     an association under Art 11. The Court held (paras 24–26 and 30–32) that the measure was
     deemed disproportionate and thus not 'necessary in a democratic society'; and further, that it
     did not properly fall within the category of lawful restriction on the exercise of rights by
     members of the administration of the state'. Cf *Salaman v United Kingdom* (dec) (15 June
     2000) (trial judge and an appeal court judge had not disclosed the fact of their membership of
     the freemasons in a case where one of the parties was also a freemason: membership of the
     freemasons was not in itself enough to cast doubt over impartiality as required by Art 6, and
     the applicant had not provided any further evidence to substantiate his fears: inadmissible).

2   9234/81, *X Association v Germany* (1981) DR 26, 270.

Assessing whether an interference with the right of association meets the requirements of Article 11(2)

7.129 Under Article 11(2), any interference must seek to achieve one of the
listed legitimate state interests, be prescribed by law, and meet the 'necessary in
a democratic society' test. The first test will not pose any difficulty to a state, as
inevitably the aim of the interference will involve public order or national security.
The 'prescribed by law' test assesses the quality of domestic law through the
foreseeability of an interference[1]. Again, the ultimate question for the Court will
be the 'necessity' of the interference. In applying the test of 'necessary in a
democratic society', association is accorded particular protection in the
maintenance of pluralist opinion and democracy, and thus the exceptions recognised
by paragraph (2) have to be construed strictly. The conclusion that Article 11 has
been violated may not be too difficult in certain cases. For example, a requirement
upon citizens who were members of an association to obtain executive approval
to participate in any meeting abroad was held to amount to in reality a general
surveillance measure which could not be deemed to be justified by national security
or public safety grounds[2].

1   See paras **3.62–3.72** above. See also *Djavit An v Turkey* 2003-III, paras 58–69 (refusal to allow
     the applicant to cross the 'green line' in Cyprus to take part in meetings of an bi-communal
     association: violation, there being no law regulating the issue of permits and the issue not being
     limited to the right of movement); and *Koretskyy and Others v Ukraine* (3 April 2008), paras 43–
     58 (domestic law too broadly worded and thus the interference was not 'prescribed by law').

2   *Izmir Savaş Karşitlari Derneði and Others v Turkey* (2 March 2006), paras 31–39 (members
     of association of conscientious objectors); and *Association of Citizens Radko and Paunkovski
     v 'the Former Yugoslav Republic of Macedonia'* 2009-..., paras 68–78 (dissolution of public
     association considered to be contrary to the Macedonian national identity: violation).

Interferences with rights of political parties

7.130 Where action is taken against a political party or restrictions imposed such
as to funding[1], particular scrutiny is required. Here, Article 11 is read in the light
of Article 3 of Protocol no 1. In *United Communist Party of Turkey and Others
v Turkey*, the applicant association had been dissolved by the country's constitutional

court on the grounds that the party had called itself 'communist' contrary to domestic law, and further that the party was seeking to promote the division of the state by encouraging Kurdish separatism. On the first point the Court considered that choice of name could never in itself justify dissolution without other relevant and sufficient reasons; on the second, there could not be any justification for such a step simply because the party sought to stimulate public debate in the political arena. A principal characteristic of democracy is 'the possibility it offers of resolving a country's problems through dialogue, without recourse to violence, even where they are irksome'. Nor was it appropriate for the state to seek to rely upon Article 17 since the party could not be said to have had any responsibility for promoting terrorism or seeking the destruction of the rights of others[2]. In contrast, in *Refah Partisi (The Welfare Party) and Others v Turkey*, the Grand Chamber unanimously ruled that the dissolution by the constitutional court of the Welfare Party, at the time the largest single party in parliament, had not resulted in a violation of Article 11. Steps had been taken against the party because of its objectives which sought the establishment of the 'sharia', a system of Islamic law, and a theocratic government in violation of the state's strictly secular constitution. In scrutinising the 'necessity' of the interference, the Court considered that three particular issues were relevant: whether any plausible evidence existed that the party posed any imminent risk to democracy, whether the acts and statements of the leadership of the party were imputable to the party as a whole, and whether any such statements imputable to the party provided a clear picture of a society advocated by the party incompatible with a ~'democratic society'. In determining that a pressing social need for the dissolution had indeed existed, the Grand Chamber noted the real potential the party had to gain power through electoral success. Statements concerning political issues made in particular by three of its leading members could incontestably be attributed to the party. Further, a regime based upon sharia law is so incompatible with Convention values and 'democratic society' since pluralism has no place in such a system, application of sharia private law rules to the Muslim population goes beyond the freedom of individuals to observe the precepts of their religion, and the party had not disassociated itself from repeated references to the 'legitimate' use of force in order to achieve political power. In any event, the prohibition from holding political office had only been temporary and had been imposed on a handful of its leadership and had not affected its other Members of Parliament[3].

1   See *Basque National Party – Iparralde Regional Organisation v France* 2007-VII, paras 45–52 (statutory ban on financing of political party by a foreign political party: no violation, the Court noting Committee of Ministers Recommendation Rec (2003) 4).

2   *United Communist Party of Turkey and Others v Turkey* 1998-I, paras 51–61 at para 57. See too *Socialist Party and Others v Turkey* 1998-III, paras 41–54 at 47 (the fact that a separatist programme 'is considered incompatible with the current principles and structures of the Turkish State does not make it incompatible with the rules of democracy'). Cf 6741/74, *X v Italy* (1976) DR 5, 83 (repression of groups seeking to restore the fascist party may be considered necessary in a democratic society); *Freedom and Democracy Party (ÖZDEP) v Turkey* [GC] 1999-VIII, paras 37–48 (the Court could find nothing in the party's programme which could be taken to constitute a call to violence or rejection of constitutional principles, and the dissolution of the party was thus deemed a violation of Art 11); and *Yazar and Others*

v Turkey 2002-II, paras 52–60 (dissolution of party supporting Kurdish cause but not promoting terrorism or otherwise undermining democratic regime: violation). Cf *WP and Others v Poland* (dec) 2004-VII (prohibition on establishment of anti-Semitic organisation justified under Art 17).

3   *Refah Partisi (The Welfare Party) and Others v Turkey* [GC] 2003–II, paras 86–105. See also Chamber judgment (31 July 2001), paras 42–52, 63–83 (means used to seek to secure political ends had to be entirely lawful and democratic; and proposed changes had themselves to be compatible with fundamental democratic principles, and thus political parties which sought change through violent means or whose political aims were incompatible with democracy or sought to suppress democratic rights and freedoms could not rely upon the Convention; cf the dissenting judgment which stresses the importance of pluralism and the lack of any pressing danger to the Turkish state posed by the party). See also *Herri Batasuna and Batasuna v Spain* 2009-…, paras 84–95 (dissolution of political parties with links to ETA, a terrorist organisation: no violation, the social model that was envisaged and advocated through acts and speeches was in contradiction with the concept of a 'democratic society'). See Harvey 'Militant Democracy and the European Convention on Human Rights' (2004) 29 ELRev 407. For domestic discussion, see *Centre Pour 'Egalité de Chances v Vlaams Blok* [2004] JT 856, [2005] EuroCLY 1690 [Belgium] (no need to show that anti-racism legislation was being applied in a proportionate manner, merely that it was being applied lawfully to any organisation (including a political party) that manifestly instigated racial hatred).

Freedom of conscience

7.131 Article 11 must also be read in the light of other guarantees such as freedom of conscience under Article 9, and thus situations where domestic law compels an individual to join an association which is contrary to his own convictions may give rise to a violation. In such circumstances, the European Court of Human Rights will consider whether a fair balance has been struck between individual and collective interests[1]. In *Young, James and Webster v United Kingdom*, the Court noted various surveys and official reports which indicated that trade unions could still have fulfilled their purpose in furthering their members' interests without compelling non-union employees to join, thus helping establish that the dismissal of the three employees had been a disproportionate measure[2].

1   Cf *Chassagnou and Others v France* [GC] 1999-III, paras 109–117 (the obligatory membership of hunting association against the convictions of the applicant which also involved the transfer of rights over members' land to allow the hunting association to attain its objects went well beyond achieving a fair balance between conflicting interests and could not be considered as proportionate to the aim pursued; the Court (paras 118–121) also established a violation of Art 11 taken in conjunction with Art 14). See further para **8.32** below. See also *Bota v Romania* (dec) (12 October 2004) (establishment of lawyers' association contrary to legislative prohibition: inadmissible).

2   *Young, James and Webster v United Kingdom* (1981) A 44, paras 63–65.

Trade unions

7.132 Article 11(1) makes specific reference to the 'right to form and to join trade unions'[1]. A trade union must be free to determine conditions for membership, and thus to expel individuals advocating opinions incompatible with its objectives providing the trade union acts in a reasonable manner in this regard[2]. The concluding words 'for the protection of his interests' imply that trade unions not only must be permitted[3] but also in some manner be allowed to express the interests of their members[4]. This may be achieved through the use of collective agreements[5] or permitting the right to strike[6] (although Article 11 cannot be read as requiring recognition of the right to strike in domestic law)[7].

Restrictions 'that affect the essential elements of trade-union freedom, without which that freedom would become devoid of substance' are not acceptable[8]. Withdrawal of legal personality of a trade union will thus constitute an interference with Article 11[9]. In this area, the Grand Chamber in *Demir and Baykara v Turkey* has recently recognised that the right to bargain collectively is 'one of the essential elements' of the right to form and to join a trade union, thus revising earlier case law on this point[10]. Further, there may be an obligation to make some special provision for trade union representatives[11], and to provide protection for individuals against anti-union discrimination in the workplace[12]. However, the right of association may also involve recognition of a right of *non*-association which provides protection against compulsion to join any association, as in the case of *Young, James and Webster v United Kingdom* discussed above[13]. In *Sørensen and Rasmussen v Denmark*, the Grand Chamber considered whether an individual could be deemed to have renounced his negative right (that is, not to be forced to join a trade union) by accepting a contract of employment where membership is a precondition. The first applicant had wished to join a union other than the one stipulated, while the second applicant claimed he had only joined the specified union in order to obtain employment, even although he did not agree with the union's political stance. The Court took into account the special features of the Danish labour market in which individual and collective agreements regulated the relationships between employers and employees, but also noted that there was 'little support' now in Europe for 'closed shop agreements', and that their use was 'not an indispensable tool for the enjoyment of trade union rights[14].

1   In consequence, a trade union may qualify as a 'victim' for the purposes of Art 11: *Federation of Offshore Workers' Trade Unions and Others v Norway* (dec) 2002-VI. Cf 6094/73, *Association X v Sweden* (1977) DR 9, 5 (students' union not a 'trade union').

2   *Associated Society of Locomotive Engineers and Firemen (ASLEF) v United Kingdom* 2007-III, paras 47–53 (determination by Employment Appeal Tribunal that the trade union was prohibited from expelling a member on account of his membership of the BNP: violation).

3   Cf *Tüm Haber Sen and Çinar v Turkey* 2006-II, paras 35–40 (absolute prohibition on civil servants from joining a trade union had not been shown to have met a pressing social need). Article 11 includes the right for a trade union to draw up its own rules: 10550/83, *Cheall v United Kingdom* (1985) DR 42, 178.

4   *Wilson, National Union of Journalists and Others* 2002-V, para 44. See also 7361/76, *Trade Union X v Belgium* (1978) DR 14, 40. Cf 7990/77, *X v United Kingdom* (1981) DR 24, 57 (no duty upon prison authorities to assist a prisoner on a pre-release employment scheme to have his trade union rights respected).

5   *National Union of Belgian Police v Belgium* (1975) A 19, paras 38 and 39; *Swedish Engine Drivers' Union v Sweden* (1976) A 20, paras 39 and 40.

6   *Schmidt and Dahlström v Sweden* (1976) A 21, para 36 (noting the right to strike contained in the European Social Charter).

7   See 28910/95, *National Association of Teachers in Further and Higher Education v United Kingdom* (1998) DR 93, 63 (the right to strike is not expressly provided for in the ECHR, and may be regulated by domestic law; and a requirement that a trade union disclose the names of its members entitled to vote on whether to take industrial action was not in the circumstances a disproportionate interference with Art 11 rights); *UNISON v United Kingdom* (dec) 2002-I (court injunction prohibiting strike action after failing to obtain assurances that employees' rights would be maintained with the transfer of business activities to a private company: inadmissible, as Art 11 does not include the right to strike); and *Federation of Offshore Workers' Trade Unions and Others v Norway* (dec) 2002-VI.

8   *Demir and Baykara v Turkey* [GC] 2008-…, at para 144.

9   *Demir and Baykara v Turkey* [GC] 2008-…, paras 117–127 and 140–170 (refusal to accord legal personality in absence of evidence of threat to society and retrospective annulment of collective bargaining agreement with local authority after it had been in force for three years: violation).

10   *Demir and Baykara v Turkey* [GC] 2008-…, paras 153–154. For earlier case law, see *Schmidt and Dahlström v Sweden* (1976) A 21, para 34; *Syndicat Suédois des Travailleurs des Transports v Sweden* (dec) (30 November 2004) (no guarantee for a trade union that a longstanding collective agreement would be maintained indefinitely); and *UNISON v United Kingdom* (dec) 2002-I (Art 11 does not require an employer enter into or remain in any particular collective bargaining agreement).

11   Cf *Sanchez Navajas* (dec) 2001-VI (deduction of salary for time spent by a trade union representative on study of new legislation concerning trade union elections on the basis that the study was to further the representative's interests rather than those of members of the union: while it was possible to deduce from Art 11 when read with Art 28 of the (revised) European Social Charter a limited right of trade union representatives to such facilities to allow the effective discharge of their union responsibilities, in this case it could not be shown that the study had been strictly necessary, and non-payment of salary did not affect the substance of the right guaranteed by Art 15: inadmissible).

12   *Danilenkov and Others v Russia* 2009-…, paras 12–123 at para 123: '[Art 11] obviously includes a right not to be discriminated against for choosing to avail oneself of the right to be protected by a trade union, given also that Article 14 forms an integral part of each of the Articles laying down rights and freedoms whatever their nature. Thus, the totality of the measures implemented to safeguard the guarantees of Article 11 should include protection against discrimination on the ground of trade union membership.… [In consequence] States are required under Articles 11 and 14 of the Convention to set up a judicial system that ensures real and effective protection.'

13   See para **7.126** above.

14   *Sørensen and Rasmussen v Denmark* [GC] 2006-I, paras 59–77 at para 75.

Members of the armed forces, police, and civil servants

7.133 Article 11(2) further provides that lawful restrictions may be placed on the exercise of these rights by 'members of the armed forces, of the police or the administration of the state'. The categories, particularly the latter, should be interpreted narrowly[1]. For example, in *Grande Oriente d'Italia de Palazzo Giustiniani v Italy*, the Court could not accept that the adoption of a law requiring candidates for public office to declare that they were not freemasons involved the imposition of lawful restrictions on members of the administration of the state since the categories subject to the requirement went beyond the narrow meaning of the term[2]. However, this provision will imply a wide margin of appreciation for states if national security considerations exist. In *Council of Civil Service Unions v United Kingdom*, where the right of employees at the government's communications monitoring centre to join a trade union had been removed, the Commission considered that there had been no violation of Article 11. 'Administration of the state' was to be read in the context of references to the armed forces and police, and the Commission was satisfied that the employees in question could be considered to fall within the category covered by the second sentence of paragraph (2). 'Restrictions' could also include a complete prohibition; and even if the qualification 'lawful' included not only the requirement of having some basis in domestic law but also protection against arbitrariness, both of these conditions had been met. In any case, states had to be given 'a wide discretion when securing the protection of their national security'[3]. Similarly, in *Rekvényi v Hungary*, a general constitutional ban on political activities by police officers and members of the security services which also involved a prohibition on membership of any political party was accepted as having the intended aim of depoliticising these services and thereby helping consolidate pluralist democracy. The Court took particular account of the recent history of the state which had only recently emerged from a totalitarian system of government in which the direct commitment of police officers to the ruling party's values had been expected[4].

1   Cf *Vogt v Germany* (1995) A 323, paras 66–68 at para 67 ('administration of the state' to be interpreted narrowly; issue of whether teacher who was civil servant included avoided in the particular case).

2   *Grande Oriente d'Italia de Palazzo Giustiniani v Italy (no 1)* 2001-VIII, paras 30–32.

3   11603/85 *Council of Civil Service Unions v United Kingdom* (1987) DR 50, 228, at 241. Cf 12719/87, *Frederiksen v Denmark* (1988) DR 56, 237 (payment of reasonable compensation for dismissal on account of trade union membership deprives the individual of status of 'victim').

4   *Rekvényi v Hungary* [GC] 1999-III, paras 58–62 (application concerned both Arts 10 and 11 (cf paras 46–50) and police officers could still articulate political opinions under Art 10 and thus the measure was not disproportionate). Cf *Enerjï Yapi-Yol Sen v Turkey* (21 April 2009), paras 31–34 (disciplinary action against civil servants following industrial action: violation).

Decisions of the domestic courts on whether interferences with association meet the requirements of Article 11(2)

7.134 Article 11(2) has been applied in a number of domestic cases concerned with freedom of association. In addition to those discussed above in the context of freedom of assembly, they have also concerned the proscription of organisations[1].

1   *R (Kurdistan Workers' Party) v Secretary of State for the Home Department* [2002] EWHC 644 (Admin).

ARTICLE 3 OF PROTOCOL NO 1: THE RIGHT TO FREE ELECTIONS

The scope of Article 3 of Protocol no 1

7.135 The Preamble to the ECHR acknowledges that the maintenance of justice and peace is dependent not only upon a shared understanding and observance of human rights, but also upon 'effective political democracy'[1]. Article 3 of Protocol no 1 complements other guarantees of thought, conscience and religion (Article 9), free expression (Article 10), and assembly and association (Article 11) in protecting political democracy by requiring that appointment to the legislature is by 'free' elections at 'reasonable intervals' through a 'secret ballot' and 'under conditions which will ensure the free expression of the opinion of the people'[2]. The right to vote is regarded by the Court as the 'active' element of the rights guaranteed by the provision (in contrast to the 'passive' nature of the right to stand as a candidate for election), and implies that exclusion of any groups or categories of the general population from exercising the franchise has to be reconcilable with the underlying purposes of the guarantee[3]. This provision initially was considered more as of symbolic importance in confirming the importance of institutional arrangements than as a provision which conferred individual rights[4], but it is now clear that this guarantee can be relied upon by individuals in a wide range of circumstances[5]. As the Grand Chamber has observed:

> '[the Court] has to satisfy itself that the conditions do not curtail the rights in question to such an extent as to impair their very essence and deprive them of their effectiveness; that they are imposed in pursuit of a legitimate aim; and that the means employed are not disproportionate. In particular, any conditions imposed must not thwart the free expression of the people in the choice of the legislature – in other words, they must reflect, or not run counter to, the concern to maintain the integrity and effectiveness of an electoral procedure aimed at identifying the will of the people through universal suffrage ... Any departure from the principle of universal suffrage risks undermining the democratic validity of the legislature thus elected and the laws it promulgates. Exclusion of any groups or categories of the general population must accordingly be reconcilable with the underlying purposes of Article 3 of Protocol No 1'[6].

1   See generally Council of Europe *Electoral Law* (2008). The promotion of democratic institutions is furthered by other Council of Europe bodies, and in particular by the European Commission for Democracy through Law ('the Venice Commission', the advisory body on constitutional matters) and by the Council for Democratic Elections which coordinates activities between the Venice Commission and the Parliamentary Assembly and the Congress of Local and Regional Authorities in election-monitoring. Guidelines, opinions and studies of the Venice Commission are available at: www.venice.coe.int.

2   *Ždanoka v Latvia* [GC] 2006–IV, para 115.

3   *Ždanoka v Latvia* [GC] 2006–IV, para 115.

4   See eg 1028/61, *X v Belgium* (1961) YB 4, 260; and 3321–3/67 and 3344/67, Greek case (1969) YB 12 at 179 (provision 'presupposes the existence of a representative legislature, elected at reasonable intervals'). But note that these rights are not 'civil' rights for the purposes of Art 6's guarantees of fair hearings: see para **5.24** above.

5   The first consideration by the Court is found in *Mathieu-Mohin and Clerfayt v Belgium* (1987) A 113. See for later Commission discussion 6745/74 and 6746/74, *W, X, Y and Z v Belgium* (1975) DR 2, 110; and 9267/81, *Moureaux and Others v Belgium* (1983) DR 33, 97. Up until 2009, 39 violations of Prot 1, Art 3 have been found. The majority have concerned Italy (15), followed by Turkey (5), Latvia (3) and the United Kingdom (3): European Court *Annual Report 2009* (2010), pp 150–151.

6   *Hirst v United Kingdom (no 2)* [GC] 2005-IX, at para 62.

7.136 The article primarily requires the discharge of positive obligations by states. In *Mathieu-Mohin and Clerfayt v Belgium*, the Court confirmed as inappropriate any suggestion that the article should be given a restrictive interpretation and rejected the argument that individual rights could not be derived from the provision. The 'inter-state colouring of the wording ... does not reflect any difference of substance from the other substantive clauses in the Convention and Protocols' and could be explained by the 'desire to give greater solemnity to the commitment undertaken and ... the fact that the primary obligation in the field concerned is not one of abstention or non-interference, as with the majority of the civil and political rights, but one of adoption by the state of positive measures to "hold" democratic elections'[1]. More recently, however, the Court has been called upon to rule upon denial of the franchise to prisoners[2] and to persons suffering from mental disabilities[3], and restrictions upon or refusal to allow individuals to stand as candidates in elections[4].

1   *Mathieu-Mohin and Clerfayt v Belgium* (1987) A 113, paras 48–54 at para 50.

2   Eg *Hirst v United Kingdom (no 2)* [GC] 2005-IX, discussed at para **7.142** below.

3   *Alajos Kiss v Hungary* 2010-..., paras 39–44, noted at para **7.141**, fn 8 below.

4   Eg *Ždanoka v Latvia* 2006-IV, discussed at para **7.137** below.

7.137 In interpreting the phrase 'effective political democracy', there is probably no implicit suggestion of the notion of the right to self-determination which is found in international law[1], although the court in *Incal v Turkey* did accept that Article 10 also protected expression which called for the dissolution of an existing state[2], and in *Tănase v Moldova*, the Grand Chamber also acknowledged that any requirement of loyalty to the state cannot be taken as precluding the ability of MPs to represent the views of any constituents wishing to pursue a political programme incompatible with 'current principles and structure'[3]. The provision is clearly closely related to safeguards for civic and political rights such as Articles 10 and 11. However, the particular textual formulation of the guarantee is phrased in collective and general terms in light of its particular relevance to a state's institutional order, in turn implying that its requirements are less stringent than those applied under Articles 8–11 of the Convention. Indeed, 'where an interference with Article 3 of Protocol No 1 is at issue the Court should not automatically adhere to the same criteria as those applied with regard to the interference permitted by the second paragraphs of Articles 8 to 11 of the Convention, and it should not necessarily base its conclusions under Article 3 of Protocol No 1 on the principles derived from the application of Articles 8–11 of the Convention'[4]. In *Ždanoka v*

Latvia, the Grand Chamber also noted that the concept of 'implied limitations' is of considerable importance in interpretation given that the provision is not limited by a specific list of legitimate aims but merely the requirement that state action is motivated by an end compatible with the principle of the rule of law and the general objectives of the Convention. In consequence, the Court does not apply the traditional tests of 'necessity' or 'pressing social need' but rather focuses on two criteria: 'whether there has been arbitrariness or a lack of proportionality, and whether the restriction has interfered with the free expression of the opinion of the people'[5].

1   Franck 'The Emerging Right to Democratic Governance' (1992) 86 AJIL 46.

2   *Incal v Turkey* 1998-IV, discussed at para **7.39** above. Similarly, the Court has found violations of Art 11 in respect of the dissolution of political parties which advocate the dissolution of a state using non-violent means: eg *United Communist Party of Turkey and Others v Turkey* 1998-I, discussed at para **7.130** above.

3   *Tănase v Moldova* [GC] 2010-..., at para 167.

4   *Ždanoka v Latvia* [GC] 2006–IV, para 115.

5   *Ždanoka v Latvia* [GC] 2006–IV, para 115.

Meaning of 'legislature'

7.138 The rights secured by Article 3 of Protocol no 1 apply in relation to the 'legislature', a term which is interpreted in the light of political institutions established by the constitution of each state[1]. The key question appears to be the level of law-making power entrusted to the institution: a 'legislature' must have the powers both to initiate legislation as well as to adopt it. Municipal councils cannot be considered as legislative bodies[2] but regional legislatures within a federal constitutional structure will so qualify[3]. In *Booth-Clibborn v United Kingdom,* the Commission had to consider whether English metropolitan county councils constituted 'legislatures' for the purposes of the Convention. Although they were able to make byelaws, this power was delegated by the national parliament which had complete control over the extent and nature of the councils' powers, and thus councils were not legislatures within the meaning of the Convention[4]. The guarantee is inapplicable to presidential elections[5].

1   6745/74 and 6746/74, *X, Y and Z v Belgium* (1975) DR 2, 110; 9267/81, *Moureaux and Others v Belgium* (1983) DR 33, 97. Cf 4982/71 *X v Austria* (1972) YB 15, 468 (compulsory voting did not constitute a violation of Art 9, even if presidential elections were covered).

2   5155/71, *X v United Kingdom* (1976) DR 6, 13. See also *Ahmed and Others v United Kingdom* 1998-VI, para 76 (no need to consider whether local government elections are covered by the provision).

3   7008/75, *X v Austria* (1976) DR 6, 120; 27311/95; *Jan Timke v Germany* (1995) DR 82, 158; 23450/94, *Polacco and Garofala v Italy* (1997) DR 90, 5; *Malarde v France* (dec) (5 September 2000).

4   11391/85, *Booth-Clibborn v United Kingdom* (1985) DR 43, 236.

5   *Guliyev v Azerbaijan* (dec) (27 May 2004); and *Paksas v Lithuania* [GC] (6 January 2011), para 72. See also *Sejdić and Finci v Bosnia and Herzegovina* [GC] 2009-..., discussed at paras **3.86** and **3.104** above.

Elections to the European Parliament

7.139 These principles have been applied to questions concerning elections to the European Parliament. In early decisions, the Commission considered that the drafters of the ECHR had only intended to cover elections to national legislatures, and also doubted whether in any case the European Parliament had the requisite powers and functions to qualify as a 'legislature': it was primarily an advisory body with only limited legislative authority[1]. However, the entry into force of the Single European Act 1986 enhanced the Parliament's status, as acknowledged by the Commission in *Fournier v France*[2]. The leading case is now *Matthews v United Kingdom* in which the Court was asked to consider whether Britain's failure to extend the right to vote in elections to the European Parliament to residents of Gibraltar raised any issue under this provision. The application also raised the wider question of whether states which were bound by the ECHR had positive responsibilities under this treaty in determining the manner in which they discharged their duties under EU law. EU law itself limited the franchise for European parliamentary elections, but the United Kingdom could have chosen to extend relevant EU legislation to become part of domestic law in Gibraltar. For the Court, since EU legislation can affect the population of Gibraltar 'in the same way as legislation which enters the domestic legal order ... there is no difference between European and domestic legislation', and thus the European Parliament fell to be considered as a 'legislature' on account of the supremacy of EU law over national law. No reason had been made out which could justify exclusion of the European Parliament from the scope of the guarantee simply 'on the ground that it is a supranational, rather than a purely domestic, representative organ'. Examination of the European Parliament's powers after the Maastricht Treaty of 1992 indicated that it was now 'sufficiently involved' both in legislative processes leading to the passage of certain EU legislation and also in the general democratic supervision of the activities of EU institutions to such an extent that it could be taken to constitute part of the 'legislature' of Gibraltar. Further, there was 'no reason why the United Kingdom should not be required to 'secure' the rights [under Article 1] ... in respect of European legislation, in the same way as those rights are required to be 'secured' in respect of purely domestic legislation'. The provision 'enshrines a characteristic of an effective political democracy', but there was no indication that steps had been taken to ensure the representation of the population of Gibraltar in the European Parliament. While the choice of electoral system is covered by a wide margin of appreciation, the 'very essence of the applicant's right to vote' had been completely denied leading to the conclusion that there has been a violation of Article 3 of Protocol no 1[3].

1   8364/78, *Lindsay and Others v United Kingdom* (1979) DR 15, 247; and 8612/79, *Alliance des*

Belges de la CEE v Belgium (1979) DR 15, 259 (question not resolved in either application); cf 11123/84, *Tête v France* (1987) DR 54, 52 (European Parliament could not yet be considered a 'legislature').

2   11406/85, *Fournier v France* (1988) DR 55, 130.

3   *Matthews v United Kingdom* [GC] 1999-I, paras 34–65 at paras 44 and 65.

Elections to the Scottish Parliament

7.140 Elections to the Scottish Parliament are covered by the provision. In *Smith v Scott*, it was accepted by both parties that the Scottish Parliament was a 'legislature' within the meaning of the provision[1], and in *Greens and MT v United Kingdom* the Court proceeded upon a similar assumption when determining that its 'pilot judgment' procedure should be applied following a further challenge to the incompatibility of a blanket ban on the right of convicted prisoners to vote[2].

1   *Smith v Scott* 2007 SC 345. It is probable that the Welsh Assembly will similarly now qualify in light of recent enhancement of its legislative authority in the area of health, education, social services and local government by virtue of the Government of Wales Act 2006.

2   *Greens and MT v United Kingdom* 2010-…, paras 116–122, discussed at para **2.81** above.

Ensuring the 'free expression of the opinion of the people': the right to vote

Restrictions and conditions upon exercise of the franchise

7.141 In relation to the franchise, the general principle is that 'any conditions imposed must not thwart the free expression of the people in the choice of the legislature – in other words, they must reflect, or not run counter to, the concern to maintain the integrity and effectiveness of an electoral procedure aimed at identifying the will of the people through universal suffrage'[1]. This does not, though, preclude states from imposing conditions on the right to vote[2] such as those relating to age[3], residency[4], inclusion on electoral list[5] or exercise of the franchise on national territory[6], or imposing disqualification from voting for conviction of offences deemed incompatible with civic duties[7], provided in each case that the measure is adequately regulated by domestic law[8], that the means employed are not disproportionate, and the very essence of the right to vote is not denied[9]. Weighty reasons will be required to justify restrictions on the rights of particularly vulnerable groups in society (for example, mentally disabled persons) without an individualised evaluation of each person's capacities and needs[10].

In carrying out an assessment of any interference with the right to vote, the Court may consider the specific political context of a case. In *Mathieu-Mohin and Clerfayt v Belgium*, the Court indeed acknowledged that assessment of arrangements for exercise of the franchise had to involve consideration of the political evolution of the state concerned: 'features that would be unacceptable in the context of one system may accordingly be justified in the context of another, at least so long as the chosen system provides for conditions which will ensure the 'free expression of the opinion of the people in the choice of the legislature'. This case concerned Belgium's rather fragile stability and a requirement placed upon a French-speaking linguistic minority to vote for candidates willing to use Flemish. The Court found no violation of the article on the grounds that French-speaking voters had the same rights as Flemish-speaking voters, and any linguistic requirement was not such a disproportionate limitation so as to thwart the 'free expression of the opinion of the people'[11]. The avoidance of inappropriate judicial involvement in political questions is thus achieved by recognising a wide margin of appreciation on the part of states in determining voting arrangements. However, 'any departure from the principle of universal suffrage risks undermining the democratic validity of the legislature thus elected and the laws it promulgates', and thus 'exclusion of any groups or categories of the general population must accordingly be reconcilable with the underlying purposes' of the guarantee[12].

1   *Hirst v United Kingdom (no 2)* [GC] 2005-IX, at para 62.

2   6745/74 and 6746/74, *W, X, Y, Z v Belgium* (1975) DR 2, 110.

3   *Hilbe v Liechtenstein* (dec) 1999-VI (ensuring the maturity of those participating in the electoral process).

4   7566/76, *X v United Kingdom* (1976) DR 9, 121 (the residence requirement in UK electoral law was not unreasonable or arbitrary, and was thus compatible with Prot 1, Art 3); 8612/79, *Alliance des Belges de la CEE v Belgium* (1979) DR 15, 259 (Belgian legislation governing participation of Belgian nationals in elections was not inconsistent with Prot 1, Art 3); *Py v France* 2005-I, paras 47–53 (ten-year residency requirement imposed as part of peace process: no violation). There is no obligation to allow expatriates the right to vote: *Doyle v United Kingdom* (dec) (6 February 2007) (denial of vote to national resident abroad for 15 years: inadmissible). See also *Sitaropoulos and Giakoumopoulos v Greece*, case pending before the Grand Chamber (failure to introduce legislation to permit expatriates to vote in parliamentary elections as provided for in the Constitution). [Chamber judgment (8 July 2010), paras 35–47: while Prot 1, Art 3 does not require that national authorities guarantee the right to vote to expatriates, the Greek Constitution itself imposed such an obligation, and the failure for more than 30 years to introduce legislation constituted a violation.]

5   *Benkaddour v France* (dec) (18 November 2003) (failure of elector to take steps necessary to change inclusion on electoral list: inadmissible).

6   7730/76, *X v United Kingdom* (1979) DR 15, 137 (non-residents less likely to have understanding of electoral issues and contact with candidates); 8987/80, *X and Association Y v Italy* (1981) DR 24, 192.

7   8701/79, *X v Belgium* (1979) DR 18, 250 (deprivation of right to vote for collaborating with German occupying forces during the 1939–45 war and thus for uncitizenlike conduct does not violate free expression of the opinion of the electorate in the choice of the legislature); 9914/82, *H v Netherlands* (1983) DR 33, 242 (restriction on right of persons convicted for refusing to serve in the military on the grounds of conscience where the individual refused to comply with formalities allowing acquisition of objector status); but cf *Thlimmenos v Greece* [GC] 2000-IV, discussed at para **7.12** above.

8   *Paksas v Lithuania* [GC] (6 January 2011), para 97.

9   *Hirst v United Kingdom (no 2)* [GC] 2005-IX, at para 62.

10 *Alajos Kiss v Hungary* 2010-…, paras 39–44 (absolute bar on voting by any person under partial guardianship irrespective of his or her actual mental faculties: violation). See also

Albanese v Italy (23 March 2006), paras 45–49 (automatic suspension of bankrupt's right to vote was essentially punitive and merely sought to belittle persons declared bankrupt: violation).

11   *Mathieu-Mohin and Clerfayt v Belgium* (1987) A 113, paras 46–59 at para 54. Cf 8873/80, *X v United Kingdom* (1982) DR 28, 99 (ratification of Prot 1 by the UK could not have been intended to interfere with the settled relationship between Westminster and Jersey so as to allow Channel Island residents the right to vote in British parliamentary elections). See also *Aziz v Cyprus* 2004-V, paras 26–30 and 36–38 (impossibility for Turkish-Cypriot to vote in parliamentary elections as only Greek-Cypriots could be registered on account of the Constitution, an anomalous provision in light of the partition of the island: the deprivation of the right to vote in parliamentary elections constituted a violation of Prot 1 Art 3 itself and in conjunction with Art 14).

12   *Hirst v United Kingdom (no 2)* [GC] 2005-IX, at para 62.

Prisoners and restrictions on the right to vote

7.142 The trend towards recognition that prisoners should continue to enjoy as far as is consistent with imprisonment those civil and political rights of general applicability in society does suggest that automatic prohibitions on convicted prisoners from voting in parliamentary elections call for careful examination. It must be stressed that the guarantee does not exclude that restrictions on electoral rights may be imposed on an individual who has, for example, seriously abused a public position or whose conduct threatens to undermine the rule of law. However, restrictions must not be disproportionate. In *Hirst v United Kingdom (no 2)*, the applicant, who was serving a sentence of life imprisonment for manslaughter, had been statutorily barred from voting in parliamentary or local elections, a decision upheld by the domestic courts as reflecting the predominant view that convicted prisoners have forfeited their legal and moral right to vote during their period in prison. In determining that there had been a breach of Article 3 of Protocol no 1, the Grand Chamber stressed that this provision was crucial to establishing and maintaining the foundations of an effective and meaningful democracy governed by the rule of law. While the rights protected by the guarantee were not absolute and there was room for implied limitations with states having some margin of appreciation in determining arrangements as long as any limitations on the right to vote were imposed in pursuit of a legitimate aim and were proportionate, British arrangements were found wanting. In the present case, in the absence of proof of any substantive debate by members of the legislature on the continued justification for maintaining such a general restriction on the right of prisoners to vote in the light of modern day penal policy and of current human rights standards, it was considered that the blanket restriction on the right to vote had been a disproportionate measure since it applied to all convicted prisoners irrespective of the length of their sentence and irrespective of the nature or gravity of their offence and of their individual circumstances[1]. In Scotland, this judgment was subsequently followed by the Inner House in *Smith v Scott*[2]. Subsequently, in *Frodl v Austria,* the Court reaffirmed the principle in *Hirst (no 2)*, noting that franchise restrictions must be very narrow and clearly defined. In this case, however, the Court additionally considered that any disenfranchisement decision should only be made by a judge[3].

1   *Hirst v United Kingdom (no 2)* [GC] 2005–IX, paras 72–85. Cf 24827/94, *Patrick Holland v Ireland* (1998) DR 93, 15; and *MDU v Italy* (dec) (28 January 2003). See further European Commission for Democracy through Law (the Venice Commission) *Code of Good Practice in Electoral Matters* (2002): deprivations of the right to vote and to be elected 'must be provided for by law; the proportionality principle must be observed; conditions for depriving individuals of the right to stand for election may be less strict than for disenfranchising them; the deprivation must be based on mental incapacity or a criminal conviction for a serious offence … [and] the withdrawal of political rights or finding of mental incapacity may only be imposed by express decision of a court of law'. See also Resolution (62) 2 on electoral, civil and social rights of prisoners. Cf *Iwańczuk v Poland* (15 November 2001), paras 53–60 (denial of the right to vote to a prisoner on account of his refusal to strip naked was held to constitute a violation of Art 3).

2   *Smith v Scott* 2007 SC 345 (challenge by convicted prisoners of statutory exclusion from the electoral roll: declaration of incompatibility in respect of the same statutory provision at issue in *Hirst v United Kingdom (no 2)* granted).

3   *Frodl v Austria* (8 April 2010), paras 27–36 at para 34 (exclusion of franchise in respect of persons serving sentences of more than one year for crimes committed with intent: violation); but cf *Greens and MT v United Kingdom* 2010-…, paras 113–115 (the choice of means for addressing the incompatibility is one for states, not for the Court to prescribe: application of 'pilot-judgment' procedure). The issue whether disqualifications must be group-based (ie, prisoners convicted of particular crimes, or sentenced to a minimum number of years) or imposed on a case-by-case basis remains unclear. A further case on voting rights for prisoners (*Scoppola v Italy (no 3)*) was pending before the Grand Chamber at the time of writing, and provides an opportunity for greater clarity.

Ensuring the 'free expression of the opinion of the people': electoral arrangements

7.143 Article 3 of Protocol no 1 does not require the adoption of a particular voting system, such as one based upon proportional representation, to ensure that each vote is of equal value[1]. Thus the use of different electoral systems in the United Kingdom with a view to protecting the interests of a minority does not interfere with the free expression of democratic opinion[2]. Elsewhere in Europe, a requirement for a minimum level of electoral support before a candidate may be returned is likely to be deemed permissible[3]. Nor is a state precluded from providing financial support to political parties[4]. In short, the provision comfortably accommodates the wide variety of arrangements for electoral and parliamentary systems found across the continent. However, there is some indication of heightened expectations in this area: for example, there may be some obligation upon a state to ensure that demographic changes in the electorate are taken into account in electoral arrangements[5].

1   8364/78, *Lindsay v United Kingdom* (1979) DR 15, 24; 78765/79, *The Liberal Party v United Kingdom* (1980) DR 21, 211 (both the simple majority system and proportional representation are compatible with Prot 1, Art 3). See also *Matthews v United Kingdom* [GC] 1999-I, at para 64: 'the choice of electoral system by which the free expression of the opinion of the people

in the choice of the legislature is ensured whether it be based on proportional representation, the "first-past-the-post" system or some other arrangement – is a matter in which the State enjoys a wide margin of appreciation'; 8941/80, *X v Iceland* (1981) DR 27, 145 (a system which results in return of successful candidate in one constituency with fewer votes than in other constituencies does not infringe 'free expression of the opinion of the people'); and *Federación Nacionalista Canaria v Spain* (dec) (7 June 2001) (challenge to rule requiring a party to secure a minimum percentage of votes cast in order to obtain a seat in Parliament: inadmissible).

2   8364/78, *Lindsay v United Kingdom* (1979) DR 15, 247.

3   Cf *Yumak and Sadak v Turkey* [GC] 2008-..., paras 116–148 at para 148 (candidates securing just over 45% of the vote in a province not elected as the party had not reached the 10% threshold nationally: while a 10% electoral threshold appeared excessive and 'compels political parties to make use of stratagems which do not contribute to the transparency of the electoral process', bearing in mind the specific political context and the correctives and other guarantees in place, there was no violation of Prot 1, Art 3).

4   6850/74, *X, Y and Z v Germany* (1976) DR 5, 90. Cf *Basque National Party – Iparralde Regional Organisation v France* 2007-VII, paras 45–52 (prohibition on donations from a foreign political party: no violation of Art 11).

5   *Bompard v France* (dec) 2006-IV.

The right to stand as a candidate

7.144 The right to stand as a candidate for the legislature[1] is considered to be the 'passive' aspect of Article 3 of Protocol no 1[2], with the result that stricter requirements may be imposed than in relation to exercise of the franchise. Recognition that states have considerable latitude in deciding the establishment of constitutional rules on the regulation of eligibility to stand for election as well as the status of members of the legislature is the consequence of the need to take into account the specific historical and political background of the state in question[3]. In practice, the Court's supervision over such matters as requirement of registration as a political party[4], of securing a minimum level of support from registered electors[5], of payment of a deposit[6] or of enrolment of candidacy in a particular language[7], was restricted initially to consideration whether there has been an absence of arbitrariness in the domestic procedures leading to disqualification of an individual from standing as a candidate[8]. More recent jurisprudence again suggests a more critical approach, particularly where arrangements may be perceived as reducing (rather than enhancing) pluralism and democracy[9]. Thus, for example, electoral registration procedures are expected to be effective[10].

1   For the meaning of 'legislature' see paras **7.138–7.140** above.

2   *Ždanoka v Latvia* [GC] 2006–IV, paras 105 and 106.

3   *Mathieu-Mohin and Clerfayt v elgium* (1987) A 113, at para 54. See also *Ždanoka v Latvia* [GC] 2006–IV, at para 106: 'although [there is a] need to ensure both the independence of elected representatives and the freedom of choice of electors, these criteria vary in accordance with the historical and political factors specific to each State. The multiplicity of situations provided for in the constitutions and electoral legislation of numerous member States of the Council of Europe shows the diversity of possible approaches in this area. Therefore, for the

purposes of applying Article 3 [of Prot 1], any electoral legislation must be assessed in the light of the political evolution of the country concerned'.

4 6850/74, *X, Y and Z v Germany* (1976) DR 5, 90. Article 11 may also be relevant: see para **7.64** above. See too *Refah Partisi (The Welfare Party) and Others v Turkey* [GC] 2003–II, para 139 (the dissolution of the Welfare Party and the imposition of disqualification from sitting in Parliament or holding other political offices on the party's leaders had been justified in terms of Art 11 and were only secondary effects, and thus did not give rise to a violation of Prot 1, Art 3).

5 7008/75, *X v Austria* (1976) DR 6, 120; and 25035/94, *Magnago and Südtiroler Volkspartei v Italy* (1996) DR 85, 112 (requirement that a political party must secure a minimum of the national vote as a condition for allocation of seats pursues the legitimate aim of promoting a legislature which contains sufficiently representative opinion and is not discriminatory).

6 *Sukhovetskyy v Ukraine* 2006-VI, paras 65–73 (inability to pay deposit as this exceeded the candidate's annual income, but the required deposit was one of the lowest in Europe, and was not excessive nor constituted an insurmountable barrier: no violation).

7 *Ždanoka v Latvia* [GC] 2006–IV, para 115.

8 *Mathieu-Mohin and Clerfayt v Belgium* (1987) A 113, para 57.

9 See *Tnase v Moldova* [GC] 2010-…, paras 168 and 177 (reference to Venice Commission Code of Practice and the Council of Europe's Honouring of Obligations Committee's and the Parliamentary Assembly's concerns).

10 *Russian Conservative Party of Entrepreneurs v Russia* 2007-I, paras 51–67 (disqualification of party list candidates on account of supposedly incorrect details supplied by one candidate, but neither the party nor the candidate had violated electoral law: violation).

7.145 Restrictions on the right to stand for election must pursue a legitimate aim[1] and meet the test of legal certainty to prevent the possibility of arbitrariness in the application of the law[2]. Otherwise, a wide margin of appreciation is recognised in relation to qualifications for candidacy[3]. However, a state must still be able to justify disqualifications from candidature[4]. Where significant restrictions are imposed on the right to vote or to stand for election, particularly where changes are introduced shortly before elections take place or 'where the measure has a significant detrimental effect on the ability of opposition parties to participate effectively in the political process', the respondent state must provide 'the relevant evidence to support their claim as to the intended aim of the impugned measure'[5]. In *Tănase v Moldova*, the Grand Chamber ruled that the disqualification of a candidate solely on account of dual nationality could not be justified. Leaving open the question whether the purported aim of securing 'loyalty' to the state could be met by the prohibition, the Court was concerned by 'the disproportionate effect of the law on political parties which were at the time of its introduction in opposition'. The Court thus had to 'examine with particular care any measure which appears to operate solely, or principally, to the disadvantage of the opposition, especially where the nature of the measure is such that it affects the very prospect of opposition parties gaining power at some point in the future'[6]. However, disqualifications based upon inclusion in a designated group may be permissible, providing always that there is sufficient protection against arbitrary application of the disqualification. In *Ždanoka v Latvia*, the Grand Chamber considered that the disqualification from holding elective office and subsequent denial of registration as a candidate in parliamentary elections of a former leading member of the

Communist Party had not constituted a violation of the provision. The applicant had never distanced herself from an attempted *coup d'état* in 1991 before Latvia had secured its independence from the USSR, and the authorities had been entitled to presume that the applicant held opinions incompatible with democratic values. Measures restricting eligibility of candidates had been determined in detail by the legislature, and therefore it had been permissible to entrust domestic courts with the task of verifying whether an individual belonged to a category excluded from standing in parliamentary elections rather than having to 'fully individualise' the application of the measure in the light of the individual's specific circumstances: for a restrictive measure to comply with Article 3 of Protocol no 1, 'a lesser degree of individualisation may be sufficient, in contrast to situations concerning an alleged breach of Articles 8–11 of the Convention'[7].

1   Cf *Tănase v Moldova* [GC] 2010-…, para 170 (question whether the prohibition on multiple nationals taking seats in Parliament pursued a legitimate aim left open).

2   See eg *Podkolzina v Latvia* 2002-II paras 35–38 (while language qualification for parliamentary candidates pursued a legitimate aim, the determination of eligibility had to avoid arbitrariness: here, the process was neither fair nor transparent and there were doubts as to the legal base for the treatment); *Krasnov and Skuratov v Russia* 2007-IX, paras 48–51 and 55–67 (disqualification of candidature on basis of submission of wrong information concerning employment and political affiliation: no violation in respect of the first applicant who had knowingly submitted untruthful details on a matter of potential concern to voters, but violation in respect of the second applicant as the disqualification lacked the requisite degree of lawfulness and foreseeability); *Petkov and Others v Bulgaria* (11 June 2009), paras 59–67 (failure of electoral authorities to abide by court judgments requiring reinstatement of candidates on an electoral list: violation); and *Seyidzade v Azerbaijan* (3 December 2009), paras 31–40 (lack of clarity in domestic legislation allowed an excessively wide discretion to electoral authorities and thus an unacceptable scope for arbitrariness in applying the restrictions on persons involved in conduct comprised under the (undefined) headings of 'clergyman' and 'professional religious activity').

3   *Melnychenko v Ukraine* 2004-X, paras 54–67 (language and residence requirements for candidacy, but since the applicant had an objective fear of persecution and his physical integrity may have been endangered were he to have stayed in the country and neither law nor practice required habitual or continuous residence: violation). Cf 8348/78 and 8406/78, *Glimmerveen and Hagenbeek v Netherlands* (1979) DR 18, 187 (leaders of a proscribed organisation with racist and xenophobic tendencies refused permission to stand for election: inadmissible, the Commission referring to Art 17 and noting that the standard of tolerance did not prevent the taking of steps to protect democratic society against activities intended to destroy Convention rights).

4   Eg *Etxeberria and Others v Spain* (30 June 2009), paras 51–56 (refusal to permit candidacy on account of links with terrorism: no violation); cf *Russian Conservative Party of Entrepreneurs and Others v Russia* 2007-I, paras 51–67 (disqualification of all (closed) party list candidates on account of supposedly incorrect details supplied by a candidate placed high in the list: violation, neither the party nor the candidate having been found to have violated electoral law, the sanction related to factors outwith their control).

5   *Tănase v Moldova* [GC] 2010-…, at para 169.

6   *Tănase v Moldova* [GC] 2010-…, paras 155–180. See also See also *Paksas v Lithuania* [GC] (6 January 2011), paras 97–112 (permanent and irreversible prohibition on candidature for legislature of a former president removed from office following impeachment proceedings was disproportionate).

7   *Ždanoka v Latvia* [GC] 2006-IV, paras 115–136 at para 115 (and at para 113: 'It is thus largely immaterial for the Court's assessment of the compatibility of the impugned measures with the Convention whether or not the applicant in that case could have requested the domestic courts to scrutinise whether his own political involvement represented a possible danger to the democratic order'). Here, the specific historical and political background was of importance, for while such a measure may be regarded as unacceptable in the context of an established democracy, it could not be deemed arbitrary or disproportionate in a newly-emerged democracy only some nine years after a failed *coup*. See also *Podkolzina v Latvia* 2002-II, para 33 (the margin of appreciation is limited by the obligation to respect the fundamental principle of 'the free expression of the opinion of the people in the choice of the legislature'), and paras 33–38 (a language proficiency qualification was permissible, but the examination procedure had lacked fundamental guarantees of fairness); but note *Adamsons v Latvia* 2008-..., paras 123–128 (with the passage of time, general restrictions on electoral rights are more difficult to justify and measures must be 'individualised' to address any real risk posed by an identified individual). Cf *Antonenko v Russia* (dec) (23 May 2006) (disqualified candidate removed from ballot papers on eve of polling day: no violation).

The right to sit in the legislature

7.146 The provision also guarantees the right of a candidate duly elected to sit in the legislature[1], but this right may be made subject to restrictions providing these are not unreasonable[2]. The issue may arise in the context either of the right to take a seat in the legislature, or in a legislator's subsequent removal. In *Gitonas and Others v Greece,* the election of five MPs had been annulled on account of their disqualification as holders of public office. The Court confirmed that the right to sit in a legislature was not absolute, but was subject to such limitations as a state considered necessary taking into account the historical and political development of the country with a view to ensuring the proper functioning of democratic institutions. The disqualification of civil servants and other categories of holders of public office from standing as candidates and from sitting in the legislature was a feature found in many other European states and helped ensure that candidates enjoyed 'equal means of influence'; further, it also 'protect[ed] the electorate from pressure from such officials who, because of their position, are called upon to take many – and sometimes important – decisions and enjoy substantial prestige in the eyes of the ordinary citizen'. Accordingly, there had been no violation of Article 3 of Protocol no 1[3]. In contrast, in *Selim Sadak and Others v Turkey (no 2)*, Members of Parliament had found that their mandate had been terminated upon the dissolution of the political party of which they were members. For the Court, such a measure had constituted an extremely harsh and disproportionate penalty since this had not been imposed on account of the applicants' political activities as individuals but merely on account of their collective membership of the party, a penalty incompatible with the very essence of the rights to stand for election and to hold parliamentary office[4].

1   For the meaning of 'legislature' see paras **7.138–7.140** above.

2   *Grosaru v Romania* 2010-..., paras 45–57 (candidate in legislative elections denied the right to take up his seat despite the fact that the applicant received the highest number of votes on

a national scale: violation, both as domestic electoral law lacked clarity, and also on account of suggestions of partiality in decision-making such as to constitute an attack on the very substance of the rights protected). See too *Buscarini and Others v San Marino* [GC] 1999-I, paras 34–41 at para 39 ('interference' with Art 9 rights where applicants who were elected to parliament were required to take a religious oath on the Bible as a condition of sitting; making the 'exercise of a mandate intended to represent different views of society within Parliament subject to a prior declaration of commitment to a particular set of beliefs' was contradictory and thus a violation of Art 9); but cf 10316/83, *M v United Kingdom* (10316/83) (1984) DR 37, 129 (disqualification on the basis of membership of another legislature); *McGuiness v United Kingdom* (dec) 1999-V (elected representatives required to take an oath of allegiance to the monarch; application declared inadmissible under Art 10 since oath could be viewed simply as an affirmation of loyalty to the UK's constitutional principles); and *Gaulieder v Slovakia* (dec) (18 May 2000) (member of parliament elected in respect of a party list had his office terminated upon his resignation from the parliamentary group: friendly settlement).

3   *Gitonas and Others v Greece* 1997-IV, paras 39–44 at para 40.

4   *Selim Sadak and Others v Turkey (no 2)* 2002-IV, paras 31–40.

Disputed elections

7.147 The resolution of disputes concerning exercise of the rights to vote or to stand as a candidate do not involve the determination of 'civil' rights for the purposes of Article 6[1]. Nevertheless, certain procedural requirements arise under Article 3 of Protocol no 1. Thus electoral irregularities should be appropriately investigated[2] and resolved[3] by the relevant authorities in an impartial and transparent manner.

1   See para **5.24** above.

2   *Namat Aliyev v Azerbaijan* (8 April 2010), paras 70–93 (failure to investigate allegations of electoral irregularity properly through an overly formalistic approach: violation); and *Kerimova v Azerbaijan* (30 September 2010), paras 42–55 (invalidation by the Election Commission of return of a candidate who had secured the largest share of the constituency vote on the basis of irregularities without considering the possibility of recounting the votes and attempting to determine in whose favour the alleged irregularities had worked as required by the election code: violation).

3   *The Georgian Labour Party v Georgia* 2008-…, paras 118–142 (annulment of election results in two districts had not been made in a transparent and consistent manner, nor were relevant and sufficient reasons given by the electoral commission for its decision, nor were there adequate procedural safeguards against an abuse of power).

Domestic cases on Article 3 of Protocol no 1

7.148 Article 3 of Protocol no 1 has been considered in a small number of domestic cases. In *Smith v Scott*, following the judgment of the European Court of Human Rights in *Hirst v United Kingdom (no 2)*[1], the court granted a declaration of incompatibility in repect of the statutory ban on voting by convicted prisoners serving sentences[2]. In *XY v Scottish Ministersr:*, on the other hand, the court refused an application for judicial review of a decision to recall to prison a prisoner who had been released on licence, the argument being that the recall was incompatible with the prisoner's right to vote. The court considered that the connection between the ministers' decision to revoke the prisoner's licence, on the one hand, and his inability to vote by virtue of the statutory ban, on the other hand, was insufficiently direct for Article 3 of Protocol no 1 to be engaged by the decision[3].

In *R (Barclay) v Lord Chancellor*, the claimants challenged a reform of the electoral law of Sark, under which the Seigneur of Sark (who holds the island as a Royal fief) and the Seneschal (who is the president of the legislature and also the chief judge of the island) would sit as non-voting unelected members of the legislature, and aliens were prohibited from standing for election. It was argued that the arrangements were incompatible with Article 3 of Protocol no 1 read alone or in conjunction with Article 14. The argument was rejected by the Supreme Court, which emphasised that contracting states had a wide margin of appreciation in the sphere of electoral arrangements. Those arrangements could reflect the relevant historical and political factors, so long as the system provided for conditions which would ensure the free expression of the opinion of the people in the choice of their legislature. The existence of unelected members of a legislature did not necessarily contravene Article 3; nor did a requirement that voters must be citizens. Having regard to the particular situation of Sark (which has no separate citizenship), the arrangements in question did not violate the guarantee[4].

In *Miller v Bull*, the claimant was a candidate for a parish council election whose nomination had been held by the returning officer to be invalid. He wished to challenge that decision and presented the appropriate petition to the court, but failed to comply timeously with a requirement under the Election Petition Rules to serve on the respondents to the petition notice of the amount and nature of the security which he had given. The Rules, ordinarily construed, precluded an extension of the time limit for compliance. It was held that, so construed, the Rules were incompatible with Article 6 and with Article 3 of Protocol no 1, and that the court was therefore bound to disregard the prohibition upon the granting of an extension of time for compliance[5].

The case of *R (Robertson) v Wakefield Metropolitan District Council* concerned the practice of selling the data contained in the electoral register to commercial organisations. It was held that the refusal of the electoral registration officer to ensure that personal details would not be supplied to commercial organisations imposed an unjustifiable condition on the claimant's right to vote, in contravention of Protocol 1, Article 3[6].

---

1   *Hirst v United Kingdom (no 2)* [GC] 2005–IX, discussed at para **7.142** above.

2   *Smith v Scott* 2007 SC 345.

3   *XY v Scottish Ministers* 2007 SC 631.

4   *R (Barclay) v Lord Chancellor* [2010] 1 AC 464.

5   *Miller v Bull* [2010] 1 WLR 1861.

6   *R (Robertson) v Wakefield Metropolitan District Council* [2002] QB 1052

Chapter 8

Property rights

INTRODUCTION: ARTICLE 1 OF PROTOCOL NO 1

8.01 The 'right to property' is normally taken to mean either a guarantee of eligibility to hold property[1], or protection against improper state expropriation or restriction on the use of property[2]. It is primarily in this second sense that the ECHR protects property rights[3], for while the text of Article 1 of Protocol no 1 provides for the right of peaceful enjoyment of property, at the same time the text recognises that the public interest may justify deprivation or control over the use of possessions[4]. Indeed, the inclusion of a right to property proved to be of some controversy at the time of drafting of the ECHR, a period when several west European states (including the United Kingdom) were taking steps to nationalise significant aspects of economic activities[5]. For this reason, the provision was not included as one of the substantive guarantees in the ECHR, but only in the first optional protocol some two years later. This background also helps explain the Court's recognition of a rather wide margin of appreciation in the case law, particularly in respect to matters such as taxation[6] and planning determinations[7].

---

1   Cf Universal Declaration of Human Rights, Art 17(1): 'Everyone has the right to own property alone as well as in association with others.' The UN Covenant on Civil and Political Rights, however, contains no similar provision.

2   See further Waldron *The Right to Private Property* (1988), pp 16–27.

3   Protection of the right to hold property is not entirely absent, however: see eg *Bozcaada Kimisis Teodoku Ortodoks Kilisesi Vakfi v Turkey (no 1)* (3 March 2009), paras 40–54 (refusal to enter religious foundation in land register as owner of property held by it without interruption for more than 20 years: violation).

4   *Sporrong and Lönnroth v Sweden* (1982) A 52, para 61. For comprehensive studies, see Çoban *Protection of Property Rights within the ECHR* (2004), pp 123–259; and International Institute for Human Rights *La Protection du Droit de Propriété par la Cour Européenne des Droits de l'Homme* (2005). See also Ress 'Reflections on the Protection of Property under the European Convention on Human Rights' in Breitenmoser et al (eds) *Human rights, Democracy and the Rule of Law: Liber Amicorum Luzius Wildhaber* (2007), pp 625–645.

5   See further Robertson 'The European Convention on Human Rights: Recent Developments' (1951) 28 BYBIL 359. See also *James and Others v United Kingdom* (1986) A 98, at para 64: 'Confronted with a text whose interpretation has given rise to such disagreement, the Court considers it proper to have recourse to the travaux préparatoires as a supplementary means of interpretation'.

6   Cf *Joubert v France* (23 July 2009), paras 57–69 (margin of appreciation available to the authorities, even although broader in a dispute concerning taxes, had been overstepped).

7   See para **8.27** below.

8.02 The guarantee has been of increasing practical importance in recent years[1], and certain judgments indicate a growing complexity in the legal issues raised, often on account of the exceptional political background to many applications[2]. Property rights have also given rise to several 'pilot judgments' on account of underlying systemic problems caused by 'a malfunctioning of [domestic] legislation and administrative practice' in satisfying compensation claims for property[3]. Other developments in case law are obvious, including a more rigorous application of the test of proportionality in respect of interferences[4]. Findings of violations of the right to property can also have considerable financial implications, reflected in determinations concerning 'just satisfaction' awards[5].

1   Between 1999 and 2005, there were 755 findings of violations of Prot 1, Art 1; between 2006 and 2009, violations were established in a further 1,460 cases, and in purely numerical terms, the provision now accounts for the second highest number of findings against states (after Art 6). Many such judgments are 'repetitive' cases involving a handful of states including Italy (291), Romania (373), Russia (386), Turkey (544) and Ukraine (289): *European Court of Human Rights, Annual Report 2009* (2010), p 151. Only one violation involving Prot 1, Art 1 itself has been established against the United Kingdom (*Stretch v United Kingdom* (24 June 2003), discussed at para **8.30** below; but several cases have involved determinations under Art 14 in respect to discrimination in the provision of welfare entitlements (eg *Willis v United Kingdom* 2002-IV, paras 39–43 (non-entitlement to a widow's payment and a widowed mother's allowance).

2   In particular, following the fall of communism in many central and east European states: see eg *Malhous v Czech Republic* (dec) [GC] 2000-XII (proceedings for restitution of land seized by the communist state: no legitimate expectation that the post-communist legislation would result in the return of the property); *Strin and Others v Romania* 2005-VII, paras 51–59 (restitution proceedings to recover nationalised property); *Prodan v Moldova* 2004-III, paras 59–62 (failure of the domestic authorities to take the necessary measures to enforce judicial decisions ordering the eviction of occupants from houses in relation to which the applicants' ownership rights were recognised and delay in enforcing a judicial decision awarding the applicant compensation); *Jahn and Others v Germany* [GC] 2005-VI, paras 100–117 (decisions taken by the East German State in respect of agricultural land expropriated after the partition of Germany in 1945), discussed at para **8.40**, below; and *Lyubomir Popov v Bulgaria* (7 January 2010), paras 112–131 (restitution of collectivised agricultural land).

3   *Broniowski v Poland* [GC] 2004-V, paras 189–194 at para 189 (failure to satisfy entitlement to compensatory property in respect of land lost at the time of the 'repatriation' of individuals and the redefinition of the Polish state's boundaries at the end of World War II: the potential number of applicants was some 80,000 individuals, leading to the Court's first 'pilot' judgment), discussed at para **8.41** below. For discussion of 'pilot judgments', see paras **2.80–2.81** above. See also *Von Maltzan and Others v Germany* (dec) [GC] 2005-V (refusal of restitution or adequate compensation in respect of property expropriated in the former GDR); *Hutten-Czapska v Poland* [GC] 2006-VIII, paras 170–184 (law affecting some 100,000 landlords through the imposition of significant restrictions upon rental income); *Viaşu v Romania* (9 December 2008), paras 58–73 (inability to secure enforcement of decisions or compensation for land or for delays on account of changes to legislation governing the restitution process and which had created a climate of legal uncertainty and thereby a whole category of individuals had been or were being deprived of the peaceful enjoyment of their possessions); and *Suljagić v Bosnia and Herzegovina* (3 November 2009), paras 49–57 (significant delays in implementation of repayment scheme for foreign currency deposited before the dissolution of Yugoslavia).

4   See Bîrsan 'La Protection du Droit de Propriété; Développements Récents de la Jurisprudence de la Cour Européenne des Droits de l'Hommè, in Caflisch, Callewaert, Liddell, Mahoney and Villiger (eds) *Liber Amicorum Luzius Wildhaber: Human Rights – Strasbourg Views* (2007), p 5 at p 23.

5   There can often be considerable difficulties in calculating just satisfaction awards in respect of pecuniary damage, and the Court regularly reserves this question in cases involving Prot 1, Art 1. Awards for pecuniary damage can be substantial: see eg *The Former King of Greece and Others v Greece* (just satisfaction) [GC] (28 November 2002) (€13.2 million); and *Motais de Narbonne v France* (just satisfaction) (27 May 2003) (failure following an expropriation to carry out a proposed development within a reasonable period: €3 million). See further Myjer 'Article 1 Protocol 1 and the Entitlement of Just Satisfaction' in Vandenberghe et al (eds) *Propriété et Droits de l'Homme* (2006), pp 99–128.

8.03 Article 1 of Protocol no 1 is also often invoked in conjunction with Article 6 since interference with property rights frequently also raises issues of the fair determination of civil rights and obligations[1]. However, a tendency on the part of the European Court of Human Rights to avoid discussion of property issues on the ground that that the merits of the application can be disposed of under Article 6 alone can, on occasion, threaten to blur the boundaries of the guarantee[2]. The provision also has a clear relationship with Article 8's requirement for respect for home life[3], and additionally on occasion with Article 10's protection of freedom of expression[4].

1   Eg *Sporrong and Lönnroth v Sweden* (1982) A 52, para 79; *G L v Italy* (3 August 2000), paras 20–26 and 31–41 (failure to implement court decision concerning recovery of possession of a flat). For cases concerning the failure of domestic authorities to implement judicial decisions, see eg *Timofeyev v Russia* (23 October 2003), paras 44–48; and *Frascino v Italy* (11 December 2003), paras 32–34 (failure of the authorities to comply with a court order to grant a building permit). See also *Papastavrou and Others v Greece* 2003-IV, paras 36–39 (indication by the Court that a fresh reassessment of the situation should have been made, but not for the Court to do so: violations of Art 6(1) and Prot 1, Art 1); and *Yagtzilar and Others v Greece* 2001-XII, paras 41–42 (violation of Art 6 on account of length of proceedings and of impossibility to obtain compensation for expropriation). Cf *Brigandì v Italy* (1991) A 194-B, paras 31–32 (question whether the length of proceedings had resulted in a deprivation of property avoided in light of the finding under Art 6); and *British-American Tobacco v Netherlands* (1995) A 331, para 91 (issue whether a patent application was a 'possession' was avoided as the question of availability of judicial remedy was considered under Art 6(1)).

2   Cf *Lobo Machado v Portugal* 1996-I (dissenting opinion of the President of the Commission) (report of 19 May 1994): the conclusion that no distinct question arises in relation to Prot 1, Art 1 may lead to the misunderstanding that a possible violation of the guarantee for property rights was covered by a finding of violation of Art 6, and thus a specific finding that there was no violation of this provision was appropriate.

3   See eg *Selçuk and Asker v Turkey* 1998-II, para 86 (deliberate burning of homes by security forces; violation of both Art 8 and Prot 1, Art 1); and *Khamidov v Russia* 2007-XII, paras 119–132 (denial of access to the applicant's property in the Chechen Republic). Eviction from rented property more readily falls within the scope of Art 8: see eg *Larkos v Cyprus* [GC] 1999-1, paras 28–36.

4   See eg *Handyside v United Kingdom* (1976) A 24, paras 43–59 and 62–63 (seizure of books considered under both Arts 10 and Prot 1, Art 1); but cf *Öztürk v Turkey* [GC] 1999-VI, paras 48–49 and 76 (destruction of publication considered only under Art 10).

8.04 The article comprises three distinct but connected rules[1]: first, a rule of general applicability found in the first sentence that 'every natural or legal person is entitled to the peaceful enjoyment of property'; secondly, a rule found in the second sentence which states that 'no one shall be deprived of his possessions except in the public interest and subject to the conditions provided for by law and by the general principles of international law'; and, thirdly, explicit recognition (in the second paragraph) that a state may seek to control the use of property since a state continues to enjoy the right without impairment 'to enforce such laws as it deems necessary to control the use of property in accordance with the general interest or to secure the payment of taxes or other contributions or penalties'.

Under Article 15, a state may take measures derogating from its obligations in time of emergency[2].

1   *Sporrong and Lönnroth v Sweden* (1982) A 52, para 61; *James and Others v United Kingdom* (1986) A 98, para 37; *Erkner and Hofauer v Austria* (1987) A 117, para 73; *Poiss v Austria* (1987) A 117, para 63; *Air Canada v United Kingdom* (1995) A 316-A, paras 29–30.

2   For further discussion of Art 15, see paras **3.23–3.25** and **4.147** above.

8.05 Assessment of whether there has been a violation of Article 1 of Protocol no 1 thus involves consideration firstly of whether a recognised property right exists; next, whether there has been an 'interference' with such a right; and thereafter the particular nature of this 'interference'. Attention then will turn to whether the interference constitutes a violation: the interference must be shown to have a basis in domestic law and thus meet the test of legal certainty; to be justified by the general or public interest; and to have a reasonable degree of proportionality between the means selected and the ends sought to be achieved. This final question focuses upon the question whether a fair balance has been struck between individual and collective interests. However, property rights have a strong claim to be considered more akin to economic rather than to civil rights, and Strasbourg supervision in this area is covered by recognition of a wide margin of appreciation on the part of state authorities. In consequence, consideration of the proportionality test may in practice involve no more than ascertaining whether there have been adequate safeguards against arbitrary decision-making and whether a reasonable scheme for compensation has been established.

Positive obligations

8.06 Article 1 of Protocol no 1 will only be engaged if the facts complained of involve an exercise of governmental authority rather than exclusively concern relationships of a private nature[1]. However, a state may also have certain positive obligations to take measures to secure the effective protection of the right to property, and thus an interference with the peaceful enjoyment of possessions may also be constituted by a failure to take necessary measures where a positive obligation to do so exists[2]. These responsibilities may include the taking of prompt action to address obvious defects in domestic law[3]. At the very least, domestic law should be sufficiently certain so as to protect property rights[4]. The positive obligation upon the authorities to ensure property rights are sufficiently protected is, however, one of means and not of result[5]. However, 'the boundaries between the State's positive and negative obligations under Article 1 of Protocol no 1 do not lend themselves to precise definition', and in any event, 'the applicable principles are nonetheless similar [for] whether the case is analysed in terms of a positive duty of the State or in terms of an interference by a public authority which needs to be justified, the criteria to be applied do not differ in substance'[6].

---

1   *Gustafsson v Sweden* 1996-II, para 60 (stoppage in deliveries between the applicant and his suppliers or deliverers did not involve a question under Prot 1, Art 1); cf 12947/ 87, *Association of General Practitioners v Denmark* (1989) DR 62, 226 (contractual rights to fee adjustments constituted a 'possession').

2   See eg *Öneryÿldÿz v Turkey* [GC] 2004-XII, para 133–138 (negligent accumulation of omissions by administrative authorities who had failed to take all measures necessary to prevent the risk of explosion); but cf *Budayeva and Others v Russia* 2008-…, paras 174–185 (town situated in an area knowingly susceptible to mudslides, but it was unclear that proper maintenance of defence infrastructures could have mitigated the exceptional force of particular mudslides, and in consequence it had not been shown that damage to applicants' possession could be solely attributed to the state).

3   *Păduraru v Romania* 2005–XII, paras 94–113 (nationalisation and sale of property to third party: violation on account of the failure to discharge the positive obligation to react speedily and coherently to a problem of general concern); and *Plechanow v Poland* (7 July 2009), paras 99–112 (failure to pay compensation for loss caused by unlawful administrative act on grounds that applicants had sued the wrong authority: constantly changing interpretation had resulted in domestic case law that was often contradictory, and the supreme court's failure to address divergences in jurisprudence had resulted in a failure to discharge the state's positive obligation to provide measures safeguarding the applicants' right to the effective enjoyment of their possessions). In such instances, the use of 'pilot judgments' by the Court may also be appropriate: see paras **2.80–2.81** above.

4   *Plechanow v Poland* (7 July 2009), paras 99–112 (failure to pay compensation for loss caused by unlawful administrative act on grounds that applicants had sued the wrong authority: constantly changing interpretation had resulted in domestic case law that was often contradictory, and the Supreme Court's failure to address divergences in jurisprudence had resulted in a failure to discharge the state's positive obligation to provide measures safeguarding the applicants' right to the effective enjoyment of their possessions).

5   *Blumberga v Latvia* (14 October 2008), paras 67–73 (the failure to bring successful criminal proceedings against the perpetrators of housebreaking had not disclosed any flagrant or serious deficiencies in the authorities' conduct: no violation).

6   *Broniowski v Poland* [GC] 2004–V, paras 143–144 at 144 (and at para 146, examination of case 'regardless of whether that conduct may be characterised as an interference or as a failure to act, or a combination of both').

The status of 'victim'

8.07 The text of the guarantee makes clear that an applicant may be either a natural or a legal person, but in each case the applicant must satisfy the requirement of being a 'victim'[1]. Where there has been an interference with a company's rights, it is thus the company itself that is the victim. However, individual shareholders may in certain cases qualify as 'victims' where there is no practical difference between the company and its owner[2], or where an individual has a direct personal interest by virtue of a substantial majority shareholding and where the company itself is unable to assert its rights. In *Agrotexim and Others v*

Greece, a company holding shares in a brewery that had gone into liquidation complained that the expropriation measures taken by the city council had involved a violation of Article 1 of Protocol no 1. The respondent government sought to argue that the applicants as mere shareholders of the brewery were not 'victims'. The Commission, noting that the measures had caused a fall in the value of the company's shares on account of the impact of the measures on the brewery, determined that the company so qualified. The Court, however, disagreed, for shareholders seeking to challenge state action taken against companies can do so:

> 'only in exceptional circumstances, in particular where it is clearly established that it is impossible for the company to apply to the Convention institutions through the organs set up under its articles of incorporation or – in the event of liquidation – through its liquidation.'[3]

1   See eg *Gayduk and Others v Ukraine* (dec) 2002-VI (complaints concerned repayment of deposits, but applicants had not sought to withdraw deposits and could not claim to be 'victims'). Prot 1, Art 1 provides the sole reference to 'legal persons' in the text of the Convention. For further discussion of 'victim', see paras **2.64–2.74** above

2   *Ankarcrona v Sweden* (dec) 2000-VI (sole owner of a company recognised as a 'victim': 'no risk of differences of opinion among shareholders or between shareholders and a board of directors').

3   *Agrotexim and Others v Greece* (1995) A 330-A, para 66. See also 8588/79 and 8589/79, *Bramelid and Malmström v Sweden* (1982) DR 29, 76 (minority shareholders complained of being compelled to surrender their shareholdings at less than their market value on account of legislation permitting a dominant shareholder to compel minority shareholders to sell their shares at the price determined either by arbiters or at the price that would have been paid if it had purchased the shares through a public offer). Cf *Olczac v Poland* (dec) 2002-X (cancellation of company's shares allowed shareholder to qualify as 'victim'); *Pine Valley Developments v Ireland* (1991) A 222, at para 42 (first applicant company was a wholly-owned subsidiary of the second, and the third applicant was the managing director of the second applicant company and its sole beneficial shareholder: the two applicant companies 'were no more than vehicles through which [the third applicant] proposed to implement the development for which outline planning permission had been granted [and thus] it would be artificial to draw distinctions between the three applicants as regards their entitlement to claim to be "victims" of a violation'); and for domestic discussion, see *Humberclyde Finance Group Ltd v Hicks* (14 November 2001, unreported), Ch D (following *Agrotexim*, shareholders' Convention rights were not infringed on account of decisions taken by the state). For more general discussion, see Emberland *The Human Rights of Companies: Exploring the Structure of ECHR Protection* (2006).

THE SCOPE OF ARTICLE 1 OF PROTOCOL NO 1

The meaning of 'possessions'

8.08 The text of Article 1 of Protocol no 1 refers to 'possessions' rather than to 'property', but in substance the two terms are synonymous[1]. In any case, 'possessions' is given an autonomous meaning and will include a wide and varied range of economic interests and assets, including social welfare benefits[2] and intellectual property. Such interests and assets may include ownership of a house[3] or of other rights associated with heritable property[4] including non-registered title[5] or disputed title[6], the goodwill of a business[7], entitlement to rent[8], a security right *in rem*[9], an enforceable award made under arbitration[10] or by a court[11], a patent[12], a claim for the registration of a trade mark[13], and a concession to work land owned by others[14]. Similarly, a licence or other permission necessary for the carrying out of a business or other economic interest will suffice to constitute a 'possession'[15], providing the conditions attached to it are respected[16]. Thus domestic classification of property rights may be relevant but will not be conclusive as the term has an autonomous meaning for the purposes of the ECHR[17].

The key factor is thus the actual existence of some economic interest. In *Öneryÿldÿz v Turkey*, for example, for some five years the applicant had occupied land belonging to the state without legal title. He had constructed a slum dwelling in which he and his family had lived and which had contained all of the family's household and personal effects. While the Grand Chamber could not accept that the hope of having the land legally transferred at some point in the future was sufficient to constitute an enforceable claim sufficient to amount to a 'possession', the fact that the authorities had tolerated the construction of the dwelling (even although this had been contrary to planning regulations) supported a conclusion 'that the authorities also acknowledged de facto that the applicant and his close relatives had a proprietary interest in their dwelling and movable goods'. This was sufficient to constitute a recognised interest for the purposes of the guarantee[18].

---

1   *Marckx v Belgium* (1979) A 31, para 63. In the French version of the text, the references are to 'biens', 'propriété, and 'usage des biens', thus supporting such an approach.

2   See para **8.10** below.

3   *Akdivar and Others v Turkey* 1996-IV, para 88; and *Selçuk and Asker v Turkey* 1998-II, para 86 (deliberate burning of homes by security forces; violations of both Art 8 and Prot 1, Art 1); *Zwierzyński v Poland*, 2001-VI, paras 63 ('possessions' on account of recognition as owner of expropriated property and payment of rates and taxes); *The Former King of Greece and Others v Greece* [GC] 2000-XII, paras 60–66 (estates owned by the applicants as private persons rather than as members of the royal family considered 'possessions'); cf 19217/91, *Durini v Italy* (1994) DR 76, 76 (the right to live in a home which is not owned is not a 'possession').

4   *Wittek v Germany* 2002-X, para 43 right of property in a dwelling house coupled with a usufruct over land belonging to the state on which it stood). The Abolition of Feudal Tenure etc (Scotland) Act 2000 made provision for the payment of compensation to superiors for the loss of the right to feu duties and for the loss of the right to certain real burdens which reserve development value, but not for the loss of the bare superiority interest itself.

5   *Holy Monasteries v Greece* (1994) A 301-A, paras 58–66.

6   *Iatridis v Greece* [GC] 1999-II, paras 54–55 (the applicant inherited three-quarters of a tract of land and subsequently purchased the remaining quarter) but the state refused to recognise him as the owner and he was ordered to vacate the premises he had built without compensation: while it was not for the European Court of Human Rights to take the place of the national courts and determine whether the land in question belonged to the state or not, it noted that as the applicant had operated a cinema on the land for 11 years under a formally valid lease, and as he had built up a regular clientele, this constituted an asset for the purposes of Prot 1, Art 1).

7 *Van Marle and Others v Netherlands* (1986) A 101, para 41 (goodwill of business conducted by chartered accountants). See also *Buzescu v Romania* (24 May 2005), paras 81–83 (state responsibility engaged for actions of a professional association, the loss of goodwill of a law practice constituting a 'possession'). However, the 'goodwill' must relate to the present valuation of a business, not to expectation of future income: see *Edgar v United Kingdom* (dec) (25 January 2000) (restrictions on the trade of firearms had an impact upon the goodwill of a business: while goodwill may be an element in the valuation of a professional practice, if the loss of goodwill is based upon a claim of entitlement to future income, this will fall outwith the scope of Prot 1, Art 1).

8 *Mellacher and Others v Austria* (1989) A 169, paras 40–41.

9 *Gasus Dosier- und Födertechnik v Netherlands* (1995) A 306-B, para 53.

10 *Stran Greek Refineries v Greece* (1994) A 301–B, paras 59–62.

11 *Sciortino v Italy* (18 October 2001), para 31.

12 12633/87, *Smith Kline and French Laboratories v Netherlands* (1990) DR 66, 70.

13 *Anheuser-Busch Inc v Portugal* [GC] 2007-I, paras 62–78.

14 *Matos e Silva and Others v Portugal* 1996-IV, para 75 (unchallenged rights over land had existed for over a century, and the applicants derived revenue from the land: sufficient to establish a 'possession').

15 *Tre Traktörer Aktiebolag v Sweden* (1989) A 159, para 53.

16 10438/83, *Batelaan and Huiges v Netherlands* (1985) DR 41, 170.

17 *Gasus Dosier- und Födertechnik v Netherlands* (1995) A 306-B, para 53 (immaterial whether a right to a concrete mixer was considered a right of ownership or as a security right *in rem*). Cf *British-American Tobacco v Netherlands* (1995) A 331, para 91 (issue of whether a patent application was a 'possession' was avoided).

18 *Öneryÿldÿz v Turkey* [GC] 2004-XII, paras 124–129 at para 127.

8.09 Certain matters do not involve 'possessions'. An application which in effect involves a claim to pursue a hobby or interest will fall outwith the scope of the provision[1]. Nor does the imposition of a duty to provide professional services without remuneration involve interference with the peaceful enjoyment of property[2], even although in discharging the responsibility outlays are incurred or the opportunity cost involved may result in a loss of revenue. Further, the provision cannot be interpreted as providing any guarantee of a particular quality of environment surrounding a property[3]. Nor can the Article be used as a basis for a claim to indexation of savings[4] or to a higher level of earnings (for example, by requiring an employer to comply with minimum wage requirements without reference to tips included in cheque and credit card payments and subsequently repaid as 'additional pay' after deduction of tax)[5]. Rights arising from protected tenancies generally do not involve 'possessions' for the purposes of the guarantee[6].

1 See eg 37664–37665/97, *RC and AWA and Others v United Kingdom* (1998) DR 94, 119 (prohibition of possession of small-calibre pistols prevented the applicants from continuing with their hobby which they claimed was a 'possession': application inadmissible as manifestly ill-founded). See also *London Armoury Ltd and Others v United Kingdom* (dec) (26 September 2000) (failure to compensate loss of goodwill to dealers' businesses following strengthened controls on firearms: inadmissible).

2 *Van der Mussele v Belgium* (1983) A 70, paras 47–49.

3 9310/81, *Rayner v United Kingdom* (1986) DR 47, 5; 13728/88, *S v France* (1990) DR 65, 250 (construction of a nuclear power plant close to a residence: application inadmissible).

4   *Gayduk and Others v Ukraine* (dec) (2 July 2002).

5   *Nerva and Others v United Kingdom* 2002-VIII, paras 40–44 (the fact that the domestic courts had ruled that the tips at issue represented 'remuneration' within the meaning of minimum wage legislation could not in itself engage the liability of the respondent state as this conclusion could not be considered arbitrary or manifestly unreasonable, bearing in mind that the interpretation and application of domestic legislation in a given dispute is essentially a matter for the domestic courts; and the suggestion that the applicants had a legitimate expectation that the tips at issue would not count towards remuneration was too imprecise a basis for a 'possession').

6   *Larkos v Cyprus* [GC] 1999-I, paras 28–36. See also 11716/85, *S v United Kingdom* (1986) DR 47, 274 (surviving partner occupying a house after the death of the tenant had no contractual right in domestic law and thus no 'possession' within the meaning of Prot 1, Art 1); *Kovalenok v Latvia* (dec) 15 February 2001 (right to live as a tenant in a home does not involve a 'possession'); *Gaćeša v Croatia* (dec) (1 April 2008) (legitimate expectation of buying a socially-owned protected tenancy was in effect a 'claim' rather than an 'existing possession', and in any event the statutory time-limit to purchase the flat had expired).

Entitlements to social welfare benefits and pensions

8.10 An entitlement to a social welfare benefit or to a pension will generally fall within the scope of Article 1 of Protocol no 1. The initial approach adopted by the Court was that the right to a pension based on employment could be assimilated to a property right where special contributions had been paid or where an employer had given a more general undertaking to pay a pension on conditions which could be considered to be part of the employment contract[1]. Until recently, case law still maintained a not entirely consistent distinction between entitlements funded by contributions and those met out of general taxation, a distinction removed in *Stec and Others v United Kingdom*. In its decision on admissibility, the Grand Chamber considered that 'possessions' now required to be interpreted in a way 'consistent with the concept of pecuniary rights under Article 6(1)' so as to avoid 'inequalities of treatment based on distinctions which, at the present day, appear illogical or unsustainable', noting that 'to exclude benefits paid for out of general taxation would be to disregard the fact that many claimants under this latter type of system also contribute to its financing, through the payment of tax'. Thus an individual who has an 'assertable right' created by domestic law to a welfare benefit, whether contributory or not, may now also rely upon Article 1 of Protocol no 1, although the provision 'places no restriction on the Contracting State's freedom to decide whether or not to have in place any form of social security scheme, or to choose the type or amount of benefits to provide under any such scheme'[2]. However, an individual must still show that conditions for entitlement have been met[3]. Further, as the Court noted in *JM v United Kingdom*, 'in particular in the context of entitlement to social security benefits, a claim may fall within the ambit of Article 1 of Protocol No. 1 so as to attract the protection of Article 14 of the Convention even in the absence of any deprivation of, or other interference with, the existing possessions' of an individual, and thus the statutory obligation on an absent parent to pay money to the parent with custody can be regarded as an interference with the right to the peaceful enjoyment of possessions'[4].

1   Eg *Gaygusuz v Austria* 1996-IV, paras 39–41. See further Kenny 'ECHR and Social Welfare' (2010) 5 EHRLRev 495.

2   *Stec and Others v United Kingdom* (dec) [GC] 2005-X (discriminatory treatment in the pensionable age for men and women resulting in reduced payments under non-contributory benefits for work-related injuries). This principle was applied in *Carson and Others v United Kingdom* [GC] 2010-..., paras 64 and 65. See also *Kopecky v Slovakia* [GC] 2004-IX, para 35. For the judgment in *Stec,* see [GC] 2006-VI, paras 54–67 (no violation). Cf *Meindel v Sweden* (7 April 2009), at para 42: 'if the subject of the national proceedings was a discretionary decision as to whether the applicant was to receive certain benefits or was entitled to actions by the authorities, the Court has held that unfettered discretion or even a wide margin of discretion on the part of the domestic authorities indicated that no "right" to those benefits or actions is recognised under domestic law [and thus] Article 6 is not applicable to those proceedings'.

3   *Wieczorek v Poland* (8 December 2009), paras 61–74 (entitlement to disability pension revoked on the basis that the appellant was no longer incapable of work: no violation). Cf *Kjartan Ásmundsson v Iceland* 2004–IX, paras 32–45 (disability pension reduced for the applicant and some 50 others following changes to conditions for entitlement from inability to perform the same work to work in general although the disability remained at the same level: violation).

4   *JM v United Kingdom* (28 September 2010), at para 46 (paras 46–49: child-maintenance regulations that discriminated on grounds of sexual orientation fell within the ambit of Art 14 in conjunction with Prot 1, Art 1: the approach adopted by the House of Lords in *M v Secretary of State for Work and Pensions* [2006] 2 AC 91 treating maintenance contributions as falling outwith the scope of the guarantee as it concerned the expropriation of assets for a public purpose, rather than the enforcement of personal obligations of absent parents, was too narrow a view).

Legitimate expectations

8.11 The scope of the Article extends only to existing rights and assets and not to future claims[1] since the 'possession' in question must be sufficiently established in its existence[2]. In other words, an applicant must be able to demonstrate that he has a claim that is sufficiently established to be enforceable[3]. In other words, mere conditional entitlement does not give rise to a right under the provision. However, the Article will be applicable where an applicant can be said to have a legitimate expectation of obtaining effective enjoyment of a property right that is sufficiently established to be enforceable[4]. There is, though, a crucial difference between a mere hope (however understandable such a hope may be in the circumstances) and a 'legitimate expectation' of a more concrete nature with a sufficient basis for the interest in domestic law[5]. The case of *Kopecký v Slovakia* concerned the dismissal of a claim for the recovery of confiscated coins on the ground of failure to comply with a statutory provision. While the Chamber had found that this requirement had placed an excessive burden on the applicant, the Grand Chamber held that there was no violation since there had been no 'possessions' within the meaning of the Article: the text of the guarantee could neither be interpreted as imposing any general obligation to restore property which was transferred to a state before it had ratified the ECHR, nor as placing restrictions on the state's power to determine the scope of or conditions for property restitution.

A wide margin of appreciation was recognised in regard to domestic determinations concerning the exclusion of certain categories of former owners from entitlements to recover property, and where such exclusions existed, claims by owners for such restitution could not provide the basis for a 'legitimate expectation' attracting the protection of the guarantee. In other words, the notion of 'legitimate expectation' does not 'contemplate the existence of a 'genuine dispute' or of an 'arguable claim', with the consequence that 'where the proprietary interest is in the nature of a claim it may be regarded as an "asset" only where it has a sufficient basis in national law, for example where there is settled case-law of the domestic courts confirming it'. Here, the applicant's restitution claim had been a conditional one from the outset, and in domestic proceedings the courts had found that he had not complied with the statutory requirements. In consequence, the claim had not been sufficiently established to qualify as an 'asset' to attract the protection of the guarantee[6].

1   *Marckx v Belgium* (1979) A 31, at para 50 (the guarantee does not apply to the acquisition of possessions 'whether on intestacy or through voluntary dispositions'); *Inze v Austria* (1987) A 126, paras 37–38. See also *Hadžić v Croatia* (dec) (13 September 2001) (failure of the applicant to fulfil the conditions for a pension as prescribed by domestic law: manifestly ill-founded); and *Nerva and Others v United Kingdom* 2002-VIII, paras 40–44 (suggestion that tips would not count towards remuneration was too imprecise a basis on which to found a legitimate expectation which could give rise to 'possessions').

2   *Stran Greek Refineries and Stratis Andreadis v Greece* (1994) A 301-B, paras 58–62 (question was whether an arbitration award was 'sufficiently established to be enforceable' rather than 'merely to furnish the applicants with the hope that they would secure recognition of the claim put forward': here, the final and binding nature of the award constituted a 'possession'). Cf *National and Provincial Building Society v United Kingdom* 1997-VII, paras 62–70 (the Court proceeded on the assumption that claims for restitution were 'possessions').

3   *Glaser v Czech Republic* 2008-..., paras 53–60 (failure to prove with sufficient certainty either that the applicant was the original owner of works of art, or that the objects in the possession of a museum were the same ones deposited by him before his emigration in 1948: no violation).

4   *Saggio v Italy* (25 October 2001), paras 24–25 (the applicant's right to payment had been acknowledged and thus the expectation of future income constituted a 'possession'). See also *Pressos Compania Naviera and Others v Belgium* (1995) A 332, para 31 (right of legal action arose when damage occurred in domestic law, and retroactive extinction of right by statute did not affect nature of the claim as an asset); and *National and Provincial Building Society v United Kingdom* 1997-VII, paras 56–70 (the Court proceeded on the assumption that claims for restitution were possessions).

5   *Von Maltzan and Others v Germany* (dec) [GC] 2005-V (refusal of restitution or adequate compensation in respect of property expropriated in the former GDR: at the time of reunification, the actual principle of compensation payments and the question of the amount had been deliberately left open and mere belief that the laws then in force would be changed to the advantage of the applicants was not a form of legitimate expectation, and thus there were no 'possessions' as no legitimate expectation existed that the property would be restored or be paid compensation commensurate with its value.)

6   *Kopecký v Slovakia* [GC] 2004-IX, paras 53–61. See also *Broniowski v Poland* [GC] 2004-V, paras 124–125, discussed at para **8.41** below; *Draon v France* [GC] (6 October 2005), paras 61–69; and *Maurice v France* [GC] 2005-IX, paras 86–94 (retrospective amendment of medical negligence compensation law after initiation of proceedings against hospital authorities

and the provisional award of damages: since settled case law of the domestic courts indicated that the applicants had a claim in respect of which they could legitimately expect to obtain compensation for damage in accordance with existing law before its amendment, the applicants had enjoyed 'possessions' within the meaning of Prot 1, Art 1); *Nacaryan and Deryan v Turkey* (8 January 2008), paras 44–57 (refusal to allow Greeks to inherit property located in Turkey as the criterion of reciprocity between Greece and Turkey had not been met: there had been a legitimate expectation that rights to inherit immovable property would be recognised, and as the application of the impugned statutory provision could not be considered to have been sufficiently foreseeable, the interference was incompatible with the requirement of lawfulness); and *Plechanow v Poland* (7 July 2009), paras 83–87 (domestic law expressly recognised the entitlement with case law confirming the existence of a causal link between a flawed administrative decision and loss sustained, and thus the applicants had a 'legitimate expectation' that their claim would be dealt with in accordance with the applicable laws). Cf 19819/92, *Størksen v Norway* (1994) DR 78, 88 (revocation of a fishing licence upon a firm's insolvency and refusal to grant a new licence to the applicant who had been a shareholder did not involve an interference with 'possessions': future loss of earnings does not constitute a 'possession' unless income has been earned or an enforceable claim to income exists); *Malhous v Czech Republic* (dec) [GC] 2000-XII (proceedings for restitution of land seized by the communist state: the hope of recognition of the survival of a property right some 50 years after expropriation could not be a 'possession'; and no legitimate expectation that the post-communist legislation would result in the return of the property: inadmissible under Prot 1, Art 1); and *Prince Hans-Adam II of Liechtenstein v Germany* [GC] 2001-VIII, at para 83 ('hope of recognition of the survival of an old property right which it has long been impossible to exercise effectively cannot be considered as a "possession" ... nor can a conditional claim which lapses as a result of the non-fulfilment of the condition').

8.12 Thus where a settled for a claim to a proprietary interest basis is lacking, no legitimate expectation can be said to arise. Such a situation may exist where there is a dispute as to the correct interpretation and application of domestic law and where the applicant's submissions have been rejected by national courts. In *Anheuser-Busch Inc v Portugal,* the domestic courts had upheld the cancellation of the American applicant company's 'Budweiser' trade mark following an agreement between Portugal and Czechoslovakia that the appellation of origin must indicate a product from a particular region. While the Grand Chamber confirmed that applications for the registration of trade marks could fall within the scope of protection of the Article (even where proprietary rights were revocable under certain conditions) in light of 'the bundle of financial rights and interests that arise upon an application for the registration of a trade mark', it was not prepared to accept in this case that there had been an interference with the applicant company's right to the peaceful enjoyment of its possessions. In this instance, the complaint mainly concerned 'the manner in which the national courts interpreted and applied domestic law in proceedings essentially between two rival claimants to the same name', the applicant company contending in particular that the domestic courts had wrongly given retrospective effect to the agreement between the two states, 'rather than about the application of a law which was on its face retrospective to deprive them of their pre-existing possessions'. This was crucial: the Court's jurisdiction is not to deal with errors of fact or law but 'to verify that domestic law has been correctly interpreted and applied.' Thus it is not the Court's function 'to take the place of the national courts, its role being rather to ensure that the decisions of those courts are not flawed by arbitrariness or otherwise manifestly unreasonable', particularly as in this case the issues involved difficult questions of the interpretation of domestic law[1].

---

1   *Anheuser-Busch Inc v Portugal* [GC] 2007-I, paras 83–86.

Decisions of the domestic courts on 'possessions'

8.13 The domestic courts have applied the jurisprudence of the Strasbourg Court. The concept of 'possessions' has been treated as including real rights in moveable or immoveable property[1], contractual and other personal rights[2], legally enforceable rights to receive social security or welfare benefits, whether contributory or non-contributory[3], and other statutory entitlements to payment[4]. Non-transferable licences and equivalent permissions to provide services to the public have generally not been treated as possessions for the purposes of Article 1 of Protocol no 1, in the absence of any right to the licence or any legitimate expectation that it would be granted. Where however the licence relates to the use of an underlying asset or economic interest, the Article may in some circumstances be engaged in respect of the impact upon that asset or interest[5]. The refusal of an application for the variation of a planning condition limiting the opening hours of a bar was held not to engage Article 1, on the basis that the refusal did not encroach on any existing right of the applicant or infringe any legitimate expectation[6]. Different views have been expressed by the Scottish and English courts as to whether a person's economic interest in earning his livelihood constitutes a 'possession' for the purposes of the Article[7]. It has been accepted that a legitimate expectation, even if arising from an ultra vires act by a public authority, can constitute a 'possession'[8]. On the other hand, a claim to be considered in the exercise of an administrative discretion has been held not to amount to a possession[9]. Differing views were expressed in the House of Lords in *Wilson v First County Trust Ltd* as to whether a creditor's right to enforce a regulated agreement which was improperly executed constituted a 'possession' for the purposes of the Article, having regard to the fact that the agreement had been unenforceable from the outset[10]. The imposition under statutory powers of financial provisions in contracts between private parties has been treated as engaging Article 1 of Protocol no 1.[11] The inability of a person who took part in a fatal accident inquiry to recover legal expenses did not engage the provision, since the proceedings were unrelated to any possessions or property of that person[12].

---

1   See eg *Aston Cantlow and Wilmcote with Billesley Parochial Church Council v Wallbank* [2004] 1 AC 546 (ownership of land); *R (Countryside Alliance) A-G* [2008] 1 AC 719 (ownership of land, animals, equipment, businesses and shares); *Howard de Walden Estates Ltd v Aggio* [2009] 1 AC 39 (rights of freeholder).

2   *Wilson v First County Trust Ltd* [2004] 1 AC 816 (rights of creditor under consumer credit agreement).

3   *R (RJM) v Secretary of State for Work and Pensions* [2009] 1 AC 311. See also *R (Carson) v Secretary of State for Work and Pensions* [2006] 1 AC 173 (refusal to award cost of living

increase to persons in receipt of the state retirement pension who were living abroad: no violation of Art 14 taken with Prot 1, Art 1 as emigration was voluntary, and in any case different treatment could be justified); and *R (Hooper) v Secretary of State for Works and Pensions* [2005] 1 WLR 1681 (denial of payment to widowers of widows' payments: non-payment objectively justified). For consideration of these cases by the European Court of Human Rights, see *Carson and Others v United Kingdom* [GC] 2010-..., paras 83–90, discussed at para **3.92** above; and *JM v United Kingdom* (28 September 2010), discussed at para **3.117** above.

4   See eg *McCall v Scottish Ministers* 2006 SC 266 (counsel's fees for work carried out under legal aid scheme).

5   See the discussion in *R (Nicholds) v Security Industry Authority* [2007] 1 WLR 2067; *Security Industry Authority v Stewart* [[2009] 1 WLR 466 (non-statutory permission to work as a door steward); and *R (Malik) v Waltham Forest NHS Primary Care Trust* [2007] 1 WLR 2092 (a personal right of a doctor to practise in the NHS arising from inclusion in a list of doctors was not a 'possession' since it constituted a future rather than a vested right to income, and monetary loss in respect of future livelihood, unless based on loss of some professional or business goodwill or other present legal entitlement, did not attract Prot 1, Art 1 protection), approved in *R (Countryside Alliance) v A-G* [2008] 1 AC 719 at para 21 per Lord Bingham of Cornhill. These decisions can be contrasted with the earlier Scottish case of *Catscratch Ltd v City of Glasgow Licensing Board (No 2)* 2002 SLT 503 (see also *Adams v South Lanarkshire Council* 2003 SLT 145).

6   *Di Ciacca v Scottish Ministers* 2003 SLT 1031.

7   Contrast *Adams v Scottish Ministers* 2004 SC 665 (where Prot 1, Art 1 was held to be engaged) with *R (Countryside Alliance) v A-G* [2007] QB 305 (where it was not). The latter decision (upholding that of the Divisional Court, reported at [2006] UKHRR 73) appears to reflect the Strasbourg case law more closely. For subsequent Strasbourg discussion, see *Friend and Others v United Kingdom* (dec) (24 November 2009) (it was unnecessary to establish the extent to which Prot 1, Art 1 was engaged as the hunting ban served a legitimate aim and was proportionate). See also *R (Malik) v Waltham Forest Primary Care Trust* [2007] 1 WLR 2092.

8   *Rowland v Environment Agency* [2005] Ch 1 (challenge to removal of signage purporting to prohibit public navigation in the Thames: the interference was justified and proportionate, and it was conceded that the public authority could not in any event be required to act ultra vires in order to give effect to the legitimate expectation). Cf *R (Carvill) v Inland Revenue Commissioners (No 2)* [2003] STC 1539 (claim for discretionary repayment of lawfully due sum not a 'possession'). The point was left undecided in *Fayed v Commissioners of Inland Revenue* 2004 SC 745.

9   *R (Carvill) v Inland Revenue Commissioners (No 2)* [2003] STC 1539.

10 *Wilson v First County Trust Ltd* [2004] 1 AC 816.

11 See *R (London and Continental Stations and Property Ltd v Rail Regulator* [2003] EWHC 2607 (Admin) (imposition by Rail Regulator of provisions for the calculation of compensation in contract between owner of railway station and train operating company); *R (Middlebrook Mushrooms Ltd) v Agricultural Wages Board of England and Wales* [2004] EWHC 1447 (Admin) (imposition of a minimum wage).

12 *Global Santa Fe Drilling (North Sea) Ltd v Lord Advocate* 2009 SC 575.

DETERMINING WHETHER THERE HAS BEEN AN INTERFERENCE: THE THREE RULES

The first rule: peaceful enjoyment of property

8.14 The three rules established by Article 1 of Protocol no 1 are closely connected. 'The first rule, set out in the first paragraph, is of a general nature and enunciates the principle of the peaceful enjoyment of property'. However, 'before enquiring whether the first general rule has been complied with, [the Court] must determine whether the last two are applicable' since these latter rules involve particular categories of interference with property rights[1]. This first rule, while subsidiary, is still of importance, for even if the facts do not support a finding of deprivation of or control over property, there may still be an interference with the peaceful enjoyment of property[2]. For example, in *Stran Greek Refineries and Statis v Greece*, an arbitration award which was final and binding in favour of the applicants had been subsequently annulled by legislation, thus rendering it impossible for the applicants to secure enforcement of the award made. While the legislative measure was neither an expropriation of property nor a measure to control the use of property, the European Court of Human Rights accepted that it nevertheless constituted an interference with the applicants' right of property, and this in turn called for an assessment of whether a fair balance had been struck between community interests and individual rights[3]. Similarly, where the applicability of the second or third rule is in doubt, the issue may be considered under this first rule concerning the peaceful enjoyment of possessions[4].

---

1   *James and Others v United Kingdom* (1986) A 98, at paras 37 and 71.

2   Eg *Sporrong and Lönnroth v Sweden* (1982) A 52, para 65; *Poiss v Austria* (1987) A 117, paras 62–64; *Katte Klitsche de la Grange v Italy* (1994) A 293-B, para 40. For recent discussion, see *Köktepe v Turkey* (22 July 2008), paras 81–93 (considerable reduction in the applicant's ability to enjoy land to which he had a valid title but which had been classified as public forest thus rendering his rights devoid of any substance: violation).

3   *Stran Greek Refineries and Statis v Greece* (1994) A 301-B, paras 61–69.

4   *Beyeler v Italy* [GC] 2000-I, paras 100–106 (the painting 'Portrait of a Young Peasant' by Vincent Van Gogh had been purchased by the applicant and had remained in his possession for several years before the state had exercised a right of pre-emption, but under domestic law the sale had been held to be null and void: the Commission was of the opinion that the applicant had never become the owner of the painting and thus could not assert a right under the ECHR, Prot 1, Art 1, but the Court accepted that the applicant had a proprietary interest recognised under domestic law which constituted a 'possession', and further that the factual complexity of the case was such that it could not be classified in a precise category but instead fell to be considered in light of the general rule requiring peaceful enjoyment of possessions).

8.15 Article 1 of Protocol no 1 protects against interference with the *enjoyment* of possessions, and thus a broad range of state activity which interferes with any of the normal consequences arising out of ownership or possession will be recognised as giving rise to an issue under the guarantee. This may include the seizure of books considered obscene[1], limitations placed on the right to dispose of possessions after death[2], expropriation permits or prohibition on construction[3] or protracted building prohibitions[4], nationalisation of private property[5], forfeiture of smuggled goods[6], adoption of development plans[7], inability to obtain repayment of tax wrongly paid on account of a failure to bring domestic law into compliance with a EU directive[8], failure to ensure reasonable consistency between interrelated decisions concerning the same property[9], and revocation of a licence to sell alcohol in a restaurant[10] or of a land exploitation permit[11] or planning consents[12]. Further, a hindrance can amount to a violation of the peaceful enjoyment of possessions just as much as a legal impediment. In *Loizidou v Turkey*, the applicant, a Cypriot national, had claimed to be the owner of several plots of land in northern Cyprus to which she had been denied access by the Turkish occupying forces. The European Court of Human Rights held that the continuous denial of access to her property must be regarded as an interference with her rights under Protocol 1, Article 1, and, while this interference could not be regarded as either a deprivation of property or a control of use within the meaning of the first and second paragraphs of the provision, it clearly fell within the ambit of an interference with the peaceful enjoyment of possessions[13]. On the other hand, the interference must be sufficiently definite. The provisional transfer of property which is not designed to restrict or control its use will not constitute an interference with property rights[14], nor will the provisional confiscation of property[15].

1   *Handyside v United Kingdom* (1976) A 24, para 61.

2   *Marckx v Belgium* (1979) A 31, para 63.

3   *Sporrong and Lönnroth v Sweden* (1982) A 52, paras 60–61; *Papamichalopoulos and Others v Greece* (1993) A 260-B, para 41.

4   *Allan Jacobsson v Sweden (no 1)* (1989) A 163, para 52.

5   *Lithgow and Others v United Kingdom* (1986) A 102, para 105.

6   *AGOSI v United Kingdom* (1986) A 108, para 49. See also *Jucys v Lithuania* (8 January 2008), para 34 (confiscation of property on suspicion of smuggling and auctioning of seized goods).

7   *Phocas v France* 1996-II, paras 49–52.

8   *S A Dangerfield v France* (16 April 2002), paras 43–62 (impossibility for the applicant company to secure reimbursement of VAT payments wrongly made: Prot 1, Art 1 was applicable as the sum owed to the applicant by the state amounted to a pecuniary right in the nature of a possession).

9   *Jokela v Finland* 2002-IV, paras 44–65 (discrepancy between the market value of property for the purposes of calculating compensation for expropriation and for the payment of inheritance tax: while the compensation payable in respect of the expropriation and the inheritance tax when examined separately did not exceed the state's margin of appreciation even though the respective proceedings were independent of one another and took place at different times, the general right of peaceful enjoyment of possessions included an expectation of reasonable consistency).

10 *Tre Traktörer v Sweden* (1989) A 159, para 53; cf *Catscratch Ltd v City of Glasgow Licensing Board (No 1)* 2002 SLT 503.

11 *Fredin v Sweden (no 1)* (1991) A 192, para 40.

12 *Pine Valley Developments and Others v Ireland* (1991) A 222, para 51.

13 *Loizidou v Turkey* 1996-VI, paras 60–64 (the Court took a much wider view than the Commission which had considered the application as essentially involving freedom of movement).

14   *Erkner and Hofauer v Austria* (1987) A 117, paras 73–79; *Poiss v Austria* (1987) A 117, paras 62–69; *Prötsch v Austria* 1996-V, 1812, para 42.

15   *Raimondo v Italy* (1994) A 281-A, para 36.

The second rule: deprivation of property

8.16 Deprivation of property is the most radical form of interference with property rights[1]. The second sentence of Article 1 of Protocol no 1 provides that deprivation of possessions may occur only where it is 'in the public interest and subject to the conditions provided for by law and by the general principles of international law'. 'Deprivation' includes expropriation and other loss of rights which flow from the legal consequences of property[2]. This will include, for example, property taken under compulsory powers[3]. It may also include the retroactive removal of liability for acts of negligence and which has the effect of depriving individuals of legal claims for compensation[4]. The deprivation must be definitive and involve an irrevocable expropriation or transfer of property rights[5]. Mere provisional seizure of goods[6] or of heritable property[7] is insufficient to give rise to a 'deprivation'. A legal obligation to make financial contributions of a modest amount does not involve a 'deprivation' of property[8], nor does the revocation of a licence or the imposition of planning controls which leads to a detrimental impact on a business[9].

1   *James and Others v United Kingdom* (1986) A 98, para 71.

2   Eg *James and Others v United Kingdom* (1986) A 98, para 38 (conversion of leasehold properties into freehold properties in favour of former tenants); *Lithgow and Others v United Kingdom* (1986) A 102, paras 105–107 (nationalisation of private property); *AGOSI v United Kingdom* (1986) A 108, para 51 (forfeiture of coins); *Håkansson and Sturesson v Sweden* (1990) A 171-A, paras 42–43 (compulsory sale of heritable property); *Hentrich v France* (1994) A 296-A, para 35 (exercise of the right of pre-emption); *Holy Monasteries v Greece* (1994) A 301-A, paras 61–66 (statutory transfer of land to the state; even although no administrative eviction order had been yet made against the applicants, this was no guarantee that none would be issued in light of the attitude of the authorities to the matter: and a deprivation of possessions had occurred).

3   *Zubani v Italy* 1996-IV, paras 45–49; *Katikaridis and Others v Greece* 1996-V, paras 45–51; and *Tsomtsos and Others v Greece* 1996-V, para 36 (irrebuttable presumption that the owners of the properties on major roads benefited when the roads were widened and requirement upon owners to contribute to the costs of expropriation).

4   *Pressos Compania Naviera and Others v Belgium* (1995) A 332, para 34 (statutory exemption of providers of pilot services from delictual liability).

5   *Raimondo v Italy* (1994) A 281-A, para 29 (confiscation of property did not have the effect in domestic law of transferring property rights until an irrevocable decision had been taken, and no such decision had been taken on account of the applicant's legal challenge).

6   *Handyside v United Kingdom* (1976) A 24, para 62.

7   *Erkner and Hofauer v Austria* (1987) A 117, para 74; *Poiss v Austria* (1987) A 117, para 64; *Wiesinger v Austria* (1991) A 213, para 72.

8   *Langborger v Sweden* (1989) A 155, paras 40–41.Cf *JM v United Kingdom* (28 September 2010), para 48 (requirement to pay child maintenance towards the upkeep of children constitute 'contributions' within the meaning of the second para of Prot 1, Art 1).

9   *Tre Traktörer v Sweden* (1989) A 159, para 55 (licence for the sale of alcohol); *Fredin v Sweden (no 1)* (1991) A 192, paras 43–47 (revocation of licence to exploit a gravel pit); *Pine Valley Developments Ltd and Others v Ireland* (1991) A 222, para 56 (imposition of planning controls).

8.17 Since the ECHR seeks to guarantee rights that are practical and effective, a deprivation of property may include de facto expropriation as well as formal expropriation[1]. In each instance, the particular facts of the case will call for close examination. In *Sporrong and Lönnroth v Sweden*, for example, the European Court of Human Rights considered that the permits granted to the municipal authorities to allow them to expropriate the applicants' property had imposed limitations on their right of property which had become precarious and thus affected the value of the premises in question. However, and crucially, the right of property had not disappeared, and the grant of the permits could not be said to have amounted in substance to a de facto deprivation of property since the applicants had continued to utilise their property and could even have disposed of it through sale. In consequence, there had been no 'deprivation of possessions' within the meaning of the second sentence[2]. In contrast, in *Papamichaelopoulos and Others v Greece*, the Court considered that there had been a clear 'deprivation' of property through the occupation of land belonging to the applicants by the military authorities who had established a naval base and holiday resort on the land. Although ownership of the land had not passed to the state, the loss of all ability on the part of the applicants to dispose of it had resulted in a de facto expropriation of the property[3].

1   *Sporrong and Lönnroth v Sweden* (1982) A 52, para 63; *Raimondo v Italy* (1994) A 281-A, para 29.

2   *Sporrong and Lönnroth v Sweden* (1982) A 52, at para 63. See too *Allan Jacobsson v Sweden (no 1)* (1989) A 163, para 54 (protracted building prohibitions); and *Mellacher and Others v Austria* (1989) A 169, paras 43–44 (imposition of system of fixed rents was not a de facto appropriation); and *Brumrescu v Romania* [GC] 1999-VII, paras 74–80 at 77 (nationalisation of property originally built by the applicant's parents and subsequently resold to tenants: the Court accepted this was a case of de facto expropriation).

3   *Papamichalopoulos and Others v Greece* (1993) A 260-B, paras 41–46.

Decisions of domestic courts on deprivation of property

8.18 Domestic courts have considered the application of Article 1 of Protocol no 1 to a wide variety of situations. It has been held that a liability which arises as an incident of the ownership of land is not, ordinarily at least, an interference with that property: the peaceful enjoyment of land involves the discharge of burdens which are attached to it[1]. Similarly, the expiry of a limited interest such as a licence in accordance with its terms does not engage the provision[2]. Nor does the enforcement of a personal obligation, such as the obligation of a non-resident parent to contribute towards the maintenance of her children[3]. On the other hand, deprivation of property in accordance with domestic law will engage the provision, even where the law in question was applicable at the time when the property was acquired[4]. It has been observed that whether legislation should be characterised as depriving a person of rights or as delimiting the extent of his rights should be considered as a matter of substance rather than form[5]. The imposition by legislation of a retroactive liability on employers, the intention and effect being to impose a consequent liability on the employers' insurers, was held to be an interference with the property of the insurers[6]. The periodical flooding of a person's property has been treated, in the context of a scheme establishing statutory sewerage undertakers, as an interference with his entitlement to the peaceful enjoyment of his possessions[7]. The imposition on a doctor of conditions requiring him to abstain from alcohol, to submit to random blood and urine tests and to attend Alcoholics Anonymous did not deprive him of any property rights[8]. Anti-avoidance tax legislation which increased the tax liabilities of service companies was not an interference with the peaceful enjoyment of possessions[9]. Nor was the non-availability of judicial review to challenge the failure of a criminal court to make a compensation order[10].

1   *Aston Cantlow and Wilmcote with Billesley Parochial Church Council v Wallbank* [2004] 1 AC 546.

2   *Wilson v First County Trust Ltd (No 2)* [2004] 1 AC 816 at para 42 per Lord Nicholls of Birkenhead.

3   *M v Secretary of State for Work and Pensions* [2006] 2 AC 91.

4   See for example *Wilson v First County Trust Ltd (No 2)* [2004] 1 AC 816, which concerned a statutory provision preventing the enforcement of a consumer credit agreement. Many other statutes empower the executive or the courts to make orders depriving a person of some of his possessions: for example, in the context of compulsory acquisition, or financial provision on divorce. The exercise of powers such as these prima facie engages Prot 1, Art 1: *Wilson* at para 42 per Lord Nicholls of Birkenhead.

5   *Wilson v First County Trust Ltd (No 2)* [2004] 1 AC 816 at para 44 per Lord Nicholls of Birkenhead. For other illustrations, see *Pennycook v Shaws (EAL) Ltd* [2004] Ch 296 (statutory restriction on right to renew tenancy); *Horsham Properties Group Ltd v Clark* [2009] 1 WLR 1255 (mortgagor's power of sale).

6   *Axa General Insurance Ltd v Lord Advocate* 2011 SLT 439. An appeal was heard by the Supreme Court in June 2011.

7   *Marcic v Thames Water Utilities Ltd* [2004] 2 AC 42.

8   *Whitefield v General Medical Council* [2003] IRLR 39.

9   *R (Professional Contractors Group Ltd) v Inland Revenue Commissioners* [2001] STC 629. The point was not pursued on appeal: [2002] STC 165.

10   *R (Faithfull) v Crown Court at Ipswich* [2008] 1 WLR 1636.

The third rule: control over the use of property

8.19 The third sentence which forms the second paragraph of Article 1 of Protocol no 1[1] provides that the first and second rules do not 'in any way impair the right of a state to enforce such laws as it deems necessary to control the use of property in accordance with the general interest or to secure the payment of taxes or other contributions or penalties'[2]. The purpose of the state action is thus of considerable relevance[3]. Many cases under this rule involve confiscation or forfeiture for statutory purposes. Control of the use of property may involve the seizure of goods by state authorities[4], the prohibition on the importation of goods[5], imposition of rent control[6] or of planning controls[7], a requirement that hunting rights are transferred to an association[8], and revocation or suspension of a licence which has an economic impact on the conduct of a business[9]. However, initial steps taken by public authorities which do not have the purpose or consequence of limiting or controlling the use of property will not fall within the scope of the second paragraph[10].

1   For discussion, see Tulkens 'La Réglementation de l'Usage des Biens dans l'Intérêt Général: la Troisième Norme de l'Article 1er du premier Protocole de la Convention Européenne des Droits de l'Homme' in Vandenberghe et al (eds) *Propriété et Droits de l'Homme* (2006), pp 61–97.

2   Litigation costs are 'contributions': 15434/89, *Antoniades v United Kingdom* (1990) DR 64, 232; as are child support payments required by statute: *JM v United Kingdom* (28 September 2010), para 48.

3   For recent applications, see *Tas v Belgium* (dec) (12 May 2009) (confiscation of premises used for purposes relating to the trafficking and exploitation of vulnerable foreign nationals made with the aim of preventing the use of property for the commission of other offences and fell within the definition of 'control of the use of property'); and *Bowler International Unit v France* (23 July 2009), paras 29–47 (confiscation from a bona fide owner of goods used to conceal drugs by a third party concerned deprivation of property).

4   Eg *Handyside v United Kingdom* (1976) A 24, para 62; *Air Canada v United Kingdom* (1995) A 316-A, paras 33–34; see also *Saggio v Italy* (25 October 2001), paras 26–29 (institution of extraordinary liquidation designed to ensure the fair administration of the assets of a company involved control of the use of property); *Riela and Others v Italy* (dec) (4 September 2001) (proceeds of crime legislation permitting confiscation of property constituted control of the use of property rather than a deprivation of possessions); and *Honecker and Others v Germany* (dec) 2001-XII (confiscation following determination that assets acquired by East German dignitaries had originated from savings acquired by a misuse of power constituted control over use).

5   *AGOSI v United Kingdom* (1986) A 108, para 51 (forfeiture of smuggled coins formed a constituent element of the procedures for control of use of gold coins, and thus was better considered as involving control of use rather than deprivation of property).

6   *Mellacher and Others v Austria* (1989) A 169, paras 43–45; *Spadea and Scalabrino v Italy* (1995) 315-B, paras 26–28; *Scollo v Italy* (1995) A 315-C, paras 27–28 (emergency measures regulating residential property leases); and *Velosa Barreto v Portugal* (1995) A 334, para 35 (termination of lease). See also 15434/89, *Antoniades v United Kingdom* (1990) DR 64, 232 (determination that an agreement is a protected tenancy rather than an occupation under licence does not constitute a deprivation of possessions).

7   *Pine Valley Developments and Others v Ireland* (1991) A 222, para 56.

8   *Chassagnou and Others v France* [GC] 1999-III, para 74.

9   *Tre Traktörer v Sweden* (1989) A 159, para 55 (revocation of licence to sell alcohol in a restaurant); *Fredin v Sweden (no 1)* (1991) A 192, paras 43–47 (revocation of permit to exploit a gravel pit); *Vendittelli v Italy* (1994) A 293-A, para 38 (sequestration of flat); *Spadea and Scalabrino v Italy* (1995) A 315-B, paras 26–28, and *Scollo v Italy* (1995) A 315-C, paras 27–28 (emergency housing controls); and *Megadat.com SRL v Moldova* 2008-..., paras 67–79 (suspension of licence by a regulatory authority for six months on account of purely formal breach of requirements).

10   *Sporrong and Lönroth v Sweden* (1982) A 52, paras 64–65; *Erkner and Hofauer v Austria*
     (1987) A 117, para 74; *Poiss v Austria* (1987) A 117, para 64.

Decisions of domestic courts on control of use

8.20 In *R (Countryside Alliance) v Attorney-General*, the House of Lords accepted that there were claimants who had suffered a loss of control over their possessions, in consequence of anti-hunting legislation, which engaged Article 1 of Protocol no 1: landowners who could not hunt over their own land or permit others to do so, those who could not use their horses and hounds to hunt, the farrier who could not use his equipment to shoe horses to be used for hunting, owners of businesses which had lost their marketable goodwill, and a shareholder whose shares had lost their value[1]. A restraint on a person's ability to dispose of his property was held to engage the guarantee[2]. So too does the system of listing buildings of special architectural or historic interest[3]. The imposition under statutory powers of provisions in contracts between private parties, relating (even indirectly) to the use of land owned by one of the parties, has been treated as engaging Article 1[4]. On the other hand, traffic regulations restricting certain vehicles from driving on certain roads do not interfere materially with the possession of the vehicle or with any trade with which the vehicle may be connected[5].

---

1   *R (Countryside Alliance) A-G* [2008] 1 AC 719 at para 20 per Lord Bingham of Cornhill.

2   *Karl Construction Ltd v Palisade Properties plc* 2002 SC 270.

3   *Cannell v Scottish Ministers* 2003 SC 404.

4   See *R (London and Continental Stations and Property Ltd v Rail Regulator* [2003] EWHC
    2607 (Admin) (imposition by Rail Regulator of provisions for the calculation of compensation
    in contract between owner of railway station and train operating company relating to access to
    the station); *R (Middlebrook Mushrooms Ltd) v Agricultural Wages Board of England and
    Wales* [2004] EWHC 1447 (Admin) (imposition of a minimum wage in employment contracts
    of mushroom pickers.

5   *Phillips v Director of Public Prosecutions* [2003] RTR 8.

ASSESSING WHETHER AN INTERFERENCE IS JUSTIFIED

8.21 Under Article 1 of Protocol no 1, any interference with property rights must satisfy three tests:

(i)   the state interference must meet the test of legal certainty;

(ii) it must be justified by the general or public interest; and

(iii) there must be a reasonable degree of proportionality between the means selected and the ends sought to be achieved to ensure that a fair balance between individual and collective interests has been maintained.

These tests apply to all interferences with property rights falling within the Article's scope. In *Handyside v United Kingdom*, the European Court of Human Rights had initially drawn a distinction between the concept of 'necessity' as it appears elsewhere in the ECHR (as, for example, in the context of Article 10(2)) and that found in the second paragraph of Article 1 of Protocol no 1, and had concluded that in respect of this latter provision that states were recognised as having exclusive authority for judging the 'necessity' of any state action giving rise to an interference. The Court had thus restricted its responsibilities under the guarantee to 'supervising the lawfulness and the purpose of the restriction in question'[1]. In subsequent cases, however, the Court reconsidered this approach and clarified that the second paragraph of the article must also be interpreted in accordance with the principles applying in any assessment carried out under the first paragraph since the text 'must be construed in the light of the principles laid down in the article's first sentence'[2].

1 *Handyside v United Kingdom* (1976) A 24, at para 62.
2 *Gasus Dosier- und Fördertechnik v Netherlands* (1995) A 306-B, at para 62.

Examining the lawfulness of state action

8.22 Deprivation of property may take place only 'subject to the conditions provided for by law and by the general principles of international law'. However, as noted, scrutiny of the lawfulness of state action will apply to all forms of interference with property rights, and not just to those falling within the second rule. Unless there is an interference with the property rights of non-nationals, the focus is likely to be on domestic rather than international law, for, in relation to the taking by a state of property belonging to its own nationals, general principles of international law will not be applicable[1].

1 See further *James and Others v United Kingdom* (1986) A 98, paras 64–66; *Lithgow and Others v United Kingdom* (1986) A 102, para 112. Cf *Blečić v Croatia* [GC] 2006–III paras 45–91 (issue when termination of tenancy took place considered with respect to international law and general principle concerning non-retroactivity); and see also Cases T–306/01 and T–315/01 *Ahmed Ali Yusuf and Al Barakaat International Foundation and Yassin Abdullah Kadi v Council of the European Union and Commission of the European Communities* [Court of First Instance] [2005] ECR II–3533 (competence of EU to order freezing of individuals' funds as part of states' actions against international terrorism upheld). For domestic discussion, see *Al-Kishtaini v Shanshal* [2001] 2 All ER (Comm) 601 (inability to recover payment made in contravention of regulations implementing UN sanctions against Iraqi Government). See Cameron 'European Union Anti-Terrorist Blacklisting – Manifestly Deficient?' (2003) 3 HRLR 225. Cf *Loizidou v Turkey* 1996-VI, paras 39–47 (international law did not recognise the 'Turkish Republic of Northern Cyprus' as a state; the Turkish state which was occupying northern Cyprus was thus responsible for the interference with property rights); and similarly, *Cyprus v Turkey* [GC] 2001-IV, para 61; and *Nacaryan and Deryan v Turkey* (8 January 2008), paras 58–60 (refusal to allow Greeks to inherit property located in Turkey as the criterion of reciprocity between Greece and Turkey had not been met: there had been a legitimate expectation that rights to inherit immovable property would be recognised, and as the application of the impugned statutory provision could not be considered to have been sufficiently foreseeable, the interference was incompatible with the requirement of lawfulness).

8.23 Where an interference occurs as the result of compliance with legal obligations flowing from EU law, the legal basis for the action will be accepted as being European law rather than as the result of an exercise of discretion by domestic authorities, either under EU or domestic law[1].

---

1   *Bosphorus Hava Yollar Turizm ve Ticaret Anonim Şirketi v Ireland* [GC] 2005–VI, paras 145–148, discussed at para **3.18** above.

8.24 Clearly, the test of lawfulness requires that an interference which is not authorised by domestic law will be considered a violation of the Article[1]. For example, in *Vasilescu v Romania*, the applicant's house had been searched by the police without a warrant in connection with a police investigation into the unlawful possession of valuables by her husband. The police had seized a substantial number of gold coins which had been deposited into a bank and retained these even after all charges had been dropped. In Strasbourg, the state conceded that the reasons for removal of the coins had been unlawful. In these circumstances, the Court held that the continuing retention of the items in question had amounted to a de facto confiscation not authorised by law and thus incompatible with the applicant's rights to the peaceful enjoyment of her possessions[2]. The importance of promoting the goal of legal certainty was also emphasised in *JA Pye (Oxford) Ltd and JA Pye (Oxford) Land Ltd v United Kingdom*, a case concerning the loss of ownership of land by virtue of application of the doctrine of adverse possession. Notice to vacate agricultural land owned by the applicants had been served on neighbouring proprietors on the expiry of a grazing agreement, but the neighbours had continued to use the land for grazing without permission and eventually had obtained title to the land by virtue of adverse possession for the statutory period. The Chamber, by a narrow majority, determined that the applicants had been deprived of their possessions, and that the lack of compensation combined with the lack of procedural guarantees – and in particular, the absence of any requirement of notification – had imposed an individual and excessive burden that upset the fair balance between the public interest and the applicants' right to peaceful enjoyment of their possessions. However, the Grand Chamber (perhaps by a less than convincing majority) determined that there had been no violation, instead holding that the applicants had lost their title to the land in question after the expiry of the period of adverse possession. The legal rules had been in operation for many years, and to require the payment of compensation in these circumstances would sit uneasily beside the concept of limitation periods in domestic law, the aim of which was to further legal certainty[3].

---

1   *Iatridis v Greece* [GC] 1999-II, paras 54–62 (while the applicant's eviction had had a basis in domestic law, the eviction order had been subsequently quashed as the conditions for issuing it had not been fulfilled; since no appeal lay against that decision, from then on occupation of the property by the state was unlawful: violation of Prot 1, Art 1). See also *Kotov v Russia,* case pending before the Grand Chamber (distribution of assets of private bank by liquidator) [Chamber judgment (14 January 2010), paras 47–61: violation as distribution had been without lawful basis)].

2   *Vasilescu v Romania* 1998-III, paras 48–53.

3   *JA Pye (Oxford) Ltd and JA Pye (Oxford) Land Ltd v United Kingdom* [GC] 2007-X, paras 75–85 (majority of 10 to 7).

8.25 However, as with the interpretation given to 'law' or 'lawful' elsewhere in the ECHR, this requirement relates not only to the conformity of a measure with the provisions of domestic law[1] but also as to whether the quality of domestic law is compatible with the rule of law[2]. In particular, under this provision, the legal justification for an interference with property rights must be sufficiently clear and precise to allow individuals to be aware of the possibility of such an interference, and further the law must not be applied unfairly. The aim is to prevent any arbitrary application of domestic law. In *Hentich v France*, for example, the European Court of Human Rights considered that a power of pre-emption which was available to the tax authorities to substitute themselves for any purchaser of property had operated 'arbitrarily and selectively and was scarcely foreseeable', and further that 'as applied to the applicant, did not sufficiently satisfy the requirements of precision and foreseeability implied by the concept of law within the meaning of the European Convention on Human Rights'[3]. In *Belvedere v Italy*, the applicant company owned a hotel and adjacent land which gave patrons of the hotel direct access to the sea. The local authority had approved a road building scheme over this land, and subsequently had taken possession and started work. The Court found that domestic law on constructive expropriation had evolved in such a way as to lead to the rule being applied inconsistently, and that this could in turn result in unforeseeable or arbitrary outcomes and thus deprive litigants of effective protection of their rights. The scheme was considered in consequence not to have met the test of lawfulness[4]. In contrast, in *Spacek v Czech Republic*, the Court accepted that the implementation of income tax legislation had sufficient legal basis in domestic law and met the requirements of accessibility and foreseeability. While the rules and regulations were not published in any official gazette in the form of a decree or ruling and so could not amount to binding legislation, the Court noted that 'the term "law" is to be understood in its substantive sense and not in its formal one'; and, further, that the ECHR did not lay down any 'specific requirements as to the degree of publicity to be given to a particular legal provision'. Here, the applicant company had been aware of the ways in which the Ministry of Finance published its accounting principles, and thus at the least should have consulted specialists about any transitional problems. Accordingly, no violation of the guarantee was established[5].

1   Cf *Pine Valley Developments and Others v Ireland* (1991) A 222, para 57 (not disputed that an interference was in conformity with planning law); *Raimondo v Italy* (1994) A 281-A, para 36 (significant delay in regularising the legal status of some of the applicant's possessions, and thus the interference was not provided for by law).

2   *James and Others v United Kingdom* (1986) A 98, para 67.

3   *Hentrich v France* (1994) A 296-A, at para 42.

4   *Belvedere Alberghiera Srl v Italy* 2000-VI, paras 56–58. See too *Carbonara and Ventura v Italy* 2000-VI, paras 61–72); *Khamidov v Russia* 2007-..., paras 133–148 (denial of access to the applicant's property in the Chechen Republic following a counter-terrorist operation: the counter-terrorism law could not serve as a sufficient legal basis for such drastic interferences

on account of its vague and general terms); *Islamic Republic of Iran Shipping Lines v Turkey*
2007-..., paras 92–103 (continued refusal to release a ship seized on suspicion of smuggling
weapons following a finding the cargo did not pose a threat to Turkish security had been
arbitrary, and the refusal of a claim for compensation disproportionate); and *Sud Fondi SRL
and Others v Italy* (20 January 2009), paras 130–142 (confiscation of development following
acquittal by domestic courts for unlawful construction since there had been 'inevitable and
excusable error' caused by 'vague and poorly formulated' regulations: the offence for which
the properties had been confiscated had no basis in law and the penalty imposed had been
arbitrary).

5   *Spacek v Czech Republic* (9 November 1999), paras 54–61 at para 57.

The existence of a general or public interest

8.26 The text of Article 1 of Protocol no 1 specifies that deprivation of property
must be in the 'public interest', while controls over the use of property are to be
'in accordance with the general interest' or otherwise to secure the payment of
taxes or other contributions or penalties. The two phrases – 'public interest' and
'general interest' – are best considered as expressing the same idea[1]. A wide
margin of appreciation is appropriate in applying these tests, since what an applicant
is likely to be challenging in effect is the social or economic policy behind a
decision affecting his property rights. The elimination of social injustice is properly
a responsibility of the legislature; and in any case policy-making of this nature is
not amenable to international judicial scrutiny. In relation to taxation, the margin
of appreciation available to the authorities is even broader[2]. In consequence,
assessment of whether action has been in the 'general' interest in practice is
restricted to assessment of whether state action can be deemed to be 'manifestly
unreasonable'[3]. Thus

> 'the taking of property effected in pursuance of legitimate economic, social, economic
> or other policies may be "in the public interest", even if the community at large has
> no direct use or enjoyment of the property taken.'[4]

1   *James and Others v United Kingdom* (1986) A 98, para 43.

2   *Joubert v France* (23 July 2009), para 68.

3   *James and Others v United Kingdom* (1986) A 98, at para 49.

4   *James and Others v United Kingdom* (1986) A 98, at para 45.

8.27 Policy decisions such as the need for import controls[1] or rent restrictions[2] or
for measures to deal with tax evasion[3] or the collection of taxes[4] or drug smuggling[5],
or action to prevent illegal sales or uncontrolled development of land[6] or the seizure
of property which appears to be the proceeds of organised crime[7], are thus
invariably respected unless the interference with property rights is manifestly
without reasonable foundation. This approach also applies to implementation of
planning and other infrastructure decisions in the areas of housing[8], licensing[9],
town planning[10], road improvements[11] and rationalisation of the use of agricultural
land[12], and decisions taken in the course of legal proceedings[13] such as forfeiture
of bail for failure to appear before the courts[14]. Similarly, action taken in order to

secure the proper functioning of international organisations will constitute a legitimate general interest objective, particularly when it is taken in order to secure compliance with EU law[15]. Yet the 'general interest' is not unlimited. The failure by public authorities to respect a judicial determination concerning property (as, for example, by continuing to occupy premises despite a judicial order recognising rights of private ownership[16]) is unlikely to satisfy the test of 'public interest'.

1   *AGOSI v United Kingdom* (1986) A 108, para 52.

2   *Mellacher and Others v Austria* (1989) A 169, paras 45–47.

3   *Hentrich v France* (1994) A 296-A, para 39; *Gasus Dosier und Fördertechnik v Netherlands* (1995) A 306-B, para 61.

4   *National and Provincial Building Society v United Kingdom* 1997-VII, para 79.

5   *Air Canada v United Kingdom* (1995) A 316-A, paras 41–42. See also *Bowler International Unit v France* (23 July 2009), paras 29–47 (confiscation from a bona fide owner of goods used to conceal drugs by a third party: the confiscation order had pursued the legitimate aims of combating international drug-trafficking and making owners more responsible in their choice of transporters).

6   *Holy Monasteries v Greece* (1994) A 301-A, para 69.

7   *Raimondo v Italy* (1994) A 281-A, paras 27–30; and *Tas v Belgium* (dec) (12 May 2009) (confiscation of premises used for purposes relating to the trafficking and exploitation of vulnerable foreign nationals: inadmissible as manifestly ill-founded).

8   *James and Others v United Kingdom* (1986) A 98, at para 47 (housing is a 'prime social need' which cannot simply be left to the operation of market forces); *Spadea and Scalabrino v Italy* (1995) A 315-B, paras 30–32; *Scolla v Italy* (1995) A 315-C, paras 29–30.

9   *Tre Traktörer v Sweden* (1989) A 159, para 57. See also the domestic case of *Crompton v Department of Transport North Western Area* [2003] RTR 34.

10 *Allan Jacobbson v Sweden (no 1)* (1989) A 163, para 57; *Phocas v France* 1996-II, paras 54–55.

11 *Phocas v France* 1996-II, para 55; *Katikaridis and Others v Greece* 1996-V, para 45; *Tsomtsos and Others v Greece* 1996-V, para 36.

12 *Håkansson and Sturesson v Sweden* (1990) A 171-A, para 44; *Prötsch v Austria* 1996-V, para 44.

13 Cf *Saggio v Italy* (25 October 2001), paras 30–35 (control of the use of property by means of liquidation pursued legitimate aims that were consistent with the general interest, namely the proper administration of justice and the protection of the rights of others).

14 10577/83, *G v Germany* (1985) DR 42, 195.

15 *Bosphorus Hava Yollar Turizm ve Ticaret Anonim Şirketi v Ireland* [GC] 2005-VI, para 150.

16 *Zwierzyński v Poland* 2001-VI, paras 68–74 (no conceivable 'public interest' in such circumstances; and public authorities had a particular moral responsibility to lead by example in observing legal decisions). See also *Timofeyev v Russia* (23 October 2003), paras 44–48; and *Frascino v Italy* (11 December 2003), paras 32–34 (failure of the authorities to comply with a court order to grant a building permit).

Environmental protection

8.28 The Court has now explicitly recognised that protection of the environment is a matter of considerable and constant concern to public opinion[1]. In consequence, economic imperatives (and even certain fundamental rights such as the right of property) cannot be placed before considerations relating to environmental protection[2].

1   For other cases relating to environmental protection, see paras **4.28–4.30** and **6.125–6.129** above.

2   See *Hamer v Belgium* 2007-XIII, para 79. Note the comments in *Turgut & Others v Turkey* 2008-…, paras 86–93 at para 90 (absence of right of compensation following determination that land owned by families for more than three generations was public forest, and applicants' good faith was not in dispute: where there was a deprivation of property some form of compensation should be provided for in domestic legislation: 'des impératifs économiques et même certains droits fondamentaux, comme le droit de propriété, ne devraient pas se voir accorder la primauté face à des considérations relatives à la protection de l'environnement, en particulier lorsque l'Etat a légiféré en la matière'). See also *Pindstrup Mosebrug A/S v Denmark* (dec) (3 June 2008) (interference with contract allowing peat extraction as the bog in question was geologically and biologically unique: inadmissible, the domestic courts having examined the issue carefully and finding the applicant's interests had not been affected particularly severely). For earlier consideration, see *Fredin v Sweden (no 1)* (1991) A 192, para 48; *Pine Valley Developments and Others v Ireland* (1991) A 222, para 57; *Matos e Silva and Others v Portugal* 1996-IV, paras 87–88; and *The Former King of Greece and Others v Greece* [GC] 2000-XII, paras 87–99 (protection of forests and agricultural sites formerly owned by the royal family as well as interest in protecting the country as a republic).

Proportionality and the 'fair balance' test

8.29 An interference with property under Article 1 of Protocol no 1 requires to satisfy the test of proportionality: that is, there must be 'a reasonable relationship of proportionality between the means employed and the aim sought to be realised'[1]. This allows the European Court of Human Rights to assess 'whether a fair balance was struck between the demands of the general interest of the community and the requirements of the protection of the individual's fundamental rights'[2]. The test also applies to the reference in the second paragraph to 'securing the payment of taxes' which explicitly recognises the power of states to enact such fiscal legislation as they consider desirable, for such measures must not 'amount to arbitrary confiscation'[3]. As noted, determination of what is in the public interest is covered by a wide margin of appreciation, and while an interference which is of benefit only to certain individuals or to a minority sector of the public may still qualify as in the general interest, the requirement of proportionality will protect an applicant from having to bear what may be considered 'an individual and excessive burden'[4]. However, the Court will be reluctant to establish that the implementation of measures considered appropriate to deal with pressing social problems such as housing shortages are disproportionate[5]. Entrepreneurs cannot avoid financial risk[6]. In practice, it will often restrict its considerations to whether there are adequate safeguards to protect the individual from arbitrary decision-making and whether a right of compensation exists.

1   *James and Others v United Kingdom* (1986) A 98, para 50. See also *Chapman v United Kingdom* [GC] 2001-I, para 120; and the related cases of *Coster v United Kingdom* [GC] (18 January 2001), para 133; *Lee v United Kingdom* [GC] (18 January 2001), para 121; and *Jane*

Smith v United Kingdom [GC] (18 January 2001), para 125 (planning enforcement notices served against the applicants: measures were necessary to protect the environment, and not disproportionate in striking a fair balance: no violation of Prot 1, Art 1 in light of the Court's disposal of these issues under Art 8).

2   *Sporrong and Lönnroth v Sweden* (1982) A 52, para 69.

3   *Gasus Dosier- und Fördertechnik v Netherlands* (1995) A 306-B, paras 59–74 at para 59 (citing relevant travaux préparatoires). See also *Allianz-Slovenská poist'ovňa as and Others v Slovakia* (dec) (9 November 2010) (statutory obligation upon private insurers to pay 8% of premiums collected for road-traffic insurance for the benefit of the emergency services and other road-safety bodies: inadmissible, the applicants not having submitted any arguments that the scope of the statutory duty was prohibitive, oppressive or disproportionate).

4   *James and Others v United Kingdom* (1986) A 98, para 50. Cf 20471/92, *Kustannus Oy Vapaa Ajattelija AB and Others v Finland* (1996) DR 85, 29 (a rule providing that tax incorrectly collected would not be reimbursed if below a certain amount did not impose an excessive burden); *S A Dangerfield v France* (16 April 2002), paras 43–62 (impossibility to secure reimbursement of VAT payments wrongly made in consequence of the legislature's failure to bring domestic law into compliance with an EU directive: the interference with the applicant company's enjoyment of its property had been disproportionate since the applicant should not have had to bear the consequences of difficulties in applying EU law at the domestic level).

5   Eg *Spadea and Scalabrino v Italy* (1995) A 315-B, paras 36–41; *Scollo v Italy* (1995) A 315-C, paras 35–40; Cf *Immobiliare Saffi v Italy* [GC] 1999-V; and *Hutten-Czapska v Poland* [GC] 2006–VIII, paras 150–151 (operation of rent-control legislation prevented landlords from receiving rent reasonably commensurate with the general costs of maintaining let properties considered to impose a disproportionate and excessive burden upon landlords: violation).

6   See eg 23773/94, *Bäck v Finland* (9 April 1996) (virtual extinction of a guarantor's claim against the principal debtor as a result of debt adjustment: no violation as the readjustment policy served a legitimate economic purpose during a period of recession and the applicant had accepted a risk of financial loss); *Fredin v Sweden* (1991) A 192, paras 54–55 (applicants were reasonably aware that a permit to exploit a gravel pit would possibly be withdrawn in the future and thus had no legitimate expectations that they would be able to carry on operations for anything other than a short period of time); and *Pine Valley Developments and Others v Ireland* (1991) A 222, para 59 (applicants were engaged on a commercial venture which carried a certain amount of risk, and were aware of a relevant zoning plan and the opposition of the local authority to their proposed development, and thus the annulment of the permission could not be regarded as disproportionate).

8.30 The cumulative effect of a range of circumstances may indeed suggest that a 'fair balance' has not been struck. For example, the loss of pension rights as an automatic consequence of dismissal from the civil service will fail to achieve the appropriate balance between the protection of the individual's right of property and public interest requirements as the automatic forfeiture of pension rights cannot be considered to serve any commensurate purpose bearing in mind the harshness of the consequences for the applicant and his family in being deprived of their means of subsistence[1]. Certainly, too narrow an application of domestic law may conflict with the overriding principle of proportionality. In *Stretch v United Kingdom,* the applicant had been unable to renew a lease of land from the local authority since the authority considered that it did not have the power to agree to such an option, even although the original lease had contained an option to renew. For the Court, the applicant had a legitimate expectation of exercising the option to renew and of deriving future return on the investment, particularly since the option to renew had been an important factor in view of the building obligations the applicant had entered into and the otherwise limited period in which he could recoup his expenditure. This legitimate expectation had been interfered with by the local authority through an overly strict application of the law. It had not been shown that any public or third party interest would have been adversely affected were the lease to have been renewed, nor had there been anything inappropriate in including the renewal option in the lease. In consequence, the refusal to renew had constituted a disproportionate interference with the applicant's right to the peaceful enjoyment of property[2].

---

1   *Apostolakis v Greece* (22 October 2009), paras 35–43 (automatic loss of pension rights and welfare benefits as a result of a criminal conviction with no causal link with retirement rights: violation, as total forfeiture of any right to a pension and social cover both amounted to a double punishment and extinguished the principal means of subsistence of a person). See also *Banfield v United Kingdom* (dec) 2005-XI, approving *Azinas v Cyprus* (20 June 2002), paras 35–46 (*Azinas* was ultimately declared inadmissible before the Grand Chamber: *Azinas v Cyprus* [GC] 2004-III).

2   *Stretch v United Kingdom* (24 June 2003), paras 37–41.

8.31 Each application thus calls for careful consideration of the particular facts[1]. Outwardly similar cases may differ as to their merits. This is illustrated by two cases concerning the adoption of general development plans which had not been subsequently implemented. In *Cooperativa La Laurentina v Italy*, the applicant company had been aware that exploitation of its land was conditional upon the adoption by the authorities of a further detailed development plan but, for some 35 years, the council had taken no action. However, it would also have been possible for the company to have sought to enter into a development agreement, an opportunity which the company had not pursued. Further, at that stage the land could only have been used for building houses, the rights of the company had largely been preserved since it could still have sold the land, the value of the property had considerably increased and the company had been able to continue receiving rent. In these circumstances the Court held that the 'fair balance' between public and private interests had not been upset[2]. In contrast, in *Elia Srl v Italy*, the Court found that there had been a violation of the guarantee. A general development plan adopted in 1974 had set aside the applicant company's land for the creation of a public park and, to this end, the council had imposed an absolute ban on building which continued until the adoption of a detailed development plan more than 20 years later when the land was finally expropriated. For the Court, the combination of the situation of complete uncertainty the company found itself in as regards the future of its property (despite repeated requests for information and the raising of legal action), the considerable diminution in its prospects of being able to sell its land, and the lack of compensation in domestic law all suggested that the 'fair balance' on this occasion had not been met[3].

---

1   For further examples of findings of violations, see eg *Stockholms Försäkrings- och Skadeståndsjuridik AB v Sweden* (16 September 2003), paras 51–54 (requirement to pay fees of the receiver appointed on the basis of a declaration of bankruptcy which was subsequently found to have been erroneous, a wholly unjustifiable requirement); *Allard v Sweden* 2003-VII

(demolition of applicant's house built without the consent of all joint owners of the land while court proceedings relating to the division of ownership were pending: violation, particularly in view of the irreparable effects of the demolition of a house used exclusively by the applicant and immediate family and where the interests of the other joint owners could not be considered to be particularly great); *Kliafas and Others v Greece* (8 July 2004), paras 21-30 (obligation to remit earnings to the state following the annulment of a law liberalising the accountancy profession: violation); and *Bugajny and Others v Poland* (6 November 2007) paras 67–75 (designation of certain plots in a housing development for construction roads and requirement that the applicant company had to bear the costs of building and maintaining these roads but as public property: violation on account of a failure to strike a fair balance between general and individual interests).

2   *Cooperativa La Laurentina v Italy* (2 August 2001), paras 58–64 and 93–115.

3   *Elia Srl v Italy* 2001-IX, paras 76–84.

Implementation of policies which affect other ECHR rights

8.32 The margin of appreciation of state authorities in relation to the implementation of policies affecting other rights guaranteed by the ECHR may be less generous. In *Chassagnou and Others v France*, the applicants were farmers in a region where the owners of smallholdings below a certain size were required to transfer hunting rights over their properties to an approved hunters' association. Following upon the transfer of these rights, the owners became members of the association and were entitled to hunt anywhere on lands over which the association had hunting rights, but only in exceptional cases would compensation be available where landowners could show that they had suffered loss of profits. As members of an anti-hunting movement, the applicants complained that the compulsory transfer of the hunting rights over their land interfered with their right to peaceful enjoyment of their possessions. For the European Court of Human Rights, while the state enjoyed a wide margin of appreciation in such matters, there still had to be a 'reasonable relationship' of proportionality between the means employed and the aim pursued. However, while the legislation was in the general interest in avoiding unregulated hunting and attempting to encourage the rational management of game stocks, 'compelling small landowners to transfer hunting rights over their land so that others can make use of them in a way which is totally incompatible with their beliefs imposes a disproportionate burden' which could not be justified under the Article[1]. A case giving rise to similar considerations – *Herrmann v Germany* – is currently pending before the Grand Chamber[2].

1   *Chassagnou and Others v France* [GC] 1999-III, para 74 at paras 75 and 85. The decision is in contrast with the Commission's opinion in 11763/85, *Banér v Sweden* (1989) DR 60, 128 (extension of public rights of fishing in Swedish waters, but no evidence of economic loss). See also *Apostolakis v Greece* (22 October 2009), paras 35–43 (automatic loss of pension rights and welfare benefits as a result of a criminal conviction with no causal link with retirement rights: violation, as total forfeiture of any right to a pension and social cover both amounted to a double punishment and extinguished the principal means of subsistence of a person). For domestic application, see eg *Barca v Mears* [2005] 2 FLR 1 (requirement that Insolvency Act 1986 should be read in a manner compatible with a bankrupt's rights under the ECHR meant that it might be necessary to recognise in certain cases that creditors' rights do not always prevail against all other interests: here, however, the claim that the education and development of a child who had special educational needs would be disrupted was unsubstantiated).

2 *Herrmann v Germany,* case referred to the Grand Chamber (a landowner who was opposed to hunting on ethical grounds had automatically become a member of a hunting association by virtue of his ownership, and thereby had been required to tolerate hunting on his land). In the Chamber judgment (20 January 2011), paras 45–56 and 68–70 the interference with the right to the peaceful enjoyment of property had been considered as serving the general interest in maintaining game populations and avoiding game damage, Germany being in one of the most densely populated areas in Central Europe thereby making it necessary to allow area-wide hunting on all suitable premises. *Chassagnou* was distinguishable as in France only 29 of the 93 *départements* in the country had been subject to the regime of compulsory membership; further, the applicant had enjoyed a statutory right to a share of the profit of the lease corresponding to the size of his property, and even although this was not a substantial sum, it did mean that others did not draw a financial profit from the use of the applicant's land; while there had been no exemption for owners of land suitable for hunting, in contrast to *Schneider v Luxembourg* (10 July 2007), para 50).

Safeguards against arbitrary decision-making

8.33 In assessing whether a fair balance has been struck between individual and collective interests, the Court will evaluate the extent to which domestic proceedings have given the applicant a reasonable opportunity of putting his case and have allowed due consideration to be taken of factors of relevance. In cases involving a dispute over property rights between private parties, the state must thus ensure that adequate procedural guarantees are available to litigants such as to 'enable the domestic courts and tribunals to adjudicate effectively and fairly in the light of [applicable domestic law]'[1]. The absence of a right to challenge an interference by public authorities will also be of significance. For example, in *AGOSI v United Kingdom*, the Court examined whether British law, which provided for the confiscation of gold coins smuggled into the country, allowed reasonable account to be taken of relevant considerations such as the degree of fault of the legal owners of the coins[2]. Thus the proportionality of an interference with property rights must also take into account the degree to which the proceedings in a case have afforded protection against arbitrary decision-making[3]. In *Hentrich v France*, the Court considered that a power of pre-emption which was available to the tax authorities to substitute themselves for any purchaser of property belonging to an individual suspected of tax evasion had not been accompanied by sufficient protection against arbitrariness. As a 'selective victim' of this power of pre-emption, the applicant 'bore an individual and excessive burden' which could only have been regarded as legitimate were she not to have been denied the possibility of challenging the measure[4]. Of relevance in such an assessment is the extent to which the authorities have made information available to relevant parties[5].

1 *Sovtransavto Holding v Ukraine* 2002-VII, at para 96. For domestic discussion, see *Crompton v Department of Transport North Western Area* [2003] RTR 34 (traffic commissioner's decision that a road haulage operator should have his licence revoked interfered with Prot 1, Art 1 rights and therefore the decision-maker should have been guided by the need for proportionality between the finding and the sanction: appeal allowed, for while the commissioner did initially ask herself whether the operator's behaviour related to his fitness to hold a licence, she then became more concerned with the unacceptability of the behaviour and failed to give mature

consideration to the question of whether that behaviour really did demonstrate a loss of good repute).

2   *AGOSI v United Kingdom* (1986) A 108, paras 54–55 at para 55 (in confiscation cases, there is a trend in European domestic practice that the behaviour of the owner of goods is taken into account in considering whether smuggled goods should be returned; any such assessment should involve consideration of the degree of fault or care displayed by the owner: no violation established). See also *Tsironis v Greece* (6 December 2001), paras 36–42 (bank wholly owned by the state and which had not yet become a joint-stock company had repossessed and sold the applicant's property in his absence and without his knowledge: violation on account of the inability to challenge the decision); *Megadat.com SRL v Moldova* 2008-…, paras 67–79 (suspension of licence by a regulatory authority for six months on account of purely formal breach of requirements but without any opportunity to appear or explain its position: violation as the measures were disproportionately harsh); *Družstevní Záložna Pria and Others v Czech Republic* (31 July 2008) paras 90–96 (refusal to allow access to documents needed for appeal against decision to place credit union into receivership for allegedly engaging in activities outwith its remit: violation, as any interference had to accompanied by procedural guarantees affording a reasonable opportunity to effectively challenge such measures); and *Joubert v France* (23 July 2009), paras 50–69 (tax inspections challenged on the ground that the body carrying them out had not been authorised were subsequently deemed retrospectively by statute to have been lawful: violation, as the removal of the right to complain of ultra vires action had deprived the applicants of a possession and compensation rights).

3   *Hentrich v France* (1994) A 296-A, para 45. Cf *Riela and Others v Italy* (dec) (4 September 2001) (proceeds of crime legislation permitting confiscation of property was provided for by law and pursued a legitimate aim, was proportionate in view of the wide margin of appreciation as regards policy for crime prevention, and domestic proceedings had afforded the applicants a reasonable opportunity to put forward their case and the facts had been examined objectively and not based upon mere suspicion: inadmissible);

4   *Hentrich v France* (1994) A 296-A, paras 45–49 at para 49. See also *Glaser v Czech Republic* 2008-…, paras 53–60 (no appearance of arbitrariness in the way in which the domestic courts had examined whether the applicant had a claim that was sufficiently established to be enforceable to amount to a 'possession').

5   *Fredin v Sweden (no 1)* (1991) A 192, paras 54–55 (applicants were reasonably aware that a permit to exploit a gravel pit would possibly be withdrawn in the future and thus had no legitimate expectations that they would be able to carry on operations for anything other than a short period of time); cf *Terazzi Sas v Italy* (17 October 2002), paras 82–92 (uncertainty resulting from a prolonged prohibition on building due to the inertia of the local authority and inability to take steps to challenge the situation in legal proceedings: violation).

8.34 An applicant will be expected to make use of procedures provided by domestic law to safeguard his interests[1], but fair hearing defects (such as delay in the decision-making process which results in considerable and prolonged uncertainty) may themselves lead to a finding that there has been a disproportionate burden placed on the applicant[2]. This assessment, however, also calls for consideration of the applicant's own behaviour. For example, in *Phocas v France*, the applicant had owned and run commercial premises at the spot where one road crossed another. A scheme for improving the crossroads had been adopted and, on this basis, the applicant had transferred his greengrocery business to other premises. Some years later, he asserted that he could not have reasonably have let his property to another trader since in the event of expropriation he would have been liable for the payment of compensation. He had also been prevented from converting the building to other uses, but had refused to sell the building to the authorities because of the derisory price that they had offered. For the Commission, the applicant's right of property had been rendered so unstable and uncertain over a lengthy period of time that the conclusion was that no fair balance had been struck between the public interest and the private interest. In contrast, a majority of the Court concluded that there had been no violation. Domestic law had afforded the applicant a remedy, but he had not followed the appropriate procedures available to him, and so eventually had found this remedy time-barred. Since the applicant was responsible for this situation, the conclusion was that there was no violation of the guarantee[3].

---

1   Eg *Air Canada v United Kingdom* (1995) A 316-A, paras 44–48 (the scope of judicial review could have provided the applicants with sufficient safeguards to challenge the confiscation of an aircraft in which drugs had been found; further, the requirement to pay £50,000 to secure the release of the aircraft was not considered a disproportionate measure in view of the aim of preventing the importation of drugs).

2   *Matos e Silva and Others v Portugal* 1996-IV, paras 92–93 (no progress in proceedings for some 13 years); cf *Prötsch v Austria* 1996-V, paras 46–48 (provisional transfer of property lasted some six years, but this was not regarded as unreasonably long in all the circumstances since the applicants had enjoyed an opportunity to challenge the lawfulness of the allotment and the domestic court had concluded that the applicants had suffered no damage and in fact had benefited from the transfer); *Beyeler v Italy* [GC] 2000-I, paras 114–122 (delay in determining whether to exercise a power of pre-emption in respect of a painting had resulted in the authorities deriving an unjust enrichment from the uncertainty that existed during the period and to which they had largely contributed: this was incompatible with the requirement of a fair balance); *Immobiliare Saffi v Italy* [GC] 1999-V, paras 47–59 (failure to enforce eviction of a tenant accepted in the circumstances as having the legitimate aim of preventing social tension and public disorder, but system of staggering enforcement orders over a six-year period had resulted in a state of uncertainty for the applicant company which was disproportionate); and similarly *AO v Italy* (30 May 2000), and *GL v Italy* (3 August 2000).

3   *Phocas v France* 1996-II, paras 56–60.

Decisions of the domestic courts on whether an interference is justified

8.35 At domestic level, it was observed in *Wilson v First County Trust Ltd (No 2)*:

'Inherent in article 1 is the need to hold a fair balance between the public interest and the protection of ... fundamental rights ... The fairness of a system of law governing the contractual or property rights of private persons is a matter of public concern. Legislative provisions intended to bring about such fairness are capable of being in the public interest, even if they involve the compulsory transfer of property from one person to another ...

There must also be a reasonable relationship of proportionality between the means employed and the aim sought to be achieved. The means chosen to cure the social mischief must be appropriate and not disproportionate in its adverse impact.'[1]

In that case, a majority of the House of Lords held that a statutory provision which prevented the enforcement of a consumer credit agreement, where requirements designed for the protection of debtors had not been complied with, constituted an interference with the creditor's possessions within the meaning of Article 1 of Protocol no 1, but was legally certain, justified in the public interest, and proportionate. The approach to be taken by the courts in assessing whether Parliament has acted in a proportionate manner was considered in detail[2].

1   *Wilson v First County Trust Ltd (No 2)* [2004] 1 AC 816.

2   The correct approach to the assessment of proportionality has also been considered in many other cases, notably in *R (Countryside Alliance) A-G* [2008] 1 AC 719. See generally paras **3.73–3.82** above.

8.36 In most cases, the courts have accepted the assessment of Parliament as to the social or economic justification for legislation interfering with possessions. For example, the seizure of property under proceeds of crime legislation was held to constitute a justified interference with property rights[1]. So also was the recovery of evidence and its provision to a foreign country for the purposes of a criminal investigation[2]. The statutory right of a tenant to acquire a new lease, subject to the payment of compensation to the freeholder, was also upheld[3]. So also was anti-hunting legislation[4]. So too was the introduction of a statutory scheme for the regulation of door stewards, which had the effect of barring stewards who had relevant criminal convictions[5]. Following Strasbourg case law[6], it has been held that Article 1 of Protocol no 1 is engaged but not violated by the law under which, in England and Wales, title to land is extinguished by adverse possession[7]. The guarantee was also held not to be violated by a refusal to repay tax which had been paid in consequence of a mistake of law (and which would have been repayable at common law), the refusal being in accordance with statutory provisions governing repayment: the public interest underlying the provisions was the protection of public finances from the risk of substantial amounts becoming repayable many years after the tax had been spent[8]. A similar conclusion was reached in a case concerned with anti-avoidance tax legislation which operated retrospectively so as to undo artificial arrangements[9]. An increase in air passenger duty which was effectively retroactive in its application to package tour operators, since they could not pass on the increase to their pre-booked customers, was also held not to violate the Article, there being legitimate financial and environmental reasons for bringing in the increase without delay, and there being practical reasons why it was difficult to treat tour operators differently from airlines[10]. The controls imposed upon a property owner under the system of listing buildings of special architectural or historic interest were not disproportionate, notwithstanding the absence of any provision for the recovery of wasted legal expenses which he might incur[11]. A statutory scheme regulating the activities of sewerage undertakers and establishing priorities for the provision of new sewers was held to be compatible with the rights of a householder under Article 1 of Protocol no 1 whose house and garden had been periodically affected by flooding as a consequence of the inadequacy of the existing sewer.[12] More controversially, legislation which retroactively imposed a liability upon employers to pay damages to employees who had developed an asbestos-related condition which had not previously constituted a compensatable 'injury', with the intention and effect that the liability would be met by the insurers whose employers' liability policies had been in force at the time of the exposure to asbestos, was held to be a justifiable interference with the insurers' property rights[13]. On the other hand, legislation which provided for the imposition of fixed fines and the temporary seizure of vehicles found to contain individuals seeking to enter the United Kingdom illegally was deemed excessively rigid and thus disproportionate[14]. The retrospective alteration of counsel's fees for work carried out under the legal aid scheme did not strike a fair balance between the public interest and the interests of those affected[15].

1   *R v Benjafield* [2003] 1 AC 1099; *R v May* [2008] 1 AC 1028. See also *HM Advocate v McSalley* 2000 JC 485, *HM Advocate v McIntosh* 2001 SC (PC) 89 and *Phillips v United Kingdom* 2001-VII, paras 50–54 (a confiscation order fell within the scope of Prot 1, Art 1 but was compatible with the article). As to the possibility that Prot 1, Art 1 might limit the extent to which costs and expenses were recoverable from assets in which third parties held the beneficial interest, see *Sinclair v Glatt* [2009] 1 WLR 1845.

2   *Calder v Frame* 2007 JC 4.

3   *Howard de Walden Estates Ltd v Aggio* [2009] 1 AC 39.

4   *R (Countryside Alliance) A-G* [2008] 1 AC 719; *Whaley v Lord Advocate* 2008 SC (HL) 107.

5   *R (Nicholds) v Security Industry Authority* [2007] 1 WLR 2067; *Security Industry Authority v Stewart* [2009] 1 WLR 466.

6   *JA Pye (Oxford) Ltd v United Kingdom* [GC] 2007-X. The application to Strasbourg sought unsuccessfully to challenge the decision of the House of Lords in *JA Pye (Oxford) Ltd v Graham* [2003] 1 AC 419.

7   *Ofulue v Bossert* [2009] Ch 1.

8   *Monro v Revenue and Customs Commissioners* [2009] Ch 69. Different views were expressed as to whether Prot 1, Art 1 was engaged.

9   *R (Huitson) v Revenue and Customs Commissioners* [2011] QB 174.

10   *R (Federation of Tour Operators) v HM Treasury* [2008] STC 2524.

11   *Cannell v Scottish Ministers* 2003 SC 404.

12   *Marcic v Thames Water Utilities Ltd* [2004] 2 AC 42.

13   *Axa General Insurance Ltd v Lord Advocate* 2011 SLT 439. An appeal was heard by the Supreme Court in June 2011.

14   *International Transport Roth GmbH v Secretary of State for the Home Department* [2003] QB 728.

15   *McCall v Scottish Ministers* 2006 SC 266.

8.37 The courts have tended to undertake a more searching examination in cases concerned with the exercise of discretionary powers. A policy of seizing vehicles found to contain smuggled goods and returning them only in exceptional circumstances was held to be disproportionate, as it prevented any consideration being given to relevant distinctions between different types of case[1]. On the other hand, the court upheld the refusal, on environmental grounds, of a licence which had previously been granted, effectively putting the applicant out of business[2]. The court also upheld a statutory direction issued by a regulatory body requiring the compulsory transfer of a non-profit making housing co-operative's stock of long leases to another social landlord[3].

1   *Lindsay v Customs and Excise Commissioners* [2002] 1 WLR 1766. See also *Fox v Customs and Excise Commissioners* [2003] 1 WLR 1331 (forfeiture legislation interpreted in light of Prot 1, Art 1 so as to allow forfeiture to be challenged by owner of goods seized).

2   *Catscratch Ltd v City of Glasgow Licensing Board (No 2)* 2002 SLT 503. See also *Adamso: v South Lanarkshire Council* 2003 SLT 145; *Di Ciacca v Scottish Ministers* 2003 SLT 1031.

3   *R (Clays Lane Housing Cooperative Ltd) v The Housing Corporation* [2005] 1 WLR 2229.

8.38 A number of cases have concerned common law rules and practices. In *Karl Construction Ltd v Palisade Properties plc*, the automatic grant of a warrant for inhibition on the dependence of proceedings, with minimal regard to either the merits of the claim or the defender's financial position, and without any right to compensation for the wrongful use of the diligence, was held to constitute a disproportionate interference with property rights[1]. In *Hanchett-Stamford v Attorney General,* it was held that when an unincorporated association ceased to exist by reason of the membership falling below two, the assets vested under English law in the sole remaining member rather than in the Crown as *bona vacantia,* since to deprive the member of his share of the assets would violate Article 1 of Protocol no 1[2].

The rescinding of an ultra vires forward tax agreement was held to be justified, since the Revenue were pursuing a legitimate aim, namely to apply the tax system fairly between taxpayers, and a fair balance had been struck between the interests of the community and the protection of the taxpayer's rights[3].

1   *Karl Construction Ltd v Palisade Properties plc* 2002 SC 270. See also *Barry D Trentham Ltd v Lawfield Investments Ltd* 2002 SLT 1094, where the use of diligence on the dependence was held to be justified; and *Advocate General v Taylor* 2004 SC 339.

2   *Hanchett-Stamford A-G* [2009] Ch 173.

3   *Fayed v Commissioners of Inland Revenue* 2004 SC 745.

Compensation for interferences with property rights

8.39 Any interference with property rights should in principle be redressed by the provision of a right to compensation. This applies not only to formal or de facto expropriation of property[1], but also to other interferences with the peaceful enjoyment of possessions[2]. The scheme of compensation payable will be material to the assessment of whether a fair balance has been struck between community and individual interests, and failure to pay compensation of an amount reasonably related to the value of the property taken or otherwise subject to interference will normally constitute a disproportionate interference with property rights[3]. In *Holy Monasteries v Greece*, the Greek legislature had expropriated land belonging to the applicants without making provision for compensation. The Commission had accepted that there had been exceptional circumstances justifying the lack of compensation, including the manner in which the property had been acquired and used and the dependency of the applicants on the Greek Orthodox Church which in turn had been dependent upon the state. For the Court, however, the expropriation had imposed too excessive a burden on the applicants, and thus a fair balance between their interests and those of the community had not been achieved[4]. In *Pressos Compania Naviera and Others v Belgium*, the retrospective extinguishing by statute of claims available to victims of pilot accidents for high awards of damages for negligence following a judicial decision, without payment by way of compensation of an amount reasonably related to the value of the claims, was similarly considered a disproportionate interference with property rights[5]. In *Perdigão v Portugal*, the amount awarded by the courts by way of compensation for the expropriation of land taken to build a motorway had been less than the court fees payable, despite expert assessments valuing the land and the potential profit from a quarry significantly higher. For the Grand Chamber, the situation had not achieved a fair balance between the general interest and the property rights of the applicants: neither the conduct of the applicants nor their legal proceedings could justify the imposition of such high court fees in relation to the amount that had been awarded as compensation for the expropriation[6].

---

1   *James and Others v United Kingdom* (1986) A 98, paras 54–56 at para 54 (the taking of property without compensation can only be justified in exceptional circumstances since otherwise the right would be 'largely illusory and ineffective'); *The Former King of Greece and Others v Greece* [GC] 2000-XII, paras 84–99 (deprivation of property by statute without compensation considered a violation); cf *Katte Klitsche de la Grange v Italy* (1994) A 293-B, paras 47–48 (no compensation payable under domestic law since the applicant's property had not been subject to expropriation: no breach of Prot 1, Art 1). For further discussion, see eg *Yagtzilar and Others v Greece* 2001-XII, paras 40–42 (no convincing explanation for the failure to pay compensation at the outcome of proceedings in respect of appropriated land: violation); *Pincová and Pinc v Czech Republic* 2002-VIII, paras 52–64, and *Zvolský and Zvolská v Czech Republic* 2002-IX, paras 70–74 (effect of restitution on the rights of third parties who had acquired the property in good faith from the state: violation on account of minimal compensation payable); *Azas v Greece* (19 September 2002), paras 45–57 (adequacy of the compensation received in light of application of an irrebuttable presumption of benefit accruing from an expropriation: violation); *Karagiannis and Others v Greece* (16 January 2003), paras 36–44 (occupation of land in 1967 followed by expropriation of land in 1999 without any account taken of the lengthy period during which the applicants had been deprived of the use of their property); *IRS and Others v Turkey* (27 July 2004), paras 52–56 (prescription of property rights following lengthy adverse possession by the state but without compensation payment: violation); *Buffalo Srl in liquidation v Italy* (3 July 2003), paras 34–37 (length of time taken to reimburse overpaid taxes in a tax system requiring advance payment of an estimated liability: violation); *NA and Others v Turkey* 2005-X, paras 36–43 (deprivation in favour of the state but without compensation of title to inherited property which had been previously registered in the name of a private individual and on which a hotel had been constructed on the ground that the land formed part of the coastal belt and could not be held in private ownership: violation on account of the total absence of compensation); *Draon v France* [GC] 2006-IX, paras 78–86 (retrospective amendment of medical negligence compensation law resulting in denial of a substantial portion of the damages they had claimed: failure to strike a fair balance since the applicants had been required to bear an individual and excessive burden without sufficient compensation); *Urbárska Obec Trenčianske Biskupice v Slovakia* (27 November 2007) paras 116–133 and 140–146 (in the context of the move to the free market state, land was transferred back to private owners but the land given by way of compensation disregarded the actual market value of the association's land at the time of transfer, and the rent payable to the association was set at such a low level for which there was no justification: violation); *Jucys v Lithuania* (8 January 2008) paras 34–39 (confiscation of

property on suspicion of smuggling and auctioning of seized goods: delays in obtaining compensation which was also significantly below market value: violation); *Ismayilov v Russia* (6 November 2008) paras 32–39 (confiscation of USD 20,000 following failure to declare the cash upon entry to the country deemed unnecessary as the lawful origin of money was not in dispute and had not caused any pecuniary damage and the applicant had already been punished for smuggling: violation); *Kozacioglu v Turkey* [GC] 2009-..., paras 65–73 (special characteristics of a listed building not taken into account when assessing compensation: violation); and *Grifhorst v France* 2009-..., paras 87–106 (customs penalty consisting of automatic confiscation and an additional fine held to be disproportionate).

2   Eg *Sporrong and Lönnroth v Sweden* (1982) A 52, para 73 (individual and excessive burden could only have been rendered legitimate were the applicants to have had the opportunity of seeking a reduction of applicable time limits or the payment of compensation); *Erkner and Hofauer v Austria* (1987) A 117, paras 76–79 (applicants still awaited clarification of the final fate of their property after 16 years and the resultant compensation: this amounted to a disproportionate burden, and thus a violation of the guarantee); *Strin and Others v Romania* 2005–VII, paras 51–59 (unlawful nationalisation of and lack of compensation for property subsequently sold to a third party while restitution proceedings were pending: violation as domestic law did not foresee with sufficient clarity and certainty the consequences for individuals' property rights of the sale of their property by the state to a third party acting in good faith; the state had sold the property despite the fact that proceedings were pending; there had been discrimination in the treatment of the applicants; and no compensation had been payable).

3   Eg *Platakou v Greece* 2001-I, paras 55–57. See also *Meidanis v Greece* (22 May 2008), paras 26–32 (default interest rates in relation to public corporations were much lower than for debts with private individuals or private corporations, but the public hospital was acting as a private employer and it could thus not be shown that the difference in default interest rates was essential for the proper functioning of the hospital: violation); *Kozaciolu v Turkey* [GC] 2009-..., paras 65–73 (compensation calculation did not take into account historical value of building: violation); *Zouboulidis v Greece (no 2)* (25 June 2009), paras 26–37 (insufficient public-interest grounds for different limitation periods and starting dates for automatic interest as between state and private parties in a labour dispute: a mere abstract reference to public interest in settling debts owed to the state promptly was not sufficient justification for granting preferential treatment to the state); and *Zaharievi v Bulgaria* (2 July 2009), paras 35–44 (execution of judgment in the applicant's favour had resulted in a smaller amount of compensation and refusal to review the situation as the judgment had become final: violation). Cf *Sud Parisienne de Construction v France* (11 February 2010), paras 35–45 (retrospective amendment of rate of default interest applicable to public-works contracts: no violation).

4   *Holy Monasteries v Greece* (1994) A 301-A, paras 71–75.

5   *Pressos Compania Naviera and Others v Belgium* (1995) A 332, paras 38–44.

6   *Perdigão v Portugal* [GC] 2010-..., paras 67–79.

8.40 In exceptional circumstances, however, it may be justifiable to make no provision for compensation for deprivation of property. Several judgments have considered the economic and political upheaval caused by the introduction of free markets upon the demise of communist regimes. The reunification of Germany has provided one context in which a failure by the state to pay compensation for property expropriation has been excused. In *Jahn and Others v Germany*, the applicants had become the owners of property as heirs of 'new settled farmers'. These farmers had obtained land specifically allocated for agricultural use in 1946 in the then Soviet-occupied zone of Germany. Prior to reunification, the parliament of the GDR (that is, of East Germany) had adopted a new land-reform law in 1990 which in turn had been incorporated into the legal order of the new German state upon reunification. In essence, this statute abolished certain restrictions on disposal of land to which these 'new farmers' had been subject by making the farmers the outright owners of land allocated to them irrespective of the use to which the land was being put at this time. Subsequently, in 1992 and after reunification, a new land-reform law resulted in the applicants having to assign their property to the tax authorities without the right to obtain compensation, the law seeking to redress a perceived injustice that individuals who had failed to meet the original condition that land not being used for agriculture had to be returned to the authorities had unfairly benefited by becoming outright owners. The Chamber and Grand Chamber diverged on whether a 'fair balance' had been achieved, the Grand Chamber, by a majority, finding that a number of exceptional circumstances could be identified which served to justify the expropriation of the applicants' property in the absence of any compensation: in particular, the 1990 law had been enacted by a parliament that had not been democratically elected and during a transitional period marked by upheaval and uncertainty. This supported the conclusion that the intention of the legislature in passing the 1992 law could not be deemed to have been unreasonable in considering that reasons of social justice required correction of the effects of the 1990 law[1].

---

1   *Jahn and Others v Germany* [GC] 2005-VI, paras 100–117. See McCarthy 'Deprivation without Compensation: the Exceptional Circumstances of *Jahn v Germany*' [2007] EHRLR 295. Cf *Honecker and Others v Germany* (dec) 2001-XII (confiscation of assets acquired by dignitaries of GDR through a misuse of power to the detriment of the public interest had been examined in detail upon appeal; and having regard to the exceptional circumstances linked to German reunification, the respondent state had not exceeded its margin of appreciation or failed to strike a fair balance between the interests of the applicants and the general interest: manifestly ill-founded). See also *Credit Bank and Others v Bulgaria* (dec) 30 April 2002 (purchase and subsequent assignment of debts of state-owned companies and subsequent judicial determination of the lawfulness of retrospective legislation seeking to influence court proceedings in a period of transition from a centrally-planned economy to a market economy, an exceptional factor which had to be taken into account, and the judgment could not be considered arbitrary nor based on retrospective legislation: manifestly ill-founded); and *Forrer-Niedenthal v Germany* (20 February 2003), paras 37–49 (refusal to order restitution of property or offer compensation following reunification: no violation).

8.41 However, a distinction may be drawn between cases where a legal right to compensation is provided for but is unenforceable on account of a lack of funds or other means, and situations in which domestic law makes no such provision. In the former instance, inability to pay compensation cannot be argued as a justification. In *Broniowski v Poland,* the Court had to consider the compensation scheme affecting some 80,000 individuals following upon the redrawing of the state boundaries of Poland after 1945. Successive undertakings to provide compensation in the form of discounted entitlement to property had been rendered in the opinion of the Polish courts entirely illusory on account of deliberate decisions to reduce the amount of available property designated for compensation. This 'exceptionally difficult situation, involving complex, large-scale policy decisions' involving not only the 'particular historical and political background of the case, as well as the importance of the various social, legal and economic considerations' and the high number of persons affected together with the considerable sum at stake were all factors to be taken into the assessment of whether a 'fair balance' had been struck. However, while the national authorities had considerable discretion in determining the choice of measures and the timing of their implementation, there had been no satisfactory explanation for the continuous failure over many years to implement compensation rights: indeed, the deliberate actions designed to prevent the implementation of enforceable rights could not, in the opinion of the Court, 'be explained in terms of any legitimate public interest or the interests of the community as a whole'[1].

1   *Broniowski v Poland* [GC] 2004-V, paras 162–187, paras 162 and 175. For further cases involving 'pilot judgments' in cases alleging violation of Prot 1, Art 1, see para **8.02**, fn 3 above, and more generally, paras **2.80–2.81** above.

Domestic decisions on the availability of compensation

8.42 In *Adams v Scottish Ministers*, a statute prohibiting the hunting of wild mammals was found not to have involved a de facto expropriation of property rights but merely control of use. The Inner House agreed with the Lord Ordinary that it was open to the Scottish Parliament in controlling the use of the petitioners' property in the interest of preventing cruelty to wild mammals to decide not to confer a right to compensation, observing that the legislature had conducted inquiries into the likely effects of a prohibition on the wider community in areas in which foxhunting took place, and clearly had taken these factors into account[1]. In other cases in which Article 1 of Protocol no 1 has been engaged, the availability of damages at common law[2] or the existence of a statutory compensation scheme[3] has been held to be sufficient. Strasbourg jurisprudence in relation to compensation was also discussed in *Booker Aquaculture Ltd v Secretary of State for Scotland*, which concerned a requirement to destroy diseased fish in terms of EU law[4].

1   *Adams v Scottish Ministers* 2004 SC 665. See also *R (Countryside Alliance) v A-G and Secretary of State for the Environment, Food and Rural Affairs* [2005] EWHC 1677.

2   See eg *Dennis v Ministry of Defence* [2003] EWHC 793 (QB) (effective defence of the realm involving the training of pilots did not prevent a noise nuisance from arising, but was relevant to remedy: there had been an interference with D's human rights under Art 8 and Prot 1, Art 1 and damages at common law would provide 'just satisfaction').

3   Eg *R (MWH and H Ward Estates Ltd) v Monmouthshire County Council* [2002] EWCA Civ 1915 (entry upon land to carry out drainage scheme: statutory compensation payable); *R (London and Continental Stations and Property Ltd) v The Rail Regulator* [2003] EWHC 2607 (unsuccessful challenge to the lawfulness of a decision on the ground that the approach to compensation had led to the imposition of a disproportionate burden); and *Howard de Walden Estates Ltd v Aggio* [2009] 1 AC 39 (statutory right of tenant to grant of new lease on payment of compensation to freeholder).

4   *Booker Aquaculture Ltd v Secretary of State for Scotland* 2000 SC 9.

QUANTIFICATION

8.43 In determining the amount of compensation payable, it is legitimate for the state to take into account any material benefits derived by others such as adjacent proprietors of land which has been expropriated[1]. However, as the European Court of Human Rights made clear in *Lithgow and Others v United Kingdom* and later in *Holy Monasteries v Greece*, there is no guarantee of a right to full compensation since there may be legitimate public interest objectives in play which 'may call for less than reimbursement of the full market value'[2]. In the *Lithgow* case, state nationalisation of shipbuilding and aircraft concerns on the Clyde and elsewhere in Britain had been challenged by eight individuals and companies, principally upon the issue of calculation of the compensation which fell to be paid. The Court held that a right to compensation was implied by Article 1 of Protocol no 1, but did not accept that any scheme adopted must meet the full market cost of any property affected since state interests in achieving social justice or economic reform had also to be taken into account[3].

1   Cf *Katikaridis and Others v Greece* 1996-V, paras 45–51, and *Tsomtsos and Others v Greece* 1996-V, paras 40–42 (Greek law created an irrebuttable presumption that the owners of the properties on major roads benefited when roads are widened and required the owners to contribute to the costs of expropriation; while it was legitimate to take into account the benefit derived from the works by the adjoining owners, the system of compensation was too inflexible and did not take into account the diversity of situations in which an owner may have received little or no benefit or caused varying degrees of loss: thus the system was 'manifestly without reasonable foundation').

2   *Lithgow and Others v United Kingdom* (1986) A 102, para 121; *Holy Monasteries v Greece* (1994) A 301-A, para 71.

3   *Lithgow and Others v United Kingdom* (1986) A 102, paras 120–22. See too *Phocas v France* 1996-II, paras 59–60 (applicant had accepted expropriation compensation, and thus domestic law afforded a remedy sufficient to meet the article's requirements).

8.44 The European Court of Human Rights will be critical of compensation terms which appear unreasonable because of undue delay in the payment of compensation[1]. In particular, the Court has shown itself prepared to take into account the impact of inflation on claims for damages and compensation. For example, in *Akkus v Turkey*, the Turkish water board had expropriated agricultural land belonging to the applicant in order to construct a hydroelectric dam, but had initially paid in compensation only one quarter of the value of the land (a figure increased on appeal) and with payment of statutory default interest set at a rate of 30% per annum. The applicant sought to argue that the calculation of interest should have been based upon the prevailing rate of inflation (some 70% per annum) rather than upon the rate of statutory interest. The Court reiterated that the adequacy of compensation would be diminished if it were not to be paid within a reasonable time since any delay would reduce its real value. In the instant case, it had taken the state authorities 17 months after the court judgment to pay the additional compensation together with interest at a rate less than half of the annual rate of inflation. The difference between the value of the applicant's compensation as finally determined and the value when paid had thus caused the applicant to sustain a further loss in addition to that caused by the expropriation, and by deferring payment for such a period the authorities had rendered the compensation inadequate[2]. In *Aka v Turkey*, the applicant's complaint concerned the insufficiency of the statutory interest intended to compensate for the high monetary depreciation during the period since the commencement of the proceedings for compensation, rather than the delay in paying additional compensation which had been the issue in the *Akkus* case. The Court again acknowledged that the national authorities have a margin of appreciation in determining compensation, and even 'that it may be important for them to limit the amount of interest payable on debts due by the state', but it was still incumbent upon the Court to 'verify whether the "fair balance" between the demands of the general interest and the requirements of the protection of the individual's fundamental rights has been preserved'. Once more, the conclusion was that the difference between the real value of the amounts due to the applicant when the land was expropriated and when they were actually paid had caused the applicant to sustain an additional and separate loss which, when taken together with the loss of his land, could be said to have upset the fair balance that should have been maintained[3].

---

1   See eg *Zubani v Italy* 1996-IV, paras 45–49 (the law providing for compensation did not enter into force until some eight years after the land was taken, and thus a fair balance between protecting the right of property and the demands of the general interest had not been struck); *Guillemin v France* 1997-I, paras 53–56 (compensation for loss sustained can only constitute adequate reparation where it also takes into account the damage arising from the length of the deprivation, and further must be paid within a reasonable time; here, proceedings were still continuing after five years and compensation had not begun to be paid: violation of the guarantee); *Almeida Garrett and Others v Portugal* 2000-I, paras 49–55 (period of 24 years without final compensation having been paid: violation of Art 6). See also *Nastou v Greece (no 1)* (16 January 2003), paras 30–35 (failure to pay compensation in respect of an expropriation which had taken place in 1973 as proceedings were still pending: violation); and *Solodyuk v Russia* (12 July 2005), paras 31–36 (entitlement to pension in the month for which it was due had been established by law and indirectly confirmed by court decisions, but during an 11-month period and at a time when inflation was very unstable, pension payments had been delayed for up to four months resulting in a significant loss of purchasing power: violation);

2   *Akkuş v Turkey* 1997-IV, paras 27–30.

3   *Aka v Turkey* 1998-VI, paras 42–50 at para 47. For recent discussion, see *Yetiş and Others v Turkey* (6 July 2010), paras 41–60 (significant depreciation in value between date of assessment and date of settlement: violation).

Appendix I

Human Rights Act 1998

An Act to give further effect to rights and freedoms guaranteed under the European Convention on Human Rights; to make provision with respect to holders of certain judicial offices who become judges of the European Court of Human Rights; and for connected purposes.

[9th November 1998]

BE IT ENACTED by the Queen's most Excellent Majesty, by and with the advice and consent of the Lords Spiritual and Temporal, and Commons, in this present Parliament assembled, and by the authority of the same, as follows:—

INTRODUCTION

1 The Convention Rights

(1) In this Act "the Convention rights" means the rights and fundamental freedoms set out in—

    (a)   Articles 2 to 12 and 14 of the Convention,

    (b)   Articles 1 to 3 of the First Protocol, and

    (c)   [Article 1 of the Thirteenth Protocol][1],

as read with Articles 16 to 18 of the Convention.

(2) Those Articles are to have effect for the purposes of this Act subject to any designated derogation or reservation (as to which see sections 14 and 15).

(3) The Articles are set out in Schedule 1.

(4) The Secretary of State may by order make such amendments to this Act as he considers appropriate to reflect the effect, in relation to the United Kingdom, of a protocol.

(5) In subsection (4) "protocol" means a protocol to the Convention—

    (a)   which the United Kingdom has ratified; or

    (b)   which the United Kingdom has signed with a view to ratification.

(6) No amendment may be made by an order under subsection (4) so as to come into force before the protocol concerned is in force in relation to the United Kingdom.

---

1   Substituted by Human Rights Act 1998 (Amendment) Order 2004/1574, art 2(1).

---

2 Interpretation of Convention rights

(1) A court or tribunal determining a question which has arisen in connection with a Convention right must take into account any—

    (a)   judgment, decision, declaration or advisory opinion of the European Court of Human Rights,

    (b)   opinion of the Commission given in a report adopted under Article 31 of the Convention,

    (c)   decision of the Commission in connection with Article 26 or 27(2) of the Convention, or

(d) decision of the Committee of Ministers taken under Article 46 of the Convention,

whenever made or given, so far as, in the opinion of the court or tribunal, it is relevant to the proceedings in which that question has arisen.

(2) Evidence of any judgment, decision, declaration or opinion of which account may have to be taken under this section is to be given in proceedings before any court or tribunal in such manner as may be provided by rules.

(3) In this section "rules" means rules of court or, in the case of proceedings before a tribunal, rules made for the purposes of this section—
  (a) by [the Lord Chancellor or]¹ the Secretary of State, in relation to any proceedings outside Scotland;
  (b) by the Secretary of State, in relation to proceedings in Scotland; or
  (c) by a Northern Ireland department, in relation to proceedings before a tribunal in Northern Ireland—
  (i) which deals with transferred matters; and
  (ii) for which no rules made under paragraph (a) are in force.

---

1   Inserted by Transfer of Functions (Lord Chancellor and Secretary of State) Order 2005/3429, Sch 1 para 3.

LEGISLATION

3 Interpretation of legislation

(1) So far as it is possible to do so, primary legislation and subordinate legislation must be read and given effect in a way which is compatible with the Convention rights.

(2) This section—
  (a) applies to primary legislation and subordinate legislation whenever enacted;
  (b) does not affect the validity, continuing operation or enforcement of any incompatible primary legislation; and
  (c) does not affect the validity, continuing operation or enforcement of any incompatible subordinate legislation if (disregarding any possibility of revocation) primary legislation prevents removal of the incompatibility.

4 Declaration of incompatibility

(1) Subsection (2) applies in any proceedings in which a court determines whether a provision of primary legislation is compatible with a Convention right.

(2) If the court is satisfied that the provision is incompatible with a Convention right, it may make a declaration of that incompatibility.

(3) Subsection (4) applies in any proceedings in which a court determines whether a provision of subordinate legislation, made in the exercise of a power conferred by primary legislation, is compatible with a Convention right.

(4) If the court is satisfied—
  (a) that the provision is incompatible with a Convention right, and
  (b) that (disregarding any possibility of revocation) the primary legislation concerned prevents removal of the incompatibility,

it may make a declaration of that incompatibility.

(5) In this section "court" means —
  (a) the [Supreme Court]¹;

(b) the Judicial Committee of the Privy Council;

(c) the [Court Martial Appeal Court][2];

(d) in Scotland, the High Court of Justiciary sitting otherwise than as a trial court or the Court of Session;

(e) in England and Wales or Northern Ireland, the High Court or the Court of Appeal [;][3]

[(f) the Court of Protection, in any matter being dealt with by the President of the Family Division, the Vice-Chancellor or a puisne judge of the High Court.][3]

(6) A declaration under this section ("a declaration of incompatibility")—

(a) does not affect the validity, continuing operation or enforcement of the provision in respect of which it is given; and

(b) is not binding on the parties to the proceedings in which it is made.

1   Substituted by Constitutional Reform Act 2005 c 4 Sch 9(1) para 66(2).

2   Words substituted by Armed Forces Act 2006 c 52 Sch 16 para 156.

3   Inserted by Mental Capacity Act 2005 c 9, Sch 6 para 43.

5 Right of Crown to intervene

(1) Where a court is considering whether to make a declaration of incompatibility, the Crown is entitled to notice in accordance with rules of court.

(2) In any case to which subsection (1) applies—

(a) a Minister of the Crown (or a person nominated by him),

(b) a member of the Scottish Executive,

(c) a Northern Ireland Minister,

(d) a Northern Ireland department,

is entitled, on giving notice in accordance with rules of court, to be joined as a party to the proceedings.

(3) Notice under subsection (2) may be given at any time during the proceedings.

(4) A person who has been made a party to criminal proceedings (other than in Scotland) as the result of a notice under subsection (2) may, with leave, appeal to the [Supreme Court][1] against any declaration of incompatibility made in the proceedings.

(5) In subsection (4)—

"criminal proceedings" includes all proceedings before the [Court Martial Appeal Court][2]; and

"leave" means leave granted by the court making the declaration of incompatibility or by the [Supreme Court][1].

1   Words substituted by Constitutional Reform Act 2005 c 4 Sch 9(1) para 66(3).

2   Words substituted by Armed Forces Act 2006 c 52 Sch 16 para 157.

PUBLIC AUTHORITIES

6 Acts of public authorities

(1) It is unlawful for a public authority to act in a way which is incompatible with a Convention right.

(2) Subsection (1) does not apply to an act if—

(a) as the result of one or more provisions of primary legislation, the authority could not have acted differently; or

(b) in the case of one or more provisions of, or made under, primary legislation which cannot be read or given effect in a way which is compatible with the Convention rights, the authority was acting so as to give effect to or enforce those provisions.

(3) In this section "public authority" includes—

(a) a court or tribunal, and

(b) any person certain of whose functions are functions of a public nature,

but does not include either House of Parliament or a person exercising functions in connection with proceedings in Parliament.

(4) ...[1]

(5) In relation to a particular act, a person is not a public authority by virtue only of subsection (3)(b) if the nature of the act is private.

(6) "An act" includes a failure to act but does not include a failure to—

(a) introduce in, or lay before, Parliament a proposal for legislation; or

(b) make any primary legislation or remedial order.

---

1 Repealed by Constitutional Reform Act 2005 c 4 Sch 18(5) para 1.

---

7 Proceedings

(1) A person who claims that a public authority has acted (or proposes to act) in a way which is made unlawful by section 6(1) may—

(a) bring proceedings against the authority under this Act in the appropriate court or tribunal, or

(b) rely on the Convention right or rights concerned in any legal proceedings,

but only if he is (or would be) a victim of the unlawful act.

(2) In subsection (1)(a) "appropriate court or tribunal" means such court or tribunal as may be determined in accordance with rules; and proceedings against an authority include a counterclaim or similar proceedings.

(3) If the proceedings are brought on an application for judicial review, the applicant is to be taken to have a sufficient interest in relation to the unlawful act only if he is, or would be, a victim of that act.

(4) If the proceedings are made by way of a petition for judicial review in Scotland, the applicant shall be taken to have title and interest to sue in relation to the unlawful act only if he is, or would be, a victim of that act.

(5) Proceedings under subsection (1)(a) must be brought before the end of—

(a) the period of one year beginning with the date on which the act complained of took place; or

(b) such longer period as the court or tribunal considers equitable having regard to all the circumstances,

but that is subject to any rule imposing a stricter time limit in relation to the procedure in question.

(6) In subsection (1)(b) "legal proceedings" includes—

(a) proceedings brought by or at the instigation of a public authority; and

(b) an appeal against the decision of a court or tribunal.

(7) For the purposes of this section, a person is a victim of an unlawful act only if he would

be a victim for the purposes of Article 34 of the Convention if proceedings were brought in the European Court of Human Rights in respect of that act.

(8) Nothing in this Act creates a criminal offence.

(9) In this section "rules" means —

(a) in relation to proceedings before a court or tribunal outside Scotland, rules made by the [the Lord Chancellor or]¹ Secretary of State for the purposes of this section or rules of court,

(b) in relation to proceedings before a court or tribunal in Scotland, rules made by the Secretary of State for those purposes,

(c) in relation to proceedings before a tribunal in Northern Ireland—

(i) which deals with transferred matters; and

(ii) for which no rules made under paragraph (a) are in force,

rules made by a Northern Ireland department for those purposes,

and includes provision made by order under section 1 of the Courts and Legal Services Act 1990.

(10) In making rules, regard must be had to section 9.

(11) The Minister who has power to make rules in relation to a particular tribunal may, to the extent he considers it necessary to ensure that the tribunal can provide an appropriate remedy in relation to an act (or proposed act) of a public authority which is (or would be) unlawful as a result of section 6(1), by order add to—

(a) the relief or remedies which the tribunal may grant; or

(b) the grounds on which it may grant any of them.

(12) An order made under subsection (11) may contain such incidental, supplemental, consequential or transitional provision as the Minister making it considers appropriate.

(13) "The Minister" includes the Northern Ireland department concerned.

---

1   Inserted by Transfer of Functions (Lord Chancellor and Secretary of State) Order 2005/3429, Sch 1 para 3.

---

8 Judicial remedies

(1) In relation to any act (or proposed act) of a public authority which the court finds is (or would be) unlawful, it may grant such relief or remedy, or make such order, within its powers as it considers just and appropriate.

(2) But damages may be awarded only by a court which has power to award damages, or to order the payment of compensation, in civil proceedings.

(3) No award of damages is to be made unless, taking account of all the circumstances of the case, including—

(a) any other relief or remedy granted, or order made, in relation to the act in question (by that or any other court), and

(b) the consequences of any decision (of that or any other court) in respect of that act,

the court is satisfied that the award is necessary to afford just satisfaction to the person in whose favour it is made.

(4) In determining—

(a) whether to award damages, or

(b) the amount of an award,

the court must take into account the principles applied by the European Court of Human Rights in relation to the award of compensation under Article 41 of the Convention.

(5) A public authority against which damages are awarded is to be treated—
- (a) in Scotland, for the purposes of section 3 of the Law Reform (Miscellaneous Provisions) (Scotland) Act 1940 as if the award were made in an action of damages in which the authority has been found liable in respect of loss or damage to the person to whom the award is made;
- (b) for the purposes of the Civil Liability (Contribution) Act 1978 as liable in respect of damage suffered by the person to whom the award is made.

(6) In this section—
"court" includes a tribunal;
"damages" means damages for an unlawful act of a public authority; and "unlawful" means unlawful under section 6(1).

9 Judicial acts

(1) Proceedings under section 7(1)(a) in respect of a judicial act may be brought only—
- (a) by exercising a right of appeal;
- (b) on an application (in Scotland a petition) for judicial review; or (c) in such other forum as may be prescribed by rules.

(2) That does not affect any rule of law which prevents a court from being the subject of judicial review.

(3) In proceedings under this Act in respect of a judicial act done in good faith, damages may not be awarded otherwise than to compensate a person to the extent required by Article 5(5) of the Convention.

(4) An award of damages permitted by subsection (3) is to be made against the Crown; but no award may be made unless the appropriate person, if not a party to the proceedings, is joined.

(5) In this section—
"appropriate person" means the Minister responsible for the court concerned, or a person or government department nominated by him;
"court" includes a tribunal;
"judge" includes a member of a tribunal, a justice of the peace and a clerk or other officer entitled to exercise the jurisdiction of a court;
"judicial act" means a judicial act of a court and includes an act done on the instructions, or on behalf, of a judge; and
"rules" has the same meaning as in section 7(9).

REMEDIAL ACTION

10 Power to take remedial action

(1) This section applies if—
- (a) a provision of legislation has been declared under section 4 to be incompatible with a Convention right and, if an appeal lies—
  - (i) all persons who may appeal have stated in writing that they do not intend to do so;
  - (ii) the time for bringing an appeal has expired and no appeal has been brought within that time; or
  - (iii) an appeal brought within that time has been determined or abandoned; or

(b) it appears to a Minister of the Crown or Her Majesty in Council that, having regard to a finding of the European Court of Human Rights made after the coming into force of this section in proceedings against the United Kingdom, a provision of legislation is incompatible with an obligation of the United Kingdom arising from the Convention.

(2) If a Minister of the Crown considers that there are compelling reasons for proceeding under this section, he may by order make such amendments to the legislation as he considers necessary to remove the incompatibility.

(3) If, in the case of subordinate legislation, a Minister of the Crown considers—

(a) that it is necessary to amend the primary legislation under which the subordinate legislation in question was made, in order to enable the incompatibility to be removed, and

(b) that there are compelling reasons for proceeding under this section,

he may by order make such amendments to the primary legislation as he considers necessary.

(4) This section also applies where the provision in question is in subordinate legislation and has been quashed, or declared invalid, by reason of incompatibility with a Convention right and the Minister proposes to proceed under paragraph 2(b) of Schedule 2.

(5) If the legislation is an Order in Council, the power conferred by subsection (2) or (3) is exercisable by Her Majesty in Council.

(6) In this section "legislation" does not include a Measure of the Church Assembly or of the General Synod of the Church of England.

(7) Schedule 2 makes further provision about remedial orders.

OTHER RIGHTS AND PROCEEDINGS

11 Safeguard for existing human rights

A person's reliance on a Convention right does not restrict—

(a) any other right or freedom conferred on him by or under any law having effect in any part of the United Kingdom; or

(b) his right to make any claim or bring any proceedings which he could make or bring apart from sections 7 to 9.

12 Freedom of expression

(1) This section applies if a court is considering whether to grant any relief which, if granted, might affect the exercise of the Convention right to freedom of expression.

(2) If the person against whom the application for relief is made ("the respondent") is neither present nor represented, no such relief is to be granted unless the court is satisfied—

(a) that the applicant has taken all practicable steps to notify the respondent; or

(b) that there are compelling reasons why the respondent should not be notified.

(3) No such relief is to be granted so as to restrain publication before trial unless the court is satisfied that the applicant is likely to establish that publication should not be allowed.

(4) The court must have particular regard to the importance of the Convention right to freedom of expression and, where the proceedings relate to material which the respondent claims, or which appears to the court, to be journalistic, literary or artistic material (or to conduct connected with such material), to—

(a) the extent to which—
(i)the material has, or is about to, become available to the public; or
(ii)it is, or would be, in the public interest for the material to be published;
(b) any relevant privacy code.

(5) In this section—
"court" includes a tribunal; and
"relief" includes any remedy or order (other than in criminal proceedings).

13 Freedom of thought, conscience and religion

(1) If a court's determination of any question arising under this Act might affect the exercise by a religious organisation (itself or its members collectively) of the Convention right to freedom of thought, conscience and religion, it must have particular regard to the importance of that right.

(2) In this section "court" includes a tribunal.

DEROGATIONS AND RESERVATIONS

14 Derogations

(1) In this Act "designated derogation" means any derogation by the United Kingdom from an Article of the Convention, or of any protocol to the Convention, which is designated for the purposes of this Act in an order made by the [Secretary of State][1].

(3) If a designated derogation is amended or replaced it ceases to be a designated derogation.

(4) But subsection (3) does not prevent the [Secretary of State][2] from exercising his power under subsection (1) to make a fresh designation order in respect of the Article concerned.

(5) The [Secretary of State][3] must by order make such amendments to Schedule 3 as he considers appropriate to reflect—
(a) any designation order; or
(b) the effect of subsection (3).

(6) A designation order may be made in anticipation of the making by the United Kingdom of a proposed derogation.

---

1   Substituted by Secretary of State for Constitutional Affairs Order 2003/1887, Sch 2 para 10(1).

2   Substituted by Secretary of State for Constitutional Affairs Order 2003/1887, Sch 2 para 10(1).

3   Substituted by Secretary of State for Constitutional Affairs Order 2003/1887, Sch 2 para 10(1).

15 Reservations

(1) In this Act "designated reservation" means—
(a) the United Kingdom's reservation to Article 2 of the First Protocol to the Convention; and
(b) any other reservation by the United Kingdom to an Article of the Convention, or of any protocol to the Convention, which is designated for the purposes of this Act in an order made by the [Secretary of State][1].

(2) The text of the reservation referred to in subsection (1)(a) is set out in Part II of Schedule 3.

(3) If a designated reservation is withdrawn wholly or in part it ceases to be a designated reservation.

(4) But subsection (3) does not prevent the [Secretary of State][2] from exercising his power under subsection (1)(b) to make a fresh designation order in respect of the Article concerned.

(5) The [Secretary of State][3] must by order make such amendments to this Act as he considers appropriate to reflect—
  (a) any designation order; or
  (b) the effect of subsection (3).

---

1   Substituted by Secretary of State for Constitutional Affairs Order 2003/1887 Sch 2 para 10(1).

2   Substituted by Secretary of State for Constitutional Affairs Order 2003/1887 Sch 2 para 10(1).

3   Substituted by Secretary of State for Constitutional Affairs Order 2003/1887 Sch 2 para 10(1).

---

16 Period for which designated derogations have effect

(1) If it has not already been withdrawn by the United Kingdom, a designated derogation ceases to have effect for the purposes of this Act, at the end of the period of five years beginning with the date on which the order designating it was made.

(2) At any time before the period—
  (a) fixed by subsection (1), or
  (b) extended by an order under this subsection,

comes to an end, the [Secretary of State][1] may by order extend it by a further period of five years.

(3) An order under section 14(1) ceases to have effect at the end of the period for consideration, unless a resolution has been passed by each House approving the order.

(4) Subsection (3) does not affect—
  (a) anything done in reliance on the order; or
  (b) the power to make a fresh order under section 14(1).

(5) In subsection (3) "period for consideration" means the period of forty days beginning with the day on which the order was made.

(6) In calculating the period for consideration, no account is to be taken of any time during which—
  (a) Parliament is dissolved or prorogued; or
  (b) both Houses are adjourned for more than four days.

(7) If a designated derogation is withdrawn by the United Kingdom, the [Secretary of State][2] must by order make such amendments to this Act as he considers are required to reflect that withdrawal.

---

1   Substituted by Secretary of State for Constitutional Affairs Order 2003/1887, Sch 2 para 10(1).

2   Substituted by Secretary of State for Constitutional Affairs Order 2003/1887, Sch 2 para 10(1).

---

17 Periodic review of designated reservations

(1) The appropriate Minister must review the designated reservation referred to in section 15(1)(a)—
  (a) before the end of the period of five years beginning with the date on which section 1(2) came into force; and

(b) if that designation is still in force, before the end of the period of five years beginning with the date on which the last report relating to it was laid under subsection (3).

(2) The appropriate Minister must review each of the other designated reservations (if any)—

(a) before the end of the period of five years beginning with the date on which the order designating the reservation first came into force; and

(b) if the designation is still in force, before the end of the period of five years beginning with the date on which the last report relating to it was laid under subsection (3).

(3) The Minister conducting a review under this section must prepare a report on the result of the review and lay a copy of it before each House of Parliament.

JUDGES OF THE EUROPEAN COURT OF HUMAN RIGHTS

18 Appointment to European Court of Human Rights

(1) In this section "judicial office" means the office of—

(a) Lord Justice of Appeal, Justice of the High Court or Circuit judge, in England and Wales;

(b) judge of the Court of Session or sheriff, in Scotland;

(c) Lord Justice of Appeal, judge of the High Court or county court judge, in Northern Ireland.

(2) The holder of a judicial office may become a judge of the European Court of Human Rights ("the Court") without being required to relinquish his office.

(3) But he is not required to perform the duties of his judicial office while he is a judge of the Court.

(4) In respect of any period during which he is a judge of the Court—

(a) a Lord Justice of Appeal or Justice of the High Court is not to count as a judge of the relevant court for the purposes of section 2(1) or 4(1) of the [Senior Court Act 1981][1] (maximum number of judges) nor as a judge of the [Senior Courts][2] for the purposes of section 12(1) to (6) of that Act (salaries etc.);

(b) a judge of the Court of Session is not to count as a judge of that court for the purposes of section 1(1) of the Court of Session Act 1988 (maximum number of judges) or of section 9(1)(c) of the Administration of Justice Act 1973 ("the 1973 Act") (salaries etc.);

(c) a Lord Justice of Appeal or judge of the High Court in Northern Ireland is not to count as a judge of the relevant court for the purposes of section 2(1) or 3(1) of the Judicature (Northern Ireland) Act 1978 (maximum number of judges) nor as a judge of the [Court of Judicature][3] Northern Ireland for the purposes of section 9(1)(d) of the 1973 Act (salaries etc.);

(d) a Circuit judge is not to count as such for the purposes of section 18 of the Courts Act 1971 (salaries etc);

(e) a sheriff is not to count as such for the purposes of section 14 of the Sheriff Courts (Scotland) Act 1907 (salaries etc.);

(f) a county court judge of Northern Ireland is not to count as such for the purposes of section 106 of the County Courts Act (Northern Ireland) 1959 (salaries etc).

(5) If a sheriff principal is appointed a judge of the Court, section 11(1) of the Sheriff Courts (Scotland) Act 1971 (temporary appointment of sheriff principal) applies, while he holds that appointment, as if his office is vacant.

(6) Schedule 4 makes provision about judicial pensions in relation to the holder of a judicial office who serves as a judge of the Court.

(7) The Lord Chancellor or the Secretary of State may by order make such transitional provision (including, in particular, provision for a temporary increase in the maximum number of judges) as he considers appropriate in relation to any holder of a judicial office who has completed his service as a judge of the Court.

[(7A) The following paragraphs apply to the making of an order under subsection (7) in relation to any holder of a judicial office listed in subsection (1)(a)—
    (a) before deciding what transitional provision it is appropriate to make, the person making the order must consult the Lord Chief Justice of England and Wales;
    (b) before making the order, that person must consult the Lord Chief Justice of England and Wales.

(7B) The following paragraphs apply to the making of an order under subsection (7) in relation to any holder of a judicial office listed in subsection (1)(c)—
    (a) before deciding what transitional provision it is appropriate to make, the person making the order must consult the Lord Chief Justice of Northern Ireland;
    (b) before making the order, that person must consult the Lord Chief Justice of Northern Ireland.

(7C) The Lord Chief Justice of England and Wales may nominate a judicial office holder (within the meaning of section 109(4) of the Constitutional Reform Act 2005) to exercise his functions under this section.

(7D) The Lord Chief Justice of Northern Ireland may nominate any of the following to exercise his functions under this section—
    (a) the holder of one of the offices listed in Schedule 1 to the Justice (Northern Ireland) Act 2002;
    (b) a Lord Justice of Appeal (as defined in section 88 of that Act).][4]

---

1   Words substituted by Constitutional Reform Act 2005 c 4 Sch 11(1) para 1(2).

2   Words substituted by Constitutional Reform Act 2005 c 4 Sch 11(2) para 4(1).

3   Words substituted by Constitutional Reform Act 2005 c 4 Sch 11(3) para 6(1).

4   Inserted by Constitutional Reform Act 2005 c 4, Sch 4(1) para 278.

PARLIAMENTARY PROCEDURE

19 Statements of compatibility

(1) A Minister of the Crown in charge of a Bill in either House of Parliament must, before Second Reading of the Bill—
    (a) make a statement to the effect that in his view the provisions of the Bill are compatible with the Convention rights ("a statement of compatibility"); or
    (b) make a statement to the effect that although he is unable to make a statement of compatibility the government nevertheless wishes the House to proceed with the Bill.

(2) The statement must be in writing and be published in such manner as the Minister making it considers appropriate.

SUPPLEMENTAL

20 Orders etc. under this Act

(1) Any power of a Minister of the Crown to make an order under this Act is exercisable by statutory instrument.

(2) The power of the Lord Chancellor or the Secretary of State to make rules (other than rules of court) under section 2(3) or 7(9) is exercisable by statutory instrument.

(3) Any statutory instrument made under section 14, 15 or 16(7) must be laid before Parliament.

(4) No order may be made by [the Lord Chancellor or]¹ the Secretary of State under section 1(4), 7(11) or 16(2) unless a draft of the order has been laid before, and approved by, each House of Parliament.

(5) Any statutory instrument made under section 18(7) or Schedule 4, or to which subsection (2) applies, shall be subject to annulment in pursuance of a resolution of either House of Parliament.

(6) The power of a Northern Ireland department to make—
    (a)   rules under section 2(3)(c) or 7(9)(c), or
    (b)   an order under section 7(11),

is exercisable by statutory rule for the purposes of the Statutory Rules (Northern Ireland) Order 1979.

(7) Any rules made under section 2(3)(c) or 7(9)(c) shall be subject to negative resolution; and section 41(6) of the Interpretation Act (Northern Ireland) 1954 (meaning of "subject to negative resolution") shall apply as if the power to make the rules were conferred by an Act of the Northern Ireland Assembly.

(8) No order may be made by a Northern Ireland department under section 7(11) unless a draft of the order has been laid before, and approved by, the Northern Ireland Assembly.

---

1   Inserted by Transfer of Functions (Lord Chancellor and Secretary of State) Order 2005/3429, Sch 1 para 3

---

21 Interpretation, etc

(1) In this Act—
    "amend" includes repeal and apply (with or without modifications);
    "the appropriate Minister" means the Minister of the Crown having charge of the appropriate authorised government department (within the meaning of the Crown Proceedings Act 1947);
    "the Commission" means the European Commission of Human Rights;
    "the Convention" means the Convention for the Protection of Human Rights and Fundamental Freedoms, agreed by the Council of Europe at Rome on 4th November 1950 as it has effect for the time being in relation to the United Kingdom;
    "declaration of incompatibility" means a declaration under section 4;
    "Minister of the Crown" has the same meaning as in the Ministers of the Crown Act 1975; "Northern Ireland Minister" includes the First Minister and the deputy First Minister in Northern Ireland;
    "primary legislation" means any—
        (a)   public general Act;
        (b)   local and personal Act;
        (c)   private Act;

    (d)   Measure of the Church Assembly;

    (e)   Measure of the General Synod of the Church of England;

    (f)   Order in Council—

        (i)   made in exercise of Her Majesty's Royal Prerogative;

        (ii)   made under section 38(1)(a) of the Northern Ireland Constitution Act 1973 or the corresponding provision of the Northern Ireland Act 1998; or

        (iii) amending an Act of a kind mentioned in paragraph (a), (b) or (c);

        and includes an order or other instrument made under primary legislation (otherwise than by the Welsh Ministers, the First Minister for Wales, the Counsel General to the Welsh Assembly Government, a member of the Scottish Executive, a Northern Ireland Minister or a Northern Ireland department) to the extent to which it operates to bring one or more provisions of that legislation into force or amends any primary legislation;

"the First Protocol" means the protocol to the Convention agreed at Paris on 20th March 1952;

"the Eleventh Protocol" means the protocol to the Convention (restructuring the control machinery established by the Convention) agreed at Strasbourg on 11th May 1994;

"the Thirteenth Protocol" means the protocol to the Convention (concerning the abolition of the death penalty in all circumstances) agreed at Vilnius on 3rd May 2002; "remedial order" means an order under section 10;

"subordinate legislation" means any—

    (a)   Order in Council other than one—

        (i)   made in exercise of Her Majesty's Royal Prerogative;

        (ii)   made under section 38(1)(a) of the Northern Ireland Constitution Act 1973 or the corresponding provision of the Northern Ireland Act 1998; or

        (iii) amending an Act of a kind mentioned in the definition of primary legislation;

    (b)   Act of the Scottish Parliament;

    (ba) Measure of the National Assembly for Wales;

    (bb) Act of the National Assembly for Wales;

    (c)   Act of the Parliament of Northern Ireland;

    (d)   Measure of the Assembly established under section 1 of the Northern Ireland Assembly Act 1973;

    (e)   Act of the Northern Ireland Assembly;

    (f)   order, rules, regulations, scheme, warrant, byelaw or other instrument made under primary legislation (except to the extent to which it operates to bring one or more provisions of that legislation into force or amends any primary legislation);

    (g)   order, rules, regulations, scheme, warrant, byelaw or other instrument made under legislation mentioned in paragraph (b), (c), (d) or (e) or made under an Order in Council applying only to Northern Ireland;

    (h)   order, rules, regulations, scheme, warrant, byelaw or other instrument made by a member of the Scottish Executive, [Welsh Ministers, the First Minister for Wales, the Counsel General to the Welsh Assembly Government,][1] a Northern Ireland Minister or a Northern Ireland department in exercise of prerogative or other executive functions of Her Majesty which are exercisable by such a person on behalf of Her Majesty;

"transferred matters" has the same meaning as in the Northern Ireland Act 1998; and

"tribunal" means any tribunal in which legal proceedings may be brought.

(2) The references in paragraphs (b) and (c) of section 2(1) to Articles are to Articles of the Convention as they had effect immediately before the coming into force of the Eleventh Protocol.

(3) The reference in paragraph (d) of section 2(1) to Article 46 includes a reference to Articles 32 and 54 of the Convention as they had effect immediately before the coming into force of the Eleventh Protocol.

(4) The references in section 2(1) to a report or decision of the Commission or a decision of the Committee of Ministers include references to a report or decision made as provided by paragraphs 3, 4 and 6 of Article 5 of the Eleventh Protocol (transitional provisions).

(5) [...][2]

---

1   Inserted by Government of Wales Act 2006 c 32, Sch 10 para 56(4).

2   'Repealed by Armed Forces Act 2006 Sch 17 para 1.

22 Short title, commencement, application and extent

(1) This Act may be cited as the Human Rights Act 1998.

(2) Sections 18, 20 and 21(5) and this section come into force on the passing of this Act.

(3) The other provisions of this Act come into force on such days as the Secretary of State may by order appoint; and different days may be appointed for different purposes.

(4) Paragraph (b) of subsection (1) of section 7 applies to proceedings brought by or at the instigation of a public authority whenever the act in question took place; but otherwise that subsection does not apply to an act taking place before the coming into force of that section.

(5) This Act binds the Crown.

(6) This Act extends to Northern Ireland.

(7) [...][1]

---

1   'Repealed by Armed Forces Act 2006 Sch 17 para 1.

SCHEDULE 1
THE ARTICLES[1]

---

[1]   Not reproduced here. For text of ECHR, see Appendix III.

SCHEDULE 2
REMEDIAL ORDERS

Section 10

ORDERS

1 (1) A remedial order may—
  (a) contain such incidental, supplemental, consequential or transitional provision as the person making it considers appropriate;
  (b) be made so as to have effect from a date earlier than that on which it is made;
  (c) make provision for the delegation of specific functions;
  (d) make different provision for different cases.

(2) The power conferred by sub-paragraph (1)(a) includes—

    (a) power to amend primary legislation (including primary legislation other than that which contains the incompatible provision); and

    (b) power to amend or revoke subordinate legislation (including subordinate legislation other than that which contains the incompatible provision).

(3) A remedial order may be made so as to have the same extent as the legislation which it affects.

(4) No person is to be guilty of an offence solely as a result of the retrospective effect of a remedial order.

PROCEDURE

2 No remedial order may be made unless—

    (a) a draft of the order has been approved by a resolution of each House of Parliament made after the end of the period of 60 days beginning with the day on which the draft was laid; or

    (b) it is declared in the order that it appears to the person making it that, because of the urgency of the matter, it is necessary to make the order without a draft being so approved.

ORDERS LAID IN DRAFT

3 (1) No draft may be laid under paragraph 2(a) unless—

    (a) the person proposing to make the order has laid before Parliament a document which contains a draft of the proposed order and the required information; and

    (b) the period of 60 days, beginning with the day on which the document required by this sub-paragraph was laid, has ended.

(2) If representations have been made during that period, the draft laid under paragraph 2(a) must be accompanied by a statement containing—

    (a) a summary of the representations; and

    (b) if, as a result of the representations, the proposed order has been changed, details of the changes.

URGENT CASES

4 (1) If a remedial order ("the original order") is made without being approved in draft, the person making it must lay it before Parliament, accompanied by the required information, after it is made.

(2) If representations have been made during the period of 60 days beginning with the day on which the original order was made, the person making it must (after the end of that period) lay before Parliament a statement containing—

    (a) a summary of the representations; and

    (b) if, as a result of the representations, he considers it appropriate to make changes to the original order, details of the changes.

(3) If sub-paragraph (2)(b) applies, the person making the statement must—

    (a) make a further remedial order replacing the original order; and

    (b) lay the replacement order before Parliament.

(4) If, at the end of the period of 120 days beginning with the day on which the original

order, was made, a resolution has not been passed by each House approving the original or replacement order, the order ceases to have effect (but without that affecting anything previously done under either order or the power to make a fresh remedial order).

DEFINITIONS

5 In this Schedule—

"representations" means representations about a remedial order (or proposed remedial order) made to the person making (or proposing to make) it and includes any relevant Parliamentary report or resolution; and

"required information" means—

    (a) an explanation of the incompatibility which the order (or proposed order) seeks to remove, including particulars of the relevant declaration, finding or order; and

    (b) a statement of the reasons for proceeding under section 10 and for making an order in those terms.

CALCULATING PERIODS

6 In calculating any period for the purposes of this Schedule, no account is to be taken of any time during which—

    (a) Parliament is dissolved or prorogued; or

    (b) both Houses are adjourned for more than four days.

[7 (1) This paragraph applies in relation to—

    (a) any remedial order made, and any draft of such an order proposed to be made,—

    (i)   by the Scottish Ministers; or

    (ii) within devolved competence (within the meaning of the Scotland Act 1998) by Her Majesty in Council; and

    (b) any document or statement to be laid in connection with such an order (or proposed order).

(2) This Schedule has effect in relation to any such order (or proposed order), document or statement subject to the following modifications.

(3) Any reference to Parliament, each House of Parliament or both Houses of Parliament shall be construed as a reference to the Scottish Parliament.

(4) Paragraph 6 does not apply and instead, in calculating any period for the purposes of this Schedule, no account is to be taken of any time during which the Scottish Parliament is dissolved or is in recess for more than four days.][1]

---

1   In relation to Scotland para 7 is inserted by Scotland Act 1998 (Consequential Modifications) Order 2000/2040, Sch 1(I) para 21.

SCHEDULE 3
DEROGATION AND RESERVATION

Sections 14 and 15

PART I
DEROGATION

[...][1]

1   RepeaLed by Human Rights Act 1998 (Amendment) Order 2005/1071, art 2.

PART II
RESERVATION

At the time of signing the present (First) Protocol, I declare that, in view of certain provisions of the Education Acts in the United Kingdom, the principle affirmed in the second sentence of Article 2 is accepted by the United Kingdom only so far as it is compatible with the provision of efficient instruction and training, and the avoidance of unreasonable public expenditure.

Dated 20 March 1952. Made by the United Kingdom Permanent Representative to the Council of Europe.

SCHEDULE 4
JUDICIAL PENSIONS

Section 18(6)

DUTY TO MAKE ORDERS ABOUT PENSIONS

1 (1) The appropriate Minister must by order make provision with respect to pensions payable to or in respect of any holder of a judicial office who serves as an ECHR judge.

(2) A pensions order must include such provision as the Minister making it considers is necessary to secure that—
   (a) an ECHR judge who was, immediately before his appointment as an ECHR judge, a member of a judicial pension scheme is entitled to remain as a member of that scheme;
   (b) the terms on which he remains a member of the scheme are those which would have been applicable had he not been appointed as an ECHR judge; and
   (c) entitlement to benefits payable in accordance with the scheme continues to be determined as if, while serving as an ECHR judge, his salary was that which would (but for section 18(4)) have been payable to him in respect of his continuing service as the holder of his judicial office.

CONTRIBUTIONS

2 A pensions order may, in particular, make provision—
   (a) for any contributions which are payable by a person who remains a member of a scheme as a result of the order, and which would otherwise be payable by deduction from his salary, to be made otherwise than by deduction from his salary as an ECHR judge; and
   (b) for such contributions to be collected in such manner as may be determined by the administrators of the scheme.

AMENDMENTS OF OTHER ENACTMENTS

3 A pensions order may amend any provision of, or made under, a pensions Act in such manner and to such extent as the Minister making the order considers necessary or expedient to ensure the proper administration of any scheme to which it relates.

DEFINITIONS

4 In this Schedule—

"appropriate Minister" means—

(a)in relation to any judicial office whose jurisdiction is exercisable exclusively in relation to Scotland, the Secretary of State; and

(b)otherwise, the Lord Chancellor;

"ECHR judge" means the holder of a judicial office who is serving as a judge of the Court; "judicial pension scheme" means a scheme established by and in accordance with a pensions Act;

"pensions Act" means—

(a)the County Courts Act (Northern Ireland) 1959;

(b)the Sheriffs' Pensions (Scotland) Act 1961;

(c)the Judicial Pensions Act 1981; or

(d)the Judicial Pensions and Retirement Act 1993; and

"pensions order" means an order made under paragraph 1.

This text is based on a version originally published by Westlaw UK.

Appendix II

Scotland Act 1998

1998 CHAPTER 46

An Act to provide for the establishment of a Scottish Parliament and Administration and other changes in the government of Scotland; to provide for changes in the constitution and functions of certain public authorities; to provide for the variation of the basic rate of income tax in relation to income of Scottish taxpayers in accordance with a resolution of the Scottish Parliament; to amend the law about parliamentary constituencies in Scotland; and for connected purposes.

[19th November 1998]

Be it enacted by the Queen's most Excellent Majesty, by and with the advice and consent of the Lords Spiritual and Temporal, and Commons, in this present Parliament assembled, and by the authority of the same, as follows:—

ss 1–27, 37–43, 59–97, 104–106, 108–125, 128, Schs 1–5, 7–9 (*outside the scope of this work*)

PART I
THE SCOTTISH PARLIAMENT

LEGISLATION

28 Acts of the Scottish Parliament

(1) Subject to section 29, the Parliament may make laws, to be known as Acts of the Scottish Parliament.

(2) Proposed Acts of the Scottish Parliament shall be known as Bills; and a Bill shall become an Act of the Scottish Parliament when it has been passed by the Parliament and has received Royal Assent.

(3) A Bill receives Royal Assent at the beginning of the day on which Letters Patent under the Scottish Seal signed with Her Majesty's own hand signifying Her Assent are recorded in the Register of the Great Seal.

(4) The date of Royal Assent shall be written on the Act of the Scottish Parliament by the Clerk, and shall form part of the Act.

(5) The validity of an Act of the Scottish Parliament is not affected by any invalidity in the proceedings of the Parliament leading to its enactment. $

(6) Every Act of the Scottish Parliament shall be judicially noticed.

(7) This section does not affect the power of the Parliament of the United Kingdom to make laws for Scotland.

29 Legislative competence

(1) An Act of the Scottish Parliament is not law so far as any provision of the Act is outside the legislative competence of the Parliament.

1049

(2) A provision is outside that competence so far as any of the following paragraphs apply—
- (a) it would form part of the law of a country or territory other than Scotland, or confer or remove functions exercisable otherwise than in or as regards Scotland,
- (b) it relates to reserved matters,
- (c) it is in breach of the restrictions in Schedule 4,
- (d) it is incompatible with any of the Convention rights or with [EU][1] law,
- (e) it would remove the Lord Advocate from his position as head of the systems of criminal prosecution and investigation of deaths in Scotland.

(3) For the purposes of this section, the question whether a provision of an Act of the Scottish Parliament relates to a reserved matter is to be determined, subject to subsection (4), by reference to the purpose of the provision, having regard (among other things) to its effect in all the circumstances.

(4) A provision which—
- (a) would otherwise not relate to reserved matters, but
- (b) makes modifications of Scots private law, or Scots criminal law, as it applies to reserved matters,

is to be treated as relating to reserved matters unless the purpose of the provision is to make the law in question apply consistently to reserved matters and otherwise.

---

1   Word substituted by Treaty of Lisbon (Changes in Terminology) Order 2011/1043 Pt 2 art 6(2)(a).

---

30 Legislative competence: supplementary

(1) Schedule 5 (which defines reserved matters) shall have effect.

(2) Her Majesty may by Order in Council make any modifications of Schedule 4 or 5 which She considers necessary or expedient.

(3) Her Majesty may by Order in Council specify functions which are to be treated, for such purposes of this Act as may be specified, as being, or as not being, functions which are exercisable in or as regards Scotland.

(4) An Order in Council under this section may also make such modifications of—
- (a) any enactment or prerogative instrument (including any enactment comprised in or made under this Act), or
- (b) any other instrument or document,

as Her Majesty considers necessary or expedient in connection with other provision made by the Order.

31 Scrutiny of Bills before introduction

(1) A member of the Scottish Executive in charge of a Bill shall, on or before introduction of the Bill in the Parliament, state that in his view the provisions of the Bill would be within the legislative competence of the Parliament.

(2) The Presiding Officer shall, on or before the introduction of a Bill in the Parliament, decide whether or not in his view the provisions of the Bill would be within the legislative competence of the Parliament and state his decision.

(3) The form of any statement, and the manner in which it is to be made, shall be determined under standing orders, and standing orders may provide for any statement to be published.

32 Submission of Bills for Royal Assent

(1) It is for the Presiding Officer to submit Bills for Royal Assent.

(2) The Presiding Officer shall not submit a Bill for Royal Assent at any time when—

    (a) the Advocate General, the Lord Advocate or the Attorney General is entitled to make a reference in relation to the Bill under section 33,

    (b) any such reference has been made but has not been decided or otherwise disposed of by the [Supreme Court][1], or

    (c) an order may be made in relation to the Bill under section 35.

(3) The Presiding Officer shall not submit a Bill in its unamended form for Royal Assent if—

    (a) the [Supreme Court has][2] decided that the Bill or any provision of it would not be within the legislative competence of the Parliament, or

    (b) a reference made in relation to the Bill under section 33 has been withdrawn following a request for withdrawal of the reference under section 34(2)(b).

(4) In this Act—

    "Advocate General" means the Advocate General for Scotland,

    ...[3].

---

1   Words substituted by Constitutional Reform Act 2005 c 4 Sch 9(2) para 95(a).

2   Words substituted by Constitutional Reform Act 2005 c 4 Sch 9(2) para 95(b).

3   Definition repealed by Constitutional Reform Act 2005 c 4 Sch 18(5) para 1.

---

33 Scrutiny of Bills by the [Supreme Court][1]

(1) The Advocate General, the Lord Advocate or the Attorney General may refer the question of whether a Bill or any provision of a Bill would be within the legislative competence of the Parliament to the [Supreme Court][2] for decision.

(2) Subject to subsection (3), he may make a reference in relation to a Bill at any time during—

    (a) the period of four weeks beginning with the passing of the Bill, and

    (b) any period of four weeks beginning with any subsequent approval of the Bill in accordance with standing orders made by virtue of section 36(5).

(3) He shall not make a reference in relation to a Bill if he has notified the Presiding Officer that he does not intend to make a reference in relation to the Bill, unless the Bill has been approved as mentioned in subsection (2)(b) since the notification.

---

1   Words substituted by Constitutional Reform Act 2005 c 4 Sch 9(2) para 96(1).

2   Words substituted by Constitutional Reform Act 2005 c 4 Sch 9(2) para 96(2).

---

34 ECJ references

(1) This section applies where—

    (a) a reference has been made in relation to a Bill under section 33,

    (b) a reference for a preliminary ruling has been made by the [Supreme Court][1] in connection with that reference, and

    (c) neither of those references has been decided or otherwise disposed of.

(2) If the Parliament resolves that it wishes to reconsider the Bill—

    (a) the Presiding Officer shall notify the Advocate General, the Lord Advocate and the Attorney General of that fact, and

(b) the person who made the reference in relation to the Bill under section 33 shall request the withdrawal of the reference.

(3) In this section "a reference for a preliminary ruling" means a reference of a question to the European Court under Article 177 of the Treaty establishing the European Community, Article 41 of the Treaty establishing the European Coal and Steel Community or Article 150 of the Treaty establishing the European Atomic Energy Community.

1   Words substituted by Constitutional Reform Act 2005 c 4 Sch 9(2) para 97.

35 Power to intervene in certain cases

(1) If a Bill contains provisions—
(a) which the Secretary of State has reasonable grounds to believe would be incompatible with any international obligations or the interests of defence or national security, or
(b) which make modifications of the law as it applies to reserved matters and which the Secretary of State has reasonable grounds to believe would have an adverse effect on the operation of the law as it applies to reserved matters,

he may make an order prohibiting the Presiding Officer from submitting the Bill for Royal Assent.

(2) The order must identify the Bill and the provisions in question and state the reasons for making the order.

(3) The order may be made at any time during—
(a) the period of four weeks beginning with the passing of the Bill,
(b) any period of four weeks beginning with any subsequent approval of the Bill in accordance with standing orders made by virtue of section 36(5),
(c) if a reference is made in relation to the Bill under section 33, the period of four weeks beginning with the reference being decided or otherwise disposed of by the [Supreme Court][1].

(4) The Secretary of State shall not make an order in relation to a Bill if he has notified the Presiding Officer that he does not intend to do so, unless the Bill has been approved as mentioned in subsection (3)(b) since the notification.

(5) An order in force under this section at a time when such approval is given shall cease to have effect.

1   Words substituted by Constitutional Reform Act 2005 c 4 Sch 9(2) para 98.

36 Stages of Bills

(1) Standing orders shall include provision—
(a) for general debate on a Bill with an opportunity for members to vote on its general principles,
(b) for the consideration of, and an opportunity for members to vote on, the details of a Bill, and
(c) for a final stage at which a Bill can be passed or rejected.

(2) Subsection (1) does not prevent standing orders making provision to enable the Parliament to expedite proceedings in relation to a particular Bill.

(3) Standing orders may make provision different from that required by subsection (1) for the procedure applicable to Bills of any of the following kinds—

(a) Bills which restate the law,

(b) Bills which repeal spent enactments,

(c) private Bills.

(4) Standing orders shall provide for an opportunity for the reconsideration of a Bill after its passing if (and only if)—

(a) the [Supreme Court decides][1] that the Bill or any provision of it would not be within the legislative competence of the Parliament,

(b) a reference made in relation to the Bill under section 33 is withdrawn following a request for withdrawal of the reference under section 34(2)(b), or

(c) an order is made in relation to the Bill under section 35.

(5) Standing orders shall, in particular, ensure that any Bill amended on reconsideration is subject to a final stage at which it can be approved or rejected.

(6) References in subsection (4), sections 28(2) and 38(1)(a) and paragraph 7 of Schedule 3 to the passing of a Bill shall, in the case of a Bill which has been amended on reconsideration, be read as references to the approval of the Bill.

---

1   Words substituted by Constitutional Reform Act 2005 c 4 Sch 9(2) para 99.

PART II
THE SCOTTISH ADMINISTRATION

MINISTERS AND THEIR STAFF

44 The Scottish Executive

(1) There shall be a Scottish Executive, whose members shall be—

(a) the First Minister,

(b) such Ministers as the First Minister may appoint under section 47, and

(c) the Lord Advocate and the Solicitor General for Scotland.

(2) The members of the Scottish Executive are referred to collectively as the Scottish Ministers.

(3) A person who holds a Ministerial office may not be appointed a member of the Scottish Executive; and if a member of the Scottish Executive is appointed to a Ministerial office he shall cease to hold office as a member of the Scottish Executive.

(4) In subsection (3), references to a member of the Scottish Executive include a junior Scottish Minister and "Ministerial office" has the same meaning as in section 2 of the House of Commons Disqualification Act 1975.

45 The First Minister

(1) The First Minister shall be appointed by Her Majesty from among the members of the Parliament and shall hold office at Her Majesty's pleasure.

(2) The First Minister may at any time tender his resignation to Her Majesty and shall do so if the Parliament resolves that the Scottish Executive no longer enjoys the confidence of the Parliament.

(3) The First Minister shall cease to hold office if a person is appointed in his place.

(4) If the office of First Minister is vacant or he is for any reason unable to act, the

functions exercisable by him shall be exercisable by a person designated by the Presiding Officer.

(5) A person shall be so designated only if—
    (a) he is a member of the Parliament, or
    (b) if the Parliament has been dissolved, he is a person who ceased to be a member by virtue of the dissolution.

(6) Functions exercisable by a person by virtue of subsection (5)(a) shall continue to be exercisable by him even if the Parliament is dissolved.

(7) The First Minister shall be the Keeper of the Scottish Seal.

46 Choice of the First Minister

(1) If one of the following events occurs, the Parliament shall within the period allowed nominate one of its members for appointment as First Minister.

(2) The events are—
    (a) the holding of a poll at a general election,
    (b) the First Minister tendering his resignation to Her Majesty,
    (c) the office of First Minister becoming vacant (otherwise than in consequence of his so tendering his resignation),
    (d) the First Minister ceasing to be a member of the Parliament otherwise than by virtue of a dissolution.

(3) The period allowed is the period of 28 days which begins with the day on which the event in question occurs; but—
    (a) if another of those events occurs within the period allowed, that period shall be extended (subject to paragraph (b)) so that it ends with the period of 28 days beginning with the day on which that other event occurred, and
    (b) the period shall end if the Parliament passes a resolution under section 3(1)(a) or when Her Majesty appoints a person as First Minister.

(4) The Presiding Officer shall recommend to Her Majesty the appointment of any member of the Parliament who is nominated by the Parliament under this section.

47 Ministers

(1) The First Minister may, with the approval of Her Majesty, appoint Ministers from among the members of the Parliament.

(2) The First Minister shall not seek Her Majesty's approval for any appointment under this section without the agreement of the Parliament.

(3) A Minister appointed under this section—
    (a) shall hold office at Her Majesty's pleasure,
    (b) may be removed from office by the First Minister,
    (c) may at any time resign and shall do so if the Parliament resolves that the Scottish Executive no longer enjoys the confidence of the Parliament,
    (d) if he resigns, shall cease to hold office immediately, and
    (e) shall cease to hold office if he ceases to be a member of the Parliament otherwise than by virtue of a dissolution.

48 The Scottish Law Officers

(1) It is for the First Minister to recommend to Her Majesty the appointment or removal of

a person as Lord Advocate or Solicitor General for Scotland; but he shall not do so without the agreement of the Parliament.

(2) The Lord Advocate and the Solicitor General for Scotland may at any time resign and shall do so if the Parliament resolves that the Scottish Executive no longer enjoys the confidence of the Parliament.

(3) Where the Lord Advocate resigns in consequence of such a resolution, he shall be deemed to continue in office until the warrant of appointment of the person succeeding to the office of Lord Advocate is granted, but only for the purpose of exercising his retained functions.

(4) Subsection (3) is without prejudice to section 287 of the Criminal Procedure (Scotland) Act 1995 (demission of office by Lord Advocate).

(5) Any decision of the Lord Advocate in his capacity as head of the systems of criminal prosecution and investigation of deaths in Scotland shall continue to be taken by him independently of any other person.

(6) In Schedule 2 to the House of Commons Disqualification Act 1975 (Ministerial offices) and Part III of Schedule 1 to the Ministerial and other Salaries Act 1975 (salaries of the Law Officers), the entries for the Lord Advocate and the Solicitor General for Scotland are omitted.

49 Junior Scottish Ministers

(1) The First Minister may, with the approval of Her Majesty, appoint persons from among the members of the Parliament to assist the Scottish Ministers in the exercise of their functions.

(2) They shall be known as junior Scottish Ministers.

(3) The First Minister shall not seek Her Majesty's approval for any appointment under this section without the agreement of the Parliament.

(4) A junior Scottish Minister—
   (a) shall hold office at Her Majesty's pleasure,
   (b) may be removed from office by the First Minister,
   (c) may at any time resign and shall do so if the Parliament resolves that the Scottish Executive no longer enjoys the confidence of the Parliament,
   (d) if he resigns, shall cease to hold office immediately, and
   (e) shall cease to hold office if he ceases to be a member of the Parliament otherwise than by virtue of a dissolution.

50 Validity of acts of Scottish Ministers etc

The validity of any act of a member of the Scottish Executive or junior Scottish Minister is not affected by any defect in his nomination by the Parliament or (as the case may be) in the Parliament's agreement to his appointment.

51 The Civil Service

(1) The Scottish Ministers may appoint persons to be members of the staff of the Scottish Administration.

(2) Service as—
   (a) the holder of any office in the Scottish Administration which is not a ministerial office, or

(b) a member of the staff of the Scottish Administration,

shall be service in the [civil service of the State]¹ .

[(3) See Part 1 of the Constitutional Reform and Governance Act 2010 (in particular, sections 3 and 4) for provision affecting—
(a) subsection (1), and
(b) any other enactment about the appointment of persons mentioned in subsection (2).]²

[(4) See also section 1 of the Civil Service (Management Functions) Act 1992 under which functions conferred on the Minister for the Civil Service by section 3 of the Constitutional Reform and Governance Act 2010 may be delegated to the Scottish Ministers etc.]³

(5) Any salary or allowances payable to or in respect of the persons mentioned in subsection (2) (including contributions to any pension scheme) shall be payable out of the Scottish Consolidated Fund.

(6) Section 1(2) and (3) of the Superannuation Act 1972 (delegation of functions relating to civil service superannuation schemes etc.) shall have effect as if references to a Minister of the Crown (other than the Minister for the Civil Service) included the Scottish Ministers.

(7) The Scottish Ministers shall make payments to the Minister for the Civil Service, at such times as he may determine, of such amounts as he may determine in respect of—
(a) the provision of pensions, allowances or gratuities by virtue of section 1 of the Superannuation Act 1972 to or in respect of persons who are or have been in such service as is mentioned in subsection (2), and
(b) any expenses to be incurred in administering those pensions, allowances or gratuities.

(8) Amounts required for payments under subsection (7) shall be charged on the Scottish Consolidated Fund.

[...]⁴

---

1   Words substituted by Constitutional Reform and Governance Act 2010 c 25 Sch 2(1) para 9(2).

2   Substituted by Constitutional Reform and Governance Act 2010 c 25 Sch 2(1) para 9(3).

3   Substituted by Constitutional Reform and Governance Act 2010 c 25 Sch 2(1) para 9(4).

4   Repealed by Constitutional Reform and Governance Act 2010 c 25 Sch 2(1) para 9(5).

MINISTERIAL FUNCTIONS

52 Exercise of functions

(1) Statutory functions may be conferred on the Scottish Ministers by that name.

(2) Statutory functions of the Scottish Ministers, the First Minister or the Lord Advocate shall be exercisable on behalf of Her Majesty.

(3) Statutory functions of the Scottish Ministers shall be exercisable by any member of the Scottish Executive.

(4) Any act or omission of, or in relation to, any member of the Scottish Executive shall be treated as an act or omission of, or in relation to, each of them; and any property acquired, or liability incurred, by any member of the Scottish Executive shall be treated accordingly.

(5) Subsection (4) does not apply in relation to the exercise of—

(a) functions conferred on the First Minister alone, or

(b) retained functions of the Lord Advocate.

(6) In this Act, "retained functions" in relation to the Lord Advocate means—

(a) any functions exercisable by him immediately before he ceases to be a Minister of the Crown, and

(b) other statutory functions conferred on him alone after he ceases to be a Minister of the Crown.

(7) In this section, "statutory functions" means functions conferred by virtue of any enactment.

53 General transfer of functions

(1) The functions mentioned in subsection (2) shall, so far as they are exercisable within devolved competence, be exercisable by the Scottish Ministers instead of by a Minister of the Crown.

(2) Those functions are—

(a) those of Her Majesty's prerogative and other executive functions which are exercisable on behalf of Her Majesty by a Minister of the Crown,

(b) other functions conferred on a Minister of the Crown by a prerogative instrument, and

(c) functions conferred on a Minister of the Crown by any pre-commencement enactment,

but do not include any retained functions of the Lord Advocate.

(3) In this Act, "pre-commencement enactment" means—

(a) an Act passed before or in the same session as this Act and any other enactment made before the passing of this Act,

(b) an enactment made, before the commencement of this section, under such an Act or such other enactment,

(c) subordinate legislation under section 106, to the extent that the legislation states that it is to be treated as a pre-commencement enactment.

(4) This section and section 54 are modified by Part III of Schedule 4.

54 Devolved competence

(1) References in this Act to the exercise of a function being within or outside devolved competence are to be read in accordance with this section.

(2) It is outside devolved competence—

(a) to make any provision by subordinate legislation which would be outside the legislative competence of the Parliament if it were included in an Act of the Scottish Parliament, or

(b) to confirm or approve any subordinate legislation containing such provision.

(3) In the case of any function other than a function of making, confirming or approving subordinate legislation, it is outside devolved competence to exercise the function (or exercise it in any way) so far as a provision of an Act of the Scottish Parliament conferring the function (or, as the case may be, conferring it so as to be exercisable in that way) would be outside the legislative competence of the Parliament.

55 Functions exercisable with agreement

(1) A statutory provision, or any provision not contained in an enactment, which provides

for a Minister of the Crown to exercise a function with the agreement of, or after consultation with, any other Minister of the Crown shall cease to have effect in relation to the exercise of the function by a member of the Scottish Executive by virtue of section 53.

(2) In subsection (1) "statutory provision" means any provision in a pre-commencement enactment other than paragraph 5 or 15 of Schedule 32 to the Local Government, Planning and Land Act 1980 (designation of enterprise zones).

56 Shared powers

(1) Despite the transfer by virtue of section 53 of any function under—
  (a) section 17(1) of the Ministry of Transport Act 1919 (power to make advances for certain purposes),
  (b) any Order in Council under section 1 of the United Nations Act 1946 (measures to give effect to Security Council decisions),
  (c) section 9 of the Industrial Organisation and Development Act 1947 (levies for scientific research, promotion of exports, etc.),
  (d) section 5 of the Science and Technology Act 1965 (funding of scientific research),
  (e) section 1 of the Mineral Exploration and Investment Grants Act 1972 (contributions in respect of mineral exploration),
  (f) sections 10 to 12 of the Industry Act 1972 (credits and grants for construction of ships and offshore installations),
  (g) sections 2, 11(3) and 12(4) of the Employment and Training Act 1973 (power to make arrangements for employment and training etc. and to make certain payments),
  (h) sections 7 to 9 and 11 to 13 of the Industrial Development Act 1982 (financial and other assistance for industry), and
  (i) sections 39 and 40 of the Road Traffic Act 1988 (road safety information and training),

the function shall be exercisable by a Minister of the Crown as well as by the Scottish Ministers.

(2) Despite the transfer of any other function by virtue of section 53, the function shall, if subordinate legislation so provides, be exercisable (or be exercisable so far as the legislation provides) by a Minister of the Crown as well as by the Scottish Ministers.

(3) Subordinate legislation under subsection (2) may not be made so as to come into force at any time after the function in question has become exercisable by the Scottish Ministers.

(4) Any power referred to in section 53(2)(a) to establish, maintain or abolish a body, office or office-holder having functions which include both—
  (a) functions which are exercisable in or as regards Scotland and do not relate to reserved matters, and
  (b) other functions,

shall, despite that section, be exercisable jointly by the Minister of the Crown and the Scottish Ministers.

(5) In subsection (4), "office-holder" includes employee or other post-holder.

57 [EU]¹ law and Convention rights

(1) Despite the transfer to the Scottish Ministers by virtue of section 53 of functions in relation to observing and implementing obligations under [EU]¹ law, any function of a Minister of the Crown in relation to any matter shall continue to be exercisable by him as regards Scotland for the purposes specified in section 2(2) of the European Communities Act 1972.

(2) A member of the Scottish Executive has no power to make any subordinate legislation, or to do any other act, so far as the legislation or act is incompatible with any of the Convention rights or with [EU][1] law.

(3) Subsection (2) does not apply to an act of the Lord Advocate—
   (a) in prosecuting any offence, or
   (b) in his capacity as head of the systems of criminal prosecution and investigation of deaths in Scotland,

which, because of subsection (2) of section 6 of the Human Rights Act 1998, is not unlawful under subsection (1) of that section.

---

1   Word substituted by Treaty of Lisbon (Changes in Terminology) Order 2011/1043 Pt 2 art 6(2)(a).

---

58 Power to prevent or require action

(1) If the Secretary of State has reasonable grounds to believe that any action proposed to be taken by a member of the Scottish Executive would be incompatible with any international obligations, he may by order direct that the proposed action shall not be taken.

(2) If the Secretary of State has reasonable grounds to believe that any action capable of being taken by a member of the Scottish Executive is required for the purpose of giving effect to any such obligations, he may by order direct that the action shall be taken.

(3) In subsections (1) and (2), "action" includes making, confirming or approving subordinate legislation and, in subsection (2), includes introducing a Bill in the Parliament.

(4) If any subordinate legislation made or which could be revoked by a member of the Scottish Executive contains provisions—
   (a) which the Secretary of State has reasonable grounds to believe to be incompatible with any international obligations or the interests of defence or national security, or
   (b) which make modifications of the law as it applies to reserved matters and which the Secretary of State has reasonable grounds to believe to have an adverse effect on the operation of the law as it applies to reserved matters,

the Secretary of State may by order revoke the legislation.

(5) An order under this section must state the reasons for making the order.

PART IV

THE TAX VARYING POWER

JUDICIAL

98 Devolution issues

Schedule 6 (which makes provision in relation to devolution issues) shall have effect.

99 Rights and liabilities of the Crown in different capacities

(1) Rights and liabilities may arise between the Crown in right of Her Majesty's Government in the United Kingdom and the Crown in right of the Scottish Administration by virtue of a contract, by operation of law or by virtue of an enactment as they may arise between subjects.

(2) Property and liabilities may be transferred between the Crown in one of those capacities and the Crown in the other capacity as they may be transferred between subjects; and they may together create, vary or extinguish any property or liability as subjects may.

(3) Proceedings in respect of—
  (a) any property or liabilities to which the Crown in one of those capacities is entitled or subject under subsection (1) or (2), or
  (b) the exercise of, or failure to exercise, any function exercisable by an office-holder of the Crown in one of those capacities,

may be instituted by the Crown in either capacity; and the Crown in the other capacity may be a separate party in the proceedings.

(4) This section applies to a unilateral obligation as it applies to a contract.

(5) In this section—
  "office-holder", in relation to the Crown in right of Her Majesty's Government in the United Kingdom, means any Minister of the Crown or other office-holder under the Crown in that capacity and, in relation to the Crown in right of the Scottish Administration, means any office-holder in the Scottish Administration,
  "subject" means a person not acting on behalf of the Crown.

100 Human rights

(1) This Act does not enable a person—
  (a) to bring any proceedings in a court or tribunal on the ground that an act is incompatible with the Convention rights, or
  (b) to rely on any of the Convention rights in any such proceedings,

unless he would be a victim for the purposes of Article 34 of the Convention (within the meaning of the Human Rights Act 1998) if proceedings in respect of the act were brought in the European Court of Human Rights.

(2) Subsection (1) does not apply to the Lord Advocate, the Advocate General, the Attorney General or the Attorney General for Northern Ireland.

(3) This Act does not enable a court or tribunal to award any damages in respect of an act which is incompatible with any of the Convention rights which it could not award if section 8(3) and (4) of the Human Rights Act 1998 applied.

[(3A) Subsection (3B) applies to any proceedings brought on or after 2 November 2009 by virtue of this Act against the Scottish Ministers or a member of the Scottish Executive in a court or tribunal on the ground that an act of the Scottish Ministers or a member of the Scottish Executive is incompatible with the Convention rights.

(3B) Proceedings to which this subsection applies must be brought before the end of—
  (a) the period of one year beginning with the date on which the act complained of took place, or
  (b) such longer period as the court or tribunal considers equitable having regard to all the circumstances,

but that is subject to any rule imposing a stricter time limit in relation to the procedure in question.

(3C) Subsection (3B) does not apply to proceedings brought by the Lord Advocate, the Advocate General, the Attorney General, the Attorney General for Northern Ireland or the Advocate General for Northern Ireland.

(3D) In subsections (3A) and (3B) "act" does not include the making of any legislation but it does include any other act or failure to act (including a failure to make legislation).

(3E) The reference in subsection (3A) to proceedings brought on or after 2 November 2009 includes proceedings relating to an act done before that date.]¹

(4) In this section "act" means—
    (a) making any legislation,
    (b) any other act or failure to act, if it is the act or failure of a member of the Scottish Executive.

---

1   Modified by Convention Rights Proceedings (Amendment) (Scotland) Act 2009 s 1.

---

101 Interpretation of Acts of the Scottish Parliament etc –:

(1) This section applies to—
    (a) any provision of an Act of the Scottish Parliament, or of a Bill for such an Act, and
    (b) any provision of subordinate legislation made, confirmed or approved, or purporting to be made, confirmed or approved, by a member of the Scottish Executive,

which could be read in such a way as to be outside competence.

(2) Such a provision is to be read as narrowly as is required for it to be within competence, if such a reading is possible, and is to have effect accordingly.

(3) In this section "competence"—
    (a) in relation to an Act of the Scottish Parliament, or a Bill for such an Act, means the legislative competence of the Parliament, and
    (b) in relation to subordinate legislation, means the powers conferred by virtue of this Act.

102 Powers of courts or tribunals to vary retrospective decisions

(1) This section applies where any court or tribunal decides that—
    (a) an Act of the Scottish Parliament or any provision of such an Act is not within the legislative competence of the Parliament, or
    (b) a member of the Scottish Executive does not have the power to make, confirm or approve a provision of subordinate legislation that he has purported to make, confirm or approve.

(2) The court or tribunal may make an order—
    (a) removing or limiting any retrospective effect of the decision, or
    (b) suspending the effect of the decision for any period and on any conditions to allow the defect to be corrected. to:

(3) In deciding whether to make an order under this section, the court or tribunal shall (among other things) have regard to the extent to which persons who are not parties to the proceedings would otherwise be adversely affected.

(4) Where a court or tribunal is considering whether to make an order under this section, it shall order intimation of that fact to be given to—
    (a) the Lord Advocate, and
    (b) the appropriate law officer, where the decision mentioned in subsection (1) relates to a devolution issue (within the meaning of Schedule 6),

unless the person to whom the intimation would be given is a party to the proceedings.

(5) A person to whom intimation is given under subsection (4) may take part as a party in the proceedings so far as they relate to the making of the order.

(6) Paragraphs 36 and 37 of Schedule 6 apply with necessary modifications for the purposes of subsections (4) and (5) as they apply for the purposes of that Schedule.

(7) In this section—
"intimation" includes notice,
"the appropriate law officer" means—
    (a) in relation to proceedings in Scotland, the Advocate General,
    (b) in relation to proceedings in England and Wales, the Attorney General,
    (c) in relation to proceedings in Northern Ireland, the Attorney General for Northern Ireland.

103 ... [1]

---

1   Repealed by Constitutional Reform Act 2005 c 4 Sch 18(5) para 1.

SUPPLEMENTARY POWERS

104 Power to make provision consequential on legislation of, or scrutinised by, the Parliament

(1) Subordinate legislation may make such provision as the person making the legislation considers necessary or expedient in consequence of any provision made by or under any Act of the Scottish Parliament or made by legislation mentioned in subsection (2).

(2) The legislation is subordinate legislation under an Act of Parliament made by—
    (a) a member of the Scottish Executive,
    (b) a Scottish public authority with mixed functions or no reserved functions, or
    (c) any other person (not being a Minister of the Crown) if the function of making the legislation is exercisable within devolved competence.

105 Power to make provision consequential on this Act

Subordinate legislation may make such modifications in any pre-commencement enactment or prerogative instrument or any other instrument or document as appear to the person making the legislation necessary or expedient in consequence of this Act.

106 Power to adapt functions

(1) Subordinate legislation may make such provision (including, in particular, provision modifying a function exercisable by a Minister of the Crown) as the person making the legislation considers appropriate for the purpose of enabling or otherwise facilitating the transfer of a function to the Scottish Ministers by virtue of section 53 or 63.

(2) Subordinate legislation under subsection (1) may, in particular, provide for any function which—
    (a) is not exercisable separately in or as regards Scotland to be so exercisable, or
    (b) is not otherwise exercisable separately within devolved competence to be so exercisable.

(3) The reference in subsection (1) to the transfer of a function to the Scottish Ministers shall be read as including the sharing of a function with the Scottish Ministers or its other adaptation.

(4) No recommendation shall be made to Her Majesty in Council to make, and no Minister of the Crown shall make, subordinate legislation under this section which modifies a

function of observing or implementing an obligation mentioned in subsection (5) unless the Scottish Ministers have been consulted about the modification.

(5) The obligation is an international obligation, or an obligation under [EU][1] law, to achieve a result defined by reference to a quantity (whether expressed as an amount, proportion or ratio or otherwise), where the quantity relates to the United Kingdom (or to an area including the United Kingdom or to an area consisting of a part of the United Kingdom which includes the whole or part of Scotland).

(6) If subordinate legislation under this section modifies a function of observing or implementing such an international obligation so that the function to be transferred to the Scottish Ministers relates only to achieving so much of the result to be achieved under the obligation as is specified in the legislation, references in section 58 to the international obligation are to be read as references to the requirement to achieve that much of the result.

(7) If subordinate legislation under this section modifies a function of observing or implementing such an obligation under [EU][1] law so that the function to be transferred to the Scottish Ministers relates only to achieving so much of the result to be achieved under the obligation as is specified in the legislation, references in sections 29(2)(d) and 57(2) and paragraph 1 of Schedule 6 to [EU][1] law are to be read as including references to the requirement to achieve that much of the result.

1   Word substituted by Treaty of Lisbon (Changes in Terminology) Order 2011/1043 Pt 2 art 6(2)(a).

107 Legislative power to remedy ultra vires acts

Subordinate legislation may make such provision as the person making the legislation considers necessary or expedient in consequence of—

(a)   an Act of the Scottish Parliament or any provision of an Act of the Scottish Parliament which is not, or may not be, within the legislative competence of the Parliament, or

(b)   any purported exercise by a member of the Scottish Executive of his functions which is not, or may not be, an exercise or a proper exercise of those functions.

FINAL PROVISIONS

126 Interpretation

(1) In this Act—

"body" includes unincorporated association,

"constituencies" and "regions", in relation to the Parliament, mean the constituencies and regions provided for by Schedule 1,

"constituency member" means a member of the Parliament for a constituency,

"the Convention rights" has the same meaning as in the Human Rights Act 1998,

"document" means anything in which information is recorded in any form (and references to producing a document are to be read accordingly),

"enactment" includes an Act of the Scottish Parliament, Northern Ireland legislation (within the meaning of the Northern Ireland Act 1998) and an enactment comprised in subordinate legislation, and includes an enactment comprised in, or in subordinate legislation under, an Act of Parliament, whenever passed or made,

"financial year" means a year ending with 31st March,

"functions" includes powers and duties, and "confer", in relation to functions, includes impose, "government department" means any department of the Government of the United Kingdom,

"the Human Rights Convention" means—

  (a) the Convention for the Protection of Human Rights and Fundamental Freedoms, agreed by the Council of Europe at Rome on 4th November 1950, and

  (b) the Protocols to the Convention,

as they have effect for the time being in relation to the United Kingdom,

"Minister of the Crown" includes the Treasury,

"modify" includes amend or repeal,

"occupational pension scheme", "personal pension scheme" and "public service pension scheme" have the meanings given by section 1 of the Pension Schemes Act 1993, but as if the reference to employed earners in the definition of personal pension scheme were to any earners,

"the Parliament" means the Scottish Parliament,

"parliamentary", in relation to constituencies, elections and electors, is to be taken to refer to the Parliament of the United Kingdom,

"prerogative instrument" means an Order in Council, warrant, charter or other instrument made under the prerogative,

"the principal appointed day" means the day appointed by an order under section 130 which is designated by the order as the principal appointed day,

"proceedings", in relation to the Parliament, includes proceedings of any committee or sub-committee,

"property" includes rights and interests of any description,

"regional member" means a member of the Parliament for a region,

"Scotland" includes so much of the internal waters and territorial sea of the United Kingdom as are adjacent to Scotland,

"Scottish public authority" means any public body (except the Parliamentary corporation), public office or holder of such an office whose functions (in each case) are exercisable only in or as regards Scotland,

"the Scottish zone" means the sea within British fishery limits (that is, the limits set by or under section 1 of the Fishery Limits Act 1976) which is adjacent to Scotland,

"standing orders" means standing orders of the Parliament,

"subordinate legislation" has the same meaning as in the Interpretation Act 1978 and also includes an instrument made under an Act of the Scottish Parliament,

"tribunal" means any tribunal in which legal proceedings may be brought.

(2) Her Majesty may by Order in Council determine, or make provision for determining, for the purposes of this Act any boundary between waters which are to be treated as internal waters or territorial sea of the United Kingdom, or sea within British fishery limits, adjacent to Scotland and those which are not.

(3) For the purposes of this Act—

  (a) the question whether any function of a body, government department, office or office-holder relates to reserved matters is to be determined by reference to the purpose for which the function is exercisable, having regard (among other things) to the likely effects in all the circumstances of any exercise of the function, but

  (b) bodies to which paragraph 3 of Part III of Schedule 5 applies are to be treated as if all their functions were functions which relate to reserved matters.

(4) References in this Act to Scots private law are to the following areas of the civil law of Scotland—

  (a) the general principles of private law (including private international law),

  (b) the law of persons (including natural persons, legal persons and unincorporated bodies),

(c) the law of obligations (including obligations arising from contract, unilateral promise, delict, unjustified enrichment and negotiorum gestio),

(d) the law of property (including heritable and moveable property, trusts and succession), and

(e) the law of actions (including jurisdiction, remedies, evidence, procedure, diligence, recognition and enforcement of court orders, limitation of actions and arbitration),

and include references to judicial review of administrative action.

(5) References in this Act to Scots criminal law include criminal offences, jurisdiction, evidence, procedure and penalties and the treatment of offenders.

(6) References in this Act and in any other enactment to the Scottish Administration are to the office-holders in the Scottish Administration and the members of the staff of the Scottish Administration.

(7) For the purposes of this Act—

(a) references to office-holders in the Scottish Administration are to—
    (i) members of the Scottish Executive and junior Scottish Ministers, and
    (ii) the holders of offices in the Scottish Administration which are not ministerial offices, and

(b) references to members of the staff of the Scottish Administration are to the staff of the persons referred to in paragraph (a).

(8) For the purposes of this Act, the offices in the Scottish Administration which are not ministerial offices are—

(a) the Registrar General of Births, Deaths and Marriages for Scotland, the Keeper of the Registers of Scotland and the Keeper of the Records of Scotland, and

(b) any other office of a description specified in an Order in Council made by Her Majesty under this subsection.

(9) In this Act—

(a) all those rights, powers, liabilities, obligations and restrictions from time to time created or arising by or under the Community Treaties, and

(b) all those remedies and procedures from time to time provided for by or under the Community Treaties,

are referred to as ["EU law"][1].

(10) In this Act, "international obligations" means any international obligations of the United Kingdom other than obligations to observe and implement Community law or the Convention rights.

(11) In this Act, "by virtue of" includes "by" and "under".

---

1   Word substituted by Treaty of Lisbon (Changes in Terminology) Order 2011/1043 Pt 2 art 6(2)(a).

---

127 Index of defined expressions

In this Act, the expressions listed in the left-hand column have the meaning given by, or are to be interpreted in accordance with, the provisions listed in the right-hand column.

Expression	Provision of this Act
Act of the Scottish Parliament	Section 28(1)
Advocate General	Section 32(4)
Auditor General for Scotland	Section 69
Body	Section 126(1)
By virtue of	Section 126(11)

Expression	Provision of this Act
Clerk, and Assistant Clerk	Section 20 and paragraph 3 of Schedule 2
[EU][1] law	Section 126(9)
Constituencies and constituency member	Section 126(1)
The Convention rights	Section 126(1)
Cross-border public authority	Section 88(5)
Devolved competence(in relation to the exercise of functions)	Section 54
Document	Section 126(1)
Enactment	Sections 113(6) and 126(1)
Financial year	Section 126(1)
Functions	Section 126(1)
Government department	Section 126(1)
The Human Rights Convention	Section 126(1)
International obligations	Section 126(10)
...[2]	
Legislative competence	Section 29
Member of the Scottish Executive	Section 44(1)
Members of the staff of the Scottish Administration	Section 126(7)
Minister of the Crown	Section 126(1)
Modify	Section 126(1)
Occupational pension scheme, personal pension scheme and public service pension scheme	Section 126(1)
Office-holders in the Scottish Administration	Section 126(7)
Offices in the Scottish Administration which are not ministerial offices	Section 126(8)
Open power	Section 112(3)
The Parliament	Section 126(1)
"parliamentary" (in relation to constituencies, elections and electors)	Section 126(1)
The Parliamentary corporation	Section 21(1)
Pre-commencement enactment	Section 53(3)
Prerogative instrument	Section 126(1)
Presiding Officer	Section 19
Principal appointed day	Section 126(1)
Proceedings	Section 126(1)
Property	Section 126(1)
Regional list (in relation to a party)	Section 5(4)
Regional returning officer	Section 12(6)
Regional vote	Section 6(2)
Regions and regional member	Section 126(1)
Registered political party	Section 5(9)
Reserved matters	Schedule 5
Retained functions (in relation to the Lord Advocate)	Section 52(6)
Scotland	Section 126(1) and (2)
Scots criminal law	Section 126(5)
Scots private law	Section 126(4)
Scottish Administration	Section 126(6)
Scottish Ministers	Section 44(2)
Scottish public authority	Section 126(1)

Expression	Provision of this Act
Scottish public authority with mixed functions or no reserved functions	Paragraphs 1 and 2 of Part III of Schedule 5
Scottish Seal	Section 2(6)
The Scottish zone	Section 126(1)
Staff of the Parliament	Paragraph 3 of Schedule 2
Standing orders	Section 126(1)
Subordinate legislation	Section 126(1)
Tribunal	Section 126(1)

1 Word substituted by Treaty of Lisbon (Changes in Terminology) Order 2011/1043 Pt 2 art 6(2)(a).

2 Entry repealed by Constitutional Reform Act 2005 c 4 Sch 18(5) para 1.

128 Expenses

(1) There shall be paid out of money provided by Parliament—
  (a) any expenditure incurred by a Minister of the Crown by virtue of this Act, and
  (b) any increase attributable to this Act in the sums payable out of money so provided under any other enactment.

(2) There shall be paid into the Consolidated Fund any sums received by a Minister of the Crown by virtue of this Act which are not payable into the National Loans Fund.

129 Transitional provisions etc

(1) Subordinate legislation may make such provision as the person making the legislation considers necessary or expedient for transitory or transitional purposes in connection with the coming into force of any provision of this Act.

(2) If any of the following provisions come into force before the Human Rights Act 1998 has come into force (or come fully into force), the provision shall have effect until the time when that Act is fully in force as it will have effect after that time: sections 29(2)(d), 57(2) and (3), 100 and 126(1) and Schedule 6.

Schedule 6
Devolution issues

Part I Preliminary

1 In this Schedule "devolution issue" means—
  (a) a question whether an Act of the Scottish Parliament or any provision of an Act of the Scottish Parliament is within the legislative competence of the Parliament,
  (b) a question whether any function (being a function which any person has purported, or is proposing, to exercise) is a function of the Scottish Ministers, the First Minister or the Lord Advocate,
  (c) a question whether the purported or proposed exercise of a function by a member of the Scottish Executive is, or would be, within devolved competence,
  (d) a question whether a purported or proposed exercise of a function by a member of the Scottish Executive is, or would be, incompatible with any of the Convention rights or with Community law,
  (e) a question whether a failure to act by a member of the Scottish Executive is incompatible with any of the Convention rights or with [EU][1] law,

(f) any other question about whether a function is exercisable within devolved competence or in or as regards Scotland and any other question arising by virtue of this Act about reserved matters.

2 A devolution issue shall not be taken to arise in any proceedings merely because of any contention of a party to the proceedings which appears to the court or tribunal before which the proceedings take place to be frivolous or vexatious.

1   Word substituted by Treaty of Lisbon (Changes in Terminology) Order 2011/1043 Pt 2 art 6(2)(a).

PART II
PROCEEDINGS IN SCOTLAND

APPLICATION OF PART II

3 This Part of this Schedule applies in relation to devolution issues in proceedings in Scotland.

INSTITUTION OF PROCEEDINGS

4 (1) Proceedings for the determination of a devolution issue may be instituted by the Advocate General or the Lord Advocate.

(2) The Lord Advocate may defend any such proceedings instituted by the Advocate General.

(3) This paragraph is without prejudice to any power to institute or defend proceedings exercisable apart from this paragraph by any person.

INTIMATION OF DEVOLUTION ISSUE

5 Intimation of any devolution issue which arises in any proceedings before a court or tribunal shall be given to the Advocate General and the Lord Advocate (unless the person to whom the intimation would be given is a party to the proceedings).

6 A person to whom intimation is given in pursuance of paragraph 5 may take part as a party in the proceedings, so far as they relate to a devolution issue.

REFERENCE OF DEVOLUTION ISSUE TO HIGHER COURT

7 A court, other than the [Supreme Court][1] or any court consisting of three or more judges of the Court of Session, may refer any devolution issue which arises in proceedings (other than criminal proceedings) before it to the Inner House of the Court of Session.

1   Words substituted by Constitutional Reform Act 2005 c 4 Sch 9(2) para 103(2).

8 A tribunal from which there is no appeal shall refer any devolution issue which arises in proceedings before it to the Inner House of the Court of Session; and any other tribunal may make such a reference.

9 A court, other than any court consisting of two or more judges of the High Court of

Justiciary, may refer any devolution issue which arises in criminal proceedings before it to the High Court of Justiciary.

REFERENCES FROM SUPERIOR COURTS TO [SUPREME COURT][1]

10 Any court consisting of three or more judges of the Court of Session may refer any devolution issue which arises in proceedings before it (otherwise than on a reference under paragraph 7 or 8) to the [Supreme Court][1].

1   Words substituted by Constitutional Reform Act 2005 c 4 Sch 9(2) para 103(4).

11 Any court consisting of two or more judges of the High Court of Justiciary may refer any devolution issue which arises in proceedings before it (otherwise than on a reference under paragraph 9) to the [Supreme Court][1].

1   Words substituted by Constitutional Reform Act 2005 c 4 Sch 9(2) para 103(5).

APPEALS FROM SUPERIOR COURTS TO [SUPREME COURT][1]

12 An appeal against a determination of a devolution issue by the Inner House of the Court of Session on a reference under paragraph 7 or 8 shall lie to the [Supreme Court][1].

1   Words substituted by Constitutional Reform Act 2005 c 4 Sch 9(2) para 103(7).

13 An appeal against a determination of a devolution issue by—
  (a) a court of two or more judges of the High Court of Justiciary (whether in the ordinary course of proceedings or on a reference under paragraph 9), or
  (b) a court of three or more judges of the Court of Session from which there is no appeal to the [Supreme Court apart from this paragraph][1] ,

shall lie to the [Supreme Court][2] , but only with [permission][3] of the court [from which the appeal lies][4] or, failing such [permission][3] , with [permission][5] of the [Supreme Court][2] .

1   Words substituted by Constitutional Reform Act 2005 c 4 Sch 9(2) para 103(8)(a).
2   Words substituted by Constitutional Reform Act 2005 c 4 Sch 9(2) para 103(8)(b).
3   Word substituted by Constitutional Reform Act 2005 c 4 Sch 9(2) para 103(8)(c).
4   Word substituted by Constitutional Reform Act 2005 c 4 Sch 9(2) para 103(8)(d).
5   Words substituted by Constitutional Reform Act 2005 c 4 Sch 9(2) para 103(8)(e).

PART III
PROCEEDINGS IN ENGLAND AND WALES

APPLICATION OF PART III

14 This Part of this Schedule applies in relation to devolution issues in proceedings in England and Wales.

INSTITUTION OF PROCEEDINGS

15 (1) Proceedings for the determination of a devolution issue may be instituted by the Attorney General.

(2) The Lord Advocate may defend any such proceedings.

(3) This paragraph is without prejudice to any power to institute or defend proceedings exercisable apart from this paragraph by any person.

NOTICE OF DEVOLUTION ISSUE

16 A court or tribunal shall order notice of any devolution issue which arises in any proceedings before it to be given to the Attorney General and the Lord Advocate (unless the person to whom the notice would be given is a party to the proceedings).

17 A person to whom notice is given in pursuance of paragraph 16 may take part as a party in the proceedings, so far as they relate to a devolution issue.

REFERENCE OF DEVOLUTION ISSUE TO HIGH COURT OR COURT OF APPEAL

18 A magistrates' court may refer any devolution issue which arises in proceedings (other than criminal proceedings) before it to the High Court.

19(1) A court may refer any devolution issue which arises in proceedings (other than criminal proceedings) before it to the Court of Appeal.

(2) Sub-paragraph (1) does not apply to—
  (a) a magistrates' court, the Court of Appeal or the [Supreme Court][1], or
  (b) the High Court if the devolution issue arises in proceedings on a reference under paragraph 18.

---

1   Words substituted by Constitutional Reform Act 2005 c 4 Sch 9(2) para 104(2).

20 A tribunal from which there is no appeal shall refer any devolution issue which arises in proceedings before it to the Court of Appeal; and any other tribunal may make such a reference.

21 A court, other than the [Supreme Court][1] or the Court of Appeal, may refer any devolution issue which arises in criminal proceedings before it to—
  (a) the High Court (if the proceedings are summary proceedings), or
  (b) the Court of Appeal (if the proceedings are proceedings on indictment).

---

1   Words substituted by Constitutional Reform Act 2005 c 4 Sch 9(2) para 104(3).

REFERENCES FROM COURT OF APPEAL TO [SUPREME COURT][1]

22 The Court of Appeal may refer any devolution issue which arises in proceedings before it (otherwise than on a reference under paragraph 19, 20 or 21) to the [Supreme Court][1].

---

1 Words substituted by Constitutional Reform Act 2005 c 4 Sch 9(2) para 104(5).

APPEALS FROM SUPERIOR COURTS TO [SUPREME COURT][1]

23 An appeal against a determination of a devolution issue by the High Court or the Court of Appeal on a reference under paragraph 18, 19, 20 or 21 shall lie to the [Supreme Court][1], but only with [permission][2] of the High Court or (as the case may be) the Court of Appeal or, failing such [permission][2], with [permission][3] of the [Supreme Court][1].

1   Words substituted by Constitutional Reform Act 2005 c 4 Sch 9(2) para 104(7)(a).

2   Word substituted by Constitutional Reform Act 2005 c 4 Sch 9(2) para 104(7)(b).

3   Words substituted by Constitutional Reform Act 2005 c 4 Sch 9(2) para 104(7)(c).

PART IV
PROCEEDINGS IN NORTHERN IRELAND

APPLICATION OF PART IV

24 This Part of this Schedule applies in relation to devolution issues in proceedings in Northern Ireland.

INSTITUTION OF PROCEEDINGS

25 (1) Proceedings for the determination of a devolution issue may be instituted by the Attorney General for Northern Ireland.

(2) The Lord Advocate may defend any such proceedings. re:

(3) This paragraph is without prejudice to any power to institute or defend proceedings exercisable apart from this paragraph by any person.

NOTICE OF DEVOLUTION ISSUE

26 A court or tribunal shall order notice of any devolution issue which arises in any proceedings before it to be given to the Attorney General for Northern Ireland and the Lord Advocate (unless the person to whom the notice would be given is a party to the proceedings).

27 A person to whom notice is given in pursuance of paragraph 26 may take part as a party in the proceedings, so far as they relate to a devolution issue.

REFERENCE OF DEVOLUTION ISSUE TO COURT OF APPEAL

28 A court, other than the [Supreme Court][1] or the Court of Appeal in Northern Ireland, may refer any devolution issue which arises in any proceedings before it to the Court of Appeal in Northern Ireland.

1   Words substituted by Constitutional Reform Act 2005 c 4 Sch 9(2) para 105(2).

29 A tribunal from which there is no appeal shall refer any devolution issue which arises in any proceedings before it to the Court of Appeal in Northern Ireland; and any other tribunal may make such a reference.

REFERENCES FROM COURT OF APPEAL TO [SUPREME COURT][1]

30 The Court of Appeal in Northern Ireland may refer any devolution issue which arises in proceedings before it (otherwise than on a reference under paragraph 28 or 29) to the [Supreme Court][2].

1   Words substituted by Constitutional Reform Act 2005 c 4 Sch 18 para 1.

2 Words substituted by Constitutional Reform Act 2005 c 4 Sch 9(2) para 105(4).

APPEALS FROM COURT OF APPEAL TO [SUPREME COURT]

31 An appeal against a determination of a devolution issue by the Court of Appeal in Northern Ireland on a reference under paragraph 28 or 29 shall lie to the [Supreme Court][1], but only with [permission][2] of the Court of Appeal in Northern Ireland or, failing such [permission][2], with [permission][3] of the [Supreme Court][1].

1 Words substituted by Constitutional Reform Act 2005 c 4 Sch 9(2) para 105(6)(a).

2 Word substituted by Constitutional Reform Act 2005 c 4 Sch 9(2) para 105(6)(b).

3 Words substituted by Constitutional Reform Act 2005 c 4 Sch 9(2) para 105(6)(c).

PART V
GENERAL

PROCEEDINGS IN THE HOUSE OF LORDS

32 ...

1 Repealed by Constitutional Reform Act 2005 c 4 Sch 18(5) para 1.

DIRECT REFERENCES TO [SUPREME COURT][1]

33 The Lord Advocate, the Advocate General, the Attorney General or the Attorney General for Northern Ireland may require any Court or tribunal to refer to the [Supreme Court][1] any devolution issue which has arisen in proceedings before it to which he is a party.

1 Words substituted by Constitutional Reform Act 2005 c 4 Sch 9(2) para 106(4).

34 The Lord Advocate, the Attorney General, the Advocate General or the Attorney General for Northern Ireland may refer to the [Supreme Court][1] any devolution issue which is not the subject of proceedings.

1 Words substituted by Constitutional Reform Act 2005 c 4 Sch 9(2) para 106(5).

35 (1) This paragraph applies where a reference is made under paragraph 34 in relation to a devolution issue which relates to the proposed exercise of a function by a member of the Scottish Executive.

(2) The person making the reference shall notify a member of the Scottish Executive of that fact.

(3) No member of the Scottish Executive shall exercise the function in the manner proposed during the period beginning with the receipt of the notification under sub-paragraph (2) and ending with the reference being decided or otherwise disposed of.

(4) Proceedings relating to any possible failure by a member of the Scottish Executive to comply with sub-paragraph (3) may be instituted by the Advocate General.

(5) Sub-paragraph (4) is without prejudice to any power to institute proceedings exercisable apart from that sub-paragraph by any person.

EXPENSES

36 (1) A court or tribunal before which any proceedings take place may take account of any additional expense of the kind mentioned in sub-paragraph (3) in deciding any question as to costs or expenses.

(2) In deciding any such question, the court or tribunal may award the whole or part of the additional expense as costs or (as the case may be) expenses to the party who incurred it (whatever the decision on the devolution issue).

(3) The additional expense is any additional expense which the court or tribunal considers that any party to the proceedings has incurred as a result of the participation of any person in pursuance of paragraph 6, 17 or 27.

PROCEDURE OF COURTS AND TRIBUNALS

37 Any power to make provision for regulating the procedure before any court or tribunal shall include power to make provision for the purposes of this Schedule including, in particular, provision—
  (a) for prescribing the stage in the proceedings at which a devolution issue is to be raised or referred,
  (b) for the sisting or staying of proceedings for the purpose of any proceedings under this Schedule, and
  (c) for determining the manner in which and the time within which any intimation or notice is to be given.

INTERPRETATION

38 Any duty or power conferred by this Schedule to refer a devolution issue to a court shall be construed as a duty or (as the case may be) power to refer the issue to the court for decision.

This text is based on a version originally published by Westlaw UK.

Appendix III

Convention for the Protection of Human Rights and Fundamental Freedoms

as amended by Protocol Nos 11 and 14

with Protocol Nos. 1, 4, 6, 7, 12 and 13

The text of the Convention is presented as amended by the provisions of Protocol No. 14 (CETS no. 194) as from its entry into force on 1 June 2010.

The text of the Convention had previously been amended according to the provisions of Protocol No. 3 (ETS no. 45), which entered into force on 21 September 1970, of Protocol No. 5 (ETS no. 55), which entered into force on 20 December 1971, and of Protocol No. 8 (ETS no. 118), which entered into force on 1 January 1990, and comprised also the text of Protocol No. 2 (ETS no. 44) which, in accordance with Article 5 § 3 thereof, had been an integral part of the Convention since its entry into force on 21 September 1970. All provisions which had been amended or added by these Protocols were replaced by Protocol No. 11 (ETS no. 155), as from the date of its entry into force on 1 November 1998. As from that date, Protocol No. 9 (ETS no. 140), which entered into force on 1 October 1994, was repealed and Protocol No. 10 (ETS no. 146) lost its purpose.

The current state of signatures and ratifications of the Convention and its Protocols as well as the complete list of declarations and reservations are available at http://conventions.coe.int.

Registry of the European Court of Human Rights June 2010

Convention for the Protection of Human Rights and Fundamental Freedoms

Rome, 4.XI.1950 The governments signatory hereto, being members of the Council of Europe,

Considering the Universal Declaration of Human Rights proclaimed by the General Assembly of the United Nations on 10 December 1948; Considering that this Declaration aims at securing the universal and effective recognition and observance of the Rights therein declared; Considering that the aim of the Council of Europe is the achievement of greater unity between its members and that one of the methods by which that aim is to be pursued is the maintenance and further realisation of human rights and fundamental freedoms; Reaffirming their profound belief in those fundamental freedoms which are the foundation of justice and peace in the world and are best maintained on the one hand by an effective political democracy and on the other by a common understanding and observance of the human rights upon which they depend; Being resolved, as the governments of European countries which are likeminded and have a common heritage of political traditions, ideals, freedom and the rule of law, to take the first steps for the collective enforcement of certain of the rights stated in the Universal Declar-ation, Have agreed as follows:

Article 1
Obligation to respect human rights

The High Contracting Parties shall secure to everyone within their jurisdiction the rights and freedoms defined in Section I of this Convention.

SECTION I
RIGHTS AND FREEDOMS

Article 2
Right to life

1. Everyone's right to life shall be protected by law. No one shall be deprived of his life intentionally save in the execution of a sentence of a court following his conviction of a crime for which this penalty is provided by law.

2. Deprivation of life shall not be regarded as inflicted in contravention of this Article when it results from the use of force which is no more than abso-lutely necessary:
   (a) in defence of any person from unlawful violence;
   (b) in order to effect a lawful arrest or to prevent the escape of a person lawfully detained;
   (c) in action lawfully taken for the purpose of quelling a riot or insurrection.
   (c) in action lawfully taken for the purpose of quelling a riot or insurrection.

Article 3
Prohibition of torture

No one shall be subjected to torture or to inhuman or degrading treatment or punishment.

Article 4
Prohibition of slavery and forced labour

1. No one shall be held in slavery or servitude.

2. No one shall be required to perform forced or compulsory labour.

3. For the purpose of this Article the term "forced or compulsory labour" shall not include:
   (a) any work required to be done in the ordinary course of detention imposed according to the provisions of Article 5 of this Convention or during conditional release from such detention;
   (b) any service of a military character or, in case of conscientious objectors in countries where they are recognised, service exacted instead of compulsory military service;
   (c) any service exacted in case of an emergency or calamity threatening the life or well-being of the community;
   (d) any work or service which forms part of normal civic obligations.

Article 5
Right to liberty and security

1. Everyone has the right to liberty and security of person. No one shall be deprived of his liberty save in the following cases and in accordance with a procedure prescribed by law:
   (a) the lawful detention of a person after conviction by a competent court;
   (b) the lawful arrest or detention of a person for non-compliance with the lawful order of a court or in order to secure the fulfilment of any obligation prescribed by law;
   (c) the lawful arrest or detention of a person effected for the purpose of bringing him before the competent legal authority on reasonable suspicion of having committed

an offence or when it is reasonably considered necessary to prevent his committing an offence or fleeing after having done so;

   (d) the detention of a minor by lawful order for the purpose of educational supervision or his lawful detention for the purpose of bringing him before the competent legal authority;

   (e) the lawful detention of persons for the prevention of the spreading of infectious diseases, of persons of un-sound mind, alcoholics or drug addicts or vagrants;

   (f) the lawful arrest or detention of a person to prevent his effecting an unauthorised entry into the country or of a person against whom action is being taken with a view to deportation or extradition.

2. Everyone who is arrested shall be informed promptly, in a language which he understands, of the reasons for his arrest and of any charge against him.

3. Everyone arrested or detained in accordance with the provisions of paragraph 1 (c) of this Article shall be brought promptly before a judge or other officer authorised by law to exercise judicial power and shall be entitled to trial within a reasonable time or to release pending trial. Release may be conditioned by guarantees to appear for trial.

4. Everyone who is deprived of his liberty by arrest or detention shall be entitled to take proceedings by which the lawfulness of his detention shall be decided speedily by a court and his release ordered if the detention is not lawful.

5. Everyone who has been the victim of arrest or detention in contravention of the provisions of this Article shall have an enforceable right to compensation.

Article 6
Right to a fair trial

1. In the determination of his civil rights and obligations or of any criminal charge against him, everyone is entitled to a fair and public hearing within a reasonable time by an independent and impartial tribunal established by law. Judgment shall be pronounced publicly but the press and public may be excluded from all or part of the trial in the interests of morals, public order or national security in a democratic society, where the interests of juveniles or the protection of the private life of the parties so require, or to the extent strictly necessary in the opinion of the court in special circumstances where publicity would prejudice the interests of justice. :

2. Everyone charged with a criminal offence shall be presumed innocent until proved guilty according to law.

3. Everyone charged with a criminal offence has the following minimum rights:
   (a) to be informed promptly, in a language which he understands and in detail, of the nature and cause of the accusation against him;
   (b) to have adequate time and facilities for the preparation of his defence;
   (c) to defend himself in person or through legal assistance of his own choosing or, if he has not sufficient means to pay for legal assistance, to be given it free when the interests of justice so require;
   (d) to examine or have examined witnesses against him and to obtain the attendance and examination of wit-nesses on his behalf under the same conditions as witnesses against him;
   (e) to have the free assistance of an interpreter if he cannot understand or speak the language used in court.

Article 7
No punishment without law

1. No one shall be held guilty of any criminal offence on account of any act or omission

which did not constitute a criminal offence under national or international law at the time when it was committed. Nor shall a heavier penalty be imposed than the one that was applicable at the time the criminal offence was committed.

2. This Article shall not prejudice the trial and punishment of any person for any act or omission which, at the time when it was committed, was criminal according to the general principles of law recognised by civilised nations.

Article 8
Right to respect for private and family life

1. Everyone has the right to respect for his private and family life, his home and his correspondence.

2. There shall be no interference by a public authority with the exercise of this right except such as is in accordance with the law and is necessary in a democratic society in the interests of national security, public safety or the economic well-being of the country, for the prevention of disorder or crime, for the protection of health or morals, or for the protection of the rights and freedoms of others.

Article 9
Freedom of thought, conscience and religion

1. Everyone has the right to freedom of thought, conscience and religion; this right includes freedom to change his religion or belief and freedom, either alone or in community with others and in public or private, to manifest his religion or belief, in worship, teaching, practice and observance.

2. Freedom to manifest one's religion or beliefs shall be subject only to such limitations as are prescribed by law and are necessary in a democratic society in the interests of public safety, for the protection of public order, health or morals, or for the protection of the rights and freedoms of others.

Article 10
Freedom of expression

1. Everyone has the right to freedom of expression. This right shall include freedom to hold opinions and to receive and impart information and ideas without interference by public authority and regardless of frontiers. This Article shall not prevent States from requiring the licensing of broadcasting, television or cinema enterprises.

2. The exercise of these freedoms, since it carries with it duties and responsibilities, may be subject to such formalities, conditions, restrictions or penalties as are prescribed by law and are necessary in a democratic society, in the interests of national security, territorial integrity or public safety, for the prevention of disorder or crime, for the protection of health or morals, for the protection of the reputation or rights of others, for preventing the disclosure of information received in confidence, or for maintaining the authority and impartiality of the judiciary.

Article 11
Freedom of assembly and association

1. Everyone has the right to freedom of peaceful assembly and to freedom of association with others, including the right to form and to join trade unions for the protection of his interests.

2. No restrictions shall be placed on the exercise of these rights other than such as are prescribed by law and are necessary in a democratic society in the interests of national

security or public safety, for the prevention of disorder or crime, for the protection of health or morals or for the protection of the rights and freedoms of others. This Article shall not prevent the imposition of lawful restrictions on the exercise of these rights by members of the armed forces, of the police or of the administration of the State.

Article 12
Right to marry

Men and women of marriageable age have the right to marry and to found a family, according to the national laws governing the exercise of this right.

Article 13
Right to an effective remedy

Everyone whose rights and freedoms as set forth in this Convention are violated shall have an effective remedy before a national authority notwithstanding that the violation has been committed by persons acting in an official capacity.

Article 14
Prohibition of discrimination

The enjoyment of the rights and freedoms set forth in this Convention shall be secured without discrimination on any ground such as sex, race, colour, language, religion, political or other opinion, national or social origin, association with a national minority, property, birth or other status.

Article 15
Derogation in time of emergency

1. In time of war or other public emergency threatening the life of the nation any High Contracting Party may take measures derogating from its obligations under this Convention to the extent strictly required by the exigencies of the situation, provided that such measures are not inconsistent with its other obligations under international law.

2. No derogation from Article 2, except in respect of deaths resulting from lawful acts of war, or from Articles 3, 4 § 1 and 7 shall be made under this provision.

3. Any High Contracting Party availing itself of this right of derogation shall keep the Secretary General of the Council of Europe fully informed of the measures which it has taken and the reasons therefor. It shall also inform the Secretary General of the Council of Europe when such measures have ceased to operate and the provisions of the Convention are again being fully executed.

Article 16
Restrictions on political activity of aliens

Nothing in Articles 10, 11 and 14 shall be regarded as preventing the High Contracting Parties from imposing restrictions on the political activity of aliens.

Article 17
Prohibition of abuse of rights

Nothing in this Convention may be interpreted as implying for any State, group or person any right to engage in any activity or perform any act aimed at the destruction of any of the rights and freedoms set forth herein or at their limitation to a greater extent than is provided for in the Convention.

Article 18
Limitation on use of restrictions on rights

The restrictions permitted under this Convention to the said rights and freedoms shall not be applied for any purpose other than those for which they have been prescribed.

SECTION II
EUROPEAN COURT OF HUMAN RIGHTS

Article 19
Establishment of the Court

To ensure the observance of the engagements undertaken by the High Contracting Parties in the Convention and the Protocols thereto, there shall be set up a European Court of Human Rights, hereinafter referred to as "the Court". It shall function on a permanent basis.

Article 20
Number of judges

The Court shall consist of a number of judges equal to that of the High Contracting Parties.

Article 21
Criteria for office

1. The judges shall be of high moral character and must either possess the qualifications required for appointment to high judicial office or be jurisconsults of recognised competence.

2. The judges shall sit on the Court in their individual capacity.

3. During their term of office the judges shall not engage in any activity which is incompatible with their independence, impartiality or with the demands of a full-time office; all questions arising from the application of this paragraph shall be decided by the Court.

Article 22
Election of judges

The judges shall be elected by the Parliamentary Assembly with respect to each High Contracting Party by a majority of votes cast from a list of three candidates nominated by the High Contracting Party.

Article 23
Terms of office and dismissal

1. The judges shall be elected for a period of nine years. They may not be re-elected.

2. The terms of office of judges shall expire when they reach the age of 70.

3. The judges shall hold office until replaced. They shall, however, continue to deal with such cases as they already have under consideration.

4. No judge may be dismissed from office unless the other judges decide by a majority of two-thirds that that judge has ceased to fulfil the required conditions.

Article 24
Registry and rapporteurs

1. The Court shall have a Registry, the functions and organisation of which shall be laid down in the rules of the Court.

2. When sitting in a single-judge formation, the Court shall be assisted by rapporteurs who shall function under the authority of the President of the Court. They shall form part of the Court's Registry.

Article 25
Plenary Court

The plenary Court shall
   (a) elect its President and one or two Vice-Presidents for a period of three years; they may be re-elected;
   (b) set up Chambers, constituted for a fixed period of time;
   (c) elect the Presidents of the Chambers of the Court; they may be re-elected;
   (d) adopt the rules of the Court;
   (e) elect the Registrar and one or more Deputy Registrars;
   (f) make any request under Article 26 § 2.

Article 26
Single-judge formation, Committees, Chambers and Grand Chamber

1. To consider cases brought before it, the Court shall sit in a single-judge formation, in Committees of three judges, in Chambers of seven judges and in a Grand Chamber of seventeen judges. The Court's Chambers shall set up Committees for a fixed period of time.

2. At the request of the plenary Court, the Committee of Ministers may, by a unanimous decision and for a fixed period, reduce to five the number of judges of the Chambers.

3. When sitting as a single judge, a judge shall not examine any application against the High Contracting Party in respect of which that judge has been elected.

4. There shall sit as an *ex officio* member of the Chamber and the Grand Chamber the judge elected in respect of the High Contracting Party concerned. If there is none or if that judge is unable to sit, a person chosen by the President of the Court from a list submitted in advance by that Party shall sit in the capacity of judge.

5. The Grand Chamber shall also include the President of the Court, the Vice-Presidents, the Presidents of the Chambers and other judges chosen in accordance with the rules of the Court. When a case is referred to the Grand Chamber under Article 43, no judge from the Chamber which rendered the judgment shall sit in the Grand Chamber, with the exception of the President of the Chamber and the judge who sat in respect of the High Contracting Party concerned.

Article 27
Competence of single judges

1. A single judge may declare inadmissible or strike out of the Court's list of cases an application submitted under Article 34, where such a decision can be taken without further examin-ation.

2. The decision shall be final.

3. If the single judge does not declare an application inadmissible or strike it out, that judge shall forward it to a Committee or to a Chamber for further examination.

Article 28
Competence of Committees

1. In respect of an application sub-mitted under Article 34, a Committee may, by a unanimous vote,

   (a) declare it inadmissible or strike it out of its list of cases, where such decision can be taken without further examination; or

   (b) declare it admissible and render at the same time a judgment on the merits, if the underlying question in the case, concerning the interpretation or the application of the Convention or the Protocols thereto, is already the subject of well-established case-law of the Court.

2. Decisions and judgments under paragraph 1 shall be final.

3. If the judge elected in respect of the High Contracting Party concerned is not a member of the Committee, the Committee may at any stage of the proceedings invite that judge to take the place of one of the members of the Committee, having regard to all relevant factors, including whether that Party has contested the application of the pro-cedure under paragraph 1 (b).

Article 29
Decisions by Chambers on admissibility and merits

1. If no decision is taken under Article 27 or 28, or no judgment rendered under Article 28, a Chamber shall decide on the admissibility and merits of individual applications submitted under Article 34. The decision on admissibility may be taken separately.

2. A Chamber shall decide on the admissibility and merits of inter-State applications submitted under Article 33. The decision on admissibility shall be taken separately unless the Court, in exceptional cases, decides otherwise.

Article 30
Relinquishment of jurisdiction to the Grand Chamber

Where a case pending before a Chamber raises a serious question affecting the interpretation of the Convention or the Protocols thereto, or where the resolution of a question before the Chamber might have a result inconsistent with a judgment previously delivered by the Court, the Chamber may, at any time before it has rendered its judgment, relinquish jurisdiction in favour of the Grand Chamber, unless one of the parties to the case objects.

Article 31
Powers of the Grand Chamber

The Grand Chamber shall

   (a) determine applications submitted either under Article 33 or Article 34 when a Chamber has relinquished jurisdiction under Article 30 or when the case has been referred to it under Art-icle 43;

   (b) decide on issues referred to the Court by the Committee of Ministers in accordance with Article 46 § 4; and

   (c) consider requests for advisory opinions submitted under Article 47.

Article 32
Jurisdiction of the Court

1. The jurisdiction of the Court shall extend to all matters concerning the interpretation and application of the Convention and the Protocols thereto which are referred to it as provided in Articles 33, 34, 46 and 47.

2. In the event of dispute as to whether the Court has jurisdiction, the Court shall decide.

Article 33
Inter-State cases

Any High Contracting Party may refer to the Court any alleged breach of the provisions of the Convention and the Protocols thereto by another High Contracting Party.

Article 34
Individual applications

The Court may receive applications from any person, non-governmental organisa-tion or group of individuals claiming to be the victim of a violation by one of the High Contracting Parties of the rights set forth in the Convention or the Protocols thereto. The High Contracting Parties undertake not to hinder in any way the effective exercise of this right.

Article 35
Admissibility criteria

1. The Court may only deal with the matter after all domestic remedies have been exhausted, according to the generally recognised rules of inter-national law, and within a period of six months from the date on which the final decision was taken.

2. The Court shall not deal with any application submitted under Article 34 that
   (a) is anonymous; or
   (b) is substantially the same as a matter that has already been examined by the Court or has already been submitted to another procedure of international investigation or settlement and contains no relevant new infor-mation.

3. The Court shall declare inadmissible any individual application submitted under Article 34 if it considers that:
   (a) the application is incompatible with the provisions of the Convention or the Protocols thereto, manifestly ill-founded, or an abuse of the right of individual application; or
   (b) the applicant has not suffered a significant disadvantage, unless respect for human rights as defined in the Convention and the Protocols thereto requires an examination of the application on the merits and provided that no case may be rejected on this ground which has not been duly considered by a domestic tribunal.

4. The Court shall reject any application which it considers inadmis-sible under this Article. It may do so at any stage of the proceedings.

Article 36
Third party intervention

1. In all cases before a Chamber or the Grand Chamber, a High Contracting Party one of whose nationals is an applicant shall have the right to submit written comments and to take part in hearings.

2. The President of the Court may, in the interest of the proper administration of justice, invite any High Contracting Party which is not a party to the proceedings or any person concerned who is not the applicant to submit written comments or take part in hearings.

3. In all cases before a Chamber or the Grand Chamber, the Council of Europe Commissioner for Human Rights may submit written comments and take part in hearings.

Article 37
Striking out applications

1. The Court may at any stage of the proceedings decide to strike an appli-cation out of its list of cases where the circumstances lead to the conclusion that

    (a) the applicant does not intend to pursue his application; or

    (b) the matter has been resolved; or

    (c) for any other reason established by the Court, it is no longer justified to continue the examination of the application. However, the Court shall continue the examination of the application if respect for human rights as defined in the Convention and the Protocols thereto so requires.

2. The Court may decide to restore an application to its list of cases if it considers that the circumstances justify such a course.

Article 38
Examination of the case

The Court shall examine the case together with the representatives of the parties and, if need be, undertake an investigation, for the effective conduct of which the High Contracting Parties concerned shall furnish all necessary facilities.

Article 39
Friendly settlements

1. At any stage of the proceedings, the Court may place itself at the disposal of the parties concerned with a view to securing a friendly settlement of the matter on the basis of respect for human rights as defined in the Convention and the Protocols thereto.

2. Proceedings conducted under para-graph 1 shall be confidential.

3. If a friendly settlement is effected, the Court shall strike the case out of its list by means of a decision which shall be confined to a brief statement of the facts and of the solution reached.

4. This decision shall be transmitted to the Committee of Ministers, which shall supervise the execution of the terms of the friendly settlement as set out in the decision.

Article 40
Public hearings and access to documents

1. Hearings shall be in public unless the Court in exceptional circumstances decides otherwise.

2. Documents deposited with the Registrar shall be accessible to the public unless the President of the Court decides otherwise.

Article 41
Just satisfaction

If the Court finds that there has been a violation of the Convention or the Protocols thereto, and if the internal law of the High Contracting Party concerned allows only partial reparation to be made, the Court shall, if necessary, afford just satisfaction to the injured party.

Article 42
Judgments of Chambers

Judgments of Chambers shall become final in accordance with the provisions of Article 44 § 2.

Article 43
Referral to the Grand Chamber

1. Within a period of three months from the date of the judgment of the Chamber, any party to the case may, in exceptional cases, request that the case be referred to the Grand Chamber.

2. A panel of five judges of the Grand Chamber shall accept the request if the case raises a serious question affecting the interpretation or application of the Convention or the Protocols thereto, or a serious issue of general importance.

3. If the panel accepts the request, the Grand Chamber shall decide the case by means of a judgment.

Article 44
Final judgments

1. The judgment of the Grand Chamber shall be final.

2. The judgment of a Chamber shall become final
   (a) when the parties declare that they will not request that the case be referred to the Grand Chamber; or
   (b) three months after the date of the judgment, if reference of the case to the Grand Chamber has not been requested; or
   (c) when the panel of the Grand Chamber rejects the request to refer under Article 43.

3. The final judgment shall be pub-ished.

Article 45
Reasons for judgments and decisions

1. Reasons shall be given for judg-ments as well as for decisions declaring applications admissible or inadmissible.

2. If a judgment does not represent, in whole or in part, the unanimous opinion of the judges, any judge shall be entitled to deliver a separate opinion.

Article 46
Binding force and execution of judgments

1. The High Contracting Parties under-take to abide by the final judgment of the Court in any case to which they are parties.

2. The final judgment of the Court shall be transmitted to the Committee of Ministers, which shall supervise its execution.

3. If the Committee of Ministers considers that the supervision of the execution of a final judgment is hindered by a problem of interpretation of the judgment, it may refer the matter to the Court for a ruling on the question of interpretation. A referral decision shall require a majority vote of two thirds of the representatives entitled to sit on the Committee.

4. If the Committee of Ministers considers that a High Contracting Party refuses to abide by a final judgment in a case to which it is a party, it may, after serving formal notice on that Party and by decision adopted by a majority vote of two-thirds of the representatives entitled to sit on the Committee, refer to the Court the question whether that Party has failed to fulfil its obligation under paragraph 1.

5. If the Court finds a violation of paragraph 1, it shall refer the case to the Committee of Ministers for consideration of the measures to be taken. If the Court finds no violation of

paragraph 1, it shall refer the case to the Committee of Ministers, which shall close its examination of the case.

Article 47
Advisory opinions

1. The Court may, at the request of the Committee of Ministers, give advisory opinions on legal questions concerning the interpretation of the Convention and the Protocols thereto.

2. Such opinions shall not deal with any question relating to the content or scope of the rights or freedoms defined in Section I of the Convention and the Protocols thereto, or with any other question which the Court or the Committee of Ministers might have to consider in consequence of any such proceedings as could be instituted in accordance with the Convention.

3. Decisions of the Committee of Ministers to request an advisory opinion of the Court shall require a majority vote of the representatives entitled to sit on the Committee.

Article 48
Advisory jurisdiction of the Court

The Court shall decide whether a request for an advisory opinion submitted by the Committee of Ministers is within its competence as defined in Article 47.

Article 49
Reasons for advisory opinions

1. Reasons shall be given for advisory opinions of the Court.

2. If the advisory opinion does not represent, in whole or in part, the unanimous opinion of the judges, any judge shall be entitled to deliver a separate opinion.

3. Advisory opinions of the Court shall be communicated to the Committee of Ministers.

Article 50
Expenditure on the Court

The expenditure on the Court shall be borne by the Council of Europe.

Article 51
Privileges and immunities of judges

The judges shall be entitled, during the exercise of their functions, to the privileges and immunities provided for in Article 40 of the Statute of the Council of Europe and in the agreements made thereunder.

SECTION III
MISCELLANEOUS PROVISIONS

Article 52
Inquiries by the Secretary General

On receipt of a request from the Secretary General of the Council of Europe any High Contracting Party shall furnish an explanation of the manner in which its internal law ensures the effective implementation of any of the provisions of the Convention.

Article 53
Safeguard for existing human rights

Nothing in this Convention shall be construed as limiting or derogating from any of the human rights and funda-mental freedoms which may be ensured under the laws of any High Contracting Party or under any other agreement to which it is a party.

Article 54
Powers of the Committee of Ministers

Nothing in this Convention shall prejudice the powers conferred on the Committee of Ministers by the Statute of the Council of Europe.

Article 55
Exclusion of other means of dispute settlement

The High Contracting Parties agree that, except by special agreement, they will not avail themselves of treaties, conventions or declarations in force between them for the purpose of submitting, by way of petition, a dispute arising out of the interpretation or application of this Convention to a means of settlement other than those provided for in this Convention.

Article 56
Territorial application

1. Any State may at the time of its ratification or at any time thereafter declare by notification addressed to the Secretary General of the Council of Europe that the present Convention shall, subject to paragraph 4 of this Article, extend to all or any of the territories for whose international relations it is responsible.

2. The Convention shall extend to the territory or territories named in the notification as from the thirtieth day after the receipt of this notification by the Secretary General of the Council of Europe.

4. The provisions of this Convention shall be applied in such territories with due regard, however, to local requirements.

5. Any State which has made a declaration in accordance with para-graph 1 of this Article may at any time thereafter declare on behalf of one or more of the territories to which the declaration relates that it accepts the competence of the Court to receive applications from individuals, non-governmental organisations or groups of individuals as provided by Article 34 of the Convention.

Article 57
Reservations

1. Any State may, when signing this Convention or when depositing its instrument of ratification, make a reservation in respect of any particular provision of the Convention to the extent that any law then in force in its territory is not in conformity with the provision. Reservations of a general character shall not be permitted under this Article.

2. Any reservation made under this Article shall contain a brief statement of the law concerned.

Article 58
Denunciation

1. A High Contracting Party may denounce the present Convention only after the expiry

of five years from the date on which it became a party to it and after six months' notice contained in a notification addressed to the Secretary General of the Council of Europe, who shall inform the other High Contracting Parties.

2. Such a denunciation shall not have the effect of releasing the High Contracting Party concerned from its obligations under this Convention in respect of any act which, being capable of constituting a violation of such obligations, may have been performed by it before the date at which the denunciation became effective.

3. Any High Contracting Party which shall cease to be a member of the Council of Europe shall cease to be a party to this Convention under the same conditions.

4 The Convention may be denounced in accordance with the provisions of the preceding paragraphs in respect of any territory to which it has been declared to extend under the terms of Article 56.

Article 59
Signature and ratification

1. This Convention shall be open to the signature of the members of the Council of Europe. It shall be ratified. Ratifications shall be deposited with the Secretary General of the Council of Europe.

2. The European Union may accede to this Convention.

3. The present Convention shall come into force after the deposit of ten instruments of ratification.

4. As regards any signatory ratifying subsequently, the Convention shall come into force at the date of the deposit of its instrument of ratification.

5. The Secretary General of the Council of Europe shall notify all the members of the Council of Europe of the entry into force of the Convention, the names of the High Contracting Parties who have ratified it, and the deposit of all instruments of ratification which may be effected subsequently.

Done at Rome this 4th day of November 1950, in English and French, both texts being equally authentic, in a single copy which shall remain deposited in the archives of the Council of Europe. The Secretary General shall transmit certified copies to each of the signatories.

Protocol to the Convention for the Protection of Human Rights and Fundamental Freedoms

Paris, 20.III.1952 The governments signatory hereto, being members of the Council of Europe, Being resolved to take steps to ensure

the collective enforcement of certain rights and freedoms other than those already included in Section I of the Convention for the Protection of Human Rights and Fundamental Freedoms signed at Rome on 4 November 1950 (hereinafter referred to as "the Convention"), Have agreed as follows:

Article I
Protection of property

Every natural or legal person is entitled to the peaceful enjoyment of his possessions. No one shall be deprived of his possessions except in the public interest and subject to the conditions provided for by law and by the general principles of international law. The preceding provisions shall not, however, in any way impair the right of a State to enforce such laws as it deems necessary to control the use of property in accordance with the general interest or to secure the payment of taxes or other contributions or penalties.

Article 2
Right to education

No person shall be denied the right to education. In the exercise of any functions which it assumes in relation to education and to teaching, the State shall respect the right of parents to ensure such education and teaching in conformity with their own religious and philosophical convictions.

Article 3
Right to free elections

The High Contracting Parties undertake to hold free elections at reasonable intervals by secret ballot, under conditions which will ensure the free expression of the opinion of the people in the choice of the legislature.

Article 4
Territorial application

Any High Contracting Party may at the time of signature or ratification or at any time thereafter communicate to the Secretary General of the Council of Europe a declaration stating the extent to which it undertakes that the provisions of the present Protocol shall apply to such of the territories for the international relations of which it is responsible as are named therein. Any High Contracting Party which has communicated a declaration in virtue of the preceding paragraph may from time to time communicate a further declaration modifying the terms of any former declaration or terminating the application of the provisions of this Protocol in respect of any territory. A declaration made in accordance with this Article shall be deemed to have been made in accordance with para-graph 1 of Article 56 of the Convention.

Article 5
Relationship to the Convention

As between the High Contracting Parties the provisions of Articles 1, 2, 3 and 4 of this Protocol shall be regarded as additional Articles to the Convention and all the provisions of the Convention shall apply accordingly.

Article 6
Signature and ratification

This Protocol shall be open for signature by the members of the Council of Europe, who are the signatories of the Convention; it shall be ratified at the same time as or after the ratification of the Convention. It shall enter into force after the deposit of ten instruments of ratification. As regards any signatory ratifying subsequently, the Protocol shall enter into force at the date of the deposit of its instrument of ratification. The instruments of ratification shall be deposited with the Secretary General of the Council of Europe, who will notify all members of the names of those who have ratified.

Done at Paris on the 20th day of March 1952, in English and French, both texts being equally authentic, in a single copy which shall remain deposited in the archives of the Council of Europe. The Secretary General shall transmit certified copies to each of the signatory governments.

Protocol No. 4 to the Convention for the Protection of Human Rights and Fundamental Freedoms securing certain rights and freedoms other than those already included in the Convention and in the first Protocol thereto

Strasbourg, 16.IX.1963

The governments signatory hereto, being members of the Council of Europe,

Being resolved to take steps to ensure the collective enforcement of certain rights and freedoms other than those already included in Section I of the Convention for the Protection of Human Rights and Fundamental Freedoms signed at Rome on 4 November 1950 (hereinafter referred to as the "Convention") and in Articles 1 to 3 of the First Protocol to the Convention, signed at Paris on 20 March 1952, Have agreed as follows:

Article I
Prohibition of imprisonment for debt

No one shall be deprived of his liberty merely on the ground of inability to fulfil a contractual obligation.

Article 2
Freedom of movement

1. Everyone lawfully within the territory of a State shall, within that territory, have the right to liberty of movement and freedom to choose his residence.

2. Everyone shall be free to leave any country, including his own.

3. No restrictions shall be placed on the exercise of these rights other than such as are in accordance with law and are necessary in a democratic society in the interests of national security or public safety, for the maintenance of *ordre public*, for the prevention of crime, for the protection of health or morals, or for the protection of the rights and freedoms of others.

4. The rights set forth in paragraph 1 may also be subject, in particular areas, to restrictions imposed in accordance with law and justified by the public interest in a democratic society.

Article 3
Prohibition of expulsion of nationals

1. No one shall be expelled, by means either of an individual or of a collective measure, from the territory of the State of which he is a national.

2. No one shall be deprived of the right to enter the territory of the State of which he is a national.

Article 4
Prohibition of collective expulsion of aliens

Collective expulsion of aliens is pro-hibited.

Article 5
Territorial application

1. Any High Contracting Party may, at the time of signature or ratification of this Protocol, or at any time thereafter, communicate to the Secretary General of the Council of Europe a declaration stating the extent to which it undertakes that the provisions of this Protocol shall apply to such of the territories for the international relations of which it is responsible as are named therein.

2. Any High Contracting Party which has communicated a declaration in virtue of the preceding paragraph may, from time to time, communicate a further declaration modifying the terms of any former declaration or terminating the application of the provisions of this Protocol in respect of any territory.

3. A declaration made in accordance with this Article shall be deemed to have been made in accordance with paragraph 1 of Article 56 of the Convention.

4. The territory of any State to which this Protocol applies by virtue of ratification or acceptance by that State, and each territory to which this Protocol is applied by virtue of a declaration by that State under this Article, shall be treated as separate territories for the purpose of the references in Articles 2 and 3 to the territory of a State.

5. Any State which has made a declaration in accordance with para-graph 1 or 2 of this Article may at any time thereafter declare on behalf of one or more of the territories to which the declaration relates that it accepts the competence of the Court to receive applications from individuals, non-governmental organisations or groups of individuals as provided in Article 34 of the Convention in respect of all or any of Articles 1 to 4 of this Protocol.

Article 6
Relationship to the Convention

As between the High Contracting Parties the provisions of Articles 1 to 5 of this Protocol shall be regarded as additional Articles to the Convention, and all the provisions of the Convention shall apply accordingly.

Article 7
Signature and ratification

1. This Protocol shall be open for signature by the members of the Council of Europe who are the signatories of the Convention; it shall be ratified at the same time as or after the ratification of the Convention. It shall enter into force after the deposit of five instruments of ratification. As regards any signatory ratifying subsequently, the Protocol shall enter into force at the date of the deposit of its instrument of ratification.

2. The instruments of ratification shall be deposited with the Secretary General of the Council of Europe, who will notify all members of the names of those who have ratified.

In witness whereof the undersigned, being duly authorised thereto, have signed this Protocol. Done at Strasbourg, this 16th day of September 1963, in English and in French, both texts being equally authoritative, in a single copy which shall remain deposited in the archives of the Council of Europe. The Secretary General shall transmit certified copies to each of the signatory States.

Protocol No. 6 to the Convention for the Protection of Human Rights and Fundamental Freedoms concerning the abolition of the death penalty

Strasbourg, 28.IV.1983

The member States of the Council of Europe, signatory to this Protocol to the Convention for the Protection of Human Rights and Fundamental Freedoms, signed at Rome on 4 November 1950 (hereinafter referred to as "the Convention"),

Considering that the evolution that has occurred in several member States of the Council of Europe expresses a general tendency in favour of abolition of the death penalty; Have agreed as follows:

Article 1
Abolition of the death penalty

The death penalty shall be abolished. No one shall be condemned to such penalty or executed.

Article 2
Death penalty in time of war

A State may make provision in its law for the death penalty in respect of acts committed in time of war or of imminent threat of war; such penalty shall be applied only in the instances laid down in the law and in accordance with its provisions. The State shall communicate to the Secretary General of the Council of Europe the relevant provisions of that law.

Article 3
Prohibition of derogations

No derogation from the provisions of this Protocol shall be made under Article 15 of the Convention.

Article 4
Prohibition of reservations

No reservation may be made under Article 57 of the Convention in respect of the provisions of this Protocol.

Article 5
Territorial application

1. Any State may at the time of signature or when depositing its instrument of ratification, acceptance or approval, specify the territory or territories to which this Protocol shall apply.

2. Any State may at any later date, by a declaration addressed to the Secretary General of the Council of Europe, extend the application of this Protocol to any other territory specified in the declar-ation. In respect of such territory the Protocol shall enter into force on the first day of the month following the date of receipt of such declaration by the Secretary General.

3. Any declaration made under the two preceding paragraphs may, in respect of any territory specified in such declaration, be withdrawn by a notification addressed to the Secretary General. The withdrawal shall become effective on the first day of the month following the date of receipt of such notification by the Secretary General.

Article 6
Relationship to the Convention

As between the States Parties the provisions of Articles 1 and 5 of this Protocol shall be regarded as additional Articles to the Convention and all the provisions of the Convention shall apply accordingly.

Article 7
Signature and ratification

The Protocol shall be open for signature by the member States of the Council of Europe, signatories to the Convention. It shall be subject to ratification, accept-ance or approval. A member State of the Council of Europe may not ratify, accept or approve this Protocol unless it has, simultaneously or previously, ratified the Convention. Instruments of ratification, acceptance or approval shall be de-posited with the Secretary General of the Council of Europe.

Article 8
Entry into force

1. This Protocol shall enter into force on the first day of the month following the date on which five member States of the Council of Europe have expressed their consent to be bound by the Protocol in accordance with the pro-visions of Article 7.

2. In respect of any member State which subsequently expresses its con-sent to be bound by it, the Protocol shall enter into force on the first day of the month following the date of the deposit of the instrument of ratification, accept-ance or approval.

Article 9
Depositary functions

The Secretary General of the Council of Europe shall notify the member States of the Council of:
    (a) any signature;
    (b) the deposit of any instrument of ratification, acceptance or approval;
    (c) any date of entry into force of this Protocol in accordance with Articles 5 and 8;
    (d) any other act, notification or communication relating to this Protocol.

In witness whereof the undersigned, being duly authorised thereto, have signed this Protocol.

Done at Strasbourg, this 28th day of April 1983, in English and in French, both texts being equally authentic, in a single copy which shall be deposited in the archives of the Council of Europe. The Secretary General of the Council of Europe shall transmit certified copies to each member State of the Council of Europe.

Protocol No. 7 to the Convention for the Protection of Human Rights and Fundamental Freedoms

Strasbourg, 22.XI.1984 The member States of the Council of Europe signatory hereto,

Being resolved to take further steps to ensure the collective enforcement of certain rights and freedoms by means of the Convention for the Protection of Human Rights and Fundamental Freedoms signed at Rome on 4 Nov-ember 1950 (hereinafter referred to as "the Convention"), Have agreed as follows:

Article 1
Procedural safeguards relating to expulsion of aliens

1. An alien lawfully resident in the territory of a State shall not be expelled therefrom except in pursuance of a decision reached in accordance with law and shall be allowed:
    (a) to submit reasons against his expulsion,
    (b) to have his case reviewed, and
    (c) to be represented for these pur-poses before the competent authority or a person or persons designated by that authority.

2. An alien may be expelled before the exercise of his rights under paragraph 1 (a), (b) and (c) of this Article, when such expulsion is necessary in the interests of public order or is grounded on reasons of national security.

Article 2
Right of appeal in criminal matters

1. Everyone convicted of a criminal offence by a tribunal shall have the right to have his conviction or sentence reviewed by a higher tribunal. The exercise of this right, including the grounds on which it may be exercised, shall be governed by law.

2. This right may be subject to exceptions in regard to offences of a minor character, as prescribed by law, or in cases in which the person concerned was tried in the first instance by the highest tribunal or was convicted following an appeal against acquittal.

Article 3
Compensation for wrongful conviction

When a person has by a final decision been convicted of a criminal offence and when subsequently his conviction has been reversed, or he has been pardoned, on the ground that a new or newly discovered fact shows conclusively that there has been a miscarriage of justice, the person who has suffered punishment as a result of such conviction shall be compensated according to the law or the practice of the State concerned, unless it is proved that the non-disclosure of the unknown fact in time is wholly or partly attributable to him.

Article 4
Right not to be tried or punished twice

1. No one shall be liable to be tried or punished again in criminal proceedings under the jurisdiction of the same State for an offence for which he has already been finally acquitted or convicted in accordance with the law and penal procedure of that State.

2. The provisions of the preceding paragraph shall not prevent the reopening of the case in accordance with the law and penal procedure of the State concerned, if there is evidence of new or newly discovered facts, or if there has been a fundamental defect in the previous proceedings, which could affect the outcome of the case.

3 No derogation from this Article shall be made under Article 15 of the Convention.

Article 5
Equality between spouses

Spouses shall enjoy equality of rights and responsibilities of a private law character between them, and in their relations with their children, as to marriage, during marriage and in the event of its dissolution. This Article shall not prevent States from taking such measures as are necessary in the interests of the children.

Article 6
Territorial application

1. Any State may at the time of signature or when depositing its instrument of ratification, acceptance or approval, specify the territory or territories to which the Protocol shall apply and state the extent to which it undertakes that the provisions of this Protocol shall apply to such territory or territories.

2. Any State may at any later date, by a declaration addressed to the Secretary General of the Council of Europe, extend the application of this Protocol to any other territory specified in the declar-ation. In respect of such territory the Protocol shall enter into force on the first day of the month following the expiration of a period of two months after the date of receipt by the Secretary General of such declaration.

3. Any declaration made under the two preceding paragraphs may, in respect of any territory specified in such declaration, be withdrawn or modified by a notification addressed to the Secretary General. The withdrawal or modification shall become effective on the first day of the month following the expiration of a period of two months after the date of receipt of such notification by the Secretary General.

4. A declaration made in accordance with this Article shall be deemed to have been made in accordance with paragraph 1 of Article 56 of the Convention.

5. The territory of any State to which this Protocol applies by virtue of ratification, acceptance or approval by that State, and each territory to which this Protocol is applied by virtue of a declaration by that State under this Article, may be treated as separate territories for the purpose of the reference in Article 1 to the territory of a State.

6. Any State which has made a declaration in accordance with paragraph 1 or 2 of this Article may at any time thereafter declare on behalf of one or more of the territories to which the declaration relates that it accepts the competence of the Court to receive applications from individuals, non-governmental organisations or groups of individuals as provided in Article 34 of the Convention in respect of Articles 1 to 5 of this Protocol.

Article 7
Relationship to the Convention

As between the States Parties, the provisions of Article 1 to 6 of this Protocol shall be regarded as additional Articles to the Convention, and all the provisions of the Convention shall apply accordingly.

Article 8
Signature and ratification

This Protocol shall be open for signature by member States of the Council of Europe which have signed the Convention. It is subject to ratification, acceptance or approval. A member State of the Council of Europe may not ratify, accept or approve this Protocol without previously or simultaneously ratifying the Convention. Instruments of ratification, acceptance or approval shall be deposited with the Secretary General of the Council of Europe.

Article 9
Entry into force

1. This Protocol shall enter into force on the first day of the month following the expiration of a period of two months after the date on which seven member States of the Council of Europe have expressed their consent to be bound by the Protocol in accordance with the provisions of Article 8.

2. In respect of any member State which subsequently expresses its consent to be bound by it, the Protocol shall enter into force on the first day of the month following the expiration of a period of two months after the date of the deposit of the instrument of ratification, acceptance or approval.

Article 10
Depositary functions

The Secretary General of the Council of Europe shall notify all the member States of the Council of Europe of:

   (a) any signature;

   (b) the deposit of any instrument of ratification, acceptance or approval;

   (c) any date of entry into force of this Protocol in accordance with Articles 6 and 9;

   (d) any other act, notification or declaration relating to this Protocol.

In witness whereof the undersigned, being duly authorised thereto, have signed this Protocol. Done at Strasbourg, this 22nd day of November 1984, in English and French, both texts being equally authentic, in a single copy which shall be deposited in the archives of the Council of Europe. The Secretary General of the Council of Europe shall transmit certified copies to each member State of the Council of Europe.

Protocol No. 12 to the Convention for the Protection of Human Rights and Fundamental Freedoms

Rome, 4.XI.2000

The member States of the Council of Europe signatory hereto,

Having regard to the fundamental principle according to which all persons are equal before the law and are entitled to the equal protection of the law; Being resolved to take further steps to promote the equality of all persons through the collective enforcement of a general prohibition of discrimination by means of the Convention for the Protection of Human Rights and Fundamental Freedoms signed at Rome on 4 November 1950 (hereinafter referred to as "the Convention"); Reaffirming that the principle of non-discrimination does not prevent States Parties from taking measures in order to promote full and effective equality, provided that there is an objective and reasonable justification for those measures, Have agreed as follows:

Article I
General prohibition of discrimination

1. The enjoyment of any right set forth by law shall be secured without dis-crimination on any ground such as sex, race, colour, language, religion, political or other opinion, national or social origin, association with a national minority, property, birth or other status.

2. No one shall be discriminated against by any public authority on any ground such as those mentioned in paragraph 1.

Article 2
Territorial application

1. Any State may, at the time of signature or when depositing its instrument of ratification, acceptance or approval, specify the territory or territories to which this Protocol shall apply.

2. Any State may at any later date, by a declaration addressed to the Secretary General of the Council of Europe, extend the application of this Protocol to any other territory specified in the declar-ation. In respect of such territory the Protocol shall enter into force on the first day of the month following the expiration of a period of three months after the date of receipt by the Secretary General of such declaration.

3. Any declaration made under the two preceding paragraphs may, in respect of any territory specified in such declar-ation, be withdrawn or modified by a notification addressed to the Secretary General of the Council of Europe. The withdrawal or modification shall become effective on the first day of the month following the expiration of a period of three months after the date of receipt of such notification by the Secretary General.

4. A declaration made in accordance with this Article shall be deemed to have been made in accordance with paragraph 1 of Article 56 of the Convention.

5. Any State which has made a declaration in accordance with para-graph 1 or 2 of this Article may at any time thereafter declare on behalf of one or more of the territories to which the declaration relates that it accepts the competence of the Court to receive applications from individuals, non-governmental organisations or groups of individuals as provided by Article 34 of the Convention in respect of Article 1 of this Protocol.

Article 3
Relationship to the Convention

As between the States Parties, the provisions of Articles 1 and 2 of this Protocol shall be regarded as additional Articles to the Convention, and all the provisions of the Convention shall apply accordingly.

Article 4
Signature and ratification

This Protocol shall be open for signature by member States of the Council of Europe which have signed the Convention. It is subject to ratification, acceptance or approval. A member State of the Council of Europe may not ratify, accept or approve this Protocol without previously or simultaneously ratifying the Convention. Instruments of ratifi-cation, acceptance or approval shall be deposited with the Secretary General of the Council of Europe.

Article 5
Entry into force

1. This Protocol shall enter into force on the first day of the month following the expiration of a period of three months after the date on which ten member States of the Council of Europe have expressed their consent to be bound by the Protocol in accordance with the provisions of Article 4.

2. In respect of any member State which subsequently expresses its con-sent to be bound by it, the Protocol shall enter into force on the first day of the month following the expiration of a period of three months after the date of the deposit of the instrument of ratifi-cation, acceptance or approval.

Article 6
Depositary functions

The Secretary General of the Council of Europe shall notify all the member States of the Council of Europe of: ve:
  (a) any signature;
  (b) the deposit of any instrument of ratification, acceptance or approval;
  (c) any date of entry into force of this Protocol in accordance with Articles 2 and 5;
  (d) any other act, notification or communication relating to this Protocol.

In witness whereof the undersigned, being duly authorised thereto, have signed this Protocol. Done at Rome, this 4th day of November 2000, in English and in French, both texts being equally authentic, in a single copy which shall be deposited in the archives of the Council of Europe. The Secretary General of the Council of Europe shall transmit certified copies to each member State of the Council of Europe.

Protocol No. 13 to the Convention for the Protection of Human Rights and Fundamental Freedoms concerning the abolition of the death penalty in all circumstances

Vilnius, 3.V.2002

The member States of the Council of Europe signatory hereto,

Convinced that everyone's right to life is a basic value in a democratic society and that the abolition of the death penalty is essential for the protection of this right and for the full recognition of the inherent dignity of all human beings; Wishing to strengthen the protection of the right to life guaranteed by the Convention for the Protection of Human Rights and Fundamental Freedoms signed at Rome on 4 November 1950 (hereinafter referred to as "the Convention"); Noting that Protocol No. 6 to the Convention concerning the abolition of the death penalty, signed at Strasbourg on 28 April 1983, does not exclude the death penalty in respect of acts com-mitted in time of war or of imminent threat of war; Being resolved to take the final step in order to abolish the death penalty in all circumstances, Have agreed as follows:

Article 1
Abolition of the death penalty

The death penalty shall be abolished. No one shall be condemned to such penalty or executed.

Article 2
Prohibitions of derogations

No derogation from the provisions of this Protocol shall be made under Article 15 of the Convention.

Article 3
Prohibitions of reservations

No reservation may be made under Article 57 of the Convention in respect of the provisions of this Protocol.

Article 4
Territorial application

1. Any State may, at the time of signature or when depositing its instrument of ratification, acceptance or approval, specify the territory or territories to which this Protocol shall apply.

2. Any State may at any later date, by a declaration addressed to the Secretary General of the Council of Europe, extend the application of this Protocol to any other territory specified in the declaration. In respect of such territory the Protocol shall enter into force on the first day of the month following the expiration of a period of three months after the date of receipt by the Secretary General of such declaration.

3. Any declaration made under the two preceding paragraphs may, in respect of any territory specified in such declar-ation, be withdrawn or modified by a notification addressed to the Secretary General. The withdrawal or modification shall become effective on the first day of the month following the expiration of a period of three months after the date of receipt of such notification by the Secretary General.

Article 5
Relationship to the Convention

As between the States Parties the provisions of Articles 1 to 4 of this Protocol shall be regarded as additional Articles to the Convention, and all the provisions of the Convention shall apply accordingly.

Article 6
Signature and ratification

This Protocol shall be open for signature by member States of the Council of Europe which have signed the Convention. It is subject to ratification, acceptance or approval. A member State of the Council of Europe may not ratify, accept or approve this Protocol without previously or simultaneously ratifying the Convention. Instruments of ratifi-cation, acceptance or approval shall be deposited with the Secretary General of the Council of Europe.

Article 7
Entry into force

1. This Protocol shall enter into force on the first day of the month following the expiration of a period of three months after the date on which ten member States of the Council of Europe have expressed their consent to be bound by the Protocol in accordance with the provisions of Article 6.

2. In respect of any member State which subsequently expresses its con-sent to be bound by it, the Protocol shall enter into force on the first day of the month following the expiration of a period of three months after the date of the deposit of the instrument of ratifi-cation, acceptance or approval.

Article 8
Depositary functions

The Secretary General of the Council of Europe shall notify all the member States of the Council of Europe of:
    (a) any signature;
    (b) the deposit of any instrument of ratification, acceptance or approval;
    (c) any date of entry into force of this Protocol in accordance with Articles 4 and 7;
    (d) any other act, notification or communication relating to this Protocol;

In witness whereof the undersigned, being duly authorised thereto, have signed this Protocol. Done at Vilnius, this 3rd day of May 2002, in English and in French, both texts being equally authentic, in a single copy which shall be deposited in the archives of the Council of Europe. The Secretary General of the Council of Europe shall transmit certified copies to each member State of the Council of Europe

Index

All references are to paragraph numbers.
Preparation of the table is based upon HURIDOCS thesauri of human rights.